D0370832

PACIFIC NORTHWEST HIKING

SCOTT LEONARD & SEAN PATRICK HILL

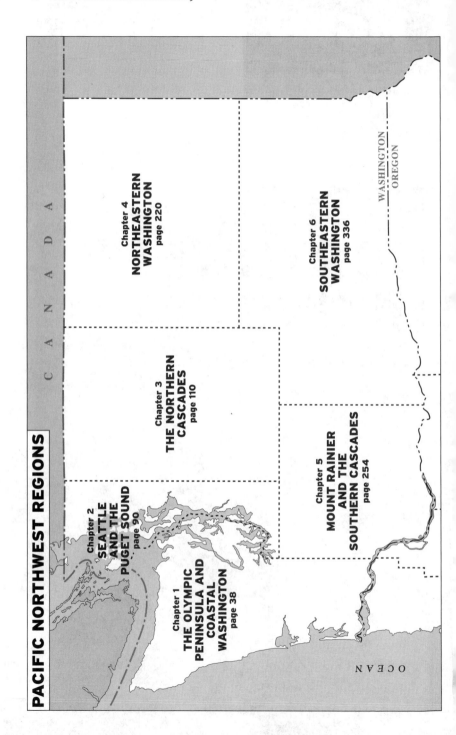

PACIFIC NORTHWEST REGIONS

CANADA

WASHINGTON
OREGON

Chapter 4
NORTHEASTERN WASHINGTON
page 220

Chapter 6
SOUTHEASTERN WASHINGTON
page 336

Chapter 3
THE NORTHERN CASCADES
page 110

Chapter 5
MOUNT RAINIER AND THE SOUTHERN CASCADES
page 254

Chapter 2
SEATTLE AND THE PUGET SOUND
page 90

Chapter 1
THE OLYMPIC PENINSULA AND COASTAL WASHINGTON
page 38

OCEAN

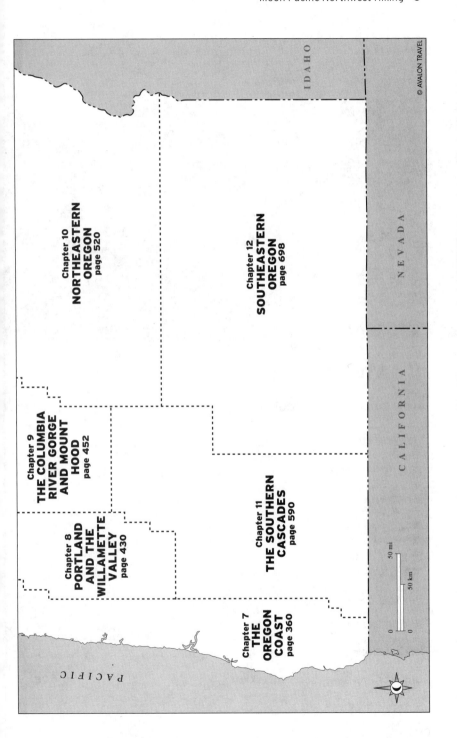

Chapter 10
NORTHEASTERN OREGON
page 520

Chapter 12
SOUTHEASTERN OREGON
page 698

Chapter 9
THE COLUMBIA RIVER GORGE AND MOUNT HOOD
page 452

Chapter 8
PORTLAND AND THE WILLAMETTE VALLEY
page 430

Chapter 11
THE SOUTHERN CASCADES
page 590

Chapter 7
THE OREGON COAST
page 360

IDAHO

NEVADA

CALIFORNIA

PACIFIC

© AVALON TRAVEL

0   50 mi

0   50 km

Contents

Washington

How to Use This Book

ABOUT THE TRAIL PROFILES

Each hike in this book is listed in a consistent, easy-to-read format to help you choose the ideal hike. From a general overview of the setting to detailed driving directions, the profile will provide all the information you need. Here is a sample profile:

Map number and hike number →

1 SOMEWHERE USA HIKE

Round-trip mileage → **9.0 mi/5.0 hrs** (unless otherwise noted) and the approximate amount of time needed to complete the hike (actual times can vary widely, especially on longer hikes)

Difficulty and quality ratings ←

at the mouth of the Somewhere River ←

General location of the trail, named by its proximity to the nearest major town or landmark →

Map on which the trailhead can be found and page number on which the map can be found →

Map 1.2, page 24   **BEST (** ←

Symbol indicating that the hike is listed among the author's top picks →

Each hike in this book begins with a brief overview of its setting. The description typically covers what kind of terrain to expect, what might be seen, and any conditions that may make the hike difficult to navigate. Side trips, such as to waterfalls or panoramic vistas, in addition to ways to combine the trail with others nearby for a longer outing, are also noted here. In many cases, mile-by-mile trail directions are included.

User Groups: This section notes the types of users that are permitted on the trail, including hikers, mountain bikers, horseback riders, and dogs. Wheelchair access is also noted here.

Permits: This section notes whether a permit is required for hiking, or, if the hike spans more than one day, whether one is required for camping. Any fees, such as for parking, day use, or entrance, are also noted here.

Maps: This section provides information on how to obtain detailed trail maps of the hike and its environs. Whenever applicable, names of U.S. Geologic Survey (USGS) topographic maps and national forest maps are also included; contact information for these and other map sources are noted in the Resources section at the back of this book.

Directions: This section provides mile-by-mile driving directions to the trail head from the nearest major town.

Contact: This section provides an address and phone number for each hike. The contact is usually the agency maintaining the trail but may also be a trail club or other organization.

ABOUT THE ICONS

The icons in this book are designed to provide at-a-glance information on the difficulty and quality of each hike.

The **difficulty rating** (rated **1-5** with **1** being the lowest and **5** the highest) is based on the steepness of the trail and how difficult it is to traverse

The **quality rating** (rated **1-10** with **1** being the lowest and **10** the highest) is based largely on scenic beauty, but also takes into account how crowded the trail is and whether noise of nearby civilization is audible

ABOUT THE DIFFICULTY RATINGS

Trails rated 1 are very easy and suitable for hikers of all abilities, including young children.

Trails rated 2 are easy-to-moderate and suitable for most hikers, including families with active children 6 and older.

Trails rated 3 are moderately challenging and suitable for reasonably fit adults and older children who are very active.

Trails rated 4 are very challenging and suitable for physically fit hikers who are seeking a workout.

Trails rated 5 are extremely challenging and suitable only for experienced hikers who are in top physical condition.

MAP SYMBOLS

▭▭▭ Expressway	🅸🅾	Interstate Freeway	✕	Airfield
▭▭▭ Primary Road	⟨101⟩	U.S. Highway	✕	Airport
▭▭▭ Secondary Road	⟨21⟩	State Highway	○	City/Town
▭▭▭ Unpaved Road	⟨66⟩	County Highway	▲	Mountain
⋯⋯ Ferry		Lake	⬧	Park
─ · ─ National Border		Dry Lake	⟋⟋	Pass
─ ·· ─ State Border		Seasonal Lake	◉	State Capital

ABOUT THE MAPS

This book is divided into chapters based on major regions in each state; an overview map of these regions precedes the table of contents. Each chapter begins with a map of the region, which is further broken down into detail maps. Trailheads are noted on the detail maps by number.

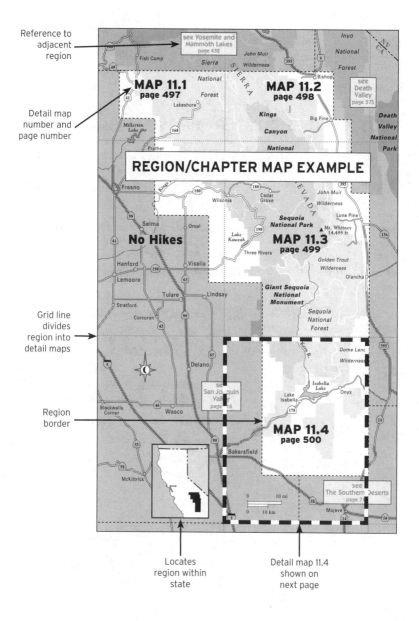

Reference to adjacent region

Detail map number and page number

REGION/CHAPTER MAP EXAMPLE

Grid line divides region into detail maps

Region border

Locates region within state

Detail map 11.4 shown on next page

Indicates adjacent detail maps within region

Locates detail map within region

Map number → **Map 11.4**

Hikes shown on detail map and the page range where those hikes are listed → **Hikes 105-117**
Pages 564-570

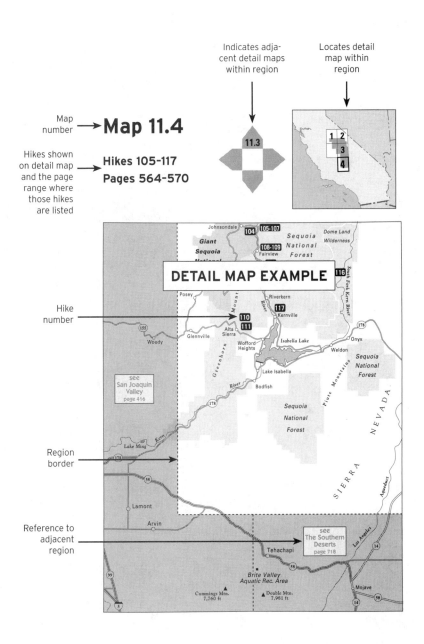

INTRODUCTION

Author's Note

If you love the outdoors, Washington has everything you could ever ask for. In any given season, you'll find Washingtonians outdoors in our beloved wildernesses. First and foremost in our hearts are the mountains, where we hike, ski, snowshoe, rock climb, mountain bike, and camp year-round. The Olympics, slick with nearly 200 inches of annual rainfall, reign over the northwestern corner of the state. The Cascades divide Washington into its wet and dry halves and are home to some of America's most scenic peaks, like Mount Rainier and Mount Baker, and countless alpine meadows and glaciers. One of the world's most restless mountains, Mount Saint Helens, is here as well, still continuing to re-build from its major eruption in 1980. Washington's moun-

Scott Leonard

tains are places of peace and quiet, where the worries of city life quickly give way to the delights of wild natural beauty.

But Washington is more than just mountains. Any trail in the state is a grand trip, from the beaches and sea stacks of the coast to the expansive alpine meadows of the high country. With lush old-growth forests on its western side and dry deserts at its eastern end, Washington contains a wide range of plant life and terrain within its 71,303 square miles. We have rumbling rivers, gurgling streams, and breathtaking waterfalls left and right—many of which start as glaciers, something that Washington has more of than the rest of the United States combined (excluding Alaska). Washington is an incredibly diverse state, and as the ultimate trail authority, *Moon Pacific Northwest Hiking* will help you explore every inch of it.

More than 400 trails throughout Washington are included in this book, and during my time with Earthcorps, a Seattle nonprofit, I even helped build some of them. Every trail is different, and you can find the perfect trek for any region or time frame. One weekend you may be looking for a quick hike close to Seattle (try the Alpine Lakes Wilderness), while on another weekend you may want to spend a few days exploring Washington's backcountry (like Glacier Peak Wilderness). And when your mother-in-law is in town, scenic Mount Rainier is the quintessential place to go (or you can just show her the mountain on a state license plate).

In the process of writing this book, I spent over three months camping under the stars. My trusty Subaru packed on over 12,000 miles while carrying me back and forth across the state. On the trail, deer became regular companions and elk crossed my path. And my, oh my, the bears I've seen—though, admittedly, no creature was quite as ter-rorizing as the ravenous camp mouse. I shook off 9 inches of rain in 24 hours on one trip, and battled snowstorms in more than one season. Hiking in Washington is always a guaranteed adventure.

Author's Note

Oregon can feel as populous as California or as wild as Idaho. With its proximity to Portland, a day-trip on Mount Hood, a Cape Falcon exploration, or a survey of waterfalls in the Columbia River Gorge can bring a hiker in contact with many urbanites. On the other hand, wandering the Siskiyous, or the extensive gorges whittled away from Steens Mountain, or even into the depths of Hell's Canyon can be an experiment in solitude. This is a landscape that quickly changes from cities housing thousands to an occasional lonesome ranch.

Sean Patrick Hill

Oregon is divided into distinct regions, each with its various opportunities for hiking. The maritime region, known simply as "the coast," offers rocky capes, towering sand dunes, and forests thick with Sitka spruce. The Willamette Valley is home to its namesake river, a rolling countryside of fish-laden creeks, wetlands, and steep buttes. The Columbia River Gorge, a National Scenic Area, is rich with waterfalls, wildflowers, and wild mushrooms. Towering above the Gorge is Mount Hood, Oregon's tallest peak, girdled by the famous Timberline Trail and part of the Cascade Mountains, where old-growth forests and rivers are born. To the southeast lies the high desert, and to the northeast, the pine and larch forests of the Blue Mountains and the awesome chasm of the Snake River.

Oregon is a destination for skiers, kayakers, mountain bikers, and Olympic athletes in training—and, of course, hikers. In Oregon, you can climb to the peak of the Tillamook Head and stand exactly where explorers Lewis and Clark overlooked the Pacific Ocean. You can visit stone shelters built by the Civilian Conservation Corps on Mount Hood and Cape Perpetua, or poke around miners' cabins along the upper reaches of the John Day River. With the right determination, you can even climb South Sister—Oregon's third-highest peak—and see nearly half the state of Oregon around you. No wonder old license plates here read "Pacific Wonderland."

In this book are the best hikes in the state of Oregon. From abandoned cabins to mountain lookouts to decrepit mines, there is plenty of history to see. From mountain lakes to lazy rivers, there are plenty of holes to swim. Bring your camera and pack your gear; with places carrying names like the Painted Hills, the Big Obsidian Flow, and the Devil's Punchbowl, you know you're in for the most memorable of experiences.

Best Hikes

◖ Best Beach and Coastal Walks

Shi Shi Beach, The Olympic Peninsula and Coastal Washington, page 45.

Dungeness Spit, The Olympic Peninsula and Coastal Washington, page 52.

Second Beach, The Olympic Peninsula and Coastal Washington, page 52.

Cape Disappointment State Park, The Olympic Peninsula and Coastal Washington, page 85.

Deception Pass State Park, Seattle and the Puget Sound, page 99.

Cape Falcon, The Oregon Coast, page 369.

Cape Lookout, The Oregon Coast, page 376.

Baker Beach, The Oregon Coast, page 393.

Umpqua Dunes, The Oregon Coast, page 401.

Sunset Bay to Cape Arago, The Oregon Coast, page 402.

Umpqua Dunes in the Oregon Dunes National Recreation Area

◖ Best Hikes for Kids

Little Cranberry Lake, Seattle and the Puget Sound, page 96.

Twin Falls, The Northern Cascades, page 188.

Cedar Flats, Mount Rainier and the Southern Cascades, page 265.

Ape Cave, Mount Rainier and the Southern Cascades, page 267.

Paradise Nature Trails, Mount Rainier and the Southern Cascades, page 286.

Willamette Mission State Park, Portland and the Willamette Valley, page 439.

McDowell Creek Falls, Portland and the Willamette Valley, page 444.

Latourell Falls, The Columbia River Gorge and Mount Hood, page 458.

Timothy Lake, The Columbia River Gorge and Mount Hood, page 498.

Shevlin Park, The Southern Cascades, page 629.

◖ Best Hikes for Views

Moran State Park, Seattle and the Puget Sound, page 94.

Mount Pilchuck, The Northern Cascades, page 139.

Granite Mountain, The Northern Cascades, page 194.

Mount Fremont Lookout, Mount Rainier and the Southern Cascades, page 274.

Oregon Butte, Southeastern Washington, page 348.

Saddle Mountain, The Oregon Coast, page 368.

Zigzag Canyon and Paradise Park, The Columbia River Gorge and Mount Hood, page 487.

Jefferson Park, The Columbia River Gorge and Mount Hood, page 512.

The Obsidian Trail, The Southern Cascades, page 621.

Green Lakes via Fall Creek, The Southern Cascades, page 625.

◖ Best Hikes Through Old-Growth Forests

Hoh River, The Olympic Peninsula and Coastal Washington, page 61.

tide pools at Cape Alava along the Ozette Triangle, Olympic Peninsula, Washington

Seward Park, Seattle and the Puget Sound, page 103.
Lake 22, The Northern Cascades, page 140.
Cedar Flats, Mount Rainier and the Southern Cascades, page 265.
Grove of the Patriarchs, Mount Rainier and the Southern Cascades, page 293.
Valley of the Giants, The Oregon Coast, page 382.
Shrader Old-Growth Trail, The Oregon Coast, page 414.
Redwood Nature Trail, The Oregon Coast, page 424.
Opal Creek, The Columbia River Gorge and Mount Hood, page 505.
Lookout Creek Old-Growth Trail, The Southern Cascades, page 605.

❰ Best Self-Guided Nature Walks
Bridle Trails State Park, Seattle and the Puget Sound, page 102.
Nisqually National Wildlife Refuge, Seattle and the Puget Sound, page 105.
Rainy Lake Nature Trail, The Northern Cascades, page 147.
Iron Goat, The Northern Cascades, page 185.
Trail of Two Forests, Mount Rainier and the Southern Cascades, page 267.
Cascade Head Nature Conservancy Trail, The Oregon Coast, page 380.
Big Pine Interpretive Loop, The Oregon Coast, page 415.
Tryon Creek State Park, Portland and the Willamette Valley, page 438.
McDonald Research Forest, Portland and the Willamette Valley, page 442.
Lava Cast Forest, The Southern Cascades, page 663.

❰ Best Short Backpacking Trips
Ozette Triangle, The Olympic Peninsula and Coastal Washington, page 46.
Oval Lakes, The Northern Cascades, page 169.
Necklace Valley, The Northern Cascades, page 181.

Middle North Falls in Silver Falls State Park, Oregon

© SEAN PATRICK HILL

〖 Best Hikes for Waterfalls

〖 Best Wheelchair-Accessible Trails

Hiking Tips

HIKING ESSENTIALS

Hiking essentials are just that—indispensable items that you should carry every time you hit the trail. No matter where you're headed, you never know what you're going to come across (or what's going to come across you); being prepared can help to prevent problems before they start.

Food

The lore of the backcountry is filled with tales of folks who head out for a quick day hike and end up spending a night (or more) in the wilderness. Planning on just an afternoon away from the kitchen, they don't bring enough food to last into the night or morning. Not only is an empty stomach a restless stomach, it can be dangerous as well. A full stomach provides energy to help ward off hypothermia and keeps the mind clear for the task at hand: Not getting even more lost.

When packing food for an outing, include a little extra gorp or an extra energy bar. This will come in extremely handy if you find yourself wandering back to the trailhead later than planned. A grizzled old veteran of the backcountry once passed on a helpful tip for packing extra food. Extra food is meant for an emergency; the last thing you want to do is eat it in a nonemergency and then need it later. So, he packed something nutritious that he'd consider eating only in an emergency: canned dog food.

Water

Be sure to drink lots of water, even if it's not that hot out. Staying properly hydrated can prevent heat exhaustion. Symptoms of heat exhaustion include excessive sweating, gradual weakness, nausea, anxiety, and eventually loss of consciousness. Usually the skin becomes pale and clammy or cold, the pulse slows, and blood pressure may drop. Heat exhaustion is often unexpected but very serious; someone experiencing heat exhaustion will have difficulty getting out of a wilderness setting and will need assistance—not always an easy task.

When day hiking, you can probably carry from the trailhead all the water you'll need for the hike. Two liters per person is a good rule of thumb. Carrying water with you or having a method of filtering water is important—never drink untreated water in the wild. A stream may look crystal clear and be ice cold, but it can also be full of nasty parasites and viruses. If you catch a case of *giardia* or *cryptosporidia,* you could be incapacitated for a full week. Carrying a stove or a filter can be impractical on day hikes. The best back-up method is to carry iodine and chlorine tablets that quickly and easily purify water. They're lightweight and come in handy in a pinch. If you don't mind a strange taste in your water, these will do the trick.

Map and Compass

You need to carry a map and compass on your person *every* time you hit the trail, whether you're going up Mount Si with the rest of Seattle or venturing into the vacant backcountry of North Cascades National Park. No matter how familiar you think you are with a trail, you can get lost. Not only should you carry a map and compass, but you also need to know how to use them.

A map is not always a map. You can't rely on the map that AAA gave you out on the trail. Instead, it's best to purchase a quality topographic map for use on the trail. A quality topographic map allows hikers to follow their steps more accurately and is infinitely more helpful for figuring out where you are when you're lost. Green Trails of Seattle makes high-quality topo maps for 90 percent of Washington trails and has expanded into Oregon as well, covering much of the Cascades throughout the state. The USGS and National Geographic also make good topo maps, although Green Trails maps have supplanted USGS topographical maps as the authority for hikers in Oregon and Washington.

Now that it's the 21st century, GPS devices are becoming more popular. These are great toys to play with while out on the trail. Some folks even swear by them. But a GPS device often won't work in a thick forest canopy. A good old-fashioned compass, on the other hand, is significantly cheaper and won't ever die on you when the batteries run out.

Extra Clothing

Here in the Pacific Northwest, the weather can turn at the drop of a hat. In every season, rain is an inevitability. We didn't get a reputation for wet weather for nothing. During the summer, sudden thundershowers or snowstorms can give even experienced hikers a surprise. So it's best to bring extra clothing for those unexpected weather fronts.

Clothing that can ward off the cold is extremely important. Most accidents in the wilderness are the result of, or complicated by, hypothermia, which can set in quickly and with little warning. Once a person starts getting cold, the ability to think and troubleshoot heads downhill. Symptoms of hypothermia include fatigue, drowsiness, unwillingness to go on, a feeling of deep cold or numbness, poor coordination, and mumbling. To avoid this, bring clothes that are easily layered. During the summer, that can be as simple as a warm fleece. During the winter, wool or synthetic fleeces are effective against the cold. A stocking cap is extremely helpful since a big chunk of body heat is lost through the head. Extra socks are helpful for keeping feet warm and comfortable. Remember that you can be vulnerable even in the summer—bitter July snowstorms are not unprecedented.

Rain gear, such as a waterproof jacket, pants, and a hat or hood, is equally important during all seasons, but especially during the fall and spring when it's practically impossible to head outdoors without rain. Even if there is no rain in the forecast, be prepared for it. (Local weather reporters are forecasting for the cities, not the mountains.) And short but serious rainstorms are the year-round norm, not the exception, in the Pacific Northwest.

Light Source

Even veteran hikers who intend to go out only for a "quick" day hike can end up finishing in the dark. There were just too many things to see, too many lakes to swim in, and too many peaks to bag on that "short" hike. Often, getting back to the car or camp before it's dark requires the difficult task of leaving a beautiful place while it's still light out. Or perhaps while out on an easy forest hike, you're on schedule to get back before dark, but the thick forest canopy brings on night an hour or two early. There are lots of ways to get stuck in the outdoors in the dark. And what good are a map and compass if you can't see them? Plan ahead and bring an adequate light source. The market is flooded these days with cheap (and not so cheap) headlamps. Headlamps are basically small flashlights that fit around your head. They're great because they're bright and they keep your hands free, so you're better able to beat back brush on the trail or fend off hungry fellow campers around the dinner stove.

Sun Protection

Most hikers don't think that fierce sunburns are a serious concern in the notoriously gray Pacific Northwest. But during the summer, the sun can be extremely brutal, especially at higher altitudes where a few thousand feet of atmosphere can be sorely missed. A full day in the blazing sun is hard on the eyes as well.

Don't let the sun spoil an otherwise great day in the outdoors. Sunscreen is worth its weight in gold out on the trail. Be sure to apply it regularly, and keep kids lathered up as well. It helps to bring a hat and lightweight clothing with long sleeves, both of which can make sunscreen almost unnecessary. Finally, many hikers swear by a good pair of sunglasses. Perhaps obvious during the summer, sunglasses are also a snowshoer's best friend. Snow blindness is a serious threat on beautiful sunny days during the winter.

All of these measures will make a trip not only safer but more enjoyable as well. Avoiding sunburn is also extremely helpful in warding off heat stroke, a serious condition in the backcountry.

First-Aid Kit

A first-aid kit is an important essential to carry while out on the trail. With twigs, rocks, and bears lurking around every corner, hiking can be dangerous business. Injuries can range from small abrasions to serious breaks, and a simple but well-stocked first-aid kit can be a lifesaver. It's best to purchase a first-aid kit at an outdoors store. Kits come in different sizes, depending on intended use, and include the fundamentals. Also, a number of organizations provide medical training for backcountry situations. Courses run from one-day seminars in simple first aid all the way to month-long classes for wilderness EMT certification. Outdoors enthusiasts who venture out on a regular basis should consider a course in Wilderness First Aid (WOOFA) or Wilderness First Response (WOOFER).

Band-aids come in every kit but are only helpful for small, nonserious cuts or abrasions. Here are a few things that are especially important and can come in handy in an emergency:

- Ibuprofen: It works very well to combat swelling. Twist an ankle or suffer a nasty bruise and reducing the swelling quickly becomes an important consideration.
- Athletic tape and gauze: These are helpful in treating twisted or strained joints. A firm wrap with athletic tape will make the three-mile hobble to the car less of an ordeal.
- Travel-size supplies of general medicines: Items like Alka-Seltzer or NyQuil are multipurpose and practical.

Finally: The only thing better than having a first-aid kit on the trail is not needing one.

Emergency Kit

You'll probably have a hard time finding a pre-prepared emergency kit for sale at any store. Instead, this is something that you can quickly and inexpensively assemble yourself.

- Space blanket: Find these at any outdoor store or army surplus store. They're small, shiny blankets that insulate extremely well, are highly visible, and will make do in place of a tent when needed.
- Signal mirror: A signal mirror is handy when you're lost. Catch the glare of the sun, and you can signal your position to search-and-rescue hikers or planes. The small mirror that comes attached to some compasses works perfectly.
- Whistle: Again, if you get really lost, don't waste your breath screaming and hollering. You'll lose your voice quickly, and it doesn't carry far anyhow. Blow your whistle all day or night long, and you'll still be able to talk to the trees (or yourself).

Fire Starter

Some people prefer matches while others choose to bring along a lighter. Either way, it's important to have something with which to start a fire. Don't think that you can start your fire by rubbing two sticks together. Even when it's dry, sticks don't like to start up easily. So be certain to purchase some quality waterproof matches (you can make your own with paraffin wax and wooden matches), or carry a couple of lighters. Regardless of your choice, keep them packed away in a safe and dry place (like a plastic sandwich baggie). Besides a starter, bring along something to keep the fire going for a bit. Fire pellets are available at any outdoor store. Do-it-yourselfers will be glad to know that toilet paper is highly flammable, as are cotton balls dipped in Vaseline. Starting a fire when it's cold, dark, and wet can save your life.

Multipurpose Knife

For outdoors enthusiasts, the multipurpose Swiss Army knife is one of the greatest things since sliced bread. Handy utility knives come in all shapes and sizes and are made by about a hundred different companies. A high-quality utility knife will come in handy in a multitude of situations. The features available include big knives and little knives, saws and scissors, corkscrews and screwdrivers, and about 30 other fun little tools. They are useful almost everywhere, except at the airport.

HIKING GEAR

You don't need to break the bank to be prepared for a hiking trip. However, it is important to make sure you are properly outfitted and clothed before embarking for the outdoors. When planning for a hike, be sure to know the general climate and expected weather for that part of the state; the length of the hike and the expected time of day that you will be out on the trail; the range of elevation on the trail you have selected; and any special needs of the hiker. A properly prepared hiker is a hiker likely to return home in one piece and with a good experience.

Clothing

First, know what the expected weather is for the time and place of your planned trip. The climate on the west side of the Cascades is far different than that of the east side. Elevation plays a major factor in weather as well, affecting both precipitation and temperature.

The best approach to clothing is to wear layers. This means you have several items of clothing that you can layer, taking things on and off while hiking. For example, you might start your hike in the morning with a t-shirt and fleece when it's colder, put the fleece in your pack during the hot part of the day, and then pile on a t-shirt, fleece, and rain jacket during that unexpected evening rain shower. The longer your hike, the more layers are recommended.

When dressing for a hike, it's important to avoid cotton clothing, especially if rain is a possibility. Clothing made from cotton can be dangerous when wet because it does not dry easily or quickly. While wet, cotton draws a significant amount of warmth from your body and can quickly lead to hypothermia. Stick to natural fabrics such as wool or synthetic fabrics such as polyester or polypropylene. T-shirts, pants (especially denim jeans), and sweatshirts made from cotton are not recommended when venturing out on the trail.

Shoes and Socks

A good pair of footwear is perhaps the most important piece of gear for any hiker. Footwear should accomplish several goals at once. First, footwear should protect the ankles. Twisted ankles are common occurrences while hiking; sturdy boots that cover and lace up to the ankle are recommended. Second, footwear should keep your feet dry. Feet face all kinds of wet obstacles in the woods, from rain, puddles, and mud to stream crossings small and large. Boots are best at keeping your feet dry. Third, footwear should be comfortable. It's important to break in new boots or shoes before venturing out. Replace insoles regularly to maintain cushion. Regularly apply an approved water-proofing agent to leather boots and maintain the seams. If you pick the right footwear, your feet will thank you.

As important as good footwear is to comfortable hiking, the socks you wear can be just as important. Thick hiking socks are preferred because of their extra padding. Liner socks are thin socks that are worn under hiking socks. They aid in preventing blisters, and when it comes to blisters, the best approach is to keep them from forming in the first place. Once blisters form, an excellent remedy is moleskin, a soft adhesive pad that goes right on top of blisters and provides welcome relief. Moleskin is available at drug stores and most outdoors stores.

Equipment

A trip to the local outdoor store will prove that there is an amazing amount of gear produced for the hiking market. There may be dozens of items to choose from when buying a backpack, sleeping bag, or rain gear. And there is no end to the specialty items, such as titanium forks, portable espresso machines, and bells to ward off bears. Is all of this really necessary? Probably not. To be prepared, ask yourself a few simple questions in preparation. First, how long is your trip expected to last. A day hike may not need more than a daypack, some water and food, an extra layer of clothing, a small first aid kit, and navigational aids (map, compass, GPS). An overnight trip requires much more. Second, think through your trip and picture the activities you'll be doing. Sleeping? Picture a tent, a sleeping bag, and a sleeping pad. Cooking? Picture a stove, fuel, a lighter, cookware, utensils, and food. Third, how much can you carry? The idea is not to reach that theoretical limit (it can be expected to change one mile into your hike), but to make the pack weight comfortable. Each hiking trip is an opportunity to learn what you do and don't need in your pack. Finally, consider items that may be helpful for you. Trekking poles are extremely helpful when hiking down a long descent or for people with "more experienced" knees. Water filters are sometimes preferred to treating water with chemicals. A field guide and binoculars can add a lot to a wilderness experience. The basic rule to equipment is: Pack only what you need and can carry.

CLIMATE AND WEATHER PROTECTION

As parts of the Pacific Northwest, Oregon and Washington share very similar climates. The two states are generally broken into two parts, with the north-south Cascade Mountain Range as a dividing line. Generally, weather systems move off of the Pacific Ocean and move inland to the east. The Cascades generally act as a barrier, wringing out much of the systems' moisture over the western sides of the states. As a result, the eastern portions of our states are considerably dryer with more sunshine. Hikes located east of the Cascades are often good alternatives when the weather on the Westside is not cooperating.

Seasons

Each of the seasons are distinct in the Pacific Northwest. It is important to select a hike for the proper season, as the winter snows turn many trails from easy hikes to difficult or impossible.

Spring is a time of warming temperatures and frequent rainfall. The mountain snowpack experiences a significant melt but can easily last into July in certain years and locations. Many hikes begin to open up east of the Cascades during this season.

Summer rarely starts on time in the Pacific Northwest. By late June, hikers can finally expect the return of warmer temperatures and sunny days to the west sides of the states. On the east sides, temperatures are significantly warmer and regularly break 100 degrees Fahrenheit. The air is much dryer, too, making dehydration and heat exhaustion a concern. At night, significant drops in the temperature are common on the east side as well as at higher elevations.

Fall is my favorite hiking season. September and October bring cooler temperatures to both sides of the states, but the rains generally lag behind. By November, nightly lows begin reaching the freezing point in many parts of the Northwest, especially at higher elevations.

During the winter, lower elevations west of the Cascades see frequent rain and cooler temperatures while the mountains receive heavy snowfall. East of the Cascades, snow is common and the temperature regularly drops below the freezing point.

Rain Gear

Yes, it rains in the Pacific Northwest. In some places, it rains over 100 inches each year. So is rain gear important? Absolutely. Staying dry is the key to staying warm and avoiding hypothermia. In the northwest, hypothermia is just as likely in wet, cool weather as during dry, very cold weather. A rain jacket and even rain pants are highly recommended for hiking in the Northwest anytime outside of summer. Know the expected weather and prepare accordingly. Personally, I carry a light rain jacket on every hike I take in every season; it also doubles as a good extra layer if the temperature drops.

SAFETY AND FIRST AID

A hiking trip rarely goes exactly as planned. Sometimes, injuries or other hazards are encountered. Since hiking trips often remove you from immediate medical care or rescue, it is important to be prepared.

Plants

The Pacific Northwest does not have many dangerous plants. In drier parts of Oregon and Washington, including the southern Cascades in Oregon, hikers should be on the lookout for poison oak. The plant often grows as a thick shrub and more rarely as a vine. The leaves are green and may appear glossy; the sheen is the toxin of the plant. Each leaf actually looks like three smaller leaves, leading to the warning, "Leaves of three, let it be." The oils from poison oak are extremely irritating to the skin and should be treated with a cleanser such as Tecnu.

Insects

Spring and early summer are the prime seasons for insects in the Pacific Northwest. Mosquitoes and other biting insect populations peak in the weeks following the spring snowmelt. They are particularly abundant at high elevations during this time. Bug spray is recommended. During this time, parts of

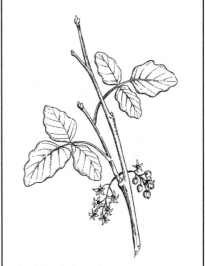

Avoiding Poison Oak: Remember the old Boy Scout saying: "Leaves of three, let them be."

Eastern Oregon and Washington also experience outbreaks of ticks. These pesky insects occasionally carry Lyme disease. It is a good idea to carry tick repellent when hiking on the east side during spring and summer.

First Aid

A first aid kit is never more appreciated than when it is needed. Unfortunately, it's impossible to know when it will come in handy. So it is important to always carry at least a small first aid kit on every hike. A decent first aid kit should have items to dress and bandage cuts or scrapes; wraps or other items to wrap sprains; medicine to address pain or swelling (ibuprofen is ideal); and moleskin to treat blisters. Additionally, some safety items are worth carrying on every trip. This includes a safety blanket (for warmth), a signal mirror and whistle for getting found when lost, and materials to start a fire if needed.

Some first aid issues deserve special consideration. First, hypothermia is a critical concern and can quickly lead to serious trouble on the trail. The best way to avoid hypothermia is to stay dry with rain gear and to stay warm with appropriate clothing. Aggressively treat hypothermia by attempting to raise body temperature, whether through physical activity, warm liquids, or getting into a dry clothes and a sleeping bag. Second, dehydration is just as serious a concern in warmer weather. Carrying enough water is important in warding off dehydration and other effects, such as heat exhaustion.

Third, our bodies need water to keep on hiking, but that water needs to be free of bacteria and parasites. If you plan on obtaining water from a source in the wild, it is important to treat it by boiling it, collecting it with a filter, or treating with chemicals (chlorination or iodination). Fourth, sunburn can occur quickly during the summer. Hiking at higher elevations with thinner air can decrease the amount of exposure before becoming sunburned. If hiking during the summer, especially on the east sides of our states, sunscreen is important and should always be carried.

Navigational Tools

You may know where you want to go on your trip, but do you know how to get there? This is where carrying proper navigational tools comes in. First, it is highly recommended to carry a map on all trips. With only a map, it is often possible to orientate yourself and return to a trail or trailhead. Conversely, other navigational tools are worthless without a map. Second, a compass or GPS unit is recommended. Whether you choose a simple compass or purchase a high-end GPS unit, it is important to know how to use them. Each device has advantages and disadvantages over the other, but both items will do little to help you find your way if you don't understand how to use them. Third, carrying a headlamp is always recommended in case you are unexpectedly still on the trail when it becomes dark. Negotiating a trail in the dark is dangerous and likely to lead to injury or becoming further lost.

ON THE TRAIL

It's Friday afternoon, work has been a trial all week, and there's only one thing on your mind: getting outdoors and hitting the trail for the weekend. For many of us, nature is a getaway from the confines of urban living. The irony of it all, however, is that the more people head to the backcountry, the less wild it truly is. That means that it takes a collective effort from all trail users to keep the outdoors as pristine as it was 100 years ago. This effort is so important, in fact, that the organization Leave No Trace has created an ideology for low-impact use of our wilderness. (For more information on the Leave No Trace Center for Outdoor Ethics and their values, check out their website at www.lnt.org.) Here are a few principles that we all can follow to ensure that the great outdoors continues to be great.

Planning Your Trip

A little careful planning and preparation not only makes your trip safer, but it also makes it easy to minimize resource damage. Make sure you know the regulations, such as group size limits or campfire regulations, before hitting the trail. Prepare for any special circumstances an area may have, such as the need for ice axes or water filters. Many places are visited heavily during summer weekends. Schedule your trip for a weekday or off-season, and you'll encounter far fewer fellow bipeds.

Hiking and Camping

One of the most important principles for hikers and campers here in the Pacific Northwest is to minimize our impact on the land. Many of our greatest and most heavily used trails visit fragile environments, such as alpine meadows and lakeshores. These ecosystems are easily injured by hikers and campers. Take care to travel only on the main trail, never cut a switchback, and avoid the social trails—small, unofficial trails

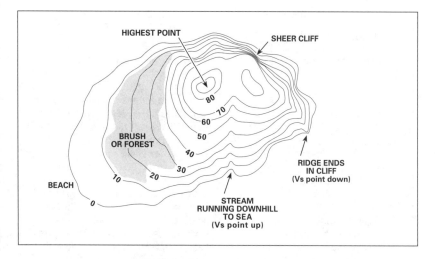

that are made over years by hikers cutting trails—that spiderweb through many a high meadow. When camping, pitch camp in already established sites, never on a meadow. Take care in selecting a site for a camp kitchen and when heading off for the bathroom. Being aware of how your impact not only improves the experience for yourself but also for those who follow you.

Packing Out Your Trash

It goes without saying that trash does not belong in the great outdoors. That goes for all trash, regardless of whether it's biodegradable or not. From food packaging to the food itself, it has to go out the way it came in: on your back. Ditto for toilet paper. As far as human waste goes, dig a cat hole for your waste, and pack all toilet paper and hygiene products in bags. It may be gross, but it's only fair for others.

Leaving What You Find

The old saying goes, "Take only photographs and leave only footprints." Well, if you're walking on durable surfaces such as established trails, you won't even leave footprints. And it's best to leave the artifacts of nature where they belong: in nature. By doing so, you ensure that others can enjoy them as well. If you see something interesting, remember that it is only there because the hiker in front of you left it for you to find. The same goes for attractive rocks, deer and elk antlers, and wildflowers. Avoid altering sites by digging trenches, building lean-tos, or harming trees.

Lighting Campfires

Thanks to Smokey the Bear, we all know the seriousness of forest fires. If you're going to have a fire, make sure it's out before going to sleep or leaving camp. But there are other important considerations for campfires. In Washington and Oregon, many national forests and wildernesses have fire bans above 3,500 feet. At these higher altitudes, trees grow slowly and depend greatly on decomposition of downed trees. Burning downed limbs and trees robs the ecosystems of much-needed nutrients, an impact that lasts centuries. Carry a camp stove any time you plan on cooking while backpacking.

HIKING ETIQUETTE

1. Leave no trace. We love hiking for the opportunity to leave civilization behind and enjoy nature. Thus, we all need to leave the trail as nice – or nicer – than we found it. Pack all litter out (even litter that others may have left behind, if you're so inclined). Do not leave graffiti or other marks on trees or rocks. Let wildlife stay wild by not feeding or harassing animals. If you find something interesting, it's likely that someone else will also find it interesting: Be sure to leave rocks, flowers, and other natural objects where you find them.

2. Stay on the trail. Pacific Northwest trails are heavily used. While just one person cutting a switchback or zipping off trail through a meadow has little consequence, the cumulative damage from many hikers wandering off trail is all too easy to spot. Avoid erosion and unsightly way-trails by hiking only on established trails.

3. Yield to uphill hikers. Hikers who are headed up an incline have the right-of-way. After all, uphill hikers have built up momentum and are working hard to put trail beneath their feet. Downhill hikers should find a safe place to step off the trail and allow others to pass.

4. Keep dogs under control. Yes, we all love to take our best friends out on the trail. But they need to stay on the trail. Out-of-control dogs can easily end up lost in the woods. While a leash is not always necessary, one should be carried at all times and used when on a busy trail. Where dogs are not permitted, it is bad form and even dangerous to take them along.

5. Be respectful of others. Be aware of your noise level, and make way for others. Common courtesy creates community on the trail and enhances everyone's experience. Remember, our public lands belong to no one and everyone at the same time.

Encountering Wildlife

Hiking is all about being outdoors. Fresh air, colorful wildflowers, expansive mountain views, and a little peace and quiet are what folks are after as they embark on the trail. The great outdoors is also home to creatures big and small. Remember, you are in their home: No chasing the deer. No throwing rocks at the chipmunks. No bareback riding the elk. And no wrestling the bears. In all seriousness, the most important way we can respect wildlife is by not feeding them. Chipmunks may be cute, but feeding them only makes them fat and dependent on people for food. Keep a clean camp without food on the ground, and be sure to hang food anytime you're separated from it. A good bear hang is as much about keeping the bears out of the food as it is about keeping the mice and squirrels from eating it.

Nearly all wildlife in the Pacific Northwest is completely harmless to hikers; bears and cougars are the only wildlife that pose a danger to us humans. Fortunately, the vast majority of encounters with these big predators result in nothing more than a memorable story. Coming across bears and cougars may be frightening, but these encounters don't need to be dangerous as long as you follow a few simple precautions.

BEARS

Running into a bear is the most common worry of novice hikers when they hit the trail. Bears are big, furry, and naturally a bit scary at first sight. But in reality, bears want little to do with people and much prefer to avoid us altogether. The chance of getting into a fistfight with a bear is rare in the Pacific Northwest. In our region, there have only been a handful of attacks, most of them non-fatal. As long as you stay away from bear cubs and food, bears will almost certainly leave you alone.

What kind of bear will you see out on the trail? Most likely, you won't see one at all, but if you do, it will almost certainly be a black bear. Grizzlies occasionally visit some remote parts of Washington, but black bears, whose thick coats range from light tan to cinnamon to black, are by far the most numerous. Grizzly bears are primarily located along the Canadian border in the Pasayten Wilderness and Selkirk Mountains. Grizzlies have a distinctive hump between their shoulders.

The old image of Yogi the Bear stealing picnic baskets is not that far off. Bears love to get ahold of human food, so proper food storage is an effective way to avoid an unwanted bear encounter. When camping, be sure to use a bear hang. Collect all food, toiletries, and anything else with scent; place it all in a stuff sack and hang the sack in a tree. The sack should be at least 12 feet off the ground and eight feet from the tree trunk.

Should you come across a bear on the trail, stay calm. It's okay to be scared, but with a few precautions, you will be completely safe. First, know that your objective is not to intimidate the bear but simply to let it know you are not easy prey. Make yourself look big by standing tall, waving your arms, or even holding open your jacket. Second, don't look it in the eye. Bears consider eye contact to be aggressive and an invitation to a confrontation. Third, speak loudly and firmly to the bear. Bears are nearsighted and can't make out objects from afar. But a human voice means humans, and a bear is likely to retreat from your presence. If a bear advances, it is very likely only trying to get a better look. Finally, if the bear doesn't budge, go around it in a wide circle. In case the unlikely should occur and the bear attacks, curl up in a ball, stay as still as possible, and wait for the attack to end. If the bear bites, take a cheap shot at the nose. Bears hate being hit on their sensitive noses. Trying to hit a bear from this position is difficult. It can work if you can cover your neck with one hand and swing with the other. Protecting yourself is first priority. If the bear is especially aggressive, it's necessary to fight back. Most important, don't let fear of bears prevent you from getting out there; it's rare to see a bear and even rarer to have a problem with one.

COUGARS

With millions of acres of wilderness, the Pacific Northwest is home to cougars, bobcats, and lynx. Bobcats and lynx are small and highly withdrawn. If you encounter one of these recluses, you're in a small minority. Cougars are also very shy, and encounters with these big cats are rare. Cougar attacks are extremely uncommon. You're more likely to be struck by lightning than attacked by a cougar. In most circumstances, sighting a cougar will just result in having a great story to tell.

If you should encounter a cougar in the wild, make every effort to intimidate it. First, don't run! A cougar views something running from it as dinner. Second, make yourself bigger by waving your arms, jumping around, and spreading open a jacket. Cougars have very little interest in a tough fight. Third, don't bend down to pick up a rock; you'll only look smaller to the cougar. Fourth, stare the cougar down—a menacing stare-down is intimidating for a cougar. Finally, should a cougar attack, fight back with everything you have and as dirtily as possible.

Respecting Other Hikers

If you are considerate of others on the trail, they are likely to return the favor. This includes such simple things as yielding right-of-way to those who are trudging uphill, keeping noise to a minimum, and observing any use regulations, such as no mountain bikes and no fires. If possible, try to set up camp off trail and out of sight. Together, everyone can equally enjoy the beauties of hiking in the Pacific Northwest.

Hiking with Dogs

Though not everyone may have a dog, nearly everyone has an opinion about dogs on the trail. Hiking with canine friends can be a great experience, not only for us but for them, as well. What dog doesn't love being out on the trail, roaming the wild and in touch with his ancestral roots? That's great, but there are a few matters that must be considered before taking a dog on a hike.

First, be aware that national parks do not allow dogs on any trail at any time. However, dogs are allowed throughout national forests and any wildernesses contained within them. Second, dogs should remain on the trail at all times. Dogs can create an enormous amount of erosion when roaming off trail, and they're frequent switchback cutters. Third, dogs must be under control at all times. Leashes are not always mandatory because many dogs are obedient and do very well while unleashed. But if you're not going to use a leash, your dog should respond to commands well and not

HIKING WITH KIDS

1. Prepare, prepare, prepare. Heading out on the trail with kids calls for extra preparation. Hiking essentials are more important than ever. And be ready for the unexpected: Bring something extra to drink and eat, and bring proper rain/sun protection. And don't hesitate to involve them – kids often love to help pack.

2. Pick the right hike. Kids are much more likely to enjoy hiking if the trail is appropriate for their age and ability. And don't assume the trail will need to include peaks and summits for kids to enjoy the journey: From bugs and animals to streams and forests, kids will find something in nature to interest them (if they aren't wiped from the hike).

3. Gear up. Hiking with children doesn't mean you have to drop a week's pay at REI. But making sure you and your little hiker have the proper gear is important for safety and enjoyment. Comfortable footwear and weather-appropriate clothing are musts. A backpack for your child helps them feel involved in the "work" of hiking; just make sure it's not too heavy. And parents should be carrying extra water and food for all.

4. Be flexible. Hiking is not mandatory. Our parents may have insisted that discomfort builds character, but kids often know when enough is enough for their bodies. Accommodating a request to turn around before the intended destination can be rewarded by a request for another trip soon. Remember, the point is for each hiker to enjoy the journey.

5. Be attentive. When hiking with children, there are more factors to keep in mind. Kids may be getting wet or cold, sunburned or overheated. Many hikes have inherent danger, such as cliffs, snakes, poison oak, or slippery ground. Keep an eye on your little hikers and they will be around for many hikes to come.

bother other hikers. Finally, be aware that dogs and wildlife don't mix well. Dogs love to chase chipmunks, rabbits, deer, and anything else that moves. But from the chipmunk's point of view, a big, slobbering beast chasing you is stressful and unequivocally bad. Not only that, but dogs can incite aggression in bears or cougars. An unleashed dog can quickly transform a peaceful bear into a raging assault of claws and teeth. Plus, bears and cougars find dogs to be especially tasty. Don't hesitate to bring your dog out on the trail as long as you take the dog's interests, as well as other hikers' interests, into consideration.

PERMITS

You've got your pack ready, done your food shopping, purchased the right maps, and even wrestled the kids into the car. But do you have the right permits? Here in the Pacific Northwest, there are several permits that you may need before you can hit the trail. Headed for a national forest? Read up on the Northwest Forest Pass. Driving down to Mount Rainier or the Olympics? You probably need a National Parks Pass. Backpacking in a national park? Don't forget your backcountry camping permit.

Northwest Forest Pass

The Northwest Forest Pass (NWFP) is the most widely used permit in our states. The pass is accepted at 680 day-use recreation sites in Washington and Oregon. Almost every trailhead in every national forest in Washington requires a NWFP for parking. Remarkably, a Northwest Forest Pass is all that is required in the North Cascades National Park. The Colville National Forest is the one agency that does not participate in the NWFP program; access to trailheads in the Colville is free.

In Oregon, each National Forest follows its own rules regarding the NWFP. Most of the national forests here require a pass at a majority of their trailheads, such as Mount Hood and Willamette National Forests. In contrast, Ochoco and Malheur National Forests do not require the pass at any trailheads.

Senior citizens take note: In lieu of a NWFP, the federal Golden Eagle, Golden Access, and Golden Age passes are accepted.

The Northwest Forest Pass costs $30 and is valid for one year from date of purchase. It's interchangeable between vehicles in the same household. Day passes may also be purchased at a cost of $5 per day. More than 240 vendors across the northwest offer the pass, including all ranger stations, most outdoor stores, and many service stations in recreational areas. Passes can also be ordered online through Nature of the Northwest at www.naturenw.org. Proceeds from Northwest Forest Passes go toward improvements at recreational sites, including refurbishing trailheads, trail maintenance and construction, and environmental education. There is a lot of controversy over the pass, as critics contend that national forests are public lands and already paid for by federal taxes. They have a point, but the revenue serves to supplement ever-dwindling forest service budgets.

National Parks Passes and Permits

No question, the United States has the world's premier national park system. From Acadia National Park in Maine to Denali National Park in Alaska, the United States has taken care to preserve our most important ecosystems for future generations to enjoy.

In Washington, we have the North Cascades, Olympic, and Mount Rainier National Parks to savor, and in Oregon, we have Crater Lake. Any of the national parks passes are good for one year at all national parks in the United States. National parks passes include: the National Parks Pass ($50 and good at any national park in the United States for one year), the Golden Access Pass (available for people who are blind or permanently disabled and allows lifetime admittance to any national park for free), and the Golden Age Pass (available to people 62 years or older and allows lifetime admittance to any national park for a one-time fee of $10).

Washington

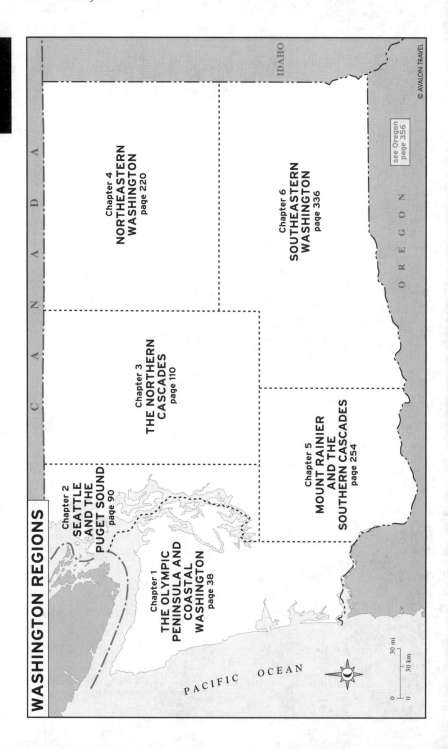

WASHINGTON REGIONS

Chapter 2
SEATTLE AND THE PUGET SOUND
page 90

Chapter 1
THE OLYMPIC PENINSULA AND COASTAL WASHINGTON
page 38

Chapter 3
THE NORTHERN CASCADES
page 110

Chapter 4
NORTHEASTERN WASHINGTON
page 220

Chapter 5
MOUNT RAINIER AND THE SOUTHERN CASCADES
page 254

Chapter 6
SOUTHEASTERN WASHINGTON
page 336

CANADA

IDAHO

OREGON

see Oregon page 356

© AVALON TRAVEL

PACIFIC OCEAN

30 mi
30 km
0
0

THE OLYMPIC PENINSULA AND COASTAL WASHINGTON

© SCOTT LEONARD

BEST HIKES

◖ **Beach and Coastal Walks**
Shi Shi Beach, **page 45.**
Dungeness Spit, **page 52.**
Second Beach, **page 52.**
Cape Disappointment State Park, **page 85.**

◖ **Hikes Through Old-Growth Forests**
Hoh River, **page 61.**

◖ **Short Backpacking Trips**
Ozette Triangle, **page 46.**

◖ **Hikes for Waterfalls**
Sol Duc Falls/Lover's Lane, **page 55.**

There may be drier regions of Washington – the

Olympic Mountains get more than 200 inches a year – but the Olympic Peninsula is one of the United States' most unique places. Three distinct and beautiful environments grace this isolated and lightly inhabited peninsula.

On the west side is the Pacific Ocean and the Olympic Coast Wilderness, where picturesque sea stacks and tidal pools bless one of the West Coast's finest stretches of coastline. Protected by wilderness and wildlife designations, the Olympic Coast is environmentally rich. Bald eagles patrol the skies, while sea otters play in the surf. Trails run the length of the Olympic Coast: good day hikes, overnighters, and longer trips.

Farther inland are the area's famous rainforests: giant trees, and moss seemingly blanketing anything that will sit still for a minute. If you've never visited the Olympic rainforest, you're in for a treat. One of the country's few rainforests, the west side of the peninsula grows some of the earth's largest trees. Western hemlock, Sitka spruce, and western red cedar tower some 200-300 feet overhead, forming giant canopies over dense understories of vine maple, elderberry, devil's club, and salmonberry. On the rare dry spring or fall day, humidity hangs in the air, wetting everything it touches – even Gore-Tex. The Bogachiel, Hoh, and Quinault River Valleys are full of trails that explore this great area.

Finally, the wild and beautiful Olympic Mountains, with their subalpine meadows and flowing glaciers, which spread down the valleys for miles, producing distinctive U-shaped valleys. The Olympics are profoundly unique in that they have a circular shape, known as a radial formation. The river drainages start in the center of the range and flow outward. The mountains got their start as deposits of lava and sedimentation under the Pacific Ocean. Gradually they were bent out of shape by the Juan de Fuca plate colliding offshore with the continental plate. The light sedimentary rocks, driven below the heavier continental plate, eventually broke through and sprang like a cork to the surface, creating the circular shape. More recently, the Ice Age left its mark on the range. The Cordilleran ice sheet scraped past and around the mountains, creating the picturesque Hood Canal. To say the least, the Olympics are a great place to geek out on geology.

Several unique species call these forests home, including Roosevelt elk, Olympic salamanders, and Olympic marmots. Late summer in the high country is practically a bear mecca, when the sedate creatures gorge themselves into a stupor on ripe huckleberries. Of the Olympics' many rivers, the longest is the glacier-fed Elwha River, which once bore populations of all five Northwest salmon species. Also on the north peninsula are trails out of Hurricane Ridge, an outstanding visitors center at 6,000 feet.

The northeastern portion of the range is distinguishable by its relatively light rainfall: The mountains receive as little as 20 inches of annual rainfall – an anomaly in this rainy region. Most fronts move off the Pacific in a southwest to northeast direction, and as wet air from the ocean crosses the range, the water is squeezed out over the western side. By the time the air reaches the east side, much of the rain has fallen already, leaving the "rain shadow" dry. All of the retirees flocking to Sequim couldn't be happier. While this region is noticeably drier (tell that to someone hiking here in October), it has some extraordinary richness in landscape and forests.

Moving southward, the rest of the eastern side of the range is comprised of rivers dropping quickly from high mountain crests to the Hood Canal, including the Dosewallips, Duckabush, Hamma Hamma, and Skokomish Rivers. This area receives its fair share of rain, certainly more than the rain shadow.

Whether you're looking for a quiet stroll among tidal pools or a long, satisfying climb to an alpine summit, the Olympic Peninsula satisfies.

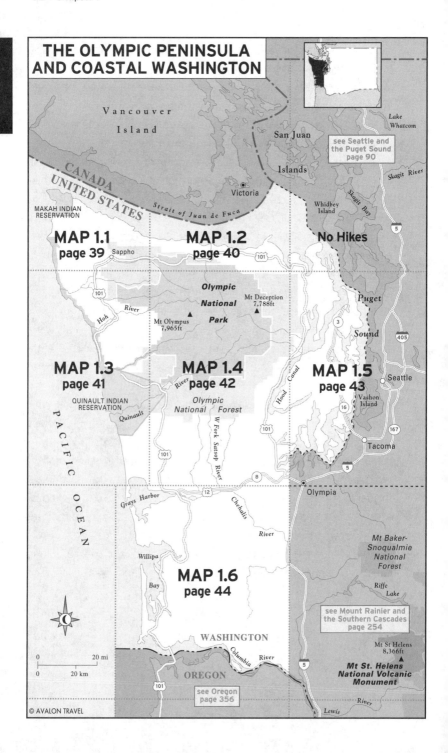

THE OLYMPIC PENINSULA AND COASTAL WASHINGTON

Vancouver Island

San Juan Islands

Lake Whatcom

see Seattle and the Puget Sound page 90

Skagit River

CANADA
UNITED STATES

Victoria

Strait of Juan de Fuca

Whidbey Island

Skagit Bay

MAKAH INDIAN RESERVATION

MAP 1.1
page 39   Sappho

MAP 1.2
page 40   101

No Hikes

5

Olympic

National

Park

Mt Deception 7,788ft

Mt Olympus 7,965ft

Puget

3

Sound

405

Hoh   River

MAP 1.3
page 41

QUINAULT INDIAN RESERVATION

Quinault

River

MAP 1.4
page 42

Olympic National Forest

W Fork Satsop River

Hood Canal

MAP 1.5
page 43   Seattle

Vashon Island

16

167

101

101

Tacoma

5

8

P A C I F I C   O C E A N

Grays Harbor

12

Chehalis

River

Olympia

Mt Baker-Snoqualmie National Forest

Willipa

Bay

MAP 1.6
page 44

Riffe Lake

see Mount Rainier and the Southern Cascades page 254

0   20 mi
0   20 km

WASHINGTON

Columbia   River

Mt St Helens 8,366ft

Mt St. Helens National Volcanic Monument

OREGON

101

see Oregon page 356

Lewis   River

© AVALON TRAVEL

Map 1.1

Hikes 1-4
Pages 45-48

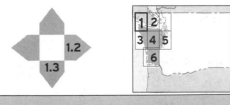

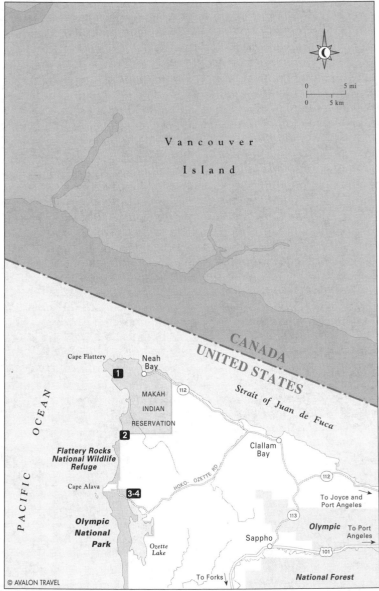

© AVALON TRAVEL

Map 1.2

Hikes 5-10
Pages 48-52

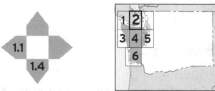

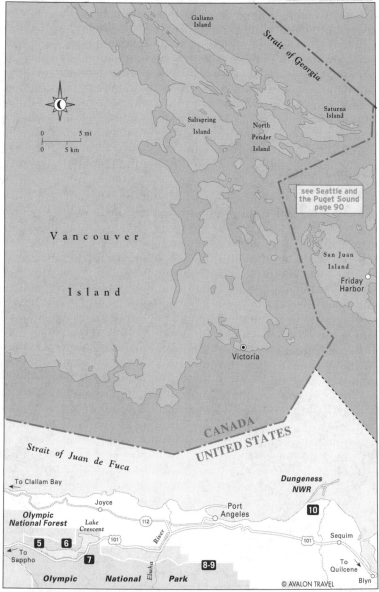

Galiano Island

Strait of Georgia

Saltspring Island

North Pender Island

Saturna Island

see Seattle and the Puget Sound page 90

San Juan Island

Friday Harbor

V a n c o u v e r

I s l a n d

Victoria

CANADA

UNITED STATES

Strait of Juan de Fuca

0   5 mi
0   5 km

To Clallam Bay

Dungeness NWR

Joyce

Port Angeles

10

Olympic National Forest

Lake Crescent

(112)

(101)

Sequim

5   **6**

To Sappho

7

Elwha River

(101)

To Quilcene

8-9

Olympic   National   Park

Blyn

© AVALON TRAVEL

Map 1.3

Hikes 11-14
Pages 52-54

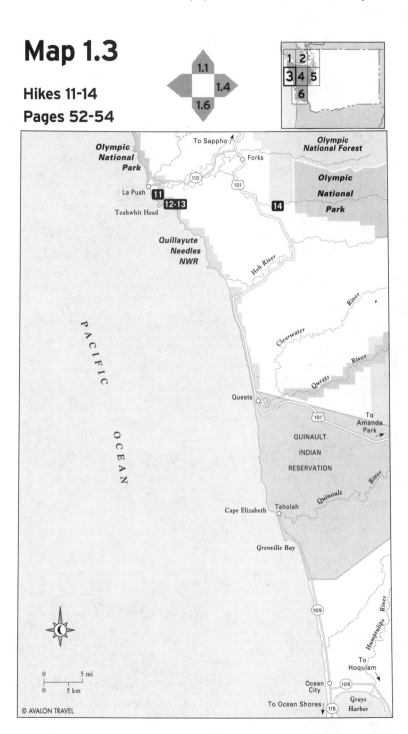

Map 1.4

Hikes 15-57
Pages 55-83

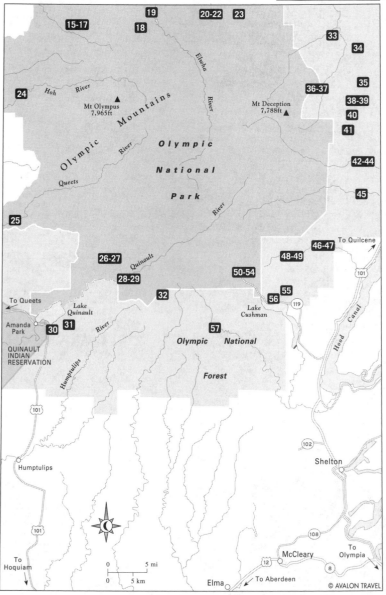

Map 1.5

Hike 58
Page 84

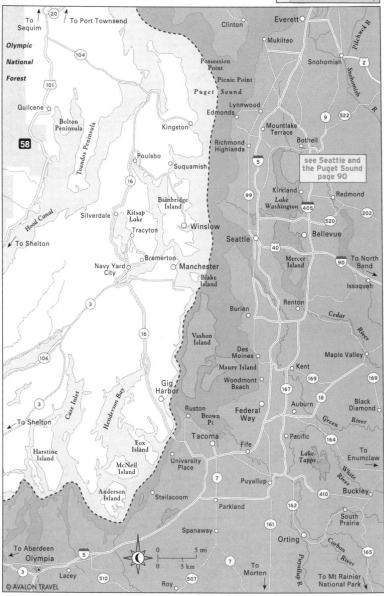

Map 1.6

Hikes 59-61

Pages 84-85

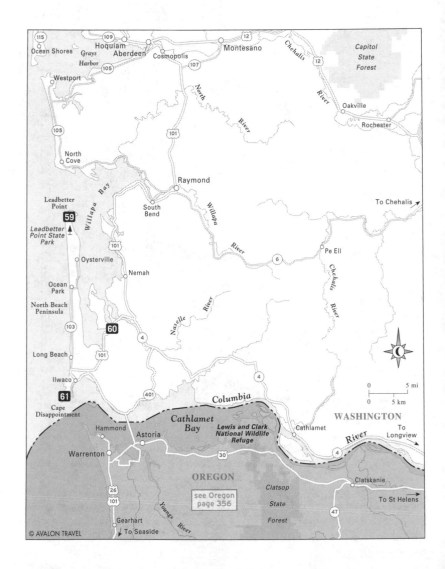

Ocean Shores
115
Hoquiam
109
Aberdeen
Cosmopolis
Montesano
12
Chehalis
Capitol State Forest

Grays Harbor
105
107
12
River

Westport

North River

Oakville

Rochester

105
101

North Cove

Raymond

Leadbetter Point
Willapa Bay
South Bend
To Chehalis

59
Leadbetter Point State Park

Oysterville
101
Nemah
Willapa River
6
Pe Ell
Chehalis River

Ocean Park

North Beach Peninsula
103
60
4
Naselle River

Long Beach
101

Ilwaco
4

61
401
Columbia River

Cape Disappointment

Hammond
Astoria
Cathlamet Bay
Lewis and Clark National Wildlife Refuge
Cathlamet
WASHINGTON
To Longview

Warrenton
30
4

OREGON
Clatsop State Forest
Clatskanie
To St Helens

26
101
see Oregon page 356
47

Gearhart
Youngs River
To Seaside

0   5 mi
0   5 km

© AVALON TRAVEL

1 CAPE FLATTERY
1.5 mi/1.0 hr   🚶1 ⛰9

northwest of Neah Bay on the Makah Indian Reservation

Map 1.1, page 39

A newly refurbished trail leads through great coastal forest to one of the Washington Coast's most scenic places. The Makah Nation rebuilt Cape Flattery Trail several years back, taking a dangerous, muddy trail to near perfection. Four observation decks hover above sea cliffs overlooking the cape, providing views of ocean and wildlife. Birds and sea creatures flock to the area year-round. During the spring and fall, it's possible to sight gray whales.

Cape Flattery Trail works its way through a coastal forest of large old-growth cedars and firs. Many boardwalks and bridges along the way keep feet dry on this once infamously muddy trail. The trail pops out of the forest at the cape, above the Olympic Coast National Marine Sanctuary. The sanctuary designation provides protection for numerous animals. Scores of cormorants and tufted puffins make their way in and out of their homes in the sea cliffs. Below in the water, sea lions swim from cove to cove on the prowl for a meal. From mid-March through mid-April, Cape Flattery is a prime location for spotting migrating gray whales; binoculars are a must. Cape Flattery may be a long way from the rest of Washington, but North America's most northwestern point is awesome.

User Groups: Hikers and leashed dogs. No horses or mountain bikes are allowed. No wheelchair access.

Permits: This trail is accessible year-round. A Makah Recreation Pass is required to park here. An annual pass costs $10 and is available at most businesses in Neah Bay.

Maps: For topographic maps, ask Green Trails for No. 98S, Cape Flattery, or ask the USGS for Cape Flattery.

Directions: From Port Angeles, drive 5 miles west on U.S. 101 to Highway 112. Turn right (north) onto Highway 112 and drive 63 miles to Neah Bay. At the west end of town, turn left on Cape Flattery Road and drive to Cape Loop Road. Turn right and drive to the signed trailhead at road's end.

Contact: Makah Tribe, P.O. Box 115, Neah Bay, WA 98357, 360/645-2201.

2 SHI SHI BEACH
4.0–9.6 mi/2.0 hr–2 days   🚶1 ⛰10

south of the Makah Indian Reservation in Olympic National Park

Map 1.1, page 39   **BEST (**

Protected from development by wilderness designations, more than 75 miles of Olympic Coast remain in pristine condition, untamed by humans. This rich habitat sustains a biodiversity that offers unparalleled opportunities for seeing wildlife. And its most beautiful section lies here, from the wide, sandy shores of Shi Shi Beach to the rugged sea stacks at Point of the Arches.

The Makah Tribe recently began rebuilding Shi Shi Beach Trail from its reservation, providing new and easier access to this beach. The trail travels 2 muddy miles through forest before breaking out onto Shi Shi Beach. Two miles of beach stretching southward offer great strolling, even when the weather fails to cooperate (which is often). The beach is a good point to turn around, for those looking for a shorter hike.

Shi Shi Beach ends where Point of the Arches begins. Here, a large grouping of enormous sea stacks spread out into the sea off a point. Tidal pools abound here, offering excellent chances for seeing starfish and urchins. Sea otters often play in the water while bald eagles soar overhead in perpetual wind.

The trip to Point of the Arches (4.8 miles) can easily be done in one day, but camping is a popular activity along Shi Shi. Permits, however, must be obtained from the park service. Good sites are found regularly along the shore. Water should be obtained at Petroleum Creek (3.3 miles), which must be forded to

© SCOTT LEONARD

The views along the Olympic Coast are first-rate.

access Point of the Arches. It is an easy crossing made easier by low tides. Traveling south of Point of the Arches brings hikers to Cape Alava and the Ozette Triangle, not a recommended approach.

User Groups: Hikers only. No dogs, horses, or mountain bikes are allowed. No wheelchair access.

Permits: This trail is accessible year-round. A Makah Recreation Pass is required to park here. An annual pass costs $10 and is available at most businesses in Neah Bay. Overnight stays within the national park require backcountry camping permits, which are available at the Wilderness Information Center in Port Angeles.

Maps: For a map of Olympic National Park, contact the Outdoor Recreation Information Center at the downtown Seattle REI. For topographic maps, ask Green Trails for No. 98S, Cape Flattery, or ask the USGS for Makah Bay and Ozette.

Directions: From Port Angeles, drive 5 miles west on U.S. 101 to Highway 112. Turn right (north) onto Highway 112 and drive 63 miles to Neah Bay. At the west end of town, turn

left on Cape Flattery Road and drive 3 miles to Hobuck Beach Road. Turn left, cross the Waatch River, and drive to Sooes River. Here, Hobuck Beach Road becomes Sooes Beach Road. Cross the Sooes River and drive to the clearly marked trailhead on the right. The parking area here is for day use only. Overnight visitors can pay local homeowners (who have signs advertising parking) to park on their private property (where their cars will be secure).

Contact: Makah Tribe, P.O. Box 115, Neah Bay, WA 98357, 360/645-2201; Olympic Wilderness Information Center, located in the Olympic National Park, Wilderness Information Center, 3002 Mount Angeles Rd., Port Angeles, WA 98362-6798, 360/565-3130.

❸ OZETTE TRIANGLE
9.0 mi/1-2 days   🚶1 ⛺10

northwest of Forks in Olympic National Park

Map 1.1, page 39	BEST (

No route in Washington claims a heritage quite like the Ozette Triangle. Three trails form this triangle, with the leg along the beach home to Wedding Rocks. Wedding Rocks bear petroglyphs carved by Native Americans hundreds of years ago. Their illustrations depict orcas, the sun and moon, and even a ship of explorers. Even without Wedding Rocks, this beach would be highly popular. Large sea stacks set among larger islands, countless tide pools brimming with sea life, bald eagles aplenty, and possible sightings of gray whales make this a pleasurable trip.

Cape Alava and Sand Point Trails lead to the beach from Lake Ozette. Each trail is 3 miles long, flat, and forested by big trees. Boardwalk covers most of each trail and can be slippery; watch out! Starting on the northern route (Cape Alava) will drop you off at a coastline full of sea stacks and wildlife. The numerous campsites near Cape Alava require reservations (from the Port Angeles Wilderness Information Center) because of large summer crowds.

Head south from Cape Alava among countless tidal pools, brimming with life. Wedding Rocks are 1 mile south from Cape Alava, scattered around a jutting point; they are above the high tide line. The site is legendary for attracting cultists and other New Age folk, but you're more likely to run across sea otters floating offshore in beds of kelp. The beach extends south 2 miles before intersecting Sand Point Trail. Here, a large headland juts into the sea and provides an excellent vantage point from atop it. The Ozette Triangle is rightfully one of the peninsula's most beautiful hikes.

User Groups: Hikers only. No dogs, horses, or mountain bikes are allowed. No wheelchair access.

Permits: This trail is accessible year-round. There is a $1 daily parking fee here, payable at the trailhead. Overnight stays within the national park require backcountry camping permits, which are available at the Wilderness Information Center in Port Angeles.

Maps: For a map of Olympic National Park, contact the Outdoor Recreation Information Center at the downtown Seattle REI. For topographic maps, ask Green Trails for No. 135S, Ozette, or ask the USGS for Ozette.

Directions: From Port Angeles, drive east 5 miles on U.S. 101 to Highway 112. Turn right (west) and drive 49 miles to Hoko/Ozette Lake

© SCOTT LEONARD

tide pools at Cape Alava along the Ozette Triangle

Road. Turn left and drive 21 miles to the well-signed trailhead at Lake Ozette.

Contact: Olympic National Park, Wilderness Information Center, 3002 Mount Angeles Rd., Port Angeles, WA 98362, 360/565-3100.

◪ NORTH WILDERNESS BEACH

19.7 mi one-way/2–3 days 🏃3 ⛰10

west of Forks in Olympic National Park

Map 1.1, page 39

This stretch of the Olympic coastline is one of the wildest and most scenic beaches anywhere in the United States. North Wilderness Beach features countless tidal pools packed with creatures crawling, swimming, or simply affixed to the rocks. Unremitting waves roll in through the fog to break apart on the sea stacks jutting into the Pacific Ocean. Sea otters, eagles, herons, cormorants, and ducks are all likely sightings.

Access to North Wilderness Beach Route is via Sandpoint Trail, 3 miles of virgin coastal forest. The travelway heads south along sandy beaches, but at times may test ankles with stretches of cobbles and boulders. Several times the trail is driven on land because of impassibility around a point. Circular signs (painted like bull's-eyes and visible from the shore) indicate these points. Also, it is important to carry a tide table, as 12 sections of trail require passage at low or medium tides. Green Trails maps indicate points that require passages during low tides.

The route encounters the tall cliffs of Yellow Bank (4.5 miles). A pair of memorials stand along the route; Norwegian Memorial (9.9 miles), marked by an obelisk, and Chilean Memorial (16.5 miles). The travelway crosses Cedar Creek (11.3 miles), a necessary ford, and rounds Cape Johnson (15 miles). South of Cape Johnson is Hole in the Wall, a rock formation forming a natural arch, where hikers can capture a postcard moment. The route ends at the sea stacks of Rialto Beach.

Throughout the route, camping is plentiful, with numerous sites on the shore. Campfires are not permitted along the beach between Wedding Rocks (north of Sand Point) and Yellow Banks. Elsewhere, be sure to gather only driftwood from the beach.

User Groups: Hikers only. No dogs, horses, or mountain bikes are allowed. No wheelchair access.

Permits: This trail is accessible year-round. There is a $1 daily parking fee here, payable at the trailhead. Reservations are required for camping between Norwegian Memorial and Point of the Arches May 1 through September 30. Overnight stays within the national park require backcountry camping permits, which are available at the Wilderness Information Center in Port Angeles.

Maps: For a map of Olympic National Park, contact the Outdoor Recreation Information Center at the downtown Seattle REI. For topographic maps, ask Green Trails for No. 130S, Lake Ozette, or ask the USGS for Ozette, Allens Bay, and La Push.

Directions: From Port Angeles, drive east 5 miles on U.S. 101 to Highway 112. Turn right (west) and drive 49 miles to Hoko/Ozette Lake Road. Turn left and drive 21 miles to the well-signed trailhead at Lake Ozette.

Contact: Olympic National Park, Wilderness Information Center, 3002 Mount Angeles Rd., Port Angeles, WA 98362, 360/565-3100.

◱ PYRAMID MOUNTAIN

7.0 mi/3.5 hr 🏃3 ⛰6

north of Lake Crescent in Olympic National Park

Map 1.2, page 40

Pyramid Mountain Trail provides a good workout through old-growth forest culminating at a wonderful cabin lookout. From the top, peer out over the Strait of Juan de Fuca to Canada and over Lake Crescent to the Olympics. The lookout was built during World War II so the army could watch for incoming enemy aircraft. Fortunately, none arrived, but the lookout remained. The cabin on stilts perches atop the 3,100-foot peak, not high by Olympic standards, but good enough to work up a sweat on the way up.

Pyramid Mountain Trail starts off in a previously logged forest but soon enters old-growth forest. Mixed with the large conifers are numerous Pacific madrona, the Northwest's distinctive broad-leaved evergreen. Madrona is known for its uniquely papery bark that comes off in ragged shreds to reveal fine, smooth wood. These handsome trees produce small, bell-shaped flowers in the spring. Madrona trees deserve close inspection and always garner admiration.

The trail climbs through forest, crossing June Creek, which often runs below ground at this spot. It's a good idea to bring your own water on this hike, especially on warm days. The trail eventually reaches the ridgeline, where devastating clear-cuts have revealed views of the strait. After several false summits, the trail finally reaches the lookout. Be a bit careful up here; the north side of the mountain features a precipitous drop. The views extend in every direction. Lake Crescent is a beautiful green jewel to the south, while the strait is wide and large to the north.

User Groups: Hikers only. No dogs, horses, or mountain bikes are allowed. No wheelchair access.

Permits: This trail is accessible April–October. Parking and access are free. Overnight stays within the national park require backcountry camping permits, which are available at the Wilderness Information Center in Port Angeles.

Maps: For a map of Olympic National Park, contact the Outdoor Recreation Information Center at the downtown Seattle REI. For topographic maps, ask Green Trails for No. 101, Lake Crescent, or ask the USGS for Lake Crescent.

Directions: From Port Angeles, drive west 28 miles on U.S. 101 to North Shore Road. Turn right and drive about 3 miles to the well-signed trailhead on the left side of the road.

Contact: Olympic National Park, Wilderness Information Center, 3002 Mount Angeles Rd., Port Angeles, WA 98362, 360/565-3100.

6 SPRUCE RAILROAD
8.0 mi/4.0 hr

north shore of Lake Crescent in Olympic National Park

Map 1.2, page 40

Anyone who has ever navigated the twisty section of U.S. 101 as it passes Lake Crescent knows the beauty of the emerald lake. With lush green forests and high mountain ridges encircling the waters, Lake Crescent often stands out in the memories of passing motorists. That is to say nothing of the memories it leaves with hikers who walk the shores of Lake Crescent on the Spruce Railroad Trail.

Four miles of trail edge the lake along a former railroad built by the U.S. Army. This rail route once carried high-quality spruce timber to Seattle and eastward for production of World War I airplanes. Metal eventually replaced wood in aircraft production and the army sold the route, allowing the railway to be successfully converted into a level, easy-to-walk trail. The highlight is Devil's Punchbowl, 1.1 miles from the east trailhead. Here, a small cove from the lake is ringed by cliffs of pillow basalt. The depth of this popular swimming hole is reportedly more than 300 feet. Spruce Railroad Trail continues another 3 miles below towering cliffs where Pacific madrona cling to the walls. Lush forest covers parts of the trail, but Lake Crescent rarely leaves your sight. A trailhead exists at the west end, also. This hike is extremely well suited for families and for the off-season. It's a local winter favorite.

User Groups: Hikers, horses, and bicycles allowed. No dogs are allowed. No wheelchair access.

Permits: This trail is accessible year-round. Parking and access are free. Overnight stays within the national park require backcountry camping permits, which are available at the Wilderness Information Center in Port Angeles.

Maps: For a map of Olympic National Park, contact the Outdoor Recreation Information Center at the downtown Seattle REI. For topographic maps, ask Green Trails for No. 101, Lake Crescent, or ask the USGS for Lake Crescent.

Directions: From Port Angeles, drive west 28 miles on U.S. 101 to North Shore Road. Turn right and drive 5 miles to the well-signed trailhead.

Contact: Olympic National Park, Wilderness Information Center, 3002 Mount Angeles Rd., Port Angeles, WA 98362, 360/565-3100.

⁊ MARYMERE FALLS

1.4 mi/1.0 hr

south of Lake Crescent in Olympic National Park

Map 1.2, page 40

Marymere Falls Trail offers hikers of all ages and abilities a great view of the Olympics' best waterfall. A short stroll through old forest and a climb up a large series of crib steps presents visitors with a vantage point well positioned for the showcase cascade. Falls Creek shoots over Marymere Falls and tumbles more than 100 feet. With adequate flow, the creek plummets so fiercely that surrounding trees and ferns sway. A delicate mist covers all who lean over the railing. Marymere is a beautiful spot and is popular in the summer with the many people passing by on U.S. 101. Ferns and mosses grow upon everything in the forest, a great example of what the Olympic forests are all about. The route starts at Storm King Ranger Station, follows the Barnes Creek Trail for 0.5 mile, then cuts off by crossing Barnes Creek and Falls Creek before ascending to the viewpoint.

User Groups: Hikers only. No dogs, horses, or mountain bikes are allowed. No wheelchair access.

Permits: This trail is accessible year-round. Permits are not required. Parking and access are free.

Maps: For a map of Olympic National Park, contact the Outdoor Recreation Information Center at the downtown Seattle REI. For topographic maps, ask Green Trails for No. 101, Lake Crescent, or ask the USGS for Lake Crescent.

Directions: From Port Angeles, drive west 20 miles on U.S. 101 to the well-signed Storm King Ranger Station. Turn right and drive 200 yards to Lake Crescent Road. Turn right for the trailhead at Storm King Ranger Station.

Contact: Olympic National Park, Wilderness Information Center, 3002 Mount Angeles Rd., Port Angeles, WA 98362, 360/565-3100.

⁊ HEATHER PARK/MOUNT ANGELES

10.0 mi one-way/5.5 hr

south of Port Angeles in Olympic National Park

Map 1.2, page 40

A popular route for Port Angeles visitors, Heather Park Trail delivers grand views into the Olympics from along windswept ridges. Meadows are the name of the game along the upper sections. An outstanding parkland basin is found at Heather Park, while several accessible peaks offer views stretching over the heart of the Olympic Range. The route can also be completed from Hurricane Ridge Visitor Center, a less strenuous but busier choice.

Heather Park Trail leaves Heart o' the Hills in pleasant but unspectacular second-growth forest and climbs steadily to timberline and Heather Park (4.1 miles). The wide-open basin rests between the pinnacles of First Peak and Second Peak. Meadows of heather and lupine fill in the voids between scattered subalpine fir trees, and several campsites are to be had. This is a good turnaround point.

Heather Park Trail continues, climbing below the base of Mount Angeles (6 miles), whose summit is accessible by an easy social trail. Beyond, the trail drops to a junction with Sunrise Trail (6.3 miles), a highly used route that leads west to Hurricane Ridge Visitor Center. It's 3.5 miles of ridgeline hiking through open forest and meadows. Sunrise Trail gains less elevation and has its own social trail to the top of Mount Angeles. Campfires are not allowed at Heather Park.

User Groups: Hikers and horses. No dogs or mountain bikes are allowed. No wheelchair access.

Permits: This trail is accessible mid-June–October. Parking and access are free. Overnight stays within the national park require backcountry camping permits, which are available at the Wilderness Information Center in Port Angeles.

Maps: For a map of Olympic National Park, contact the Outdoor Recreation Information Center at the downtown Seattle REI. For topographic maps, ask Green Trails for No. 103, Port Angeles, and No. 135, Mount Angeles, or ask the USGS for Port Angeles and Mount Angeles.

Directions: From Port Angeles, drive north 2 miles on Race Street as it turns into Mount Angeles Road. Veer right at the well-signed fork and continue on Mount Angeles Road 5 miles to the trailhead immediately prior to the national park entrance booth. The trailhead is down a short access road.

Contact: Olympic National Park, Wilderness Information Center, 3002 Mount Angeles Rd., Port Angeles, WA 98362, 360/565-3100.

9 KLAHHANE RIDGE
13.0 mi/6.5 hr   3   △ 9

south of Port Angeles in Olympic National Park

Map 1.2, page 40

Klahhane Ridge Trail offers much more than just Klahhane Ridge. For starters, the trail passes Lake Angeles, one of the peninsula's larger subalpine lakes, set beneath cliffs. Talk about picturesque. Second, it makes an outstanding loop when combined with Mount Angeles Trail. This 12.9-mile round-trip samples all of the best of the North Olympics.

And the trail leads out along Klahhane Ridge, a place where open meadows and small trees give way to sweeping views of the interior Olympics. It may well be the best sampler of the Olympics around.

Klahhane Ridge Trail leaves Heart o' the Hills and climbs steadily through forest to Lake Angeles (3.7 miles). The lake is very popular with visitors to the North Peninsula, particularly on weekends. One would think the steep trip would weed folks out, but apparently not enough. A few camps are found around the lake. The trail continues up to Klahhane Ridge (5 miles), where distant vistas make their appearance, extending in every direction. The cities of Port Angeles and Victoria are visible to the north. Klahhane Ridge Trail ends at a junction with Mount Angeles Trail (6.5 miles), where turning north takes you through spectacular Heather Park and back to Heart o' the Hills.

User Groups: Hikers and horses. No dogs or mountain bikes are allowed. No wheelchair access.

Permits: This trail is accessible mid-June–October. Parking and access are free. Overnight stays within the national park require backcountry camping permits, which are available at the Wilderness Information Center in Port Angeles.

Maps: For a map of Olympic National Park, contact the Outdoor Recreation Information Center at the downtown Seattle REI. For topographic maps, ask Green Trails for No. 103, Port Angeles, and No. 135, Mount Angeles, or ask the USGS for Port Angeles and Mount Angeles.

Directions: From Port Angeles, drive north 2 miles on Race Street as it turns into Mount Angeles Road. Veer right at the well-signed fork and continue on Mount Angeles Road 5 miles to the trailhead immediately prior to the national park entrance booth. The trailhead is down a short road on the right.

Contact: Olympic National Park, Wilderness Information Center, 3002 Mount Angeles Rd., Port Angeles, WA 98362, 360/565-3100.

🔟 DUNGENESS SPIT
10.0 mi/5.0 hr 🥾1 ⛰️8

north of Sequim on the northeast tip of the
Olympic Peninsula

Map 1.2, page 40   **BEST (**

Set within Dungeness National Wildlife Refuge, Dungeness Spit is undoubtedly one of the state's premier sites for watching wildlife. The refuge hosts a rich and diverse ecosystem that is home to birds, critters of land and sea, and numerous fish and shellfish. The trail is more of a walk on a great beach than it is a traditional hike.

Dungeness Spit juts into the Strait of Juan de Fuca 5.5 miles, creating a quiet harbor and bay of tide flats. The spit is constantly growing, as nearby bluffs erode sandy sediments into the strait. At the end of the spit stands a historic lighthouse that was built in 1857 and is still open to the public.

The refuge sees more than 250 species of birds each year—mainly shorebirds and waterfowl, but some migratory and some permanent residents. It's definitely a bird-watcher's dream. More than 50 species of mammals of both land and sea live here, too. Harbor seals occasionally use the tip of the spit as a pup-raising site. In the bay, eelgrass beds provide a nursery for young salmon and steelhead adjusting to saltwater. This is a wonderful place to enjoy regional wildlife.

User Groups: Hikers only. No dogs or mountains bikes are allowed. The trail is wheelchair accessible (to several lookouts, not the spit).

Permits: Most of this area is accessible year-round (some parts are closed seasonally to protect wildlife feeding and nesting). The entrance fee is $3 per family daily. Admission is free with a federal duck stamp, a Golden Eagle Pass, a Golden Age Pass, or a Golden Access passport.

Maps: For a topographic map, ask the USGS for Dungeness.

Directions: From U.S. 101, go just west of Sequim and turn north on Kitchen-Dick Road. Continue for 3 miles to the Dungeness Recreation Area. Go through the recreation area to the refuge parking lot at the end of the road. The well-marked trailhead is located immediately prior to the parking area.

Contact: Dungeness National Wildlife Refuge, Washington Maritime NWR Complex, 33 South Barr Rd., Port Angeles, WA 98362, 360/457-8451.

🔟🔟 SECOND BEACH
2.4 mi/2.0 hr 🥾1 ⛰️9

south of La Push on the central Olympic Coast

Map 1.3, page 41   **BEST (**

Second Beach is a place to do some thinking. Sit and stare at the many sea stacks out among the waves. Watch waves crash through the large archway to the north. Spy eagles and gulls tangling high overhead. During the months of March, April, and October you may glimpse migrating whales not far offshore. When you tire of resting, walk along the sandy beach. It is in pristine condition, save for a little garbage that floats in from the ocean. Well over a mile long, Second Beach provides lots to see: driftwood, crabs, eagles, sea otters, and who knows what else. The trail down to the beach (0.7 mile) is easy to negotiate; it's flat and wide the whole way save for the last few hundred yards. A wide pile of driftwood stands between the trail and beach, requiring a bit of scrambling, but it's nothing much. Second Beach is well worth a couple of extra hours for anyone on the way to La Push.

User Groups: Hikers and leashed dogs. No horses or mountain bikes are allowed. No wheelchair access.

Permits: This trail is accessible year-round. Permits are not required. Parking and access are free.

Maps: For a map of Olympic National Park, contact the Outdoor Recreation Information Center at the downtown Seattle REI. For topographic maps, ask Green Trails for No. 163S, La Push, or ask the USGS for Toleak Point.

Directions: From Port Angeles, drive west 54 miles on U.S. 101 to La Push Road (Highway 110; just before the town of Forks). Turn right and drive 8 miles to a Y, where the road splits. Stay left, on La Push Road, and drive 4.5 miles to the signed trailhead on the left.

Contact: Olympic National Park, Wilderness Information Center, 3002 Mount Angeles Rd., Port Angeles, WA 98362, 360/565-3100.

12 THIRD BEACH
2.6 mi/2.0-3.0 hr

south of La Push on the central Olympic Coast

Map 1.3, page 41

Snaking its way through a nice lowland forest, Third Beach Trail accesses a long strip of extravagant Olympic coast. The beach is wide and sandy for nearly its entire length, well over a mile, and bends inward slightly to make a crescent. The resulting bay was named Strawberry Bay for the ubiquitous strawberry plant in the coastal forests. Tall, rocky cliffs mark the north end of the crescent and are impassable, no matter your skill level. As you look to the south, beyond Taylor Point, a number of sea stacks are visible in the distance. It's easy for hikers of all abilities to enjoy all this, as the trail down to the beach loses very little elevation and is wide and well maintained. As you hike through the forest, the increasing roar of the ocean signals your progress, as does the increasing size of massive cedar trees. Although some may say that Second Beach is more scenic, Third Beach is a great trip as well.

User Groups: Hikers and leashed dogs. No horses or mountain bikes are allowed. No wheelchair access.

Permits: This trail is accessible year-round. Permits are not required. Parking and access are free.

Maps: For a map of Olympic National Park, contact the Outdoor Recreation Information Center at the downtown Seattle REI. For topographic maps, ask Green Trails for No.

163S, La Push, or ask the USGS for Toleak Point.

Directions: From Port Angeles, drive west 54 miles on U.S. 101 to La Push Road (Highway 110; just before the town of Forks). Turn right and drive 8 miles to a Y, where the road splits. Stay left, on La Push Road, and drive 3 miles to the signed trailhead on the left.

Contact: Olympic National Park, Wilderness Information Center, 3002 Mount Angeles Rd., Port Angeles, WA 98362, 360/565-3100.

13 CENTRAL WILDERNESS BEACH
16.7 mi one-way/2 days

south of La Push on the central Olympic Coast

Map 1.3, page 41

As beautiful as the other long beach routes, Third Beach to Oil City provides a bit more of a hiking challenge. This is the South Coast Beach Travelway, and it requires that several overland bypasses and three creeks be crossed. Not that any of these obstacles is too much to overcome. The South Travelway has some great scenery, including Giants Graveyard, Alexander Island, and an extraordinary abundance of birds and sea life. Bald eagles and blue herons regularly sweep the shores in search of dinner, while sea otters play it cool, reclining in the water and eating shellfish off their stomachs.

Access the route via Third Beach, hiking south above Taylor's Point, impassable along the water. Many times hikers must avoid impassable coastline by hiking trails on land; it's important to carry a map to properly identify these sections. Five miles of great beach present views of Giants Graveyard (4.2 miles), Strawberry Point (6.5 miles), and Toleak Point (7.2 miles), appropriate images of the rugged coastline.

The middle section of Southern Travelway requires fords of Falls Creek (8.5 miles), Goodman Creek (9 miles), and Mosquito Creek (11.5 miles). If it's been wet recently, expect them to be difficult. The lower section of Southern Travelway uses beach, with Alexander Island offshore, and a long 3.5-mile overland route bypassing Hoh Head. This leaves you just north of the trailhead at Oil City (16.7 miles), near the mouth of the Hoh River. Campsites are spread throughout the trip, usually tucked away on shore but visible from the beach.

User Groups: Hikers only. No dogs, horses, or mountain bikes are allowed. No wheelchair access.

Permits: This trail is accessible year-round. Permits are not required. Parking and access are free.

Maps: For a map of Olympic National Park, contact the Outdoor Recreation Information Center at the downtown Seattle REI. For topographic maps, ask Green Trails for No. 163, La Push, or ask the USGS for Toleak Point and Hoh Head.

Directions: From Port Angeles, drive west 54 miles on U.S. 101 to La Push Road (Highway 110; just before the town of Forks). Turn right and drive 8 miles to a Y, where the road splits. Stay left, on La Push Road, and drive 3 miles to the signed trailhead on the left.

Contact: Olympic National Park, Wilderness Information Center, 3002 Mount Angeles Rd., Port Angeles, WA 98362, 360/565-3100.

14 BOGACHIEL RIVER
41.6 mi/4 days   👫3 ⛺9

southeast of Forks in Olympic National Park

Map 1.3, page 41

Let the masses drive the road up the Hoh River and visit the overpopulated Hoh River Valley. Follow the wiser hikers who access the Bogachiel River for the same gargantuan trees covered in moss, the same cascading streams filled with juvenile salmon, and the same forests teeming with wildlife—but with considerably more solitude.

While the Bogachiel River Trail is a fine day hike, the route increasingly gets wilder as it heads into the mountains, making it an outstanding overnight trip. Beginning along an old logging road, the trail soon enters the national park and virgin rainforest (2 miles). Massive trees fill the forests, awash in green from the heavy rains off the Pacific Ocean. The mostly flat trail moves in and out of the forest, regularly nearing the river and passing camps. Maintenance on the trail often fails to keep up with the regular washouts from heavy winter rains, so be ready for some route-finding along the way.

After Flapjack Camp (10 miles), Bogachiel River Trail leaves the main branch of the river and slowly climbs with North Fork Bogachiel River toward High Divide. This is the trail's best section, where at 15 Mile Shelter (14.5 miles) the river surges through a deep gorge. After Hyak Camp (17.6 miles) and 21 Mile Camp (20.8 miles), the trail overlooks the Bogachiel and vast meadows. Those who plan for it can connect this trail to Mink Lake or Deer Lake Trails (25.5 miles) for through-hikes via the Sol Duc Valley. This route is truly wild country, where elk and ancient trees far outnumber bipeds.

User Groups: Hikers and horses. No dogs or mountain bikes are allowed. No wheelchair access.

Permits: This trail is usually accessible year-round (up to about 15 Mile Camp, where the winter snowpack becomes quite deep). A federal Northwest Forest Pass is required to park here. Overnight stays within the national park require backcountry camping permits, which are available at the Wilderness Information Center in Port Angeles.

Maps: For a map of Olympic National Park, contact the Outdoor Recreation Information Center at the downtown Seattle REI. For topographic maps, ask Green Trails for No. 132, Spruce Mountain, No. 133, Mount Tom, and No. 134, Mount Olympus, or ask the USGS for Reade Hill, Indian Pass, Hunger Mountain, Slide Peak, and Bogachiel Peak.

Directions: From Forks, drive south 6 miles on U.S. 101 to Undie Road. Turn left (east) and drive 4 miles to the trailhead at road's end.

Contact: Olympic National Park, Wilderness Information Center, 3002 Mount Angeles Rd., Port Angeles, WA 98362, 360/565-3100.

15 SOL DUC FALLS/ LOVER'S LANE

5.6 mi/3.0 hr

south of Lake Crescent in Olympic National Park

| Map 1.4, page 42 | BEST |

This is not an exclusive trail for sweethearts. Sure, a couple in love are apt to find this the perfect stroll. But those even more likely to find this a great trail are those who love an easy hike along a great trail through the forest. That group includes couples and kids, seasoned hikers, singles, groups, and anyone between. Add to the pleasure of Lover's Lane the excitement of Sol Duc Falls, one of the Olympics' premier photo ops, and you have a widely agreed-upon fun hike.

The trail departs from the Sol Duc Hot Springs Resort, where folks can relax weary muscles in a number of springs, and starts off into an old-growth forest. The Sol Duc River is never far away and calls out with its incessant rushing. The trail crosses three streams on easy-to-negotiate footbridges, each a nice interruption in the scenery.

Before 3 miles are underfoot, the trail arrives at Sol Duc Falls. Here, the river makes an abrupt turn and cascades from three notches into a narrow gorge. The forest is incredibly green in these parts and moss seems omnipresent. Regardless of your romantic pursuits, Lover's Lane is a trail for all.

User Groups: Hikers only. No dogs, horses, or mountain bikes are allowed. No wheelchair access.

Permits: This trail is accessible year-round. A federal National Parks Pass is required to park here.

Maps: For a map of Olympic National Park, contact the Outdoor Recreation Information Center at the downtown Seattle REI. For topographic maps, ask Green Trails for

Sol Duc Falls is a popular and easy hike to access.

No. 133, Mount Tom, or ask the USGS for Bogachiel Peak.

Directions: From Port Angeles, drive west 30 miles on U.S. 101 to well-signed Sol Duc Hot Springs Road. Turn left (south) and drive 14 miles to the trailhead at road's end.

Contact: Olympic National Park, Wilderness Information Center, 3002 Mount Angeles Rd., Port Angeles, WA 98362, 360/565-3100.

16 SEVEN LAKES BASIN LOOP

20.1 mi/2 days

south of Lake Crescent in Olympic National Park

| Map 1.4, page 42 |

This is one of the peninsula's greatest hikes, a exceptional journey into one of the best lake basins in Washington. This is one of the peninsula's greatest hikes, an exceptional journey into the heart of the Olympic Mountains. The trip revels in the views of High Divide and

Seven Lakes Basin offers some of the Olympic Mountains' best lake fishing.

offers great camping and fishing in the Seven Lakes Basin. The divide is more than 5,000 feet in elevation, making this meadow territory. Views open wide to the south, revealing Mount Olympus at close range. Wildlife is plentiful in this part of the park, where regular sightings include black bear, ravens, Roosevelt elk, picas, and Olympic marmots. If you have a camera, you'd best bring it. During July, wildflowers are prolific and difficult not to trample underfoot.

The trail makes a loop by heading up the Sol Duc River to High Divide, then coming back via Deer Lake and Canyon Creek. The trail up the Sol Duc River is a trip through pristine old-growth forests along a river that makes constant cascades and falls. After the Appleton Pass Trail cuts off at 4.8 miles, the Sol Duc Trail climbs vigorously up Bridge Creek to High Divide. Camps are frequent, but Sol Duc Park and Heart Lake are highly recommended.

From High Divide, Mount Olympus and the Bailey Range ring the Hoh Valley. Head north on the High Divide to the Seven Lakes Basin, a series of not seven but actually eight subalpine lakes. The lakes lie on a gentle slope facing the north, meaning snow can linger well into July. To curb overuse, campsites here must be reserved with the Wilderness Information Center. The trail leaves the basin and drops to Deer Lake. Here, one trail leads down to the trailhead via Canyon Creek, another long string of waterfalls.

User Groups: Hikers only. No dogs, horses, or mountain bikes are allowed. No wheelchair access.

Permits: This trail is accessible July–October. A National Parks Pass is required to park here. Overnight stays within the national park require backcountry camping permits, which are available at the Wilderness Information Center in Port Angeles.

Maps: For a map of Olympic National Park, contact the Outdoor Recreation Information Center at the downtown Seattle REI. For topographic maps, ask Green Trails for No. 133, Mount Tom, and No. 134, Mount Olympus, or ask the USGS for Bogachiel Peak and Mount Carrie.

Directions: From Port Angeles, drive west 30 miles on U.S. 101 to well-signed Sol Duc Hot Springs Road. Turn left (south) and drive 14 miles to the trailhead at road's end.

Contact: Olympic National Park, Wilderness Information Center, 3002 Mount Angeles Rd., Port Angeles, WA 98362, 360/565-3100.

🏷17 APPLETON PASS
14.8 mi/8.0 hr   🏃3 ⛺8

south of Lake Crescent in Olympic National Park

Map 1.4, page 42

Appleton Pass Trail provides a crossing from the Sol Duc to the Elwha drainages. It's also an alternate route up to Boulder Lake and a great entry to acres of open meadows and parkland. The Sol Duc Valley is full of waterfalls, and this route passes by several of them.

From the trailhead, the route uses Sol Duc River Trail for the first 4.8 miles. Along the way is Sol Duc Falls, a popular day hike. This section of trail passes through cool forests of old-growth timber. Appleton Pass Trail climbs steeply via a tiring number of switchbacks to the pass. Just before the pass, it reaches the timberline, and spacious meadows break out in abundance.

The diminutive Oyster Lake is a short side trail from the pass and well recommended. Mount Appleton stands to the north, cloaked in wildflowers and heather during the early summer. For through-hikers, the trail continues beyond the pass down the South Fork of Boulder Creek. Just before the trail converges with North Fork Trail, Boulder Creek makes a tremendous leap into a deep pool, followed by several smaller cascades—a wonderful sight.

User Groups: Hikers and horses. No dogs or mountain bikes are allowed. No wheelchair access.

Permits: This trail is accessible July–October. A National Parks Pass is required to park here. Overnight stays within the national park require backcountry camping permits, which are available at the Wilderness Information Center in Port Angeles.

Maps: For a map of Olympic National Park, contact the Outdoor Recreation Information Center at the downtown Seattle REI. For topographic maps, ask Green Trails for No. 133, Mount Tom, and No. 134, Mount Olympus, or ask the USGS for Bogachiel Peak and Mount Carrie.

Directions: From Port Angeles, drive west 30 miles on U.S. 101 to well-signed Sol Duc Hot Springs Road. Turn left (south) and drive 14 miles to the trailhead at road's end.

Contact: Olympic National Park, Wilderness Information Center, 3002 Mount Angeles Rd., Port Angeles, WA 98362, 360/565-3100.

18 BOULDER LAKE

11.2 mi/6.0 hr

southwest of Port Angeles in Olympic National Park

Map 1.4, page 42

Although Boulder Lake is a great destination, it's often overlooked for the soothing waters of Olympic Hot Springs. The hot springs draw the majority of visitors (understandably), but those soakers miss out on a great hike. The hike is a relatively easy one, climbing gradually through virgin forests. At the base of Boulder Peak, the small Boulder Lake sits within open forests of subalpine fir and mountain hemlock. In spite of the lake's beauty, you're more likely to remember your soak in the Olympic Hot Springs if you take it on your way back down the trail.

The first 2.2 miles of the trail are old roadbed, terminating at Boulder Creek Camp. The hot springs are just across Boulder Creek. Consisting of several pools collecting hot mineral water, the springs feel primitive and natural. Save it for your muscles on the way down, when they'll be more thankful. The trail splits 0.5 mile beyond the camp; the left fork goes to Appleton Pass, the right fork travels another 2 miles to Boulder Lake. Campsites can be found around the lake within the open forest. View seekers can scramble Boulder Peak.

At the lake, the trail turns into Happy Lake Ridge Trail, an optional return of 10 miles to Hot Springs Road, 2 miles below the trailhead. Most of the hike is on the ridge, within open spreads of subalpine meadows. Happy Lake sits at the midpoint of the ridge, perfect for longer stays. It's nice, but most prefer the hot springs.

User Groups: Hikers and horses. No dogs or mountain bikes are allowed. No wheelchair access.

Permits: This trail is accessible June–October. A National Parks Pass is required to park here. Overnight stays within the national park require backcountry camping permits, which are available at the Wilderness Information Center in Port Angeles.

Maps: For a map of Olympic National Park, contact the Outdoor Recreation Information Center at the downtown Seattle REI. For topographic maps, ask Green Trails for No. 134, Mount Olympus, or ask the USGS for Mount Carrie.

Directions: From Port Angeles, drive west 8 miles on U.S. 101 to Elwha Hot Springs Road. Turn left (south) and drive 10 miles, into the national park, to the road's end at a barrier with a well-signed trailhead.

Contact: Olympic National Park, Wilderness Information Center, 3002 Mount Angeles Rd., Port Angeles, WA 98362, 360/565-3100.

19 ELWHA RIVER

54.2 mi/3-5 days

southwest of Port Angeles in Olympic National Park

Map 1.4, page 42

The Elwha River serves as the main artery of the Olympic Mountains. For more than 25 miles, the trail closely follows a historic and well-traveled route deep into the heart of the range. The Elwha was used for ages by local tribes to delve into the mountains for hunting and ceremonial reasons. In the late 1800s, the Press Expedition (a contingent of newspapermen and explorers) followed it on their trek across the mountain range. It has been an often-visited trail by backpackers and hikers for decades and is thought of as the spirit of the Olympics. The glacially fed waters boom through magnificent forests, a setting for many a backcountry tale. Sounds like a great place, doesn't it?

Elwha Trail travels deep into the Olympics to Low Divide. There are many campsites and shelters, and they receive heavy use in the summer. Old-growth forest breaks to reveal the river in stands of alder and maple. The trail forks at Chicago Camp (25 miles). The north fork heads to Elwha Basin, while the south fork proceeds up

to Low Divide and the North Fork Quinault. It's an amazing trek for those who complete it, and especially great when done with a friend.

Day hikers will also find much to see and do within several miles of the trailhead. Side trails (1.2 miles in) lead down to Goblin's Gate (1.7 miles), where the Elwha passes through a narrow gorge. From here, a small network of trails finds the sites of old homesteads and large meadows. These are great places to see deer, elk, and even black bears.

User Groups: Hikers and horses. No dogs or mountain bikes are allowed. No wheelchair access.

Permits: The lower part of this trail is usually accessible year-round (upper part is accessible May–October). A National Parks Pass is required to park here. Overnight stays within the national park require backcountry camping permits, which are available at the Wilderness Information Center in Port Angeles.

Maps: For a map of Olympic National Park, contact the Outdoor Recreation Information Center at the downtown Seattle REI. For topographic maps, ask Green Trails for No. 134, Mount Olympus, No. 135, Mount Angeles, No. 166, Mount Christie, and No. 167, Mount Steel, or ask the USGS for Hurricane Hill, Mount Angeles, McCartney Peak, Chimney Peak, and Mount Christie.

Directions: From Port Angeles, drive west 8 miles on U.S. 101 to Elwha Hot Springs Road. Turn left (south) and drive 4 miles to the cutoff for Whiskey Bend Road. Turn left and drive 5 miles to the trailhead at road's end.

Contact: Olympic National Park, Wilderness Information Center, 3002 Mount Angeles Rd., Port Angeles, WA 98362, 360/565-3100.

20 HURRICANE HILL

3.2 mi/2.0 hr

south of Port Angeles in Olympic National Park

Map 1.4, page 42

Visitors to Hurricane Ridge should and very often do hike this trail. Why? Because no trail in the Olympics offers such easy access to such exceptional views. The trail is completely within the high country, where windswept ridges are covered in lush, green meadows. The open trail offers nonstop views to the north and south, and the summit of Hurricane Hill is one giant panoramic vista. The hike is relatively easy and can be made by hikers of all abilities at their own pace.

Hurricane Hill Trail starts off on a cleared roadbed and gently climbs for its entire length. Wildflowers are in full gear during late June, while the last vestiges of the winter's snowpack hang on. Eventually the roadbed ends, but the trail remains wide and easy to hike. At the top of Hurricane Hill are wide knolls, perfect for a picnic or extended rest before heading back to the car. It's likely you'll want to stick around for awhile, mostly for the views. Much of the Olympic interior is revealed, including the Bailey Range and most of the Elwha drainage. The views to the north include the Strait of Juan de Fuca, Vancouver Island, and to the east, the Cascades. If there is any one trail that will endear the Olympics to its visitors, this is surely it.

User Groups: Hikers only. No dogs, horses, or mountain bikes are allowed. No wheelchair access.

Permits: This trail is accessible June–October. A National Parks Pass is required to park here.

Maps: For a map of Olympic National Park, contact the Outdoor Recreation Information Center at the downtown Seattle REI. For topographic maps, ask Green Trails for No. 134, Mount Olympus, or ask the USGS for Hurricane Hill.

Directions: From Port Angeles, drive north 2 miles on Race Street as it turns into Mount Angeles Road. Veer right at the well-signed fork and continue on Mount Angeles Road 19 miles, past the lower and upper visitors centers, to the well-signed trailhead.

Contact: Olympic National Park, Wilderness Information Center, 3002 Mount Angeles Rd., Port Angeles, WA 98362, 360/565-3100.

21 GRAND RIDGE
8.0 mi/4.0 hr

south of Port Angeles in Olympic National Park

Map 1.4, page 42

The National Park Service was once crazy about cars. It hoped to build a road through the park connecting Obstruction Point to Deer Park. Fortunately, the park service realized it would be insane to destroy such a beautiful area and abandoned the idea after surveying the route. Survey markers from the Bureau of Public Roads still line the trail, the intended course. Barren, open, and windy, Grand Ridge offers views of the Gray Wolf River drainage and many northern Olympic peaks. It's a great trip for those visiting Obstruction Point and the Hurricane Ridge area.

The trail primarily follows the southern side of Grand Ridge. This area is extremely barren, where even krummholz (small, distorted trees that look more like bushes) struggle to establish a foothold. Thin soils and intense winds work together to keep this area devoid of trees and full of views. A couple of high points offer good scramble opportunities and panoramic views of Elk Mountain (1.5 miles) and Maiden Peak (4 miles). Be sure to bring water, as hot days are even hotter on this south-facing slope. And be aware that when the wind picks up, which is often, you can expect 50–60 mph gusts to knock you around. Usually the wind blows you into the mountain, a good thing, because the drop down the mountain is precipitous.

User Groups: Hikers only. No dogs, horses, or mountain bikes are allowed. No wheelchair access.

Permits: This trail is usually accessible May–October. A National Parks Pass is required to park at Hurricane Hill; parking at Deer Park is free. Camping is limited between May 1 and September 30. Obtain permits at the WIC in Port Angeles during business hours.

Maps: For a map of Olympic National Park, contact the Outdoor Recreation Information Center at the downtown Seattle REI. For topographic maps, ask Green Trails for No. 135, Mount Angeles, or ask the USGS for Mount Angeles and Maiden Peak.

Directions: From Port Angeles, drive north 2 miles on Race Street as it turns into Mount Angeles Road. Veer right at the well-signed fork and continue on Mount Angeles Road 17 miles to Obstruction Point Road. Turn left and drive 7 miles to the road's end and Obstruction Point Trailhead.

Contact: Olympic National Park, Wilderness Information Center, 3002 Mount Angeles Rd., Port Angeles, WA 98362, 360/565-3100.

22 GRAND PASS
12.0 mi/1-2 days

south of Port Angeles in Olympic National Park

Map 1.4, page 42

There's good reason that this is one of the Olympics' most popular destinations. Easily accessible and very beautiful, Grand and Moose Lakes are favorite campgrounds. Farther up Grand Valley are plentiful subalpine meadows and rough, rocky slopes leading to Grand Pass, where views reach for miles around. Throw in two routes to the valley from Obstruction Peak (each of which is terrific), and you have a popular and well-visited spot in the North Olympics.

Leaving Obstruction Point, you are faced with two possible routes. Grand Pass Trail traverses Lillian Ridge, well above 6,000 feet and awash in mountain views, before dropping to Grand Lake. Alternatively, Badger Valley Trail makes its way through meadows and Alaskan cedar groves before climbing to Grand Lake. The best option is to make this a small loop, along the ridge on the way in and up the valley on the way out.

Overnight guests to Grand and Moose Lakes are required to secure a permit and reservation from the Wilderness Information Center. While there are numerous sites, they often fill up in the summer. The lakes are bordered by beautiful forests and rocky

valley hillsides. Beyond, Grand Pass Trail passes small Gladys Lake and climbs steeply to Grand Pass. The rocky and barren territory is a testament to the snowpacks that linger well into summer along these north-facing inclines. From Grand Pass, the Olympics are at hand and breathtaking.

User Groups: Hikers only. No dogs, horses, or mountain bikes are allowed. No wheelchair access.

Permits: This trail is usually accessible June–October. A National Parks Pass is required to park here. Overnight stays at Grand or Moose Lake require reservations and backcountry camping permits, which are available at the Wilderness Information Center in Port Angeles.

Maps: For a map of Olympic National Park, contact the Outdoor Recreation Information Center at the downtown Seattle REI. For topographic maps, ask Green Trails for No. 135, Mount Angeles, or ask the USGS for Mount Angeles, Maiden Peak, and Wellesley Peak.

Directions: From Port Angeles, drive north 2 miles on Race Street as it turns into Mount Angeles Road. Veer right at the well-signed fork and continue on Mount Angeles Road 17 miles to Obstruction Point Road. Turn left and drive 7 miles to the road's end and Obstruction Point Trailhead.

Contact: Olympic National Park, Wilderness Information Center, 3002 Mount Angeles Rd., Port Angeles, WA 98362, 360/565-3100.

23 CAMERON CREEK
32.0 mi/4 days

south of Sequim in Olympic National Park

Map 1.4, page 42

The best backcountry locations often require an extra bit of effort to reach. Perhaps it is that extra exertion that makes some places so special and memorable. Cameron Creek is one of those places. It requires more than a few miles of approach hiking before you even embark on the long trail itself. Don't fret, time-conscious hikers; the journey along the trail and the vast mountain meadows deep within Cameron Basin are reward enough.

Cameron Creek Trail begins at Three Forks, where the creek joins Grand Creek and Gray Wolf River. The best access is via Three Forks Trail, a steep drop from Deer Park. While it's possible to hike up from the Lower Gray Wolf, river crossings are necessary and difficult. Cameron Creek Trail heads up the valley 7 miles, passing through beautiful forests of Douglas fir. Lower Cameron Camp (4 miles from Three Forks) is the primary campground.

Cameron Trail becomes more rugged near its headwaters, sometimes blown out by the creek. The upper basin is pure parkland, where wildflowers and waterfalls cover the landscape. Although it's a tough climb, Cameron Pass rewards with deep wilderness views. Mount Claywood and Sentinel Peak beckon from across Lost River Basin, one of the wildest places on the peninsula. The trail eventually drops to Dosewallips River. Campsites for the second night are scattered along the trail and throughout Cameron Basin.

User Groups: Hikers only. No dogs, horses, or mountain bikes are allowed. No wheelchair access.

Permits: This trail is accessible June–early October. Parking and access are free. Overnight stays within the national park require backcountry camping permits, which are available at the Wilderness Information Center in Port Angeles.

Maps: For a map of Olympic National Park, contact the Outdoor Recreation Information Center at the downtown Seattle REI. For topographic maps, ask Green Trails for No. 135, Mount Angeles, and No. 136, Tyler Peak, or ask the USGS for Tyler Peak, Maiden Peak, and Wellesley Peak.

Directions: From Port Angeles, drive east 5 miles on U.S. 101 to Deer Park Road. Turn right (south) and drive 17 miles to the well-signed trailhead.

Contact: Olympic National Park, Wilderness Information Center, 3002 Mount Angeles Rd., Port Angeles, WA 98362, 360/565-3100.

24 HOH RIVER

34.0 mi/1–4 days   🏃2 ⛺10

southeast of Forks in Olympic National Park

Map 1.4, page 42   **BEST (**

The Hoh Valley is world famous for the enormous size of its forests. Known as a cathedral forest, the massive trees' canopy stands more than 200 feet above the trail, filtering sunlight onto numerous ferns and draping mosses. This trail is also popular because it is the route for those seeking the pinnacle of the Olympic Mountains, Mount Olympus. Never mind the herds of people (or elk)—trees with trunks that wouldn't fit in your living room focus your attention upward.

The entire trail is outstanding. The first 12 miles are flat and well laid out, avoiding many ups and downs. It's a constant biology lesson in growth limits, as behemoth trees compete to outgrow each other. Many places along the trail allow for full appreciation of a river's ecology. Eagles and ravens stand atop trees looking for salmon or steelhead within the river. American dippers patrol the waterline while herds of Roosevelt elk graze along the forest floor. There are several well-interspersed campgrounds throughout. At 9.5 miles is Hoh Lake Trail cutoff, a trip for another day.

After 12 miles, the trail begins to slowly climb. The river courses through a spectacular canyon more than 100 feet deep by the time a hiker reaches the 13-mile mark. Hoh Trail crosses the canyon on a well-built bridge and begins its true ascent. Through a series of switchbacks, the trail passes through the forest and into a deep ravine. Beyond lies Glacier Meadows, where Olympus stands tall above terminating glaciers, revealing fields of blooming wildflowers among piles of glacial moraine. There are numerous camps here; all sites must be reserved at the Wilderness Information Center and may fill up quickly with backpackers and mountain climbers. This is the climax of the Olympics, standing between mighty Olympus above and miles and miles of rainforest below. Enjoy your hike out.

User Groups: Hikers and horses. No dogs or mountain bikes are allowed. No wheelchair access.

Permits: This trail is usually accessible April–October. A National Parks Pass is required to park here. Overnight stays within the national park require backcountry camping permits, which are available at the Hoh Ranger Station (at the end of Hoh River Road, 360/374-6925). Permits are limited May 1 through September 30. Reservations are recommended once the lake is snow free. For reservations call 360/565-3100.

Maps: For a map of Olympic National Park, contact the Outdoor Recreation Information Center at the downtown Seattle REI. For topographic maps, ask Green Trails for No. 133, Mount Tom, and No. 134, Mount Olympus, or ask the USGS for Owl Mountain, Mount Tom, Bogachiel Peak, Mount Carrie, and Mount Olympus.

Directions: From Port Angeles, drive south 14 miles on U.S. 101 to Upper Hoh River Road. Turn left (east) and drive 18 miles to the Hoh Ranger Station and trailhead.

Contact: Olympic National Park, Wilderness Information Center, 3002 Mount Angeles Rd., Port Angeles, WA 98362, 360/565-3100.

25 QUEETS RIVER
30.8 mi/2-3 days

south of Forks in Olympic National Park

Map 1.4, page 42

Queets River Trail is all about two things: forests chock-full of enormous trees and total seclusion. Trees here grow to tremendous sizes, with Sitka spruce, western hemlock, western red cedar, and Douglas fir creating a community of giants. In fact, the Queets is home to the world's largest living Douglas fir, a monster with a trunk 14.5 feet in diameter

and a broken top 221 feet above the ground. While as impressive as the Hoh, this valley receives just a fraction of the visitors. That's because of a necessary river ford just beyond the trailhead. The river can be forded only during times of low water (late summer or fall) and should be undertaken with care at any time; once you're past it, though, traveling is easy.

The trail travels roughly 15 miles along the river. The forest often gives way to glades of big leaf maple and the cutting river. Bears outnumber people here. The world's largest Douglas fir is 2 miles in, just off Kloochman Rock Trail heading north. There are three established camps along the trail, easily providing sufficient camping for the few backpackers on this trail. The first is Spruce Bottom (6 miles). Sticking on the trail will eventually take you to the Pelton Creek Shelter (15 miles), where the trail ends. It is certainly possible to carry on farther to Queets Basin, but it's a bushwhack. It's enough to sit down, enjoy the permeating quiet of the wilderness, and smile.

User Groups: Hikers and horses. No dogs or mountain bikes are allowed. No wheelchair access.

Permits: This trail is usually accessible May–October. Parking is free. Overnight stays within the national park require backcountry camping permits, which are available at the Wilderness Information Center in Port Angeles.

Maps: For a map of Olympic National Park, contact the Outdoor Recreation Information Center at the downtown Seattle REI. For topographic maps, ask Green Trails for No. 165, Kloochman Rock, or ask the USGS for Stequaleho Creek, Kloochman Rock, and Bob Creek.

Directions: From Forks, drive south on U.S. 101 to Forest Service Road 21. Turn left and drive about 10 miles north to Upper Queets Road. Turn right and drive about 2 miles to the trailhead at road's end.

Contact: Olympic National Park, Wilderness

Information Center, 3002 Mount Angeles Rd., Port Angeles, WA 98362, 360/565-3100.

26 SKYLINE RIDGE
45.0 mi/5-6 days ⛹4 ⛺10

northeast of Quinault in Olympic National Park
Map 1.4, page 42

Sure to test even the toughest hikers, Skyline Ridge rewards with one of the most beautiful hikes on the peninsula. The trail never leaves the high country as it follows the ridge separating the large Quinault and Queets Valleys. The views up here are unbelievable, with Mount Olympus standing just one ridge away. From this high perch, watch the sun set or the fog roll in from the Pacific Ocean, which is visible in the distance. And stay on your toes, as this is the perfect place to spot black bears as they drunkenly wolf down huckleberries. The Quinault is said to sport some of the highest black bear concentrations in the state, so be ready for some excitement. Mile after mile, Skyline Ridge consistently offers the best of the Olympics.

The route must be accessed by Three Lakes Trail (6.5 miles) or North Fork Quinault Trail (16 miles; see listing in this chapter). The best route is via North Fork Quinault, making a loop. Climbing out of Low Divide, Skyline Trail skirts several basins of meadows and rises to Beauty Pass (7.4 miles from Low Divide). A side trail heads to Lake Beauty and campsites with views of Olympus.

Beyond, the trail is difficult to follow and marked by rock cairns. Excellent map and route-finding skills are needed here. Skyline Trail heads for Three Prune Camp (18 miles), switching between the Quinault and Queets Valleys several times. Water can be difficult to find here until Three Prune. The trail begins its decent to Three Lakes, the last spot for camping, and Three Lakes Trail back to the trailhead. By the time you get back to the car, you'll already be planning next year's trip.

User Groups: Hikers only. No dogs, horses, or mountain bikes are allowed. No wheelchair access.

Permits: This trail is usually accessible August–September (depending on the previous winter's snowpack). Parking is free. Overnight stays within the national park require backcountry camping permits, which are available at Quinault Ranger Station.

Maps: For a map of Olympic National Park, contact the Outdoor Recreation Information Center at the downtown Seattle REI. For topographic maps, ask Green Trails for No. 166, Mount Christie, or ask the USGS for Bunch Lake, Kimta Peak, and Mount Christie.

Directions: From Forks, travel south on U.S. 101 to North Shore Road at Lake Quinault. Turn left (east) and drive 17 miles to North Fork Ranger Station at road's end.

Contact: Olympic National Park, Wilderness Information Center, 3002 Mount Angeles Rd., Port Angeles, WA 98362, 360/565-3100.

27 NORTH FORK QUINAULT
31.4 mi/3-4 days ⛹2 ⛺8

northeast of Quinault in Olympic National Park
Map 1.4, page 42

With headwaters at Low Divide, North Fork Trail provided the way for many a party of explorers. From this popular junction, used by the Press Expedition, Army Lieutenant Joseph P. O'Neil, and others, the river flows more than 30 miles to the Pacific through beautiful high country and forests of enormous size in the lowlands. Its link to Low Divide makes it a well-used route for folks coming or going to the Elwha River. It also makes a great counterpart to Skyline Trail, which skirts the North Fork's upper ridge. There's no end to things to see as the trail crosses numerous beautiful creeks and even the river itself. It passes through superb forests of trees swollen to rainforest dimensions, and hikers often encounter wildlife.

The trail follows the river all the way to its source at Low Divide. Campsites and shelters occur regularly throughout this section of trail, including Wolf Bar (2.5 miles), Halfway House (5.2 miles), Elip Creek (6.5 miles), Trapper Shelter (8.5 miles), and 12 Mile (11.5 miles). Be prepared for several easy creek crossings. The ascent up the valley is modest, making these 12 miles pass quickly underfoot.

After a good day's hike, the trail crosses the North Fork at 16 Mile Camp (12.3 miles). This river crossing can be difficult if not impassable during times of high flow. If coming from the Elwha, beware. A U-turn here makes the return trip more than 40 miles. Beyond, the trail climbs to Low Divide, an open meadow surrounded by waterfalls. Low Divide Ranger Station lies just beyond the Skyline Trail junction.

User Groups: Hikers and horses. No dogs or mountain bikes are allowed. No wheelchair access.

Permits: This trail is accessible May–October. No fee is required to park here. Overnight stays within the national park require backcountry camping permits, which are available at the Wilderness Information Center in Port Angeles.

Maps: For a map of Olympic National Park, contact the Outdoor Recreation Information Center at the downtown Seattle REI. For topographic maps, ask Green Trails for No. 166, Mount Christie, or ask the USGS for Bunch Lake, Kitma Peak, and Mount Christie.

Directions: From Forks, travel south on U.S. 101 to North Shore Road at Lake Quinault. Turn left (east) and drive 17 miles to North Fork Ranger Station at road's end.

Contact: Olympic National Park, Wilderness Information Center, 3002 Mount Angeles Rd., Port Angeles, WA 98362, 360/565-3100.

28 ENCHANTED VALLEY
36.0 mi/4 days

🥾3 ⛺10

east of Quinault in Olympic National Park

Map 1.4, page 42

Undoubtedly one of Washington's most beautiful places, Enchanted Valley leaves visitors reminiscing about their trip here for years to come. East Fork Quinault Trail travels through old-growth forests of giant trees to the steep cliffs and waterfalls of Enchanted Valley. The wide and wild valley offers miles of exploration and loads of views of the tall peaks enclosing the Quinault. The trail eventually finds the high-country playground of Anderson Pass, home to glaciers and acres of meadows.

East Fork Quinault Trail immediately crosses Graves Creek, then travels 13 level and easy miles among ancient trees growing in a lush and humid forest. Elk and deer roam the thick understory. The forest gives way to clearings as the trail nears Enchanted Valley. A ford of the river is required here, difficult at times of high water. Countless waterfalls cascade from the vertical cliffs on both sides of the valley. The valley is home to a ranger station and old chalet, now closed to visitors except in emergencies.

East Quinault Trail continues out of Enchanted Valley and finally begins climbing to reach Anderson Pass and several glaciers. This high country is home to huckleberries and their biggest fans: black bears. Good places to pitch a tent are found at O'Neil Creek Camp (6.7 miles), Enchanted Valley Camp (13.1 miles), and Anderson Pass Camp (18 miles).

User Groups: Hikers and horses. No dogs or mountain bikes are allowed. No wheelchair access.

Permits: This trail is accessible May–September. Parking is free. Overnight stays within the national park require backcountry camping permits, which are available at the Wilderness Information Center in Port Angeles.

Maps: For a map of Olympic National Park, contact the Outdoor Recreation Information Center at the downtown Seattle REI. For topographic maps, ask Green Trails for No. 166, Mount Christie, and No. 167, Mount Steel, or ask the USGS for Mount Hoquiam, Mount Olson, Mount Steel, and Chimney Peak.

Directions: From Forks, drive south on U.S. 101 to South Shore Road. Turn left (east) and drive 18.5 miles to Graves Creek Ranger Station and the signed trailhead.

Contact: Olympic National Park, Wilderness Information Center, 3002 Mount Angeles Rd., Port Angeles, WA 98362, 360/565-3100.

29 GRAVES CREEK
18.0 mi/2 days   🏃3 ⛰8

northeast of Quinault in Olympic National Park

Map 1.4, page 42

Sometimes the itch to visit the Quinault area cannot be denied. The desire to see big trees, experience high-country meadows, and hear the boom of a roaring creek must be met. Fortunately, Graves Creek Trail scratches these itches without the considerable crowds of people found in the Enchanted Valley.

Graves Creek Trail begins soon after crossing Graves Creek on Quinault River Trail. It climbs gently above Graves Creek, which roars from within a box canyon for most of its descent. The trail makes a lot of ups and downs, but the overall trend is definitely up. At 3.2 miles the trail crosses Graves Creek, which can be difficult at times of high water (fall and spring). The forest breaks as meadows take over, a place where most hikers linger to fill up on huckleberries. The trail reaches Sundown Lake, set within a small glacial cirque complete with campsites. The trail eventually winds up at Six Ridge Pass and continues as Six Ridge Trail.

User Groups: Hikers only. No dogs, horses, or mountain bikes are allowed. No wheelchair access.

Permits: This trail is accessible July–October. No permits are needed for parking. Overnight stays within the national park require backcountry camping permits, which are available at the Wilderness Information Center in Port Angeles.

Maps: For a map of Olympic National Park, contact the Outdoor Recreation Information Center at the downtown Seattle REI. For topographic maps, ask Green Trails for No. 166, Mount Christie, or ask the USGS for Mount Hoquim.

Directions: From Forks, drive south on U.S. 101 to South Shore Road. Turn left (east) and drive 18.5 miles to Graves Creek Ranger Station and the signed trailhead.

Contact: Olympic National Park, Wilderness Information Center, 3002 Mount Angeles Rd., Port Angeles, WA 98362, 360/565-3100.

30 LAKE QUINAULT TRAILS
0.6-4.0 mi/0.5-2.0 hr   🏃1 ⛰9

on the shores of Lake Quinault in Olympic National Forest

Map 1.4, page 42

Lake Quinault Loop is one of three trails on the south side of the lake. Built within exceptional old-growth forests, the three trails offer two loops and a creek hike. The shortest of the three is Rain Forest Trail, a loop that finds its way into a stand of 500-year-old Douglas firs. Signs are placed along the path to enlighten hikers on the forest's ecology. The trail also passes a great stretch of Willaby Creek running through a gorge.

Rain Forest Trail is a larger undertaking of 4 miles. It ventures farther into the forest, crossing a swamp on well-built puncheons and passing Cascade Falls on Falls Creek. It returns to the trailhead via Lake Quinault Shoreline Trail. The final hike is into Willaby Creek. A steady forest of immense proportions follows hikers to a granddaddy of cedars. The trail crosses the creek, which can be tricky, and eventually peters out. All three trails offer typically large Olympic forests full of moss and ferns. These are trails for the whole family to relish, regardless of age or hiking ability.

User Groups: Hikers and leashed dogs. No horses or mountain bikes are allowed. No wheelchair access.

Permits: This area is accessible year-round. No permit is needed to park. Parking is free.

Maps: For a map of Olympic National Forest, contact the Outdoor Recreation Information Center at the downtown Seattle REI. For topographic maps, ask Green Trails for No.

197, Quinault Lake, or ask the USGS for Lake Quinault East.

Directions: From Forks, drive south on U.S. 101 to South Shore Road. Turn left (east) and drive 1.5 miles to the signed trailhead on the right side of the road.

Contact: Olympic National Forest, Quilcene Ranger Station, 295142 U.S. 101 South, Quilcene, WA 98376, 360/765-2200.

31 COLONEL BOB MOUNTAIN
14.4 mi/8.0 hr

east of Quinault in the Colonel Bob Wilderness of Olympic National Forest

Map 1.4, page 42

It's a hard climb from the bottoms of the Quinault Valley to the peaks of the southern ridge, the home of Colonel Bob Mountain. The overall elevation gain is greater than 4,000 feet, much of which is covered twice on this hike. The trail climbs out of the rainforests of the lower valley to subalpine meadows, where ridges and views seem to extend for days on end. While crowds of folks bump into each other down in the Enchanted Valley, far fewer people are to be found up here. Trips to Colonel Bob during June and July are absolutely wonderful, when the wildflowers are in full bloom and snowfields linger on distant mountains.

Colonel Bob Trail is a true scaling of the peak, starting directly from the Quinault River. The trail heads up through a forest of Douglas fir and western red cedar. Mosses, lichens, and ferns grow on anything that can support them. The trail eventually reaches the camps of Mulkey Shelter (4 miles) and Moonshine Flats (6 miles).

The trail now climbs steeply to a ridge and dishearteningly drops down the other side. Take courage in knowing that while you must give back some elevation, open meadows await you. The trail navigates between the surrounding peaks before ascending Colonel Bob. The views are grand from on top, revealing much of the southern Olympics.

User Groups: Hikers and leashed dogs. No horses or mountain bikes are allowed. No wheelchair access.

Permits: This trail is accessible mid-June–October. No permit is required to park. Parking is free.

Maps: For a map of Olympic National Forest, contact the Outdoor Recreation Information Center at the downtown Seattle REI. For topographic maps, ask Green Trails for No. 197, Quinault Lake, and No. 198, Griswold, or ask the USGS for Lake Quinault East and Colonel Bob.

Directions: From Forks, drive south on U.S. 101 to South Shore Road. Turn left (east) and drive 6 miles to the signed trailhead on the right side of the road.

Contact: Olympic National Forest, Quilcene Ranger Station, 295142 U.S. 101 South, Quilcene, WA 98376, 360/765-2200.

32 WYNOOCHEE PASS
7.2 mi/4.0 hr

east of Quinault in Olympic National Park

Map 1.4, page 42

This is not a long trail, and that's the beauty of it. Smart hikers know that Wynoochee Pass provides easy access to Sundown Lake and the incredible high country of the area. These spots add many additional miles and feet of elevation when accessed via two other converging trails. The few hikers who visit this trail each year find superb forests of mountain hemlock and silver fir along the route. It's nearly the perfect trail; not too long, incredibly scenic, and rarely used.

Wynoochee Pass Trail begins along an old logging road within the national forest before quickly entering the pristine confines of the national park. The trail is set high above the Wynoochee River, which at this location has neared the end of its journey. The trail makes a few switchbacks up to the small meadow at Wynoochee Pass; at just over 2 miles from the trailhead, the elevation is 3,600 feet. From here, hikers should follow a lightly used footpath for 1 mile to Sundown Lake and meadowy Sundown Pass. Since it's so far out of the way, it's understandable that so few people visit this part of the Olympics. But others' loss is your gain on Wynoochee Pass Trail. In the best sense of the term, it really is a getaway.

User Groups: Hikers only. No dogs, horses, or mountain bikes are allowed. No wheelchair access.

Permits: This trail is accessible May–November. Permits are not required. Parking and access are free.

Maps: For a map of Olympic National Park, contact the Outdoor Recreation Information Center at the downtown Seattle REI. For topographic maps, ask Green Trails for No. 166, Mount Christie, or ask the USGS for Mount Hoquim.

Directions: This road has experienced washouts in recent years. Call the WIC before choosing this hike to find out current road status, because alternative routes may be available. From Aberdeen, drive east 9 miles to Wynoochee Valley Road (just before Montesano). Turn left (north) and drive 33 miles to Forest Service Road 2270 (at a four-way intersection). Go straight on Forest Service Road 2270 and drive 12 miles to Forest Service Road 2270-400. Turn right and drive 2 miles to the signed trailhead.

Contact: Olympic National Park, Wilderness Information Center, 3002 Mount Angeles Rd., Port Angeles, WA 98362, 360/565-3100.

33 GRAY WOLF RIVER
30.2 mi/3-4 days

south of Sequim in Olympic National Park

Map 1.4, page 42

When the rain gives you pause about your planned trip to the west side of the peninsula, the little-visited Gray Wolf may be one of your better options. It's conveniently situated in the rain shadow of the Olympics, where much less rain falls than in other parts of the peninsula. So when it's raining on the west side, you're likely to luck out and stay dry in the rain shadow. This hike is quite long with the best parts, of course, far up the trail. The lower section of Gray Wolf is lowland river hiking.

© SCOTT LEONARD

enjoying the rumble of the Gray Wolf River

It's only above Three Forks, where Cameron and Grand Creeks join Gray Wolf, that the trail develops real personality.

Skip the lower half of the river and access Gray Wolf via Three Forks Trail (5.5 miles). From here, Gray Wolf Trail passes through beautiful forests of hemlock, cedar, and Douglas fir. A shelter is at Falls Camp (10.7 miles). From here, one can hike a way trail 3 miles up to Cedar Lake, a very large subalpine lake set within a large meadow. This little-visited spot alone is well worth a trip of several days.

Gray Wolf Trail continues by crossing the river several times and then beginning its real ascent. The basin at the head of the Gray Wolf is rather large and expansive. Several high tarns are set amid groves of mountain hemlocks and bare slides of shale. The basin is surrounded by high peaks, including the Needles as they extend from Mount Deception. The trail continues by steeply descending to Dosewallips River Trail.

User Groups: Hikers only. No dogs, horses, or mountain bikes are allowed. No wheelchair access.

Permits: This trail is usually accessible May–October. A federal Northwest Forest Pass is required to park here. Overnight stays require backcountry camping permits, which are available at the Quilcene Ranger Station.

Maps: For a map of Olympic National Park, contact the Outdoor Recreation Information Center at the downtown Seattle REI. For topographic maps, ask Green Trails for No. 135, Mount Angeles, and No. 136, Tyler Peak, or ask the USGS for Tyler Peak, Maiden Peak, and Wellesley Peak.

Directions: From Sequim, drive 3 miles east on U.S. 101 to Palo Alto Road. Turn right (south) and drive 7.5 miles to Forest Service Road 2880. Turn right and drive 1 mile to Forest Service Road 2870. Turn right and drive 0.5 mile to the signed trailhead.

Contact: Olympic National Forest, Quilcene Ranger Station, 295142 U.S. 101 South, Quilcene, WA 98376, 360/765-2200.

34 MOUNT ZION
3.6 mi/2.0 hr   2 8

west of Quilcene in Olympic National Forest

Map 1.4, page 42

This is one of the Olympics' easier, more accessible peaks. It's not one of the tallest peaks, yet it offers its fair share of views from the northeast corner of the peninsula. A forested trail deposits hikers at a fairly flat, open summit. In comparison with the rest of the Olympics, it is in close proximity to Seattle, making it a great day hike for those with an itch for the Olympics.

The trail's best attraction is the plethora of rhododendrons that grace the forest blanketing the route. They are in full bloom during June and will make for one of the lasting memories of the hike. The trail gains just 1,300 feet on its ascent, pretty light fare for summit hikes. The forest eventually gives way near the summit to grand views of Olympic ranges and peaks. Mount Baker and the Cascades are visible beyond Puget Sound on clear days. On days that aren't so clear, fear not. Mount Zion is in the Olympic rain shadow, a corner of the mountain range that receives much less rain than the other parts of the peninsula. So when it's raining elsewhere, Mount Zion will be much drier. In sum, Mount Zion is a wonderful trail for easy hiking and basking in the sun.

User Groups: Hikers, leashed dogs, horses, mountain bikes, and motorcycles are permitted. No wheelchair access.

Permits: This trail is accessible mid-May–November (accessible nearly year-round with snowshoes). A federal Northwest Forest Pass is required to park here.

Maps: For a map of Olympic National Forest, contact the Outdoor Recreation Information Center at the downtown Seattle REI. For topographic maps, ask Green Trails for No. 136, Tyler Peak, or ask the USGS for Mount Zion.

Directions: From Quilcene, drive north 1.5 miles on U.S. 101 to Lords Lake Road. Follow

Lords Lake Road to the lake and turn left onto Forest Service Road 28. Drive to Bon Jon Pass and turn right onto Forest Service Road 2810. The trailhead is 2 miles ahead on the left.

Contact: Olympic National Forest, Hood Canal Ranger Station, 295142 U.S. 101 South, Quilcene, WA 98376 (2 miles from Highway 101 on South Shore Quinault Road), 360/765-2200.

35 TUBAL CAIN
17.4 mi/2 days   🥾3 ⛰9

west of Quilcene in the Buckhorn Wilderness of Olympic National Forest

Map 1.4, page 42

Tubal Cain Trail is more than a secluded forest or place of expansive mountain views. Unlike most wilderness settings, the route features a good deal of evidence of mankind. Along the route are a pair of easy-to-find old mines. Here, copper, manganese, and other minerals were extracted from the flanks of Iron and Buckhorn Mountains. But another unexpected find is made along a side trail, deep within a high basin. Tull Canyon is the final resting place for an old Air Force B-17. The plane crashed here more than 50 years ago and has been left intact.

The trail immediately crosses Silver Creek to climb the valley within thick growth of rhododendrons, in full bloom in June. At 3.2 miles is the junction with Tull Canyon Trail. Tubal Cain Mine (and campground) lies on the east side of the creek a short 0.5 mile later. The shaft of the mine ventures into the mountain for a distance of nearly 3,000 feet. Although the mine shaft is unsafe for exploration, there are many old relics left outside the mine. From Tubal Cain Mine, the trail becomes more scenic as it climbs to Buckhorn Lake (5.5 miles). This is a good turnaround point for day hikers. Buckhorn and Iron Mountains stand imposingly across the valley at this point, guarding their treasures. The trail ends at Marmot Pass, where meadows are awash in wildflowers during July.

User Groups: Hikers, leashed dogs, and horses. No mountain bikes are allowed. No wheelchair access.

Permits: This trail is accessible June–October. Permits are not required, parking and access are free.

Maps: For a map of Olympic National Forest, contact the Outdoor Recreation Information Center at the downtown Seattle REI. For topographic maps, ask Green Trails for No. 136, Tyler Peak, or ask the USGS for Mount Townsend and Mount Deception.

Directions: From Sequim, drive 3 miles east on U.S. 101 to Palo Alto Road. Turn right (south) and drive 7.5 miles to Forest Service Road 28. Stay left and drive 1 mile to Forest Service Road 2860. Turn right and drive a long 14.5 miles to the signed trailhead.

Contact: Olympic National Forest, Quinault Wilderness Information Office, 295142 U.S. 101 South, Quilcene, WA 98376 (2 miles from Highway 101 on South Shore Quinault Road), 360/288-0232.

36 ROYAL BASIN
16.2 mi/2 days   🥾3 ⛰10

south of Sequim in Olympic National Park

Map 1.4, page 42

Unrivaled in beauty, Royal Basin Trail travels miles of old-growth forest before reaching acres of parkland meadows beneath towering peaks. This is one trail that guidebook authors prefer to keep mum about.

Royal Basin Trail begins along Dungeness River Trail 1 mile from the trailhead, where Royal Creek enters the river. Stay to the right on Royal Basin Trail. Easy to follow and well maintained, the trail serves hikers of all abilities as it courses through forest and avalanche tracks. Progress up the trail is easy to gauge as the forest changes from Douglas firs and western hemlocks to silver firs, yellow cedars, and finally subalpine firs. Campsites are found at the first meadow; these make a good alternative to the traditional campground a mile farther at Royal Lake.

The trail clambers over a terrace to reach Royal Lake. The large basin reveals Mount Deception, the Olympics' second-highest peak, and the always-impressive Needles, a long, jagged ridge. Explore to your heart's content, but stay on established trails, please. Parkland and meadows abound here, with wildflowers that burst with color in early summer. At the top of the basin is Royal Glacier, which you can walk on, while a trip to the shoulder below Mount Deception is also possible, revealing the Elwha River drainage. Royal Basin is sure to capture your heart. So hike Royal Basin and then lie about where you've been to anyone who asks.

User Groups: Hikers only. No dogs, horses, or mountain bikes are allowed. No wheelchair access.

Permits: This trail is usually accessible mid-June–October. A federal Northwest Forest Pass is required to park here. Overnight stays require backcountry camping permits, which are available at the Port Angeles Wilderness Information Center. Camping is limited between May 1 and September 30. Reservations are required.

Maps: For a map of Olympic National Park, contact the Outdoor Recreation Information Center at the downtown Seattle REI. For topographic maps, ask Green Trails for No. 136, Tyler Peak, or ask the USGS for Mount Deception.

Directions: From Sequim, drive 3 miles east on U.S. 101 to Palo Alto Road. Turn right (south) and drive 7.5 miles to Forest Service Road 28. Stay left and drive 1 mile to Forest Service Road 2860. Turn right and drive 11 miles to the signed Dungeness Trailhead.

Contact: Olympic National Park, Wilderness Information Center, 3002 Mount Angeles Rd., Port Angeles, WA 98362, 360/565-3100; Olympic National Forest, Quinault Wilderness Information Office, 295142 U.S. 101 South, Quilcene, WA 98376 (2 miles from Highway 101 on South Shore Quinault Road), 360/288-0232.

37 UPPER DUNGENESS
12.4 mi/6.0 hr

west of Quilcene in the Buckhorn Wilderness of Olympic National Forest

Map 1.4, page 42

The Upper Dungeness River is one of the most picturesque of the Olympics' many rivers, and this trail captures much of its scenic beauty. The trail follows the Dungeness as it passes through outstanding forests and eventually reaches a major junction, high within a mountain basin. Along the way is Heather Creek Trail, a nonmaintained route heading directly into the Olympics' wild interior. Add the fact that the Dungeness receives less rain than most of the peninsula, and you have a popular off-season hike.

The trail makes its way along the valley bottom for the first mile to a junction with Royal Basin Trail. Cross Royal Creek to stay on Dungeness Trail. The forest here is superb, with large Douglas firs, red cedars, and western hemlocks towering over an open understory. The trail eventually crosses the Dungeness to the east side and comes to Camp Handy, at 3.2 miles. Great camps are found within this slightly wooded meadow.

From Camp Handy, Heather Creek Trail continues up the valley alongside the Dungeness for another 4 miles. This stretch is not maintained and is fairly undisturbed wilderness. Dungeness Trail leaves Camp Handy to begin climbing out of the valley and into parkland meadows. The trail ends at Boulder Camp, the junction with Constance Pass Trail and Big Quilcene Trail.

User Groups: Hikers, leashed dogs, and horses. No mountain bikes are allowed. No wheelchair access.

Permits: This trail is accessible June–October. A federal Northwest Forest Pass is required to park here. Overnight stays require backcountry camping permits, which are available at the Port Angeles Wilderness Information Center.

Maps: For a map of Olympic National Forest, contact the Outdoor Recreation Information Center at the downtown Seattle REI. For topographic maps, ask Green Trails for No. 136, Tyler Peak, or ask the USGS for Mount Deception, Tyler Peak, and Mount Zion.

Directions: From Sequim, drive 3 miles east on U.S. 101 to Palo Alto Road. Turn right (south) and drive 7.5 miles to Forest Service Road 28. Stay left and drive 1 mile to Forest Service Road 2860. Turn right and drive 11 miles to the signed Dungeness Trailhead.

Contact: Olympic National Forest, Hood Canal Ranger Station, 295142 U.S. 101 South, Quilcene, WA 98376, 360/765-2200.

38 MOUNT TOWNSEND
7.8 mi/4.5 hr   3   9

west of Quilcene in Buckhorn Wilderness of Olympic National Forest

Map 1.4, page 42

Upon reaching the top of Mount Townsend, hikers may be hard-pressed to decide if they're in the midst of mountains or perched above long stretches of Puget waterways. This lofty summit strategically puts you smack-dab in the middle of the two settings. The grand, competing vistas are likely to vie for your attention during the length of your stay here. Be thankful. High mountain meadows scrubbed by forceful winds, complete with requisite berries, complement the experience. It's no wonder that Mount Townsend is one of the peninsula's more popular day hikes.

Mount Townsend Trail climbs steadily throughout its length. The first couple of miles pass through forest punctuated by rhododendrons (catch them blooming in June). At 2.5 miles lies Camp Windy (not nearly as windy as Townsend's summit), and the trail soon reaches a junction with Silver Lakes Trail. Mount Townsend Trail harshly climbs through opening meadows, full of late summer's huckleberries. Snow and wind limit the growth of the subalpine trees, leaving vistas for hikers. The summit is long and flat with superb views. Nearly the full range of the Cascades lines the east, while Mount Deception and The Needles are highlights of the Olympic Range. The trail continues for another 1.4 miles down to Little Quilcene River Trail.

User Groups: Hikers, leashed dogs, and horses are permitted. No mountain bikes are allowed. No wheelchair access.

Permits: This trail is accessible June–October. A federal Northwest Forest Pass is required to park here.

Maps: For a map of Olympic National Forest, contact the Outdoor Recreation Information Center at the downtown Seattle REI. For topographic maps, ask Green Trails for No. 136, Tyler Peak, or ask the USGS for Mount Townsend.

Directions: From Quilcene, drive 1 mile south on U.S. 101 to Penny Creek Road. Turn right (west) and drive 1.5 miles to Big Quilcene Road. Stay to the left at this Y and drive 3 miles to the Forest Service boundary and paved Forest Service Road 27. Drive 9 miles to Forest Service Road 2760. Drive 1 mile to the trailhead at road's end.

Contact: Olympic National Forest, Quinault Wilderness Information Office, 295142 U.S. 101 South, Quilcene, WA 98376 (2 miles from Highway 101 on South Shore Quinault Road), 360/288-0232.

39 SILVER LAKES
10.8 mi/6.0 hr   4   8

west of Quilcene in the Buckhorn Wilderness of Olympic National Forest

Map 1.4, page 42

It takes a harsh rainstorm to ruin a trip to Silver Lakes. And that's a less-than-likely proposition since this trail is snugly tucked away in the peninsula's rain shadow. Silver Lakes nestle within a large basin rimmed with jagged peaks. Subalpine firs are amply spread around the lakes, mingling with meadows of heather. Alpine flowers add strokes of color and are likely to provide great memories and photo ops. Throw in some good scrambles at the end to an extremely pleasant hike and you have yourself a thoroughly agreeable trip.

Silver Lakes Trail begins on Mount Townsend Trail, 2.9 miles from the trailhead (see listing in this chapter). The trail immediately drops into the forested valley, crosses Silver Creek, and makes a quick ascent to the larger Silver Lake. The smaller and less visited lake is just before the larger one, to the west off a visible side trail.

Parkland surrounds the lake, with large meadows of wildflowers mingling with small stands of subalpine fir. There are several campsites for overnight guests. The lake is favored by swimmers and anglers alike. Be sure to scramble the slope rising to the south, between rocky peaks, for more wildflowers and the prime views.

User Groups: Hikers, leashed dogs, and horses. No mountain bikes are allowed. No wheelchair access.

Permits: This trail is accessible July–October. Permits are not required, parking and access are free.

Maps: For a map of Olympic National Forest, contact the Outdoor Recreation Information Center at the downtown Seattle REI. For topographic maps, ask Green Trails for No. 136, Tyler Peak, or ask the USGS for Mount Townsend.

Directions: From Quilcene, drive 1 mile south on U.S. 101 to Penny Creek Road. Turn right (west) and drive 1.5 miles to Big Quilcene Road. Stay to the left at this Y and drive 3 miles to the Forest Service boundary and paved Forest Service Road 27. Drive 9 miles to Forest Service Road 2760. Drive 1 mile to the trailhead at road's end.

Contact: Olympic National Forest, Quinault Wilderness Information Office, 295142 U.S. 101 South, Quilcene, WA 98376 (2 miles from Highway 101 on South Shore Quinault Road), 360/288-0232.

40 UPPER BIG QUILCENE
10.6 mi/5.5 hr   🥾3 ⛰️9

west of Quilcene in the Buckhorn Wilderness of Olympic National Forest

Map 1.4, page 42

Rarely can hikers get to such an outstanding viewpoint, with so much wild country spread before them, than with Upper Big Quilcene Trail. Passing through virgin timber and open, pristine meadows, the trail delivers hikers to Marmot Pass. This is an opportunity to view many of the Olympics' most impressive peaks, including Mount Mystery and Mount Deception. The trail is one of the best on the peninsula's east side and perfect for an outing with the dog.

The trail follows the river for several miles, where the forest consists of old-growth Douglas fir, western hemlock, and western red cedar. In June, rhododendrons light up the understory with fragrant blossoms. The trail then climbs gently but steadily out of the valley. Good camps are at Shelter Rock (2.6 mi) and Camp Mystery (4.6 mi), each next to water. The trail eventually broaches the confines of forest and finds itself at Marmot Pass, where one can finally see all that is to the north of the ridge. Grand views of near and far mountains are plentiful. The trail junctions here with Tubal Cain Trail before dropping to Boulder Camp. Constance Pass and Upper Dungeness Trails meet at Boulder Camp.

User Groups: Hikers and leashed dogs. No horses or mountain bikes are allowed. No wheelchair access.

Permits: This trail is accessible July–October. A federal Northwest Forest Pass is required to park here.

Maps: For a map of Olympic National Forest, contact the Outdoor Recreation Information Center at the downtown Seattle REI. For topographic maps, ask Green Trails for No. 136, Tyler Peak, or ask the USGS for Mount Townsend and Mount Deception.

Directions: From Quilcene, drive 1 mile south on U.S. 101 to Penny Creek Road. Turn right (west) and drive 1.5 miles to Big Quilcene Road. Stay left at this Y and drive 3 miles to the Forest Service boundary and paved Forest Service Road 27. Drive 6 miles to Forest Service Road 2750. Stay to the left and drive 4.5 miles to the signed trailhead.

Contact: Olympic National Forest, Hood Canal Ranger Station, 295142 U.S. 101 South, Quilcene, WA 98376 (2 miles from Highway 101 on South Shore Quinault Road), 360/765-2200.

41 TUNNEL CREEK
8.2 mi/4.5 hr

west of Quilcene in the Buckhorn Wilderness of Olympic National Forest

Map 1.4, page 42

The trail up Tunnel Creek leads to a pair of subalpine lakes and a pass with far-reaching views. It's a popular day hike, whisking hikers from old-growth forests along the valley floor to open meadows and views up high. Never mind the steep final ascent to the lakes and 50-50 Pass, as you'll have plenty of time to rest while surveying the mountainous horizon.

The trail ventures easily through great forests of Douglas fir and western red cedar accompanied by numerous rhododendrons (blooming in June) for 2.7 miles. Here, the trail encounters Tunnel Creek Shelter, where a few campsites can be found. Beyond this point, the route steeply climbs to the Twin Lakes (3.7 miles). The lakes are situated in a tiny basin and bounded by mountain hemlocks, an appealing setting. The trail climbs a bit more to 50-50 Pass, at elevation 5,050 feet. This is mostly just a rocky promontory, but the views are grand during clear weather. Nowhere is Mount Constance better seen, with

pockets of snow often finding refuge among the many crags and faces. Views toward Puget Sound stand out as well. This is the ideal place to turn around; otherwise, a sharp descent awaits, into a valley other than the one where your car is parked.

User Groups: Hikers, leashed dogs, and horses are permitted. No mountain bikes are allowed. No wheelchair access.

Permits: This trail is accessible mid-June–October. Permits are not required. Parking and access are free.

Maps: For a map of Olympic National Forest, contact the Outdoor Recreation Information Center at the downtown Seattle REI. For topographic maps, ask Green Trails for No. 136, Tyler Peak, and No. 168, The Brothers, or ask the USGS for Mount Townsend.

Directions: From Quilcene, drive 1 mile south on U.S. 101 to Penny Creek Road. Turn right (west) and drive 1.5 miles to Big Quilcene Road. Stay left at this Y and drive 3 miles to the Forest Service boundary and Forest Service Road 2740. Stay to the left at this Y and drive 6.5 miles to the signed trailhead.

Contact: Olympic National Forest, Quinault Wilderness Information Office, 295142 U.S. 101 South, Quilcene, WA 98376 (2 miles from Highway 101 on South Shore Quinault Road), 360/288-0232.

42 WEST FORK DOSEWALLIPS
31.0 mi/3-4 days

south of Quilcene in Olympic National Park

Map 1.4, page 42

West Fork Dosewallips Trail is half of one of the premier routes for trekking across the Olympic Range. Making its way along the west fork of its namesake, the trail reaches Anderson Pass and connects to the legendary Enchanted Valley. This route has had its troubles in recent years. A suspension bridge has been repeatedly washed out and then rebuilt, only to be washed out again. Currently, a bridge is in place, but be sure to call the Wilderness Information Center for current access status.

West Fork Dosewallips Trail begins 1.4 miles up Dosewallips River Trail (actually 6.5 miles because the road is permanently out 5 miles below the trailhead) at a signed junction. After a short distance lies the troubled bridge crossing over a beautiful canyon. Beyond, the trail weaves through grand old-growth forest. Big Timber Camp is at 4.2 miles (from the Dosewallips Ranger Station) and Diamond Meadows is at 6.6 miles.

The trail climbs to Honeymoon Meadows, wide open meadows of grass and flowers, and eventually to Anderson Pass (access to the Enchanted Valley). This low pass is a real playground, with a trail leading to Anderson Glacier and its craggy home, the highlight of the trip. A final camp is just below the pass.

User Groups: Hikers and horses. No dogs or mountain bikes are allowed. No wheelchair access.

Permits: This trail is accessible June–October. Low elevations are usually accessible April through October, sometimes year-round. No permit is required to park here. Parking is free. Overnight stays within the national park require backcountry camping permits, which are available at the Wilderness Information Center in Port Angeles.

Maps: For a map of Olympic National Park, contact the Outdoor Recreation Information Center at the downtown Seattle REI. For topographic maps, ask Green Trails for No. 168, The Brothers, and No. 167, Mount Steel, or ask the USGS for The Brothers and Mount Steel.

Directions: From Quilcene, drive south 11.5 miles on U.S. 101 to Dosewallips River Road. Turn right (west) and drive about 10 miles to the road's end at a washout. The trail is on the right side of the road and climbs above the washout before returning to the road, 5 miles from Dosewallips Ranger Station.

Contact: Olympic National Park, Wilderness Information Center, 3002 Mount Angeles Rd., Port Angeles, WA 98362, 360/565-3100.

43 MAIN FORK DOSEWALLIPS RIVER

40.0 mi/4 days

south of Quilcene in Olympic National Park

Map 1.4, page 42

This exceptionally beautiful river valley has suddenly become much more remote. A few years back, the river wiped out the road to the trailhead, adding roughly 5 miles to the hike. This has weeded out a considerable number of visitors, and now the hike is a wilderness lover's dream come true. But don't worry about hiking an extra 5 miles, all of it on the old road. The trek is easily worth it.

After 5 miles along the old road, the abandoned car camp of Muscott Flats appears. The trail begins here at the ranger station. Dosewallips River Trail follows the river before splitting at 1.5 miles. Stay on the right fork to continue along the main Dosewallips Trail. Dosewallips Trail makes a long journey through typically grand forests of Douglas fir, hemlock, and cedar and passes three established camps on its way to Dose Meadows Camp, 12.5 miles from the end of the road.

The final 2.5 miles is the best part as it breaks out into spacious meadows. The trail begins a more steady ascent from here to Hayden Pass. Along the way is 1,000 Acre Meadow, a wildflower mecca off trail to the southeast for adventurous types. Those who make it to the pass will be rewarded. Countless peaks outline several valleys streaking away from this point. And, of course, Mount Olympus shines from the west.

User Groups: Hikers and horses are permitted. No dogs or mountain bikes are allowed. No wheelchair access.

Permits: This trail is usually accessible mid-May–October. No permit is required to park here. Parking is free. Overnight stays within the national park require backcountry camping permits, which are available at the Wilderness Information Center in Port Angeles.

Maps: For a map of Olympic National Park, contact the Outdoor Recreation Information

Center at the downtown Seattle REI. For topographic maps, ask Green Trails for No. 135, Mount Angeles, No. 136, Tyler Peak, and No. 168, The Brothers, or ask the USGS for The Brothers, Mount Deception, and Wellesley Peak.

Directions: From Quilcene, drive south 11.5 miles on U.S. 101 to Dosewallips River Road. Turn right (west) and drive about 10 miles to the road's end at a washout. The trail is on the right side of the road and climbs above the washout before returning to the road, 5 miles from Dosewallips Ranger Station.

Contact: Olympic National Park, Wilderness Information Center, 3002 Mount Angeles Rd., Port Angeles, WA 98362, 360/565-3100.

44 LAKE CONSTANCE
10.0 mi/6.0 hr

south of Quilcene in Olympic National Park

Map 1.4, page 42

You're likely to hear two things about Lake Constance. First, folks always mention the incredible beauty of the lake. Craggy Mount Constance towers above mountain hemlocks and subalpine firs that border the deep blue lake. But there's a catch, which you're also likely to hear about Lake Constance. The trail is unbelievably steep—3,300 feet in just 2 miles. That's steep enough to be the toughest climb in the Olympics and steep enough that you can forget about switchbacks. The trail heads straight up the ridge. Your arms will get as much of a workout as your legs as you grab onto roots and branches, pulling yourself up what barely qualifies as a trail. It's a very difficult climb and should not be undertaken by those unprepared for a strenuous ascent.

Camping is available at the lake, but because of heavy use, a permit and reservation are required for overnight stays. There are lots of opportunities to explore around the lake, but staying on established trails is important to prevent further ecosystem damage. Also, don't forget that the road up the Dosewallips is out

and requires about 3 miles of hiking on the old road to get to the trail. For those in shape enough to make it up to Lake Constance, it is well worth the effort.

User Groups: Hikers only. No dogs, horses, or mountain bikes are allowed. No wheelchair access.

Permits: This trail is usually accessible June–October. No permit is required to park here. Parking is free. Overnight stays at Lake Constance require reservations and backcountry camping permits.

Maps: For a map of Olympic National Park, contact the Outdoor Recreation Information Center at the downtown Seattle REI. For topographic maps, ask Green Trails for No. 168, The Brothers, or ask the USGS for The Brothers.

Directions: From Quilcene, drive south 11.5 miles on U.S. 101 to Dosewallips River Road. Turn right (west) and drive about 10 miles to the road's end at a washout. The trail is on the right side of the road and climbs above the washout before returning to the road, 3 miles from Lake Constance Trail.

Contact: Olympic National Park, Wilderness Information Center, 3002 Mount Angeles Rd., Port Angeles, WA 98362, 360/565-3100.

45 DUCKABUSH RIVER
43.6 mi/3-4 days

south of Quilcene in the Brothers Wilderness of Olympic National Forest and Olympic National Park

Map 1.4, page 42

The Duckabush ranks as one of the longest river valley trails on the peninsula. It starts just 6 miles from Hood Canal and makes a long trek up to the river's headwaters. Much of the forest is big old-growth, and wildlife is regularly seen throughout the valley. Yet Duckabush Trail receives only moderate use, tapering off significantly farther up the lengthy valley. As wilderness lovers would say, "Other people's loss is our gain."

The main reasons few people venture far into the Duckabush are Little Hump and Big Hump. Elevation gains of 500 feet and 1,100 feet weed out many a noncommitted day hiker. Thank Big Hump, however, for preventing timber-cutting in the upper river valley. This obstacle kept much of the valley forested in old-growth, the main theme of the trail.

Good spots to throw down for the night are found at 5 Mile and 10 Mile Camps. The trail finally reaches the steep walls of Duckabush Basin after 20 miles. The trail makes a steep ascent to La Crosse Basin, a beautiful collection of high-country lakes, and O'Neil Pass. O'Neil Pass features scenery so spectacular that it's pretty much beyond compare to anything else in the Olympics. Magnificent mountains, valleys, and rivers sum it up best. It may be a lot of hard work to get very far on Duckabush Trail, but it will be well remembered.

User Groups: Hikers and horses. No dogs or mountain bikes are allowed. No wheelchair access.

Permits: The lower part of this trail is accessible year-round (the upper part is accessible July–October). A federal Northwest Forest Pass is required to park here. Overnight stays require backcountry camping permits, which are available at the Wilderness Information Center in Port Angeles.

Maps: For a map of Olympic National Park, contact the Outdoor Recreation Information Center at the downtown Seattle REI. For topographic maps, ask Green Trails for No. 167, Mount Steel, and No. 168, The Brothers, or ask the USGS for Mount Steel, The Brothers, and Mount Jupiter.

Directions: From Quilcene, drive 16 miles south on U.S. 101 to the Duckabush River Road (Forest Service Road 2510). Turn right (west) and drive 5.5 miles to Forest Service Road 2510-060. Turn right and drive 0.1 mile to a large parking lot and the signed trailhead.

Contact: Olympic National Park, Wilderness Information Center, 3002 Mount Angeles Rd., Port Angeles, WA 98362, 360/565-3100; Olympic National Forest, Hoodsport Ranger District, 150 N. Lake Cushman Rd., Hoodsport, WA 98548, 360/877-5254.

46 LENA LAKES

6.0–12.0 mi/3.5 hr-2 days 🏃5 ⛰10

south of Quilcene in Olympic National Park

Map 1.4, page 42

Upper Lena Lake may possibly render hikers speechless with its beauty and open views. Meanwhile, the trail up to Lena Lake will certainly leave hikers breathless with its intense steep ascent and sections that require something more akin to scrambling than hiking. Lower Lena Lake is a much less strenuous excursion. Both lakes are great day hikes but also feature many campsites for overnight visits.

Lena Lake Trail climbs gently but steadily through 3 miles of shady forest to Lower Lena Lake. Dogs and mountain bikes are allowed up to this point, where numerous camps encircle the large lake. Upper Lena Lake Trail continues from the northeast corner of the lake and climbs strenuously for another 3 miles. This section features switchback after switchback as it ascends the steep valley. Be prepared for a rocky, narrow, and brushy trip.

The upper lake sits among some of the Olympics' best parkland meadows. Mount Bretherton stands to the south while Mount Lena fills the northern horizon. The National Park Service maintains numerous campsites around the eastern and southern shores of the lake. Footpaths create weblike patterns into the lakeside meadows. Be careful of treading into revegetation plots, where the park is aiding regrowth of the very sensitive meadow ecosystem. Although Upper Lena Lake receives many visitors during the summer, it is worthy of all the attention it receives.

User Groups: Hikers only. No dogs, horses, or mountain bikes are allowed. No wheelchair access.

Permits: This trail is accessible July–October.

A federal Northwest Forest Pass is required to park here. Overnight stays require backcountry camping permits, which are available at the park boundary.

Maps: For a map of Olympic National Park, contact the Outdoor Recreation Information Center at the downtown Seattle REI. For topographic maps, ask Green Trails for No. 168, The Brothers, or ask the USGS for Mount Washington and The Brothers.

Directions: From Quilcene, drive south 24 miles on U.S. 101 to Forest Service Road 25. Turn right and drive 8 miles to the Lena Lakes Trailhead.

Contact: Olympic National Park, Wilderness Information Center, 3002 Mount Angeles Rd., Port Angeles, WA 98362, 360/565-3100.

47 THE BROTHERS
3.0 mi/2.0 hr

south of Quilcene in the Brothers Wilderness of Olympic National Forest

Map 1.4, page 42

While The Brothers are the most easily recognized Olympic peaks from Seattle, visitors to the peninsula rarely hike this trail. That's because The Brothers Trail is primarily used by climbers to reach the base camp for a shot at the mountain's summit. The trail to the base camp is hikable for almost anyone, but since you won't see much, it's hardly worth it. To really appreciate The Brothers, you would have to go beyond the trail and ascend the mountain, which is not a job for amateurs. So unless you're ready for some real mountaineering, The Brothers Trail is best left as a through-way for climbers.

The trail begins near the northwest corner of Lena Lake, where Lena Creek empties into the lake. It is rocky and overcome with roots in places. It even requires some careful maneuvering over boulder fields. The trail enters the Valley of Silent Men, named for the climbers from Lena Lake passing through before the sun rises or the conversation heats

up. The trail passes back and forth over East Lena Creek several times and after 3 miles crosses one last time, skirts a small pond, and ends at The Brothers base camp. Most hikers should turn around here.

Beyond the base camp, climbing The Brothers is recommended only with the proper gear and training. It's a pretty serious ascent, not a scramble for novices. Hikers intending to go up to the summit should consult climbing guides that cover this peak or contact the ranger station in Quilcene.

User Groups: Hikers, leashed dogs, and horses. No mountain bikes are allowed. No wheelchair access.

Permits: This trail is accessible June–October. A Federal Northwest Forest Pass is required to park here.

Maps: For a map of Olympic National Forest, contact the Outdoor Recreation Information Center at the downtown Seattle REI. For topographic maps, ask Green Trails for No. 168, The Brothers, or ask the USGS for Mount Washington and The Brothers.

Directions: From Quilcene, drive south 24 miles on U.S. 101 to Forest Service Road 25. Turn right and drive 8 miles to the Lena Lakes Trailhead.

Contact: Olympic National Forest, Hoodsport Ranger Station, 150 N. Lake Cushman Rd., Hoodsport, WA 98548, 360/877-5254.

48 PUTVIN
8.0 mi/4.0 hr   4   9

south of Quilcene in Mount Skokomish Wilderness of Olympic National Forest and in Olympic National Park

Map 1.4, page 42

Putvin Trail includes much of what is great about the Olympics. There are forests full of trees big enough to test the limits of how far you can crane your neck, and there are prime subalpine meadows, full of heather and huckleberries, enough to make your mouth water. And, of course, there are outstanding views, enough to make you rub your eyes. It's a steep trail, gaining 3,400 feet in just 4 miles. But as the pilgrims once said, there's redemption in suffering.

Putvin Trail starts off in the river bottom of the Hamma Hamma, climbing through an old logging tract. The trail eventually enters the Mount Skokomish Wilderness (1.5 miles) and a land of big trees. After briefly leveling out, Putvin resumes climbing, arriving at several small tarns. Keep going, as this is not Lake of the Angels. It is farther yet, set within a small glacier cirque called the Valley of Heaven. Heaven indeed. The lake is absolutely beautiful, surrounded by meadows and craggy peaks. Mount Skokomish and Mount Stone flank the valley's two ends. For outstanding views, hike the small footpath up to the long ridge separating the two peaks. From here, Putvin Trail's anonymity is hard to understand.

User Groups: Hikers and leashed dogs. No horses or mountain bikes are allowed. No wheelchair access.

Permits: This trail is accessible mid-June–November. Parking permit not required. Overnight stays require backcountry camping permits, which are available at Hoodsport Ranger Station.

Maps: For a map of Olympic National Park and Olympic National Forest, contact the Outdoor Recreation Information Center at the downtown Seattle REI. For topographic maps, ask Green Trails for No. 167, Mount Steel, and No. 168, The Brothers, or ask the USGS for Mount Skokomish.

Directions: From Hoodsport, drive 14 miles north on U.S. 101 to Forest Service Road 25 (Hamma Hamma Recreation Area). Turn left (west) and drive 12 miles to the Putvin Historical Marker. The trail is on the right side of the road. High clearance vehicles are recommended to access this trailhead.

Contact: Olympic National Forest, Hoodsport Ranger Station, 150 N. Lake Cushman Rd., Hoodsport, WA 98548, 360/877-5254; Olympic National Park, Wilderness Information Center, 3002 Mount Angeles Rd., Port Angeles, WA 98362, 360/565-3100.

49 MILDRED LAKES
9.8 mi/6.0 hr

northwest of Hoodsport in Mount Skokomish Wilderness of Olympic National Forest

Map 1.4, page 42

Although Mildred Lakes is gaining in popularity, you're likely to experience fewer fellow hikers here than elsewhere in the Olympics. The Forest Service provides little maintenance on the trail to help keep this sensitive area in good condition, as an easy trail would likely lead to overuse. Nonetheless, Mildred Lakes are still out there and very much worth visiting.

The trail climbs through an old logging tract before entering virgin forest. The trail is relatively easy to follow through the pleasant forest of hemlock and fir. Before long, however, the trail becomes increasingly infested with rocks and roots. At about 3 miles, you must cross a ravine more than 20 feet deep. Now the trail becomes really rough. Head straight up the steep mountainside, pulling yourself up by rocks and roots. At 4.9 miles, crest the ridge to find the Mildred Lakes Basin.

The basin holds three lakes bordered by subalpine firs and meadows of heather. The Sawtooth Range runs along the north and western part of the basin, with Mount Cruiser and Mount Lincoln acting as bookends to the jagged ridge. There are a fair number of campsites up here, but Leave-No-Trace principles are to be emphasized, as heavy use has been detrimental to the area in the past.

User Groups: Hikers and leashed dogs. No horses or mountain bikes are allowed. No wheelchair access.

Permits: This trail is accessible July–October. A federal Northwest Forest Pass is required to park here.

Maps: For a map of Olympic National Forest, contact the Outdoor Recreation Information Center at the downtown Seattle REI. For topographic maps, ask Green Trails for No. 167, Mount Steel, or ask the USGS for Mount Skokomish.

Directions: From Hoodsport, drive north 14 miles on U.S. 101 to Forest Service Road 25 (Hamma Hamma Recreation Area). Turn left (west) and drive 14 miles to Mildred Lakes Trailhead at road's end.

Contact: Olympic National Forest, Hoodsport Ranger Station, 150 N. Lake Cushman Rd., Hoodsport, WA 98548, 360/877-5254.

50 STAIRCASE RAPIDS
2.0 mi/1.0 hr

northwest of Hoodsport in Olympic National Park

Map 1.4, page 42

Walks through the forest rarely get better than this. Set along the North Fork Skokomish River within an old-growth forest, Staircase Rapids Trail is perfect for families and older hikers. The flat, level trail encounters several sites where the river pours over bedrock or rumbles over rapids. And it all occurs within one of the eastern Olympics' most beautiful old-growth forests. The trail has a bit of history, as well, as it was part of the original route taken by the O'Neil Expedition in 1890. This is either an excellent destination or just a great side trip to a bigger excursion.

The trail starts at Staircase Ranger Station on the west side of the river. The exceptional old-growth forest is highlighted by Big Cedar (accessible by a side trail signed "Big Cedar"). Definitely check it out. Along the way to the rapids are Red Reef, an outcropping of red limestone that does its best to hold back the rushing river, and Dolly Varden Pool, where rocky cliffs loom over the river as it rumbles between large boulders. The climax of the walk is Staircase Rapids, a series of regularly spaced terraces over which the river spills. This is easily one of the Olympics' most scenic stretches of river and well worth a visit.

User Groups: Hikers only. No dogs, horses, or mountain bikes are allowed. No wheelchair access.

Permits: This trail is accessible year-round. A National Parks Pass is required to park here.

Maps: For a map of Olympic National Park, contact the Outdoor Recreation Information Center at the downtown Seattle REI. For topographic maps, ask Green Trails for No. 167, Mount Steel, or ask the USGS for Mount Skokomish.

Directions: From Hoodsport, drive west 9 miles on Lake Cushman Road (Highway 119) to Forest Service Road 24 (a T intersection). Turn left and drive 6.5 miles to Staircase Ranger Station for the trailhead and trailhead parking.

Contact: Olympic National Park, Wilderness Information Center, 3002 Mount Angeles Rd., Port Angeles, WA 98362, 360/565-3100.

51 NORTH FORK SKOKOMISH
25.2 mi/2-3 days

northwest of Hoodsport in Olympic National Park

Map 1.4, page 42

The western rivers of the Olympic Mountains rightfully share reputations for forests of enormous proportions. While the North Fork Skokomish remains out of this limelight, it's no less impressive. The trail follows the North Fork Skokomish for 10 miles at relative ease, passing through a virgin forest full of massive trees. This route is historical, as well, having been blazed by Army Lieutenant Joseph P. O'Neil on the first east—west expedition of the Olympics in the winter of 1890.

The trail leaves Staircase Ranger Station along an old roadbed. It quickly encounters the Beaver Fire of 1985, where new firs are growing up among towering burned snags. At 5 miles, the trail crosses the Skokomish via a bridge where the slate-gray water passes through a beautiful box canyon bordered by colossal Douglas firs. The trail crosses several large streams, two of which lack a bridge and may be tricky in times of heavy runoff.

Camp Pleasant (6.4 miles) and Nine Stream Camp (9.3 miles) make for great places to spend the night and build a fire. After Nine Stream, the trail begins its ascent to First Divide through large mountain hemlocks and Douglas firs. After 3.5 miles of climbing, the trail reaches First Divide and several small tarns. Views into the upper Duckabush reward the long trek. Just beyond the pass, Home Sweet Home (13.5 miles) offers another great site for camping in a meadow setting.

User Groups: Hikers and horses. No dogs or mountain bikes are allowed. No wheelchair access.

Permits: The lower part of this trail is accessible year-round. The upper part is accessible June–October. A National Parks Pass is required to park here. Overnight stays in the national park require backcountry camping permits, which are available at the Wilderness Information Center in Port Angeles or at the Hoodsport Ranger Station.

Maps: For a map of Olympic National Park, contact the Outdoor Recreation Information Center at the downtown Seattle REI. For topographic maps, ask Green Trails for No. 167, Mount Steel, or ask the USGS for Mount Skokomish, Mount Olson, and Mount Steel.

Directions: From Hoodsport, drive west 9 miles on Lake Cushman Road (Highway 119) to Forest Service Road 24 (a T intersection). Turn left and drive 6.5 miles to Staircase Ranger Station for the trailhead and trailhead parking.

Contact: Olympic National Park, Wilderness Information Center, 3002 Mount Angeles Rd., Port Angeles, WA 98362, 360/565-3100; Olympic National Forest, Hoodsport Ranger Station, 150 N. Lake Cushman Rd., Hoodsport, WA 98548, 360/877-5254.

52 WAGONWHEEL LAKE
5.8 mi/3.5 hr

northwest of Hoodsport in Olympic National Park

Map 1.4, page 42

When people mention Wagonwheel Lake, they mostly condemn it to being nothing more than a conditioning hike. Consider that neither an insult nor compliment; it's mostly just the truth. After all, the trail makes a brutal ascent of 3,200 feet in less than 3 miles. For most hikers, a pace of 1,000 feet per mile is considered "difficult." Throw in the fact that there are few views to be had along the way or at the lake and you get only the diehards or the foolhardy on the trail.

Nearly the entire length of the trail is a steep climb through the forest. The lower part of the trail climbs via switchback through second-growth forest tamed by fire before eventually reaching some old-growth hemlock. After nearly 3 miles of huffing and puffing, hikers are delivered to Wagonwheel Lake, set within a small basin on the north side of Copper Mountain and bounded by a dense forest offering relatively no views. With all the hard work, why come here? Because a day in the woods is always a good day.

User Groups: Hikers only. No dogs, horses, or mountain bikes are allowed. No wheelchair access.

Permits: This trail is accessible July–November. A National Parks Pass is required to park here. Overnight stays in the national park require backcountry camping permits, which are available at Hoodsport Ranger Station.

Maps: For a map of Olympic National Park, contact the Outdoor Recreation Information Center at the downtown Seattle REI. For topographic maps, ask Green Trails for No. 167, Mount Steel, or ask the USGS for Mount Skokomish.

Directions: From Hoodsport, drive west 9 miles on Lake Cushman Road (Highway 119) to Forest Service Road 24 (a T intersection). Turn left and drive 6.5 miles to Staircase

Ranger Station for the trailhead and trailhead parking.

Contact: Olympic National Park, Wilderness Information Center, 3002 Mount Angeles Rd., Port Angeles, WA 98362, 360/565-3100; Olympic National Forest, Hoodsport Ranger Station, 150 N. Lake Cushman Rd., Hoodsport, WA 98548, 360/877-5254.

53 FLAPJACK LAKES
16.0 mi/2 days

northwest of Hoodsport in Olympic National Park

Map 1.4, page 42

Flapjack Lakes is one of the most scenic and popular destinations in Olympic National Park. So popular, in fact, that the Park Service instituted a permit system limiting the number of overnight campers here. Don't let that deter you, however, as it's a must-hike on any to-do list of Olympic trails. Plus, Flapjack Lakes are easily accessible, especially for families on a weekend excursion.

The route follows North Fork Skokomish Trail for 3.5 miles, where Flapjack Lake Trail takes off to the east. The trail steadily ascends through a forest of impressively large trees while following Donahue Creek. At 7 miles, the trail splits, with the left fork heading to Black and White Lakes. Stay to the right and find old mountain hemlocks, subalpine firs, and yellow cedars surrounding the two lakes. Mount Cruiser and the jagged ridge leading to Mount Lincoln enclose the eastern view; a way trail leading up to the Gladys Divide is a great side trip.

If the thought of crowds at Flapjacks is unappealing, an attractive alternative is Black and White Lakes. From the fork in the trail (7 miles), a mile of walking brings hikers to an open ridge below Mount Gladys. The lakes are small and have fewer campsites, but they are much more open and offer outstanding views of the entire North Fork Skokomish drainage. With several options for exploration, the Flapjack Lakes area is definitely a destination for Olympic enthusiasts to undertake.

User Groups: Hikers only. No dogs, horses, or mountain bikes are allowed. No wheelchair access.

Permits: This trail is accessible mid-May–October. A National Parks Pass is required to park at North Fork Skokomish Trailhead. Overnight stays in the national park require backcountry camping permits, which are available at Staircase Ranger Station. Camping permits are limited between May 1 and September 30th. Call 360/565-3100 for reservations.

Maps: For a map of Olympic National Park, contact the Outdoor Recreation Information Center at the downtown Seattle REI. For topographic maps, ask Green Trails for No. 167, Mount Steel, or ask the USGS for Mount Skokomish and Mount Olson.

Directions: From Hoodsport, drive west 9 miles on Lake Cushman Road (Highway 119) to Forest Service Road 24 (a T intersection). Turn left and drive 6.5 miles to Staircase Ranger Station for the trailhead and trailhead parking.

Contact: Olympic National Park, Wilderness Information Center, 3002 Mount Angeles Rd., Port Angeles, WA 98362, 360/565-3100.

54 SIX RIDGE
32.8 mi/3-4 days

northwest of Hoodsport in Olympic National Park

Map 1.4, page 42

If you are considering hiking Six Ridge, you are to be commended. You have a thirst for adventure and are undeterred by difficult ascents. You appreciate grand mountain views, love mountain meadows full of blooming wildflowers, and enjoy wilderness best when it's solitary. Six Ridge Trail is all that and more.

To access Six Ridge, one must first travel North Fork Skokomish Trail 5.6 miles, a flat and easy walk. Skokomish Trail crosses the river here and Six Ridge turns south. After crossing Seven Stream, the trail climbs gradually through forest to achieve the eastern end of Six Ridge. From here are 8 miles of ridge walking. The trail passes through exceptional subalpine meadows for much of the route, although fields of scree, talus, and even snow are common. There are several camps on the ridge, most notably McGravey Lakes at 8.5 miles up the ridge. The trail technically ends at Six Ridge Pass, where it becomes Graves Creek Trail but continues to Lake Sundown in 1.2 miles.

User Groups: Hikers only. No dogs, horses, or mountain bikes are allowed. No wheelchair access.

Permits: This trail is accessible mid-July–October. A National Parks Pass is required to park here. Overnight stays in the national park require backcountry camping permits, which are available at the Staircase Ranger Station.

Maps: For a map of Olympic National Park, contact the Outdoor Recreation Information Center at the downtown Seattle REI. For topographic maps, ask Green Trails for No. 166, Mount Christie, and No. 167, Mount Steel, or ask the USGS for Mount Skokomish, Mount Olson, and Mount Hoquim.

Directions: From Hoodsport, drive west 9 miles on Lake Cushman Road (Highway 119) to Forest Service Road 24 (a T intersection). Turn left and drive 6.5 miles to Staircase Ranger Station for the trailhead and trailhead parking.

Contact: Olympic National Park, Wilderness Information Center, 3002 Mount Angeles Rd., Port Angeles, WA 98362, 360/565-3100.

55 MOUNT ELLINOR
6.2 mi/3.0 hr   🏃4 ⛰8

northwest of Hoodsport in Mount Skokomish
Wilderness of Olympic National Forest

Map 1.4, page 42

Tucked away in the southeastern corner of the Olympic Peninsula, Mount Ellinor is rarely high on peoples' radar when they are looking for a hike. It gets less attention than other nearby spots, such as Mount Rose or Flapjack Lakes. But the trip is no less beautiful and actually features some the area's best views.

The trail has two trailheads, the lower one adding about 1.5 miles and 800 feet elevation gain to the trip. Since it's not much farther, the lower trailhead is the better choice, as it follows a well-forested ridge that should not be missed. The trail is a steady climb, rarely leveling out for more than a few yards. The forest breaks into avalanche chutes and meadows about 0.5 mile from the summit. At the top, views of Hood Canal, Lake Cushman, and neighboring Olympic peaks can be found. Neither well known nor frequently visited, Mount Ellinor makes for a perfect one-day getaway.

User Groups: Hikers and leashed dogs. No horses or mountain bikes are allowed. No wheelchair access.

Permits: This trail is accessible mid-June–November (accessible year-round with ice ax). A federal Northwest Forest Pass is required to park here.

Maps: For a map of Olympic National Forest, contact the Outdoor Recreation Information Center at the downtown Seattle REI. For topographic maps, ask Green Trails for No. 167, Mount Steel, and No. 168, The Brothers, or ask the USGS for Mount Washington and Mount Skokomish.

Directions: From Hoodsport, drive east 9 miles on Hoodsport Road (County Road 44) to Forest Service Road 24. Turn right and drive 1.5 miles to Forest Service Road 2419 (Big Creek Road). Turn left and drive 6 miles to Forest Service Road 2419-014. Turn left and drive 1 mile to the signed trailhead at road's end.

Contact: Olympic National Forest, Hoodsport Ranger Station, 150 N. Lake Cushman Rd., Hoodsport, WA 98548, 360/877-5254.

56 MOUNT ROSE

6.4 mi/3.5 hr

northwest of Hoodsport in Mount Skokomish Wilderness of Olympic National Forest

Map 1.4, page 42

Mount Rose is one of the more popular summits in the southeastern Olympic Mountains. Which means it must be awfully scenic, as it is certainly not an easy route. The trail is unique for a summit route in that it is a loop. Laid out like a lasso, the trail ascends straight to the summit and then makes a circle along the ridge to the trail again. Overall elevation gain is 3,500 feet in just about 3 miles.

The trail navigates a mile of second-growth timber before entering the wilderness. The rise to the junction (1.8 miles) is rather steep despite the many switchbacks. Head to the right for the more gradual route along the ridge. The trail has peek-a-boo views of neighboring peaks and drainages. The summit is forested save for a small chuck of basalt that reaches up roughly 30 feet. From the top are grand, panoramic views of Hood Canal and numerous Olympic peaks. Good luck, and enjoy the workout.

User Groups: Hikers and leashed dogs. No horses or mountain bikes are allowed. No wheelchair access.

Permits: This trail is accessible July–October. Permits are not required. Parking and access are free.

Maps: For a map of Olympic National Forest, contact the Outdoor Recreation Information Center at the downtown Seattle REI. For topographic maps, ask Green Trails for No. 167, Mount Steel, or ask the USGS for Lightning Peak and Mount Skokomish.

Directions: From Hoodsport, drive west 9 miles on Lake Cushman Road (Highway 119) to Forest Service Road 24 (a T intersection). Turn left and drive 3 miles to the signed trailhead on the right side of the road.

Contact: Olympic National Forest, Hoodsport Ranger Station, 150 N. Lake Cushman Rd., Hoodsport, WA 98548, 360/877-5254.

57 UPPER SOUTH FORK SKOKOMISH

15.0 mi/1-2 days

west of Hoodsport in the Wonder Mountain Wilderness and Olympic National Park

Map 1.4, page 42

Upper South Fork Skokomish Trail is a great route through a typically great Olympic river valley. Unfortunately, an extension of the access road has made this hike much shorter than it was once. This trail has just what one could want out of Olympic river hike: a forest composed of large trees, a river carving occasional canyons, and meadows at the river's headwaters along a high mountain ridge. And throw in an absence of people on the trail, which is all right with the folks who know of this place.

The trail leaves the road and sets off into a forest of large cedars, firs, and hemlocks, all old-growth and of good size. Streams and creeks regularly cross the trail, but few give any trouble. The trail crosses the river twice via bridges and makes a detour into the Startup Creek valley. Soon after the route enters the national park, it becomes little more than a beaten footpath. It's not exceptionally difficult to follow as long as snow isn't lingering on the ground (after mid-June). The trail climbs gradually through the headwaters of the South Fork of the Skokomish, eventually reaching Sundown Pass and Lake Sundown, a remote place of meadows and open subalpine forests. Backpackers will find overnight spots at Camp Riley (5.4 miles) and Sundown Pass.

User Groups: Hikers and horses. No dogs or mountain bikes are allowed. No wheelchair access.

Permits: This trail is accessible mid-June–October. Permits are not required. Parking and access are free.

Maps: For a map of Olympic National Park and Olympic National Forest, contact the Outdoor Recreation Information Center at the downtown Seattle REI. For topographic maps, ask Green Trails for No. 166, Mount

Christie, No. 167, Mount Steel, and No. 199, Mount Tebo, or ask the USGS for Lightning Peak, Mount Tebo, Mount Olson, and Mount Hoquim.

Directions: From Hoodsport, drive south 7 miles to Skokomish Valley Road. Turn right (west) and drive 5.5 miles to Forest Service Road 23. Turn right and drive 13 miles to Forest Service Road 2361. Turn right and drive 5.5 miles to the signed trailhead at road's end.

Contact: Olympic National Forest, Hoodsport Ranger Station, 150 N. Lake Cushman Rd., Hoodsport, WA 98548, 360/877-5254.

58 RAINBOW CANYON
1.0 mi/0.5 hr   👫1 ⛺8

south of Quilcene in the Buckhorn Wilderness of Olympic National Forest

Map 1.5, page 43

This is a great leg-stretcher for those making a long trek along U.S. 101. Just outside Rainbow Campground (which is right off the highway), a short 0.5-mile hike accesses a nice waterfall on the way to Rainbow Canyon on the Big Quilcene River. The trail's drop is not much to speak of, making it easily accessible to hikers of all abilities.

Forests of Douglas fir tower over an understory that includes vine maple, a tangle of brilliant colors in September. An overlook peers into Elbo Creek, where the waterfall cascades into a small pool. The trail continues down to the Big Quilcene River, where it makes a gentle turn within the canyon walls. Moss and ferns line the sides. When the kids are getting antsy in the back seat, Rainbow Canyon is just the thing to burn off a little energy. Total distance for the round-trip excursion is just 1 mile.

User Groups: Hikers and leashed dogs. No horses or mountain bikes are allowed. No wheelchair access.

Permits: This trail is accessible year-round. Permits are not required. Parking and access are free.

Maps: For a map of Olympic National Forest, contact the Outdoor Recreation Information Center at the downtown Seattle REI. For topographic maps, ask the USGS for Mount Walker.

Directions: From Quilcene, drive 5 miles south on U.S. 101 to Rainbow Campground. While the trail begins from within the campground, it is a group site and the gate will be locked. Park across Highway 101 and walk into the site. The trailhead is at the back of the campground.

Contact: Olympic National Forest, Hood Canal Ranger Station, 295142 U.S. 101 South, Quilcene, WA 98376 (2 miles from Highway 101 on South Shore Quinault Road), 360/765-2200.

59 LEADBETTER POINT
2.6-8.3 mi/1.5-4.5 hr   👫1 ⛺9

northern tip of Long Beach in southwestern Washington

Map 1.6, page 44

It may not appear as though there is much going on at Leadbetter Point, but in fact the tip of Long Beach is extremely rich in wildlife. Comprising sand dunes and miles of grasses waving in the strong breeze, the area can look barren and a bit forbidding. On closer inspection, however, you'll see that hundreds of thousands of seabirds and shorebirds make this place home for a part of each year. Leadbetter Point is a bird-watcher's dream, home to snowy plovers, grouse, bald eagles, great herons, and woodpeckers. Although it's a good visit anytime of the year, winter is the peak of bird season. Just be ready for soggy trail in places.

A small network of trails courses around the ever-changing peninsula. Taken altogether, they make an 8.3-mile loop that includes sand dunes, coastal forest, Willapa Bay, and a stretch along the beach. Shorter hikes include Blue Trail, a 2.6-mile round-trip out to the Pacific Ocean. All of the trails are fairly level, climbing only over sand dunes and grassy knolls. The park is managed by State Parks but is also a National Wildlife Refuge because of its importance as a migratory stop for birds. Dogs are not allowed on any trails.

User Groups: Hikers only. No dogs, horses, or mountain bikes are allowed. No wheelchair access.

Permits: This trail is accessible year-round. No permits are required. Parking and access are free.

Maps: For topographic maps, ask the USGS for Oysterville and North Cove.

Directions: From Long Beach, drive north 18 miles on Highway 103 (Pacific Way) to Leadbetter Point State Park. The route passes through Oysterville and is well signed. The trailhead is at the end of the road within the Leadbetter Point State Park.

Contact: Willapa National Wildlife Refuge, 3888 U.S. 101, Ilwaco, WA 98624-9707, 360/484-3482.

60 LONG ISLAND
1.0–5.0 mi/2.0–5.0 hr

in Willapa Bay in Southwestern Washington

Map 1.6, page 44

Talk about secluded. As the name implies, this is an island, and it's one with no bridges. One reaches Long Island by boat or kayak, with no other options. If that's not a problem (it actually makes the trip all the more special), then Long Island is a real gem.

Roughly 5 miles of trail and even more old road crisscross the island, 2 miles wide by 7 miles long. Hiking along the shore is a real wildlife getaway, with a plethora of seabirds and shorebirds stopping by on their yearly migrations. Bald eagles, grouse, great herons, and snowy plovers are just a few of the many winged inhabitants. Inland, deer, bear, and elk are some of the bigger mammals to be found.

The highlight of the island is the ancient cedar grove in the center of the island. After crossing the bay to the island by boat (the crossing is about 200 feet and can be done only at high tide), hike north on the old logging road about 2.5 miles to the signed "Trail of the Ancient Cedars." Turn left and in 0.5 mile you will be among a large grove of massive cedars. Spared from logging because of its hard-to-reach locale, the stand is certain to instill a sense of awe for a forest that once covered the entire island. There are a number of primitive campgrounds around the lake, although there is no water during the summer.

User Groups: Hikers only. No dogs, horses, or mountain bikes are allowed. No wheelchair access.

Permits: This trail is accessible year-round. Permits are not required. Parking and access are free.

Maps: For topographic maps, ask the USGS for Long Island.

Directions: From Long Beach, drive north 13 miles on U.S. 101 to the signed Refuge Headquarters and trailhead.

Contact: Willapa National Wildlife Refuge, 3888 U.S. 101, Ilwaco, WA 98624-9707, 360/484-3482.

61 CAPE DISAPPOINTMENT STATE PARK
0.5–9.0 mi /0.5–4.5 hr 🏃1 ⛰10

southwest of Ilwaco in southwest Washington

Map 1.6, page 44   BEST (

A network of trails through Cape Disappointment State Park makes for a great combination of forest and coastal hiking. All of the trails are extremely easy and highly scenic, providing parents a prime locale to take the kids on the weekend. Formerly known as Fort Canby, the state park covers the grounds where Lewis and Clark spent a wet winter. On Cape Disappointment, Washington's most southwestern point, the park overlooks both the Columbia River and Pacific Ocean.

The main route through the park is Washington Coast Trail, a long trek that gets its southern start here. Patched together from several trails, this 4.5-mile segment bisects the park through old-growth forest to link a pair of old lighthouses. Folks spending a full day here will want to hike the length of it, the best way to see the park.

Families looking for a shorter trip should hike to Beard's Hollow. The trail travels just 0.5 mile through coastal forest and sand dunes before finding the secluded cove, a gateway to more than 20 miles of beach to the north. Another beauty is Cape Disappointment Lighthouse Trail, 1.4 miles to the West Coast's oldest working lighthouse. Be sure to check out the Lewis and Clark Interpretive Center, atop a pair of enormous gun emplacements from World Wars I and II. The center features a cornucopia of artifacts from the Corps of Discovery's journey 200 years ago.

User Groups: Hikers, leashed dogs, and mountain bikes. No horses are allowed. Parts of the trails are wheelchair accessible.

Permits: This area is accessible year-round. No permits are required. Parking and access are free.

Maps: For topographic maps, ask the USGS for Cape Disappointment.

Directions: From Long Beach, drive south 3.5 miles on Pacific Way to Ilwaco. Turn right on North Head Road and drive 2.5 miles to North Head Lighthouse Road. Turn right and drive 0.5 miles to the well-signed park entrance. The main trailhead is located at the Lewis and Clark Interpretive Center, inside the park entrance.

Contact: Cape Disappointment State Park, P.O. Box 488, Ilwaco WA, 98624, 360/642-3078.

SEATTLE AND THE PUGET SOUND

© SCOTT LEONARD

BEST HIKES

Who says you have to go far from Seattle to

enjoy the great outdoors? The Puget Sound area is undoubtedly one of the United States' most scenic locales for a major urban area, which is great for Seattleites. The North Cascades may be just a one- or two-hour drive from Seattle, but the secluded parks and beaches of this region are even closer. Stretching from the San Juan Islands in Puget Sound (accessible only by ferry, one of the prettiest boat rides you'll ever embark upon) down to Seattle and Olympia, a strong network of state and city parks have preserved a bit of the wilderness for people to enjoy quickly and easily. Thanks to easy trails and loads of wildlife, these places are excellent trips for young hikers in training.

A number of great parks line the Sound, many located on the San Juans. Moran State Park is the best, not simply among these, but among all of Washington's state parks. Situated on horseshoe-shaped Orcas Island, the park boasts Mount Constitution as its highlight. From the lofty height of 2,409 feet, Mount Constitution lays Puget Sound and the Strait of Juan de Fuca below you. This makes a great hike, but the peak is accessible on four wheels as well. In Anacortes, Little Cranberry and Whistle Lakes are local favorites. They're convenient to access loop hikes for people passing through Anacortes on their way to other places – you'd be wise to be one of the few to stop and explore the trails and shoreline of this city park. On Whidbey Island are Deception Pass, Fort Ebey, and South Whidbey State Parks. These are great destinations any time of the year, with miles of trail along the water. Lucky visitors may spot sea lions or orcas swimming and playing in the sound.

Back on the mainland are several great wildlife refuges. The Puget Sound region sees millions of birds pass through the area each spring and fall on their way to warmer climes. Refuges like Tennant Lake near Bellingham, Padilla Bay near Mount Vernon, and Nisqually Wildlife Refuge near Olympia offer exceptional opportunities for quiet walks and wildlife sightings. Ducks and geese might be lounging in the marshlands while goshawks and falcons patrol the air in search of dinner.

And let's not forget the wealth of forests and trails within the city limits, either; Seattle's city park system rivals any in the nation. Carkeek Park overlooks Puget Sound from high bluffs and is home to one of Seattle's few remaining salmon streams (fall runs of salmon can still be seen in Piper Creek). Seward Park covers Bailey Peninsula in Lake Washington and still boasts some old-growth timber. At Discovery Park on the Sound, hikers can enjoy sunsets from on the hill or explore the tidal pools of Puget Sound during low tides. There's a lot to do in Seattle's own backyard.

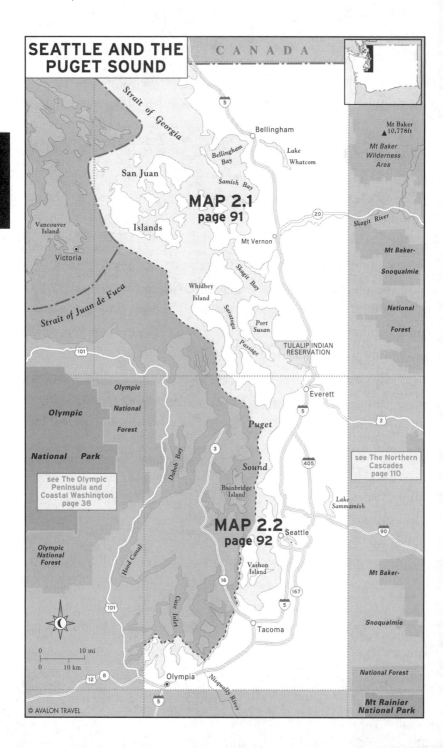

Map 2.1

Hikes 1-13
Pages 93-100

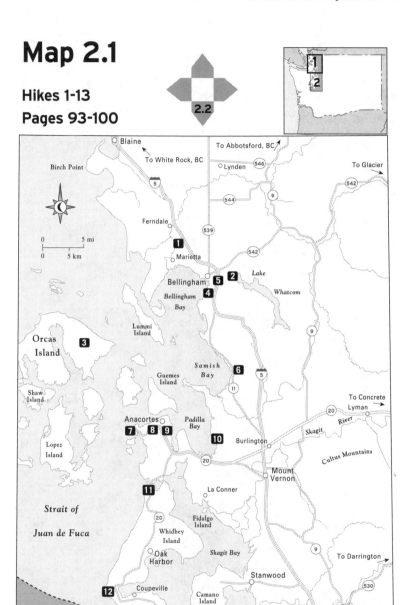

Map 2.2

Hikes 14-22
Pages 101-105

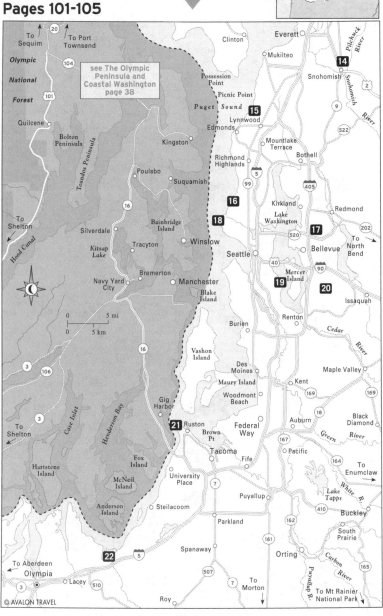

1 TENNANT LAKE
0.8-4.4 mi/1.0-2.5 hr 🏃1 ⛰9

south of Ferndale in Tennant Lake County Park

Map 2.1, page 91

Pristine wetlands are hard to come by within the lower Nooksack River Valley, inundated by suburban sprawl and the spreading fields of agriculture. Fortunately, Tennant Lake Wildlife Area has preserved a chunk of these lands that are so important to wildlife. Spread over 624 acres, this protected land is an important spring and fall stopover for thousands of migratory birds who make extensive use of the shallow lake and surrounding wetlands, fields, and forest. Three flat, easy trails meander through the park, a prime winter walk.

Tennant Lake Marsh Boardwalk is a 1.4-mile loop that explores most of the park. A well-built boardwalk helps to keep feet dry as the trail explores the marshes and wetlands. The route passes a 50-foot observation tower, which provides an awesome panoramic view of the area. At its top, a pair of binoculars comes in handy. A longer hike can be made by following River Dike Trail (2.2 miles one-way). The trail follows the meandering Nooksack River through forest, wetlands, and neighboring farmlands. Finally, Hovander Park Trail (0.4 mile one-way) visits the historic Hovander Homestead along a wooded boardwalk.

User Groups: Hikers and mountain bikes. No dogs or horses are allowed. Two of the trails are wheelchair accessible.

Permits: This area is accessible year-round. Permits are not required. Parking and access are free.

Maps: Maps of the trail system are posted at trailheads. For a topographic map, ask the USGS for Ferndale.

Directions: From Seattle, drive north on I-5 to Ferndale (exit 262). Turn left (west) on Main Street and drive 0.5 mile to Hovander Road. Turn left and drive to Nielsen Avenue. Turn right and follow signs to Tennant Lake Interpretive Center (at the end of Nielsen Avenue). The trailhead is at the interpretive center.

Contact: Tennant Lake Interpretive Center, 5236 Nielsen Ave., Ferndale, WA 98248, 360/384-3064.

2 WHATCOM FALLS
0.5-2.0 mi/0.5-1.0 hr 🏃1 ⛰8

in Bellingham

Map 2.1, page 91   **BEST (**

Residents of Bellingham are lucky to have Whatcom Falls in their own backyard. In one of Washington's best municipal parks, several miles of trail explore Whatcom Creek and its large sets of falls. The park is ideal for rambling as the network of trails weaves along the creek and through the forest. Pipeline Trail is the main artery of the park, running for several miles along Whatcom Creek. This park was once the scene of a tragic accident. In the late 1990s, several people were killed when a natural-gas pipeline exploded, igniting a fire along half of the park. Burned trees and denuded slopes are a testament to this sad misfortune, but the area is quickly revegetating. A fish hatchery in the center of the park is open to the public. The hatchery can be accessed via an old stone bridge constructed by the Depression-era Works Progress Administration. The scenic bridge overlooks Whatcom Falls, just one in a series of cascades. A short distance downstream are another set of falls, viewable from Pipeline Trail.

User Groups: Hikers, leashed dogs, and mountain bikes. No horses are allowed. Parts of the trails are wheelchair accessible.

Permits: This area is accessible year-round. Permits are not required. Parking and access are free.

Maps: Maps of the trail system are posted at trailheads. For a topographic map, ask the USGS for Bellingham South.

Directions: From downtown Bellingham, drive east on Lakeway Drive to Electric Avenue. Turn right and drive 0.25 mile to Silver Beach Road. Turn left into the park entrance.

The trailhead is on the west side of the parking lot.

Contact: Bellingham City Parks, 3424 Meridian St., Bellingham, WA 98225, 360/778-7000.

❸ MORAN STATE PARK
0.5-7.4 mi/0.5-4.0 hr 🏃2 ⛰10

on Orcas Island in Moran State Park

Map 2.1, page 91   **BEST(**

One of Washington's most beautiful and most popular state parks, Moran State Park rarely fails to impress. Situated on Orcas Island, the park is crowned by 2,409-foot Mount Constitution. It's the highest point in the San Juan Island chain, and the views from the summit are unbelievable. More than 30 miles of hiking trails lie within the park, exploring everything from forested lakes to the historic stone tower at Constitution's peak. Whether you're visiting Orcas Island for a day or staying overnight at the campground, the trails of Moran State Park are well worth hiking.

The diversity of trails allows visitors to find a hike that suits them best. Many trails are short and flat. Among the best of the easy trails is Cascade Falls Trail, a quick 0.5-mile hike to the large waterfall on Cascade Creek. This is a real gusher during the springtime. Longer but just as flat is Mountain Lake Loop Trail, a 3.9-mile route around the park's largest body of water. Mountain Lake Trail starts at the large campground along the lake's shores.

The most popular destination for many visitors is the summit of Mount Constitution. Although one can drive to the top, Twin Lakes Trail is a survey of the park. Twin Lakes Trail skirts Mountain Lake before following a creek to Twin Lakes (1.5 miles), where loops circle both small lakes. The latter half of the trail switchbacks steeply to the summit (3.7 miles), where an old stone watchtower provides a panorama. The San Juans and Puget Sound are revealed in full glory, while Mount Baker rests behind the growing city of Bellingham.

User Groups: Hikers, leashed dogs, and mountain bikes (mountain bikes allowed September 15–May 15). No horses are allowed. No wheelchair access.

Permits: This area is accessible year-round. A $5 day-use fee is required to park here and is payable at the trailhead, or you can get an annual State Parks Pass for $30; contact Washington State Parks and Recreation, 360/902-8500.

Maps: Maps of the trail system are available at trailheads. For a topographic map, ask the USGS for Mount Constitution.

Directions: From the ferry terminal on Orcas Island, drive 13 miles on Horseshoe Highway (Orcas Road) to the park entrance. There are several trailheads within the park, all of them well signed.

Contact: Moran State Park, Star Route Box 22, Eastsound, WA, 98245, 360/376-2326.

❹ LARRABEE STATE PARK
0.5-8.0 mi/1.0-4.0 hr 🏃3 ⛰9

south of Bellingham on Chuckanut Mountain

Map 2.1, page 91

Spanning an area from the shores of Puget Sound to the crest of Chuckanut Mountain, Larrabee State Park is a treasure for hikers. Larrabee was Washington's first state park and today remains one of its largest. A diverse mix of trails varies from a beach ramble to a hike to several high, forested lakes. Trails to Clayton Beach and Teddy Bear Cove (each about 0.5 mile round-trip, accessible from Highline Road) drop to the sandy shores of Chuckanut Bay and Puget Sound. The beaches are strewn with boulders and driftwood. Best of all, this area lies within the rain shadow of the Olympic Peninsula, meaning it receives about half the rain of the Seattle area.

Longer trails lead up the western slopes of Chuckanut Mountain to Fragrance Lake (2 miles) and Lost Lake (4 miles). Surrounded by lush forests, these large lakes are favorite haunts for both campers and anglers. Along the way to the lakes are numerous viewpoints of the San Juan Islands and the Strait of Juan de Fuca.

User Groups: Hikers, leashed dogs, horses, and mountain bikes. No wheelchair access.

Permits: This area is accessible year-round. A $5 day-use fee is required to park here and is payable at the trailhead, or you can get an annual State Parks Pass for $30; contact Washington State Parks and Recreation, 360/902-8500.

Maps: For a topographic map, ask the USGS for Bellingham South.

Directions: From Seattle, drive north on I-5 to Chuckanut Drive (exit 231). Turn left (west) and drive 14.5 miles to the park entrance. The trailhead is just inside the park entrance.

Contact: Larrabee State Park, 245 Chuckanut Dr., Bellingham, WA 98226, 360/676-2093.

5 PINE AND CEDAR LAKES
4.8 mi/3.0 hr 👫3 ⛰9

south of Bellingham on Chuckanut Mountain

Map 2.1, page 91

Although it's best known as a great place to take a colorful drive during the fall, Chuckanut Mountain also has some great trails. Here, on the eastern end of the long mountain ridge, are Pine and Cedar Lakes. These are a pair of mountain lakes well regarded for their views and fishing. A single trail leads to both of them, just a few hundred yards apart. Pine and Cedar Lakes Trail climbs steeply for the first 1.5 miles through a terrific forest of broadleafed trees. It's hikable year-round, but October is a grand time to visit, when the forest is alive with autumn color. The trail reaches a junction—Cedar Lake to the left and Pine Lake to the right. Both lakes are forested and have a subalpine feel to them, odd given that the altitude here is 1,600 feet. Several campsites are also found at each lake. A loop trail encircles Cedar Lake, which also has a side trail leading to a high viewpoint.

User Groups: Hikers, leashed dogs, horses, and mountain bikes. No wheelchair access.

Permits: This area is accessible year-round. Permits are not required. Parking and access are free.

Maps: For a topographic map, ask the USGS for Bellingham South.

Directions: From Bellingham, drive south on I-5 to North Lake Samish exit. Turn right (west) onto North Lake Samish Drive and drive to Old Samish Road. Turn left and drive 2.5 miles to the signed trailhead on the left.

Contact: Whatcom County Parks and Recreation, 3373 Mount Baker Hwy., Bellingham, WA 98226, 360/733-2900.

6 OYSTER DOME
6.2 mi/4.0 hr 👫4 ⛰9

south of Bellingham in the Chuckanut Mountains

Map 2.1, page 91

Around the Seattle area, the Chuckanut Mountains may be an afterthought to other destinations in the Cascade and Olympic Mountain ranges. Of course, the Chuckanuts don't reach as high or boast subalpine meadows. But at Oyster Dome, the Chuckanuts reveal the best views of the upper Puget Sound. With views from Vancouver Island, over the San Juans, and out to Whidbey Island and the Olympics, Puget Sound is clearly laid out in all its glory. Of course, the best views along this hike are reserved for the hardiest of hikers who make it to the top of this challenging day hike.

The hike to Oyster Dome begins on the Pacific Northwest Trail (PNT), which spans more than 1,200 miles, from the Continental Divide in Montana to the Pacific Ocean on the Olympic Peninsula. After years of effort from local groups, the PNT was finally designated a National Scenic Trail by the U.S. Congress and President Obama in 2009, joining the likes of the Appalachian and Pacific Crest Trails.

From the trailhead, climb steadily along the PNT through a shady second-growth forest of firs and Pacific madronas. At 1.8 miles, the PNT junctions with the Samish Connector Trail. Turn left on the Samish Connector Trail. At 2.4 miles, stay right on the Samish Connector Trail where it merges with the Old Oyster Trail. At 2.9 miles, turn left and make the final steep ascent to the top of Oyster Dome (3.2 miles). This last part can be rooty and rocky, often with one side dropping sharply. Take care on the final stretch. From the top of Oyster Dome, it's more than 2,000 feet down to Samish Bay below. Enjoy the wide-open views from north to south, an amazing and well-earned vista of Puget Sound and beyond.

User Groups: Hikers and leashed dogs. No mountain bikes or horses are allowed.

Permits: This area is accessible year-round. Permits are not required. Parking and access are free.

Maps: Maps of the trail system are posted at trailheads. For a topographic map, ask the USGS for Bellingham South and Bow.

Directions: From Seattle, drive north on I-5 to exit 231/Larrabee State Park/Chuckanut Drive. Drive north on State Route 11/Chuckanut Drive toward Samish Bay. Just beyond milepost 10 is the signed Pacific Northwest Trailhead. Parking is limited along both shoulders of the road.

Contact: Washington Department of Natural Resources, P.O. Box 47001, 1111 Washington St. SE, Olympia, WA 98504-7000, 360/902-1000.

◼ WASHINGTON PARK
2.6 mi/1.5 hr   🏃1 ⛰9

in Anacortes on Puget Sound

Map 2.1, page 91

On the shores of Puget Sound and within the city limits of Anacortes, Washington Park gets far less attention than it deserves. Thousands of people pass right by the park on their way to the ferry to the San Juan Islands. But Washington Park is just as great, with more than 40,000 feet of shoreline and a 220-acre forest

of cedar, fir, and madrona. Washington Park sits on a rocky point of Fidalgo Head, a large peninsula surrounded by saltwater and views. Although a road rounds the park, the best views are from Fidalgo Head Loop Trail, the main route through the park.

Fidalgo Head Loop Trail explores the perimeters of the park with frequent views of Puget Sound and the San Juan Islands. Numerous small side trails depart from this main artery, so it's a good idea to check out a trail map at the trailhead. Juniper Point and Burrows Trail are good, quick add-ons to Loop Trail. Elevation gains are modest, and the trail is easy enough for hikers of all abilities. Wildlife is plentiful, especially waterfowl. Brant, loons, murrelets, scoters, grebes, and hooded mergansers are frequently sighted, so a camera or binoculars are handy.

User Groups: Hikers, leashed dogs, and mountain bikes. No horses are allowed. No wheelchair access.

Permits: This area is accessible year-round. Permits are not required. Parking and access are free.

Maps: For a topographic map, ask the USGS for Anacortes North.

Directions: From Seattle, drive north on I-5 to Highway 20 (exit 230). Head west on Highway 20 to Anacortes. Take Commercial Street to 12th Street. Turn left and drive 3 miles to Washington Park. The trailhead is located at the parking lot, just inside the park entrance.

Contact: Anacortes Parks and Recreation, P.O. Box 547, 904 Sixth St., Anacortes, WA 98221, 360/299-1918.

◼ LITTLE CRANBERRY LAKE
1.7 mi/1.5 hr   🏃1 ⛰7

in the Anacortes Community Forest

Map 2.1, page 91   BEST (

The community of Anacortes takes real pride in the green spaces on Fidalgo Island. Anacortes may be better known as a sleepy port

© SCOTT LEONARD

Little Cranberry Lake is home to a family-friendly day hike.

town providing ferry service to the San Juan Islands. But tucked away in the island's quiet places are nearly 2,800 acres of city-owned forest land. The Anacortes Community Forest Lands (ACFL) protects a diverse array of forests, wetlands, lakes, and meadows with more than 50 miles of trails. The hike around Little Cranberry Lake is one of the island's best hikes, an easy loop around the beautiful lake.

Little Cranberry Lake is a great hike for families with children of any age. The hike gains very little elevation, always in modest amounts. While the trail network in the ACFL is usually confusing, making the loop around Little Cranberry Lake is easy to follow (turn left), is well signed, and does not require a map.

Little Cranberry Lake is a great place to see wildlife, with increased bird activity during the spring and fall. Mornings and evenings are also good times to see great blue herons, eagles, and migratory birds taking a rest. Trails on Fidalgo Island also make for great winter destinations, as the island sits within the Olympic rain shadow, receiving less rain than Seattle and having little chance of snow.

In any season, Little Cranberry Lake is a recommended hike.

User Groups: Hikers, leashed dogs, mountain bikes, and horses are allowed.

Permits: This area is accessible year-round. Permits are not required. Parking and access are free.

Maps: For a map of this hike, ask Green Trails for No. 41S, Deception Pass/ACFL.

Directions: From Seattle, drive north on I-5 to Highway 20 in Mount Vernon. Drive west on Highway 20 toward the town of Anacortes. As the freeway ends at a large traffic circle, turn right onto Commercial Avenue, and drive 1.4 miles to 12th Street. Turn left, following signs for the San Juan Ferries, and drive 1.6 miles to Georgia Avenue, a residential street. Turn left and drive 0.2 mile to Little Cranberry Lake Road. Turn right and drive 0.3 mile to the signed trailhead at the end of the road.

Contact: Anacortes Parks and Recreation, P.O. Box 547, 904 Sixth St., Anacortes, WA 98221, 360/299-1918. ACFL maps are also sold at local retailers, including Skagit Cycle Center, 1620 Commercial Ave., Anacortes, WA, 360/588-8776.

9 WHISTLE LAKE
3.5 mi/2 hr   👣2 ⛰6

in the Anacortes Community Forest

Map 2.1, page 91

The Anacortes Community Forrest Lands (ACFL) offer more than 50 miles of hiking trails. Located on Fidalgo Island, between Whidbey Island and the San Juan Islands, these city-owned parks are a pride of the Island. Rightfully so, because the ACFL encompasses multiple lakes and some old-growth forest as well. For those of us who don't live on the island, the loop hike around Whistle Lake is a great introduction to the ACFL, a scenic loop around the lake with multiple views of the lake.

The hike around Whistle Lake is more difficult than its companion ACFL Little Cranberry Lake in two ways. First, the multitude of side trails and junctions make a map a very handy thing to have with you on the trail. While every trail junction is meticulously signed, this hike is easier to follow with a map in hand. Second, this hike takes in more elevation change than Little Cranberry Lake. There are a number of ups and downs along the hike. None are that difficult, but they will be sure help to break a sweat. Older children (8+ years old) should have few problems completing the hike.

Like its ACFL partner, Whistle Lake makes a great hike option during the winter. Fidalgo Island receives less rain than Seattle or the Cascades. Rain in those places can mean only cloudy skies over the island. And snow is rarely a barrier to hiking in the colder months. Also, Whistle Lake sees a lot of migratory birds during the spring and fall. Morning and evening visits usually encounter herons, eagles, or deer (yes, there are deer on the island).

User Groups: Hikers, leashed dogs, and mountain bikes are allowed.

Permits: This area is accessible year-round. Permits are not required. Parking and access are free.

Maps: For a map of this hike, ask Green Trails for No. 41S, Deception Pass/ACFL.

Directions: From Seattle, drive north on I-5 to Highway 20 in Mount Vernon. Drive west on Highway 20 toward the town of Anacortes. As the freeway ends at a large traffic circle, turn left onto Commercial Avenue (a 3/4 drive around the circle), and drive 0.3 mile to Fidalgo Avenue. Turn left and drive 0.2 mile to St. Mary's Drive. Turn left and drive 0.3 mile as St. Mary's Drive becomes Hillcrest Drive. Turn right at Whistle Lake Road and drive 1.1 miles to the signed trailhead at the end of the road.

Contact: Anacortes Parks and Recreation, P.O. Box 547, 904 Sixth St., Anacortes, WA 98221, 360/299-1918. ACFL maps are also sold at local retailers, including Skagit Cycle Center, 1620 Commercial Ave., Anacortes, WA, 360/588-8776.

10 PADILLA BAY
0.8-4.6 mi/0.5-2.5 hr   👣1 ⛰8

west of Mount Vernon on Puget Sound

Map 2.1, page 91   **BEST (**

On the shores of the expansive Padilla Bay, this wildlife refuge provides excellent walks through important wildlife habitat. Although the area was disturbed for agricultural use more than 100 years ago, it flourishes as a bird habitat today. Thousands of migrating marsh and shore birds stop through the reserve during the spring and fall. The area is also an important habitat for many marine animals. Open year-round, Padilla Bay makes a great place to stretch the legs during winter.

A pair of trails explores the federally protected reserve. Upland Trail, a short 0.8-mile loop, leaves from the Breazeale Center to explore open meadows and sparse forest. Interpretive guides are available from the Breazeale Center, explaining different sightings along the way. The beginning of the trail reaches a viewing platform and is accessible to wheelchairs.

A longer hike can be made along Shore Trail, a 2.3-mile graveled path along a dike bordering Padilla Bay. The route explores the tidal slough and open mudflats of the bay, a good place to see wildlife. Views of the Olympics and even Mount Baker can be had while enjoying the salty marine air of Puget Sound. The path ends at Bayview State Park, home to a large campground.

User Groups: Hikers, leashed dogs, and mountain bikes (dogs and mountain bikes allowed only on Shore Trail). No horses are allowed. Parts of the trails are wheelchair accessible.

Permits: This area is accessible year-round. Permits are not required. Parking and access are free.

Maps: Maps of the trail system are posted at trailheads. For a topographic map, ask the USGS for Anacortes South and LaConner.

Directions: From Seattle, drive north on I-5 to Highway 20 (exit 230). Turn left (west) and drive 5 miles to Farm to Market Road. Turn right (north) and drive 2 miles to Josh Wilson Road. Turn left and drive 1.5 miles to Bayview-Edison Road. Turn right and drive 0.5 mile to Breazeale Interpretive Center, where the trailhead is located.

Contact: Padilla Bay National Estuarine Research Reserve, 10441 Bayview-Edison Rd., Mount Vernon, WA 98273, 360/428-1558.

▥ DECEPTION PASS STATE PARK

1.0-12.0 mi/1.0-6.0 hr   🏃1 ⛰9

on northern Whidbey Island in Deception Pass State Park

Map 2.1, page 91   **BEST (**

A wide network of trails winds throughout this park, one of Washington State's most beautiful. More than 35 miles of trails lead through great forests to loads of seashore exploring. Tides rush water through the pass between Skagit Bay and Rosario Strait as though it were a river. Beaches edged by contorted pines and madronas offer chances to see orcas and sea otters in the water. Numerous upland trails offer great opportunities for runs and more extended hiking.

The park is split between Fidalgo Island and Whidbey Island. A large bridge spans the pass to connect the two islands. The best beach hiking is along Rosario Beach, on Fidalgo Island, where the Samish legend of the Maiden of Deception Pass is recounted. Signed reader boards provide maps for a number of trails around Rosario Beach and Bowman Bay. Be sure to pick up a map, which shows trails and distances, to see the route and distance of the hike you wish to take.

On Whidbey Island, trails of interest include one running from West Point, on Rosario Strait, along the pass channel to Haypus Point and Goose Rock. The many upland trails on this side of the island are often visited by mountain cyclists. In all, there are nine islands within the state park, some of which can be reached only by canoe. More than 250 campsites are here for those wishing to spend the night, but they go quickly, because nearly three million people a year visit the park. Finally, it pays to be cautious when hiking here. The park staff spends a considerable amount of time performing first aid and rescue for folks, especially kids, who wander too close to cliff edges.

User Groups: Hikers, leashed dogs, and mountain bikes. No horses are allowed. Some trails are wheelchair accessible.

Permits: This area is accessible year-round. A $5 day-use fee is required to park here and is payable at the trailhead, or you can get an annual State Parks Pass for $30; contact Washington State Parks and Recreation, 360/902-8500.

Maps: Maps of the trail system are available at trailheads. For a topographic map, ask the USGS for Deception Pass.

Directions: From Mount Vernon, drive west 18 miles on Highway 20 toward Oak Harbor. Entrances to the park, before and after crossing

Deception Pass by way of a high bridge, are along Highway 20 and well signed. Trail maps at each entrance show the exact locations of each trailhead.

Contact: Deception Pass State Park, 5175 N. Hwy. 20, Oak Harbor, WA 98277, 360/675-2417.

12 FORT EBEY
6.0 mi/3.0 hr

south of Oak Harbor on Whidbey Island

Map 2.1, page 91

Shake those wintertime blues and enjoy the drier climate of Whidbey Island. Situated in the rain shadow of the Olympic Mountains, America's longest island gets less than half the annual rainfall of Seattle. Fort Ebey is a great alternative to the crowds of people visiting the better-known Deception Pass State Park. A large network of more than 20 miles of trail spreads out over the forested park, popular with mountain cyclists. The highlight of Fort Ebey is Bluff Trail, 6 miles of wide, level trail extending along the high cliffs bordering the water. This is the most popular and scenic trail in the park, with outstanding views of the Olympic Mountains and Strait of Juan de Fuca. Lucky hikers may see a pod of orcas in the water below. Although rain is sparse here, wind isn't; remember an extra layer in all seasons. The park has several large cannon emplacements along the hillside overlooking the Strait of Juan de Fuca. Together with similar emplacements at Fort Worden and Fort Casey, these cannons formed a "Triangle of Fire," rendering Puget Sound invulnerable to invasion during World War II. Fortunately, the invasion never arrived. There is a large car campground in the park; it's bordered by Kettles Park with even more trails to explore.

User Groups: Hikers, leashed dogs, and mountain bikes. No horses are allowed. No wheelchair access.

Permits: This area is accessible year-round. A $5 day-use fee is required to park here

and is payable at the trailhead, or you can get an annual State Parks Pass for $30; contact Washington State Parks and Recreation, 360/902-8500.

Maps: Maps of the trail system are posted at trailheads. For a topographic map, ask the USGS for Port Townsend North.

Directions: From the ferry terminal in Clinton, on Whidbey Island, drive north 30 miles on Highway 525 to Libby Road. Turn left (west) and drive 1 mile to Valley Drive. Turn left and drive right into the park entrance. The trailhead is inside the park entrance and marked by a sign.

Contact: Fort Ebey State Park, 395 North Fort Ebey Rd., Coupeville, WA 98239, 360/678-4636.

13 SOUTH WHIDBEY STATE PARK
1.0-1.5 mi/1.0 hr

north of Clinton on Whidbey Island

Map 2.1, page 91

South Whidbey State Park remains far less known than its sister to the north, Deception Pass, but its scenery is just as great. On Admiralty Inlet, between Bush and Lagoon Points, the park offers great strolling along the peaceful beach and hiking within a stand of old-growth forest. From the day-use parking area, an unnamed path leads down to the water. The sandy beach stretches nearly a mile along Smugglers Cove. Wind-swept trees appear gnarly and stunted, growing out of the sides of the steep hillsides. Don't be surprised to spot sea otters playing and feeding offshore. A 1-mile signed nature loop investigates the cliffs overlooking Admiralty Inlet, where lucky hikers can spot orcas in the water. For a quick and shady hike, Wilbert Trail winds 1.5 miles through an old, large forest of fir and cedar. All trails are family friendly. South Whidbey State Park is also home to a large car campground.

User Groups: Hikers and leashed dogs. No

horses or mountain bikes are allowed. No wheelchair access.

Permits: This area is accessible year-round. A $5 day-use fee is required to park here and is payable at the trailhead, or you can get an annual State Parks Pass for $30; contact Washington State Parks and Recreation, 360/902-8500.

Maps: Maps of the trail system are posted at trailheads. For a topographic map, ask the USGS for Freeland.

Directions: From the ferry terminal in Clinton, drive north 10.5 miles on Highway 525 to Bush Point Road. Turn left and drive 5 miles (as the road becomes Smugglers Cove Road) to the park entrance on the left. The trailhead is inside the park entrance and marked by a sign.

Contact: South Whidbey State Park, 4128 Smugglers Cove Rd., Freeland, WA 98249, 360/331-4559.

14 SNOHOMISH CENTENNIAL TRAIL
1.0–17.0 mi/1.0 hr–1 day   👣1 ⛰8

in Snohomish County

Map 2.2, page 92   BEST (

One of Washington's many rails-to-trails projects, Snohomish Centennial Trail runs along 17 miles of old railroad line. The original segment of trail ran from Lake Stevens to Snohomish, but recent years have seen lengthy additions (an extra 10 miles between Lake Stevens and Arlington). Total length of the trail now runs 17 miles and is likely to continue growing. The trail rambles through the rural countryside of Snohomish County, through open fields into dense, shady forest. Views of the surrounding Cascade Mountains are nearly constant (except when in the woods, of course). This is a very popular mountain bike and equestrian trail. The 7 miles between Lake Stevens and Snohomish are paved. Hikers can take the trail for as long as they please; since the views are fairly consistent, they can turn around at any point.

User Groups: Hikers, leashed dogs, horses, and mountain bikes. The trail is wheelchair accessible (the trail is a mix of gravel and pavement).

Permits: This area is accessible year-round. Permits are not required. Parking and access are free.

Maps: For topographic maps, ask the USGS for Snohomish and Lake Stevens.

Directions: From Seattle, drive north on I-5 to Highway 2 (exit 194). Drive east to the town of Snohomish. The trailhead is at the intersection of Maple Street and Pine Avenue.

Contact: Snohomish County Parks and Recreation, 9623 32nd St. SE, Everett, WA 98205, 425/388-6600.

15 MEADOWDALE BEACH
2.5 mi/1.5 hr   👣2 ⛰7

in Meadowdale Beach Park in Edmonds

Map 2.2, page 92

It is surprising to find a place as quiet as Meadowdale Beach Park in such an urban area. But the trail to Meadowdale Beach is a little-known jewel in our Puget Sound region. Operated by Snohomish County Parks, this hike drops down into Lund's Gulch and follows Lund's Creek to Meadowdale Beach on Puget Sound. This park is a success in other ways, too. In recent years, Lund's Creek has seen the return of spawning salmon in the spring and fall. This is a rare urban hike that will have you feeling miles from the city. Keep this hike in mind during the winter season, when many trails are snowbound or too exposed for hiking. Unless Seattle is buried under snow, this hike is open for business.

Snohomish County Parks has constructed a wide, well-maintained trail through Meadowdale Beach Park. Although the trail has only 425 feet of elevation change, this occurs in the first half-mile as the trail drops into Lund's Gulch. The trail passes under a tall canopy of alder, maple, hemlock, and fir. It then encounters the stream (0.5 mile) and follows it through the forest to Puget Sound. At 1.0 mile, the trail forks around the meadow and park ranger house, reconvening at the railroad track (1.25 miles). Walk through a tunnel under the tracks and emerge at Meadowdale Beach. Numerous picnic tables and views of the Olympics encourage a stay.

User Groups: Hikers and leashed dogs. No mountain bikes or horses are allowed.

Permits: This hike is accessible year-round. The park is open daily, 7:00 A.M. to dusk. Permits are not required. Parking and access are free.

Maps: A map of the trail system is posted at the trailhead, and online at the Snohomish County Parks Department website.

Directions: From Seattle, drive north on I-5 to exit 183, 164th Street. Turn left off the freeway onto 164th Street and drive 2.2 miles to 52nd Avenue, crossing Highway 99 along this stretch. Turn right on 52nd Avenue and drive 0.2 mile to 160th Street. Turn left and drive 0.2 mile to 56th Avenue West. Turn right and drive 0.3 mile to 156th Avenue West. Drive 0.3 mile to the signed park entrance, parking area, and signed trailhead.

Contact: Snohomish County Parks and Recreation, 6705 Puget Park Dr., Snohomish, WA 98296, 425/388-6600.

16 CARKEEK PARK
0.5-3.0 mi/0.5-2.0 hr 🥾1 ⛰9

in Seattle on Puget Sound

Map 2.2, page 92

A flurry of recent work at Carkeek Park has turned it into one of Seattle's best in-city destinations for hiking. Trail work combined with revegetative plantings along several routes has shored up eroded areas and erased evidence of overuse and abuse. Stream restoration work has turned Piper Creek, which runs through the park, into one of Seattle's most promising salmon streams. Visit Carkeek in the spring or fall and you're likely to see salmon struggling up the short creek on their way to spawn.

Wetland Trail is made of well-constructed boardwalk and explores Piper Creek for 0.5 mile. Other trails head up into the young forest covering the slopes of Carkeek Park. North Bluff Trail hits several great viewpoints overlooking Puget Sound and the wide beach below. Carkeek is a wonderful hideaway within the city limits.

User Groups: Hikers, leashed dogs, and mountain bikes. No horses are allowed. No wheelchair access.

Permits: This area is accessible year-round. Permits are not required. Parking and access are free.

Maps: Maps of the trail system are available at the trailhead kiosk.

Directions: From I-5 in Seattle, exit at Northgate Way (exit 173). Head west on Northgate Way (it becomes 105th Street) to Greenwood Avenue. Turn right and drive to 110th Street. Turn left and drive about 1 mile as the street becomes Northwest Carkeek Park Road and curves down to the park entrance. The trailhead is located at the main parking lot within the park, at the end of the road.

Contact: Seattle City Parks and Recreation, 100 Dexter Ave. N., Seattle, WA 98109, 206/684-4075.

17 BRIDLE TRAILS STATE PARK
1.0-4.8 mi/1.0-2.5 hr 🥾1 ⛰8

in Bellevue

Map 2.2, page 92   BEST (

In the heart of Bellevue, Bridle Trails State Park is like stepping into a vortex. As busy shoppers crowd into the nearby shopping mall, a small oasis of lush forest crisscrossed by miles of trails offers a peaceful getaway. Hikers be forewarned, however, as this is a popular and heavily used equestrian park. Encounters with the occasional piles of horse apples are a small price to pay for such an accessible forest getaway. Nearly 30 miles of trail form a large network within the 500 acres of park. Few specific routes exist; the best strategy is to just start rambling through the woods. A popular choice is to hike the perimeter of the park, a 4.8-mile loop. All trails within the park are relatively flat, wide, and easy to negotiate, and some are as short as 1 mile. Bridle Trails offers great springtime hiking, when the Cascades are full of snow but trillium and other flowers are blooming within the park.

User Groups: Hikers, leashed dogs, and horses. No mountain bikes are allowed. No wheelchair access.

Permits: This area is accessible year-round. A $5 day-use fee is required to park here and is payable at the trailhead, or you can get an annual State Parks Pass for $30; contact Washington State Parks and Recreation, 360/902-8500.

Maps: Maps of the trail system are posted at trailheads. For a topographic map, ask the USGS for Bellevue North.

Directions: From I-405 in Bellevue, take exit 17. Turn right onto 116th Avenue and drive to Northeast 53rd Street. The park entrance is on the left. The main trailhead is near the park entrance at the main parking area.

Contact: Washington State Parks and Recreation, P.O. Box 42650, Olympia, WA 98504-2669, 360/902-8844.

18 DISCOVERY PARK
2.8 mi/1.5 hr   🏃1 ⛰9

in Seattle along Puget Sound

Map 2.2, page 92

Discovery Park is a perfect example of how an abandoned military base can be reclaimed and released for public use. Seattle City Parks took over the former Fort Lawton years ago and has turned it into one of the city's premier open spaces. The park sits on a high bluff overlooking Puget Sound. Watching the sun set over the Olympic Mountains from here makes for an evening to remember. Seven miles of trail explore the park, but the highlight is the 2.8-mile Nature Loop Trail. The route enjoys a

little bit of everything, passing old army barracks, weaving through old forest, and hitting a number of great viewpoints. Several steep side trails offer access to the sandy beach. The beach is well worth exploring during low tide, when tidal pools and their inhabitants (crabs, mussels, and tiny fish) are exposed. Although Discovery Park is in the midst of Washington's largest city, it's easy to feel as though you're miles away.

User Groups: Hikers, leashed dogs, and mountain bikes. No horses are allowed. No wheelchair access.

Permits: This area is accessible year-round. Permits are not required. Parking and access are free.

Maps: Maps of the trail system are posted at trailheads. For a topographic map, ask the USGS for Seattle North.

Directions: From Ballard (in Seattle), drive south on 15th Avenue NW to Emerson Street. Turn right and drive to West Gilman Street. Turn right and drive 2 miles to the park entrance. The main trailhead at the visitors center is 0.2 mile inside the entrance on the left.

Contact: Seattle City Parks and Recreation, 100 Dexter Ave. N., Seattle, WA 98109, 206/684-4075.

19 SEWARD PARK
1.8 mi/1.0 hr   🏃1 ⛰8

in Seattle on Lake Washington

Map 2.2, page 92   BEST (

One doesn't have to go far from Seattle to enjoy a stand of magnificent old-growth forest. In fact, one needn't even leave the city limits. On Bailey Peninsula, which juts into Lake Washington in South Seattle, Seward Park contains the largest stand of forest in the city. A wide, flat trail explores the forest and makes a loop along the waterfront. The forest has many large, towering Douglas firs and beautiful madronas with their peeling bark. A rich understory of salal, thimbleberry, and salmonberry creates a cool, peaceful interior. Although there is a network of small social trails, it's best to stick to the established path to avoid getting lost. The trail cuts through the park to the shore of Lake Washington. From here, hikers can walk the shore back to the parking area.

User Groups: Hikers, leashed dogs, and mountain bikes. No horses are allowed. The trails are wheelchair accessible.

Permits: This area is accessible year-round. Permits are not required. Parking and access are free.

Maps: Maps of the trail system are posted at trailheads. For a topographic map, ask the USGS for Seattle South.

Directions: From I-5 northbound, take Swift Avenue (exit 161) toward Albro Place. Turn right onto Swift Avenue and drive to Eddy Street. Turn left and drive to Beacon Avenue South. Turn left and drive to Orcas Street; turn right and follow this street as it becomes Lake Washington Boulevard and hits the well-signed Seward Park. The trailhead is at the main parking area at the end of the park entrance road.

Contact: Seattle City Parks and Recreation, 100 Dexter Ave. N., Seattle, WA 98109, 206/684-4075.

20 COUGAR MOUNTAIN
0.5-6.0 mi/0.5-3.0 hr 🏃2 ⛰8

south of Bellevue in Cougar Mountain Regional Park

Map 2.2, page 92

The most western of the Issaquah Alps, Cougar Mountain is sanctuary in Seattle's backyard. Now encroached upon by development on all sides, the county park has become a near island of forest. Despite the close proximity of the city, Cougar Mountain and its large network of trails can feel like a step into the wilderness. A pair of trailheads offers access to roughly 30 miles of trail crisscrossing the 3,000 acres of Cougar Mountain.

Red Town lies near the bottom on the south side while a second trailhead exists atop the mountain at Anti-Aircraft Peak. This area is great for wintertime hiking, when snow covers much of the Cascades. Pick up a map, available at trailheads, to choose which hike you want to do.

From Red Town, a number of hikes can be custom-made. Coal Creek Trail runs through an open forest of big-leaf maple and red alder, encountering numerous mining artifacts. This area was heavily mined for coal until as recently as the 1960s. Be sure to carry a map, for many trails venture off the main artery. Good side trips include Bagley Seam Trail, Wildside Trail, and Rainbow Town Trail.

From Anti-Aircraft Peak, Anti-Aircraft Trail delves into the open forest that covers the mountain. Deer make common company along the way, as do coyotes and mountain beavers. Again, bring a map when hiking here. The trails are unmarked and it's easy to get turned around. The trails provide several opportunities for easy or challenging loops.

User Groups: Hikers, leashed dogs, horses, and mountain bikes. No wheelchair access.

Permits: This area is accessible year-round. Permits are not required. Parking and access are free.

Maps: Maps of the trail system are posted at trailheads. For a topographic map, ask the USGS for Bellevue South.

Directions: For Red Town, take exit 13 off I-90 and turn south on Lakemount Boulevard. Drive 3 miles to the signed entrance on the left.

For Radar Park, which allows access to Anti-Aircraft Peak, take exit 11 off I-90. Drive south on Southeast Newport Way to 164th Avenue. Turn right and drive to Cougar Mountain Drive. Turn right and drive 1 mile to the signed entrance.

Contact: Cougar Mountain Regional Wildland Park, King County Parks and Recreation, 201 South Jackson St., Ste. 700, Seattle, WA 98104, 206/296-8687.

21 POINT DEFIANCE
1.2-4.1 mi/2.0-4.0 hr

in Tacoma on Puget Sound

Map 2.2, page 92

The feather in Tacoma's cap, Point Defiance is a rare respite from the noise of the city. Secluded on a large point jutting into Commencement Bay, Point Defiance lays claim to miles of waterfront and some of Puget Sound's best views. While its exact ranking is left open to debate, Point Defiance is unquestionably one of the largest urban parks in North America. Large conifer forests grace nearly 20 miles of trail, a welcome change of scenery from Tacoma's industrial core. Point Defiance is also home to the city's zoo and aquarium; the roar of an elephant shouldn't be a surprise. Tacoma locals dearly love Point Defiance.

There are several options for exploring Point Defiance. Short walks can be made along Waterfront Promenade, stretching from Owen Beach to a small assortment of restaurants. This short trail (0.6 mile) is paved and accessible to wheelchairs. Other trails take on more natural forms (dirt pathways) through the forest. Running along the cliffs that mark the edge of much of the park, Square Trail Outer Loop (4.1 miles) is by far the most scenic. It visits numerous overlooks of the sound, and scenes of the Tacoma Narrow Bridge are especially great. Triangle Trail Inner Loop (3.3 miles) makes a shorter trip with a couple of viewpoints of the sound, but it mostly stays within the forest. The most popular route is Spine Trail (2.1 miles), which runs straight through the park to a commanding viewpoint of Gig Harbor and The Narrows. Whatever your choice, enjoy the shady forest and rich ecosystem; even deer live within the park.

User Groups: Hikers, leashed dogs, and mountain bikes. No horses are allowed. The Waterfront Promenade is wheelchair accessible.

Permits: This area is accessible year-round. Permits are not required. Parking and access are free.

Maps: Maps of the trail system are posted at trailheads. For a topographic map, ask the USGS for Gig Harbor.

Directions: From I-5 in Tacoma, drive west on Highway 16 to the Pearl Street exit. Turn right (north) and drive about 6 miles to the road's end at Point Defiance Park. Parking and trailheads are throughout the park.

Contact: Metro Parks Tacoma, 4702 S. 19th St., Tacoma, WA 98405, 253/305-1006.

22 NISQUALLY NATIONAL WILDLIFE REFUGE
1.0-5.0 mi/0.5-2.5 hr

north of Olympia on Puget Sound

Map 2.2, page 92   **BEST (**

One of Western Washington's largest undisturbed estuaries, Nisqually National Wildlife Refuge is an unnoticed treasure along I-5. Here, where freshwater meets saltwater, a rich habitat exists for animals of all sorts, but especially birds. Thousands of migratory birds pass through the refuge each spring and fall on their way to warming climates or feeding grounds. Mallards, widgeons, teal, Canada geese, red-tailed hawks, and great blue heron are regular sightings. Fortunately for those of us stuck on the ground, two loop trails explore this area.

Much of the refuge is an expansive collection of marshes. The wide, slow-flowing Nisqually runs through the middle, but where the river ends and the sound begins is difficult to discern. The two loop trails that run through the refuge both feature viewing platforms and blinds, where visitors can spy on wildlife without being noticed. It's a good idea to bring a pair of binoculars. A nice visitors center is open Wednesday–Sunday year-round.

Twin Barns Trail is a short 1-mile loop with many interpretive signs explaining the history and ecology of the area. It's a great introduction to the refuge and the animals that live here. The trail is completely built of wooden boardwalk, making it accessible to all.

A longer hike can be made by hiking Brown Farm Dike Trail, a 5-mile loop around the perimeter of the refuge. This flat trail gets users close to the Nisqually River, Puget Sound, and McAllister Creek.

User Groups: Hikers only. No dogs, horses, or mountain bikes are allowed. The shorter of the two loops is wheelchair accessible.

Permits: This area is accessible year-round. A $3 day-use fee is required to park here and is payable at the trailhead.

Maps: Maps of the trail system are available at the visitor center. For a topographic map, ask the USGS for Nisqually.

Directions: From Seattle, drive south on I-5 to Nisqually (exit 114). Turn right (west) onto Brown Farm Road and drive 0.3 mile to the well-signed trailhead.

Contact: Nisqually National Wildlife Refuge, 100 Brown Farm Rd., Olympia, WA 98516, 360/753-9467.

© SCOTT LEONARD

Nisqually National Wildlife Refuge, along the boardwalk

THE NORTHERN CASCADES

© SCOTT LEONARD

BEST HIKES

It's truly hard to go wrong when setting out in the

North Cascades. From ancient old-growth forests to alpine meadows, from wild and rushing rivers to enormous glaciers – there are more glaciers here than in the rest of the lower 48 states combined! – the North Cascades are the playground of the Puget Sound region. This region is home to a sizable chunk of Washington's greatest forests, mountains, and rivers. Hundreds of trails crisscross the enormous region, and nearly every one of them is great and exciting.

Thanks to careful and diligent conservation, much of the North Cascades' natural beauty remains for us to enjoy. The region is home to one national park (North Cascades) and eight federally protected wildernesses (Alpine Lakes, Boulder River, Glacier Peak, Henry M. Jackson, Lake Chelan-Sawtooth, Mount Baker, Noisy-Diobsud, Pasayten, and Wild Sky). Together, they make more than 2.5 million acres of protected land. The latest is the Wild Sky Wilderness, near Skykomish, created in 2007 after a long, hard fight in Congress. These protected lands in the North Cascades make hiking and backpacking in Washington the attraction that it is.

The Alpine Lakes Wilderness offers the most easily accessed trails. Situated between Interstate 90 and Highway 2, many of these trailheads are less than a 90-minute drive from Seattle. Alpine Lakes is home to – you guessed it – hundreds of alpine lakes (technically subalpine). When you're itching to get outdoors for a quick hike, Alpine Lakes is a great place to start your search.

On the north side of Highway 2 are Henry M. Jackson and Glacier Peak Wildernesses. These two areas take up much of the North Cascades' central portion, about 670,000 acres. With glistening white glaciers covering its 10,541-foot summit, Glacier Peak is naturally the central focus of the area. Cady Ridge (both of them), Image Lake, and Buck Creek Pass are just a few of the excellent hikes in these wildernesses. These areas are also easily accessed by the Mountain Loop Highway. Cutting into the Cascades from Darrington, the route makes a large loop around the Boulder River Wilderness. This area is home to easy trails (Lake 22, Heather Lake, Goat Flats) and difficult trails alike (Mount Dickerson, Stujack Pass, Poodle Dog Pass).

Even with all these attractions, this isn't even half of what the North Cascades have to offer. The Mount Baker Wilderness, for one, contains alpine meadows that are absolutely amazing in July (when they're alive with wildflowers) and completely delicious in late August (when they're smothered in huckleberries). The insane beauty of Mount Baker and Mount Shuksan can almost go without saying. Head up Route 542 out of Bellingham for access to trails like Lake Ann, Hannegan Pass, and Chain Lakes.

Although North Cascades National Park and the Pasayten Wilderness are actually neighbors, they seem to be one entity. These two areas extend along a 70-mile stretch of the Canadian border, totaling 1,150,000 acres. Access is via Route 20, where glacier-capped mountains and old forests are regular sights from the road. Such a big area requires longer trips, and there are plenty to be found here. Day hikes to Driveway Butte and Desolation Peak are certainly possible, but such a short taste will definitely leave you wanting to spend at least four or five days on the trail. Copper Ridge, Whatcom Pass, Devil's Dome Loop, Boundary Trail, and Cathedral Basin are classics of the region. Folks on their way to the Pasayten will love the town of Winthrop, where the theme is Old West. A stop at Winthrop Brewing Company's local brewpub is a must, especially after your hike!

Finally, the east side of the Cascades is drier and often a great destination when the west side is rainy. (Like the Olympics, the Cascades act like a big squeegee, forcing moist air from the ocean to release most of its rain on the west side.) Many of the wilderness areas stretch across the Cascade Crest and have portions that benefit from this rain shadow effect. U.S. 97 runs along the east side of the Cascades and provides access to many of these dry trails. The Lake Chelan–Sawtooth Wilderness is the heart and soul of the east side, with high, craggy peaks and mind-boggling views.

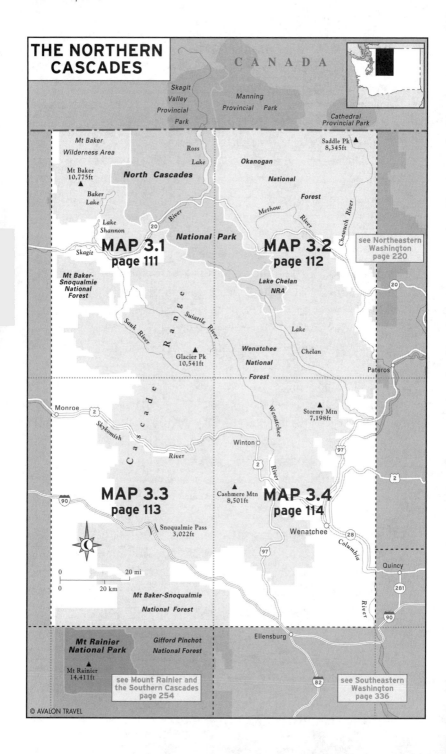

THE NORTHERN CASCADES

CANADA

Skagit Valley Provincial Park

Manning Provincial Park

Cathedral Provincial Park

Mt Baker Wilderness Area

Ross Lake

Saddle Pk ▲ 8,345ft

Mt Baker 10,775ft ▲

North Cascades

Okanogan National Forest

Baker Lake

Lake Shannon

River

Methow River

Chewuch River

MAP 3.1 page 111

National Park

20

MAP 3.2 page 112

Skagit

see Northeastern Washington page 220

Mt Baker-Snoqualmie National Forest

Lake Chelan NRA

20

Sauk River

Suiattle River

Range

Glacier Pk 10,541ft ▲

Wenatchee National Forest

Lake Chelan

Pateros

Cascade

Monroe 2

Skykomish River

Wenatchee

Stormy Mtn 7,198ft ▲

Winton

MAP 3.3 page 113

2

97

2

90

Cashmere Mtn 8,501ft ▲

MAP 3.4 page 114

Snoqualmie Pass 3,022ft

Wenatchee 28

Columbia

0 ___ 20 mi
0 ___ 20 km

97

Quincy

281

Mt Baker-Snoqualmie National Forest

90

River

Mt Rainier National Park

Gifford Pinchot National Forest

Ellensburg

Mt Rainier 14,411ft ▲

see Mount Rainier and the Southern Cascades page 254

82

see Southeastern Washington page 336

© AVALON TRAVEL

Map 3.1

Hikes 1-45
Pages 115-144

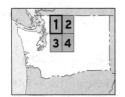

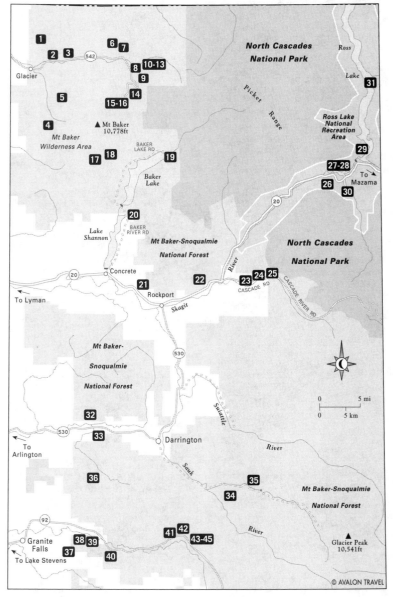

Map 3.2

Hikes 46-94
Pages 145-176

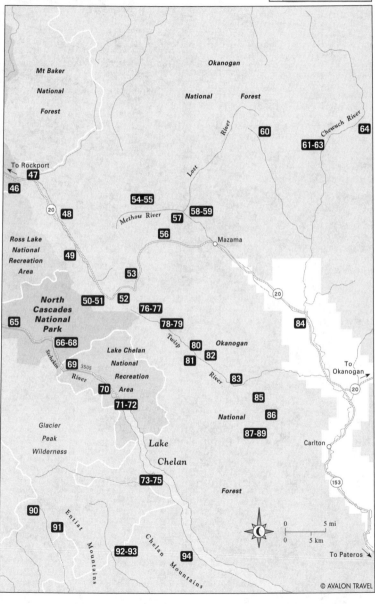

Map 3.3

Hikes 95-139
Pages 177-206

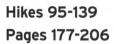

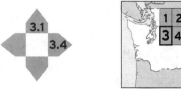

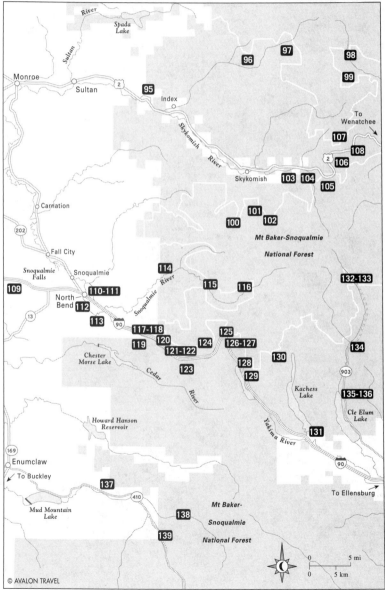

Map 3.4

Hikes 140-154
Pages 206-216

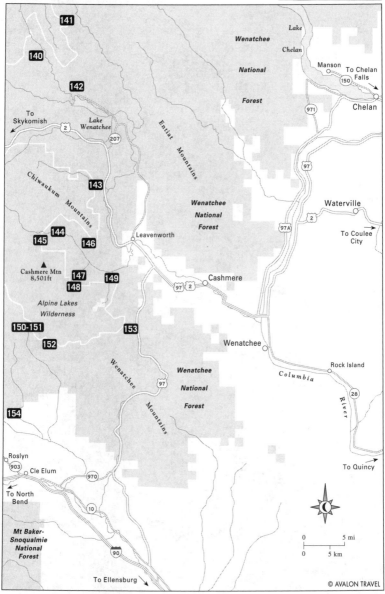

1 DAMFINO LAKES

1.4–19.6 mi/1.0–5.0 hr

east of Bellingham in Mount Baker–
Snoqualmie National Forest

Map 3.1, page 111

Damfino Lakes are merely a starting point for hiking and exploration, as the area serves as a junction to several beautiful hikes. Canyon Ridge, regarded highly by the few who know of it, is accessible only via this trail. Excelsior Ridge, normally a long, steep climb, is achieved much more easily via Damfino Lakes Trail. Damfino Lakes Trail is more about what lies beyond the lakes than the lakes themselves.

Damfino Lakes Trail climbs gently through forest to the pair of lakes (0.7 mile). From here, turn north and encounter the high meadow run of Canyon Ridge Trail (up to 9.8 miles one-way). Turn north at the lakes to head to Cowap Peak (elevation 5,658 feet), a summit for great views. A map and compass are highly recommended for these two trails.

Turn south at the lakes to climb gradually to the vast meadows of Excelsior Ridge (3 miles). This is a quicker and much easier shortcut to the ridge (one-third of the elevation gain and half the distance than from the traditional trailhead). So don't head for Damfino Lakes and stop there; the two small lakes are just the beginning.

User Groups: Canyon Ridge Trail is open to hikers, leashed dogs, horses, llamas, bicycles, and motorcycles. South of Damfino Lakes is open to hikers and leashed dogs only. Boundary Way Trail is open to hikers, leashed dogs, and llamas. No wheelchair access.

Permits: This area is usually accessible July–October. A federal Northwest Forest Pass is required to park here.

Maps: For a map of Mount Baker–Snoqualmie National Forest, contact the Outdoor Recreation Information Center at the downtown Seattle REI. For topographic maps, ask Green Trails for No. 13, Mount Baker, or ask the USGS for Bearpaw Mountain.

Directions: From Bellingham, drive 36 miles east on Highway 542 (Mount Baker Highway) to Canyon Creek Road (Forest Service Road 31). Turn left (north) and drive 14.5 miles to the trailhead, on the right side at a sharp turn in the road.

Contact: Mount Baker–Snoqualmie National Forest, Glacier Public Service Center, Glacier, WA 98244, 360/599-2714.

2 CHURCH MOUNTAIN

8.4 mi/6.0 hr

east of Bellingham in Mount Baker–
Snoqualmie National Forest

Map 3.1, page 111

One of the North Fork Nooksack River's finest hikes is fittingly the first and easiest trail to access. Church Mountain Trail rises through old-growth forest to an enormous basin and peak with views over the broad river valley to Mount Baker, Mount Shuksan, and much of Canada. It's not an easy height to achieve, as the 3,600-foot climb in just over 4 miles will attest. The trail offers enough wonder and inspiring views to more than make up for any weariness in the legs.

Church Mountain Trail starts off in a mean fashion, with a breath-stealing climb of switchbacks. These first 2 miles are mostly deep within virgin forest, with big trees providing welcome shade on warm, sunny days. The trail breaks out into the mountain's large glacial cirque, covered in subalpine meadows and streams. During July and early August, basin walls come alive with blooming wildflowers while heather and lupine thrive in the basin. This is a good turnaround point for some, with Mount Baker directly across the basin, a real postcard view.

The final 2 miles are a steep ascent up basin walls, at times on tricky footing. This section is hot, dry, and exposed; plenty of water is a must. From atop Church Mountain, the views are panoramic and a topographic map is a necessity to identify the numerous mountains.

User Groups: Hikers and leashed dogs. No

horses or mountain bikes are allowed. No wheelchair access.

Permits: This trail is usually accessible mid-July–early October. A federal Northwest Forest Pass is required to park here.

Maps: For a map of Mount Baker–Snoqualmie National Forest, contact the Outdoor Recreation Information Center at the downtown Seattle REI. For topographic maps, ask Green Trails for No. 13, Mount Baker, or ask the USGS for Bearpaw Mountain.

Directions: From Bellingham, drive east 38 miles on Highway 542 (Mount Baker Highway) to Church Mountain Road (Forest Service Road 3040). Turn left (north) and drive 2.5 miles to the trailhead at road's end.

Contact: Mount Baker–Snoqualmie National Forest, Glacier Public Service Center, Glacier, WA 98244, 360/599-2714.

❸ EXCELSIOR RIDGE
11.2 mi/8.0 hr

east of Bellingham in Mount Baker Wilderness of Mount Baker-Snoqualmie National Forest

Map 3.1, page 111

In a land where tough ascents and endless switchbacks are an accepted way of life on the trail, this hike makes others look tame. Excelsior Trail and Welcome Pass Trail climb from the valley floor to Excelsior Ridge, covered in meadows with views of mountains in every direction. Connecting them is High Divide Trail, 4.5 miles of ridgeline meadows. There's very little you won't see along this outstanding route.

To complete the whole loop, you must arrange a drop-off between the two trailheads. Better yet, drop off mountain bikes at the upper trailhead (Welcome Pass) and pick them up after hiking for an easy ride back to the car. For a one-way up-and-back trip, Welcome Pass is the best bet. Excelsior and Welcome Pass Trails both entail many switchbacks at an excruciating grade. The trails are mostly engulfed by old-growth forest, but they are nonetheless dry and hot.

The two trails are connected by High Divide Trail, which runs for 4.5 miles along the ridge. Views of Mount Baker and Mount Shuksan, just across the Nooksack River, are outstanding. The trail runs through seemingly endless meadows of wildflowers. Tomyhoi, Border Peaks, and a lot of Canada are visible from up here. Its south-facing orientation means that snow melts sooner here, making this one of the first trails to open in the valley.

User Groups: Hikers, leashed dogs, horses (horses allowed August 1–November 1), and llamas. No mountain bikes are allowed. No wheelchair access.

Permits: This trail is usually accessible mid-June–early October. A federal Northwest Forest Pass is required to park here.

Maps: For a map of Mount Baker–Snoqualmie National Forest, contact the Outdoor Recreation Information Center at the downtown Seattle REI. For topographic maps, ask Green Trails for No. 13, Mount Baker, and No. 14, Mount Shuksan, or ask the USGS for Bearpaw Mountain.

Directions: From Bellingham, drive east 41 miles on Highway 542 (Mount Baker Highway) to an unsigned trailhead on the left (north) side of the highway. This is Excelsior Pass Trailhead and is immediately past Nooksack Falls.

For Welcome Pass Trailhead, drive another 4.5 miles to Forest Service Road 3060. Turn left and drive 1 mile to the trailhead at road's end.

Contact: Mount Baker–Snoqualmie National Forest, Glacier Public Service Center, Glacier, WA 98244, 360/599-2714.

❹ HELIOTROPE RIDGE
5.0 mi/3.0 hr

east of Bellingham in Mount Baker Wilderness of Mount Baker-Snoqualmie National Forest

Map 3.1, page 111

One of the best opportunities to see and hear a living glacier lies at the end of this popular trail. Heliotrope Ridge Trail ascends through beautiful forests to the terminus of the Coleman Glaciers. This is the most popular route for climbers who seek the summit of Mount Baker, which towers above the route. Huge glacial moraines shape the terrain above timberline, including the brightly layered Chromatic Moraine at the head of Glacier Creek. There's no shortage of hikers along the trail, but that should not detract from the great views and the ability to comprehend the mass of the slowly moving glaciers.

The trail leaves the trailhead and steadily ascends through beautiful forests of old-growth timber, crossing several ice-cold creeks. After 2 miles, the trail forks. The left fork crosses Heliotrope Creek and scrambles up to an overlook near an arm of the Coleman Glacier, where it terminates into a morass of mud and ice. Colorful Chromatic Moraine is just across the way.

The right fork at the junction climbs to a rocky terrain of wildflowers and whistling marmots. Mount Baker towers above a wide-open area of scrambling opportunities. Climbers continue from here to the Coleman Glacier base camp. Be aware that the trickle of a stream you crossed in the morning may be a river by the afternoon. Plan carefully. Also, exploration on glaciers is not recommended without proper equipment and expertise—glacial crevasses prefer to swallow the foolish.

User Groups: Hikers and leashed dogs. No horses or mountain bikes are allowed. No wheelchair access.

Permits: This trail is accessible August–early October. A federal Northwest Forest Pass is required to park here.

Maps: For a map of Mount Baker–Snoqualmie National Forest, contact the Outdoor Recreation Information Center at the downtown Seattle REI. For topographic maps, ask Green Trails for No. 13, Mount Baker, or ask the USGS for Mount Baker and Goat Mountain.

Directions: From Bellingham, drive east 34 miles on Highway 542 (Mount Baker Highway) to Glacier Creek Road (Forest Service Road 39). Turn right (south) and drive 8.5 miles to the signed trailhead on the left.

Contact: Mount Baker–Snoqualmie National Forest, Glacier Public Service Center, Glacier, WA 98244, 360/599-2714.

⑤ SKYLINE DIVIDE

7.0 mi/4.0 hr

east of Bellingham in Mount Baker Wilderness of Mount Baker-Snoqualmie National Forest

Map 3.1, page 111

Catch a sunset from Skyline Divide, and you'll never stop talking about it. This long ridge extending from Mount Baker is covered in meadows. Views stretch from the North Cascades to Puget Sound and from Mount Baker to British Columbia. The Skyline Trail truly lives in the sky.

Skyline Trail climbs 2 miles through a grand forest of Pacific silver fir and western hemlock. The grade is constant and not difficult. Before long, the trail reaches the divide, and Mount Baker seems close enough to touch. The North Cascades unfold to the east for miles, and there is no end to the peaks one can identify. The ridge is dry and hot, so bring plenty of water.

Skyline Trail carries on south for another 1.5 miles, going up and down with the ridge and heading ever closer to Baker. To the west are the San Juan Islands in the sound, and Vancouver, British Columbia, is also discernible. Sunsets from here dazzle and are well worth the night hike down. Very little camping is found on the ridge; consider a hike by moonlight another part of a remarkable experience.

User Groups: Hikers, leashed dogs, horses, and llamas. No mountain bikes are allowed. No wheelchair access.

Permits: This trail is accessible July–early October. A federal Northwest Forest Pass is required to park here.

Maps: For a map of Mount Baker–Snoqualmie

National Forest, contact the Outdoor Recreation Information Center at the downtown Seattle REI. For topographic maps, ask Green Trails for No. 13, Mount Baker, or ask the USGS for Mount Baker and Bearpaw Mountain.

Directions: From Bellingham, drive east 34 miles on Highway 542 (Mount Baker Highway) to Glacier Creek Road (Forest Service Road 39). Turn right (south) and quickly turn left onto Forest Service Road 37. Drive 15 miles to the trailhead at road's end.

Contact: Mount Baker–Snoqualmie National Forest, Glacier Public Service Center, Glacier, WA 98244, 360/599-2714.

6 YELLOW ASTER BUTTE
7.2 mi/3.5 hr   🏃3 ⛰8

east of Bellingham in Mount Baker Wilderness of Mount Baker-Snoqualmie National Forest

Map 3.1, page 111

This trail to the high country offers just about everything one could ask for in a trail. Wildflowers and huckleberries fill wide-open meadows. A basin of subalpine lakes opens to reveal outstanding views of Baker and Shuksan, and a scramble yields Tomyhoi Peak. Best of all, the trail starts high, preserving your energy for high-country rambling. Bring your swimsuit, as the lakes are too enticing to turn down. It's hard to imagine what's missing in this great subalpine parkland.

The route begins on Tomyhoi Lake Trail, which switchbacks through avalanche chutes and thick brush to a signed junction (1.4 miles). Take a left and climb through open meadows with nonstop views to the lake basin. Indian paintbrush, monkey flowers, and penstemon are just a few of the flowers you'll find blooming in late July. Facing south toward the sun, this trail can be very hot; bring extra water or a filter.

The basin features various small lakes, perfect for taking a dip. The meadows are delicate and suffer from deterioration because of heavy use; camp only at designated sites and follow strict Leave-No-Trace principles. For the hardy, a well-used path leads to the top of Yellow Aster Butte and big views of Mount Larrabee, Border Peaks, and Mount Baker. Yellow Aster Butte is a must-do for dedicated North Cascades hikers.

User Groups: Hikers and leashed dogs. No horses or mountain bikes are allowed. No wheelchair access.

Permits: This trail is accessible July–early October. A federal Northwest Forest Pass is required to park here.

Maps: For a map of Mount Baker–Snoqualmie National Forest, contact the Outdoor Recreation Information Center at the downtown Seattle REI. For topographic maps, ask Green Trails for No. 14, Mount Shuksan, or ask the USGS for Mount Larrabee.

Directions: From Bellingham, drive east 46 miles on Highway 542 (Mount Baker Highway) to Twin Lakes Road (Forest Service Road 3065), just beyond the Department of Transportation facility. Turn left (north) and drive 5 miles to the signed trailhead (where the road makes several switchbacks on an exposed slope).

Contact: Mount Baker–Snoqualmie National Forest, Glacier Public Service Center, Glacier, WA 98244, 360/599-2714.

7 WINCHESTER MOUNTAIN
3.8 mi/2.5 hr   🏃3 ⛰8

east of Bellingham in Mount Baker Wilderness of Mount Baker-Snoqualmie National Forest

Map 3.1, page 111

Winchester Mountain is home to a backcountry favorite: an abandoned fire lookout. Built in 1935, the lookout is no longer used by the Forest Service but receives regular maintenance from a dedicated volunteer group. From up here, much of the North Cascades, in Washington and Canada, are revealed. Add to the spectacular views an enjoyable trail, flush with ripe huckleberries in September, and you have a great hike.

Winchester Mountain Trail is accessible at

Twin Lakes (elevation 5,200 feet), an old base camp for miners and prospectors. The trail climbs steeply through meadows and patches of alpine trees. Be aware that the upper part of the trail is home to a hazardous snowfield that does not melt until late summer. Don't cross it without an ice ax. Otherwise it's best to drop below the snowfield and reconnect to the trail at the other side. The trail is a constant climb, but it's only 1,300 feet gain in about 2 miles. Bring water and a tolerance for other hikers.

User Groups: Hikers and leashed dogs. No horses or mountain bikes are allowed. No wheelchair access.

Permits: This trail is usually accessible late July–early October. (September is the ideal month to hike the trail, with the best chances of avoiding the snow field.) A federal Northwest Forest Pass is required to park here.

Maps: For a map of Mount Baker–Snoqualmie National Forest, contact the Outdoor Recreation Information Center at the downtown Seattle REI. For topographic maps, ask Green Trails for No. 14, Mount Shuksan, or ask the USGS for Mount Larrabee.

Directions: From Bellingham, drive east 46 miles on Highway 542 (Mount Baker Highway) to Twin Lakes Road (Forest Service Road 3065), just beyond the Department of Transportation facility. Turn left (north) and drive 7 miles to the signed trailhead at road's end. The last 2 miles are not recommended for passenger cars. A four-wheel-drive vehicle with high clearance is highly recommended.

Contact: Mount Baker–Snoqualmie National Forest, Glacier Public Service Center, Glacier, WA 98244, 360/599-2714.

8 GOAT MOUNTAIN

6.4 mi/4.5 hr   🥾5 ⛰8

east of Bellingham in Mount Baker Wilderness of Mount Baker-Snoqualmie National Forest

Map 3.1, page 111

When June rolls around and the urge to explore the high country is strong, Goat Mountain is your sanctuary. The trail to this former lookout site lies on the south side of the mountain, making it one of the first to melt out in the summer. With views of Mount Shuksan and countless other peaks and ridges, this is a great first hike of the season. The climb is extremely strenuous, with more than 2,900 feet of elevation gain in just 3 miles, so it's a sure way to test your fitness for the coming summer of hiking.

Goat Mountain Trail is a steady climb up the side of the mountain. The first part passes through typically great forests of the Nooksack Valley. The trail enters Mount Baker Wilderness (2 miles) just as the forest gives way to open meadows. Huckleberries are as plentiful as the views of Shuksan and Baker. Be sure to bring water on this taxing ascent, as you won't find any on the way other than old patches of snow.

Below the summit sits an old lookout site, abandoned and torn down long ago. The views are excellent, and a long lunch break is well deserved after the hike. Those who are feeling adventurous and have the extra energy can continue scrambling up the ridge to the true summit, where the views only get better.

User Groups: Hikers, leashed dogs, llamas, and horses (horses allowed August 1–November 1). No mountain bikes are allowed. No wheelchair access.

Permits: This trail is accessible late-June–October. A federal Northwest Forest Pass is required to park here.

Maps: For a map of Mount Baker–Snoqualmie National Forest, contact the Outdoor Recreation Information Center at the downtown Seattle REI. For topographic maps, ask Green Trails for No. 14, Mount Shuksan, or ask the USGS for Mount Larrabee.

Directions: From Bellingham, drive east 46 miles on Highway 542 (Mount Baker Highway) to Hannegan Pass Road (Forest Service Road 32). Turn left and drive 2.5 miles to the trailhead on the left side. Parking is on the left immediately before the trailhead.

Contact: Mount Baker–Snoqualmie National

Forest, Glacier Public Service Center, Glacier, WA 98244, 360/599-2714.

9 NOOKSACK CIRQUE
9.0 mi/5.0 hr   🥾2 ⛰7

east of Bellingham in Mount Baker Wilderness
of Mount Baker-Snoqualmie National Forest

Map 3.1, page 111

Unlike any other trail in this valley, Nooksack Cirque Trail is an easy river hike with little elevation gain. This is a welcome respite from the area's straight-up, straight-down trails. Miles of forest rambling delivers hikers to Nooksack Cirque, one of the most easily accessible and largest glacial cirques you'll ever lay eyes upon.

Nooksack Cirque Trail starts by fording Ruth Creek (cross downed logs for a drier experience) and follows an old logging road. It's second-growth forest until the road ends at the wilderness boundary (3 miles), where old-growth forest starts. The two forests are hugely different. Enormous western hemlocks and Pacific silver firs give the feeling that one has been suddenly transported to the Olympic rainforests. Look for colonnades, straight lines of three or four ancient trees growing from a decomposed log.

The final mile is not maintained and becomes brushier as one goes along. Several times the trail breaks out onto the riverbed and route-finding is necessary (but not difficult—head upstream!). At the end sits the large, open cirque beneath the Nooksack Glacier. The ice-scraped cliffs covered in waterfalls are impressive if you're willing to endure the bushwhack. There are two large campsites about 0.5 mile inside the wilderness boundary.

User Groups: Hikers and leashed dogs. No horses or mountain bikes are allowed. No wheelchair access.

Permits: This trail is usually accessible year-round. A federal Northwest Forest Pass is required to park here.

Maps: For a map of Mount Baker–Snoqualmie

National Forest, contact the Outdoor Recreation Information Center at the downtown Seattle REI. For topographic maps, ask Green Trails for No. 14, Mount Shuksan, or ask the USGS for Mount Larrabee, Mount Sefrit, and Mount Shuksan.

Directions: From Bellingham, drive east 46 miles on Highway 542 (Mount Baker Highway) to Forest Service Road 32, just before you cross the Nooksack River. Turn left and drive 2 miles to Forest Service Road 34. Turn right and drive 1.5 miles to the trailhead at road's end.

Contact: Mount Baker–Snoqualmie National Forest, Glacier Public Service Center, Glacier, WA 98244, 360/599-2714.

10 HANNEGAN PASS
10.0 mi/5.0 hr   🥾3 ⛰9

east of Bellingham in Mount Baker Wilderness
of Mount Baker-Snoqualmie National Forest

Map 3.1, page 111

More than a backcountry entrance to North Cascades National Park, Hannegan Trail is absolutely beautiful to boot. Passing beneath the looming Nooksack Ridge up to Hannegan Pass and down to Boundary Camp, the trail is one of the most scenic valley hikes anywhere. Leading to Copper Ridge, Chilliwack River, and Whatcom Pass, Hannegan Trail is a popular segment of longer treks. But the trail reaches Hannegan Peak, one of the best vistas in all of the North Cascades.

Hannegan Trail follows Ruth Creek back to its headwaters beneath Ruth Mountain. Much of the route features open avalanche chutes, revealing the enormous, vertical ridges on either side. Soon, the 7,100-foot Ruth Mountain appears with its enormous glacier and glacially polished walls. Beneath Ruth is Hannegan Camp (3.5 miles), a large and picturesque campground.

Hannegan Trail climbs to the meadows of Hannegan Pass (4 miles) and down to Boundary Camp (5 miles). At the pass is Hannegan

Peak Trail, a steep pitch through meadows to the 6,186-foot peak. The views are grand, including Ruth, Mount Shuksan, Mount Baker, the Picketts, and countless other Cascade peaks. Just about every footstep along this hike is unbelievably beautiful. To hike this trail and not visit Hannegan Peak is a missed opportunity.

User Groups: Hikers, leashed dogs, llamas, and horses. No mountain bikes are allowed. No wheelchair access.

Permits: This trail is usually accessible July–early October. A federal Northwest Forest Pass is required to park here. Overnight stays within the national park (Boundary Camp or beyond) require backcountry camping permits, which are available at Glacier Public Service Center. No permit is required for staying at Hannegan Camp.

Maps: For a map of Mount Baker–Snoqualmie National Forest, contact the Outdoor Recreation Information Center at the downtown Seattle REI. For topographic maps, ask Green Trails for No. 14, Mount Shuksan, or ask the USGS for Mount Sefrit.

Directions: From Bellingham, drive east 46 miles on Highway 542 (Mount Baker Highway) to Hannegan Pass Road (Forest Service Road 32). Turn left and drive 5 miles to the signed trailhead at road's end.

Contact: Mount Baker–Snoqualmie National Forest, Glacier Public Service Center, Glacier, WA 98244, 360/599-2714.

11 COPPER RIDGE LOOP
34.5 mi/4-5 days

east of Bellingham in North Cascades National Park

Map 3.1, page 111

Strike up a conversation with a North Cascades hiking veteran and you'll invariably be asked, "Have you done Copper Ridge yet?" This backcountry trek maintains cultlike popularity, thanks to being one of the most scenic and beloved routes in the state. Views and meadows

abound along this high-country route. Several lakes highlight the ridge run, which also leads to an old lookout. The wild ridge is isolated in the upper national park and makes an excellent loop with Chilliwack Trail.

Copper Ridge is accessible via Hannegan Pass (see previous listing). At Boundary Camp (5 miles) the trail splits—up to Copper Ridge and down to Chilliwack River (see listing in this chapter). Your direction will depend upon available camp reservations (the National Park Service requires permits to camp within the park). Much of the trail enjoys open meadows. Great views, but it's hot and dry, too; come prepared for these conditions by packing plenty of water.

Copper Ridge Trail leaves Boundary Camp and climbs around Hells Gorge to the ridge. Silesia Camp and Egg Lake Camp (8.2 miles) offer great camps and a refreshing dip in Egg Lake. An old lookout offers the route's highest point at 6,260 feet (10.7 miles). Below the long arm of Copper Mountain lies Copper Lake Camp (11.9 miles). The trail continues four additional miles on the ridge before dropping to Chilliwack River (19.4 miles). Become a North Cascades veteran and make plans for Copper Ridge.

User Groups: Hikers only. No horses, dogs, or mountain bikes are allowed. No wheelchair access.

Permits: This trail is usually accessible August–September. No permits are required. Parking and access are free. Overnight stays within the national park require backcountry camping permits, which are available at Glacier Public Service Center.

Maps: For a map of North Cascades National Park, contact the Outdoor Recreation Information Center at the downtown Seattle REI. For a topographic map, ask Green Trails for No. 14, Mount Shuksan, and No. 15, Mount Challenger, or ask the USGS for Mount Sefrit and Copper Mountain.

Directions: From Bellingham, drive east 46 miles on Highway 542 (Mount Baker Highway) to Hannegan Pass Road (Forest Service Road 32). Turn left and drive 5 miles to the signed trailhead at road's end.

Contact: North Cascades National Park, Wilderness Information Center, 7280 Ranger Station Rd., Marblemount, WA 98267, 360/854-7245; Mount Baker–Snoqualmie National Forest, Glacier Public Service Center, Glacier, WA 98244, 360/599-2714.

12 WHATCOM PASS
34.0 mi/4 days

east of Bellingham in North Cascades
National Park

Map 3.1, page 111

The legend of Whatcom Pass frequently and quickly makes its way around hiking circles. It's not a legend of Sasquatch or a miner's ghost, but instead true accounts of the beauty found at Whatcom Pass. Nestled at the base of the Picket Range, Whatcom Pass enjoys the North Cascades' most impressive range. Some old-timers even proclaim Whatcom Pass the king of all backcountry destinations. That sounds about right.

The route follows the beautiful Hannegan Pass and Chilliwack River Trails (see listings in this chapter) to Brush Creek (12.3 miles). By this point, the scenery should have knocked your boots off. Brush Creek Trail splits from the Chilliwack and climbs 5 miles to the subalpine splendor of Whatcom Pass. Graybeal Camp sits at 12.3 miles, but pass it up for a camp near the pass. Take care in this delicate ecosystem by staying on established trails and avoiding campfires. Appreciate the view of Mount Challenger and its enormous glacier. Make great side trips by scrambling north to Tapto Lakes or south along the Whatcom Arm.

User Groups: Hikers and horses (horses allowed up to Brush Creek Trail only). No dogs, horses, or mountain bikes are allowed. No wheelchair access.

Permits: This trail is accessible August–September. No permits are required. Parking and access are free. Overnight stays within the national park require reservations and backcountry camping permits, which are available at Glacier Public Service Center.

Maps: For a map of North Cascades National Park, contact the Outdoor Recreation Information Center at the downtown Seattle REI. For topographic maps, ask Green Trails for No. 14, Mount Shuksan, and No. 15, Mount Challenger, or ask the USGS for Mount Sefrit, Copper Mountain, Mount Redoubt, Mount Challenger, and Mount Blum.

Directions: From Bellingham, drive east 46 miles on Highway 542 (Mount Baker Highway) to Hannegan Pass Road (Forest Service Road 32). Turn left and drive 5 miles to the signed trailhead at road's end.

Contact: North Cascades National Park, Wilderness Information Center, 7280 Ranger Station Rd., Marblemount, WA 98267, 360/854-7245; Mount Baker–Snoqualmie National Forest, Glacier Public Service Center, Glacier, WA 98244, 360/599-2714.

13 CHILLIWACK RIVER
40.0 mi/4 days

east of Bellingham in North Cascades
National Park

Map 3.1, page 111

As the miles pass underfoot on Chilliwack River Trail, the solitude of the wilderness grows ever more lonely. Most often hiked to reach Copper Ridge or Whatcom Pass, Chilliwack River Trail is grand by itself, too. Miles of large old-growth forest tower over the trail, pleasantly following the rambling river. This is real wilderness, where bears and elk are regular hiking partners. Regardless of one's destination, Chilliwack River Trail is an enjoyable journey.

Chilliwack Trail is accessible via Boundary Camp on Hannegan Pass Trail (5 miles). Chilliwack Trail drops through ever-thickening forest to Copper Creek Camp (8.5 miles) and U.S. Cabin Camp (11.1 miles). The trail crosses the river at one of the state's unique river crossings: A cable car whisks hikers above the river to the opposite shore.

Brush Creek Trail (12.9 miles) ventures south up to Whatcom Pass (12.9 miles) while Copper Ridge Trail climbs to the west (16.5 miles). Beyond this point, the trail rambles through beautiful lowland river forests, where green dominates the scenery. Bear Creek Camp (18.3 miles) and Little Chilliwack Camp (20.7 miles) offer campsites before entering Canada (24 miles one-way). Few ever make it so deep into this wild place.

User Groups: Hikers and horses (horses allowed up to Brush Creek trail only). No dogs or mountain bikes are allowed. No wheelchair access.

Permits: This trail is accessible from Hannegan Pass July–September and from Canada nearly year-round. No permits are required. Parking and access are free. Overnight stays within the national park require backcountry camping permits.

Maps: For a map of North Cascades National Park, contact the Outdoor Recreation Information Center at the downtown Seattle REI. For topographic maps, ask Green Trails for No. 14, Mount Shuksan, and No. 15, Mount Challenger, or ask the USGS for Mount Sefrit and Copper Mountain.

Directions: From Bellingham, drive east 46 miles on Highway 542 (Mount Baker Highway) to Hannegan Pass Road (Forest Service Road 32). Turn left and drive 5 miles to the signed trailhead at road's end.

Contact: North Cascades National Park, Wilderness Information Center, 7280 Ranger Station Rd., Marblemount, WA 98267, 360/854-7245.

14 LAKE ANN
8.6 mi/6.0 hr   🏃3 ⛰10

east of Bellingham in Mount Baker Wilderness of Mount Baker-Snoqualmie National Forest

Map 3.1, page 111

When you finally crest the meadowy pass and spot Lake Ann lying beneath Mount Shuksan, you will know that you have arrived

someplace special. Rocky alpine meadows surround this high-country lake, while the towering cliffs and glaciers of Mount Shuksan stand above. The journey is through 4 miles of old-growth forest and berry-filled meadows. This is one of the best hikes in an area full of beautiful country.

Lake Ann Trail quickly drops through forest into Swift Creek Basin (1.5 miles). Despite an average of 700 inches of snow each winter, mountain hemlocks swell massively. In the basin, acres of meadows brim with huckleberries, making this a sweet hike in August. The trail crosses Swift Creek (look downstream to Mount Baker) and climbs 2 miles through more meadows to a pass above Lake Ann.

Surrounded by alpine meadows and mountain views, Lake Ann presents a nice place to rest awhile. Take a dip in the cool water while watching marmots play in the meadows. On Mount Shuksan, the Curtis Glaciers can be heard breaking and settling in the summer heat. There is plenty of camping space, but it can go quickly. This trail is a perfect midweek or late-season trip.

User Groups: Hikers and leashed dogs. No horses or mountain bikes are allowed. No wheelchair access.

Permits: This area is usually accessible July–early October. A federal Northwest Forest Pass is required to park here.

Maps: For a map of Mount Baker–Snoqualmie National Forest, contact the Outdoor Recreation Information Center at the downtown Seattle REI. For topographic maps, ask Green Trails for No. 14, Mount Shuksan, or ask the USGS for Shuksan Arm.

Directions: From Bellingham, drive east 56 miles on Highway 542 (Mount Baker Highway) to the signed trailhead on the left, past Heather Meadows Visitor Center.

Contact: Mount Baker–Snoqualmie National Forest, Glacier Public Service Center, Glacier, WA 98244, 360/599-2714.

15 GALENA CHAIN LAKES
6.5 mi/4.0 hr   🏃3 ⛰8

east of Bellingham in Mount Baker Wilderness
of Mount Baker-Snoqualmie National Forest

Map 3.1, page 111

Galena Chain Lakes have been a backcountry destination for hikers and backpackers for generations. Nestled among towering mountains, these four lakes are picturesque examples of the subalpine. Chain Lakes are immersed in meadows and huckleberries and offer lots of great camping. They can be fished for dinner as well. This trail is great for families and is accessible for both day hikers visiting Heather Meadows as well as overnight backpackers.

The route is best done as a loop, starting at Artist Point. Chain Lakes Trail heads toward Ptarmigan Ridge before turning right at a signed junction (1 mile). Before you know it, you've reached Mazama Lake (2 miles). There are four choice camps here, set on the small ridge between the lake and Mount Baker. The trail makes its way to large Iceberg Lake, which sits below the vertical walls of Table Mountain. Reportedly, the fish are biggest here. A side trail leads to four camps along Hayes Lake, which requires a bit of up and down.

To exit the basin, the trail climbs to a saddle between Table and Mazama Dome, the best vista of the trail, and drops two steep miles to the visitors center. Wild Goose Trail returns hikers to Artist Point, but drivers passing through here are always happy to pick up a few riders for the 2-mile drive. This is a popular trail in season.

User Groups: Hikers and leashed dogs. No horses or mountain bikes are allowed. No wheelchair access.

Permits: This trail is usually accessible July–September. A federal Northwest Forest Pass is required to park here.

Maps: For a map of Mount Baker–Snoqualmie National Forest, contact the Outdoor Recreation Information Center at the downtown Seattle REI. For topographic maps, ask Green Trails for No. 14, Mount Shuksan, or ask the USGS for Shuksan Arm.

Directions: From Bellingham, drive east 58 miles on Highway 542 (Mount Baker Highway) to Artist's Point at the end of the highway. The trailhead is on the northwest side of the parking lot.

Contact: Mount Baker–Snoqualmie National Forest, Glacier Public Service Center, Glacier, WA 98244, 360/599-2714.

16 PTARMIGAN RIDGE
8.0 mi/4.0 hr   🏃3 ⛰9

east of Bellingham in Mount Baker Wilderness
of Mount Baker-Snoqualmie National Forest

Map 3.1, page 111

Just as one might expect from an arm of Mount Baker, Ptarmigan Ridge Trail revels in an excess of natural beauty. Wildflowers paint miles of meadows while even more miles of views extend in all directions. Mount Shuksan looms from the east, and Mount Baker towers directly above. Marmots and picas are local residents, living it up with location, location, location. You can't ask too much of Ptarmigan Ridge on a sunny, summer day.

Before hitting the trail, be aware of several safety issues. Snowfields linger along the route well into summer, sometimes all year long. They are steep and should be crossed only by the most experienced hikers. Along this precipitous ridge, a misstep can have grave consequences. Mount Baker's weather changes rapidly, so be ready to use a map and compass should a storm blow in and create a whiteout. That said, Ptarmigan Ridge Trail presents an exciting trip for those prepared for it.

The route uses Chain Lakes Trail before cutting left at a signed junction (1 mile). Ptarmigan Ridge Trail follows the cusp of the ridge as it ascends to Coleman Pinnacle (4.5 miles). Along the way are miles of wildflower meadows and fields of rock. Summer days are blistering hot in the sun, so extra water is a must. A scramble to the top of Coleman Pinnacle rewards with close views of Rainbow Glacier and Mount Baker. Climbers use this route to approach Mount Baker from Camp Kiser.

User Groups: Hikers and leashed dogs. No horses or mountain bikes are allowed. No wheelchair access.

Permits: This trail is accessible August–September. A federal Northwest Forest Pass is required to park here.

Maps: For a map of Mount Baker–Snoqualmie National Forest, contact the Outdoor Recreation Information Center at the downtown Seattle REI. For topographic maps, ask Green Trails for No. 14, Mount Shuksan (No. 13, Mount Baker, is helpful in identifying ridges and peaks on the mountain), or ask the USGS for Shuksan Arm.

Directions: From Bellingham, drive east 58 miles on Highway 542 (Mount Baker Highway) to Artist's Point at the end of the highway. The trailhead is on the northwest side of the parking lot.

Contact: Mount Baker–Snoqualmie National Forest, Glacier Public Service Center, Glacier, WA 98244, 360/599-2714.

🔟 BELL PASS/CATHEDRAL PASS/MAZAMA PARK

17.0 mi/1-2 days

east of Bellingham in Mount Baker Wilderness of Mount Baker-Snoqualmie National Forest

Map 3.1, page 111

On the southwestern slopes of Washington's youngest volcano, Bell Pass Trail offers a more reclusive entry into the wonders of the Mount Baker high country. The trail presents a longer route into a parkland of expansive meadows, crackling glaciers, and wide vistas. That means fewer people travel along it than on the Park Butte and Scott Paul Trails, an enticing consideration.

Bell Pass Trail begins along Elbow Lake Trail, cutting switchbacks through the forest on its way to a junction (3.5 miles); Bell Pass Trail heads to the right. Elk sightings

are an ordinary occurrence here. The trail departs the forest to find itself at Bell Pass (5.5 miles), where views of the Twin Sister Range are great. The trail levels out while it traverses above Ridley Creek. The meadows of Mazama Park (8.5 miles) are exceptional throughout the summer, but especially in July during full bloom. Campsites are located here. The trail continues up through Cathedral Pass to meet Park Butte Trail. A great lookout sits atop Park Butte, well worth the extra effort.

User Groups: Hikers and leashed dogs. No mountain bikes or horses are allowed. No wheelchair access.

Permits: This area is accessible July–October. No permits are required. Parking and access are free.

Maps: For a map of Mount Baker–Snoqualmie National Forest, contact the Outdoor Recreation Information Center at the downtown Seattle REI. For topographic maps, ask Green Trails for No. 45, Hamilton, or ask the USGS for Twin Sisters Mountain and Mount Baker.

Directions: From Sedro-Woolley, drive east 16 miles on Highway 20 to Mile Marker 82. Turn left (north) on Baker Lake Highway (Forest Service Road 11) and drive 12 miles to Forest Service Road 12. Turn left and drive 14 miles to a signed spur road on the left. Turn left on this road and drive 0.25 mile to Elbow Lake Trailhead.

Contact: Mount Baker–Snoqualmie National Forest, Mount Baker Ranger District Office, 810 Hwy. 20, Sedro-Woolley, WA 98284, 360/856-5700.

🔢 PARK BUTTE/ RAILROAD GRADE/ SCOTT PAUL TRAIL

7.0-8.0 mi/4.0 hr 🥾3 ⛰10

east of Bellingham in Mount Baker Wilderness of Mount Baker-Snoqualmie National Forest

Map 3.1, page 111

This is arguably the finest terrain in all of the North Cascades. Three trails lead to high subalpine meadows set at the foot of Mount Baker, where glaciers crumble off the mountain and the sky opens up around you. Spend days roaming the high country here, spotting wildflowers and wildlife. The three trails form a network offering wide exploration, so it's best to have a map when picking your route through this area. Campsites spread throughout the area offer magical overnight stays. This place attracts lots of visitors, so come for the scenery, not the solitude.

Park Butte Trail (7 miles round-trip, up and back) climbs through forest to open meadows and Park Butte lookout. The trail crosses Sulphur and Rocky Creeks (clear in the morning but milky white with glacial flour by afternoon). Marmots whistle from meadows while picas peep from atop boulders. The trail splits in Morovitz Meadow (2 miles); the left fork climbs a ridge to the lookout, with views of the mountain and Twin Sisters.

Scott Paul Trail (8 miles round-trip loop) leaves the Park Butte Trail in Morovitz Meadow to climb up Metcalf Moraine and meet the interesting terminus of Easton Glacier. The moraine exposes barren rock and mud, detailing an infant landscape before mountain meadows encroach. The trail continues east through meadows to climb a high crest with views of Mount Shuksan and the North Cascades before dropping through forest to the trailhead. Railroad Grade (6 miles round-trip, up and back) is a side trail shooting up to the mountain out of Morovitz Meadow. The trail is on a moraine created by the Easton Glacier and brings you close to the living glacier.

User Groups: Hikers, leashed dogs, and horses. No mountain bikes are allowed. No wheelchair access.

Permits: This area is accessible July–October. A federal Northwest Forest Pass is required to park here.

Maps: For a map of Mount Baker–Snoqualmie National Forest, contact the Outdoor Recreation Information Center at the downtown Seattle REI. For topographic maps, ask Green

Trails for No. 45, Hamilton, or ask the USGS for Baker Pass.

Directions: From Sedro-Woolley, drive east 16 miles on Highway 20 to Mile Marker 82. Turn left (north) on Baker Lake Highway (Forest Service Road 11) and drive 12 miles to Forest Service Road 12. Turn left and drive 3.5 miles to Forest Service Road 13. Turn right and drive 5.5 miles to the trailhead at road's end.

Contact: Mount Baker–Snoqualmie National Forest, Mount Baker Ranger District Office, 810 Hwy. 20, Sedro-Woolley, WA 98284, 360/856-5700.

🔢19 BAKER LAKE AND BAKER RIVER

3.6-28.6 mi/2.0 hr-2 days   👥1   ⛰7

east of Sedro-Woolley in Mount Baker–Snoqualmie National Forest

> **Map 3.1, page 111**

For year-round forest wandering, Mount Baker presents hikers with these two trails. Baker Lake Trail meanders 14.3 miles along the eastern shore of the large, dogleg-shaped lake. Baker River Trail continues from the north part of the lake and ventures 8 miles up the river into North Cascades Park. Exceptional old-growth forests line the lengths of both trails, and water is always at hand. These are great trails for both day hikes and more extended adventures.

Short hikes along Baker Lake Trail are best begun from the south end. The trail contours along the eastern shores of the lake through stands of large trees. Anderson Point, a good turnaround, juts into the lake with campsites (1.8 miles); there are also three other campgrounds. The grade is level and easy, perfect for families with small children.

At the north end of the lake is Baker River Trail. Baker River Trail passes through terrific stands of virgin timber and even a beaver pond as it follows the river. In contrast to wildlife, people are relatively scarce here. The maintained trail ends when it crosses Sulphide

Creek, impassable during times of high water. If you ford the river, a social trail continues beside the milky river 5 miles before truly petering out. For the adventurous, solitude and an enjoyable time are highly likely.

User Groups: Baker Lake Trail is open to hikers, leashed dogs, horses, llamas, bicycles, and motorcycles. The Baker River trail is open to hikers and leashed dogs only. No wheelchair access.

Permits: This trail is accessible year-round. A federal Northwest Forest Pass is required to park here. Overnight stays within the national park (Sulphide Camp or beyond) require backcountry camping permits, which are available at Glacier Public Service Center.

Maps: For a map of Mount Baker–Snoqualmie National Forest, contact the Outdoor Recreation Information Center at the downtown Seattle REI. For topographic maps, ask Green Trails for No. 46, Lake Shannon, or ask the USGS for Welker Peak, Bacon Peak, and Mount Shuksan.

Directions: From Sedro-Woolley, drive east 16 miles on Highway 20 to Mile Marker 82. Turn left (north) on Baker Lake Highway (Forest Service Road 11). For Baker Lake Trailhead, drive 14 miles to Baker Dam Road. Turn right and drive across Upper Baker Dam to Forest Service Road 1107. Turn left and drive 1 mile to the trailhead on the left side. For Baker River Trailhead, drive 25.5 miles on Forest Service Road 11 to the trailhead at road's end.

Contact: Mount Baker–Snoqualmie National Forest, Mount Baker Ranger District Office, 810 Hwy. 20, Sedro-Woolley, WA 98284, 360/856-5700.

20 ANDERSON AND WATSON LAKES

2.5 mi/2.0 hr   🏃2 ⛰8

east of Bellingham in Noisy-Diobsud Wilderness of Mount Baker–Snoqualmie National Forest

Map 3.1, page 111

High in the Noisy-Diobsud Wilderness is a trail with several options. Watson Lakes

Trail passes Anderson Butte, a former lookout site full of views, on its way to two sets of picturesque subalpine lakes. Accessible to hikers of all abilities, these lakes present grand views of distant peaks and offer superb fishing for those with dinner in mind. Throw in old-growth forest and subalpine meadows, and this is a day hike or overnight trip that has it all.

Watson Lakes Trail leaves the lofty trailhead (elevation 4,200 feet) and proceeds through virgin timber and meadows to Anderson Butte junction (0.9 mile). A 0.5-mile climb achieves the summit, a great place to see Mount Baker and North Cascade peaks. Include this side trip in a hike to the lakes.

Watson Lakes Trail soon arrives at another junction (1.5 miles). To the right are Anderson Lakes (2 miles), three small subalpine lakes surrounded by meadows and trees. The left fork in the trail leads over a shoulder and down to Watson Lakes (2.5 miles), a larger pair of lakes with more mountain views. Both lakes are ringed by big trees and meadows. Camping at both lakes is in designated sites only. Also, both lake basins are notoriously buggy. Access to both sets of lakes is easy and hikers of all abilities will enjoy visiting them.

User Groups: Hikers and leashed dogs. No horses or mountain bikes are allowed. No wheelchair access.

Permits: This area is accessible mid-June–October. A federal Northwest Forest Pass is required to park here.

Maps: For a map of Mount Baker–Snoqualmie National Forest, contact the Outdoor Recreation Information Center at the downtown Seattle REI. For topographic maps, ask Green Trails for No. 46, Lake Shannon, or ask the USGS for Bacon Peak.

Directions: From Sedro-Woolley, drive east 16 miles on Highway 20 to Mile Marker 82. Turn left (north) on Baker Lake Highway (Forest Service Road 11). Drive 14 miles to Baker Dam Road. Turn right and drive across Upper Baker Dam to Forest Service Road 1107. Turn left and drive 10 miles to Forest Service Road

022. Turn left and drive to the trailhead at road's end.

Contact: Mount Baker–Snoqualmie National Forest, Mount Baker Ranger District Office, 810 Hwy. 20, Sedro-Woolley, WA 98284, 360/856-5700.

21 SAUK MOUNTAIN
4.2 mi/4.0 hr

west of Marblemount in Mount Baker-Snoqualmie National Forest

Map 3.1, page 111

This is a great short day hike that offers outstanding vistas the entire way. Sauk Mountain Trail starts and ends in meadows smothered with alpine flowers. Most would say that it's difficult to find anything better than that. Of course, the terrific nature of the trail attracts loads of folks, but solitude is always difficult to find so close to Highway 20.

The trail is well laid out, with many switchbacks cutting the 1,300 feet of elevation gain to a much easier grade. This is exclusive meadow country, and in midsummer, flower enthusiasts will find themselves in heaven. Expect to find paintbrush, phlox, tiger lilies, aster, columbine, and lupine on display. Sauk Mountain Trail splits (1.5 miles), with the left fork heading to the summit and the right fork leading down to Sauk Lake, which is set between the rocky slopes of Sauk and Bald Mountains. The summit is a former fire lookout site with panoramic views. Gaze from the San Juans to the rugged North Cascades, from Mount Baker and Mount Shuksan all the way south to Mount Rainier. This trail gets a lot of use, so please stick to the path and don't cut switchbacks.

User Groups: Hikers and leashed dogs. No horses or mountain bikes are allowed. No wheelchair access.

Permits: This trail is accessible mid-June–October. A federal Northwest Forest Pass is required to park here.

Maps: For a map of Mount Baker–Snoqualmie

National Forest, contact the Outdoor Recreation Information Center at the downtown Seattle REI. For topographic maps, ask Green Trails for No. 46, Lake Shannon, or ask the USGS for Sauk Mountain.

Directions: From Sedro-Woolley, drive east on Highway 20 for 32 miles. At Mile Marker 96, turn left on Sauk Mountain Road (Forest Service Road 1030). Follow Forest Service Road 1030 for 7 miles to the junction of Forest Service Road 1036. Turn right on Road 1036 and follow to the road's end, where the trailhead is located.

Contact: Mount Baker–Snoqualmie National Forest, Mount Baker Ranger District Office, 810 Hwy. 20, Sedro-Woolley, WA 98284, 360/856-5700.

22 THORNTON LAKES
9.5 mi/5.0 hr

west of Newhalem in North Cascades National Park

Map 3.1, page 111

The three Thornton Lakes are high in an outstretched arm of Mount Triumph along the western side of North Cascades National Park. The trail does not offer much until near the very end, where Mount Triumph and Thornton Lakes come into view along a ridge crest. Here, Mount Triumph towers over the lakes while Eldorado Peak stands to the south. The best views are not at the lake but rather atop Trappers Peak to the north.

Thornton Lakes Trail was never actually built by a trail crew but instead was fashioned over time simply by boots. The first half of the trail follows an old logging road, brushy with alders, before finding the makeshift trail. It climbs steeply through second-growth forest before breaking out into open meadows.

The trail reaches a ridge (4.5 miles) above Lower Thornton Lake, where hikers have three options. For access to the lower lake, the biggest of the three, drop down the ridge along the obvious trail. The upper lakes, often covered with snow and ice well into summer, are reached by traversing the west slopes of the lower lake along small footpaths. And finally, view seekers should follow the ridge crest to the north to scramble Trappers Peak. From up here, the close Pickett Range comes into full view along with much of the surrounding North Cascades. There are not many sites for camping here, so the trip is definitely recommended as a day hike.

User Groups: Hikers only. No dogs, horses, or mountain bikes are allowed. No wheelchair access.

Permits: This trail is accessible July– October. A federal Northwest Forest Pass is required to park here.

Maps: For a map of North Cascades National Park, contact the Outdoor Recreation Information Center at the downtown Seattle REI. For topographic maps, ask Green Trails for No. 47, Marblemount, or ask the USGS for Mount Triumph.

Directions: Drive east on Highway 20 from Marblemount. Look for the Thornton Lakes Trail sign near Mile Marker 117. Turn north on the gravel road and drive 5 miles to the road's end, where the trailhead is located.

Contact: North Cascades National Park, Wilderness Information Center, 7280 Ranger Station Road, Marblemount, WA 98267, 360/854-7245.

23 MONOGRAM LAKE/ LOOKOUT MOUNTAIN
9.4 mi/5.0 hr   🥾5 ⛰10

east of Marblemount in Mount Baker-Snoqualmie National Forest and North Cascades National Park

Map 3.1, page 111

At the western edge of North Cascades National Park are two exceptional destinations accessible from one trail. Monogram Lake sits in a small cirque on a high alpine ridge, framed by meadows and high mountain views. On the other hand, the lookout atop creatively named Lookout Mountain offers scores of extraordinary vistas of North Cascade peaks. The catch is well over 4,000 feet of elevation gain from the trailhead to either point. Don't worry about reaching only one. It will still be a memorable trip, and there's something left for next weekend.

Both routes begin on Lookout Mountain Trail, a treacherously steep series of switchbacks through shady old-growth forest. The trail splits (2.8 miles), with Lookout Mountain to the left and Monogram Lake to the right. Lookout Mountain Trail continues climbing harshly but now through open meadows teeming with blooming wildflowers in July and early August. At the summit (4.7 miles, 5,719 feet) rests a functional lookout at the edge of a mighty drop-off. As expected, the views are spectacular from this height.

Monogram Lake Trail soon enters wildflower meadows and traverses open slopes to the lake (4.9 miles). This is national park territory, a place where dogs are strictly not allowed. A multitude of exploring exists around the lake, perfect for those with an itch for scrambling. Backpackers can stay at Monogram Lake Camp, but don't forget reservations with the Park Service.

User Groups: Monogram Lake Trail is open to hikers. Lookout Mountain Trail is open to hikers and leashed dogs. No horses or mountain bikes are allowed. No wheelchair access.

Permits: This trail is accessible mid-July– October. A federal Northwest Forest Pass is required to park here.

Maps: For a map of Mount Baker–Snoqualmie National Forest and North Cascades National Park, contact the Outdoor Recreation Information Center at the downtown Seattle REI. For topographic maps, ask Green Trails for No. 47, Marblemount, or ask the USGS for Big Devil Peak.

Directions: From Sedro-Woolley, drive east on Highway 20 for 39 miles to the community of Marblemount. On the east end of town, turn right on the Cascade River Road, which immediately crosses the Skagit River. Drive 6.5 miles on Cascade River Road to the signed trailhead on the north side of the road, just inside the national forest boundary.

Contact: North Cascades National Park, Wilderness Information Center, 7280 Ranger Station Rd., Marblemount, WA 98267, 360/854-7245.

24 HIDDEN LAKE PEAKS
9.0 mi/5.0 hr   👣4 ⛰9

east of Marblemount in Mount Baker-Snoqualmie National Forest and North Cascades National Park

> **Map 3.1, page 111**

An aura surrounds trails that are open for short periods each year. Thanks to heavy winter snowfall, some routes are accessible just a few fleeting months each summer. Thus trips to these destinations are rare and special. That's the case with Hidden Lake, often locked away from hikers by snow until late summer. But if you bide your time, you won't be disappointed. Hidden Lake and its accompanying lookout are high in the sky but surrounded by even higher Cascade peaks.

Hidden Lake Peaks Trail is classic North Cascades: lots of elevation gain. As usual, the 3,500 feet of climbing is well worth it. The trail climbs through a forest of Pacific silver fir before giving way to the meadows and views of Sibley Creek Basin. Sunbathing marmots on the granite boulders are as common as lingering patches of snow.

Hidden Lake Peaks Trail climbs to a saddle from which Hidden Lake is finally revealed. Hikers can either drop to the lake or climb to Hidden Lake Lookout for views. If snow lingers along either route, it's best to simply enjoy the great views from the saddle.

User Groups: Hikers and leashed dogs (up to the park boundary at the saddle). Overnight stays within the national park (Hidden Lakes) require backcountry camping permits, which are available at Marblemount National Park

Service Station. No horses or mountain bikes are allowed. No wheelchair access.

Permits: This trail is accessible August–October. A federal Northwest Forest Pass is required to park here.

Maps: For a map of Mount Baker–Snoqualmie National Forest and North Cascades National Park, contact the Outdoor Recreation Information Center at the downtown Seattle REI. For topographic maps, ask Green Trails for No. 48, Diablo Dam, and No. 80, Cascade Pass, or ask the USGS for Eldorado Peak and Sonny Boy Lake.

Directions: From Sedro-Woolley, drive east on Highway 20 for 39 miles to the community of Marblemount. On the east end of town, turn right on Cascade River Road, which immediately crosses the Skagit River. At about 10 miles, turn left onto Sibley Creek Road (Forest Service Road 1540, also signed "Hidden Lake Trail") and drive to the end, about 5 miles.

Contact: North Cascades National Park, Wilderness Information Center, 7280 Ranger Station Rd., Marblemount, WA 98267, 360/854-7245.

25 CASCADE PASS
7.4 mi/3.5 hr   👣2 ⛰10

east of Marblemount in North Cascades National Park

> **Map 3.1, page 111**

From the parking lot at the trailhead, there is little doubt that Cascade Pass Trail is one magnificent hike. With the mighty Johannesburg Mountain to the south, Cascade Pass Trail carries hikers to the Cascade Crest at the foot of several tall, massive peaks. Wildflowers and glacial views are the norm along the entire route, an entrance to the Stehekin Valley and much of North Cascades National Park.

Cascade Pass Trail climbs steadily but gently throughout its length. A grand forest of mountain hemlock and Pacific silver fir offers welcome shade before breaking into

gazing into eastern Washington from Cascade Pass, a great day hike

expansive meadows. At Cascade Pass (3.7 miles), acres of wildflowers compete for attention with the neighboring glacier-capped ridges and peaks. This is a dry trail, so bring plenty of water. Also, this area sees plenty of traffic, so stay on designated trails and make this a day hike only.

Cascade Pass is a fine turnaround, but options for further exploration do exist. Sahale Arm Trail heads north from the pass, gaining big elevation and bigger views. A less difficult path heads in the opposite direction to scale Mix-Up Peak and find a small tarn. Trekkers will be glad to know that Cascade Pass Trail continues east and drops to the Stehekin River. This route to Lake Chelan was used for thousands of years by Native American traders.

User Groups: Hikers only. No dogs, horses, or mountain bikes are allowed. No wheelchair access.

Permits: This trail is accessible July–October. A federal Northwest Forest Pass is required to park here.

Maps: For a map of North Cascades National Park, contact the Outdoor Recreation Information Center at the downtown Seattle REI.

For topographic maps, ask Green Trails for No. 80, Cascade Pass, or ask the USGS for Cascade Pass.

Directions: From the town of Marblemount on Highway 20, drive 23 miles on Cascade River Road to the trailhead at road's end.

Contact: North Cascades National Park, Wilderness Information Center, 7280 Ranger Station Rd., Marblemount, WA 98267, 360/854-7245.

26 PYRAMID LAKE

4.2 mi/2.0 hr

south of Diablo in Ross Lake National Recreation Area

Map 3.1, page 111

Pyramid Lake Trail provides easy access to a deep lake set far below the towering summit of Pyramid Peak. The trail follows the gentle Pyramid Creek through a forest of large and small trees, where a recent burn killed some trees but spared others. The trail is a popular one since it's one of the easier hikes within the park. It's a great destination for folks passing through the park along the highway and looking for a short hike to stretch the legs.

Pyramid Lake Trail gains 1,500 feet in 2 miles. Closely spaced lodgepole pine and Douglas fir compete to revegetate the forest after a slope-clearing fire. Farther on, larger trees begin appearing, particularly some western red cedars. The trail crosses the creek at the 1-mile mark, which may result in some wet feet during times of heavy flow. The trail climbs at a steady rate to the lake, bound by vertical cliffs on two sides. Pyramid Peak stands tall to the southwest, seemingly barren and without a tree to speak of. The lake lies within a National Research Area because of the high levels of biodiversity here. Camping is strictly prohibited, and exploration around the lake should be confined to clearly established trails. Please keep dogs on leashes at all times!

User Groups: Hikers and leashed dogs. No horses or mountain bikes are allowed. No wheelchair access.

Permits: This trail is accessible May–October. A federal Northwest Forest Pass is required to park here.

Maps: For a map of North Cascades National Park, contact the Outdoor Recreation Information Center at the downtown Seattle REI. For topographic maps, ask Green Trails for No. 48, Diablo Dam, or ask the USGS for Diablo Dam and Ross Dam.

Directions: From Newhalem, drive east on Highway 20 to the trailhead on the north side of the road, just beyond Mile Marker 126.

Contact: North Cascades National Park, Wilderness Information Center, 7280 Ranger Station Road, Marblemount, WA 98267, 360/854-7245.

27 SOURDOUGH MOUNTAIN
11.5 mi/6.0 hr   🥾5 ⛰9

north of Diablo in Ross Lake National Recreation Area and North Cascades National Park

Map 3.1, page 111

Sourdough Mountain Trail is all about two very simple things: unrivaled views of the North Cascades and steep pitch. Views extend in every direction—up, down, east and west, and north and south. Countless peaks are within sight, including Colonial and Snowfield Peaks and the celebrated Picket Range, often called simply "the Pickets." This vista comes with a dear cost, however, as the trail is one of the steepest you'll come across. From trailhead to summit is a grueling 5,100-foot ascent in just 5.7 miles. It's a real hoofer, but those who complete it will not soon forget it.

Sourdough Mountain Trail gets to work immediately, climbing 3,000 feet in the first 3 miles. Great forests of Douglas fir and western hemlock provide shade along the exhausting climb. The trail eventually reaches grand subalpine meadows and the sky-high summit. Sourdough Lookout sits atop the 5,985-foot summit. The panoramic views are top-notch and difficult to duplicate within the park. A pair of camps are on either side of the lookout for those wishing to recover tired legs with a night's rest.

User Groups: Hikers only. No dogs, horses, or mountain bikes are allowed. No wheelchair access.

Permits: This trail is accessible July–October. A federal Northwest Forest Pass is required to park here.

Maps: For a map of North Cascades National Park, contact the Outdoor Recreation Information Center at the downtown Seattle REI. For topographic maps, ask Green Trails for No. 48, Diablo Dam, and No. 16, Ross Lake, or ask the USGS for Diablo Dam and Ross Dam.

Directions: From Marblemount, drive east on Highway 20. Turn left at the town of Diablo, near Mile Marker 126. Sourdough Mountain Trailhead is behind the domed swimming pool near the back of the town.

Contact: North Cascades National Park, Wilderness Information Center, 7280 Ranger Station Rd., Marblemount, WA 98267, 360/854-7245.

28 DIABLO LAKE
7.6 mi/4.0 hr

near Diablo in Ross Lake National
Recreation Area

Map 3.1, page 111

By itself, Diablo Lake Trail is an excellent way to pass an afternoon, with views of emerald Diablo Lake and pristine old-growth forests. There are a multitude of activities, however, that can be enjoyed in conjunction with the trail to make the day that much more memorable. For instance, during the summer, hike the trail to Ross Dam and then take a Seattle City Light ferry on the lake back down to the trailhead. Tours of the dams are also available, allowing folks to see why their lights turn on at the flip of a switch. Several campgrounds and picnic sites are also nearby for those using their cars as a base.

Diablo Lake Trail actually never nears the lakeshore, and instead takes a higher route that provides more views. Numerous peaks and ridges of the North Cascades are visible along the trail, especially from the viewpoint halfway down the trail. The trail is a great place to bird-watch, as scores of species make the forests here their home. While there is some elevation gain along the route, few hikers will have any difficulty with it. That makes it great for families (but keep an eye on little ones near the viewpoints). The trail eventually connects to Ross Dam, the end of one lake but the beginning of another.

User Groups: Hikers and leashed dogs. No horses or mountain bikes are allowed. No wheelchair access.

Permits: This trail is accessible when Highway 20 is open. Highway 20 closure depends on seasonal snow, and it is usually closed November–April. A federal Northwest Forest Pass is required to park here.

Maps: For a map of North Cascades National Park, contact the Outdoor Recreation Information Center at the downtown Seattle REI. For topographic maps, ask Green Trails for No. 48, Diablo Dam, or ask the USGS for Diablo Dam and Ross Dam.

Directions: From Marblemount, drive east on Highway 20. Turn left at Diablo Dam. The parking area is before crossing the dam, which is closed to car traffic. The trailhead is a 0.5-mile walk down the old road.

Contact: North Cascades National Park, Wilderness Information Center, 7280 Ranger Station Rd., Marblemount, WA 98267, 360/854-7245.

29 BEAVER LOOP
32.5 mi/4 days

west of Ross Lake in North Cascades
National Park

Map 3.1, page 111

Not so long ago, glaciers a mile thick slid down the Big Beaver and Little Beaver Valleys, carving them into wide U-shaped troughs. If you need proof, the Beaver Loop through the two valleys will surely provide it. This well-known backpacking route gains little elevation but enjoys some of Washington's largest stands of old-growth forest. Beaver Pass offers grand views of enormous valleys framed by even larger peaks.

The route follows Little Beaver Creek before crossing into Big Beaver Creek Valley. It's necessary to arrange a water taxi with Ross Lake Resort to deposit yourself at the mouth of Little Beaver Creek. Little Beaver Trail threads up the valley through 11 miles of remarkable forest. Camps are situated at the boat landing, at Perry Creek at 4.6 miles, and at Stillwell Camp at 11.2 miles.

At Stillwell Camp, Big Beaver Trail cuts off and climbs to the pass. This requires a ford of Little Beaver Creek, difficult if not impossible in early summer when the snows are in full melt, so be prepared. At Big Beaver Pass (13.7 miles and home to Beaver Pass Camp), exploration will yield amazing views into the Luna Valley and its basin, while the Picketts tower over the valley. Big Beaver Trail drops into the wide, U-shaped valley and travels 13.5 miles to Ross Lake through stands of western red cedar more than 1,000 years old. The cedars alone are worth the 26.5 miles. Luna Camp is 2.7 miles from Beaver Pass, 39 Mile Camp is 7 miles from the pass, and Pumpkin Mountain Camp is at Ross Lake. To get back to the car, hike the Ross Lake Trail 6 miles or make arrangements with the water taxi for a pickup at Big Beaver.

User Groups: Hikers and horses (horses not allowed from Little Beaver to Stillwell). No dogs or mountain bikes are allowed. No wheelchair access.

Permits: This trail is accessible July–September. No permits are required. Parking and access are free. Overnight stays within the national park require reservations and backcountry camping permits, which are available at the Wilderness Information Center.

Maps: For a map of North Cascades National Park, contact the Outdoor Recreation Information Center at the downtown Seattle REI. For topographic maps, ask Green Trails for No. 15, Mount Challenger, and No. 16, Ross Lake, or ask the USGS for Pumpkin Mountain, Mount Prophet, Mount Redoubt, Mount Spickard, and Hozomeen Mountain.

Directions: From Marblemount, drive east 20 miles on Highway 20 to signed Diablo Dam. Turn left and cross the dam and turn immediately right for the parking area for Ross Lake Resort. Here, a ferry carries passengers to the Ross Lake Water Taxi for transportation to the trailheads.

Contact: North Cascades National Park, Wilderness Information Center, 7280 Ranger Station Rd., Marblemount, WA 98267, 360/873-4500; Ross Lake Resort Water Taxi, 206/386-4437.

30 THUNDER CREEK

38.8 mi/4 days

south of Diablo Lake in North Cascades National Park

Map 3.1, page 111

This is one of the North Cascades' classic routes, leading deep into the park and out to Lake Chelan. The trail is also great for short day hikes up the creek, as there is plenty to see and do within the first several miles. Immense, icy peaks line the valley ridges while massive cedars and firs fill the forest along the trail. Thunder Creek is deservedly considered one of the park's classic hikes.

Thunder Creek Trail sets off within a large forest of western red cedar and Douglas fir. Hikers looking for a short day hike will enjoy Thunder Creek Nature Loop (0.5 mile up Thunder Creek Trail), a 1-mile loop that ventures off into old-growth forest. Thunder Creek Trail stays relatively flat for 7.5 miles to McAllister Camp, a good turnaround for long day hikes. Here, a bridge spans the creek as it rushes through a small canyon of granite, a wonderful place for lunch.

Farther along Thunder Creek Trail, the wilderness grows deeper, with views of rugged, glacial peaks to the west. Enormous glaciers cover these mountains and provide the creek with much of its rock flour. The trail continues through the forested valley to Park Creek Pass, a one-way total of 19.4 miles. Stehekin lies 8 miles beyond. Numerous campsites are situated throughout the valley. Thunder Creek makes a wonderful segment of a long trek through the North Cascades.

User Groups: Hikers, leashed dogs (dogs allowed on the first 6.5 miles but not within the national park), and horses. No mountain bikes are allowed. No wheelchair access.

Permits: This trail is accessible April–November. No permits are required. Parking and access are free. Overnight stays within the national park require backcountry camping permits, which are available at the Wilderness Information Center.

Maps: For a map of North Cascades National Park, contact the Outdoor Recreation Information Center at the downtown Seattle REI. For topographic maps, ask Green Trails for No. 48, Diablo Dam, No. 49, Mount Logan, and No. 81, McGregor Mountain, or ask the USGS for Ross Dam, Forbidden Peak, and Mount Logan.

Directions: From Newhalem, drive east on Highway 20 to Mile Marker 130 and Colonial Creek Campground. Turn right and park in the lot above the boat ramp. The signed trailhead is located at the end of the parking lot.

Contact: North Cascades National Park, Wilderness Information Center, 7280 Ranger Station Road, Marblemount, WA 98267, 360/873-4500.

DESOLATION PEAK
13.6 mi/8.0 hr

east of Ross Lake in North Cascades National Park

Map 3.1, page 111

Jack Kerouac made Desolation Peak world-famous when he included the mountain in his book *Desolation Angels*. The book is based on his time with the Forest Service, when he was stationed at the still-functional lookout atop the lofty peak. Kerouac has helped to keep the peak a well-visited locale despite its truly desolate location.

Ross Lake Resort offers boat transportation to Desolation Landing near Lightning Creek. After disembarking from the boat, hike Desolation Peak Trail north along Ross Lake for 2 miles before making a very steep ascent to Desolation Peak. Although there is some shade along the way, much of the hillside was burned in a fire 75 years ago and gets a lot of sun. The views improve as the elevation increases, creating the opportunity for regular breaks. Bringing extra water is a must, as snow is the only source this high. From the open slopes of Desolation Peak, numerous peaks and ridges are visible. Ross Lake appears particularly agreeable after such a long hike. Overnight hikers will enjoy Desolation Camp, just below the tree line.

User Groups: Hikers only. No dogs, horses, or mountain bikes are allowed. No wheelchair access.

Permits: This trail is accessible mid-June–September. A federal Northwest Forest Pass is required to park here. Overnight stays within the national park require reservations and backcountry camping permits, which are available at the Wilderness Information Center.

Maps: For a map of North Cascades National Park, contact the Outdoor Recreation Information Center at the downtown Seattle REI. For topographic maps, ask Green Trails for No. 16, Ross Lake, or ask the USGS for Hozomeen Mountain.

Directions: From Marblemount, drive east 20 miles on Highway 20 to signed Diablo Dam. Turn left and cross the dam and turn immediately right for the parking area for Ross Lake Resort. Here, a ferry carries passengers to the Ross Lake Water Taxi for transportation to the trailheads.

Contact: North Cascades National Park, Wilderness Information Center, 7280 Ranger Station Rd., Marblemount, WA 98267, 360/873-4500; Ross Lake Resort Water Taxi, 206/386-4437.

32 MOUNT HIGGINS
9.0 mi/5.0 hr

west of Darrington in Mount Baker-Snoqualmie National Forest

Map 3.1, page 111

Mount Higgins is best known by Mountain Loop Highway drivers as the first big mountain they pass under. Highly visible from the road is the long band of rock capping the ridge and leading into the tilted slats of Mount Higgins. The hike up is every bit as rewarding and as strenuous as it would seem from the car.

Mount Higgins Trail endures 3,300 feet of harsh elevation gain on the way. That's a lot of climbing, and only boggy and buggy Myrtle Lake offers a little respite along the way. Weary hikers who turn back early will still have a good time, but they miss the climax that makes all the hard work worth it. After passing a clear-cut, the trail enters virgin national forest. The grade eventually levels out, and the Myrtle Lake Trail soon breaks to the left, at 3.3 miles. Myrtle Lake is a short 0.5 mile away. Mount Higgins Trail continues climbing to an abandoned lookout post, just below the summits of Mount Higgins. These peaks are best left to true rock climbers. The view from the old lookout encompasses miles of mountains, including the Olympics across Puget Sound.

User Groups: Hikers and leashed dogs. No horses or mountain bikes are allowed. No wheelchair access.

Permits: This trail is accessible July–October. No permits are required. Parking and access are free.

Maps: For a map of Mount Baker–Snoqualmie National Forest, contact the Outdoor Recreation Information Center at the downtown Seattle REI. For topographic maps, ask Green Trails for No. 77, Oso, or ask the USGS for Oso.

Directions: From Arlington, drive east 16 miles on the Mountain Loop Highway (Highway 530) to C-Post Road (just before Mile Marker 38). Turn right (north) onto C-Post Road. Continue on the road for 2.8 miles after crossing over the North Fork Stillaguamish River. The road dead-ends at the signed trailhead, and the trail is on the right side (east) of the road. Some parking is available along the road. Note that C-Post Road is often deeply rutted and a high-clearance vehicle is recommended.

Contact: Mount Baker–Snoqualmie National Forest, Darrington Ranger Station, 1405 Emmens Ave. N., Darrington, WA 98241, 360/436-1155.

33 BOULDER RIVER

8.6 mi/4.5 hr

within the Boulder River Wilderness southwest of the town of Darrington

Map 3.1, page 111   BEST (

When the snow still lingers in the alpine regions during the springtime, Boulder River

© SCOTT LEONARD

Boulder River Trail, a good year-round hike

Trail offers an excellent chance to stretch the legs and get ready for summer. The trail wanders 4 miles into the river valley to a picturesque setting of camps. Along the way are several outstanding waterfalls dropping into the river, which makes much of its way through narrow gorges. With little elevation gain, the trail is a favorite for hikers of all ages and abilities.

Boulder River Trail follows an old logging road to the wilderness boundary, where great old-growth forest begins (1 mile). The first of Boulder's two high waterfalls soon comes into view. While this is a nice turnaround spot for the less serious, it's advisable to trek the next 3 miles.

Boulder River Trail continues through exceptional old-growth forests, often high above the noisy river. Early-season hikers will encounter numerous trilliums and other understory flowers in full bloom. The trail empties out onto the river's banks (4.3 miles), where Three Fingers Peak can be seen up the valley. Expect to linger here a while. Boulder River is a great overnight trip as well, with several campsites clustered around the end of the trail.

User Groups: Hikers and leashed dogs. No horses or mountain bikes are allowed. No wheelchair access.

Permits: This trail is accessible year-round. No permits are required. Parking and access are free.

Maps: For a map of Mount Baker–Snoqualmie National Forest, contact the Outdoor Recreation Information Center at the downtown Seattle REI. For topographic maps, ask Green Trails for No. 77, Oso, and No. 109, Granite Falls, or ask the USGS for Granite Falls.

Directions: From Arlington, drive east on Mountain Loop Highway (Highway 530) to French Creek Road. Turn right and drive 4 miles to the trailhead at road's end.

Contact: Mount Baker–Snoqualmie National Forest, Darrington Ranger Station, 1405 Emmens Ave. N., Darrington, WA 98241, 360/436-1155.

🖽 MOUNT PUGH (STUJACK PASS)
7.0 mi/5.0 hr

in Mount Baker-Snoqualmie National Forest

Map 3.1, page 111

In true North Cascades form, Mount Pugh Trail makes a challenging climb (nearly 4,000 feet) to expansive views that encompass a multitude of peaks. Stujack Pass is a small saddle on the ridge below mighty Pugh Mountain. The terrain is inspiring, where patches of small, weather-beaten trees grow in gardens of rock and heather. If this isn't enough, there is a footpath that leads to the summit of Mount Pugh. The question won't be if you want to summit Mount Pugh. The question will be if you have the energy to summit.

Mount Pugh Trail is in good shape to the pass, but beyond it is not much more than a rocky path. The trail moves through old-growth forest and encounters small Lake Meten (1.5 miles). Get used to switchbacks, for they are the story of the day. The forest eventually breaks and the route provides loads of views as it scales the rocky slope. Stujack Pass is a welcome sight. It's a great reward when you hit the pass and so much is finally revealed to the east. Hearty hikers can climb another 1,500 feet (in just 1.5 miles) to the summit via a tricky footpath along the ridge. From the summit, views from Rainier to Baker embrace too much of the Cascades to absorb in just one afternoon.

User Groups: Hikers and leashed dogs. No horses or mountain bikes are allowed. No wheelchair access.

Permits: This trail is accessible August–October. A federal Northwest Forest Pass is required to park here.

Maps: For a map of Mount Baker–Snoqualmie National Forest, contact the Outdoor Recreation Information Center at the downtown Seattle REI. For topographic maps, ask Green Trails for No. 111, Sloan Peak, or ask the USGS for Pugh Mountain and White Chuck Mountain.

Directions: From Darrington, drive east 12.5 miles on Mountain Loop Highway to Forest Service Road 2095. Turn left and drive 1.5 miles to the trailhead on the right.

Contact: Mount Baker–Snoqualmie National Forest, Darrington Ranger Station, 1405 Emmens Ave. N., Darrington, WA 98241, 360/436-1155.

🖾 MEADOW MOUNTAIN
21.0 mi/2-3 days   🏃3 ⛰9

in Glacier Peak Wilderness of Mount Baker-Snoqualmie National Forest

Map 3.1, page 111

A long approach to Meadow Mountain has made it much wilder than many of its counterparts. Closure of the access road added 5.5 miles to the hike, weeding out the day-hiker crowd. That's good news for those seeking an easy but satisfying weekend trip to sublime meadows and mountain views. Huckleberries, wildflowers, and marmots are all over, indulging hikers in paradise. The trail gets only better the farther one travels, tracing an open ridge to Fire Mountain.

The first 5.5 miles are along Forest Service Road 2710, whose closure is a mixed blessing. It's never much fun to hike a road, but say goodbye to the crowds. Meadow Mountain Trail climbs steeply and quickly to a pass, where the trail forks (7.5 miles). The left route drops slightly to Meadow Lake (8.2 miles), encircled by rocky cliffs and meadows. The main trail follows the ridge east, passing through subalpine parkland. Big Glacier Peak stands almost alarmingly close. Emerald and Diamond Lakes (10.5 miles) lie to the north of the trail, requiring some easy cross-country travel. Few spots are as peaceful Meadow Mountain. Campsites are scattered along the route but the best, most established sites are found at each of the lakes.

User Groups: Hikers, leashed dogs, and horses. No mountain bikes are allowed. No wheelchair access.

Permits: This trail is accessible July–October. A federal Northwest Forest Pass is required to park here.

Maps: For a map of Mount Baker–Snoqualmie National Forest, contact the Outdoor Recreation Information Center at the downtown Seattle REI. For topographic maps, ask Green Trails for No. 111, Sloan Peak, and No. 112, Glacier Peak, or ask the USGS for Pugh Mountain and Glacier Peak.

Directions: From Darrington, drive east 9 miles on Mountain Loop Highway to White Chuck Road (Forest Service Road 23). Turn left (east) and drive 6 miles to Forest Service Road 27 (signed "Meadow Mountain Trail"). Turn left (north) and drive 2.4 miles to Forest Service Road 2710, which is gated, and the new trailhead.

Contact: Mount Baker–Snoqualmie National Forest, Darrington Ranger Station, 1405 Emmens Ave. N., Darrington, WA 98241, 360/436-1155.

36 GOAT FLATS
10.0 mi/5.0 hr   🏃3 ⛰10

in the Boulder River Wilderness, within Mount Baker-Snoqualmie National Forest

Map 3.1, page 111

It's hard to believe that such great hiking is so close to the Seattle area. Proximity to the city brings out the crowds, but the high-country beauty of Goat Flats deserves to be experienced by all. Three Fingers Trail travels 5 miles to the paradise of Goat Flats. Ancient forests surrender to views of old, craggy mountains. This is undoubtedly the best stretch of trail in Boulder River Wilderness.

Three Fingers Trail climbs through old-growth forest before encountering Saddle Lake (2.5 miles), modest in size but inviting nonetheless. Overnight guests need to make camp at least 200 feet from the lake. Three Fingers Trail continues its ascent through alpine meadows and increasingly rewarding views. Goat Flats sit in a particularly wide saddle along the ridge (5.5 miles), offering a grand perspective on the Cascades. Enjoy the meadows overflowing with flowers in mid-summer and huckleberries in the late summer. The trail continues 1 mile to Tin Can Gap and another mile to an old lookout atop Three Fingers. Tin Can Gap is too strenuous of an effort to be worthwhile and the lookout is usually reserved for climbers. Bring your lunch, stick to Goat Flats, and you'll be talking about it for months.

User Groups: Hikers and leashed dogs. No horses or mountain bikes are allowed. No wheelchair access.

Permits: This trail is accessible July–October. No permits are required. Parking and access are free.

Maps: For a map of Mount Baker–Snoqualmie National Forest, contact the Outdoor Recreation Information Center at the downtown Seattle REI. For topographic maps, ask Green Trails for No. 109, Granite Falls, and No. 110, Silverton, or ask the USGS for Granite Falls and Silverton.

Directions: From Granite Falls, drive 7 miles east to Tupso Pass Road (Forest Service Road 41). Turn right and drive this long, gravel road to its end, 18 miles later. Watch for road markers, as many small roads branch off the main road, Forest Service Road 41.

Contact: Mount Baker–Snoqualmie National Forest, Verlot Public Service Center, 33515 Mountain Loop Hwy., Granite Falls, WA 98252, 360/691-7791.

37 MOUNT PILCHUCK
6.0 mi/3.5 hr

east of Verlot in Mount Baker-Snoqualmie National Forest and Mount Pilchuck State Park

Map 3.1, page 111 **BEST (**

An outstanding hike, the greatest attraction along Mount Pilchuck Trail is undoubtedly the restored fire lookout at the summit. The lookout, which was built in 1920, was restored by the Everett Chapter of the Mountaineers to a condition that parallels the outstanding views it offers of the entire Puget Sound Basin. The views extend to reveal Seattle's buildings as distant specks, up to Mount Baker and over many North Cascade peaks to Glacier Peak. The lookout contains a full history of the site as well as a great map of visible peaks. It's all offered at the culmination of a hike through a beautiful old-growth forest and parkland meadows among the granite slabs of the mountain.

Mount Pilchuck Trail begins within a forest teeming with giant mountain hemlocks. The trail climbs steadily the entire way but never at an excruciating grade. The trail turns north and works its way around Little Pilchuck to enter the north basin. Hemlocks and Alaskan yellow cedar find ground amid enormous slabs of granite. Snow lingers late into summer along this north-facing basin, although it rarely poses a problem. The ascent to the summit is the steepest part of the trail but well worth it. On a sunny day, there is no grander view of the Puget Sound Basin. Check the

weather, as Pilchuck has a reputation for nasty fast-arriving fog, a definite view-spoiler.

User Groups: Hikers and leashed dogs. No horses or mountain bikes are allowed. No wheelchair access.

Permits: This trail is accessible June–November. A federal Northwest Forest Pass is required to park here.

Maps: For a map of Mount Baker–Snoqualmie National Forest, contact the Outdoor Recreation Information Center at the downtown Seattle REI. For topographic maps, ask Green Trails for No. 109, Granite Falls, or ask the USGS for Granite Falls.

Directions: From Granite Falls, drive east 12 miles on Mountain Loop Highway (Highway 530) to Pilchuck Road (Forest Service Road 42). Turn right and drive 7 miles to the trailhead at road's end.

Contact: Mount Baker–Snoqualmie National Forest, Verlot Public Service Center, 33515 Mountain Loop Hwy., Granite Falls, WA 98252, 360/691-7791.

38 HEATHER LAKE
3.8 mi/3.0 hr

east of Granite Falls in Mount Baker-Snoqualmie National Forest

Map 3.1, page 111

Below the north face of Mount Pilchuck, Heather Lake is one of the Mountain Loop Highway's most beautiful day hikes. A stretch among giant timber leads to Heather Lake, inviting hikers to stick around for a while with a loop around the lake. In the latter part of summer, tasty huckleberries stain your hands while lofty peaks strain your neck. For proximity to the Seattle area and overall grandeur, there are few better destinations.

Heather Lake Trail climbs steadily but at an easy grade. While the path may be overcome by roots or rocks at times, it is wide enough to easily accommodate the crowds that hike it. The first mile winds through long-ago-logged land, where enormous cedar stumps remain as a testament to the old forests. Notice several 80-foot western hemlocks growing atop cedar stumps, with roots snaking to the ground. Soon, the trail enters virgin forest set upon steep slopes, and one can begin to see the challenges the old lumberjacks faced. The trail drops into Heather Lake Basin, with views of Mount Pilchuck's steep walls and a trail with numerous structures to take you around the lake. Time your hike right (in August) and feast on berries.

User Groups: Hikers and leashed dogs. No horses or mountain bikes are allowed. No wheelchair access.

Permits: This trail is accessible mid-May–November. A federal Northwest Forest Pass is required to park here.

Maps: For a map of Mount Baker–Snoqualmie National Forest, contact the Outdoor Recreation Information Center at the downtown Seattle REI. For topographic maps, ask Green Trails for No. 109, Granite Falls, or ask the USGS for Verlot.

Directions: From Granite Falls, drive east 12 miles on the Mountain Loop Highway (Highway 530) to Pilchuck Road (Forest Service Road 42). Turn right and drive 1.5 miles to the signed trailhead.

Contact: Mount Baker–Snoqualmie National Forest, Verlot Public Service Center, 33515 Mountain Loop Hwy., Granite Falls, WA 98252, 360/691-7791.

39 LAKE 22

5.4 mi/4.0 hr   🥾3 ⛰9

east of Granite Falls in Mount Baker–Snoqualmie National Forest

Map 3.1, page 111   BEST (

The designation of Lake 22 Research Natural Area preserved the landscape around this trail, making it the jewel of the southern Mountain Loop Highway. Climbing entirely through old-growth forest, the journey is as beautiful as the destination, which is a tall order in Lake 22's case. Along the trail, cascading waterfalls work to

draw your attention from enormous Douglas firs and western red cedars. At the lake, steep walls leading to a rugged ridge of granite compete for attention with bushes of huckleberries.

Lake 22 Trail climbs steadily along 22 Creek, rumbling with several large cascades. The tread is well maintained, and the number of log structures is impressive. Just in time, the grade flattens and Lake 22 stands before you, guarded by the towering north face of Mount Pilchuck. The lake is stocked, so a fishing pole is put to good use here. This is a great day hike from Seattle and is very popular. But no size of crowd should keep hikers from experiencing Lake 22.

User Groups: Hikers only. No dogs, horses, or mountain bikes are allowed. No wheelchair access.

Permits: This trail is accessible mid-May–November. A federal Northwest Forest Pass is required to park here.

Maps: For a map of Mount Baker–Snoqualmie National Forest, contact the Outdoor Recreation Information Center at the downtown Seattle REI. For topographic maps, ask Green Trails for No. 109, Granite Falls, or ask the USGS for Verlot.

Directions: From Granite Falls, drive east 13 miles on the Mountain Loop Highway (Highway 530) to the signed trailhead on the right.

Contact: Mount Baker–Snoqualmie National Forest, Verlot Public Service Center, 33515 Mountain Loop Hwy., Granite Falls, WA 98252, 360/691-7791.

40 ASHLAND LAKES/ BALD MOUNTAIN

4.0-9.8 mi/2.0-10.0 hr   🥾2 ⛰8

south of Verlot on Washington Department of Natural Resources land

Map 3.1, page 111

This is one of the Seattle area's lesser-known hikes. On Washington Department of Natural Resources (DNR) land, which is usually less than scenic, the Ashland Lakes and Bald

Mountain area actually retains its old-growth forests and meadows. Perhaps the nickname Department of Nothing Left is not entirely appropriate after all. A small network of trails visits several sets of lakes and rides the crest of a long ridge. Much of it is easily accessible to hikers of all ages. For just an hour out of Seattle, it doesn't get much better than this.

Hikers can access Bald Mountain from the west or east end. Bald Mountain Trail runs along the crest of Bald Mountain, more like a ridge than a mountain. On the eastern side are Cutthroat Lakes (9.8 miles), a large grouping of tarns and small lakes set in subalpine meadows. On the western end of the trail are Ashland Lakes (4 miles). These two lakes, along with Beaver Plant Lake, are immersed in grand old-growth forest. DNR constructed nice, large campsites at each of the lakes. A little farther down the trail from these lakes are Twin Falls, where Wilson Creek makes an enormous cascade off a cliff into a small lake.

User Groups: Hikers and leashed dogs. No horses or mountain bikes are allowed. No wheelchair access.

Permits: This trail is accessible May–November. A federal Northwest Forest Pass is required to park here.

Maps: For a map of this area, contact the Outdoor Recreation Information Center at the downtown Seattle REI. For topographic maps, ask Green Trails for No. 110, Silverton, and No. 142, Index, or ask the USGS for Silverton and Index.

Directions: For Ashland Lakes, drive 4.7 miles east of Verlot to Forest Serice Road 4020. Turn right (south) and drive 2.3 miles to Forest Service Road 4021. Turn right and drive 1.5 miles to Forest Service Road 4021-016. Turn left onto Forest Service Road 4021-016 and drive to the Ashland trailhead at road's end.

For Cutthroat Lakes, drive east 6 miles from Verlot to Forest Service Road 4030. Turn right (south) and drive 1 mile to Forest Service Road 4032. Turn right and drive 8 miles to the trailhead at road's end.

Contact: Mount Baker–Snoqualmie National Forest, Verlot Public Service Center, 33515 Mountain Loop Hwy., Granite Falls, WA 98252, 360/691-7791.

41 MOUNT FORGOTTEN MEADOWS

8.0 mi/5.0 hr

east of Granite Falls in Mount Baker–Snoqualmie National Forest

Map 3.1, page 111

When Perry Creek Trail breaks out of the forest onto the open ridge and Mount Forgotten stares down on you, the previous 4 miles of steep ascent become worth every step. Great mountain views are finally at hand. But the best is yet to come. Continuing to the meadows of Mount Forgotten delivers expansive and panoramic views of numerous North Cascades peaks.

At first, Perry Creek Trail climbs slowly through several open avalanche fields. As the trail enters the forest, Perry Creek Falls greets hikers as it rushes through a small gorge. From here, the trail gets mean. The route switchbacks up through old-growth forest of Alaskan yellow cedars and Pacific silver firs, whose shade and understory of huckleberries compensate for the climb.

Soon, the trail breaks out onto the ridge, with Mount Baker visible from afar and Mount Forgotten finally apparent. Just before the ridge, follow a small footpath to the right. Mount Forgotten Meadows await a few hundred yards away, with spectacular views of Glacier Peak and other surrounding mountains. There are few better picnic spots in the Mountain Loop Highway area.

User Groups: Hikers and leashed dogs. No horses or mountain bikes are allowed. No wheelchair access.

Permits: This trail is accessible June–October. A federal Northwest Forest Pass is required to park here.

Maps: For a map of Mount Baker–Snoqualmie

looking out to Glacier Peak from Mount Forgotten Meadows

© SCOTT LEONARD

National Forest, contact the Outdoor Recreation Information Center at the downtown Seattle REI. For topographic maps, ask Green Trails for No. 111, Sloan Peak, or ask the USGS for Bedal.

Directions: From Granite Falls, drive east 26 miles on Mountain Loop Highway (Highway 530) to Perry Creek Road (Forest Service Road 4063). Turn left and drive 1.5 miles (stay left at the fork) to the trailhead at road's end.

Contact: Mount Baker–Snoqualmie National Forest, Verlot Public Service Center, 33515 Mountain Loop Hwy., Granite Falls, WA 98252, 360/691-7791.

42 MOUNT DICKERMAN
8.6 mi/5.0 hr   ⛰4 ⛰9

east of Granite Falls in Mount Baker–Snoqualmie National Forest

Map 3.1, page 111

Mount Dickerman persists as a Mountain Loop Highway favorite in spite of its punishing nature. After all, prolific berry bushes and expansive mountain views have the tendency

to cancel out killer ascents. During the burly hike up countless switchbacks, keep your mind focused on the August berries that will surely revive your step. And during the final rise, keep your attention on the gradually expanding views—the climb culminates in an absolute feast of vistas at the summit.

Mount Dickerman Trail starts off as serious as a heart attack, making a full-on assault on the hillside. The valley floor disappears while you zigzag up through a cool forest with a few creeks for splashdowns. The trail levels off a bit to enter open meadows chock-full of huckleberry bushes. The trail keeps on climbing to make the final ascent to the summit. Glacier Peak is an imposing neighbor while all of the Monte Cristo peaks make their own appearances. It can be a busy trail in the summer, but as always with North Cascade summits, it's well worth it.

User Groups: Hikers and leashed dogs. No horses or mountain bikes are allowed. No wheelchair access.

Permits: This trail is accessible July–October. A federal Northwest Forest Pass is required to park here.

Maps: For a map of Mount Baker–Snoqualmie National Forest, contact the Outdoor Recreation Information Center at the downtown Seattle REI. For topographic maps, ask Green Trails for No. 111, Sloan Peak, or ask the USGS for Bedal.

Directions: From Granite Falls, drive east on the Mountain Loop Highway (Highway 530) for 27.5 miles. The signed trailhead is on the left (north) side of the highway.

Contact: Mount Baker–Snoqualmie National Forest, Verlot Public Service Center, 33515 Mountain Loop Hwy., Granite Falls, WA 98252, 360/691-7791.

43 GOTHIC BASIN
9.0 mi/5.0 hr

east of Granite Falls in Henry M. Jackson Wilderness of Mount Baker-Snoqualmie National Forest

Map 3.1, page 111

While little remains of the once-bustling mining town of Monte Cristo, the miners' trails live on. The trail up to Gothic Basin, one of many mines in the area, reveals the job's greatest perk: unbelievable views of mountains and valleys. Indeed, Gothic Basin Trail is a testament to the hardiness of the old miners. In a successful effort to get to the worksite quickly, it makes a very steep ascent to the basin, a barren moonscape save for large Foggy Lake.

Hike or bike Monte Cristo Road 1.1 miles to Gothic Basin Trail, just before the road crosses the Sauk River. It's a quick and dirty climb to the basin using steep switchbacks, but several impressive waterfalls alleviate the tough ascent. Snow lingers late within several creek gorges, making the route strongly discouraged when significant snowpack remains on the hillside. The trail eventually reaches the Gothic Basin (4.6 miles), an expansive bowl of heather meadows. Del Campo and Gothic Peaks tower above Foggy Lake on either side. For the rockhounds out there, this is a great place to explore. Numerous types of rocks are found up here, including conglomerates, granite, limestone, and sandstone. It's amazing to think that this place used to be, for miners, just another day at the office.

User Groups: Hikers, leashed dogs, and mountain bikes (mountain bikes only on Monte Cristo Road). No horses are allowed. No wheelchair access.

Permits: This trail is accessible late July–October. A federal Northwest Forest Pass is required to park here.

Maps: For a map of Mount Baker–Snoqualmie National Forest, contact the Outdoor Recreation Information Center at the downtown Seattle REI. For topographic maps, ask Green Trails for No. 111, Sloan Peak, and No. 143, Monte Cristo, or ask the USGS for Monte Cristo.

Directions: From Granite Falls, drive east 31 miles on the Mountain Loop Highway (Highway 530) to the trailhead at Barlow Pass, where the highway permanently turns to gravel.

Contact: Mount Baker–Snoqualmie National Forest, Verlot Public Service Center, 33515 Mountain Loop Hwy., Granite Falls, WA 98252, 360/691-7791.

44 POODLE DOG PASS/ TWIN LAKES
17.4 mi/1-2 days

east of Granite Falls in Henry M. Jackson Wilderness of Mount Baker-Snoqualmie National Forest

Map 3.1, page 111

Poodle Dog Pass is one of the Mountain Loop Highway's premier hikes, set about as deep as one can get within the Cascades. This is high country, where meadows of heather cover the hillsides and mountain peaks dominate the skyline. The closure of Monte Cristo Road has made this a much longer trek, subsequently helping the path ditch most of its crowds. Rugged peaks and mountains are the theme to this hike, some of the best of the Monte Cristo region.

Accessing Poodle Dog Pass requires an easy 4-mile hike or bike down Monte Cristo Road. While the road is closed to vehicles, it's not closed to mountain bikes, a popular way of cutting 8 miles off the round-trip. From Monte Cristo, Poodle Dog Pass Trail steadily climbs out of the forest and into meadows, climbing over 1,600 feet in just 1.7 miles. From Poodle Dog Pass (1.7 miles), a side trail leads to the large Silver Lake, set beneath the cliffs of Silvertip Peak. Beyond the pass, Twin Lakes Trail continues through superb terrain of meadows and rock fields, shooting right between Twin Peaks before dropping to Twin Lakes. The long ridge of Columbia Peak stands more than 2,400 feet above the lakes, creating a large, ringed basin. Established campsites are found at each of the three lakes, and camping should be restricted to these sites only.

User Groups: Hikers, leashed dogs, and mountain bikes (mountain bikes only on Monte Cristo Road). No horses are allowed. No wheelchair access.

Permits: This trail is accessible July–October. A federal Northwest Forest Pass is required to park here.

Maps: For a map of Mount Baker–Snoqualmie National Forest, contact the Outdoor Recreation Information Center at the downtown Seattle REI. For topographic maps, ask Green Trails for No. 111, Sloan Peak, and No. 143, Monte Cristo, or ask the USGS for Monte Cristo.

Directions: From Granite Falls, drive east 31 miles on the Mountain Loop Highway (Highway 530) to the trailhead at Barlow Pass, where the highway permanently turns to gravel.

Contact: Mount Baker–Snoqualmie National Forest, Verlot Public Service Center, 33515 Mountain Loop Hwy., Granite Falls, WA 98252, 360/691-7791.

45 GLACIER BASIN

12.2 mi/8.0 hr

east of Granite Falls in Henry M. Jackson Wilderness of Mount Baker–Snoqualmie National Forest

Map 3.1, page 111

Glacier Basin has the ability to make a person feel about as big as an ant. With massive mountains towering several thousand feet above the basin on every side, any understanding of "perspective" slips off into the thin mountain air. The imposing cliffs and peaks of Cadet and Monte Cristo seem to redefine scale. Glacier Basin is the perfect locale to reset the human ego.

Glacier Basin Trail departs from the old town of Monte Cristo, an easy 4-mile walk down the closed-to-vehicles Monte Cristo Road. A popular means for arriving here is via mountain bike, riding along the road and then hiking the trail. The trail sets off at a decent pace before sharply quickening in its ascent. Rising up the valley, the trail passes a dramatic waterfall on Glacier Creek before taking a turn up over Mystery Hill (6 miles), the place for overnight camps.

By now the forest has faded away and meadows fill in between talus slopes. Picas and marmots are heard frequently, just before they scuttle off beneath the rocks. The trail gradually levels out and enters the basin, which is filled with meadows and interlocked braids of creeks. This is beautiful alpine territory, not so long ago buried beneath massive glaciers.

User Groups: Hikers, leashed dogs, and mountain bikes (mountain bikes only on Monte Cristo Road). No horses are allowed. No wheelchair access.

Permits: This trail is accessible July–October. A federal Northwest Forest Pass is required to park here.

Maps: For a map of Mount Baker–Snoqualmie National Forest, contact the Outdoor Recreation Information Center at the downtown Seattle REI. For topographic maps, ask Green Trails for No. 111, Sloan Peak, and No. 143,

Monte Cristo, or ask the USGS for Monte Cristo and Blanca Lake.

Directions: From Granite Falls, drive east 31 miles on the Mountain Loop Highway (Highway 530) to the trailhead at Barlow Pass, where the highway permanently turns to gravel.

Contact: Mount Baker–Snoqualmie National Forest, Verlot Public Service Center, 33515 Mountain Loop Hwy., Granite Falls, WA 98252, 360/691-7791.

46 FOURTH OF JULY PASS
12.2 mi/5.0 hr

east of Newhalem in Ross Lake National Recreation Area and North Cascades National Park

Map 3.2, page 112

This is one of the few passes in the North Cascades that does not inspire a cold sweat in hikers. Unlike many of its kin, this is not a steep, near-vertical trail leading to the pass. On the contrary, the route along Panther Creek is extremely beautiful and easy to hike. Numerous cascades and waterfalls are the result of the creek's course over ever-present boulders. The total elevation gain of 1,800 feet is spread out over 6 miles, so Fourth of July Pass can be achieved by the whole family. Wide views of glacially capped mountains await at the top. And for those with the means for transportation, the trail continues to Thunder Creek for a great through-hike.

The best route up to the pass is definitely via Panther Creek. Panther Creek Trail stays near the gushing creek as it passes through a luxuriant forest of large western red cedars. At 3.1 miles is Panther Camp, with several sites. The trail begins to climb up the hillside when the creek makes a hard turn to the southeast to venture deep into the wilderness. Glaciers carved the pass long ago to avoid Ruby Mountain, leaving it wide and flat. Panther Potholes offer a cool respite on hot days. The best views are from Fourth of July Camp. From here are expansive views of the Neve Glacier sliding

down off Snowfield Peak and Colonial Peak. The trail continues 2.5 miles to Thunder Creek Trail (2.1 miles from the trailhead).

User Groups: Hikers and mountain bikes only. No dogs or horses are allowed. No wheelchair access.

Permits: This trail is accessible July–October. A federal Northwest Forest Pass is required to park here.

Maps: For a map of North Cascades National Park, contact the Outdoor Recreation Information Center at the downtown Seattle REI. For topographic maps, ask Green Trails for No. 48, Diablo Dam, and No. 49, Mount Logan, or ask the USGS for Crater Mountain and Ross Dam.

Directions: From Marblemount, drive east on Highway 20 to East Bank Trailhead, 8 miles beyond Colonial Creek Campground. Park at East Bank Trailhead, cross the highway, and walk 0.3 mile east to the trailhead on the south side of the highway.

Contact: North Cascades National Park, Wilderness Information Center, 7280 Ranger Station Rd., Marblemount, WA 98267, 360/873-4500.

47 DEVIL'S DOME LOOP
41.7 mi/4–5 days

east of Ross Lake in North Cascades National Park and Pasayten Wilderness

Map 3.2, page 112

The North Cascades National Park is well known for its large selection of extended backpacking trips. Devil's Dome Loop is one of its best, even trekking across part of the Pasayten Wilderness. Set along the high ridges east of Ross Lake, the loop encircles mammoth Jack Mountain while enjoying miles of far-flung vistas, acres of old-growth forests, and privacy in the deep wilderness. The route is a tough one and should be undertaken only by those ready for four or more days in the backcountry.

Heading counterclockwise, Jackita Ridge Trail climbs steeply from Canyon Creek onto the barren, rocky slopes of Crater Mountain. From here, 11 miles of trail traverses Jackita Ridge before encountering Devil's Ridge Trail at Devil's Pass. Devil's Ridge Trail heads east for another 5 miles of high-country hiking. From this point, the trail drops to Ross Lake. The East Bank Trail follows the shore 15 miles before returning to Canyon Creek Trailhead. While a four-day trip is possible, five or six days is much better.

Water is an important consideration, as the ridge is extremely dry once the snowpack has melted. Along the way are many established camps. Most notable are (from Canyon Creek Trailhead): Devil's Park (7 miles), Devil's Pass Shelter (16 miles), Skyline Camp (18 miles), Devil's Dome (20 miles), and Bear Skull (22 miles). The East Bank Trail has many camps spread along its shores. The Devil's Dome Loop is highly respected for its ability to challenge even veteran hikers.

User Groups: Hikers and horses only. No dogs or mountain bikes are allowed. No wheelchair access.

Permits: This area is accessible July–October. A federal Northwest Forest Pass is required to park here. Overnight stays within the national park require backcountry camping permits, which are available at the Wilderness Information Center.

Maps: For a map of North Cascades National Park, contact the Outdoor Recreation Information Center at the downtown Seattle REI. For topographic maps, ask Green Trails for No. 16, Ross Lake, No. 17, Jack Mountain, No. 48, Diablo Dam, and No. 49, Mount Logan, or ask the USGS for Crater Mountain, Azurite Peak, Shull Mountain, Jack Mountain, and Pumpkin Mountain.

Directions: From Marblemount, drive east on Highway 20 to the Canyon Creek Trailhead, near Mile Marker 142.

Contact: North Cascades National Park, Wilderness Information Center, 7280 Ranger Station Rd., Marblemount, WA 98267, 360/873-4500.

48 EAST CREEK
16.0 mi/2 days

west of Winthrop in North Cascades Scenic Highway and Okanogan National Forest

Map 3.2, page 112

Despite an easily accessible trailhead on Highway 20, few people bother to visit East Creek. Perhaps the trail is overshadowed by the reputations of bigger, better-known trails. Other folks' loss is your gain should you undertake East Creek. Eight miles of trail travel through terrific old-growth forest and open meadow to Mebee Pass, where views are finally afforded. From the pass, scramble to surrounding peaks, peer into the long Methow River valley, bask in the sun, and most of all, enjoy the solitude.

East Creek Trail crosses Granite Creek via footbridge before making a quick ascent along East Creek. A ford of East Creek is required (2.5 miles), a difficult endeavor when the winter's snows are still melting. Late July is best, as runoff has lowered but wildflowers are still in bloom. The trail continues up the valley, crossing numerous creeks. The last 1.5 miles is a steep climb up the side of the valley, breaking out of the forest into meadows. At the pass stands an old fire lookout, built in 1933 and recently renovated. Camps are situated at several places along the trail, but the best are just below Mebee Pass in the meadows.

User Groups: Hikers, leashed dogs, and horses. No mountain bikes are allowed. No wheelchair access.

Permits: This trail is accessible July–October. A federal Northwest Forest Pass is required to park here.

Maps: For a map of Okanogan National Forest, contact the Outdoor Recreation Information Center at the downtown Seattle REI. For topographic maps, ask Green Trails for No. 49, Mount Logan, or ask the USGS for Azurita Peak.

Directions: From Marblemount, drive east on Highway 20 to the East Creek Trailhead, near Mile Marker 146.

Contact: Okanogan National Forest, Methow Valley Ranger District, 24 W. Chewuch Rd., Winthrop, WA 98862, 509/996-4000.

49 EASY PASS/ FISHER CREEK

7.0 mi/5.0 hr 🏃5 ⛺9

east of Newhalem in Okanogan National Forest and North Cascades National Park

Map 3.2, page 112

Easy Pass is easily one of the biggest misnomers within the North Cascades, as there is nothing easy about it. After all, a rugged, rocky climb of 2,800 feet is rarely easy. It certainly isn't here. The scenery, however, is easy on the eyes. The colossal Mount Logan, cloaked in ice, stares from across the valley while Fisher Peak stands at the head of the basin. Wildflowers abound and wildlife roam freely in the wild and undisturbed valley below. The trail continues by dropping into the basin and wandering out Fisher Creek Valley to Thunder Creek, an exceptional trek.

Easy Pass Trail immediately crosses boulder-strewn Granite Creek and starts a long, arduous climb to the pass. After 2 miles, the trail breaks out of forest and enters an avalanche chute between the steep walls of Ragged Ridge. The name Easy Pass stems from the fact that this was the easiest (and only) place for a trail over Ragged Ridge. The trail finally reaches the pass after 3.5 miles. Here, subalpine larches claim whatever soil they can for a home, turning a brilliant gold in the fall. There is no camping at the pass.

For overnight trips, Easy Pass Trail continues down to Fisher Creek (within the national park). This is black-bear country; they are frequently spotted roaming the hillsides munching on huckleberries. Fisher Camp is at the lower part of the flower-filled basin and makes a great overnight resting spot. The trail proceeds down through the forested valley to Thunder Creek, 11 miles from Easy Pass.

User Groups: Hikers and leashed dogs (dogs to Easy Pass only). No horses or mountain bikes are allowed. No wheelchair access.

Permits: This trail is accessible mid-July–mid-October. A federal Northwest Forest Pass is required to park here. Overnight stays within the national park require backcountry camping permits.

Maps: For a map of Okanogan National Forest and North Cascades National Park, contact the Outdoor Recreation Information Center at the downtown Seattle REI. For topographic maps, ask Green Trails for No. 49, Mount Logan, or ask the USGS for Mount Arriva and Mount Logan.

Directions: From Winthrop, drive about 40 miles west on Highway 20 (or 46 miles east from Marblemount) to Easy Pass Trailhead. The trailhead is on the south side of the highway.

Contact: North Cascades National Park, Wilderness Information Center, 7280 Ranger Station Rd., Marblemount, WA 98267, 360/873-4500.

50 RAINY LAKE NATURE TRAIL

1.8 mi/1.0 hr 🏃1 ⛺9

west of Winthrop in Okanogan National Forest

Map 3.2, page 112 **BEST (**

The achievement of motoring up a pass is usually a call for celebration and a little leg stretching. Rainy Lake Nature Trail provides the perfect excuse to pull over and work out the cramps. Only a mile to the lake, with no elevation change, Rainy Lake Trail is easily accomplished by folks of all ages and abilities. The paved path has educational signs pointing out plant species or ecological processes. Some of the trees on the trail are downright imposing. At the end lies Rainy Lake, sitting within a glacial cirque. The Lyall Glacier sits above with its meltwater cascading into the lake. This is a great stop!

User Groups: Hikers and leashed dogs. No

horses or mountain bikes are allowed. The trail is wheelchair accessible.

Permits: This trail is accessible mid-June–October. A federal Northwest Forest Pass is required to park here.

Maps: For a map of Okanogan National Forest, contact the Outdoor Recreation Information Center at the downtown Seattle REI. For topographic maps, ask Green Trails for No. 50, Washington Pass, or ask the USGS for Washington Pass.

Directions: From Newhalem, drive Highway 20 to Mile Marker 157. Turn right into the south trailhead. The north trailhead is only for Cutthroat Pass and the Pacific Crest Trail (PCT).

Contact: Okanogan National Forest, Methow Valley Ranger District, 24 W. Chewuch Rd., Winthrop, WA 98862, 509/996-4000.

51 LAKE ANN/MAPLE PASS
3.8-7.6 mi/2.0-4.5 hr   🥾3 ⛰8

west of Winthrop in Okanogan National Forest

Map 3.2, page 112

With good reason, Lake Ann is one of Highway 20's most-often-recommended day hikes. Just 2 miles of hiking delivers a beautiful lake surrounded by towering ridges. It's a great place for bird-watching, offers the chance to do a little fishing, and makes for a nice picnic. Plus, it can be added as a side trip to Maple Pass.

Lake Ann Trail heads up through a great old-growth forest filled with Pacific silver fir and mountain hemlock. The path is well maintained and the grade climbs gently. Marmots are likely to greet you with a shrill whistle while you pass through the meadows. The trail divides (1.5 miles), with the Maple Pass Trail heading to the right. Stay to the left and soon you'll be at Lake Ann. (If you don't go back to do Maple Pass, your trip will be 3.8 miles round-trip.) Unfortunately there is no camping at Lake Ann because of previous overuse and abuse. The lake basin is a result

of glacial carving nearly a million years ago. As the glacier retreated, the rocks and dirt it deposited formed a natural dam, creating Lake Ann. Meadows abound here, even on a small island in the south part of the lake. And there is always a chance of seeing a black bear here. So keep that picnic nearby at all times.

In local hiking circles, Maple Pass is considered one of the best day hikes in the region. And rightfully so: This trail takes hikers above two shimmering blue lakes to a level with glaciers. It leads through mountain meadows teeming with marmots and visited by mountain goats and black bears. Most impressively, it takes you on even terms with so many major peaks that you need six topo maps to name them all. This really is a trail to remember and visit again and again.

The loop is best started counterclockwise. This makes the ascent a little easier to handle. In the other direction, a sign forewarns, "Trail beyond steeper but more scenic." Maple Pass Trail follows Lake Ann trail for 1.5 miles before climbing the basin wall to Heather Pass. Lake Ann glitters below and mountain heather lights up the meadows in August. Black Peak, 8,970 feet, emerges and rarely leaves your sight. The trail moves up the western ridge through high meadows. Alpine larches grace any fertile spot possible, and the northern peaks stand out. Maple Pass is a good climb, and from it an understanding of several major creek drainages can be had. On clear days, even Glacier Peak is visible. The trail, now even with the Lyall Glacier, continues down, moving between views of Rainy Lake and Lake Ann. A steep drop through a wonderful forest brings you to the car again. The experience will likely keep you coming back to Maple Pass.

User Groups: Hikers and leashed dogs (dogs are allowed on the loop but cannot complete it, as Maple Pass is in the national park). No horses or mountain bikes are allowed. No wheelchair access.

Permits: This trail is usually accessible mid-July–early October. A federal Northwest Forest Pass is required to park here.

Maps: For a map of Okanogan National Forest, contact the Outdoor Recreation Information Center at the downtown Seattle REI. For topographic maps for the Lake Ann Trail, ask Green Trails for No. 50, Washington Pass, or ask the USGS for Washington Pass. For topographic maps for Maple Pass, ask Green Trails for No. 49, Mount Logan, and No. 50, Washington Pass, or ask the USGS for Washington Pass and Mount Arriva.

Directions: From Newhalem, drive Highway 20 to Mile Marker 157. Turn right into the south trailhead. The north trailhead is only for Cutthroat Pass and the PCT.

Contact: Okanogan National Forest, Methow Valley Ranger District, 24 W. Chewuch Rd., Winthrop, WA 98862, 509/996-4000.

52 BLUE LAKE
4.4 mi/2.5 hr

west of Winthrop in Okanogan National Forest

Map 3.2, page 112

Blue Lake is a natural masterpiece. To begin, Blue Lake Trail climbs through shady old-growth forests. The destination is a short 2 miles, a lake sparkling deep turquoise, making Blue Lake a most appropriate name. Enormous craggy peaks and ridges skirted in rock and talus stand to three sides. The 7,800-foot Early Winters Spires rise to the northeast as if trying to steal the show. And the high mountain subalpine forests bring it all to life.

Blue Lake is a truly fantastic hike, considering its easy accessibility and attractiveness in all seasons. The first mile of trail climbs gradually through virgin forest. Before long, it breaks into meadows, and Cutthroat Peak is visible across the valley. The trail was built well and receives good maintenance, as it seems much shorter than its stated distance. The path finds the lake before you know it. Mountain hemlock, alpine larch, and subalpine fir find homes in the smallest crevasses and complete the scene. The alpine larch make a late-season hike here highly appealing. During autumn,

the larch seem to catch on fire, their needles turning orange and then yellow before falling off. There is no camping allowed at Blue Lake, so please keep it to a day hike.

User Groups: Hikers and leashed dogs. No horses or mountain bikes are allowed. No wheelchair access.

Permits: This trail is accessible mid-July–September. A federal Northwest Forest Pass is required to park here.

Maps: For a map of Okanogan National Forest, contact the Outdoor Recreation Information Center at the downtown Seattle REI. For topographic maps, ask Green Trails for No. 50, Washington Pass, or ask the USGS for Washington Pass.

Directions: From Winthrop, drive west on Highway 20 to Blue Lake Trailhead. The signed trailhead is on the left, about 0.5 mile west of Washington Pass.

Contact: Okanogan National Forest, Methow Valley Ranger District, 24 W. Chewuch Rd., Winthrop, WA 98862, 509/996-4000.

53 CUTTHROAT PASS
11.0 mi/6.0 hr

near Washington Pass in Okanogan National Forest

Map 3.2, page 112

Cutthroat Pass is perfect for all kinds of hikers, from beginners to the experienced, which has made it a popular destination over the years. The pass isn't a difficult journey, making it a great trip for first-timers in the North Cascades. Cutthroat Lake offers a good turnaround point for those uninterested in climbing to the pass and simply wanting a great, short day hike. Conversely, the views from the pass will inspire even the most trail-hardened of hikers, who may think they have seen it all.

Cutthroat Pass Trail leisurely climbs through the valley's forest to a junction (1.7 miles). Here, Cutthroat Lake Trail breaks to the left. The lake is a short 0.25 mile down the trail, lined by boulders, forests, and steep basin walls. Those wanting an easy overnighter will find campsites here. Make sure it's an established site, though, and at least 200 feet from the lakeshore.

Continuing on Cutthroat Pass Trail takes hikers abruptly up to the pass. Expect a lot of wildflowers in the expansive meadows during the month of July. The views are exceptional, distant, and rewarding. Visitors often return home with stories of seeing or encountering mountains goats, who regularly frequent the area. Camps are situated around the pass, although water is nonexistent once the snowpack is gone. The pass sees its fair share of traffic because the PCT runs right through it.

User Groups: Hikers, leashed dogs, and horses. No mountain bikes are allowed. No wheelchair access.

Permits: This trail is accessible July–September. A federal Northwest Forest Pass is required to park here.

Maps: For a map of Okanogan National Forest, contact the Outdoor Recreation Information Center at the downtown Seattle REI. For topographic maps, ask Green Trails for No. 50, Washington Pass, or ask the USGS for Washington Pass.

Directions: From Winthrop, drive west 26 miles on Highway 20 to Forest Service Road 400. Turn right (north) and drive 1 mile to the trailhead at road's end.

Contact: Okanogan National Forest, Methow Valley Ranger District, 24 W. Chewuch Rd., Winthrop, WA 98862, 509/996-4000.

54 WEST FORK METHOW RIVER

16.0 mi/2-6 days

northwest of Mazama in Okanogan National Forest

Map 3.2, page 112
The West Fork of the Methow River serves as an access point to one of the PCT's most

scenic sections. The trail follows the river 8 miles up the valley to the PCT. The trail along the river is well known by anglers, who come here to catch and release cutthroat and other trout. Campsites appear regularly along the way, usually directly on the river. The trail eventually leaves the riverside to reach the PCT.

From here, hikers have several options. They can join the PCT as it heads north through Brush Creek and along a high ridge to Hart's Pass (20.7 miles). Expect lots of meadows, views, and probably mountain goats. Or one can travel south on the PCT. The famous trail continues south through the river valley, up to meadowy ridges and on to Rainy Pass Trailhead via three major passes (26.4 miles). And the East Creek Trail ventures out of the Methow Valley to Mebee Pass, an old fire lookout, and eventually to East Creek Trailhead (17.9 miles). These three options require two cars, however, which is sometimes a difficult undertaking. If you have only one car, there's no shame in hiking out the same way you came in.

User Groups: Hikers, leashed dogs, horses, and mountain bikes. No wheelchair access.

Permits: This trail is accessible late June–mid-October. A federal Northwest Forest Pass is required to park here.

Maps: For a map of Okanogan National Forest, contact the Outdoor Recreation Information Center at the downtown Seattle REI. For topographic maps, ask Green Trails for No. 49, Mount Logan, and No. 50, Washington Pass, or ask the USGS for Robinson Mountain and Slate Peak.

Directions: From Winthrop, drive west 17 miles on Highway 20 to Mazama. Turn right (north) onto Mazama Road and drive 0.2 mile to Hart's Pass Road (County Road 9140/Forest Service Road 5400). Turn left and drive to Rattlesnake Trailhead, 0.3 beyond River Bend Campground.

Contact: Okanogan National Forest, Methow Valley Ranger District, 24 W. Chewuch Rd., Winthrop, WA 98862, 509/996-4000.

55 BUCKSKIN RIDGE
22.2 mi/2 days   ☖3 △10

northwest of Mazama in Pasayten Wilderness of Okanogan National Forest

Map 3.2, page 112

Thanks to Slate Pass, a trailhead conveniently situated at 6,200 feet of elevation, access to Buckskin Ridge is a piece of cake. Well, maybe a little more difficult than cake, but still, very little of the North Cascades is as accessible. Buckskin Ridge Trail runs the long, jagged ridge at a steady elevation. Major peaks of the Pasayten Wilderness are close enough to touch at times (or even climb). Buckskin Trail passes a pair of lakes before dropping to the Pasayten River, which offers a pair of excellent river hike loop options.

From Hart's Pass, hike the road up to Slate Pass (1.4 miles) and where Buckskin Ridge Trail begins. The trail enjoys open meadows for much of its length. The trail winds around the east side of the ridge to good camping at Silver Lake (6 miles) and on to Silver Pass (8 miles). The trail now runs the west side of the ridge, with all new peaks to admire. This segment has several steep and challenging sections, so be prepared for a slow time. Buckskin Lake (11.1 miles) marks the northern end of the ridge and also makes for a good campsite. The obvious return route is back along the ridge. But those seeking a loop can continue on Buckskin Trail to the Pasayten River. Here, trails up the West and Middle Forks return to Slate Peak. Each is about 35 miles in total length.

User Groups: Hikers, leashed dogs, and horses (horses permitted but strongly discouraged). No mountain bikes are allowed. No wheelchair access.

Permits: This trail is accessible July–September. A federal Northwest Forest Pass is required to park here.

Maps: For a map of Okanogan National Forest, contact the Outdoor Recreation Information Center at the downtown Seattle REI. For topographic maps, ask Green Trails for No.

18, Pasayten Peak, and No. 50, Washington Pass, or ask the USGS for Slate Peak, Pasayten Peak, and Frosty Creek.

Directions: From Winthrop, drive west 17 miles on Highway 20 to Mazama. Turn right (north) onto Mazama Road and drive 0.2 mile to Hart's Pass Road (County Road 9140/Forest Service Road 5400). Turn left and drive 18.5 miles to Hart's Pass. Turn right on Forest Service Road 5400-600 and drive 5 miles to Slate Pass at road's end. Hart's Pass Road is prone to frequent washouts; call the ranger station for current status.

Contact: Okanogan National Forest, Methow Valley Ranger District, 24 W. Chewuch Rd., Winthrop, WA 98862, 509/996-4000.

56 DRIVEWAY BUTTE
8.0 mi/5.0 hr   ☖4 △9

north of Highway 20 in Okanogan National Forest

Map 3.2, page 112

This is a steep ascent to a former lookout site atop Driveway Butte. If the Forest Service once used a peak to scan for fires, you can be certain that it has an expansive view. Indeed it does, looking out over many surrounding valleys, ridges, and peaks, all the way into the Pasayten Wilderness. Driveway Butte Trail gains about 3,000 feet, which is no easy feat. Complicating the task is a trail that can be rocky and rough at times. For those prepared for a strenuous hike, however, the vista is a wonderful reward.

Driveway Butte Trail leaves Early Winters Creek very near Highway 20. The first 2 miles are brutal, climbing steeply up Indian Creek through forest. At a small pass, the trail heads around the headwaters of McGee Creek. Subalpine meadows finally appear before the top of the Butte, with grand views of Silver Star Mountain and many other Cascade peaks. Once the snow is gone, very little water is to be found along the trail, so carrying extra water is important, especially on hot summer days. The panoramic views will be well appreciated by those who accomplish the summit.

User Groups: Hikers, leashed dogs, and horses. No mountain bikes are allowed. No wheelchair access.

Permits: This trail is accessible late-June–October. A federal Northwest Forest Pass is required to park here.

Maps: For a map of Okanogan National Forest, contact the Outdoor Recreation Information Center at the downtown Seattle REI. For topographic maps, ask Green Trails for No. 50, Washington Pass, or ask the USGS for Silverstar Mountain and Robinson Mountain.

Directions: From Winthrop, drive west on Highway 20 for 18.5 miles to Klipchuck Campground. Near the self-service fee station is a gated service road. The trail begins about 100 yards down this road.

Contact: Okanogan National Forest, Methow Valley Ranger Station, 24 W. Chewuch Rd., Winthrop, WA 98862, 509/996-4000.

57 WEST FORK PASAYTEN
31.0 mi/3-4 days   3   10

northwest of Mazama in Pasayten Wilderness of Okanogan National Forest

Map 3.2, page 112

The West Fork of the Pasayten is easily accessible via Slate Peak, a trailhead conveniently situated at an elevation of 6,800 feet. Start high and drop into the large, wide valley of the Pasayten's West Fork. The trail sticks to the river valley, passing through ancient forests of pine and fir with frequent views to the towering peaks lining the valley ridges. This trail experiences some of the Pasayten's wildest regions, where sightings of bear and other wildlife are frequent. Best of all, the trail makes two excellent loops when combined with trails that run along the top of the valley's ridges.

West Fork Pasayten Trail drops from the high vantage of Slate Peak into the river valley below. Snow lingers a little late on the north side of Slate Peak and you must ford the river (4 miles). That means late July or early August are prime times to hit this trail. Campsites are littered along the route, frequently right on the river. At 8.5 miles is a junction for Holman Creek and up to the PCT, the first of the two great loop possibilities. Hike up to Holman Pass and head south on the PCT back to Slate Peak for a total of 21 miles. Many call this the best of the PCT. Anywhere.

The main trail continues another seven miles to a major junction. Head south on the Buckskin Ridge Trail, a 16.6-mile trip back to Slate Peak. This section of trail can be obscure and difficult to find at times, but experienced route-finders will love it.

User Groups: Hikers, leashed dogs, and horses. No mountain bikes are allowed. No wheelchair access.

Permits: This trail is accessible mid-July–mid-October. A federal Northwest Forest Pass is required to park here. A free wilderness permit is also required to hike here and is available at the trailhead.

Maps: For a map of Okanogan National Forest, contact the Outdoor Recreation Information Center at the downtown Seattle REI. For topographic maps, ask Green Trails for No. 18, Pasayten Peak, and No. 50, Washington Pass, or ask the USGS for Slate Peak, Pasayten Peak, and Frosty Creek.

Directions: From Winthrop, drive west 17 miles on Highway 20 to Mazama. Turn right (north) onto Mazama Road and drive 0.2 mile to Hart's Pass Road (County Road 9140/Forest Service Road 5400). Turn left and drive 18.5 miles to Hart's Pass. Turn right on Forest Service Road 5400-600 and drive 5 miles to Slate Pass at road's end. Hart's Pass Road is prone to frequent washouts; call the ranger station for current status.

Contact: Okanogan National Forest, Methow Valley Ranger District, 24 W. Chewuch Rd., Winthrop, WA 98862, 509/996-4000.

58 ROBINSON PASS

55.0 mi/5-10 days   3   △10

north of Mazama in Pasayten Wilderness of Okanogan National Forest

Map 3.2, page 112

By no means must you hike this trail 27.5 miles in only to come out the same 27.5 miles. Instead, Robinson Creek Trail can be drastically shortened or dramatically lengthened. Heading over Robinson Pass into the Middle Fork Pasayten River valley, the trail ventures into the most secluded section of the already remote wilderness. Numerous trails intersect the trail along the Pasayten River, making hikes easily customizable. Even a straight trip up and back isn't all that bad.

Robinson Creek Trail follows the creek to Robinson Pass (8.8 miles). Campsites are scattered along the creek and are usually forested; the better ones are near the pass. The trail now drops elevation for the next 19 miles down through the Pasayten River Valley. The wide, U-shaped valley is regularly broken up by enormous avalanche chutes, revealing the tall, rounded peaks lining the valley. Campsites are abundant in this valley and are often along the river.

Trails frequently break off to head over the ridge or up another major creek drainage. Trails lead up the West Fork of Pasayten (20.5 miles), Rock Creek (21.6 miles), and Frosty Creek (22.8 miles), each more desolate than the one before it. High-country treks can be made up to Freds Lake and Doris Lake (15.7 miles) or Tatoosh Buttes (20.7 miles). The Pasayten Wilderness is a place where grizzly bears and gray wolves still roam the countryside, and Robinson Creek Trail is the gateway to all of it.

User Groups: Hikers, leashed dogs, and horses. No mountain bikes are allowed. No wheelchair access.

Permits: This trail is accessible mid-June–mid-October. A federal Northwest Forest Pass is required to park here. A free wilderness permit is also required to hike here and is available at the trailhead.

Maps: For a map of Okanogan National Forest, contact the Outdoor Recreation Information Center at the downtown Seattle REI. For topographic maps, ask Green Trails for No. 18, Pasayten Peak, and No. 50, Washington Pass, or ask the USGS for Robinson Mountain, Slate Peak, Pasayten Peak, and Mount Lago.

Directions: From Winthrop, drive west 17 miles on Highway 20 to Mazama. Turn right (north) onto Mazama Road and drive 0.2 mile to Hart's Pass Road (County Road 9140/Forest Service Road 5400). Turn left and drive 9.5 miles to Robinson Creek Trailhead. Hart's Pass Road is prone to frequent washouts; call the ranger station for current status.

Contact: Okanogan National Forest, Methow Valley Ranger District, 24 W. Chewuch Rd., Winthrop, WA 98862, 509/996-4000.

59 LOST RIVER

8.5 mi/5.0 hr   2   △8

northwest of Mazama in Pasayten Wilderness of Okanogan National Forest

Map 3.2, page 112

While the Pasayten Wilderness is best known for its long treks into the backcountry, it does have its share of great day hikes. This easy stroll through the woods leads to the convergence of two large gorges, the Lost River and Eureka Creek. Along the way, the Lost River makes for noisy company, cascading over boulders and small rapids. With very little elevation gain along the route, the trail is perfect for hikers of all abilities and families. As an additional bonus, the low-lying trail opens earlier than other high routes, making the Lost River a good springtime outing.

Monument Creek Trail follows Lost River through forests of pine and fir, regularly breaking out for views of the valley ridges. Four miles in, the trail comes to Eureka Creek. Spilling out of a deep gorge, the creek passes over impressive falls before joining the Lost River. Cross a bridge over Eureka to streamside campsites, a very pleasant place to have lunch or spend the night. The narrow Lost River Gorge is viewable from the end of the trail, although it gets even more rugged and remote up the valley—so much so that trail construction isn't possible up the gorge. Folks who are ready for serious cross-country navigation can leave the two streams' confluence and hike up to Pistol Pass and on to Monument Creek (15.4 miles), a strenuous, even hellish, up and down.

User Groups: Hikers, leashed dogs, and horses. No mountain bikes are allowed. No wheelchair access.

Permits: This trail is accessible April–October. A federal Northwest Forest Pass is required to park here.

Maps: For a map of Okanogan National Forest, contact the Outdoor Recreation Information Center at the downtown Seattle REI. For topographic maps, ask Green Trails for No. 50, Washington Pass, and No. 51, Mazama, or ask the USGS for Robinson Mountain and McLeod Mountain.

Directions: From Winthrop, drive west 17 miles on Highway 20 to Mazama. Turn right (north) onto Mazama Road and drive 0.2 mile to Hart's Pass Road (County Road 9140/Forest Service Road 5400). Turn left and drive 9.5 miles to Monument Creek Trailhead. Hart's Pass Road is prone to frequent washouts; call the ranger station for current status.

Contact: Okanogan National Forest, Methow Valley Ranger District, 24 W. Chewuch Rd., Winthrop, WA 98862, 509/996-4000.

60 BURCH MOUNTAIN
9.8 mi/5.5 hr

north of Winthrop in Okanogan National Forest

Map 3.2, page 112

From atop Burch Mountain, feel awash in a sea of rocky peaks, with waves of mountain ridges extending in every direction. The vastness of the Pasayten Wilderness is easily felt from this high point of 7,782 feet. Catch the trail during the early summer and the journey is as grand as the summit, with open forests providing cool shade and wildflowers taking over open meadows. Venture here later in the season and you're sure to experience hot, dry weather. If you come in August, bring plenty of water.

The route starts on Billy Goat Pass Trail, which gains a hefty 1,800 feet of elevation in 3 miles. At the pass, double back to the south on Burch Mountain Trail. This path scales the side of Eightmile Ridge at a less harsh pitch. Meadows and vistas are the norm along the way. After 1.5 miles, the trail has reached the base of Burch Mountain and a side trail scrambles to the summit. Big Craggy Peak lives up to its name across Eightmile Creek, while numerous other peaks and ridges shine in the not-so-far distance. Bring a map, for many of the peaks deserve to be identified.

User Groups: Hikers, leashed dogs, and horses. No mountain bikes are allowed. No wheelchair access.

Permits: This trail is accessible July–September. A federal Northwest Forest Pass is required to park here.

Maps: For a map of Okanogan National Forest, contact the Outdoor Recreation Information Center at the downtown Seattle REI. For topographic maps, ask Green Trails for No. 19, Billy Goat Mountain, or ask the USGS for Billy Goat Mountain and Sweetgrass Butte.

Directions: From Winthrop, drive north on Chewuch River Road (across Highway 20 from the visitors center) 10 miles to Forest Service Road 5140. Turn left and drive 11 miles to the trailhead at road's end.

Contact: Okanogan National Forest, Methow Valley Ranger District, 24 W. Chewuch Rd., Winthrop, WA 98862, 509/996-4000.

61 COLEMAN RIDGE
31.7 mi/3-6 days

north of Winthrop in Pasayten Wilderness of
Okanogan National Forest

Map 3.2, page 112

While Coleman Ridge Trail runs more than
20 miles along the high alpine ridge, the best
part of the trip is contained in the upper part
of ridge, near Four Point Lake. Here, scattered among glacially scraped boulders, are
meadows full of early summer wildflowers
and far-reaching vistas. Four Point Lake makes
for a wonderful camp, where captivating stars
illuminate the night sky.

Before embarking on this hike, be aware
that the Farewell Fire burned along this route
in 2004. While the trail has been maintained
by the Forest Service since that time, it's not
unusual for downed trees to block the trail.
Plan for extra time and energy on this hike.

The route follows the Chewuch River before making a lazy loop up to Coleman and
back down. Hike the Chewuch River, passing
Chewuch Falls along the way, until you reach
Fire Creek Trail (6 miles), heading off to the
left. You must ford the Chewuch, a difficult
crossing when the snowpack runoff is high.
The trail climbs up Fire Creek, eventually
becoming Coleman Ridge Trail (10.7 miles),
and finds a high mountain pass complete with
views. Campsites are scattered along the route,
with nice spots on the creek and a couple atop
the ridge.

Coleman Ridge Trail heads north on the
ridge and passes below Remmel Mountain, a
worthy peak for an easy side trip. Four Point
Lake is off a short side trail (16.5 miles). Be
sure to use the established sites at the lake. The
route then drops down Four Point Creek to
the Chewuch River, 12.9 miles from the trailhead. Good times for a trip here are July, when
wildflowers are blooming, and late September,
when larches turn gold.

User Groups: Hikers, leashed dogs, and horses.
No mountain bikes are allowed. No wheelchair access.

Permits: This trail is accessible July–September. A federal Northwest Forest Pass is
required to park here. A free wilderness permit
is also required to hike here and is available
at the trailhead.

Maps: For a map of Okanogan National Forest, contact the Outdoor Recreation Information Center at the downtown Seattle REI.
For topographic maps, ask Green Trails for
No. 20, Coleman Peak, or ask the USGS for
Coleman Peak, Mount Barney, and Bauerman Ridge.

Directions: From Winthrop, drive north on
Chewuch River Road (across Highway 20
from the visitors center) 30 miles to Thirtymile Trailhead at road's end.

Contact: Okanogan National Forest, Methow
Valley Ranger District, 24 W. Chewuch Rd.,
Winthrop, WA 98862, 509/996-4000.

62 CATHEDRAL BASIN
39.0 mi/5-6 days

north of Winthrop in Pasayten Wilderness of
Okanogan National Forest

Map 3.2, page 112

For folks seeking to experience the best of
what the Pasayten Wilderness has to offer,
this is the trail. More than 20 miles from the
nearest car lies resplendent Cathedral Basin.
Lakes are set inside basins, illuminated by
wildflowers in the summer, larches in the
fall, and multitudes of stars every night. The
Cathedral Pass journey is one of the prized
hikes of the Pasayten.

The best access is via Andrews Creek, an
excellent, although long, valley hike. It's 12.5
miles along the forested creek to Andrews Pass.
Some of the route was very recently burned
in 2003. Throughout the valley are tremendous views of surrounding peaks and ridges.
Camps are scattered regularly along the trail
here. It's another 3 miles from the pass to a
junction with Boundary Trail. Head east to
encounter Lower Cathedral Lake (18.6 miles)
and Upper Cathedral (20.5 miles). Campsites

are scarce around the lakes, so be ready to set up camp near the Boundary Trail junction or other available sites.

Above the lakes, Cathedral Peak and Amphitheater Mountain form worthy sentinels, standing on either side of the pass. Marmots rumble across the tundralike meadows while bears forage for berries. Scrambles are possible up many of the neighboring peaks, where the views extend across the wilderness to the Cascades and Canada.

User Groups: Hikers, leashed dogs, and horses. No mountain bikes are allowed. No wheelchair access.

Permits: This trail is accessible July–September. A federal Northwest Forest Pass is required to park here. A free wilderness permit is also required to hike here and is available at the trailhead.

Maps: For a map of Okanogan National Forest, contact the Outdoor Recreation Information Center at the downtown Seattle REI. For topographic maps, ask Green Trails for No. 20, Coleman Peak, or ask the USGS for Coleman Peak, Mount Barney, and Remmel Mountain.

Directions: From Winthrop, drive north on Chewuch River Road (across Highway 20 from the visitors center) 24 miles to signed Andrew's Creek Trailhead.

Contact: Okanogan National Forest, Methow Valley Ranger District, 24 W. Chewuch Rd., Winthrop, WA 98862, 509/996-4000.

63 PEEPSIGHT
28.0 mi/3-4 days

north of Winthrop in Pasayten Wilderness of Okanogan National Forest

Map 3.2, page 112

Off Andrews Creek and normally a route to other places, the trail to Peepsight Mountain and Peepsight Lake is a worthy journey in itself. The 8-mile trail leaves Andrews Creek to scale the side of Peepsight Mountain. This is high country, full of meadows and views. A trip to Peepsight Mountain, elevation 8,146 feet, is a window on the Pasayten, laying much of the vast wilderness at your tired feet. And Peepsight Lake lies on the other side of the pass, but it usually opens later in the season because of snow melting slowly on the pass. The trail winds back down to Andrews Creek to form a loop.

The route follows Andrews Creek Trail to Peepsight Trail (8.5 miles). A ford of Andrews Creek is necessary, not an easy task in the early summer. Peepsight Trail climbs to a junction (12.6 miles); to the west lies Peepsight Lake, a welcome sight when fall larches are alive with color. Peepsight Mountain is an easy scramble from this trail. The right fork in the trail skirts Peepsight Mountain and makes for Crazy Man Pass and Rock Lake before dropping back to Andrews Pass, 12.5 miles from the trailhead. Campsites are found at many places along the route; when possible, stick to established sites.

User Groups: Hikers, leashed dogs, and horses. No mountain bikes are allowed. No wheelchair access.

Permits: This trail is accessible July–September. A federal Northwest Forest Pass is required to park here. A free wilderness permit is also required to hike here and is available at the trailhead.

Maps: For a map of Okanogan National Forest, contact the Outdoor Recreation Information Center at the downtown Seattle REI. For topographic maps, ask Green Trails for No. 20, Coleman Peak, or ask the USGS for Coleman Peak and Remmel Mountain.

Directions: From Winthrop, drive north on Chewuch River Road (across Highway 20 from the visitors center) 24 miles to signed Andrew's Creek Trailhead.

Contact: Okanogan National Forest, Methow Valley Ranger District, 24 W. Chewuch Rd., Winthrop, WA 98862, 509/996-4000.

64 CHEWUCH RIVER

36.0 mi/4 days   🥾3 ⛰9

north of Winthrop in Pasayten Wilderness of
Okanogan National Forest

Map 3.2, page 112

This long, river valley trail makes connections
to several trails branching off into the Pasayten
Wilderness before arriving at some of the area's most beautiful country. But it also makes
for a good day hike, with Chewuch Falls a
short 3 miles up the trail. Those looking for
an extended trip will enjoy Remmel Lake at
the head of the Chewuch. Trips up Tungsten
Creek, Topaz Mountain, and Coleman Peak
are also begun from the Chewuch River.

Chewuch River Trail is popular with those
riding horses or driving stock, meaning that it
can be wide and dusty. Overall, the hike gains
little elevation as it passes through forests of
lodgepole pine, some of it burned in 2003.
Campsites are scattered along the length of the
trail, and water is never far away. Keep plodding and the trail eventually rises into Remmel
Basin to find Remmel Lake (18 miles), surrounded by meadows and larches. The high,
flat terrain makes the surrounding 8,000-plus-feet peaks seem like rolling hills. At the lake,
make camp at established campsites more than
200 feet from the lakeshore.

User Groups: Hikers, leashed dogs, and horses.
No mountain bikes are allowed. No wheelchair access.

Permits: This trail is accessible July–September. A federal Northwest Forest Pass is
required to park here. A free wilderness permit
is also required to hike here and is available
at the trailhead.

Maps: For a map of Okanogan National Forest, contact the Outdoor Recreation Information Center at the downtown Seattle REI.
For topographic maps, ask Green Trails for
No. 20, Coleman Peak, or ask the USGS for
Coleman Peak, Bauerman Ridge, and Remmel Mountain.

Directions: From Winthrop, drive north on
Chewuch River Road (across Highway 20

from the visitors center) 30 miles to Thirtymile Trailhead at road's end.

Contact: Okanogan National Forest, Methow
Valley Ranger District, 24 W. Chewuch Rd.,
Winthrop, WA 98862, 509/996-4000.

65 HORSESHOE BASIN (STEHEKIN)

7.8–16.4 mi/2 days   🥾2 ⛰9

north of Stehekin in North Cascades
National Park

Map 3.2, page 112

Fortunately, one of the North Cascades' most
beautiful basins is a convenient trip for folks
on both the west side and east side of the Cascades. Hikers living on the rainy side of the
state can reach Horseshoe Basin via Cascade
Pass in 8.2 up-down-and-up-again miles. Eastsiders can take a shorter route via Stehekin,
which involves a beautiful ferry ride on Lake
Chelan. On either route, the enormous cliffs
and waterfalls ringing Horseshoe Basin make
for an awesome trip.

Folks seeking access to Horseshoe Basin
from the west need to hike to Cascade Pass
(3.7 miles; see listing in this chapter) and drop
to the Stehekin River and Horseshoe Basin
Trail junction (6.7 miles). From Chelan, ride
the ferry to Stehekin and catch the shuttle to
Cottonwood Campground, at the end of Stehekin Valley. From here, the Horseshoe Basin
junction is a quick hike (2.4 miles).

Horseshoe Basin Trail wanders up Basin
Creek 1.5 miles to the head of the basin. Covered in meadows, the basin offers impressive
views of the enormous mountains and glaciers towering 4,000 feet above. Campers,
please stick to established campsites, scattered
throughout the basin. This area is dotted with
numerous mines, operated decades ago, and
their remains are worth checking out. Horseshoe Basin is a North Cascades classic.

User Groups: Hikers only. No dogs, horses, or
mountain bikes are allowed. No wheelchair
access.

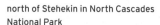

the view down Horseshoe Basin to the Stehekin River Valley

Permits: This trail is accessible July–mid-October. A federal Northwest Forest Pass is required to park at Cascade Pass, for hikers entering from the west. Overnight stays within the national park require reservations and backcountry camping permits, which are available at the Wilderness Information Center in Marblemount or the visitors center in Stehekin.

Maps: For a map of North Cascades National Park, contact the Outdoor Recreation Information Center at the downtown Seattle REI. For topographic maps, ask Green Trails for No. 80, Cascade Pass, or ask the USGS for McGregor Mountain, Goode Mountain, and Mount Logan.

Directions: For the eastern entrance, from Wenatchee, drive north 33 miles on U.S. 97 to Chelan. Lady of the Lake Ferry Terminal is on U.S. 97 Alternate just before entering downtown. Catch the passenger ferry to Stehekin and ride the shuttle to Cottonwood Camp Trailhead.

For the western entrance, from the town of Marblemount on Highway 20, drive 23 miles

on Cascade River Road to the Cascade Pass Trailhead at road's end.

Contact: North Cascades National Park, Golden West Visitor Center, Stehekin, WA, 360/854-7365, ext. 14; Lady of the Lake Ferry Service, 1418 W. Woodin Ave., Chelan, WA 98816, 509/682-4584.

66 NORTH FORK BRIDGE CREEK
19.4 mi/3 days   👣2 ⛰9

north of Stehekin in North Cascades National Park

Map 3.2, page 112

A high, rugged ridge dotted by glaciers surrounds the large basin at the head of North Fork Bridge Creek. The high peaks of Goode Mountain, Storm King, and Mount Logan stand impressively over the open, rocky expanse of North Fork Meadows. The splendor of it all is easily accessible via a gentle trail along valley floors and a trio of great camps, easy stuff for beginner backpackers.

North Fork Bridge Creek Trail is accessible through Stehekin, which requires a ride on the Lake Chelan passenger ferry. Catch the shuttle from Stehekin to Bridge Creek Trailhead. The first 3 miles are along Bridge Creek Trail. Shortly after crossing the creek, via a bridge, North Fork Trail takes off to the left (north). At 5.2 miles is Walker Park Camp, for hikers and horses, while at 6.2 miles are Grizzly Creek Camps, one each for horses and hikers. Camping beyond is now forbidden because of excessive abuse in the meadows.

North Fork Bridge Creek Trail alternates between old forests and avalanche chutes. The views from the openings get successively better. From Grizzly Camps, it's a quick hike to North Fork Meadows (8.5 miles). The bulky valley walls shoot skyward to enormous peaks. Glaciers struggle to cling to the steep slopes. Enjoy.

User Groups: Hikers and horses. No dogs or mountain bikes are allowed. No wheelchair access.

Permits: This trail is accessible July–mid-October. Overnight stays within the national park require reservations and backcountry camping permits, which are available at the visitors center in Stehekin.

Maps: For a map of North Cascades National Park, contact the Outdoor Recreation Information Center at the downtown Seattle REI. For topographic maps, ask Green Trails for No. 49, Mount Logan, and No. 81, McGregor Mountain, or ask the USGS for McGregor Mountain, Goode Mountain, and Mount Logan.

Directions: From Wenatchee, drive north 33 miles on U.S. 97 to Chelan. Lady of the Lake Ferry Terminal is on U.S. 97 Alternate just before entering downtown. Catch the passenger ferry to Stehekin and ride the shuttle to Bridge Creek Trailhead.

Contact: North Cascades National Park, Golden West Visitor Center, Stehekin, WA, 360/854-7365, ext. 14; Lady of the Lake Ferry Service, 1418 W. Woodin Ave., Chelan, WA 98816, 509/682-4584.

67 GOODE RIDGE
10.0 mi/6.0 hr

north of Stehekin in North Cascades National Park

Map 3.2, page 112

Doing things the old-fashioned way, Goode Ridge Trail starts low in the valley before climbing to a high valley ridge. Make no mistake; Goode Ridge Trail is a steep one, gaining 4,400 feet of elevation in just 5 miles. Its challenging but not overwhelming ascent is perfect for those who are craving some mean vistas but who aren't crazy enough to challenge McGregor Mountain to a fight.

Goode Ridge Trail is in the northern part of the Stehekin Valley. For that, one must hop the passenger ferry from Chelan and then a shuttle from Stehekin. All that is not possible for one day, so plan on camping in the valley somewhere at least one night. The trail makes a steady climb away from the river, passing through forests for the first half before breaking out into open meadows. Expect hot, dry weather during the summer and bring extra water. The trail eventually reaches the southern end of Goode Ridge. The views of the surrounding peaks, lakes, and valleys are impressive. McGregor, Goode, Storm King, and Glacier Peak are the most memorable from a long list of visible peaks.

User Groups: Hikers and horses only. No dogs or mountain bikes are allowed. No wheelchair access.

Permits: This trail is accessible July–September. Overnight stays within the national park require reservations and backcountry camping permits, which are available at the visitors center in Stehekin.

Maps: For a map of North Cascades National Park, contact the Outdoor Recreation Information Center at the downtown Seattle REI. For topographic maps, ask Green Trails for No. 81, McGregor Mountain, or ask the USGS for Goode Mountain.

Directions: From Wenatchee, drive north 33 miles on U.S. 97 to Chelan. Lady of the Lake

Ferry Terminal is on U.S. 97 Alternate just before entering downtown. Catch the passenger ferry to Stehekin and ride the shuttle to Goode Ridge Trailhead.

Contact: North Cascades National Park, Golden West Visitor Center, Stehekin, WA, 360/854-7365, ext. 14; Lady of the Lake Ferry Service, 1418 W. Woodin Ave., Chelan, WA 98816, 509/682-4584.

68 RAINBOW LAKE
23.8 mi/3 days 　　　 🏃3 ⛰8

north of Stehekin in North Cascades National Park and Lake Chelan National Recreation Area

Map 3.2, page 112

Since there are no car-carrying ferries to Stehekin, there are no cars in the small town. A shuttle bus is your only option for access to the valley's nine trailheads. But the lack of a car makes through-hikes extremely easy. Rainbow Lake Trail is a perfect example. Have the shuttle drop you off upriver and hike your way back to Stehekin. This route is a grand one, via four creek valleys and a stop at a high alpine lake.

The route is best done from north to south, since the north trailhead is 1,000 feet higher. Disembark from the Stehekin shuttle at Bridge Creek Trailhead and hike the famed Pacific Crest Trail to South Fork Bridge Creek junction (6.8 miles). Good first-night camps are found at Sixmile Camp (6 miles) and South Fork Camp (6.8 miles). South Fork Bridge Creek Trail climbs to Bowan Pass (13.1 miles), passing Dans Camp (9.8 miles). The pass lies directly below the rocky and sheer face of Bowan Mountain.

Rainbow Lake rests just on the other side of the pass, set within open meadows dotted by larches, which are colorful in the early fall. An established camp is found here at 14 miles, near Rainbow Lake, and two more are at 15.4 miles and 16 miles, down in the North Fork Rainbow Creek Valley. Follow the trail through forests of pine and fir, out the valley,

and down Rainbow Creek Trail to Stehekin. Enjoy a meal and a beer in Stehekin and then ride Lady of the Lake to Chelan and your unmissed auto.

User Groups: Hikers and horses. No dogs or mountain bikes are allowed. No wheelchair access.

Permits: This trail is accessible July–September. Overnight stays within the national park require reservations and backcountry camping permits, which are available at the visitors center in Stehekin.

Maps: For a map of North Cascades National Park, contact the Outdoor Recreation Information Center at the downtown Seattle REI. For topographic maps, ask Green Trails for No. 81, McGregor Mountain, and No. 82, Stehekin, or ask the USGS for McGregor Mountain, McAlester Mountain, and Stehekin.

Directions: From Wenatchee, drive north 33 miles on U.S. 97 to Chelan. Lady of the Lake Ferry Terminal is on U.S. 97 Alternate just before entering downtown. Catch the passenger ferry to Stehekin and ride the shuttle to Bridge Creek Trailhead.

Contact: North Cascades National Park, Golden West Visitor Center, Stehekin, WA, 360/854-7365, ext. 14; Lady of the Lake Ferry Service, 1418 W. Woodin Ave., Chelan, WA 98816, 509/682-4584.

69 MCGREGOR MOUNTAIN
15.4 mi/2-3 days 　　　 🏃5 ⛰9

north of Stehekin in Lake Chelan National Recreation Area

Map 3.2, page 112

It's difficult to verify, but it's my opinion that McGregor Mountain is the steepest trail in the state. And with all the steep trails in the North Cascades, Olympics, and Mount Rainier, that's a fine distinction. From trailhead to summit, McGregor Mountain Trail climbs 6,300 feet. Few care to continue counting past 50 the number of switchbacks to the top of an 8,122-foot peak. Keep in mind that pain on the trail always pays off at the top.

High Bridge Trailhead is in the Stehekin River Valley, meaning you'll need to catch the passenger ferry from Chelan to Stehekin and subsequently ride the shuttle bus to High Bridge Camp. Start on the PCT before turning right (east) onto McGregor Mountain Trail (1.3 miles). The ascent starts immediately and doesn't end until Heaton Camp at 7,000 feet. Much of the trail lies in open, rocky meadows. The trail is dry, so bring enough water for hiking and for meals at camp. Heaton Camp offers exceptional views. A short scramble reaches the ridge below McGregor's summit, revealing far-flung views to the east. Finally, before you hit the trail, ask yourself, "Are you sure you want to do this when there's a nice bakery in Stehekin instead?"

User Groups: Hikers and horses only. No dogs or mountain bikes are allowed. No wheelchair access.

Permits: This trail is accessible July–September. Permits are not required. Parking and access are free.

Maps: For a map of North Cascades National Park, contact the Outdoor Recreation Information Center at the downtown Seattle REI. For topographic maps, ask Green Trails for No. 81, McGregor Mountain, or ask the USGS for McGregor Mountain.

Directions: From Wenatchee, drive north 33 miles on U.S. 97 to Chelan. Lady of the Lake Ferry Terminal is on U.S. 97 Alternate just before entering downtown. Catch the passenger ferry to Stehekin and ride the shuttle to High Bridge Trailhead.

Contact: North Cascades National Park, Golden West Visitor Center, Stehekin, WA, 360/854-7365, ext. 14; Lady of the Lake Ferry Service, 1418 W. Woodin Ave., Chelan, WA 98816, 509/682-4584.

70 COMPANY/ DEVORE CREEKS LOOP

27.5 mi/3 days   🥾4 ⛰9

west of Stehekin in Glacier Peak Wilderness of Wenatchee National Forest

Map 3.2, page 112

This is another excellent through-hike within Stehekin Valley. The route heads up long, wide Company Creek Valley and circles around a sharp ridge of craggy peaks before dropping through Fourth of July Basin on the way to Stehekin. The crowds are rather thin along the trail, having been drawn to other, better-known trails farther up the valley. That's good news for those who venture here, a wild place full of things to see.

The route begins on Company Creek Trail with a long but scenic climb to Hilgard Pass (11.3 miles). Avalanche chutes expose Tupshin and Devore Peaks for long distances. You must ford Company Creek 5 miles in; this is difficult during times of heavy runoff. Well-established campsites are found at 3.5 miles, 10 miles, and 11.5 miles. At 6,600 feet, Hilgard Pass offers some scenic views.

The route now drops 1,900 feet before gaining 1,800 back on the way to Tenmile Pass (15.8 miles). If it sounds like a lot of work, it is. But enormous Fourth of July Basin awaits on the other side. This is premier high country, with sweeping views of the Devore Creek drainage. Bears and coyotes are frequent visitors, but they rarely approach close enough for mug shots. Excellent second-night camps are found at Tenmile Pass and within Fourth of July Basin. The trail drops to Bird Creek Camp (20 miles) and Weaver Point Camp (25 miles) before arriving at Devore Creek Trailhead.

User Groups: Hikers, leashed dogs, and horses (hikers only on Devore Creek trail). No mountain bikes are allowed. No wheelchair access.

Permits: This trail is accessible July–September. Permits are not required. Parking and access are free.

Maps: For a map of Wenatchee National Forest, contact the Outdoor Recreation Information Center at the downtown Seattle REI. For topographic maps, ask Green Trails for No. 81, McGregor Mountain, No. 82, Stehekin, No. 113, Holden, and No. 114, Lucerne, or ask the USGS for Stehekin, Mount Lyall, and Holden.

Directions: From Wenatchee, drive north 33 miles on U.S. 97 to Chelan. Lady of the Lake Ferry Terminal is on U.S. 97 Alternate just before entering downtown. Catch the passenger ferry to Stehekin and ride the shuttle to Company Creek Trailhead.

Contact: North Cascades National Park, Golden West Visitor Center, Stehekin, WA, 360/854-7365, ext. 14; Lady of the Lake Ferry Service, 1418 W. Woodin Ave., Chelan, WA 98816, 509/682-4584.

71 STEHEKIN TRAILS
0.5-9.0 mi/0.5-5.0 hr

around Stehekin north of Lake Chelan

Map 3.2, page 112

Accessible only by passenger ferry or plane, Stehekin is as remote as it gets. The small village consists of resorts and cabins, several small restaurants and bakeries, and no fewer than 12 campgrounds. Scattered around town and valley are 18 different trails, many of which are full-scale adventures (covered elsewhere in this chapter). Some are perfect day hikes for families, including Agnes Gorge, Bullion Loop (a section of PCT), and Rainbow Loop Trail.

Agnes Gorge Trail, on the north side of Agnes Creek (a different trail), travels 2.5 easy miles up the creek as it runs through a tight chasm. At the end, the trail finds the creek as it passes over a small waterfall. Rainbow Loop Trail goes 5 miles along the eastern ridge above Stehekin. The trail gains little elevation and gets in a couple of views of Lake Chelan. The PCT also runs through the upper valley. Using the shuttle, make a 6.5-mile through-hike from Bullion Camp past Coon Lake up to Bridge Creek Camp. The Stehekin Valley is beautiful, and now you can say you've hiked the PCT.

User Groups: Hikers, leashed dogs, and horses. No mountain bikes are allowed. No wheelchair access.

Permits: This area is accessible March–

Mountain peaks tower over the Stehekin River Valley.

© SCOTT LEONARD

November. Permits are not required. Parking and access are free.

Maps: For a map of North Cascades National Park, contact the Outdoor Recreation Information Center at the downtown Seattle REI. For topographic maps, ask Green Trails for No. 82, Stehekin, and No. 81, McGregor Mountain, or ask the USGS for Stehekin.

Directions: From Wenatchee, drive north 33 miles on U.S. 97 to Chelan. Lady of the Lake Ferry Terminal is on U.S. 97 Alternate just before entering downtown. Catch the passenger ferry to Stehekin and ride the shuttle to the various trailheads.

Contact: North Cascades National Park, Golden West Visitor Center, Stehekin, WA, 360/854-7365, ext. 14; Lady of the Lake Ferry Service, 1418 W. Woodin Ave., Chelan, WA 98816, 509/682-4584.

72 CHELAN LAKESHORE
16.9 mi one-way/2-4 days

south of Stehekin in Lake Chelan-Sawtooth Wilderness of Okanogan National Forest

Map 3.2, page 112

April and May are great times to hike Lake Chelan Lakeshore Trail, before the summer's heat makes it unbearable. Besides, summers should be reserved for the alpine. Lakeshore Trail travels 17 miles along the eastern bank to the hamlet of Stehekin, soaking up much of the lake's scenery.

Park in the town of Chelan and ride the passenger ferry to the landing of Prince Creek, on the eastern shore. After your hike, catch lunch in Stehekin and a returning ferry to Chelan. The trail follows the lakeshore, often climbing a few hundred yards above the waterline. Open forests of enormous ponderosa pine and Douglas fir line the hillside, and snowy peaks appear across the lake.

A number of established camps lie along the trail, including Prince Creek, Cascade Creek (5.5 miles), Meadow Creek (7.6 miles), Moore Point (10.6 miles), Flick Creek (13.5 miles),

and Purple Point, in Stehekin. The trail can be done in two days, but three or four days is best, allowing for great side trips. Spend a day hiking up Fish Creek to Boulder Lake or Prince Creek to the Sawtooth Range. It may be only a lakeshore trail, but those who hike it know there is much more to it than that.

User Groups: Hikers only. No dogs, horses, or mountain bikes are allowed. No wheelchair access.

Permits: This trail is accessible year-round. Permits are not required. Parking and access are free.

Maps: For a map of Okanogan National Forest, contact the Outdoor Recreation Information Center at the downtown Seattle REI. For topographic maps, ask Green Trails for No. 82, Stehekin, No. 114, Lucerne, and No. 115, Prince Creek, or ask the USGS for Prince Creek, Lucerne, and Stehekin.

Directions: From Wenatchee, drive north 33 miles on U.S. 97 to Chelan. Lady of the Lake Ferry Terminal is on U.S. 97 Alternate just before entering downtown. Catch the passenger ferry to Stehekin and ride the shuttle to Prince Creek Landing.

Contact: North Cascades National Park, Golden West Visitor Center, Stehekin, WA, 360/854-7365, ext. 14; Lady of the Lake Ferry Service, 1418 W. Woodin Ave., Chelan, WA 98816, 509/682-4584.

73 LYMAN LAKES
18.2 mi/3-4 days

west of Lake Chelan in Glacier Peak Wilderness of Wenatchee National Forest

Map 3.2, page 112

For years, this has been one of the state's most frequented glaciers. Dropping off into the upper lake, Lyman Glacier displays the workings of the Ice Age, albeit on a smaller scale. The hike is a great trip up Railroad Creek Valley to large Lyman Lake, an outstanding place to spend the night. Further adventures and wide-open meadows await up the trail in this high-country parkland. The lakes are often visited as a stop along a larger loop, but they make for a great trip in themselves.

The trailhead is accessible via passenger ferry from Chelan. Disembark at Lucerne and catch a ride on a privately operated bus to the village of Holden. Railroad Creek Trail ascends the forested valley to Hart Lake (3.5 miles) and Lyman Lake (8.1 miles). Camps are scattered along the way and at Lyman Lake. Lyman Spur Trail (8.1 miles) climbs to Spider Gap, a steep but scenic ascent.

Deep within Glacier Peak Wilderness, wildlife is found everywhere. Mountain goats roam the high ridges while deer and bear roam the valleys. Be sure to hang bear sacks when camping. The trail continues south another mile to the upper lake and meadow bliss. Lyman Glacier is safe for careful exploration. For those on an extended stay, a trip up to Cloudy Pass (12.1 miles) and Suiattle Pass (13.1 miles) delivers grand views of the Cascades.

User Groups: Hikers, leashed dogs, and horses. No mountain bikes are allowed. No wheelchair access.

Permits: This trail is accessible July–September. Permits are not required. Parking and access are free.

Maps: For a map of Wenatchee National Forest, contact the Outdoor Recreation Information Center at the downtown Seattle REI. For topographic maps, ask Green Trails for No. 113, Holden, or ask the USGS for Holden.

Directions: From Wenatchee, drive north 33 miles on U.S. 97 to Chelan. Lady of the Lake Ferry Terminal is on U.S. 97 Alternate just before entering downtown. Catch the passenger ferry to Lucerne, the drop-off for Holden. Take the bus to the town of Holden. The trailhead is located at Holden Campground.

Contact: North Cascades National Park, Golden West Visitor Center, Stehekin, WA, 360/856-5700, ext. 340; Lady of the Lake Ferry Service, 1418 W. Woodin Ave., Chelan, WA 98816, 509/682-4584.

⁊⁊ DOMKE LAKE
7.0 mi/4.0 hr–2-plus days

west of Lake Chelan in Wenatchee National Forest

Map 3.2, page 112

This large lake sits within a small valley above and away from Lake Chelan. More than a mile long, the lake is a favorite stop for hikers, anglers, and families looking to do some camping. While the lake is accessible only by passenger ferry, it still receives a fair amount of traffic. Domke Lake isn't as large as Lake Chelan, but its water is warmer and thus more inviting for extended swims.

Domke Lake is just 3.5 miles from Lucerne, the boat drop-off point. The trail ascends just 1,000 feet to the forested lake. Camps are at the northeast and southeast corners while yet another camp is reached by boat on the western shore. Make the lake a base camp to explore the area on Domke Mountain Trail. Its junction is just below the lake on the main trail. Three miles of trail gain nearly 3,000 feet to a grand viewpoint of the lakes and imposing mountains.

User Groups: Hikers, leashed dogs, horses, and mountain bikes and motorcycles. No wheelchair access.

Permits: This trail is accessible mid-May–November. Permits are not required. Parking and access are free.

Maps: For a map of Wenatchee National Forest, contact the Outdoor Recreation Information Center at the downtown Seattle REI. For topographic maps, ask Green Trails for No. 114, Lucerne, or ask the USGS for Lucerne.

Directions: From Wenatchee, drive north 33 miles on U.S. 97 to Chelan. Lady of the Lake Ferry Terminal is on U.S. 97 Alternate just before entering downtown. Catch the passenger ferry to Lucerne. The trailhead is located at the ferry stop.

Contact: North Cascades National Park, Golden West Visitor Center, Stehekin, WA, 360/856-5700, ext. 340; Lady of the Lake Ferry Service, 1418 W. Woodin Ave., Chelan, WA 98816, 509/682-4584.

75 EMERALD PARK

14.2 mi/1-3 days 　　　🏃3 △9

within Glacier Peak Wilderness west of
Lake Chelan

Map 3.2, page 112

Below the high summits of the Chelan Mountains is a lush escape from the surrounding dry
climate. Green meadows sit within a deep,
rocky basin, where Emerald Peak and Pinnacle Peak tower 3,000 feet above Emerald
Park. The trail can be accomplished as a full
day of hiking, but two or three days is best.
The basin deserves exploration and a trip up
to Millham Pass is well recommended. The
area is remote and belongs mostly to coyotes
and the stars.

A passenger ferry is the only option to the
trailhead at Lucerne, three-quarters of the way
up Lake Chelan on the western shore. The
route spends 1.6 miles on Domke Lake Trail
before heading off on Emerald Park Trail. A
short 0.5 mile later the trail splits again; head
to the left, saving Railroad Creek for another
day. Five miles of trail slowly makes its way
up the valley, gaining 3,000 feet. The trail is
often far above the creek, making water scarce.
At Emerald Park, the forest gives way to green,
open meadows and astounding views of the
basin. Emerald Park Camp is 7.1 miles from
Lucerne.

User Groups: Hikers, leashed dogs, and horses.
No mountain bikes are allowed. No wheelchair access.

Permits: This trail is accessible July–September. Permits are not required. Parking and access are free.

Maps: For a map of Wenatchee National Forest, contact the Outdoor Recreation Information Center at the downtown Seattle REI. For
topographic maps, ask Green Trails for No.
114, Lucerne, or ask the USGS for Holden,
Pinnacle Mountain, and Lucerne.

Directions: From Wenatchee, drive north 33
miles on U.S. 97 to Chelan. Lady of the Lake
Ferry Terminal is on U.S. 97 Alternate just before entering downtown. Catch the passenger
ferry to Lucerne. The trailhead is located at
the ferry stop.

Contact: North Cascades National Park,
Golden West Visitor Center, Stehekin, WA,
360/856-5700, ext. 340; Lady of the Lake
Ferry Service, 1418 W. Woodin Ave., Chelan,
WA 98816, 509/682-4584.

76 TWISP PASS

4.2 mi/3.0 hr 　　　🏃4 △9

northwest of Twisp in Lake Chelan-Sawtooth
Wilderness of Okanogan National Forest

Map 3.2, page 112

The upper Sawtooth Mountain Range is full of
natural beauty; wildflowers envelop mountain
meadows in color in the early summer while
subalpine larches light up the hillsides during
the fall. The trail to Twisp Pass encounters
both, as well as impressive views of crowded
mountain peaks in all directions. It's one of
the best day hikes in the Twisp Valley, but
it also serves hikers looking for longer trips.
The trail is a major route into the North Cascades National Park, on the western side of the
pass. An additional 4.3 miles delivers hikers
to Bridge Creek and a junction of four major
trails. Day hikers will be content with the pass
and Dagger Lake, just inside the park.

The trail is a steep one, gaining 2,400 feet
on the way to the pass. The first 2 miles are
well forested and come to a trail junction. The
right fork heads up to Copper Pass, an equally
impressive gap within the mighty Sawtooths.
A great loop can be made via Copper Pass and
Bridge Creek for 20.5 miles. Stay to the left
for Twisp Pass, climbing steeply through rocky
meadows to Twisp Pass. Water is scarce after
the junction, so bring plenty. Lincoln Butte
and Twisp Mountain stand tall on either side
of the pass, while Dagger Lake sparkles from
below. A quick mile's descent into the park
arrives at an established camp at Dagger Lake.
A backcountry permit from the national park
is required for overnight stays here.

User Groups: Hikers, leashed dogs (up to

Twisp Pass, but not beyond), and horses. No mountain bikes are allowed. No wheelchair access.

Permits: This trail is accessible July–September. A federal Northwest Forest Pass is required to park here.

Maps: For a map of Okanogan National Forest, contact the Outdoor Recreation Information Center at the downtown Seattle REI. For topographic maps, ask Green Trails for No. 82, Stehekin, or ask the USGS for Gilbert.

Directions: From Twisp, drive east 26 miles on Twisp River Road (Forest Service Road 44 becomes Forest Service Road 4440) to the trailhead at road's end.

Contact: Okanogan National Forest, Methow Valley Ranger Station, 24 W. Chewuch Rd., Winthrop, WA 98862, 509/996-4000.

7 7 NORTH CREEK
9.2 mi/4.5 hr

northwest of Twisp in Lake Chelan–Sawtooth Wilderness of Okanogan National Forest

Map 3.2, page 112

North Creek presents one of the Twisp Valley's more gentle and accessible lake hikes. The trail climbs just 2,200 feet over 4.6 miles, a relative cakewalk compared to the routes for some other lakes in the valley. The valley nearly encircles Gilbert Mountain, offering a chance to view the rugged peak from nearly every side. To add color to the scenery, wildflowers light up the open meadows around the lake during July.

After passing through an old timber harvest, the trail climbs through a forest of Douglas fir and ponderosa pine. The trail occasionally passes through avalanche chutes where snow can stick around into July some years. When it does, passage is difficult. Despite the arid conditions of Eastern Cascades, this valley received a fair amount of carving by Ice Age glaciers, leaving it flat and wide. The trail follows the creek for the most part, following the natural loop of the valley, eventually turning

south before encountering the lake. Gilbert Mountain looms high above from the south, more than 2,000 feet overhead. Exploration above the lake is best avoided; vertical shafts and loose rock remain from previous mining activity, as well as fragile meadows that don't endure hiking boots well.

User Groups: Hikers, leashed dogs, and horses. No mountain bikes are allowed. No wheelchair access.

Permits: This trail is accessible June–mid-October. A federal Northwest Forest Pass is required to park here.

Maps: For a map of Okanogan National Forest, contact the Outdoor Recreation Information Center at the downtown Seattle REI. For topographic maps, ask Green Trails for No. 82, Stehekin, or ask the USGS for Gilbert.

Directions: From Twisp, drive east 26 miles on Twisp River Road (Forest Service Road 44 becomes Forest Service Road 4440) to the trailhead at road's end.

Contact: Okanogan National Forest, Methow Valley Ranger Station, 24 W. Chewuch Rd., Winthrop, WA 98862, 509/996-4000.

7 8 LOUIS LAKE
11.4 mi/6.0 hr

northwest of Twisp in Lake Chelan–Sawtooth Wilderness of Okanogan National Forest

Map 3.2, page 112

Louis Lake is one of the best deals in the Twisp Valley. Less grueling than other routes in the valley, Louis Lake Trail visits the most scenic lakes in the Sawtooth Range. Grand examples of Englemann spruce, Douglas fir, and whitebark pine battle with mountain views for your attention. It's an epic bout, although the great ridges dominating the skyline win out. To top it all off, Louis Lake sits within a narrow, rugged valley surrounded by some of the range's most jagged ridges. Visitors to the Twisp area are well advised to consider Louis Lake for a day trip, as this challenging trail is one of the area's best and most scenic hikes.

The route begins along South Creek Trail before Louis Lake Trail cuts to the south (2.1 miles). The trail travels straight toward the ridge before the valley turns 90 degrees, revealing a narrow slot. The forest breaks into meadows often, revealing South Creek Butte and Crescent Mountain. Louis Lake (5.3 miles) sits in a picturesque setting, surrounded by meadows of heather and harboring a small, tree-covered island. Steep valley walls lead to a sharp ridge around the basin, highlighted by a tall peak of 8,142 feet. Despite its popularity during the summer, Louis Lake is an outstanding Twisp Valley destination.

User Groups: Hikers, leashed dogs, and horses. No mountain bikes are allowed. No wheelchair access.

Permits: This trail is accessible mid-June–October. A federal Northwest Forest Pass is required to park here.

Maps: For a map of Okanogan National Forest, contact the Outdoor Recreation Information Center at the downtown Seattle REI. For topographic maps, ask Green Trails for No. 82, Stehekin, or ask the USGS for Gilbert.

Directions: From Twisp, drive east 22 miles on Twisp River Road (Forest Service Road 44 becomes Forest Service Road 4440) to South Creek Trailhead on the right.

Contact: Okanogan National Forest, Methow Valley Ranger Station, 24 W. Chewuch Rd., Winthrop, WA 98862, 509/996-4000.

79 SCATTER CREEK
8.6 mi/6.0 hr

northwest of Twisp in Lake Chelan-Sawtooth Wilderness of Okanogan National Forest

Map 3.2, page 112

The prime time to visit Scatter Lake is fall, when wildly colorful larches mark the perimeter of this deep blue pool. To add to the array of colors, afternoon sunlight brings out the deep red of high Abernathy Peak. Scatter Lake offers lots of color to make up for the punishing hike. In fact, punishing may be a light

word for 3,800 feet of elevation gain contained within four short miles. But that's the way of the Twisp Valley. The scenery around Scatter Lake easily makes up for it.

The route begins along Twisp River Trail but quickly turns onto Scatter Creek Trail (0.2 mile). The trail begins a short series of switchbacks before abandoning them altogether for the alternative of a straight ascent up the valley. Scatter Creek is always at hand offering cool refreshment. Scatter Creek Trail crosses the creek before climbing the final mile to the lake. Wildflowers are prolific in the open meadows during July. Abernathy Peak, at 8,321 feet, looks down from the talus-strewn ridge around the lake basin.

User Groups: Hikers, leashed dogs, and horses. No mountain bikes are allowed. No wheelchair access.

Permits: This trail is accessible June–October. A federal Northwest Forest Pass is required to park here.

Maps: For a map of Okanogan National Forest, contact the Outdoor Recreation Information Center at the downtown Seattle REI. For topographic maps, ask Green Trails for No. 82, Stehekin, or ask the USGS for Gilbert and Midnight Mountain.

Directions: From Twisp, drive east 22 miles on Twisp River Road (Forest Service Road 44 becomes Forest Service Road 4440) to South Creek Trailhead on the right.

Contact: Okanogan National Forest, Methow Valley Ranger Station, 24 W. Chewuch Rd., Winthrop, WA 98862, 509/996-4000.

80 SLATE CREEK
10.2 mi/6.0 hr

northwest of Twisp in Lake Chelan-Sawtooth Wilderness of Okanogan National Forest

Map 3.2, page 112

Slate Lake is the most brutal of the Twisp Valley lake hikes. Other appropriate descriptions include terrorizing, demanding, and exceptionally beautiful. Such words go along with

3,800-foot elevation gains laid out over just 3 miles. The lake is set back within a recess along the Abernathy Ridge, nearly becoming a part of the Wolf Creek drainage. Instead, the lake drains into Little Slate Creek and down to Twisp River. The terrain is fairly open, as the forest struggles to thicken for lack of much precipitation. This makes for good views and excellent scrambling.

Slate Creek Trail gets all the work out of the way in the first 3 miles. In this stretch, the trail climbs straight up to a knob on the west side of the creek. This ascent is dry and extremely demanding on hot summer days. From this point, however, the views are outstanding. The rugged Sawtooth Range stretches out across from the entire length of the Twisp River. Midnight and 3 A.M. Mountains are directly across from Little Slate Creek. From here, the trail follows at a nearly even grade along the ridge enclosing Slate Lake. Those with energy left can take advantage of the great scrambling opportunities around the lake. Despite the treacherous ascent up, Slate Lake is the best lake in the valley for those with an adventurous spirit.

User Groups: Hikers, leashed dogs, and horses. No mountain bikes are allowed. No wheelchair access.

Permits: This trail is accessible June–October. A federal Northwest Forest Pass is required to park here.

Maps: For a map of Okanogan National Forest, contact the Outdoor Recreation Information Center at the downtown Seattle REI. For topographic maps, ask Green Trails for No. 83, Buttermilk Butte, or ask the USGS for Midnight Mountain.

Directions: From Twisp, drive east 18 miles on Twisp River Road (Forest Service Road 44 becomes Forest Service Road 4440) to Slate Creek Trailhead on the right.

Contact: Okanogan National Forest, Methow Valley Ranger Station, 24 W. Chewuch Rd., Winthrop, WA 98862, 509/996-4000.

81 WILLIAMS CREEK
13.6 mi/8.0 hr   🏃4 ⛰️7

northwest of Twisp in Lake Chelan-Sawtooth Wilderness of Okanogan National Forest

Map 3.2, page 112

Williams Creek Trail starts low and ends high. Make no mistake about that. If you're into difficult 3,700-foot elevation gains, then perhaps this is the perfect trail for you. The most distinctive facet of the route is its passage through an old forest burn. Although the fire occurred decades ago, the forest remains open. Significant regenerative growth has taken place, staging an interesting example of forest dynamics.

Williams Lake is set within a great bowl, where Williams Butte and War Creek Ridge rim the basin. Meadows are prolific around the lake, with July flowers as bright as the sky. The trail to the lake follows the creek the entire way, staying to the north side. The trail is popular with equestrians, as there is a horse camp just before the lake. While the lake is stocked, fishing reviews are mixed. If you're going to hike almost 7 miles, though, you might as well bring your pole and try to catch some lunch.

User Groups: Hikers, leashed dogs, and horses. No mountain bikes are allowed. No wheelchair access.

Permits: This trail is accessible June–October. A federal Northwest Forest Pass is required to park here.

Maps: For a map of Okanogan National Forest, contact the Outdoor Recreation Information Center at the downtown Seattle REI. For topographic maps, ask Green Trails for No. 82, Stehekin, and No. 83, Buttermilk Butte, or ask the USGS for Gilbert, Midnight Mountain, and Sun Mountain.

Directions: From Twisp, drive east 19 miles on Twisp River Road (Forest Service Road 44) to Mystery Campground. Turn left on Forest Service Road 4430, cross the river, and stay left for 0.5 mile to Williams Creek Trailhead on the right.

Contact: Okanogan National Forest, Methow Valley Ranger Station, 24 W. Chewuch Rd., Winthrop, WA 98862, 509/996-4000.

82 NORTH WAR CREEK

19.0 mi/2 days

west of Twisp in Lake Chelan-Sawtooth Wilderness of Okanogan National Forest

Map 3.2, page 112

North War Creek Trail is the most northern and scenic route to Chelan Summit Trail. The trail makes a long gradual ascent to War Creek Pass, where the high-country Lake Juanita awaits. A side trail leads to the summit of Boulder Butte, where the views of much of the North Cascades are superb. Most hikers on this trail are completing the longer Chelan Summit Loop and wish to exit via the Twisp River. Nonetheless, War Creek is a great excursion for those wanting to see what the Sawtooth Ridge has to offer.

North War Creek Trail parallels the stream for nearly its entire length. The grade is gentle until the end, where the last mile rises to the pass. Forests of old-growth pine and spruce blanket the valley, adding shade on hot days, although parts of the forest are scarred from a 1994 fire. The trail crests at War Creek Pass in a subalpine setting, where meadows cover the crest and views extend in many directions. Lake Juanita is below with a hiker and horse camp. The trail up to Boulder Butte is highly recommended and not to be missed by any who have ventured this far. From War Creek Pass, trails lead down Purple Creek to Stehekin, up Boulder Creek, and down the crest of the Sawtooth Mountains.

User Groups: Hikers, leashed dogs, and horses. No mountain bikes are allowed. No wheelchair access.

Permits: This trail is accessible late June–October. A federal Northwest Forest Pass is required to park here.

Maps: For a map of Okanogan National Forest, contact the Outdoor Recreation Information Center at the downtown Seattle REI. For topographic maps, ask Green Trails for No. 82, Stehekin, and No. 83, Buttermilk Butte, or ask the USGS for Sun Mountain and Oval Peak.

Directions: From Twisp, drive east 15 miles on Twisp River Road (Forest Service Road 44) to Forest Service Road 4430. Turn left on Forest Service Road 4430, cross the river, and stay right for 1 mile to Forest Service Road 100. Turn left and drive 1.5 miles to the trailhead at road's end.

Contact: Okanogan National Forest, Methow Valley Ranger Station, 24 W. Chewuch Rd., Winthrop, WA 98862, 509/996-4000.

83 OVAL LAKES

15.0-22.6 mi/2-3 days

west of Twisp in Lake Chelan-Sawtooth Wilderness of Okanogan National Forest

Map 3.2, page 112   **BEST (**

The Sawtooth Range east of Lake Chelan is full of great adventures and destinations. Situated along the high mountainous crest, Oval Lakes are one of the range's most beautiful locales. These three lakes lie within small, rocky basins at the head of Oval Creek. Subalpine larches eke out an existence here, at nearly 7,000 feet. The lakes have great camping and offer great exploration, with loads of views from Oval Pass.

The route begins on Eagle Creek Trail but soon cuts off on Oval Creek Trail (1.9 miles). The old forest provides welcome shade for a while but begins to break into meadows and views. West Oval Lake is achieved via a short side trail (at 7.2 miles) but is not open to camping. Check it out, get a taste of what's ahead, and continue to Middle Oval Lake (8.9 miles) or East Oval Lake (9.4 miles). The fishing's good but the camping's even better. One look at the rocky ridges ringing the lakes, and you'll know why this is called the Sawtooth Wilderness.

Between West Oval and Middle Oval Lakes,

be sure to hike a quick 0.25 mile to Oval Pass and views of Tuckaway Basin. Adventurous hikers with a map can initially follow Eagle Creek Trail to Eagle Pass and around Tuckaway Lake to Oval Pass, a lasso-shaped loop of 22.6 miles.

User Groups: Hikers, leashed dogs, and horses. No mountain bikes are allowed. No wheelchair access.

Permits: This trail is accessible July–mid-October. A federal Northwest Forest Pass is required to park here.

Maps: For a map of Okanogan National Forest, contact the Outdoor Recreation Information Center at the downtown Seattle REI. For topographic maps, ask Green Trails for No. 83, Buttermilk Butte, or ask the USGS for Sun Mountain and Oval Peak.

Directions: From Twisp, drive east 15 miles on Twisp River Road (Forest Service Road 44) to Forest Service Road 4430. Turn left on Forest Service Road 4430, cross the river, and stay to the left for 1 mile to Forest Service Road 080. Turn right and drive 1.5 miles to the trailhead at road's end.

Contact: Okanogan National Forest, Methow Valley Ranger Station, 24 W. Chewuch Rd., Winthrop, WA 98862, 509/996-4000.

84 WOLF CREEK

19.8 mi/2 days

west of Winthrop in Lake Chelan-Sawtooth Wilderness of Okanogan National Forest

Map 3.2, page 112

Gardner Meadows caps one of the region's most beautiful valley treks. Wolf Creek Trail ventures 10 miles into Wolf Creek valley, ending where Abernathy Ridge and Gardner Mountain loom high above the open parkland. Although the trail is popular with equestrians and hunters during fall, an abundance of wildlife awaits to be seen. Lupine and glacier lilies paint the meadows with color during early summer while deer and coyotes roam the open expanse. And there's no end to exploring off the main trail, as several nonmaintained trails lead into side valleys.

Wolf Creek Trail ascends gently over 10 miles to Gardner Meadows. The trail never strays far from the creek, which is locally known for booming bull trout populations. Most of the route passes through forests of huge Douglas fir and ponderosa pines. Side trails include one up the North Fork Wolf Creek at 2.7 miles, one up the South Fork Wolf Creek at 6.5 miles, and another up Hubbard Creek at 7.2 miles; none of them are maintained. Less maintenance, however, usually means more adventure.

Gardner Meadows is set upon wide-open rolling hills. Patches of trees litter the terrain, which runs up to steep, scree-covered slopes. Scrambles farther up to Abernathy Lake or to the top of Abernathy Ridge are well advised for those looking for off-trail travel. Rumors continue to persist regarding gray wolves within the appropriately named valley. Reported sightings have not been confirmed and are most likely coyotes, which are abundant here. Sightings of gray wolves in the North Cascades have been confirmed only north of Highway 20.

User Groups: Hikers, leashed dogs, and horses. No mountain bikes are allowed. No wheelchair access.

Permits: This trail is accessible June–September. A federal Northwest Forest Pass is required to park here.

Maps: For a map of Okanogan National Forest, contact the Outdoor Recreation Information Center at the downtown Seattle REI. For topographic maps, ask Green Trails for No. 83, Buttermilk Butte, or ask the USGS for Thompson Ridge, Gilbert, and Midnight Mountain.

Directions: From Winthrop, drive east on Highway 20 to Twin Lakes Road (County Road 9120). Turn right (west) and drive 1.5 miles to Wolf Creek Road (County Road 1145). Turn right and drive 5 miles to the trailhead at road's end.

Contact: Okanogan National Forest, Methow

Valley Ranger Station, 24 W. Chewuch Rd., Winthrop, WA 98862, 509/996-4000.

85 EAST FORK BUTTERMILK CREEK
15.0 mi/1-2 days   👥2 ⛰5

west of Twisp in Lake Chelan-Sawtooth Wilderness of Okanogan National Forest

Map 3.2, page 112

East Fork Buttermilk Creek is much like the West Fork. It's a hike through a forest that really isn't worth the time it takes to hike it. It's always nice to get out and enjoy nature, but there are many other trails within the area that are far more deserving of your time. That said, there are still some good things about this trail. Those good things are mainly limited to large forests near the creek and some great views at Hoodoo Pass. Unless you've hiked many other trails in the area and are looking for a new experience, East Fork Buttermilk Creek just isn't all that special.

The trail is laid out on an old mining road for the first 4 miles. Forests of Englemann spruce and lodgepole pine cover the valley and occasionally provide glimpses of surrounding ridges. The trail is not steep until it reaches the headwaters of the creek in Hoodoo Basin. Here, it abruptly ascends to Hoodoo Pass (7.5 miles). Views to the north and south are well worth a long stop here. The trail drops to Chelan Summit Trail (8.8 miles). Backpackers should plan on camping at Hoodoo Pass or at the junction of Chelan Summit Trail.

User Groups: Hikers, leashed dogs, and horses. No mountain bikes are allowed. No wheelchair access.

Permits: This trail is accessible mid-June–October. A federal Northwest Forest Pass is required to park here.

Maps: For a map of Okanogan National Forest, contact the Outdoor Recreation Information Center at the downtown Seattle REI. For topographic maps, ask Green Trails for No. 83, Buttermilk Butte, and No. 115, Prince Creek, or ask the USGS for Hoodoo Peak and Martin Peak.

Directions: From Twisp, drive east 11 miles on Twisp River Road to Forest Service Road 43. Turn left and drive 6 miles to Forest Service Road 400. Turn right and drive 3.5 miles to the trailhead on the left.

Contact: Okanogan National Forest, Methow Valley Ranger Station, 24 W. Chewuch Rd., Winthrop, WA 98862, 509/996-4000.

86 LIBBY CREEK
10.4 mi/6.0 hr   👥4 ⛰8

southwest of Twisp in Lake Chelan-Sawtooth Wilderness of Okanogan National Forest

Map 3.2, page 112

Libby Lake sits within its own amphitheater. Large, towering walls of granite ringing the high lake give way to large slopes of boulders and talus. But the lake is not easy to reach. Several elevation drops along the way are relentlessly followed by difficult climbs. But Libby Lake is well regarded and always enjoyable.

Libby Creek Trail begins on an old logging road and climbs steadily before becoming a real trail. The path eventually drops to cross the North Fork of Libby Creek, a great time to dip one's head in the cold water and cool off. The trail remains within the wide, forested valley bottom, crossing another pair of small creeks, sometimes dry. Tall Hoodoo Peak is to the north. The trail makes a final charge upward just before the lake. Remnants of a very old cabin can be seen to the side of the trail, beaten up by heavy winter snowfalls. There are several campsites below the lake, a quiet and inviting overnight stay. The lake itself is ringed by broken talus and subalpine larches, subsisting in this harsh, almost barren, mountain hideaway.

User Groups: Hikers, leashed dogs, and horses. No mountain bikes are allowed. No wheelchair access.

Permits: This trail is accessible May–October.

No permits are required. Parking and access are free.

Maps: For a map of Okanogan National Forest, contact the Outdoor Recreation Information Center at the downtown Seattle REI. For topographic maps, ask Green Trails for No. 83, Buttermilk Butte, and No. 115, Prince Creek, or ask the USGS for Hoodoo Peak.

Directions: From Twisp, drive east 3 miles on Highway 20 to Highway 153. Turn right onto Okanogan County Road 1045 and drive to Forest Service Road 43. Turn left and drive 5.5 miles to Forest Service Road 4340. Turn left and drive 1.5 miles to Forest Service Road 4340-700. Turn right and drive 1.5 miles to Forest Service Road 4340-750. Turn left and drive to the signed trailhead.

Contact: Okanogan National Forest, Methow Valley Ranger Station, 24 W. Chewuch Rd., Winthrop, WA 98862, 509/996-4000.

87 MARTIN LAKES
14.2 mi/2 days

southwest of Twisp in Lake Chelan-Sawtooth Wilderness of Okanogan National Forest

Map 3.2, page 112

Martin Lakes are a great first experience of the Sawtooths, a place of high lakes and higher peaks. Surrounded on three sides by woods and on another by the larch-dotted base of Martin Peak, the lakes offer a lot of peace, quiet, and most likely, solitude. Dinner's never more than a few casts away, either, as the lakes sport a good deal of healthy trout. It's enough to make hungry hikers curse forgotten poles.

The trail is in good condition and makes a steady, modest incline. The route begins on Eagle Lakes Trail but splits onto Martin Creek Trail (2.3 miles). The trail regularly opens to provide views of the opposing ridge and beyond, preventing feelings of forest claustrophobia. The two Martin Lakes are down a short and signed side trail at 6.3 miles. Several good campsites are found at the lower

lake. High peaks and ridges surround the large basin. Clark's nutcrackers swoop about the whitebark pines, and hawks give the numerous chipmunks chase.

User Groups: Hikers, leashed dogs, horses, mountain bikes, and motorcycles (motorcycles most of the way). No wheelchair access.

Permits: This trail is accessible July–mid-October. A federal Northwest Forest Pass is required to park here.

Maps: For a map of Okanogan National Forest, contact the Outdoor Recreation Information Center at the downtown Seattle REI. For topographic maps, ask Green Trails for No. 115, Prince Creek, or ask the USGS for Martin Peak.

Directions: From Pateros, drive north on Highway 153. Turn left onto Gold Creek Loop Road, south of the town of Carlton. Turn left (west) onto Forest Service Road 4340. Drive about 6 miles to Forest Service Road 4340-300. Turn left and drive for about 5 miles to the trailhead at road's end.

Contact: Okanogan National Forest, Methow Valley Ranger Station, 24 W. Chewuch Rd., Winthrop, WA 98862, 509/996-4000.

88 CRATER LAKE
7.4 mi/4.0 hr

southwest of Twisp in Lake Chelan-Sawtooth Wilderness of Okanogan National Forest

Map 3.2, page 112

Crater Lake is not the result of a large meteor hitting the Sawtooths. Nor was it created by a long-ago volcanic eruption. So erase the image of a crater from your mind, and replace it with tall, jagged ridges, craggy peaks, colorful larches, and blue mountain water. Voilà, you have a picture of the real Crater Lake. It's a good day hike and shows what the Sawtooths have to offer.

The route begins on Eagle Lake Trail, cutting to the right just after crossing Crater Creek (0.5 mile). It moves quickly up the valley at a moderate grade. Crossing the creek again, it climbs more steeply. Before long, you'll be swearing the trail feels like more than the posted 3 miles from the junction. After a large granite outcrop, which reveals most of Eastern Washington, the trail levels off and hits the lake. There are several spots for camping at the outlet of the lake. This is a favorite spot for high-country anglers.

User Groups: Hikers, leashed dogs, horses, and mountain bikes. No wheelchair access.

Permits: This trail is accessible July–mid-October. A federal Northwest Forest Pass is required to park here.

Maps: For a map of Okanogan National Forest, contact the Outdoor Recreation Information Center at the downtown Seattle REI. For topographic maps, ask Green Trails for No. 115, Prince Creek, or ask the USGS for Martin Peak.

Directions: From Pateros, drive north on Highway 153. Turn left onto Gold Creek Loop Road, south of the town of Carlton. Turn left (west) onto Forest Service Road 4340. Drive about 6 miles to Forest Service Road 4340-300. Turn left and drive for about 5 miles to the trailhead at road's end.

Contact: Okanogan National Forest, Methow Valley Ranger Station, 24 W. Chewuch Rd., Winthrop, WA 98862, 509/996-4000.

89 EAGLE LAKES
12.3 mi/1-2 days

southwest of Twisp in Lake Chelan-Sawtooth Wilderness of Okanogan National Forest

Map 3.2, page 112

Take a trip to Eagle Lakes and you are likely to run into folks who have been coming here for 35 years or more. They enthusiastically call it home, and it's easy to understand why. Set below the towering granite walls of Mount Bigelow, Upper Eagle Lake enjoys a grand forest of subalpine larch and fir. A beautiful trail to the lakes and pretty decent fishing make this a popular choice in the South Sawtooth Range.

Eagle Lakes Trail climbs for much of its length but never too steeply. After Martin Lakes junction (2.5 miles), the forest begins to open up along Eagle Lakes Trail, providing a welcome view and appreciation of how far one has come. The trail passes granite outcroppings and very large Douglas firs and ponderosa pines. The junction for Upper Eagle Lake arrives first (5.8 miles) and climbs a short 0.5 mile to the lake. Campsites ring the eastern shore, opposite the rocky slopes of the western shore. Upper Lake is definitely the better choice. Lower Eagle Lake Trail drops to the left (6.1 miles) to the more forested and larger lake, home to a horse camp.

User Groups: Hikers, leashed dogs, horses, mountain bikes, and motorcycles. No wheelchair access.

Permits: This trail is accessible July–mid-October. A federal Northwest Forest Pass is required to park here.

Maps: For a map of Okanogan National Forest, contact the Outdoor Recreation Information Center at the downtown Seattle REI. For topographic maps, ask Green Trails for No. 115, Prince Creek, or ask the USGS for Martin Peak.

Directions: From Pateros, drive north on Highway 153. Turn left onto Gold Creek Loop Road, south of the town of Carlton. Turn left (west) onto Forest Service Road 4340. Drive about 6 miles to Forest Service Road 4340-300. Turn left and drive for about 5 miles to the trailhead at road's end.

Contact: Okanogan National Forest, Methow Valley Ranger Station, 24 W. Chewuch Rd., Winthrop, WA 98862, 509/996-4000.

90 BUCK CREEK PASS
20.5 mi/2 days

north of Trinity in Glacier Peak Wilderness of Wenatchee National Forest

Map 3.2, page 112

Great by itself, Buck Creek Pass is also the means to grander ends. The pass is between three high peaks, each of them offering exceptional views of surrounding peaks and mountain ranges. The views are first-rate, but the wildflower meadows are what draw crowds of folks up the trail each year. In fact, Flower Dome could not be better named, for a blanket of flowers covers it entirely during July. Glacier Peak is a regular fixture, its mighty glaciers well revealed.

Buck Creek Trail leaves the town of Trinity along the road but quickly enters Glacier Peak Wilderness. The trail splits (2 miles), so stick to the left, cross the Chiwawa River via bridge, and head up Buck Creek Valley through large forests of Douglas fir, Englemann spruce, and hemlock.

Buck Creek Pass is achieved after a tiring 10 miles. Numerous campsites line the trail and are widespread at the pass. Once camp is set up, the exploration can begin. Absolutely necessary is a 1-mile trip up Flower Dome, awash in wildflower color. Another trail climbs to the top of Liberty Cap. For the hearty, a difficult trail heads toward High Pass and barren Triad Lake. Much of the area is delicate and receives heavy traffic, so be sure to take care where you step.

User Groups: Hikers, leashed dogs, and horses. No mountain bikes are allowed. No wheelchair access.

Permits: This trail is accessible July–September. A federal Northwest Forest Pass is required to park here.

Maps: For a map of Wenatchee National Forest, contact the Outdoor Recreation Information Center at the downtown Seattle REI. For topographic maps, ask Green Trails for No. 113, Holden, or ask the USGS for Trinity, Clark Mountain, and Suiattle Pass.

Directions: From Leavenworth, drive west on Highway 2 to Highway 207, at Coles Corner. Veer left to Fish Lake and drive 1 mile to Chiwawa Valley Road (Forest Service Road 62). Turn left and drive to Trinity. The trailhead is at road's end, just beyond Phelps Creek Campground.

Contact: Wenatchee National Forest, Lake Wenatchee Ranger District, 22976 Hwy. 207, Leavenworth, WA 98826, 509/548-2550.

91 PHELPS CREEK (SPIDER MEADOW)

17.0 mi/2 days

north of Lake Wenatchee in Glacier Peak Wilderness of Wenatchee National Forest

Map 3.2, page 112

Officially, the route is named Phelps Creek Trail. But within Washington hiking circles, it is better known as Spider Meadow, after the enormous meadows within the elongated valley. At the head of the valley slides Spider Glacier, Washington's easiest glacier to explore. Nearly a mile long but not more than 150 feet across, Spider Glacier ends at scenic Spider Gap, with views of the North Cascades. Few trails this scenic are this easy.

Phelps Creek Trail follows an old logging road but soon enters Glacier Peak Wilderness (1 mile). The forest grows older and larger, and edible mushrooms are regularly spotted. Chicken-of-the-woods and bear's head tooth fungus are easily identifiable by beginners, but be sure to leave trailside specimens alone for others to enjoy. The trail breaks into Spider Meadow (4 miles). The obvious U shape to the valley is the work of the valley's previous tenant, a glacier. Camping must only be done at established campsites; there are about 30 throughout the lower valley.

After climbing out of the meadow (5 miles), the trail climbs to Spider Glacier, to the east. This glacier is completely nontechnical and can be traversed easily by all. At the top is Spider Gap, with views to the north of the larger Lyman Glacier and various North Cascade peaks. There are an additional 10 campsites within this upper basin. Expect a lot of people here on summer weekends.

User Groups: Hikers, leashed dogs, and horses (horses allowed up to Spider Meadow only). No mountain bikes are allowed. No wheelchair access.

Permits: This trail is accessible mid-June–September. A federal Northwest Forest Pass is required to park here.

Maps: For a map of Wenatchee National Forest, contact the Outdoor Recreation Information Center at the downtown Seattle REI. For topographic maps, ask Green Trails for No. 113, Holden, or ask the USGS for Trinity, Holden, and Suiattle Pass.

Directions: From Leavenworth, drive west on Highway 2 to Highway 207, at Coles Corner. Turn left and drive to Fish Lake and drive 1 mile to Chiwawa Valley Road (Forest Service Road 62). Turn left and drive toward Trinity. Just before Trinity, turn right on Forest Service Road 6211 and drive to the trailhead at road's end.

Contact: Wenatchee National Forest, Lake Wenatchee Ranger District, 22976 Hwy. 207, Leavenworth, WA 98826, 509/548-2550.

92 ENTIAT MEADOWS
29.6 mi/3-4 days

northwest of Entiat in Glacier Peak Wilderness of Wenatchee National Forest

Map 3.2, page 112

After 15 miles, a trail needs to offer something special. I'm talking large peaks or glaciers, wide-open meadows with wildflowers, or lots of wildlife. Actually, that's what Entiat River Trail delivers, making its easy but long route well worth the trip.

Entiat River Trail quietly follows the Entiat River to its headwaters, making little substantial change in elevation. The first 10 miles are forested by large Englemann spruce, silver fir, and Douglas fir. Soon, the valley opens into meadows, and Tin Pan Mountain welcomes you to true backcountry. The trail turns west with the valley and Seven Fingered Jack beckons from the end of the valley, encouraging hikers to keep moving. There are good camps throughout this section of the trail for resting tired feet. Many hours from the car, Entiat River Trail arrives at its terminus among meadows and enormous piles of glacier moraine.

Entiat Glacier covers the backside of Maude Mountain, breaking and crackling during warm summer days. Mountain goats regularly patrol the steep valley walls in pursuit of dinner. Their bright white coats are easy to spot. There are many deer in the valley, and there is always a good chance of seeing a cougar or bobcat. This spot is far from any civilization, a very welcome bargain indeed.

User Groups: Hikers, leashed dogs, horses, and mountain bikes (horses and mountain bikes not allowed in wilderness area). No wheelchair access.

Permits: This trail is accessible June–October. A federal Northwest Forest Pass is required to park here.

Maps: For a map of Wenatchee National Forest, contact the Outdoor Recreation Information Center at the downtown Seattle REI. For topographic maps, ask Green Trails for No. 113, Holden, and No. 114, Lucerne, or ask the USGS for Holden and Saska Peak.

Directions: From Wenatchee, drive north along U.S. 97 Alternate to Entiat. Turn left on Entiat River Road and drive 38 miles to the road's end, where the trailhead is located.

Contact: Wenatchee National Forest, Entiat Ranger Station, 2108 Entiat Way, P.O. Box 476, Entiat, WA 98822, 509/784-1511.

93 ICE LAKES
25.6 mi/2-3 days

northwest of Entiat in Glacier Peak Wilderness of Wenatchee National Forest

Map 3.2, page 112

Ice Lakes are true high country. Other than subalpine larches and big mountains, there is little else here. No worries, because Ice Lakes is phenomenally beautiful. Think of the Enchantments, but without the crowds or discouraging permit process. The upper Entiat Mountains rise above Ice Valley and surround the lakes. Hike up here in late

September and the larches will add radiant yellows and oranges to the landscape. Best of all, this trail is not exceptionally well known.

The journey to Ice Lakes is no piece of cake. First, hike 8 miles up Entiat River Trail. Cross the Entiat (troublesome in the spring) and wind up Ice Creek Valley through a forest filled with large Englemann spruce. First-night spots can be found on either side of the Entiat River crossing (8 miles), where Pomas Creek runs into Ice Creek (8.8 miles), and at Ice Camp (12.7 miles).

At Ice Camp, the trail turns downright nasty, scaling the valley wall (a 1,300-foot climb in 1 mile). This section often requires 90 minutes or more, so don't be discouraged. At the top is Lower Ice Lake, and a short mile farther is Upper Ice Lake. There is lots of camping to be had at the lakes, particularly the lower one. Plan for time to kick back and relax here, as it's time well spent. There are lots of scrambles to be had from here, including an ascent of 9,082-foot Mount Maude.

User Groups: Hikers, leashed dogs, and horses (horses up to Ice Camp; they won't be able to make it farther). No mountain bikes are allowed. No wheelchair access.

Permits: This trail is usually accessible mid-July–October. No permits are required. Parking and access are free.

Maps: For a map of Wenatchee National Forest, contact the Outdoor Recreation Information Center at the downtown Seattle REI. For topographic maps, ask Green Trails for No. 113, Holden, and No. 114, Lucerne, or ask the USGS for Holden, Saska Peak, and Pinnacle Mountain.

Directions: From Wenatchee, drive north along U.S. 97 Alternate to Entiat. Turn left on Entiat River Road and drive 38 miles to the road's end, where the well-signed trailhead is located.

Contact: Wenatchee National Forest, Entiat Ranger Station, 2108 Entiat Way, P.O. Box 476, Entiat, WA 98822, 509/784-1511.

94 PYRAMID MOUNTAIN
18.4 mi/1-2 days

west of Lake Chelan in Wenatchee National Forest

Map 3.2, page 112

Pyramid Mountain is for hikers looking to seemingly stand atop the state. From the lofty elevation of 8,243 feet, Pyramid Mountain provides a panorama rarely matched in the region. From the high ridge and even higher peak, one can see much of Lake Chelan, surrounding mountain ranges, and much of the Cascades. To attain such a high vantage is relatively easy thanks to a trailhead at 6,500 feet. Vistas this grand don't come this cheaply very often.

Pyramid Mountain Trail spends the length of its time along the Chelan Mountains' ridgeline among sparse meadows and subalpine trees. Passing Crow Hill, the trail hits a junction (2.7 miles); stay right to skirt below Graham Mountain. You'll endure a pair of elevation losses before climbing Pyramid Mountain, where an old fire lookout once stood. Camping can be done in accordance with Leave-No-Trace principles, but fires are never a good idea in this dry climate. Carrying extra water is important here, where the summer sun is scorching.

User Groups: Hikers, leashed dogs, horses, and mountain bikes. No wheelchair access.

Permits: This trail is accessible mid-July–September. No permits are required. Parking and access are free.

Maps: For a map of Wenatchee National Forest, contact the Outdoor Recreation Information Center at the downtown Seattle REI. For topographic maps, ask Green Trails for No. 114, Lucerne, or ask the USGS for Pyramid Mountain and Saksa Peak.

Directions: From Entiat, drive east on Entiat River Road to Forest Service Road 5900, just beyond Lake Creek Campground. Turn right and drive 8.5 miles to Forest Service Road 113 at Shady Pass. Turn left and drive 2 miles to the trailhead at road's end. This is a rough road and a high-clearance vehicle is recommended.

Contact: Wenatchee National Forest, Entiat Ranger Station, 2108 Entiat Way, P.O. Box 476, Entiat, WA 98822, 509/784-1511.

95 WALLACE FALLS
5.6 mi/3.0 hr   👣2 ⛺9

north of Gold Bar in Wallace Falls State Park

Map 3.3, page 113   **BEST (**

There are few better trails within such easy reach of Seattle. Wallace Falls are some of the Cascades' best-known waterfalls, with more than nine drops of at least 50 feet. The tallest cascade, with a drop of 265 feet, is visible from Highway 2. Why see something from the highway when you can check it out up close?

There are two options for reaching the falls, thanks to the hard work of volunteers. A direct route to the falls is achieved in 2.8 miles while a longer, gentler loop adds a mile. Either way, Wallace Falls is certainly made for the whole family and for all hikers. The trail leaves the trailhead before splitting into Woody Trail and Railroad Grade (the longer of the two). Traveling through forests of alder and fir, the trails meet near the bridge over the North Wallace River. Another mile up the trail reveals the numerous falls. It's wonderful during the spring, when snowmelt turns Wallace River into a torrent and adds spectacular drama to the falls. Also during the spring, many forest plants and flowers are in bloom, adding much color to the setting. The trail gets its fair share of visitors during the summer, but it's understandable why.

User Groups: Hikers and leashed dogs. No horses or mountain bikes are allowed. No wheelchair access.

Permits: This trail is accessible year-round. No permits are required. Parking and access are free.

Maps: For topographic maps, ask Green Trails for No. 142, Index, or ask the USGS for Gold Bar and Wallace Lake.

Directions: From Everett, drive east on U.S. 2 to the town of Gold Bar. Turn left (north) on 1st Street and follow the signs to the park entrance. The well-signed trailhead is near the main parking area in the park.

Contact: Wallace Falls State Park, 14503 Wallace Lake Rd., P.O. Box 230, Gold Bar, WA 98251, 360/793-0420.

96 BLANCA LAKE
7.0 mi/4.0 hr   👣4 ⛺9

northeast of Index in Henry M. Jackson Wilderness of Mount Baker-Snoqualmie National Forest

Map 3.3, page 113

Below a trio of towering peaks, Blanca Lake makes a scenic trip. With the large Columbia Glacier feeding the lake a steady stream of silt-filled runoff, the lake turns an intense turquoise that's perfect for photographs. The beauty of the lake and its surroundings are not without grinding effort. The trail makes a steep ascent to a pass at Virgin Lake before steeply dropping to the lake. From amid parkland meadows, however, views of Glacier Peak help to ease the leg-numbing switching.

Blanca Lake Trail dances the switchback shuffle, ascending 2,700 feet in just 3 miles. Forests of red cedar, Douglas fir, and western hemlock shade the way. Near the crest (2.7 miles), enjoy views of the inner peaks and ridges of the Cascades. Pass Virgin Lake and drop to Blanca Lake. Columbia Peak, Monte Cristo Peak, and Kyes Peak ring the large basin. Trails for exploration wander around the lake, but Columbia Glacier should be treated as off-limits. A number of good campsites ring the lake, but they see a lot of use, especially on summer weekends. Blanca Lake is well worth writing home about.

User Groups: Hikers and leashed dogs. No horses or mountain bikes are allowed. No wheelchair access.

Permits: This trail is accessible July–October. A federal Northwest Forest Pass is required to park here.

Maps: For a map of Mount Baker–Snoqualmie

National Forest, contact the Outdoor Recreation Information Center at the downtown Seattle REI. For topographic maps, ask Green Trails for No. 143, Monte Cristo, or ask the USGS for Blanca Lake.

Directions: From Everett, drive east on U.S. 2 until 0.5 mile east of the town of Skykomish. Turn left (north) onto the Beckler River Road (Forest Service Road 65) and drive over Jack Pass and to the road's end at a junction with North Fork Skykomish River Road (Forest Service Road 63). Turn right and drive about 3 miles to the clearly marked trailhead.

Contact: Mount Baker–Snoqualmie National Forest, Skykomish Ranger Station, 74920 NE Stevens Pass Hwy., Skykomish, WA 98288, 360/677-2414.

97 WEST CADY RIDGE
7.0-17.0 mi/1-2 days

north of Skykomish in Henry M. Jackson Wilderness of Mount Baker-Snoqualmie National Forest

Map 3.3, page 113

West Cady Ridge is blessed with miles of wide-open big-sky meadows. The views are supreme from nearly every inch of the trail, which rides the crest of the ridge straight to the PCT. Meadows of heather and wildflower aplenty cover the ridge, making July the time to hit this trail. Splendor this grand rarely comes at so easy a price. And topping it all off is the panoramic vista from atop Benchmark Mountain.

West Cady Ridge Trail reaches meadows in a quick but steep hike through great Cascade old-growth forest. The trees shrink before your eyes as you steadily climb higher. The trail finds the crest (3.5 miles, a good turnaround point for a shorter hike) and follows it to the PCT (8.5 miles). There are some ups and downs, but at all times the trail is easy to follow. Huckleberries line the route, an encouragement to take things slowly. A side trail (at 7 miles) shoots up Benchmark Mountain

to the summit. Backpackers are encouraged to explore this trail. At 5,816 feet, the summit reveals much of the Cascades. Hiking north on the PCT brings hikers to Pass Creek Trail, which can be used to make a loop out of West Cady Ridge.

User Groups: Hikers, leashed dogs, and horses. No mountain bikes are allowed. No wheelchair access.

Permits: This trail is accessible July–October. A federal Northwest Forest Pass is required to park here.

Maps: For a map of Mount Baker–Snoqualmie National Forest, contact the Outdoor Recreation Information Center at the downtown Seattle REI. For topographic maps, ask Green Trails for No. 143, Monte Cristo, and No. 144, Benchmark Mountain, or ask the USGS for Blanca Lake and Benchmark Mountain.

Directions: From Everett, drive east on U.S. 2 until 0.5 mile east of the town of Skykomish. Turn left (north) onto the Beckler River Road (Forest Service Road 65) and drive over Jack Pass and to the road's end at a junction with North Fork Skykomish River Road (Forest Service Road 63). Turn right and drive about 5 miles to the clearly marked trailhead at road's end.

Contact: Mount Baker–Snoqualmie National Forest, Skykomish Ranger Station, 74920 NE Stevens Pass Hwy., Skykomish, WA 98288, 360/677-2414.

98 CADY CREEK/LITTLE WENATCHEE LOOP
19.0 mi/2-3 days

north of Lake Wenatchee in Henry M. Jackson Wilderness of Wenatchee National Forest

Map 3.3, page 113

This is an excellent trip along the PCT. Using Cady Creek and Little Wenatchee River Trails, the route offers access to a pair of superb highcountry destinations. Meadows of wildflowers and sweeping vistas are the name of the game here, one of the PCT's most beautiful stretches. While the loop can be made in two days, three is far better. A more relaxed pace allows for side trips and more time in this exceptional place.

The route begins along Cady Creek, a gradual climb through old-growth forests to Cady Pass (5.2 miles). Cady Creek must be forded, but the cool water is refreshing on hot summer days. Hike north on the PCT through terrific meadows to Lake Sally Ann (10 miles) below Skykomish Peak. Lake Sally Ann has several great campsites.

The PCT continues north to Meander Meadow (12.3 miles), a large, flat basin overflowing with wildflowers. Several great camps are near the outlet of the meadow. Kodak Peak stands over the basin, offering panoramic views from the summit. Much of Glacier Peak and Henry M. Jackson Wildernesses are within sight. The route returns to the trailhead via Little Wenatchee River Trail, which is full of great forests and waterfalls. Much of the PCT is along north-facing slopes, where snow lingers late into summer, a consideration. All in all, this is an outstanding three-day weekend.

User Groups: Hikers, leashed dogs, and horses. No mountain bikes are allowed. No wheelchair access.

Permits: This trail is accessible mid-July–October. A federal Northwest Forest Pass is required to park here.

Maps: For a map of Wenatchee National Forest, contact the Outdoor Recreation Information Center at the downtown Seattle REI. For topographic maps, ask Green Trails for No. 144, Benchmark Mountain, or ask the USGS for Poe Mountain and Benchmark Mountain.

Directions: From Leavenworth, drive west on U.S. 2 to Highway 207, at Coles Corner. Turn left and drive to Little Wenatchee Road (Forest Service Road 65). Veer left and drive to the signed trailhead at road's end.

Contact: Wenatchee National Forest, Lake Wenatchee Ranger Station, 22976 Hwy. 207, Leavenworth, WA 98826, 509/763-3103.

99 FORTUNE PONDS
17.0 mi/1-2 days

north of Skykomish in Henry M. Jackson Wilderness of Mount Baker-Snoqualmie National Forest

Map 3.3, page 113

Don't be fooled by the name of the hike. Tradition dictates that the hike be called Fortune Ponds, even though they are but a small feature of this wonderful route. The bigger features are Pear and Peach Lakes, two large high-country lakes enclosed by parkland meadows and outstanding views. And for those seeking even more adventure, a climb to the top of Fortune Mountain is easy and well recommended.

Meadow Creek Trail immediately climbs a steep valley wall through a burned-out forest. The trail levels out and gradually climbs along Meadow Creek. The creek must be crossed twice, a wet ordeal during the early summer. By the time the forest thins and eventually breaks, you reach Fortune Ponds. Benchmark Mountain stands to the north, framed nicely behind the lakes. The trail continues another mile to Pear Lake and an intersection with the PCT. Peach Lake is to the south and over a small ridge. Subalpine fir and mountain hemlocks line the lakes, where established camps can be found. This is the high country, where huckleberries madly grow before bears can madly eat them. A side trail leads up Fortune Mountain, which at 5,903 feet presents the best of what the surrounding wilderness has to offer.

User Groups: Hikers, leashed dogs, and horses. No mountain bikes are allowed. No wheelchair access.

Permits: This trail is accessible July–October. No permits are required. Parking and access are free.

Maps: For a map of Wenatchee National Forest, contact the Outdoor Recreation Information Center at the downtown Seattle REI. For topographic maps, ask Green Trails for No. 144, Benchmark Mountain, or ask the USGS for Captain Point and Benchmark Mountain.

Directions: From Everett, drive east on U.S. 2 until 0.5 mile east of the town of Skykomish. Turn left (north) onto Beckler River Road (Forest Service Road 65) and drive for 6 miles to the junction with Rapid River Road (Forest Service Road 6530). Turn right and continue for 4.5 miles to the trailhead.

Contact: Mount Baker–Snoqualmie National Forest, Skykomish Ranger Station, 74920 NE Stevens Pass Hwy., Skykomish, WA 98288, 360/677-2414.

100 SNOQUALMIE AND DOROTHY LAKES

4.0-15.0 mi/2.5 hr-2 days 👣2 ⛰️8

south of Skykomish in Alpine Lakes Wilderness of Mount Baker-Snoqualmie National Forest

Map 3.3, page 113

There are two ways to experience this great route. Snoqualmie and Dorothy Lake Trails make a long, east–west journey through the Alpine Lakes Wilderness, progressing from the Taylor River in the Snoqualmie drainage over to the Miller River in the Skykomish drainage. Along the way are a number of great waterfalls and no fewer than five large lakes. There's a lot to explore here, and a lot of ways for hikers of all abilities to experience it.

Snoqualmie, Dear, Bear, and Dorothy Lakes lie within 2.5 miles of each other. These big lakes feature grand forests reaching to the shores, with big peaks visible over the basin's gentle ridges. Quick and easy access is gained from Miller River Trailhead, just 2 miles from enormous Lake Dorothy. This access point is preferred by families and those interested in visiting the lakes without a long trek. From the west trailhead, the route makes a longer (15 miles round-trip), more scenic trek to the lakes. Also, a steep side trail (6.3 miles) shoots up to isolated Nordrum Lake. Campsites are located at each of the lakes.

User Groups: Hikers, leashed dogs, horses, and mountain bikes (horses and mountain bikes allowed on the first 6 miles of Taylor River Road). No wheelchair access.

Permits: This trail is accessible mid-May–November. A federal Northwest Forest Pass is required to park here. A free wilderness permit is also required to hike here and is available at the trailhead.

Maps: For a map of Mount Baker–Snoqualmie National Forest, contact the Outdoor Recreation Information Center at the downtown Seattle REI. For topographic maps, ask Green Trails for No. 175, Skykomish, or ask the USGS for Snoqualmie Lake and Big Snow Mountain.

Directions: Taylor River Trailhead: From Seattle, drive east on I-90 to exit 34. Turn left onto 468th Avenue North. At 0.6 mile, turn right onto Middle Fork Road (Forest Service Road 56). Stay on Forest Service Road 56 for 12.5 miles to the Taylor River Trailhead. Forest Service Road 56 splits just after it crosses the Taylor River; stay to the left. The trailhead is 0.5 mile farther, at a gate.

East Miller River Trailhead: From Everett, drive east on U.S. 2 to Money Creek Campground, 2.8 miles prior to the town of Skykomish. Turn south onto the Old Cascade Highway. The road is just west of the highway tunnel. Drive the Old Cascade Highway for 1 mile, then turn right (south) onto the Miller River Road (Forest Service Road 6410). Continue on Forest Service Road 6410 for 9.5 miles to the road's end at the trailhead.

Contact: Mount Baker–Snoqualmie National Forest, North Bend Ranger Station, 902 SE North Bend Way, Bldg. 1, North Bend, WA 98045, 425/888-1421 x200.

101 FOSS LAKES

13.6 mi/2 days 👣3 ⛰️8

east of Skykomish in Alpine Lakes Wilderness of Mount Baker-Snoqualmie National Forest

Map 3.3, page 113

This classic Alpine Lakes Wilderness trail takes in no fewer than five lakes, offering a day hike or overnighter that never gets boring. The upper lakes are set among a rugged landscape once dominated by glaciers. Even today, it sees a lot of winter snow. But be forewarned: Within two hours of Seattle and with easy accessibility up to even the farthest lake, this trail sees a lot of use, even bordering on abuse. If you're willing to forgo solitude, then Foss Lakes is a must-visit.

The trail begins very easily, with little elevation gain along the first 1.5 miles to Trout Lake. Along the way, the trail passes one of the biggest Douglas firs you'll ever see. Only the largest of families will be able to wrap their arms around this one. Surrounded by forest, Trout Lake whets the appetite for the alpine lakes to come. This is a good turnaround point for less serious hikers.

From Trout Lake, West Fork Foss Trail climbs steeply to Lake Malachite, cruising in and out of forest alongside a beautiful cascading stream that offers much-needed refreshment on hot days. This is the trail's big climb, gaining 1,800 feet in 2 miles. From Lake Malachite, another three lakes (Copper, Little Heart, and Big Heart) lie within 3 miles' distance. The lakes seem to get better as you progress, with the blues of the lakes getting deeper and the rocky ridges getting steeper and higher. From Big Heart Lake, trails lead to Lake Angeline and the many ridges and lakes beyond. There is camping at each of the lakes, although it goes quickly during the summer season. These are true alpine lakes, sure to stick in your hiking memory.

User Groups: Hikers and leashed dogs. No horses or mountain bikes are allowed. No wheelchair access.

Permits: This trail is usually accessible June–October. A federal Northwest Forest Pass is required to park here. A free wilderness permit is also required to hike here and is available at the trailhead.

Maps: For a map of Mount Baker–Snoqualmie National Forest, contact the Outdoor Recreation Information Center at the downtown Seattle REI. For topographic maps, ask Green Trails for No. 175, Skykomish, or ask the USGS for Big Snow Mountain and Skykomish.

Directions: From Everett, drive east on U.S. 2 to 1.7 miles east of the town of Skykomish. Turn right (south) onto Foss River Road (Forest Service Road 68). Stay on this main road, avoiding any turnoffs, to the trailhead at road's end.

Contact: Mount Baker–Snoqualmie National Forest, Skykomish Ranger Station, 74920 NE Stevens Pass Hwy., Skykomish, WA 98288, 360/677-2414.

102 NECKLACE VALLEY
16.0 mi/1-2 days   🏃5 △10

west of Stevens Pass in Alpine Lakes Wilderness of Mount Baker-Snoqualmie National Forest

Map 3.3, page 113   **BEST (**

It's a long, hard hike into Necklace Valley. After 5 miles of river valley, the trail climbs 2,500 feet in a little more than 2 miles. Not exactly the stuff for beginners. For those who endure the challenge of reaching the Necklace Valley, however, ample compensation awaits. The Necklace Valley hosts a string of handsome lakes dotting a narrow, high valley. On nearly all sides are rocky slopes and ridges, where patches of snow linger late into summer. The upper valley is wide and very open, leaving lots of room to explore.

Necklace Valley Trail quickly enters the wilderness (1.5 miles) and enjoys 4 miles of old-growth forest along the East Fork Foss River. From here, the trail shoots up through the forest quickly and mercilessly into Necklace Valley (7 miles). A map is a necessity up here, as there are a number of lakes and lots of ways to get lost. The best plan of action is to just start wandering, as there is no such thing as a bad section of the Necklace Valley. The lower lakes are forested and provide good shelter, while the upper lakes are open with meadows. All of the lakes here have established campsites. The scenery only gets better as the trail follows the valley up past La Bohn Lakes to La Bohn Gap. From here, Mount Hinman and Bears Breast Mountain stand tall to the south and north.

User Groups: Hikers and leashed dogs. No horses or mountain bikes are allowed. No wheelchair access.

Permits: This trail is accessible June–October. A federal Northwest Forest Pass is required to park here. A free wilderness permit is also required to hike here and is available at the trailhead.

Maps: For a map of Mount Baker–Snoqualmie National Forest, contact the Outdoor Recreation Information Center at the downtown Seattle REI. For topographic maps, ask Green Trails for No. 175, Skykomish, and No. 176, Stevens Pass, or ask the USGS for Skykomish, Big Snow Mountain, and Mount Daniel.

Directions: From Everett, drive east on U.S. 2 to 1.7 miles east of the town of Skykomish. Turn right (south) onto Foss River Road (Forest Service Road 68) and drive 4.2 miles to the trailhead.

Contact: Mount Baker–Snoqualmie National Forest, Skykomish Ranger Station, 74920 NE Stevens Pass Hwy., Skykomish, WA 98288, 360/677-2414.

103 TONGA RIDGE
9.2 mi/5.0 hr

west of Stevens Pass in Alpine Lakes
Wilderness of Mount Baker-Snoqualmie
National Forest

Map 3.3, page 113

This is a great opportunity for the whole family to experience the high country. Starting out at a lofty 4,300 feet elevation, the trail rides out Tonga Ridge for more than 4 miles, offering Mount Sawyer and Fisher Lake for excellent side trips. The route stays below 5,000 feet for its entire length, making for very little climbing yet excellent mountain views. The trail is popular

with hikers because of its extensive meadows overflowing with huckleberries. Never mind the late August crowds; stay focused on the terrific views of nearby peaks.

Tonga Ridge Trail travels 4.6 miles along Tonga Ridge, connecting at each end to a part of Forest Service Road 6830-310. The first and closest trailhead is recommended, save for those looking for a shorter hike to Fisher Lake. Subalpine meadows dominate the route, as do great views of Mounts Hinman and Daniel. During August, hikers quickly take note of the plentiful huckleberry bushes. A side trail leads to the summit of Mount Sawyer for a 360-degree view of the surrounding peaks and much of the Cascades. A side trail also leads to Fisher Lake. The rough trail heads up and over a small crest to the large and impressive lake, set beneath towering cliffs.

User Groups: Hikers, leashed dogs, and horses. No mountain bikes are allowed. No wheelchair access.

Permits: This trail is accessible June–October. A federal Northwest Forest Pass is required to park here. A free wilderness permit is also required to hike here and is available at the trailhead.

Maps: For a map of Mount Baker–Snoqualmie National Forest, contact the Outdoor Recreation Information Center at the downtown Seattle REI. For topographic maps, ask Green Trails for No. 175, Skykomish, and No. 176, Stevens Pass, or ask the USGS for Skykomish and Scenic.

Directions: From Everett, drive east on U.S. 2 to 1.7 miles east of the town of Skykomish. Turn right (south) onto Foss River Road (Forest Service Road 68). Drive on Forest Service Road 68 for 3.5 miles to Forest Service Road 6830. Turn left onto Forest Service Road 6830 and drive for 6 miles to Forest Service Road 6830-310. Turn right onto Forest Service Road 6830-310 and drive 1 mile to the end of the road.

Contact: Mount Baker–Snoqualmie National Forest, Skykomish Ranger Station, 74920 NE Stevens Pass Hwy., Skykomish, WA 98288, 360/677-2414.

104 DECEPTION CREEK
20.6 mi/2 days

west of Stevens Pass in Alpine Lakes
Wilderness of Mount Baker-Snoqualmie
National Forest

Map 3.3, page 113

Some trips into the wilderness need not culminate at a vista or high alpine lake. Sometimes, simple travel within giant forests and along a cool, murmuring creek is the end in itself. That is certainly the case with Deception Creek, a great stroll through shady cool Cascade forest with access to high-country lakes.

Deception Creek Trail parallels the stream for 6 miles. It crosses the swirling creek below a nice waterfall (0.5 mile). The route features a bit of up and down as it slowly climbs up the valley. This is Cascadia at its best, with the forest full of large Douglas firs, western red cedars, and western hemlocks. Moss grows on most everything while the forest floor becomes a carpet of ferns at times.

Deception Creek Trail eventually leaves the valley floor to ascend the valley wall. A connector trail (7.3 miles) leads up to Deception Lakes, a good option as a destination. Deception Pass (10.3 miles) is a junction for the PCT and Marmot and Hyas Lakes. Campsites are scattered liberally along the trail.

User Groups: Hikers, leashed dogs, and horses. No mountain bikes are allowed. No wheelchair access.

Permits: This trail is accessible April–November. A federal Northwest Forest Pass is required to park here. A free wilderness permit is also required to hike here and is available at the trailhead.

Maps: For a map of Mount Baker–Snoqualmie National Forest, contact the Outdoor Recreation Information Center at the downtown Seattle REI. For topographic maps, ask Green Trails for No. 176, Stevens Pass, or ask the USGS for Scenic and Mount Daniel.

Directions: From Everett, drive east on U.S. 2 to Forest Service Road 6088, immediately beyond the Deception Falls picnic area. Turn right and drive 0.3 mile to the trailhead at road's end.

Contact: Mount Baker–Snoqualmie National Forest, Skykomish Ranger Station, 74920 NE Stevens Pass Hwy., Skykomish, WA 98288, 360/677-2414.

105 SURPRISE LAKE
8.0 mi/4.0 hr

near Stevens Pass in Alpine Lakes Wilderness
of Mount Baker-Snoqualmie National Forest

Map 3.3, page 113

By the time one has hiked a mile up Surprise Creek, the surprise should be over. Within the first half hour, it is readily evident that this is a beautiful hike. It gets only better as it progresses. But perhaps a surprise does exist, because the view from Pieper Pass seems almost too good to be true. This is a great part of the Alpine Lakes Wilderness, with many lakes and lots of stunning scenery.

Surprise Creek Trail quickly says good-bye to civilization and enters old-growth forest. Surprise Creek makes a number of small falls and cascades. The grade is gentle until the trail makes a quick rise to a narrow gap between two ridges. Reach the notch and Surprise Lake (4 miles); Glacier Lake is a bit farther up the long, narrow basin (5 miles). Forest and meadow fringe the lakes, and the tall cliffs of Surprise Mountain drop to Glacier Lake. Numerous campsites are found around each lake.

For additional exploration, hike the PCT up to 6,000-foot Pieper Pass to view the large glaciers on Mount Hinman and Mount Daniel. Spark Plug and Thunder Mountains are good scrambles as well. There is a lot of high country to explore around here, and likely more than a few extra surprises.

User Groups: Hikers and leashed dogs. No horses or mountain bikes are allowed. No wheelchair access.

Permits: This trail is accessible July–October. A federal Northwest Forest Pass is required to park here. A free wilderness permit is also required to hike here and is available at the trailhead.

Maps: For a map of Mount Baker–Snoqualmie National Forest, contact the Outdoor Recreation Information Center at the downtown Seattle REI. For topographic maps, ask Green Trails for No. 176, Stevens Pass, or ask the USGS for Scenic.

Directions: From Everett, drive east on U.S. 2 to Mile Marker 58. Turn right (south) onto an unmarked road to the service center for the Burlington Northern Railroad. Cross the railroad tracks and turn onto the spur road on the far right. Continue for 0.2 mile to the trailhead.

Contact: Mount Baker–Snoqualmie National Forest, Skykomish Ranger Station, 74920 NE Stevens Pass Hwy., Skykomish, WA 98288, 360/677-2414.

106 CHAIN LAKES
22.0 mi/2 days

near Stevens Pass in Alpine Lakes Wilderness of Wenatchee National Forest

Map 3.3, page 113

Chain Lakes are tucked way, way back in the Alpine Lakes Wilderness. Eleven miles from the nearest trailhead, there are few people back in these parts. Great old-growth forest lines much of the route before it breaks into subalpine meadows and views, with several spectacular lakes. Chain Lakes are an excellent destination for a long weekend. They definitely deserve three days for exploration rather than two cramped days spent mostly hiking.

Chain Lakes are accessible by either Stevens Pass or Icicle Creek out of Leavenworth. These are two different approaches to the shared segment of Chain Lakes Trail. From near Stevens Pass, the PCT climbs above Josephine Lake

and Lake Susan Jane before dropping into the Icicle Creek drainage and Chain Lakes Trail (5 miles). Traveling from Icicle Creek (6.5 miles) takes you through a more typical east-side forest, drier with more pines.

The two routes converge at Chain Lakes Trail, which climbs quickly to the lakes. Chain Lakes lie within a narrow basin, filled with parkland and meadows along the upper lakes, where jagged crags line the rim of the basin. There are several established campsites near the lower two lakes. The trail heads over the jagged ridge through a gap and drops to Doelle Lakes, two more great high lakes with camping.

User Groups: Hikers, leashed dogs, and horses (horses allowed day use of Chain Lakes). No mountain bikes are allowed. No wheelchair access.

Permits: This trail is accessible July–October. A federal Northwest Forest Pass is required to park here. A free wilderness permit is also required to hike here and is available at the trailhead.

Maps: For a map of Mount Baker–Snoqualmie National Forest, contact the Outdoor Recreation Information Center at the downtown Seattle REI. For topographic maps, ask Green Trails for No. 176, Stevens Pass, and No. 177, Chiwaukum Mountains, or ask the USGS for Stevens Pass.

Directions: From Everett, drive east on U.S. 2 to Forest Service Road 6960 (about 4 miles east of Stevens Pass). Turn right and drive 4 miles to the parking lot at the road's gated end. Turn right (south) onto an unmarked road to the service center for the Burlington Northern Railroad. Cross the railroad tracks and turn onto the spur road on the far right. Continue for 0.2 mile to the trailhead.

Contact: Mount Baker–Snoqualmie National Forest, Skykomish Ranger Station, 74920 NE Stevens Pass Hwy., Skykomish, WA 98288, 360/677-2414.

107 NASON RIDGE

6.0–22.1 mi/3.5 hr–2 days 🏃🏃4 ⛰9

east of Stevens Pass in Wenatchee National Forest

Map 3.3, page 113

This subalpine ridge provides hikers with a lot of trail and several excellent destinations. Running the length of Nason Ridge, Nason Ridge Trail passes three lakes and an alpine lookout, summits several peaks more than 6,000 feet in elevation, and features five different access points. It is not, however, an easy ascent to any part of Nason Ridge. Every trailhead has at least 2,000 feet of climbing to the ridge. The splendor of Nason Ridge is well worth it.

The main attractions along the ridge are Rock Mountain and Rock Lake (9.2 miles round-trip), Merritt Lake (6 miles round-trip), and Alpine Lookout (10.4 miles). Rock Mountain (6,852 feet) stands on the western end of Nason Ridge. Rock Lake sits below, in a small cirque and surrounded by subalpine forest. Farther east are Crescent and Merritt Lakes. Merritt is accessible by its own trail right off U.S. 2. The lakes on the ridge have established campsites; overnight campers must use these at all times. Alpine Lookout is a staffed Forest Service fire watchtower, about 5 miles from Butcher Creek Trailhead. Spread out on the ridge between these points are 20 miles of trail threading through high meadow, the perfect place for mountain goats. The two ends of the trail also have trailheads, on Butcher Creek and Snowy Creek. These are accessible from U.S. 2 and Lake Wenatchee. There is much to do and see on Nason Ridge, and it gets better later in the season.

User Groups: Hikers, leashed dogs, and mountain bikes. No horses are allowed. No wheelchair access.

Permits: This trail is open mid-July–October. A federal Northwest Forest Pass is required to park here.

Maps: For a map of Wenatchee National Forest, contact the Outdoor Recreation Information Center at the downtown Seattle REI. For topographic maps, ask Green Trails for No.

145, Lake Wenatchee, or ask the USGS for Labyrinth Mountain, Mount Howard, and Lake Wenatchee.

Directions: From Leavenworth, drive west about 18 miles on U.S. 2 to Forest Service Road 6910 for Alpine Lookout. For Merritt Lake and the recommended Rock Mountain Trailhead, drive west about 23 miles on U.S. 2 to Forest Service Road 657.

Contact: Wenatchee National Forest, Lake Wenatchee Ranger Station, 22976 Hwy. 207, Leavenworth, WA 98826, 509/763-3103.

108 IRON GOAT

12.0 mi one-way/6.0 hr 🏃🏃2 ⛰8

west of Stevens Pass along U.S. 2

Map 3.3, page 113   BEST 🌑

Iron Goat Trail is the result of a lot of volunteer labor. Volunteers for Outdoor Washington have led the effort to remake an old railway into one of Washington's best rails-to-trails projects. The route follows the old path of the Great Northern Railway, the first rail service to cross Stevens Pass back in the late 1800s. Volunteers have done an excellent job of cleaning up debris, refurbishing the trail, and adding many interesting interpretive signs along the way. The route is great for families and hikers of all abilities—you can turn around at any point having had a satisfying hike. Along the way are many old artifacts from the railway. Several tunnels lead off into the hillside, appearing as deep, dark caverns. As a railway, the route was plagued by trouble from the uncooperative Cascades. Snowslides and avalanches were frequent problems, as were fires. The trail is accessible at its two ends, each of which is on the west side of Stevens Pass. This is an excellent trip not only for families with young children, but for anyone crossing the pass and needing a break.

User Groups: Hikers and leashed dogs. No horses or mountain bikes are allowed. Part of the trail is wheelchair accessible (near Martin Creek).

Permits: This trail is usually accessible April–November. A federal Northwest Forest Pass is required to park at the trailheads.

Maps: Maps of this trail are best obtained at the trailheads. Current Green Trails and USGS maps do not show the Iron Goat.

Directions: From Everett, drive east on U.S. 2 beyond the town of Skykomish. At Mile Marker 55 (6 miles east of the town of Skykomish), turn left (north) onto the Old Cascade Highway (Forest Service Road 67). Drive 2.3 miles to Forest Service Road 6710 and turn left onto Forest Service Road 6710. Drive 1.4 miles to the Martin Creek Trailhead.

To get to Wellington Trailhead, drive to Mile Marker 64.3, just west of Stevens Pass, and turn left (north) onto the Old Cascade Highway. Drive 2.8 miles to Road 050. Turn right onto Road 050. Turn right and drive to the trailhead.

Contact: Mount Baker–Snoqualmie National Forest, Skykomish Ranger Station, 74920 NE Stevens Pass Hwy., Skykomish, WA 98288, 360/677-2414.

109 TIGER MOUNTAIN
1.0–5.2 mi/1.0–5.0 hr   🏃1 ⛰7

within Tiger Mountain State Forest

Map 3.3, page 113

Tiger Mountain State Forest is a shining example of what a great place Seattle is to live. More than 80 miles of trail lie within 13,000 acres of this wooded park less than a half hour from the city. That makes it the state's busiest trailhead, with cars often parked along the entrance all the way to the freeway. But don't be dismayed by the parking, as the miles of wandering trails offer many chances for casual forest strolling or intensive hiking. The park's easy accessibility makes it extremely popular with hikers of all abilities and especially with families.

There are many trails to explore here. The best strategy is to peruse the signboard at the trailhead and pick one that suits your mood.

Your own map will also be handy in navigating the vast network of trails. The most popular is West Tiger 3, which leads to the western summit. With an elevation gain of more than 2,000 feet in just 2.6 miles, it satisfies even serious hikers. It offers grand views of the Seattle and Puget Sound region, the adjacent Issaquah Alps, and even Mount Rainier. Other favorites with less climbing include Poo Poo Point Trail and Seattle View Trail. Easier, more level hikes include Around the Lake Trail, leading to Tradition Lake, and Bus Road Trail. Children will love Swamp Monster Trail, a level interpretive trail with signboards telling the story of a lovable raccoon.

User Groups: Hikers, leashed dogs, horses, and mountain bikes. No wheelchair access.

Permits: This area is usually accessible year-round. Permits are not required. Parking and access are free.

Maps: For topographic maps, ask Green Trails for No. 204S, Tiger Mountain, or ask the USGS for Fall City and Hobart.

Directions: From Seattle, drive east on I-90 to exit 20, High Point Road. Take a right, and then another quick right, following the sign for Tradition Lake Trailhead. The gate is open seven days a week dawn–8 P.M.

Contact: Washington Department of Natural Resources, P.O. Box 47001, Olympia, WA 98504-7001, 360/902-1375.

110 MOUNT SI
8.0 mi/4.0 hr   🏃4 ⛰8

north of North Bend in Mount Si Natural Resources Conservation Area

Map 3.3, page 113

Mount Si is like the Disneyland of Seattle hiking: more crowds than you can shake a stick at. Busloads of folks from the metropolitan area descend upon this mountain, the closest high peak to Seattle. It's literally the most heavily used trail in the state. Experienced and novice hikers alike come here for the views of the Cascades, Seattle, and Puget Sound Basin.

The trail is steep and at times rocky, often used by folks as a late-spring training hike for the upcoming summer. It's certainly not an ideal trail for those seeking wilderness exploration, but it scratches the itch for wooded hikes and commanding views.

Mount Si Trail is a continuous climb through the forest. Views into the Snoqualmie River Valley are few until the top. A good stop is at Snag Flats (2 miles), where giant Douglas fir offer a great rest. This is the only level section of the trail, where extensive puncheon and turnpike has been installed by EarthCorps crews. A few interpretive signs discuss a fire that hit the area almost a century ago.

From Snag Flats is yet more incline, eventually turning into serious switchbacks. The summit, best left for those with rock-climbing experience, is marked by a haystack. The views from up here are wide, from Puget Sound to deep into the Cascades. Mount Rainier is often visible to the south. It's a great hike if you don't mind hiking with half of Seattle.

User Groups: Hikers and leashed dogs. No horses or mountain bikes are allowed. No wheelchair access.

Permits: This trail is usually accessible May–November. Permits are not required. Parking and access are free.

Maps: For topographic maps, ask Green Trails for No. 206S, Mount Si, or ask the USGS for Mount Si.

Directions: From Seattle, drive east on I-90 to exit 32. Turn left on 436th Avenue and drive to North Bend Way. Turn left and drive to Mount Si Road. Turn right and drive 2.4 miles to the signed trailhead entrance and parking lot on the left.

Contact: Washington Department of Natural Resources, P.O. Box 47001, Olympia, WA 98504-7001, 360/902-1375.

111 LITTLE SI
5.0 mi/2.5 hr

north of North Bend in Mount Si Natural Resources Conservation Area

Map 3.3, page 113

Appropriately named, Little Si is Mount Si in a nutshell. A shorter hike, less of an incline, and fewer people all make this a nice early- or late-season hike when other, more intriguing trails are out of reach because of snow. The trail offers a pretty good workout nonetheless, making an ascent for most of its length. There are a number of side trails, so it's best to have a map and a good memory of which direction you came. The views from the top extend across the Snoqualmie Valley to Rattlesnake Mountain and up to Mount Si and Mount Washington.

Little Si Trail immediately climbs an outcropping of exposed rock. The main trail goes straight ahead while spur trails stray to the sides. These side trails can be good extracurricular journeys, and some great new ones have been built by EarthCorps crews. Most side trails lead to exposed rock heavily used by local climbers. Mostly second-growth forest covers the trail, although some granddaddy trees can be seen in places. The summit of the Little Si is exposed to reveal the surrounding countryside, quickly becoming "North Bend: The Strip Mall." In all, it's a fun and manageable hike for the whole family.

User Groups: Hikers and leashed dogs. No horses or mountain bikes are allowed. No wheelchair access.

Permits: This area is usually accessible March–December. Permits are not required. Parking and access are free.

Maps: For topographic maps, ask Green Trails for No. 206S, Mount Si, or ask the USGS for North Bend.

Directions: From Seattle, drive east on I-90 to exit 32. Turn left on 436th Avenue and drive to North Bend Way. Turn left and drive to Mount Si Road. Turn right and drive 0.5 mile to the signed trailhead and parking lot on the left.

Contact: Washington Department of Natural Resources, P.O. Box 47001, Olympia, WA 98504-7001, 360/902-1375.

112 RATTLESNAKE MOUNTAIN
3.0-11.3 mi/1.5 hr   🥾2 ⛰8

within the Cedar River Municipal Watershed and on Washington Department of Natural Resources Land

Map 3.3, page 113

One of the most popular hikes in the Seattle area is the trail to Rattlesnake Ledge, an immense outcropping of rock that offers great views of the surrounding area. But unbeknownst to most hikers, Rattlesnake Mountain Trail is actually an 11.3-mile trail that spans nearly the entire east-to-west length of the mountain. The trail was recently re-routed and constructed by Washington Trails Association and EarthCorps crews in conjunction with Mountains to Sound Greenway Trust and the City of Seattle. The new trail is a vast improvement over the old, which was essentially a straight-up assault on the hill, ending just past the ledge. Now a consistent, manageable, wide grade whisks hundreds of hikers to the ledge and beyond each day.

The hike to Rattlesnake Ridge is 3 miles round-trip. Starting in the Cedar River watershed, the trail passes through second-growth forest rich in undergrowth flowers and ferns before arriving at the ledge (1.5 miles). The ledge literally drops straight down, so take care with dogs and children. Views extend across the Snoqualmie Valley to Mount Si and eastward into the watershed, the source of Seattle's drinking water.

A longer option encompasses the whole of Rattlesnake Trail 11.3 miles one-way. A car-drop at the southern trailhead is highly recommended. From Rattlesnake Ledge, the trail steadily climbs up the ridge. The view into the watershed grows bigger, and on clear days Mount Rainier looms surreally large to the south. The trail is a makeshift collection of trails and old logging roads, although a more continuous replacement is being built. At 4.9 miles, the trail reaches Grand Prospect, looking over the town of North Bend. The trail ends at Snoqualmie Point 11.3 miles later.

User Groups: Hikers and leashed dogs. No horses or mountain bikes are allowed. No wheelchair access.

Permits: This trail is usually accessible year-round. Permits are not required. Parking and access are free.

Maps: For topographic maps, ask Green Trails for No. 205S, Rattlesnake Mountain, or ask the USGS for North Bend.

Directions: Main trailhead for Rattlesnake Ledge: From Seattle, drive east on Interstate 90 to exit 32. Turn right on 436th Avenue (becomes Southeast Edgewick Road) and drive 3 miles to the signed trailhead and parking lot at Rattlesnake Lake, on the right side of the road. South trailhead: From Seattle, drive east on Interstate 90 to exit 27. Turn right onto Winery Road and drive 0.5 miles to the large parking area at the end of the road.

Contact: Cedar River Watershed Education Center, 425/831-6780.

113 TWIN FALLS
2.6 mi/1.5 hr   🥾1 ⛰8

east of North Bend in Twin Falls State Park

Map 3.3, page 113   BEST (

Twin Falls Trail makes an excellent winter hike, when high-country trails are covered with the excessive white of winter's work and the rivers are flowing with Washington's most ordinary commodity: rain. Twin Falls are much more than just a pair of cascades; rather, the South Fork of the Snoqualmie River makes a series of falls that concludes with an impressive plummet of more than 150 feet. The trail is manageable for hikers of all abilities. The journey is something special, too, as it passes through old-growth forest and one particular granddaddy of a tree.

A well-maintained trail ambles alongside the Snoqualmie River to the falls. Several enormous cedars line the trail, having been spared the long, cutting arm of the timber industry. A number of boardwalks and bridges are strategically placed to keep feet dry in even the wettest of weather. At the falls (1.3 miles), a platform offers misty views of the falls. Above, a bridge spans the river in the midst of the cascades. The optimum time to visit is the winter and spring, when more than 75,000 gallons of water flow over the falls each minute. During dry summers, this torrent vanishes to just 200 gallons per minute. The trail continues to connect to John Wayne Pioneer Trail, which provides access to a trailhead at exit 38.

User Groups: Hikers and leashed dogs. No horses or mountain bikes are allowed. No wheelchair access.

Permits: This trail is accessible year-round. No permits are required. Parking and access are free.

Maps: For topographic maps, ask Green Trails for No. 206, Bandera, or ask the USGS for Chester Morse Lake.

Directions: From Seattle, drive east on I-90 to exit 34. Turn right off the freeway on 468th Avenue Southeast and drive south 0.5 mile to Southeast 159th Street. Drive 0.5 mile to the trailhead at road's end.

Contact: Washington State Parks and Recreation, 1111 Israel Rd. SW, P.O. Box 42650, Olympia, WA 98504-2669, 360/902-8844.

114 MIDDLE FORK SNOQUALMIE RIVER

1.0-10.0 mi/0.5-5.0 hr

northeast of North Bend in Mount Baker–Snoqualmie National Forest

Map 3.3, page 113

The Middle Fork of the Snoqualmie River is a fantastic trail close to the Seattle area and accessible year-round. Much of the trail passes through old-growth forests that survived the saw or ax. Along the upper reaches of trail

are the privately operated Goldmeyer Hot Springs, one of the best in Washington. The trail has been undergoing an intense amount of reconstruction by the Forest Service in the past few years, opening up many more miles of trail along the river.

Middle Fork Trail works its way through the river valley for roughly 12 miles along the south shore. It is accessible at two trailheads, one near the Taylor River and another near Dingford Creek. Customize your hike by turning around when the mood strikes—even a stroll of just 1 mile out and back will feel satisfying. Near the Taylor River, at Middle Fork Trailhead, Middle Fork Trail crosses the river on a new, extraordinary wooden bridge and meanders up the river valley, swooping near and away from the river. Above Dingford Trailhead, the trail encounters routes up to Snow, Gem, and Wildcat Lakes. Goldmeyer Hot Springs are roughly 5 miles from the trailhead and require reservations. The Middle Fork rarely gets snow, making it an excellent escape during the winter.

User Groups: Hikers, leashed dogs, horses (horses allowed July 15–October 31), and mountain bikes (mountain bikes permitted only on odd-numbered calendar days April 15–October 31). No wheelchair access.

Permits: This trail is accessible year-round. A federal Northwest Forest Pass is required to park at the trailheads.

Maps: For a map of Mount Baker–Snoqualmie National Forest, contact the Outdoor Recreation Information Center at the downtown Seattle REI. For topographic maps, ask Green Trails for No. 174, Mount Si, No. 175, Skykomish, and No. 207, Snoqualmie Pass, or ask the USGS for Lake Phillipa and Snoqualmie Lake.

Directions: From Seattle, drive east on I-90 to exit 34. Turn left onto 468th Avenue North and drive 0.6 mile to Middle Fork Road. Turn right and drive 3 miles to Forest Service Road 56. Turn left and drive 11 miles to Middle Fork Snoqualmie Trailhead.

To reach the upper trailhead at Dingford,

continue on Forest Service Road 56 for 6 miles.

Contact: Mount Baker–Snoqualmie National Forest, North Bend Ranger Station, 902 SE North Bend Way, Bldg. 1, North Bend, WA 98045, 425/888-1421 x200.

115 DINGFORD CREEK
11.0 mi/6.0 hr

northeast of North Bend in Alpine Lake Wilderness of Mount Baker-Snoqualmie National Forest

Map 3.3, page 113

Hester and Myrtle Lakes are just two of many wonderful high-country lakes off Dingford Creek Trail. Hester and Myrtle are the largest and best known, attracting a majority of Dingford Trail's visitors. The hikes to the lakes are exceptional and offer miles of further exploration in the high-country meadows. Old-growth forest of hemlock, cedar, and fir make the journey along rumbling Dingford Creek an excellent day hike.

Dingford Creek Trail makes a quick ascent through second-growth forest before leveling out and strolling through ancient forests. At 3 miles the trail splits; head right for Hester Lake (5.5 miles). Hester Lake is large and encircled by forests of subalpine fir and mountain hemlock. Anglers love the lake for its stocked trout. From here, adventurous folks can reach Little Hester Lake and explore Mount Price.

Dingford Creek Trail continues following the stream up to Myrtle Lake (5.5 miles), fringed with forest and talus shores. Folks with off-trail experience can get to three small lakes to the west or climb up to Big Snow Lake, which sits directly under Big Snow Mountain. The trail grows faint from Myrtle Lake but does head up to Little Myrtle Lake and two other, smaller lakes. Regardless of destination, any route up Dingford Creek Trail is outstanding.

User Groups: Hikers and leashed dogs. No horses or mountain bikes are allowed. No wheelchair access.

Permits: This trail is accessible June–early November. A federal Northwest Forest Pass is required to park here.

Maps: For a map of Mount Baker–Snoqualmie National Forest, contact the Outdoor Recreation Information Center at the downtown Seattle REI. For topographic maps, ask Green Trails for No. 175, Skykomish, or ask the USGS for Snoqualmie Lake and Big Snow Mountain.

Directions: From Seattle, drive east on I-90 to exit 34. Turn left onto 468th Avenue North and drive 0.5 mile to Middle Fork Road. Turn right and drive 3 miles (via the left fork in the road). Turn left on Forest Service Road 56 and drive 14 miles to Dingford Trailhead. Park in the wide turnout on the right; the trailhead is on the left.

Contact: Mount Baker–Snoqualmie National Forest, North Bend Ranger Station, 902 SE North Bend Way, Bldg. 1, North Bend, WA 98045, 425/888-1421 x200.

116 DUTCH MILLER GAP
30.0 mi/2-3 days

northeast of North Bend in Alpine Lake Wilderness of Mount Baker-Snoqualmie National Forest

Map 3.3, page 113

A trip to Dutch Miller Gap is a trip to the headwaters of the mighty Middle Fork Snoqualmie River. Here, deep within the river's valley, wilderness reigns supreme in the old-growth forests and meadows. Tall, rocky peaks dominate the wild landscape. As a bonus, there are several options for exploration in the high country, including Williams Lake and beautiful La Bohn Gap and La Bohn Lakes.

This hike has been made much more remote by the permanent closure of Forest Service Road 56 at Dingford Creek. This closure adds 7.5 miles of road hiking in and out. Those miles pass quickly, though, alongside the river and through quiet forest. From the old trailhead (7.5 miles), Middle Fork Snoqualmie Trail gradually climbs 4 miles up the valley alongside the river. The river makes a number of cascades and creates lots of pools for dipping. A short but noticeable rise, where the trail climbs a glacial step, delivers hikers into subalpine meadows with frequent rock slides. Camp Pedro is at 13.5 miles and has several great campsites.

After Camp Pedro, the trail splits, with the right fork climbing to Dutch Miller Gap through meadows and talus (15 miles). The surrounding peaks tower over hikers at the pass. Expect lots of ripe huckleberries in August. The other fork leads up to Williams Lake, set within meadows in a glacial cirque. Footpaths lead up to La Bohn Gap, which features views as great as those of Dutch Miller, and down to the Necklace Valley. With so many excellent places up here, hikers can't go wrong.

User Groups: Hikers, leashed dogs, horses, and mountain bikes are allowed. No wheelchair access.

Permits: This trail is accessible June–October. A federal Northwest Forest Pass is required to park here.

Maps: For a map of Mount Baker–Snoqualmie National Forest, contact the Outdoor Recreation Information Center at the downtown Seattle REI. For topographic maps, ask Green Trails for No. 175, Skykomish, and No. 176, Stevens Pass, or ask the USGS for Big Snow Mountain and Mount Daniel.

Directions: From Seattle, drive east on I-90 to exit 34. Turn left onto 468th Avenue North and drive 0.5 mile to Middle Fork Road. Turn right and drive 3 miles (via the left fork in the road). Turn left on Forest Service Road 56 and drive 12.5 miles to the Dingford Creek Trailhead at the road's closure. Forest Service Road 56 is often very rough and may require a high-clearance vehicle.

Contact: Mount Baker–Snoqualmie National Forest, North Bend Ranger Station, 902 SE North Bend Way, Bldg. 1, North Bend, WA 98045, 425/888-1421 x200.

117 MOUNT DEFIANCE/ MASON LAKES

16.6 mi/8.0 hr   4   9

east of North Bend in Alpine Lakes Wilderness of Mount Baker–Snoqualmie National Forest

Map 3.3, page 113

New Ira Spring Trail couples great high lakes with a high peak chock-full of views. Recently rebuilt, the trail to Mount Defiance and Mason Lakes commemorates one of Washington's strongest wilderness advocates, trail guide guru Ira Spring. Fields of heather and huckleberries are prolific along this route, as are the blackflies and mosquitoes in early summer. This trail encounters numerous lakes stocked with trout and is complemented with a scramble atop Mount Defiance.

Ira Spring Trail travels 2 miles on an old road before the new section of trail begins with spectacular results. Lazy switchbacks climb through open meadows before it tops a crest and descends to a wide, forested basin and Mason Lake. The main trail continues east to Rainbow Lake, filled to the brim with what else, rainbow trout. A side trail leads to Island Lake, the prime swimming hole (deep, cool, and sunny). All of the lakes have several campsites, although they fill up quickly.

Just beyond Mason Lake lies the Mount Defiance Trail junction. Turn left and climb through huckleberry meadows to the great views atop the summit. Cascade peaks line the horizons to the north, east, and south, while Puget Sound Basin and the Olympics stand out to the west. It's a great viewpoint.

User Groups: Hikers and leashed dogs. No horses or mountain bikes are allowed. No wheelchair access.

Permits: This trail is accessible June–October. A federal Northwest Forest Pass is required to park here. A free wilderness permit is also required to hike here and is available at the trailhead.

Maps: For a map of Mount Baker–Snoqualmie National Forest, contact the Outdoor Recreation Information Center at the downtown

Seattle REI. For topographic maps, ask Green Trails for No. 206, Bandera, or ask the USGS for Bandera.

Directions: From Seattle, drive east on I-90 to exit 45. Turn left (north, over the freeway) to Forest Service Road 9030. Turn left and drive left 1 mile to Forest Service Road 9031. Veer left on Forest Service Road 9031 and drive 4 miles to the trailhead at road's end.

Contact: Mount Baker–Snoqualmie National Forest, North Bend Ranger Station, 902 SE North Bend Way, Bldg. 1, North Bend, WA 98045, 425/888-1421 x200.

118 BANDERA MOUNTAIN
7.0 mi/4.0 hr   🏃4 ⛰8

east of North Bend in Alpine Lakes Wilderness of Mount Baker-Snoqualmie National Forest

Map 3.3, page 113

Bandera has a reputation for two things: a steep, difficult ascent and breathtaking panoramic views. The second feature far outweighs the first. A new trail built by the Forest Service makes access to Bandera Trail much easier and should encourage even more folks to visit this great place. That's good for everyone, since Bandera is less than an hour from Seattle. The trail is awash in mountain views in every direction, offering one of Washington's best sunsets.

The route to Bandera follows Mason Lakes Trail for 2.5 miles before splitting off to the right at a signed junction. By this point, hikers are out of the woods and immersed in wide-open mountain meadows, kept in check by heavy snowpacks and regular (every 100 years or so) fires. The views are grand along the way and only get better as the trail reaches the summit of Bandera. Mount Rainier is enormous to the south, behind McClellan Butte. Miles and miles of forest and mountain ridges give way to Glacier Peak to the east and Mount Baker to the north. Total elevation gain is about 3,000 feet, a rough day's work, but the memories of the great views will outlast any soreness.

User Groups: Hikers and leashed dogs. No horses or mountain bikes are allowed. No wheelchair access.

Permits: This trail is accessible June–mid-November. A federal Northwest Forest Pass is required to park here. A free wilderness permit is also required to hike here and is available at the trailhead.

Maps: For a map of Mount Baker–Snoqualmie National Forest, contact the Outdoor Recreation Information Center at the downtown Seattle REI. For topographic maps, ask Green Trails for No. 206, Bandera, or ask the USGS for Bandera.

Directions: From Seattle, drive east on I-90 to exit 45. Turn left (north, over the freeway) to Forest Service Road 9030. Turn left and drive left 1 mile to Forest Service Road 9031. Veer left on Forest Service Road 9031 and drive 4 miles to the trailhead at road's end.

Contact: Mount Baker–Snoqualmie National Forest, North Bend Ranger Station, 902 SE North Bend Way, Bldg. 1, North Bend, WA 98045, 425/888-1421 x200.

119 MCCLELLAN BUTTE
9.2 mi/5.0 hr   🏃4 ⛰8

east of North Bend in Mount Baker-Snoqualmie National Forest

Map 3.3, page 113

A tough, steep, rocky path leads to the top of McClellan Butte. Few hikers will have kind words for a trail that asks so much. That is, until they reach the top with miles of forests and peaks stretching out before them. Adversity is often just an exercise in building character (thanks, Dad). McClellan Butte may be a difficult climb, but it's an excellent alternative to other trails that are busier and just as difficult (Mount Si, for instance).

McClellan Butte Trail climbs through forest for nearly its entire length. After 0.6 mile it intersects the Iron Horse Trail; follow it west 0.4 mile, then turn south on

McClellan Butte Trail. A great number of steep switchbacks scale the hillside, crossing several avalanche chutes that can remain filled with snow until July. Be aware that when filled with snow, they are dangerous because of avalanches. Overuse has exposed many frustrating rocks and roots.

The trail eventually finds the southern edge of the butte at the border of the Cedar River watershed. The trail ends below the true summit, a rocky point with vertical walls best left to experienced rock climbers. Nevertheless, there are great views just below the summit, with Mount Rainier in the distance and Chester Morse Lake directly below. Think of all the character you just built after that treacherous climb. Cheers!

User Groups: Hikers and leashed dogs. Horses and mountain bikes are allowed for the first mile to the Iron Horse Trail only. No wheelchair access.

Permits: This trail is accessible July–October. A federal Northwest Forest Pass is required to park here.

Maps: For a map of Mount Baker–Snoqualmie National Forest, contact the Outdoor Recreation Information Center at the downtown Seattle REI. For topographic maps, ask Green Trails for No. 206, Bandera, or ask the USGS for Bandera.

Directions: From Seattle, drive east on I-90 to exit 42 (Tinkham Road). Turn right (south) and then turn left onto Forest Service Road 55. Drive 0.3 mile to a signed gravel road. Turn right and drive 0.2 mile to the trailhead at road's end.

Contact: Mount Baker–Snoqualmie National Forest, North Bend Ranger Station, 902 SE North Bend Way, Bldg. 1, North Bend, WA 98045, 425/888-1421 x200.

120 TALAPUS AND OLALLIE LAKES

4.0–6.0 mi/2.0–3.0 hr   🏃🏃₂ 🛆₇

east of North Bend in Alpine Lakes Wilderness of Mount Baker–Snoqualmie National Forest

Map 3.3, page 113

Although they're not showy or flashy, this pair of forested lakes can offer the perfect respite from the city. Talapus and Olallie Lakes are greatly accessible, situated within an hour's drive of Seattle. The easy trail gains less than 1,000 feet, perfect for hikers both young and old. The result during the summer is swarms of families to match the swarms of bugs. Regardless, the lakes make great overnight destinations with many nice campsites. And forests of virgin Douglas fir and western hemlock surround the lakes to offer shade for those not inclined to jump in the water.

Talapus Lake Trail begins on an old cat track but soon becomes a true trail. The trail dances a laid-back switchback shuffle through a cool, shady forest. Alpine Lakes Wilderness is entered just before a marshy area, below Talapus Lake. Many paths diverge from here, leading to good camping spots around Talapus. This trail is very busy, so the camping spots fill up early during the summer.

For Olallie Lake, continue 0.5 mile along the main trail to a junction; veer left for 0.5 mile to the forested shores of Olallie. Again, there are many camps along the lake for the many visitors. Keep in mind that both lakes harbor a lot of mosquitoes. Olallie visitors should follow Pratt Lake Trail above the lake for a picturesque view of Mount Rainier.

User Groups: Hikers and leashed dogs. No horses or mountain bikes are allowed. No wheelchair access.

Permits: This trail is accessible June–October. A federal Northwest Forest Pass is required to park here. A free wilderness permit is also required to hike here and is available at the trailhead.

Maps: For a map of Mount Baker–Snoqualmie National Forest, contact the Outdoor

Recreation Information Center at the downtown Seattle REI. For topographic maps, ask Green Trails for No. 206, Bandera, or ask the USGS for Bandera.

Directions: From Seattle, drive east on I-90 to exit 45. From the off-ramp, turn north (left) onto Forest Service Road 9031 for 1 mile. Turn right onto Forest Service Road 9030 and drive 2 miles to road's end, where the trailhead is located.

Contact: Mount Baker–Snoqualmie National Forest, North Bend Ranger Station, 902 SE North Bend Way, Bldg. 1, North Bend, WA 98045, 425/888-1421 x200.

121 GRANITE MOUNTAIN
8.6 mi/5.0 hr

east of North Bend in Alpine Lakes Wilderness of Mount Baker-Snoqualmie National Forest

Map 3.3, page 113   **BEST (**

Let's not mince words: Granite Mountain Trail is a hell of a climb to one of the best summit views in the region. The trail ascends nearly 4,000 feet in just over 4 miles but rewards with broad meadows of huckleberries and copious views of surrounding peaks. The summit is home to the last functioning fire lookout operated by the Forest Service in the area. If the Forest Service is here, you know it has views.

Granite Mountain Trail begins 1.3 miles up Pratt Lake Trail. As the hum of the freeway fades away, Granite Mountain Trail takes off to the right. The ascent is certainly steep, making numerous switchbacks up through the forest. Be thankful for the shade, as there is unlikely to be any water on the route. The trail eventually emerges into open meadows with Mount Rainier off in the distance.

This south-facing slope melts out early in the year, but the trail soon levels out and jumps to the north slope of the hill. Here, snow lingers late and avalanche danger persists even into June. Head-turning views will likely

slow your ascent and help to keep your heart rate reasonable. All of the Snoqualmie-area peaks are on display as are Mount Baker and Glacier Peak on clear days.

User Groups: Hikers, leashed dogs, llamas, and goats. No horses or mountain bikes are allowed. No wheelchair access.

Permits: This trail is accessible July–October. A federal Northwest Forest Pass is required to park here.

Maps: For a map of Mount Baker–Snoqualmie National Forest, contact the Outdoor Recreation Information Center at the downtown Seattle REI. For topographic maps, ask Green Trails for No. 207, Snoqualmie Pass, or ask the USGS for Snoqualmie Pass.

Directions: From Seattle, drive east on I-90 to exit 47. Turn left (north) from the off-ramp and turn left at the T in the road. Drive 0.3 mile to the signed trailhead.

Contact: Mount Baker–Snoqualmie National Forest, North Bend Ranger Station, 902 SE North Bend Way, Bldg. 1, North Bend, WA 98045, 425/888-1421 x200.

122 PRATT LAKE
11.4 mi/6.0 hr

east of North Bend in Alpine Lakes Wilderness of Mount Baker-Snoqualmie National Forest

Map 3.3, page 113

Pratt Lake is one of the nicest but least-visited destinations in Alpine Lakes Wilderness. The journey to the lake is just as enjoyable as the destination. Great forests, views of Mount Rainier, berries for everyone, and lots of lakeshore to explore make this an exceptional hike. What's more is that there are often few people along this route. That's amazing, since it is easily one of the best loops anywhere near I-90 and Seattle.

Pratt Lake Trail begins in the shade of forest, much needed during summer days. The trail climbs gently, crossing several small creeks on its way to Olallie Lake. It passes signed junctions for Granite Mountain and

© SCOTT LEONARD

Ollalie Lake as seen from the trail to Pratt Lake

Talapus Lake. As the trail contours above Olallie Lake, the forest breaks for an amazing view of Mount Rainier.

The trail splits along a ridge; the left fork leads to Mount Defiance, so head right, down to Pratt Lake through fields of granite boulders. The chirping you hear comes from picas, saying hello. Mount Roosevelt stands out across from the basin, above Pratt Lake. Numerous campsites are located at the north end of the lake, where it drains into the Pratt River. Remnants of abandoned Pratt River Trail are on the western shore, ripe for exploration. At night, with the moon and stars at play in the sky, this place seems very far away from everything, yet it is less than an hour from Seattle.

User Groups: Hikers, leashed dogs, llamas, and goats. No horses or mountain bikes are allowed. No wheelchair access.

Permits: This trail is accessible mid-June–October. A federal Northwest Forest Pass is required to park here. A free wilderness permit is also required to hike here and is available at the trailhead.

Maps: For a map of Mount Baker–Snoqualmie

National Forest, contact the Outdoor Recreation Information Center at the downtown Seattle REI. For topographic maps, ask Green Trails for No. 206, Bandera, and No. 207, Snoqualmie Pass, or ask the USGS for Bandera and Snoqualmie Pass.

Directions: From Seattle, drive east on I-90 to exit 47. Turn left (north) from the off-ramp and turn left at the T in the road. Drive 0.3 mile to the signed trailhead.

Contact: Mount Baker–Snoqualmie National Forest, North Bend Ranger Station, 902 SE North Bend Way, Bldg. 1, North Bend, WA 98045, 425/888-1421 x200.

123 ANNETTE LAKE

7.0 mi/4.0 hr   2   9

in the Mount Baker-Snoqualmie National Forest, south of Snoqualmie Pass

Map 3.3, page 113

Nothing is especially unique about Annette Lake. Then again, Annette is another beautiful alpine lake, set between large peaks, with waterfalls and beautiful forest. Add it all up, and it's definitely a great place to spend the day. The trail up to Annette Lake is fairly easy to hike, and that's never a bad thing.

Annette Lake Trail proceeds through dense forest on its way to the lake. In the beginning, the trail follows an old service road and soon crosses an old railway line (now Iron Horse Trail). Switchbacks rise steeply on the side of Silver Peak, high above Humpback Creek. Avalanche chutes open the canopy in places, providing some views of Humpback Mountain. The trail continues smoothly for the last mile, arriving at Annette Lake.

Annette Lake sits directly between Silver Peak and Abiel Peak. Steep cliffs drop into the woods and lingering snowfields that surround the lake. It's not your typically deep blue alpine lake, but it does make for some decent fishing. There is some camping around the lake for those seeking an overnighter.

User Groups: Hikers and leashed dogs. Horses and mountain bikes are allowed for first 0.7 mile to Iron Horse Trail only. No wheelchair access.

Permits: This trail is accessible June–mid-November. A federal Northwest Forest Pass is required to park here. A free wilderness permit is also required to hike here and is available at the trailhead.

Maps: For a map of Mount Baker–Snoqualmie National Forest, contact the Outdoor Recreation Information Center at the downtown Seattle REI. For topographic maps, ask Green Trails for No. 207, Snoqualmie Pass, or ask the USGS for Snoqualmie Lake and Lost Pass.

Directions: From Seattle, drive east on I-90 to exit 47. Turn right (south) and then left on Forest Service Road 55. Drive 0.5 mile to the signed trailhead at road's end.

Contact: Mount Baker–Snoqualmie National Forest, North Bend Ranger Station, 902 SE North Bend Way, Bldg. 1, North Bend, WA 98045, 425/888-1421 x200.

124 DENNY CREEK AND LAKE MELAKWA

9.0 mi/4.5 hr   🏃3 ⛰10

east of North Bend in Alpine Lakes Wilderness of Mount Baker-Snoqualmie National Forest

Map 3.3, page 113   **BEST (**

This may well be the most beautiful hike in the I-90 corridor. Two series of incredible waterfalls parallel the trail. After crossing Hemlock Pass, Lake Melakwa sits within a beautiful, large basin, rimmed by jagged peaks giving way to forests of subalpine trees. This is a perfect introduction to all that the Alpine Lakes Wilderness has to offer; accordingly, it attracts flocks of people during the summer. Don't be dismayed, as there is plenty to see for all.

Denny Creek Trail begins along Denny Creek as cars and trucks pass overhead on I-90. The highway overpass preserves important corridors, allowing wildlife to move uninhibited through the forests. The trail encounters Keekwulee Falls at 1.5 miles; at 2 miles are Snowshoe Falls. These cascades form large pools on slabs of granite with lots of nooks and crannies.

The trail switchbacks up through avalanche chutes and fields of huckleberries to Hemlock Pass; Lake Melakwa lies another 0.3 mile beyond. There are many campsites at the lake, on both the eastern and western shores. Be sure to stay on footpaths, as the meadows here have taken a beating. Sharp-toothed Chair Peak is the tallest peak of the jagged rim around the basin. More great lakes lie beyond Lake Melakwa for the adventurous. The trail drops with Melakwa Creek to Lower Tuscohatchie Lake, a favorite backcountry swimming hole.

User Groups: Hikers and leashed dogs. No horses or mountain bikes are allowed. No wheelchair access.

Permits: This trail is accessible July–October. A federal Northwest Forest Pass is required to park here. A free wilderness permit is also required to hike here and is available at the trailhead.

Maps: For a map of Mount Baker–Snoqualmie National Forest, contact the Outdoor Recreation Information Center at the downtown Seattle REI. For topographic maps, ask Green Trails for No. 207, Snoqualmie Pass, or ask the USGS for Snoqualmie Pass.

Directions: From Seattle, drive east on I-90 to exit 47. Turn left (north) from the off-ramp and turn right at the T in the road. Drive 0.2 mile to Forest Service Road 58. Turn left and drive 2.6 miles to Forest Service Road 5830. Turn left and drive 0.2 mile to the signed trailhead at road's end.

Contact: Mount Baker–Snoqualmie National Forest, North Bend Ranger Station, 902 SE North Bend Way, Bldg. 1, North Bend, WA 98045, 425/888-1421 x200.

125 SNOW LAKE

6.0 mi/3.0 hr

north of Snoqualmie Pass in Alpine Lakes Wilderness of Mount Baker-Snoqualmie National Forest

Map 3.3, page 113

Everything about this place seems super-sized. Snow Lake is remarkably large, especially for an alpine lake. The basin itself is enormous, easily absorbing the large crowds that trek to the area. Big meadows satisfy appetites with large numbers of prime huckleberries. And of course the surrounding peaks and ridges are large, looming over the lake and making for some striking vistas. It's all large and all exceptionally grand.

Snow Lake Trail gently works its way toward tiny Source Lake. This section is mostly open, providing great views of the jagged valley ridges. Switchbacks climb steeply to a ridge looking down on Snow Lake. The trail is occasionally rocky, mostly because of the high use. The ridge is a turnaround point for many, as the trail then drops about 500 feet in 0.5 mile to Snow Lake. Unless you're on a strict time schedule (you shouldn't be), it's worth the effort to continue.

Snow Lake is cloaked in typical Alpine Lakes Wilderness beauty. The cliffs of Chair Peak tower over meadows and groves of mountain hemlock surrounding the lake. Camping at Snow Lake is discouraged because of the heavy use of the trail; alpine meadows have delicate makeups. If you're not satisfied with stopping here, then you're in for a treat. A climb over a steep ridge ends up at Gem and Wildcat Lakes.

User Groups: Hikers, leashed dogs, llamas, and goats. No horses or mountain bikes are allowed. No wheelchair access.

Permits: This trail is accessible April–October. A federal Northwest Forest Pass is required to park here. A free wilderness permit is also required to hike here and is available at the trailhead.

Maps: For a map of Mount Baker–Snoqualmie National Forest, contact the Outdoor Recreation Information Center at the downtown Seattle REI. For topographic maps, ask Green Trails for No. 207, Snoqualmie Pass, or ask the USGS for Bandera and Snoqualmie Pass.

Directions: From Seattle, drive east on I-90 to exit 52 (West Summit). Turn left (under the freeway) and left again on Alpental Road. Drive 0.2 mile and turn right on Forest Service Road 9040. Drive 1.2 miles to a large gravel parking lot on the left at Alpental Ski Area. The trailhead is on the right.

Contact: Mount Baker–Snoqualmie National Forest, North Bend Ranger Station, 902 SE North Bend Way, Bldg. 1, North Bend, WA 98045, 425/888-1421 x200.

126 COMMONWEALTH BASIN/RED PASS

10.0 mi/5.0 hr

near Snoqualmie Pass in Alpine Lakes Wilderness of Mount Baker-Snoqualmie National Forest

Map 3.3, page 113

This is one of the better trails out of the Snoqualmie Pass area. The trailhead literally starts at Snoqualmie Pass and climbs 5 miles to a spectacular viewpoint atop Red Pass. Along the way are old-growth forests of enormous mountain hemlocks that give way to wide-open meadows and fields of blueberry bushes. The trail needn't be hiked its entire length to be fully enjoyed. That makes this trail a great family hike, in case little ones get tuckered out early.

The first half of the route follows the PCT. Along this stretch, the trail gently and gradually climbs through shady forest to reach a junction (2.5 miles). Stick to the left on Commonwealth Basin Trail as the basin opens into parkland, meadows mixed with pockets of forest. You must make a crossing of Commonwealth Creek (4 miles), but it is unlikely to be much trouble by mid-July. The last mile is a descent climb of about 1,200 feet. Halfway up is Red Pond and a nice campsite. Finally, after more switchbacks, Red Pass is achieved. Views extend in nearly all directions, taking in countless peaks of the Alpine Lakes Wilderness.

User Groups: Hikers and leashed dogs. No horses or mountain bikes are allowed. No wheelchair access.

Permits: This trail is accessible June–October. A federal Northwest Forest Pass is required to park here.

Maps: For a map of Mount Baker–Snoqualmie National Forest, contact the Outdoor Recreation Information Center at the downtown Seattle REI. For topographic maps, ask Green Trails for No. 207, Snoqualmie Pass, or ask the USGS for Snoqualmie Pass.

Directions: From Seattle, drive east on I-90 to exit 52. Turn left (north) at the exit ramp and take the first right into the PCT-North parking area. The lot to the left is intended for stock; hikers can continue straight to the main parking lot. The trail starts at the east end of the parking lot.

Contact: Mount Baker–Snoqualmie National Forest, North Bend Ranger Station, 902 SE North Bend Way, Bldg. 1, North Bend, WA 98045, 425/888-1421 x200.

127 KENDALL KATWALK
11.0 mi/6.0 hr   👫3 ⛰10

north of Snoqualmie Pass in Alpine Lakes Wilderness of Mount Baker–Snoqualmie National Forest

Map 3.3, page 113

Without a doubt, Kendall Katwalk is one of the most unforgettable and exciting stretches of the PCT. Heading north from Snoqualmie Pass, the PCT encounters a long granite wall on the side of Kendall Peak, with a slope of roughly 75 degrees. That's pretty close to vertical. With a little ingenuity and even more dynamite, trail engineers blasted a 100-yard stretch of trail into the slope. Named Kendall Katwalk, it's now famous across the country.

The PCT leaves Snoqualmie Pass and wastes little time before beginning the ascent to the high country. Shady and well graded, the trail passes underfoot quickly. Stay right at Commonwealth Basin junction (2.5 miles) and continue climbing with the PCT. The forest soon breaks, and numerous neighboring peaks and ridges come into view. In August, ripe huckleberries fuel the climb to Katwalk (5.5 miles). This is a crowded segment of the PCT, but take the time to walk Katwalk a couple of times anyway. Although the trail is plenty wide, watch your step; Silver Creek Valley is a good 1,200-foot drop. Campers will need to hike an extra 2 miles to Gravel and Ridge Lakes.

User Groups: Hikers and leashed dogs only. No horses or mountain bikes are allowed. No wheelchair access.

Permits: This trail is accessible mid-June–September. A federal Northwest Forest Pass is required to park here.

Maps: For a map of Mount Baker–Snoqualmie National Forest, contact the Outdoor Recreation Information Center at the downtown Seattle REI. For topographic maps, ask Green Trails for No. 207, Snoqualmie Pass, or ask the USGS for Snoqualmie Pass.

Directions: From Seattle, drive east on I-90 to exit 52. Turn left (north) at the exit ramp and take the first right into the PCT-North parking area. The lot to the left is intended for stock; hikers can continue straight to the main parking lot. The trail starts at the east end of the parking lot.

Contact: Mount Baker–Snoqualmie National Forest, North Bend Ranger Station, 902 SE North Bend Way, Bldg. 1, North Bend, WA 98045, 425/888-1421 x200.

128 GOLD CREEK VALLEY
8.0 mi/4.0 hr   🏃1 ⛰9

north of Snoqualmie Pass in Alpine Lakes Wilderness of Mount Baker-Snoqualmie National Forest

Map 3.3, page 113

Gold Creek Trail is an easy venture through old-growth forest on the east side of the crest. The trail gains just 400 feet of elevation in 4 miles of maintained trail, making it accessible by hikers of all abilities. Meadows and avalanche chutes are numerous, providing ample views of the surrounding peaks and ridges. Although it is along the Cascade Crest, the trail sits low in the valley. It is often one of the first trails in the area to be snow free. That makes it a great selection in June. Hikers looking for a challenge can continue on nonmaintained trails to Alaska or Joe Lakes, each situated high on the valley's ridges.

Gold Creek Trail travels for a mile before crossing into Alpine Lakes Wilderness. An old-growth forest of fir and hemlock provides needed shade as Gold Creek gushes with the winter's snowmelt. The trail crosses several streams along the way, including Gold Creek, and may be difficult or even impassable when stream flow is high. The route eventually crosses Silver Creek, where maintenance of the trail ends. From here, audacious hikers can bushwhack it to steep footpaths up to Alaska and Joe Lakes. These high lakes in small cirques are set within subalpine parkland. A specific destination is not required on Gold Creek Trail, as the entire length of the trail makes for excellent hiking.

User Groups: Hikers and leashed dogs. No horses or mountain bikes are allowed. No wheelchair access.

Permits: This trail is accessible mid-May–November. A federal Northwest Forest Pass is required to park here.

Maps: For a map of Mount Baker–Snoqualmie National Forest, contact the Outdoor Recreation Information Center at the downtown Seattle REI. For topographic maps, ask Green Trails for No. 207, Snoqualmie Pass, or ask the USGS for Chikamin Peak.

Directions: From Seattle, drive east on I-90 to exit 54 (Hyak/Gold Creek). Turn left and drive 0.2 mile to Forest Service Road 4832. Turn right and drive 1 mile to Forest Service Road 142. Turn left and drive 0.4 mile to the signed trailhead and parking lot at the road's closure.

Contact: Mount Baker–Snoqualmie National Forest, North Bend Ranger Station, 902 SE North Bend Way, Bldg. 1, North Bend, WA 98045, 425/888-1421 x200.

129 MARGARET AND LILLIAN LAKES
9.2-10.6 mi/5.0-6.0 hr   🏃4 ⛰9

northeast of Snoqualmie Pass in Alpine Lakes Wilderness of Wenatchee National Forest

Map 3.3, page 113

Margaret and Lillian Lakes are just two in a series of high-country lakes within the south end of Rampart Ridge. These subalpine lakes enjoy knockout views of the inner Cascade Crest. You'd never guess from the jumble of cars at the trailhead that this trail is a steep one or that it endures a stretch of road hiking for the first 2 miles. Never mind, for this is a great hike just 90 minutes from Seattle.

The signed trailhead is just uphill from the parking lot on Forest Service Road 4934. Passing through the gates, hike the old road for nearly 2 miles before finding true trail. Subalpine fir and mountain hemlock provide welcome shade on this hot, dry trail. Extra water will be appreciated during the summer heat. The trail soon splits at a saddle (3.5 miles), with the right fork dropping to Margaret Lake (4.6 miles). Rocky meadows surround the cool lake below Mount Margaret.

For a slightly longer hike, stay left at the junction, continuing to follow Rampart Ridge Trail down to Twin Lakes (4.5 miles) and on to Lake Lillian (5.3 miles). Both lakes revel in wildflower blooms in July, and views across Gold Creek to Kendall Peak are awesome. Campers need to stay away from lakeshores and find established sites. Adhere to the trails at all times, for these are fragile environs.

User Groups: Hikers only. No dogs, horses, or mountain bikes are allowed. No wheelchair access.

Permits: This trail is accessible mid-June–mid-October. A federal Northwest Forest Pass is required to park here.

Maps: For a map of Wenatchee National Forest, contact the Outdoor Recreation Information Center at the downtown Seattle REI. For topographic maps, ask Green Trails for No. 207, Snoqualmie Pass, or ask the USGS for Chikamin Peak and Stampede Pass.

Directions: From Seattle, drive east on I-90 to exit 54 (Hyak/Gold Creek). Turn left and drive 0.2 mile to Forest Service Road 4832. Turn right and drive 4.5 miles to Forest Service Road 4934 (signed for Trail 1332). Turn left and drive 0.5 mile to the parking area. The signed trailhead is a short walk up Forest Service Road 4934 behind a gated road.

Contact: Wenatchee National Forest, Cle Elum Ranger Station, 803 W. 2nd St., Cle Elum, WA 98922, 509/852-1100.

130 RACHEL LAKE

7.6 mi/4.0 hr

northeast of Snoqualmie Pass in Alpine Lakes Wilderness of Wenatchee National Forest

Map 3.3, page 113

Rachel Lake is one of the most popular destinations along the I-90 corridor. Crowds are a given on just about any day of the week, a testament to the accessibility and beauty of the lakes basin. Rachel Lake Trail is perfect for folks looking for an undemanding but beautiful hike a little more than an hour from Seattle. The enjoyable hike leads to a basin of lakes neighbored by craggy peaks.

The first 3 miles of Rachel Lake Trail are relatively flat and pass quickly. This section passes through forest and occasional avalanche chutes, where colorful fireweed dominates the openings. The last mile gets interesting and much tougher, climbing steeply through a classic box canyon. The views begin to appear as you enter the high country. Rachel Lake is the largest of three lakes and many small tarns beneath Rampart Ridge, each tempting with their cool water.

Rampart Ridge and the lakes have seen a lot of use, with denuded areas abounding. This is unfortunate, as beautiful alpine meadows used to be prolific here. Alta Mountain stands tall to the north and offers a good scramble to the top. There is a lot of country to explore from Rachel Lake, and much of it already has been covered. Yet Rachel Lake is a beautiful destination and will always be a solidly popular day hike.

User Groups: Hikers Only. No dogs, horses, or mountain bikes are allowed. No wheelchair access.

Permits: This trail is accessible June–October. A federal Northwest Forest Pass is required to park here. A free wilderness permit is also required to hike here and is available at the trailhead.

Maps: For a map of Wenatchee National Forest, contact the Outdoor Recreation Information Center at the downtown Seattle REI. For topographic maps, ask Green Trails for No. 207, Snoqualmie Pass, or ask the USGS for Snoqualmie Pass.

Directions: From Seattle, drive east on I-90 to exit 62. Turn left on Kachess Lake Road and drive 5.5 miles to Forest Service Road 4930. Turn right and drive 3.5 miles to the trailhead at road's end.

Contact: Wenatchee National Forest, Cle Elum Ranger District, 803 W. 2nd St., Cle Elum, WA 98922, 509/852-1100.

131 KACHESS RIDGE

13.1 mi one-way/7.0 hr 🏃3 ⛰8

north of Easton in Wenatchee National Forest

Map 3.3, page 113

High above two large reservoirs, Kachess Ridge Trail traverses more than 13 miles along a high, meadowy ridge. One of the best trails to this outstanding trail is via French Cabin Creek Trail, which reaches the ridge by passing through a large meadow on its way to bigger meadows and great views. From here, hikers have an easy option to enjoy the meadows of Silver Creek Basin. A longer option to the summit of Thorp Mountain is also possible with this hike.

Located on the east side of the Cascade Crest, the hike through French Cabin Basin often opens up to hiking earlier than many other trails in the Interstate 90 corridor. This is a great place to catch wildflowers in bloom in June. Later in summer, however, the hike can be quite hot and draining in the hot sun. Be sure to bring sunscreen and extra water in hot weather, as there is little to no water to be found along the route.

From the recommended parking area, hike 0.5 miles up Forest Service Road 4308-132 to the official trailhead on the left. From here, French Cabin Creek Trail steadily climbs through the forest until it reaches the open expanse of French Cabin Basin (1.5 miles). The trail continues climbing to a junction with Kachess Ridge Trail. The easier option is to turn left (south) at this junction and hike 1.5 miles along Kachess Ridge Trail as it passes through a notch of French Cabin Mountain to Silver Creek Basin. The recommended turn-around is at a second junction with Silver Creek Tie Trail (3.5 miles).

A second, more challenging option is to turn right (north) on Kachess Ridge Trail and hike to Thorp Mountain. At 4 miles from the car, stay left on Kachess Ridge Trail as it passes above Thorp Lake. At 5 miles, the trail passes beneath Thorp Mountain and a well-used side trail climbs to the summit (5.3 miles) for some of the area's best views. At 5,854 feet, you'll see much of the surrounding Cascades, most spectacularly Mount Rainier.

User Groups: Hikers, leashed dogs, horses, and mountain bikes. No wheelchair access.

Permits: This trail is accessible April–October. A federal Northwest Forest Pass is required to park here.

Maps: For a map of Wenatchee National Forest, contact the Outdoor Recreation Information Center at the downtown Seattle REI. For topographic maps, ask Green Trails for No. 208, Kachess Lake, or ask the USGS for Kachess Lake.

Directions: From Seattle, drive east on Interstate 90 to exit 80 (Roslyn/Salman la Sac). Drive north over the freeway and turn left on Bullfrog Road. Drive 4 miles to Highway 903 and turn left (north) toward Roslyn. Drive about 12 miles to French Cabin Creek Road (Forest Service Road 4308), located just past Cle Elem Lake. Turn left and drive 6.5 miles to Forest Service Road 4308-132. This junction is the recommended parking area. The official trailhead is 0.5 mile up Road 4308-132.

132 DECEPTION PASS LOOP

14.7 mi/1-3 days 🏃2 ⛰8

north of Cle Elum in Alpine Lakes Wilderness of Wenatchee National Forest

Map 3.3, page 113

The climax of the trip is not at Deception Pass but instead beneath the amazing Cathedral Rock and the parkland surrounding its base. Cathedral Rock looms high above the PCT, with towering rock cliffs that somehow sing and make cathedral the only word fit to describe the peak. Throw in great views of the Wenatchee Mountains and Mount Stuart, and you have the makings for a great weekend of hiking.

The hike works either clockwise or counterclockwise, but the latter makes for less strenuous climbing and is described here. Start at Tucquala Lake and head north through Cle Elum Valley to the pass, which is wooded and offers few views. Here, Marmot Lake and Lake Clarice are 4 miles to the north along a down-and-up trail, each with campsites.

From Deception Pass, the route follows the PCT south past impressive mountain hemlocks before arriving at the base of Cathedral Rock. A pair of stream crossings may be difficult in times of heavy runoff. At Cathedral Rock, the trail climbs to beautiful parkland meadows of huckleberries, heather, and small trees. Peggy's Pond lies a short 0.5 mile around the base of Cathedral Rock and is worth visiting. The route drops steeply to the trailhead via Cathedral Rock Trail, passing Squaw Lake along the way.

User Groups: Hikers, leashed dogs, and horses (horses will be unable to cross a blown-out ford on a stream along the PCT). No mountain bikes are allowed. No wheelchair access.

Permits: This trail is accessible June–October. A federal Northwest Forest Pass is required to park here.

Maps: For a map of Wenatchee National Forest, contact the Outdoor Recreation Information Center at the downtown Seattle REI. For topographic maps, ask Green Trails for No. 176, Stevens Pass, or ask the USGS for Mount Daniel and The Cradle.

Directions: From Seattle, drive east on I-90 to exit 80 (Roslyn). Turn left on Bullfrog Cutoff Road and drive to Highway 903. Turn left and drive to Salmon La Sac and Forest Service Road 4330. Continue straight on Forest Service Road 4330 to Tucquala Meadows Trailhead at road's end.

Contact: Wenatchee National Forest, Cle Elum Ranger District, 803 W. 2nd St., Cle Elum, WA 98922, 509/852-1100.

133 TUCK AND ROBIN LAKES
12.8 mi/1–2 days 🥾3 ⛰9

north of Cle Elum in Alpine Lakes Wilderness of Wentachee National Forest

Map 3.3, page 113

These two picturesque lakes are classics among folks who regularly hike this area. Set high on the west side of the Wenatchee Ridge, Robin Lake reveals typical but never-tiring beauty of mountain hemlocks, heather, and huckleberries. This is a great destination, but with a little more effort, Tuck Lake delivers an outstanding high-mountain landscape uncommon in the Northwest. At an elevation of 6,100 feet, vegetation becomes scarce, large bare slabs of Granite Mountain beg for exploration, and a feeling of high alpine is always in the air.

The trail begins on Deception Pass Trail. The first 3 miles are flat and easy as the trail moves up the upper reaches of the Cle Elum River Valley. From here, the trail climbs well up through lazy switchbacks and at 4.5 miles is the cutoff for Tuck and Robin Lakes. Turning right, the trail ascends steeply, 1,100 feet in 2 miles, on sometimes rocky and difficult trail. After 2 miles, you've arrived at Robin Lake in subalpine forest. Bare slabs of granite mix with patches of mountain hemlocks and heather. Tuck Lake is about 1.5 miles farther on a way path that can provide some difficulty, as it climbs another 900 feet. At Tuck, the landscape is barren, with large slabs of granite exposed for lack of any decent soil at such an altitude. Blue sky and massive peaks fill the horizon.

While camping is available at both lakes, don't count on getting a spot if you show up late. This is a popular trail, and established campsites fill early; disappearing vegetation is a concern, so setting up camp outside of the designated sites is discouraged. During the summer and early fall, it is best as a day hike.

User Groups: Hikers only. No dogs, horses, or mountain bikes are allowed. No wheelchair access.

Permits: This trail is accessible late June–early October. A federal Northwest Forest Pass is required to park here.

Maps: For a map of Wenatchee National Forest, contact the Outdoor Recreation Information Center at the downtown Seattle REI. For topographic maps, ask Green Trails for No. 176, Stevens Pass, or ask the USGS for Mount Daniel and The Cradle.

Directions: From Seattle, drive east on I-90 to exit 80 (Roslyn). Turn left on Bullfrog Cutoff Road and drive to Highway 903. Turn left and drive to Salmon La Sac and Forest Service Road 4330. Continue straight on Forest Service Road 4330 to Tucquala Meadows Trailhead at road's end.

Contact: Wenatchee National Forest, Cle Elum Ranger District, 803 W. 2nd St., Cle Elum, WA 98922, 509/852-1100.

134 PADDY-GO-EASY PASS

6.0 mi/3.5 hr

north of Roslyn in Alpine Lakes Wilderness of Wenatchee National Forest

Map 3.3, page 113

Trailblazers must be sarcastic folk, especially when it comes to naming their new trails. Experienced hikers know as a general rule of thumb that when the word "easy" is used in a trail name, that trail is usually anything but easy. Regardless of the effort, hikers are often pleased with the outstanding views of many nearby peaks and ridges. The route travels outstanding high-country terrain, full of meadows covered in wildflowers. To top off the trip is Sprite Lake, an all-star lake set before The Cradle.

French Creek Trail makes a steady and steep ascent to the pass. Forest lines most of the way up before thinning to great meadows. This is a very colorful place in early July, when wildflowers are in full bloom. The trail gains roughly 2,700 feet in 3 miles. The pass is superb, with views of numerous peaks. Mounts Daniel, Stuart, and Rainier are particularly memorable. The pass lies at the crest of the Wenatchee Mountains, a beautiful ridge in its own right.

For further exploration, Sprite Lake lies a short distance over the pass within a small glacial cirque, with rocky slopes and scrubby subalpine trees. Across the valley below stands The Cradle, a tall, rocky, and barren peak. No, Paddy, it's not an easy hike, but it certainly is spectacular.

User Groups: Hikers, leashed dogs, and horses. No mountain bikes are allowed. No wheelchair access.

Permits: This trail is accessible July–mid-October. A federal Northwest Forest Pass is required to park here.

Maps: For a map of Wenatchee National Forest, contact the Outdoor Recreation Information Center at the downtown Seattle REI. For topographic maps, ask Green Trails for No. 176, Stevens Pass, or ask the USGS for The Cradle.

Directions: From Seattle, drive east on I-90 to exit 80 (Roslyn). Turn left on Bullfrog Cutoff Road and drive to Highway 903. Turn left and drive to Salmon La Sac and Forest Service Road 4330. Continue straight on Forest Service Road 4330 to Paddy-Go-Easy Pass, 1 mile before road's end.

Contact: Wenatchee National Forest, Cle Elum Ranger Station, 803 W. 2nd St., Cle Elum, WA 98922, 509/852-1100.

135 WAPTUS RIVER VALLEY

29.6 mi/4 days

north of Salmon La Sac in Alpine Lakes Wilderness of Wenatchee National Forest

Map 3.3, page 113

Waptus River Valley is not an end in itself. The trail leads to a number of high-country destinations, including Spade Lake and Dutch Miller Gap, two highlights of the Alpine Lakes Wilderness. It's a bit like those old books in which you can choose your own adventure. Take a number of trips up the river, each with different destinations and results. Of course, Waptus River and Waptus Lake are not to be overlooked. The route up the valley is beautiful, while Waptus Lake is the Alpine Lakes' largest lake, with excellent camping.

Waptus River Trail follows the river closely within surrounding forests. Waptus Lake (8.5 miles) has campsites and views of massive Summit Chief and Bears Breast Mountains. The main trail skirts the lake and continues to the head of the valley, where it makes for Dutch Miller Gap. Near the top of the tough ascent to the pass lies Lake Ivanhoe, a high lake set within shores of granite. Dutch Miller Gap leads down into the Middle Fork Snoqualmie.

One of the most popular side trips is Spade Lake. From Waptus Lake, Spade Lake Trail climbs steeply to Spade Lake. The views are good until the lake, where they become excellent. Other adventures along Waptus River Trail include trails up gentle Trail Creek, Waptus Pass over to Escondido Creek, and the PCT, which crosses the valley just above Waptus Lake.

User Groups: Hikers, leashed dogs, and horses. No mountain bikes are allowed. No wheelchair access.

Permits: This trail is accessible July–October. A federal Northwest Forest Pass is required to park here.

Maps: For a map of Wenatchee National Forest, contact the Outdoor Recreation Information Center at the downtown Seattle REI. For topographic maps, ask Green Trails for No. 176, Stevens Pass, and No. 208, Kachess Lake, or ask the USGS for Mount Daniel and Polallie Ridge.

Directions: From Seattle, drive east on I-90 to exit 80 (Roslyn). Turn left on Bullfrog Cutoff Road and drive to Highway 903. Turn left and drive to Salmon La Sac Campground. Waptus Trailhead is on the right, just after you cross Cle Elum River.

Contact: Wenatchee National Forest, Cle Elum Ranger Station, 803 W. 2nd St., Cle Elum, WA 98922, 509/852-1100.

136 JOLLY MOUNTAIN
12.4 mi/8.0 hr

north of Cle Elum in Wenatchee National Forest

Map 3.3, page 113

At 6,443 feet elevation, Jolly Mountain is well capable of delivering excellent views of surrounding ridges and mountains. On clear days, which are easier to come by here on the east side of the Cascades, the tall peak delivers. The route climbs up along Salmon La Sac Creek to a ridge before making the final ascent to Jolly Mountain. The way is extremely steep, gaining more than 4,000 feet in just 6 miles of trail. This trail is definitely for the well conditioned, except for those traveling by mountain bike or motorcycle, which are allowed on the trail.

Jolly Mountain Trail makes a steady and steep climb up the creek valley, crossing it at 2.6 miles (difficult ford when the snows are still melting, until mid-July). The views are plentiful, as are the wildflowers blooming in early summer. The trail makes a final steep rise to the summit of Jolly Mountain. The peak provides wide views in all directions, and the vast size of Mount Stuart is readily apparent. The trail is very dry, so be sure to carry lots of water.

User Groups: Hikers, leashed dogs, horses, mountain bikes, and motorcycles. No wheelchair access.

Permits: This trail is accessible June–November. A federal Northwest Forest Pass is required to park here.

Maps: For a map of Wenatchee National Forest, contact the Outdoor Recreation Information Center at the downtown Seattle REI. For topographic maps, ask Green Trails for No. 208, Kachess Lake, or ask the USGS for Davis Peak.

Directions: From Seattle, drive east on I-90 to exit 80 (Roslyn). Turn left on Bullfrog Cutoff Road and drive to Highway 903. Turn left and drive to Salmon La Sac. Jolly Mountain Trailhead is on the right, just beyond Cayuse Horse Camp.

Contact: Wenatchee National Forest, Cle

Elum Ranger Station, 803 W. 2nd St., Cle Elum, WA 98922, 509/852-1100.

137 SUMMIT LAKE/ BEARHEAD MOUNTAIN

5.0-6.0 mi/3.0 hr   👫2 ⛰9

south of Enumclaw in Clearwater Wilderness of Mount Baker-Snoqualmie National Forest

Map 3.3, page 113

One trailhead provides access to these two destinations, one a high, subalpine lake and the other an even higher mountain summit. Most folks pick one and take it easy, rather than cram both hikes into one long, strenuous day. A trip to Summit Lake, an ideal midsummer swimming hole, is 2.5 miles one-way and a 1,000-foot elevation gain. A trip to the panoramic viewpoint of Bearhead Mountain is 3 miles one-way, climbing 1,700 feet.

The routes follow Summit Lake Trail into Clearwater Wilderness, climbing to Twin Lake (0.8 mile). The trail splits here; Summit Lake Trail turns left while Carbon Trail heads right to Bearhead Mountain. The climb to Bearhead traverses the base of the mountain before turning to climb straight up the shoulder on Bearhead Mountain Trail (2.2 miles). From 6,089 feet, the views are stupendous. Mountains to the north, mountains to the east, and mountains to the south.

A slight majority of hikers turn toward Summit Lake and its meadow shores. Wildflowers arrive in July while huckleberries wait until late August. Mount Rainier is easily seen from the shore, an incredible dream. Those with an itch for views will enjoy knowing that an easy scramble leaves from the lake to a peak rising west of the lake with great views.

User Groups: Hikers, leashed dogs, and horses. No mountain bikes are allowed. No wheelchair access.

Permits: This trail is accessible mid-June–September. A federal Northwest Forest Pass is required to park here.

Maps: For a map of Mount Baker-Snoqualmie National Forest, contact the Outdoor Recreation Information Center at the downtown Seattle REI. For topographic maps, ask Green Trails for No. 237, Enumclaw, or ask the USGS for Bearhead Mountain.

Directions: From Enumclaw, drive west 5 miles to Highway 165 (on the west side of Buckley). Turn left (south) and drive 10.5 miles to Carbon River Highway. Turn left and drive 7.7 miles to Cayada Creek Road (Forest Service Road 7810). Turn left and drive 7 miles to the trailhead at road's end.

Contact: Mount Baker–Snoqualmie National Forest, Enumclaw Ranger Station, 450 Roosevelt Avenue East, Enumclaw, WA 98022, 360/825-6585.

138 GREENWATER RIVER

15.2 mi/1-2 days   👫2 ⛰9

south of Enumclaw in Norse Peak Wilderness of Mount Baker-Snoqualmie National Forest

Map 3.3, page 113

In one of the few virgin river valleys left in the southern Mount Baker–Snoqualmie National Forest, Greenwater River Trail explores it all. Coursing more than 10 miles to Corral Pass, its highlights are several lakes gracing the route. Being rather flat and certainly easy, this is a great full day hike or overnight trip for young or beginner backpackers, especially early or late in the year, when snow still blankets the high country.

Greenwater River Trail never ventures far from the beautiful, lively river. Endure a quick spell of old logging before immersing yourself in an ancient forest of Douglas fir, western hemlock, and western red cedar. A pair of small lakes (Meeker and Upper Greenwater) appear at two and 2.4 miles. These lakes are good turnarounds for a short day hike. Continuing up, the trail passes a pair of signed junctions to Echo Lake (6.9 miles). A number of campgrounds are found at the south end of the lake (7.4 miles). Don't forget the fly rod, because the trout in this lake make a sizable dinner.

User Groups: Hikers, leashed dogs, and horses. No mountain bikes are allowed. No wheelchair access.

Permits: This trail is accessible April–November. A federal Northwest Forest Pass is required to park here.

Maps: For a map of Mount Baker–Snoqualmie National Forest, contact the Outdoor Recreation Information Center at the downtown Seattle REI. For topographic maps, ask Green Trails for No. 239, Lester, or ask the USGS for Lester SW.

Directions: From Enumclaw, drive east on Highway 410 20.5 miles to Greenwater Road (Forest Service Road 70). Turn left (north) and drive 10 miles to Forest Service Road 7033. Turn right and drive 0.5 mile to the signed trailhead on the right.

Contact: Mount Baker–Snoqualmie National Forest, Enumclaw Ranger Station, 450 Roosevelt Avenue East, Enumclaw, WA 98022, 360/825-6585.

139 NOBLE KNOB

7.4 mi/4.0 hr

south of Enumclaw in Norse Peak Wilderness of Mount Baker-Snoqualmie National Forest

Map 3.3, page 113

Tally it all up: $10 national park fee? No. Pure meadow bliss, complete with wildflowers in July? Yes. Long, taxing climb? No. Miles and miles of brilliant views? Yes. If you're not sold already, keep reading. The trail to Noble Knob is one of ease and excitement, a glorious ramble through the high country to a magnificent viewpoint. Noble Knob Trail starts high, at 5,700 feet elevation, an altitude that changes little throughout the hike. Skirting the base of Mutton Mountain and the slopes of Dalles Ridge, the trail arrives at the base of Noble Knob, a small rounded peak. A short side trail leads to the summit, the former site of a fire lookout. Mountain views appear from every direction (Olympics to the northwest), but of course Mount Rainier steals the show. Expect

to see a lot of company on Noble Knob Trail, especially on summer weekends.

User Groups: Hikers, leashed dogs, horses, and mountain bikes. No wheelchair access.

Permits: This trail is accessible June– September. A federal Northwest Forest Pass is required to park here.

Maps: For a map of Mount Baker–Snoqualmie National Forest, contact the Outdoor Recreation Information Center at the downtown Seattle REI. For topographic maps, ask Green Trails for No. 239, Lester, or ask the USGS for Suntop and Lester SW.

Directions: From Enumclaw, drive east 32 miles on Highway 410 to Corral Pass Road (Forest Service Road 7174). Turn left (east) and drive 6.7 miles to the trailhead just before Corral Pass Campground.

Contact: Mount Baker–Snoqualmie National Forest, Enumclaw Ranger Station, 450 Roosevelt Avenue East, Enumclaw, WA 98022, 360/825-6585.

140 MOUNT DAVID

14.0 mi/8.0 hr

north of Lake Wenatchee in Glacier Peak Wilderness of Wenatchee National Forest

Map 3.4, page 114

This is about as high as one can get in the Glacier Peak Wilderness, other than Glacier Peak itself. It certainly feels that way. Tucked up north of Lake Wenatchee, Mount David towers over surrounding peaks for miles and miles. That leaves unmatched panoramic views for those who summit the challenging peak. Neighboring ridges and peaks fall away from beneath, melting into scores of other ridges as far as the eye can see. Challenging is an understatement for this trail. Make no mistake, this is a long, taxing ascent to the top. Alpine ridges and never-ending views make all the hard work worthwhile.

The route begins on Panther Creek Trail but Mount David Trail takes off to the right (west) after 1 mile. Here, the climbing begins. It's a steady assault on the mountain, but thanks to the excellent layout of the trail, it's never too much. The total elevation gain is 5,100 feet, or what is known as a "full day." No water is to be found along the trail, so be sure to bring several liters per person. From the ridge, the views open up as the trail contours on or just below the sharp ridge. The mountain falls away precipitously at your feet, down to the valley bottom far below. The trail seems to become steeper nearer the end, but that is likely because of complaints from weary legs. A small scramble conquers the summit. There's no end to the visible peaks, certainly too many to list here. At 7,431 feet tall, Mount David feels like the top of the world.

User Groups: Hikers and leashed dogs. No horses or mountain bikes are allowed. No wheelchair access.

Permits: This trail is accessible August–October. A federal Northwest Forest Pass is required to park here.

Maps: For a map of Wenatchee National Forest, contact the Outdoor Recreation Information Center at the downtown Seattle REI. For topographic maps, ask Green Trails for No. 145, Wenatchee Lake, or ask the USGS for Wenatchee Lake.

Directions: From Leavenworth, drive west on U.S. 2 to Highway 207 (at Coles Corner). Turn right and drive to White River Road, north of Lake Wenatchee (Forest Service Road 6400). Turn right and drive to the trailhead at road's end.

Contact: Wenatchee National Forest, Lake Wenatchee Ranger Station, 22976 Hwy. 207, Leavenworth, WA 98826, 509/548-2550.

141 LITTLE GIANT PASS
10.0 mi/7.0 hr

north of Lake Wenatchee in Glacier Peak Wilderness of Wenatchee National Forest

Map 3.4, page 114

From Little Giant Pass, the views are nearly indescribable. From the pass, enjoy expansive views stretching miles to dozens of mountains and ridges. Don't forget to look down, as well, for the perspective of not one but two immense, glacially carved valleys at your feet. This is one knee-knocking, lung-busting, hellraiser of a hike—3,800 vertical feet in a brisk 5 miles. In addition to the breathtaking vistas, you'll view vast wildflower meadows within beautiful basins during summer.

Little Giant Trail begins with a ford of Chiwawa River, a wet ordeal in the summer and fall but an impassable obstacle any other time. The trail wastes no time and immediately begins a long series of switchbacks out of the valley. Old-growth forest covers the trail and keeps hikers cool with shade. The trail crosses Little Giant Creek (other than remnant snowpack, the route's only water source) and begins entering exposed meadows. The climbing isn't done until you reach the pass. The wide, U-shaped valleys of the Chiwawa and Napeequa Rivers reveal their glacial origins. Snowcapped peaks and ridges line the horizon in every direction. Remember extra water or a water filter on this trip; you'll definitely need it.

User Groups: Hikers, leashed dogs, and horses (horses not recommended). No mountain bikes are allowed. No wheelchair access.

Permits: This trail is accessible June–October. No permits are required. Parking and access are free.

Maps: For a map of Wenatchee National Forest, contact the Outdoor Recreation Information Center at the downtown Seattle REI. For topographic maps, ask Green Trails for No. 113, Holden, or ask the USGS for Trinity and Clark Mountain.

Directions: From Leavenworth, drive west on U.S. 2 to Highway 207, at Coles Corner. Turn left, drive to Fish Lake, and drive 1 mile to Chiwawa Valley Road (Forest Service Road 62). Turn left and drive toward Trinity to Little Giant Trailhead on the left, 1.5 miles beyond Nineteenmile Campground.

Contact: Wenatchee National Forest, Lake Wenatchee Ranger Station, 22976 Hwy. 207, Leavenworth, WA 98826, 509/548-2550.

142 DIRTY FACE
9.0 mi/5.0 hr   🏃5 ⛰8

north of Lake Wenatchee in Wenatchee
National Forest

Map 3.4, page 114

We won't throw around terms such as cruel or nasty, but Dirty Face is not a stroll in the park. This trail is a straight-up assault on the mountain. Fair enough, for hikers are armed with endless switchbacks and canteens of water to help reach the top. A successful hiker is rewarded with views of Lake Wenatchee and numerous peaks of the Glacier Peak Wilderness. The site formerly hosted a Forest Service lookout to take advantage of the wide vista. Don't be discouraged if the hike sounds difficult. It is challenging, but it is beautiful as well.

Dirty Face Trail changes little over its length, composed entirely of switchbacks—reports vary between 70 and 90. After about 25 or so, the simple act of counting becomes easier said than done. The trail runs into an abandoned logging road (1.5 miles), which must be followed to its end—there the trail begins again. Ponderosa pine provides poor shade along the trail before patches of subalpine trees begin to offer even less. The trail reaches a ridge, then switchbacks up even more to the former lookout site. The views are grand to the east and west, encompassing much of the Glacier Peak Wilderness. Lake Wenatchee glimmers in the sunshine below.

User Groups: Hikers, leashed dogs, horses, and mountain bikes. No wheelchair access.

Permits: This trail is accessible mid-June–October. A federal Northwest Forest Pass is required to park here.

Maps: For a map of Wenatchee National Forest, contact the Outdoor Recreation Information Center at the downtown Seattle REI. For topographic maps, ask Green Trails for No. 145, Wenatchee Lake, or ask the USGS for Wenatchee Lake.

Directions: From Leavenworth, drive west on U.S. 2 to Highway 207 (at Coles Corner). Turn right and drive to the trailhead at Lake Wenatchee Ranger Station.

Contact: Wenatchee National Forest, Lake Wenatchee Ranger Station, 22976 Hwy. 207, Leavenworth, WA 98826, 509/548-2550.

143 CHIWAUKUM CREEK
24.4 mi/2-3 days   🏃3 ⛰10

near Leavenworth in Alpine Lakes Wilderness of Wenatchee National Forest

Map 3.4, page 114

Little-known Chiwaukum Creek is a trail corridor with all sorts of options. Several decades ago the road to the trailhead closed, adding a couple of miles to the hike in. Apparently an old road is grounds for dismissal of a trail, perhaps because there are so many other great hikes in the area. But fewer people adds to its appeal. The options exist because the trail starts up the valley before splitting into North and South Forks. Each of these trails then splits again. It can quickly amount to a full summer of weekends trying to hike it all. The crown jewel of the valley is Larch Lake, attained via 12 miles on North Fork Trail.

Chiwaukum Trail heads up the valley for 6 miles before splitting, staying close to the cool water of the creek among great forests of pine and fir. The beautiful and rarely traveled South Fork heads left, eventually splitting to reach Icicle Ridge Trail at Ladies Pass or Index Creek. The route via Ladies Pass travels between Lake Brigham and Lake Flora, outstanding high-country lakes. Also on the South Fork is a trail up Palmer Creek, to the Badlands and Icicle Ridge again.

North Fork Trail crosses Glacier Creek (8 miles) before climbing to reach the forested shores of Chiwaukum Lake (10 miles). Rocky mountain ridges surround the cool, blue water of the lake, as do numerous campsites. The trail continues to Larch Lake (12.2 miles), an area of meadows and jagged ridges. Larches and subalpine firs cover the landscape.

User Groups: Hikers, leashed dogs, and horses

(horses allowed only to Glacier Creek). No mountain bikes are allowed. No wheelchair access.

Permits: This trail is accessible late July–October. A federal Northwest Forest Pass is required to park here.

Maps: For a map of Wenatchee National Forest, contact the Outdoor Recreation Information Center at the downtown Seattle REI. For topographic maps, ask Green Trails for No. 177, Chiwaukum Mountains, or ask the USGS for Winton, Big Jim Mountain, and Chiwaukum Mountain.

Directions: From Stevens Pass, drive 25 miles east on U.S. 2 to Mile Marker 89. Turn right onto Chiwaukum Creek Road (Forest Service Road 7908) just beyond the marker. Drive to a junction and stay to the right. Drive to the road's end and the trailhead.

Contact: Wenatchee National Forest, Leavenworth Ranger Station, 600 Sherbourne, Leavenworth, WA 98826, 509/548-2550.

144 CHATTER CREEK/ LAKE EDNA

11.5 mi/8.0 hr

near Leavenworth in Alpine Lakes Wilderness of Wenatchee National Forest

Map 3.4, page 114

Some folks hike the Alpine Lakes for a relaxing time away from home. Others come here looking for a relentless workout that offers killer views. Chatter Creek Trail up to Lake Edna is definitely for the latter type of hiker. It gains nearly 4,000 feet in just over 5 miles. That is undoubtedly considered a workout. As steep as the trail may be, however, it pays off with a terrific lake set in parkland and panoramic views of the Cascades. Lake Edna is situated along Icicle Ridge Trail, making Chatter Creek a quick but grueling access route to the high ridge trail.

Chatter Creek Trail quickly begins climbing, where old forests provide welcome shade on hot days. The trail crosses the creek (tricky

before June) and continues its relentless ascent to the ridgeline (5 miles). At least it spends its last half among wide-open meadows. The views begin to really emerge at this point.

Chatter Creek Trail contours a basin before making a final climb to the lake at 6,735 feet. The lake lies within a north-side basin, so snow may linger well into August. The shores are fairly barren of trees; only scrubs and meadow endure this high up. The best vistas are found atop Cape Horn, a steep scramble to the west. At over 7,000 feet, much of the Cascades can be seen. Those planning to camp at the lake or along the ridge must use established campsites and refrain from camping on the fragile meadows.

User Groups: Hikers only, no dogs. Not recommended for horse travel. No mountain bikes are allowed. No wheelchair access.

Permits: This trail is accessible July–October. A federal Northwest Forest Pass is required to park here. A free wilderness permit is also required to hike here and is available at the trailhead.

Maps: For a map of Wenatchee National Forest, contact the Outdoor Recreation Information Center at the downtown Seattle REI. For topographic maps, ask Green Trails for No. 177, Chiwaukum Mountains, or ask the USGS for Jack Ridge and Chiwaukum Mountain.

Directions: From Leavenworth, drive south on Icicle Creek Road (Forest Service Road 7600) 16 miles to Chatter Creek Campground and Trailhead, on the right.

Contact: Wenatchee National Forest, Leavenworth Ranger Station, 600 Sherbourne, Leavenworth, WA 98826, 509/548-2550.

145 JACK CREEK

23.2 mi/1-3 days

near Leavenworth in Alpine Lakes Wilderness of Wenatchee National Forest

Map 3.4, page 114

A lot awaits off Jack Creek Trail. Several trails lead off from Jack Creek, connecting to other major drainages of Icicle Creek and thereby creating spectacular loops for backpacking. Alone, the trail travels more than 11 miles to Stuart Pass and exceptional subalpine parkland. Most of the route is forested, the trail surrounded by old-growth forests of Douglas fir, Englemann spruce, and pines. The full length of the trail is rarely traveled, making Jack Creek a preferred backcountry route.

Jack Creek Trail follows the stream closely for most of its length. The trail to Trout Lake cuts off just over a mile in. This is a great loop when connected to Eightmile Lake (see listing in this chapter). A couple of miles later another trail leads to Trout Lake, much more steeply. Meadow Creek heads off to the west, providing a pair of loops; one climbs to Blackjack Ridge and Cradle Lake, an excellent high-country route, while the other crosses Meadow Creek Pass and drops into French Creek. Any of these routes are well chosen.

Jack Creek Trail slowly but surely gains in elevation to Stuart Pass (11.6 miles, 6,400 feet). Mount Stuart looms large to the east, and the Esmerelda Peaks are in view. The trail is a great valley hike, with plenty of camping along the way. It's an excellent trail to simply see where you end up.

User Groups: Hikers, leashed dogs, and horses. No mountain bikes are allowed. No wheelchair access.

Permits: This trail is accessible mid-June–November. A federal Northwest Forest Pass is required to park here. A free wilderness permit is also required to hike here and is available at the trailhead.

Maps: For a map of Wenatchee National Forest, contact the Outdoor Recreation Information Center at the downtown Seattle REI. For topographic maps, ask Green Trails for No. 177, Chiwaukum Mountains, and No. 210, Liberty, or ask the USGS for Jack Ridge and Mount Stuart.

Directions: From Leavenworth, drive south on Icicle Creek Road (Forest Service Road 7600) 16 miles to Trout/Jack Creek Trailhead on the left, just beyond Rock Island Campground.

Contact: Wenatchee National Forest, Leavenworth Ranger Station, 600 Sherbourne, Leavenworth, WA 98826, 509/548-2550.

146 ICICLE RIDGE
10.0-25.0 mi/3.5 hr-4 days

near Leavenworth in Alpine Lakes Wilderness of Wenatchee National Forest

Map 3.4, page 114

This long ridge trail is a favorite among Leavenworth locals. Extending for 25 miles and more, the trail takes in a wide variety of high country. Alpine meadows full of early summer flowers dominate nearly the entire route, while a number of high lakes occupy the western end. The route has a number of access points, both from Icicle Creek Road and the backcountry. Views are as prolific as the wildflowers, extending over much of the Alpine Lakes Wilderness and south to Mount Stuart and Mount Daniel. This high country is outstanding and, thankfully, preserved by the Alpine Lakes Wilderness.

At the eastern trailhead, Icicle Ridge Trail seemingly starts right in the town of Leavenworth. Little time is wasted in reaching the ridge, as the trail climbs quickly and steeply and then runs the crest. A steep trail from Icicle Creek Road via Fourth of July Creek reaches the ridge in this section. It's extremely dry in the summer, and the snow melts here before the rest of the trail, providing early access.

Icicle Ridge Trail drops off the ridge to cross Cabin Creek and reach large Lake Augusta, at 6,854 feet. Set beneath Big Jim Mountain, this is a great place for camping. The stars at night are surreal. The trail meanders along the north side of the ridge for a while, making junctions with Palmer Creek Trail and Index Creek Trail. Another ascent delivers Lakes Edna and craggy Cape Horn. Chatter Creek Trail accesses the ridge here in a 10-mile trip. The trail stays at or above

7,000 feet for several miles before dropping to Mary and Margaret Lakes. Hikers have access to Frosty or Whitehorse Creek Trails, both backcountry exits.

User Groups: Hikers, leashed dogs, and horses. Mountain bikes are allowed up to the wilderness boundary (near Fourth of July trail intersection). No wheelchair access.

Permits: This trail is accessible July–October (the eastern end opens in late May). A federal Northwest Forest Pass is required to park here. A free wilderness permit is also required to hike here and is available at the trailhead.

Maps: For a map of Wenatchee National Forest, contact the Outdoor Recreation Information Center at the downtown Seattle REI. For topographic maps, ask Green Trails for No. 177, Chiwaukum Mountains, and No. 178, Leavenworth, or ask the USGS for Big Jim Mountain, Cashmere Mountain, and Leavenworth.

Directions: From Leavenworth, drive south on Icicle Creek Road (Forest Service Road 7600) 16 miles to Chatter Creek Campground and Trailhead, on the right.

Contact: Wenatchee National Forest, Leavenworth Ranger Station, 600 Sherbourne, Leavenworth, WA 98826, 509/548-2550.

147 EIGHTMILE AND TROUT LAKE LOOP
18.0 mi/2 days   🥾4   ⛰10

near Leavenworth in Alpine Lakes Wilderness of Wenatchee National Forest

Map 3.4, page 114

This is an outstanding loop through tall, rocky ridges and mountains in the Alpine Lakes Wilderness. Windy Pass connects Trout Lake to Eightmile Lake via miles of excellent high-country hiking, achieving lakes and views that will not soon be forgotten. Windy Pass stands at 7,300 feet, revealing much of the surrounding wilderness. Cashmere Mountain stands to the east, Mount Stuart to the south,

and countless other peaks and ridges line the horizon. Trout and Eightmile Lakes are excellent destinations by themselves for day hikes or overnighters.

The loop requires a car drop or hitchhike from a friendly passerby. Starting from Eightmile Creek, the trail climbs moderately to Little Eightmile Lake and Eightmile Lake (3.3 miles), each dwarfed by the surrounding mountains. Camping along this route requires hikers to obtain a permit at the Leavenworth Ranger Station. The trail next reaches open parkland meadows and Lake Caroline (6.8 miles).

The prime moment of the hike comes at Windy Pass (7,200 feet), one of the best panoramic views on any trail in the region. Flowers and larches add color to the scene, each at their own times of the year. The trail descends three miles from Windy Pass to Trout Lake (12.3 miles), surrounded by trees and even more high ridges and peaks. From Trout Lake, the trail drops to Icicle Creek (18 miles).

User Groups: Hikers, leashed dogs (no dogs south of Windy Pass), and horses (horses day use only). No mountain bikes are allowed. No wheelchair access.

Permits: This trail is accessible July–early November. A federal Northwest Forest Pass is required to park here. Overnight stays require backcountry camping permits ($5 per person per day), which are available at Leavenworth Ranger Station.

Maps: For a map of Wenatchee National Forest, contact the Outdoor Recreation Information Center at the downtown Seattle REI. For topographic maps, ask Green Trails for No. 177, Chiwaukum Mountains, or ask the USGS for Cashmere Mountain and Jack Ridge.

Directions: From Leavenworth, drive south on Icicle Creek Road (Forest Service Road 7600) 7 miles to Forest Service Road 7601 (Bridge Creek Campground). Turn left and drive 3 miles to the signed trailhead on the right.

Contact: Wenatchee National Forest, Leavenworth Ranger Station, 600 Sherbourne, Leavenworth, WA 98826, 509/548-2550.

148 COLCHUCK AND STUART LAKES

9.0 mi/6.0 hr

near Leavenworth in Alpine Lakes Wilderness of Wenatchee National Forest

Map 3.4, page 114

These are two favorite destinations for many Alpine Lakes hikers. Each lake is a beautiful turquoise and is surrounded by great subalpine forests. Massive, rocky mountains enclose the lakes, and typically awesome mountain views are encountered along the trails. The lakes are great to hike no matter what your timeframe for the trip, as they are challenging day hikes as well as excellent overnighters. The trails can be fairly busy during the summer with day hikers, but an overnight permitting system keeps campers to a reasonable number. Colchuck and Stuart Lakes are wonderful and wild mountain lakes.

The route to the two lakes follows cool and refreshing Mountaineer Creek before splitting (2.5 miles). The left fork climbs to Colchuck Lake, a steep grade of switchbacks. A cool waterfall eases the pain. Colchuck Lake sits within patches of forest, directly beneath the enormous walls of Dragontail and Colchuck Peaks. Their rocky cliffs drop straight to the water.

From the junction, Stuart Lake Trail makes an easy and gentle climb through meadows to Stuart Lake. The way is full of views of the surrounding ridges and peaks, with Mount Stuart towering 4,000 feet above the lake. Impressive stuff, indeed. At both lakes, camping is grand. Regardless of which lake you choose, it's difficult to go wrong once you've stepped foot onto this trail.

User Groups: Hikers only. No dogs, horses, or mountain bikes are allowed. No wheelchair access.

Permits: This area is accessible July–October. A federal Northwest Forest Pass is required to park here. Overnight stays require backcountry camping permits ($5 per person per day), which are available at Leavenworth Ranger Station.

Maps: For a map of Wenatchee National Forest, contact the Outdoor Recreation Information Center at the downtown Seattle REI. For topographic maps, ask Green Trails for No. 177, Chiwaukum Mountains, and No. 209, Mount Stuart, or ask the USGS for Cashmere and Enchantment Lakes.

Directions: From Leavenworth, drive south on Icicle Creek Road (Forest Service Road 7600) 7 miles to Forest Service Road 7601 (Bridge Creek Campground). Turn left and drive 3 miles to the signed trailhead on the left.

Contact: Wenatchee National Forest, Leavenworth Ranger Station, 600 Sherbourne, Leavenworth, WA 98826, 509/548-2550.

149 THE ENCHANTMENTS

16.8 mi/2-4 days

south of Leavenworth in Alpine Lakes Wilderness of Wenatchee National Forest

Map 3.4, page 114   BEST ☾

Ahh, the Enchantments. Just the thought of this spectacular playground of high country warms the heart. Nowhere is quite like the Enchantments; this is the Shangri-la of Washington hiking. This series of high basins is filled with lakes of unsurpassed quality, with acres of subalpine parkland. Larches are everywhere, making late September a time not to miss. These high ridges have the craggiest rock you've seen. No trail description can ever do justice to the true beauty of the Enchantments.

The Enchantments are best reached via Snow Lakes. An excellent loop can be made by hiking down Aasgard Pass to Colchuck Lake. This requires a car-drop, however. So this description will stick to the Snow Lakes access. Because of large crowds of people visiting the area, folks planning on staying overnight—which is recommended— must obtain a permit from the Leavenworth Ranger Station.

Snow Lakes Trail crosses Icicle Creek and immediately climbs to Snow Lakes (6.5 miles).

Fortunately, much of the route is in old-growth forest. Snow Lakes are a common first-night camp for those unable to make it all the way to the Lower Enchantments. Between Snow Lakes and the first basin, the trail makes a very steep, rugged climb. The trees gradually give way, and hikers finally find themselves within the Enchantments (8 miles).

The Enchantments are a series of basins filled with lakes. A good map is necessary, as a network of trails laces the area. Marmots frolic in the meadows and sun themselves on the boulders while wind rustles the needles of subalpine firs and larches. The basins are rimmed by a number of ridges jutting into the sky with their sharp, craggy peaks. The main trail passes lake after lake on its way farther up and deeper into the basin. Glaciers overhang many of the upper lakes and are often heard cracking and breaking. The trail reaches Aasgard Pass (10.7 miles) before dropping steeply to Colchuck Lake, far below. Backpackers looking to spend a night or two in the Enchantments have numerous campsite options. Dozens of sites are located at nearly every lake. Just remember to pitch camp on a hard, durable, and established spot.

User Groups: Hikers only. No dogs, horses, or mountain bikes are allowed. No wheelchair access.

Permits: This trail is accessible mid-July–October. A federal Northwest Forest Pass is required to park here. Overnight stays within the Enchantments require backcountry camping permits, which are awarded by lottery at the Leavenworth Ranger Station.

Maps: For a map of Wenatchee National Forest, contact the Outdoor Recreation Information Center at the downtown Seattle REI. For topographic maps, ask Green Trails for No. 209S, The Enchantments, or ask the USGS for Cashmere, Enchantment Lakes, and Blewett.

Directions: From Leavenworth, drive south on Icicle Creek Road (Forest Service Road 7600) 4 miles to Snow Creek Trailhead on the left.

Contact: Wenatchee National Forest, Leavenworth Ranger Station, 600 Sherbourne, Leavenworth, WA 98826, 509/548-2550.

150 ESMERELDA BASIN
4.5 mi/3.0 hr

northwest of Cle Elum in Wenatchee National Forest

Map 3.4, page 114

The lazy trail to Esmerelda Basin is perfectly suited for those seeking subalpine meadows and rocky peaks without the difficulty of a major climb. Esmerelda Basin is filled with meadows of wildflowers set among rock. Total elevation gain is 1,700 feet, making it easy to understand the popularity of the trail. From the basin, several attractive options await. Fortune Creek Pass offers distant views of mountains. Alternatively, the trail meanders on the ridgeline to find the small Lake Ann, set on the barren slopes of Ingalls Peak, an outstanding destination.

Esmerelda Basin Trail begins at a lofty elevation of 4,300 feet, providing an easy journey to a grand landscape. The route pleases immediately and consistently, passing back and forth between subalpine forests and open meadows. The rocky Esmerelda Peaks line the route to the south. Esmerelda Basin is about two miles from the trailhead. At this junction, head left to climb to Fortune Creek Pass, where the views become sublime. Turn right at the junction for another adventure, a trail riding the crest toward Fortune Peak and Lake Ann. These are highly recommended as extended day hikes.

User Groups: Hikers, leashed dogs, and horses. No mountain bikes are allowed. No wheelchair access.

Permits: This trail is accessible July–October. A federal Northwest Forest Pass is required to park here.

Maps: For a map of Wenatchee National Forest, contact the Outdoor Recreation Information Center at the downtown Seattle REI.

For topographic maps, ask Green Trails for No. 209, Mount Stuart, or ask the USGS for Mount Stuart.

Directions: From Seattle, drive east on I-90 to exit 86. Turn left on Highway 970 and drive 6.5 miles to Teanaway River Road. Turn left and drive 13 miles to Forest Service Road 9737. Drive 10 miles to the trailhead at road's end.

Contact: Wenatchee National Forest, Cle Elum Ranger Station, 803 W. 2nd St., Cle Elum, WA 98922, 509/852-1100.

151 LONGS PASS AND LAKE INGALLS
6.0-10.8 mi/3.5-6.0 hr 🏃3 ⛰9

northwest of Cle Elum in Wenatchee National Forest

Map 3.4, page 114

Longs Pass and Lake Ingalls are two of the Cle Elum area's best destinations. Larches are ablaze in the fall while amazing views of Mount Stuart linger year-round. The high elevation trailhead makes it easy to achieve the best of the eastern Cascades. Open subalpine forests provide constant views of surrounding peaks, valleys, and forests on a steady climb to Longs Pass and Lake Ingalls. From Longs Pass, the view of Mount Stuart is unbeatable, with the massive mountain staring directly at hikers from across Ingalls Creek. Lake Ingalls is bound by glacially scraped granite and patches of meadows. Day hikes as good as this are hard to come by so easily.

The route starts high, at 4,400 feet, on Esmerelda Basin Trail. At the first junction (0.4 mile), veer right for Ingalls Way Trail. Two miles of switchbacks end at another junction; left for Lake Ingalls, right for Longs Pass. Both trails are moderately steep and exposed, so bring plenty of water. Open meadows are scattered with larches brightening the slopes in the fall. Longs Pass (3 miles) has the Cascades' best view of Stuart, set among superb meadows with larches to boot. Ingalls Lake (5.4

miles) rests directly beneath its own craggy mountain, Ingalls Peak. While they get quite dry and scorching hot in the dead of summer, both of these trails are wonderful during early summer and fall trips.

User Groups: Hikers and leashed dogs. No horses or mountain bikes are allowed. No wheelchair access.

Permits: This trail is accessible July–October. A federal Northwest Forest Pass is required to park here.

Maps: For a map of Wenatchee National Forest, contact the Outdoor Recreation Information Center at the downtown Seattle REI. For topographic maps, ask Green Trails for No. 209, Mount Stuart, or ask the USGS for Mount Stuart.

Directions: From Seattle, drive east on I-90 to exit 86. Turn left on Highway 970 and drive 6.5 miles to Teanaway River Road. Turn left and drive 13 miles to Forest Service Road 9737. Drive 10 miles to the trailhead at road's end.

Contact: Wenatchee National Forest, Cle Elum Ranger Station, 803 W. 2nd St., Cle Elum, WA 98922, 509/852-1100.

152 BEVERLY TURNPIKE
6.4 mi/3.5 hr 🏃2 ⛰9

northeast of Cle Elum in Wenatchee National Forest

Map 3.4, page 114

Connecting the Teanaway River to Ingalls Creek, Beverly and Turnpike Trails meet in the most beautiful of circumstances. At 5,800 feet, Beverly-Turnpike Pass is endowed with excellent views of mountain ridges and peaks, particularly the nearby and impressive Mount Stuart. Like most high-country routes, this trail passes through miles of subalpine meadows and revels in swaths of wildflowers. The route drops to the Ingalls Creek Trail, making for a good loop if a car-drop can be arranged.

Beverly Turnpike Trail climbs steadily from Teanaway River Valley up along Beverly Creek. It's not very impressive at first, as it travels an old road and passes through a clear-cut. As the trail progresses, however, unspoiled forests and meadows enter the scene. Rocky ridges line the way, their slopes covered in meadows. A trail cuts off to the right to Fourth Creek, also an access to Ingalls Creek. Stay left and follow the main trail to the pass. The best views are achieved here, where Mount Stuart appears to the north. A steep side trip up to Iron Peak, just before the pass, is well recommended for panoramic views. The route then follows Turnpike Creek through old-growth forest to Ingalls Creek and a necessary ford to reach that trail.

User Groups: Hikers, leashed dogs, and horses. No mountain bikes are allowed. No wheelchair access.

Permits: This trail is accessible July–October. A federal Northwest Forest Pass is required to park here.

Maps: For a map of Wenatchee National Forest, contact the Outdoor Recreation Information Center at the downtown Seattle REI. For topographic maps, ask Green Trails for No. 209, Mount Stuart, or ask the USGS for Red Top Mountain, Enchantment Lakes, and Mount Stuart.

Directions: From Seattle, drive east on I-90 to exit 86. Turn left on Highway 970 and drive 6.5 miles to Teanaway River Road. Turn left and drive 13 miles to Forest Service Road 9737. Drive 3 miles to Forest Service Road 112. Turn right and drive 1.5 miles to the trailhead at road's end.

Contact: Wenatchee National Forest, Cle Elum Ranger Station, 803 W. 2nd St., Cle Elum, WA 98922, 509/852-1100.

▌153▐ INGALLS CREEK

32.0 mi/3-4 days   3 ⚠10

southeast of Leavenworth in Alpine Lakes Wilderness of Wenatchee National Forest

Map 3.4, page 114

The longest river hike in the Alpine Lakes Wilderness, this valley route leads to unbelievably beautiful country. Set below massive Mount Stuart and numerous other craggy peaks and mountains, Ingalls Creek makes an impressive trek through eastside forest to superb subalpine meadows. An early summer hike reveals untold treasures in melting snowfields and natural bouquets of wildflowers. Few treks left in the Alpine Lakes area can boast of such remoteness and wildness. That makes this a very special place to those who visit it.

Ingalls Creek Trail rarely strays far from the banks of Ingalls Creek. The route is mostly old-growth ponderosa pines and Douglas firs. Campsites are numerous along the trail, which keeps an easy grade for most of its path.

At Porcupine Creek (10 miles), the trail begins climbing, emerging from the forest into excellent subalpine parkland. Surrounding ridges and peaks break out into view. The Wenatchee Mountains, while quite big, pale in comparison to Mount Stuart directly to the north. Ingalls Lake is a favorite site, set among larches on granite slabs. While camping is not allowed at the lake, plentiful campsites are to be found nearby. The trail ends by climbing to Stuart Pass at 6,400 feet.

User Groups: Hikers, leashed dogs, and horses. No mountain bikes are allowed. No wheelchair access.

Permits: This trail is accessible June–November. A federal Northwest Forest Pass is required to park here.

Maps: For a map of Wenatchee National Forest, contact the Outdoor Recreation Information Center at the downtown Seattle REI. For topographic maps, ask Green Trails for No. 209, Mount Stuart, and No. 210, Liberty, or ask the USGS for Mount Stuart, Enchantment Lakes, and Blewett.

Directions: From Seattle, drive east on I-90 to Highway 970 (exit 86). Drive north to U.S. 97. Drive north to Ingalls Creek Road, 14 miles north of Blewett Pass. Turn left and drive 1 mile to the trailhead at road's end.

Contact: Wenatchee National Forest, Leavenworth Ranger Station, 600 Sherbourne, Leavenworth, WA 98826, 509/548-2550.

154 YELLOW HILL AND ELBOW PEAK

6.0-10.0 mi/4.0-6.0 hr 🥾 3 ⛰ 9

northeast of Cle Elum in Wenatchee
National Forest

Map 3.4, page 114

Yellow Hill and Elbow Peak are all about
views. Situated in the Teanaway drainage,
these two mountaintops offer wide vistas of
the surrounding Cascades. The route itself is
not anything special, being mainly composed
of roads and dirt tracks fit for bikes. Nothing
keeps hikers from enjoying these trails other
than the steep climbs, but that's what trails
offering breathtaking views are all about.

Yellow Hill Trail follows a logging road
high above the Teanaway Valleys. Second-
growth forests offer shade on this dry trail as
it switchbacks up a ridge. The trees gradually
thin out along the path, giving hikers great
views of neighboring ridges and peaks. The
trail makes it to Yellow Hill at 3 miles and
5,527 feet elevation. Mount Stuart appears
surprisingly close while Mount Rainier stands
to the south. Elbow Peak is another 2 miles of
hiking along a high ridge, definitely a pleasant
way to spend a few hours. The views are not
much different from those at Yellow Hill, but
people are much more scarce. From their lofty
perches, both peaks provide a proper outlook
on the numerous ridges and valleys of the Teanaway Valleys.

User Groups: Hikers, leashed dogs, horses,
mountain bikes, and motorcycles. No wheelchair access.

Permits: This trail is accessible mid-June–
October. No permits are required. Parking
and access are free.

Maps: For a map of Wenatchee National For-
est, contact the Outdoor Recreation Infor-
mation Center at the downtown Seattle REI.
For topographic maps, ask Green Trails for
No. 208, Kachess Lake, and No. 209, Mount
Stuart, or ask the USGS for Cle Elum Lake,
Teanaway Butte, and Davis Peak.

Directions: From Seattle, drive east on I-90
to exit 86. Turn left on Highway 970 and
drive 6.5 miles to Teanaway River Road. Turn
left and drive 7 miles to West Fork Teanaway
Road. Turn left and drive 1 mile to Middle
Fork Teanaway Road. Turn right and drive 6
miles to the signed trailhead on the right.

Contact: Wenatchee National Forest, Cle
Elum Ranger Station, 803 W. 2nd St., Cle
Elum, WA 98922, 509/852-1100.

NORTHEASTERN WASHINGTON

It's easy to find folks who are experts on hiking

in the Alpine Lakes or Glacier Peak Wildernesses. The same goes for finding authoritative voices on North Cascades National Park or even the desolate Pasayten Wilderness. But hikers with an intricate knowledge of northeastern Washington are few and far between. Sure, westsiders have plenty to keep them occupied with the Cascades and Olympic Mountains. But never visiting or exploring Colville National Forest is a missed opportunity.

Locals from places like Republic, Colville, or Metaline Falls don't mind this lack of attention because that means they have nearly two million acres of national forest practically to themselves. The likelihood of running into a crowd out here is pretty much zilch. In fact, except for hunting season, you're unlikely to see other folks in the backcountry.

The wild Kettle and Selkirk Ranges are two major subregions of northeast Washington, and they are crisscrossed by great trails. Hit the trail in the Kettle Range and don't be surprised by elk, deer, or even moose. When hiking in the Selkirks, be on the lookout for caribou, gray wolves, or even grizzlies. Transecting northeast Washington, Highway 20 from Anacortes to Newport is easily the state's most scenic highway. Expect to come across places like Republic, Kettle Falls, Colville, and Metaline Falls. Never heard of them? Most folks haven't.

The Kettle Mountains are located east of the Cascades proper but west of the mighty Columbia River rise. The range runs south to north, and most peaks top 7,000 feet of elevation. Many of the trails networking the mountains start low and work their way up to the main travelway, the Kettle Crest Trail, which runs along the length of the ridge. The Columbia Mountain Trail offers a great and quick experience of the Kettles. With a trailhead at Sherman Pass right on Highway 20, the trail climbs quickly to the peak of Columbia Mountain, giving up views for miles. The southwest side of the range was burned severely in 1988, but the Edds Mountain and Barnaby Butte Trails are still great trails despite the charred forest lining their routes.

Great trails are found in the low country, as well. Outside of Republic (another great small town, complete with a co-op grocery) are Fish and Swan Lakes. In addition to great fishing and a good car campground, trails loop each lake. On the east side of the Kettle Range is Hoodoo Canyon, a short hike through a narrow gorge, complemented by a lake and a good campground.

Farther east (much farther east) lie the Selkirk Mountains. Many of the peaks in the Selkirks, like Grassy Top, Thunder Mountain, and Shedroof Mountain, fall in the 6,000- to 7,000-foot range. The most popular adventures in this area occur at Sullivan Lake, a large, glacially cut lake bordered by old forests. A pair of great campgrounds makes this a regular summer destination for families and boaters.

Tucked away into Washington's borders with Canada and Idaho, the Salmo-Priest Wilderness protects 40,000 acres of the Colville National Forest. The wilderness is shaped like a horseshoe and protects the high ridges framing Sullivan Creek. Several great trails explore the peaks and meadows of the Salmo-Priest. Crowell Ridge, Grassy Top, and Shedroof Divide are all fine trails.

In short, if you don't know the Selkirks or the Kettles, you should. It's well worth the trip from west of the Cascades to see how the other half plays.

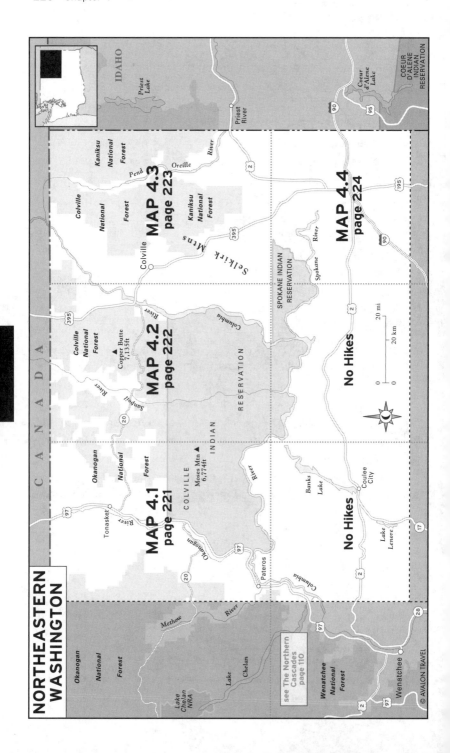

NORTHEASTERN WASHINGTON

MAP 4.1 page 221

MAP 4.2 page 222

MAP 4.3 page 223

MAP 4.4 page 224

No Hikes

No Hikes

see The Northern Cascades page 110

IDAHO

CANADA

Priest Lake

Priest River

Kaniksu National Forest

Colville National Forest

Pend Oreille River

Kaniksu National Forest

Colville

Selkirk Mtns

Colville National Forest

Copper Butte 7,135ft

Okanogan National Forest

Sanpoil River

Columbia River

Tonasket

Okanogan River

Moses Mtn 6,774ft

COLVILLE INDIAN RESERVATION

SPOKANE INDIAN RESERVATION

Spokane River

Coeur d'Alene Lake

COEUR D'ALENE INDIAN RESERVATION

Banks Lake

Coulee City

Lake Lenore

Pateros

Methow River

Lake Chelan NRA

Lake Chelan

Columbia River

Wenatchee National Forest

Wenatchee

20 mi

20 km

0

0

© AVALON TRAVEL

Map 4.1

Hikes 1-10
Pages 225-230

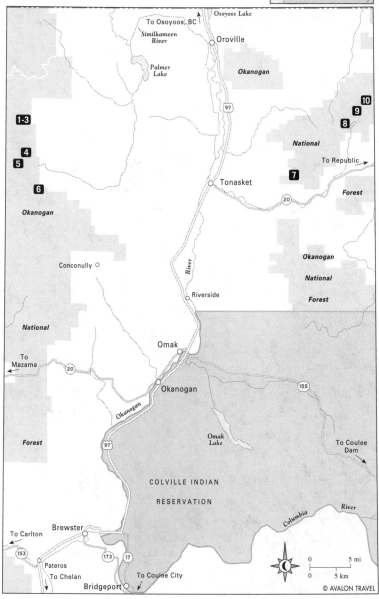

Map 4.2

**Hikes 11-29
Pages 231-241**

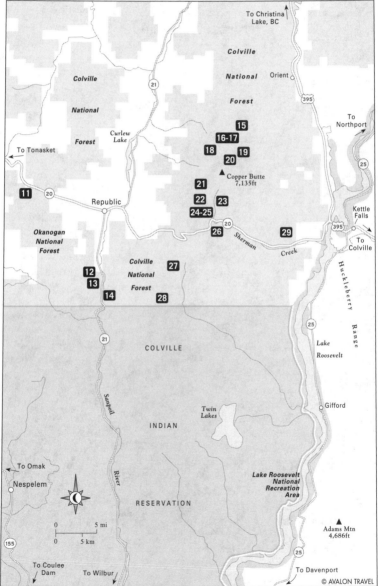

Map 4.3

Hikes 30-43
Pages 241-249

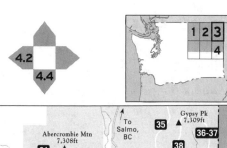

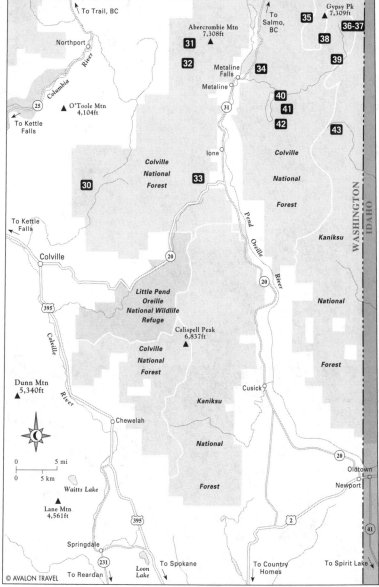

Map 4.4

Hike 44
Page 249

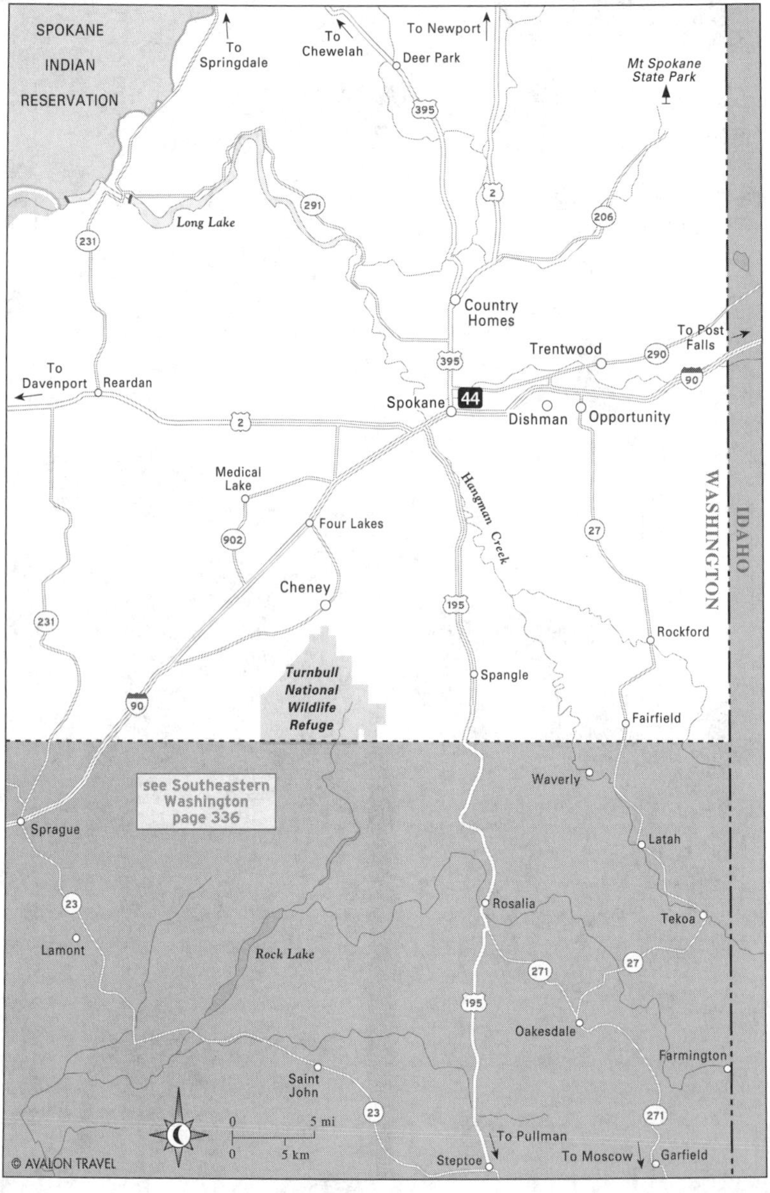

4.3

1	2	3
		4

SPOKANE
INDIAN
RESERVATION

To Springdale

To Chewelah

To Newport

Deer Park

Mt Spokane State Park

395

291

2

206

Long Lake

231

Country Homes

395

Trentwood

290

To Post Falls

90

To Davenport   Reardan

2

Spokane   44

Dishman   Opportunity

WASHINGTON

IDAHO

Medical Lake

Four Lakes

902

Hangman Creek

27

Cheney

231

195

Rockford

90

Turnbull National Wildlife Refuge

Spangle

Fairfield

see Southeastern Washington page 336

Waverly

Sprague

Latah

23

Rosalia

Tekoa

Lamont

Rock Lake

271

27

195

Oakesdale

Farmington

Saint John

23

271

To Pullman

Steptoe   To Moscow   Garfield

0   5 mi
0   5 km

© AVALON TRAVEL

1 BOUNDARY TRAIL

98.0 mi/9-10 days

near the Canadian border in Pasayten
Wilderness of Okanogan National Forest

Map 4.1, page 221

One of Washington's granddaddy trails, Boundary Trail runs across the entirety of America's largest wilderness, the Pasayten. The route follows the Canadian border, hence the name. It is an extremely high route, much of it occurring at 6,000 feet or more. The area is completely wild and one of the few places in the lower 48 where grizzly bears and gray wolves still roam. The route needn't be hiked end to end; there are many great trips accessing just a part of the trail. At least eight major trails provide access for small loops.

The Boundary Trail begins at Castle Pass on the Pacific Crest Trail (PCT). Start at Hart's Pass and hike north 18 miles to Castle Pass and "Ol' 533," the trail's number. From here, it heads east 73 miles to Iron Gate Trailhead, in the middle of nowhere. Along the way it climbs dozens of high passes and ridges, crosses the Pasayten River, and basks in endless views of mountains. The summer is a prime time to visit, when wildflowers are in bloom, as is the fall, when larches do their thing. Established camps are littered along the route, and off-trail camping is OK as long as it's low impact. Also, if you hike this route without the maps, you likely won't come back. Good luck.

User Groups: Hikers, leashed dogs, and horses. No mountain bikes are allowed. No wheelchair access.

Permits: This trail is accessible July–September. A federal Northwest Forest Pass is required to park here. A free wilderness permit is also required to hike here and is available at the trailhead.

Maps: For a map of Okanogan National Forest, contact the Outdoor Recreation Information Center at the downtown Seattle REI. For topographic maps, ask Green Trails

for No. 17, Jack Mountain, No. 18, Pasayten Peak, No. 19, Billy Goat Mountain, No. 20, Coleman Peak, and No. 21, Horseshoe Basin, or ask the USGS for Horseshoe Basin, Bauerman Ridge, Remmel Mountain, and Ashnola Pass.

Directions: Harts Pass: From Winthrop, drive west 17 miles on Highway 20 to Mazama. Turn right (north) onto Mazama Road and drive 0.2 mile to Hart's Pass Road (County Road 9140/Forest Service Road 5400). Turn left and drive to Rattlesnake Trailhead, 0.3 mile beyond River Bend Campground.

Iron Gate: From Tonasket, drive north on Tonasket–Oroville Westside Road to Loomis-Oroville Road. Turn left and drive through Enterprise and Loomis to Sinlahekin Valley Road (County Road 9425). Turn right and drive 2 miles to Touts Coulee Road (Forest Service Road 39). Turn left and drive 14 miles to Iron Gate Road. Turn right and drive 5 miles to the trailhead at road's end.

Contact: Okanogan National Forest, Methow Valley Ranger District, 24 W. Chewuch Rd., Winthrop, WA 98862, 509/996-4000.

2 HORSESHOE BASIN (PASAYTEN)

13.0 mi/2-4 days

north of Winthrop in Pasayten Wilderness of
Okanogan National Forest

Map 4.1, page 221

This is not the well-known Horseshoe Basin trail at the head of the Stehekin River. Instead, this is a much more remote and hence lesser-known Horseshoe Basin deep within the Pasayten Wilderness. The terrain, high rolling hills covered in tundralike meadows, is unlike that anywhere else in Washington. Many of the peaks top out over 8,000 feet, an impressive height. One of the best trails the Pasayten has to offer, Horseshoe Basin is appropriate for backpackers with moderate experience.

Starting at Iron Gate Trailhead, follow Boundary Trail as it climbs through scenic forest and meadow to Sunny Pass (5.2 miles). Boundary Trail turns north and finds expansive Horseshoe Pass and Basin (6.7 miles). Incredible camps are found at Sunny Pass, Horseshoe Pass, Louden Lake, and Smith Lake. The ecosystem is delicate at this elevation and necessitates strict Leave-No-Trace camping.

The basin is ripe for exploration. Each of the many peaks is an easy walk, little more than 1,000 feet above the high pass. Armstrong Mountain lines the Canadian border while Arnold Peak and Horseshoe Mountain are worthy American peaks. Any side trip is highly recommended. Although the snowpack is gone by Memorial Day, be prepared for adverse weather—even a snowstorm—well into summer.

User Groups: Hikers, leashed dogs, and horses. No mountain bikes are allowed. No wheelchair access.

Permits: This trail is accessible mid-May–October. A federal Northwest Forest Pass is required to park here. A free wilderness permit is also required to hike here and is available at the trailhead.

Maps: For a map of Okanogan National Forest, contact the Outdoor Recreation Information Center at the downtown Seattle REI. For topographic maps, ask Green Trails for No. 21, Horseshoe Basin, or ask the USGS for Horseshoe Basin.

Directions: From Tonasket, drive north on Tonasket–Oroville Westside Road to Loomis-Oroville Road. Turn left and drive through Enterprise and Loomis to Sinlahekin Valley Road (County Road 9425). Turn right and drive 2 miles to Touts Coulee Road (Forest Service Road 39). Turn left and drive 14 miles to Iron Gate Road. Turn right and drive 5 miles to the trailhead at road's end.

Contact: Okanogan National Forest, Methow Valley Ranger District, 24 W. Chewuch Rd., Winthrop, WA 98862, 509/996-4000.

3 WINDY PEAK
12.8 mi/6.5 hr

north of Winthrop in Pasayten Wilderness of Okanogan National Forest

Map 4.1, page 221

The tallest point in the area, Windy Peak makes an attractive summit on clear days. There are no fewer than four different routes to the peak, but this wilderness trail up Windy Creek is the shortest and best. Passing through old-growth forests, it climbs to the vast open meadows along the flanks of Windy Peak. Wildflowers, views, and indeed a little wind is about all you'll find at 8,334 feet. This is one of Washington's most expansive views.

From Iron Gate Trailhead, begin on Boundary Trail but turn left on Clutch Creek Trail (0.7 mile). Climbing the ridge through forests of fir and pine, the route turns right on Windy Peak Trail (4.4 miles). The trail climbs straight up, but it's a meadow walk from here on to the top. At the summit (6.4 miles), much of the Pasayten is laid bare at your feet, spread out in front of the Cascades Mountains. Don't forget extra water and food on this dry, strenuous trip.

User Groups: Hikers, leashed dogs, and horses. No mountain bikes are allowed. No wheelchair access.

Permits: This trail is accessible July–October. A federal Northwest Forest Pass is required to park here. A free wilderness permit is also required to hike here and is available at the trailhead.

Maps: For a map of Okanogan National Forest, contact the Outdoor Recreation Information Center at the downtown Seattle REI. For topographic maps, ask Green Trails for No. 21, Horseshoe Basin, or ask the USGS for Horseshoe Basin.

Directions: From Tonasket, drive north on Tonasket–Oroville Westside Road to Loomis-Oroville Road. Turn left and drive through Enterprise and Loomis to Sinlahekin Valley Road (County Road 9425). Turn right and drive 2 miles to Touts Coulee Road (Forest Service

Road 39). Turn left and drive 20 miles to the trailhead at Long Swamp Campground.
Contact: Okanogan National Forest, Methow Valley Ranger District, 24 W. Chewuch Rd., Winthrop, WA 98862, 509/996-4000.

4 TIFFANY MOUNTAIN
8.2 mi/4.5 hr

east of Winthrop in Okanogan National Forest

Map 4.1, page 221

The roadless area surrounding Tiffany Mountain is distinct from the rest of the North Cascades. High, rolling hills dominate the horizons, while wetlands and meadows populate many of the valleys. Open forests of fir and pine create beautiful parkland on the slopes of mountains, while their summits are covered in wildflowers, grasses, and mosses. It's a more subtle beauty than the jagged peaks of the North Cascades. If you're here in July, expect a lot of green for such an easterly locale.

Tiffany Mountain is reachable via four routes, making a loop trip easy and promising. Pick or choose, but Tiffany Lake Trail is the best choice. This route passes the timbered Tiffany Lake (an excellent base camp) before climbing to Whistler Pass. The four trails converge here and may be confusing, so bring a map and compass. A scramble to the top of Tiffany Mountain yields vistas extending for miles. Peer into the vast Pasayten Wilderness, then turn and survey much of the Cascade Range. A walk along flowered Freezeout Ridge is an easier but equally great side trip. The area is protected as a botanical reserve, so if camping here, stick to established camps and observe strict Leave-No-Trace principles.

User Groups: Hikers, leashed dogs, horses, and mountain bikes. No wheelchair access.

Permits: This trail is accessible mid-June–September. A federal Northwest Forest Pass is required to park here.

Maps: For a map of Okanogan National Forest, contact the Outdoor Recreation Information Center at the downtown Seattle REI. For topographic maps, ask Green Trails for No. 53, Tiffany Mountain, or ask the USGS for Tiffany Mountain.

Directions: From the town of Conconully, drive Okanogan County Road 2017 around the reservoir for 3 miles. Turn right onto Forest Service Road 37 and continue for 21 miles. After crossing Bernhardt Creek, turn right onto Forest Service Road 39 and drive 8 miles north to Tiffany Springs Campground and the trailhead.

Contact: Okanogan National Forest, Methow Valley Ranger District, 24 W. Chewuch Rd., Winthrop, WA 98862, 509/996-4000.

5 BERNHARDT MINE
5.0 mi/3.0 hr

northeast of Winthrop in Okanogan National Forest

Map 4.1, page 221

Mention the word "mine" to a hiker, and you're likely to get a nasty scowl in return. After all, who wants to toil along a trail just to check out a big hole? Well, Bernhardt Mine Trail is really much more than a field trip to an old mine. The trail passes several old, barely standing cabins along the way, testaments to the hardy living of the old settlers. And there's the mine itself, a tame model of extraction compared to modern practices, when bulldozers rip up entire hillsides and chemical solutions strip streams into lifelessness. Enjoy the mine, but keep hiking to Clark Peak, where you'll forget all about industry thanks to sweeping meadows of wildflowers that reveal distant mountain ranges.

The route to the mine is steep but only 2 miles. Pass through soggy wetlands and climb almost straight up to the miner's cabin and an accompanying mine. Hike a little higher to intersect North Summit Trail. This trail runs north to Tiffany Mountain and makes possible an 11-mile loop (hike Freezeout Ridge Trail to Forest Service Road 39 and walk the road 2 miles to your car). If you're looking for something shorter, just scramble to the top of Clark Peak. Expansive views and grassy meadows will be your reward.

User Groups: Hikers, leashed dogs, horses, and mountain bikes. No wheelchair access.

Permits: This trail is accessible July–mid-October. A federal Northwest Forest Pass is required to park here.

Maps: For a map of Okanogan National Forest, contact the Outdoor Recreation Information Center at the downtown Seattle REI. For topographic maps, ask Green Trails for No. 53, Tiffany Mountain, or ask the USGS for Tiffany Mountain.

Directions: From the town of Conconully, drive Okanogan County Road 2017 around the reservoir 3 miles. Turn right onto Forest Service Road 37 and continue for 21 miles. After crossing Bernhardt Creek, turn right onto Forest Service Road 39 and drive 1 mile north to the trailhead on the right.

Contact: Okanogan National Forest, Methow Valley Ranger District, 24 W. Chewuch Rd., Winthrop, WA 98862, 509/996-4000.

6 GRANITE MOUNTAIN
11.0 mi/6.0 hr   🚶4 ⛰️8

northeast of Winthrop in Okanogan National Forest

Map 4.1, page 221

In the early 1990s, more than 700 local residents sent letters to the U.S. Forest Service, objecting to plans to build more than 30 miles of road through the Granite Mountain Roadless Area. The roads were to help log thousands of acres of forest, spoiling one of the Okanogan's best forests. Fortunately for hikers today, their efforts were successful. Granite Mountain Trail climbs steeply to Granite's 7,366-foot summit, surveying the protected forests as well as many distant peaks and ranges. If you're not into a full hike, you can still obtain views from Little Granite Mountain, a 6-mile round-trip.

Granite Mountain Trail climbs steeply through forests of lodgepole pine and fir to a small ridge. A side trail leads north to the top of Little Granite (2 miles). The main trail continues toward much larger Granite Mountain through a gap between ridges. A stiff scramble almost straight up leads to the summit and the requisite views. Although it passes near Little Granite Creek, the trail is usually very dry once the snowpack has disappeared, so extra water is a must.

User Groups: Hikers, leashed dogs, horses, and mountain bikes. No wheelchair access.

Permits: This trail is accessible July–mid-October. A federal Northwest Forest Pass is required to park here.

Maps: For a map of Okanogan National Forest, contact the Outdoor Recreation Information Center at the downtown Seattle REI. For topographic maps, ask Green Trails for No. 53, Tiffany Mountain, and No. 85, Loup Loup, or ask the USGS for West Conconully and Loup Loup Summit.

Directions: From Conconully, drive southwest 2 miles on Okanogan County Road 2017. The road branches to Forest Service Road 42 and Forest Service Road 37; turn right onto Road 37. Drive 1 mile and turn left onto Forest Service Road 37-100. Drive 4 miles and turn right onto Forest Service Road 37-120. The trailhead is 0.5 mile ahead, on the right.

Contact: Okanogan National Forest, Methow Valley Ranger District, 24 W. Chewuch Rd., Winthrop, WA 98862, 509/996-4000.

7 FOURTH OF JULY RIDGE
9.0 mi/5.0 hr   🚶3 ⛰️8

northwest of Tonasket in Okanogan National Forest

Map 4.1, page 221

Fourth of July Ridge is less about big views than it is a trip back into time. Along the trail are several old cabins built more than 100 years ago by some of the region's first settlers. In the 19th century, folks slowly moved into the upper Okanogan for the deceptively rich natural resources of the area. Although the forests and prairies appear dry during much of the summer, this area is really an ideal place to raise cattle. Geologically, the land of the Okanogan is very old and composed of metamorphic rocks, a type of rock that is often home to vast mineral deposits. That attracted miners to these parts. The cabins along the ridge have long ago been abandoned, yet old artifacts can still found among their remains. After passing the cabins (1.5 miles), Fourth of July Trail slowly traverses Mount Bonaparte by climbing the southeast slope. At 3.5 miles is Lightning Spring, usually dry by June, and at 4.5 miles the trail intersects Southside Trail, access to Mount Bonaparte's summit (see listing for South Side Bonaparte in this chapter).

User Groups: Hikers, leashed dogs, and horses. No mountain bikes are allowed. No wheelchair access.

Permits: This trail is accessible May–November. Permits are not required. Parking and access are free.

Maps: For a map of Okanogan National Forest, contact the Outdoor Recreation Information Center at the downtown Seattle REI. For topographic maps, ask the USGS for Havillah and Mount Bonaparte.

Directions: From Tonasket, drive north 15 miles on County Road 9467 (Tonasket-Havillah Road) to Forest Service Road 3230. Turn right and drive 4 miles to the signed trailhead.

Contact: Okanogan National Forest, Tonasket Ranger Station, 1 W. Winesap, Tonasket, WA 98855, 509/486-2186.

of spectacular views of distant mountains in every direction. South Side Trail is the shortest and easiest way to reach the summit out of four possible options. While much of the route is forested, the upper parts of the trail are fairly open, cloaked in meadows and steep slopes. The summit of Mount Bonaparte is rounded like a large dome, meaning trees obscure most views until one climbs the 90-year-old fire lookout stationed atop the mountain. That the lookout still stands is a testament to its hardy construction in 1914. The snow-capped North Cascades are readily visible to the west while the Kettle River Range stands to the east. Rarely seen mountains of Canada stand to the north.

User Groups: Hikers, leashed dogs, and horses. No mountain bikes are allowed. No wheelchair access.

Permits: This trail is accessible May–November. Permits are not required. Parking and access are free.

Maps: For a map of Okanogan National Forest, contact the Outdoor Recreation Information Center at the downtown Seattle REI. For a topographic map, ask the USGS for Mount Bonaparte.

Directions: From Tonasket, drive east 20 miles on Highway 20 to County Road 4953. Turn left (north) and drive 9 miles to Forest Service Road 33. Turn left and drive 7 miles to Forest Service Road 33-100. Turn left and drive 3.5 miles to the trailhead.

Contact: Okanogan National Forest, Tonasket Ranger Station, 1 W. Winesap, Tonasket, WA 98855, 509/486-2186.

8 SOUTH SIDE BONAPARTE

11.2 mi/6.0 hr   🚶3 ⛰9

northwest of Tonasket in Okanogan National Forest

Map 4.1, page 221

Mount Bonaparte registers as one of eastern Washington's tallest summits, standing tall at 7,257 feet. Being that the peak is in the north-central part of the state, you're assured

9 STRAWBERRY MOUNTAIN

3.0 mi/1.5 hr   🚶2 ⛰9

northwest of Tonasket in Okanogan National Forest

Map 4.1, page 221

While the summit of big brother Mount Bonaparte towers over little brother Strawberry Mountain, the latter boasts the easier and more enjoyable hike. Strawberry Trail climbs from a great campground on Lost Lake up through some magnificent old-growth forest. Enormous ponderosa pines, Douglas firs, and western larches highlight the trip to Strawberry Mountain's summit. These trees have survived through the centuries thanks to strong natural defenses against fire (thick bark, wide spacing). The trail climbs the north side of the mountain steadily but gently all the way to the top. Although the summit is more than 2,500 feet below the peak of Mount Bonaparte, the forest breaks open to reveal great views of Lost and Bonaparte Lakes below. Strawberry Trail is a definite must-hike trail for anyone camping at Lost Lake or in the general area. And proving that life is truly sweet, you can expect to find strawberries (small ones) along the route.

User Groups: Hikers, leashed dogs, and horses. No mountain bikes are allowed. No wheelchair access.

Permits: This trail is accessible May–November. Permits are not required. Parking and access are free.

Maps: For a map of Okanogan National Forest, contact the Outdoor Recreation Information Center at the downtown Seattle REI. For a topographic map, ask the USGS for Mount Bonaparte.

Directions: From Tonasket, drive east 20 miles on Highway 20 to Bonaparte Lake Road (County Road 4953). Turn left (north) and drive 9 miles to Forest Service Road 33. Turn left and drive 5.5 miles to Lost Lake Campground. The trailhead is 50 yards down the small side road (Forest Service Road 33-050) immediately before the campground (but park in the campground's day-use area).

Contact: Okanogan National Forest, Tonasket Ranger Station, 1 W. Winesap, Tonasket, WA 98855, 509/486-2186.

10 BIG TREE BOTANICAL LOOP
0.7 mi/0.5 hr

northwest of Tonasket in Okanogan National Forest

Map 4.1, page 221

Big trees indeed. This easy-to-navigate trail shows that the east side of the Cascades can grow enormous evergreens much like the west side does. The short loop trail, with a wide, flat, and graveled path for wheelchair access, walks through an old-growth forest of ponderosa pine, Douglas fir, Englemann spruce, and western larch. Many of the trees are upward of 300 years old. Although the forest underwent selective logging about 40 years ago (to remove trees doomed to die by bark beetles), the forest is a great example of eastern climax forests. The trees are widely spaced with a sparse undergrowth of grasses and small shrubs. These understory plants are meant to burn regularly, at low intensities. The fire burns quickly with little chance to ignite the large trees. At the end of the loop is the highlight of the hike, where two gigantic western larches grow in a small depression. These two granddaddy tamaracks are more than 900 years old, on par with some of the biggest trees in the Olympics. Here's to another 900 years!

User Groups: Hikers and leashed dogs. No horses or mountain bikes are allowed. This trail is wheelchair accessible.

Permits: This trail is accessible year-round. Permits are not required. Parking and access are free.

Maps: For a map of Okanogan National Forest, contact the Outdoor Recreation Information Center at the downtown Seattle REI. For a topographic map, ask the USGS for Mount Bonaparte.

Directions: From Tonasket, drive east on Highway 20 to Bonaparte Lake Road (County Road 4953). Turn left (north) and drive 9 miles to Forest Service Road 33. Turn left and drive 3.5 miles to the well-signed trailhead and parking area on the right side of the road.

Contact: Okanogan National Forest, Tonasket Ranger Station, 1 W. Winesap, Tonasket, WA 98855, 509/486-2186.

⓫ FIR MOUNTAIN
4.0 mi/2.5 hr

east of Tonasket in Okanogan National Forest

Map 4.2, page 222

Although the route up Fir Mountain is nothing to write home about, much of your sweat is paid off with a great summit view. Fir Mountain Trail shows no qualms about its intention of climbing straight up the hillside to the summit, a long craggy mass of exposed rock. The trail is mostly forested until it reaches the summit, meaning you'll have to wait until you're well invested in the hike to achieve any views. This is a good place to see deer or elk browsing in the forest, or to hear the whoomp-whoomp-whoomp of grouse. The summit has good vistas of the Kettle River Range and the white-capped North Cascades to the east. Expect the trail to be hot and dry with no water to be found along the way. The trailhead is across Highway 20 from Sweat Creek Campground, a nice place to call home for the night.

User Groups: Hikers and leashed dogs. No horses or mountain bikes are allowed. No wheelchair access.

Permits: This trail is accessible May–October. Permits are not required. Parking and access are free.

Maps: For a map of Okanogan National Forest, contact the Outdoor Recreation Information Center at the downtown Seattle REI. For a topographic map, ask the USGS for Wauconda Summit.

Directions: From Republic, drive west 9 miles on Highway 20 to Forest Service Road 31. Turn left (south) and drive 1.5 miles to the signed trailhead.

Contact: Okanogan National Forest, Tonasket Ranger Station, 1 W. Winesap, Tonasket, WA 98855, 509/486-2186.

⓬ SWAN AND LONG LAKE LOOPS
1.3-1.8 mi/1.0 hr

south of Republic in Colville National Forest

Map 4.2, page 222

These are a pair of outstanding lakeshore loops leaving from a pair of great campgrounds. The two trails encircle Swan Lake (1.8 miles) and Long Lake (1.3 miles), passing through old-growth ponderosa pine forest with steady views of the lakes. Swan Lake is large and open atop a high plateau. Long Lake lies in a narrow valley between two rocky cliffs. The trails are flat and easy, perfect for hikers of all ages and abilities. Moose and elk are often heard calling out from around the lake during late evening, while loons, geese, and ducks fill the woods with sound during the morning. The two campgrounds are great for casual campers, as they feature full car-camping amenities. Anglers in pursuit of the well-stocked trout in the lakes will most appreciate the trails since they pass countless secluded fishing holes.

User Groups: Hikers, leashed dogs, and mountain bikes. No horses are allowed. No wheelchair access.

Permits: This trail is accessible March–November. Permits are not required. Parking and access are free.

Maps: For a map of Colville National Forest, contact the Outdoor Recreation Information Center at the downtown Seattle REI. For a topographic map, ask the USGS for Swan Lake.

Directions: From Republic, drive south 7.5 miles on Highway 21 to Scatter Creek Road. Turn right (west) and drive 7 miles to Swan Lake Campground. The trailhead is in the day-use area.

Contact: Colville National Forest, Republic Ranger Station, 650 E. Delaware Ave., Republic, WA 99166, 509/775-7400.

13 TENMILE
5.0 mi/2.5 hr

south of Republic in Colville National Forest

Map 4.2, page 222

Unlike many of the summit hikes in the area, Tenmile Trail hikes through a small, rugged canyon up into nice parkland forests of fir and pine. The route leaves San Poil Campground (conveniently situated alongside Highway 21) and climbs through the lightly forested canyon. Ponderosa pines line the steep walls while cottonwoods inhabit the wet canyon bottom. This is a great place to see deer, hear elk, and maybe even stumble across a moose. Don't forget about bears or the possibility of a rattlesnake. Tenmile Trail climbs 1.5 miles in the canyon before reaching the plateau above, a good turnaround point. The last mile works its way up through a draw to Tenmile Road, a good access point for those staying at Swan or Long Lake Campgrounds.

User Groups: Hikers and leashed dogs. No horses or mountain bikes are allowed. No wheelchair access.

Permits: This trail is accessible June–October. Permits are not required. Parking and access are free.

Maps: For a map of Colville National Forest, contact the Outdoor Recreation Information Center at the downtown Seattle REI. For topographic maps, ask the USGS for Bear Mountain and Swan Lake.

Directions: From Republic, drive 10 miles south on Highway 21 to San Poil Campground. Turn right (west) into the campground. The trailhead is near the day-use parking area.

For the upper trailhead, turn right onto Scatter Creek Road (7.5 miles from Republic) and drive 4 miles to Tenmile Road. Turn left and drive 2.5 miles to the signed trailhead.

Contact: Colville National Forest, Republic Ranger Station, 650 E. Delaware Ave., Republic, WA 99166, 509/775-7400.

14 THIRTEEN MILE
16.5 mi one-way/8.0 hr

southeast of Republic in Colville National Forest

Map 4.2, page 222

A trail with options is Thirteen Mile, making for a great trek through the southern reach of the Kettle River Range. The route has three trailheads, making the entire stretch of trail (more than 16 miles) easily accessible. The views are unbeatable from the high ridge, whether they be looking out to other Kettle peaks or out over San Poil Valley.

All three trailheads offer something different and worthwhile. From Thirteen Mile Campground, the trail climbs quickly to views of the beautiful San Poil River canyon. Hawks and eagles looking for dinner are commonly seen high above the valley. The trail intersects Forest Service Road 2054 and the middle trailhead at about 4 miles. Thirteen Mile Trail continues east to grassy meadows along the south slopes of Thirteen Mile Mountain before dropping into a creek valley. Deer and elk are frequently encountered on this lightly used section of the route. The high point (in elevation) is achieved when the trail reaches the saddle between Fire and Seventeen Mile Mountains, just 2.5 miles from the east trailhead. The great thing about Thirteen Mile Trail is that with three trailheads, it's like three trails in one and each is equally fun. Water sources are undependable (especially in late summer) along this high route, so be sure to carry an adequate supply. A few camps are dispersed throughout, but best bets are to find a flat spot 50 yards from the trail and to call it home for the night.

User Groups: Hikers, leashed dogs, horses, and mountain bikes. No wheelchair access.

Permits: This trail is accessible June–October. Permits are not required. Parking and access are free.

Maps: For a map of Colville National Forest, contact the Outdoor Recreation Information Center at the downtown Seattle REI. For topographic maps, ask the USGS for

Thirteenmile Creek, Bear Mountain, and Edds Mountain.

Directions: West access: From Republic, drive 13 miles south on Highway 21 to Thirteen Mile Campground on the left (east) side of the road. The Thirteen Mile Trailhead is within the campground.

East access: From Republic, drive east 7 miles to Hall Creek Road (County Road 99, which turns into Forest Service Road 2054). Turn right (south) and drive 5.5 miles to Forest Service Road 600. Turn left onto Forest Service Road 600 and drive 5 miles to the signed trailhead on the right (west) side of the road.

Middle Access: From Republic, drive east 7 miles to Hall Creek Road (County Road 99). Turn right (south) and drive 1.5 miles to County Road 233. Turn right and drive 1.5 miles to Forest Service Road 2053. Veer left and drive 1 mile to Forest Service Road 2054. Turn right and drive 5.5 miles to Cougar Trailhead.

Contact: Colville National Forest, Republic Ranger Station, 650 E. Delaware Ave., Republic, WA 99166, 509/775-7400.

15 TAYLOR RIDGE
8.0 mi/4.0 hr

northwest of Kettle Falls in Colville National Forest

Map 4.2, page 222

Taylor Ridge Trail has just about everything you could ask for from a trail. The route traverses the high ridge, frequently leaving the timber to take in good views of the surrounding peaks and valleys. Water is frequently available along the route and there are several good campsites, making overnight ventures a good bet. The trail is also split in half by a Forest Service road, making upper sections of the ridge easily accessible. From the bisecting road, the two segments are each about 4 miles in length. Head east on Taylor Ridge Trail to follow the ridge for a short while before dropping sharply to Boulder Creek. The trail to the

west gently climbs higher, passing through meadows and vistas as the ridge works its way toward the Kettle Crest. Find camps near the road and up higher on the trail. Water can be found from several streams and springs along the route.

User Groups: Hikers, leashed dogs, horses, mountain bikes, and motorcycles. No wheelchair access.

Permits: This trail is accessible May–October. Permits are not required. Parking and access are free.

Maps: For a map of Colville National Forest, contact the Outdoor Recreation Information Center at the downtown Seattle REI. For topographic maps, ask the USGS for Mount Leona and Bulldog Mountain.

Directions: From Kettle Falls, drive north 22 miles to Boulder–Deer Creek Road (Forest Service Road 6100). Turn left (west) and drive 8 miles to Forest Service Road 6113. Turn left (south) and drive 7 miles to the signed trailhead.

Contact: Colville National Forest, Kettle Falls Ranger Station, 255 W. 11th Ave., Kettle Falls, WA 99141, 509/738-7700.

16 PROFANITY
6.0 mi/3.5 hr

northeast of Republic in Colville National Forest

Map 4.2, page 222

Rarely used by anyone other than hunters, Profanity Peak Trail offers a firsthand glimpse at the impact of forest fires on dry, east-side forests. The Leona Fire roared through this area in 2001, destroying much of the forest. Already, the area has begun to regenerate. Ground covers revealed by the now-gone canopy are doing extremely well in the sunlight. Seedlings have already taken root in many places and are working on creating a forest of their own. It's a welcome sight to see nature taking care of itself, especially after the doomsday coverage forest fires often receive.

The first half of Profanity Trail climbs

through parts of the fire on its way up to Kettle Crest Trail. At this point, the views are grand to the east and west. Those with a cursing streak can exercise it by heading south on Kettle Crest Trail and scaling the summit of Profanity Peak. Grand vistas await those who do.

User Groups: Hikers, leashed dogs, horses, and mountain bikes. No wheelchair access.

Permits: This trail is accessible May–October. Permits are not required. Parking and access are free.

Maps: For a map of Colville National Forest, contact the Outdoor Recreation Information Center at the downtown Seattle REI. For a topographic map, ask the USGS for Mount Leona.

Directions: From Republic, drive east 2.5 miles on Highway 20 to Highway 21. Turn left (north) and drive 13 miles to Aeneas Creek Road (County Road 566). Turn right and drive 8 miles (the road becomes Forest Service Road 2160) to the trailhead at road's end.

Contact: Colville National Forest, Republic Ranger Station, 650 E. Delaware Ave., Republic, WA 99166, 509/775-7400.

17 STICK PIN
2.6 mi/2.0 hr

northwest of Kettle Falls in Colville National Forest

Map 4.2, page 222

Stick Pin, one of the many trails offering access to Kettle Crest Trail, is unique in that water is readily available nearly the length of the trail. Thanks go out to the trail engineer who laid out Stick Pin, as it follows the South Fork of Boulder Creek up to its headwaters in the Kettle River Range. The cool water is refreshing on hot summer days. Most of Stick Pin Trail is covered by thick forests of Douglas fir, western larch, and lodgepole pine. Deer and elk are plentiful in this area, as are easy-to-startle grouse. The trail threads between Ryan Hill and Stickpin Hill to make a steep climb up to Kettle Crest Trail and the requisite meadow views.

User Groups: Hikers, leashed dogs, horses, and mountain bikes. No wheelchair access.

Permits: This trail is accessible May–October. Permits are not required. Parking and access are free.

Maps: For a map of Colville National Forest, contact the Outdoor Recreation Information Center at the downtown Seattle REI. For a topographic map, ask the USGS for Mount Leona.

Directions: From Kettle Falls, drive west approximately 22 miles on Highway 20 to Albian Hill Road. Turn right (north) and drive 12.1 miles to Forest Service Road 2030-921, a small side road. Follow this road 0.5 mile to its end and the signed trailhead. A primitive camp is at the trailhead.

Contact: Colville National Forest, Kettle Falls Ranger Station, 255 W. 11th Ave., Kettle Falls, WA 99141, 509/738-7700.

18 LEONA
3.2 mi/1.5 hr

northeast of Republic in Colville National Forest

Map 4.2, page 222

It may be hard to distinguish between the many trails leading up to Kettle Crest Trail, but Leona is one of the best. Much of the trail features glorious views of Curlew Valley and out to the North Cascades. And when you reach Kettle Crest Trail, you can gaze out over the Columbia River Valley and up and down the Kettle River Range. Leona Trail climbs steadily, but the grade is easily managed, especially since this is such a short trail. At the halfway point is Leona Spring, a rare source of water at this elevation. At the crest, hike north along signed Leona Loop Trail, which combines with Kettle Crest Trail to a make a 6-mile loop (total). Cutting off from the loop is a trail to the summit of Leona, a well-recommended vista.

User Groups: Hikers, leashed dogs, horses, and mountain bikes. No wheelchair access.

Permits: This trail is accessible May–October.

Permits are not required. Parking and access are free.

Maps: For a map of Colville National Forest, contact the Outdoor Recreation Information Center at the downtown Seattle REI. For a topographic map, ask the USGS for Mount Leona.

Directions: From Republic, drive east 2.5 miles on Highway 20 to Highway 21. Turn left (north) and drive 11.5 miles to St. Peter's Creek Road (County Road 584). Turn right (east) and drive 7 miles (it will turn into Forest Service Road 2157) to a roadblock and road's end. The trailhead is to the right of the roadblock.

Contact: Colville National Forest, Republic Ranger Station, 650 E. Delaware Ave., Republic, WA 99166, 509/775-7400.

19 US MOUNTAIN
5.2 mi/3.0 hr

northeast of Kettle Falls in Colville National Forest

Map 4.2, page 222

One of the few trails in this region not connecting to Kettle Crest Trail, US Mountain Trail instead undertakes a summit of the 6,200-foot peak. As can be expected, the summit opens to reveal meadows and spectacular views. Most notable is that from this vantage it is possible to see much of the Kettle River Range. US Mountain is set off to the east side of the divide, thus making the northern half of the mountains well discernable. US Mountain Trail makes a steady ascent on the mountain but is not terribly steep. The forest can be pretty thick in places, but parts of the trail are covered in swaths of meadows (and flowers during the early summer). Although the trail continues down into the South Fork Boulder Creek Valley, hikers are well advised to turn back after reaching the top of US Mountain. This is a hot and dry trail, so extra water is an important consideration.

User Groups: Hikers, leashed dogs, horses,

mountain bikes, and motorcycles. No wheelchair access.

Permits: This trail is accessible May–October. Permits are not required. Parking and access are free.

Maps: For a map of Colville National Forest, contact the Outdoor Recreation Information Center at the downtown Seattle REI. For a topographic map, ask the USGS for Copper Butte.

Directions: From Kettle Falls, drive west approximately 22 miles on Highway 20 to Albian Hill Road. Turn right (north) and drive 7.3 miles to a difficult-to-find trailhead on the right (east) side of the road.

Contact: Colville National Forest, Kettle Falls Ranger Station, 255 W. 11th Ave., Kettle Falls, WA 99141, 509/738-7700.

20 OLD STAGE ROAD
3.2-10.6 mi/1.5-6.0 hr

northeast of Republic in Colville National Forest

Map 4.2, page 222

As far as unique histories go, Old Stage Road Trail takes the cake. This is the last remaining section of the first Washington state highway. Well, highway is hardly the proper word. How about calling it a bumpy, dusty, rocky route over the mountains? Today it's not so bad, thanks to lots of volunteer work from the Inland Empire Chapter of Backcountry Horsemen of Washington. The trail is popular with folk on horseback but is perfectly suited for families on foot.

In 1892, the Washington legislature commissioned a road to be built from Marblemount, west of the Cascades, to Marcus on the Columbia River. The old road came up from the west to the Kettle River Range and crossed it via this route. It lasted only about six years before a better route over Sherman Pass was recognized and built. Much of the hike is forested as the trail gently climbs to Kettle Crest Trail. The trail stretches up to the crest (1.6 miles), a good turnaround point for shorter excursions, before dropping down through forest. Hikers today will find a trail much more suited for boots than wagon wheels, but it is amazing to see what folks once went through just to get across the state.

User Groups: Hikers, leashed dogs, horses, and mountain bikes. No wheelchair access.

Permits: This trail is accessible mid-May–October. Permits are not required. Parking and access are free.

Maps: For a map of Colville National Forest, contact the Outdoor Recreation Information Center at the downtown Seattle REI. For a topographic map, ask the USGS for Copper Butte.

Directions: From Kettle Falls, drive 25 miles west on Highway 20 to Albian Hill Road (Forest Service Road 2030). Turn right (north) and drive 7.1 miles to Forest Service Road 2030-380. The signed trailhead lies a few hundred yards up Forest Service Road 2030-380.

Contact: Colville National Forest, Republic Ranger Station, 650 E. Delaware Ave., Republic, WA 99166, 509/775-7400.

21 MARCUS
7.0 mi/3.5 hr   👥2 ⛰9

northeast of Republic in Colville National Forest

Map 4.2, page 222

To say the least, Marcus Trail provides an easy and extremely beautiful access to Kettle Crest Trail. What should really be known about the trail is that leads to the foot of Copper Butte, the tallest point in the Kettle River Range. Parts of Copper Butte were burned by a 1996 fire. Marcus makes a steady ascent to Kettle Crest Trail. After 2 miles of old, open forest, the trail breaks out into open meadows, alive with wildflower color during the early summer. The trail traverses a south-facing slope, making it accessible a little earlier than others in the area, but hot and dry, without water. Once you reach Kettle Crest Trail, don't miss the highlight of the trip, a summit of Copper Butte. At 7,135 feet, the peak soaks up the

views of numerous distant mountain ranges within two countries and two states, with Glacier Peak to the west.

User Groups: Hikers, leashed dogs, horses, and mountain bikes. No wheelchair access.

Permits: This trail is accessible May–October. Permits are not required. Parking and access are free.

Maps: For a map of Colville National Forest, contact the Outdoor Recreation Information Center at the downtown Seattle REI. For topographic maps, ask the USGS for Cooke Mountain and Copper Butte.

Directions: From Republic, drive east on Highway 20 about 3 miles to Highway 21. Turn left (north) and drive 2.5 miles to County Road 284. Turn right and drive 2.5 miles until it turns into Forest Service Road 2152. Continue on Forest Service Road 2152 for 2.7 miles to Forest Service Road 2040. Turn left and drive 5.2 miles to Forest Service Road 250. Turn right and drive 1.5 miles to the signed trailhead. A primitive campsite is at the trailhead.

Contact: Colville National Forest, Republic Ranger Station, 650 E. Delaware Ave., Republic, WA 99166, 509/775-7400.

22 SHERMAN
2.6 mi/1.5 hr   👥4 ⛰7

east of Republic along SR20 in Colville National Forest

Map 4.2, page 222

Sherman Trail provides quick but difficult access to the northern section of Kettle Crest Trail. By itself, the trail is rather miserable. But Kettle Crest Trail is prime country for exploration, and it lends itself well to making longer trips possible. Sherman gains nearly 1,600 feet of elevation in a short 1.3 miles. Much of the route is within a thick, young forest. Although the views are eaten up by the surrounding thicket of trees, at least they provide shade on this normally hot and dry route. Not until you reach the end of the trail, along the crest of the range, does the forest break and the views come out. For hikers looking to continue along Kettle Crest Trail, Jungle Hill lies to the south (2 total miles) and Wapaloosie to the north (3.5 total miles).

User Groups: Hikers, leashed dogs, horses, and mountain bikes. No wheelchair access.

Permits: This trail is accessible June–October. Permits are not required. Parking and access are free.

Maps: For a map of Colville National Forest, contact the Outdoor Recreation Information Center at the downtown Seattle REI. For topographic maps, ask the USGS for Cooke Mountain and Copper Butte.

Directions: From Republic, drive east approximately 12 miles to Forest Service Road 2040. Turn left (north) and drive 2.5 miles to Forest Service Road 065. Turn right (east) and drive 2 miles to the signed trailhead.

Contact: Colville National Forest, Republic Ranger Station, 650 E. Delaware Ave., Republic, WA 99166, 509/775-7400.

23 WAPALOOSIE
5.5 mi/3.0 hr   👫2 ⛰10

northwest of Kettle Falls in Colville National Forest

Map 4.2, page 222

More than a worthy candidate for a tongue-twister contest, Wapaloosie is an excellent scenic route to North Kettle Crest Trail. The summit of Wapaloosie itself is a grand adventure, challenging for some hikers and just right for others. Wapaloosie Trail takes advantage of numerous switchbacks to make a slow but steady ascent on the mountain. The trail gains roughly 2,000 feet of elevation in a short 2.75 miles, not an effort to snicker at. After 1.5 miles, the trail breaks out into open slopes covered in grasses and wildflowers. Deer and elk are likely to be seen in the early mornings or late evenings. Hawks are regularly soaring above, keeping an eye on all below. Wapaloosie Trail reaches Kettle Crest Trail

just below Wapaloosie Mountain. A short side trail leads to the summit, offering panoramic views of the surrounding countryside. This is a great way to get in some views and exercise at the same time.

User Groups: Hikers, leashed dogs, horses, and mountain bikes. No wheelchair access.

Permits: This trail is accessible June–October. Permits are not required. Parking and access are free.

Maps: For a map of Colville National Forest, contact the Outdoor Recreation Information Center at the downtown Seattle REI. For a topographic map, ask the USGS for Copper Butte.

Directions: From Kettle Falls, drive west approximately 22 miles on Highway 20 to Albian Hill Road. Turn right (north) and drive 3.2 miles to the signed trailhead.

Contact: Colville National Forest, Kettle Falls Ranger Station, 255 W. 11th Ave., Kettle Falls, WA 99141, 509/738-7700.

24 COLUMBIA MOUNTAIN
7.1 mi/3.5 hr   👫2 ⛰10

east of Republic along SR20 in Colville National Forest

Map 4.2, page 222

Columbia Mountain offers the most easily accessible and most encompassing viewpoint within the Kettle River Range. Directly off Highway 20, Columbia Mountain Trail cuts off from Kettle Crest Trail to create a loop encircling the 6,700-foot butte. Within the loop is a side trail leading to an abandoned lookout and the summit of Columbia Mountain. This is one of the best vantages in the Kettle River Range, with long views of the divide to the north and south. The devastation of the 1988 White Mountain fire is readily apparent, with much of the southern mountain range nothing but miles of dead snags.

The route follows Kettle Crest Trail 2 miles through forest and eventually open

view from Columbia Mountain (in Kettle River Range), looking north

meadows. On clear days, the North Cascades are well visible to the west. At Columbia Spring, a seasonal source of water, Columbia Mountain Trail cuts right and backtracks up the slopes. The trail diverges after 0.5 mile to create a loop around the mountain, much like a lasso. On the north side of the loop you'll find the trail up to the peak. Mountains appear across the distant horizons, with snow-capped peaks in Canada and Idaho joining in. Outside of the North Cascades, nowhere else along Highway 20 will you find a better hike.

User Groups: Hikers, leashed dogs, horses, and mountain bikes. No wheelchair access.

Permits: This trail is accessible June–October. Permits are not required. Parking and access are free.

Maps: For a map of Colville National Forest, contact the Outdoor Recreation Information Center at the downtown Seattle REI. For a topographic map, ask the USGS for Sherman Peak.

Directions: From Republic, drive 17 miles east on Highway 20 to Sherman Pass. On the east side of the pass, turn left (north) into the signed trailhead.

Contact: Colville National Forest, Republic Ranger Station, 650 E. Delaware Ave., Republic, WA 99166, 509/775-7400.

25 KETTLE CREST NORTH
30.3 mi one-way/3 days   🥾3   ⛰10

northeast of Republic in Colville National Forest

Map 4.2, page 222

This is a long, rugged, and popular route through the high country of the Kettle River Range. Stretching 30 miles from Sherman Pass all the way to Deer Creek Summit, North Kettle Crest Trail starts high and stays that way. The trail climbs or skirts the base of numerous mountains and buttes, including Columbia (2 miles from Sherman Pass), Wapaloosie (7 miles), Copper (13 miles), Ryan Hill (20 miles), Profanity (22 miles), and Sentinel (28 miles). Each peak along the way can be scrambled to the top to reveal expansive views in all directions. Much of the route is swathed in open meadows of grass and wildflowers. June is usually a great month to enjoy some color on the trail.

Although parts of Kettle Crest North Trail are relatively well traveled, much of the trail has few visitors most of the year (hunting season in the fall brings increased use). That means animals are aplenty in these parts, with deer, elk, and moose spotted along the trail regularly. Signs of bear and cougar are frequently seen along the trail; these big predators scratch trees to mark their territory, leaving behind stripped bark and exposed trunk. Campsites are scattered throughout the length of the trail. Water is a less dependable commodity. There are some springs and streams along the route, but by late summer they are not reliable; rationing of water is smart planning. The best bet is to set up a through-hike with a car at each end. Many access trails lead to the Kettle Crest, so many options exist for a customized hike. For a decent backpacking experience, there's no better trail in this area.

User Groups: Hikers, leashed dogs, horses, and mountain bikes. No wheelchair access.

Permits: This trail is accessible June–October. Permits are not required. Parking and access are free.

Maps: For a map of Colville National Forest, contact the Outdoor Recreation Information Center at the downtown Seattle REI. For topographic maps, ask the USGS for Sherman Peak, Copper Butte, and Mount Leona.

Directions: South access: From Republic, drive 17 miles east on Highway 20 to Sherman Pass. On the east side of the pass, turn left (north) into the signed trailhead.

North access: From Republic, drive north approximately 20 miles to the town of Curlew. Turn east on County Road 602 and drive 12 miles to Deer Creek Summit Trailhead.

Contact: Colville National Forest, Republic Ranger Station, 650 E. Delaware Ave., Republic, WA 99166, 509/775-7400.

26 KETTLE CREST SOUTH
13.3 mi one-way/8.0 hr   3   10

east of Republic along Highway 20 in Colville National Forest

Map 4.2, page 222

The southern leg of Kettle Crest Trail is highly memorable for two reasons. Most of this high route is along the crest of the Kettle River Range and thus offers expansive views of the surrounding country, from the North Cascade Mountains in the west to the Columbia River Valley to the east. Even more remarkable is the charred forest that covers much of the route. In 1988, eight lightning strikes created six fires. Because of extremely dry conditions, the fires merged to create the White Mountain Complex. The fire eventually burned more than 20,000 acres of forest, leaving behind miles of dead trees, known as snags. The fire burned along much of Kettle Crest Trail but did leave pockets of older forest. Where the fire burned, it burned hot and left little. As nature tends to do, the area is quickly recovering. Small pines and lush ground cover are filling in the area, well on the way to creating a forest of their own.

Kettle Crest South Trail truly follows the crest of this large range for much of its length. From Sherman Pass, it climbs around Sherman Peak and Snow Peak, each of which is tall and reached via side trails. Bald Mountain, Barnaby Buttes, and White Mountain are other peaks easily bagged along the way. It's best done as a through-hike, with a second car positioned at White Mountain Trailhead. Water can be obtained via several springs and streams scattered along the route. Campsites are strewn consistently along the route.

User Groups: Hikers, leashed dogs, horses, and mountain bikes. No wheelchair access.

Permits: This trail is accessible June–October. Permits are not required. Parking and access are free.

Maps: For a map of Colville National Forest, contact the Outdoor Recreation Information Center at the downtown Seattle REI. For a topographic map, ask the USGS for Sherman Peak.

Directions: North access: From Republic, drive 17 miles east on Highway 20 to Sherman Pass. On the east side of the pass, turn left (north) into the signed trailhead.

South access: From Republic, drive 20 miles east on Highway 20 to Forest Service Road 2020 (about 3 miles beyond Sherman Pass). Turn right (south) and drive 5 miles to Forest Service Road 2014. Turn right and drive 4 miles to Forest Service Road 2020-250. Turn right and drive 3.5 miles to White Mountain Trailhead.

Contact: Colville National Forest, Kettle Falls Ranger Station, 255 W. 11th Ave., Kettle Falls, WA 99141, 509/738-7700.

27 EDDS MOUNTAIN
8.4 mi/4.0 hr   🥾4 ⛰8

southeast of Republic in Colville National Forest

Map 4.2, page 222

Edds Mountain Trail offers the most scenic route to South Kettle Crest Trail. The route passes below Edds Mountain and Bald Mountain, a pair of 6,800-foot peaks, each of which is an easy scramble to broad views. The North Cascades line the western horizon over Sanpoil Valley, while the Kettle River Range fills the east. Parts of the route are in forest, other parts are in open meadows. June is a great time to see wildflowers covering these south-facing slopes. The trail offers a great firsthand look at the White Mountain Complex fire of 1988, passing through several sections of charred forest that is once again teeming with plant life. Although the trail gains just 1,000 feet over 4 miles, parts of the path are steep and rocky. Extra water is a must on this hot and dry trail.

User Groups: Hikers, leashed dogs, horses, and mountain bikes. No wheelchair access.

Permits: This trail is accessible June–October. Permits are not required. Parking and access are free.

Maps: For a map of Colville National Forest, contact the Outdoor Recreation Information Center at the downtown Seattle REI. For a topographic map, ask the USGS for Edds Mountain.

Directions: From Republic, drive east 7 miles on Highway 20 to Hall Creek Road (County Road 99, which turns into Forest Service Road 2054). Turn right (south) and drive 4 miles to Forest Service Road 300. Turn left and drive 1.5 miles to road's end and the trailhead.

Contact: Colville National Forest, Republic Ranger Station, 650 E. Delaware Ave., Republic, WA 99166, 509/775-7400.

28 BARNABY BUTTE
14.0 mi/8.0 hr   🥾4 ⛰9

southeast of Republic in Colville National Forest

Map 4.2, page 222

Barnaby Butte Trail offers a lot more than just a summit of the two rounded peaks. For starters, it offers a good workout. The trail climbs more than 3,000 feet over the course of 7 miles, a decent day's work for anyone. It also passes through a wide variety of ecosystems, most notably recently burned areas of forests. These patches were engulfed by the White Mountain Fire of 1988 and are now home to stands of small young pines. Animals are never far from this seldom-used route. These open areas make for a great wildlife habitat, providing open space for deer to graze and countless snags from which hawks conduct their hunt. And, of course, the trail makes a grand summit of Barnaby Buttes, the site of a former lookout. The view of the southern Kettle River Range is great, and the bird's-eye view of the fire's impact is incredible. It's important to carry extra water and sunscreen on this trail because of its long and exposed (hot) nature. Water will likely not be available along the way.

User Groups: Hikers, leashed dogs, horses, and mountain bikes. No wheelchair access.

Permits: This trail is accessible June–October. Permits are not required. Parking and access are free.

Maps: For a map of Colville National Forest, contact the Outdoor Recreation Information Center at the downtown Seattle REI. For a topographic map, ask the USGS for Sherman Peak.

Directions: From Republic, drive east 7 miles on Highway 20 to Hall Creek Road (County Road 99, which turns into Forest Service Road 2054). Turn right (south) and drive 5.5 miles to Forest Service Road 600. Turn left onto Forest Service Road 600 and drive 7 miles to the signed trailhead on the left (east) side of the road. The first 2 miles of trail is old Road 680.

Contact: Colville National Forest, Republic Ranger Station, 650 E. Delaware Ave., Republic, WA 99166, 509/775-7400.

29 HOODOO CANYON
4.5 mi/2.5 hr

west of Kettle Falls in Colville National Forest

Map 4.2, page 222

Hoodoo Canyon provides one of the best day hikes in northeastern Washington. Departing from a great campground on a well-stocked fishing lake, Hoodoo Canyon Trail climbs the wall of a narrow canyon to a viewpoint. The way is steep and rough at times, but always well worth the effort. And it can all be done in a morning or afternoon hike, with enough time to make s'mores at Trout Lake under the stars.

Hoodoo Canyon Trail departs Trout Lake Campground and quickly switchbacks up the canyon wall. It then traverses the length of the canyon with Trout and Emerald Lakes reflecting from far below. The forest mingles with open slopes along the way, making the hike especially scenic. The trail can be rocky and narrow at points; be careful. The trail climbs to a bluff overlooking the glacially carved canyon. To the north are the eastern peaks of the Kettle River Range. The trail continues 2 miles down to Deadman Creek and a northern trailhead. The much better option is to return to Trout Lake and catch yourself some dinner.

User Groups: Hikers, leashed dogs, horses, and mountain bikes are allowed. No wheelchair access.

Permits: This trail is accessible April–November. Permits are not required. Parking and access are free.

Maps: For a map of Colville National Forest, contact the Outdoor Recreation Information Center at the downtown Seattle REI. For topographic maps, ask the USGS for Bangs Mountain, Boyds, and Jackknife Mountain.

Directions: From Kettle Falls, drive west 8 miles on Highway 20 to Trout Lake Road (Forest Service Road 020). Turn right (north) and drive 5 miles to Trout Lake Campground. The trailhead is within the campground.

Contact: Colville National Forest, Kettle Falls Ranger Station, 255 W. 11th Ave., Kettle Falls, WA 99141, 509/738-7700.

30 GILLETTE RIDGE
12.5 mi/6.0 hr

north of Colville in Colville National Forest

Map 4.3, page 223

Gillette Ridge provides something of a rarity in the state: an easy-to-access and easy-to-complete ridge run. Starting at 4,700 feet, Gillette Ridge Trail traverses the crest of the ridge and tops out on the north section at 5,775 feet. Although there are a few saddles in which to lose hard-earned elevation, don't fret. Instead, munch on some huckleberries. The trail makes a good tour of the ridge, with plenty of views along the way. Various mountains appear from near and far on the horizons, but far more scenic is the valley below. It's hard to miss the distinctive U shape of the valley, sculpted roughly 12,000 years ago by glaciers. Even more impressive is that the glaciers that ground out Deep Creek Valley also smoothed out the ridge you're on. Back in 10,000 B.C., you'd be under hundreds of feet of ice. That's a refreshing thought on hot summer days, which accounts for most of them up here. Water isn't to be found along the route, so bring plenty of your own to wash down the huckleberries you'll harvest.

User Groups: Hikers, leashed dogs, horses, and mountain bikes. No wheelchair access.

Permits: This trail is accessible mid-May–October. Permits are not required. Parking and access are free.

Maps: For a map of Colville National Forest, contact the Outdoor Recreation Information Center at the downtown Seattle REI. For topographic maps, ask the USGS for Aladdin and Gillette Mountain.

Directions: From Colville, drive north approximately 14.5 miles on Alladin Road (County Road 9435) to Forest Service Road 500. Turn left (west) and drive 6 miles to the trailhead on the left side of the road.

Contact: Colville National Forest, Colville Ranger Station, 765 S. Main, Colville, WA 99114, 509/684-7000.

31 ABERCROMBIE MOUNTAIN

6.5 mi/3.5 hr

north of Colville in Colville National Forest

Map 4.3, page 223

From the high vantage point afforded by Abercrombie Mountain, one can seemingly peer into infinity. At 7,308 feet, the peak is one of the tallest in eastern Washington. On clear days, visitors can literally look out over hundreds of square miles, well into Canada and Idaho. Just 5 miles from the Canadian border, the peak towers above the surrounding country. Trails scale Abercrombie from the east and west, but the road to the west trailhead is more accessible. Abercrombie Trail cuts steep switchbacks up the hillside, passing through a variety of environments, from forests of lodgepole pine to clear-cuts to forests long ago ravaged by fire. The remains of an old fire lookout lie strewn about the summit, remnants of a once-awesome place to wake up and go to work. Bring plenty of water, as this is hot and dry country with no refreshment along the way.

User Groups: Hikers, leashed dogs, horses, and mountain bikes are allowed. No wheelchair access.

Permits: This trail is accessible June–October. Permits are not required. Parking and access are free.

Maps: For a map of Colville National Forest, contact the Outdoor Recreation Information Center at the downtown Seattle REI. For topographic maps, ask the USGS for Leadpoint and Abercrombie Mountain.

Directions: From Colville, drive north 25 miles on Alladin Road (County Road 9435) to Deep Creek Road (County Road 9445). Turn right and drive 7 miles to County Road 4720. Turn right and drive 2 miles to Forest Service Road 070. Drive 3.5 miles to road's end and the signed trailhead.

Contact: Colville National Forest, Colville Ranger Station, 765 S. Main, Colville, WA 99114, 509/684-7000.

32 SHERLOCK PEAK

2.5 mi/2.0 hr

north of Colville in Colville National Forest

Map 4.3, page 223

Abercrombie's little brother to the south, Sherlock Peak, is on par when it comes to bragging rights. While not as tall as Abercrombie Mountain, Sherlock Peak delivers a better journey to the final destination. The route starts high, resulting in a less strenuous hike. A seasonal cold-water spring is found along the route, providing a refresher early in the summer. And best of all, much of the route is in open forest and meadows. That may make the hike hotter, but it makes it more scenic, too. Just munch on some of the huckleberries found along the trail to make up for any sunburn. From the top of Sherlock, gaze east to the Selkirk Range running into Idaho and Canada or west to the Columbia River Valley.

User Groups: Hikers, leashed dogs, horses, and mountain bikes are allowed. No wheelchair access.

Permits: This trail is accessible June–October. Permits are not required. Parking and access are free.

Maps: For a map of Colville National Forest, contact the Outdoor Recreation Information Center at the downtown Seattle REI. For topographic maps, ask the USGS for Leadpoint and Deep Lake.

Directions: From Colville, drive north 25 miles on Alladin Road (County Road 9435) to Deep

Creek Road (County Road 9445). Turn right and drive 7 miles to County Road 4720. Turn right and drive 2 miles to Forest Service Road 070. Turn right and drive 0.5 mile to Forest Service Road 075, a rough dirt road. Drive 4 miles to road's end and the trailhead.

Contact: Colville National Forest, Colville Ranger Station, 765 South Main, Colville, WA 99114, 509/684-7000.

33 TIGER/ COYOTE ROCK LOOPS

1.8–4.8 mi/1.0–2.5 hr

west of Ione in Colville National Forest

Map 4.3, page 223

This pair of nice and easy loops makes for an excellent break from a long drive across Highway 20. With little elevation gain, Tiger and Coyote Rock Loops can be tackled by hikers of all abilities, particularly little ones. The two loops are situated in a small basin filled with wildlife. Beavers swim in Frater Lake while deer, elk, and moose often feed in the open meadows. Tiger Loop is the smaller of the two (1.8 miles) and takes only an hour to complete. It follows the shore of Frater Lake before journeying over to the waving grasses of Tiger Meadows. The trail junctions with Coyote Loop; turn left to return to the trailhead. Coyote Loop is just under 5 miles long, a more moderate distance for a full morning or afternoon. The trail passes through stands of Douglas fir and lodgepole pine to reach several viewpoints of the surrounding valley, at Coyote Rock and Shelter Rock. Be sure to bring water with you, as it won't be found along the way.

User Groups: Hikers, leashed dogs, mountain bikes, and motorcycles. No horses are allowed. No wheelchair access. Cross-country skiing and snowshoeing permitted during winter.

Permits: This area is accessible April–November. Permits are not required. Parking and access are free.

Maps: For a map of Colville National Forest,

contact the Outdoor Recreation Information Center at the downtown Seattle REI. For a topographic map, ask the USGS for Ione.

Directions: From Ione, drive south on Highway 31 to the junction with Highway 20. Turn right (west) and drive approximately 15 miles to the well-signed trailhead on the right (north) side of the highway.

Contact: Colville National Forest, Colville Ranger Station, 765 S. Main, Colville, WA 99114, 509/684-7000.

34 HALLIDAY/NORTH FORK

19.0 mi/2 days

east of Metaline Falls in the Salmo-Priest Wilderness of Colville National Forest

Map 4.3, page 223

This pair of trails combines to make a well-used route up to Crowell Ridge, in the northern arm of the Salmo-Priest Wilderness. Unfortunately, this promising route into the high country is actually a bit of a disappointment. For such a long trip, little water is to be found along the way. Much of the route is in the deep forest, revealing little of the surrounding mountains or valleys. And there's a big drop in the middle, resulting in a dreaded loss of hard-earned elevation. However, the trail offers an excellent opportunity to come across a large sampling of wildlife. Most folks have seen deer or grouse when out hiking. But how about moose or caribou? Or the symbol of wilderness, grizzly bears? You're likely to find them here.

The first trail is Halliday, which starts from Slate Creek and soon passes a marsh and ponds, a likely place to find moose feeding. Halliday then climbs the shoulder of Crowell Mountain before dropping sharply to North Fork Sullivan Trail. This trail doesn't get near the refreshing creek, which is rather annoying on hot days. Desperate hikers will have to bushwhack through underbrush for a cooldown. North Fork Trail climbs steeply in its last 2 miles to reach Crowell Ridge and spectacular payoff views. Inconveniently, the only campsite is a few miles below Crowell Ridge; reaching it extends a long and tiring day. With so much working against it, one might question why this backcountry route gets any use. Hunters love it.

User Groups: Hikers, leashed dogs, horses, and mountain bikes are allowed. No wheelchair access.

Permits: This trail is accessible May–October. Permits are not required. Parking and access are free.

Maps: For a map of Colville National Forest, contact the Outdoor Recreation Information Center at the downtown Seattle REI. For topographic maps, ask the USGS for Boundary Dam and Gypsy Peak.

Directions: From Metaline Falls, drive north 6.5 miles on Highway 31 to Forest Service Road 180. Turn right and the trailhead is 200 yards down a dirt road, on the left of the large clearing.

Contact: Colville National Forest, Sullivan Lake Ranger Station, 12641 Sullivan Lake Rd., Metaline Falls, WA 99153, 509/446-7500.

mostly used during the fall hunting seasons, so the animals are unlikely to be expecting you. A campsite and the trail's only water are at Uncas Gulch Creek. The trail ends after 4.3 miles at a junction with North Fork Sullivan Trail, where the forest finally opens to reveal the surrounding mountains.

User Groups: Hikers, leashed dogs, and horses. No mountain bikes are allowed. No wheelchair access.

Permits: This trail is accessible June–October. Permits are not required. Parking and access are free.

Maps: For a map of Colville National Forest, contact the Outdoor Recreation Information Center at the downtown Seattle REI. For a topographic map, ask the USGS for Gypsy Peak.

Directions: From Metaline Falls, drive north on Highway 31 for 9 miles to Forest Service Road 3155. Turn right and drive 5.5 miles to the trailhead on the right side of the road.

Contact: Colville National Forest, Sullivan Lake Ranger Station, 12641 Sullivan Lake Rd., Metaline Falls, WA 99153, 509/446-7500.

35 SLATE CREEK
8.6 mi/4.5 hr   🚶4 ⛺8

east of Metaline Falls in Colville National Forest

Map 4.3, page 223

Slate Creek is one of the more difficult trails in the Sullivan Lake area. After crossing its namesake, Slate Creek Trail climbs steeply through the forest to a small depression within a small ridge. From there, lace your boots tightly for a quick descent into Uncas Gulch, only to climb right out of it again. It's a significant up and down of about 500 feet and is likely to leave you a bit spent for the extra effort. Plenty of good things will more than make up for your effort. Hikers who walk quietly are likely to encounter wildlife, whether it be as small as a rabbit or grouse, or as large as an elk, caribou, or grizzly bear. The trail is

36 SALMO LOOP
17.8 mi/2-3 days   🚶3 ⛺10

east of Metaline Falls in the Salmo-Priest Wilderness of Colville National Forest

Map 4.3, page 223

Backcountry trekkers, this is the hike for you. Salmo Loop explores the old-growth forests of Salmo River while also climbing to the peak of Snowy Top, a 7,500-foot peak that's actually in Idaho. The route feels as if it's some of the deepest wilderness in the country for a reason: It is. The symbol of wilderness in North America, the grizzly bear, still lives here. Not to mention herds of deer, elk, caribou, and moose. The trail encounters old-growth western hemlock and western red cedar within the Salmo Basin but passes through sublime alpine meadows near the peak of Little Snowy

Top. This is one trail that certainly makes the long drive out to this little-known corner of the state worthwhile.

Salmo Basin Trail drops from Salmo Divide Trailhead steeply to South Salmo River (3.1 miles). The bridge may or may not be passable when you get there, so be sure to consider carefully before fording this river during times of high snow runoff. The trail then follows the South Salmo River up to the ridgeline between Snowy Top and Little Snowy Top (8.8 miles). It may be out of the way to hike the side trail up to Snowy Top, but it's the perfect spot for a long break. Possession of a camera is recommended here. The route then follows Shed-roof Divide Trail back down to Salmo Divide Trail (14.8 miles), three miles from the car.

Campsites are scattered liberally throughout the trip, most notably along the South Salmo River. A pair are also up on the Shed-roof Divide. Water is plentiful in the Salmo Basin, but may be tricky if not impossible to secure once you're on the ridge. Be sure to top off your water before leaving the river. Other than that, be prepared for an amazing trip.

User Groups: Hikers, leashed dogs, and horses. No mountain bikes are allowed. No wheelchair access.

Permits: This trail is accessible mid-June–October. Permits are not required. Parking and access are free.

Maps: For a map of Colville National Forest, contact the Outdoor Recreation Information Center at the downtown Seattle REI. For topographic maps, ask the USGS for Salmo Mountain and Continental Mountain (Idaho).

Directions: From Metaline Falls, drive north 2 miles on Highway 31. Turn right onto County Road 9345 and drive 5 miles to Forest Service Road 22. Turn left and drive 20 miles (the road becomes Forest Service Road 2220 at 6.5 miles) to the road's end and the trailhead.

Contact: Colville National Forest, Sullivan Lake Ranger Station, 12641 Sullivan Lake Rd., Metaline Falls, WA 99153, 509/446-7500.

③⑦ SHEDROOF DIVIDE
18.7 mi one-way/2 days

east of Metaline Falls in the Salmo-Priest Wilderness of Colville National Forest

Map 4.3, page 223

Cutting through the heart of Salmo-Priest Wilderness, Shedroof Divide Trail revels in open meadows and expansive views of the surrounding Selkirk Mountains. This high route along the crest of a long ridge is practically unequaled in its beauty, making for a backpacker's dream. Big game abounds in this high country, with scores of deer, elk, and even caribou roaming the hillsides. Hikers may encounter a bear (both black bears and grizzly bears live here) or a more elusive cougar. Don't worry, these big predators prefer to mind their own business; just remember to look big if you come across one.

Shedroof Divide Trail is accessible via several trails and trailheads, including Shedroof Mountain (the northern trailhead), Pass Creek Pass (southern trailhead), Thunder Creek Trail, and Shedroof Cutoff Trail. A through-hike is recommended to take in all of the route, but bringing two cars to this remote part of Washington can prove problematic. Single-car hikers are best advised to start at the northern trailhead and hike in from there as time allows. Shedroof Divide Trail follows the crest, passing below a number of peaks, including Shedroof, Thunder, and Round Top Mountains. Side trails to their peaks are a must-do diversion. Much of the route is awash in open meadows and grand views deep into Idaho and Canada. Water may be difficult to find along the trail, but there are a couple of seasonal cold-water springs for help. Camps are dispersed along the route, with good, established sites just north of Round Top and just south of Thunder Mountain. Shedroof Divide Trail is the way best way to experience the vastness of the Selkirk Mountains.

User Groups: Hikers, leashed dogs, and horses. No mountain bikes are allowed. No wheelchair access.

Permits: This trail is accessible mid-June–October. Permits are not required. Parking and access are free.

Maps: For a map of Colville National Forest, contact the Outdoor Recreation Information Center at the downtown Seattle REI. For topographic maps, ask the USGS for Salmo Mountain, Helmer Mountain, and Pass Creek.

Directions: North access: From Metaline Falls, drive north 2 miles on Highway 31. Turn right onto County Road 9345 and drive 5 miles to Forest Service Road 22. Turn left and drive 20.5 miles to the end of the road and the signed trailhead.

South access: From Metaline Falls, drive north 2 miles on Highway 31. Turn right onto County Road 9345 and drive 5 miles to Forest Service Road 22. Turn left and drive 6.5 miles to a signed junction. Stay to the right on Forest Service Road 22 and drive 7.5 miles to Pass Creek Pass and the signed trailhead.

Contact: Colville National Forest, Sullivan Lake Ranger Station, 12641 Sullivan Lake Rd., Metaline Falls, WA 99153, 509/446-7500.

38 CROWELL RIDGE
12.0 mi/8.0 hr 🏃3 ⛰10

east of Metaline Falls in the Salmo-Priest Wilderness of Colville National Forest

Map 4.3, page 223

Visitors to Crowell Ridge will think they have accidentally hiked into the North Cascades. Glacial basins and snowy peaks greet hikers as they traverse this high ridge in the northern arm of Salmo-Priest Wilderness. Undisturbed forests of subalpine fir and Englemann spruce give way to big meadows and bigger vistas. Expect to see a large assortment of wildlife, from bald eagles patrolling the skies for a meal to deer, elk, and bighorn sheep grazing along the steep hillsides.

Crowell Ridge Trail leaves Bear Pasture Trailhead and immediately climbs to Crowell Ridge. The trees quickly disappear from the rocky ridge and open meadows. At more than 7,300 feet, Gypsy Peak stands as a beacon from the north with a large glacial basin and lakes at the bottom of steep slopes. If you're interested in seeing wildflowers, try late June and early July, when the winter's snowpack has finally melted out. The trail heads south and makes a junction with North Fork Sullivan Trail at 3.7 miles. Here is the trail's only campsite, a grand place to set up camp. Crowell Ridge Trail continues 4.1 miles through open meadow over to Sullivan Mountain Trailhead, the trail's end. If you had only one day to spend in the Sullivan Lake area, this would be the trail to hike.

User Groups: Hikers, leashed dogs, and horses. No mountain bikes are allowed. No wheelchair access.

Permits: This trail is accessible mid-June–October. Permits are not required. Parking and access are free.

Maps: For a map of Colville National Forest, contact the Outdoor Recreation Information Center at the downtown Seattle REI. For a topographic map, ask the USGS for Gypsy Peak.

Directions: A high-clearance vehicle is recommend to access this trailhead. From Metaline Falls, drive north 2 miles on Highway 31. Turn right onto County Road 9345 and drive 5 miles to Forest Service Road 22. Turn left and drive 8 miles (the road becomes Forest Service Road 2220 at 6.5 miles) to Forest Service Road 2212. Turn left and drive 3 miles to Forest Service Road 200. Turn right and drive 6 miles to the road's end and Bear Pasture Trailhead.

Contact: Colville National Forest, Sullivan Lake Ranger Station, 12641 Sullivan Lake Rd., Metaline Falls, WA 99153, 509/446-7500.

39 THUNDER CREEK
10.2 mi/5.0 hr

east of Metaline Falls in the Salmo-Priest Wilderness of Colville National Forest

Map 4.3, page 223

Less traveled than many other trails in the region, Thunder Creek Trail serves as an excellent way to step into the heart of Shedroof Divide. The first half of the trail follows an old road through the forest, passing many small streams and wet spots. After 2.2 miles, the road ends and the trail becomes a true footpath as it crosses into Salmo-Priest Wilderness. Old-growth western hemlock and western red cedar fill the forests, making prime habitat for a variety of big game animals. Deer, elk, bear, and even caribou are found in these forests. Thunder Creek Trail finds Shedroof Divide Trail after 5.1 miles, complete with open meadows and encouraging views. From here, hikers can head north or south along the backbone of Salmo-Priest Wilderness. Although the trail can often be wet, suitable drinking water may be difficult to find. Folks looking to make a night out of it will want to pitch their tents up on the divide in previously used spots.

User Groups: Hikers, leashed dogs, and horses. No mountain bikes are allowed. No wheelchair access.

Permits: This trail is accessible mid-June–October. Permits are not required. Parking and access are free.

Maps: For a map of Colville National Forest, contact the Outdoor Recreation Information Center at the downtown Seattle REI. For topographic maps, ask the USGS for Salmo Mountain and Helmer Mountain.

Directions: From Metaline Falls, drive north 2 miles on Highway 31. Turn right onto County Road 9345 and drive 5 miles to Forest Service Road 22. Turn left and drive 13 miles (the road becomes Forest Service Road 2220 at 6.5 miles) to Gypsy Meadows. The signed trailhead is on the right side of Forest Service Road 2220.

Contact: Colville National Forest, Sullivan Lake Ranger Station, 12641 Sullivan Lake Rd., Metaline Falls, WA 99153, 509/446-7500.

40 SULLIVAN LAKESHORE
8.4 mi/4.0 hr

east of Metaline Falls in Colville National Forest

Map 4.3, page 223

Situated between two national forest campgrounds, Sullivan Lakeshore Trail is a great hike for families. Four miles of level hiking along Sullivan Lake is highlighted by a great self-guided nature trail at one end. The trail runs between East Sullivan and Noisy Creek Campgrounds along the eastern shore of Sullivan Lake, making for two easily accessible trailheads. The better bet is to start from East Sullivan, where a short 0.5-mile nature loop cuts off the main trail into the heart of the forest. Hikers can pick up a brochure to follow as they hike, learning about different processes of the forest ecosystem. This short trail is ideal for little ones.

Sullivan Lakeshore Trail runs along the edge of Sullivan Lake, passing in and out of a mixed forest of hardwoods and conifers. The trail frequently breaks out to views of the lake and Sand Creek Mountain to the west. Often, hikers will turn around and peer up from the foot of Hall Mountain to see mountain goats scaling the rocky cliffs. Hikers young and old will appreciate this lakeside trail.

User Groups: Hikers and leashed dogs. No horses or mountain bikes are allowed. The nature trail is wheelchair accessible.

Permits: This trail is accessible year-round. Permits are not required. Parking and access are free.

Maps: For a map of Colville National Forest, contact the Outdoor Recreation Information Center at the downtown Seattle REI. For a topographic map, ask the USGS for Metaline Falls.

Directions: From Metaline Falls, drive north 2

miles on Highway 31. Turn right onto County Road 9345 and drive 5 miles to Forest Service Road 22. Turn left and drive 0.5 mile to East Sullivan Campground. Turn right and drive 0.3 mile to the well-signed trailhead on the left.

Contact: Colville National Forest, Sullivan Lake Ranger Station, 12641 Sullivan Lake Rd., Metaline Falls, WA 99153, 509/446-7500.

41 HALL MOUNTAIN
5.0 mi/2.5 hr
🏃2 ⛰9

east of Metaline Falls in Colville National Forest

Map 4.3, page 223

Hall Mountain Trail is one of the best day hikes in the Sullivan Lake area. The trail up Hall Mountain is relatively short, never too steep for even younger hikers, and ends at an old lookout site, an obvious spot for views of the surrounding mountains. Hall Mountain Trail starts along an old road before arriving at a junction with Noisy Creek Trail (0.7 mile). Take a right and keep climbing through the forest of subalpine fir and Englemann spruce. Big-game encounters are possible, with scores of deer, elk, and even caribou filling the woods during different seasons. More likely, you'll be startled by the sudden noise of a grouse taking off from under your feet. Hall Mountain Trail breaks out of the forest to find old remains of the Hall Mountain fire lookout. Sand Creek Mountain stands opposite the deep, blue water of Sullivan Lake, a tempting refresher for the end the day. Lucky hikers will peer down the steep slopes of Hall Mountain to find bighorn sheep scaling the hillside.

User Groups: Hikers, leashed dogs, horses, and mountain bikes. No wheelchair access.

Permits: This trail is accessible June–October. Permits are not required. Parking and access are free.

Maps: For a map of Colville National Forest, contact the Outdoor Recreation Information Center at the downtown Seattle REI. For topographic maps, ask the USGS for Metaline Falls and Pass Creek.

Directions: From Metaline Falls, drive north 2 miles on Highway 31. Turn right onto County Road 9345 and drive 5 miles to Forest Service Road 22. Turn left and drive 3.5 miles to Forest Service Road 500. Turn right and drive 7 miles to the road's end and the trailhead. This road is open only July 1–August 14, to minimize disturbances to wildlife habitat. Hall Mountain is accessible via Grassy Top or Noisy Creek during other times of the year.

Contact: Colville National Forest, Sullivan Lake Ranger Station, 12641 Sullivan Lake Rd., Metaline Falls, WA 99153, 509/446-7500.

42 NOISY CREEK
10.6 mi/4.0 hr
🏃2 ⛰8

east of Metaline Falls in Colville National Forest

Map 4.3, page 223

In a region of high mountains, Noisy Creek Trail offers an easier hike perfectly suited for more laid-back hikers. The trail follows Noisy Creek, an appropriate name for the gushing stream during the spring snowmelt, for 5 miles through forests new and old. The first 1.3 miles climbs gently through the valley up to a vista of Sullivan Lake. This is a great turnaround for those seeking a shorter day hike, as it's about the only view you're going to find. More serious hikers will want to follow the trail farther up the creek valley as it makes its way through a forest of western hemlock, western red cedar, grand fir, and western larch, a hard-to-find species in Washington. Watch for camp robbers (not bandits, just gray jays) following you from the trailhead, hoping for a trail-mix handout. Woodpeckers pound away on dead snags while deer and elk frequently cross hikers' paths. Noisy Creek Trail crosses its namesake once (1.8 miles), a wet and even troublesome ford when the stream is running strongly. The trail makes a steep, mile-long climb out of the valley before ending at a junction with Hall Mountain Trail, at 5.3 miles.

User Groups: Hikers, leashed dogs, horses, and mountain bikes. No wheelchair access.

Permits: This trail is accessible year-round. Permits are not required. Parking and access are free.

Maps: For a map of Colville National Forest, contact the Outdoor Recreation Information Center at the downtown Seattle REI. For topographic maps, ask the USGS for Metaline Falls and Pass Creek.

Directions: From Metaline Falls, drive north 2 miles on Highway 31. Turn right onto County Road 9345 and drive 9.8 miles to Noisy Creek Campground. The well-signed trailhead is between the group and individual camp sections.

Contact: Colville National Forest, Sullivan Lake Ranger Station, 12641 Sullivan Lake Rd., Metaline Falls, WA 99153, 509/446-7500.

43 PASS CREEK/ GRASSY TOP

7.6 mi/4.0 hr   🏃2 ⛰9

east of Metaline Falls in Colville National Forest

Map 4.3, page 223

A mountain summit covered in grass means few trees. Few trees means expansive views of the surrounding mountains. One of the easier and more beautiful peaks to bag in the Sullivan Lake area is Grassy Top, a challenging but not overwhelming trail to the summit of the same name. All of this lies just outside of the Salmo-Priest Wilderness, but that is no harm to the appeal of this hike.

Grassy Top Trail begins at lofty Pass Creek Pass, a low point in the Shedroof Divide. The trail heads south along the ridge and steadily climbs toward Grassy Top. The forest of subalpine fir, Englemann spruce, and whitebark pine breaks open into expansive meadows of wildflowers (during the early summer) and waves of grass. These meadows are great places

to catch deer grazing or bears scavenging. The trail passes just below Grassy Top, but a side trail leads to the summit. The surrounding Selkirk Range is in full splendor from this vantage, a delight on clear days. Remember to pack enough water, as it's nonexistent along the trail. Overnight hikers will need to find an off-trail place to camp, as there are no developed sites. I recommend atop Grassy Top.

User Groups: Hikers, leashed dogs, horses, and mountain bikes. No wheelchair access.

Permits: This trail is accessible mid-June–October. Permits are not required. Parking and access are free.

Maps: For a map of Colville National Forest, contact the Outdoor Recreation Information Center at the downtown Seattle REI. For a topographic map, ask the USGS for Pass Creek.

Directions: From Metaline Falls, drive north 2 miles on Highway 31. Turn right onto County Road 9345 and drive 5 miles to Forest Service Road 22. Turn left and drive 6.5 miles to a signed junction. Stay to the right on Forest Service Road 22 and drive 7.5 miles to Pass Creek Pass and the signed trailhead.

Contact: Colville National Forest, Sullivan Lake Ranger Station, 12641 Sullivan Lake Rd., Metaline Falls, WA 99153, 509/446-7500.

44 LITTLE SPOKANE RIVER NATURAL AREA

7.5 mi/4.0 hr   🏃1 ⛰9

east of Spokane in Little Spokane River Natural Area

Map 4.4, page 224

Little Spokane River Natural Area provides a great escape from the city into an undisturbed wilderness. Contrasting greatly with the dry pine forests common to the Spokane area, the lowland bordering the river is abundant with life. It's a prime spot to see animals normally viewed only on wildlife television shows. The river ecosystem is fertile habitat for wildlife, including beaver, muskrat, porcupines, raccoons, coyotes, white-tailed deer, and even the occasional moose. The river also serves as important habitat for birds, including woodpeckers, bald eagles, red-tailed hawks, mergansers, and wood ducks. During the spring, this area serves as a rookery (nesting site) for great blue herons. The Little Spokane River is also a great place to cast a fishing line, and the trail offers access to many secluded fishing holes where rainbow and cutthroat trout lurk below the surface.

From the central Painted Rocks Trailhead, the main trail runs to the east and west along the river. An informative brochure is available at the trailhead, providing a natural-history lesson as one wanders the trails. There is no true destination along the trail; a hike of any length is certain to be great trip. Be sure to investigate rock outcroppings for ancient Indian pictographs; these paintings are found all along the trail. Hikers who lead a double life as river rats will be happy to know that the Little Spokane River is a favorite haunt for canoeists and kayakers.

User Groups: Hikers only. No dogs, horses, or mountain bikes are allowed. No wheelchair access.

Permits: This trail is accessible year-round. Permits are not required. Parking and access are free.

Maps: For topographic maps, ask the USGS for Dartford and Ninemile Falls.

Directions: From Spokane, drive north on Highway 291 to Rutter Parkway. Turn right (east) and drive to the trailhead, on the left just after you cross the river.

Contact: Riverside State Park, 9711 W. Charles St., Nine Mile Falls, WA 99026, 509/465-5064.

MOUNT RAINIER AND THE SOUTHERN CASCADES

© SCOTT LEONARD

BEST HIKES

By far the Northwest's tallest point, Mount Rainier

never seems to be far from view. At 14,411 feet, the towering mass of The Mountain looms over life in Puget Sound, southern Washington, and a good chunk of the east side as well. Perhaps because Mount Rainier is such familiar sight, many of the forests and mountains to her south go unnoticed. That's a shame, for the South Cascades of Washington are home to some excellent adventures in waiting. This area not only contains the living outdoor laboratory that is Mount St. Helens, it also has the glaciers and meadows of Mount Adams and Goat Rocks.

First and foremost on the agenda of most visitors to the region is Mount Rainier, since it is, to say the least, the embodiment of hiking in the Evergreen State. From old-growth forest to alpine meadows, from icy glaciers to milky white rivers, Mount Rainier has it all. A total of 26 glaciers grace the slopes of Takhoma (which, in the Puyallup language, means "breast of the milk-white waters"). These glistening masses of ice give birth to opalescent rivers flowing in every direction.

There are several points of access: Route 410 and 123 transect the eastern side of the park, accessing Sunrise (6,400 feet), where great day hikes and longer trips exploring the north and east sides of Mount Rainier begin. Along the south side of the park, Nisqually and Stevens Canyon Roads meet at the glorious high country of Paradise. Again, numerous trails branch out from the visitors center and historic Park Lodge, exploring the meadows and glaciers of the area. Skyline Trail is a mecca for wildflowers. Although the west side of the park is inaccessible by car, Mowich Lake and Carbon River in the northwest corner can still be reached by road, the easiest park access from Seattle.

To the south is the Cascades' most restless sister, Mount St. Helens. Once one of the nation's most majestic mountains, it erupted in a mighty explosion in 1980, drastically altering its figure. Cubic miles of rock and mud slid off the mountain, and many square miles of forest were completely leveled. Today, life around the mountain is making a comeback. Shrubs and wildflowers are taking hold, and trees are even popping up here and there. But the devastation of the eruption is still readily evident. Johnston Ridge Visitor Center is a great stop, with trails leading into the blast zone. Or you can drive right into the blast zone at Windy Ridge Viewpoint, on the east side. Hikes along Plains of Abraham or Meta Lake make for great day trips.

Not to be outdone, the Gifford Pinchot National Forest boasts two beautiful wildernesses. Near White Pass are the snowcapped and rocky peaks of Goat Rocks. Numerous trails access this complex of obsolete volcanoes. Snowgrass Flats and Goat Ridge are the most scenic – and popular – routes into the area. Farther south is Indian Heaven, another group of high peaks and ridges left over from old volcanoes. Thomas Lake and Indian Heaven Trails are great routes to explore the meadows and get good views of Mounts Hood, Adams, St. Helens, and even Rainier.

The rest of the Gifford Pinchot National Forest is crisscrossed by a large network of paved and unpaved roads. Mount Adams stands as Washington's second-tallest peak and enjoys a wealth of trails and campgrounds. Although Round-the-Mountain doesn't actually make it all the way around, it's a great through-hike amongst meadows and waterfalls. Mount Adams is another fun one to climb. Many ridge trails are perfect for those on wheels (check out Langille Ridge, Boundary Trail, or Badger Ridge). Thanks to all the volcanic soil of the South Cascades, huckleberries are a plentiful backcountry harvest; Juniper Ridge, Dark Meadows, and Hidden Lakes are great berry-picking trails. Rounding out the hiking selection is every kid's favorite school field trip: Ape Cave, a long underground lava tube. For water lovers, there's the White Salmon River, a very popular white-water rafting river, and while driving along the Columbia River Gorge, perhaps on your way to hike Beacon Rock, you're sure to notice hundreds of windsurfers on the river near Hood River.

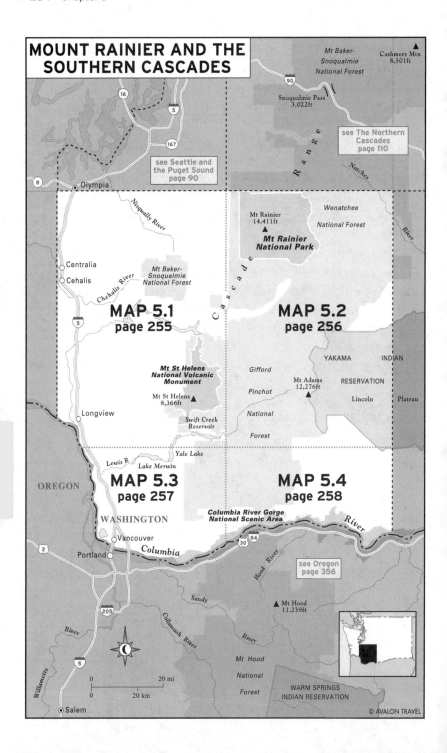

MOUNT RAINIER AND THE SOUTHERN CASCADES

Mt Baker-Snoqualmie National Forest

Cashmere Mtn
8,501ft

90

Snoqualmie Pass
3,022ft

Range

see The Northern
Cascades
page 110

Natches

16

5

167

see Seattle and
the Puget Sound
page 90

8

Olympia

Nisqually River

Mt Rainier
14,411ft

Wenatchee

National Forest

**Mt Rainier
National Park**

Centralia

Cehalis

Cascade

Chehalis River

Mt Baker-
Snoqualmie
National Forest

5

**MAP 5.1
page 255**

**MAP 5.2
page 256**

River

YAKAMA   INDIAN

Gifford

RESERVATION

**Mt St Helens
National Volcanic
Monument**

Pinchot

Mt Adams
12,276ft

Lincoln   Plateau

Mt St Helens
8,366ft

National

Longview

Swift Creek
Reservoir

Forest

Yale Lake

Lewis R   Lake Merwin

**MAP 5.3
page 257**

**MAP 5.4
page 258**

OREGON

WASHINGTON

**Columbia River Gorge
National Scenic Area**

River

Vancouver

2

Columbia

30   84

Portland

see Oregon
page 356

Hood River

River

205

Mt Hood
11,239ft

River

Sandy

River

Clackamas River

Willamette

5

0   20 mi

0   20 km

Mt Hood

National

Forest

WARM SPRINGS
INDIAN RESERVATION

Salem

© AVALON TRAVEL

Map 5.1

Hikes 1-17
Pages 259-268

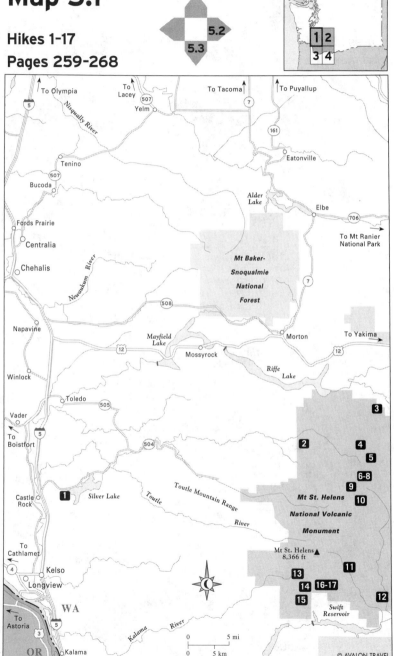

Map 5.2

Hikes 18-110
Pages 269-327

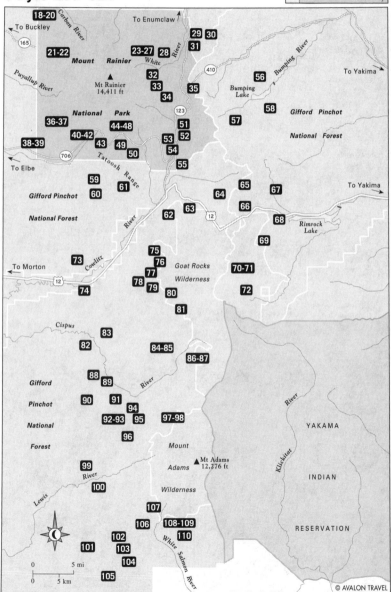

Map 5.3

Hikes 111-112
Page 328

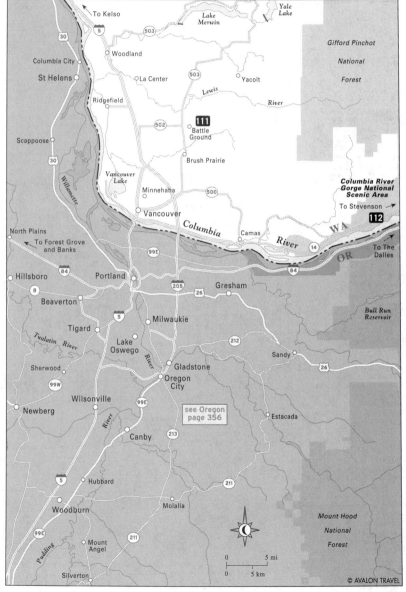

Map 5.4

Hikes 113-119
Pages 329-332

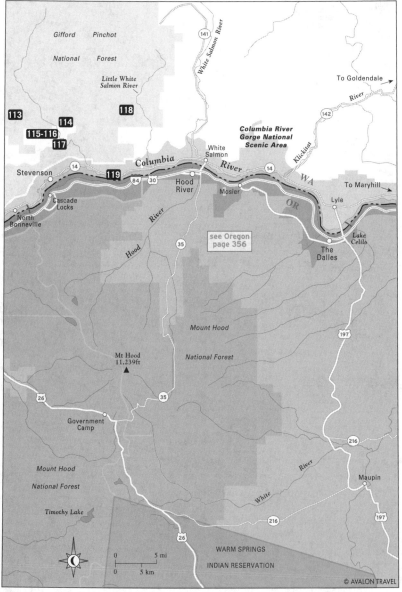

Gifford   Pinchot

National   Forest

Little White
Salmon River

White Salmon River

To Goldendale

141

142

River

113

114

118

115-116

117

Columbia   River

Columbia River
Gorge National
Scenic Area

Klickitat

WA

Stevenson

14

119

84   30

Hood
River

White
Salmon

Mosier

14

To Maryhill

Lyle

OR

Cascade
Locks

North
Bonneville

River

Hood

35

see Oregon
page 356

Lake
Celilo

The
Dalles

Mount Hood

197

Mt Hood
11,239ft

National Forest

26

35

Government
Camp

216

Mount Hood

National Forest

River

Maupin

Timothy Lake

White

216

197

26

WARM SPRINGS

INDIAN RESERVATION

0   5 mi

0   5 km

© AVALON TRAVEL

1 SILVER LAKE

1.0 mi/0.5 hr   👫1 ⛰8

east of Castle Rock in Silver Lake State Park

Map 5.1, page 255

The quick, one-mile loop of Silver Lake Trail is a great leg stretcher for folks hitting up the Silver Lake Visitor Center. The trail delves into the growing wetlands that in turn are slowly shrinking Silver Lake. The lake itself was formed by lava flows more than 2,000 years ago and is now on its last legs. Although the outlook may not be good for the lake, wildlife is abundant around the lake. This is a favorite winter haunt for deer and elk, while spring and fall bring loads of migrating waterfowl. On clear days, Mount St. Helens is visible across Silver Lake. The trail is barrier free and accessible to wheelchairs.

User Groups: Hikers and leashed dogs. No horses or mountain bikes are allowed. The trail is wheelchair accessible.

Permits: This trail is accessible year-round. A federal Northwest Forest Pass is not required to park here.

Maps: For a topographic map, ask the USGS for Silver Lake.

Directions: From Castle Rock, drive east 5 miles on Highway 504 to Silver Lake Mount St. Helens Visitor Center. The trailhead is on the south side of the visitors center.

Contact: Gifford Pinchot National Forest, Mount St. Helens National Volcanic Monument, 42218 Yale Bridge Rd., Amboy, WA 98601, 360/449-7871.

2 COLDWATER LAKE

5.5 mi/3.0 hr   👫2 ⛰9

east of Castle Rock in Mount St. Helens National Volcanic Monument of Gifford Pinchot National Forest

Map 5.1, page 255

Hikers along the shores of Coldwater Lake can thank the 1980 eruption of Mount St. Helens for the trail they're enjoying. That's because before the blast, there was no Coldwater Lake. Massive amounts of mud and debris rushed down from the erupting volcano and created a large natural dam on Coldwater Creek, slowly filling up to become Coldwater Lake.

Coldwater Lake Trail follows the shores of this lake before climbing abruptly to the ridge above. The trail is easy to reach, beginning at the Coldwater Ridge Visitor Center. The trail follows the shores, now regenerating with small shrubs and plants. Although the gray, ashen hillsides look unfit for survival, many species of wildlife are spotted here, including deer, elk, squirrels, and frogs, and trout have been stocked in the lake. The trail hugs the shoreline for nearly 3 miles before climbing steeply. It's best to turn around and enjoy the walk back before the steep ascent.

User Groups: Hikers only. No dogs, horses, or mountain bikes are allowed. No wheelchair access.

Permits: This trail is accessible April–November. A federal Northwest Forest Pass, or an $8.00 day-use pass, is required to park here.

Maps: For a map of Gifford Pinchot National Forest, contact the Outdoor Recreation Information Center at the downtown Seattle REI. For a topographic map, ask Green Trails for No. 364, Mount St. Helens, or ask the USGS for Elk Rock and Spirit Lake West.

Directions: From Castle Rock, drive east 35 miles to the Coldwater Visitor Center in Mount St. Helens National Monument. The signed trailhead appears immediately following the visitors center on the left.

Contact: Gifford Pinchot National Forest, Mount St. Helens National Volcanic Monument, 42218 Yale Bridge Rd., Amboy, WA 98601, 360/449-7871.

3 STRAWBERRY MOUNTAIN
12.0 mi/6.0 hr 　　　　🏃2 ⛰9

south of Randle in Mount St. Helens National Volcanic Monument of Gifford Pinchot National Forest

Map 5.1, page 255

Running south to north along the edge of Mount St. Helens' blast zone, Strawberry Mountain tells a great story of the effects of the 1980 eruption. Strawberry Mountain Trail rides the crest of the long mountain (which is more a ridge than a mountain). Along the western side, entire forests were leveled by a wave of searing gas and ash. The blast leveled the trees like blades of grass, leaving them arranged in neat rows. On the eastern side, it's business as usual. Subalpine meadows filled with wildflowers now dominate the southern part of the route, which climbs to a pair of open peaks.

Strawberry Mountain Trail runs the length of the ridge, 11 miles in all. The southern trailhead saves a lot of elevation gain and is more open and scenic. Thus it's the preferred route. Start at Bear Meadows and hike Boundary Trail to Strawberry Mountain Trail (0.4 mile). Turn left and follow Strawberry Mountain Trail north. Old-growth forest is mixed with open meadows. A short side trail (2.7 miles) cuts off to the west and quickly finds an expansive viewpoint. Views of the alpine Mount Margaret backcountry and the crater within Mount St. Helens are terrific. The trail continues into open meadows of heather and lupine (5 miles). It's a good time to turn around and retrace your steps to the car when you've had your fill of views. Don't expect to find any water along this high route.

User Groups: Hikers, leashed dogs, horses, and mountain bikes. No wheelchair access.

Permits: This trail is accessible June–October. A federal Northwest Forest Pass is not required to park here.

Maps: For a map of Gifford Pinchot National Forest, contact the Outdoor Recreation Information Center at the downtown Seattle REI.

For a topographic map, ask Green Trails for No. 332, Spirit Lake, or ask the USGS for Cowlitz Falls and Vanson Peak.

Directions: From Randle, drive south 1 mile on Highway 131 to Forest Service Road 25. Stay to the right and drive 19 miles to Forest Service Road 99. Turn right and drive 6 miles to Bear Meadow Trailhead. The trail starts on the north side of Road 99.

Contact: Gifford Pinchot National Forest, Mount St. Helens National Volcanic Monument, 42218 NE Yale Bridge Rd., Amboy, WA 98601, 360/449-7871.

4 QUARTZ CREEK BIG TREES
0.5 mi/0.5 hr 　　　　🏃1 ⛰9

southwest of Randle in Gifford Pinchot National Forest

Map 5.1, page 255 　　　　**BEST (**

So close to such devastated landscape, it's amazing to see what much of the forest near Mount St. Helens previously looked like. Not far from the blast zone, Quartz Creek Big Trees Trail is a short loop into an ancient forest of Douglas fir, western hemlock, and western red cedar. Mosses and ferns blanket every branch and inch of ground, a moist contrast to the barren landscapes just a few miles away over the ridge. Quartz Creek Big Trees Trail is flat, level, and barrier free, perfect for hikers of all ages and abilities. The trail makes a short 0.5-mile loop within this old-growth forest.

User Groups: Hikers and leashed dogs. No horses or mountain bikes are allowed. The trail is wheelchair accessible.

Permits: This trail is accessible year-round. A federal Northwest Forest Pass is required to park here.

Maps: For a map of Gifford Pinchot National Forest, contact the Outdoor Recreation Information Center at the downtown Seattle REI. For a topographic map, ask Green Trails for No. 332, Spirit Lake, or ask the USGS for Cowlitz Falls.

Directions: From Randle, drive south 1 mile on Highway 131 to Forest Service Road 25. Stay to the right and drive 8 miles to Forest Service Road 26. Turn right and drive 8 miles to Forest Service Road 2608. Turn left and drive 1.5 miles to the signed trailhead on the right.

Contact: Gifford Pinchot National Forest, Cowlitz Valley Ranger Station, 10024 U.S. 12, Randle, WA 98377, 360/497-1100.

5 GOAT MOUNTAIN
8.0 mi/5.0 hr

north of Mount St. Helens in Gifford Pinchot National Forest

Map 5.1, page 255

Situated 12 miles north of Mount St. Helens (as the crow flies), Goat Mountain managed to escape much of the eruption's devastating impact. Thank goodness, because Goat Mountain is a subalpine wonderland. Covered in open meadows, this rocky ridge provides great views of the eruption's impact to the south. Goat Mountain is an excellent way to see the altered landscape yet still enjoy a hike among lush meadows.

Goat Mountain Trail climbs from Ryan Lake, zigzaging in and out of affected forest, now a graveyard of standing dead trees. The trail reaches the ridge (1.5 miles) and navigates a mix of meadows and rocky bluffs, each awash in wildflowers (bear grass, lupine, spirea, and stonecrop, to name a few). The towering slopes of Mount Margaret loom from the south.

Goat Mountain Trail traverses the ridge for three spectacular miles, eventually dropping to Deadman Lake (4.8 miles) and on to Vanson Lake (8.1 miles). Unless you're looking for a long hike or tough climb back, the best turnaround is before the trail drops to Deadman Lake. You'll see that Goat Mountain is an appropriate name. Fluffy white goats are a common sight, scrambling along the rocky cliffs.

User Groups: Hikers, leashed dogs, horses, and mountain bikes. No wheelchair access.

Permits: This trail is accessible June–September. A federal Northwest Forest Pass is not required to park here.

Maps: For a map of Gifford Pinchot National Forest, contact the Outdoor Recreation Information Center at the downtown Seattle REI. For a topographic map, ask Green Trails for No. 332, Spirit Lake, or ask the USGS for Cowlitz Falls and Vanson Peak.

Directions: From Randle, drive south 1 mile on Highway 131 to Forest Service Road 25. Stay to the right and drive 8 miles to Forest Service Road 26. Turn right and drive 14 miles to Forest Service Road 2612. Turn right and drive 0.5 mile to the trailhead on the right.

Contact: Gifford Pinchot National Forest, Mount St. Helens National Volcanic Monument, 42218 NE Yale Bridge Rd., Amboy, WA 98601, 360/449-7871.

6 BOUNDARY, WEST END
12.0 mi/5.0-6.0 hr

in Mount St. Helens National Volcanic Monument

Map 5.1, page 255

This western end of Boundary Trail is the most glorious stretch of trail in Mount St. Helens National Monument. Every step is better than the one before it, as you experience beautiful meadows of wildflowers with expansive views of the eruption's impact. This section of Boundary Trail runs 13.8 miles (one-way) between Johnston Ridge Observatory and Norway Pass, near Winder Ridge Viewpoint. A car-drop between these two points involves hundreds of miles of driving and is hardly worthwhile. No worries, because each trailhead offers access to a great peak in about 12 miles.

Visitors to Johnston Ridge Observatory can hike to Coldwater Peak (12.2 miles round-trip), an up-close look at the crater. From the observatory, hike east on Boundary Trail above sprawling plains of ash and mud. The trail heads north and climbs above St. Helens Lake, a site of total devastation. A side trail leads to the summit (elevation 5,727 feet).

From Forest Service Road 99, a hike to Mount Margaret (11.6 miles round-trip) makes for an incredible trip through alpine meadows and views of sparkling lakes. From Norway Pass Trailhead, hike west on Boundary Trail to Norway Pass (2.2 miles). The trail travels through the heart of the blast zone, but lush meadows survived to the north. A side trail leads to Margaret's summit.

Both hikes are exposed and dry, with no water to be found. They also have rocky sections along steep slopes; care is necessary at times.

User Groups: Hikers only. No dogs, horses, or mountain bikes are allowed. No wheelchair access.

Permits: This trail is accessible June–mid-October. A federal Northwest Forest Pass is required to park here.

Maps: For a map of Gifford Pinchot National Forest, contact the Outdoor Recreation Information Center at the downtown Seattle REI. For a topographic map, ask Green Trails for No. 332, Spirit Lake, or ask the USGS for Spirit Lake West and Spirit Lake East.

Directions: From Randle, drive south 1 mile on Highway 131 to Forest Service Road 25. Stay to the right and drive 19 miles to Forest Service Road 99. Turn right and drive 11 miles to Forest Service Road 26. Turn right and drive 1.5 miles to Norway Pass Trailhead.

Contact: Gifford Pinchot National Forest, Mount St. Helens National Volcanic Monument, 42218 NE Yale Bridge Rd., Amboy, WA 98601, 360/449-7871.

7 BOUNDARY TRAIL
27.8 mi one-way/3.0 days

across Gifford Pinchot National Forest
> **Map 5.1, page 255**

Boundary Trail is a long through-hike traversing Gifford Pinchot National Forest west

to east. The trail previously began near the Mount Margaret backcountry, but the 1980 eruption destroyed the western trailhead and made the western 6 miles an adventuresome and entirely new out-and-back hike (see previous listing). The eastern contiguous section of Boundary Trail gets in miles of meadow rambling and even some old-growth shade. Views of surrounding valleys and peaks are nonstop in the middle segment.

The best place to start is Elk Pass, an easy access on Forest Service Road 25. From here, Boundary Trail travels alternating patches of old-growth and clear-cuts for about 7 miles. The trail gets interesting as it skirts Badger and Craggy Peaks, where meadows and views reign supreme. The trail leads to the southern ends of Langille and Juniper Ridges, an exposed and beautiful 11-mile segment. The remainder of the trail (9 miles) sticks mostly to forest, ending at Council Lake.

Many so-called feeder trails offer access to Boundary Trail, making numerous segments of the route accessible for day hikes. Water is often scarce along the route, so plan well and bring your full capacity. Campsites are rarely designated; low-impact cross-country camping is necessary. Although few hikers complete the whole trip in one go, occasional crowds are likely because of the many access points. Also, be ready for noisy motorcycles on summer weekends.

User Groups: Hikers, leashed dogs, horses, mountain bikes, and motorcycles. No wheelchair access.

Permits: This trail is accessible July–mid-October. A federal Northwest Forest Pass is required to park at the trailheads.

Maps: For a map of Gifford Pinchot National Forest, contact the Outdoor Recreation Information Center at the downtown Seattle REI. For a topographic map, ask Green Trails for No. 332, Spirit Lake, No. 333, McCoy Peak, and No. 334, Blue Lake, or ask the USGS for French Butte, McCoy, Spirit Lake East, and Spirit Lake West.

Directions: From Randle, drive south 1 mile

on Highway 131 to Forest Service Road 25. Stay to the right and drive 23 miles to the well-signed trailhead.

Contact: Gifford Pinchot National Forest, Cowlitz Valley Ranger Station, 10024 U.S. 12, Randle, WA 98377, 360/497-1100.

8 META LAKE
0.5 mi/0.5 hr

northeast of Mount St. Helens in Mount St. Helens National Volcanic Monument in Gifford Pinchot National Forest

Map 5.1, page 255

Lying behind a small ridge, Meta Lake received less than a death blow from Mount St. Helens' eruption despite being squarely in the blast zone. It helped that a snowpack lingered around the still-frozen lake, providing plants and trees a modest insulation from the searing heat and gas. With such protection in place, Meta Lake survived the blast and today provides a great example of the regeneration of life after the 1980 eruption.

Meta Lake Trail makes a quick trip to the lake (just 0.25 mile one-way). Several interpretive signs line the route, filling visitors in on the ability of life to survive and thrive here. Firs and hemlocks are once again creating a forest among blown-down logs, with lots of huckleberry bushes filling in the holes. Brook trout are still found in the lake, as are salamanders and frogs. The path is paved and is one of the best in the area for wheelchair access.

User Groups: Hikers only. No dogs, horses, or mountain bikes are allowed. The trail is wheelchair accessible.

Permits: This trail is accessible June–September. A federal Northwest Forest Pass is required to park here.

Maps: For a map of Gifford Pinchot National Forest, contact the Outdoor Recreation Information Center at the downtown Seattle REI. For a topographic map, ask Green Trails for No. 332, Spirit Lake, or ask the USGS for Spirit Lake East.

Directions: From Randle, drive south 1 mile on Highway 131 to Forest Service Road 25. Stay to the right and drive 19 miles to Forest Service Road 99. Turn right and drive 11.5 miles to the signed trailhead on the right.

Contact: Gifford Pinchot National Forest, Mount St. Helens National Volcanic Monument, 42218 NE Yale Bridge Rd., Amboy, WA 98601, 360/449-7871.

9 HARMONY FALLS
2.0 mi/1.5 hr

northeast of Mount St. Helens in Mount St. Helens National Volcanic Monument in Gifford Pinchot National Forest

Map 5.1, page 255

Before the 1980 eruption of Mount St. Helens, Spirit Lake was home to houses and lodges, campgrounds, and an old, lush forest. All of that was quickly destroyed by the eruption, which left behind a surreal landscape. Harmony Trail passes right through this devastated area down to Spirit Lake, surveying the enormously changed scene.

Harmony Trail provides the only access to Spirit Lake, reaching the lakeshore where Harmony Falls drops in. The trail drops 600 feet to the lake, a considerable climb out. Bare trees lie scattered on the hillsides in neat rows, leveled by the searing gases of the eruption. Part of Spirit Lake is covered by dead trees, neatly arranged in the northern arm. On the hillsides, now covered in fine ash, small plants and shrubs work hard to revegetate the land. With a significant chunk of the mountain now lying at the bottom of the lake, the shores of Spirit Lake were raised 200 feet. This significantly enlarged the lake and cut off much of the height of Harmony Falls. Harmony Trail is a great way to experience one of the most affected areas of the blast zone.

User Groups: Hikers only, horses, and mountain bikes are allowed. No wheelchair access.

Mount Rainier stands in the distance, with Spirit Lake in the foreground.

Permits: This trail is accessible June–September. A federal Northwest Forest Pass is required to park here.

Maps: For a map of Gifford Pinchot National Forest, contact the Outdoor Recreation Information Center at the downtown Seattle REI. For a topographic map, ask Green Trails for No. 332, Spirit Lake, or ask the USGS for Spirit Lake West and Spirit Lake East.

Directions: From Randle, drive south 1 mile on Highway 131 to Forest Service Road 25. Stay to the right and drive 19 miles to Forest Service Road 99. Turn right and drive 16 miles to the signed trailhead on the right.

Contact: Gifford Pinchot National Forest, Mount St. Helens National Volcanic Monument, 42218 NE Yale Bridge Rd., Amboy, WA 98601, 360/449-7871.

10 PLAINS OF ABRAHAM
9.0 mi/5.0 hr   2   10

south of Randle in Mount St. Helens National Volcanic Monument in Gifford Pinchot National Forest

Map 5.1, page 255

Other than Loowit Trail, a round-the-mountain trek, no route gets closer to Mount St. Helens

than Abraham Trail. Even better, Plains of Abraham makes a loop, with only 2 miles of trail hiked twice. The route, shaped like a lasso, spends its entirety within the blast zone, a barren landscape leveled by the 1980 eruption. During summer, when wildflowers speckle the slopes with color, this is undoubtedly the best option for a longer day hike near Mount St. Helens.

The route begins at popular Windy Ridge Viewpoint and follows the ridge on Truman Trail. Turn left on Abraham Trail (1.7 miles) as the path rounds five narrow draws (3 miles) to Loowit Trail (4 miles), within the Plains of Abraham. The plains are a wide, barren landscape repeatedly pounded by mud and landslides. Other than the smallest of plants and mosses, life is absent. It's an eerie but impressive scene.

Turn right on Loowit Trail to climb to Windy Pass (5 miles), an appropriate name on most days. The loop returns to the car via Truman Trail (6 miles) and Windy Ridge. July and August are great months to hike Abraham Trail, when wildflowers are at their peak. Water and shade are not found at any time along the trail, so consider packing extra water and sunscreen.

User Groups: Hikers only. No dogs, horses, or mountain bikes are allowed. No wheelchair access.

Permits: This trail is accessible June–October. A federal Northwest Forest Pass is required to park here.

Maps: For a map of Gifford Pinchot National Forest, contact the Outdoor Recreation Information Center at the downtown Seattle REI. For a topographic map, ask Green Trails for No. 364S, Mount St. Helens NW, or ask the USGS for Spirit Lake East.

Directions: From Randle, drive south 1 mile on Highway 131 to Forest Service Road 25. Stay to the right and drive 19 miles to Forest Service Road 99. Turn right and drive to Windy Ridge Trailhead at road's end.

Contact: Gifford Pinchot National Forest, Mount St. Helens National Volcanic Monument, 42218 NE Yale Bridge Rd., Amboy, WA 98601, 360/449-7871.

11 LAVA CANYON

2.0 mi/1.5 hr

northeast of Cougar in Mount St. Helens National Volcanic Monument in Gifford Pinchot National Forest

Map 5.1, page 255

Spared from the blast zone of the 1980 eruption, Sheep Canyon nonetheless felt a few effects. The eruption created a raging torrent of mud and debris that gushed through the narrow gorge. The violent flow scoured the canyon bottom clean, leaving only barren bedrock for the Muddy River. That was a good thing, as it created a colorful river canyon with numerous pools and cascades. The trail through the gorge is one of the coolest places in Mount St. Helens National Volcanic Monument.

The first section of Lava Canyon Trail descends a steep series of switchbacks to several views of the canyon (0.5 mile). Platforms are in place with interpretive signs. This section is paved and accessible to wheelchairs, although it's very steep and assistance is usually needed. From here, a signed loop crosses the river via a bridge and follows the river down. This section of river has many pools and channels carved

into the bedrock. The loop crosses back over the river via a high suspension bridge (1 mile). Although Lava Canyon Trail continues to a lower trailhead (2.5 miles), the lower suspension bridge marks a good place to turn around.

User Groups: Hikers and leashed dogs. No horses or mountain bikes are allowed. Part of the trail is wheelchair accessible (for the first 0.5 mile, down to a viewpoint of the canyon, although very steep).

Permits: This trail is accessible June–November. A federal Northwest Forest Pass is required to park here.

Maps: For a map of Gifford Pinchot National Forest, contact the Outdoor Recreation Information Center at the downtown Seattle REI. For a topographic map, ask Green Trails for No. 364, Mount St. Helens, or ask the USGS for Smith Creek Butte.

Directions: From Vancouver, drive north on I-5 to Highway 503 (Woodland, exit 21). Drive east 35 miles to Forest Service Road 83. Turn left and drive 10 miles to the signed trailhead at road's end.

Contact: Gifford Pinchot National Forest, Mount St. Helens National Volcanic Monument, 42218 NE Yale Bridge Rd., Amboy, WA 98601, 360/449-7871.

12 CEDAR FLATS

1.0 mi/0.5 hr   👣1 ⛰9

north of Cougar in Gifford Pinchot National Forest

Map 5.1, page 255   **BEST (**

Quick and easy, Cedar Flats Trail ventures through Southern Washington's most impressive old-growth forest. It's easy to imagine you've been transported to the Olympic Peninsula when wandering among these giants. Douglas fir, western hemlock, and western red cedar create a forest of immense proportions. The area is preserved as part of Cedar Flats Natural Area, which was set aside in the 1940s. This area serves as important, undisturbed habitat for a variety of animals. Herds of elk winter in this area and deer are year-round inhabitants. Cedar Flats Trail makes a short and flat loop, arranged like a lasso, making this a great walk for families and hikers who prefer to avoid difficult hikes. Part of the trail nears the steep cliffs overlooking the Muddy River (inaccessible from the trail). The trail can be easily walked in a half hour, but it's well worth spending an afternoon in this peaceful setting.

User Groups: Hikers and leashed dogs. No horses or mountain bikes are allowed. No wheelchair access.

Permits: This trail is accessible year-round. A federal Northwest Forest Pass is required to park here.

Maps: For a map of Gifford Pinchot National Forest, contact the Outdoor Recreation Information Center at the downtown Seattle REI. For a topographic map, ask Green Trails for No. 364, Mount St. Helens, or ask the USGS for Cedar Flat.

Directions: From Cougar, drive east on Highway 503 (Forest Service Road 90) to Forest Service Road 25, at Pine Creek Information Station. Turn left and drive 6 miles to the trailhead on the right.

Contact: Gifford Pinchot National Forest, Mount St. Helens National Volcanic Monument, 42218 NE Yale Bridge Rd., Amboy, WA 98601, 360/449-7871.

13 SHEEP CANYON
4.4 mi/3.0 hr

north of Cougar in Mount St. Helens National Volcanic Monument of Gifford Pinchot National Forest

Map 5.1, page 255

Not all of Mount St. Helens' destruction in May 1980 was the result of searing gas and ash. Areas not directly in the line of fire were instead affected by torrents of mud, water, and debris. That's what happened along Sheep Creek, a muddy, ashen stream running

through a steep canyon. The trail provides access to Loowit Trail, the route running around the mountain, home to impressive views of the flattened volcano.

Sheep Canyon Trail quickly leaves a patch of clear-cut land to enter an old-growth forest of noble fir. The route climbs much of its length, gaining more than 1,400 feet, rendering the shady, old forest a welcome friend. The highlight of the trail is Sheep Canyon, where Sheep Creek flows between vertical rock walls. Raging mudflows scoured the bottom of the canyon, leaving debris scattered over bare bedrock. Finally, the trail climbs harshly to Loowit Trail, where hikers can add extra miles by exploring to the north or south.

User Groups: Hikers and leashed dogs. No horses or mountain bikes are allowed. No wheelchair access.

Permits: This trail is accessible June–October. A federal Northwest Forest Pass is required to park here.

Maps: For a map of Gifford Pinchot National Forest, contact the Outdoor Recreation Information Center at the downtown Seattle REI. For a topographic map, ask the USGS for Mount St. Helens and Goat Mountain.

Directions: From Vancouver, drive north on I-5 to Highway 503 (Woodland, exit 21). Drive east 35 miles to Forest Service Road 83. Turn left and drive 3.5 miles to Forest Service Road 81. Turn left and drive to Forest Service Road 8123. Turn right and drive to the signed trailhead at road's end.

Contact: Gifford Pinchot National Forest, Mount St. Helens National Volcanic Monument, 42218 NE Yale Bridge Rd., Amboy, WA 98601, 360/449-7871.

14 APE CAVE
2.5 mi/3.0 hr

north of Cougar in Mount St. Helens National
Volcanic Monument in Gifford Pinchot
National Forest

Map 5.1, page 255   **BEST (**

The name Ape Cave conjures images of Sasquatch huddled in a narrow underground passage, hiding from people and their cameras. Sorry to disappoint. The caves were first explored by members of a local outdoors club, "The Apes," hence the name. Ape Cave is a long, large cave (known as a lava tube) naturally carved into the basalt by lava and water through thousands of years. Explored by thousands of visitors each year (including busloads of schoolchildren), these deep, pitch-black tunnels make for an eerie and memorable experience.

From the main entrance, the cave heads in two directions. The Lower Passage is easier and shorter. It delves about 0.7 mile past a number of formations, including a Lava Ball and mudflow floor. The Upper Passage is 1.3 miles long underground with a 1.3-mile trail aboveground that returns to the trailhead. Upper Passage is more challenging, with segments that climb over rock piles and a small lava ledge. Near the upper exit, a large hole in the ceiling of the cave creates a natural skylight.

Be prepared for a chilly hike. Year-round temperature is a steady 42°F. Imagine that, 85 outside but 42 inside! Two sources of light are recommended, and headlamps don't count. The deep darkness of the caves requires very strong flashlights or, preferably, large gas lanterns. Parts of the upper passage are rocky, so sturdy shoes and pants are also recommended.

User Groups: Hikers only. No dogs, horses, or mountain bikes are allowed. Wheelchair accessible.

Permits: This trail is accessible year-round. A federal Northwest Forest Pass is required to park here.

Maps: For a map of Gifford Pinchot National Forest, contact the Outdoor Recreation Information Center at the downtown Seattle REI. For a topographic map, ask Green Trails for No. 364, Mount St. Helens, or ask the USGS for Mount Mitchell.

Directions: From Vancouver, drive north on I-5 to Highway 503 (Woodland, exit 21). Drive east 35 miles to Forest Service Road 83. Turn left and drive 2 miles to Forest Service Road 8303. Turn left and drive 1.5 miles to the signed trailhead on the right.

Contact: Gifford Pinchot National Forest, Mount St. Helens National Volcanic Monument, 42218 NE Yale Bridge Rd., Amboy, WA 98601, 360/449-7871.

15 TRAIL OF TWO FORESTS
0.3 mi/0.5 hr

northeast of Cougar in Mount St. Helens
National Volcanic Monument in Gifford
Pinchot National Forest

Map 5.1, page 255   **BEST (**

Trail of Two Forests is a quick nature loop into one of the most unlikely natural phenomena in the Northwest. Nearly two millennia ago, Mount St. Helens sent a wave of molten lava down her south flank. This wave of lava consumed everything in its path before eventually cooling and stopping. Trail of Two Forests is perfectly situated near the bottom of the flow, where the lava still moved but was not hot enough to immediately destroy trees. Here, lava cooled around the trees, which eventually decomposed and left small tunnels, caves, and pits as a testament to the old forest. The second of the two forests is the one that stands today. Interpretive signs do a great job of explaining the story in depth. Conveniently, boardwalk lines the entire route, making Trail of Two Forests accessible to wheelchairs. The boardwalk also protects the fragile forest ground, so please stay on the trail. The one chance visitors have to get off-trail is a chance to crawl through a tunnel, or lava tube, nearly 30 feet long. It's a trip!

User Groups: Hikers and leashed dogs. No horses or mountain bikes are allowed. Wheelchair accessible.

Permits: This trail is accessible March–November. A federal Northwest Forest Pass is required to park here.

Maps: For a map of Gifford Pinchot National Forest, contact the Outdoor Recreation Information Center at the downtown Seattle REI. For a topographic map, ask Green Trails for No. 364, Mount St. Helens, or ask the USGS for Mount Mitchell.

Directions: From Vancouver, drive north on I-5 to Highway 503 (Woodland, exit 21). Drive east 35 miles to Forest Service Road 83. Turn left and drive 2 miles to Forest Service Road 8303. Turn left and drive 0.1 mile to the signed trailhead on the left.

Contact: Gifford Pinchot National Forest, Mount St. Helens National Volcanic Monument, 42218 NE Yale Bridge Rd., Amboy, WA 98601, 360/449-7871.

16 JUNE LAKE
2.8 mi/2.0 hr

northeast of Cougar in Mount St. Helens National Volcanic Monument in Gifford Pinchot National Forest

Map 5.1, page 255

June Lake achieves recognition by being the only subalpine lake on the slopes of Mount St. Helens. As the volcano forms a nice, neat cone, few basins are created to host a beautiful lake. Well, that's what Mount St. Helens has done here, nestling a great lake below a cliff of basalt, complete with waterfall. Subalpine forest and meadow ring the lake, which has a sandy beach perfect for summer afternoon lounging.

June Lake Trail gains just 500 feet in 1.4 miles and is ideal for families. It courses its way through young forest with views of a gorge before emerging upon a large field of basalt boulders (1 mile). The trail sticks to

the forest and soon finds June Lake. For a view of Mount St. Helens, hike past the lake a few hundred yards on Loowit Trail. Several campsites are scattered around the lake, and campers are expected to follow strict Leave-No-Trace principles.

User Groups: Hikers, leashed dogs, and mountain bikes are allowed. No horses are allowed. No wheelchair access.

Permits: This trail is accessible May–November. A federal Northwest Forest Pass is required to park here.

Maps: For a map of Gifford Pinchot National Forest, contact the Outdoor Recreation Information Center at the downtown Seattle REI. For a topographic map, ask Green Trails for No. 364S, Mount St. Helens NW, or ask the USGS for Mount St. Helens.

Directions: From Vancouver, drive north on I-5 to Highway 503 (Woodland, exit 21). Drive east 35 miles to Forest Service Road 83. Turn left and drive 6 miles to the signed trailhead on the left.

Contact: Gifford Pinchot National Forest, Mount St. Helens National Volcanic Monument, 42218 NE Yale Bridge Rd., Amboy, WA 98601, 360/449-7871.

17 LOOWIT TRAIL
30.5 mi/3-4 days

around the mountain in Mount St. Helens National Volcanic Monument in Gifford Pinchot National Forest

Map 5.1, page 255

Loowit Trail is the grand loop encircling Mount St. Helens. It was an interesting trip before 1980, and the eruption of the volcano turned this trek into an unforgettable outing. Loowit experiences everything imaginable— old-growth forest, alpine meadows, and barren, ravaged landscapes. Compared to Wonderland Trail, elevation changes along the route are modest. Still, many sections of the trail are difficult and rocky.

Loowit Trail has no definite trailhead.

Instead, several feeder trails lead to the 27.7-mile loop. Among these trails are June Lake in the south (1.7 miles one-way), Truman Trail at Windy Ridge (3 miles), and Sheep Canyon on the west side (2.2 miles). Diligent planning is a must before setting out on Loowit Trail. Water sources and campsites are limited throughout the route and often change year to year. The Forest Service suggests that you call ahead to get the current scoop. Finally, be ready for ash, lots and lots of ash. The fine, gray particles will invade everything you own. Bring a coffee filter to tie around your water filter and protect it. Also, take special care with cameras, binoculars, or eyeglasses, all easily damaged by ash.

Loowit Trail is often hiked counterclockwise. From June Lake, the trail climbs beneath the rocky toe of the Worm Flows to Shoestring Glacier, from the barren Plains of Abraham to Loowit Falls and impressive views of the crater. Loowit Trail traverses the blast zone, a real lesson in the magnitude of the destructive blast, before crossing the mud-ravaged Toutle River. Meadow and old-growth forest line the route as it returns to June Lake.

User Groups: Hikers and mountain bikes (not in the blast zone) only. No dogs or horses are allowed. No wheelchair access.

Permits: This trail is accessible June–October. A federal Northwest Forest Pass is required to park here.

Maps: For a map of Gifford Pinchot National Forest, contact the Outdoor Recreation Information Center at the downtown Seattle REI. For a topographic map, ask Green Trails for No. 364S, Mount St. Helens NW, or ask the USGS for Mount St. Helens, Smith Creek Butte, and Goat Mountain.

Directions: From Vancouver, drive north on I-5 to Highway 503 (Woodland, exit 21). Drive east 35 miles to Forest Service Road 83. Turn left and drive 6 miles to the signed trailhead on the left for June Lake (the shortest access on the south side).

Contact: Gifford Pinchot National Forest, Mount St. Helens National Volcanic Monument, 42218 NE Yale Bridge Rd., Amboy, WA 98601, 360/449-7871.

18 GREEN LAKE
9.6 mi/5.0 hr

in northwest Mount Rainier National Park

Map 5.2, page 256

You don't need amnesia to forget about Mount Rainier when hiking the trail to Green Lake. Grabbing your attention from the start are granddaddy Douglas firs and western hemlocks as the hike gets better each step of the way. This hike has been considerably lengthened (by 6 miles) due to the closure of Carbon River Road. The extra 3 miles from the park entrance to the trailhead are easy hiking. The Park Service also allows mountain bikes along the road, making this an outstanding bike-and-hike option on the weekend.

From the old trailhead, the hike wanders beneath giant trees towering over the trail that are estimated to be more than 800 years of age. The trail then climbs alongside Ranger Creek, within earshot but mostly out of sight. A must-see stop is a small side trail to Ranger Falls (4 miles). During the spring snowmelt, this large series of cascades creates a thunderous roar heard throughout the forest. The trail switchbacks 0.5 mile before leveling and crossing the creek. Green Lake sits among pristine forest and a little meadow. Anglers can try their luck here for trout. South of the lake and peeking through a large valley stands Tolmie Peak. Green Lake is a great day hike during the summer but also makes a good snowshoe trek during the winter. Old-growth forest, big waterfalls, and a serene mountain lake—now what was the name of that mountain everyone keeps talking about?

User Groups: Hikers only. No dogs or horses are allowed. Mountain bikes are permitted on the Carbon River Road, the first 3 miles of the hike. No wheelchair access.

Permits: This area is usually accessible April–November. A National Parks Pass is required to enter the park.

Maps: For a map of Mount Rainier National Park, contact the Outdoor Recreation Information Center at the downtown Seattle REI. For a topographic map, ask Green Trails for No. 269, Mount Rainier West, or ask the USGS for Mowich Lake.

Directions: From Tacoma, drive east on Highway 410 to Buckley. Turn south on Highway 165 and drive 14 miles to Carbon River Road. Turn left and drive 8 miles to Carbon River Entrance Station, where Carbon River Road is closed to motor vehicles.

Contact: Mount Rainier National Park, Longmire Wilderness Information Center, Tahoma Woods, Star Route, Ashford, WA 98304, 360/569-4453.

19 WINDY GAP
23.0-27.0 mi/2-3 days

in northern Mount Rainier National Park

Map 5.2, page 256

Mount Rainier grabs the most attention (it stands more than 14,000 feet tall, after all). But the park holds miles of amazing terrain, tucked away from the mountain's view. Windy Gap is a perfect example. The enjoyable trail climbs into a high-country playground of meadows and rocky peaks, with plenty to see and do. Hikes to Lake James and the Natural Bridge (a large rock arch) start here. Unfortunately, flooding closed a section of the access road, adding a total of 10 extra road miles, which is easy hiking and is also open to mountain bikes. Fortunately, Windy Gap features two great backcountry camps for overnight visits.

First, hike or bike 5 miles along the closed Carbon River Road to Ipsut Creek Campground. Here, the trail begins and joins Wonderland Trail (5.5 miles), eventually leaving to cross the Carbon River (7.4 miles). Turn left and do the switchback shuffle up

Northern Loop Trail to Windy Gap. The sighting of colorful Yellowstone Cliffs (10.1 miles) signals the arrival of parkland meadows, reflective tarns, and craggy horizons. Boulder-strewn Windy Gap (11.4 miles), a good place to turn around, is truly a blustery experience, and mountain goats roam the surrounding ridges.

Beyond Windy Gap, Northern Loop Trail drops 1.5 miles to lightly visited Lake James, clad in subalpine meadows. Beyond Windy Gap 0.25 mile, a signed trail leads to Natural Bridge. Rising out of the forest, the large rock formation seems lost from the sea. After crossing the Carbon, the trail is dry; bring plenty of water. Beautiful backcountry camps are situated at Yellowstone Cliffs and Lake James and require camping permits.

User Groups: Hikers only. No dogs, horses, or mountain bikes are allowed. No wheelchair access.

Permits: This area is usually accessible mid-July–September. A National Parks Pass is required to enter the park. Overnight stays within the national park require backcountry camping permits, which are available at Carbon River Ranger Station.

Maps: For a map of Mount Rainier National Park, contact the Outdoor Recreation Information Center at the downtown Seattle REI. For a topographic map, ask Green Trails for No. 269, Mount Rainier West, and No. 270, Mount Rainier East, or ask the USGS for Mowich Lake and Sunrise.

Directions: From Tacoma, drive east on Highway 410 to Buckley. Turn south on Highway 165 and drive 14 miles to Carbon River Road. Turn left and drive 8 miles to Carbon River Entrance Station, where Carbon River Road is closed to motor vehicles.

Contact: Mount Rainier National Park, Longmire Wilderness Information Center, Tahoma Woods, Star Route, Ashford, WA 98304, 360/569-4453.

20 CARBON GLACIER/ MYSTIC LAKE

25.5 mi/2 days   4 △10

north of The Mountain in Mount Rainier
National Park

Map 5.2, page 256

Situated on the famed Wonderland Trail, there isn't a lake closer to Mount Rainier than Mystic Lake. This hike visits a 7-mile stretch of Washington's most esteemed trail is incredibly diverse. It travels through old-growth forest on the Carbon River, past Rainier's lowest and longest glacier, and upward to rocky alpine meadows and a majestic lake. This is one of the park's premier hikes.

The first 5 miles are spent hiking or biking along the now-closed Carbon River Road to Ipsut Campground, the former trailhead. From here, the length of the route follows the Wonderland Trail. The trail starts mildly, cruising through ancient forests. After crossing Carbon River on an impressive suspension bridge (8 miles), however, the trail climbs unrelentingly to Mystic Lake. Somehow, the trail finds a path between Carbon Glacier and the valley wall. Those cracking noises you hear are the glacier giving way to the hot summer sun; walking on the glacier is ill advised without an ice ax and proper training.

Wonderland Trail parts ways with the glacier as it enters Moraine Park (10.5 miles), featuring acres of wildflower meadows. A welcome sight on hot days, Mystic Lake lies just below Mineral Mountain. Although it stands 800 feet above the lake, Mineral Mountain can do little to block Mount Rainier and its ragged Willis Wall. Backcountry camps are situated at Dick Creek (9 miles) and Mystic Lake (12.7 miles); they require permits and are frequented by Wonderland trekkers.

User Groups: Hikers only. No dogs, horses, or mountain bikes are allowed. No wheelchair access.

Permits: This area is usually accessible mid-July–September. A National Parks Pass is required to enter the park. Overnight stays within the national park require backcountry camping permits, which are available at Carbon River Ranger Station.

Maps: For a map of Mount Rainier National Park, contact the Outdoor Recreation Information Center at the downtown Seattle REI. For a topographic map, ask Green Trails for No. 269, Mount Rainier West, or ask the USGS for Mowich Lake.

Directions: From Tacoma, drive east on Highway 410 to Buckley. Turn south on Highway 165 and drive 14 miles to Carbon River Road. Turn left and drive 8 miles to Carbon River Entrance Station, where Carbon River Road is closed to motor vehicles.

Contact: Mount Rainier National Park, Longmire Wilderness Information Center, Tahoma Woods, Star Route, Ashford, WA 98304, 360/569-4453.

21 TOLMIE PEAK LOOKOUT

6.5 mi/3.5 hr   [🥾]2 △10

northwest of Tahoma in Mount Rainier
National Park

Map 5.2, page 256

The best job in the United States is a summer spent staffing the Tolmie Peak Lookout. The job description includes: a 3-mile commute through pristine subalpine forest, picturesque Eunice Lake surrounded in parkland meadows, and panoramic views from the office, encompassing The Mountain and miles of national forest. Ready to sign up?

Tolmie Peak Trail begins at Mowich Lake, a spectacular setting itself. The trail leaves the large, forested lake and rises gently to Ipsut Pass (1.5 miles), a junction with Carbon River Trail. Stay to the left and continue climbing to Eunice Lake (2.3 miles), where meadows reach to the lake's edges. The trail then climbs steeply 1 more mile to Tolmie Lookout (elevation 5,939 feet) atop the windswept peak. Mount Rainier is the obvious attraction, but Mount St. Helens and the North Cascades make appearances as well. Talk about your prime picnic spots. If the final steep climb to the lookout sounds unappealing, stopping short at Eunice Lake is a good hike as well. In late July, wildflowers fill the meadows bordering Eunice, and views of Mount Rainier are still to be had.

User Groups: Hikers only. No dogs, horses, or mountain bikes are allowed. No wheelchair access.

Permits: This area is accessible June–October. A National Parks Pass is required to enter the park.

Maps: For a map of Mount Rainier National Park, contact the Outdoor Recreation Information Center at the downtown Seattle REI. For a topographic map, ask Green Trails for No. 269, Mount Rainier West, or ask the USGS for Mowich Lake and Golden Lakes.

Directions: From Tacoma, drive east on Highway 410 to Buckley. Turn south on Highway 165 and drive 14 miles to Carbon River Road junction. Stay to the right on Mowich Lake Road and drive 17 miles to Mowich Lake Campground at road's end. The trailhead is well marked.

Contact: Mount Rainier National Park, Longmire Wilderness Information Center, Tahoma Woods, Star Route, Ashford, WA 98304, 360/569-4453.

22 SPRAY PARK
8.8 mi/4.5 hr   2   10

northwest of The Mountain in Mount Rainier National Park

Map 5.2, page 256

Spray Park is without a doubt one of the most beautiful places on Mount Rainier. Meadows measured by the square mile cover the upper reaches of this trail, dominated by the imposing stature of The Mountain. Wildflowers erupt and blanket the high country in late July, while black bears in search of huckleberries roam in late August. The trail is one of the greats in the national park and receives heavy use.

Spray Park Trail leaves from Mowich Lake,

© SCOTT LEONARD

Spray Falls cascades near the trail to Spray Park

an inviting dip after a hot summer day on the trail. The trail meanders through the forest to Eagle Cliff (1.5 miles), where the trail follows the precipitous slope. A side trail wanders over to Spray Falls (1.9 miles) before making a steep ascent on switchbacks. The reward for the effort is a breakout from forest into open meadow. Spray Park Trail wanders through this open country, past tarns and rock fields to a saddle (elevation 6,400 feet) with views of even more meadows. The saddle is a good turnaround point, as the trail drops beyond it to Carbon River. Be sure to bring ample water, a rarity beyond Spray Falls. And remember, the meadows here are very fragile; please stay on established trails.

User Groups: Hikers only. No dogs, horses, or mountain bikes are allowed. No wheelchair access.

Permits: This area is usually accessible July–September. A National Parks Pass is required to enter the park. Overnight stays within the national park require backcountry camping permits, which are available at Longmire Wilderness Information Center.

Maps: For a map of Mount Rainier National Park, contact the Outdoor Recreation Information Center at the downtown Seattle REI. For a topographic map, ask Green Trails for No. 269, Mount Rainier West, or ask the USGS for Mowich Lake.

Directions: From Tacoma, drive east on Highway 410 to Buckley. Turn south on Highway 165 and drive 14 miles to Carbon River Road junction. Stay to the right on Mowich Lake Road and drive 17 miles to Mowich Lake Campground at road's end. The trailhead is well marked.

Contact: Mount Rainier National Park, Longmire Wilderness Information Center, Tahoma Woods, Star Route, Ashford, WA 98304, 360/569-4453.

23 SUNRISE NATURE TRAILS
1.5-3.2 mi/0.5-1.5 hr

near Sunrise in Mount Rainier National Park

Map 5.2, page 256

The beauty of Sunrise's high placement means that hikers don't have to venture far for an incredible hike. Although the views start at the parking lot, pavement is usually something we're trying to avoid. Several great options are well suited to hikers of all abilities. Options vary from trips to Shadow Lake or Frozen Lake to a nature trail and a walk through a silver forest. These are perfect trails for families with little ones or for folks conducting an auto tour around the park.

Although the network of trails surrounding Sunrise seems like a jumbled cobweb, every junction is well signed and easy to navigate. Trails to the two lakes are easy walks. Shadow Lake is a level 3-mile round-trip, with meadows and views of Rainier all the way. Frozen Lake gains a little more elevation and peers out over the colorful meadows of Berkeley Park (3.2 miles round-trip).

The west end of Sourdough Ridge Trail features a self-guided nature trail, a 1.5-mile loop with some elevation gain. Lupine and bistort are on full display in July. On the south side of the visitors center is Silver Forest Trail (2.4 miles), a unique path through a forest of bare snags, long ago killed but not toppled by fire.

User Groups: Hikers only. No dogs, horses, or mountain bikes are allowed. No wheelchair access.

Permits: This area is usually accessible July–September. A National Parks Pass is required to enter the park.

Maps: For a map of Mount Rainier National Park, contact the Outdoor Recreation Information Center at the downtown Seattle REI. For a topographic map, ask Green Trails for No. 270, Mount Rainier East, or ask the USGS for Sunrise.

DBirections: From Puyallup, drive east 52 miles on Highway 410 to Sunrise Road in Mount Rainier National Park. Turn right and drive 15 miles to the trailhead at Sunrise Visitor Center.

Contact: Mount Rainier National Park, White River Wilderness Information Center, 70004 Hwy. 410 E., Enumclaw, WA 98022, 360/569-221 x6030.

24 BERKELEY AND GRAND PARKS
7.6-15.2 mi/4.0-8.0 hr

out of Sunrise in Mount Rainier National Park

Map 5.2, page 256

A grand destination indeed—wide, flat Grand Park stretches for more than a mile with incredible views of Mount Rainier. On the way, Berkeley Park dazzles with its own wildflower displays and beautiful stream. In a land of many high-country meadows, this is a dandy of a choice.

The route leaves the high country of Sunrise and gently wanders through meadows to Frozen Lake (1.5 miles), tucked beneath Mount Fremont and Burroughs Mountain. Follow the Wonderland Trail for 1 mile to Northern Loop Trail and drop into Berkeley Park (2.5 miles), where streams crisscross the lush meadows. This is a good turnaround spot for hikers uninterested in making the longer trip to Grand Park.

Northern Loop Trail leaves Berkeley Park and travels through open subalpine forest to Grand Park (7.6 miles). Grand Park and its meadows stretch more than a mile to the north. Deer and elk are frequent visitors to the meadows, where they find an abundance of summer grazing. Although Grand Park is preferably accomplished in a day, hikers hoping to spend the night can pitch camp at Berkeley Camp (3.8 miles) or hike 3.3 miles beyond Grand Park to Lake Eleanor (11.4 miles one-way). Access to Lake Eleanor via an unofficial trail from national forest land is frowned upon by the Park Service; besides, it misses out on the best sections of the route.

User Groups: Hikers only. No dogs, horses, or mountain bikes are allowed. No wheelchair access.

Permits: This area is usually accessible mid-July–September. A National Parks Pass is required to enter the park.

Maps: For a map of Mount Rainier National Park, contact the Outdoor Recreation Information Center at the downtown Seattle REI. For a topographic map, ask Green Trails for No. 270, Mount Rainier East, or ask the USGS for Sunrise.

Directions: From Puyallup, drive east 52 miles on Highway 410 to Sunrise Road in Mount Rainier National Park. Turn right and drive 15 miles to the trailhead at Sunrise Visitor Center.

Contact: Mount Rainier National Park, White River Wilderness Information Center, 70004 Hwy. 410 E., Enumclaw, WA 98022, 360/569-2211 x6030.

25 MOUNT FREMONT LOOKOUT

6.0 mi/3.0 hr   🏃2 ⛰9

out of Sunrise in Mount Rainier National Park

Map 5.2, page 256   BEST (

Where there's a lookout, there are views. And there's no lookout closer to Mount Rainier than the one atop Mount Fremont. Never mind that the lookout doesn't sit on Fremont's summit. There are still plenty of views along this great trail. Hiking in Rainier high country is all about meadows, and this trail is no different. It travels exclusively through open meadows, and as long as the weather is clear (never a guarantee around The Mountain), you can expect knock-your-boots-off views. Best of all, Mount Fremont is an easy trail to navigate for hikers, gaining just 1,200 feet in about 3 miles.

Mount Fremont Trail leaves the popular Sunrise Visitor Center and quickly climbs to Sourdough Ridge. Mount Rainier is almost too close, crowding much of the southern horizon. Pass picturesque Frozen Lake at 1.5 miles as the trail encounters a large but well-signed junction. Mount Fremont Trail heads north along the rocky ridge, tops out in elevation, and drops to the lookout, built in the 1930s. Although it's hard to take your eyes off Tahoma and its glaciers, the Cascades and Olympics will call from distant horizons. The vast meadows of Grand Park below the lookout are a painter's palette of color in July. Be sure to carry enough water for the trip; there's none to be found along the way.

User Groups: Hikers only. No dogs, horses, or mountain bikes are allowed. No wheelchair access.

Permits: This trail is accessible mid-July–September. A National Parks Pass is required to enter the park.

Maps: For a map of Mount Rainier National Park, contact the Outdoor Recreation Information Center at the downtown Seattle REI. For a topographic map, ask Green Trails for No. 270, Mount Rainier East, or ask the USGS for Sunrise.

Directions: From Puyallup, drive east 52 miles on Highway 410 to Sunrise Road in Mount Rainier National Park. Turn right and drive 15 miles to the trailhead at Sunrise Visitor Center.

Contact: Mount Rainier National Park, White River Wilderness Information Center, 70004

Hwy. 410 E., Enumclaw, WA 98022, 360/569-2211 x6030.

26 SOURDOUGH RIDGE/ DEGE PEAK
2.5 mi/1.5 hr   👫2 ⛰9

near Sunrise in Mount Rainier National Park

Map 5.2, page 256

Sourdough Ridge Trail covers more than 4 miles of immaculate subalpine meadows immersed in grand views of Mount Rainier and much more. The trail follows Sourdough Ridge from Sunrise Visitor Center out to Dege Peak and Sunrise Point on the east end. A visit here in July will yield acre upon acre of blooming wildflowers, with swaths of paintbrush, lupine, and daisies on the mountainside. This is a popular and heavily used trail near the Sunrise Visitor Center, and rightfully so. There may be no easier or quicker way to get a view of Tahoma.

Sourdough Ridge Trail quickly climbs away from Sunrise Visitor Center into meadows. Every step leads to a better view. Of course The Mountain is impressively big, but the Cowlitz Chimneys and Sarvent Glaciers are seen best from this route. Those who survive the ascent of the first mile have seen the worst. The trail follows the ridge beneath Antler Peak and Dege Peak, the trail's highlight (a side trail leads to its summit). Look north over meadowy ridges to the Palisades and all the way up to Glacier Peak. This is a great hike for families visiting Sunrise; the trail gains less than 600 feet.

User Groups: Hikers only. No dogs, horses, or mountain bikes are allowed. No wheelchair access.

Permits: This area is usually accessible mid-June–September. A National Parks Pass is required to enter the park.

Maps: For a map of Mount Rainier National Park, contact the Outdoor Recreation Information Center at the downtown Seattle REI. For a topographic map, ask Green Trails

for No. 270, Mount Rainier East, or ask the USGS for Sunrise.

Directions: From Puyallup, drive east 52 miles on Highway 410 to Sunrise Road in Mount Rainier National Park. Turn right and drive 15 miles to the trailhead at Sunrise Visitor Center.

Contact: Mount Rainier National Park, White River Wilderness Information Center, 70004 Hwy. 410 E., Enumclaw, WA 98022, 360/569-2211 x6030.

27 BURROUGHS MOUNTAIN LOOP
5.5 mi/3.0 hr   👫3 ⛰10

near Sunrise in Mount Rainier National Park

Map 5.2, page 256

One of Mount Rainier's best day hikes, Burroughs Mountain is also one of its most challenging. Many hikers set out on this hike only to be turned back by snowfields that linger well into August. It's best to check in with the ranger at Sunrise and get a trail report. Snow or not, there's definitely lots to see along the way. You'll find meadows of flowers and marmots before reaching the tundralike expanses atop Burroughs Mountain. Add to it a lake for a lunch break and views of glaciers, and Burroughs Loop seems to have it all.

Burroughs Mountain Trail makes a 5-mile loop up to the high, rocky plateau of Burroughs Mountain. A clockwise direction is best, especially if the north side is still snowy. From the visitors center, the trail crosses over crystal streams and colorful meadows to Shadow Lake and an overlook of Emmons Glacier and the White River (1.4 miles). Hikers start dropping off as the trail climbs 900 feet to First Burroughs Mountain (2.8 miles). Guaranteed: Mount Rainier has never looked so big in your life.

Burroughs Mountain Trail wanders the wide, flat plateau and drops to Frozen Lake (3.6 miles). Snowfields like to linger along this northern half of the loop. These steep slopes can be crossed when snowy, but an ice ax is highly, highly recommended. The well-signed trail heads back to the visitors center.

User Groups: Hikers only. No dogs, horses, or mountain bikes are allowed. No wheelchair access.

Permits: This area is usually accessible July–September. A National Parks Pass is required to enter the park.

Maps: For a map of Mount Rainier National Park, contact the Outdoor Recreation Information Center at the downtown Seattle REI. For a topographic map, ask Green Trails for No. 270, Mount Rainier East, or ask the USGS for Sunrise.

Directions: From Puyallup, drive east 52 miles on Highway 410 to Sunrise Road in Mount Rainier National Park. Turn right and drive 15 miles to the trailhead at Sunrise Visitor Center.

Contact: Mount Rainier National Park, White River Wilderness Information Center, 70004 Hwy. 410 E., Enumclaw, WA 98022, 360/569-2211 x6030.

28 PALISADES LAKES
6.6 mi/3.5 hr-2 days

near Sunrise in Mount Rainier National Park

Map 5.2, page 256

There is no easier lake hike in Mount Rainier National Park than Palisades Lakes Trail. It has no big views of Tahoma; those are blocked by the rugged Sourdough Mountains. But Palisades Lakes Trail offers seven subalpine lakes and many smaller tarns, each among acres of meadows and rocky ridges. The trail is up and down but never significantly, making this a perfect hike for younger hikers. The short length of the trail means it's easily hiked in an afternoon, but a pair of backcountry camps are enticing enough to warrant an overnight visit.

Palisades Lakes Trail leaves Sunrise Road and quickly climbs to Sunrise Lake (0.4 mile), where a short side trail leads to the small,

forested lake. Palisades Trail continues past Clover Lake (1.4 miles) and Hidden Lake (2.5 miles), each surrounded by subalpine groves and meadows. Another mile of trail through acres of meadows, brimming with wildflowers in early August, arrives at Upper Palisades Lake. The lake gets its name from the rocky ridge, known as the Palisades, framing the basin. Marmots and picas are sure to be heard whistling from the talus slopes, and mountain goats are residents of the area too. For an overnight stay, you must make camp at either Dicks Lake or Upper Palisades.

User Groups: Hikers only. No dogs, horses, or mountain bikes are allowed. No wheelchair access.

Permits: This area is usually accessible mid-June–September. A National Parks Pass is required to enter the park. Overnight stays within the national park require backcountry camping permits, which are available at Sunrise Visitor Center.

Maps: For a map of Mount Rainier National Park, contact the Outdoor Recreation Information Center at the downtown Seattle REI. For a topographic map, ask Green Trails for No. 270, Mount Rainier East, or ask the USGS for White River Park.

Directions: From Puyallup, drive east 52 miles on Highway 410 to Sunrise Road in Mount Rainier National Park. Turn right and drive 13 miles to Sunrise Point and the trailhead.

Contact: Mount Rainier National Park, White River Wilderness Information Center, 70004 Hwy. 410 E., Enumclaw, WA 98022, 360/569-2211 x6030.

29 CRYSTAL MOUNTAIN
9.0 mi/4.5 hr

near Crystal Mountain Ski Resort in Mount Baker-Snoqualmie National Forest

Map 5.2, page 256

Better known for ski runs, Crystal Mountain features a good hiking trail. Getting there isn't quite as easy as using a ski lift, however, unless you actually ride the resort's chair lift, which is possible. Crystal Mountain Trail spends a fair amount of time in unimpressive woods before breaking out into miles of more-than-wonderful ridge hiking. This is a great place to view Mount Rainier and munch on huckleberries.

Crystal Mountain Trail begins with little flair, enduring clear-cuts and second-growth forest for 3 miles as it ascends 1,600 feet. That's the requirement to achieve Crystal Ridge and any notable rewards. At the ridge, Mount Rainier appears above the White River Valley. The trail climbs another 3 miles along the ridge through wide, rounded meadows mixed with steep, rocky slopes. Wildflowers are in full gear during early June while huckleberries make the trip twice as sweet in early August. Any place along the ridge makes for a good turnaround spot. Water is nonexistent, so carry an extra supply.

Crystal Mountain Trail can be completed several other ways, but they aren't as enjoyable. The trail forms a loop back to the ski resort, passing several small mountain lakes (a total of 13.8 miles, 2.5 on the road). An all-downhill version can be had by riding a ski lift up to the ridge and hiking back down.

User Groups: Hikers, leashed dogs, horses, and mountain bikes. No wheelchair access.

Permits: This trail is accessible June–September. A federal Northwest Forest Pass is required to park here.

Maps: For a map of Mount Baker–Snoqualmie National Forest, contact the Outdoor Recreation Information Center at the downtown Seattle REI. For topographic maps, ask Green Trails for No. 270, Mount Rainier East, and No. 271, Bumping Lake, or ask the USGS for Bumping Lake and White River.

Directions: From Puyallup, drive east 47 miles on State Highway 410 to Crystal Mountain Road (Forest Service Road 7190). Turn left (east) and drive 4.4 miles to Forest Service Road 7190-510. Turn right and drive 0.4 mile to Sand Flats camping area and the trailhead.

Contact: Mount Baker–Snoqualmie National Forest, Enumclaw Ranger Station, 450 Roosevelt Ave. E., Enumclaw, WA 98022, 360/825-6585.

⊞ NORSE PEAK

11.2-13.8 mi/6.0-7.5 hr

near Crystal Mountain Ski Resort in Mount Baker-Snoqualmie National Forest

Map 5.2, page 256

Ignored by the masses at Mount Rainier, Norse Peak and Cascade Crest are equally deserving of attention. Although steep, Norse Peak Trail travels miles of meadows to a former lookout site west of Rainier. Conveniently, the trail offers a detour of even more meadowy hiking on the way. When in this region, it's often hard to justify not visiting the national park. Not here. Norse Peak is worth it.

Norse Peak Trail spends all of its time climbing, gaining 2,900 feet to the lookout. It's well laid out and never too steep, but it's certainly tiring under a hot summer sun. Most of the trail is exposed in high-country meadows, so bringing plenty of water and sunscreen are good ideas. Norse Peak Trail spends less than 2 miles in the forest before emerging into the open. As the trail climbs, Tahoma rises from behind Crystal Mountain. At 3.6 miles lies Goat Lake junction and at 4.9 miles is Norse Peak Lookout junction; stay to the right both times for the lookout, 6,856 feet of views. Tahoma is its usual magnificent self, but numerous other peaks are noteworthy too.

You can make a loop to visit beautiful Big Crow Basin. Descend from the lookout to the upper junction. Turn right and pass through the large basin of meadows to the Pacific Crest Trail (PCT) and back again via Goat Lake Trail. Even with a trip to the lookout, the loop is less than 14 miles.

User Groups: Hikers, leashed dogs, horses, and mountain bikes (no mountain bikes in Big Crow Basin). No wheelchair access.

Permits: This trail is accessible mid-June–September. A federal Northwest Forest Pass is required to park here.

Maps: For a map of Mount Baker–Snoqualmie National Forest, contact the Outdoor Recreation Information Center at the downtown Seattle REI. For a topographic map, ask Green Trails for No. 271, Bumping Lake, or ask the USGS for Norse Peak.

Directions: From Puyallup, drive east 47 miles on State Highway 410 to Crystal Mountain Road (Forest Service Road 7190). Turn left (east) and drive 4 miles to Forest Service Road 7190-410. Parking is on the right side of Crystal Mountain Road (Forest Service Road 7190); the signed trailhead is several hundred yards up Forest Service Road 7190-410.

Contact: Mount Baker–Snoqualmie National Forest, Enumclaw Ranger Station, 450 Roosevelt Ave. E., Enumclaw, WA 98022, 360/825-6585.

31 CRYSTAL LAKES
6.0 mi/3.5 hr 🥾3 ⛰9

near Sunrise in Mount Rainier National Park
Map 5.2, page 256

Crystal Lakes Trail presents hikers a choice between two inspiring destinations. One route heads to Crystal Lakes, a pair of sublime subalpine lakes cloaked in wildflower meadows. As the lakes are in a large basin beneath Sourdough Gap and Crystal Peak, the distant views are limited (but hardly missed). The second option bypasses the two lakes and climbs to Crystal Peak Lookout. Naturally, the views of The Mountain are great. Either way, a great trip is assured.

Crystal Lakes Trail leaves Highway 410 and hastily climbs the valley wall within the forest. At 1.3 miles lies the decisive junction. Left for the lakes, right for the lookout. Crystal Lakes Trail keeps climbing, soon entering the open subalpine and Lower Crystal Lake (2.3 miles). Upper Crystal Lake is just a short climb away (3 miles). Acres of wildflowers light up the basins in early August. Backcountry camps are at each lake

and require a camping permit. For those itching to get to a high viewpoint, the Crystal Peak Trail climbs 2.5 miles from the junction along a dry, open slope to the lookout (elevation 6,615 feet). On a clear day, five Cascades volcanoes are within view, not to mention much of the national park and surrounding national forest.

User Groups: Hikers only. No dogs, horses, or mountain bikes are allowed. No wheelchair access.

Permits: This trail is usually accessible mid-July–September. A National Parks Pass is required to enter the park. Overnight stays within the national park require backcountry camping permits, which are available at Sunrise Visitor Center.

Maps: For a map of Mount Rainier National Park, contact the Outdoor Recreation Information Center at the downtown Seattle REI. For a topographic map, ask Green Trails for No. 270, Mount Rainier East, or ask the USGS for White River Park.

Directions: From Puyallup, drive east 51 miles on Highway 410 to Crystal Lakes Trailhead, just before the White River Wilderness Information Center.

Contact: Mount Rainier National Park, White River Wilderness Information Center, 70004 Hwy. 410 E., Enumclaw, WA 98022, 360/569-2211 x6030.

32 GLACIER BASIN
3.8-7.0 mi/2.0-3.5 hr 🥾2 ⛰8

near Sunrise in Mount Rainier National Park
Map 5.2, page 256

Mount Rainier may be known best for the immense glaciers covering its slopes. More than two dozen massive ice sheets radiate from the mountain's summit, sculpting entire valleys and ridges. Glacier Basin Trail provides a close look at two of Mount Rainier's glaciers, Emmons Glacier and Inter Glacier, hard at work. If you find glaciers boring, then shift your attention to the hillsides and look for mountain goats among the meadows.

Here's a little geology lesson first. Glaciers are massive sheets of ice produced over thousands of years. Snowfall slowly accumulates through the years and becomes compacted into a sheet of ice. Enter gravity, which slowly pulls the glacier down the valley, scraping and sculpting the terrain as it moves. It may take a while (millennia), but glaciers are heavy-duty landscapers. When glaciers retreat (melt faster than they form, as happens now), they leave a denuded valley filled with moraine (piles of rock and dirt), which you'll see here. Got it? You're ready for Glacier Basin Trail.

The trail has two forks: Glacier Basin Trail (7 miles round-trip) and Emmons Glacier Trail (3.8 miles). The trail departs White River Campground and gently climbs to the junction (0.9 mile): Head left for Emmons Glacier (the largest in the lower 48 states), right for Inter Glacier. Both trails provide great views of the glaciers. Being a glacier is dirty work, apparent from the enormous piles of rock and mud covering the ice. Glacier Basin is most popular with mountaineers seeking a summit of The Mountain.

User Groups: Hikers only. No dogs, horses, or mountain bikes are allowed. No wheelchair access.

Permits: This trail is usually accessible mid-July–September. A National Parks Pass is required to enter the park.

Maps: For a map of Mount Rainier National Park, contact the Outdoor Recreation Information Center at the downtown Seattle REI. For a topographic map, ask Green Trails for No. 270, Mount Rainier East, or ask the USGS for White River Park.

Directions: From Puyallup, drive east 52 miles on Highway 410 to Sunrise Road in Mount Rainier National Park. Turn right and drive 5.5 miles to White River Road. Turn left and drive 2 miles to White River Campground and signed trailhead.

Contact: Mount Rainier National Park, White River Wilderness Information Center, 70004 Hwy. 410 E., Enumclaw, WA 98022, 360/569-2211 x6030.

33 SUMMERLAND/ PANHANDLE GAP

8.6–11.4 mi/4.5–6.0 hr   🏃3   ⛰10

near Sunrise in Mount Rainier National Park

Map 5.2, page 256

Many hikers who have completed Wonderland Trail, a 93-mile trek around The Mountain, claim the country surrounding Panhandle Gap as their favorite. The meadows of Summerland and Ohanapecosh Park lie on either side of Panhandle Gap. Above, the ancient volcano of Little Tahoma stands before its big sister, Mount Rainier. Traveling this high country via Wonderland Trail at White River is a diverse and scenic trip.

The route leaves White River Campground and follows Wonderland through old-growth forest of large western hemlock, western red cedar, and Douglas fir. Little Tahoma, with Fryingpan Glacier hanging off its side, signals your arrival in the meadows and wildflowers of Summerland (4.3 miles). Large herds of mountain goats are frequently seen on the rocky slopes surrounding Summerland.

The curious and energetic can follow Wonderland Trail another 1.4 miles as it ascends steeply to the wind-swept terrain of Panhandle Gap. From this high point, the meadows of Ohanapecosh Park unfold beneath several high waterfalls. A word of caution: This high country is rocky and fairly barren. In many places, the trail is designated by rock cairns. No matter the season, be prepared for adverse weather. Tahoma has a system of its own, one that changes rapidly and unexpectedly, so bring warm clothes and know how to use your compass.

User Groups: Hikers only. No dogs, horses, or mountain bikes are allowed. No wheelchair access.

Permits: This area is usually accessible August–September. A National Parks Pass is required to enter the park.

Maps: For a map of Mount Rainier National Park, contact the Outdoor Recreation Information Center at the downtown Seattle

REI. For a topographic map, ask Green Trails for No. 270, Mount Rainier East, or ask the USGS for Sunrise and White River Park.

Directions: From Puyallup, drive east 52 miles on Highway 410 to Sunrise Road in Mount Rainier National Park. Turn right and drive 4.5 miles to Fryingpan Trailhead on the left.

Contact: Mount Rainier National Park, White River Wilderness Information Center, 70004 Hwy. 410 E., Enumclaw, WA 98022, 360/569-2211 x6030.

34 OWYHIGH LAKES
7.6 mi/4.0 hr

east of Tahoma in Mount Rainier National Park

Map 5.2, page 256

With such a dominating presence, Mount Rainier makes it easy to miss some of the other outstanding scenery in the park. Plenty of great hiking is to be had that doesn't include bulky views of the massive volcano. Owyhigh Lakes Trail is one such hike, traveling up through old but dense forest to parkland lakes. Meadows of wildflowers surround the several lakes and light up the scenery during early August. If you're worried about missing out on seeing rocky peaks and ridges, don't fret. The lakes are situated between craggy Governors Ridge and stately Tamanos Mountain, home of four prominent pinnacles known as the Cowlitz Chimneys.

Adding to Owyhigh Trail's allure is its lack of people. When the crowds at the park visitors centers make you begin to think it's holiday shopping season at the mall, Owyhigh Lakes is likely to be vacant. Folks hoping to spend the night can pitch their shelters at Tamanos Creek Camp, 0.5 mile before the lakes; just remember to pick up your permit. The trail continues beyond the lakes, crests a pass, and drops 5 miles to Deer Creek Trailhead, requiring a car-drop. Day hikers should turn around at Owyhigh Lakes.

User Groups: Hikers only. No dogs, horses, or mountain bikes are allowed. No wheelchair access.

Permits: This trail is accessible mid-July–September. A National Parks Pass is required to enter the park.

Maps: For a map of Mount Rainier National Park, contact the Outdoor Recreation Information Center at the downtown Seattle REI. For a topographic map, ask Green Trails for No. 270, Mount Rainier East, or ask the USGS for White River Park and Chinook Pass.

Directions: From Puyallup, drive east 52 miles on Highway 410 to Sunrise Road in Mount Rainier National Park. Turn right and drive 3 miles to the signed trailhead on the left.

Contact: Mount Rainier National Park, White River Wilderness Information Center, 70004 Hwy. 410 E., Enumclaw, WA 98022, 360/569-2211 x6030.

35 CHINOOK PASS HIKES
1.0-13.0 mi/0.5-6.0 hr

at Chinook Pass in Mount Baker-Snoqualmie National Forest

Map 5.2, page 256

Chinook Pass is one of the most beautiful of Washington's Cascade passes. So it comes as no surprise that it is a starting point for some amazing hiking. Three great hikes originate here, two of them routes along the famed PCT. Tipsoo Lake Trail is extremely easy, perfect for families with little ones. Naches Loop is longer but also easy, full of big-time views. Sourdough Gap and Pickhandle Point offer views and meadows along the PCT.

Tipsoo Lake is a short 1-mile walk around the high mountain lake. Wildflowers light up the meadows in July, with views of Mount Rainier. The trail around Tipsoo Lake is flat with many picnic sites.

Making a 4-mile loop around Naches Peak, the PCT connects to Naches Trail among acres of wildflower-filled meadows. The preferred route is clockwise, so as to keep Mount Rainier in front of you. The trail gains just 400 feet but is exposed and dry, becoming hot on summer afternoons.

A longer trip from Chinook Pass heads along the PCT to Sourdough Gap and Pickhandle Point. This is one of the PCT's most beautiful segments, traveling through open meadows to Sourdough Gap (3 miles one-way) and Pickhandle Point (6.5 miles). Pickhandle Point lies south and above the lifts of the local ski resort; skiers accustomed to a snowy landscape will be just as pleased with the summertime look.

User Groups: Hikers, leashed dogs, and horses. No mountain bikes are allowed. Tipsoo Lake Trail is wheelchair accessible.

Permits: This area is accessible June–mid-October. A federal Northwest Forest Pass is required to park here.

Maps: For a map of Mount Baker–Snoqualmie National Forest, contact the Outdoor Recreation Information Center at the downtown Seattle REI. For a topographic map, ask Green Trails for No. 270, Mount Rainier East, and No. 271, Bumping Lake, or ask the USGS for Chinook Pass.

Directions: From Puyallup, drive east 60 miles on Highway 410 to Tipsoo Lake Trailhead, on the west side of Chinook Pass.

Contact: Wenatchee National Forest, Naches Ranger Station, 10237 U.S. 12, Naches, WA 98937, 509/653-1401.

36 KLAPATCHE PARK

21.0 mi/2 days

near Longmire in Mount Rainier National Park

Map 5.2, page 256

The one sure way to instantly turn a popular backcountry destination into a remote and lonely journey is to close the access road. That's exactly what happened to Klapatche Park, now mostly enjoyed by trekkers on Wonderland Trail. A washout on Westside Road extended a trip into Klapatche from 5 miles round-trip into 21 miles. That's 16 miles of road—but don't miss out on the miles of meadows and high country lakes of Klapatche Park. Instead, hop on a mountain bike and turn this into Washington's best ride and hike.

The best access to Klapatche Park is via Klapatche Ridge Trail, eight miles up Westside Road. The trail climbs through old-growth forest to the high meadows of Klapatche Park and Aurora Lake (2.5 miles). Mount Rainier towers above fields of lupine, aster, and penstemon. The giant meadows of St. Andrew's Park make for a must-do side trip, just a mile south on Wonderland Trail. This certainly qualifies as some of the park's best high country. Return back via Klapatche Ridge Trail or make a loop of it via South Puyallup Trail. Camping is allowed only at Klapatche Park Camp or South Puyallup Camp and requires reservations. Road or not, this is a gorgeous hike.

User Groups: Hikers and mountain bikes (mountain bikes on Westside Road). No dogs or horses are allowed. No wheelchair access.

Permits: This trail is accessible July–mid-October. A National Parks Pass is required to enter the park. Overnight stays within the national park require backcountry camping permits, which are available at Longmire Wilderness Information Center.

Maps: For a map of Mount Rainier National Park, contact the Outdoor Recreation Information Center at the downtown Seattle REI. For a topographic map, ask Green Trails for No. 269, Mount Rainier West, or ask the USGS for Mount Wow and Mount Rainier West.

Directions: From Tacoma, drive south 40 miles on Highway 7 to Elbe. Turn east on Highway 706 and drive 10 miles to the Nisqually Entrance Station. Continue 1 mile to Westside Road. Turn left and drive to the trailhead at the washout. Hike or bike 8 miles on the closed road to the trailhead on the right.

Contact: Mount Rainier National Park, Longmire Wilderness Information Center, Tahoma Woods, Star Route, Ashford, WA 98304, 360/569-4453.

37 EMERALD RIDGE LOOP

16.2 mi/1-2 days   👣3 ⛰10

near Longmire in Mount Rainier National Park

Map 5.2, page 256

More remote and less accessible than other faces, Mount Rainier's western side features few trails outside of Mowich. And the trails that do explore The Mountain's western slopes are fading into obscurity thanks to the closure of Westside Road. That's a shame, as Emerald Ridge is a beauty of a trail. With old-growth forest, alpine meadows, and an almost-close-enough-to-touch encounter with Tahoma Glacier, there's little left to desire.

Westside Road once provided easy access to the trailheads. But after a washout, the Park Service decided not to reopen it. That has kept the crowds out and the animals wild. It also means some road walking, about 8.3 miles of road out of a 16.2-mile total loop. The park does allow mountain bikes on the road; the smart hiker bikes to the upper trailhead, hikes the loop, and coasts back to the car.

On the trail, the loop follows Round Pass Trail and South Emerald Ridge Trail up to Wonderland Trail (2.1 miles). An interesting outcrop of columnar basalt (hexagonal columns formed as erupted lava cooled) is found just before the junction. Wonderland Trail climbs to emerald meadows and Tahoma Glacier (4.3 miles). Glacier Island, encircled by glaciers as recently as the 1930s, stands before the towering bulk of Mount Rainier. The loop drops to Tahoma Creek Trail (5.8 miles) and to the lower trailhead (7.9 miles). Backpackers need to plan on setting up for the night at South Puyallup Camp (the only site along the trail), located at the junction of South Emerald Ridge and Wonderland Trails.

User Groups: Hikers and mountain bikes (mountain bikes on Westside Road). No dogs or horses are allowed. No wheelchair access.

Permits: This trail is accessible July–mid-October. A National Parks Pass is required to enter the park.

Maps: For a map of Mount Rainier National

Park, contact the Outdoor Recreation Information Center at the downtown Seattle REI. For a topographic map, ask Green Trails for No. 269, Mount Rainier West, or ask the USGS for Mount Wow and Mount Rainier West.

Directions: From Tacoma, drive south 40 miles on Highway 7 to Elbe. Turn east on Highway 706 and drive 10 miles to the Nisqually Entrance Station. Continue 1 mile to Westside Road. Turn left and drive to the trailhead at the washout. Hike or bike 5 miles on the closed road to the trailhead on the right.

Contact: Mount Rainier National Park, Longmire Wilderness Information Center, Tahoma Woods, Star Route, Ashford, WA 98304, 360/569-4453.

38 GLACIER VIEW WILDERNESS

1.5-7.0 mi/1.0-3.5 hr   👣1 ⛰9

west of Mount Rainier in Glacier View Wilderness of Gifford Pinchot National Forest

Map 5.2, page 256

Excluded from the national park but protected by wilderness designation, Glacier View Wilderness is a gem hidden from the masses. This small enclave on the west side of Mount Rainier National Park features several pristine mountain lakes and a pair of gorgeous viewpoints. When you want to see The Mountain in all its glory but don't want to bump elbows with the crowds at Sunrise or Paradise, head to Glacier View Wilderness.

The wilderness is bisected by Glacier View Trail, which runs north to south and has two trailheads. The southern trailhead provides easy access to Lake Christine. The trail climbs gently to the mountain lake (0.75 mile), cloaked by mountain hemlock and subalpine fir. There are several great campsites, and the fishing is supposedly not half bad either. From the lake, a side trail leads 1 mile to the summit of Mount Beljica, awash in big views of Rainier.

The northern trailhead provides access to Glacier View Lookout. Glacier View Trail runs north along a forested ridge to Glacier View Lookout (2 miles; elevation 5,450). This high forest is chock-full of ancient trees and bear grass with its huge blooms. The lookout provides great views of Rainier and surrounding countryside. Beyond the lookout are Lake West (2.3 miles) and Lake Helen (3.5 miles). Both lakes have several campsites. You'll likely be able to count on one hand the people you run across.

User Groups: Hikers, leashed dogs, and horses are allowed. No mountain bikes are allowed. No wheelchair access.

Permits: This area is accessible mid-June–October. A federal Northwest Forest Pass is required to park here.

Maps: For a map of Gifford Pinchot National Forest, contact the Outdoor Recreation Information Center at the downtown Seattle REI. For a topographic map, ask Green Trails for No. 269, Mount Rainier West, or ask the USGS for Mount Wow.

Directions: From Tacoma, drive south 40 miles on Highway 7 to Elbe. Turn east on Highway 706 and drive to Copper Creek Road (Forest Service Road 59). Turn left and drive 4.5 miles to Forest Service Road 5920. Turn right and drive to the unsigned trailhead at road's end.

Contact: Gifford Pinchot National Forest, Cowlitz Valley Ranger Station, 10024 U.S. 12, Randle, WA 98377, 360/497-1100.

39 GOBBLER'S KNOB/ LAKE GEORGE

6.4-8.8 mi/3.5-4.5 hr

west of Mount Rainier in Glacier View Wilderness and Mount Rainier National Park

Map 5.2, page 256

Gobbler's Knob is the best deal in the Mount Rainier area. Pristine old-growth forest blankets this grand route as it passes a beautiful mountain lake on its way to the national park,

a viewpoint, and another impressive lake. From atop Gobbler's Knob, Mount Rainier looms large with its impressive stature. Lake George lies beneath Mount Wow. Wow means "goat" in the Salish, the language of local American Indians in the Puget Sound region, and it's likely what you'll be mouthing as you watch mountain goats rambling along the steep slopes.

The preferred route to Gobbler's Knob and Lake George crosses Glacier View Wilderness. A washout on Westside Road increased access via the national park by 3 miles (all on old road). Avoid park fees and an unsightly road walk by hiking through the wilderness. Puyallup Trail meanders through Beljica Meadows to the junction with Lake Christine Trail (0.9 mile). Head left as the trail drops through old-growth mountain hemlock and subalpine fir to Goat Lake (2.3 miles). Campsites are scattered around the lake and require no backcountry permits.

Puyallup Trail then climbs to a saddle between Gobbler's Knob and rocky Mount Wow (3.2 miles). A side trail leads to Gobbler's Knob Lookout and its drop-dead views of Mount Rainier and its glaciers. What a place to watch a sunset! Lake George lies 1,200 feet below, surrounded by forest and rocky slopes. Lake George Camp requires backcountry permits from the National Park Service. The trail continues 0.8 mile to the abandoned Westside Road.

User Groups: Hikers only. No dogs, horses, or mountain bikes are allowed. No wheelchair access.

Permits: This area is accessible mid-June–October. A federal Northwest Forest Pass is required to park here. Overnight stays within the national park require backcountry camping permits, which are available at Longmire Wilderness Information Center.

Maps: For a map of Mount Rainier National Park and Gifford Pinchot National Forest, contact the Outdoor Recreation Information Center at the downtown Seattle REI. For a topographic map, ask Green Trails for No.

269, Mount Rainier West, or ask the USGS for Mount Wow.

Directions: From Tacoma, drive south 40 miles on Highway 7 to Elbe. Turn east on Highway 706 and drive to Copper Creek Road (Forest Service Road 59). Turn left and drive 4.5 miles to Forest Service Road 5920. Turn right and drive to the unsigned trailhead at road's end. (For access via the national park, follow directions for the Emerald Ridge listing in this chapter.)

Contact: Mount Rainier National Park, Longmire Wilderness Information Center, Tahoma Woods, Star Route, Ashford, WA 98304, 360/569-4453.

40 INDIAN HENRY'S HUNTING GROUND

11.4 mi/7.0 hr   🥾3 ⛰9

near Longmire in Mount Rainier National Park

Map 5.2, page 256

Home to some of Mount Rainier's most beautiful scenery, Kautz Creek Trail to Indian Henry's Hunting Ground has it all. The trail passes through old-growth forest, where Douglas firs, western hemlocks, and western red cedars have been standing together for centuries. Upper sections of the route are enveloped in subalpine meadows, where bear, deer, and marmots roam the parkland. And of course, The Mountain makes a grand appearance, towering above the high country with rocky arms and glistening glaciers. It's a full day of hiking, but enjoyable every step of the way.

There are three ways into Indian Henry's Hunting Ground, the best being via Kautz Creek, described below. Other options include Wonderland Trail out of Longmire (an up-and-down 13.8 miles) and Tahoma Creek Trail (a steeper, less scenic 10 miles). Kautz Creek Trail quickly crosses its namesake on an old floodplain. The trail then climbs through stands of old-growth forest on its way to high-country meadows (3.5 miles).

The grade becomes more gentle in its final 2 miles, providing plenty of time to snack on huckleberries in the fall. A great side trip is Mirror Lakes (an extra 1.2 miles round-trip), where Tahoma reflects in the small subalpine tarns. At Indian Henry's Hunting Ground stands a historic patrol cabin still staffed by the Park Service. The only campground within the area is Devils Dream Camp (reservations required), usually full with Wonderland Trail trekkers.

User Groups: Hikers only. No dogs, horses, or mountain bikes are allowed. No wheelchair access.

Permits: This area is usually accessible year-round. A National Parks Pass is required to enter the park. Overnight stays within the national park require backcountry camping permits, which are available at Longmire Wilderness Information Center in Ashford.

Maps: For a map of Mount Rainier National Park, contact the Outdoor Recreation Information Center at the downtown Seattle REI. For a topographic map, ask Green Trails for No. 269, Mount Rainier West, and No. 301, Randle, or ask the USGS for Mount Rainier West.

Directions: From Tacoma, drive south 40 miles on Highway 7 to Elbe. Turn east on Highway 706 and drive 10 miles to the Nisqually Entrance Station. Continue 7 miles to Longmire Wilderness Information Center. The trailhead is across the street in Kautz Creek Picnic Area.

Contact: Mount Rainier National Park, Longmire Wilderness Information Center, Tahoma Woods, Star Route, Ashford, WA 98304, 360/569-4453.

41 RAMPART RIDGE LOOP

4.5 mi/2.5 hr   🥾2 ⛰8

near Longmire in Mount Rainier National Park

Map 5.2, page 256

Climbing atop one of Rainier's ancient lava flows, Rampart Ridge Trail delivers the requisite views and meadows needed in any hike. The trail offers some of the best views of Tahoma (Mount Rainier) from the Longmire Visitor Center. Included in the deal are old-growth forests and some likely encounters with wildlife. Deer, grouse, squirrels, and woodpeckers are regular residents of the area. Gaining little more than 1,100 feet, it's a great trail for all hikers.

The loop is best done clockwise, hiking along the ridge toward the mountain. Rampart Ridge Trail begins on Trail of the Shadows, just 300 yards from the parking lot. From there, it switchbacks at a moderate but steady grade around the steep cliffs of Rampart Ridge. The forest here is great old-growth mountain hemlocks and subalpine firs, decked out in gowns of moss and lichens. The trail finds the top of the ridge (1.5 miles) and follows the level plateau for more than a mile. Forest is regularly broken up by meadows of wildflowers (try the month of July) and huckleberries (usually ripe in August). Although The Mountain dominates the skyline, Rampart Ridge offers a great view of the large, U-shaped Nisqually River Valley (thank you, glaciers). The trail circles back to Longmire via Wonderland Trail.

User Groups: Hikers only. No dogs, horses, or mountain bikes are allowed. No wheelchair access.

Permits: This trail is usually accessible July–mid-October. A National Parks Pass is required to enter the park.

Maps: For a map of Mount Rainier National Park, contact the Outdoor Recreation Information Center at the downtown Seattle REI. For a topographic map, ask Green Trails for No. 269, Mount Rainier West, or ask the USGS for Mount Rainier West.

Directions: From Tacoma, drive south 40 miles on Highway 7 to Elbe. Turn east on Highway 706 and drive 10 miles to the Nisqually Entrance Station. Continue 18 miles to the National Park Inn at Paradise. The trailhead is behind the inn.

Contact: Mount Rainier National Park, Longmire Wilderness Information Center, Tahoma Woods, Star Route, Ashford, WA 98304, 360/569-4453.

42 COMET FALLS/ VAN TRUMP PARK
6.2 mi/3.5 hr   🥾3 △10

near Longmire in Mount Rainier National Park

Map 5.2, page 256   BEST (

Two of the most scenic spots in Mount Rainier National Park are conveniently on the same trail. One of Rainier's highest waterfalls, Comet Falls, plunges off a rocky cliff more than 320 feet. It's the largest of several cascades along the route. As great as Comet Falls may be, Van Trump Park is arguably even better. Acre upon acre of meadow unfolds beneath behemoth Tahoma, with wildflowers coloring the entire scene during the summer. That rumbling is just Kautz and Van Trump Glaciers doing their thing, cracking and breaking in the summer heat.

You can bet that with so much to see, the trail will be busy. In fact, this is one of the park's most popular hikes. Unfortunately, it has a small trailhead with no alternate parking; be ready to choose another hike if the parking lot is full. Van Trump Park Trail leaves the trailhead and briskly climbs alongside the constantly cascading Van Trump Creek. Christine Falls is a short 10-minute walk from the trailhead. Old-growth forest provides shade all the way to Comet Falls. Shutterbugs rejoice, but save some film for later. From the falls, Van Trump Park Trail switchbacks up to open meadows and prime views. Clear days reveal the Tatoosh Range, Mount Adams, and Mount St. Helens to the south. Be sure to stick to established trails; in such a heavily used area, meadows are quickly destroyed by wayward feet.

User Groups: Hikers only. No dogs, horses, or mountain bikes are allowed. No wheelchair access.

Permits: This trail is usually accessible

July–mid-October. A National Parks Pass is required to enter the park.

Maps: For a map of Mount Rainier National Park, contact the Outdoor Recreation Information Center at the downtown Seattle REI. For a topographic map, ask Green Trails for No. 269, Mount Rainier West, or ask the USGS for Mount Rainier West.

Directions: From Tacoma, drive south 40 miles on Highway 7 to Elbe. Turn east on Highway 706 and drive 10 miles to the Nisqually Entrance Station. Continue 12 miles to the signed trailhead on the left.

Contact: Mount Rainier National Park, Longmire Wilderness Information Center, Tahoma Woods, Star Route, Ashford, WA 98304, 360/569-4453.

43 EAGLE PEAK
7.2 mi/4.0 hr   🥾3 ⛰️8

near Longmire in Mount Rainier National Park

Map 5.2, page 256

Directly out of Longmire, Eagle Peak Trail climbs skyward through old-growth forest and meadows to Eagle Peak Saddle on the north side of Tatoosh Range. At an elevation of 5,700 feet, Mount Rainier looms large while several other Cascade volcanoes are well within sight. The trail is fairly steep, gaining 2,700 feet in just 3.6 miles. Despite its close proximity to Longmire, the ascent keeps the trail less traveled than those near Sunrise or Paradise Visitor Centers.

Eagle Peak Trail climbs quickly and steeply through the mature forest. Douglas fir and mountain hemlock quickly give way to their relatives, mountain hemlock and subalpine fir. The forest covers the trail for 3 miles, keeping it relatively cool; the only water is found when the trail crosses a small stream (2 miles). The final 0.5 mile is a steep ascent in flower-clad meadows, with Eagle Peak towering above. The trail ends in a large saddle between Eagle and Chutla Peaks. Scrambles to either peak are recommended only for experienced and

outfitted climbers. From this outpost of the Tatoosh Range, miles and miles of surrounding countryside (some forested, some denuded) are revealed. Hikers who neglect to bring a camera never fail to regret it.

User Groups: Hikers only. No dogs, horses, or mountain bikes are allowed. No wheelchair access.

Permits: This area is usually accessible mid-July–September. A National Parks Pass is required to enter the park.

Maps: For a map of Mount Rainier National Park, contact the Outdoor Recreation Information Center at the downtown Seattle REI. For a topographic map, ask Green Trails for No. 269, Mount Rainier West, and No. 301, Randle, or ask the USGS for Mount Rainier West and Wahpenayo.

Directions: From Tacoma, drive south 40 miles on Highway 7 to Elbe. Turn east on Highway 706 and drive 10 miles to the Nisqually Entrance Station. Continue 7 miles to Longmire Museum for parking. The signed trailhead is on the opposite side of the suspension bridge crossing the Nisqually River, on the left.

Contact: Mount Rainier National Park, Longmire Wilderness Information Center, Tahoma Woods, Star Route, Ashford, WA 98304, 360/569-4453.

44 PARADISE NATURE TRAILS
1.5-2.8 mi/0.7-1.5 hr   🥾1 ⛰️9

near Paradise in Mount Rainier National Park

Map 5.2, page 256   BEST (

World-famous and Mount Rainier's most visited setting, Paradise fails to disappoint even the highest expectations. Directly below The Mountain among acres of subalpine meadows, Paradise sports a striking visitors center as well as the historic Paradise Inn. Folks have been coming here to experience Mount Rainier for well over 100 years. And Paradise is a great place to become acquainted with Washington's tallest peak on a number of easy and highly scenic trails. From glacier viewpoints to wildflower rambles, the trails of Paradise easily put visitors into seventh heaven.

The large network of trails near Paradise may appear confusing on a map, but all junctions are well signed. The meadows of this high country are extremely fragile and wither away quickly under the stomp of a boot. Be sure to stick to designated trails at all times. For a view of enormous Nisqually Glacier and its expansive moraine, hike from the visitors center to Nisqually Vista (1.6 miles). This level and wide trail makes a loop (shaped like a lasso) and is perfect for hikers of any ability. Also accessible from the visitors center is Alta Vista Trail (1.5 miles), a gentle climb to a viewpoint. From this small knob, Rainier's bulk astounds even the most veteran of hikers. Look south to take in views of southern Washington's other volcanic peaks, Mount St. Helens and Mount Adams.

Paradise Inn also offers an array of trails, easily customized to any length desired. A good hike is to Golden Gate (2.8 miles) and the vast meadows of Edith Creek Basin. Also beginning in Paradise but long enough to warrant their own listings in this chapter are Skyline Loop, Mazama Ridge, and Paradise Glacier Trails (see next listings).

User Groups: Hikers only. No dogs, horses, or mountain bikes are allowed. No wheelchair access.

Permits: This area is accessible mid-June–October. A National Parks Pass is required to enter the park.

Maps: For a map of Mount Rainier National Park, contact the Outdoor Recreation Information Center at the downtown Seattle REI. For a topographic map, ask Green Trails for No. 270S, Paradise, or ask the USGS for Mount Rainier East.

Directions: From Tacoma, drive south 40 miles on Highway 7 to Elbe. Turn east on Highway 706 and drive 10 miles to the Nisqually Entrance Station. Continue 17.5 miles to the Henry M. Jackson Visitor Center or 18 miles to the Paradise National Park Inn. The trails emanate from the visitors center and the lodge. Consult a map to see which trailhead to access.

Contact: Mount Rainier National Park, Longmire Wilderness Information Center, Tahoma Woods, Star Route, Ashford, WA 98304, 360/569-4453.

45 PARADISE GLACIER
6.0 mi/3.0 hr

near Paradise in Mount Rainier National Park

Map 5.2, page 256

To discover what millions of tons of ice look and sound like, take scenic Paradise Glacier Trail, which gently climbs through wide, open meadows, rock fields, and snowfields to the living Paradise Glacier. Centuries of snowfall built up this massive block of ice slowly sliding down Mount Rainier. The upper reaches of the trail reveal the barren landscapes that are trademarks of retreating glaciers. Paradise Glacier Trail is the park's best chance to view up close the mountain's most famous features.

The route to Paradise Glacier follows Skyline Trail (counterclockwise from Paradise Inn) 1.9 miles to Paradise Glacier Trail junction, just above Sluiskin Falls. Also here is Stevens–Van Trump Historical Memorial, commemorating the 1870 ascent of Mount Rainier, one of the first by white men. Paradise Glacier Trail begins here and heads directly for the glacier (3 miles), cracking, creaking, and breaking apart before your very eyes and ears. Although the terrain appears barren, it is very fragile; be sure to stick to designated trails. The high country here is pretty close to true tundra, with tiny plants doing their best to survive on the barren slopes. Streams cascade all around. Paradise Glacier used to sport several large ice caves that could be explored, but warm weather through the last few decades has left them destroyed or unsafe. Walking on the glacier is also unsafe and prohibited.

User Groups: Hikers only. No dogs, horses, or

mountain bikes are allowed. No wheelchair access.

Permits: This trail is accessible mid-June–October. A National Parks Pass is required to enter the park.

Maps: For a map of Mount Rainier National Park, contact the Outdoor Recreation Information Center at the downtown Seattle REI. For a topographic map, ask Green Trails for No. 270S, Paradise, or ask the USGS for Mount Rainier East.

Directions: From Tacoma, drive south 40 miles on Highway 7 to Elbe. Turn east on Highway 706 and drive 10 miles to the Nisqually Entrance Station. Continue 18 miles to the National Park Inn at Paradise. The trailhead is behind the inn.

Contact: Mount Rainier National Park, Longmire Wilderness Information Center, Tahoma Woods, Star Route, Ashford, WA 98304, 360/569-4453.

46 MAZAMA RIDGE
5.4 mi/2.5 hr   👣2 ⛰10

near Paradise in Mount Rainier National Park

Map 5.2, page 256

Walking away from The Mountain, Mazama Ridge avoids the mall-like crush of visitors along other Paradise trails. Such a beautiful hike still gets plenty of use, however, and for good reason. The easy trail spends its entirety wandering amid subalpine meadows with big views of the big mountain. To the south stands the jagged Tatoosh Range. And to cap it all off is a series of small tarns, idyllic spots for lunch.

The theme of Mazama Ridge Trail is meadows, meadows, meadows. The route leaves Paradise Inn and follows Skyline Trail 1.5 miles to a signed junction; to the right is Mazama Ridge Trail. The trail follows the wide, flat ridgeline south. During July, lupine, daisies, and countless other wildflowers add shrouds of color to green meadows.

The trail reaches a number of small lakes

and tarns (2.5 miles) along the flat top of Faraway Rock. Below its steep slopes lie Louise and Reflection Lakes and Wonderland Trail. With little elevation change, this is a great trail for families with little ones.

User Groups: Hikers only. No dogs, horses, or mountain bikes are allowed. No wheelchair access.

Permits: This trail is accessible mid-June–October. A National Parks Pass is required to enter the park.

Maps: For a map of Mount Rainier National Park, contact the Outdoor Recreation Information Center at the downtown Seattle REI. For a topographic map, ask Green Trails for No. 270S, Paradise, or ask the USGS for Mount Rainier East.

Directions: From Tacoma, drive south 40 miles on Highway 7 to Elbe. Turn east on Highway 706 and drive 10 miles to the Nisqually Entrance Station. Continue 18 miles to the National Park Inn at Paradise. The trailhead is behind the inn.

Contact: Mount Rainier National Park, Longmire Wilderness Information Center, Tahoma Woods, Star Route, Ashford, WA 98304, 360/569-4453.

47 SKYLINE LOOP
5.0 mi/3.0 hr   👣2 ⛰10

out of Paradise in Mount Rainier National Park

Map 5.2, page 256

Skyline Trail may well be the premier hike in Mount Rainier National Park. The trail delivers miles of alpine meadows, peers over the enormous Nisqually Glacier, and summits Panorama Point. This high vista is as close to The Mountain as you can get without ropes and a harness. Acres of blooming wildflowers line the trail in late July, and if big-time views bore you, several streams and waterfalls are thrown in for good measure. This is a popular trip for folks visiting the Paradise Visitor Center. The overall elevation gain is 1,400 feet, a respectable but not strenuous workout.

The best route is a clockwise one. Although numerous trails crisscross this area, Skyline Trail is well signed at every junction. Starting at Paradise, the trail skirts Alta Vista Peak and climbs through meadows to the ridge above Nisqually Glacier (1.3 miles). On hot summer days, the silence of the high country is broken only by whistling marmots and the cracking glacier.

Panorama Point (2.5 miles; elevation 6,800 feet) is an appropriate name for this high vista. Mount Rainier towers above the viewpoint, and the rocky and jagged Tatoosh Range stands to the south. On clear days, Mount Adams, Goat Rocks, Mount St. Helens, and even Mount Hood in Oregon make appearances. Panorama indeed! Because you definitely packed your camera, save some film for the last half of the trail. Descending to Paradise, Skyline Trail passes Stevens–Van Trump Memorial (commemorating an ascent of Mount Rainier), Sluiskin Falls, and Myrtle Falls. Camping is not permitted in the Paradise area.

User Groups: Hikers only. No dogs, horses, or mountain bikes are allowed. Part of the trail is wheelchair accessible (but somewhat steep).

Permits: This trail is accessible mid-July–September. A National Parks Pass is required to enter the park.

Maps: For a map of Mount Rainier National Park, contact the Outdoor Recreation Information Center at the downtown Seattle REI. For a topographic map, ask Green Trails for No. 270S, Paradise, or ask the USGS for Mount Rainier East.

Directions: From Tacoma, drive south 40 miles on Highway 7 to Elbe. Turn east on Highway 706 and drive 10 miles to the Nisqually Entrance Station. Continue 18 miles to the National Park Inn at Paradise. The trailhead is behind the inn.

Contact: Mount Rainier National Park, Longmire Wilderness Information Center, Tahoma Woods, Star Route, Ashford, WA 98304, 360/569-4453.

48 WONDERLAND TRAIL
93.0 mi/10 days   5   10

around Tahoma in Mount Rainier National Park

Map 5.2, page 256

Wonderland Trail is considered by many to be the be-all and end-all of Washington hiking. The long, demanding trek makes a full circle around the behemoth mountain, exploring old-growth forest, high alpine meadows, and everything in between. Tahoma (Mount Rainier's Native American name) is the center of attention at almost every turn, towering above the trail with massive glaciers and windswept snowfields. The Wonderland passes through the park's most beautiful terrain. Acres and acres of wildflower meadows dominate Spray Park, Indian Henry's Hunting Ground, and Summerland. Outstanding lakes and streams are repeat encounters, with Mowich Lake, Carbon River, and Martha Falls a sampling of many highlights.

Wonderland Trail is certainly one of the most demanding hikes in the state. The route repeatedly climbs out of low river valleys to high ridges radiating from Tahoma. Although some folks complete the hike in as few as seven or eight days, plan for at least 10 full days. This makes for a leisurely pace of about 10 miles per day. Besides, there's far too much to see to rush through it. The best starting points include Longmire, Sunrise, or Paradise Visitor Centers. Smart hikers plan carefully and leave a food cache at a visitors center halfway through the route. Because of the trail's popularity, the Park Service requires reservations for all backcountry camps (cross-country camping—that is, selecting a temporary site somewhere off-trail, is not allowed). Spots are limited and regularly fill up in April (reservations can be made after April 1). And finally, be prepared for adverse weather in any season. Tahoma creates its own weather systems, sometimes in just minutes. Set out upon this epic trail and you will not be disappointed, guaranteed!

User Groups: Hikers only. No dogs, horses, or mountain bikes are allowed. No wheelchair access.

Permits: This trail is accessible mid-July–September. A National Parks Pass is required to enter the park. Overnight stays within the national park require backcountry camping permits, which are available at Longmire Wilderness Information Center in Ashford. Hikers doing the complete Wonderland Trail are limited to camping in designated camps only—the use of cross-country zones is not permitted.

Maps: For a map of Mount Rainier National Park, contact the Outdoor Recreation Information Center at the downtown Seattle REI. For a topographic map, ask Green Trails for No. 269, Mount Rainier West, and No. 270, Mount Rainier East, or ask the USGS for Mount Rainier West, Mount Rainier East, Mowich Lake, Sunrise, Golden Lakes, Mount Wow, White River Park, and Chinook Pass.

Directions: From Tacoma, drive south 40 miles on Highway 7 to Elbe. Turn east on Highway 706 and drive 10 miles to the Nisqually Entrance Station. Continue 18 miles to the National Park Inn at Paradise. The well-signed trailhead is beside the inn. Other access points include Sunrise Visitor Center or Mowich Lake.

Contact: Mount Rainier National Park, Longmire Wilderness Information Center, Tahoma Woods, Star Route, Ashford, WA 98304, 360/569-4453.

49 PINNACLE SADDLE
2.6 mi/2.5 hr

near Paradise in Mount Rainier National Park

Map 5.2, page 256

Pinnacle Peak Trail is one of the park's steepest trails. An elevation gain of 1,050 feet passes underfoot in a short 1.3 miles, delivering hikers to a wonderful viewpoint. The steep, rocky path keeps the crowds at bay, leaving the route for only the most determined hikers and view junkies. Although it starts gently, much of the trail does little but climb skyward. Mount Rainier remains visible the entire way. Because the trail is situated on the north-facing slopes of the Tatoosh Range, snow lingers here late, sometimes into August. Marmots and picas whistle and scurry about the rocky meadows while mountain goats frequently patrol the jagged ridge. The trail eventually reaches Pinnacle Saddle, between Pinnacle and Denham Peaks, in the heart of the Tatoosh Range. To the north stands The Mountain, above Paradise Meadows; to the south, snowy Goat Rocks and Mount Adams are visible. The truly adventurous can undertake a rocky scramble to the summit of Pinnacle Peak. It's a gain of 600 feet, but few views are to be gained for the extra effort. Other than snowmelt, little water is to be found along the way; be sure to pack your own.

User Groups: Hikers only. No dogs, horses, or mountain bikes are allowed. No wheelchair access.

Permits: This area is accessible August–September. A National Parks Pass is required to enter the park.

Maps: For a map of Mount Rainier National Park, contact the Outdoor Recreation Information Center at the downtown Seattle REI. For a topographic map, ask Green Trails for No. 270, Mount Rainier East, or ask the USGS for Mount Rainier East.

Directions: From Tacoma, drive south 40 miles on Highway 7 to Elbe. Turn east on Highway 706 and drive 10 miles to the Nisqually Entrance Station. Continue 16 miles to Stevens Canyon Road. Turn right and drive 2.5 miles to the signed trailhead on the right.

Contact: Mount Rainier National Park, Longmire Wilderness Information Center, Tahoma Woods, Star Route, Ashford, WA 98304, 360/569-4453.

50 SNOW AND BENCH LAKES
2.6 mi/1.5 hr

near Paradise in Mount Rainier National Park

Map 5.2, page 256

Short, flat, and beautiful best describe Snow Lake Trail. The perfect hike for folks young and old, Snow Lake Trail features a pair of subalpine lakes enclosed by meadows and rocky peaks. The total elevation gain is about 200 feet, practically unnoticeable. Away from the bustle of the Paradise area, Snow Lake offers visitors prime hiking without the crowds.

Snow Lake Trail leaves Stevens Canyon Road and quickly reaches The Bench, a wide, flat meadow with perfect views of Mount Rainier. Bear grass occupies the large meadows, sending its large blooms skyward during August. Bench Lake occupies part of the large meadow. The trail continues another 0.5 mile to Snow Lake, tucked away within a large basin. The lake got its name from the heavy snowpack that lingers around the lake (and on the trail) until late July. Craggy Unicorn Peak rises above the lake and talus slopes from the south. Visitors interested in spending the night will appreciate Snow Lake Camp, the park's most accessible backcountry campground (permits required).

User Groups: Hikers only. No dogs, horses, or mountain bikes are allowed. No wheelchair access.

Permits: This trail is usually accessible August–September. A National Parks Pass is required to enter the park. Overnight stays within the national park require backcountry camping permits, which are available at Sunrise Visitor Center.

Maps: For a map of Mount Rainier National Park, contact the Outdoor Recreation Information Center at the downtown Seattle REI. For a topographic map, ask Green Trails for No. 270, Mount Rainier East, or ask the USGS for Mount Rainier East.

Directions: From Tacoma, drive south 40 miles on Highway 7 to Elbe. Turn east on Highway 706 and drive 10 miles to the Nisqually Entrance Station. Continue 16 miles to Stevens Canyon Road. Turn right and drive 4 miles to the signed trailhead on the right.

Contact: Mount Rainier National Park, Longmire Wilderness Information Center, Tahoma Woods, Star Route, Ashford, WA 98304, 360/569-4453.

51 SHRINER PEAK LOOKOUT
8.4 mi/5.0 hr -2 days

near Stevens Canyon entrance in Mount Rainier National Park

Map 5.2, page 256

Probably nothing is more beautiful than waking to Mount Rainier basking in the glow of the rising sun. And probably there is no better place to behold such a sight than Shriner Peak. But this extraordinary place requires extraordinary effort. Shriner Peak Trail gains extensive elevation in open terrain, made hot by the afternoon sun. Easily done in a day, Shriner Camp invites hikers to spend the night and enjoy the daybreak view.

Shriner Peak Trail is not for the faint of heart. The trail gains more than 3,400 feet in just 4.2 miles, a steep ascent by any standard. Plus, much of the route lies on an exposed, south-facing slope (the hottest of them all). As you sweat and trudge uphill, keep in mind that nature rewards those who work the hardest. The trail winds its way through shady forest before entering an old burn area and eventually open meadows (2.5 miles). The upper half of the route is awash in views of Mount Rainier and surrounding valleys. Shriner Camp is just below the summit off a short side trail; unfortunately it's a dry camp. Shriner Peak is best undertaken early in the day, before the sun is high. Finally, be sure to carry extra water; even if it's cloudy and cool, you'll need it.

User Groups: Hikers only. No dogs, horses, or mountain bikes are allowed. No wheelchair access.

Permits: This area is accessible August–September. A National Parks Pass is required to enter the park. Overnight stays within the national park require backcountry camping permits, which are available at the Longmire and White River Wilderness Information Centers.

Maps: For a map of Mount Rainier National Park, contact the Outdoor Recreation Information Center at the downtown Seattle REI. For a topographic map, ask Green Trails for No. 270, Mount Rainier East, or ask the USGS for Chinook Pass.

Directions: From Puyallup, drive east 56 miles on Highway 410 to Highway 123. Turn right (south) and drive 7.5 miles to the trailhead on the left side of the road.

Contact: Mount Rainier National Park, White River Wilderness Information Center, 70004 Hwy. 410 E., Enumclaw, WA 98022, 360/569-2211 x6030.

52 LAUGHINGWATER CREEK
11.4 mi/6.0 hr-2 days   🏃2 ⛰8

near Stevens Canyon entrance in Mount Rainier National Park

Map 5.2, page 256

A rarity in this national park, Laughingwater Creek Trail forsakes mountain meadows and views of Mount Rainier. Instead, this lightly used trail makes a grand trip through old-growth forest to Three Lakes, set among open subalpine forest. The trail provides a quiet reintroduction to the Cascade Mountains after the crowds of Mount Rainier's visitors centers. The only sounds around these parts are the noisy rumbling of Laughingwater Creek and the bellows of elk.

Laughingwater Creek Trail gains more than 2,500 feet between the trailhead and Three Lakes. Most of the climb is spread moderately along the route, easy enough for hikers young and old. The trail sticks close to the creek and passes within view of a waterfall at 2.5 miles. Western hemlocks give way to mountain hemlocks and subalpine fir replaces Douglas fir as the trail nears the crest of the hike.

Three Lakes lie in a small basin atop the ridge. A wonderful backcountry camp is situated here with an aged shelter. This is an out-of-the-way section of the national park (if any remain these days), with few visitors spending the night at Three Lakes Camp. If you have an itch to see The Mountain, continue on the trail past Three Lakes toward the PCT and meadow vistas.

User Groups: Hikers and horses. No dogs or mountain bikes are allowed. No wheelchair access.

Permits: This area is usually accessible July–September. A National Parks Pass is required to enter the park. Overnight stays within the national park require backcountry camping permits, which are available at White River Wilderness Information Center in Enumclaw.

Maps: For a map of Mount Rainier National Park, contact the Outdoor Recreation Information Center at the downtown Seattle REI. For a topographic map, ask Green Trails for No. 270, Mount Rainier East, and No. 271, Bumping Lake, or ask the USGS for Chinook Pass.

Directions: From Puyallup, drive east 56 miles on Highway 410 to Highway 123. Turn right (south) and drive 10.5 miles to the trailhead on the left side of the road, just south of Stevens Canyon entrance.

Contact: Mount Rainier National Park, White River Wilderness Information Center, 70004 Hwy. 410 E., Enumclaw, WA 98022, 360/569-2211 x6030.

53 SILVER FALLS LOOP
3.0 mi/1.5 hr   🏃1 ⛰8

out of Ohanapecosh in Mount Rainier National Park

Map 5.2, page 256

Silver Falls Loop is one of Mount Rainier's best river trails, perfect for families and hikers of all abilities. The route is a gentle grade along the bustling river to one of the park's most impressive cascades. Silver Falls Trail follows Ohanapecosh River a gentle 1.5 miles to Silver Falls. Old-growth trees dominate the forest found along the route, making the trail a cool and shady respite from hot and sunny meadows. Squirrels and woodpeckers are often found scurrying among the timber while deer and elk browse the forest floor. Anglers are frequent visitors to the trail, thanks to its easy access to the trout-laden river.

Silver Falls is a thunderous waterfall, where the glacial-fed Ohanapecosh makes a series of cascades. The climax is a 70-foot drop into a large punch bowl. The trail crosses a deep gorge via a bridge immediately below the falls, showering hikers in mist when the river is roaring. Although beautiful, the falls are dangerous if explored off-trail. Keep a short leash on little ones and stick to the established trail. The loop heads directly back to Ohanapecosh Campground along the opposite bank of the river, a quick and easy outing.

User Groups: Hikers only. No dogs, horses, or mountain bikes are allowed. No wheelchair access.

Permits: This trail is accessible year-round. A National Parks Pass is required to enter the park.

Maps: For a map of Mount Rainier National Park, contact the Outdoor Recreation Information Center at the downtown Seattle REI. For a topographic map, ask Green Trails for No. 270, Mount Rainier East, or ask the USGS for Ohanapecosh Hot Springs and Chinook Pass.

Directions: From Puyallup, drive east 56 miles on Highway 410 to Highway 123. Turn right (south) and drive 13 miles to Ohanapecosh Campground. Turn left into the campground; the trailhead is near the visitor center.

Contact: Mount Rainier National Park, White River Wilderness Information Center, 70004 Hwy. 410 E., Enumclaw, WA 98022, 360/569-2211 x6030.

54 GROVE OF THE PATRIARCHS
1.5 mi/1.0 hr   🏃1 ⛰9

near Stevens Canyon entrance in Mount Rainier National Park

Map 5.2, page 256   **BEST (**

Competing with Olympic rainforests, here, in the low valley of the Ohanapecosh River, is one of Washington's most impressive stands of old-growth timber. On a small island in the middle of the river, this grove of Douglas fir, western hemlock, and western red cedar has been growing undisturbed for nearly 1,000 years. That's right, a full millennium. Isolated by the river from the surrounding forest, Grove of the Patriarchs has been able to avoid fire and other natural disturbances, living up to its full potential. This is a true climax forest. The trail to Grove of the Patriarchs is flat and easily navigated. The trail heads upstream for 0.5 mile through an impressive (yet comparatively small) forest. The trail crosses the river via bridge and loops around the island. Many of the trees measure more than 25 feet around the trunk, with one granddaddy fir rounding out at 35 feet in circumference. In this ancient place, the only hazard is a strained neck.

User Groups: Hikers only. No dogs, horses, or mountain bikes are allowed. No wheelchair access.

Permits: This area is accessible mid-May–October. A National Parks Pass is required to enter the park.

Maps: For a map of Mount Rainier National Park, contact the Outdoor Recreation Information Center at the downtown Seattle REI. For a topographic map, ask Green Trails for No. 270, Mount Rainier East, or ask the USGS for Ohanapecosh Hot Springs.

Directions: From Puyallup, drive east 56 miles on Highway 410 to Highway 123. Turn right (south) and drive 11 miles to Stevens Canyon Road/entrance. Turn right and the trailhead is just beyond the guard station on the right.

Contact: Mount Rainier National Park, White River Wilderness Information Center, 70004

Hwy. 410 E., Enumclaw, WA 98022, 360/569-2211 x6030.

55 EAST SIDE TRAIL
3.0–5.0 mi/1.5–3.5 hr

near Stevens Canyon entrance in Mount
Rainier National Park

Map 5.2, page 256

East Side Trail follows Chinook Creek and
Ohanopecosh River as they wind their ways
through exceptional old-growth forests. The
trail has three trailheads, including near Cayuse Pass and Ohanapecosh Campgrounds.
The distance between these two endpoints
is 12 miles. The best access, however, is via
Deer Creek in the middle of the route. This
0.5-mile access trail joins East Side Trail
within a mile of spectacular waterfalls to the
north and south. Deer Creek Trail drops to
East Side Trail at the backcountry camp of
Deer Creek. The best option is to turn left
(south) and follow the level trail 1 mile to
where it crosses Chinook Creek. Here, the
stream cascades through a narrow gorge directly below the footbridge. Bigger Stafford
Falls is another mile down the trail. From
Deer Creek Camp, the trail climbs kindly
toward Cayuse Pass, passing more falls and
cascades. This is a great trail for families with
little ones; just keep a short leash on them
near all stream crossings.

User Groups: Hikers only. No dogs, horses, or
mountain bikes are allowed. No wheelchair
access.

Permits: This area is usually accessible April–
October. Permits are not required. Parking
and access are free.

Maps: For a map of Mount Rainier National
Park, contact the Outdoor Recreation In-
formation Center at the downtown Seattle
REI. For a topographic map, ask Green Trails
for No. 270, Mount Rainier East, or ask the
USGS for Ohanapecosh Hot Springs and
Chinook Pass.

Directions: From Puyallup, drive east 56 miles

on Highway 410 to Highway 123. Turn right
(south) and drive 4 miles to the signed trailhead on the right side of the road.

Contact: Mount Rainier National Park, White
River Wilderness Information Center, 70004
Hwy. 410 E., Enumclaw, WA 98022, 360/569-
2211 x6030.

56 AMERICAN RIDGE
10.2–26.2 mi/5.0 hr–3 days

in William O. Douglas Wilderness of Wenatchee
National Forest

Map 5.2, page 256

A major route bisecting the northern William
O. Douglas Wilderness, American Ridge Trail
offers hikers many options to customize a hike.
From the Bumping River all the way up to the
PCT, American Ridge stretches more than 26
miles. Eight different access trails, including
the PCT, create a whole slew of opportunities. The eastern end is primarily high forests;
the middle third reaches into high ridgeline
meadows with lots of views; the western end
offers access to a number of high-country lakes
and meadows (see the next listing).

Four trails reach American Ridge from
Highway 410, with Mesatchee Creek Trail
a favorite. Mesatchee Trail climbs 5.3 miles
and 2,200 feet through forest and intermittent
meadows to the ridge. East of this junction
delivers more than 5 miles of meadows. Also
from Highway 410, Goat Peak Trail climbs
3,000 feet in 4 miles to a lookout.

Three trails reach the ridge from Bumping
River, Goose Prairie Trail being the preferred
route. This is a 5.1-mile ascent to the ridge.
Hike west for tiny Kettle Lake and miles of
meadows. All of these trails are very hot in
the late summer and always lack any water, an
important consideration. They're also lonely
routes into a beautiful backcountry.

User Groups: Hikers, leashed dogs, and horses.
No mountain bikes are allowed. No wheelchair access.

Permits: This trail is accessible April–October.

A federal Northwest Forest Pass is required to park here.

Maps: For a map of Wenatchee National Forest, contact the Outdoor Recreation Information Center at the downtown Seattle REI. For a topographic map, ask Green Trails for No. 271, Bumping Lake, and No. 272, Old Scab Mountain, or ask the USGS for Norse Peak, Cougar Peak, Bumping Lake, Goose Prairie, and Old Scab Mountain.

Directions: From Yakima, drive west on Highway 410 to Forest Service Road 460, just west of Lodgepole Campground. Turn left and drive 0.3 mile to the trailhead at road's end.

Contact: Wenatchee National Forest, Naches Ranger Station, 10237 U.S. 12, Naches, WA 98937, 509/653-1401.

57 COUGAR LAKES
12.0–20.0 mi/6.0 hr–2 days

in William O. Douglas Wilderness of Wenatchee National Forest

Map 5.2, page 256

Cougar Lakes lie at the western end of American Ridge, directly below the Cascade Crest. They make a great day hike or easy overnighter. Also in the area is the PCT, which lends itself to an excellent loop hike connecting to Cougar Lakes. This is a great weekend hike, encompassing one of the best sections of PCT in southern Washington. Meadows and mountain lakes are prominent themes on both routes. Each route is great for hikers of all abilities, gaining moderate elevation gently.

To reach Cougar Lakes, the route begins with Swamp Lake Trail, a gradual, forested ascent to Swamp Lake (4 miles) and American Ridge Trail (4.6 miles). Hike west toward PCT; Cougar Lakes junction (5.2 miles) cuts south to the two lakes (6 miles). Around the lakes, subalpine meadows unfold beneath tall, rocky cliffs. Numerous campsites are around the basin. Whether on a day hike or overnighter, be sure to scramble the crest for a view of Mount Rainier.

To hike the longer loop on PCT, continue west on American Ridge Trail toward PCT (6.7 miles). The loop route goes south on PCT, passing Two Lakes, Crag Lake, and Buck Lake. This is meadow country with prime viewing of Mount Rainier and many other mountains. The route intersects Bumping River Trail (13.1 miles) and turns east to return to the trailhead (20 miles). All lakes along the way offer camping and are the sole sources of water.

User Groups: Hikers, leashed dogs, and horses. No mountain bikes are allowed. No wheelchair access.

Permits: This trail is accessible June–mid-October. A federal Northwest Forest Pass is required to park here.

Maps: For a map of Wenatchee National Forest, contact the Outdoor Recreation Information Center at the downtown Seattle REI. For a topographic map, ask Green Trails for No. 271, Bumping Lake, or ask the USGS for Cougar Lake.

Directions: From Yakima, drive west on Highway 410 to Bumping Lake Road (Forest Service Road 1800). Turn left and drive 17 miles to the trailhead at road's end.

Contact: Wenatchee National Forest, Naches Ranger Station, 10237 U.S. 12, Naches, WA 98937, 509/653-1401.

58 MOUNT AIX
11.0 mi/6.0 hr

in William O. Douglas Wilderness of Wenatchee National Forest

Map 5.2, page 256

Steep, rocky, and downright treacherous at times, Mount Aix does its best to discourage visitors. It stands at 7,766 feet, and hikers must scale 4,000 feet in just 5.5 miles to reach the summit. And the mountain offers no water to aid the trek, a harsh slight on the hot, exposed slopes. Demanding as it may be, Mount Aix rewards with much more than it asks. Miles of meadows chock-full of wildflowers highlight the upper half as do exceptional views of Mount Rainier and surrounding mountains. Mount Aix is definitely best for seasoned hikers who are looking for a good workout.

Mount Aix Trail rests on the east side of the Cascade Crest, meaning the route receives less snow than trails just a few miles west. This is one of the earliest high-country routes to open in the state. Switchbacks are the name of the game, rising out of the forest into the open meadows. At 3.7 miles is a junction with Nelson Ridge Trail. This is a nice option, offering several miles of ridgeline meadows before dozens of miles in the William O. Douglas Wilderness. Head right and climb another 2 miles to the summit. This last effort to the trail's climax is rocky and sometimes a scramble.

User Groups: Hikers, leashed dogs, and horses. No mountain bikes are allowed. No wheelchair access.

Permits: This trail is accessible mid-May–mid-October. A federal Northwest Forest Pass is required to park here.

Maps: For a map of Wenatchee National Forest, contact the Outdoor Recreation Information Center at the downtown Seattle REI. For a topographic map, ask Green Trails for No. 271, Bumping Lake, or ask the USGS for Timberwolf Mountain and Bumping Lake.

Directions: From Yakima, drive west on Highway 410 to Bumping Lake Road (Forest Service Road 1800). Turn left and drive 14 miles to Forest Service Road 1808. Turn left and drive 1.5 miles to the signed trailhead on the left side.

Contact: Wenatchee National Forest, Naches Ranger Station, 10237 U.S. 12, Naches, WA 98937, 509/653-1401.

59 SAWTOOTH LAKES
7.0 mi/4.0 hr 👫2 ⛰8

south of Mount Rainier in Gifford Pinchot National Forest

Map 5.2, page 256

Along the north side of Sawtooth Ridge lie four high lakes among forest and meadows. Just outside the national park boundary, these lakes are highly ignored by the masses headed for Mount Rainier. That's good news for peace and quiet, at least until July 1. After that date motorcycles are allowed on the trail. Visit here in late May or June, and you'll have these great swimming holes all to yourself. Old forest and peek-a-boo views of The Mountain vie for attention along the way. And to cap off the hike is a neck-straining view of High Rock's 600-foot vertical cliff.

The best route to Sawtooth Lakes is via Teeley Creek Trail. After a quick climb past Pothole Lake, the trail levels out completely. At Osborne Mountain Trail junction (0.7 mile), stay left on Teeley Creek Trail and soon reach the two largest and best lakes, Bertha May (1.2 miles) and Granite (1.8 miles). The trail continues along the north side of Sawtooth Ridge to meadows directly beneath the cliffs of High Rock (3.1 miles). Although the trail continues 2 miles to Cora Lake and additional trailheads, the meadows below High Rock are a great turnaround. On hot summer days, a dip in the lakes will be calling your name.

User Groups: Hikers, leashed dogs, horses, mountain bikes, and motorcycles (motorcycles allowed after June 30). No wheelchair access.

Permits: This trail is accessible mid-June–October. No permits are required. Parking and access are free.

Maps: For a map of Gifford Pinchot National Forest, contact the Outdoor Recreation Information Center at the downtown Seattle REI. For a topographic map, ask Green Trails for No. 301, Randle, or ask the USGS for Sawtooth Ridge.

Directions: From Tacoma, drive south 40

miles on Highway 7 to Elbe. Turn east on Highway 706 and drive 7 miles to Forest Service Road 52. Turn right and drive 4.5 miles to Forest Service Road 84. Turn right and drive 1.5 miles to Forest Service Road 8410. Turn right and drive 4.5 miles to the trailhead on the left.

Contact: Gifford Pinchot National Forest, Cowlitz Valley Ranger Station, 10024 U.S. 12, Randle, WA 98377, 360/497-1100.

60 HIGH ROCK LOOKOUT
3.2 mi/2.0 hr

south of Mount Rainier in Gifford Pinchot National Forest

Map 5.2, page 256

Towering over the adjacent Sawtooth Ridge at 5,685 feet, this peak is certainly high. And with a sheer 600-foot drop on its north face, it definitely qualifies as a rock. And yet the name is an understatement. High Rock might be an imposing sight from below, but the Forest Service Lookout stationed on the summit boasts some of the best views in the Gifford Pinchot. The mountain is separated from Mount Rainier National Park only by Nisqually Valley. Thus, broad views but sparse crowds.

Atop the tallest peak in Sawtooth Range, High Rock Lookout Trail endures a short but sharp climb: 1,600 feet in just 1.5 miles. It wastes little time reaching high meadows and glorious views along High Rock's southern arm. Southern-oriented meadows means sunny, exposed, and dry. Bring water. The lookout stands at 5,685 feet and revels in views of Goat Rocks, Mount Adams, and Mount St. Helens. That enormous mountain just a stone's throw away is Mount Rainier. The northern edge is a sharp drop, so watch your step. Over the edge lie three high lakes along Sawtooth Ridge (see previous listing).

User Groups: Hikers and leashed dogs. No horses or mountain bikes are allowed. No wheelchair access.

Permits: This trail is accessible mid-June–October. No permits are required. Parking and access are free.

Maps: For a map of Gifford Pinchot National Forest, contact the Outdoor Recreation Information Center at the downtown Seattle REI. For a topographic map, ask Green Trails for No. 301, Randle, or ask the USGS for Sawtooth Ridge.

Directions: From Tacoma, drive south 40 miles on Highway 7 to Elbe. Turn east on Highway 706 and drive 7 miles to Forest Service Road 52. Turn right and drive 1 mile to Forest Service Road 85. Continue straight and drive 5 miles to Forest Service Road 8440. Stay to the left and drive 4.5 miles to the trailhead on the left at Towhead Gap.

Contact: Gifford Pinchot National Forest, Cowlitz Valley Ranger Station, 10024 U.S. 12, Randle, WA 98377, 360/497-1100.

61 TATOOSH RIDGE
5.0 mi/3.5 hr

south of Mount Rainier in Tatoosh Wilderness of Gifford Pinchot National Forest

Map 5.2, page 256

Tatoosh Range stands less than 10 miles from Mount Rainier (as the crow flies), practically a smaller sister to the dominating mountain. And Tatoosh Ridge Trail boasts incredible views of The Mountain, yet it seems so far away—far away from the crowds in the national park, that is. Just south of the park boundary but protected by its own wilderness, Tatoosh Range receives just a fraction of the visitors that trails inside the park do. It's good habitat for lonely views, high lakes, and mountain meadows.

Tatoosh Ridge Trail runs along the southern spine of Tatoosh Ridge, with trailheads at either end. Both ends are steep switchback shuffles, but the northern trailhead offers access to much more scenic terrain. Tackle 2,600 feet of elevation in just 2 miles before reaching Tatoosh Lakes junction. This side trail (1 mile round-trip) leads up to a saddle of epic views and down to Tatoosh Lakes, lying among rocky slopes and meadows. Several great camps are found along the lakeshore.

From the first junction, Tatoosh Ridge Trail continues over rocky and exposed terrain to another junction (3.9 miles), this time leading up to Tatoosh Lookout. At 6,310 feet, here are your epic views. The trail drops from the second junction, below Butter Peak and to the southern trailhead (9 miles one-way). Pack sunscreen and extra water, as the trail is hot, often exposed, and without water, save for the lakes.

User Groups: Hikers and horses only. No dogs or mountain bikes are allowed. No wheelchair access.

Permits: This trail is accessible July–September. No permits are required. Parking and access are free.

Maps: For a map of Gifford Pinchot National Forest, contact the Outdoor Recreation Information Center at the downtown Seattle REI. For a topographic map, ask Green Trails for No. 302, Packwood, or ask the USGS for Tatoosh Lakes.

Directions: To the northern trailhead: From Packwood, drive north 4 miles on Skate Creek Road (Forest Service Road 52) to Forest Service Road 5270. Turn right and drive 6 miles to the signed trailhead on the right.

To the southern trailhead: From Packwood, drive north on Skate Creek Road and turn right on Forest Service Road 5290. Drive 5 miles, staying on the main gravel road, then veer left, remaining on Forest Service Road 5290 for 3.5 miles to the trailhead at road's end.

Contact: Gifford Pinchot National Forest, Cowlitz Valley Ranger Station, 10024 U.S. 12, Randle, WA 98377, 360/497-1100.

62 CLEAR FORK
19.2 mi/8.0 hr

east of Packwood in Goat Rocks Wilderness of Gifford Pinchot National Forest

Map 5.2, page 256

Clear Fork Trail offers something rarely found south of the North Cascades: a long, undisturbed river valley hike up to the PCT. Although many river valleys in the area were logged long ago, the upper Clear Fork of Cowlitz River survived the ax and saw. That's a good thing, for the bubbling water of this stream makes for a serene scene. This is an ideal hike for families, with lots to see and very little elevation change in the first 7 miles.

Clear Fork Trail begins on a level, timbered plateau above the river. Situated in an open meadow, Lily Lake (1.5 miles) makes a great swimming hole and turnaround for hikers seeking a shorter hike. Beyond, Clear Fork rambles through old-growth forest and meets the river (5.5 miles). Anglers will note that trout inhabit this wild, rarely fished water. The forests are full of deer and elk, and maybe even a black bear or two. The trail eventually fords the river (7 miles) and climbs to the PCT (9.6 miles).

User Groups: Hikers, and horses only. No dogs or mountain bikes are allowed. No wheelchair access.

Permits: This trail is accessible year-round. No permits are required. Parking and access are free.

Maps: For a map of Gifford Pinchot National Forest, contact the Outdoor Recreation Information Center at the downtown Seattle REI. For a topographic map, ask Green Trails for No. 303, White Pass, or ask the USGS for White Pass and Packwood.

Directions: From Randle, drive east 21 miles on Highway 12 to Forest Service Road 46. Turn right (south) and drive 9 miles to the trailhead at road's end.

Contact: Gifford Pinchot National Forest, Cowlitz Valley Ranger Station, 10024 U.S. 12, Randle, WA 98377, 360/497-1100.

63 BLUFF LAKE
3.0-13.2 mi/2.0-8.0 hr

east of Packwood in Goat Rocks Wilderness
of Gifford Pinchot National Forest

Map 5.2, page 256

On the map, Bluff Lake fails to muster much excitement, appearing as nothing more than a small body of water atop a low ridge. Once boots hit trail, however, it's apparent that a great trip is in store. Bluff Lake Trail climbs to its namesake and beyond, running 6.6 miles along the crest of Coal Creek Mountain. Old-growth forest gives way to subalpine meadows. No map mentions that your most likely traveling companions will be deer, elk, and mountain goats. And the map's biggest secret is huckleberries, acres of them.

Bluff Lake Trail gets under way in a mean way, quickly rising 1,000 feet to Bluff Lake (1.5 miles) in the forest atop the ridge. The lake is a good place to turn around for a short hike, but the best is yet to come. The trail maintains its ascent to the crest of Coal Creek Mountain and mellows out along the ridge. The forest grows increasingly sparse, giving way to meadows full of views and huckleberries. This is a good place to see the Goat Rocks, several miles to the southeast. At 6.6 miles, Bluff Lake Trail ends atop a high butte, at a junction with Clear Lost Trail (dropping to Lost Hat Lake, 1 mile) and Packwood Lake Trail (dropping to Lost Lake, 1.4 miles). Trips to these lakes can make your hike slightly longer. Other than Bluff Lake, there's no water to be found along the route.

User Groups: Hikers and horses only. No dogs or mountain bikes are allowed. No wheelchair access.

Permits: This trail is accessible mid-May–October. No permits are required. Parking and access are free.

Maps: For a map of Gifford Pinchot National Forest, contact the Outdoor Recreation Information Center at the downtown Seattle REI. For a topographic map, ask Green Trails

for No. 302, Packwood, or ask the USGS for Ohanapecosh.

Directions: From Randle, drive east 21 miles on Highway 12 to Forest Service Road 46. Turn right (south) and drive 2 miles to Forest Service Road 4610. Turn right and drive 2 miles to Forest Service Road 4612. Turn left and drive 3 miles to the trailhead at a sharp left turn in the road.

Contact: Gifford Pinchot National Forest, Cowlitz Valley Ranger Station, 10024 U.S. 12, Randle, WA 98377, 360/497-1100.

64 DUMBBELL LAKE LOOP
15.8 mi/2 days

southeast of Mount Rainier in William O.
Douglas Wilderness of Gifford Pinchot
National Forest

Map 5.2, page 256

Dumbbell Lake knows how to treat a hiker well. It offers not only beautiful scenery but the opportunity for lots of exploring. It's situated on a high plateau, where the firs are plentiful and form a nice surrounding forest. On the north side, a connected chain of small islands extends into the lake and encourages lots of investigation.

The hike to Dumbbell begins along the PCT out of White Pass. Follow PCT for 6.5 miles as it climbs gently onto the plateau. The trail passes small Sand Lake before dropping to Buesch Lake, where good camping is to be had. Abandon PCT and join Trail 56, where Dumbbell lies just 0.5 mile away. The best camping is found near the middle of the lake on the north side, beyond the burned section at the west end. The trail continues past Cramer Lake while gradually dropping elevation back to the trailhead.

On these high flatlands, dense groves of subalpine firs and mountain hemlocks frequently give way to open meadows. The many small lakes and large open meadows on this high plateau make for great day excursions. If you try this hike in the summer, expect people and bugs. Both can be pesky, but don't miss this hike.

User Groups: Hikers and horses only. No dogs or mountain bikes are allowed. No wheelchair access.

Permits: This trail is usually accessible July–mid-October. No permits are required. Parking and access are free.

Maps: For a map of Gifford Pinchot National Forest, contact the Outdoor Recreation Information Center at the downtown Seattle REI. For topographic maps, ask Green Trails for No. 303, White Pass, or ask the USGS for White Pass and Spiral Lake.

Directions: From Randle, drive east on Highway 12 to White Pass Campground, on the north side of the highway just east of the pass. The trailhead is located just before the campground entrance and is signed as the Pacific Crest Trail.

Contact: Gifford Pinchot National Forest, Cowlitz Valley Ranger Station, 10024 U.S. 12, Randle, WA 98377, 360/497-1100.

65 TWIN SISTERS
2.4 mi/1.5 hr

southeast of Mount Rainier in William O. Douglas Wilderness of Gifford Pinchot National Forest

Map 5.2, page 256

It's almost too easy to get to Twin Sisters. A place so beautiful usually loses out when access is so easy, and that's nearly the case here. A pair of large, stunning high lakes are the Twin Sisters, surrounded by a wilderness of firs and hemlocks. The lakes are popular destinations for folks of all types because of their easy accessibility, great camping, and extensive opportunities for side trips, including the great Tumac Mountain.

This hike serves well both as a day hike or as an extended backpacking trip. The grade up Deep Creek is short and never taxing. The lakes are surrounded by forests of subalpine fir and mountain hemlock. To the north, almost

between the lakes, lies a small butte. Most of the terrain in this area is gentle, rolling hills. At the lakes, excessive use through the years created numerous campsites. Camping must now be at least 200 feet from the lakeshore to keep damage to a minimum. If the crowds feel too thick at Twin Sisters, many other small lakes are worth seeking out.

A necessary side trip is Tumac Mountain, a relatively small and young High Cascades volcano. Just 2 miles from the east lake, the 6,340-foot summit of Tumac includes a crater and stunning views of Mount Rainier. Other easy expeditions are to Fryingpan Lake, Snow Lake, or Blakenship Lakes, and the PCT is not far.

User Groups: Hikers, leashed dogs, and horses. No mountain bikes are allowed. No wheelchair access.

Permits: This area is usually accessible July–early October. A federal Northwest Forest Pass is required to park here.

Maps: For a map of Gifford Pinchot National Forest, contact the Outdoor Recreation Information Center at the downtown Seattle REI. For a topographic map, ask Green Trails for No. 303, White Pass, or ask the USGS for Spiral Lake, Bumping Lake, and White Pass.

Directions: From Yakima, drive west on Highway 410 to Bumping Lake Road (Forest Service Road 1800). Turn left and drive 13 miles to Forest Service Road 1808. Turn left and drive 6.5 miles to Deer Creek Campground and the trailhead at road's end.

Contact: Gifford Pinchot National Forest, Cowlitz Valley Ranger Station, 10024 U.S. 12, Randle, WA 98377, 360/497-1100.

66 SPIRAL BUTTE
12.0 mi/6.0 hr

southeast of Mount Rainier in William O. Douglas Wilderness of Gifford Pinchot National Forest

Map 5.2, page 256

Forget all the gear, time, and trouble it takes to summit Mount Rainier or Mount Adams.

Getting atop a High Cascades volcano can be done in a day with nothing more than a sturdy pair of hiking boots. That's the allure of Spiral Butte, a small peak just north of Highway 12 near White Pass. The scene from the top is panoramic, offering views of Mount Rainier, Goat Rocks, and other surrounding peaks and ridges.

The trail is a steady climb nearly all the way, gaining 2,500 feet. Sand Ridge Trail climbs through a typical east-side forest. Take a left onto Shellrock Lake Trail (3 miles) and another left on Spiral Butte Trail (4 miles). Here, western larches begin to appear and add some needed color on autumn days. Spiral Butte is so named because of a long, twisting arm of the mountain that swings out from the north. It is on this arm that the trail climbs, providing a great alternative to switchbacks but nevertheless gaining 1,100 feet in the final 2 miles.

Spiral Butte is relatively young, about one million years old, and consists of andesite, a volcanic rock that breaks into large and beautiful gray chunks. Large slopes of talus are visible, revealing the difficulty vegetation can encounter when trying to pioneer such tough terrain.

User Groups: Hikers, leashed dogs, mountain bikes, and horses. No wheelchair access.

Permits: This trail is usually accessible mid-June–early October. A federal Northwest Forest Pass is required to park here.

Maps: For a map of Gifford Pinchot National Forest, contact the Outdoor Recreation Information Center at the downtown Seattle REI. For topographic maps, ask Green Trails for No. 303, White Pass, or ask the USGS for Spiral Butte.

Directions: From Randle, drive east on Highway 12 to White Pass. Continue east on Highway 12 for 6 miles to the trailhead (signed "Sand Ridge") on the north side of the highway.

Contact: Gifford Pinchot National Forest, Cowlitz Valley Ranger Station, 10024 U.S. 12, Randle, WA 98377, 360/497-1100.

67 IRONSTONE MOUNTAIN

11.0 mi/6.0 hr   🏃2 △9

north of White Pass in William O. Douglas Wilderness of Wenatchee National Forest

Map 5.2, page 256

Aided by a high trailhead (elevation 6,300 feet), Ironstone Mountain presents the easiest ridge hike in the area. Sparse, open forest regularly gives way to open meadows and great views. Ironstone Mountain Trail leaves Forest Service Road 199 and follows the ups and downs of the ridge to Ironstone Mountain. Along the way are several trail junctions, including Burnt Mountain Trail (2.5 miles) and Shellrock Peak (4.5 miles). These two side trails can be combined to form a loop option down (way down) to Rattlesnake Creek and back. A full trip out to Ironstone Mountain is nearly 20 miles round-trip. The best option is to hike the ridge to Shellrock Peak Trail and head north on this trail. Within a mile is easy access to Shellrock Peak, a panoramic vista at 6,835 feet. This is a great viewpoint to see Mount Rainier, the Cascade Crest, and Goat Rocks. Remember to carry plenty of water. This trail is on the east side of the Cascades and can be extremely hot and dry.

User Groups: Hikers, leashed dogs, and horses. No mountain bikes are allowed. No wheelchair access.

Permits: This trail is accessible June–October. A federal Northwest Forest Pass is required to park here.

Maps: For a map of Wenatchee National Forest, contact the Outdoor Recreation Information Center at the downtown Seattle REI. For a topographic map, ask Green Trails for No. 304, Rimrock, or ask the USGS for Spiral Butte and Rimrock Lake.

Directions: From White Pass, drive east 18 miles to Bethel Ridge Road (Forest Service Road 1500) at Bethel Ridge Sno-Park. Turn left and drive 9.5 miles to Forest Service Road 199. Turn left and drive 2.5 miles to the trailhead at road's end.

Contact: Wenatchee National Forest, Naches

Ranger Station, 10237 U.S. 12, Naches, WA 98937, 509/653-1401.

68 ROUND MOUNTAIN

5.0 mi/3.0 hr

south of White Pass in Goat Rocks Wilderness of Wenatchee National Forest

Map 5.2, page 256

Short but steep, Round Mountain Trail climbs to an abandoned lookout and onward over Twin Peaks to the PCT. This rugged trail shows few qualms about reaching its destination, gaining 1,600 feet in just 2.5 miles. Round Mountain Trail begins in open forest, but the timber gives way to rocky meadows near the top of Round Mountain. This is a good place to see elk and deer foraging in the forest. At the summit, 5,970 feet, stands an old, shuttered lookout no longer in use by the Forest Service. The views, looking out over miles of the Cascade Crest, are grand—north to Spiral Butte and Mount Rainier and south to Goat Rocks. Beyond the summit, Round Mountain Trail continues over Twin Peaks (4.5 miles) to the PCT (6.5 miles). Be sure to carry plenty of water and sunscreen, as this is a hot and dry trail.

User Groups: Hikers, leashed dogs, and horses. No mountain bikes are allowed. No wheelchair access.

Permits: This trail is accessible June–October. A federal Northwest Forest Pass is required to park here.

Maps: For a map of Gifford Pinchot National Forest, contact the Outdoor Recreation Information Center at the downtown Seattle REI. For a topographic map, ask Green Trails for No. 303, White Pass, or ask the USGS for Spiral Butte.

Directions: From White Pass, drive east 7.5 miles on Highway 12 to Tieton Road (Forest Service Road 1200). Turn right (south) and drive 3 miles to Forest Service Road 830. Turn right and drive 4.5 miles to the trailhead on the left side.

Contact: Wenatchee National Forest, Naches Ranger Station, 10237 U.S. 12, Naches, WA 98937, 509/653-1401.

69 SHOE LAKE

13.5 mi/8.0 hr

south of White Pass in Goat Rocks Wilderness of Gifford Pinchot National Forest

Map 5.2, page 256

Some of the best stretches of the PCT are here in Goat Rocks Wilderness. Though not as celebrated as the rocky crags of the Goat Rocks peaks, Shoe Lake is a scenic hike and certainly carries its own weight. Starting directly from Highway 12, the PCT traverses 7 miles of open forest and wide open meadows to reach refreshing Shoe Lake.

The PCT leaves White Pass and progressively climbs through open forest, passing small Ginette Lake (2.2 miles). The PCT eventually finds itself swamped in meadows (5 miles) and awash in wildflower color in late June. For those who have made it this far, the best is still to come. Mount Rainier comes into view as the PCT skirts Hogback Mountain and ascends to a high saddle (6.3 miles) overlooking the basin of Shoe Lake with Pinegrass Ridge in the distance. Reaching Shoe Lake requires a steep, short drop into the basin.

The hike to Shoe Lake is very hot and dry, especially during late summer. Until you reach the lake, water is nonexistent, an important consideration when packing before your trip. Camping is highly discouraged in Shoe Lake Basin because of heavy use in the past. Overnight hikers must continue to Hidden Spring (8.5 miles) or cross-country camp more than 200 yards from the trail.

User Groups: Hikers, leashed dogs, and horses. No mountain bikes are allowed. No wheelchair access.

Permits: This trail is accessible June–October. A federal Northwest Forest Pass is required to park here.

Maps: For a map of Gifford Pinchot National

Forest, contact the Outdoor Recreation Information Center at the downtown Seattle REI. For a topographic map, ask Green Trails for No. 303, White Pass, or ask the USGS for White Pass.

Directions: From White Pass, drive east 0.7 mile on Highway 12 to the Pacific Crest Trailhead at White Pass Campground. Park here, on the north side of the highway. The trailhead is on the south side.

Contact: Gifford Pinchot National Forest, Cowlitz Valley Ranger Station, 10024 U.S. 12, Randle, WA 98377, 360/497-1100.

70 NORTH FORK TIETON

14.0 mi/1-2 days

south of White Pass in Goat Rocks Wilderness of Wenatchee National Forest

Map 5.2, page 256

North Fork Tieton Trail makes a terrific run up to the PCT and an amazing basin below the glaciers of Goat Rocks. This is one of the best ways to reach PCT, just before it climbs into the Goat Rocks. Although this isn't Mount Rainier, Goat Rocks still gets fairly crowded on a summer weekend. This northern side of Goat Rocks, however, sees a fraction of the use compared to the western side.

North Fork Tieton Trail climbs at a steady grade before making a steep rise to Tieton Pass (4.9 miles). Old-growth forests line the trail, with large timber despite being east of the Cascade Crest. Along the way are views of enormous Tieton Valley, ringed by tall, snowy peaks. Gilbert Peak and Old Snowy tower from the heart of the Goat Rocks, at the head of the basin. To the east stand the rugged, rocky slopes of Tieton Peak and Devils Horns.

The PCT runs north-south from Tieton Pass. Head south to reach a junction for McCall Basin (6.5 miles). Break south along McCall Basin Trail and wander into a subalpine wonderland. Acres of meadows run into rocky slopes. Large herds of mountain goats

are regular visitors in the area. Since McCall Basin makes a long day hike, campsites are scattered about, ideal for Leave-No-Trace camping.

User Groups: Hikers, leashed dogs, and horses. No mountain bikes are allowed. No wheelchair access.

Permits: This trail is accessible mid-June–mid-October. A federal Northwest Forest Pass is required to park here.

Maps: For a map of Wenatchee National Forest, contact the Outdoor Recreation Information Center at the downtown Seattle REI. For a topographic map, ask Green Trails for No. 303, White Pass, or ask the USGS for Pinegrass Ridge and Old Snowy Mountain.

Directions: From White Pass, drive east 7.5 miles on Highway 12 to Tieton Road (Forest Service Road 1200). Turn right (south) and drive 3 miles to Forest Service Road 1207. Continue straight onto Road 1207 and drive 4.5 miles to the trailhead at road's end.

Contact: Wenatchee National Forest, Naches Ranger Station, 10237 U.S. 12, Naches, WA 98937, 509/653-1401.

71 BEAR CREEK MOUNTAIN

12.8 mi/8.0 hr   ☒4 ◩10

southeast of White Pass in Goat Rocks Wilderness of Wenatchee National Forest

Map 5.2, page 256

As far as forgotten and ignored trails in the Goat Rocks go, this is it. Bear Creek Mountain Trail makes a steep trip to the summit along the ridge dividing the North and South Fork Tieton Rivers. Because of an elevation gain of more than 3,000 feet, most hikers select other trails in the area. That's a shame, because high-country meadows full of wildflowers, maybe even mountain goats, reward those who make the trip.

Bear Creek Mountain Trail wastes little time before starting a steep ascent out of the South Fork Tieton Valley. The trees are big, but this being the east side of the Cascade

Crest, the forest is open. Meadows begin to appear as the trail reaches a junction with Tieton Meadows Trail (5.4 miles). The views are grand from this north-facing vista, including Mount Rainier, which outshines any other peak.

To gain panoramic views, one must turn south and scramble nearly 1,000 feet in 1 mile to the summit of Bear Creek Mountain. To say the least, this is an impressive location from which to study Goat Rocks. Hikers who pack a pair of binoculars this far will be glad they did. Bear Creek Mountain Trail passes no water along the way, so plan to carry plenty.

User Groups: Hikers, leashed dogs, and horses, and mountain bikes are allowed. No wheelchair access.

Permits: This trail is accessible July–October. A federal Northwest Forest Pass is required to park here.

Maps: For a map of Wenatchee National Forest, contact the Outdoor Recreation Information Center at the downtown Seattle REI. For a topographic map, ask Green Trails for No. 303, White Pass, or ask the USGS for Pinegrass Ridge.

Directions: From White Pass, drive east 7.5 miles on Highway 12 to Tieton Road (Forest Service Road 1200). Turn right (south) and drive 12 miles to Forest Service Road 1000. Turn right and drive 12 miles to the trailhead at road's end.

Contact: Wenatchee National Forest, Naches Ranger Station, 10237 U.S. 12, Naches, WA 98937, 509/653-1401.

72 SOUTH FORK TIETON RIVER

13.9 mi/1-2 days   🥾2   ⛰10

southeast of White Pass in Goat Rocks Wilderness of Wenatchee National Forest

> **Map 5.2, page 256**

Free from the crowds that pack much of the Goat Rocks Wilderness in summer, South Fork Tieton River Trail offers access to one of the mountains' most beautiful basins. The trail follows the river upstream before splitting to make a loop around the top of the expansive basin. The beauty of this trail layout (it's shaped like a lasso) is that very little of the trail is walked twice. Rocky peaks of Gilbert Peak and Klickitat Divide loom over the loop, home to fields of wildflowers and herds of mountain goats.

South Fork Tieton Trail remains exceptionally level and easy for the first several miles. Open Conrad Meadows features some very large timber. Elk and deer are common. The trail comes to a junction (4.3 miles), where the loop begins. This is also where the climbing starts. Either side of the loop climbs quickly to the upper slopes of the basin before leveling out. Long, narrow Surprise Lake is truly a surprise along the forested slopes, and it makes a great place to pitch camp. Mountain goats are frequent along the rocky rim bordering the basin. Hikers can make great excursions among the rocky meadows to the crest of Klickitat Divide for views of the surrounding Goat Rocks.

User Groups: Hikers, leashed dogs, and horses. No mountain bikes are allowed. No wheelchair access.

Permits: This trail is accessible July–October. A federal Northwest Forest Pass is required to park here.

Maps: For a map of Wenatchee National Forest, contact the Outdoor Recreation Information Center at the downtown Seattle REI. For a topographic map, ask Green Trails for No. 303, White Pass, or No. 335, Walupt Lake, or ask the USGS for Jennies Butte and Pinegrass Ridge.

Directions: From White Pass, drive east 7.5 miles on Highway 12 to Tieton Road (Forest Service Road 1200). Turn right (south) and drive 12 miles to Forest Service Road 1000. Turn right and drive 12 miles to the trailhead at road's end.

Contact: Wenatchee National Forest, Naches Ranger Station, 10237 U.S. 12, Naches, WA 98937, 509/653-1401.

73 PURCELL MOUNTAIN
7.4-15.4 mi/4.0-8.0 hr 4 ⛰9

north of Randle in Gifford Pinchot National Forest

Map 5.2, page 256

Conveniently situated along Highway 12 near Randle, Purcell Mountain reaches into the high country and snags meadows and views. It's not an easy trip, however, despite two separate access trails. Expect some significant climbing along either end, with switchbacks the name of the game. The reward for such efforts? Expansive meadows of flowers spread before vast mountain vistas.

Purcell Mountain Trail runs the ridge of the long mountain, almost 8 miles from end to end with a total elevation gain of 4,500 feet. From Highway 12, the trail wastes no time and quickly climbs among old timber. The forest provides welcome shade but breaks occasionally for valley views. Meadows appear before Prairie Mountain (5 miles) and dominate the eastern slopes at Little Paradise (6 miles). The trail ends atop Purcell Mountain (7.7 miles).

A shorter but more strenuous option is Purcell Lookout Trail to the upper ridge. The trail climbs from a logging road to the top of Purcell Mountain (elevation 5,442 feet), gaining 2,400 feet in 3.7 miles. The lookout is long gone, but the views stuck around. Across miles of logged national forest land, Mount Rainier, Mount St. Helens, and Goat Rocks make inspiring neighbors.

On either route, water is a scarce commodity; be sure to carry adequate supplies. Campsites are also scarce, but a couple may be found below Little Paradise Meadows and at the two trails' junction.

User Groups: Hikers, leashed dogs, horses, and mountain bikes. No wheelchair access.

Permits: This trail is accessible mid-June–October. A federal Northwest Forest Pass is required to park here.

Maps: For a map of Gifford Pinchot National Forest, contact the Outdoor Recreation Information Center at the downtown Seattle REI. For a topographic map, ask Green Trails for No. 301, Randle, or ask the USGS for Randle.

Directions: Lower trailhead: From Randle, drive east 6 miles on Highway 12 to the signed trailhead, on the left (north) side.

Upper trailhead: From Randle, drive east 6 miles to Davis Creek Road. Turn left and drive 1 mile to Forest Service Road 63. Turn left and drive 4.5 miles to Forest Service Road 6310. Turn left and drive 1 mile to the trailhead on the right.

Contact: Gifford Pinchot National Forest, Cowlitz Valley Ranger Station, 10024 U.S. 12, Randle, WA 98377, 360/497-1100.

74 POMPEY PEAK
3.2 mi/2.0 hr 🥾3 ⛰8

southwest of Packwood in Gifford Pinchot National Forest

Map 5.2, page 256

Pompey Peak Trail offers a quick, beautiful, but steep trip to a high viewpoint overlooking the Cowlitz River Valley. The trailhead actually bisects the trail, eliminating 2,500 feet of knee-knocking elevation gain along Kilborn Creek. That sounds good. From Kilborn Springs at the trailhead, Pompey Peak Trail climbs quickly and steadily through shady old-growth forest. Douglas fir and western hemlock give way to silver fir as the trail climbs. A social trail breaks off from the main trail (1.5 miles) and makes a short scramble to the summit (elevation 5,180 feet). Mount Rainier towers above the Tatoosh Range, while the peaks of Goat Rocks peek out from the east. Those with a hankering to put more trail underfoot can wander along Pompey Peak Trail another 2.8 miles along the ridge to Klickitat Trail, near Twin Sisters Mountain. And for a bit of history: Pompey Peak was named for a pack mule belonging to an old settler. The mule fell to its death on the upper part of the trail in the 1890s.

User Groups: Hikers, leashed dogs, horses, and mountain bikes. No wheelchair access.

Permits: This trail is accessible June–October. No permits are required. Parking and access are free.

Maps: For a map of Gifford Pinchot National Forest, contact the Outdoor Recreation Information Center at the downtown Seattle REI. For a topographic map, ask Green Trails for No. 301, Randle, or ask the USGS for Purcell Mountain.

Directions: From Randle, drive south 1 mile on Highway 131 to Forest Service Road 23. Turn left and drive 3.5 miles to Forest Service Road 2404. Turn left and drive to the trailhead at road's end.

Contact: Gifford Pinchot National Forest, Cowlitz Valley Ranger Station, 10024 U.S. 12, Randle, WA 98377, 360/497-1100.

75 PACKWOOD LAKE
9.2 mi/5.0 hr 🥾2 ⛰️7

east of Packwood in Goat Rocks Wilderness of Gifford Pinchot National Forest

Map 5.2, page 256

Here's a hike the whole family can enjoy. Packwood Lake Trail skirts the base of Snyder Mountain through a forest of big trees to the large, scenic lake. Peaks of the Goat Rocks are visible to the south and Mount Rainier's summit to the north. The lake's crystal-blue water is inviting to swimmers and anglers alike; it holds a healthy population of trout. Elk are frequent visitors during the winter. The idyllic setting is punctuated by a small forested island in the middle.

Although Packwood Lake Trail is forested and shady, little water is to be found along the way. The elevation gain of 900 feet is barely noticeable, well spread over the 4.6 miles of trail. Clear-cuts and second-growth forests are quickly passed by before you enter stands of old timber. The lake is a favorite overnight destination for families, with campsites found around the shores of the lake. A trail winds

around the east shore, with trails leading to Mosquito (6.8 miles) and Lost Lakes (8.8 miles).

User Groups: Hikers and horses only. No dogs or mountain bikes are allowed. No wheelchair access.

Permits: This trail is accessible year-round. A federal Northwest Forest Pass is required to park here.

Maps: For a map of Gifford Pinchot National Forest, contact the Outdoor Recreation Information Center at the downtown Seattle REI. For a topographic map, ask Green Trails for No. 302, Packwood, or ask the USGS for Packwood.

Directions: From Randle, drive east 16 miles to Packwood. Turn right on Forest Service Road 1260 (near the ranger station) and drive south 5 miles to the trailhead at road's end.

Contact: Gifford Pinchot National Forest, Cowlitz Valley Ranger Station, 10024 U.S. 12, Randle, WA 98377, 360/497-1100.

76 LILY BASIN
12.0 mi/6.0 hr 🥾2 ⛰️9

south of Mount Rainier in Goat Rocks Wilderness of Gifford Pinchot National Forest

Map 5.2, page 256

Lily Basin Trail is full of great views of the South Cascade volcanoes and blooming wildflowers. Contouring around the head of Glacier Creek, the trail gives a bird's-eye view of Lily Basin, where bugling elk and howling coyotes are frequently heard. Johnson Peak towers above the trail before Heart Lake, set within subalpine meadows, comes into view below the trail. Many hikers leave with a camera full of great pictures.

The trail begins quite high, at 4,200 feet, and quickly enters Goat Rocks Wilderness. The trees along the ridge fight the heavy winter snowpack to attain large girths. The trail follows the ridge for 4 miles before arriving high above Lily Basin. Large populations of elk often graze in Lily Basin. The trail becomes tricky as it contours around the basin through avalanche chutes and talus. The slope falls away quickly, and hikers should take care when tackling this section. Wildflowers are abundant in these high open slopes.

At 6 miles is the junction with Angry Mountain Trail. From here, one can gaze down onto either side of the ridge, and no fewer than three of the major volcanoes are within view. A couple of possible camps lie along the trail, with the best camping a quick descent to Heart Lake.

User Groups: Hikers, leashed dogs, and horses (horses may have difficulty navigating the last couple of miles around the basin). No mountain bikes are allowed. No wheelchair access.

Permits: This area is accessible July–October. A federal Northwest Forest Pass is required to park here.

Maps: For a map of Gifford Pinchot National Forest, contact the Outdoor Recreation Information Center at the downtown Seattle REI. For a topographic map, ask Green Trails for No. 302, Packwood, or ask the USGS for Packwood.

Directions: From Randle, drive east 14 miles on Highway 12 to Forest Service Road 48. Turn right (south) and drive 9.5 miles to the trailhead on the right. This is shortly after a sharp left-hand turn in a creek bottom.

Contact: Gifford Pinchot National Forest, Cowlitz Valley Ranger Station, 10024 U.S. 12, Randle, WA 98377, 360/497-1100.

77 SOUTH POINT LOOKOUT
7.0 mi/4.0 hr   🥾5 ⛰️7

south of Randle in Gifford Pinchot National Forest

Map 5.2, page 256

The lookout may be long gone, but the far-reaching views remain. South Point Lookout Trail makes a rugged assault on South Point Mountain, gaining 3,200 feet in just 3.5 miles. That's steep by anyone's standards. The payoff

is grand, though, with views of Mount Rainier, Mount St. Helens, and Goat Rocks, not to mention many surrounding ridges and peaks. Much of the trail climbs within an open forest burned long ago. The resulting forest of snags provides increasingly better vistas along the ascent but also makes the hike a hot one (and dry, so bring extra water). The trail ends at the summit, where the lookout once stood. Adventurous folk will enjoy scrambling south along the rocky, meadowy ridge.

User Groups: Hikers, leashed dogs, horses, and mountain bikes. No wheelchair access.

Permits: This trail is accessible June–October. No permits are required. Parking and access are free.

Maps: For a map of Gifford Pinchot National Forest, contact the Outdoor Recreation Information Center at the downtown Seattle REI. For a topographic map, ask Green Trails for No. 302, Packwood, or ask the USGS for Packwood.

Directions: From Randle, drive east 11 miles on Highway 12 to Forest Service Road 20. Turn right (south) and drive 4 miles (crossing Smith Creek) to the signed trailhead on the left.

Contact: Gifford Pinchot National Forest, Cowlitz Valley Ranger Station, 10024 U.S. 12, Randle, WA 98377, 360/497-1100.

78 GLACIER LAKE
4.0 mi/2.0 hr   🥾2 ⛰️7

south of Mount Rainier in Goat Rocks Wilderness of Gifford Pinchot National Forest

Map 5.2, page 256

The trail to Glacier Lake is short, has just 800 feet of gain, and leads to a great lake full of trout. The name is misleading, as there are no glaciers near the lake. Instead, beautiful forests of old-growth fir and hemlock encase the lake with a small meadow at the west end making for a great picnicking spot. Elk roam Lily Basin farther up the creek and often make it down to the lake.

Glacier Lake Trail starts off from the trailhead in a young forest logged several decades ago. Within a mile the trail enters the wilderness and virgin forests. The trail is well maintained and never very steep, making easy access for all. A footpath skirts the large lake for exploration by anglers and families alike.
User Groups: Hikers, leashed dogs, and horses. No mountain bikes are allowed. No wheelchair access.

Permits: This trail is accessible May–November. A federal Northwest Forest Pass is required to park here.

Maps: For a map of Gifford Pinchot National Forest, contact the Outdoor Recreation Information Center at the downtown Seattle REI. For a topographic map, ask Green Trails for No. 302, Packwood, or ask the USGS for Packwood.

Directions: From Randle, drive east 12 miles on Highway 12 to Forest Service Road 21. Turn right (south) and drive 5 miles to Forest Service Road 2110. Turn left and drive 0.5 mile to the trailhead on the right.

Contact: Gifford Pinchot National Forest, Cowlitz Valley Ranger Station, 10024 U.S. 12, Randle, WA 98377, 360/497-1100.

79 ANGRY MOUNTAIN
16.8 mi/8.0 hr   🧍4 ▲7

south of Mount Rainier in Goat Rocks Wilderness of Gifford Pinchot National Forest

Map 5.2, page 256

Despite the name of the mountain, few people leave Angry Mountain in a foul mood. Out of breath and quite tired, but angry, not likely. The trail climbs 3,400 feet along the long ridge of the mountain with the help of plenty of switchbacks. Mount Rainier seems never to be far off, constantly in view to the north. The route ventures deep into the Goat Rocks Wilderness, ending at Heart Lake, a beautiful high lake sure to calm flared tempers and sore feet.

Angry Mountain Trail is difficult from the get-go. It quickly switchbacks up the west end

of the mountain through nice forests of Douglas fir and hemlock. The forest soon opens, with large trees spaced farther apart because of heavy winter snowpacks. The trail follows the ridge, which drops steeply to the south. The severe cliffs along the south side of the mountain are a likely source of the name Angry Mountain. Or maybe it's the steep ascent.

Angry Mountain Trail continues by making another series of steep switchbacks, nearing the high point of the mountain and a viewpoint. The trail enters its prime from here, meandering along the ridge. Wildflowers go crazy during June and July. The trail eventually connects to Lily Basin Trail, near the head of Jordan Basin. A great overnight stay is found at Heart Lake (9 miles).

User Groups: Hikers, leashed dogs, and horses. No mountain bikes are allowed. No wheelchair access.

Permits: This area is usually accessible mid-June–October. A federal Northwest Forest Pass is required to park here.

Maps: For a map of Gifford Pinchot National Forest, contact the Outdoor Recreation Information Center at the downtown Seattle REI. For topographic maps, ask Green Trails for No. 302, Packwood, or ask the USGS for Packwood Lake.

Directions: From Randle, drive east 12 miles on Highway 12 to Forest Service Road 21. Turn right (south) and drive 7.5 miles to Forest Service Road 2120. Turn left and drive 0.5 mile to the trailhead on the right.

Contact: Gifford Pinchot National Forest, Cowlitz Valley Ranger Station, 10024 U.S. 12, Randle, WA 98377, 360/497-1100.

80 GOAT RIDGE
11.0 mi/6.0 hr   🧍3 ▲9

south of Mount Rainier in Goat Rocks Wilderness of Gifford Pinchot National Forest

Map 5.2, page 256   BEST (

This is one of the most popular trails in Goat Rocks and for good reason. After climbing into

© SCOTT LEONARD

Mount Adams from Goat Lake

the subalpine with miles of views, the trail finds the beautiful but cold Goat Lake. Guarantees are rare, but it's likely that you'll see mountain goats on the high ridges surrounding the lake in the evening. So if you're after goats, wildflowers, or views, Goat Ridge is your hike.

The trail begins from Berry Patch Trailhead and climbs quickly through the forest. A loop option is available (1.2 miles) and is highly recommended. It climbs to the site of a former lookout, where three Cascade volcanoes sit close by. The loop returns to the main Goat Ridge Trail and adds little distance to the hike.

Scaling the slopes of Jordan Basin, the trail passes through wide-open meadows that ignite with wildflower blooms in the summer. The trail intercepts Jordan Basin Trail (5.1 miles), a great side trip. Goat Lake lies another 0.5 mile on Goat Ridge Trail, set deep among high alpine ridges, home to white fuzzy goats.

Goat Ridge makes a great loop. Beyond Goat Lake, hike to Snowgrass Flats (7.8 miles), where hikers can drop back to the trailhead (13.3 miles) via Snowgrass Trail. This is an outstanding overnight trip.

User Groups: Hikers, leashed dogs, and horses. No mountain bikes are allowed. No wheelchair access.

Permits: This trail is usually accessible July–September. A federal Northwest Forest Pass is required to park here.

Maps: For a map of Gifford Pinchot National Forest, contact the Outdoor Recreation Information Center at the downtown Seattle REI. For topographic maps, ask Green Trails for No. 334, Blue Lake, and No. 303, White Pass, or ask the USGS for Hamilton Butte and Old Snowy Mountain.

Directions: From Randle, drive east 12 miles on Highway 12 to Forest Service Road 21. Turn right (south) and drive 13 miles to Forest Service Road 2150 (the second left). Turn left and drive 3.5 miles. Stay left at the first Chambers Lake sign, stay right at the Chambers Lake turnoff, and then left to the north Berry Patch Trailhead. (There are two trailheads named Berry Patch—check signboards to verify you're at the one you want.)

Contact: Gifford Pinchot National Forest, Cowlitz Valley Ranger Station, 10024 U.S. 12, Randle, WA 98377, 360/497-1100.

81 SNOWGRASS FLATS

8.4 mi/5.0 hr

south of Mount Rainier in Goat Rocks
Wilderness of Gifford Pinchot National Forest

Map 5.2, page 256

Some trails feature smile-inducing views or open vistas. Others showcase beautiful vegetation or wildlife. When a trail delivers both, it enters a realm reserved for few hikes. Snowgrass Flats is one of those hikes. The trail starts with a diverse forest featuring trees of inspiring size. Next are a pair of beautiful streams. And at the top lies Snowgrass Flats, a wide-open parkland featuring more than acres of meadow. And last, the towering peaks of the Goat Rocks.

Snowgrass Trail leaves Berry Patch Trailhead and climbs over the end of Goat Ridge. It crosses Goat Creek on a nice bridge, where the stream cascades and courses over bedrock. Giant yellow cedars, Douglas firs, silver firs, and mountain hemlocks grow here. The trail passes another cascading stream, and the scenery only gets better. Numerous trees cost hikers time on the trail to ponder their ages.

After fairly steady climbing, the trail reaches Snowgrass Flats. This is open parkland for the most part, with meadows spreading far and wide. Here the trail runs into the PCT. Hiking about 2 miles south on PCT is well worth the effort, as the trail climbs to the base of Old Snowy and the views north become wide open. Old Snowy, at almost 8,000 feet, beckons you to climb farther with a very steep but trouble-free way trail to the summit. This is a hike to remember. Unfortunately, camping is prohibited within Snowgrass Flats.

User Groups: Hikers, and horses only. No dogs or mountain bikes are allowed. No wheelchair access.

Permits: This trail is usually accessible July–September. No permits are required. Parking and access are free.

Maps: For a map of Gifford Pinchot National Forest, contact the Outdoor Recreation Information Center at the downtown Seattle REI.

For topographic maps, ask Green Trails for No. 334, Blue Lake, No. 335, Walupt Lake, and No. 303, White Pass, or ask the USGS for Hamilton Butte and Walupt Lake.

Directions: From Randle, drive east 12 miles on Highway 12 to Forest Service Road 21. Turn right (south) and drive 14 miles to Forest Service Road 2150. Turn left and drive 3.5 miles. Stay right at Chambers Lake turnoff and then right on Forest Service Road 2150-405, toward the south Berry Patch Trailhead. (There are two trailheads named Berry Patch—check signboards to verify you're at the one you want.)

Contact: Gifford Pinchot National Forest, Cowlitz Valley Ranger Station, 10024 U.S. 12, Randle, WA 98377, 360/497-1100.

82 CISPUS BRAILLE

0.5 mi/0.5 hr

south of Randle in Gifford Pinchot
National Forest

Map 5.2, page 256

This nature trail at the Cispus Environmental Learning Center investigates a forest recovering from fire. The trail is level and easy to negotiate, an ideal outing for families or those using a wheelchair. Interpretive signs lead the way and describe the flora and fauna helping to recreate a forest. The folks at the Learning Center have also designed this trail to be accessible to the visually impaired, with Braille markings and roping to guide hikers around the loop. This is a wonderful place to find elk or deer grazing the understory, especially in the winter when the high country lies under several feet of wet snow.

User Groups: Hikers, leashed dogs, horses, and mountain bikes are allowed. No wheelchair access.

Permits: This trail is accessible year-round. No permits are required. Parking and access are free.

Maps: For a map of Gifford Pinchot National Forest, contact the Outdoor Recreation

Information Center at the downtown Seattle REI. For a topographic map, ask Green Trails for No. 333, McCoy Peak, or ask the USGS for Tower Rock.

Directions: From Randle, drive south 1 mile on Highway 131 to Forest Service Road 23. Veer left and drive 8 miles to Forest Service Road 28. Turn right and drive 1.5 miles to Forest Service Road 76. Stay to the right and drive 1 mile to the Cispus Environmental Learning Center. The trailhead is on the opposite side of Road 76.

Contact: Gifford Pinchot National Forest, Cowlitz Valley Ranger Station, 10024 U.S. 12, Randle, WA 98377, 360/497-1100.

83 KLICKITAT TRAIL

17.1 mi one-way/9.0 hr   4 ⛰9

south of Packwood in Gifford Pinchot National Forest

Map 5.2, page 256

Following an ancient Native American trail through the high country, Klickitat Trail makes an excellent ridge run. Bathed in summer sun, with miles of huckleberry bushes and mountain views, Klickitat Trail makes for an ideal day (or two) in the Gifford Pinchot. The length and orientation of the trail make an out-and-back hike very unappealing; a car-drop is best if it can be arranged. If not, the two trailheads are supplemented with several additional access points. Although the trail starts and ends high, the route encounters numerous ups and downs, making for some challenging elevation changes. Because much of the trail rides the crest of a ridge, snowfields are common on north slopes well into August.

From west to east, the trail skirts the rocky masses of Twin Sisters and Castle Butte. A side trail leads to the summit of Cispus Lookout (3.2 miles). Huckleberries and views of Mount Rainier dominate the scenery on the way to Horseshoe Point (7.5 miles), Cold Spring Butte (9 miles), and Mission Mountain (12.4 miles).

The ridge (and trail) head south to the eastern trailhead, below Elk Peak (17.1 miles). The trail is dry except for Jackpot Lake (4.4 miles) and St. Michael Lake (off-trail below Cold Springs Butte).

User Groups: Hikers, leashed dogs, horses, and mountain bikes. No wheelchair access.

Permits: This trail is accessible mid-July–October. A federal Northwest Forest Pass is required to park here.

Maps: For a map of Gifford Pinchot National Forest, contact the Outdoor Recreation Information Center at the downtown Seattle REI. For a topographic map, ask Green Trails for No. 334, Blue Lake, or ask the USGS for Tower Rock, Hamilton Butte, and Blue Lake.

Directions: From Randle, drive south 1 mile on Highway 131 to Forest Service Road 25. Stay to the right and drive 21 miles to Forest Service Road 28. Turn left and drive 2.5 miles to the signed trailhead.

Contact: Gifford Pinchot National Forest, Cowlitz Valley Ranger Station, 10024 U.S. 12, Randle, WA 98377, 360/497-1100.

84 HAMILTON BUTTES

5.6 mi/3.0 hr   2 ⛰8

south of Randle in Gifford Pinchot National Forest

Map 5.2, page 256

Hamilton Buttes Trail features a pair of trailheads, one low and one high. Pick the starting location that's right for you, but the upper trailhead is 1.5 miles shorter and saves 1,000 feet of elevation gain. Hamilton Buttes Trail leads to the twin peaks on a route primarily cloaked in carpets of wildflower meadows and huckleberries.

From the upper trailhead, Hamilton Buttes Trail scales the side of a forested basin to reach a small ridgeline and junction (2.2 miles). Turning right drops to the lower trailhead, so don't do that. Head left, uphill, and climb to the top of the two peaks. This is divine country, with outstanding views of Goat Rocks and Mount Adams. August is the prime month to find ripe huckleberries. Carry plenty of water, as none is to be found once you leave the car.

User Groups: Hikers, leashed dogs, horses, mountain bikes, and motorcycles. No wheelchair access.

Permits: This trail is accessible June–October. No permits are required. Parking and access are free.

Maps: For a map of Gifford Pinchot National Forest, contact the Outdoor Recreation Information Center at the downtown Seattle REI. For a topographic map, ask Green Trails for No. 334, Blue Lake, or ask the USGS for Hamilton Butte.

Directions: From Randle, drive south 1 mile on Highway 131 to Forest Service Road 23. Veer left and drive 12 miles to Forest Service Road 22. Turn left and drive 6 miles to Forest Service Road 78. Turn right and drive 8.5 miles to the trailhead at the pass.

Contact: Gifford Pinchot National Forest, Cowlitz Valley Ranger Station, 10024 U.S. 12, Randle, WA 98377, 360/497-1100.

85 YOZOO
8.0 mi/4.0 hr

south of Randle in Gifford Pinchot National Forest

Map 5.2, page 256

Don't ask where the name came from, just enjoy the huckleberries and views of Mount Rainier. That's easy enough, because Yozoo Trail spends a big chunk of its length in open meadows along the high ridge. Through large, old forest, the trail skirts a ridge and climbs through the small valley of Grouse Creek (1.5 miles). This is the last chance for water before Yozoo Trail enters the high country with open meadows of small trees and huckleberry bushes. The trail runs just below the rim of Yozoo Basin, where views of Mount Rainier are constant. Several peaks frame the basin

and make great scrambles to even bigger views. Mountain goats, elk, and black bear are all regular visitors to this area during the summer and early fall. Just be mindful of the most annoying of beasts, roaring motorbikes. Yozoo Trail ends at Bishop Ridge Trail (4 miles), overlooking the sparkling and tempting water of Blue Lake.

User Groups: Hikers, leashed dogs, horses, mountain bikes, and motorcycles. No wheelchair access.

Permits: This trail is accessible April– October. No permits are required. Parking and access are free.

Maps: For a map of Gifford Pinchot National Forest, contact the Outdoor Recreation Information Center at the downtown Seattle REI. For a topographic map, ask Green Trails for No. 334, Blue Lake, or ask the USGS for Hamilton Butte.

Directions: From Randle, drive south 1 mile on Highway 131 to Forest Service Road 23. Veer left on Forest Service Road 23 and drive 12 miles to Forest Service Road 22. Turn left and drive 6 miles to Forest Service Road 78. Turn right and drive 5 miles to the signed trailhead.

Contact: Gifford Pinchot National Forest, Cowlitz Valley Ranger Station, 10024 U.S. 12, Randle, WA 98377, 360/497-1100.

86 NANNIE RIDGE
9.0 mi/5.5 hr

south of White Pass in Goat Rocks Wilderness of Gifford Pinchot National Forest

Map 5.2, page 256

Nannie Ridge Trail, in the southern Goat Rocks Wilderness, makes a scenic trip along the high crest. Nannie Ridge is between the craggy peaks of Goat Rocks and the commanding presence of Mount Adams. The trail passes an old lookout site on its way to the meadows of Sheep Lake and the PCT. Understandably, Nannie Ridge is a popular trail in the Gifford Pinchot.

Beginning from the shores of Walupt Lake, Nannie Ridge Trail climbs steadily and steeply to the crest of the ridge. A social trail leads to Nannie Peak (2.5 miles, elevation 6,106), the first but not last opportunity for expansive views. The trail traverses the ridge beneath tall, rocky cliffs and over open meadows of heather. This is hot and dry country, demanding that hikers pack extra water and sunscreen. Nannie Ridge Trail ends at Sheep Lake, a favorite campsite and swimming hole for hikers passing through on the PCT. If Sheep Lake doesn't tempt you into the water, Walupt Lake will.

User Groups: Hikers and horses only. No dogs or mountain bikes are allowed. No wheelchair access.

Permits: This trail is accessible June–October. No permits are required. Parking and access are free.

Maps: For a map of Gifford Pinchot National Forest, contact the Outdoor Recreation Information Center at the downtown Seattle REI. For a topographic map, ask Green Trails for No. 335, Walupt Lake, or ask the USGS for Walupt Lake.

Directions: From Randle, drive east 12 miles on Highway 12 to Forest Service Road 21. Turn right (south) and drive 18.5 miles to Forest Service Road 2160. Turn left and drive 5.5 miles to Walupt Lake Trailhead.

Contact: Gifford Pinchot National Forest, Cowlitz Valley Ranger Station, 10024 U.S. 12, Randle, WA 98377, 360/497-1100.

87 WALUPT CREEK
8.6-13.5 mi/4.5 hr-2 days 👤👥2 ⛰️8

south of White Pass in Goat Rocks Wilderness of Gifford Pinchot National Forest

Map 5.2, page 256

Short, easy, and not exceptionally scenic, Walupt Creek Trail is about more than just the creek. The up-and-back along the trail is a great hike, with pleasant forest and meadows,

and even a few high tarns thrown in at the end. But more importantly, Walupt Creek Trail provides two great loops along the PCT.

Walupt Creek Trail provides great access to the PCT, gaining just 1,000 feet in more than 4 miles. The trail spends its first 1.5 miles along the shores of Walupt Lake. Good luck getting past here on a hot summer day without a quick dip to cool off. The trail briefly follows the creek before leaving it to climb out of the glacially shaped valley (notice the U shape) to a large, flat basin. Here are your open sub-alpine meadows and small tarns. Campsites are found along Walupt Creek and here, near the tarns and PCT.

Walupt Creek is the starting leg to a pair of great loops. From the end of Walupt Creek Trail, head north on the PCT to Sheep Lake and along Nannie Ridge (see previous listing) to Walupt Lake (12.3 miles). This route has the most views, especially along Nannie Ridge. Or head south on the PCT (13.5 miles), through a large basin and the meadows of Coleman Weedpatch. Both loops turn Walupt Creek from mundane into terrific.

User Groups: Hikers and horses only. No dogs or mountain bikes are allowed. No wheelchair access.

Permits: This trail is accessible June–October. No permits are required. Parking and access are free.

Maps: For a map of Gifford Pinchot National Forest, contact the Outdoor Recreation Information Center at the downtown Seattle REI. For a topographic map, ask Green Trails for No. 335, Walupt Lake, or ask the USGS for Walupt Lake.

Directions: From Randle, drive east 12 miles on Highway 12 to Forest Service Road 21. Turn right (south) and drive 18.5 miles to Forest Service Road 2160. Turn left and drive 5.5 miles to Walupt Lake Trailhead.

Contact: Gifford Pinchot National Forest, Cowlitz Valley Ranger Station, 10024 U.S. 12, Randle, WA 98377, 360/497-1100.

88 LANGILLE RIDGE

8.4 mi/5.0 hr 🏃3 ⛰9

south of Randle in Gifford Pinchot
National Forest

Map 5.2, page 256

In the heart of Gifford Pinchot National Forest, Langille Ridge stands as a lonely place. Because of a road washout at one end and a steep, rocky access trail, few hikers have the pleasure of hiking this high ridge. Thus the spoils of Langille Ridge are left to the few, a tantalizing prospect for hikers looking for solitude. The jagged ridge runs more than 10 miles from end to end, but the best spots are close to the car.

With the washout of the northern trailhead, Langille Ridge Trail is best reached via Rough Trail. Appropriately named, Rough Trail climbs 2,000 feet over a rocky path to Langille Ridge Trail (1.7 miles). This is the worst of it, however. From the junction, Langille Ridge Trail runs north and south, making some ups and downs along the jagged ridge. A hike south travels through rocky meadows, complete with huckleberries, to Boundary Trail (5.6 miles one-way).

The preferred option is to head north from the Rough Trail junction along Langille Ridge to McCoy Peak (4.2 miles) and Langille Peak (5.9 miles). Both peaks offer panoramic views of the surrounding countryside and forests. The northern half of Langille Ridge features uninterrupted views of Juniper Ridge and Mount Adams. This is a great place to see mountain goats along the rocky slopes and to hear elk bellowing from the basins below. Plan on packing plenty of water, as much of the ridge is exposed and dry.

User Groups: Hikers, leashed dogs, horses, mountain bikes, and motorcycles. No wheelchair access.

Permits: This trail is accessible May– October. No permits are required. Parking and access are free.

Maps: For a map of Gifford Pinchot National Forest, contact the Outdoor Recreation Information Center at the downtown Seattle REI.

For a topographic map, ask Green Trails for No. 333, McCoy Peak, or ask the USGS for Tower Rock and McCoy Peak.

Directions: From Randle, drive south 1 mile on Highway 131 to Forest Service Road 23. Veer left on Forest Service Road 23 and drive 8 miles to Forest Service Road 28. Turn right and drive 1.5 miles to Forest Service Road 29. Turn left and drive 12 miles to Forest Service Road 29-116. Turn right and drive 0.5 mile to the signed trailhead.

Contact: Gifford Pinchot National Forest, Cowlitz Valley Ranger Station, 10024 U.S. 12, Randle, WA 98377, 360/497-1100.

89 TONGUE MOUNTAIN

3.4 mi/2.0 hr 🏃2 ⛰9

south of Randle in Gifford Pinchot
National Forest

Map 5.2, page 256

Standing slightly apart from Juniper Ridge, Tongue Mountain towers over lush Cispus River Valley. Although the peak looks as if it belongs to the neighboring ridge, Tongue Mountain is actually the remains of an old volcano. Tongue Mountain Trail makes a gentle climb through old-growth forest to an open saddle (1 mile). Folks interested in views but not a workout can enjoy looking out over the valley to Mount Adams and Mount Rainier from here. More determined hikers can make the sharp and steep ascent to the peak's summit (1.7 miles, elevation 4,838 feet). This section of trail is a tough climb, but it's over quickly and is certainly rewarding. Cascades volcanoes tower over the Gifford Pinchot, and the noisy Cispus River roars from below. Lucky hikers will spot fluffy white mountain goats along the peaks' sheer cliffs.

User Groups: Hikers, leashed dogs, horses, mountain bikes, and motorcycles. No wheelchair access.

Permits: This trail is accessible April–October. No permits are required. Parking and access are free.

Maps: For a map of Gifford Pinchot National Forest, contact the Outdoor Recreation Information Center at the downtown Seattle REI. For a topographic map, ask Green Trails for No. 333, McCoy Peak, or ask the USGS for Tower Rock.

Directions: From Randle, drive south 1 mile on Highway 131 to Forest Service Road 23. Veer left on Forest Service Road 23 and drive 8 miles to Forest Service Road 28. Turn right and drive 1.5 miles to Forest Service Road 29. Turn left and drive 4 miles to Forest Service Road 2904. Turn left and drive 4 miles to the signed trailhead.

Contact: Gifford Pinchot National Forest, Cowlitz Valley Ranger Station, 10024 U.S. 12, Randle, WA 98377, 360/497-1100.

90 BADGER PEAK
2.0 mi/1.5 hr

south of Randle in Gifford Pinchot National Forest

Map 5.2, page 256

Such easy access to a former lookout point is hard to come by, but Badger Ridge Trail delivers. It's just one short mile to the summit of Badger Peak (elevation 5,664 feet), where a lookout stood until the 1960s. Even harder to find is a refreshing lake nearby to enjoy after the climb to the summit, but that is found here also. Badger Ridge Trail starts high and climbs to the crest of Badger Ridge (0.6 mile). Already, the views of Mount St. Helens are grand. They have competition, however, from fields of huckleberries. The trail now splits, dropping slightly to Badger Lake or climbing to Badger Peak. From the summit, volcanoes new and old dominate the landscape. Mount St. Helens, Mount Rainier, and Mount Adams represent the new school, still busy at building themselves up. Older, extinct volcanoes include craggy Pinto Rock, jagged Langille Ridge, and other surrounding peaks. Your best bet is to climb the summit before dipping into Badger Lake.

User Groups: Hikers, leashed dogs, horses, mountain bikes, and motorcycles. No wheelchair access.

Permits: This trail is accessible May–October. No permits are required. Parking and access are free.

Maps: For a map of Gifford Pinchot National Forest, contact the Outdoor Recreation Information Center at the downtown Seattle REI. For a topographic map, ask Green Trails for No. 333, McCoy Peak, or ask the USGS for French Butte.

Directions: From Randle, drive south 1 mile on Highway 131 to Forest Service Road 25. Stay to the right and drive 21 miles to Forest Service Road 28. Turn left (east) and drive 2.5 miles to Forest Service Road 2816 (a bit rocky). Turn right and drive 5 miles to the trailhead at road's end.

Contact: Gifford Pinchot National Forest, Cowlitz Valley Ranger Station, 10024 U.S. 12, Randle, WA 98377, 360/497-1100.

91 JUNIPER RIDGE
6.4-8.8 mi/5.0 hr

south of Randle in Gifford Pinchot National Forest

Map 5.2, page 256

High, open, and awash in huckleberries and views, Juniper Ridge Trail is a southern Washington favorite. The long ridge run follows the crest of Juniper Ridge over Juniper, Sunrise, and Jumbo Peaks. The hiker's reward is miles of huckleberries and views of Mount Adams, Mount Rainier, Mount St. Helens, and even Mount Hood. Between gazing and grazing, be sure not to bump into the numerous elk, mountain goats, deer, or bear that live here. Juniper Ridge is tremendously scenic and wild (except for the occasional dirt bike roaring through).

Juniper Ridge Trail runs 11.4 miles along the crest of the high ridge. Fortunately, the trail is bisected by Sunrise Trail, a short access trail (1.4 miles) conveniently starting at

4,500 feet. From Sunrise, hikers have options to head north to two separate peaks or south to miles of huckleberry meadows. Backpackers thinking of spending the night here will need to pack extra water; the ridge is dry.

The southern half of Juniper Ridge is certainly the best. The route is one big meadow ramble. Huckleberries are ripest in August. Juniper Ridge Trail skirts Jumbo Peak (3.2 miles), a good turnaround, before dropping to Dark Meadows and Boundary Trail.

The northern half of Juniper Ridge Trail leaves Sunrise Trailhead and climbs Sunrise Peak (1.4 miles), a steep but manageable endeavor. This is Juniper Ridge's highest point. The trail follows the rocky ridge north to Juniper Peak (4.4 miles), a good turnaround, before dropping into clear-cuts.

User Groups: Hikers, leashed dogs, horses, mountain bikes, and motorcycles. No wheelchair access.

Permits: This trail is accessible May–October. No permits are required. Parking and access are free.

Maps: For a map of Gifford Pinchot National Forest, contact the Outdoor Recreation Information Center at the downtown Seattle REI. For a topographic map, ask Green Trails for No. 333, McCoy Peak, and No. 334, Blue Lake, or ask the USGS for McCoy Peak and Tower Rock.

Directions: From Randle, drive south 1 mile on Highway 131 to Forest Service Road 23. Veer left on Forest Service Road 23 and drive 24 miles to Forest Service Road 2324. Turn right and drive 5 miles to Forest Service Road 2324-063. Turn left and drive 0.3 mile to the trailhead at road's end.

Contact: Gifford Pinchot National Forest, Cowlitz Valley Ranger Station, 10024 U.S. 12, Randle, WA 98377, 360/497-1100.

92 YELLOWJACKET PASS/ HAT ROCK

5.4 mi/3.0 hr

south of Randle in Gifford Pinchot National Forest

Map 5.2, page 256

Hat Rock is but one of many things to see or travel to from this trailhead. Yellowjacket Trail is merely a shortcut to other trails, heading in every direction through the high country. This is also known as a cheater trail; that is, quick and easy access to terrain normally approached by longer, more traditional routes. In this instance, Yellowjacket Trail provides a quick route to Boundary Trail's scenic eastern segment and Langille Ridge.

Yellowjacket Trail climbs sharply to Boundary Trail, gaining 800 feet in just 1 mile. Head left for Langille Ridge junction (1.2 miles from the trailhead) or to follow Boundary Trail to the huckleberry riches of Dark Meadow. Turning right from Yellowjacket Trail leads through open meadows with stunning views of Mount Adams to Hat Rock (2.4 miles from the trailhead) and Yellowjacket Pass (2.7 miles). A boot-beaten path leads to the top of Hat Rock (elevation 5,599 feet) and a remarkable view of Badger Peak, Craggy Peak, Langille Ridge, and Juniper Ridge. The flattened top of Mount St. Helens rises to the west. Although short, this is an exposed and dry hike; remember plenty of water.

User Groups: Hikers, leashed dogs, horses, mountain bikes, and motorcycles. No wheelchair access.

Permits: This trail is accessible June–October. No permits are required. Parking and access are free.

Maps: For a map of Gifford Pinchot National Forest, contact the Outdoor Recreation Information Center at the downtown Seattle REI. For a topographic map, ask Green Trails for No. 333, McCoy, or ask the USGS for McCoy Peak.

Directions: From Randle, drive south 1 mile on Highway 131 to Forest Service Road 23.

Veer left on Forest Service Road 23 and drive 8 miles to Forest Service Road 28. Turn right and drive 11 miles to Forest Service Road 2810. Stay to the left and drive 9 miles to trailhead at road's end.

Contact: Gifford Pinchot National Forest, Mount St. Helens National Volcanic Monument, 42218 NE Yale Bridge Rd., Amboy, WA 98601, 360/449-7871.

93 CRAGGY PEAK

8.8 mi/5.0 hr

northeast of Cougar in Gifford Pinchot National Forest

Map 5.2, page 256

Craggy Peak Trail makes a great ridge run in the heart of the Gifford Pinchot, with meadow views to craggy peaks (including Craggy Peak!) and distant volcanoes. Enjoy the virgin forest shading the trail before it breaks out into spectacular meadows. Craggy Peak Trail also offers great access to Boundary Trail. With lots of campsites, this is a great day hike or an easy overnighter. Elk, deer, and mountain goats are frequent visitors to the area, and black bears appear in late summer to browse the huckleberries.

Craggy Peak Trail gets most of the climbing done early, ascending through an old forest of fir trees, dominated on the ground by bear grass. Quick glimpses of Mount Adams can be had through the trees, but the real views are reserved until the meadows (3 miles). The trail continues through prime huckleberry habitat to Boundary Trail, at the base of Craggy Peak (4.4 miles). Exploration along Boundary Trail is a meadow delight, north to Shark Rock or east to Yellowjacket Pass. The peaks tower over the deep, glaciated valleys, lush with old forests. Great campsites are situated along the trail, often down faint boot-worn paths to big views. Basin Camp is 0.5 mile east on Boundary Trail. Just be prepared for a dry trip with extra packed water.

User Groups: Hikers, leashed dogs, horses, mountain bikes, and motorcycles. No wheelchair access.

Permits: This trail is accessible June–October. A federal Northwest Forest Pass is required to park here.

Maps: For a map of Gifford Pinchot National Forest, contact the Outdoor Recreation Information Center at the downtown Seattle REI. For a topographic map, ask Green Trails for No. 333, McCoy Peak, and No. 365, Lone Butte, or ask the USGS for Spencer Butte, Quartz Creek, and McCoy Peak.

Directions: From Vancouver, drive north on I-5 to Highway 503 (Woodland, exit 21). Drive east 45 miles to Forest Service Road 25. Continue straight on Forest Service Road 25 and drive 6 miles to Forest Service Road 93, just beyond the Muddy River. Turn right and drive 13 miles to Forest Service Road 93-040. Turn left and drive 0.5 mile to the signed trailhead on the right.

Contact: Gifford Pinchot National Forest, Mount St. Helens National Volcanic Monument, 42218 NE Yale Bridge Rd., Amboy, WA 98601, 360/449-7871.

94 SUMMIT PRAIRIE

17.8 mi/1-2 days

northeast of Cougar in Gifford Pinchot National Forest

Map 5.2, page 256

Miles from the nearest trailhead, Summit Prairie is isolated, to say the least. Access to the open meadows, chock-full of huckleberry bushes, requires a long climb of nearly 3,000 feet. That keeps the crowds out of Summit Prairie and the wildlife wild, despite the occasional motorbike (they're still allowed in this "roadless" area). Herds of elk and mountain goats live in Quartz Creek Ridge and Summit Prairie, one of the Gifford Pinchot's most remote places.

In honor of full disclosure, a cheater trail does offer access to Summit Prairie (Boundary Trail, via Table Mountain). It's a little shorter, but nowhere near as scenic. Better access is via Summit Prairie Trail, which climbs Quartz Creek Ridge and runs the long, open ridgeline to Summit Prairie. Leaving from Forest Service Road 90, Summit Prairie Trail climbs harshly to the ridgeline (4 miles). The only water on the route is found in this first segment. Open subalpine forest and frequent meadows cover the ridge to Summit Prairie (8.9 miles) and Boundary Trail.

This is a tough trip to complete in one day, but campsites are few and far between. Overnight campers should plan on cross-country camping without a water source. If you've made it this far, the best option is to turn the trip into a 20.7-mile loop on Boundary Trail, Quartz Creek Trail (see listing in this chapter), and Quartz Creek Butte Trail (a 1.5-mile trail that serves as connector between Summit Prairie and Quartz Creek Big Trees).

User Groups: Hikers, leashed dogs, horses, mountain bikes, and motorcycles. No wheelchair access.

Permits: This trail is accessible mid-June–October. A federal Northwest Forest Pass is required to park here.

Maps: For a map of Gifford Pinchot National Forest, contact the Outdoor Recreation Information Center at the downtown Seattle REI. For a topographic map, ask Green Trails for No. 334, Blue Lake, No. 365, Lone Butte, and No. 366, Mount Adams West, or ask the USGS for Steamboat Mountain and East Canyon Ridge.

Directions: From Vancouver, drive north on I-5 to Highway 503 (Woodland, exit 21). Drive east 45 miles to Pine Creek Information Center. Turn right and continue on Forest Service Road 90 for 25 miles to the signed trailhead on the left (1.5 miles before Forest Service Road 88).

Contact: Gifford Pinchot National Forest, Mount St. Helens National Volcanic Monument, 42218 NE Yale Bridge Rd., Amboy, WA 98601, 360/449-7871.

95 DARK MEADOW

8.4 mi/4.5 hr

south of Randle in Gifford Pinchot National Forest

Map 5.2, page 256

Yet another locale with an ill-fitting name, the only thing dark in Dark Meadows are black huckleberries, juicy and ripe in August. In fact, these open meadows are lit up with summer sun, revealing great views of Jumbo Peak, Langille Ridge, and Mount Adams. Dark Meadow Trail endures several miles of shady forest before emerging into the dueling glories of huckleberry fields and vistas.

Dark Meadow Trail begins by gently wandering up the level valley of Dark Creek. The forest here is old Douglas fir and western hemlock, a perfect home for elk. After 1 mile, the trail climbs steeply to a junction with Juniper Ridge Trail (3.2 miles). The forest opens occasionally to reveal views of the valleys below. A short mile south on Juniper Ridge Trail finds Dark Meadow. Black huckleberry bushes fill the open meadows, attracting hikers and black bears alike. A short footpath leads through the meadow to the summit of Dark Mountain for a panoramic viewpoint (Mount Adams, wow!).

User Groups: Hikers, leashed dogs, horses, mountain bikes, and motorcycles. No wheelchair access.

Permits: This trail is accessible May–October. No permits are required. Parking and access are free.

Maps: For a map of Gifford Pinchot National Forest, contact the Outdoor Recreation Information Center at the downtown Seattle REI. For a topographic map, ask Green Trails for No. 333, McCoy Peak, and No. 334, Blue Lake, or ask the USGS for McCoy Peak and East Canyon Ridge.

Directions: From Randle, drive south 1 mile on Highway 131 to Forest Service Road 23. Veer left on Forest Service Road 23 and drive 25 miles to the signed trailhead on the right.

Contact: Gifford Pinchot National Forest, Cowlitz Valley Ranger Station, 10024 U.S. 12, Randle, WA 98377, 360/497-1100.

96 QUARTZ CREEK

21.2 mi/1-2 days

northeast of Cougar in Gifford Pinchot National Forest

Map 5.2, page 256

Lesser known for old-growth forests than other forests of Washington, Gifford Pinchot features forests as magnificent as any other. Quartz Creek Trail is a wonderful example of these ancient timberlands, where towering Douglas fir, western hemlock, and western red cedar grow to immense proportions. Quartz Creek Trail spends more than 10 miles wandering up the valley. Numerous streams enter Quartz Creek, including Straight Creek and its waterfalls. Regardless of how far one ventures up Quartz Creek Trail, the trip is sure to be grand.

Although Quartz Creek Trail gains 2,500 feet net elevation, numerous ups and downs make total elevation change more than twice that amount. The trail encounters Straight Creek (2 miles), home to a beautiful series of waterfalls. The occasional sections of logged forest are worth tolerating, balanced by the many miles of ancient old-growth forest. Campsites dot the trail as it wanders up the valley, passing Quartz Creek Butte Trail (a 1.5-mile connector between Summit Prairie and Quartz Creek Big Trees) junction at 4.5 miles. The upper section of the trail passes through forest burned long ago and now replaced by a subalpine setting. The trail connects to Boundary Trail (10.6 miles).

Folks who decide to hike the length of the trail are well advised to turn the trip into a loop. Summit Prairie Trail (see listing in this chapter) traverses Quartz Creek Ridge, awash in distant views and berry bushes. At the junction with Boundary Trail, hike east 2.3 miles to Summit Prairie Trail and turn south

toward Quartz Creek Butte Trail, descending to Quartz Creek. Total mileage is 22 miles.

User Groups: Hikers only. Wheelchair accessible the first 0.3 miles of trail.

Permits: This trail is accessible mid-June–October. A federal Northwest Forest Pass is required to park here.

Maps: For a map of Gifford Pinchot National Forest, contact the Outdoor Recreation Information Center at the downtown Seattle REI. For a topographic map, ask Green Trails for No. 333, McCoy Peak, No. 334, Blue Lake, No. 365, Lone Butte, and No. 366, Mount Adams West, or ask the USGS for Quartz Creek Butte, East Canyon Ridge, and Steamboat Mountain.

Directions: From Vancouver, drive north on I-5 to Highway 503 (Woodland, exit 21). Drive east 45 miles to Pine Creek Information Center. Turn right and continue on Forest Service Road 90 for 20 miles to the signed trailhead on the left (just beyond Forest Service Road 93).

Contact: Gifford Pinchot National Forest, Mount St. Helens National Volcanic Monument, 42218 NE Yale Bridge Rd., Amboy, WA 98601, 360/449-7871.

97 HIGH LAKES

8.0 mi/3.5 hr

south of Packwood in Gifford Pinchot National Forest

Map 5.2, page 256

Take much of what is great about the Gifford Pinchot, combine it into one trail, and High Lakes Trail is the result. The trail does indeed visit several high, meadow-rimmed lakes along the way. Views of Mount Adams make regular appearances along the route. And during the later summer, delicious, ripe huckleberries make this trip an appetizing day hike.

High Lakes Trail connects Olallie and Horseshoe Lakes. Save for a small segment in the middle, much of the route is easy to negotiate with little elevation gain. From the western end, the trail travels the dense forest around Olallie Lake to the open forest and meadows of Chain Lakes (1.3 miles). The trail crosses a large lava flow punctuating the valley of Adams Creek (2.8 miles) and climbs to Horseshoe Lake and campground. August is usually the best month to harvest mouthfuls of huckleberries along the way. These juicy berries constitute a large part of the summer diets for local black bears.

User Groups: Hikers, leashed dogs, horses, mountain bikes, and motorcycles. No wheelchair access.

Permits: This trail is accessible May–November. No permits are required. Parking and access are free.

Maps: For a map of Gifford Pinchot National Forest, contact the Outdoor Recreation Information Center at the downtown Seattle REI. For a topographic map, ask Green Trails for No. 334, Blue Lake, or ask the USGS for Green Mountain.

Directions: From Randle, drive south 1 mile on Highway 131 to Forest Service Road 23. Veer left on Forest Service Road 23 and drive 33 miles to Forest Service Road 2329. Turn left and drive 1 mile to the signed trailhead on the left.

Contact: Gifford Pinchot National Forest, Cowlitz Valley Ranger Station, 10024 U.S. 12, Randle, WA 98377, 360/497-1100.

98 TAKHLAKH LAKE AND MEADOWS
2.6 mi/1.5 hr 🥾1 ⛰8

north of Trout Lake in Gifford Pinchot National Forest

Map 5.2, page 256

Families on the lookout for an easy but scenic hike will want to pay attention to this one. Two trails combine to enjoy Takhlakh Lake, a 1.1-mile loop, and Takhlakh Meadows, a 1.5-mile loop situated off the first trail (imagine a

figure eight). Both trails are flat and extremely level, perfect for hikers of any age. The trails are even barrier free, making them accessible for folks in wheelchairs, although in a few sections assistance will be appreciated. Both trails enjoy views of Mount Adams to the southeast. Takhlakh Lake Trail loops around the lake. From the southeast part of this loop, Takhlakh Meadows Trail makes a separate loop. In August, these open meadows are full of delicious, ripe huckleberries.

User Groups: Hikers and leashed dogs. No horses or mountain bikes are allowed. These trails are wheelchair accessible.

Permits: This trail is accessible May–November. No permits are required. Parking and access are free.

Maps: For a map of Gifford Pinchot National Forest, contact the Outdoor Recreation Information Center at the downtown Seattle REI. For a topographic map, ask Green Trails for No. 334, Blue Lake, or ask the USGS for Green Mountain.

Directions: From Randle, drive south 1 mile on Highway 131 to Forest Service Road 23. Veer left on Forest Service Road 23 and drive 33 miles to Forest Service Road 2329. Turn left and drive 2 miles to the signed trailhead at road's end.

Contact: Gifford Pinchot National Forest, Mount Adams Ranger District, 2455 Highway 141, Trout Lake, WA 98650, 509/395-3400.

99 SPENCER BUTTE
3.8 mi/2.0 hr 🥾2 ⛰8

north of Cougar in Gifford Pinchot National Forest

Map 5.2, page 256

Spencer Butte Trail leads to one of the most beautiful views of a volcano you're likely to find anywhere. From atop Spencer Butte, a natural rock arch frames Mount St. Helens, a memorable and picturesque view. Short and accessible, with trailheads at either end of the 3-mile route, Spencer Butte is a great trip for folks looking for views on a quick day hike.

The best access is from the upper (north) trailhead in Spencer Meadows. It's not unlikely that you'll spot a herd of elk before you've even hit the trail. Spencer Butte Trail climbs steadily from the open meadows along a wide ridge. White pines give way to noble fir as the trail ascends through an open forest with regular views of the surrounding valleys. The trail crests atop Spencer Butte (elevation 4,247 feet). On the south side, a side trail drops slightly to a cold-water spring and the natural archway. Bring a camera, and you'll have a picture to display for years.

User Groups: Hikers, leashed dogs, horses, mountain bikes, and motorcycles. No wheelchair access.

Permits: This trail is accessible May–November. A federal Northwest Forest Pass is required to park here.

Maps: For a map of Gifford Pinchot National Forest, contact the Outdoor Recreation Information Center at the downtown Seattle REI. For a topographic map, ask Green Trails for No. 365, Lone Butte, or ask the USGS for Spencer Butte.

Directions: From Vancouver, drive north on I-5 to Highway 503 (Woodland, exit 21). Drive east 45 miles to Forest Service Road 25. Continue straight on Forest Service Road 25 and drive 6 miles to Forest Service Road 93, just beyond the Muddy River. Turn right and drive 9 miles to the signed trailhead on the left. This road is accessible for a passenger car but a high-clearance vehicle is recommended.

Contact: Gifford Pinchot National Forest, Mount St. Helens National Volcanic Monument, 42218 NE Yale Bridge Rd., Amboy, WA 98601, 360/449-7871.

100 BIG CREEK FALLS
1.4 mi/0.5 hr

north of Cougar in Gifford Pinchot National Forest

Map 5.2, page 256

This is one of the best and easiest trails in the Gifford Pinchot National Forest. Big Creek Falls Trail follows the steep cliffs alongside Big Creek to an overlook with an excellent view of the 110-foot cascade. Big Creek is exactly that, a thunderous gusher of a stream. The sound alone of Big Creek dropping into a pool beside the Lewis River is impressive, not to say anything of the enormous cloud of mist the fall generates. The trail has some interpretive signs discussing the old-growth forest through which the trail travels. Granddaddy Douglas firs and western hemlocks dominate the forest, draped in shrouds of ferns and mosses. The trail ends at a viewpoint over the falls, overlooking the Lewis River and Hemlock Falls on the opposite side. This is an ideal trail for young hikers-in-training.

User Groups: Hikers, leashed dogs, horses, mountain bikes and motorcycles (no motorized use March to July) are allowed. Part of this trail (a loop to a viewpoint) is wheelchair accessible.

Permits: This trail is accessible year-round. No permits are required. Parking and access are free.

Maps: For a map of Gifford Pinchot National Forest, contact the Outdoor Recreation Information Center at the downtown Seattle REI. For a topographic map, ask Green Trails for No. 365, Lone Butte, or ask the USGS for Burnt Peak.

Directions: From Vancouver, drive north on I-5 to Highway 503 (Woodland, exit 21). Drive east 45 miles to Pine Creek Information Center. Turn right and continue on Forest Service Road 90 for 11 miles to the signed trailhead on the left.

Contact: Gifford Pinchot National Forest, Mount St. Helens National Volcanic Monument, 42218 NE Yale Bridge Rd., Amboy, WA 98601, 360/449-7871.

101 THOMAS LAKE

6.6 mi/3.0 hr

north of Carson in Indian Heaven Wilderness
of Gifford Pinchot National Forest

Map 5.2, page 256

The high country of Indian Heaven is covered by small lakes in beautiful subalpine settings. Thomas Lake Trail encounters more of these lakes than any other trail in Indian Heaven Wilderness. It's also one of the easiest trails here, gaining just 600 feet in 3 miles. That makes Thomas Lake Trail a popular route into the huckleberry fields and wildflower meadows that characterize this high, volcanic plateau.

Thomas Lake Trail gets much of the work out of the way early, quickly climbing through dense forest to Thomas, Dee, and Heather Lakes (0.6 mile). The forest begins to break frequently, revealing meadows full of lupine and huckleberries in August. Elk and deer are frequently seen in this area, grazing in the meadows or wallowing in the small lakes and tarns. The trail ascends gently through meadows, passing yet more lakes. It crests at Rock Lake before dropping slightly to Blue Lake and the PCT. Although the trail is easily accomplished in a morning, it's advisable to plan on spending a full day exploring the many meadows and lakes. Just remember a fly rod or swimsuit.

User Groups: Hikers, leashed dogs, and horses. No mountain bikes are allowed. No wheelchair access.

Permits: This trail is accessible July–October. A federal Northwest Forest Pass is required to park here.

Maps: For a map of Gifford Pinchot National Forest, contact the Outdoor Recreation Information Center at the downtown Seattle REI. For a topographic map, ask Green Trails for No. 365S, Indian Heaven, or ask the USGS for Gifford Peak and Lone Butte.

Directions: From Vancouver, drive east 55 miles on Highway 14 to the town of Carson. Turn north on Wind River Road and drive 5 miles to Forest Service Road 65. Turn right

and drive 17 miles to the signed trailhead on the right.

Contact: Gifford Pinchot National Forest, Mount Adams Ranger District, 2455 Hwy. 141, Trout Lake, WA 98650, 509/395-3400.

102 HIDDEN LAKES

0.4 mi/0.5 hr

west of Trout Lake in Indian Heaven
Wilderness of Gifford Pinchot National Forest

Map 5.2, page 256

Hidden Lakes is a short and easy hike for everyone. Traveling around several small subalpine lakes, Hidden Lakes Trail provides a great sampler of this scenic area. On the northeast side of Indian Heaven Wilderness, the lakes are home to a primitive car campground. Small forest and open meadows dominate this area of the Gifford Pinchot National Forest, famous for its berry fields. Hidden Lakes is no different, basking in large fields of huckleberries, with peak season typically arriving in early August. Enjoy the berries, but leave some for others. A view of Mount Adams completes the scene.

User Groups: Hikers, leashed dogs, mountain bikes, and horses. No wheelchair access.

Permits: This trail is accessible June–October. No permits are required. Parking and access are free.

Maps: For a map of Gifford Pinchot National Forest, contact the Outdoor Recreation Information Center at the downtown Seattle REI. For a topographic map, ask Green Trails for No. 365S, Indian Heaven, or ask the USGS for Sleeping Lady.

Directions: From Vancouver, drive east 70 miles on Highway 14 to Highway 141. Turn north and drive 22 miles to Trout Lake. Continue north on Highway 141 as it becomes Forest Service Road 24 for 16 miles (past Little Goose Campground) to the trailhead on the right.

Contact: Gifford Pinchot National Forest, Mount Adams Ranger District, 2455 Hwy. 141, Trout Lake, WA 98650, 509/395-3400.

103 INDIAN HEAVEN
6.6 mi/3.5 hr

west of Trout Lake in Indian Heaven
Wilderness of Gifford Pinchot National Forest

Map 5.2, page 256

Strewn with high country lakes and subalpine meadows, Indian Heaven is heavenly indeed. A visit to this volcanic highland in August is divine, when ripe black huckleberries are ubiquitous. Indian Heaven Trail is the best way to the meadows and lakes of this subalpine playground. The short and accessible trail delivers every step of the way, whether it be old-growth forest, wildflower meadows, or scenic vistas.

Indian Heaven Trail wastes no time in reaching the high plateau of Indian Heaven. The trail climbs steadily through superb old-growth forest of subalpine fir, mountain hemlock, Englemann spruce, and white pine. Peek-a-boo views of Mount Adams whet the appetite for the meadows to come. The arrival into the high country is signaled when the trail reaches Cultus Lake, directly next to the trail (2.3 miles). A signed side trail leads a few hundred yards to Deep Lake. The trail junctions with Lemei Trail (2.5 miles) and bypasses Clear Lake before continuing to the PCT (3.3 miles). Rambling along any of these trails is well recommended.

Hikers looking for a little variety can turn Indian Heaven Trail into part of a great loop. The 6.7-mile loop uses the PCT to encircle Bird Mountain, passing numerous lakes along the way. Hike east on Indian Heaven Trail to the PCT (3.3 miles). Turn north and hike to Cultus Creek Trail (5.2 miles), which quickly descends back to Cultus Creek Campground and trailhead.

User Groups: Hikers, leashed dogs, and horses. No mountain bikes are allowed. No wheelchair access.

Permits: This trail is accessible June–October. A federal Northwest Forest Pass is required to park here.

Maps: For a map of Gifford Pinchot National Forest, contact the Outdoor Recreation Information Center at the downtown Seattle REI. For a topographic map, ask Green Trails for No. 365S, Indian Heaven, or ask the USGS for Lone Butte.

Directions: From Vancouver, drive east 70 miles on Highway 14 to Highway 141. Turn north and drive 22 miles to Trout Lake. Continue north on Highway 141 as it becomes Forest Service Road 24 for 18 miles to the signed trailhead within Cultus Creek Campground.

Contact: Gifford Pinchot National Forest, Mount Adams Ranger District, 2455 Hwy. 141, Trout Lake, WA 98650, 509/395-3400.

104 LEMEI
10.6 mi/5.0 hr

west of Trout Lake in Indian Heaven
Wilderness of Gifford Pinchot National Forest

Map 5.2, page 256

Lemei Trail provides a scenic route to the volcanic plateau of Indian Heaven Wilderness. The trail is a decent workout, ascending through much of its length. Views, huckleberries, and lakes are ample reward for the effort. After enjoying the meadows teeming with wildflower displays and feasting on August-ripe huckleberries, hikers will find that the waters of Lake Wapiki make a refreshing dip. One of the prettiest lakes in the high country of Indian Heaven, Lake Wapiki is enclosed by the area's tallest peak, jagged Lemei Rock.

Lemei Trail spends its first mile in dense second-growth forest. As the trail enters the wilderness (1 mile), the timber becomes old and large, in a more open forest. An understory of huckleberry bushes helps to ease the sting of the continuous climb. A side trail (3 miles) leads 0.5 mile to Lake Wapiki in the basin of Lemei Rock. Small forest and meadow fill the basin under craggy Lemei Rock. Lemei Trail continues beyond the junction to Indian Heaven Trail (5.3 miles) and miles of meadow exploration.

User Groups: Hikers, leashed dogs, and horses. No mountain bikes are allowed. No wheelchair access.

Permits: This trail is accessible mid-July–October. A federal Northwest Forest Pass is required to park here.

Maps: For a map of Gifford Pinchot National Forest, contact the Outdoor Recreation Information Center at the downtown Seattle REI. For a topographic map, ask Green Trails for No. 365S, Indian Heaven, or ask the USGS for Sleeping Beauty and Lone Butte.

Directions: From Vancouver, drive east 70 miles on Highway 14 to Highway 141. Turn north and drive 22 miles to Trout Lake. Continue north on Highway 141 as it becomes Forest Service Road 24 for 13 miles to the trailhead on the left (before Little Goose Campground).

Contact: Gifford Pinchot National Forest, Mount Adams Ranger District, 2455 Hwy. 141, Trout Lake, WA 98650, 509/395-3400.

105 RACE TRACK
6.2 mi/3.5 hr

west of Trout Lake in Indian Heaven
Wilderness of Gifford Pinchot National Forest

Map 5.2, page 256

Huckleberries and history are the story of this trail. Race Track Trail delves into the southern section of Indian Heaven Wilderness, a former meeting place for Native Americans. Each year, thousands of people from Yakama, Klickitat, and Columbia River nations gathered here during the height of the berry-harvesting season (August). The huckleberry bushes that flourish in this volcanic soil were a major source of food for Native Americans. And as it's situated along an important cross-Cascades trade route, it's easy to see how this area came to be known as an "Indian Heaven." During their time here, Native Americans entertained themselves by staging pony races, hence the name Race Track. The dirt track they used is still visible today within an open meadow.

A popular trail into the wilderness, Race Track Trail climbs steadily but gently, emerging from large timber to open subalpine meadows. During August, huckleberries will be sure to be the main attraction. But don't let them keep you from spotting the abundant wildlife, including deer, elk, hawk, and even black bear. Race Track Trail reaches Race Track Lake (2.3 miles), where the dirt track can be seen, and then ascends to the peak of Red Mountain. This lofty peak with big views is home to one of Gifford Pinchot's three remaining fire lookouts.

User Groups: Hikers, leashed dogs, and horses. No mountain bikes are allowed. No wheelchair access.

Permits: This trail is accessible June–October. A federal Northwest Forest Pass is required to park here.

Maps: For a map of Gifford Pinchot National Forest, contact the Outdoor Recreation Information Center at the downtown Seattle REI. For a topographic map, ask Green Trails for No. 365S, Indian Heaven, or ask the USGS for Gifford Peak.

Directions: From Vancouver, drive east 55 miles on Highway 14 to the town of Carson. Turn north on Wind River Road and drive 5 miles to Forest Service Road 65. Turn right and drive 13 miles to the signed trailhead at Falls Creek Horse Camp.

Contact: Gifford Pinchot National Forest, Mount Adams Ranger District, 2455 Hwy. 141, Trout Lake, WA 98650, 509/395-3400.

106 SLEEPING BEAUTY
2.8 mi/2.0 hr

north of Trout Lake in Gifford Pinchot
National Forest

Map 5.2, page 256

As close to Mount Adams as one can be without actually scaling its slopes, Sleeping Beauty offers a grand view of the mountain. A tall outcrop of craggy rock sticking out above the surrounding forest, Sleeping Beauty gazes at the mass of Mount Adams from just 8 miles distant. Access to the rocky peak is a steep but quick trip through dense second-growth forest. The trail finds the edge of logging and enjoys old timber for a short time. Any views are reserved until the very end.

Sleeping Beauty is so named because it apparently resembles the profile of a sleeping woman; we'll let you decide. All personifications aside, the view from the top is spectacular. Rainier, St. Helens, and Hood dot the distant horizons. The peaks of Indian Heaven rise on the western skyline. The peak was formerly home to a Forest Service lookout.

User Groups: Hikers and leashed dogs. No horses or mountain bikes are allowed. No wheelchair access.

Permits: This trail is accessible May–November. No permits are required. Parking and access are free.

Maps: For a map of Gifford Pinchot National Forest, contact the Outdoor Recreation Information Center at the downtown Seattle REI. For a topographic map, ask Green Trails for No. 366, Mount Adams West, or ask the USGS for Sleeping Beauty.

Directions: From Vancouver, drive east 70 miles on Highway 14 to Highway 141. Turn north and drive 22 miles to Forest Service Road 88, just beyond the town of Trout Lake. Turn right on Forest Service Road 88 and drive 5 miles to Forest Service Road 8810. Turn right and drive 5 miles to Forest Service Road 8810-040. Turn right and drive 0.5 mile to the trailhead on the left.

Contact: Gifford Pinchot National Forest, Mount Adams Ranger District, 2455 Hwy. 141, Trout Lake, WA 98650, 509/395-3400.

107 STAGMAN RIDGE
8.0–12.8 mi/4.0–7.0 hr

north of Trout Lake in Mount Adams Wilderness of Gifford Pinchot National Forest

Map 5.2, page 256

Stagman Ridge Trail provides great access to the high-country meadows flanking the western slopes of Mount Adams. The trail steadily but gently climbs to Horseshoe Meadows, home of juicy huckleberries, roaming mountain goats, and some pretty spectacular views. A trip to Horseshoe Meadows is indeed a great day, but hikers looking to throw in a subalpine lake (think refreshing swim) can continue an extra 2.4 miles to Lookingglass Lake.

Stagman Ridge Trail begins at a lofty elevation of 4,200 feet and gains about 1,600 feet over 4 miles. The forested trail quickly opens to reveal tremendous views of the mountain. It crosses several small streams, and Stagman Ridge Trail intersects the PCT (4 miles) on the lower slopes of Horseshoe Meadows. Although you could turn around here, hikers are well advised to continue on the PCT in either direction for at least a mile; the meadows are full of huckleberries in late summer and offer outstanding views year-round.

If the cold and refreshing water of Lookingglass Lake entices you to continue (it's well worth it), turn right on PCT, turn right again on Round the Mountain Trail (4.4 miles), and one more right turn onto Lookingglass Trail (5.5 miles). The lake (6.4 miles) is situated within high meadows, underneath the mountain.

User Groups: Hikers, leashed dogs, and horses. No mountain bikes are allowed. No wheelchair access.

Permits: This trail is accessible June–October. A federal Northwest Forest Pass is required to park here.

Maps: For a map of Gifford Pinchot National Forest, contact the Outdoor Recreation Information Center at the downtown Seattle REI. For a topographic map, ask Green Trails for No. 367S, Mount Adams, or ask the USGS for Mount Adams West.

Directions: From Vancouver, drive east 70 miles on Highway 14 to Highway 141. Turn north and drive 22 miles to Forest Service Road 23 (Buck Creek Road), near the town of Trout Lake. Turn right and drive 8 miles to Forest Service Road 8031. Turn right and drive 0.5 mile to Forest Service Road 070. Turn left and drive 3.5 miles to Forest Service Road 120. Turn right and drive 0.5 mile to the trailhead at road's end.

Contact: Gifford Pinchot National Forest, Mount Adams Ranger District, 2455 Hwy. 141, Trout Lake, WA 98650, 509/395-3400.

108 ROUND-THE-MOUNTAIN
22.2 mi one-way/2 days   🥾4   ⛰10

north of Trout Lake in Mount Adams
Wilderness of Gifford Pinchot National Forest

Map 5.2, page 256

Like Washington's other big volcanoes, Mount Adams is circumnavigated by a long, demanding trail. Set high in the subalpine meadows gracing the slopes of Mount Adams, Round-the-Mountain Trail is the best way to fully experience Washington's second-tallest peak. Here's the catch. The east side of Mount Adams is managed by the Yakima Indian Nation, and special permits are required to hike within the reservation (a vexing process). Additionally, this section of trail is extremely difficult. East-side streams turn into dangerous glacial torrents during the summer, and no maintained trail exists over enormous lava fields. Thus, Round-the-Mountain is best completed as a through-hike, along the western side of Mount Adams.

Round-the-Mountain Trail is best begun from Cold Springs on the south side of Mount Adams. Hike South Climb Trail to Round-the-Mountain Trail (1.3 miles) and turn north. The scenery is supreme every step of the way, with alpine meadows and distant mountain views the norm. Expect to see an abundance of wildflowers in midsummer and huckleberries in early fall. The trail encounters the PCT (7 miles) and follows it to Muddy Meadows Trail (19.8 miles). Turn north to reach the northern trailhead at Keenee Campground (22.2 miles).

Highlights along the way include Lookingglass Lake (5.9 miles), Horseshoe Meadows (7 miles), Sheep Lake (11 miles), and Adams Meadows (14.5 miles, below Adams Glacier). Campsites are frequent along the route; stick to already established sites to minimize damage to fragile meadows. The views of Mount Adams improve with progress around the peak, with great looks at the glaciers. If a true circumnavigation of the mountain is an unshakable goal, please contact the Mount Adams Ranger Station for full details on trail conditions.

User Groups: Hikers, leashed dogs, and horses. No mountain bikes are allowed. No wheelchair access.

Permits: This trail is accessible mid-July–October. A federal Northwest Forest Pass is required to park here.

Maps: For a map of Gifford Pinchot National Forest, contact the Outdoor Recreation Information Center at the downtown Seattle REI. For a topographic map, ask Green Trails for No. 367S, Mount Adams, or ask the USGS for Mount Adams West, Mount Adams East, and Green Mountain.

Directions: From Vancouver, drive east 70 miles on Highway 14 to Highway 141. Turn north and drive 22 miles to Forest Service Road 23 (Buck Creek Road), near the town of Trout Lake. Turn right and drive 3 miles to Forest Service Road 82. Turn right and drive 0.5 mile to Forest Service Road 80. Turn left and drive 4 miles to Forest Service Road 8040. Continue 5 miles on Road 8040 to Morrison Creek Campground and Forest Service Road 500. Turn right and drive 2 miles to the trailhead at road's end.

Contact: Gifford Pinchot National Forest, Mount Adams Ranger District, 2455 Hwy. 141, Trout Lake, WA 98650, 509/395-3400.

109 KILLEN CREEK
6.2 mi/4.0 hr   🥾3   ⛰10

north of Trout Lake in Mount Adams
Wilderness of Gifford Pinchot National Forest

Map 5.2, page 256

By the time the first views of Mount Adams emerge (which is quickly), hikers on Killen Creek Trail know they've selected a beauty of a hike. This popular route on the north side of Mount Adams climbs steadily through open forest to wide-open meadows beneath towering glaciers. This is undoubtedly great rambling country, where the hike gets better every step of the way. Day hikes this grand are hard to come by in southern Washington, and this is one of the best in the state.

Killen Creek Trail starts high (4,600 feet) and climbs slowly but steadily to the PCT (3.1 miles). Much of the trail traverses open forest with repeated views of Mount Adams, but the last mile or so revels in meadows. Wildflowers take turns blooming throughout the summer. Rambling in either direction along the PCT is highly recommended to soak up the scenery. Hikers hoping to approach even closer to the mountain are welcome to do so along High Camp Trail, a continuation of Killen Creek Trail on the uphill side of the PCT. This is a 1-mile trail to High Camp, one of Adams' best, among rocky meadows and glacier moraine.

User Groups: Hikers, leashed dogs, and horses. No mountain bikes are allowed. No wheelchair access.

Permits: This trail is accessible mid-July–mid-October. A federal Northwest Forest Pass is required to park here.

Maps: For a map of Gifford Pinchot National Forest, contact the Outdoor Recreation Information Center at the downtown Seattle REI. For a topographic map, ask Green Trails for No. 367S, Mount Adams, or ask the USGS for Green Mountain and Mount Adams West.

Directions: From Vancouver, drive east 70 miles on Highway 14 to Highway 141. Turn north and drive 22 miles to Forest Service Road 23 (Buck Creek Road), near the town of Trout Lake. Turn right and drive about 30 miles to Forest Service Road 2329. Turn right and drive 5 miles (around Takhlakh Lake) to the trailhead on the right.

Contact: Gifford Pinchot National Forest, Mount Adams Ranger District, 2455 Hwy. 141, Trout Lake, WA 98650, 509/395-3400.

110 SOUTH CLIMB
6.8 mi/4.5 hr

north of Trout Lake in Mount Adams Wilderness of Gifford Pinchot National Forest

Map 5.2, page 256

Not for the faint of heart, South Climb is exactly what the name implies: an ascent of Mount Adams from the south side. The summit needn't be one's goal to embark on this beautiful trail, but well-conditioned legs certainly are always helpful. South Climb Trail assaults the mountain straight on and reaches 8,500 feet of elevation before petering out beside Crescent Glacier. From here, it's a mad scramble to the top. Stopping at Crescent Glacier reveals spectacular views of the surrounding valleys, forests, and distant mountain ridges. If the wildflower meadows alongside the trail and beautiful views don't take your breath away, the steep pitch of South Climb will.

Should a summit of Mount Adams be on your wish list, keep several things in mind. One, it's steep as hell and strenuous. Experienced climbers take at least 6–8 hours to reach the summit from Cold Springs, an elevation gain of 6,700 feet. Visibility decreases after early morning, so smart mountaineers camp at Cold Springs Car Campground and hit the trail by 3 A.M. That's 3 o'clock in the morning. And the climb requires permits from the ranger station in Trout Lake. The summit is certainly achievable and is relatively easy compared to Mount Hood or Mount Rainier. Novices frequently reach the peak. At the top are views conceivable only if you've been there.

User Groups: Hikers, leashed dogs, and horses. No mountain bikes are allowed. No wheelchair access.

Permits: This trail is accessible July–September. A federal Northwest Forest Pass is required to park here. Climbing permits are required for summits of Mount Adams. The $15 permits are available at Trout Lake Ranger Station.

Maps: For a map of Gifford Pinchot National

Forest, contact the Outdoor Recreation Information Center at the downtown Seattle REI. For a topographic map, ask Green Trails for No. 367S, Mount Adams, or ask the USGS for Mount Adams West.

Directions: From Vancouver, drive east 70 miles on Highway 14 to Highway 141. Turn north and drive 22 miles to Forest Service Road 23 (Buck Creek Road), near the town of Trout Lake. Turn right and drive 3 miles to Forest Service Road 82. Turn right and drive 0.5 mile to Forest Service Road 80. Turn left and drive 4 miles to Forest Service Road 8040. Continue 5 miles on Road 8040 to Morrison Creek Campground and Forest Service Road 500. Turn right and drive 2 miles to the trailhead at road's end.

Contact: Gifford Pinchot National Forest, Mount Adams Ranger District, 2455 Hwy. 141, Trout Lake, WA 98650, 509/395-3400.

111 BATTLE GROUND LAKE LOOP
7.0 mi/3.5 hr

north of Vancouver in Battle Ground Lake State Park

Map 5.3, page 257

There's no need to drive all the way to southern Oregon to see Crater Lake. Washington has its own miniature version here in Battle Ground Lake. Like Crater Lake, Battle Ground Lake was created by a massive volcanic explosion. The resulting crater filled with spring water and created Battle Ground Lake. Today, conifer forests of Douglas fir and western hemlock surround the lake, creating peaceful and quiet surroundings. The trail circles the lake within the shady forest, never venturing far from the lakeshore. Anglers will appreciate the access to solitary fishing holes, where monster trout hide out. The state park has a large car campground, but it fills quickly on summer weekends.

User Groups: Hikers, leashed dogs, and horses. No mountain bikes are allowed. No wheelchair access.

Permits: This trail is accessible year-round.

No permits are required. Parking and access are free.

Maps: For a topographic map, ask the USGS for Battleground and Wacolt.

Directions: From Vancouver, drive north on I-5 to exit 14. Turn right on Northeast 179th Street and drive to the city of Battle Ground. Drive to the east end of town and turn left on Grace Avenue. Drive 3 miles to Battle Ground Lake State Park. The signed trailhead is near the day-use area within the park.

Contact: Battle Ground Lake State Park, 18002 NE 249th St., Battle Ground, WA, 98604, 360/687-4621.

112 BEACON ROCK
2.0 mi/2.0 hr

east of Vancouver in Beacon Rock State Park

Map 5.3, page 257

Visible from miles away and towering over the Columbia River, Beacon Rock offers an unbeatable view of the Columbia River Gorge. Geologically speaking, Beacon Rock is a true rock. That is, it's one solid piece of rock, not a conglomeration of different types of rock like many mountains are. That makes Beacon Rock the second tallest "rock" in the world! Beacon Rock is actually the core of an old volcano, exposed when the Missoula Floods eroded softer rock encasing it. The resulting hulk towers 848 feet over the mighty Columbia. It's quite a perch from the top.

Beacon Rock State Park offers nearly 20 miles of trail and road to explore, but the most popular and scenic is the trail to the summit. It's a little under 1 mile to the top, but don't let the short distance fool you. It's a steep climb every step of the way. Old forest shades the trail where trees can find a small ledge to grow, but many areas are on steep, exposed cliffs. Boardwalks, stairways, and handrails have been installed to present a safer experience. The summit is an ideal picnic spot, with great views of the gorge and Mount Hood.

User Groups: Hikers and leashed dogs. No

horses or mountain bikes are allowed. No wheelchair access.

Permits: This trail is accessible March–November. No permits are required. Parking and access are free.

Maps: For a topographic map, ask the USGS for Bonneville Dam and Tanner Butte.

Directions: From Vancouver, drive east on Highway 14 to Beacon Rock State Park (near Mile Marker 35). The trailhead is on the right side of the highway.

Contact: Beacon Rock State Park, 34841 State Road 14, Stevenson, WA, 98648-6081, 509/427-8265.

113 SIOUXON

8.0 mi/4.0 hr

east of Cougar in Gifford Pinchot National Forest

Map 5.4, page 258

Deep within old forest, Siouxon Trail journeys alongside the noisy creek. Waterfalls and deep pools are regular highlights, making this a great winter hike when higher routes are closed due to snow. Siouxon Trail quickly descends from the trailhead to the creek. Large and gushing West Creek is crossed by a large wooden bridge (0.5 mile). Peer downstream to see the first of many waterfalls. The trail encounters another cascade on Siouxon Creek (4 miles), where the creek empties into a large emerald pool. During the summer, good luck avoiding the urge for a quick dip in the cold water. This is a common turnaround point for many day hikers, but Siouxon Trail travels along the creek for a total of 5.5 miles through grand forest the entire length. This is a great place to spend a night with little ones or first-time backpackers. Numerous campsites are on the stream banks, where the noisy stream lulls one to sleep.

User Groups: Hikers, leashed dogs, horses, and mountain bikes. No wheelchair access.

Permits: This trail is accessible year-round. No permits are required. Parking and access are free.

Maps: For a map of Gifford Pinchot National Forest, contact the Outdoor Recreation Information Center at the downtown Seattle REI. For a topographic map, ask Green Trails for No. 396, Lookout Mountain, or ask the USGS for Siouxon Peak and Bear Mountain.

Directions: From Vancouver, drive north on I-5 to Highway 503 (Woodland, exit 21). Drive east 45 miles to Pine Creek Information Center. Turn right and continue on Forest Service Road 90 to Northeast Healy Road, in the town of Clehatchie. Turn right and drive 10 miles to Forest Service Road 57. Turn left and drive 1.5 miles to Forest Service Road 5701. Turn left and drive 4 miles to the trailhead at road's end.

Contact: Gifford Pinchot National Forest, Mount Adams Ranger District, 2455 Hwy. 141, Trout Lake, WA 98650, 509/395-3400.

114 LOWER FALLS CREEK

3.4 mi/2.0 hr

north of Carson in Gifford Pinchot National Forest

Map 5.4, page 258

About the only thing keeping the masses from Lower Falls Creek is the short length of the trail. It's not a destination in itself. But anyone visiting the town of Carson should certainly spend the time to visit Lower Falls Creek. The trail follows this beautiful stream as it passes through a narrow gorge and ends at the base of a large waterfall. On hot summer days, the forest is cool and shady, and the water of Falls Creek is especially appealing.

Lower Falls Creek Trail climbs gently throughout its short length. Deer and elk are frequently seen browsing in the forest, filled with the sounds of woodpeckers and wrens. The trail crosses Falls Creek as it gushes through a rock gorge; fortunately, a suspension bridge spans the gap. Falls Creek Trail ends at the base of a large waterfall, where Falls Creek cascades down a steep wall.

User Groups: Hikers, leashed dogs, and mountain bikes. No horses are allowed. No wheelchair access.

Permits: This trail is accessible year-round. A federal Northwest Forest Pass is required to park here.

Maps: For a map of Gifford Pinchot National Forest, contact the Outdoor Recreation Information Center at the downtown Seattle REI. For a topographic map, ask Green Trails for No. 397, Wind River, or ask the USGS for Termination Point.

Directions: From Vancouver, drive east 55 miles on Highway 14 to the town of Carson. Turn north on Wind River Road and drive 9 miles to Forest Service Road 30. Turn right and drive 3 miles to the signed trailhead on the right.

Contact: Gifford Pinchot National Forest, Mount Adams Ranger District, 2455 Hwy. 141, Trout Lake, WA 98650, 509/395-3400.

115 TRAPPER CREEK
9.5 mi/4.5 hr

north of Carson in Trapper Creek Wilderness of Gifford Pinchot National Forest

Map 5.4, page 258

Any opportunity to hike in old-growth forest should be seized, sooner rather than later. Trapper Creek, one of the least-known wildernesses in the state of Washington, preserves a small chunk of ancient timberland just north of the Columbia River Gorge. Trapper Creek Trail makes a full immersion into the wilderness, following the beautiful, restless creek to its headwaters as it flows over waterfalls and through narrow gorges. Trapper Creek Trail connects to Observation Trail (see next listing), so if you're itching for views, you can have them by making a large loop.

Trapper Creek Trail spends much of its length alongside the noisy creek. The forest is a diverse mix of giants, with Douglas fir, western hemlock, and western red cedar, all draped with mosses and lichens, growing to immense proportions. Trapper Creek Trail junctions with Observation Peak Trail (1 mile) but continues alongside the creek. The creek is a long sequence of cascades and pools, but Trapper Creek Falls

(4.5 miles) are the highlight of the trip and a good turnaround point. The trail ends at another junction with Observation Trail, the option for a loop trip (about 12 miles).

User Groups: Hikers, leashed dogs, and horses. No mountain bikes are allowed. No wheelchair access.

Permits: This trail is accessible year-round. A federal Northwest Forest Pass is required to park here.

Maps: For a map of Gifford Pinchot National Forest, contact the Outdoor Recreation Information Center at the downtown Seattle REI. For a topographic map, ask the USGS for Bare Mountain.

Directions: From Vancouver, drive east 55 miles on Highway 14 to the town of Carson. Turn north on Wind River Road and drive 10 miles to Forest Service Road 3065. Turn left and drive 1.5 miles to the signed trailhead at Government Mineral Springs.

Contact: Gifford Pinchot National Forest, Mount Adams Ranger District, 2455 Hwy. 141, Trout Lake, WA 98650, 509/395-3400.

116 OBSERVATION PEAK
6.0-13.0 mi/3.0-7.0 hr   2   10

north of Carson in Trapper Creek Wilderness of Gifford Pinchot National Forest

Map 5.4, page 258

Options, options, options. Observation Peak provides great views from the heart of Trapper Creek Wilderness, over lush, green valleys out to several snowcapped volcanic peaks. Best of all, there are several ways to enjoy this pristine and unlogged section of the Gifford Pinchot. A trip to Observation Peak can be a short hike (5.6 miles), a long up and down (13 miles), or one of two loop trips (12 miles). These loops are by far the best way to experience the wilderness, where misty forests are full of ancient timber.

Observation Trail runs from the valley bottom up along a high ridge to Observation Peak and out to Forest Service Road 58. For a short hike, park on Forest Service Road 58 and hike south through Sister Rocks Natural Area (big trees!) to the peak (2.8 miles). Reaching Observation Peak from the south is certainly longer and more strenuous, but remember that rule: no pain, no gain.

From Government Mineral Springs, Observation Trail climbs steadily from old-growth lowland forest into a mix of subalpine trees. Views are frequent along the lightly forested ridge, as are huckleberries and deer. Hearty hikers can pass the peak and descend back to the trailhead via Trapper Creek Trail (see previous listing) or Dry Creek (Big Hollow Trail, another big tree and beautiful creek route).

User Groups: Hikers, leashed dogs, and horses. No mountain bikes are allowed. No wheelchair access.

Permits: This trail is accessible July–October. A federal Northwest Forest Pass is required to park here.

Maps: For a map of Gifford Pinchot National Forest, contact the Outdoor Recreation Information Center at the downtown Seattle REI. For a topographic map, ask Green Trails for No. 396, Lookout Mountain, and No. 397, Wind River, or ask the USGS for Bare Mountain.

Directions: From Vancouver, drive east 55 miles on Highway 14 to the town of Carson. Turn north on Wind River Road and drive 10 miles to Forest Service Road 3065. Turn left and drive 1.5 miles to the signed trailhead at Government Mineral Springs.

Contact: Gifford Pinchot National Forest, Mount Adams Ranger District, 2455 Hwy. 141, Trout Lake, WA 98650, 509/395-3400.

117 BUNKER HILL

3.6 mi/1.5 hr

north of Carson in Gifford Pinchot National Forest

Map 5.4, page 258

Great for folks in Carson with a couple of hours to kill, Bunker Hill Trail is a quick but strenuous climb to the summit. The first

0.5 mile of the route follows the PCT north. Most folks on the PCT are through-hikers coming from Oregon and on their way to big, grand country in the coming months. Turn left onto Bunker Hill Trail and do the switchback shuffle up to the summit. Views are reserved until the very top, where a fire lookout once stood. Views of the Wind River Valley are revealed, as are numerous surrounding ridges.

User Groups: Hikers and leashed dogs. No horses or mountain bikes are allowed. No wheelchair access.

Permits: This trail is accessible April–December. No permits are required. Parking and access are free.

Maps: For a map of Gifford Pinchot National Forest, contact the Outdoor Recreation Information Center at the downtown Seattle REI. For a topographic map, ask Green Trails for No. 397, Wind River, or ask the USGS for Stabler.

Directions: From Vancouver, drive east 55 miles on Highway 14 to the town of Carson. Drive north 5.5 miles on Wind River Road to Hemlock Road. Turn left and drive 1.5 miles to Forest Service Road 43. Turn right and drive 0.5 mile to Forest Service Road 43-417. Turn right and drive 0.2 mile to the Pacific Crest Trailhead. Head to the right (north) on the PCT.

Contact: Gifford Pinchot National Forest, Mount Adams Ranger District, 2455 Hwy. 141, Trout Lake, WA 98650, 509/395-3400.

118 LITTLE HUCKLEBERRY

5.0 mi/3.0 hr

west of Trout Lake in Gifford Pinchot National Forest

Map 5.4, page 258

One of the more accessible viewpoints from Highway 14, Little Huckleberry Trail makes a quick and at times steep trip to an old lookout site. Views of Mount Adams and Mount Hood, across the Columbia River, are quite nice. And a feast of huckleberries along the way sweetens the deal on August trips to the mountain. This is a nice trail for a weekend morning, if you're coming from Vancouver or Portland.

Little Huckleberry Trail gains 1,800 feet in just 2.5 miles, a steady and soon tiring ascent within a small draw. Enjoy the old forest and take your time. Early in the summer, a cold-water spring runs (2 miles), offering a great place to break. The final 0.5 mile climbs through open berry fields and rock slopes to the summit. A lookout once stood atop this rounded top, perched over a wide expanse of the Gifford Pinchot. With room for a tent, this is a fun overnighter for beginning backpackers (think of the stars).

User Groups: Hikers, leashed dogs, horses, and mountain bikes. No wheelchair access.

Permits: This trail is accessible April–November. A federal Northwest Forest Pass is required to park here.

Maps: For a map of Gifford Pinchot National Forest, contact the Outdoor Recreation Information Center at the downtown Seattle REI. For a topographic map, ask Green Trails for No. 398, Willard, or ask the USGS for Sleeping Beauty.

Directions: From Vancouver, drive east 70 miles on Highway 14 to Highway 141. Turn north and drive 22 miles to Trout Lake. Continue north on Highway 141 as it becomes Forest Service Road 24 for 10 miles to Forest Service Road 66. Turn left (south) and drive 5 miles to the trailhead on the left.

Contact: Gifford Pinchot National Forest, Mount Adams Ranger District, 2455 Hwy. 141, Trout Lake, WA 98650, 509/395-3400.

119 DOG MOUNTAIN

6.0 mi/3.5 hr

east of Carson in Gifford Pinchot National Forest

Map 5.4, page 258

Getting to Dog Mountain, with a trailhead directly on Highway 14, is no problem. Getting up Dog Mountain is a bit more of a workout, however. Dense forest mixes with open wildflower meadows along the trail, cresting at the open summit of Dog Mountain. The views of the Columbia River Gorge are outstanding, with snowcapped Mount Hood standing across the way. This is a very popular hike with folks coming from Vancouver or Portland, especially on the weekends. Expect to see a neighbor or two.

Dog Mountain Trail makes the best of what it has been given, forming a loop instead of a straight up and down. The loop is arranged like a lasso. Climb steeply to the loop junction (0.5 mile). Head to the right for a more gradual and scenic route to the top. Regular breaks in the forest provide room for open meadows of wildflowers (May is a great month here). This is dry country, meaning water is nonexistent; pack plenty, because overall elevation gain is 2,700 feet. Do be on the lookout for poison oak and rattlesnakes, things that most hikers don't care to mess with. The summit is the former home to a Forest Service lookout. The loop returns to the junction via a steep, densely forested route.

User Groups: Hikers and leashed dogs. No horses or mountain bikes are allowed. No wheelchair access.

Permits: This trail is accessible March–December. No permits are required. A federal Northwest Forest Pass is required to park here, and access is free.

Maps: For a map of Gifford Pinchot National Forest, contact the Outdoor Recreation Information Center at the downtown Seattle REI. For a topographic map, ask the USGS for Mount Defiance.

Directions: From Vancouver, drive east on Highway 14 to Mile Marker 53 and the signed trailhead.

Contact: Gifford Pinchot National Forest, Mount Adams Ranger District, 2455 Hwy. 141, Trout Lake, WA 98650, 509/395-3400.

SOUTHEASTERN WASHINGTON

© SCOTT LEONARD

BEST HIKES

◖ **Hikes for Views**
Oregon Butte, **page 348.**

What's that? You didn't know that there was

any hiking in the southeast portion of our state? There surely is, and most of it is unlike anything else found in a state famous for cloudy and rainy days. Better known for its agricultural base, this region offers up some beautiful and wild places for hiking, although not much. This is the sparsest region for trails, and most of them are concentrated in the very southeastern corner of the state in the Blue Mountains. That's a long drive for most Washington residents, especially those living on the west side of the Cascades. Still, thanks to the warm weather that makes wheat, hops, and wine grapes major crops in the region, some great trails exist for spring hiking, when snow still blankets the high country of the Cascades.

Near Yakima, the Cascades devolve into a mass of rolling foothills. Just a few dozen miles from the rain forests on the west side of the Cascades, this is dry country for sure. Much of this region receives just 20 inches or less of rain each year, so you can almost always count on sunny skies. Yakima Rim Trail is a hike for the first outing of the year. While snow measured by the foot still lingers in the Cascades, wildflowers are beginning to blossom in this desert-steppe environment. Yakima Rim runs along Umtanum Ridge, delivering views of the snow-capped Stuart Range on the horizon, colorful blossoms, and dry, moderate temperatures in April and May. Umtanum Creek Trail wanders up a low valley, one of the few places to find water year-round. Each of these hikes is located on the Yakima River, a world-class trout river and a pretty good river raft, too.

Spread amidst miles of agricultural land are several unlikely environments for Washington. Potholes Sand Dunes are an expansive landscape in the middle of our state. Countless small lakes and the larger Potholes reservoir break up large dunes of sand. Near the Tri-Cities are Juniper Dunes Wilderness, another desertlike landscape seemingly out of place in Washington. In fact, it's so unusual that it is affectionately known as "Washington's Sahara," where vast dunes spread out over the high desert, dotted by small shrubs and the occasional tree. You may even come across an grove of ancient juniper trees, many of them centuries old and subsisting on just inches of rain each year. Coyotes, deer, and owls far outnumber bipeds in this area. This is one of the region's best places to set out and explore cross-country. Folks who don't want to venture far from the car will love the easy access to Palouse Falls, Washington's version of Niagara Falls. Smack-dab in the middle of nowhere (ever heard of Washtucna?), the Palouse River makes a mighty and vociferous drop into a large bowl. The falls are just one of the many land features left by the Missoula Glacial Floods, when billions of gallons of water rushed from Montana to the Pacific, scouring eastern Washington along the way.

The jackpot of hiking in southeast Washington is the Wenaha-Tucannon Wilderness. This federally protected wilderness envelops more than 177,000 acres of the Blue Mountains, stretching across the border of Washington and Oregon. The Blue Mountains are an untamed, rarely visited place, where bighorn sheep, deer, and elk are plentiful and draw hundreds of hunters in the fall. The Wenaha-Tucannon Wilderness is unique in that access points start from on high, usually around 5,000 feet, and require hikers to drop down into the vast canyons and gorges to explore. The lookout atop Oregon Butte is a popular (and easy) place to visit here, where you can get a panoramic view of the arid mountains and valleys. Longer trips can be made along Crooked Creek or Smooth Ridge down to the Wenaha River, an excellent trout and salmon river. Despite its remote location, the Wenaha-Tucannon Wilderness is a beautiful Washington landscape and should be visited at least once by all devout hikers.

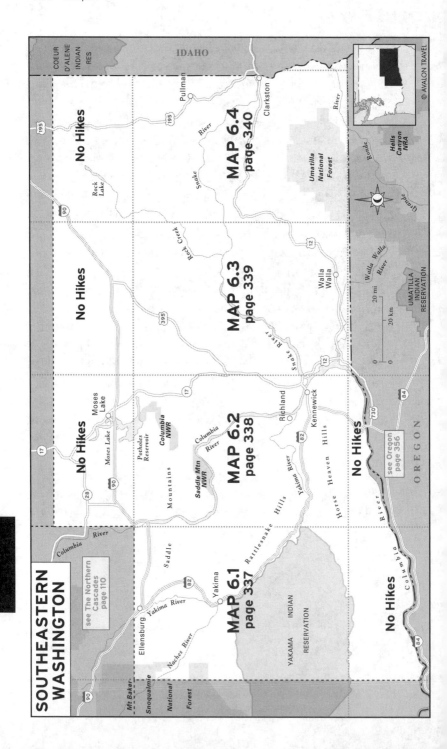

SOUTHEASTERN WASHINGTON

see The Northern Cascades page 110

MAP 6.1 page 337

MAP 6.2 page 338

MAP 6.3 page 339

MAP 6.4 page 340

No Hikes

see Oregon page 356

© AVALON TRAVEL

Map 6.1

Hikes 1-2
Page 341

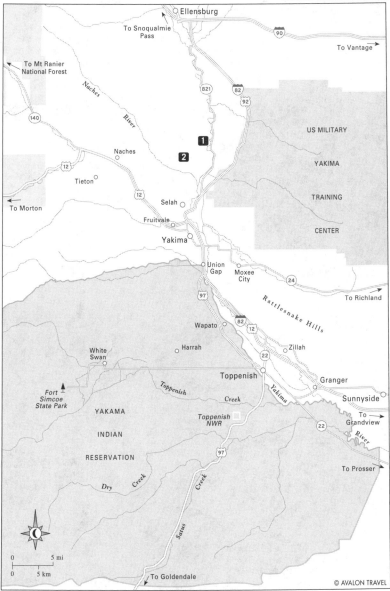

Map 6.2

Hike 3
Page 342

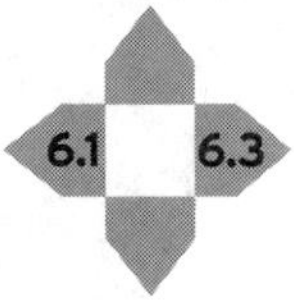

6.1   6.3

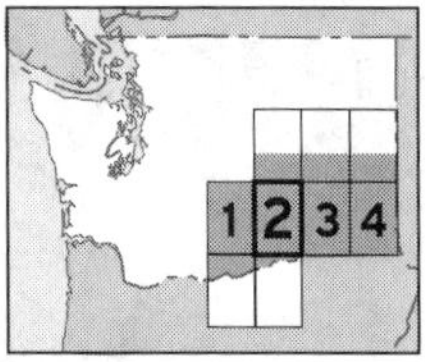

1 2 3 4

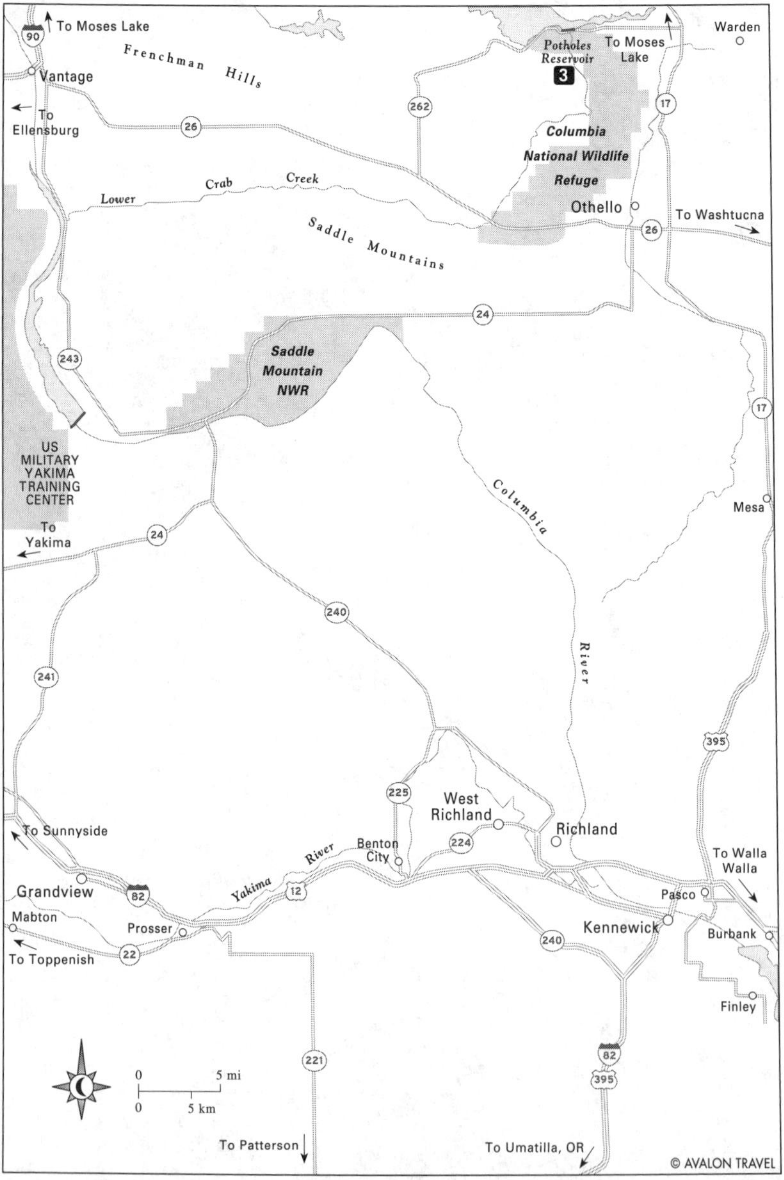

To Moses Lake

90

Frenchman Hills

Vantage

To Ellensburg

26

Lower   Crab   Creek

Saddle   Mountains

243

Saddle
Mountain
NWR

US
MILITARY
YAKIMA
TRAINING
CENTER

To Yakima

24

240

241

262

Potholes
Reservoir
3

To Moses Lake

Warden

17

Columbia
National Wildlife
Refuge

Othello

26

To Washtucna

24

Columbia

17

Mesa

River

395

225

West Richland

Richland

224

To Walla Walla

To Sunnyside

Yakima   River

Benton
City

12

Grandview

82

Mabton

Prosser

To Toppenish

22

Pasco

Kennewick

Burbank

240

Finley

221

82

395

N

0   5 mi
0   5 km

To Patterson

To Umatilla, OR

© AVALON TRAVEL

Map 6.3

Hikes 4-5
Page 344

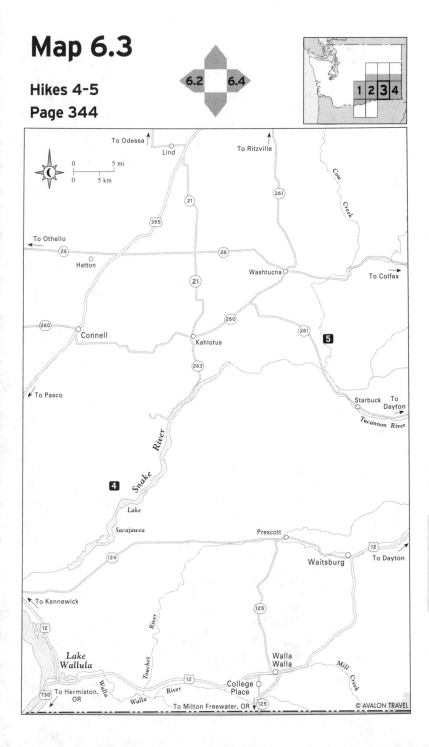

Map 6.4

Hikes 6-19
Pages 345-353

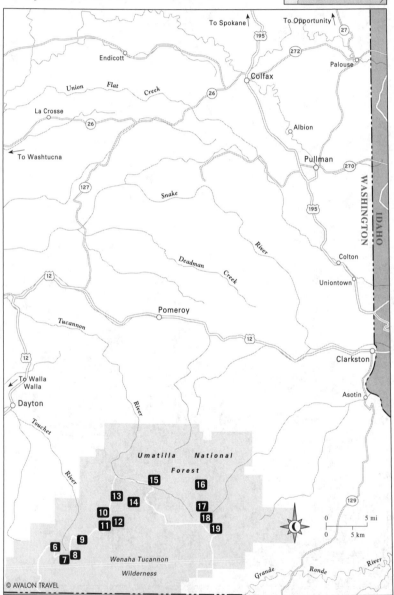

1 UMTANUM CREEK

4.0 mi/2.0 hr

north of Yakima in L. T. Murray Wildlife Refuge

Map 6.1, page 337

Umtanum Creek offers the ideal early season hike. You know that time of year, when Cle Elum and Yakima are hitting 75°F but Seattle is still mired in May showers, and snow blankets the Cascades. This is the trail to hit. Umtanum Creek Trail begins within one of Washington's most beautiful canyons, home to the Yakima River. Basalt cliffs and large rounded mountains dominate the valley, with small creek drainages running in between. Umtanum Creek Trail follows the creek through rarely experienced east-side meadows, a rich habitat for wildlife. Spring is the best season to hike here, especially in May, when wildflowers smother the hillsides in color.

The trail begins by crossing the Yakima River on a suspension bridge and quickly crosses railroad tracks, entering the L. T. Murray Wildlife Refuge. Although it gets extremely dry in summer, this area is home to an array of wildlife, including deer, eagles, hawks, coyotes, amphibians, snakes, and, some say, bighorn sheep. Umtanum Creek Trail follows the gently flowing creek up the valley. Willows and cottonwoods mark the creek, a sharp contrast to the meadows on the hillsides. The maintained trail ends about 2 miles upstream. If a longer hike is your intention, it's only a short scramble to the top of the bordering ridges. From on top, views stretch from the valley below to the Stuart Range.

User Groups: Hikers, leashed dogs, horses, and mountain bikes. No wheelchair access.

Permits: This trail is accessible March–November. The Washington Department of Fish and Wildlife requires an annual Vehicle Use Permit to park here. Permits are issued free with the purchase of a hunting or fishing license; additional permits are $11 each. Permits are available anywhere hunting or fishing licenses are sold, by telephone at 866/246-9453, or online at fishhunt.dfw.wa.gov.

Maps: For topographic maps, ask the USGS for Wymer and The Cottonwoods.

Directions: From Ellensburg, drive south 16.5 miles on Highway 821 to the signed trailhead and parking area on the right (west) side of the road.

Contact: Washington Department of Fish and Wildlife, 201 N. Pearl St., Ellensburg, WA 98926, 509/925-6746.

2 YAKIMA RIM

4.0-18.0 mi/2.0 hr-2 days

north of Yakima in L. T. Murray Wildlife Refuge

Map 6.1, page 337

When snow still blankets the high country and the rains are still drenching the west side (that is, much of the spring), there is no better trail than Yakima Rim. It's an east-side gem, especially considering that you can tally on one hand the number of trees you encounter. The route traverses a high, rolling ridge with views of the surrounding countryside and far-off mountains. Wildflowers are everywhere, bringing much-needed life to a normally brown and dry terrain. It's a completely different world from the forests of the Cascades and every bit as beautiful.

Yakima Rim Trail is more of a route than a trail. Often following an old road through the L. T. Murray Wildlife Refuge, the trail makes a long loop, with half along a high ridge and the other half through a narrow valley. From the lower trailhead, head to the left and climb along the old, abandoned, but signed Jacob Durr Road to the crest of the ridge, about 4.5 miles, and an upper trailhead. Mount Rainier pokes up from the southwest while the Stuart Range is visible in all its glory to the north. A closed dirt road heads east along the ridge, dropping to the Yakima River in about 10 miles. The way back to the trailhead is 4 miles through the lush Rosa Creek Valley, full of grasses, willows, snakes, and deer.

Spring is by far the best time to visit, when the daytime air is still cool. Be sure to carry

Yakima Rim Trail is easily accessible from Seattle.

water, especially on the ridge, as water is found only in Rosa Creek. The best campsite is on Rosa Creek 1.5 miles from the Yakima River at Birdsong Tree, an old locust tree planted nearly 150 years ago by homesteaders. For a shorter and less demanding trip, head to the left from the trailhead to find Birdsong Tree (2.0 miles). Deer are a frequent companion within the willow groves alongside Rosa Creek.

User Groups: Hikers, leashed dogs, horses, and mountain bikes. No wheelchair access.

Permits: This trail is accessible March–November. The Washington Department of Fish and Wildlife requires an annual Vehicle Use Permit to park here. Permits are issued free with the purchase of a hunting or fishing license; additional permits are $11 each. Permits are available anywhere hunting or fishing licenses are sold, by telephone at 866/246-9453, or online at fishhunt.dfw.wa.gov.

Maps: For topographic maps, ask the USGS for Wymer and The Cottonwoods.

Directions: From Selah, drive 5 miles on Wenas Road to Sheep Company Road. Turn right and drive 5 miles (enter the wildlife refuge at Mile 2.6) to the unsigned trailhead. The key to finding the start of the trail is a small sign at a junction naming the Jacob Durr Road. Head left on the road to reach the ridge. Head right to find Rosa Creek Valley.

Contact: Washington Department of Fish and Wildlife, 201 N. Pearl St., Ellensburg, WA 98926, 509/925-6746.

₃ SEEP LAKES
1.0-6.0 mi/1.0-3.0 hr

south of Moses Lake in Columbia Basin Wildlife Area

Map 6.2, page 338

As you drive through this dry part of Eastern Washington, with sagebrush and rolling scablands all around, you may not expect to find many lakes in the area. But take a hike through Seep Lakes Wildlife Area, and you will be amazed at the lakes you'll stumble upon. The small lakes were created thousands of years ago when the low, flat land was flooded by the massive Missoula Floods. The floods carved channels in the land and left pockets of lakes amongst tall basalt cliffs. Grasses and juniper grow thickly, supporting a rich population of wildlife—mule deer, coyotes, and a vast abundance of birds. The area is also popular with fishermen, who hike into remote lakes for impressive trout and bass.

Hiking here is best done with a good topo map and a compass. There are clear trails criss-crossing the area, but few are marked. In many places, the trail may seem more like a game trail than anything made by man. But the vague trail system makes for a multitude of possibilities, and full-on cross-country trips here make for great adventure. The best bet is to head out south from the Soda Lake parking area (about 2 miles down Seep Lakes Road) and hike roughly 2.5 miles south to Long and Hampton Lakes. Bring water, as the area is quite hot during summer, and the potholes aren't recommended for drinking. Wide-open horizons make this a great place for a night hike. Set out under a full moon and witness the night shift of wildlife at work.

User Groups: Hikers, leashed dogs, horses, and mountain bikes. No wheelchair access.

Permits: This area is accessible year-round.

The Washington Department of Fish and Wildlife requires an annual Vehicle Use Permit to park here. Permits are issued free with the purchase of a hunting or fishing license; additional permits are $11 each. Permits are available anywhere hunting or fishing licenses are sold, by telephone at 866/246-9453, or online at fishhunt.dfw.wa.gov.

Maps: For topographic maps, ask the USGS for Royal Camp and Mae.

Directions: From Moses Lake, go south on State Route 17 to County Road M SE. Turn south on County Road M SE and proceed 6 miles to State Highway 262. Turn east (left) on Highway 262 and go a half-mile to the gravel road on the south (right). This gravel road is known as "the Seep Lakes Road" and it provides public access through the Seep Lakes Unit to the McManamon Road on the south end.

Contact: Washington Department of Fish and Wildlife, 6653 Road K NE, Moses Lake, WA 98837, 509/765-6641.

© SCOTT LEONARD

Rocky outcroppings frame many of the Seep Lakes in eastern Washington.

◢ JUNIPER DUNES
5.5 mi/4.0 hr

northeast of Pasco in Juniper Dunes Wilderness

Map 6.3, page 339

One of Washington's smallest and certainly most isolated wildernesses, Juniper Dunes promises to be unique. Covering more than 7,100 acres of pristine high desert, the Juniper Dunes preserve a small gem in the middle of Eastern Washington. Sagebrush and desert grasses do their best to hold together the large mounds of sand, some more than 100 feet high. This layer of vegetation keeps the dunes in place and provides habitat for wildlife. Mule deer, coyotes, porcupines, and mice do their business on the ground while red-tailed hawks and owls work from the skies. The highlight of a trip to Juniper Dunes is surely the six small groves of juniper trees found near the center of the wilderness. From the trailhead, walk the road roughly 1.5 miles before turning due north for 1 mile. These groves of juniper trees have existed here in relative isolation for thousands of years; many individual trees have grown for two or three centuries. The trees are surprisingly big and seem fairly out of place, in light of the fact that the region receives on average only 12 inches of rain a year. Special considerations include water (there is none to be found here) and a map and compass (other than the jeep trail bisecting the wilderness, there are no discernable trails). A field guide and binoculars will also prove helpful, for wildlife is sure to be a part of your trip to Juniper Dunes.

User Groups: Hikers, leashed dogs, and horses. No mountain bikes are allowed. No wheelchair access.

Permits: This trail is accessible year-round. No permits are needed. Parking and access are free.

Maps: For topographic maps, ask the USGS for Levey, Levey SW, and Levey NE.

Directions: From Pasco, drive east 2 miles on Highway 12 to Pasco/Kahlotus Highway. Turn left and drive 5.5 miles to Peterson Road. Turn left and drive 4.5 miles to a large sandy parking area, where the jeep trail starts.

Contact: Bureau of Land Management, Spokane District Office, 1103 N. Fancher St., Spokane, WA 99212-1275, 509/536-1200.

◢ PALOUSE FALLS
0.2 mi/0.5 hr

north of Walla Walla on the Palouse River

Map 6.3, page 339

The trail may be short, but the falls are big. From a high viewpoint, watch the Palouse River make a thunderous plummet nearly 200 feet into a large bowl before rolling downstream to the Snake River. Adding to the scenic beauty are enormous cliffs and columns of basalt stationed around the falls. The enormous falls were created by the Missoula Floods more than 15,000 years ago. Mile-thick sheets of ice in Montana blocked glacial meltwater, creating an enormous lake. When the dams eventually broke (dozens of times through thousands of years), the torrents they released raced from Montana down through the Columbia Basin of Washington. Much of Eastern Washington was scoured and altered, as were Eastern Oregon and the Willamette Valley. Palouse Falls is just one of the more interesting and noisy changes the floods left behind. The heavy flows of water quickly eroded the basalt, producing the falls. The official trail is short, but there are several nonofficial side trails leading (safely) to viewpoints upriver from the parking lot. A trail is visible down around the falls, but it is dangerous and should not be attempted. It's not a destination hike (don't drive from Seattle just to see it), but Palouse Falls is a good stopover when passing through the area. A number of trees provide welcome shade for picnics and lounging. The only safety consideration is an important one: This is rattlesnake country, so be cautious at all times, and be mindful of canine companions, who should be leashed at all times. Rattlers enjoy basking on side trails, in the grass, and even in the parking lot.

User Groups: Hikers and leashed dogs. No horses or mountain bikes are allowed. This trail is wheelchair accessible.

Permits: This trail is accessible year-round. No permits are needed. Parking and access are free.

Maps: For a topographic map, ask the USGS for Palouse Falls.

Directions: From Kennewick, drive north on U.S. 395 to Highway 260. Head east for 25 miles to Highway 261. Turn north and drive 14.5 miles to Palouse Falls Road. Turn left and drive 2 miles to the parking area where the trail starts.

Contact: Palouse Falls State Park, Hwy. 261, Washtucna, WA, 509/549-3551.

6 SAWTOOTH RIDGE
28.0 mi/3-4 days

east of Walla Walla in the Wenaha-Tucannon Wilderness of Umatilla National Forest

Map 6.4, page 340

The trail along Sawtooth Ridge is the epitome of the Wenaha-Tucannon Wilderness—long and high, dry and secluded, but chock-full of gorgeous views of the surrounding country. The trail makes a long traverse of Sawtooth Ridge, passing in and out of forests and meadows on its way into Oregon and down to the Wenaha River. The trail's placement along the ridge means that you shouldn't expect to find any water until the Wenaha. On such a long trail, it's necessary to plan carefully and carry plenty of extra fluids. Much of the path is rocky and difficult, not surprising for a ridge named Sawtooth. As far as camping is concerned, set up camp in the scenic meadow of your choice, as long as it's low impact. Wildlife in the forms of deer, bighorn sheep, and elk abound, while other hikers certainly do not (save for hunting seasons). In May and early June, Sawtooth Ridge will pleasantly surprise hikers with a grand display of wildflowers.

User Groups: Hikers, leashed dogs, and horses.

No mountain bikes are allowed. No wheelchair access.

Permits: This trail is accessible mid-June–October. No permits are required. Parking and access are free.

Maps: For a map of Umatilla National Forest, contact the Outdoor Recreation Information Center at the downtown Seattle REI. For topographic maps, ask the USGS for Godman Spring and Wenaha Forks.

Directions: From Dayton, drive south on North Fork Touchet River Road (following signs toward Bluewood Ski Area). This road becomes Forest Service Road 64 and eventually intersects Forest Service Road 46. Turn left on Forest Service Road 46 and drive 0.5 mile to the signed trailhead on the right side of the road.

Contact: Umatilla National Forest, Pomeroy Ranger District, 71 W. Main St., Pomeroy, WA 99347, 509/843-1891.

7 SLICK EAR
12.0 mi/7.0 hr

east of Walla Walla in the Wenaha-Tucannon Wilderness of Umatilla National Forest

Map 6.4, page 340

More than half of this trail actually lies within Oregon, but it would be a shame to omit such a beautiful route to the Wenaha River. Heavily used by hunters in the fall but rarely during other times of the year, Slick Ear offers hikers outstanding views of the surrounding landscape before dramatically dropping into a beautiful forested canyon ending at the Wenaha. Don't expect to find much water along the first 2 miles, where the trail rides the ridge top. At that point (a good turnaround for less serious excursions), the trail drops steeply into the canyon containing Slick Ear Creek. Down here is where you'll find water, campsites, and, unfortunately, rattlesnakes too. The trail ends at the Wenaha River, a prime spot for both trout and salmon fishing (Wenaha salmon are endangered and federally protected, so be sure to check Oregon fishing regulations). The trail works especially well as a loop if hikers travel east on the Wenaha River Trail to Grizzly Bear Trail, a total of 18.2 miles.

User Groups: Hikers, leashed dogs, and horses. No mountain bikes are allowed. No wheelchair access.

Permits: This trail is accessible June–October. A federal Northwest Forest Pass is required to park here.

Maps: For a map of Umatilla National Forest, contact the Outdoor Recreation Information Center at the downtown Seattle REI. For topographic maps, ask the USGS for Godman Spring and Wenaha Forks.

Directions: From Dayton, drive south on North Fork Touchet River Road (following signs toward Bluewood Ski Area). This road becomes Forest Service Road 64 and eventually intersects Forest Service Road 46. Turn left on Forest Service Road 46 and drive 3 miles to Forest Service Road 46-300. Turn right and drive 5 miles to Twin Buttes Trailhead at road's end.

Contact: Umatilla National Forest, Pomeroy Ranger District, 71 W. Main St., Pomeroy, WA 99347, 509/843-1891.

8 GRIZZLY BEAR RIDGE
15.0 mi/2 days

east of Walla Walla in the Wenaha-Tucannon Wilderness of Umatilla National Forest

Map 6.4, page 340

This is one more of the many great ridge hikes in the wilderness. Putting it near the top of the list is a pair of cold-water springs supplying much-needed refreshment on hot summer days and panoramic views leading to the Wenaha River. The Wenaha is an outstanding river for trout fishing with Grizzly Bear offering access to one of the most remote sections. The trail follows an old road for about 2 miles, at which point Coyote Spring can be found on the south side. The trail then follows the ridge into Oregon, slowly losing elevation for 4 miles

to Meadow Spring (on the north side of the trail). Meadow Spring is a good turnaround point for folks out for just a day hike. The descent continues as the trail makes its way to the Wenaha River. Camps are best made near Meadow Spring or preferably at the Wenaha. Hikers can make a great loop by combining Grizzly Bear Ridge with Slick Ear, a total of 18.2 miles. Actual grizzly bears may be gone from this area, but a lot of other wildlife abounds. Black bears roam the meadows, as do mule deer, elk, and bighorn sheep. Hawks and ravens soar in the skies, while trout and salmon ply the Wenaha.

User Groups: Hikers, leashed dogs, and horses. No mountain bikes are allowed. No wheelchair access.

Permits: This trail is accessible June–October. A federal Northwest Forest Pass is required to park here.

Maps: For a map of Umatilla National Forest, contact the Outdoor Recreation Information Center at the downtown Seattle REI. For topographic maps, ask the USGS for Godman Spring, Oregon Butte, and Elbow Creek.

Directions: From Dayton, drive south on North Fork Touchet River Road (following signs toward Bluewood Ski Area). This road becomes Forest Service Road 64 and eventually intersects Forest Service Road 46. Turn left on Forest Service Road 46 and drive 3 miles to Forest Service Road 46-300. Turn right and drive 5 miles to Twin Buttes Trailhead at road's end.

Contact: Umatilla National Forest, Pomeroy Ranger District, 71 W. Main St., Pomeroy, WA 99347, 509/843-1891.

9 WEST BUTTE CREEK
16.0 mi/2 days

east of Walla Walla in the Wenaha-Tucannon Wilderness of Umatilla National Forest

Map 6.4, page 340

West Butte Creek has a bit of everything. After spending several miles along a high open ridge with panoramic views of the wilderness, the trail drops through the Rainbow Creek Natural Research Area. Wildlife is extremely abundant along this route. Mule deer, elk, bighorn sheep, and black bear are frequent sightings in this wild area.

The trail begins from Godman, a Forest Service station on the edge of Wenaha-Tucannon Wilderness. Soak in the views as you slowly traverse the ridge for 2 miles. The trail then steeply drops to Rainbow Creek and some campsites (4 miles). This is in the heart of the Rainbow Creek Natural Research Area, a large section of wilderness devoted to the study of this unique and natural ecosystem. Large Douglas and grand firs provide welcome shade and lower the temperature significantly during the summer. The route ends at a junction with East Butte and Twin Buttes Trails, two primitive and rarely maintained routes back up to high ridge trailheads, which if hiked would require car-drops. The trail is hot and dry along the ridge but water is available year-round from Rainbow Creek.

User Groups: Hikers, leashed dogs, and horses. No mountain bikes are allowed. No wheelchair access.

Permits: This trail is accessible June–October. No permits are required. Parking and access are free.

Maps: For a map of Umatilla National Forest, contact the Outdoor Recreation Information Center at the downtown Seattle REI. For topographic maps, ask the USGS for Godman Spring and Oregon Butte.

Directions: From Dayton, drive 1 mile south on 4th Street to Mustard Hollow Road. Turn left and drive 28 miles (as the road turns to Eckler Mountain Road, Skyline Drive, and Forest Service Road 46) to the Godman Guard Station. The trailhead is on the left immediately after the guard station.

Contact: Umatilla National Forest, Pomeroy Ranger District, 71 W. Main St., Pomeroy, WA 99347, 509/843-1891.

10 SMOOTH RIDGE
28.0 mi one-way/3 days

east of Walla Walla in the Wenaha-Tucannon Wilderness of Umatilla National Forest

Map 6.4, page 340

Smooth Ridge is the chief high route through the Wenaha-Tucannon Wilderness, offering constant views of mountains near and far. No route through the wilderness is as scenic or as likely to provide wildlife sightings as Smooth Ridge. Numerous cold-water springs along the route provide water well into summer, and campsites are found regularly along the way, making the long journey easy. Smooth Ridge is a trekker's dream, either as an excellent through-hike or an outstanding (but extremely long) loop hike.

The best access to Smooth Ridge is via Mount Misery Trail out of Teepee Trailhead. After 2.5 miles, the trail intersects Smooth Ridge below the north slope of Oregon Butte, a quick, must-see side trip. Smooth Ridge Trail travels south over Danger Point and encounters the first set of springs at about 5 miles. From here, the trail follows the ridge through forest and meadow up to Weller Butte at 10 miles and slowly drops to the Wenaha River and the state of Oregon (18 miles). On clear days (which is nearly every day during summer), the Wallowa Range in Oregon and the Seven Devils Range in Idaho are plainly visible.

It's highly recommended to carry a map on this trip to help find the many springs (usually just off the main trail). Most springs provide water well into August, unless it's been a very dry spring. Campsites are situated throughout the route, with the best ones found next to the springs. From the Wenaha River, hike 9 miles east to Troy, Oregon, and the logical drop-off for your return ride. Another option is to hike Crooked Creek north and return via Indian Corral, a long, tiring, and beautiful loop of more than 50 miles.

User Groups: Hikers, leashed dogs, and horses. No mountain bikes are allowed. No wheelchair access.

Permits: This trail is accessible June–October. A federal Northwest Forest Pass is required to park here.

Maps: For a map of Umatilla National Forest, contact the Outdoor Recreation Information Center at the downtown Seattle REI. For topographic maps, ask the USGS for Oregon Butte, Eden, and Diamond Peak.

Directions: From Dayton, drive 1 mile south on 4th Street to Mustard Hollow Road. Turn left and drive 28 miles (as the road turns to Eckler Mountain Road, Skyline Drive, and Forest Service Road 46) to the Godman Guard Station. Turn left onto Forest Service Road 4608 and drive 5 miles to Teepee Trailhead at road's end.

Contact: Umatilla National Forest, Pomeroy Ranger District, 71 W. Main St., Pomeroy, WA 99347, 509/843-1891.

⓫ TURKEY CREEK
8.0 mi/4.5 hr   🥾4   ⛰8

east of Walla Walla in the Wenaha-Tucannon Wilderness of Umatilla National Forest

> **Map 6.4, page 340**

While much of Southeastern Washington receives little rain or snow, Turkey Creek is an exception. Turkey Creek drains to the north, meaning much of the valley gets less sunshine than other valleys. The result is that Turkey Creek holds on to a hefty snowpack well into May. With a source of water lasting so long, the creek supports a more lush forest. And that makes for great hiking scenery: many large trees with a thick, green understory. Water also means an abundance of wildlife, with deer and elk finding Turkey Creek a cool refuge from the area's dry, hot ridges.

Turkey Creek Trail drops from Teepee Trailhead, the one and only vista along the route (in the opposite direction, no less). The trail descends sharply into a valley of enormous Douglas firs and western larches. The strongly flowing creek is never out of earshot as the trail travels 4 miles to the confluence with Panjab Creek. Several camps lie along the route (mainly used by hunters in the fall), including a pair near the midpoint and the best site at the junction with Panjab Trail. Turkey Creek flows year-round, meaning water is readily available, even on hot summer days. Good on its own, the trail works especially well as part of a 16-mile loop with Panjab and Oregon Butte Trails.

User Groups: Hikers, leashed dogs, and horses. No mountain bikes are allowed. No wheelchair access.

Permits: This trail is accessible June–November. A federal Northwest Forest Pass is required to park here.

Maps: For a map of Umatilla National Forest, contact the Outdoor Recreation Information Center at the downtown Seattle REI. For topographic maps, ask the USGS for Panjab Creek and Oregon Butte.

Directions: From Dayton, drive 1 mile south on 4th Street to Mustard Hollow Road. Turn left and drive 28 miles (as the road turns to Eckler Mountain Road, Skyline Drive, and Forest Service Road 46) to the Godman Guard Station. Turn left onto Forest Service Road 4608 and drive 5 miles to Teepee Trailhead at road's end.

Contact: Umatilla National Forest, Pomeroy Ranger District, 71 W. Main St., Pomeroy, WA 99347, 509/843-1891.

⓬ OREGON BUTTE
5.5 mi/3.0 hr   🥾2   ⛰10

east of Walla Walla in the Wenaha-Tucannon Wilderness of Umatilla National Forest

> **Map 6.4, page 340**   **BEST (**

Where there are fire lookouts, there are views. Oregon Butte is no exception to this high-country rule. With easy access and knockout vistas, Oregon Butte is undoubtedly the most beautiful day hike in the Wenaha-Tucannon Wilderness. The high, open mountaintop reveals all of the surrounding wilderness, and on clear days, the jagged, snowy peaks of the Wallowa Range in Oregon and Seven Devils Range in Idaho are readily visible. And to top it off, mule deer and bighorn sheep are frequently seen along the route.

The trip to Oregon Butte follows Mount Misery Trail east out of Teepee Trailhead. At 2.5 miles, the trail passes Oregon Butte Spring, the route's only source of water. Just beyond is the junction for Smooth Ridge, along with several campsites. An easily found side trail heads straight up to the summit of Oregon Butte and the fire lookout, still staffed by the Forest Service during the summer. The views extend in every direction, with most of the wilderness's drainages easily traced back to their sources. The trail is easy to follow at all times and fairly gentle and easy. It's important to know that Mount Misery Trail lies on the north side of a ridge, meaning snow can linger along the trail well into June.

User Groups: Hikers, leashed dogs, and horses. No mountain bikes are allowed. No wheelchair access.

Permits: This trail is accessible June–October. A federal Northwest Forest Pass is required to park here.

Maps: For a map of Umatilla National Forest, contact the Outdoor Recreation Information Center at the downtown Seattle REI. For a topographic map, ask the USGS for Oregon Butte.

Directions: From Dayton, drive 1 mile south on 4th Street to Mustard Hollow Road. Turn left and drive 28 miles (as the road turns to Eckler Mountain Road, Skyline Drive, and Forest Service Road 46) to the Godman Guard Station. Turn left onto Forest Service Road 4608 and drive 5 miles to Teepee Trailhead at road's end.

Contact: Umatilla National Forest, Pomeroy Ranger District, 71 W. Main St., Pomeroy, WA 99347, 509/843-1891.

13 PANJAB
11.2 mi/6.0 hr 🏃3 ▲7

east of Walla Walla in the Wenaha-Tucannon Wilderness of Umatilla National Forest

Map 6.4, page 340

Panjab provides the best access to Indian Corral, the Wenaha-Tucannon Wilderness's largest and most popular high-country camp. Indian Corral is an intersection for several long, highly scenic trails spreading into the far reaches of the wilderness. Having such a crossroads as its end makes Panjab useful as a starting point for long treks. With wide expansive meadows, Panjab is also a great day hike.

The trail starts from large Panjab Trailhead and gently climbs alongside Panjab Creek through cool forests for 1.5 miles to an intersection with Turkey Creek Trail and the route's only camp. Notice the diverse forests, full of Douglas fir, yews, grand fir, ponderosa pine, and western larch. This a good turnaround spot for casual hikers, as the trail only gets steeper. The next 2.5 miles climb steadily through the forest to Indian Corral and wide meadows of wildflowers. Water is common along the route, important on those hot summer days. Numerous camps are available at Indian Corral, and for water Dunlap Springs is just a few hundred yards down Crooked Creek Trail. Except in the fall, during hunting season, don't expect to see many people; the Wenaha-Tucannon is desolate country.

User Groups: Hikers, leashed dogs, and horses. No mountain bikes are allowed. No wheelchair access.

Permits: This trail is accessible June–October. A federal Northwest Forest Pass is required to park here.

Maps: For a map of Umatilla National Forest, contact the Outdoor Recreation Information Center at the downtown Seattle REI. For topographic maps, ask the USGS for Panjab Creek.

Directions: From Dayton, drive east 12 miles on Highway 12 to Tucannon River Road. Turn right and drive 35 miles to a fork. Stay to the right as the road turns into Forest Service Road 4713 and drive 3 miles to the well-signed trailhead.

Contact: Umatilla National Forest, Pomeroy Ranger District, 71 W. Main St., Pomeroy, WA 99347, 509/843-1891.

14 CROOKED CREEK
29.2 mi one-way/2-3 days 🏃4 ⛰9

east of Walla Walla in the Wenaha-Tucannon Wilderness of Umatilla National Forest

Map 6.4, page 340

This is the trail for those seeking a long trek through the heart of the Wenaha-Tucannon Wilderness. Starting high at Indian Corral, overlooking the surrounding Blue Mountains, Crooked Creek Trail drops into cool, shady forests and travels 18 miles to the Wenaha River. By the time you're done, you'll be in Oregon. And you'll likely be tired. Crooked Creek Valley is full of life, passing through prime wildlife country where deer, elk, bighorn sheep, and black bears are common residents.

The route begs for a car-drop, with one vehicle stationed at Panjab Trailhead and another in Troy, Oregon. Otherwise, it's a long trip back to your car, either via the same route or via Smooth Ridge (a 52-mile loop). Start at Panjab Trailhead and hike to Indian Corral (5.6 miles). Crooked Creek Trail drops beside Trout Creek, which runs into Third Creek (12 miles), which runs into Crooked Creek (18 miles). Another 5 miles brings hikers to the Wenaha River; Troy is six miles to the east.

Much of the route is well forested, a big plus in this hot, dry region. Frequent breaks in the trees, however, reveal the high, open ridges that define this wilderness. Water is never a problem since the creeks run year-round. Camps are situated regularly along the trail as well. A fishing pole is a nice luxury, as Crooked Creek and the Wenaha are prime fishing streams. Solitude seekers will be in heaven here; except during the fall hunting seasons, you likely won't encounter another soul.

User Groups: Hikers, leashed dogs, and horses. No mountain bikes are allowed. No wheelchair access.

Permits: This trail is accessible June–October. A federal Northwest Forest Pass is required to park here.

Maps: For a map of Umatilla National Forest, contact the Outdoor Recreation Information Center at the downtown Seattle REI. For topographic maps, ask the USGS for Diamond Peak, Eden, Oregon Butte, and Panjab Creek.

Directions: From Dayton, drive east 12 miles on Highway 12 to Tucannon River Road. Turn right and drive 35 miles to a fork in the road. Veer to the left onto Forest Service Road 4712 and drive 5 miles to the well-signed trailhead at road's end.

Contact: Umatilla National Forest, Pomeroy Ranger District, 71 W. Main St., Pomeroy, WA 99347, 509/843-1891.

15 TUCANNON RIVER
8.2 mi/4.5 hr 🏃1 ⛰9

east of Walla Walla in Umatilla National Forest

Map 6.4, page 340

The Tucannon River provides the setting for the area's most laid-back hike, a gentle walk through a striking canyon among surprisingly large trees. The route gains little elevation over its 5-mile length, making it great for families and casual hikers. Though after 4.1 miles in, the trail begins a steep climb out of the valley. For a more relaxed hike, turn back after 4.1 miles. The Tucannon is well stocked with trout, making it an angler's dream. Although the trail isn't within the wilderness boundaries, there's little trace of people other than the easy-to-follow footpath. The narrow valley of the Tucannon is made of steep cliffs giving way to rounded ridges, with thick forests in the valley bottom. Ponderosa pine, yew, Douglas fir, and grand fir grow quite large here, creating a forest as impressive as those of the West Cascades, at least in light of what little precipitation the area receives. The trail ends at a junction with Jelly Springs Trail (a steep ascent to Diamond Peak) and Bear Creek (a steep ascent to Hunter's Spring). The Tucannon is a protected stream, so anglers will want to check state fishing regulations on the way in. Also keep in mind that this is rattlesnake country. They're most often found in sunny, rocky sections of the trail and are likely to warn you of their presence with a few shakes of their tails. Nevertheless, keep your eyes and ears peeled, and mind your canine companions.

User Groups: Hikers, leashed dogs, and horses. No mountain bikes are allowed. No wheelchair access.

Permits: This trail is accessible April–November. A federal Northwest Forest Pass is required to park here.

Maps: For a map of Umatilla National Forest, contact the Outdoor Recreation Information Center at the downtown Seattle REI. For a topographic map, ask the USGS for Stentz Spring.

Directions: From Dayton, drive east 12 miles on Highway 12 to Tucannon River Road. Turn right and drive 35 miles to a fork in the road. Veer to the left onto Forest Service Road 4712 and drive 5 miles to the well-signed trailhead at road's end.

Contact: Umatilla National Forest, Pomeroy Ranger District, 71 W. Main St., Pomeroy, WA 99347, 509/843-1891.

16 BEAR CREEK
6.0 mi/4.0 hr   🏃4 ⛰8

east of Walla Walla in Umatilla National Forest

Map 6.4, page 340

Bear Creek serves as a route to the wildest parts of the Tucannon River. The trail drops from Hunter's Spring atop a high ridge into a rough canyon encasing the Tucannon River. This section of the river is at least 3 miles from any road, making visitors scarce. Few visitors means even fewer anglers, which in turn

means mostly unfished water—this equals a trout angler's dream. The hike down is not easy, though, losing more than 1,600 feet along a steep and rocky descent. Although the trail is rough, the view is great. Pine, spruce, and larch create an open parkland forest with plenty of views of the rocky canyon below. The rustling in the bushes is probably mule deer or elk, both of which are plentiful in this wild area. Also present in the area are rattlesnakes, so be sure to keep your eyes and ears alert, and keep your dog leashed, as well. The trail empties on the valley floor at the shores of the Tucannon River. A couple of campsites can be found here at this junction, where trails lead down the river or up the other side of the canyon to Jelly Springs.

User Groups: Hikers, leashed dogs, and horses. No mountain bikes are allowed. No wheelchair access.

Permits: This trail is accessible June–November. No permits are required. Parking and access are free.

Maps: For a map of Umatilla National Forest, contact the Outdoor Recreation Information Center at the downtown Seattle REI. For a topographic map, ask the USGS for Stentz Spring.

Directions: From Pomeroy, drive south 10 miles on County Road 128 to Mountain Road 40. Stay to the right and drive about 16 miles to the Blue Mountain Trail sign. Turn right and drive 0.25 mile to the signed trailhead.

Contact: Umatilla National Forest, Pomeroy Ranger District, 71 W. Main St., Pomeroy, WA 99347, 509/843-1891.

17 JELLY SPRINGS
9.0 mi/5.0 hr   🏃4 ⛰7

east of Walla Walla in Umatilla National Forest

Map 6.4, page 340

Within the Blue Mountains just north of the Wenaha-Tucannon Wilderness, Jelly Springs Trail offers a unique perspective on the area. The trail is one of the few to bear due north from the wilderness, offering views not seen from the region's other trails. From Diamond Peak Trailhead, the route makes an easy traverse of a high ridge (over 6,000 feet in elevation) for 3 miles. Hawks frequently patrol the skies in search of a meal while Rocky Mountain elk and mule deer graze within the high meadows. Jelly Springs, a cold-water spring that runs well into August, serves as a good turnaround point for those not interested in making the sharp, steep descent to the Tucannon River. The trail encounters the Tucannon River Trail at 4.5 miles, a potential route for a through-hike. While most of the trail lies outside the wilderness boundary, the uppermost section is protected, keeping out noisy motorbikes.

User Groups: Hikers, leashed dogs, and horses. Motorcycles are allowed on the lower section of the trail and must turn around at the wilderness boundary. No mountain bikes are allowed. No wheelchair access.

Permits: This trail is accessible June–October. No permits are required. Parking and access are free.

Maps: For a map of Umatilla National Forest, contact the Outdoor Recreation Information Center at the downtown Seattle REI. For topographic maps, ask the USGS for Stentz Spring and Diamond Peak.

Directions: From Pomeroy, drive south 10 miles on County Road 128 to Mountain Road (Forest Service Road 40). Continue straight (on Forest Service Road 40) for 24 miles to Forest Service Road 4030. Turn right and drive 5 miles to the Diamond Trailhead at road's end. Jelly Springs Trail begins 1.5 miles west on Mount Misery Trail.

Contact: Umatilla National Forest, Pomeroy Ranger District, 71 W. Main St., Pomeroy, WA 99347, 509/843-1891.

18 MOUNT MISERY
14.7 mi one-way/2 days

east of Walla Walla in the Wenaha-Tucannon Wilderness of Umatilla National Forest

Map 6.4, page 340

It may be known as Mount Misery Trail, but in fact, it has little to do with its namesake. Mount Misery is quickly skirted in the first few miles and soon forgotten. Instead, the trail continues to Diamond Peak, the Wenaha-Tucannon Wilderness's highest point, and onward for 12 miles through exceptional meadows packed full of far-flung vistas. Some of the area's best hiking is found here, along a trail that starts high and stays there. Throw in a number of cold-water springs and scenic camps, and you have yourself a wonderful trip.

The trail is best completed as a through-hike, with a start at Diamond Peak Trailhead and ending at Teepee Trailhead. Pass on the side trip to Mount Misery (although it isn't a miserable view) and make a short side trip up Diamond Peak (at 2.5 miles) and big-time views. From there the trail travels 7 miles to Indian Corral, wandering in and out of meadows along Horse Ridge. Views extend over the whole of the Wenaha-Tucannon Wilderness, all the way to the Wallowa Range in Oregon and Seven Devils Range in Idaho. The route passes five springs along the way and campsites are plentiful, with the best spots usually near the springs. From Indian Corral, the trail heads south 3 miles to Oregon Butte (another great, short side trip) then east 2 miles to Teepee Trailhead. Expect to encounter a fair amount of wildlife, including mule deer, Rocky Mountain elk, and bighorn sheep. Don't expect to run into many other hikers, save for during the fall hunting seasons.

User Groups: Hikers, leashed dogs, and horses. No mountain bikes are allowed. No wheelchair access.

Permits: This trail is accessible June–October. No permits are required. Parking and access are free.

Maps: For a map of Umatilla National Forest, contact the Outdoor Recreation Information Center at the downtown Seattle REI. For topographic maps, ask the USGS for Panjab Creek, Diamond Peak, and Stentz Spring.

Directions: From Pomeroy, drive south 10 miles on County Road 128 to Mountain Road (Forest Service Road 40). Continue straight (on Forest Service Road 40) for 24 miles to Forest Service Road 4030. Turn right and drive 5 miles to Diamond Trailhead at road's end.

Contact: Umatilla National Forest, Pomeroy Ranger District, 71 W. Main St., Pomeroy, WA 99347, 509/843-1891.

19 MELTON CREEK
19.4 mi/2 days

east of Walla Walla in the Wenaha-Tucannon Wilderness of Umatilla National Forest

Map 6.4, page 340

It's a shame that so few people travel Melton Creek Trail, because it's packed full of exceptional views and awe-inspiring terrain. The first 5 miles traverse a high ridge immersed in panoramic views of the surrounding wilderness. There are loads of opportunities to see bighorn sheep and Rocky Mountain elk in this country. As if that weren't good enough, the trail then drops to the shady forest of Melton Creek, which flows through a stunning canyon. This is one of the more secluded spots within the Wenaha-Tucannon Wilderness, an attractive consideration for those seeking a little solitude. Water is nonexistent along the ridge but Melton Creek flows year-round. The trail intersects Crooked Creek Trail at the 10-mile mark, a decent day's travel (day hikers will want to turn around before the trail drops to Melton Creek). A few camps are spread out along the route, with the best ones in the valley. The few who set out on this trail will surely not be disappointed.

User Groups: Hikers, leashed dogs, and horses. No mountain bikes are allowed. No wheelchair access.

Permits: This trail is accessible June–October. No permits are required. Parking and access are free.

Maps: For a map of Umatilla National Forest, contact the Outdoor Recreation Information Center at the downtown Seattle REI. For a topographic map, ask the USGS for Diamond Peak.

Directions: From Pomeroy, drive south 10 miles on County Road 128 to Mountain Road (Forest Service Road 40). Continue straight (on Forest Service Road 40) for 24 miles to Forest Service Road 4030. Turn right and drive 5 miles to Diamond Trailhead at road's end. Melton Creek Trail begins 1.5 miles west on Mount Misery Trail.

Contact: Umatilla National Forest, Pomeroy Ranger District, 71 W. Main St., Pomeroy, WA 99347, 509/843-1891.

Oregon

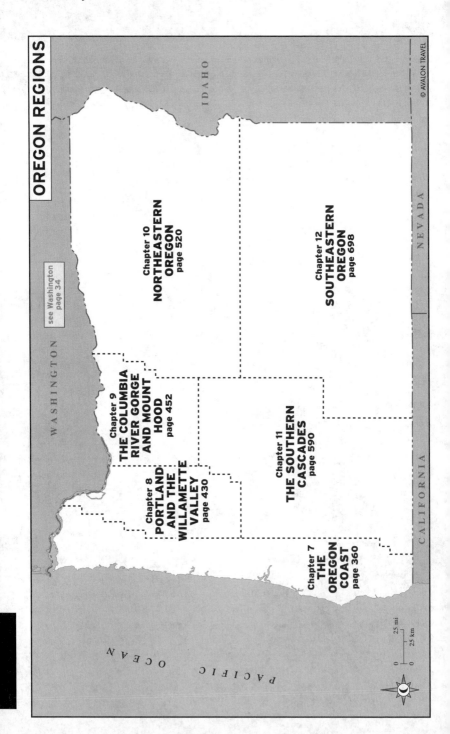

OREGON REGIONS

see Washington
page 34

WASHINGTON

IDAHO

NEVADA

CALIFORNIA

PACIFIC OCEAN

Chapter 10
NORTHEASTERN
OREGON
page 520

Chapter 12
SOUTHEASTERN
OREGON
page 698

Chapter 9
THE COLUMBIA
RIVER GORGE
AND MOUNT
HOOD
page 452

Chapter 8
PORTLAND
AND THE
WILLAMETTE
VALLEY
page 430

Chapter 11
THE SOUTHERN
CASCADES
page 590

Chapter 7
THE
OREGON
COAST
page 360

0   25 mi
0   25 km

© AVALON TRAVEL

THE OREGON COAST

© SEAN PATRICK HILL

BEST HIKES

Oregonians go to "the coast," but never to

"the beach." Sure, there are beaches here, but forget your image of the West Coast. This is not your ordinary Los Angeles beach with surfers riding the waves – though you'll see them, too. Oregon's coastline is 363 miles of rugged, awe-inspiring, and unforgettable landscape. From enormous, cliff-lined capes to windswept sand dunes, from rhododendron-sheltered coves to forested mountains, from sandy spits to towering sea stacks teeming with wildlife, Oregon's coast runs the gamut. You can see ancient Sitka spruce and redwoods, climb lava flow headlands, explore tidal pools, or just sit on a beach watching the brown pelicans skirt the surf, making Oregon's coastline by far some of the most dramatic in the country.

The Oregon state parks on the coast are among the best in the state, and many are free. There are also scores of "waysides," simple turnouts with a picnic table or two that are often the site of amazing trailheads. Many parks offer camping, swimming, and historical sites in addition to trails and beaches. You will also find National Forest land with dense forests of Douglas fir, Western red cedar, Western hemlock, and Sitka spruce. Wildlife is plentiful, from elk to deer to shorebirds. Among the parks and forestlands is the Oregon Dunes National Recreation Area, a must-see for anyone, with its stupendous dunes rising hundreds of feet and covering nearly 36 miles of coastline.

But there is more than just ocean and sand; what Oregonians know of the coast also includes the Coast Range, mountains that separate the coastline proper from the Willamette Valley. In the Coast Range, you'll find incredible mountain hikes, flowering rhododendrons, and waterfall after waterfall. The southern portion of the Coast Range gives way to the Klamath and Siskiyou Mountains, a granite landscape that geographically is one of the oldest parts of the state. The sweeping forest fire known as the Biscuit Fire, among the largest in Oregon's history, swept through here in 2002, but the area is recovering nicely. Flowers bloom and many trees were spared. Cutting through these mountains are the Rogue and Illinois Rivers, destinations for river rats and wilderness aficionados.

Many of the trails in this area follow the 360-mile Oregon Coast Trail, extending from Brookings in the south to Astoria in the north. Following this trail, you'll cross rivers, follow rocky headlands, and pass through quaint towns. As with the more well-known Pacific Crest Trail, this path can be followed for the entire distance, backpacked for shorter sequences, or just make for some great day-tripping.

In the coastal area, towering, inaccessible cliffs often hem in beaches, so be sure to check tide charts and go at low tide. Be extra careful when atop the cliffs themselves, too. Though the many capes and cliffs make for great vistas, they can also be dangerous. Make sure you don't step on anything living around sea stacks and tidepools. Many areas, like Haystack Rock on Cannon Beach, are federally protected wildlife preserves, and it is against the law to intrude on these important nesting and breeding sites. When in doubt, check with local agencies and land management.

So don't go thinking "coast" means bathing suits and sand castles, though you'll see your share of those. Instead, think of it as a real wilderness. In this regard, it is valuable to not only check the weather before you go (Oregon weather anywhere, let alone the finicky coast, can change abruptly; believe me, I know), but check the tide charts. Oregon is famous for its "sneaker waves" that come up quite unexpectedly with little forewarning. Be safe on your adventures on the Oregon coast, and you'll remember it as the rugged adventure it has always been.

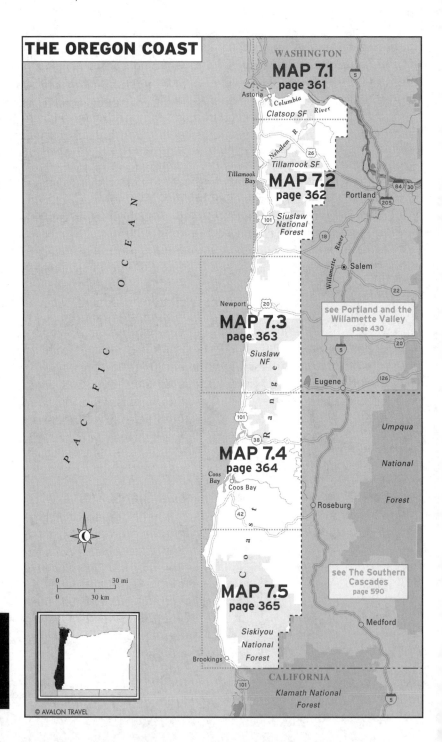

THE OREGON COAST

WASHINGTON

MAP 7.1
page 361

Astoria

Columbia River

Clatsop SF

Nehalem R.

Tillamook SF

Tillamook Bay

MAP 7.2
page 362

Portland

Siuslaw National Forest

Salem

Newport

MAP 7.3
page 363

Siuslaw NF

Coast Range

see Portland and the Willamette Valley
page 430

Eugene

MAP 7.4
page 364

Coos Bay

Coos Bay

Roseburg

Umpqua

National

Forest

PACIFIC OCEAN

see The Southern Cascades
page 590

MAP 7.5
page 365

Siskiyou National Forest

Brookings

Medford

CALIFORNIA

Klamath National Forest

0   30 mi
0   30 km

© AVALON TRAVEL

Map 7.1

Hikes 1-2
Page 366

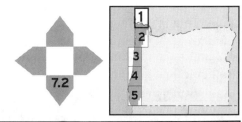

7.2

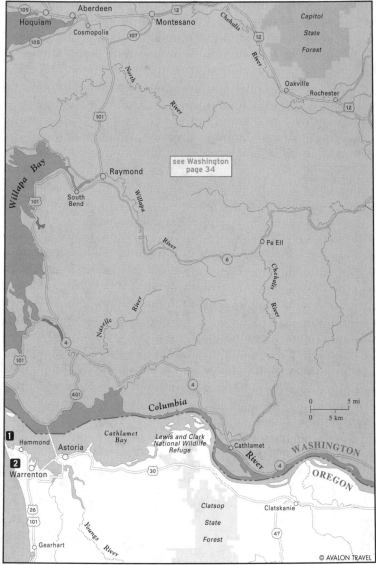

© AVALON TRAVEL

Map 7.2

Hikes 3-24
Pages 367-380

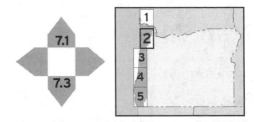

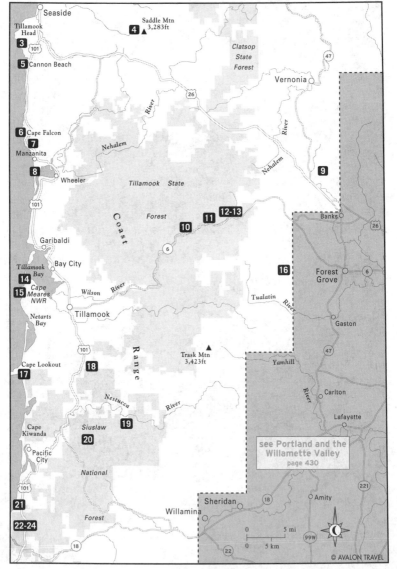

Map 7.3

Hikes 25-48
Pages 381-394

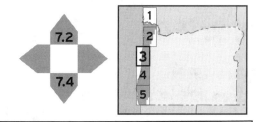

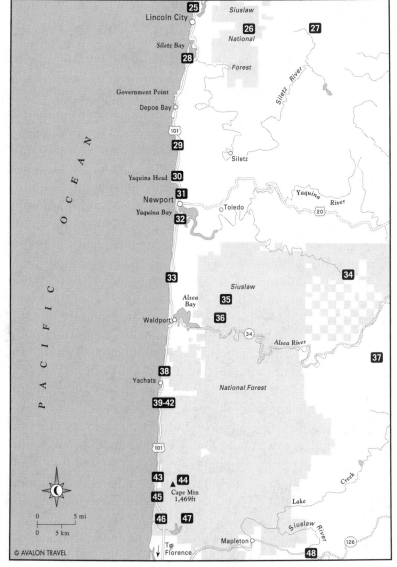

Map 7.4

Hikes 49-66
Pages 395-405

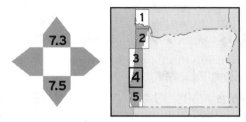

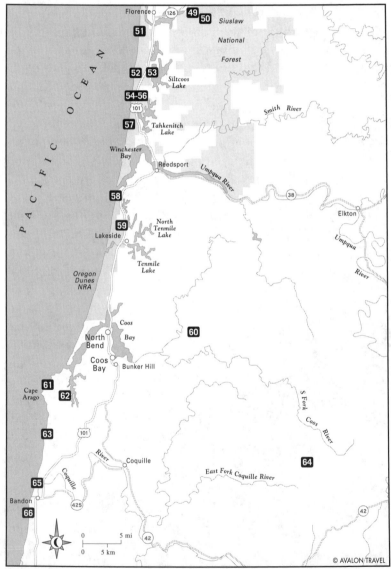

Map 7.5

Hikes 67-98
Pages 406-424

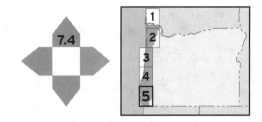

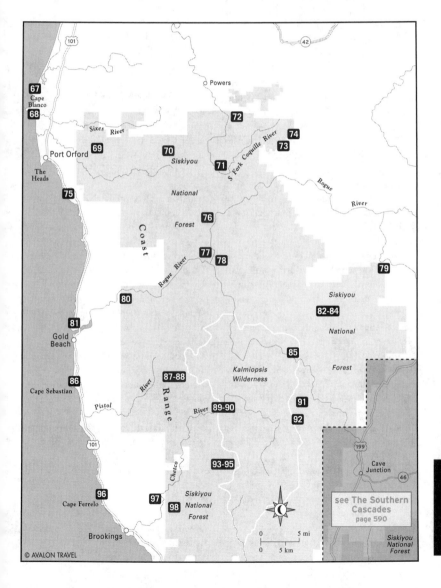

◼ CLATSOP SPIT
4.5 mi/2.0 hr

on the Columbia River in Fort Stevens State Park

Map 7.1, page 361

The Oregon coast begins at Clatsop Spit, where the Columbia River meets the Pacific Ocean. Here the fishing boats and towering barges butt their way inland, reckoning with the Columbia Bar and crazy tides. With all this water comes a lot of wildlife, too, and the Spit offers an easy way to see famous shorebirds. An easy hike begins in Area D of Fort Stevens State Park, with opportunities to get in a bit of both bird-watching and barge-watching, as enormous freighters and marine birds push against the tides and winds.

This easy exploration of the spit and the South Jetty begins at the Area D lot, with a short boardwalk leading to a bird blind overlooking Trestle Bay, an excellent place to spot coastal birds, and a trail leading through the dunes to the beach on the Columbia River. Follow the beach to the left for 2.3 miles to the massive jetty, then go left another 0.5 mile to a viewing platform. Continuing south along the top of the jetty 0.3 mile brings you to an X-junction; turn left here another 0.3 mile to the paved road, and follow it to the left, going 1.1 mile back to Area D.

User Groups: Hikers and dogs on leashes. No horses or mountain bikes. No wheelchair facilities.

Permits: Permits are not required. If you use the day-use area only, parking and access are free. Otherwise, a $3 day-use fee is collected at the camping entrance, or you can get an annual Oregon Parks and Recreation pass for $25; contact Oregon Parks and Recreation, 800/551-6949.

Maps: For a free park brochure, call Oregon Parks and Recreation, 800/551-6949, or download a free map at www.oregonstateparks.org. For a topographic map, ask the USGS for Clatsop Spit.

Directions: Drive south of Astoria on U.S. 101 for four miles and turn west at a sign for Fort Stevens State Park. Follow park signs for 4.9 miles, turning left at the day-use entrance. Drive at total of 3.9 miles, passing Battery Russell, to a fork. Go right to Area D.

Contact: Oregon Parks and Recreation Department, 1115 Commercial Street NE, Salem, OR, 97301, 800/551-6949, www.oregonstateparks.org.

◼ FORT STEVENS STATE PARK
5.3 mi/2.5 hr

northwest of Astoria in Fort Stevens State Park

Map 7.1, page 361

The tip of the Oregon coast lies between the Pacific Ocean and the Columbia River, the "Gateway to the West," at least for ships. Explorers had been trying for years to find the elusive mouth of the Columbia, which more often than not was shrouded in fog. As you can imagine, this area was heavily guarded during World War II by no less than three military installations. Fort Stevens was in use for a total of 84 years, from the Civil War to the close of World War II. Today it is an 11-square-mile state park with campgrounds, miles of bike paths, a swimmable lake, and even the rusting remains of the *Peter Iredale,* a historic 1906 shipwreck. The network of paved trails makes it that much more accessible for everyone.

To begin your exploration, park in the loop lot for Battery Russell. Behind an exhibit board, climb a stairway and walk along the concrete bunkers, site of a battery that guarded the Columbia's mouth for 40 years. When you reach a sandy trail, follow it 1.3 miles, staying right at all junctions, to Picnic Area A and the loop trail around Coffenbury Lake. At the end of the loop, and to try a different way back, head to the nearby campground to the start of the Nature Trail behind campsite B5T. This 1.4-mile trail follows a creek and joins with a paved bike path, going left 0.2 mile back to the Battery Russell lot.

User Groups: Hikers and dogs on leashes.

Bikes on designated paths only. Paved paths are wheelchair accessible.

Permits: Permits are not required. If you use the day-use area only, parking and access are free. Otherwise, a $3 day-use fee is collected at the camping entrance, or you can get an annual Oregon Parks and Recreation pass for $25; contact Oregon Parks and Recreation, 800/551-6949.

Maps: For a free park brochure, call Oregon Parks and Recreation, 800/551-6949, or download a free map at www.oregonstateparks. org. For a topographic map, ask the USGS for Warrenton.

Directions: Drive south of Astoria on U.S. 101 for four miles and turn west at a sign for Fort Stevens State Park. Follow park signs for 4.9 miles, turning left at the day-use entrance. Drive one mile to Battery Russell.

Contact: Oregon Parks and Recreation Department, 1115 Commercial Street NE, Salem, OR, 97301, 800/551-6949, www.oregonstateparks.org.

❸ TILLAMOOK HEAD

6.1 mi one-way/3.0 hr

north of Cannon Beach in Ecola State Park

Map 7.2, page 362   BEST ❰

The Oregon coast has some of the best state parks in Oregon, and this is by far one of the most scenic. The Tillamook Head, a remnant of a 15-billion-year-old Columbia River basaltic lava flow, rises over 1,000 feet above the Pacific Ocean, and it was on this headland that Lewis and Clark stood on their famous cross-country journey, their mission to find an overland route to the Pacific successful. In fact, they were crossing this head in 1806 to make their way down to nearby Cannon Beach to buy some blubber from a beached whale from some local Native Americans. No one said exploration was easy. You can re-create this journey, seeing things they never saw, like the abandoned military bunker and an unbelievable lighthouse on the island of

Tillamook Rock, which operated from 1881 to 1957. The only reason it is unmanned today is that winter storms tended to throw waves right over the top of the lighthouse. Today, it houses cremated remains taken ashore by helicopters. Consider bringing a backpack for this one—there's a handy camping area in a nook atop the head.

You can tour the entire head or take it in pieces. Start at the Ecola Point Picnic Area lot, where you can take a short walk out to the point to see a sea lion-populated rock. The hike begins in the trees at the edge of the lot, heading north on the Oregon Coast Trail. The first 1.5 miles breezes through some woods before dramatically following the cliffs over the ocean and dropping down to secluded Indian Beach, usually rife with surfers, which is a good turnaround for a short hike. If you continue on, the hike gets more difficult as it climbs 1.6 mile to a primitive campground (either on the road to the right or the trail to the left), complete with sheltered bunkhouses. From this camping area, follow a short trail toward the ocean for a look at the mossed-over bunkers. If you're up for more, you can continue as far as you like up the headland, but be ready to climb. The trail gains 200 feet in the next half-mile, then eases off for the next 2.1 miles to the summit. The remaining 1.7 miles of this stretch of the OCT descends to the beach at Seaside.

User Groups: Hikers and dogs on leashes only. No horses or mountain bikes permitted. No wheelchair facilities.

Permits: Permits are not required. A $3 day-use fee is collected at the camping entrance, or you can get an annual Oregon Parks and Recreation pass for $25; contact Oregon Parks and Recreation, 800/551-6949.

Maps: For a free park brochure, call Oregon Parks and Recreation, 800/551-6949 or download a free map at www.oregonstateparks.org. For a topographic map, ask the USGS for Tillamook Head.

Directions: From U.S. 101, take the north exit for Cannon Beach and follow Ecola State Park signs, keeping right for two miles to the entrance booth. To shuttle, drive north from the north exit to Cannon Beach on U.S. 101 toward Seaside for 5.8 miles. Turn left on Avenue U for 0.2 mile and take the first left on Edgewood Street for 0.4 mile. Continue on Edgewood Street until becomes Ocean Vista Drive, and follow it for 0.2 mile. Ocean Vista Drive turns into Sunset Boulevard. Follow Sunset Boulevard for 0.7 mile to its end at the trailhead.

Contact: Oregon Parks and Recreation Department, 1115 Commercial Street NE, Salem, OR, 97301, 800/551-6949, www.oregonstateparks.org.

4 SADDLE MOUNTAIN
5.0 mi/3.0 hr 　　　🥾3 ⛰9

east of Seaside in Saddle Mountain State Natural Area

Map 7.2, page 362　　　BEST (

Aptly named for its dipping peak, Saddle Mountain is the highest point in northwestern Oregon. It has a commanding 360-degree view reaching from the Pacific to five Cascade peaks ranging from Rainier to Jefferson. To earn that view, you must endure the difficult hike up a steep trail, though it is comforting to know that the trail has been drastically improved of late. On the other hand, the flower show here is famous: trilliums, bleeding hearts, goatsbeard, chocolate lily, candyflower, larkspur, Indian paintbrush, fawn lily, purple iris, and phlox are some of the 300-odd blooms you'll see along the trail, particularly in spring, and the peak offers refuge to the rare crucifer and Saddle Mountain bittercress, a mustard-family flower found virtually nowhere else on earth.

The first 0.2-mile portion of the Saddle Mountain Trail passes through an alder forest, passing a short side trail to the right that climbs 0.2 mile to a rocky viewpoint of the mountain itself—a worthy side trip. The next 1.1 miles climbs steeply up a series of switchbacks to

© SEAN PATRICK HILL

Saddle Mountain

the long wall of a basalt dike formed from lava poured into cracks in the ground and cooled, the ground having slowly eroded away around it leaving a wall that resembles stacked wood. The next 0.9 mile crosses the wild-flowered meadows populated by Ice Age species (stay on the trail) before reaching the saddle itself. The remaining 0.4 mile is a steep pitch lined with cables that ascends to an awe-inspiring viewpoint at the 3,283-foot peak, with vistas reaching as far as the Pacific Ocean, Cape Disappointment, the Columbia River, and the Cascades.

User Groups: Hikers and dogs on leash only. No horses or mountain bikes allowed. No wheelchair facilities.

Permits: Permits are not required. Parking and access are free.

Maps: For a topographic map, ask the USGS for Saddle Mountain.

Directions: From Portland, take U.S 26 west of Portland 66 miles and turn north at a state park sign. This winding, paved road climbs seven miles to its end at a picnic area and campground.

Contact: Oregon Parks and Recreation Department, 1115 Commercial Street NE, Salem, OR, 97301, 800/551-6949, www.oregonstateparks.org.

5 CANNON BEACH TO HUG POINT
8.6 mi/4.0 hr　🚶1　⛰7

in the Tolovana Beach State Recreation Site in Cannon Beach on the Pacific Ocean

> Map 7.2, page 362

If you wonder why the town of Cannon Beach is so named, it dates back to 1846 when a Navy ship broke up crossing the infamous Columbia River bar. An entire piece of the deck, with the cannon mounted to it, washed ashore. The town is known especially for Haystack Rock, the 235-foot sea stack that ends up on quite a few calendars.

This stretch of beach was, for the longest time, the main travel route for motorists. Getting around Hug Point during even low tide required motorists to "hug" the cliff; they decided the easiest way around it was over it, and so they dynamited their own road into the sandstone. An easy beachside stroll visits all these points, plus other sea stacks, tidepools, and a waterfall pouring right onto the beach.

Start at the Haystack Rock Parking Area, within view of Haystack Rock. Head south along the sandstone cliffs for 1.2 miles to the Tovana Beach Wayside. For the next 1.8 miles, watch for a number of sea stacks, including Silver Point, Jockey Cap, and Lion Rock. Round Humbug Point, aptly named because it is not the fabled Hug Point, and arrive at the Arcadia Wayside. Continuing another 1.3 miles brings you to Hug Point itself, with its powder-blasted road, a cave, the falls of Fall Creek, and the Hug Point Wayside.

User Groups: Hikers, dogs, and horses. No wheelchair facilities.

Permits: Permits are not required. Parking and access are free.

Maps: For a topographic map, ask the USGS for Arch Cape.

Directions: From U.S. 101 take the southern Cannon Beach exit, heading west on East Sunset Boulevard 0.2 mile to Hemlock Street. Go right on Hemlock to the Haystack Rock parking area.

Contact: Oregon Parks and Recreation Department, 1115 Commercial Street NE, Salem, OR, 97301, 800/551-6949, www.oregonstateparks.org.

6 CAPE FALCON
5.0 mi/2.5 hr　🚶2　⛰8

south of Cannon Beach in Oswald West State Park

> Map 7.2, page 362　　　　**BEST (**

Oswald West is a certain kind of hero in Oregon. As the 14th governor of Oregon, his lasting contribution was to designate the entire length of the Oregon coast as a public highway, thus forever protecting it from development. His legacy shows, in particular at the state park named for him. Dense with old-growth Sitka spruce forests, with Neahkahnie Mountain and Cape Falcon cupping the wide Smuggler Cove and a sandy beach, Oswald West State Park brings a hiker close to a coastal wilderness area. The Oregon Coast Trail goes either direction from Short Sands Beach: to the south, it climbs the cliffs and continues on to Neahkahnie Mountain (see *Neahkahnie Mountain* listing in this chapter), and to the north it climbs to raptor-shaped Cape Falcon.

For an easy exploration, follow Short Sand Creek from the parking area to the coast for 0.4 paved miles. If the view here isn't staggering enough, just wait. A moderate 2.1-mile trail following the OCT route leads up from the beach and into groves of Sitkas that rival the fabled redwoods. The trail skirts a cliff above the cove with views to lofty Neahkahnie Mountain. Watch for the side trail to the left traveling 0.2 mile out the headland of rocky Cape Falcon, the peak a dense cover of leathery salal. This makes a good turnaround point, but to add another 2.4 miles on for more rewarding views, keep going up the OCT to three astonishing viewpoints of the wave-pounded inlets. When the trail begins to steeply ascend away from the ocean, turn back.

User Groups: Hikers, dogs, horses. No mountain bikes allowed. The paved trail to Short Sands Beach is wheelchair accessible.

Permits: Permits are not required. Parking and access are free.

Maps: For a free park brochure, call Oregon Parks and Recreation, 800/551-6949, or download a free map at www.oregonstateparks.org. For a topographic map, ask the USGS for Arch Cape.

Directions: Drive 10 miles south of Cannon Beach on U.S. 101. Park in the lot on the east side of the highway a bit south of milepost 39.

Contact: Oregon Parks and Recreation Department, 1115 Commercial Street NE, Salem, OR, 97301, 800/551-6949, www.oregonstateparks.org.

7 NEAHKAHNIE MOUNTAIN

3.0 mi/2.0 hr   🏃3 ⛰8

south of Cannon Beach in Oswald West State Park

Map 7.2, page 362

Rising above the surf and breezy ocean air, Neahkahnie Mountain in Oswald West State Park is a panoramic dream. As far as climbing mountains goes, this one is fairly easy, at 1,600 feet above sea level, but enough of a haul to get your heart going. It was a coastal Indian tribe, probably the Tillamook, who named this peak to mean, roughly, "place of the gods." The hike can be extended, too, out onto a ridge with red huckleberry bushes that fan out overhead like green umbrellas, and if you're really daring, a descent down the west slope leads to Highway 101 and farther to an oceanic cliff-edge view of the Devil's Cauldron.

The hike follows the Oregon Coast Trail, an easy, single trail, that steeply switchbacks up the first 0.9 mile before leveling out on the wooded peak for 0.6 mile, arriving at the summit meadows and an easy view down to the town of Manzanita. Turning around here makes for a three-mile round-trip, though the trail continues down another two miles to Highway 101, where it crosses the roadway and continues about 100 yards to two good viewpoints over the rugged cliffs to the Pacific.

User Groups: Hikers and dogs. No mountain bikes or horses. No wheelchair facilities.

Permits: Permits are not required. Parking and access are free.

Maps: For a free park brochure, call Oregon Parks and Recreation, 800/551-6949, or download a free map at www.oregonstateparks.org. For a topographic map, ask the USGS for Nehalem.

Directions: Drive south of Cannon Beach on U.S. 101 about 13 miles to a brown hiker symbol between mileposts 41 and 42. Turn east onto a gravel road for 0.4 mile to a Trailhead Parking sign. The trail begins at a post.

Contact: Oregon Parks and Recreation Department, 1115 Commercial Street NE, Salem, OR, 97301, 800/551-6949, www.oregonstateparks.org.

8 NEHALEM BAY

5.2 mi/2.5 hr   🏃1 ⛰6

south of Manzanita in Nehalem Bay State Park

Map 7.2, page 362

The beach that lies between Neahkahnie Mountain and Nehalem Spit has seen its share of bad luck: In 1913, a drunk captain steered the British *Glenesslin,* with an astoundingly inexperienced crew, into the nearby cliffs, and rumors still abound of a wrecked Spanish galleon heavy with treasure, most of which is believed to have been buried by survivors somewhere in the area. Needless to say, people are still looking for it. There's other treasure to be found here today in a trove of seals and seabirds along the Nehalem Spit. Formed by tidal patterns, the Oregon spits make for ideal wildlife-viewing, especially of seabirds. This hike visits two distinct zones: the beach and the bay, seemingly worlds apart.

From the Nehalem Bay State Park picnic area, head out along the ocean 2.3 miles to the North Jetty, and turn right for 0.5 mile to a beach where harbor seals tend to lay around and sun themselves. It's illegal to harass them, though they'll quickly disperse if you approach at all. Return along the bay for a 2.2-mile walk, turning left at the boat ramp for a quick 0.2-mile return to the picnic area.

User Groups: Hikers, dogs, and horses. Mountain bikes allowed on loop path only. A 1.5-mile loop is wheelchair accessible.

Permits: Permits are not required. A $3 day-use fee is collected at the entrance, or you can get an annual Oregon Parks and Recreation pass for $25; contact Oregon Parks and Recreation, 800/551-6949.

Maps: For a free park brochure, call Oregon Parks and Recreation, 800/551-6949, or download a free map at www.oregonstateparks.org. For a topographic map, ask the USGS for Nehalem.

Directions: From Manzanita, follow U.S 101 to milepost 44. Turn right on Necarney City Road and follow signs for two miles to Nehalem Bay State Park. Park at the picnic area after the fee booth

Contact: Oregon Parks and Recreation Department, 1115 Commercial Street NE, Salem, OR, 97301, 800/551-6949, www.oregonstateparks.org.

9 BANKS-VERNONIA RAILROAD

5.3 mi one-way/2.5 hr 　🏃1 　⛰7

northwest of Portland in Banks Vernonia Linear Park

Map 7.2, page 362 　　　BEST (

Oregon has many fine examples of "rails-to-trails" paths, and this is certainly one of them. Totaling 21 miles in all, the former grade of this 1920s Burlington-Northern Railroad Line used primarily for lumber and, later, excursion trains, has been converted to a great pathway through the Coast Range foothills. Though there are plenty of options for journeys along the old route, a good day trip can be made by going between two old wooden trestles, either as a longer hike or with a car shuttle. The trail can accommodate just about anyone on foot, horses, bikes, and wheelchair users.

Start at the Buxton Trestle just outside the town of Buxton. An easy loop explores the area around the trestle spanning Mendenhall Creek, which is now open to trail use. From there the trail stretches north 5.3 miles to a second trailhead beneath Horseshoe Trestle, which is not to be crossed—but is a good place for a shuttle. Along the way, you'll cross Logging and Williams Creeks and stay largely out of sight of Highway 43.

User Groups: Hikers, dogs, mountain bikes, and horses. Parts of the paved path are wheelchair accessible.

Permits: Permits are not required. Parking and access are free.

Maps: For a free park brochure, call Oregon Parks and Recreation, 800/551-6949, or download a free map at www.oregonstateparks.org. For a topographic map, ask the USGS for Buxton.

Directions: From Portland, drive 28 miles west on U.S. 26 and turn right on Fisher Road. In 0.7 mile, the road becomes Baconia Road and leads to the Buxton Trailhead on the right. To shuttle to the Horseshoe Trestle, return to Highway 47 and drive 5.5 miles north to the Tophill Trailhead on the left.

Contact: Oregon Parks and Recreation Department, 1115 Commercial Street NE, Salem, OR, 97301, 800/551-6949, www.oregonstateparks.org.

10 KINGS MOUNTAIN
5.4 mi/3.5 hr

east of Tillamook in the Tillamook State Forest

Map 7.2, page 362

Between 1933 and 1951, four massive fires swept through this area of the Coast Range in what is known as the Tillamook Burn. With the help of determined locals, an equally massive campaign was waged to replant the area into what is now the Tillamook State Forest. Kings Mountain bears both the scars of the fire (those emblematic snags testify to that) and also the regrowth capable with the help of humans and nature. This hike passes through that history and ultimately rises above it to views of the Wilson River Valley and the Cascade Mountains. Granted, this hike is difficult: You'll have to climb more than 2,500 feet in 2.5 miles, but because of the burned trees—known as "gray ghosts"—it makes for good views. You'll even pass a picnic table before the last pitch, and you can leave your name in a summit registry at the top. A 1.3-mile extension connects to nearby Elk Mountain, potentially making this a daunting day.

The first mile of the Kings Mountain Trail threads through red alder and maple woods and wildflowers and then steepens dramatically for the next 1.4 miles. At the top of the 2.7-mile climb is the 3,226-foot peak of Kings Mountain, having passed through meadows of summer beargrass plumes (a type of lily). This hike can be stretched to nearby pinnacles and Elk Mountain (see *Elk Mountain* listing in this chapter) but only for the exceptionally hardy. Otherwise, return as you came.

User Groups: Hikers and dogs only. No wheelchair facilities.

Permits: Permits are not required. Parking and access are free.

Maps: For a Tillamook Forest Visitor Map & Guide, contact the Forest Grove District Office, 503/357-2191, egov.oregon.gov/ODF/TSF/about_us.shtml. For a topographic map, ask the USGS for Rogers Peak.

Directions: From Portland, drive U.S. 26 west

20 miles to Highway 6. Go west on Highway 6 for 22 miles to the trailhead and parking area near milepost 25, on the north side of the road.

Contact: Tillamook State Forest, Forest Grove District Office, 801 Gales Creek Road, Forest Grove, OR, 97116, 503/357-2191, egov.oregon.gov/ODF/TSF/about_us.shtml.

11 ELK MOUNTAIN
3.0 mi/2.5 hr

east of Tillamook in the Tillamook State Forest

Map 7.2, page 362

Because the route to loop this hike with Kings Mountain can prove arduous, it is easiest to climb Elk Mountain by its own trail. Did I say "easy"? This is also a strenuous hike, but ultimately a rewarding one, with views on a clear day as far as the Pacific Ocean and Mounts Adams, Hood, and Jefferson, due in part to the massive Tillamook Burn that swept much of this mountain clear of living trees, leaving the ghostly white snags behind. This trail is narrower than Kings Mountain, gaining 1,900 feet in 1.5 miles.

Starting from the Elk Creek Campground, the Wilson River Trail heads 0.1 mile to the junction with the Elk Mountain Trail, which climbs steeply through alder forests and onto the rocky trail for 1.4 miles to the 2,788 peak. Be sure to watch your footing and wear good boots, as much of the trail can be loose scree. Crossing four saddles, as well as vaunting a false summit, you'll arrive at the peak, which bears white Washington lilies in spring.

User Groups: Hikers and dogs only. No wheelchair facilities.

Permits: Permits are not required. Parking and access are free.

Maps: For a Tillamook Forest Visitor Map & Guide, contact the Forest Grove District Office, 503/357-2191, egov.oregon.gov/ODF/TSF/about_us.shtml. For a topographic map, ask the USGS for Cochran.

Directions: From Portland, drive U.S. 26 west

20 miles to Highway 6. Go west on Highway 6 for 19 miles to the Elk Creek Campground near milepost 28, on the north side of the road. Turn right into the campground, driving 0.6 mile to the far end of the campground and crossing a bridge. The trailhead is behind the information board.

Contact: Tillamook State Forest, Forest Grove District Office, 801 Gales Creek Road, Forest Grove, OR, 97116, 503/357-2191, egov. oregon.gov/ODF/TSF/about_us.shtml.

12 GALES CREEK
3.6 mi/1.5 hr

east of Tillamook in the Tillamook State Forest
Map 7.2, page 362

In the deep green forests of the Coast Range, Gales Creek glides swiftly in its bed. To find this creek from the highway, visiting two picturesque fern-draped creeks, begin at the Summit Trailhead and descend sharply on the Gales Creek Trail, following Low Divide Creek 1.9 miles along an old 1930s railroad grade to the Gales Creek Campground (which is suitable for picnics, as there are plenty of tables amidst the trees). Near the end of the trail, a spur trail to the left leads to the parking area and the Gales Creek Trail. Granted, the return trip to the highway will be uphill, a little more than 600 feet elevation gain, but either way this trail is remarkably wild in comparison to much of the devastation resulting from decades of forest fires.

Gales Creek, too, is entirely explorable, with a trail leading out of the campground and following Gales Creek up into the hills. Beginning from the junction with the Low Divide Creek Trail, head upstream 0.8 mile, staying right at a junction with the Storey Burn Trail. The remaining trail follows Gales Creek through forest for 5.2 miles farther, meeting Bell Camp Road; this section may be closed due to storm damage. Once open, you will be able to continue on another 3.4 miles from Bell Camp Road to the terminal trailhead at Reehers Camp.

User Groups: Hikers, dogs, and mountain bikes. Horses allowed on parts of Gales Creek Trail north of the campground. No wheelchair facilities.

Permits: Permits are not required. Parking and access are free.

Maps: For a Tillamook Forest Visitor Map & Guide, contact the Forest Grove District Office, 503/357-2191, egov.oregon.gov/ODF/TSF/about_us.shtml. For a topographic map, ask the USGS for Cochran and Timber.

Directions: From Portland, drive U.S. 26 west 20 miles to Highway 6. Go west on Highway 6 for 21 miles to milepost 33 at the Coast Range Summit. The parking area for Low Divide Creek and the Summit Trailhead is on the north side of the highway. To enter the Gales Creek Campground parking area, open mid-May through October, follow Highway 6 west of Portland 39 miles to a sign near milepost 35 reading "Gales Creek CG" and turn north through a yellow gate. If the gate is locked, park to the side and walk in 0.7 mile.

Contact: Tillamook State Forest, Forest Grove District Office, 801 Gales Creek Road, Forest Grove, OR, 97116, 503/357-2191, egov. oregon.gov/ODF/TSF/about_us.shtml.

13 UNIVERSITY FALLS
8.6 mi/4.5 hr

east of Tillamook in the Tillamook State Forest
Map 7.2, page 362

Despite the massive Tillamook Fires—particularly the 1933 fire, which torched 240,000 acres—the forest has been reborn. Now there's second-growth Douglas fir, western hemlock, red alder, and red cedar, with a sturdy undergrowth of sword ferns, Oregon grape—the state flower—and leathery salal. Wildlife has returned; you can hear grouse on occasion in the underbrush. This loop, sometimes following an old wagon road, tours the reborn forest with University Falls as the destination high in the headwaters of the Wilson River. The 65-foot falls on Elliott Creek just southwest of the Coast Range summit suffers from off-road vehicle use, particularly the motorcycles whining in the distance. You'll leave them behind eventually on this small epic tour of the rain forest.

From the Rogers Camp RV parking area, briefly follow the Fire Break 1 road uphill to the Nels Rogers Trail. The first 1.3 miles crosses two roads and reaches a junction on the Devils Lake Fork of the Wilson River. Turn left over a footbridge, cross the creek, and turn left again, staying on Nels Rogers, which ends in 0.3 mile at the Beaver Dam Road and continues as the Wilson River Wagon Road Trail on the opposite side. This trail wanders three miles, crossing roads, ducking under power lines, crossing clear-cuts and Deyoe Creek, where you'll find a bench near a footbridge, before ending at University Falls Road and another trailhead. From here follow the Gravelle Brothers Trail, arriving in 0.4 mile at the wispy University Falls, where a left-hand junction comes to a viewpoint. To complete the loop, follow the Gravelle Trail two miles to an old road, going right toward Rogers Camp. Follow a gravel road to the right to the top of the hill and a maintenance shed. Go behind the cement barriers on the Elliott Creek OHV Trail, then follow Beaver Dam Road 0.2 miles back to the trailhead.

User Groups: Hikers, dogs, mountain bikes, horses. No wheelchair facilities.

Permits: Permits are not required. Parking and access are free.

Maps: For a Tillamook Forest Visitor Map & Guide, contact the Forest Grove District Office, 503/357-2191, egov.oregon.gov/ODF/TSF/about_us.shtml. For a topographic map, ask the USGS for Woods Point.

Directions: From Portland, drive U.S. 26 west 20 miles to Highway 6. Go west on Highway 6 for 21 miles to milepost 33 at the Coast Range Summit. Watching for signs to Rogers Camp, turn left on Beaver Dam Road and go 250 feet to a T-junction. Turn left 0.1 mile to the trailhead.

Contact: Tillamook State Forest, Forest Grove District Office, 801 Gales Creek Road, Forest Grove, OR, 97116, 503/357-2191, egov.oregon.gov/ODF/TSF/about_us.shtml.

14 BAYOCEAN SPIT
8.1 mi/4.0 hr

west of Tillamook in Cape Meares State Park

Map 7.2, page 362

Cradling Tillamook Bay like a mother's arm, the Bayocean Spit is the site of a ghost town that is more ghost than town. The town formerly known as Bayocean, the "Atlantic City of the West," sold some 600 lots for excited resort types, in addition to having a bowling alley, hotel, dance hall, and grocery store. The developer apparently went mad one fateful night and disappeared. And that, as they say, was that. But what really did the town in was the construction of the South Jetty, which altered currents so that the town slowly eroded into the sea. Now it's a great place to spot wading birds in Tillamook Bay. Being a spit, you'll be able to enjoy both bird-watching and beach-strolling, and there is even the opportunity for camping. In the center of the spit, a large forested rock formation makes for a short cut and exploration, and makes a good turnaround point if you want to cut this hike in half.

Start out by following the old road for 1.6 miles. About halfway out, a well-marked trail cuts 0.5 mile through a forested bluff to the left. Follow this route to the beach, and head left 1.9 miles to the South Jetty. Watch for tufted puffins and brown pelicans. Continuing onward toward the bay for another 2.8 miles will bring you past Crab Harbor, a primitive campsite, and back to the beginning of the loop. Follow the road back 1.6 miles to your car.

User Groups: Hikers, dogs, horses. Bikes allowed on the old road. No wheelchair facilities.

Permits: Permits are not required. Parking and access are free.

Maps: For a topographic map, ask the USGS for Garibaldi.

Directions: From U.S 101 in downtown Tillamook, follow signs for Three Capes Scenic Route for seven miles. On the right, near a large wooden sign about Bayocean Spit, turn right on a gravel road along the dike for 0.9 mile to a parking area.

Contact: Oregon Parks and Recreation Department, 1115 Commercial Street NE, Salem, OR, 97301, 800/551-6949, www.oregonstateparks.org.

15 CAPE MEARES
0.6–4.0 mi/0.5–3.0 hr

west of Tillamook in Cape Meares State Park

Map 7.2, page 362

Cape Meares is a great place to take the grandparents when they come for a visit. There are a number of short trails, making it easy to experience wonders like the historic lighthouse or the Octopus Tree, a giant Sitka spruce that has to be seen to be believed. But it is also a fine place to take a longer hike over a magnificent Oregon cape, visiting a 400-year-old, 16-foot-thick spruce and descending to a pleasant cove on the Pacific. Keep an eye on those cliffs, which are home to peregrine falcons. There's also the Three Arch Rocks, an offshore wildlife refuge home to common murres, black oystercatchers, Leach's storm-petrels, and pigeon guillemots.

For two easy hikes to the lighthouse and the Octopus Tree, start at the main parking lot on Cape Meares. The 0.4-mile round-trip to the lighthouse is paved and easy, and the 0.2-mile round-trip to the Octopus Tree is mostly level dirt but just as easy. For a more challenging hike on the Big Spruce Tree Trail, park at a small lot just before the entrance to the park off Three Capes Loop Drive. From here the trail quickly splits; 0.2 mile to the left is the giant spruce, and to the right a 0.9-mile descent, dropping 500 feet, to a cove on the ocean only passable at low tide. It's a good way to get down to the beach and watch for seabirds, and provides views out to Bayocean Spit.

User Groups: Hikers and dogs only. No horses or mountain bikes allowed. Paved portions of the park are wheelchair accessible.

Permits: Permits are not required. Parking and access are free.

Maps: For a free park brochure, call Oregon Parks and Recreation, 800/551-6949, or download a free map at www.oregonstateparks.org. For a topographic map, ask the USGS for Netarts.

Directions: From U.S 101 in downtown Tillamook follow signs for Three Capes Scenic Route for 10 miles. The park entrance is on the right. Follow the paved road 0.6 mile to a parking lot turnaround.

Contact: Oregon Parks and Recreation Department, 1115 Commercial Street NE, Salem, OR, 97301, 800/551-6949, www.oregonstateparks.org.

16 HAGG LAKE
13.1 mi/6.5 hr

southwest of Forest Grove in Scoggins Valley Park

Map 7.2, page 362

Hagg Lake has been a destination for boaters and fishermen since 1975, when the Scoggins Valley Dam was built. Now hikers can get in on Hagg's unique landscape and spend anywhere from an hour to an entire day exploring the lake's weaving inlets and meadows from a plethora of access points. There are a number of creeks tumbling over smooth rock beds, and a variety of forest types from Douglas fir to white oak. Watch for poison oak along some trails. Also be aware that at times the trail joins the road for short intervals. All trails are marked by posts and along the way there are opportunities to stop at picnic areas and explore side creeks in shaded coves.

Should you decide to have a go at the entire 13.1-mile loop, you can start from the "free parking" lot by climbing the earth dam to the road, and following it to the left for 0.8 mile past a fishing dock to a lot where the official shoreline trail begins. The first 3.6 miles to Boat Ramp "C" crosses long span footbridges and scenic picnic areas. The next 1.3 miles follows the lake well past the "buoy line," thus moving away from the motorized boats and into the quieter areas of the park. The trail follows the road 0.6 mile over Scoggins Creek and another picnic area, then follows the lake 3.7 miles through grasslands and forest, over Tanner Creek and out to a grassy promontory on the lake. The remaining 3.1 miles returns along the north shore to the dam, passing more picnic areas and Boat Ramp "A."

User Groups: Hikers, dogs, and mountain bikes. Horses are not allowed. There is wheelchair access on some trails, boat ramps, and picnic areas.

Permits: Permits are not required. A $5 day-use fee is collected at the park entrance unless parking at the free parking lot beside the fee booth.

Maps: For a map, contact Washington County Facilities Management, 169 North 1st Avenue, MS 42, Hillsboro, OR, 97124, 503/846-8715. For a topographic map, ask the USGS for Gaston.

Directions: From Portland, drive U.S. 26 west 20 miles to Highway 6. Go west on Highway 6 for 2.3 miles and take the ramp for NW OR-47, following this highway south for 12.2 miles. Turn right at SW Scoggins Valley Road for 3.2 miles to the park.

Contact: Washington County Facilities Management, 169 North 1st Avenue, MS 42, Hillsboro, OR, 97124, 503/846-8715.

17 CAPE LOOKOUT
5.0 mi/2.5 hr 🚶2 ⛰9

south of Tillamook in Cape Lookout State Park

Map 7.2, page 362   **BEST (**

Of all the capes on the Oregon coast, this one stands out by sheer length: it extends two full miles to sea like an accusing finger, making it one of the best places to whale-watch and, of course, hike. Numerous viewpoints scan north, south, and west, including one viewpoint over the spot where a patrolling B-17 bomber crashed into the cliffs on a foggy 1943 day. You'll see Cape Kiwanda, Cape Foulweather, the Cascade Head, and Cape Meares from this promontory—all on a single trail that boasts enormous trees and boggy microclimates. The destination is a sheer cliff viewpoint where the shoreline tidal sounds are a distant echo.

Beginning at the main parking area, take the left-hand Cape Lookout Trail (the right descends 2.3 miles to the day-use area on Netarts Spit) and just ahead stay straight at a second junction (this left-hand trail descends two miles to a beach) and continue 2.5 miles overland, descending into a hollow and back up and crossing several wooden bridges. The trail can be muddy. At the tip of the cape, the ocean hovers 400 feet below, and the surf against the mainland is a distant white noise. Each year, 20,000 gray whales migrate around this cape between December and June. Return as you came.

User Groups: Hikers and dogs. No mountain bikes or horses allowed. No wheelchair facilities.

Permits: Permits are not required. A $3 day-use fee is collected at the camping entrance, or you can get an annual Oregon Parks and Recreation pass for $25; contact Oregon Parks and Recreation, 800/551-6949.

Maps: For a free park brochure, call Oregon Parks and Recreation, 800/551-6949, or download a free map at www.oregonstateparks.org. For a topographic map, ask the USGS for Sand Lake.

Directions: From Tillamook, drive 3rd Street west following signs for Cape Lookout State Park for 13 miles. Head 2.7 miles past the campground turnoff to the trailhead lot on the right.

Contact: Oregon Parks and Recreation Department, 1115 Commercial Street NE, Salem, OR, 97301, 800/551-6949, www.oregonstateparks.org.

18 MUNSON CREEK FALLS
0.6 mi/0.25 hr

south of Tillamook in Munson Creek State
Natural Site

Map 7.2, page 362

At 366 feet, the five-tiered Munson Creek
Falls, named for early pioneer Goran Munson, is the tallest in the Coast Range. Munson
settled near here, coming all the way from
Michigan in 1889. Today, visitors have easy
access and a short walk through old-growth
Western red cedars and Sitka spruce to see the
falls, and even eat from a picnic table viewpoint. At the right time of year, you may see
salmon spawning here. In fact, these trails are
good any time of year, even winter when ice
crystallizes around the falls.

The 0.3-mile trail begins in Munson Creek
State Natural Site and follows an easy path to
the falls. Along the way, the trail is shaded by
a variety of trees, hung heavy with mosses and
lichens. The gravel path makes this one good
for a good family trip.

User Groups: Hikers and dogs. No wheelchair
facilities.

Permits: Permits are not required. Parking
and access are free.

Maps: For a topographic map, ask the USGS
for Beaver.

Directions: Drive south of Tillamook eight
miles on U.S. 101. Just before milepost 73,
turn left at a sign for Munson Creek Falls,
following a paved road for one mile and forking right on a 0.4-mile gravel road to a small
turnaround lot.

Contact: Oregon Parks and Recreation
Department, 1115 Commercial Street NE,
Salem, OR, 97301, 800/551-6949, www.oregonstateparks.org.

19 NIAGARA FALLS
2.0 mi/1.0 hr

southeast of Tillamook in the Siuslaw National
Forest

Map 7.2, page 362

Well, it may not be as grand as *the* Niagara
Falls we all know, but then *those* Niagara Falls
don't plunge 107 feet over a magnificent lava
wall into a lush box canyon of vine maples
and yellow monkeyflower, either. Sometimes,
smaller is better. This trail also passes shimmering Pheasant Creek Falls, another 112-foot
cascade, along the way. This easy one-mile
trail crosses a gurgling creek several times to
a picnic table overlooking the amphitheatre
wall over which the falls pour. The trail makes
use of four wooden bridges and an observation
deck overlooking the lush creeks.

User Groups: Hikers and dogs. No wheelchair
facilities.

Permits: Permits are not required. Parking
and access are free.

Maps: For a map of the Siuslaw National
Forest, contact the Siuslaw National Forest
headquarters, 4077 SW Research Way, P.O.
Box 1148, Corvallis, OR, 97339, 541/750-
7000. For a topographic map, ask the USGS
for Niagara Creek.

Directions: Drive U.S. 101 south of Tillamook
15 miles to the village of Beaver near milepost
80. Turn east on Blaine Road for 6.7 miles. At
Blaine Junction, turn right on Upper Nestucca
River Road for 5.8 miles to Forest Service
Road 8533. Go south on this road 4.3 miles
to FS 8533-131. Turn right at the junction and
continue 0.7 mile to the trailhead.

Contact: Siuslaw National Forest, Hebo
Ranger District, 31525 Highway 22, Hebo,
OR, 97122, 503/392-5100.

20 MOUNT HEBO
6.5 mi/4.0 hr   🏃2 ⛰7

east of Pacific City in the Siuslaw
National Forest

Map 7.2, page 362

The Pioneer-Indian Trail is so named because
this trail, if you can believe it, was the first
developed route between the Willamette Valley and the Tillamook Valley. Why wouldn't
you believe it? Because this is a mountain, and
one tall enough to be buried in snow, a rarity
for these elevations so close to the ocean and
sea level. Native Americans first used it, likely
figuring it easier to cross this meadow plateau
rather than fighting through the deep forests.
Later, Hiram Smith and some Tillamook settlers improved the trail in 1854. This route
remained the main thoroughfare over the
Coast Range until a new wagon road was built
in 1882. The trail went forgotten until the
Forest Service reopened it as an 8-mile trail
over Mount Hebo. This 3,174-foot summit
commands a view of the Coast Range, extending to the Cascade volcanoes from Rainier to
Jefferson. And, of course, the Pacific Ocean.
Locals say the best time to see the view is late
summer, though even the valleys may be bot-
tomed out in fog. All this is likely what helps
designate the area as the Mount Hebo Special
Interest Area.

Starting at a signboard at Hebo Lake, the
Pioneer-Indian Trail climbs 2.9 miles, crossing
both a gravel road and a meadow of bracken
fern, which can grow to five feet tall, before
reaching a saddle and Road 14. Cross the
road and take a side trail on an abandoned
road to the right leading 0.3 mile up to the
peak. Here there was once a Cold War–era
radar station, but now only a bulldozed site
surrounded by steep meadows of edible thimbleberry. For those in the mood for a 16-mile
day, the Pioneer-Indian Trail continues along
the plateau, paralleling Road 14 to a primitive
campground before descending to North and
South Lakes.

User Groups: Hikers, dogs, and horses.
Mountain bikes not allowed. The trail around
Hebo Lake is wheelchair accessible.

Permits: Permits are not required. A federal
Northwest Forest Pass is required to park here;
the cost is $5 a day or $30 for an annual pass.
You can buy a day pass at the trailhead, at
ranger stations, or through private vendors.

Maps: For a map of the Siuslaw National
Forest, contact the Siuslaw National Forest
headquarters, 4077 SW Research Way, P.O.
Box 1148, Corvallis, OR, 97339, 541/750-
7000. For a topographic map, ask the USGS
for Niagara Creek and Hebo.

Directions: Drive U.S. 101 south of
Tillamook 19 miles to Hebo and turn east on
Highway 22 for 0.3 mile. Turn left at a sign
for Hebo Lake just before the Hebo Ranger
Station. Follow Road 14 for 4.7 miles, taking
the right-hand fork at the Hebo Lake campground entrance. Keep right for 0.2 mile to
the trailhead parking area. From November to mid-April, the campground is gated
closed, so you'll need to walk in 0.2 mile to
the trailhead.

Contact: Siuslaw National Forest, Hebo
Ranger District, 31525 Highway 22, Hebo,
OR, 97122, 503/392-5100.

21 KIWANDA BEACH AND PORTER POINT
9.2 mi/3.5 hr   🏃3 ⛰7

at Neskowin on the Pacific Ocean

Map 7.2, page 362

It's always interesting to see the estuaries where
a coastal river flows into the ocean; sometimes
they argue, each pushing against the other,
creating a unique landscape amenable to
birds and other wildlife. This lovely beach
trek heads up Kiwanda Beach to the mouth
of the Nestucca River. Along the way it passes
climbable Proposal Rock, where an 1800s sea
captain was said to have rowed his beloved
to ask her hand, and continues to the cliffs
of Porter Point and the river mouth opposite
the Nestucca Spit.

From the Neskowin Wayside, hike 0.3 mile along Neskowin Creek to Proposal Rock. To the south, the Cascade Head looms up. Hike 3.3 miles along a sandy beach to the base of Winema Road and Camp Winema. From there, it is one mile to the mouth of the Nestucca. Return as you came.

User Groups: Hikers, dogs, and horses. No wheelchair facilities.

Permits: Permits are not required. Parking and access are free.

Maps: For a topographic map, ask the USGS for Neskowin.

Directions: Drive south of Tillamook on U.S. 101 for 33 miles and turn west at a "Neskowin" pointer. Head straight about 100 yards to the Neskowin Wayside.

Contact: Oregon Parks and Recreation Department, 1115 Commercial Street NE, Salem, OR, 97301, 800/551-6949, www.oregonstateparks.org.

22 HARTS COVE
5.4 mi/2.5 hr

on Cascade Head in the Siuslaw National Forest

Map 7.2, page 362

The Cascade Head is a unique landform, a massive headland rising above the ocean like a fortress, capped with forests and swaths of meadow. Harts Cove is a trek that requires you to climb down 900 feet, and then back up, to see the spectacle. It's worth it: With views of the Cascade Head's jaggy cliffs, the Chitwood Creek waterfall plunging into a towering ocean cove, and a Sitka spruce and western hemlock forest, you'll see what the fuss is about. But note that the road to the trailhead is closed from January 1 to July 15 to protect endangered butterflies and rare wildflowers that thrive here. This area is part of the Cascade Head Scenic Research Area for just this reason.

Harts Cove Trail begins from the road on a series of switchbacks dropping 0.7 mile to Cliff Creek then meanders through the forest of giants another 1.4 miles before reaching a bench looking down to Harts Cove's head. Continue on the main trail 0.5 mile to Chitwood Creek, then another 0.6 mile to a former homestead meadow. A path on the left overlooks Harts Cove and its waterfall. Like many places on the coast, you can sometimes hear the sea lions barking below.

User Groups: Hikers and dogs. No horses or mountain bikes allowed. No wheelchair facilities.

Permits: Permits are not required. Parking and access are free.

Maps: For a map of the Siuslaw National Forest, contact the Siuslaw National Forest headquarters, 4077 SW Research Way, P.O. Box 1148, Corvallis, OR, 97339, 541/750-7000. For a topographic map, ask the USGS for Neskowin.

Directions: From the junction of U.S. 101 and Highway 18 north of Lincoln City, drive north on 101 for 4 miles. Just before the crest, turn left on Cascade Head Road (Road 1861) and follow Hart's Cove signs down this 4.1-mile gravel road to road's end.

Contact: Siuslaw National Forest, Hebo Ranger District, 31525 Highway 22, Hebo, OR, 97122, 503/392-5100.

23 CASCADE HEAD INLAND TRAIL
6.0 mi one-way/3.0 hr

north of Lincoln City in Cascade Head Experimental Forest

Map 7.2, page 362

The Cascade Head is a veritable museum, preserved and protected from development because of its unique ecosystem and importance to education and study. The inland trail over the head does not visit the ocean, but certainly does tour the rainforests of coastal Oregon. A path leads into the Cascade Head Experimental Forest, an area studied by foresters since 1934. It shelters a grove of six-foot-thick Sitka spruce on the headwater springs of Calkins Creek, but it's a less-traveled trail because of its lack of views. Check with the Siuslaw National Forest before heading out, as this trail may be closed due to tree hazards.

From the trailhead at Three Rocks Road, the path switchbacks up a hill of elderberry, salmonberry, and thimbleberry. The Sitka grove is 2.9 miles along the trail where a boardwalk path crosses a marsh of skunk cabbage. In another 0.7 mile the trail meets Road 1861. Go right 100 yards to find the remainder of the trail, a 2.4-mile stretch that ends at U.S. 101.

User Groups: Hikers and dogs. No horses or mountain bikes allowed. No wheelchair facilities.

Permits: Permits are not required. Parking and access are free.

Maps: For a map of the Siuslaw National Forest, contact the Siuslaw National Forest headquarters, 4077 SW Research Way, P.O. Box 1148, Corvallis, OR, 97339, 541/750-7000. For a topographic map, ask the USGS for Neskowin.

Directions: From the junction of U.S. 101 and Highway 18 north of Lincoln City, drive north on U.S. 101 for one mile and turn left on Three Rocks Road and immediately park on the right by a trail sign. To shuttle, continue north on U.S. 101 toward Neskowin for about five miles and park at a trailhead sign on the left, one mile south of Neskowin on U.S. 101.

Contact: Siuslaw National Forest, Hebo Ranger District, 31525 Highway 22, Hebo, OR, 97122, 503/392-5100.

24 CASCADE HEAD NATURE CONSERVANCY TRAIL

3.4 mi/1.5 hr 👫2 ⛰8

north of Lincoln City in Cascade Head Preserve

Map 7.2, page 362 BEST (

The steep and undulating meadows atop Cascade Head are the home of a rare

© SEAN PATRICK HILL

the Pacific Ocean from Cascade Head

checkermallow and an equally rare caterpillar of the Oregon silverspot butterfly. Because of this, this trail is considered a delicate area, and with the support of locals, the area was purchased by the non-profit Nature Conservancy. The road to the upper trailhead is closed from January 1 to July 15 to protect this fragile habitat, but the lower trailhead is open year-round. Be sure to stay on the trail and respect nature, and pay attention to seasonal closure signs. The trail is steep at times, but the expansive views are rewarding beyond belief—the ocean surges forth hundreds of feet below, and the coastline stretches out to the south as far as the eye can see.

From the boat ramp trailhead, follow the trail along the Three Rocks Road then uphill along Savage Road for 0.6 mile, passing the Sitka Arts Center. From this road, the well-marked trail climbs steadily through old-growth spruce and over several creeks for 1.1 miles to the first viewpoint down to the Salmon River estuary and Cape Foulweather. The next 0.6 mile to the top is breathtaking—both for its views and for its steepness. A marker points out the actual peak at 1,200 feet; relax and enjoy the view and the play of light on the surf in the distance. From here, the trail continues an easy mile through more woods to the trailhead on the 1861 road.

User Groups: Hikers and horses. Mountain bikes and dogs are not allowed. No wheelchair facilities.

Permits: Permits are not required. Parking and access are free.

Maps: For a map of the Siuslaw National Forest, contact the Siuslaw National Forest headquarters, 4077 SW Research Way, P.O. Box 1148, Corvallis, OR, 97339, 541/750-7000. For a topographic map, ask the USGS for Neskowin.

Directions: From the junction of U.S. 101 and Highway 18 north of Lincoln City, drive north on 101 for one mile and turn left on Three Rocks Road and immediately park on the right by a trail sign.

Contact: Siuslaw National Forest, Hebo Ranger District, 31525 Highway 22, Hebo, OR, 97122, 503/392-5100.

²⁵ ROADS END WAYSIDE
2.8 mi/1.5 hr 🏃1 ⛰7... 6

north of Lincoln City on the Pacific Ocean

Map 7.3, page 363

An easy stroll along the beach from the hidden town of Roads End leads 1.4 miles north to rough basalt cliffs and tidepools alive with barnacles, sea stars, and anemones. This is a great hike for kids, who'll enjoy poking around the lakes of seawater in the bowls of black rock. You might even see a few old guys panning for gold. If the tide is low, make your way farther north to a secret cove where stones of just about every color are washed up alongside polished agates on the beach in droves. The entire cove is hemmed in by rugged sea stacks and overhanging cliffs—there's even a cave to

poke around in. Bring the kids; they'll stay entertained for a long time. Just be sure to check the tide charts, since isolated spots like this can quickly become inundated with waves. Go at low tide and be safe.

User Groups: Hikers, dogs, and horses. No wheelchair facilities.

Permits: Permits are not required. Parking and access are free.

Maps: For a topographic map, ask the USGS for Neskowin OE W.

Directions: From Lighthouse Square on U.S. 101 in Lincoln City, turn onto Logan Road and follow it one mile to Roads End Wayside.

Contact: Oregon Parks and Recreation Department, 1115 Commercial Street NE, Salem, OR, 97301, 800/551-6949, www.oregonstateparks.org.

²⁶ DRIFT CREEK FALLS
3.0 mi/1.5 hr 🏃1 ⛰7

east of Lincoln City in the Siuslaw National Forest

Map 7.3, page 363

It's all about the numbers: Here you can overlook a 75-foot horsetail waterfall from a 240-foot-long swaying suspension bridge hung 100 feet over Drift Creek. Sound perilous? It's actually quite easy, a three-mile walk through ferns, salal, red huckleberry, and vine maple. The best time to go is in the spring and fall when the rains have powered the flow, making for a great show in this rain-forested chasm. The bridge itself is one of the more popular features of the trail, and in and of itself is an engineering marvel. Whether you dare to step foot on it is entirely up to you.

The first mile on the Drift Creek Falls Trail is an easy descent through forest to a 20-foot creek crossing. In the next 0.3 mile, the trail briefly traverses an old clear-cut before entering an old-growth grove and reaching the suspension bridge. The last 0.2 mile heads down to the waterfall's misty pool.

User Groups: Hikers and dogs. Part of the gravel trail is wheelchair accessible.

Permits: Permits are not required. A federal Northwest Forest Pass is required to park here; the cost is $5 a day or $30 for an annual pass. You can buy a day pass at the trailhead, at ranger stations, or through private vendors.

Maps: For a map of the Siuslaw National Forest, contact the Siuslaw National Forest headquarters, 4077 SW Research Way, P.O. Box 1148, Corvallis, OR, 97339, 541/750-7000. For a topographic map, ask the USGS for Devils Lake.

Directions: From Lincoln City, follow Highway 101 south of town to milepost 119 and turn east on Drift Creek Road for 1.5 miles, turn right at a T-junction and go 0.3 mile to another fork, heading uphill to the left onto Road 17/Drift Creek Camp Road. After 0.8 mile, turn uphill to the left. Go 9.1 miles to a large parking area on the right.

Contact: Siuslaw National Forest, Hebo Ranger District, 31525 Highway 22, Hebo, OR, 97122, 503/392-5100.

27 VALLEY OF THE GIANTS
4.7 mi/2.0 hr   🏃1 ⛰7

west of Falls City in the Coast Range

Map 7.3, page 363   BEST (

At one point, Oregon was renowned for its old-growth trees. Nowadays finding a trail that really brings out the big guys is not as easy as it was, say, 100 years ago. Though the drive to the Valley of the Giants requires navigating a maze of old logging roads, the end is an easy trail through some of Oregon's oldest and largest trees. This 51-acre forest preserve receives more than 180 inches of rain a year, and it shows. Douglas firs and Western hemlocks dominate the sky here. In spring and early summer, marbled murrelets roost high in these trees but build no nests, instead laying their eggs on flat branches a good 150 feet above the forest floor. They spend the rest of their lives at sea, but stands of trees like this are crucial to the birds' survival. To get here, it is crucial to get the directions right, and it is in your best interest to call the BLM's Salem District Office (503/375-5646). The route is best traveled on weekends to avoid log truck traffic.

Begin your descent into 450-year-old trees following the Valley of the Giants Trail 0.4 mile, crossing the river on a six-foot thick log. The main portion of the trail loops 0.7 mile through the area's biggest and most impressive stand of Oregon-style old-growth and wildflowers. Go right or left, either way you'll miss nothing.

User Groups: Hikers and dogs. No wheelchair facilities.

Permits: Permits are not required. Parking and access are free.

Maps: For a topographic map, ask the USGS for Warnicke Creek.

Directions: From the intersection of U.S. 99 West and OR 22, follow signs for Dallas for four miles. From Dallas, follow signs nine miles to Falls City. At the far end of town, curve left across a bridge onto Bridge Street, which becomes gravel in 0.7 mile, then becomes a one-lane log road. A total of 14.9 miles from Falls City, the road turns left at a locked gate with a Keep Out sign. At another 200 yards past this gate, turn right at a T-junction. Travel 8.2 miles past this gate, keeping right around an old lakebed, until you reach a wooden bridge over the South Fork Siletz River. At 0.2 mile past the bridge, head uphill to the right. In another 0.3 mile, go left at a fork. For the remaining 4.9 rough and potholed miles, keep left at all junctions to a bridge over the North Fork Siletz River. Continue 1.1 miles to a fork, going right 0.5 mile to the trailhead.

Contact: Bureau of Land Management, Salem District Office, 1717 Fabry Road SE, Salem, OR, 97306, 503/375-5646.

28 SALISHAN SPIT
8.0 mi/4.0 hr

north of Gleneden Beach on the Pacific Ocean

Map 7.3, page 363

Of all the sandy peninsulas in Oregon, the "spits" that guard the bays of every coastal river mouth, only the Salishan Spit has been developed for houses. Well, actually it's a resort. Though storms threatened the stability of this community and did indeed do some damage, the land has been stabilized. Why hike here? Because people aren't the only inhabitants: Harbor seals and sea otters frequent the more wild tip of the spit, away from the everyday human world. Views extend to the Cascade Head in the north and up to a gaggle of strange houses lining the ocean.

From the Gleneden Beach Wayside, a short paved trail leads down the sandstone bluffs to the beach. From here head north—that is, to the right—up the beach for a casual four-mile walk to the tip of the Salishan Spit. Be prepared for a moderately difficult hike not only for the distance, but because you'll be walking through sand.

User Groups: Hikers, dogs, and horses. No wheelchair facilities.

Permits: Permits are not required. Parking and access are free.

Maps: For a topographic map, ask the USGS for Lincoln City.

Directions: Head south from Lincoln City on U.S. 101 about 3.8 miles and turn west on Wessler Street at a sign for Gleneden Beach State Park, driving 0.2 mile to the parking lot.

Contact: Oregon Parks and Recreation Department, 1115 Commercial Street NE, Salem, OR, 97301, 800/551-6949, www.oregonstateparks.org.

29 DEVILS PUNCH BOWL
4.1 mi/2.0 hr

north of Newport in Devils Punch Bowl State Natural Area

Map 7.3, page 363

Surfers, tidepools, whale-watching, and thundering tides pounding into a series of sea caves beneath Otter Rock. Need I say more? There's a lot to see at the Devils Punch Bowl, and a number of ways to do it. An easy hike out the headland, a short saunter to its base within view of the Marine Gardens, and a hike down Beverly Beach are all possibilities at this state wayside. Winter storms are a great time to visit, as the ocean becomes vehement as it crashes into the sea-carved bowl, thundering and exploding like the devil himself. From the town of Newport, you can also spend some time on nearby Beverly Beach, going from violent to mellow in the space of a mile.

The first easy hike (0.3 mile round-trip) begins from the day-use lot and heads to a picnic area atop the rock. From a fenced overlook, you can see the churning Punch Bowl, waves pounding against sandstone and basalt. The second hike (0.4 mile one-way) goes down to the Punch Bowl itself and a series of tidepools called the Marine Gardens. To get here, return to the lot and walk C Street for two blocks to a Dead End sign and take the trail to the left to a hidden beach. Be sure to try this one at low tide, when anemones, mussels, and starfish are revealed. At the southern edge of the beach, at low tide you can slip into two caves. To access Beverly Beach, return to the lot and cross the road to a long staircase descending Otter Rock to a 1.5-mile walk along the beach to Spencer Creek.

User Groups: Hikers and dogs. No wheelchair facilities.

Permits: Permits are not required. Parking and access are free.

Maps: For a topographic map, ask the USGS for Newport North.

Directions: Drive north of Newport eight miles on U.S. 101 to the turnoff for the Otter

Crest Loop between mileposts 132 and 133. Follow signs 0.7 mile to the day-use parking area.

Contact: Oregon Parks and Recreation Department, 1115 Commercial Street NE, Salem, OR, 97301, 800/551-6949, www.oregonstateparks.org.

30 YAQUINA HEAD LIGHTHOUSE

0.1–2.6 mi/0.25–1.0 hr

north of Newport on Yaquina Head

Map 7.3, page 363

With a name like Yaquina Head Outstanding Natural Area, it ought to be good. With a historic 1873 lighthouse, whale-watching opportunities, colonies of seals, and views to seabird-populated Colony Rock, it really is one-of-a-kind. Five trails in all explore the head, with an interpretive center and viewpoints suitable for binoculars and cameras.

The centerpiece, of course, is the 93-foot lighthouse, the tallest in Oregon. The 200-yard paved Yaquina Head Lighthouse Trail leads to its base. This trail begins at the parking area located at the end of Lighthouse Drive, where the 0.4-mile Salal Hill Trail also begins. From the Quarry Cove parking area, the Quarry Cove Trail dives down 0.5 mile to a series of low-tide tidepools and the 0.5-mile Communications Hill Trails climbs to excellent viewpoints. There's even a stairway leading down to Cobble Beach. Bring a picnic and spend a day here.

User Groups: Hikers and mountain bikes. No dogs or horses allowed. There is wheelchair access to the tidepools.

Permits: Permits are not required. A $7 day-use fee is collected at the camping entrance, or you can get an annual Yaquina Head Vehicle Pass for $15; contact Bureau of Land Management, Salem District Office, 503/375-5646.

Maps: For a brochure and map, contact the Bureau of Land Management, 503/375-5646, or download a free map and brochure at www.blm.gov/or/resources/recreation/picbrochures.php. For a topographic map, ask the USGS for Newport North.

Directions: From Newport, drive two miles north on U.S. 101 to the park entrance. All

© SEAN PATRICK HILL

Yaquina Head Lighthouse

trailheads start from the parking areas and are well labeled.

Contact: Bureau of Land Management, Salem District Office, 1717 Fabry Road SE, Salem, OR, 97306, 503/375-5646.

31 NYE AND AGATE BEACH
4.0 mi one-way/2.0 hr

in Newport on the Pacific Ocean

Map 7.3, page 363

The 93-foot Yaquina Head Lighthouse is not the original lighthouse for this area; in fact, it is the Yaquina Bay Lighthouse that originally steered ships into the bay at Newport. This unique lighthouse is actually a lighthouse atop a house, making for an easy workday for past lighthouse keepers. You can visit this lighthouse and explore two beaches divided by an eroded sea stack called Jumpoff Joe; it used to have an arch beneath it, but it's been worn away by the surging tides.

Beginning from the Yaquina Bay Lighthouse picnic area, head down the stone steps to the North Jetty and views of the massive Yaquina Bay Bridge. Head to the right, going as far as you like. After 1.8 miles, you'll reach Jumpoff Joe, a good turnaround point. If you're up for more, continue along the 2.2-mile stretch of Agate Beach, so named for its abundance of agates and jaspers washed up by the tides, especially in winter.

User Groups: Hikers, dogs, and horses. No wheelchair facilities.

Permits: Permits are not required. Parking and access are free.

Maps: For a topographic map, ask the USGS for Newport North.

Directions: From the north end of Newport's Yaquina Bay Bridge (U.S. 101), follow state park signs to a picnic area at the Yaquina Bay Lighthouse. To shuttle from the Agate Beach State Wayside, drive 2.2 miles north of Yaquina Bay State Park on U.S. 101. Turn left on NW 26th Street for 0.2 mile, then right on NW Oceanview Drive for 0.2 mile

to the Agate Beach pullout. From here, you can walk 1.2 miles north along the beach to its end at the Yaquina Head, or south 2.8 miles to Yaquina Bay.

Contact: Oregon Parks and Recreation Department, 1115 Commercial Street NE, Salem, OR, 97301, 800/551-6949, www.oregonstateparks.org.

32 SOUTH JETTY TRAIL
2.1 mi/1.0 hr

south of Newport in South Beach State Park

Map 7.3, page 363

If you're looking for the perfect place to let the kids run off their energy without running off yours, South Beach State Park across the Yaquina Bay from Newport is perfect. In the course of a single hour (or more, depending on how much those kids may run in and out of the sand dunes), you'll cross a golden beach, skirting a foredune to a view of an old railroad route, and cross a deflation plain, a lowland area where the winds have stripped the sand down to hard ground.

From the day-use area, cross the foredune to the ocean shore. From here, walk to the right 0.9 mile toward the South Jetty on the Yaquina River. Climb the jetty for a look at the nearby Yaquina Bay Lighthouse and a series of pilings marking the long-lost railroad that brought the rocks here. Follow the jetty road back inland 0.3 mile, watching for a trail sign on the right. Follow the left fork path 0.2 mile to a paved trail. Go left a short distance on the paved path, then go right on a bark dust path across the deflation plain for 0.7 mile back to the day-use lot.

User Groups: Hikers, dogs, and horses. Bicycles on marked trails only. Paved paths are wheelchair accessible.

Permits: Permits are not required. Parking and access are free.

Maps: For a topographic map, ask the USGS for Newport South.

Directions: Drive U.S. 101 south of the

Yaquina Bay Bridge 1.4 miles and turn right at a sign for South Beach State Park. Drive straight on this road 0.5 mile to the day-use parking area.

Contact: Oregon Parks and Recreation Department, 1115 Commercial Street NE, Salem, OR, 97301, 800/551-6649, www.oregonstateparks.org.

⅗ SEAL ROCK
4.2 mi/2.5 hr

south of Newport in Ona Beach State Park

Map 7.3, page 363

This rock, recognized in the Chinook language as "seal home," is just that. You can reach Seal Rock, one of the southernmost remnants of a 15-million-year-old lava flow that originated somewhere near Hells Canyon, by car. You could have a sandwich in the neat little picnic area in a grove of spruce and shore pine. There's another way to enjoy it, though: For a more rewarding adventure, try a 2.1-mile beach walk from Ona Beach State Park and twisting Beaver Creek. It will make the sight of those seals, and sea lions, all the more spectacular.

From the Ona Beach State Park turnout, take the large paved trail toward the ocean. Cross the footbridge over Beaver Creek and head south toward Seal Rock. At a small creek, about 0.3 mile short of the cape, take a side trail up the bluff to the highway, and continue south about 300 yards to the Seal Rock Wayside. From there, you can descend another trail to a beach on the other side of the cape.

User Groups: Hikers and dogs. Paved paths are wheelchair accessible.

Permits: Permits are not required. Parking and access are free.

Maps: For a topographic map, ask the USGS for Newport South.

Directions: Follow U.S. 101 south of Newport seven miles to the parking area near milepost 149.

Contact: Oregon Parks and Recreation

Department, 1115 Commercial Street NE, Salem, OR, 97301, 800/551-6649, www.oregonstateparks.org.

⅗ MARY'S PEAK
4.0-10.0 mi/2.0-6.0 hr

west of Philomath in the Siuslaw National Forest

Map 7.3, page 363

From summer daisy fields to trees bowed down by winter snow, Mary's Peak is accessible all year long to some degree. Even better, it's the highest point in the Coastal Range, with views from the ocean to the Cascade Mountains. The Kalapuya sent their young men here on vision quests, naming the mountain Chateemanwi, the "place where spirits dwell." In fact, native legend has it that an angry coyote dammed up the Willamette, flooding all the world but this sole peak, which he spared as a refuge for all living things.

Mary's Peak is a designated Scenic Botanical Area, boasting a unique noble fir forest that rings many Ice Age flower species (more than 200 in all) dating back an estimated 6,000 years. A number of trails explore this unique vista, fanning out over the North and East Ridges with an easy, hikeable road to the summit.

From the observation point parking lot, an easy hike follows the East Ridge Trail out 1.2 miles, connecting to a 1.1-mile tie trail and returning on a 0.7-mile section of the North Ridge Trail. The East Ridge Trail in all is 2.2 miles, dropping 1,200 feet to a lower trailhead. The North Ridge Trail in its entirety is a more difficult 3.7 miles, switchbacking down nearly 2,000 feet to a trailhead and gate on Woods Creek Road.

The easier trails are the 4,097-foot summit, accessible from the observation point by climbing the gated road 0.6 mile to the top. From the campground, the easy Meadow Edge Trail loops 2.2 miles and connects to the summit as well.

User Groups: Hikers, dogs, mountain bikes,

and horses. The summit is wheelchair accessible.

Permits: Permits are not required. A federal Northwest Forest Pass is required to park here; the cost is $5 a day or $30 for an annual pass. You can buy a day pass at the trailhead, at ranger stations, or through private vendors.

Maps: For a map of the Siuslaw National Forest, contact the Siuslaw National Forest headquarters, 4077 SW Research Way, P.O. Box 1148, Corvallis, OR, 97339, 541/750-7000. For a topographic map, ask the USGS for Mary's Peak.

Directions: Drive U.S. 20 west of Corvallis through Philomath, then follow OR 34 for 8.8 miles and turn right onto Mary's Peak Road for 9.5 miles to its end at the observation point. For the Meadow Edge Trail, drive Mary's Peak Road from OR 34 8.8 miles up to the campground on the right, forking left to a picnic area and the trailhead.

Contact: Siuslaw National Forest, Waldport Ranger District, 1130 Forestry Lane, P.O. Box 400, Waldport, OR, 97122, 541/563-3211.

35 HORSE CREEK TRAIL
8.0 mi/4.0 hr   🏃2 ⛰7

northeast of Waldport in Drift Creek Wilderness

Map 7.3, page 363

Welcome to the northernmost and largest wilderness area in the Oregon Coastal Range: the Drift Creek Wilderness. Dropping 1,000 feet to this wilderness's namesake creek, the Horse Creek Trail wanders under moss-draped maples, passing huge and substantially bigger trees along the way, including hemlock, fir, and spruce. In spring, queen's-cup dots the forest floor, and in autumn chanterelle mushrooms poke from the duff.

From the trailhead, the path remains level the first mile or so, then descends 2.6 miles to a ford with a view of the ocean along the way. Turn right and follow the creek downstream one mile to another ford. Take the right hand-path, an unofficial trail to a campsite

and continue uphill 0.4 mile to return to the Horse Creek Trail.

User Groups: Hikers, dogs, and horses. No mountain bikes allowed. No wheelchair facilities.

Permits: Permits are not required. Parking and access are free.

Maps: For a map of the Siuslaw National Forest, contact the Siuslaw National Forest headquarters, 4077 SW Research Way, P.O. Box 1148, Corvallis, OR, 97339, 541/750-7000. For a map of Drift Creek Wilderness, ask the USFS for Drift Creek Wilderness. For a topographic map, ask the USGS for Tidewater.

Directions: Drive seven miles north of Waldport on U.S. 101 to Ona Beach State Park and turn right on North Beaver Creek Road for one mile. At a fork, head left for 2.7 miles to another junction and turn right onto the paved, one-lane North Elkhorn Road/Road 51 for 5.8 miles. At the next junction, turn left on Road 50 for 1.4 miles. Take a right fork onto gravel Road 5087 for 3.4 miles to the trailhead at a gate.

Contact: Siuslaw National Forest, Waldport Ranger District, 1130 Forestry Lane, P.O. Box 400, Waldport, OR, 97122, 541/563-3211.

36 HARRIS RANCH TRAIL
4.4 mi/2.5 hr   🏃2 ⛰7

northeast of Waldport in Drift Creek Wilderness

Map 7.3, page 363

Like the hike along Horse Creek Trail (see previous listing), this trail leads down to Drift Creek in its namesake wilderness area, though this trail is shorter and less difficult. To boot, it visits a meadow overgrown with bracken fern and blackberry and the site of an old homestead. For further adventuring, you can easily ford the creek here (especially in summer) and continue on to the Horse Creek Trail and the unmaintained Boulder Ridge Trail. Watch for wildlife in the meadow, including elk and black bear. This is also a good place to watch for bald eagles and the northern spotted owl.

In fall, the creek teems with spawning chinook and coho salmon, as well as steelhead and cutthroat trout.

From the trailhead, descend a whopping 1,200 feet on the Harris Ranch Trail, which is actually an abandoned road, down 2.2 miles to some small meadows and the remains of the pre–World War II ranch along Drift Creek. If the water is low, you can ford the creek 0.3 mile past the meadows and join the Horse Creek Trail, which connects to the Boulder Ridge Trail in one mile.

User Groups: Hikers, dogs, and horses. No mountain bikes allowed. No wheelchair facilities.

Permits: Permits are not required. Parking and access are free.

Maps: For a map of the Siuslaw National Forest, contact the Siuslaw National Forest headquarters, 4077 SW Research Way, P.O. Box 1148, Corvallis, OR, 97339, 541/750-7000. For a map of Drift Creek Wilderness, ask the USFS for Drift Creek Wilderness. For a topographic map, ask the USGS for Tidewater.

Directions: Drive east of Waldport on OR 34 for 6.9 miles to a bridge over the Alsea River. Turn north on Risley Creek Road/Road 3446 for 4.1 miles, staying on the larger road at each junction. Veer left on Road 346 for 0.8 mile to the Harris Ranch Trailhead.

Contact: Siuslaw National Forest, Waldport Ranger District, 1130 Forestry Lane, P.O. Box 400, Waldport, OR, 97122, 541/563-3211.

37 ALSEA FALLS
3.5 mi/1.5 hr

east of Waldport on the South Fork Alsea River

Map 7.3, page 363

If you've never seen a fish launch itself into the air to get itself over a waterfall, this is the place to do it. The 20-foot Alsea Falls are a bit off the beaten path on a scenic route over the Coast Range. A Boy Scout–constructed loop trail circles the South Fork Alsea River, while providing access to another span to another nearby waterfall in a lush side canyon. Along the way are the enormous stumps left from old-time logging, though the forest has had a long time to recover.

Starting from the Alsea Falls Recreation Area, take the left-hand trail beginning at a sign behind a maintenance garage. This trail follows the creek through second-growth woods for 0.6 mile to the first look at Alsea Falls and continues 0.3 mile down to the creek and over a logjam and boulder crossing beneath the pool at the base of the falls. Now the old-growth begins, as does the poison oak. At a junction, the right-hand trail continues the loop back one mile upstream and over a footbridge back to the car, but save that for the return; instead, take the left-hand trail, which joins a road to McBee Park. From here it's a short, 0.8-mile walk to Green Peak Falls. Stay on the gravel road until reaching the entrance road; turn right on that road, then take a quick right through a picnic site and follow that path to the 60-foot falls. A steep path can be scrambled down to reach a pool at the base.

User Groups: Hikers, dogs, and mountain bikes. No wheelchair facilities.

Permits: Permits are not required. Day-use fee is $3.

Maps: For a brochure and map, contact the Bureau of Land Management, Salem District Office, 503/375-5646, or go to www.blm.gov/or/resources/recreation/files/brochures/Alsea_Falls_Trail_System.pdf. For a topographic map, ask the USGS for Glenbrook.

Directions: Drive 16 miles south of Corvallis on U.S. 99W and turn west on South Fork Road at a sign for Alpine, and follow Alsea Falls signs to the camping area entrance on the right. Keep left to the trailhead.

Contact: Bureau of Land Management, Salem District Office, 1717 Fabry Road SE, Salem, OR, 97306, 503/375-5646.

38 SMELT SANDS WAYSIDE
1.4 m/0.75 hr ![hiker]1 ![difficulty]7

north of Yachats on the Pacific Ocean

Map 7.3, page 363

Smelt are a family of small fish found in many waters, including the Pacific. Just offshore of the quaint town of Yachats, a landowner blocked access to some traditional fishing rocks in the 1970s. Some locals went to the books and discovered a long-forgotten, 19th-century right of way for a road that was never built. A decade-long court battle went all the way to the Oregon Supreme Court and left us the 0.7-mile 804 Trail in a State Park wayside. You'll have the opportunity to see some "spouting horns" (waves crashing upward through cracks in the lava) and a long beach with running creeks and grassy dunes.

From the wayside, strike out on the gravel trail that eventually heads north, passing a motel and crossing a driveway before descending steps to the beach. From here, Tillicum Beach Campground is 2.7 miles ahead and Patterson State Park is 6.3 miles ahead.

User Groups: Hikers and dogs. No wheelchair facilities.

Permits: Permits are not required. Parking and access are free.

Maps: For a topographic map, ask the USGS for Yachats.

Directions: On the north end of Yachats on U.S. 101, turn west onto Lemwick Lane, driving to the end at a turnaround and parking area.

Contact: Oregon Parks and Recreation Department, 1115 Commercial Street NE, Salem, OR, 97301, 800/551-6949, www.oregonstateparks.org.

39 CAPE PERPETUA
1.0–6.8 mi/0.5–3.5 hrs ![hiker]2 ![difficulty]8

south of Yachats in Cape Perpetua Scenic Area

Map 7.3, page 363

The Cape Perpetua Scenic Area is one of the jewels of the Oregon coast. A network of trails radiates from the visitors center, offering access to a giant spruce, an ancient Native American midden, the Devil's Churn, Cooks Chasm and a spouting horn, and the centerpiece: a wonderful stone shelter atop 746-foot Cape Perpetua itself, built in 1933 by the Civilian Conservation Corps. It's easy to do three interesting trails in a single day and visit the top spots.

All trails begin at the visitors center lot. For the ocean hike, follow the "Tidepools" pointer on a paved trail, which goes 0.2 mile and under U.S. 101, then forks. The left fork circles 0.2 mile for a view to the spouting horns at Cooks Chasm, named for Captain Cook, who in turn named this cape for St. Perpetua in 1778. You'll also walk over the midden, a staggering mound of white mussel shells left by Native Americans (possibly as long as 6,000 years ago). The right fork heads out 0.5 mile to a loop around the Devil's Churn, a wave-pounded chasm in the lava.

For two inland hikes, return to the lot. First, follow "Giant Spruce" and "Viewpoint" pointers. In 0.2 mile, the trail splits: To see the 15-foot-thick, 600-year-old Sitka spruce, an Oregon Heritage Tree whose roots form a small tunnel, go to the right on the Giant Spruce Trail 0.8 mile. To climb Cape Perpetua, head left at this junction over Cape Creek to cross two paved roads and climb the switchbacks 1.3 miles up the Saint Perpetua Trail to the stone shelter, which affords views 37 miles to sea and 104 miles south to Cape Blanco. It's an excellent place to whale-watch, and you can consider how the CCC men endured winter storms and lugged buckets of sand up from the shore to make the mortar for the shelter.

User Groups: Hikers and dogs. Paved paths are wheelchair accessible.

Permits: Permits are not required. A federal Northwest Forest Pass is required to park here; the cost is $5 a day or $30 for an annual pass. You can buy a day pass at the visitors center, at ranger stations, or through private vendors.

Maps: For a map of the Siuslaw National Forest, contact the Siuslaw National Forest headquarters, 4077 SW Research Way, P.O. Box 1148, Corvallis, OR, 97339, 541/750-7000. For a topographic map, ask the USGS for Yachats.

Directions: Drive U.S. 101 south of Yachats three miles to the Cape Perpetua Visitor Center turnoff between mileposts 168 and 169.

Contact: Cape Perpetua Visitor Center, 2400 Highway 101, Yachats, OR, 97498, 541/547-3289, or Siuslaw National Forest, Waldport Ranger District, 1130 Forestry Lane, P.O. Box 400, Waldport, OR, 97122, 541/563-3211.

40 GWYNN CREEK
6.7 mi/3.5 hr

south of Yachats in Cape Perpetua Scenic Area

Map 7.3, page 363

Sitka spruce thrive on the foggy ocean climate and can only survive within three miles of the coastline. It so happens that some of the best spruce forests on the entire coast are in the canyons south of Cape Perpetua. This loop trail spans Cooks Ridge, drops into Gwynn Creek's canyon, and follows the Oregon Coast Trail back to the visitors center. Mushrooms love it here, too, including the delectable chanterelle and the poisonous panther amanita. Parts of the trail follow old logging roads and an 1895 wagon road between Yachats and Florence that ran until about 1910.

From the visitors center upper parking lot, follow signs for the Cooks Ridge Trail. In 0.4 mile, the path forks but rejoins, forming the Discovery Loop. Take either side and continue 0.3 mile to where the paths meet and continue on the Cooks Ridge Trail two

miles to a junction. Turn right on the Gwynn Creek Trail, descending 3.3 miles and 1,000 feet down the canyon. At the Oregon Coast Trail, go right for a 0.7-mile return to the visitors center.

User Groups: Hikers, dogs, and horses. No wheelchair facilities.

Permits: Permits are not required. A federal Northwest Forest Pass is required to park here; the cost is $5 a day or $30 for an annual pass. You can buy a day pass at the visitors center, at ranger stations, or through private vendors.

Maps: For a map of the Siuslaw National Forest, contact the Siuslaw National Forest headquarters, 4077 SW Research Way, P.O. Box 1148, Corvallis, OR, 97339, 541/750-7000. For a topographic map, ask the USGS for Yachats.

Directions: Drive U.S. 101 south of Yachats three miles to the Cape Perpetua Visitor Center turnoff between mileposts 168 and 169.

Contact: Cape Perpetua Visitor Center, 2400 Highway 101, Yachats, OR, 97498, 541/547-3289, or Siuslaw National Forest, Waldport Ranger District, 1130 Forestry Lane, P.O. Box 400, Waldport, OR, 97122, 541/563-3211.

41 CUMMINS CREEK
8.0 mi/4.0 hr

south of Yachats in Cape Perpetua Scenic Area

Map 7.3, page 363

Traversing the edge of the Cummins Creek Wilderness and connecting to the network of trails in the Cape Perpetua Scenic Area, this little-known trail itself never comes near the creek, but a small user trail will get you there nonetheless. A moderate-length loop offers a good tour of this area with opportunities for even longer hikes if you wish.

Beginning at the barricade, the initial part of the Cummins Creek Trail is an abandoned road. In the first 300 yards, an unofficial side trail to the right leads to two spots on the canyon, about 1.8 miles out and back. But the main Cummins Creek Trail ascends gradually up a forested ridge 1.4 miles to a junction. The Cummins Creek Loop Trail continues to the left 1.2 miles to the next junction; turn right for 0.5 mile, watching for a short spur trail to the left that offers a view. At the next junction, follow the Cummins Creek Trail to the right 1.4 miles back to the first junction, then stay to the left on the Cummins Creek Trail 1.4 miles back to the barricade.

User Groups: Hikers, dogs, and horses. No wheelchair facilities.

Permits: Permits are not required. A federal Northwest Forest Pass is required to park here; the cost is $5 a day or $30 for an annual pass. You can buy a day pass at the visitors center, at ranger stations, or through private vendors.

Maps: For a map of the Siuslaw National Forest, contact the Siuslaw National Forest headquarters, 4077 SW Research Way, P.O. Box 1148, Corvallis, OR, 97339, 541/750-7000. For a topographic map, ask the USGS for Yachats.

Directions: Drive U.S. 101 south of the Cape Perpetua Visitors Center one mile to a sign for Cummins Creek Trailhead. Turn left and drive gravel road 1050 for 0.3 mile to the barricade.

Contact: Cape Perpetua Visitor Center, 2400 Highway 101, Yachats, OR, 97498, 541/547-3289, or Siuslaw National Forest, Waldport Ranger District, 1130 Forestry Lane, P.O. Box 400, Waldport, OR, 97122, 541/563-3211.

42 CUMMINS RIDGE
12.0 mi/6.0 hr   🏃3 ⛰7

south of Yachats in Cummins Creek Wilderness

Map 7.3, page 363

With only 9,173 acres, Cummins Creek Wilderness is not huge. It has, in fact, only one trail. On the other hand, it has the only old-growth Sitka spruce forest in the entire wilderness system of Oregon, so why not visit? You'll find not only Cummins Creek but Bob Creek, both overhung with droopy maple and alder. The Cummins Ridge tops out at 2,200 feet

and bisects the wilderness. Wild salmon and trout spawn in the cold waters, and flowers like yellow monkeyflower, white candyflower, purple aster, and the tall spikes of foxglove thrive here. With 80–100 inches of rain a year here, it's no wonder that spruce in this rainforest sometimes reach nine feet in diameter.

From the barricade on the dirt road, the Cummins Ridge Trail begins at 1,000 foot elevation. Follow the abandoned road up three miles, gaining 750 feet in elevation, to a cairn, then follow the trail to the right another three miles to trail's end on Forest Service Road 5694-515. Return the way you came.

User Groups: Hikers, dogs, and horses. No mountain bikes allowed. No wheelchair facilities.

Permits: Permits are not required. A federal Northwest Forest Pass is required to park here; the cost is $5 a day or $30 for an annual pass. You can buy a day pass at the visitors center, at ranger stations, or through private vendors.

Maps: For a map of the Siuslaw National Forest, contact the Siuslaw National Forest headquarters, 4077 SW Research Way, P.O. Box 1148, Corvallis, OR, 97339, 541/750-7000. For a topographic map, ask the USGS for Yachats.

Directions: From Yachats, drive four miles south on U.S. 101 and turn inland on gravel Road 1051 for 2.2 miles to the end at a barricade.

Contact: Siuslaw National Forest, Waldport Ranger District, 1130 Forestry Ln., P.O. Box 400, Waldport, OR, 97122, 541/563-3211.

43 HECETA HEAD
6.9 mi/3.0 hr   🏃2 ⛰8

north of Florence in Carl Washburne State Park

Map 7.3, page 363

A plethora of fantastic landscapes nearly assaults the senses in this everything-and-the-kitchen-sink hike. From beaver ponds to a lighthouse on a surf-pounded rock to the strange "Hobbit Trails," there is plenty to discover here. There is even, if you believe in this sort of thing, a supposedly haunted light keeper's house. All in all, you'll get the best of all worlds in this meandering loop.

From the day-use area, follow the beach south 1.2 miles, crossing Blowout Creek, toward the looming Heceta Head, where starfish and mollusks cling in the booming waves. Piles of gravel near the base are a good place to dig around for agates. You'll spot a trail leading into the woods; take this up 0.4 mile through a network of paths called the Hobbit Trails (tunnels of a sort made by hollowed-out sand chutes and arching rhododendrons). At the top of the climb, nearing the highway, go right on the next trail, which climbs 1.3 mile over the Heceta Head itself, coming down to the lighthouse and an overlook. Just offshore, Parrot Rock and other sea stacks are roosting areas for thousands of Brandt's cormorants; it's the largest nesting colony in Oregon. Walk the last 0.5 mile toward the Heceta House, an 1893 Queen Anne–style home for the lighthouse keepers that is supposedly haunted; it's a bed-and-breakfast now, so you can find out for yourself.

To complete the loop, head back over the head to the U.S. 101 Hobbit Trail trailhead and cross the highway to the continuation of the Valley Trail, which in the course of 1.1 miles passes a number of ponds and a beaver lake before forking to the left (though you could hike a bit down China Creek if you head right). This trail returns to the Washburne Campground, where you can follow the entrance road out and across the highway to return to the day-use area.

User Groups: Horses and dogs. No wheelchair facilities.

Permits: Permits are not required. Parking and access are free.

Maps: For a free park brochure, call Oregon Parks and Recreation, 800/551-6949, or download a free map at www.oregonstateparks. org. For a topographic map, ask the USGS for Heceta Head.

Directions: Drive U.S. 101 north of Florence

one mile to milepost 176 and turn left into the Washburne State Park day-use area, parking at the far end of the picnic area. The trail begins past the restrooms.

Contact: Oregon Parks and Recreation Department, 1115 Commercial Street NE, Salem, OR, 97301, 800/551-6949, www.oregonstateparks.org.

44 CAPE MOUNTAIN
2.0 mi/1.0 hr   🚶1 ⛰7

north of Florence in the Siuslaw National Forest

Map 7.3, page 363

In a joint venture between the Forest Service and equestrian club volunteers, a network of trails was built on and around Cape Mountain. The Coast Horse Trail system is open to hikers, too. An easy two-mile loop leads to the peak, the site of a 1932 fire watchtower. Once you've done this easy loop, you can fan out into the wild network of trails going every which way, exploring Nelson and Scurvy Ridge and a number of loops. Much of the forest here was spared by previous wildfires, leaving habitat for old-growth trees and wildlife.

From the Dry Lake Trailhead, head behind the stables for the Princess Tasha Trail, climbing 0.4 mile through old-growth Douglas fir and coastal spruce to a four-way junction. Turn left on the Cape Mountain spur for 0.5 mile, keeping left at all junctions to attain the summit. For a loop option, follow the old road down, keeping left at all junctions to return directly to the car.

User Groups: Hikers, dogs, mountain bikes, and horses. No wheelchair facilities.

Permits: Permits are not required. Parking and access are free.

Maps: For a map of the Siuslaw National Forest, contact the Siuslaw National Forest headquarters, 4077 SW Research Way, P.O. Box 1148, Corvallis, OR, 97339, 541/750-7000. For a topographic map, ask the USGS for Mercer Lake.

Directions: Drive U.S, 101 north of Florence

seven miles and go right on Herman Peak Road for 2.8 miles to the Dry Lake Trailhead on the left.

Contact: Siuslaw National Forest, Mapleton Ranger District, 4480 Highway 101, Building G, Florence, OR, 97439, 541/902-8526.

45 BAKER BEACH
0.5-6.5 mi/0.25-3.5 hr

north of Florence in the Siuslaw National Forest

Map 7.3, page 363   BEST (

Baker Beach's windswept dunes sure look a lot like something from *Lawrence of Arabia,* and standing amid such colossal waves it's hard to believe we're still in Oregon. Interspersed with Sutton Creek, grassy hummocks, and perhaps even a little lupine flower or wild strawberry, it doesn't seem like other beaches. Nearby Lily Lake provides an easy 1.4-mile loop, and the beach itself is explorable (with trails and dunes). Hike from the lot 0.4 mile toward the ocean, then strike out in any direction; heading north three miles will land you at the estuary of Sutton Creek, a great place to bird-watch. But you may just want to go striding over the dunes themselves, finding a big one and rolling down the other side. Kids love this area, as do horseback riders.

User Groups: Hikers and horses. Dogs allowed on leash only. Bikes prohibited. No wheelchair facilities.

Permits: Permits are not required. A federal Northwest Forest Pass is required to park here; the cost is $5 a day or $30 for an annual pass. You can buy a day pass at the visitors center, at ranger stations, or through private vendors.

Maps: For a map of the Siuslaw National Forest, contact the Siuslaw National Forest headquarters, 4077 SW Research Way, P.O. Box 1148, Corvallis, OR, 97339, 541/750-7000. For a topographic map, ask the USGS for Mercer Lake.

Directions: Drive U.S. 101 north of Florence seven miles and turn west on gravel Baker Beach Road for 0.5 miles to its end.

Contact: Siuslaw National Forest, Mapleton Ranger District, 4480 Highway 101, Building G, Florence, OR, 97439, 541/902-8526.

46 SUTTON CREEK DUNES
4.4 mi/2.0 hr

north of Florence in the Siuslaw National Forest

Map 7.3, page 363

If you've never seen the famous Oregon rhododendrons, this is the place to do it. In the Sutton Creek Recreation Area, jungles of these sweet flowering trees line the meandering Sutton Creek, easy and warm to wade in the summer. Patches of spiny salal rustle in the wind, and blue herons wade in the water. A loop trail courses through the dunes and follows the creek. If you go to the shore, keep out of designated snowy plover nesting sites, as these birds are endangered and protected. A variety of dunes punctuate the landscape, making for a geographically and biologically diverse area. Look for the rare *Darlingtonia,* the insect-munching cobra lily.

From the Holman Vista lot, start at the trail behind the kitchen shelter in the picnic area. This trail curves 0.8 mile along the creek, passing a number of fords, to a bench and footbridge. Follow a sign upstream to the right for the Sutton Campground, following the Sutton Creek Trail. In 0.5 mile, you'll reach the campground's A Loop. Turn left along the road and cross a footbridge over the creek and stay to the left at the next two junctions (part of a 0.4-mile loop), continuing 1.4 miles out along the dunes (a right-hand trail leads to the Alder Dune Campground) before dropping down to the footbridge to Boldac's Meadow. Turn right along the creek, then left at the next junction to return the half-mile back to Holman Vista.

User Groups: Hikers, dogs on leash only, and horses. No bikes allowed. The Holman Vista Observation Deck is wheelchair accessible.

Permits: Permits are not required. A federal Northwest Forest Pass is required to park here; the cost is $5 a day or $30 for an annual pass. You can buy a day pass at the visitors center, at ranger stations, or through private vendors.

Maps: For a map of the Siuslaw National Forest, contact the Siuslaw National Forest headquarters, 4077 SW Research Way, P.O. Box 1148, Corvallis, OR, 97339, 541/750-7000. For a topographic map, ask the USGS for Mercer Lake.

Directions: From Florence, drive U.S. 101 north for five miles, turning west at the Sutton creek Recreation Area sign. Follow this paved road 2.2 miles to the Holman Vista lot.

Contact: Siuslaw National Forest, Mapleton Ranger District, 4480 Highway 101, Building G, Florence, OR, 97439, 541/902-8526.

47 ENCHANTED VALLEY
5.0 mi/2.5 hr

north of Florence in the Siuslaw National Forest

Map 7.3, page 363

This former dairy farm has been abandoned, and a host of wildlife (including deer and elk) has taken the place of the cows. The bed of Bailey Creek shimmers with bits of iron pyrite and is being restored for native coho salmon, thus making this a place to see both silver salmon and fool's gold: a real treasure. This fairly easy hike follows the creek 2.5 miles from a feeder creek for Mercer Lake along meadows teeming with horsetail and skunk cabbage, visiting an old farmhouse site and an upper homestead meadow, site of an old apple orchard. Following an old road converted to a path, there's really no way to lose your way. Return as you came.

User Groups: Hikers, dogs, and horses. No wheelchair facilities.

Permits: Permits are not required. Parking and access are free.

Maps: For a map of the Siuslaw National Forest, contact the Siuslaw National Forest headquarters, 4077 SW Research Way, P.O. Box 1148, Corvallis, OR, 97339, 541/750-

7000. For a topographic map, ask the USGS for Mercer Lake.

Directions: Drive five miles north of Florence on U.S. 101 and turn right on Mercer Lake Road for 3.7 miles. Fork left on Twin Fawn Drive for 0.3 mile to a parking area at the end of the road.

Contact: Siuslaw National Forest, Mapleton Ranger District, 4480 Highway 101, Building G, Florence, OR, 97439, 541/902-8526.

48 SIUSLAW RIDGE
2.6 mi/1.0 hr

west of Eugene in Whittaker Creek Recreation Site

Map 7.3, page 363

From the campground at the Whittaker Creek Recreation Site deep in the Coastal Range, you can watch the annual salmon run. Chinook, coho, and steelhead all push upstream to their spawning grounds. Just off the road, the Siuslaw River cuts its way through the mountains heading for the sea, and here the Siuslaw Ridge rises above it with a trail leading to a truly large Douglas fir: seven-feet thick and 500-years-old. The trail is just steep enough to give your heart a workout.

From the parking area near a dam, head across a footbridge spanning Whittaker Creek and down the campground road to a sign reading Old Growth Ridge Trail. This one-mile climb rockets up 800 feet to a junction at the peak of the ridge. Take a left for a short 0.1-mile jaunt to the giant fir, and a right for a short 0.2-mile walk to a river viewpoint.

User Groups: Hikers and dogs. No wheelchair facilities.

Permits: Permits are not required. Parking and access are free.

Maps: For a topographic map, ask the USGS for Roman Nose Mountain.

Directions: Drive west of Eugene 33 miles on OR 126 to a junction between mileposts 26 and 27. Turn south on Siuslaw River Road, following signs for "Whittaker Cr. Rec. Area" for 1.5 miles, turn right for 0.2 mile, then right again into the campground.

Contact: Bureau of Land Management, Eugene District Office, 2890 Chad Dr., Eugene, OR, 97440, 541/683-6600.

49 SWEET CREEK FALLS
5.2 mi/2.5 hr   🚶1 ⚠7

east of Florence in the Siuslaw National Forest

Map 7.4, page 364

This hike would be quite epic if not for lack of a bridge spanning the gorge at Sweet Creek Falls. No matter. Two trailheads will do fine to visit not just two different views of Sweet Creek, but Beaver Creek Falls, which is—to my understanding—the only double waterfall in Oregon made of two completely different creeks. One section of the trail follows an old wagon road through the Zarah T. Sweet homestead, the path now pioneered only by red alders, which thrive in disturbed ground. The other fans out toward both sets of waterfalls and stunning views. Rain or shine, it's beautiful. A total of four trailheads break these trails up into easy segments that pass a dozen waterfalls in all. To make it easy and worthwhile, try these two. Part of the trail, by the way, is a dramatic catwalk on a metal walkway hugging the canyon wall.

The Homestead Trailhead sets out into Punchbowl Falls Canyon 0.7 mile, joining up with the trail from the Sweet Creek Falls Trailhead for the final 0.4-mile walk to Sweet Creek Falls. It's easiest to return the way you came, though in very low water a ford is possible over slippery boulders. Instead, proceed by car to the Wagon Road Trailhead, where two trails begin. Directly across the road from the parking area, one 0.8-mile trail, a stretch of the old Sunset Wagon Road, leads down to a viewpoint of Sweet Creek Falls opposite the previous trails. The second route, Beaver Creek Trail, begins over the roadway bridge from the parking area for a 0.6-mile trail to Beaver Creek Falls.

User Groups: Hikers and dogs only. No wheelchair facilities.

Permits: Permits are not required. Parking and access are free.

Maps: For a map of the Siuslaw National Forest, contact the Siuslaw National Forest headquarters, 4077 SW Research Way, P.O. Box 1148, Corvallis, OR, 97339, 541/750-7000. For a topographic map, ask the USGS for Goodwin Peak.

Directions: Drive 15 miles east of Florence on OR 126 to Mapleton to the Siuslaw River Bridge. Cross the bridge and turn right on Sweet Creek Road for 10.2 miles. Take a paved turnoff to the right for the Homestead Trail. To get to the Wagon Road Trailhead, drive 1.3 miles farther to a parking area on the left.

Contact: Siuslaw National Forest, Mapleton Ranger District, 4480 Highway 101, Building G, Florence, OR, 97439, 541/902-8526.

50 KENTUCKY FALLS AND NORTH FORK SMITH RIVER
4.4-17.4 mi/2.0 hr-1 day   🚶2 ⚠7

west of Eugene in the Siuslaw National Forest

Map 7.4, page 364   **BEST (**

Eugenians certainly know about Kentucky Falls. It boasts an upper and lower fall, both dropping 100 feet, and this short trail visits both. The roads here may be twisty, and the hike may require you to climb back out of this rainforest canyon, but it's a must at any time of year. These falls are among the most famous in the entire Coast Range, and among the biggest. Because the drive to get here is so long, it's tempting to extend the hike along the North Fork Smith River, a trail that is only accessible in summer's low water.

From the trailhead, descend the Kentucky Falls Trail 0.8 mile to Upper Kentucky Falls, and continue another 1.4 miles to an observation deck overlooking Lower Kentucky Falls. From here, a newer trail follows the North Fork Smith River 6.5 miles. Head downstream two miles to a switchbacking descent, and in another 1.5 miles the trail fords the river for the first time, and in another 1.5 miles fords a second time. The trail leaves the river and ends at another trailhead after the last 1.5 miles. Note that this trail is accessible in summers only, and as of July 2008, there is an impassable slide about four miles north of the North Fork Smith Trailhead; contact the Mapleton Ranger District (541/902-8526) for up-to-date information.

User Groups: Hikers and dogs. No wheelchair facilities.

Permits: Permits are not required. Parking and access are free.

Maps: For a map of the Siuslaw National Forest, contact the Siuslaw National Forest headquarters, 4077 SW Research Way, P.O. Box 1148, Corvallis, OR, 97339, 541/750-7000. For a topographic map, ask the USGS for Baldy Mountain.

Directions: Drive west of Eugene 33 miles on OR 126 to a junction between mileposts 26 and 27. Turn south on Siuslaw River Road, following signs for "Whittaker Cr. Rec. Area" for 1.5 miles, then turn right over a bridge at another Whittaker sign. Follow this one-lane, paved road back into the hills 1.5 miles and fork left onto Dunn Ridge Road. Follow this fork 6.7 miles uphill to a junction at pavement's end and turn left on Knowles Creek Road for 2.7 miles, then right on Road 23 for 1.6 miles, then right on paved Road 919 for 2.6 miles to trailhead parking on the right. To make this hike an 8.7-mile one-way trip, shuttle a car at the North Fork Smith River Trailhead. From the junction of Forest Service Road 23 and Road 919, go 5.7 miles south on Road 23 to the trailhead.

Contact: Siuslaw National Forest, Mapleton Ranger District, 4480 Highway 101, Building G, Florence, OR, 97439, 541/902-8526.

51 HONEYMAN STATE PARK DUNES

1.6 mi/1.0 hr 🥾1 ⛰7

south of Florence in Honeyman State Park

Map 7.4, page 364

The Oregon Dunes, the jewel of the Northwest, begin just south of historic Florence. With nearly 40 miles of rippling coastline, this is an otherworldly place of massive sand dunes, tree islands, and quiet estuaries reached only by rugged hikes over sort and shifting sand. Honeyman State Park is the second-largest overnight camp in the state, and with its two freshwater lakes, pink rhododendrons, and fall huckleberries, there is more to the park than just sand. Yet sand is why they come in droves, and an easy loop allows you to get your first glimpse of what wind and weather can do to a landscape.

From the day-use lot, a sand trail leads out along lovely Cleawox Lake. At the edge of the lake, turn left and crest a grassy dune. Looking ahead and to the left of a tree island, you'll spot the biggest of the dunes here at 250 feet. Strike out on the trail-less dunes 0.5 mile toward that big one. Spend some time up top, as the views are extensive. Head down the slope opposite the ocean and head into one of the sandy trails that emerges in a sandy bowl circled by forest. Cross the bowl and head for a gap on the ridge which leads to the campground on the "I" loop. Go left on the paved road and left again on the main campground road, 0.4 mile in all. Just past the campground fee booth, go left on a paved trail for 0.2 mile to return to the day-use area.

User Groups: Hikers, dogs, and horses. Paved areas of the park are wheelchair accessible.

Permits: Permits are not required. A $3 day-use fee is collected at the camping entrance, or you can get an annual Oregon Parks and Recreation pass for $25; contact Oregon Parks and Recreation, 800/551-6949.

Maps: For a free park brochure, call Oregon Parks and Recreation, 800/551-6949, or download a free map at www.oregonstateparks.

org. For a topographic map, ask the USGS for Florence.

Directions: Drive south of Florence three miles on U.S. 101 and turn right into the park entrance, following signs 0.3 mile to the Sand Dunes Picnic Area.

Contact: Oregon Parks and Recreation Department, 1115 Commercial Street NE, Salem, OR, 97301, 800/551-6949, www.oregonstateparks.org.

52 SILTCOOS RIVER
2.6 mi/1.0 hr   👣1 ⚠6

in the Oregon Dunes National Recreation Area

Map 7.4, page 364

A small estuary at the mouth of the Siltcoos River is home to nesting snowy plovers, among other water-loving birds. The Waxmyrtle Beach Trail sets out toward the coastline with views of the estuary along a meandering river where kayakers glide by quietly. Note: The Estuary Trail is closed March 15 through September 15 to protect snowy plover nesting sites.

From the Stagecoach Trailhead, start out on the Waxmyrtle Trail, which runs 0.2 mile between the river and road, then turn right on the campground road over the river. After crossing the bridge, turn right on the trail and follow the river 0.7 mile (if it's snowy plover season, you'll have to instead take a sandy, gated road to the left and follow it 0.8 mile). At a junction, continue toward the ocean 0.3 mile on the sandy old road. Turn right 0.2 mile to the river's mouth.

User Groups: Hikers, dogs on a leash, and horses. No wheelchair facilities.

Permits: Permits are not required. A federal Northwest Forest Pass is required to park here; the cost is $5 a day or $30 for an annual pass. You can buy a day pass at the visitors center, at ranger stations, or through private vendors.

Maps: For a map of the Siuslaw National Forest, contact the Siuslaw National Forest headquarters, 4077 SW Research Way, P.O.

Box 1148, Corvallis, OR, 97339, 541/750-7000. For a topographic map, ask the USGS for Tahkenitch Creek.

Directions: Drive U.S. 101 south of Florence eight miles to the Siltcoos Recreation Area turnoff at milepost 198. Turn west and drive 0.9 mile to the Stagecoach Trailhead on the left.

Contact: Siuslaw National Forest, Mapleton Ranger District, 4480 Highway 101, Building G, Florence, OR, 97439, 541/902-8526, or the Oregon Dunes National Recreation Area, 855 Highway Avenue, Reedsport, OR, 97467, 541/271-6019.

53 SILTCOOS LAKE
4.3 mi/2.0 hr   👣1 ⚠7

in the Oregon Dunes National Recreation Area

Map 7.4, page 364

At 3,500 acres, Siltcoos Lake is the largest freshwater lake on the Oregon coast. A loop trail visits two isolated campsites on the lake's shore facing forested Booth Island.

From the highway, hike inland and downhill on the Siltcoos Lake Trail 0.8 mile to a junction. Go right 0.7 mile to another junction, then right for 0.2 mile to South Camp on the lake. Head back up this spur trail to the junction, then go right 0.5 mile to access North Camp, which has more spots to pitch a tent. In the jumble of trails, continue on the main one to complete the loop and return 1.1 miles back to the first junction, then right the remaining 0.8 mile to the highway.

User Groups: Hikers, dogs, horses, and mountain bikes. No wheelchair facilities.

Permits: Permits are not required. A federal Northwest Forest Pass is required to park here; the cost is $5 a day or $30 for an annual pass. You can buy a day pass at the visitors center, at ranger stations, or through private vendors.

Maps: For a map of the Siuslaw National Forest, contact the Siuslaw National Forest headquarters, 4077 SW Research Way, P.O. Box 1148, Corvallis, OR, 97339,

541/750-7000. For a topographic map, ask the USGS for Florence.

Directions: Drive U.S. 101 south of Florence eight miles and park on the east side of 101 opposite the Siltcoos Recreation Area turnoff at milepost 198.

Contact: Siuslaw National Forest, Mapleton Ranger District, 4480 Highway 101, Building G, Florence, OR, 97439, 541/902-8526, or the Oregon Dunes National Recreation Area, 855 Highway Avenue, Reedsport, OR, 97467, 541/271-6019.

54 CARTER LAKE DUNES
2.7 mi/1.5 hr   🥾2 ⛰️7

in the Oregon Dunes National Recreation Area

Map 7.4, page 364

Two lakes, Carter and Taylor, sit atop a forested ridge overlooking the Oregon Dunes. In some spots, the ocean is far away and a slogging walk just to reach the shore. From here, it's pretty easy, actually, and you can walk along beautiful Taylor Lake on your way to the big dunes. You'll have to follow blue-striped posts out over the dunes, over the deflation plain with its shore pine and Scotch broom forest and down to the beach. Just keep an eye on that trail once you reach the beach, so as not to wander off and lose it. Also keep in mind that sand-hiking can be tiring and slow-going.

The first 0.4 mile passes Taylor Lake to two view decks and a bench before dropping 0.5 mile to the dunes to join with the Carter Lake Trail. From here, follow posts 0.5 mile to the ocean. For a loop possibility, you could well follow the Carter Lake Trail back to the road, then head 0.4 mile left along the road to the Taylor Dunes Trailhead.

User Groups: Hikers, dogs, and horses. The first 0.5 mile is wheelchair accessible.

Permits: Permits are not required. A federal Northwest Forest Pass is required to park here; the cost is $5 a day or $30 for an annual pass. You can buy a day pass at the visitors center, at ranger stations, or through private vendors.

Maps: For a map of the Siuslaw National Forest, contact the Siuslaw National Forest headquarters, 4077 SW Research Way, P.O. Box 1148, Corvallis, OR, 97339, 541/750-7000. For a topographic map, ask the USGS for Tahkenitch Creek.

Directions: Drive U.S. 101 south of Florence nine miles, or north of Reedsport 12 miles, and turn west into the Carter Lake Campground entrance. The Taylor Dunes Trailhead is on the left just after the entrance.

Contact: Siuslaw National Forest, Mapleton Ranger District, 4480 Highway 101, Building G, Florence, OR, 97439, 541/902-8526, or the Oregon Dunes National Recreation Area, 855 Highway Avenue, Reedsport, OR, 97467, 541/271-6019.

55 OREGON DUNES OVERLOOK
2.2 mi/1.0 hr   🥾1 ⛰️7

in the Oregon Dunes National Recreation Area

Map 7.4, page 364

What a great view these overlooks afford: a vast sea of sand, massive tree islands swelling between the dunes, and beyond a shore pine forest, the rolling tides. Want a closer look? Then hike right past those decks and down to the sand, where blue-striped posts lead hikers to a long beach with opportunities to explore the wild-flowered deflation plain, where deer wander and the hummocks of sand cradle deep valleys where kids can play and dogs can run. This is one of the easier, meaning shorter, paths through the dunes to the shoreline.

The main trail begins as a paved path that drops 0.3 mile to the sand, though another trail begins just past the observation decks, briefly passing through the scrubby trees and out onto the peak of a dune. Once you get down to the flatter ground, the posts lead 0.8 mile to the shore.

User Groups: Hikers, dogs, and horses, No mountain bikes allowed. Viewing decks are wheelchair accessible.

Permits: Permits are not required. A federal Northwest Forest Pass is required to park here; the cost is $5 a day or $30 for an annual pass. You can buy a day pass at the visitors center, at ranger stations, or through private vendors.

Maps: For a map of the Siuslaw National Forest, contact the Siuslaw National Forest headquarters, 4077 SW Research Way, P.O. Box 1148, Corvallis, OR, 97339, 541/750-7000. For a topographic map, ask the USGS for Tahkenitch Creek.

Directions: The Oregon Dunes Overlook entrance is on the west side of U.S. 101, 10 miles south of Florence or 11 miles north of Reedsport.

Contact: Siuslaw National Forest, Mapleton Ranger District, 4480 Highway 101, Building G, Florence, OR, 97439, 541/902-8526, or the Oregon Dunes National Recreation Area, 855 Highway Avenue, Reedsport, OR, 97467, 541/271-6019.

Tahkenitch Creek

56 TAHKENITCH CREEK

4.2 mi/2.0 hr 2 8

in the Oregon Dunes National Recreation Area

Map 7.4, page 364

The Oregon Dunes are more than just sand, as the Tahkenitch Creek Trail amply demonstrates. This lazy creek, forested with Douglas fir and flowering rhododendrons, drifts toward the sea, meeting the tides at a lonely and largely unvisited estuary frequented by brown pelicans frequent and nesting snowy plovers. Thorny gorse, a particularly nasty invasive bush, grows here as well. Be mindful that winter often brings flooding in certain areas, making some of the loops impossible.

The first 0.3 mile of the Tahkenitch Creek Trail is in a coastal forest, crossing the creek on a long footbridge with views of the creek along the way. At a junction, a short loop is possible by heading to the right, hugging the creek a short distance until the next junction, where a left turn brings you to another left turn: a 1.6-mile loop in all. But continuing on along the creek to another junction, as well as a view of the estuary, taking the same two left turns, then keeping right at the next two junctions represents another loop, 2.6 miles in all. The longest loop follows the creek out a full mile past this first junction, eventually passing a few marshy lakes to a four-way junction with the Tahkenitch Dunes Trail; going hard left here to return to the Tahkenitch Creek Trail and keeping to the right at each consecutive junction makes a 4.2-mile loop. If you feel like you've got a bit more oomph, you could head right on the Tahkenitch Dunes Trail from this last junction an extra 0.3 mile, then take a right for another 0.3 mile to reach the beach; remember, though, that this much sand makes for a tiring hike, so save your energy.

User Groups: Hikers, dogs, and horses. No mountain bikes allowed. No wheelchair facilities.

Permits: Permits are not required. A federal Northwest Forest Pass is required to park here;

the cost is $5 a day or $30 for an annual pass. You can buy a day pass at the visitors center, at ranger stations, or through private vendors.

Maps: For a map of the Siuslaw National Forest, contact the Siuslaw National Forest headquarters, 4077 SW Research Way, P.O. Box 1148, Corvallis, OR, 97339, 541/750-7000. For a topographic map, ask the USGS for Tahkenitch Creek.

Directions: The Tahkenitch Creek Trailhead is located on the west side of U.S. 101 between mileposts 202 and 203, about 12 miles south of Florence or nine miles north of Reedsport.

Contact: Siuslaw National Forest, Mapleton Ranger District, 4480 Highway 101, Building G, Florence, OR, 97439, 541/902-8526, or the Oregon Dunes National Recreation Area, 855 Highway Avenue, Reedsport, OR, 97467, 541/271-6019.

57 TAHKENITCH DUNES
6.5 mi/3.0 hr   🥾3 ⛰️8

in the Oregon Dunes National Recreation Area

Map 7.4, page 364

For those who want to explore the Oregon Dunes on a far more rugged expedition, the Tahkenitch Dunes offer this kind of epic journey in excess. Along the way, you can view the Tahkenitch Creek estuary and a beach along Threemile Lake, and cross over a forested summit above the sand. Be aware that long hikes through sand can be tiring and slow-going, so plan on plenty of time and pack plenty of water.

The first 0.2 mile of the Tahkenitch Dunes Trail climbs into the forest to a junction. Go right for 1.1 miles across the open dunes, eventually entering a brushy forest of shore pine—also known as lodgepole pine. At a junction, go left for 0.3 mile along a marsh, then right for 0.3 mile to the beach. Note that ORV vehicles are allowed on this beach, so don't be surprised by the dune buggies. Heading to the right 0.9 mile will take you to the estuary,

but for a longer hike head to the left instead, going north 1.3 miles along the beach. Watch for a trail sign on the foredune, then head inland 0.4 mile to a viewpoint over a beach on Threemile Lake. Follow the Threemile Lake Trail 2.7 miles up and over a 400-foot summit of second-growth woods back to the first junction, and head right the remaining 0.2 mile back to the campground.

User Groups: Hikers, dogs, and horses, No mountain bikes allowed. No wheelchair facilities.

Permits: Permits are not required. A federal Northwest Forest Pass is required to park here; the cost is $5 a day or $30 for an annual pass. You can buy a day pass at the visitors center, at ranger stations, or through private vendors.

Maps: For a map of the Siuslaw National Forest, contact the Siuslaw National Forest headquarters, 4077 SW Research Way, P.O. Box 1148, Corvallis, OR, 97339, 541/750-7000. For a topographic map, ask the USGS for Tahkenitch Creek.

Directions: The Tahkenitch Dunes Trailhead is located in the Tahkenitch Campground on the west side of U.S. 101 about 13 miles south of Florence or eight miles north of Reedsport. Keep left at the loop and park at a small picnic area.

Contact: Siuslaw National Forest, Mapleton Ranger District, 4480 Highway 101, Building G, Florence, OR, 97439, 541/902-8526, or the Oregon Dunes National Recreation Area, 855 Highway Avenue, Reedsport, OR, 97467, 541/271-6019.

58 LAKE MARIE
1.4 mi/1.0 hr

south of Reedsport in Umpqua Lighthouse State Park

Map 7.4, page 364

High atop a bluff over Winchester Bay and the mouth of the Umpqua River stands the 65-foot lighthouse blinking its read and white warning to boats. Also beneath the fog-piercing light lie the beginning of the seven-mile stretch of the Umpqua Dunes and little Lake Marie. An easy hike around this forested lake begins at a picturesque picnic area, and proceeds to a viewpoint of the dunes themselves, a worthy goal for exploration.

From the shoreline, head on the right-hand trail following the lakeside 0.2 mile. At a junction, follow the right trail 0.2 mile to a view of the Umpqua Dunes. Head back and continue an easy 0.8 mile back to the picnic area.

User Groups: Hikers, dogs, and horses. No wheelchair facilities.

Permits: Permits are not required. Parking and access are free.

Maps: For a free park brochure, call Oregon Parks and Recreation, 800/551-6949, or download a free map at www.oregonstateparks.org. For a topographic map, ask the USGS for Winchester Bay.

Directions: Drive U.S 101 south of Reedsport five miles to milepost 217 and follow signs for Umpqua Lighthouse State Park. Travel one mile west, passing the campground entrance, and park at a picnic area on the left on the shore of Lake Marie.

Contact: Oregon Parks and Recreation Department, 1115 Commercial Street NE, Salem, OR, 97301, 800/551-6949, www.oregonstateparks.org.

59 UMPQUA DUNES

5.0 mi/2.5 hr

in the Oregon Dunes National Recreation Area

Map 7.4, page 364 **BEST (**

The sheer enormity of the Umpqua Dunes is staggering. This stretch of sand, nearly unreal in its proportions, makes this one of Oregon's most outstanding and beautiful areas. If you're going to pick any area of the Dunes to hike, make it this one. That being said, reaching the ocean on the John Dellenback Dunes Trail, named for the U.S. congressman who helped establish this recreation area, is one of the most difficult hikes on the coast. These towering

Umpqua Dunes in the Oregon Dunes National Recreation Area

dunes south of the Umpqua River are the largest and the broadest, stretching over two miles to the distant ocean. Blue-striped trail posts seem lonely in the vast waves of sand, following a valley between massive oblique dunes, sloping on one side and sharply carved by wind on the other. The otherworldly beauty is so tremendous that it's worth a day's journey just to get here, let alone hike this area.

From Eel Creek Campground, follow the 0.2-mile trail through twisting red-barked madrones to an impressive overlook, the sea a far-off rumble. Head for the long, high dune for a sweeping view to a massive tree island and mile after mile of cascading sand. Look toward the ocean to spot the tiny trail markers marching off into the sand. Follow these posts a total of 2.2-miles to reach the ocean.

User Groups: Hikers, dogs, and horses. No wheelchair facilities.

Permits: Permits are not required. A federal Northwest Forest Pass is required to park here; the cost is $5 a day or $30 for an annual pass.

You can buy a day pass at the visitors center, at ranger stations, or through private vendors.

Maps: For a map of the Siuslaw National Forest, contact the Siuslaw National Forest headquarters, 4077 SW Research Way, P.O. Box 1148, Corvallis, OR, 97339, 541/750-7000. For a topographic map, ask the USGS for Lakeside.

Directions: Drive 11 miles south of Reedsport on U.S. 101. Near milepost 222, turn west into Eel Creek Campground and keep left for 0.3 mile to a parking lot. The trailhead begins at a large signpost.

Contact: Siuslaw National Forest, Mapleton Ranger District, 4480 Highway 101, Building G, Florence, OR, 97439, 541/902-8526, or the Oregon Dunes National Recreation Area, 855 Highway Avenue, Reedsport, OR, 97467, 541/271-6019.

60 GOLDEN AND SILVER FALLS
3.0 mi/1.5 hr   👥1 ⛰8

east of Coos Bay in Golden and Silver Falls State Park

Map 7.4, page 364

Not to be confused with Silver Falls State Park just outside of the Willamette Valley, this state park has two falls that topple hundreds of feet into two canyons, the creeks joining a short distance below. Three different trails fan out here, following Glenn and Silver Creeks, and it's worth it to take them all, as they afford multiple views of both plunging falls. Along the way you'll see myrtlewood trees, common to this part of the state.

To start, go to the trailhead and take the farthest left-hand trail up 0.3 mile to a view of 160-foot Silver Falls, a good warm-up. Return to the lot and take the right-hand trail, which crosses Silver Creek. Here the trail splits. The left trail goes 0.4 mile up Silver Creek to another breathtaking view of Silver Falls, and continues up the canyon walls on a dizzying climb up 0.5 mile to a couple overlooks

over 200-foot Golden Falls. Return the way you came, and take the last of the trails, the right-hand junction after the footbridge, which heads through groves of myrtlewood along Glenn Creek to a lower view of Golden Falls.

User Groups: Hikers and dogs. No wheelchair facilities.

Permits: Permits are not required. Parking and access are free.

Maps: For a topographic map, ask the USGS for Golden Falls.

Directions: Follow U.S. 101 to the south end of Coos Bay and follow signs for Alleghany, eventually turning east on Coos River Highway. In 13.5 miles, arrive at Alleghany, then follow state park signs 9.4 miles on East Millicoma Road and Glen Creek Road to the end of the road at a picnic area.

Contact: Oregon Parks and Recreation Department, 1115 Commercial Street NE, Salem, OR, 97301, 800/551-6949, www.oregonstateparks.org.

61 SUNSET BAY TO CAPE ARAGO
9.4 mi/4.5 hr   👥3 ⛰9

west of Coos Bay in Sunset Bay/Shore Acres State Parks

Map 7.4, page 364   **BEST (**

Leave it to the Oregon State Parks to hold onto history. Cape Arago, hovering above a series of reefs, islands, and barking sea lions, was first spotted by Sir Francis Drake in the 1500s. Later, the land in what is now Shore Acres State Park was the estate for lumber baron Louis Simpson, including an unforgettable garden that is still blooming to this day. Today you can see all of this history and migrating whales, too, thanks to a stretch of the Oregon Coast Trail that passes along this rugged and wild coastline. You can pay a fee to enter the main part of the park, or you can hike your way in on a stunning trip along one of Oregon's best seaside trails.

For the full day's walk, start at Sunset Bay State Park parking area and follow an 0.8-mile stretch of the Oregon Coast Trail overlooking Sunset Bay and the Norton Gulch. The path briefly heads to the right along the road, then parallels the road before heading back into the woods for 1.3 miles before arriving in the core of Shore Acres State Park, site of the Botanical Gardens and the 1906 Simpson mansion, with an observation building suitable for whale-watching. Stay right at a sign for Simpson Beach. The next 0.3 mile leads to this beach in Simpson's Cove. In 0.2 mile, continue right on the Oregon Coast Trail one mile, crossing a creek and heads up a gully to an intersection. Go right on the OCT toward the stunning cliff viewpoints. The trail meets the road, follows it for a brief stretch before passing through a coastal forest and rejoining the road at the Sea Lion Viewpoint, where you can look out a quarter-mile to Shell Island where masses of the sea lions congregate. From here, you'll need to follow the paved road 0.7 mile to Cape Arago, where a short 0.3 mile trail leads out to views over North Cove, the Simpson Reef, and Shell Island. It is possible to arrange a shuttle from this point.

User Groups: Hikers only. Dogs are not allowed in Shore Acres State Park. No horses or mountain bikes allowed. Paved paths in Shore Acres State Park are wheelchair accessible.

Permits: Permits are not required. Parking and access are free.

Maps: For a free park brochure, call Oregon Parks and Recreation, 800/551-6949, or download a free map at www.oregonstateparks.org. For a topographic map, ask the USGS for Charleston and Cape Arago.

Directions: From Coos Bay, drive 12 miles south on Cape Arago Highway, following signs to Sunset Bay State Park. Park in the day-use area on the right. The trailhead is marked as the Oregon Coast Trail.

Contact: Oregon Parks and Recreation Department, 1115 Commercial Street NE, Salem, OR, 97301, 800/551-6949, www.oregonstateparks.org.

62 SOUTH SLOUGH ESTUARY
5.0 mi/2.0 hr   🖈1 ⬛7

south of Coos Bay in South Slough Reserve

Map 7.4, page 364

The South Slough National Estuarine Research Reserve is a 4,800-acre mix of freshwater and tidal wetlands, open-water channels, riparian areas, and coastal forest. Egrets perch in the trees, mudflats are exposed at low tide, and Pacific wax myrtle and Port Orford cedar populate the uplands. Salt marshes, sand flats, the list goes on. So why not visit?

There are a number of trails throughout the park, eight miles altogether. To try a loop trail, begin at the Interpretive Center and follow the 0.5-mile Middle Creek Trail. Cross a road and follow the 1.2-mile Hidden Creek Trail to a boardwalk over a skunk cabbage grove and a tide flats observation deck. From here, the 0.4-mile Tunnel Trail heads out a peninsula between the South Slough and Rhodes Marsh right out to the tip, near some old pilings. Head back from the point to a right-hand junction over the Rhodes Dike to the Bog Loop, continuing straight on the 2.5-mile North Creek Trail (where dogs are not permitted). This trail completes the loop, connecting with the 0.2-mile Ten-Minute Trail loop.

User Groups: Hikers. Leashed dogs are admitted on some trails. Some trails are wheelchair accessible.

Permits: Permits are not required. Parking and access are free.

Maps: A downloadable brochure and map is available at www.oregon.gov/DSL/SSNERR/maps.shtml. For a topographic map, ask the USGS for Charleston.

Directions: From U.S. 101 in Coos Bay, take the Cape Arago Highway nine miles west to Charleston. Turn left on Seven Devils Road and go 4.3 miles, turning left into the South Slough Reserve entrance road. In 0.2 mile, park on the left by the interpretive center.

Contact: South Slough Reserve, P.O. Box 5417, Charleston, OR, 97420, 541/888-5558.

63 SEVEN DEVILS WAYSIDE
3.0 mi/1.5 hr

north of Bandon on the Pacific Ocean

Map 7.4, page 364

Some towns have all the luck—and some don't. One of the ones that didn't was Randolph, a gold-rush town that once sat on Whiskey Run Beach and was all but gone in two years. The nearby town of Bandon was burned twice by fires feeding on spiny gorse, a nasty, thorny shrub that blankets areas of the Oregon coast, including the ravines above Whiskey Run Beach and the Seven Devils Wayside. The beaches, though, are thankfully free of it, and this excursion escapes the bristling bush in favor of a hike beneath sandstone cliffs around Fivemile Point. From the Seven Devils Wayside, strike out south along the ocean for 1.4 miles along Merchants Beach to the headland of Fivemile Point, easily passable if the tide is low. Another 0.8 mile beyond this leads along Whiskey Run Beach to another ravine with a beach access road.

User Groups: Hikers, dogs, and horses. No wheelchair facilities.

Permits: Permits are not required. Parking and access are free.

Maps: For a topographic map, ask the USGS for Bullards.

Directions: From Bandon, go north on U.S. 101 for five miles and turn left on Randolph Road, which becomes Seven Devils Road. Follow signs 4.2 miles to Seven Devils State Park.

Contact: Oregon Parks and Recreation Department, 1115 Commercial Street NE, Salem, OR, 97301, 800/551-6949, www.oregonstateparks.org.

64 THE DOERNER FIR
1.0 mi/0.5 hr

east of Coos Bay in the Coast Range

Map 7.4, page 364

Sometimes when you're passing through an area, or taking a nearby hike, it's worth it to get in a little side trip to see something special. The Doerner Fir is one such spectacle, and at 329 feet tall and 11 feet in diameter, maybe this side trip isn't so "small." It is, in fact, the world's largest Douglas fir—and it's somewhere between 500 and 700 years old. This is an opportunity to see how trees grow; you'll notice that on a true old-growth fir, the limbs don't even begin until hundreds of feet up, having been lost over the course of time as they grew in the darkness of other big trees' crowns. Now its own crown is about 10 stories up in the atmosphere. This easy half-mile hike is also a good tour of a coastal rainforest considered to be pristine, with abundant undergrowth of ferns, salmonberry, and vine maple. The trail begins across the road from the parking area, descending into a drainage only 200 feet to visit the massive fir.

User Groups: Hikers and dogs. No wheelchair facilities.

Permits: Permits are not required. Parking and access are free.

Maps: For a topographic map, ask the USGS for Sitkum.

Directions: From Coos Bay, take U.S. 101 south five miles then go left on OR 42 toward Roseburg 11 miles. Just before Coquille, turn left on West Central Boulevard for one mile and go left toward Fairview for 8.1 miles. At a junction, go right onto the Coos Bay Wagon Road for 3.7 miles and turn left on Middle Creek Road for 6.3 miles. At a fork go left toward the Park Creek Recreation Site for 6.6 miles, then turn to the right heading uphill on Burnt Mountain-Middle Creek Tie Road for 4.4 miles to a junction. Turn left, following a "Burnt Ridge Road" sign for 4.6 miles, then go right on gravel Road 27-9-21.0 for 4.3 miles to the trailhead.

Contact: Bureau of Land Management, Coos Bay District, 1300 Airport Lane, North Bend, OR, 97459, 541/756-0100.

65 BULLARDS BEACH STATE PARK

5.0 mi/2.0 hr

north of Bandon on the Pacific Ocean

Map 7.4, page 364

The scenic tip of the Bullards Beach peninsula passes an 1896 lighthouse, a view of Bandon (the "Storm Watching Capitol of the World"), and the estuary of the Coquille River, with views to the Bandon Marsh Wildlife Refuge. This state park even has a horse camp, so be prepared to see equestrians passing over the sand at sunset. Anglers and crabbers find this to be one of the best places to ply their trade. You'll get plenty of beach exploration here, both along the ocean and the bay.

From the beach parking area, head to the beach and go left 1.7 miles toward the north jetty and the 47-foot lighthouse. An easy 0.6-mile round-trip walk extends to the tip of the jetty. Then head east from the lighthouse along the river 0.4 mile on an old road and follow the beach 1.9 mile farther along the river to the road. Turn left along the road for 0.4 mile to return to the parking area.

User Groups: Hikers, dogs, and horses. The 1.3-mile bike trail is wheelchair accessible.

Permits: Permits are not required. Parking and access are free.

Maps: For a free park brochure, call Oregon Parks and Recreation, 800/551-6949, or download a free map at www.oregonstateparks.org. For a topographic map, ask the USGS for Bullards.

Directions: Drive U.S. 101 north of Bandon three miles and turn west at a Bullards Beach State Park sign. Drive past the campground entrance and picnic areas 1.4 miles to a junction. Turn right into the beach parking area.

Contact: Oregon Parks and Recreation Department, 1115 Commercial Street NE, Salem, OR, 97301, 800/551-6949, www.oregonstateparks.org.

66 FACE ROCK

3.8 mi/2.0 hr

in Bandon at Face Rock Wayside

Map 7.4, page 364

A Coquille tribal legend says that a maiden named Ewauna, daughter of Chief Siskiyou, decided to sneak off for a late-night swim. Unfortunately, an evil spirit named Seatka who lived in the ocean grabbed her. But she was bright enough to know that to look into his eyes was to be caught forever; to this day, she looks instead to the sky. Looking at Face Rock, the resemblance is, to say the least, uncanny. This maiden is only one of many sea stacks and rocks jutting from the ocean offshore of Bandon-by-the-Sea, and some easy hiking brings one close to this jumble of tide-worn stone.

A staircase descends down Grave Point from the Face Rock Wayside. Turn right at the beach to view Cat and Kittens Rocks, Face Rock, and Elephant Rock. Continue to jutting Coquille Point; by now you've gone 0.9 mile. The next mile continues to the south jetty, with views to the Coquille River Lighthouse and Table Rock.

User Groups: Hikers and dogs. Overlook is wheelchair accessible.

Permits: Permits are not required. Parking and access are free.

Maps: For a topographic map, ask the USGS for Bandon.

Directions: From U.S. 101 in Bandon, head west on 11th Avenue for 0.9 mile, then go left on Beach Loop Road 0.6 mile to the Face Rock Wayside on the right.

Contact: Oregon Parks and Recreation Department, 1115 Commercial Street NE, Salem, OR, 97301, 800/551-6949, www.oregonstateparks.org.

67 BLACKLOCK POINT
3.8 mi/1.5 hr

north of Port Orford in Floras Lake State
Natural Area

Map 7.5, page 365

On the way to Blacklock Point, you'll pass through a whole litany of shore shrubbery and coastal trees, including Sitka spruce and Sitka alder, pygmy shore pine, evergreen huckleberry, wax myrtle and juniper, black twinberry, salal, and wild azalea, rhododendron and black crowberry. All this leads to some serious cliffs atop Blacklock Point. In this largely undeveloped natural area, you may find some solitude; being off the beaten path, not many people even know about it. On the grassy headland, you can spot the Cape Blanco Lighthouse, a waterfall, and a number of islands.

The trail begins to the left of the gate on a dirt road that becomes a trail. Follow this 0.8 mile to a creek and trail junction, going left for 0.6 mile. Then fork left again, then right for 0.5 mile to the sheer headland of Blacklock Point. From here, trails fan out into Floras Lake State Natural Area—following the trail north along the coast leads to Floras Lake, and two side trails to the left lead back to the runway. Taking the first left after a waterfall makes for a 4.4-mile loop, and taking the next left at Floras Lake makes a 7.6-mile loop.

User Groups: Hikers, dogs on leash, horses, and mountain bikes. No wheelchair facilities.

Permits: Permits are not required. Parking and access are free.

Maps: For a topographic map, ask the USGS for Floras Lake.

Directions: Go seven miles north of Port Orford on U.S. 101 and between mileposts 293 and 294, turn west at an "Airport" sign. Follow County Road 160 for 2.8 miles to a parking area on the right at the gated entrance to the airport.

Contact: Oregon Parks and Recreation Department, 1115 Commercial Street NE, Salem, OR, 97301, 800/551-6949, www.oregonstateparks.org.

68 CAPE BLANCO
4.0 mi/2.0 mi

north of Port Orford in Cape Blanco State Park

Map 7.5, page 365

Standing at the tip of Cape Blanco, you are at the westernmost point in the state of Oregon. An 1870 lighthouse still functions here, throwing its light from a cape named on a 1602 Spanish exploration (in which the majority of the ship's crew died of scurvy). There are many trails here to explore, as well as a historic 1898 Victorian house-turned-museum. For a good opening exploratory route, a looping tour of the headland and the North Beach passes within view of islands, the Sixes River, and over the headland.

From the boat ramp, and beyond a gate, take the left-hand path 0.3 mile across a pasture, then fork to the right for 0.4 mile to the beach. Head left 1.2 miles along North Beach toward the lighthouse. Just before the end of the beach, take a trail up a slope 0.3 mile to the parking area for the lighthouse. Head left down the road 0.2 mile, then cut to the left at a trailpost, crossing a meadow 1.3 miles along the cliff's edges to return to the boat ramp.

User Groups: Hikers, dogs, horses, mountain bikes. Paved portions of the park are wheelchair accessible.

Permits: Permits are not required. Parking and access are free.

Maps: For a free park brochure, call Oregon Parks and Recreation, 800/551-6949, or download a free map at www.oregonstateparks.org. For a topographic map, ask the USGS for Bullards.

Directions: Drive U.S 101 north of Port Orford four miles and turn west at a Cape Blanco State Park sign for four miles to a fork. Go right, passing the Hughes House Museum, and park at the Sixes River Boat Ramp.

Contact: Oregon Parks and Recreation Department, 1115 Commercial Street NE, Salem, OR, 97301, 800/551-6949, www.oregonstateparks.org.

69 GRASSY KNOB
2.4 mi/1.0 hr

east of Port Orford in Grassy Knob Wilderness

Map 7.5, page 365

From an old fire watchtower that once stood atop Grassy Knob during World War II, lookouts spotted a Japanese airplane that dropped an incendiary bomb into the forest, hoping to start a fire. The bomb never went off and was never found. The watchtower is now gone, and what remains in this corner of the Siskiyou Mountains is a 17,200-acre Wilderness Area designated by Congress in 1984. The area remains short on trails, but this one trail, actually an old road, leads to a peak overlooking the mountains and the ocean.

From the end of Grassy Knob Road, follow the road behind the gate up 0.4 mile to a side trail on the right leading 0.1 mile up to Grassy Knob's summit. Then continue up the road another 0.7 mile to a gravel turnaround, with views along the way.

User Groups: Hikers and dogs. No wheelchair facilities.

Permits: Permits are not required. Parking and access are free.

Maps: For a map of the Siskiyou National Forest, contact the Rogue River–Siskiyou National Forest headquarters, 3040 Biddle Road, Medford, OR, 97504, 541/618-2200. For a topographic map, ask the USGS for Father Mountain.

Directions: From Port Orford, drive U.S. 101 north four miles and turn east on Grassy Knob Road for 3.9 paved miles and 3.8 more gravel miles to a gate and parking area. The trail begins on the road beyond the gate.

Contact: Siskiyou National Forest, Powers Ranger District, 42861 Highway 242, Powers, OR, 97466, 541/439-6200.

70 BARKLOW MOUNTAIN
2.0 mi/1.0 hr

northeast of Gold Beach in Siskiyou National Forest

Map 7.5, page 365

Due to budget cuts, many of the classic fire watchtowers have been abandoned and unmanned for a long time. Many of the relics of that age remain, including a shelter here atop Barklow Mountain. Of course, many of these sites have "remote" as their middle name. Still, if it's solitude you're looking for, you'll find it here.

The short 0.6-mile Barklow Mountain Trail climbs only 500 feet through a forest to the former lookout site here atop the 3,579-foot peak, with views over the Siskiyou Range; a 0.4-mile spur trail leads to the long-collapsed shelter at Barklow Camp. The Barklow Mountain Trail, in all, is six miles and wanders along the north ridge of the mountain, though this stretch is unmaintained, thus making for more opportunity to explore.

User Groups: Hikers and dogs. No horses or mountain bikes allowed. No wheelchair facilities.

Permits: Permits are not required. Parking and access are free.

Maps: For a map of the Siskiyou National Forest, contact the Rogue River–Siskiyou National Forest headquarters, 3040 Biddle Road, Medford, OR, 97504, 541/618-2200. For a topographic map, ask the USGS for Barklow Mountain.

Directions: From Gold Beach, drive Jerrys Flat Road 32 miles along the Rogue River to a bridge near Agness, and continue on Road 33 to Powers for 15.6 miles. From Powers, drive 11.5 miles south on Road 33 and turn right on Road 3353 for 11 miles to the trailhead just past milepost 11.

Contact: Siskiyou National Forest, Powers Ranger District, 42861 Highway 242, Powers, OR, 97466, 541/439-6200.

71 COQUILLE RIVER FALLS
1.0 mi/0.5 hr

northeast of Gold Beach in Siskiyou National Forest

Map 7.5, page 365

The Coquille River Falls Natural Area was established in 1945 to provide examples of the Port Orford cedar, and this rugged mountain canyon also plays host to the Douglas fir, myrtle, Pacific yew, grand fir, and sugar pine. Salamanders, voles, and secretive mammals like the bobcat, martin, and ermine all thrive here. The destination is the double falls on the Coquille River pouring over a bedrock edge into a stony bowl scoured into pockmarked mortars.

From the parking area, the trail abruptly switchbacks down 0.5 mile to a viewpoint of the Coquille River Falls and a series of cascades on Drowned Out Creek. It is possible to scramble around to a higher viewpoint and around the falls themselves, but it should only be attempted in the dry season. Mossy stones and wet leaves on the rocks around the base of the falls beg disaster—care should be taken on the slick rock.

User Groups: Hikers and dogs. No wheelchair facilities.

Permits: Permits are not required. Parking and access are free.

Maps: For a map of the Siskiyou National Forest, contact the Rogue River–Siskiyou National Forest headquarters, 3040 Biddle Road, Medford, OR, 97504, 541/618-2200. For a topographic map, ask the USGS for Illahe.

Directions: From Gold Beach, drive Jerrys Flat Road 32 miles along the Rogue River to a bridge near Agness, and continue on Road 33 to Powers for 15.6 miles. From Powers, travel south on FS 33 for 17 miles to paved FS 3348, turning left. Go 1.5 miles to a pullout on the left.

Contact: Siskiyou National Forest, Powers Ranger District, 42861 Highway 242, Powers, OR, 97466, 541/439-6200.

72 ELK CREEK FALLS
2.4 mi/1.0 hr

northeast of Gold Beach in Siskiyou National Forest

Map 7.5, page 365

By the time you've come this far south into Oregon, the landscape begins to change along with the trees. Here, the Port Orford cedar is impressive, and the trail past 60-foot Elk Creek Falls goes on to arrive at the world's largest Port Orford, as well as other big tree varieties. But you'll realize you're lucky to see such trees, as logging and a kind of root fungus have seriously jeopardized the survival of the handsome Port Orford.

The trail forks at the trailhead, with the left-hand fork heading a scant 0.1 mile to Elk Creek Falls, a lovely cascade in a fern-lined grotto. Then head up the right-hand fork for 1.2 miles, switchbacking up a steep ridge through flowering rhododendrons. When the trail hits an old dirt road at the one-mile mark, head to the right and watch for the continuation of the path on the left. Here you'll see big Douglas firs and bigleaf maples, and when you turn left at the next junction, you'll easily spot Big Tree, the 239-foot-tall, 12-foot-thick cedar.

User Groups: Hikers and dogs. No wheelchair facilities.

Permits: Permits are not required. Parking and access are free.

Maps: For a map of the Siskiyou National Forest, contact the Rogue River–Siskiyou National Forest headquarters, 3040 Biddle Road, Medford, OR, 97504, 541/618-2200. For a topographic map, ask the USGS for China Flat.

Directions: From Gold Beach and U.S. 101, take Jerrys Flat Road for 32 miles to the bridge over the Rogue River, then continue on Road 33, which eventually turns to gravel, toward Powers another 25.6 miles. The trailhead is between mileposts 57 and 58.

Contact: Siskiyou National Forest, Powers

Ranger District, 42861 Highway 242, Powers, OR, 97466, 541/439-6200.

🔳 PANTHER RIDGE

4.0 mi–11.2 mi one-way/2.0 hr–1 day
🏃3 ⛰8

northeast of Gold Beach in Wild Rogue Wilderness

Map 7.5, page 365

Here is your introduction to the Siskiyou Mountains: the classic Oregon trees like cedar and Douglas fir augmented by knobcone pine and tanoak, manzanita and chinquapin, and an amazing display of springtime rhododendrons. A wilderness ridge offers unparalleled views over the Rogue River Valley and its associated drainages. Most of this trail traverses the Wild Rogue Wilderness, which cradles the roaring river below. Here is a great opportunity for backpacking, but be sure to bring plenty of water. There's even a rentable lookout at Bald Knob where you may spot early morning elk and black bear. An easy way to start is to visit Hanging Rock, a dizzying edge above the canyon of the Wild Rogue, where the Devil's Backbone descends to Paradise Bar on the Rogue River.

From the Buck Point Trailhead, the Panther Ridge Trail climbs a mile-long ridge to Buck Point, and just around that point is a camping spot around the cedar-shaded spring of Buck Creek. The trail switchbacks up 0.6 mile to a junction. To the left, and 0.4 mile away, is the Hanging Rock. Returning to the trail, you could call it a day or continue on 2.3 miles through what becomes a maze of faint paths—stick to the lowest path to stay on the Panther Ridge Trail. A junction on the right leads 0.3 mile to Panther Camp, another backpacking site. From this junction, the trail continues 1.3 miles to a gravelly spot, where

you'll want to be careful to watch for the right trail. After this, the trail follows an old and overgrown road for 0.2 mile before meeting another road; follow this road to the left 0.2 mile to return to the forest path. In another 0.3 mile pass a spur trail, and enter a denser understory of rhododendron and wildflowers. The next 1.5 miles are a rough descent, then skirts clear-cuts for 1.3 miles. The trail then turns right along an abandoned road for 0.2 mile, then cuts left into the dense forest again. The Panther Ridge Trail ends at Forest Service Road 5520.020 near a gate. Go left on this road for 0.3 mile to arrive at the Bald Knob Lookout, with its expansive views.

User Groups: Hikers, dogs, and horses. No mountain bikes allowed in the wilderness area. No wheelchair facilities.

Permits: Permits are not required. Parking and access are free.

Maps: For a map of the Siskiyou National Forest and the Wild Rogue Wilderness, contact the Rogue River–Siskiyou National Forest headquarters, 3040 Biddle Road, Medford, OR, 97504, 541/618-2200. For a topographic map, ask the USGS for Marial.

Directions: From Gold Beach, drive Jerrys Flat Road 32 miles along the Rogue River to a bridge near Agness, and continue on Road 33 toward Powers for 15.6 miles. Go right on FS Road 3348 for 8.7 miles and turn right on gravel Road 5520 for 1.2 miles, then left on Road 230 to its end at the trailhead. To leave a shuttle at the Bald Knob Lookout, follow Road 3348 for two miles from the junction with Forest Service Road 33, then turn right on Road 5520. Follow this gravel road two miles to the spur road 020 on the right, and take it two miles to the Bald Knob Trailhead.

Contact: Siskiyou National Forest, Powers Ranger District, 42861 Highway 242, Powers, OR, 97466, 541/439-6200.

7.4 MOUNT BOLIVAR

2.8 mi/2.0 hr

northeast of Gold Beach in Wild Rogue
Wilderness

Map 7.5, page 365

For whatever reason, this mountain seems to be named for Simón Bolívar, though his conquests were thousands of miles away in South America. If you are of the conquistador spirit, then you'll spot your goal from the trailhead itself, a steep climb to 4,319-foot Mount Bolivar in the Wild Rogue Wilderness. Though it is a notoriously long drive to get here, it's comforting to know that from the peak you will have the commanding view from the Cascades to the California Siskiyous in a 360-degree panoramic view. The trail switchbacks up through open meadows, a Douglas fir forest, and finally onto the wildflower-covered rocky slopes, and all within 1.4 miles and over the course of 1,200 feet elevation gain. At the top, the site of a former lookout, you'll find a plaque commemorating Bolívar.

From the trailhead, begin on the Mount Bolivar Trail. The first mile meanders easily through dense woods and into a drier, sparser pine-fir forest intermingled with manzanita. The trail circles around the north face of the mountain, then begins to climb in the next 0.5 mile, growing steeper as the summit is neared. Return as you came.

User Groups: Hikers and dogs. No horses or mountain bikes allowed. No wheelchair facilities.

Permits: Permits are not required. Parking and access are free.

Maps: For a map of the Siskiyou National Forest, contact the Rogue River–Siskiyou National Forest headquarters, 3040 Biddle Road, Medford, OR, 97504, 541/618-2200. For a topographic map, ask the USGS for Mount Bolivar.

Directions: From Gold Beach, drive Jerrys Flat Road 32 miles along the Rogue River to a bridge near Agness, and continue on Road 33 to Powers for 15.6 miles. From Powers, turn right on Road 3348 for 18.7 miles to a trailhead on the right, with the final 0.9 mile in BLM land.

Contact: Siskiyou National Forest, Powers Ranger District, 42861 Highway 242, Powers, OR, 97466, 541/439-6200.

7.5 HUMBUG MOUNTAIN

5.5 mi/3.0 hr

south of Port Orford in Humbug Mountain
State Park

Map 7.5, page 365

This trail has been popular ever since settlers arrived in 1851 looking for gold. They were told that if they climbed this mountain, they would see the mountains filled with gold. Instead, what the scouts saw was more ocean, and they named the peak accordingly. On a sunny day, expect to see the hordes still arriving, looking for that as-good-as-gold view. You will earn that gold in a breathtaking 1,700 foot ascent conveniently, if not mockingly, marked every half-mile up the slope from myrtlewood groves to old-growth Douglas fir. Humbug Mountain also holds the last uncut grove of old-growth trees on the southern Oregon coast. You can even, surprisingly, take this trail as a loop.

After a mile, the path forks. The right-hand fork proves shorter but a bit steeper, and climbs 1.4 mile with views to Cape Blanco. Near the top, a short spur leads 0.1 mile to the summit. Descend by taking the opposite fork, this time to the right, descending 1.9 mile back to the first junction. Continue to the right to return to the trailhead.

User Groups: Hikers and dogs. No horses or mountain bikes allowed. No wheelchair facilities.

Permits: Permits are not required. Parking and access are free.

Maps: For a free park brochure, call Oregon Parks and Recreation, 800/551-6949, or download a free map at www.oregonstateparks.org. For a topographic map, ask the USGS for Port Orford.

Directions: Drive U.S. 101 south of Port Orford six miles and park at a large sign for "Humbug Mountain Trail Parking."

Contact: Oregon Parks and Recreation Department, 1115 Commercial Street NE, Salem, OR, 97301, 800/551-6949, www.oregonstateparks.org.

76 ROGUE RIVER TRAIL
40.0 mi one-way/4–5 days 🏃5 ⛰10

northeast of Gold Beach in Wild Rogue Wilderness

Map 7.5, page 365

In the heart of the Wild Rogue Wilderness, this 40-mile National Recreation Trail follows a stretch of the Wild and Scenic Rogue River into some serious canyonlands. Give yourself a week to do the entire length, travel time included. There are numerous opportunities for backpacking camps along the river, usually near creeks and sometimes equipped with toilets; there are even lodges along the way where you can make reservations. You'll pass rapids, waterfalls, and nice areas to relax, like Solitude Bar and the Coffeepot. If you're not up for a 40-mile journey, there are plenty of day-hike options in the first 15-mile wilderness stretch. This first portion can be hot and dry, particularly in summer, so be sure to pack enough water.

From the trailhead at Foster Bar, the first 4.3 miles rounds the river opposite Big Bend and continues to Flora Dell Falls, a good day-hike in itself. In another 1.7 miles you'll reach Clay Hill Lodge just above a series of rapids, with a primitive campsite on Tate Creek 0.8 mile beyond that. The next two miles passes a vista at Solitude Bar and another campground at Brushy Bar, beneath the long ridge of the Devil's Backbone. The next 2.9 miles rounds a bend to the Paradise Lodge and an airstrip and a primitive campsite at Blossom Bar beyond that. Another 1.4 miles climbs to a view at Inspiration Point, and the remaining 0.7 mile before a dirt road trailhead passes over the

churning Coffeepot, a boiling cauldron on the river where boaters often face disaster.

Walking along the road to Marial and the Rogue River Ranch for 1.8 miles connects to the remaining 23.2 miles of the Rogue River Trail to its end at Grave Creek, including a cabin at Winkle Bar (5.5 more miles), and campsites at Kelsey Creek (7.6 miles), Meadow Creek (9.4 miles), Copsey Creek (11.1 miles), Russian Creek (17.2 miles), Big Slide (19.3 miles), and Rainie Falls (23 miles). You'll also pass the Tyee Rapids, a narrow stretch appropriately called Slim Pickins, and the Whiskey Creek Cabin museum.

As of April 2009, the Bunker Creek Bridge nine miles downriver from Grave Creek is closed indefinitely, though a detour is in place. A slide in the Dulog area 14 miles downriver from Grave Creek has been deemed difficult to cross or impassable by managing agencies. Contact the Medford office of the BLM (503/808-6001) for updates.

User Groups: Hikers and dogs only. No mountain bikes and horses allowed. No wheelchair facilities.

Permits: Permits are not required. Parking and access are free.

Maps: For a map of the Siskiyou National Forest and the Wild Rogue Wilderness, contact the Rogue River–Siskiyou National Forest headquarters, 3040 Biddle Road, Medford, OR, 97504, 541/618-2200. For a topographic map, ask the USGS for Agness, Marial, Bunker Creek, Quosatana Butte, and Mount Reuben.

Directions: From U.S. 101, at the south end of the Gold Beach Bridge, follow Jerrys Flat Road for 32 miles along the Rogue River; the road becomes Road 33. Just after a river crossing, take a right fork at a sign for Illahe and follow this road for 3.5 paved miles to a trailhead spur on the right. To leave a shuttle at the trailhead, the Grave Creek Trailhead is located north of Galice. From Grants Pass, follow SW G Street/OR 260 west 1.2 miles, then continue on Upper River Road 2.4 miles. Turn right on Azalea Drive Cutoff 0.4 mile, and continue right on Azalea Drive 5.8 miles. Turn left on Galice Road, which becomes Merlin-Galice Road, for 10.7 miles to the town of Galice. Go about 7 miles north of Galice on BLM Road 35-8-13 to the Grave Creek Trailhead.

Contact: Siskiyou National Forest, Gold Beach Ranger District, 29279 Ellensburg Avenue, Gold Beach, OR, 97444, 541/247-3600.

77 COPPER CANYON ON THE ROGUE RIVER

12.6 mi one-way/7.0 hr

northeast of Gold Beach in Siskiyou National Forest

Map 7.5, page 365

Though the Lower Rogue River Trail can be dauntingly long and laborious, there are options for taking it easier. Or at least, shorter. For a look at a lower section of the Rogue, crossing creek after creek, dipping down to a beach, passing viewpoints of Copper Canyon and crossing the lower reaches of Adams Prairie and a camping spot on Dog Creek, try this section of trail out of the town of Agness. You'll get the best of this region's dramatic canyon scenery, creek hopping along the way on this designated Scenic and Recreational River. You'll begin the trail with a jog over gravel roads and through gates, bringing you to an access point of a beach on an eddy. From there, despite both the private residences and ruins you'll sometimes pass, things get wilder. A shorter stretch can be made out to the halfway point and back for a good 12-mile day, but the ambitious can tackle the whole canyon and even arrange for a shuttle with the myriad providers who do just that for boaters and hikers.

From the lot, walk the trail to a crossing of Rilea Creek and a junction. Here the trail becomes a road to the left, passing through farm property and several gates. Just after the road climbs, the trail picks up on the right. The next 2.1 miles passes a 400-foot elevation viewpoint of the Rogue's Copper Canyon and

Painted Rock Creek, where you'll climb at the 1.5-mile mark to a dirt road, where the trail heads left, crossing Blue Jay Creek before bearing right. You'll arrive at painted Rock creek at the 3.1-mile mark, followed by Leo, Stonehouse, Spring, and Sundown Creeks. This is a good turnaround point, but if you're up for more, the next 4.8 miles reaches a high point of 750 feet at the Adams Prairie, with a spur trail leading into an exploration of its meadows. You'll reach Auberry Creek at the 8.7-mile mark, the campground on Dog Creek at the 9.1-mile mark, and Slide Creek at the 11-mile point. The trail ends at the trailhead on Road 3533 another 2.5 miles past that.

User Groups: Hikers and dogs only. No mountain bikes or horses allowed. No wheelchair facilities.

Permits: Permits are not required. Parking and access are free.

Maps: For a map of the Siskiyou National Forest, contact the Rogue River–Siskiyou National Forest headquarters, 3040 Biddle Road, Medford, OR, 97504, 541/618-2200. For a topographic map, ask the USGS for Agness.

Directions: From U.S. 101, at the south end of the Gold Beach Bridge, follow Jerrys Flat Road for 32 miles along the Rogue River; the road becomes Road 33. Just after a river crossing, turn left at a sign for Agness. Follow this one-lane paved road three miles to the Agness Store and turn right on Cougar Lane for 0.2 mile. Park in the Agness Community Library gravel lot. Walk straight on the gravel road, following trail signs and passing two gates to the trail's start on the right. To shuttle and do the entire length of this trail, leave a vehicle at the west trailhead. To get there, take Jerrys Flat Road from Gold Beach (the road becomes FS 33) about 9.8 miles to the Lobster Creek Bridge. Cross the bridge and take the first right on FS Road 3533, continuing 3.7 miles to FS Road 340. Follow signs about three miles to the trailhead.

Contact: Siskiyou National Forest, Gold Beach Ranger District, 29279 Ellensburg Avenue, Gold Beach, OR, 97444, 541/247-3600.

78 ILLINOIS RIVER

5.0-17.2 mi/3.0 hr-2 days 🚶5 ⛰10

northeast of Gold Beach in Siskiyou National Forest

Map 7.5, page 365

A tributary of the Rogue River, the Illinois River is every bit as rugged as the famous waterway, the difference being that this National Recreation Trail never comes close to the river. Instead, this trail traverses into the Kalmiopsis Wilderness and even goes up and over Bald Mountain. The river itself holds a Wild and Scenic River designation, in no small part because of its substantial beauty—and good fishing. If the whole trail is not an option for the day, an easy hike to the Buzzards Roost is a good destination. But if you're in the mood and in tip-top shape, the strenuous hike to Silver Creek will test your endurance. When you've warmed up, then you may be ready to tackle the entire 27-mile length. This trail is located in the area charred by the 2002 Biscuit Fire burn; take caution and proceed knowingly. Along the way, look for recovering madrone, tanoak, myrtlewood, and black huckleberry.

The Illinois River Trail sets out from Oak Flat and climbs the canyon wall for 2.5 miles to Buzzards Roost, hung over 1,000 feet in the air above the river. This makes for a good day trip. Continuing 1.7 miles up the trail, you'll come to Indigo Creek and Indian Flat, with a left-hand spur trail leading into the meadows just before the creek. From there the trail descends slowly for 3.7 miles past the old Fantz Ranch, now USFS property, crossing numerous creeks before arriving at the canyon of Silver Creek.

User Groups: Hikers, dogs, and horses. No mountain bikes allowed. No wheelchair facilities.

Permits: Permits are not required. Parking and access are free.

Maps: For a map of the Siskiyou National Forest and the Kalmiopsis Wilderness, contact the Rogue River–Siskiyou National Forest headquarters, 3040 Biddle Road, Medford, OR, 97504, 541/618-2200. For a topographic map, ask the USGS for Agness.

Directions: From U.S. 101, at the south end of the Gold Beach Bridge, follow Jerrys Flat Road for 28 miles along the Rogue River to the bridge over the Illinois River. On the far side of the crossing, turn right on Oak Flat Road for three miles. The trailhead lot is on the left along a gravel road just beyond the end of the pavement.

Contact: Siskiyou National Forest, Gold Beach Ranger District, 29279 Ellensburg Avenue, Gold Beach, OR, 97444, 541/247-3600.

79 INDIAN MARY PARK

2.8 mi/1.5 hr 🚶1 ⛰7

west of Grants Pass on the Rogue River

Map 7.5, page 365

This historic park has a long history in an area known for its wars between white settlers and Native Americans. In 1855, one Umpqua Joe warned the white settlers of an impending attack, which they thwarted. For this he was awarded a piece of land from where he operated a ferry. He died in 1886, and his daughter, Indian Mary, kept operating the ferry crossing. Once she left for Grants Pass, the land changed hands several times until 1958, when Josephine County bought it and made it into the park it is today. The sole trail in the park is named for Umpqua Joe and climbs to a viewpoint over the Rogue River.

The trail starts across the highway from the campground and day parking lot. The trail alternates between steep and easy, climbing 0.8 mile to a 0.2-mile viewpoint loop fork to the left. Returning to the main trail, climb 0.5 mile through black oaks to the official trail's end high above the river.

User Groups: Hikers and dogs. No wheelchair facilities.

Permits: Permits are not required. A $2-per-car day-use pass is required, or you can purchase a $25 annual pass.

Maps: For a topographic map, ask the USGS for Galice.

Directions: From I-5, take the Merlin exit 61 north of Grants Pass and follow signs 3.6 miles to Merlin on the Merlin-Galice Road, then go straight seven miles to the park entrance on the right.

Contact: Josephine County Parks, 125 Ringuette Street, Grants Pass, OR, 97527, 541/474-5285.

80 SHRADER OLD-GROWTH TRAIL
0.8 mi/0.5 hr

northeast of Gold Beach in Siskiyou National Forest

Map 7.5, page 365   **BEST (**

This easy loop trail is the home of Laddie Gale Douglas fir, 220 feet high and 10 feet thick, named for a legendary University of Oregon basketball player who led the team to a national championship victory way back in 1939. Quite the commemoration. The wide and easy trail is perfect for families. This is a fine trail to take slowly, savoring the forest that a typical hiker may normally move through at a quick clip.

From the parking area, the loop is an easy stroll through not only stately Douglas fir and cedars, but deciduous tanoak. Just inside the forest, the trail splits for the loop. Go left and in 0.2 mile cross a stream on a footbridge. From here, follow the loop through the colossal trees another 0.6 mile, gradually ascending back to the start of the loop. Along the way you'll pass the Laddie Gale commemorative tree.

User Groups: Hikers and dogs only. No wheelchair facilities.

Permits: Permits are not required. Parking and access are free.

Maps: For a map of the Siskiyou National Forest, contact the Rogue River–Siskiyou National Forest headquarters, 3040 Biddle Road, Medford, OR, 97504, 541/618-2200. A

brochure map is available at the trailhead. For a topographic map, ask the USGS for Brushy Bald Mountain.

Directions: From U.S. 101, at the south end of the Gold Beach Bridge, follow Jerrys Flat Road for 11.2 miles. Pass Lobster Creek Campground on the left and turn right at a sign for the Frances Schrader memorial Trail. Follow Road 3300-090 for 2.1 steep miles to a lot on the left.

Contact: Siskiyou National Forest, Gold Beach Ranger District, 29279 Ellensburg Avenue, Gold Beach, OR, 97444, 541/247-3600.

81 OTTER POINT
1.4 mi/0.5 hr

north of Gold Beach on the Pacific Ocean

Map 7.5, page 365

This seldom-seen series of trails are off the beaten path a bit, though not far from nearby U.S. 101. Wind-sculpted sandstone formations and a long beach laid bare by waves are only a short distance from all the traffic—and are worth a visit. From the parking area at this State Recreation Area, it's a 0.4-mile round-trip to the headland of Otter Point, with its view out over a long southern beach, and a short scramble trail to a hidden beach on the north face. A second trail heads south from the lot, descending to a beach with plenty of room to run.

User Groups: Hikers and dogs. No wheelchair facilities.

Permits: Permits are not required. Parking and access are free.

Maps: For a topographic map, ask the USGS for Gold Beach.

Directions: From Gold Beach, drive north on U.S. 101 for three miles. Near milepost 325, take a right at a sign for "Old Coast Road" and drive west to a T-junction. Turn right for 0.6 mile, then left at a state park sign, driving to the end at a parking area.

Contact: Oregon Parks and Recreation Department, 1115 Commercial Street NE,

Salem, OR, 97301, 800/551-6949, www.oregonstateparks.org.

82 BIG PINE INTERPRETIVE LOOP

2.5 mi/1.0 hr

west of Grants Pass in Siskiyou National Forest

Map 7.5, page 365   **BEST (**

Along a stretch of Myers Creek, a network of four looping trails goes through a forest centered around "Big Pine," a 250-foot-high, double-topped ponderosa pine tree with a six-foot diameter. It's anyone's guess how many people it would take to get their arms around it. This is a great hike for the family, especially if you're staying at the Big Pine Campground. With wheelchair-friendly paths and more great trails nearby, this makes for a good launch point into the area. A second trail extending from the loop further surveys the old-growth Douglas fir and ponderosa pine in the area.

To walk the Big Pine Interpretive Loop, cross the bridge over Myers Creek and bear right. You'll find Big Pine in the first 0.1 mile. Continue around the loop 0.3 mile to find a marginally maintained spur, the Taylor Camp Trail. This trail is steeper and brushier, but makes for an added exploration of up to a mile one-way, before it ends at an old logging road. Return as you came and continue counterclockwise on the Big Pine Trail to complete the loop.

User Groups: Hikers and dogs. The path is wheelchair accessible.

Permits: Permits are not required. A federal Northwest Forest Pass is required to park here; the cost is $5 a day or $30 for an annual pass. You can buy a day pass at the trailhead, at ranger stations, or through private vendors.

Maps: For a map of the Siskiyou National Forest, contact the Rogue River–Siskiyou National Forest headquarters, 3040 Biddle Road, Medford, OR, 97504, 541/618-2200. For a topographic map, ask the USGS for Chrome Ridge.

Directions: From I-5, take the Merlin exit 61 north of Grants Pass and follow signs 3.6 miles to Merlin on the Merlin-Galice Road, then go straight 8.5 miles toward Galice and turn left on Briggs Valley Road/FS 25 for 12.5 miles. Turn right at the Big Pine Campground entrance and keep right for the day-use parking area.

Contact: Siskiyou National Forest, Wild Rivers Ranger District, 2164 Spalding Avenue, Grants Pass, OR, 97526, 541/471-6500.

83 TAYLOR CREEK

10.1 mi one-way/1-2 days

west of Grants Pass in Siskiyou National Forest

Map 7.5, page 365

Taylor Creek's watershed in the Siskiyou Mountains offers many opportunities to explore in many directions. Briggs Creek, Minnow Creek, China Creek, Dutchy Creek, and two interpretive trails, including the Big Pine Loop (see *Big Pine Interpretive Loop,* previous listing) and the Burned Timber Nature Trail all extend from Taylor Creek's trail. It is possible to hike the creek in differing lengths, as the trail ducks in an out of the forest, meeting the road. Active claims are still to be found along the way, as this area has a mining legacy going way back.

From the lower trailhead, hike into the forest of red-barked madrone, live oak, and Douglas fir. Watch for miner's claim notices tacked to trees. Within the first 1.8 miles, the path crosses Taylor Creek on a 60-foot-high bridge, passes the Burned Timber Loop, and meets up with another bridge to the Tin Can Campground. After another 1.4 miles, the trail crosses Road 052 and continues another 0.6 mile to the next trailhead. The next 2.6 miles crosses the creek twice and arrives at Lone Tree Pass. The final 3.6 miles leaves the creek and heads into the woods, passing a 0.7-mile spur trail to the Big Pine Campground before reaching the final trailhead.

User Groups: Hikers, dogs, horses, and mountain bikes. No wheelchair facilities.

Permits: Permits are not required. A federal Northwest Forest Pass is required to park here; the cost is $5 a day or $30 for an annual pass. You can buy a day pass at the trailhead, at ranger stations, or through private vendors.

Maps: For a map of the Siskiyou National Forest, contact the Rogue River–Siskiyou National Forest headquarters, 3040 Biddle Road, Medford, OR, 97504, 541/618-2200. For a topographic map, ask the USGS for Chrome Ridge and Galice.

Directions: From I-5, take the Merlin exit 61 north of Grants Pass and follow signs 3.6 miles to Merlin on the Merlin-Galice Road, then go straight 8.5 miles toward Galice and turn left on Briggs Valley Road/FS 25 for 3.1 miles to a pullout on the left marked "Taylor Creek Trailhead." Consider a shuttle at the Big Pine Campground, which connects to the Taylor Creek Trail. To find the campground from the town of Merlin, follow Galice Road 8.5 miles and go left at Road 25, continuing 12.5 miles to the campground on the right.

Contact: Siskiyou National Forest, Wild Rivers Ranger District, 2164 Spalding Avenue, Grants Pass, OR, 97526, 541/471-6500.

84 BRIGGS CREEK

9.5 mi/1 day   🥾3   ⛰️7

west of Grants Pass in Siskiyou National Forest

Map 7.5, page 365

Briggs Creek has mining history to spare, and in this section of the Siskiyous, there are even some modern mining claims continuing today. Though this trail goes on much farther, there is a great option of visiting the abandoned Courier Mine Cabin, making for a great day. This trail is easiest in low water, as several fords are required. It's also popular for its abundance of swimming holes. In the meadow at Sam Brown Campground, once the site of an entire mining town, the only thing left is the grave of Sam Brown himself, one of the first African American men in southern Oregon, shot for allegedly conferencing with the miners' wives in a way the miners didn't appreciate.

The trail sets out, alternately following dirt roads and trail, from clear-cut to forests of fir, yew, and cedar, for 2.4 miles along the creek, passing the Elkhorn Mine, with its rusty machinery still left behind, and reaching the 30-foot-wide creek ford. The trail continues another 1.5 miles past tanoak, madrone, and sugar pine to the abandoned flume of the Courier Mine and finally to the one-room cabin. From here, the trail fords the creek again, continuing on to its end at Soldier Creek.

User Groups: Hikers, dogs, horses, and mountain bikes. No wheelchair facilities.

Permits: Permits are not required. A federal Northwest Forest Pass is required to park here; the cost is $5 a day or $30 for an annual pass. You can buy a day pass at the trailhead, at ranger stations, or through private vendors.

Maps: For a map of the Siskiyou National Forest, contact the Rogue River–Siskiyou National Forest headquarters, 3040 Biddle Road, Medford, OR, 97504, 541/618-2200. For a topographic map, ask the USGS for York Butte.

Directions: From I-5, take the Merlin exit 61 north of Grants Pass and follow signs 3.6 miles to Merlin on the Merlin-Galice Road, then go straight 8.5 miles toward Galice and turn left on Briggs Valley Road/FS 25 for 13.4 miles. One mile after the Big Pine Campground, turn right on FS Road 2512 for 0.3 mile, then turn left into the Sam Brown Campground, keeping left. Park in the large trailhead lot on the right.

Contact: Siskiyou National Forest, Wild Rivers Ranger District, 2164 Spalding Avenue, Grants Pass, OR, 97526, 541/471-6500.

85 ILLINOIS RIVER TRAIL TO BALD MOUNTAIN

20.6 mi/1-2 days

northwest of Cave Junction in Kalmiopsis Wilderness

Map 7.5, page 365

Many hikers think of this trail as one of the best in southern Oregon. This entry into the Kalmiopsis Wilderness, overlooking the Wild and Scenic Illinois River, has plenty to brag about. Pounding rapids, sweet campsites, and an abundance of creeks, all crowned by 3,917-foot Bald Mountain, are enough to suit anyone's taste. Although the 2002 Biscuit Fire started with a lightning strike at Florence Creek near this trail, many of the towering trees survived. In other areas, pine are repopulating the area, slowly but surely, and scrub oak and tanoak have already made their comeback.

The Illinois River Trail begins at a 140-foot steel bridge over Briggs Creek and the site of an old homestead. The first 4.5 miles heads into the wilderness area and crosses several creeks beneath York Butte, with views to the river below. At a junction, a loop trail begins with the goal being Bald Mountain. Go left 0.8 mile on the Pine Flat Trail to get to Pine Flat, a great camping spot overlooking Boat Eater Rapids, a granite island and six-foot drop whose name speaks for itself. Continue 2.6 steep miles to a junction. If you're tired, go to the right on a spur trail for 1.3 miles to connect to and follow the Illinois River Trail to the right four miles back to the junction above Pine Flat. If not, endure another 1.8-mile climb on the Pine Flat Trail to a campsite by a spring, keeping left at a junction with the Illinois River Trail to ascend to a 0.2-mile loop around lofty Bald Mountain's summit. Then descend, following the Illinois River Trail down 5.6 miles to the junction above Pine Flat, going left on the Illinois River Trail to return to the trailhead.

User Groups: Hikers, dogs, and horses. No mountain bikes allowed. No wheelchair facilities.

Permits: Permits are not required. A federal Northwest Forest Pass is required to park here; the cost is $5 a day or $30 for an annual pass. You can buy a day pass at the trailhead, at ranger stations, or through private vendors.

Maps: For a map of the Siskiyou National Forest and the Kalmiopsis Wilderness, contact the Rogue River–Siskiyou National Forest headquarters, 3040 Biddle Road, Medford, OR, 97504, 541/618-2200. For a topographic map, ask the USGS for Agness, York Butte, and Silver Peak.

Directions: From Grants Pass, head south on U.S. 199 toward Crescent City for 20 miles to a flashing yellow light in Selma. Turn right on Illinois River Road 4103 for 18.6 miles to the end of a rough gravel road at the Briggs Creek Trailhead.

Contact: Siskiyou National Forest, Wild Rivers Ranger District, 2164 Spalding Avenue, Grants Pass, OR, 97526, 541/471-6500.

86 CAPE SEBASTIAN

3.8-5.8 mi/2.0-3.0 hr

south of Gold Beach in Cape Sebastian State Park

Map 7.5, page 365

In 1603, the Spanish explorer Sebastian Vizcaino named this cape—not so much for himself as for Saint Sebastian. The views on a clear day extend 43 miles to the north to Humbug Mountain. To the south, a 50-mile view extends all the way to California. The cape itself hosts a dense Sitka spruce forest and overlooks Hunters Cove and Hunters Island, where cormorants hang out.

From the lot, the trail heads out over the cape for 1.4 miles, descending in the last portion to a striking lookout. The next 0.5-mile section follows the headland for more views before descending to the beach. For a longer hike, follow the beach towards the sea stacks for another mile to the Myers Creek pullout, a good turnaround point.

User Groups: Hikers and dogs. Paved trails are wheelchair accessible.

Permits: Permits are not required. Parking and access are free.

Maps: For a topographic map, ask the USGS for Cape Sebastian.

Directions: Drive south of Gold Beach seven miles on U.S. 101 and near milepost 335 turn at a "Cape Sebastian Viewpoint" sign, following this road 0.6 mile up the cape to a parking area.

Contact: Oregon Parks and Recreation Department, 1115 Commercial Street NE, Salem, OR, 97301, 800/551-6949, www.oregonstateparks.org.

87 SNOW CAMP LOOKOUT
7.0 mi/3.5 hr ⛷2 ▲8

northeast of Brookings in Kalmiopsis Wilderness

Map 7.5, page 365

One of the losses of the Biscuit Fire was the original Snow Camp Lookout, a 15-by-15-foot lookout that had been restored prior to the fire. The good news is, it's been rebuilt yet again. From the new lookout, rentable for $30 a night, the ocean is visible on clear days—and in fact, this site offers a 360-degree view. The longer trail to the lookout is one of the oldest in the Siskiyou National Forest, dating at least as far back as 1911, and portions of it have been identified as an old Native American trail.

Snow Camp Trail passes through wildflower heaven in the spring and summer, including azalea, beargrass, iris, cat's ear lilies, death camas, and Indian paintbrush. The first 1.7 miles pass the ruins of an old shelter, a rocky knoll, and eventually meeting up with Windy Creek. Take the left-hand turn here, fording the deep and cold Windy Creek and continuing steeply another mile. It is not a difficult ford but is best done in summer. A left-hand junction heads to Panther Lake, but stick to the right another 0.7 mile, climbing Snow Camp Mountain. At the next junction,

go right again 0.6 mile on the Snow Camp Lookout Trail to the lookout road and head for the top.

User Groups: Hikers, dogs, and horses. No mountain bikes allowed. No wheelchair facilities.

Permits: Permits are not required. Parking and access are free.

Maps: For a map of the Siskiyou National Forest, contact the Rogue River–Siskiyou National Forest headquarters, 3040 Biddle Road, Medford, OR, 97504, 541/618-2200. For a topographic map, ask the USGS for Collier Butte.

Directions: From Brookings and the U.S. 101 bridge, take the North Bank Road east eight miles and continue straight on Road 1376 an additional eight miles to a junction after the South Fork Chetco Bridge. Turn left, following "Snow Camp Lookout" signs on Road 1376 another 13 miles to a trailhead on the left a few hundred yards after milepost 21.

Contact: Siskiyou National Forest, Chetco Ranger District, 539 Chetco Lane, Brookings, OR, 97415, 541/412-6000.

88 WINDY VALLEY
4.4 mi/2.5 hr ⛷1 ▲7

northeast of Brookings in Siskiyou National Forest

Map 7.5, page 365

The Klamath Mountains rise above the ocean at the southernmost stretch of the Oregon coast, playing host to a wild diversity of trees and wildflowers. The Windy Valley Trail, unfortunately, is located along a stretch burned by the 2002 Biscuit Fire, one of the biggest in Oregon's history. Yet, for a learning experience, trails like this are a great way to see how a forest regenerates itself. One thing that colonizes this area is the Darlingtonia californica, the carnivorous pitcher plant also known as the cobra lily, which makes a meal of local bugs. This strange flower is native to this area and is rarely found anywhere else.

The Windy Valley Trail will pass through wildflower heaven in the spring and summer, including azalea, beargrass, iris, cat's ear lilies, death camas, and Indian paintbrush. The first 1.7 miles pass the ruins of an old shelter, a rocky knoll, and eventually meeting up with Windy Creek. Stay to the right for 0.5 mile to another crossing (there may still be a log there) and continuing into Windy Valley's meadows to the foundations of an old cabin beside a pool and small waterfall. Return as you came.

User Groups: Hikers, dogs, and horses. No mountain bikes allowed. No wheelchair facilities.

Permits: Permits are not required. Parking and access are free.

Maps: For a map of the Siskiyou National Forest, contact the Rogue River-Siskiyou National Forest headquarters, 3040 Biddle Road, Medford, OR, 97504, 541/618-2200. For a topographic map, ask the USGS for Collier Butte.

Directions: From Brookings and the U.S. 101 bridge, take the North Bank Road east 8 miles and continue straight on Road 1376 an additional 8 miles to a junction after the South Fork Chetco Bridge. Turn left, following "Snow Camp Lookout" signs on Road 1376 another 13 miles to a trailhead on the left a few hundred yards after milepost 21.

Contact: Siskiyou National Forest, Chetco Ranger District, 539 Chetco Lane, Brookings, OR, 97415, 541/412-6000.

89 MISLATNAH TRAIL TO MISLATNAH PEAK

9.6 mi/4.5 hr

northeast of Brookings in Kalmiopsis Wilderness

Map 7.5, page 365

There is only one route into the Big Craggies Botanical Area deep in the Kalmiopsis Wilderness, and this is it. The Big Craggies is a rocky, densely brushed area requiring cross-country travel. On top of that, this trail also

tops Mislatnah Peak, the site of a former lookout. Access to this trail is somewhat sketchy, as there is a slide on the Tincup Trail, which provides access to this trail about 0.9 mile from the trailhead. Also, you have to watch as you cross the prairies, as the trail has a way of vanishing and reappearing like magic. Check current conditions before you go.

From the parking area, start out on the Tincup Trail, descending 0.9 mile to Mislatnah Creek and the woodsy, grassy bench of Mislatnah Camp. Follow the trail upstream 0.1 mile to a horse crossing and ford the creek. Continue downstream for 0.3 mile and turn left on the Mislatnah Trail. In 0.6 mile, you'll pass a spring and enter the Upper Mislatnah Prairie in 0.2 mile beyond that. Here is where to really watch for the trail as it crosses the prairie 0.3 mile, entering the trees on the far side. The trail continues through a dry tanoak and madrone woodland for 1.4 miles to Jacks Camp, where signs point out a spring. Beyond the camp, the Kalmiopsis Wilderness begins, and the brush grows thicker along this steep ridge. Only 1.0 mile farther, the trail ascends to the 3,124-foot Mislatnah Peak, with views to the Big Craggies.

User Groups: Hikers, dogs, and horses. No mountain bikes allowed. No wheelchair facilities.

Permits: Permits are not required. Parking and access are free.

Maps: For a map of the Siskiyou National Forest and the Kalmiopsis Wilderness, contact the Rogue River–Siskiyou National Forest headquarters, 3040 Biddle Road, Medford, OR, 97504, 541/618-2200. For a topographic map, ask the USGS for Big Craggies.

Directions: From Brookings and the U.S. 101 bridge, take North Bank Road east eight miles and continue straight on Road 1376 an additional eight miles to a junction after the South Fork Chetco Bridge. Turn left, following Road 1376 another 10 miles to milepost 18, then fork right onto Road 360 for 1.5 miles, keeping right at Road 365 for the last 0.8 mile to the Tincup Trailhead.

Contact: Siskiyou National Forest, Chetco Ranger District, 539 Chetco Lane, Brookings, OR, 97415, 541/412-6000.

90 TINCUP TRAIL TO BOULDER CREEK CAMP

7.2 mi/3.0 hr

northeast of Brookings in Kalmiopsis Wilderness

Map 7.5, page 365

The Tincup Trail makes its way into the Kalmiopsis Wilderness following the Chetco River along an old gold prospectors' trail, heading across Bronson Prairie to the confluence of the Chetco and Boulder Creek, a good turnaround for a 7.2-mile day. Note that fords are necessary and those fords can only be done in late summer. Also, access to this trail is limited due to a slide on the Tincup Trail at Mislatnah Creek 0.9 mile from the trailhead, though there are other options to get to the trail. Check current conditions before you go.

From the parking area, start out on the Tincup Trail, descending 0.9 mile to Mislatnah Creek and the woodsy, grassy bench of Mislatnah Camp. Follow the trail upstream a mile to a horse crossing and ford the creek. Continue downstream for 0.3 mile to a junction with the Mislatnah Trail. Continue 2.3 miles upstream to Boulder Creek Camp, with access to water and campsites—meaning this a great place to cool your heels. Hardy hikers can continue on the nearly 20-mile trail to its end at Darling Creek.

User Groups: Hikers, dogs, and horses. No mountain bikes allowed. No wheelchair facilities.

Permits: Permits are not required. Parking and access are free.

Maps: For a map of the Siskiyou National Forest and the Kalmiopsis Wilderness, contact the Rogue River–Siskiyou National Forest headquarters, 3040 Biddle Road, Medford, OR, 97504, 541/618-2200. For a topographic map, ask the USGS for Big Craggies.

Directions: From Brookings and the U.S. 101 bridge, take North Bank Road east eight miles and continue straight on Road 1376 an additional eight miles to a junction after the South Fork Chetco Bridge. Turn left, following Road 1376 another 10 miles to milepost 18, then fork right onto Road 360 for 1.5 miles, keeping right at Road 365 for the last 0.8 mile to the Tincup Trailhead.

Contact: Siskiyou National Forest, Chetco Ranger District, 539 Chetco Lane, Brookings, OR, 97415, 541/412-6000.

91 ILLINOIS RIVER FALLS

1.2 mi/0.5 hr

northwest of Cave Junction in Siskiyou National Forest

Map 7.5, page 365

Heavily damaged during the Biscuit Fire, the Fall Creek Trail was closed due to a burned-out bridge; check on the status of this trail with the U.S. Forest Service before attempting it. If you can get there, it's an easy hike across a bridge to the far side of the Illinois River. Go left 0.4 mile, then head cross country along the river about 300 yards to a view of the 10-foot Illinois River Falls. Watch out for poison oak, as it grows back viciously after fires.

User Groups: Hikers, dogs, and horses. No mountain bikes allowed. No wheelchair facilities.

Permits: Permits are not required. Parking and access are free.

Maps: For a map of the Siskiyou National Forest, contact the Rogue River–Siskiyou National Forest headquarters, 3040 Biddle Road, Medford, OR, 97504, 541/618-2200. For a topographic map, ask the USGS for Pearsoll Peak.

Directions: From Grants Pass, head south on U.S. 199 toward Crescent City for 20 miles to a flashing yellow light in Selma. Turn right on Illinois River Road 4103 for 11 miles. At an "End Maintenance" sign, turn left at a gravel pullout onto Road 087, a rough descent 0.5 mile to a bridge.

Contact: Siskiyou National Forest, Wild Rivers Ranger District, 2164 Spalding Avenue, Grants Pass, OR, 97526, 541/471-6500.

92 BABYFOOT LAKE
2.4-5.3 mi/1.0-2.5 hr

west of Cave Junction in Siskiyou National Forest

Map 7.5, page 365

For a firsthand look at the devastation—and survival—of flora in a wildfire, head to Babyfoot Lake. The trail passes through a ghost wilderness of black snags that nevertheless harbor new blooms of beargrass and Oregon grape, feeding on sunlight from the opened canopy. The lake itself is an oasis, and the trail passes through the Babyfoot Lake Botanical Area: Western red cedar, incense cedar, and Port Orford cedar all survived here, as did Jeffrey pine and Brewer's weeping spruce. Tanoak trees along the way simply sprout new trees from their roots. The entire hike is a valuable lesson in fire ecology. The lake itself is a high mountain lake in a glacial cirque.

From the trailhead, enter the burned forest on the Babyfoot Lake Trail, going 0.3 mile to a junction. From there, head to the right, descending gently 0.9 mile to the Kalmiopsis Wilderness border and Babyfoot Lake. For an interesting loop, continue past Babyfoot to Trail 1124, an old road, in 0.5 mile. Go left, following this Kalmiopsis Rim Trail along 1.8 miles to a rock cairn and a burned sign marking the trail to the left. Follow the Ridge Trail for another view down to Babyfoot Lake, keeping right at the next two junctions for 1.8 miles back to the trailhead.

User Groups: Hikers and dogs. No horses or mountain bikes allowed. No wheelchair facilities.

Permits: Permits are not required. A federal Northwest Forest Pass is required to park here; the cost is $5 a day or $30 for an annual pass.

You can buy a day pass at the trailhead, at ranger stations, or through private vendors.

Maps: For a map of the Siskiyou National Forest and the Kalmiopsis Wilderness, contact the Rogue River–Siskiyou National Forest headquarters, 3040 Biddle Road, Medford, OR, 97504, 541/618-2200. For a topographic map, ask the USGS for Josephine Mountain.

Directions: Drive U.S. 199 south of Grants Pass 24 miles and turn west on Eight Dollar Road, following signs for Kalmiopsis Wilderness. The road becomes Road 4201 and crosses the Illinois River in three miles then continues on gravel for 12 more miles. At a fork, follow signs for Babyfoot lake and go left on Road 140 for 0.7 mile to a trailhead spur on the right.

Contact: Siskiyou National Forest, Wild Rivers Ranger District, 2164 Spalding Avenue, Grants Pass, OR, 97526, 541/471-6500.

93 VULCAN PEAK
2.6 mi/2.0 hr

east of Brookings in Kalmiopsis Wilderness

Map 7.5, page 365

Atop Vulcan Peak lie the remains of an old fire watchtower, a few metal pieces, some bits of glass. The view is expansive across, ironically, the massive burn of the 2002 Biscuit Fire. Nonetheless, this is a straightforward climb with views extending down to Vulcan Lake (see *Vulcan Lake,* next listing) and the Chetco River drainage system.

From the trailhead, walk up an abandoned roadbed 0.2 mile to a junction with the Chetco Divide Trail. Fork left and climb 1.1 miles and nearly 1,000 feet to a view encompassing the Siskiyou Mountains, the Kalmiopsis Wilderness, and the Pacific Ocean.

User Groups: Hikers, dogs, and horses. No mountain bikes allowed. No wheelchair facilities.

Permits: A free wilderness permit is required and available at the trailhead. Parking and access are free.

Maps: For a map of the Siskiyou National Forest and the Kalmiopsis Wilderness, contact the Rogue River–Siskiyou National Forest headquarters, 3040 Biddle Road, Medford, OR, 97504, 541/618-2200. For a topographic map, ask the USGS for Chetco Peak.

Directions: From the U.S. 101 bridge in Brookings, head east on North Bank Road for eight miles, continuing straight on Road 1376 another eight miles. At a junction just beyond the South Fork Chetco Bridge, turn right on gravel Road 1909 for 13.4 miles, following signs for Kalmiopsis Wilderness. At a fork, go right into the Vulcan Peak Trailhead.

Contact: Siskiyou National Forest, Chetco Ranger District, 539 Chetco Lane, Brookings, OR, 97415, 541/412-6000.

94 VULCAN LAKE

3.7 mi/2.5 hr

east of Brookings in Kalmiopsis Wilderness

Map 7.5, page 365

Every good explorer can recount some beautiful mountain lake stumbled upon in the heat of the day, and how refreshing it was to sink down into some cold mountain water and feel all tensions slip away. Vulcan Lake is certainly one of these places, and as a destination it seems fitting: Its loop trail leads over some serious rocky country scarred by the 2002 Biscuit Fire but, all things considered, is recovering nicely. It makes for a hot hike and a cool finish. On the way, the trail passes the remains of the old Gardner Mine, the Sorvaag Bog, and two lovely lakes in the presence of Vulcan Peak. The lakes themselves lie in a prehistoric cirque, when this area was scoured down to bedrock by glaciers. Vulcan Lake is not only great for swimming on a hot day, it's also a great entry point for a backpacking exploration.

From the trailhead at road's end, head to the right on the Vulcan Lake Trail for 1.4 miles, climbing to a pass overlooking not one, but two lakes (a bit farther in the distance is Little

Vulcan Lake) before heading down to Vulcan Lake. Here you'll find a junction; go right to Vulcan Lake, straight to Little Vulcan, and to the left for a challenging loop. This left-hand trail leads 1.1 miles along a barely discernable path, so watch the cairns stacked here. You'll pass the bog and the mine—both good for exploration—before joining the Johnson Butte Trail. Go left 0.8 mile along this old roadbed to return to the trailhead.

User Groups: Hikers, dogs, and horses. No mountain bikes allowed. No wheelchair facilities.

Permits: A free wilderness permit is required and available at the trailhead. Parking and access are free.

Maps: For a map of the Siskiyou National Forest and the Kalmiopsis Wilderness, contact the Rogue River–Siskiyou National Forest headquarters, 3040 Biddle Road, Medford, OR, 97504, 541/618-2200. For a topographic map, ask the USGS for Chetco Peak and Tincup Peak.

Directions: From the U.S. 101 bridge in Brookings, head east on North Bank Road for eight miles, continuing straight on Road 1376 another eight miles. At a junction just beyond the South Fork Chetco Bridge, turn right on gravel Road 1909 for 13.4 miles, following signs for Kalmiopsis Wilderness. At a fork, go left 1.7 miles to road's end at the trailhead.

Contact: Siskiyou National Forest, Chetco Ranger District, 539 Chetco Lane, Brookings, OR, 97415, 541/412-6000.

95 JOHNSON BUTTE

12.6 mi/6.5 hr

northeast of Brookings in Kalmiopsis Wilderness

Map 7.5, page 365

The Kalmiopsis Wilderness is so named for the bug-eating blooms of the *Kalmiopsis* carnivorous plant that grow in profusion along the Johnson Butte Trail. The best times to see the flowers are May and June, about when the snows melt in this remote section of the Klamath Mountains. The trail follows an old mining road, long abandoned. But the ridge it follows offers substantive views, especially in light of the 2002 Biscuit Fire, which did a number on this part of the world. Still, the trail passes accessible, lily-covered Salamander Lake along the way, as well as a rare azalea found in patches in this wilderness area.

From the trailhead, the Johnson Butte Trail is a single run at 6.3 miles one-way. It follows a ridge on an old road for 1.5 miles before turning to trail, then crosses the ridge 0.4 mile later. After four miles, the trail rounds Dry Butte and arrives at a spur trail to Salamander Lake. About 1.1 miles beyond this lake is a spur trail on the right that leads to a spring. From here, it's a 1.2-mile run to a junction with the Upper Chetco Trail in the shadow of Johnson Butte, at a flat good for camping—but there's no water. Return as you came.

User Groups: Hikers, dogs, and horses. No mountain bikes permitted. No wheelchair facilities.

Permits: A free wilderness permit is required and available at the trailhead. Parking and access are free.

Maps: For a map of the Siskiyou National Forest and the Kalmiopsis Wilderness, contact the Rogue River–Siskiyou National Forest headquarters, 3040 Biddle Road, Medford, OR, 97504, 541/618-2200. For a topographic map, ask the USGS for Chetco Peak and Tincup Peak.

Directions: From the U.S. 101 bridge in Brookings, head east on North Bank Road for eight miles, continuing straight on Road 1376 another eight miles. At a junction just beyond the South Fork Chetco Bridge, turn right on gravel Road 1909 for 13.4 miles, following signs for Kalmiopsis Wilderness. At a fork, go left 1.7 miles to road's end at the trailhead.

Contact: Siskiyou National Forest, Chetco Ranger District, 539 Chetco Lane, Brookings, OR, 97415, 541/412-6000.

96 BOARDMAN STATE PARK
12.6 mi one-way/1-2 days 🏃5 ⛰10

north of Brookings on the Pacific Ocean

Map 7.5, page 365

Samuel Boardman—a 21-year veteran of the Oregon State Parks, and in fact the first superintendent of that newly created system back in the early 1900s—left Oregon with the firm foundations of a supreme park system as his legacy. No wonder that what is now Boardman State Park is named for him. It's grandiose, epic, and as far as the Oregon coast goes, you can get just about every pleasure out of it you could imagine: 300-year-old Sitka spruce, rock arches and natural bridges, amazing vistas, cove beaches, timbered sea stacks, and old midden mounds left by Native Americans. What's more, this park is easily sampled in short stretches, as the trail itself—part of the Oregon Coast Trail—parallels U.S. 101, with a number of pullouts for easy access. To do the whole trail, or to backpack it, you'll want to have tide charts handy, as some stretches will require some beach portages. Be prepared for wonder at a discount, as all sections are free. But where to start?

The southernmost stretch begins at the Lone Ranch Picnic Area on a nice beach and heads north immediately onto Cape Ferrelo, named for a 1542 Spanish explorer, traversing its grassy and wildflower-strewn meadows 1.2 miles to a viewpoint parking area. The next 1.4 miles provides a side trail down to a beach on the north end of the cape and continues through Sitka spruce forests over House Rock Creek to a viewpoint of the same name. The trail continues over the rocky headlands 1.3 miles then dives down for a 1.2-mile beach crossing before heading up to the Whalehead Beach Picnic Area—the "whalehead" being a sea stack that spouts water out its head when the tide comes in just right. You'll need to follow the entry road up 0.3 mile to connect with the rest of the trail. Continue 1.4 mile for some stunning viewpoints, arriving at the Indian Sands, a series of strange wind-sculpted sandstone formations. Follow the headlands north 1.4 miles to U.S. 101, where the trail briefly joins the highway to cross the highest bridge in Oregon at 345 feet over the canyon of Thomas Creek. The next 1.3 miles follows the cliffs and drops down to China Beach, passable only at low tide. Cross the beach and head back to the highway for 0.6 mile. Then in 1.1 miles, pass over the beautiful Natural Bridges with a viewpoint. The final 1.4-mile stretch again follows the cliffs with views out to Spruce Island and Arch Rock. The trail ends at Arch Rock Picnic Area.

User Groups: Hikers and dogs. The Arch Rock and Cape Ferrelo Viewpoints are wheelchair accessible.

Permits: Permits are not required. Parking and access are free.

Maps: For a free park brochure, call Oregon Parks and Recreation, 800/551-6949, or download a free map at www.oregonstateparks.org. For a topographic map, ask the USGS for Brookings.

Directions: Drive north of Brookings on U.S. 101 about four miles. The southernmost start of the trail is at the Lone Ranch Picnic Area between mileposts 352 and 353. The northernmost start of the trail at Arch Rock Picnic Area is between mileposts 344 and 345.

Contact: Oregon Parks and Recreation Department, 1115 Commercial Street NE, Salem, OR, 97301, 800/551-6949, www.oregonstateparks.org.

🗒 97 REDWOOD NATURE TRAIL
2.6 mi/1.0 hr   🥾1   ⛺7

east of Brookings in Siskiyou National Forest

Map 7.5, page 365   **BEST (**

Though California gets all the fame for its redwood trees, Oregon has its own share. They extend, in fact, about this far north into the state, and an easy tour in Loeb State Park visits the *Sequoia sempervirens* on land donated to the state by a group called Save the Myrtlewoods. That's not all they saved:

The park is also a haven for red alder, tanoak, evergreen huckleberries, and salmonberries. The Riverview Trail follows the Chetco River for some grand views of the rocky-bottomed river, as well.

From the picnic area, head out 0.7 mile along the Riverview Trail on the Chetco River, home to river otters and fish-hunting osprey. The trail ends at the North Bank Road, so cross the road to the Redwood Nature Trail parking area and follow this trail along Elk Creek. Head to the left for the 1.2-mile loop uphill into the stately redwood grove. Return along the Riverview Trail.

User Groups: Hikers and dogs. No wheelchair facilities.

Permits: Permits are not required. Parking and access are free.

Maps: A trail guide is available at the trailhead. For a topographic map, ask the USGS for Mount Emily.

Directions: From the U.S. 101 bridge in Brookings, head east on North Bank Road for 7.3 miles and turn right into Loeb State Park and drive to the trailhead parking area.

Contact: Oregon Parks and Recreation Department, 1115 Commercial Street NE, Salem, OR, 97301, 800/551-6949, www.oregonstateparks.org.

🗒 98 WHEELER RIDGE
1.6 mi/1.0 hr   🥾1   ⛺7

east of Brookings in Wheeler Creek Research Natural Area

Map 7.5, page 365

On September 9, 1942, a Japanese submarine surfaced off the coast of southern Oregon, and a small aircraft was launched by catapult. The pilot, Nobuo Fujita, carrying his family's 400-year-old samurai sword, dropped two incendiary bombs. The plan was to start massive forest fires. The plan failed, as the fires on Wheeler Ridge were quickly put out, and another bomb dropped on Grassy Knob (see *Grassy Knob* listing in this chapter) never went off—and indeed was never found. The pilot got away scot-free. Later, though, the pilot returned, first in 1962 to present his family's samurai sword to the city of Brookings, and then in 1992 as an act of reconciliation when he hiked this ridge and planted a redwood tree.

To find the bomb site, hike from the trailhead 0.8 mile into the Wheeler Creek Research Natural Area. This easy path weaves through big Douglas fir, tanoak, pine, and huge redwoods. The trail ends at an interpretive sign and the redwood seedling planted as a gesture of peace.

User Groups: Hikers and dogs. No wheelchair facilities.

Permits: Permits are not required. Parking and access are free.

Maps: For a map of the Siskiyou National Forest, contact the Rogue River–Siskiyou National Forest headquarters, 3040 Biddle Road, Medford, OR, 97504, 541/618-2200. For a topographic map, ask the USGS for Fourth of July Creek.

Directions: From the south end of the U.S. 101 bridge in Brookings, drive inland on South Bank Road five miles, then turn right on gravel Mount Emily Road, following "Bombsite Trail" signs 13 miles to the trailhead sign. Park along the road.

Contact: Siskiyou National Forest, Chetco Ranger District, 539 Chetco Lane, Brookings, OR, 97415, 541/412-6000.

PORTLAND AND THE WILLAMETTE VALLEY

© SEAN PATRICK HILL

BEST HIKES

⟨ Hikes for Kids
Willamette Mission State Park, page 439.
McDowell Creek Falls, page 444.

⟨ Self-Guided Nature Walks
Tryon Creek State Park, page 438.
McDonald Research Forest, page 442.

⟨ Hikes for Waterfalls
Silver Falls State Park, page 440.

⟨ Wheelchair-Accessible Trails
Powell Butte, page 436.

Though it's home to the majority of Oregon's population, the Willamette Valley isn't as dense as you might think. A drive up Highway 99 (East or West; there are two) takes you through pioneer towns, vast tracts of farmland, and into the center of Portland, Oregon's biggest city. But "the Valley," as it's known, is also a gateway to some of the best explorations in the state. State parks of cottonwood-lined riverbanks and stunning waterfalls are within easy distance of most cities, including Salem, Corvallis, and Eugene. In the Willamette Valley, you can climb a butte to get above winter fog, find beaver dams in the numerous wetlands, or go bird-watching in the many wildlife refuges. From Silver Falls to Forest Park to Sauvie Island, city folk – and visitors – have a wealth of hiking options.

Even Portland, smack in the middle of an urban area of more than two million people, has a lot of wilderness to offer. For one, there's Forest Park. At more than 5,000 acres, it is one of the largest urban wilderness parks in North America, and it has nearly 70 miles of trails and gravel roads open to hiking. Scattered throughout the city are a host of parks, many of them threaded with trails. Portland also has a series of trail networks; the 40-mile Springwater Corridor, for instance, offers access to some of the hikes in this book, such as Oaks Bottom Refuge and Powell Butte.

It's easy to see why so many people live here. Yet there is that grey-cloud gloomy idea of Oregon being eternally associated with rain. Don't sweat it; first of all, Western Oregon gets a lot of its precipitation in the form of a light misty rainfall – hardly a torrential downpour. Consider what Oregon would look like without the rain, anyway. It's a small price to pay for such a dense green, one that draws comparison to the fabled fields of Ireland. Still, Oregon isn't exactly all green. Western Oregon sustains a far-more interesting mix of landscapes. Much of the valley floor remains in its natural state as a white-oak savanna, a series of rolling grasslands where deer browse in the foggy mornings. The wetlands regions, though certainly marshy, are entirely open to exploring and are home to myriad native and migrating birds. The buttes and foothills of the Cascade Mountains, remnants of ancient volcanoes, offer rocky terrain and the beginnings of the dense conifer forests for which Oregon is famous.

Though the Willamette Valley is home to the majority of Oregon's population, it is somewhat of a blessing for explorers. For one, you don't have to travel far to access the coast, the Columbia River Gorge, or the Cascade Mountains. Secondly, you don't have to drive for hours and hours to get to the hikes listed in this section. These are fun and easy day trips, great for kids and adults alike.

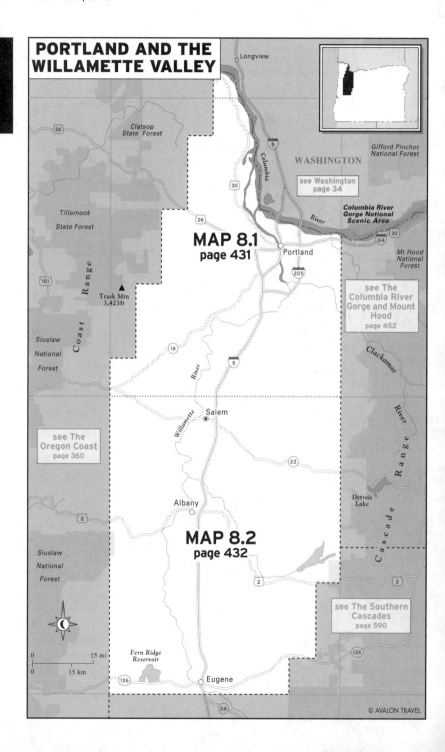

PORTLAND AND THE WILLAMETTE VALLEY

Longview

WASHINGTON

Clatsop State Forest

Tillamook State Forest

Gifford Pinchot National Forest

see Washington page 34

Columbia River Gorge National Scenic Area

MAP 8.1 page 431

Portland

Mt Hood National Forest

Trask Mtn 3,423ft

see The Columbia River Gorge and Mount Hood page 452

Clackamas River

Siuslaw National Forest

Coast Range

see The Oregon Coast page 360

Willamette River

Salem

Albany

Detroit Lake

MAP 8.2 page 432

Siuslaw National Forest

Cascade Range

see The Southern Cascades page 590

Fern Ridge Reservoir

0   15 mi
0   15 km

Eugene

© AVALON TRAVEL

Map 8.1

Hikes 1-11
Pages 433-439

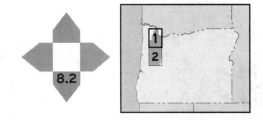

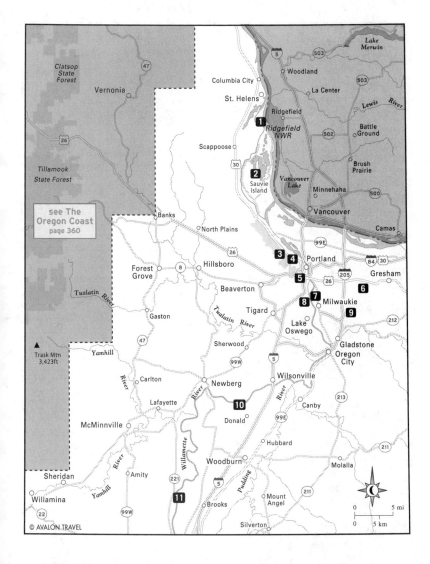

Map 8.2

Hikes 12-25
Pages 440-448

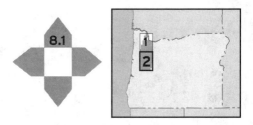

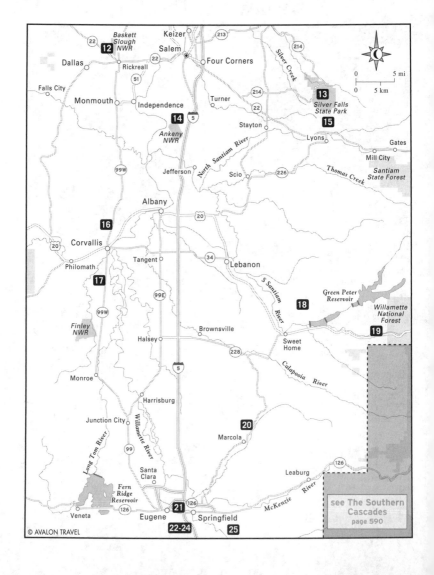

1 WARRIOR ROCK
7.0 mi/3.5 hr

on Sauvie Island, northwest of Portland

Map 8.1, page 431

Sauvie Island is Oregon's largest island. Once the home of the Multnomah tribe (who fed Lewis and Clark as the intrepid explorers threaded their way across the continent), in the 1830s it became a giant dairy farm for nearby Fort Vancouver. Though most of it remains farmed land, the island hosts a Wildlife Refuge with an impressive array of birds. The trail to a small lighthouse on Warrior Rock is a great place to start. You'll see some of the classic riverside ecology, with its cottonwoods towering overhead and wild Nootka rosebushes below. Warrior Rock Trail follows the Columbia River right out to the tip of the island, where a lighthouse, originally built in 1889 but replaced by the U.S. Coast Guard, watches over one of the largest rivers in the Western United States.

The unmarked Warrior Rock Trail starts at the edge of the parking lot and follows the massive Columbia River, passing through forests of cottonwoods for three miles, reaching the tip of the island where the white lighthouse perches on solid sandstone. Past the lighthouse, go a half-mile farther up the beach to a view of the town of St. Helens, or just sit and watch the enormous ships passing slowly on the immense river. Watch, too, for the bald eagles that make this island their home.

User Groups: Hikers and dogs on leash. No wheelchair facilities.

Permits: A daily use permit is $3.50 (or $11 a year) and is available from Oregon Department of Fish and Wildlife in Portland or Sam's Grocery on Sauvie Island Road.

Maps: For a topographic map, ask the USGS for St. Helens.

Directions: From downtown Portland, go north on U.S. 30 toward St. Helens. After about 10 miles, turn right across the Sauvie Island Bridge and continue north on Sauvie Island Road. Drive 1.8 miles past the store on Sauvie Island Road and turn right on Reeder Road, following this road 12.6 miles to its end at a parking area.

Contact: Oregon Department of Fish and Wildlife/Sauvie Island Wildlife Area, 503/621-3488, www.dfw.state.or.us/resources/visitors/sauvie_island_wildlife_area.asp.

2 OAK ISLAND
2.9 mi/1.5 hr

on Sauvie Island, northwest of Portland

Map 8.1, page 431

If it's possible to imagine an island within an island, then you'll have a fair picture of Oak Island. It's not exactly an "island," but it comes close. Surrounded on three sides by water from Sturgeon Lake, Steelman Lake, the Narrows, and Wagonwheel Hole, it is technically a peninsula, but you'll feel as if you're on an island. This loop circles a dense cottonwood and white oak forest and crosses open fields with views to the timbered ridge above the distant Multnomah Channel and an expansive sky. The best time to come, undoubtedly, is during bird migrations: This is one of the best places to see the spectacular sandhill cranes as they pass through. The trail is only open April 16 through September 30 to protect wildlife. Be sure to watch for bald eagles and explore the edges of an abandoned farm, hemmed in by walls of blackberry brambles.

Starting at the parking lot, cross the gate and go straight on the abandoned road for 0.3 mile to begin the Oak Island Nature Trail. At a junction, go to the left to begin the loop. For 1.1 miles, the trail crosses some woods and enters the vast fields, curving at the Narrows with an occasional side trail to the water. The returning 0.9 mile looks out over Sturgeon Lake toward the Cascade peaks. At a bench, continue to the right on the loop 0.3 mile back to the initial trail, going left to your car.

User Groups: Hikers and dogs on leash. No wheelchair facilities.

Permits: A daily use permit is $3.50 (or $11

a year) and is available from Oregon Department of Fish and Wildlife in Portland or Sam's Grocery on Sauvie Island Road.

Maps: For a topographic map, ask the USGS for St. Helens.

Directions: From downtown Portland, go north on U.S. 30 toward St. Helens. After about 10 miles, turn right across the Sauvie Island Bridge and continue north on Sauvie Island Road. Drive 1.8 miles past the store on Sauvie Island Road and turn right on Reeder Road, following this road 1.2 miles. Turn left on Oak Island Road, crossing a dike after 2.7 miles. Continue straight for 0.4 mile to a parking area.

Contact: Oregon Department of Fish and Wildlife/Sauvie Island Wildlife Area, 503/621-3488, www.dfw.state.or.us/resources/visitors/sauvie_island_wildlife_area.asp.

❸ WILDWOOD TRAIL

30.2 mi one-way/2 days

in Portland's Washington and Forest Parks

Map 8.1, page 431

If not for the vision of some early Portland residents, the 5,000-acre Forest Park never would have existed. You'll thank them: In a city as large and bustling as Portland, Oregon, it's hard to imagine that such easy, natural respite lies so close at hand. The Wildwood Trail, which spans Forest Park, crosses through a number of city parks, following the long forested ridge of the Tualatin Hills with a variety of side trails branching off the Wildwood Trail, not to mention the gravel Leif Erickson Road, making for nearly 70 miles in all. Here in the hills above the Willamette River and its sprawling industrial area, stands of Western maple, Douglas fir, and even wild cherry trees colonize the steep hills and wide ravines, making it a refuge for deer and birds, as well as wildflowers like the big-leafed trillium. Any time of day or on any day of the week, you're sure to find people on the trail; in order to limit some of the traffic, bikes are not allowed on footpaths (except the old Leif Erickson Road).

There are scores of possibilities for short and long day trips, and numerous access points. Depending on the season, there is ample opportunity to listen to bubbling creeks and songbirds, and to keep count of the many native flowers that bloom here. Trails weave along the steep ridges of Douglas fir and bigleaf maples. The trail officially begins in Washington Park, circling the Vietnam Veterans Memorial before launching into the Hoyt Arboretum. Once it crosses Burnside Road, passing the Pittock Mansion and an Audubon center, the trail enters the forest, continuing all the way to the northern edge of the city.

User Groups: Hikers and dogs only. No horses. Mountain bikes allowed on Leif Erickson Road only. No wheelchair facilities.

Permits: Permits are not required. Parking and access are free.

Maps: For a free trail map contact Portland Parks and Recreation, 503/823-PLAY (503/823-7529). For a topographic map, ask the USGS for Portland and Linnton.

Directions: There are a number of points of access to the Wildwood Trail. To reach the southernmost trailhead from downtown Portland, head west on U.S. 26 to Exit 72/Canyon Road. Drive past the Oregon Zoo and the World Forestry Center to a lot near the Vietnam Veterans Memorial. The trail begins to the right of the Memorial. To reach the northern trailhead, drive north on U.S. 30 to Germantown Road. Drive up the hill to a clearly marked parking area on the left.

Contact: Portland Parks and Recreation, 1120 SW 5th Avenue, Suite 1302, Portland, OR, 97204, 503/823-PLAY (503/823-7529).

▲ MACLEAY PARK

5.5 mi/2.5 hr

in Northwest Portland

Map 8.1, page 431

If you feel like showing off Portland, bring friends here to the Lower Macleay Trail. As soon as you enter the little canyon of Balch Creek, named for an early settler hanged for murder (the first man legally hanged in Oregon, by the way), you'll quickly understand why Portland is one of the premier "livable" cities in the country. The land for the park was bought by a wealthy Portland merchant named Donald Macleay, who donated it to the city. Generations later, the creek still resounds with the calls of wrens and the wind through the trees. The Wildwood Trail passes over the Lower Macleay Trail, which opens up possibilities to hike as far out as you'd like (see *Wildwood Trail,* previous listing).

Follow the paved path up the creek, which turns into a dirt trail after a viewpoint. Watch for the little sign that designates one of Portland's Heritage Trees: an enormous Douglas fir near the stream. At the intersection with the Wildwood Trail lies an old stone hut, the ruin of an old Works Project Administration effort, which makes a great playhouse for kids. Continue along the creek to a crossing, a good turnaround point for a 1.75-mile hike. Feel like more? Continue uphill to the left and stay on the Wildwood Trail, crossing Cornell Road, and up to the historic Pittock Mansion, which has an amazing view of Portland and the Cascades. When you're ready to head back, and if you're in the mood for a loop, start back down on the Wildwood Trail and take a left on the Upper Macleay Trail, strolling through the woods until it rejoins the Wildwood Trail, returning you to Balch Creek.

User Groups: Hikers and dogs only. Paved path is wheelchair accessible.

Permits: Permits are not required. Parking and access are free.

Maps: For a free trail map contact Portland Parks and Recreation, 503/823-PLAY (503/823-7529). For a topographic map, ask the USGS for Portland and Linnton.

Directions: From downtown Portland, go north on NW 23rd Street to NW Thurman Street. Go left on Thurman and continue to NW 28th, going right. Take the next left on NW Upshur and continue to the small parking area at the end. The trail begins at the lot.

Contact: Portland Parks and Recreation, 1120 SW 5th Avenue, Suite 1302, Portland, OR, 97204, 503/823-PLAY (503/823-7529).

▲ COUNCIL CREST VIA MARQUAM GULCH

3.8 mi/2.0 hr

south of downtown Portland in Marquam Nature Park

Map 8.1, page 431

Just across a busy freeway from downtown Portland lies the Marquam Nature Park. This network of forested trails climbs a canyon that runs like a cleft between neighborhoods of houses on stilts, rising to a crescendo to Council Crest, with its commanding view of the Cascade Range. From up here, you'd never know that Council Crest was once the site of an amusement park. Now it offers quiet benches and a chance to look over the city of Portland and the Willamette River. It also offers a steady climb, as well as a loop option to further explore this oasis in the midst of a city.

From the lot, follow the right-hand Sunnyside Trail for 0.4 mile up the gulch to an intersection and go right, staying on Sunnyside. From here the trail begins to climb in earnest, crossing several streets along the way. After 1.3 miles, the trail emerges from the woods into the open-air Council Crest Park. The hilltop viewpoint points out views to Mount Rainier, Mount St. Helens, Mount Adams, and Mount Hood. After soaking up the panorama, follow the trail back down 1.3 miles to the junction. From here, instead of returning on the trail you started on, go right for a 0.8-mile diversion on the Marquam Gulch Trail and Goldy Corridor Trail to complete the loop back to the lot, staying left at all junctions.

User Groups: Hikers and dogs only. The overlook at Council Crest is wheelchair accessible, but the trail from the Nature Park is not.

Permits: Permits are not required. Parking and access are free.

Maps: Maps are available at the trailhead. Parking and access are free.

Directions: From downtown Portland, go south on SW 6th Avenue, crossing the I-405 freeway. Follow blue "Hospital" signs for Oregon Health and Sciences University (OHSU) onto Terwilliger Avenue. At the intersection of Terwilliger and Sam Jackson Road, go straight on Sam Jackson. At the next bend in the road, immediately turn right into the parking area.

Contact: Portland Parks and Recreation, 1120 SW 5th Avenue, Suite 1302, Portland, OR, 97204, 503/823-PLAY (503/823-7529).

6 POWELL BUTTE
3.1 mi/1.5 hr   🥾2 ⛰️7

in Southeast Portland in Powell Butte Nature Park

Map 8.1, page 431   **BEST (**

Rising above Johnson Creek, this volcanic remnant of an ancient past offers an open meadow at its summit with views to Mount Hood and two other Cascade peaks. Perfect all year long, this loop trail wanders through the open meadows and explores the Douglas fir and red cedar slopes along its flanks. Pileated woodpeckers, deer, and, surprisingly, coyotes are all possibilities for wildlife-spotting here. The peak is the site of an old orchard, and the spiny shrubs around the meadows are hawthorn trees. Both the Mount Hood Trail and the Pioneer Orchard Trail connect to the Springwater Corridor, a marvelous 40-mile loop around the east side of Portland.

Beginning from the lot, follow the paved Mountain View Trail through fields of hawthorn and clover 0.6-mile to the walnut orchard at the summit—a good place for a picnic. Go left on the Orchard Trail Loop, following the loop around the orchard to an astonishing view of Mount Hood and waves of volcanic buttes. Staying to the right at all junctions, circle 0.8 mile almost entirely around back to the Mountain View Trail, but instead turn left on the Mount Hood Trail, diving 0.5 mile into the forest. Cross a creek and go right on the Cedar Grove Trail, staying on it for 0.3 mile, and continuing 0.3 mile on the Cougar Trail. This trail intersects with the Meadowland Trail, which you can take to the left to find the Service Road Trail, going right for 0.6 mile back to your car. Trails radiate out on Powell Butte, so feel free to explore further.

User Groups: Hikers and dogs. Horses and bicycles on designated trails only. Part of the Mountain View Trail is paved and wheelchair accessible.

Permits: No permits are required. Parking and access are free.

Maps: A brochure map is available at the trailhead. For a topographic map, ask the USGS for Gladstone.

Directions: From I-205, take Exit 19 and follow Powell Boulevard east for 3.5 miles. Turn right on 162nd Avenue, driving up to road's end at the parking lot.

Contact: Portland Parks and Recreation, 1120 SW 5th Avenue, Suite 1302, Portland, OR, 97204, 503/823-PLAY (503/823-7529).

7 OAKS BOTTOM
2.8 mi/1.5 hr   🥾1 ⛰️5

in Southeast Portland in Oaks Bottom Wildlife Refuge

Map 8.1, page 431

Nestled between the Willamette River, an amusement park, a mausoleum, and a neighborhood set atop 100-foot cliffs lies Portland's first urban wildlife refuge. If that isn't strange enough, consider the birds one can spot here: bald eagles high in the cottonwoods, great blue

© SEAN PATRICK HILL

view of Mount Hood, Powell Butte Nature Park in Southeast Portland

herons wading in a marsh, numerous geese and ducks, and an assortment of songbirds both year-round and migratory. This easy trail circles a large seasonal lake that shrinks and swells with the rainfall and goes purple with loosestrife (an invasive species) in the summer. An easy loop follows a channel of the Willamette River as it circles a branching island where fish-hunting osprey nest.

From the main Oaks Bottom parking area, a paved trail painted with icons of local animals descends 0.3 mile to a junction. Follow the paved path to the right 0.1 mile to an underpass ducking beneath a set of railroad tracks. From here, follow an excellent bike path to the left, part of the Springwater Corridor. For 0.8 mile, watch to the right for the cottonwood-lined shores of the Willamette, including views to East and Ross Islands, where birds of prey nest. To the left, you'll see the massive lake where waterfowl wade and dive year-round. At the second overpass, duck again beneath the tracks and follow a dirt path along the lake, where you'll disappear into the wooded shoreline. With a good field guide and a pair of binoculars, this trip can be particularly rewarding for spotting wildlife.

User Groups: Hikers. Dogs permitted on leash only. Bikes allowed on paved paths only. Paved paths are wheelchair accessible.

Permits: Permits are not required. Parking and access are free.

Maps: A brochure and map are available at the trailhead. For a topographic map, ask the USGS for Lake Oswego.

Directions: From the east end of the Ross Island Bridge (Highway 26) take the exit for McLaughlin Blvd/Highway 99 E. In one mile, take the exit for Milwaukie Avenue, turn right at the stop sign, and immediately turn right into a parking area for Oaks Bottom Wildlife Refuge.

Contact: Portland Parks and Recreation, 1120 SW 5th Avenue, Suite 1302, Portland, OR, 97204, 503/823-PLAY (503/823-7529).

8 TRYON CREEK STATE PARK

2.6 mi/1.0 hr   🚶2 ⛰8

in Southwest Portland

Map 8.1, page 431   **BEST (**

Cradled between the cities of Portland and Lake Oswego, this urban state park represents a quiet wilderness. Open all year, the park offers a bit of every season from wildflowers in spring to snow blankets in winter. For an easy introduction to glassy Tryon Creek, start at the nature center, where you can pick up a map. You'll need it: This state park is a weave of wonderful trails fanning out into the forested canyon. The handy map leads you through the many varieties of trees, wildflowers, and birds that are found in the park, and the nature center gives a good introduction to the ecology of the area. The centerpiece, of course, is Tryon Creek, which flows softly through this forest preserve.

Beginning at the nature center, turn right along the paved Old Main Trail 0.3 mile to the Red Fox Trail, which continues 0.2 mile to the Red Fox Bridge. After crossing the bridge, take a 0.3-mile detour to the Iron Mountain Bridge and back—it's worth it just to see this gulch. Then go back and continue left up the Cedar Trail to tour a side canyon for 0.9 mile to another intersection with a bridge. Don't be confused by the horse trails; instead, head left to the High Bridge. Linger a moment on the bridge, then follow signs to the right to the nature center for the 0.6-mile return. Once you get this loop down, you can begin to fan out on the network of trails linking the quiet neighborhoods surrounding the park.

User Groups: Hikers and dogs on six-foot or shorter leashes. Horses allowed only on designated equestrian trails. Bicycles allowed only on designated bike trail. The 0.35-mile Trillium Trail is paved and wheelchair accessible.

Permits: Permits are not required. Parking and access are free.

Maps: For a free park brochure, call Oregon Parks and Recreation, 800/551-6949, or download a free map at www.oregonstateparks.org.

For a topographic map, ask the USGS for Lake Oswego.

Directions: From I-5, take the Terwilliger Exit 297, driving south on Terwilliger Boulevard following Tryon Creek State Park signs. After 2.2 miles, turn right onto the entrance road and park at the end of the loop road.

Contact: Tryon Creek State Park, 11321 SW Terwilliger Blvd., Portland OR, 97219, 503/636-9886, or Oregon Parks and Recreation Department, 1115 Commercial Street NE, Salem, OR, 97301, 800/551-6949, www.oregonstateparks.org.

9 MOUNT TALBERT

4.2 mi/2.0 hr

in Clackamas in Mount Talbert Natural Area

Map 8.1, page 431

Within earshot of I-205, and entirely surrounded by new housing and apartment complexes, the 144-acre Mount Talbert Natural Area is a 750-foot green island in an urban sea. It is preserved as such by Metro, whose mission is to preserve jewels like this for future generations. With its Douglas fir and sword ferns, it looks like anywhere you can find in the mountain ranges of Oregon. Its stands of white oaks are home to the white-breasted nuthatch, an increasingly rare bird in this part of the world, but with the right ear you'll hear them easily enough. There are a total of 4.2 miles of trail, so why not do them all? A big signboard at the trailhead clearly labels the trails. A good start is the 2.4-mile Park Loop, which has access trails to the timbered summit.

User Groups: Hikers. Dogs and bikers are not permitted. Paved portions of the park are wheelchair accessible.

Permits: Permits are not required. Parking and access are free.

Maps: A map is available at the trailhead. For a topographic map, ask the USGS for Gladstone.

Directions: From the I-205 in Clackamas, take Exit 14 (Sunnyside Rd./Sunnybrook Blvd.).

Go east on Sunnybrook Boulevard and take a right on SE 97th Avenue, following it one mile (it becomes Mather Road after a curve) to the trailhead lot on the left.

Contact: North Clackamas Parks and Recreation District, 9101 SE Sunnybrook Boulevard, Clackamas, OR, 97015, 503/794-8041.

10 CHAMPOEG STATE PARK
3.2 mi/1.5 hr   🏃1 ⛰6

east of Newberg on the Willamette River

Map 8.1, page 431

This historic state park (pronounced sham-POO-ey) is the site of an early Oregon town that came to prominence as the home of the first provisional government of the Oregon Country. Founded by 100 white men in 1843, the new town was virtually erased by two floods in 1861 and 1890. The only remaining structure is the 1852 Newell House, situated on high ground. The rest of the town is now a quiet meadow circled by a loop trail, with posts designating the original streets. Try this park for a good dose of early Oregon history, with plenty of markers and signs pointing out what you may find.

Starting from the Riverside Day Use Area, follow signs to the Pavilion, where a monument commemorates the actual site where the 100 men debated. Start the first short loop by walking to the Willamette River and taking a paved 0.5-mile loop through enormous cottonwoods along the high banks of the river. At the end of the loop, continue east along the riverbank past the 1931 log cabin and following the road to the 1.1-mile Champoeg Townsite Trail. From this meadow you'll spot not only the ghost town site but the distant La Butte. The path skims along the Oak Grove Day Use Area and connects with the paved bike path heading right 1.1 mile back to the start of the loop. From there, return the way you came back to Riverside.

User Groups: Hikers and dogs. Bicycles are allowed only on designated bike paths. No horses allowed. Paved portions of the park are wheelchair accessible.

Permits: Permits are not required. A $3 day-use fee is collected at the park entrance, or you can get an annual Oregon Parks and Recreation pass for $25; contact Oregon Parks and Recreation, 800/551-6949.

Maps: For a free park brochure, call Oregon Parks and Recreation, 800/551-6949, or download a free map at www.oregonstateparks.org. For a topographic map, ask the USGS for Newberg.

Directions: From I-5, take Exit 278 to Donald. Turn west, following signs 5.7 miles to the entrance of the Champoeg Heritage Area. Park in the Riverside Day Use Area.

Contact: Oregon Parks and Recreation Department, 1115 Commercial Street NE, Salem, OR, 97301, 800/551-6949, www.oregonstateparks.org.

11 WILLAMETTE MISSION STATE PARK
2.7 mi/1.0 hr   🏃1 ⛰7

north of Salem on the Willamette River

Map 8.1, page 431   BEST (

Willamette Mission State Park has plenty to see. It's the site of a historic 1843 Methodist mission, home to the world's largest black cottonwood tree, plus filbert and walnut orchards, and the oldest ferry landing in Oregon, dating back to the 1844 mule-winched log barge. Start with an easy loop around the park's central meadow, hemmed in by Mission Lake—once the original channel of the Willamette River. This hike is great for kids, as most of the paths are easy and paved, and there's ample opportunity for exploration of the riverbank ecosystem.

Beginning in the Filbert Grove Day Use Area, walk 0.2 mile down to the riverbank and turn right on the paved path along the river, heading 1.2 miles to the landing for the Wheatland Ferry, which is free for pedestrians. Heading back to the loop, this time go right to walk along marshy Mission Lake. Here you'll find a monument describing the mission founded in 1834 by Jason Lee. Tired of the floods, he moved on to what is now Salem and founded what is now Willamette University. Follow this trail 0.9 mile to a road and the sign to the 155-foot black cottonwood champion (with a 26-foot circumference). Follow the road back to the Filbert Grove.

User Groups: Hikers, dogs, bikes, and horses. Paved portions of the park are wheelchair accessible.

Permits: Permits are not required. A $3 day-use fee is collected at the park entrance, or you can get an annual Oregon Parks and Recreation pass for $25; contact Oregon Parks and Recreation, 800/551-6949.

Maps: For a free park brochure, call Oregon Parks and Recreation, 800/551-6949, or download a free map at www.oregonstateparks.org. For a topographic map, ask the USGS for Mission Bottom.

Directions: From I-5, take Exit 263 towards Brooks/Gervais. Head west on Brookland Road for 1.7 miles and turn right onto Wheatland Road North for 2.4 miles to the park entrance. Drive to the Filbert Grove Day Use Area.

Contact: Oregon Parks and Recreation Department, 1115 Commercial Street NE, Salem, OR, 97301, 800/551-6949, www.oregonstateparks.org.

12 BASKETT SLOUGH REFUGE
4.7 mi/2.5 hr   🏃1 ⛰️6

east of Salem

Map 8.2, page 432

Each autumn, migrating dusky Canada geese use the Willamette Valley as a winter stomping ground from their yearly passage from Alaska. The Baskett Slough Refuge is the perfect destination if you've ever wanted to hear the sound of 20,000 geese honking and taking off in a flurry. You're likely to see and hear quite a few other birds, too, including swans, buffleheads,

and redwing blackbirds. Though part of the refuge around Morgan Lake is closed between October 1 and March 31 to protect these birds, the Baskett Butte hike is open all year.

From a parking area at the southern edge of the refuge, head in for an easy 1.5-mile loop up the butte. Go straight on the wide grassy path for 0.5 mile and then left at the junction up grass-topped Baskett Butte for a view over the Willamette Valley and out to the Coast Range. If the refuge is open, you can continue straight into the refuge through a white oak forest another 0.4 mile to a junction and an old barn colonized by darting swallows. Going right takes you to the shores of Morgan Lake, a 1.4-mile walk to a gate, where you can return via an old road for another mile back to the barn, passing a small pond of cattails and the nutria, a beaver-like rodent found throughout the Willamette Valley.

User Groups: Hikers only. Dogs are not permitted. No wheelchair facilities.

Permits: Permits are not required. Parking and access are free.

Maps: A downloadable map is available online at www.fws.gov/willamettevalley/baskett. For a topographic map, ask the USGS for Dallas.

Directions: From Salem, follow Highway 22 to Rickreall, turn north on U.S. 99 West for 1.8 miles, and turn left on gravel Colville Road 1.4 miles to the trailhead lot on the right.

Contact: U.S. Fish and Wildlife Service, Baskett Slough National Wildlife Refuge, 10995 Hwy. 22, Dallas, OR, 97338, 503/623-2749.

13 SILVER FALLS STATE PARK
7.1 mi/3.5 hr   🏃3 ⛰️8

east of Salem

Map 8.2, page 432   **BEST (**

There are many fine state parks in Oregon, and Silver Falls State Park is in the upper echelon. A rugged river canyon trail passes 10 waterfalls, half of them over 100 feet high;

© SEAN PATRICK HILL

Middle North Falls in Silver Falls State Park

it's one of the best hikes in the state. Though winter can be harsh here, closing and washing out trails, the park is open year-round. Starting from the South Falls parking area and the historic lodge built in 1940 by the Civilian Conservation Corps, head to the paved viewpoint of 177-foot South Falls and continue down the paved Canyon Trail into the canyon. What you'll see is the effect of erosion on soft ground beneath 15-million-year-old basalt, the remnants of a massive lava flow. This is why the falls go over such an overhanging lip. You'll get to see this close-up, seeing as the trail goes behind the falls.

After 0.3 mile, the trail reaches its first junction; stay left on the Canyon Trail, which turns to dirt. Continue on to the first junction past Lower South Falls, a total of 1.5 miles so far. From here, you could go right and ascend out of the canyon on the Ridge Trail another 1.3 miles to return to the lot.

Not quite ready? Then continue on 1.6 miles to viewpoints of Lower North, Double, Drake,

and Middle North Falls. At the 3.2-mile mark, a second cutoff trail to the right leads to a viewpoint of Winter Falls. Continue upstream on the Canyon Trail for some of the best falls, where another 1.5 miles will lead you to Twin Falls and finally to the grand North Falls, which you'll walk behind to continue. If you made it this far, then you may as well take the left-hand junction, which crosses under the road and brings you in only 0.2 mile to Upper North Falls. To complete the loop, head back toward North Falls and stay left this time on the Rim Trail. The remaining 2.5 miles on this trail passes through quiet woods and more views of the spectacular waterfalls before returning to South Falls.

User Groups: Hikers only. No dogs allowed on canyon trails. Paved portions of the park are wheelchair accessible.

Permits: Permits are not required. A $3 day-use fee is collected at the park entrance, or you can get an annual Oregon Parks and Recreation pass for $25; contact Oregon Parks and Recreation, 800/551-6949.

Maps: For a free park brochure, call Oregon Parks and Recreation, 800/551-6949, or download a free map at www.oregonstateparks.org. For a topographic map, ask the USGS for Drake Crossing.

Directions: From I-5, take Salem Exit 253 and drive 10 miles east on OR 22 to Highway 214. Turn left and drive 16 miles to the park entrance, following signs towards South Falls and Parking Area C.

Contact: Oregon Parks and Recreation Department, 1115 Commercial Street NE, Salem, OR, 97301, 800/551-6949, www.oregonstateparks.org.

14 ANKENY WILDLIFE REFUGE
2.2 mi/1.0 hr 🏃1 ⛰5

south of Salem

Map 8.2, page 432

One of three large tracts of land in the Willamette Valley set aside as winter habitat for dusky Canada geese, the Ankeny Wildlife

Refuge provides the opportunity to get up close and personal with wild birds using two blinds—of course, a pair of binoculars couldn't hurt, either. Unlike the Baskett Slough trails, this refuge is open all year long. Bird-watching peaks during two migrations in April and September, but the lush network of ponds and marshes provides opportunities to spot a variety of birds any time.

From the Rail Trail lot—named after a type of bird, not a guardrail or the like—head south 0.2 mile, then turn right along a 0.6-mile boardwalk through a boggy maple forest. About halfway out, a spur trail to the right leads to a blind over Wood Duck Pond. At the end of the boardwalk, and if it's dry, go right for 0.9 mile to the sound of bullfrogs and redwing blackbirds to a junction, returning 0.7 mile through the geese's wintering ground along an old road. There are other side trails to explore, including a mile-long dike trail and a half-mile Forest Trail loop, and across Wintel Road is another bird blind to spot pintails and egrets.

User Groups: Hikers only. Dogs and bicycles not allowed. No wheelchair facilities.

Permits: Permits are not required. Parking and access are free.

Maps: A map is available at the trailhead. For a topographic map, ask the USGS for Sidney.

Directions: From Salem, drive 10 miles south on I-5 to Talbot Exit 242, and go west on Talbot Road for 0.4 mile, turning right on Jorgensen Road for 0.6 mile, and then left on Wintel Road for 1.2 miles. Turn left at a sign for "Rail Trail Boardwalk."

Contact: U.S. Fish and Wildlife Service, Ankeny National Wildlife Refuge, 2301 Wintel Road, Jefferson, OR, 97352, 503/588-2701.

15 SHELLBURG FALLS
4.8 mi/2.0 hr   👫1 ⚠7

east of Salem in the Santiam State Forest

Map 8.2, page 432.

Located just outside the more famous Silver Falls State Park, this jewel of a waterfall is practically unknown. Amid stalks of foxglove and sword ferns, the Shellburg Falls Trail begins on a 1.3-mile road that crosses private land, so stay on the path. You'll cross meadows and woods before crossing Shellburg Creek on a concrete bridge over Lower Shellburg Falls, a 40-foot plummet into a green canyon. Climb the steps to the left and you'll reach Shellburg Falls in about 0.2 mile and pass behind the 100-foot cascades; there's even a bench to sit on. Continue on, switchbacking up a staircase and crossing the creek on the remaining 0.6 mile of this trail, which ends at an upper trailhead and campground. Follow the gravel road to the right, staying to the right at another junction, for a 2.3-mile descent on the August Mountain Trail to the car. Where the road turns sharply right, a 0.2-mile side trail leads to a scramble down to a viewpoint of Stassel Falls and a 200-foot deep canyon. But go no farther: This waterfall is on private land.

User Groups: Hikers and dogs only. No wheelchair facilities.

Permits: Permits are not required. Parking and access are free.

Maps: For a topographic map, ask the USGS for Lyons.

Directions: From I-5, take Salem Exit 253 and go east on OR 22. After 22.4 miles, turn left at the flashing yellow light in Mehama and follow the Fern Ridge Road 1.3 miles and take a sharp turn uphill to a locked yellow gate. The trail begins here.

Contact: Santiam State Forest, 22965 North Fork Road SE, Lyons, OR, 97358, 503/859-4344.

16 MCDONALD RESEARCH FOREST
4.8 mi/2.0 hr   👫1 ⚠7

north of Corvallis off Highway 99 West

Map 8.2, page 432   **BEST (**

There's plenty learn in this 11-square-mile research forest managed by Oregon State University. Six self-guiding nature walks overlap and mingle between the Peavy Arboretum and the McDonald Forest, between a lake and an old-growth forest. There's even a viewpoint of the Willamette Valley. If you need a place to take the kids for an educational adventure, this is it.

From the trailhead for the Forest Discovery Trail, start into the maple and fir forest. To access the popular Section 36 Loop, take the right-hand fork at the first junction, leaving the Forest Discovery Trail; follow this trail about 0.5 mile, crossing a road and passing several other trails until you arrive at the loop. Take a quick detour to the right and get a trail brochure at the Forestry Club Cabin, then head back the way you came. You'll pass through an experimental ponderosa pine forest before coming to a junction with the Powder House Trail after 1.2 miles. Climb 0.4 mile to the left to reach the 1,285-foot viewpoint across the Willamette Valley to Mount Hood, Mount Jefferson, and the Three Sisters. The trail descends 1.1 mile from here, crossing three gravel roads, passing a dynamite cap storage shed, and finally entering a forest of true old-growth Douglas fir. In another mile you'll reach Cronemiller Lake—the site of an annual logrolling competition. At the far end of the lake, watch for signs for the Forestry Club Cabin to complete the loop.

User Groups: Hikers, dogs, mountain bikes, and horses. (Section 36 Loop/Powder House Trail is for hikers only.) No wheelchair facilities.

Permits: Permits are not required. Parking and access are free.

Maps: A trail map is available at local outdoors vendors like the Oregon State University bookstore in Corvallis. A brochure is available at the Peavy Arboretum offices in the forest, or online at www.cof.orst.edu. For a topographic map, ask the USGS for Airlie South.

Directions: From Corvallis, drive north on Highway 99W for five miles and turn left onto Arboretum Road to the park entrance. Park at the day-use parking area.

Contact: Oregon State University, College of Forestry, 8692 Peavy Arboretum Road, Corvallis, OR, 97330, 541/737-2004, www.cof.orts.edu.

⓱ FINLEY WILDLIFE REFUGE
6.1 mi/3.0 hr   🏃1 ⛰6

south of Corvallis

Map 8.2, page 432

This eight-square-mile former farm was purchased in the 1960s by the U.S. Fish and Wildlife Service to protect wintering grounds for the dusky Canada goose. With its mix of ponds, meadow, and woods, it is both bird and hiker friendly. If you come, why not try all the trails? They're easy, and you could very well see some extraordinary birds. The 1.2-mile Woodpecker Loop crosses a field of wild roses and blackberry to an observation deck with views to Mount Jefferson and the Three Sisters. The next loop starts out from the Finley Refuge Road, passing a lake teeming with birds in season. Follow Mill Hill Loop signs, heading in 0.3 mile to a gravel road, turning right for another 0.2 mile to a junction at a curve. To the right, a 1.9-mile trail circles Mill Hill and follows Gray Creek. At the end of the loop, another loop continues on, though it is closed November 1 to April 30 to protect geese. If it's open, go right 0.4 mile to another junction, then take a right on a 1.2-mile trail past Beaver Pond (which has no beavers, unfortunately) and a cattail swamp back to the road. Turn right for 0.3 mile, then go left on a trail for another 0.3 mile, and finally follow the road back to your car for another 0.3 mile. As long as you're here, head up the road to see the 1855 Fiechter House, a Greek Revival clapboard farmhouse paid for with California Gold Rush money.

User Groups: Hikers only. No wheelchair facilities.

Permits: Permits are not required. Parking and access are free.

Maps: For a topographic map, ask the USGS for Greenberry.

Directions: Drive south of Corvallis 10 miles on Highway 99W to a Finley Refuge sign at milepost 93. Turn west on gravel Bellfountain Road for 0.7 mile, then left on Finley Refuge Road for 1.5 miles to the Fiechter House. Two trailheads are along Finley Refuge Road.

Contact: U.S. Fish and Wildlife Service, Finley National Wildlife Refuge, 26208 Finley Refuge Road, Corvallis, OR, 97333, 541/757-7236.

18 MCDOWELL CREEK FALLS
1.7 mi/0.75 hr   🥾1 ⛰7

east of Lebanon

Map 8.2, page 432   BEST (

Hidden back in the Cascade foothills, this lovely glen with three waterfalls makes a perfect stop on a journey into the Cascades, or a destination unto itself, especially when the mountains are snowed in for winter. This tour of the Cascade foothills makes an ideal hike for kids: It's easy, short, and fascinating.

From the lower lot, this loop traverses up McDowell Creek amid bunches of sword fern, white trilliums, bleeding hearts, and the yellow blooms of Oregon grape, the state flower. In 0.2 mile you'll spot three-tiered Royal Terrace Falls; at 119 feet, it's the largest of the cascades here. Another 0.6 mile crosses under the highway and passes the 20-foot cascade into Crystal Pool before arriving at 39-foot Majestic Falls, a great place to pick your way across the stones to the base of the falls—but beware of wet, slippery rocks. A stairway takes you to a viewpoint at the top, and another stairway to the upper lot. To make a loop of this hike, head to the lot, then follow the road down about 200 yards and take the left-hand paved road 0.2 mile. Opposite the park entrance sign, keep an eye out for the path that descends 0.4 mile back to Royal Terrace Falls.

User Groups: Hikers and dogs. No wheelchair facilities.

Permits: Permits are not required. Parking and access are free.

Maps: For a topographic map, ask the USGS for Sweet Home.

Directions: From Lebanon, go 4.5 miles east on U.S. 20, turning left on Fairview Road for two miles. Watch for signs to McDowell Creek Park, and turn on McDowell Creek Road, going seven miles to the park.

Contact: Linn County Parks and Recreation, 3010 SW Ferry St., Albany, OR, 97322, 541/967-3917.

19 CASCADIA STATE PARK
2.6 mi/1.0 hr   🥾1 ⛰7

east of Sweet Home on the South Santiam River

Map 8.2, page 432

Say you're traveling from the Willamette Valley to the Santiam Pass. Consider how long this route, now Highway 20, has been used by people doing exactly as you have done, from the Native Americans to early pioneers. All of them stopped here, at what is now Cascadia State Park. Excavations have shown that nearby Cascadia Cave (on private land) was used by Native Americans. The highway was once a for-profit wagon road between Albany and Sisters. In 1895, George and Jennie Geisendorfer bought this land, with its natural mineral springs and waterfalls, and built a resort with a hotel, store, cabins, a bathhouse, and campgrounds. When they sold it to the state, it became Cascadia State Park. Though the buildings are gone, the mineral springs and waterfall remains, and several easy loops explore Soda Creek, the springs, and the shore of the South Santiam.

For the first easy hike to see the springs, take the Soda Spring Trail from the parking lot down a paved path 100 yards to an open pipe where you'll see the bubbling iron-laden orange water. Following the paved path and keeping right at all junctions for 200 yards will bring you to the gravel beach on the river. From the restroom in the East Picnic Area, an old road becomes a bark-dust trail, making an easy 0.6 mile-loop. To hike to Lower Soda Falls, head toward the road to the East Picnic Area. The broad trail heads off to the left, following Soda Creek 0.7 mile to the falls.

User Groups: Hikers and dogs. Paved paths are wheelchair accessible.

Permits: Permits are not required. Parking and access are free.

Maps: For a free park brochure, call Oregon Parks and Recreation, 800/551-6949, or download a free map at www.oregonstateparks.org. For a topographic map, ask the USGS for Cascadia.

Directions: From Sweet Home go east on U.S. 20 for 14 miles. At a State Park sign between mileposts 41 and 42, turn left over a bridge and follow the road to a parking lot on the left.

Contact: Oregon Parks and Recreation Department, 1115 Commercial Street NE, Salem, OR, 97301, 800/551-6949, www.oregonstateparks.org.

20 SHOTGUN CREEK PARK
3.4 mi/1.5 hr ♿1 ⛰6

north of Springfield in Shotgun Creek Recreation Site

Map 8.2, page 432

Legend has it that sometime in the 1800s, a young man left his shotgun here. He came back to get it, and named the creek Shotgun. A simple story, unlike the one involving the two engineers and the Hellsgate Construction company, who took two years to build this park—and even then they ran out of the resources to complete it. Nonetheless, the park offers a couple of easy hikes and a great place to swim under moss-draped bigleaf maples. It's usually open from early June through the end of September.

From the trailhead parking area, head toward the creek on a paved path, passing a picnic shelter. Turn onto the loop following Shotgun Creek upstream. Eventually, the trail heads up into second-growth woods, and

begins to loop back. At the 2.1-mile mark, a right turn leads 0.3 mile back to the lot, but you can continue on for a longer loop. If you do, another 0.6 mile brings you to a junction. The trail to the left climbs 1.2 miles up Drury Ridge, and going right brings you back 0.7 mile to the creek and picnic grounds.

User Groups: Hikers and dogs. Paved paths are wheelchair accessible.

Permits: Permits are not required. From June through September, a $3 parking fee is collected at the entrance.

Maps: For a topographic map, ask the USGS for Marcola.

Directions: From Springfield, take Exit 194 off I-5 and drive four miles east on I-105 to the 42nd Street/Marcola exit. Turn left on 42nd Street for 0.6 mile to a junction, turning right on Marcola Road for 13.3 miles. Three miles past the town of Marcola, turn left at a "Shotgun Creek" sign onto Shotgun Creek Road, going 1.6 miles to the park entrance on the right.

Contact: Bureau of Land Management Eugene Office, 2890 Chad Drive, Eugene, OR, 97440, 541/683-6600.

21 RUTH BASCOM RIVERSIDE PATH SYSTEM
1.0-14.0 mi/0.5-7.0 hr ♿2 ⛰6

in Eugene on the Willamette River

Map 8.2, page 432

This perfectly paved, 14-mile trail system girdles the Willamette River in the city of Eugene. It provides access to many parks—including Alton Baker, Skinner Butte, Maurie Jacobs, and Rasor Parks—and passes the Owen Rose Gardens, the Delta Ponds, and Pre's Trail, where Oregon legend Steve Prefontaine used to practice running. The trail system follows the river up and downstream in the shade of cottonwood trees, where beavers and water birds are active. With so many access points, it's hard to say where to begin, but Alton Baker Park, where Pre's Trail is located, is as good a place as any.

From Alton Baker Park, head to the North Bank path at the DeFazio Pedestrian/Bike Bridge, going right downstream about 1.75 miles to the Greenway Pedestrian/Bike Bridge and crossing the river. On the other side, turn left on the South Bank Trail for a tour of Eugene's wonderful Maurie Jacobs and Skinner Butte Parks, a continuous greenway that features a community garden, the Owen Rose Garden with its 150-year old cherry tree, the towering Skinner Butte, and a bevy of playgrounds and picnic areas. Follow this path back 1.75 miles to the DeFazio Bridge. A longer loop is possible by continuing north past the Greenway Bridge 1.9 miles to the Owosso Bike Bridge, then crossing the river and going left two miles on the West Bank Trail to join the South Bank Trail.

User Groups: Hikers, dogs, and bicycles. Paved portions of the park are wheelchair accessible.

Permits: Permits are not required. Parking and access are free.

Maps: A downloadable map is available from the City of Eugene Willakenzie Parks website, www.eugene-or.gov/portal/server.pt. For a topographic map, ask the USGS for Eugene East.

Directions: From downtown Eugene, drive north over Ferry Street Bridge and turn right on Centennial Boulevard. Turn right at the first light and go a short distance to the large lot at Alton Baker Park.

Contact: City of Eugene Parks, 99 West 10th Avenue, Suite 340, Eugene, OR, 97401, 541/682-5333.

22 MOUNT PISGAH
3.0 mi/1.5 hr   👫1 ⛰7

southeast of Eugene in the Howard Buford Recreation Area

Map 8.2, page 432

From the grassy peak of Mount Pisgah, named by pioneers for the biblical hill from which Moses viewed the Promised Land, you'll get your own grand view. At the peak you'll find a bronze sighting pedestal for the nearby peaks, a memorial to Jed, the son of *One Flew Over the Cuckoo's Nest* author Ken Kesey, who lived in nearby Pleasant Hill. Numbered trails circle this 1,516-foot mound near Eugene and Springfield, and an arboretum at its base lies along the Coast Fork of the Willamette River.

From the visitors center, start uphill at a gate on Trail #1. Without veering from this path, you will arrive at the peak in 1.5 miles. Trails go off in all directions and the possibilities for exploration are numerous.

User Groups: Hikers and dogs. No bikes or horses are allowed.

Permits: Permits are not required. From May through October, a $2 parking fee is collected at the entrance.

Maps: For a free map, contact Lane County Parks, 90064 Coburg Road, Eugene, OR, 97408, 541/682-2000. For a topographic map, ask the USGS for Springfield.

Directions: From the southern end of Eugene, take I-5 south to Exit 189 (30th Street). At the second light, turn left over the freeway, turn left at the next stop sign, and turn right onto Franklin Road. In 0.25 mile, turn left onto Seavey Loop Road. Drive 1.5 miles and turn right at the park entrance. Parking is at the end of the road at the arboretum entrance.

Contact: Lane County Parks, 90064 Coburg Road, Eugene, OR, 97408, 541/682-2000.

23 SPENCER BUTTE
2.0 mi/1.0 hr   👫1 ⛰7

south of Eugene in Spencer Butte Park

Map 8.2, page 432

Looming above Eugene is the imposing Spencer Butte, a 2,054-foot knob thick with Douglas fir, ferns, poison oak, and, if one is to believe the signs, rattlesnakes. Nevertheless, there is no better hike in Eugene. A fairly easy hike ascends and descends the rocky knob, but more challenging courses can be arranged

peak of Spencer Butte in Eugene

off the Ridgeline Trail (see *Ridgeline National Recreation Trail,* next listing) to lengthen your stay on this high, forested ridge. This is the classic hike for Eugenians looking for the perfect sunset and moonrise, with views to the Three Sisters and Fern Ridge Reservoir.

From the main lot, head up the right-hand trail, which begins at a signboard and gently climbs for 0.5 mile to the first junction, a side trail leading to the Ridgeline Trail. Continue to the left; the trail gradually grows steeper as it rises from the woods onto the rocky crest. Watch out for poison oak here! A summit benchmark handily marks the top. For a more challenging hike, start at a gravel lot on Willamette Street just beyond 52nd Street on the left; from here, follow the Ridgeline Trail 1.2 miles to the first junction on the right. Go right 0.5 mile, then right again for the last 0.5-mile climb.

User Groups: Hikers and dogs only, though bikes are allowed on the Ridgeline Trail. No horses.

Permits: Permits are not required. Parking and access are free.

Maps: For a topographic map, ask the USGS for Creswell.

Directions: From downtown Eugene, drive five miles south on Willamette Street, going uphill much of the way, and turn left into the parking lot for Spencer Butte Park.

Contact: City of Eugene Parks, 99 West 10th Avenue, Suite 340, Eugene, OR, 97401, 541/682-5333.

24 RIDGELINE NATIONAL RECREATION TRAIL

6.6 mi one-way/3.5 hr   🏃1 ⛰7

in the South Hills of Eugene

Map 8.2, page 432

Designated a National Recreation Trail in 2006, Eugene's Ridgeline Trail is a pleasant stroll through patches of Douglas fir woods and out into open grasslands overlooking the city in the valley below. Along the trail, numerous access points offer a variety of options for short or long hikes. At one end lies 1,233-foot Mount Baldy, an easy climb to a view over the city. In the middle, the trail connects to a summit of Spencer Butte (see *Spencer Butte,* previous listing).

For an easy excursion in Dillard Skyline Park to Mount Baldy, start from the Dillard North Trailhead off Dillard Road. Climb 0.5 mile to a sweet view of the Willamette Valley. The trail accesses other trailheads and points from along the way. The Fox Hollow Trailhead lies at 0.8 mile, where the path heads to the right along the road before re-entering the forest. At the 1.2-mile mark, after a set of stairs, a left-hand spur connects to the Spencer Butte climbing trail. In another 1.2 miles, the trail crosses Willamette Street and continues 1.5 miles to the 52nd Avenue Trailhead.

User Groups: Hikers and dogs. Bikes on designated paths only.

Permits: Permits are not required. Parking and access are free.

© SEAN PATRICK HILL

Maps: A downloadable map is available from the City of Eugene Willakenzie Parks website, www.eugene-or.gov/portal/server.pt. For a topographic map, ask the USGS for Creswell.

Directions: From downtown Eugene, drive south on Pearl Street (it becomes Amazon Parkway) to 30th Street and go right on Hilyard Street. At the next light, go left on Amazon Drive East, driving 1.2 miles and turning left on Dillard Road for 1.5 miles to a hiker symbol on the left. To access the western trailhead from downtown Eugene, drive south on Willamette Street to Crest Drive. Go west on Crest Drive 0.6 mile, then left on Storey Boulevard for 0.3 mile, then straight onto Crest Drive for 0.2 mile. Continue onto Blanton Road for 0.5 mile to West 40th Avenue and the trailhead.

Contact: City of Eugene Parks, 99 West 10th Avenue, Suite 340, Eugene, OR, 97401, 541/682-5333.

25 ELIJAH BRISTOW STATE PARK

1.0-10.0 mi/0.5-5.0 hr

southeast of Eugene on Highway 58

Map 8.2, page 432

This state park on the Middle Fork Willamette River is named for Lane County's first settler, Elijah Bristow, who was born in Virginia in 1788 and took up residence in Oregon in 1846 in nearby Pleasant Hill. Here you can hike along a channel lake or slosh your way to Dexter Dam. This park comprises a series of wetlands and so can be quite marshy in winter, but it's nothing a good pair of big boots can't handle. Trekking here, you can see the rare Oregon ash tree (as well as western hemlock, red cedar, Douglas fir, cottonwoods, white oak, and bigleaf maple) and you may even get lucky and spot the threatened Western pond turtle.

For an easy one-mile loop, park on the left before the second bridge about 0.6 mile in from the highway. Follow the Turtle Trail around an ancient channel of the river, keeping right at all junctions. If this gets you warmed up for more, there are plenty of loops and longer hikes available throughout the park, including the 1.5-mile Heron Trail, the two-mile Elk Trail, and the five-mile River Trail.

User Groups: Hikers, dogs, bikes, and horses. No wheelchair facilities.

Permits: Permits are not required. Parking and access are free.

Maps: For a free park brochure, call Oregon Parks and Recreation, 800/551-6949, or download a free map at www.oregonstateparks.org. For a topographic map, ask the USGS for Lowell.

Directions: From Eugene, drive seven miles east on Highway 58 and turn left into the park entrance.

Contact: Oregon Parks and Recreation Department, 1115 Commercial Street NE, Salem, OR, 97301, 800/551-6949, www.oregonstateparks.org.

THE COLUMBIA RIVER GORGE AND MOUNT HOOD

© SEAN PATRICK HILL

BEST HIKES

❰ Hikes for Kids
Latourell Falls, **page 458.**
Timothy Lake, **page 498.**

❰ Hikes for Views
Zigzag Canyon and Paradise Park, **page 487.**
Jefferson Park, **page 512.**

❰ Hikes Through Old-Growth Forests
Opal Creek, **page 505.**

❰ Short Backpacking Trips
Eagle Creek, **page 469.**
Mazama Trail to Cairn Basin, **page 481.**

❰ Hikes for Waterfalls
Wahkeena Falls Loop, **page 459.**

❰ Wheelchair-Accessible Trails
Mosier Twin Tunnels, **page 474.**
Timothy Lake, **page 498.**

At 11,249, feet Mount Hood is the tallest
mountain in Oregon and towers over the city of Portland. Circled by the
Timberline Trail — built by the Civilian Conservation Corps in the 1930s —
the mountain provides easy access to some of the best alpine country in
the state. Wildflower-covered meadows, tumbling creeks, massive glaciers,
and a series of stone huts make for exciting hiking. It's as if the whole area
rises up to meet the mountain, and all trails lead to Hood, including the
Pacific Crest Trail, which skirts just behind the famous Timberline Lodge
and spans the Columbia River Gorge and the entire Cascade Range.

Then there is the massive Columbia River, which pounded its way
through the Cascade Range in a series of prehistoric floods, the grand-
est canyon by far. What the deluges left behind is not one gorge, but
many; the Oregon side of the Columbia is awash with side gorges,
waterfalls, and salmon-filled creeks extending deep into the mountains. Because of the sheer walls here, some of the most challenging

climbs in Oregon begin from the shores of the Columbia, including the prominent Mount Defiance, a nearly 5,000-foot ascent with stunning views from the Gorge to the Cascades.

Looming above the Gorge, Mount Hood broods with its glacier-clad slopes. But it's not only the mountain that dominates here; the surrounding area is just as stunning. The Sandy, Hood, and Salmon Rivers flow close by, carving out their own canyons. And ridge upon ridge of other glacier-carved mountains provide spectacular vistas and challenging hiking. With a number of wilderness areas in the area, you'll find some pristine outback lands in northwestern Oregon. Lake upon lake dots the basins, where huckleberries bloom on the shores and deer and elk come down to drink.

With the proximity of these mountains and gorges to a major urban area, it's not hard to see why people flock to Oregon to live, work, and play.

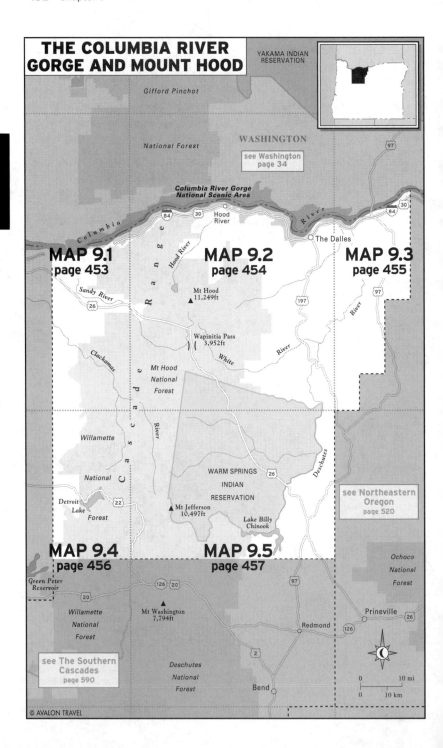

THE COLUMBIA RIVER GORGE AND MOUNT HOOD

YAKAMA INDIAN RESERVATION

Gifford Pinchot

National Forest

WASHINGTON

see Washington page 34

Columbia River Gorge National Scenic Area

Columbia

Hood River

The Dalles

MAP 9.1
page 453

MAP 9.2
page 454

MAP 9.3
page 455

Sandy River

▲ Mt Hood 11,249ft

Wapinitia Pass 3,952ft

White River

Mt Hood National Forest

Clackamas

Willamette

National

Cascade River

WARM SPRINGS

INDIAN

RESERVATION

see Northeastern Oregon page 520

Detroit Lake

Forest

▲ Mt Jefferson 10,497ft

Lake Billy Chinook

Deschutes

MAP 9.4
page 456

MAP 9.5
page 457

Ochoco National Forest

Green Peter Reservoir

Willamette

National

Forest

▲ Mt Washington 7,794ft

Prineville

Redmond

see The Southern Cascades page 590

Deschutes

National

Forest

Bend

0   10 mi
0   10 km

© AVALON TRAVEL

Map 9.1

Hikes 1-15
Pages 458-466

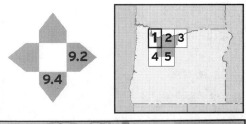

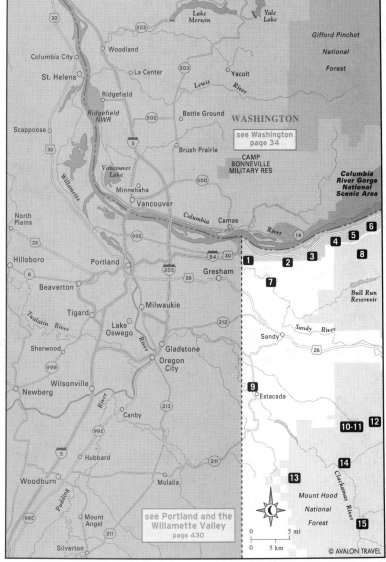

Map 9.2

Hikes 16-68
Pages 467-498

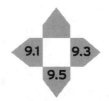

9.1 9.3
9.5

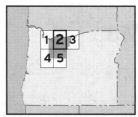

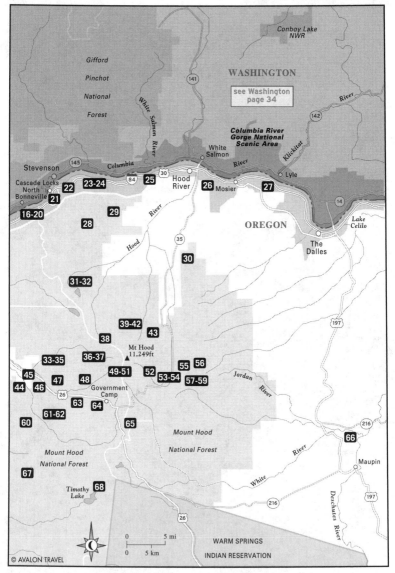

Conboy Lake NWR

Gifford

Pinchot

National

Forest

WASHINGTON

see Washington
page 34

141

White Salmon River

River

142

Columbia River
Gorge National
Scenic Area

Klickitat

Columbia

White
Salmon

River

Lyle

Stevenson 145 84 30 Hood
River

26 Mosier

27

14

Cascade Locks 22 23-24 25
North
Bonneville 21

16-20 28 29

35

River

OREGON

Lake
Celilo

Hood

The
Dalles

30

197

31-32

39-42 43

38 Mt Hood
11,249ft

33-35 36-37 55 56
49-51 52 57-59
45 53-54 Jordan River
44 46 47 48
Government 26 63 Camp
64

60 61-62 65 216

Mount Hood 66

National Forest Maupin

River 197

Mount Hood

67 National Forest White Deschutes River

Timothy 68
Lake

216

26

WARM SPRINGS

0   5 mi
0   5 km

INDIAN RESERVATION

© AVALON TRAVEL

Map 9.3

Hike 69
Page 499

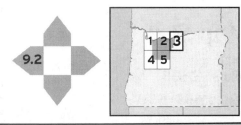

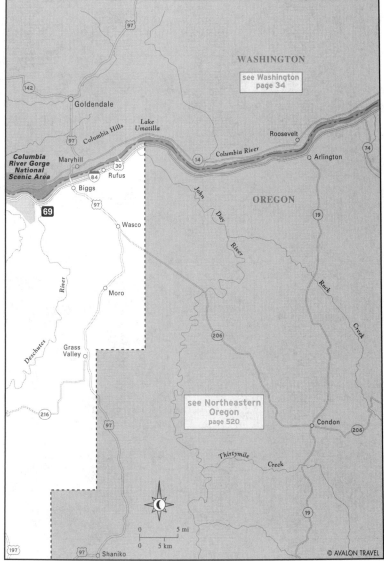

Map 9.4

Hikes 70-86
Pages 499-508

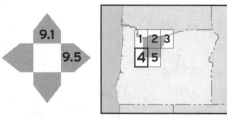

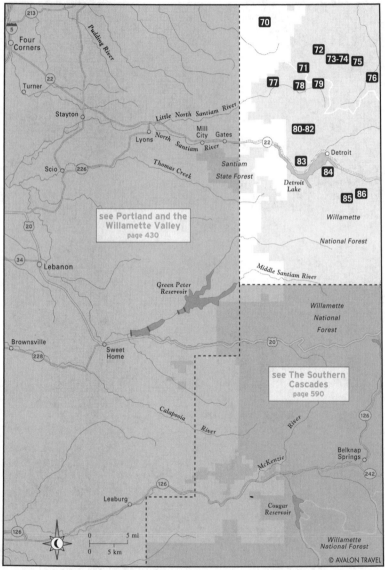

Map 9.5

Hikes 87-98
Pages 509-515

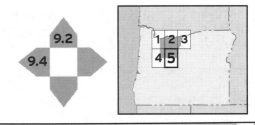

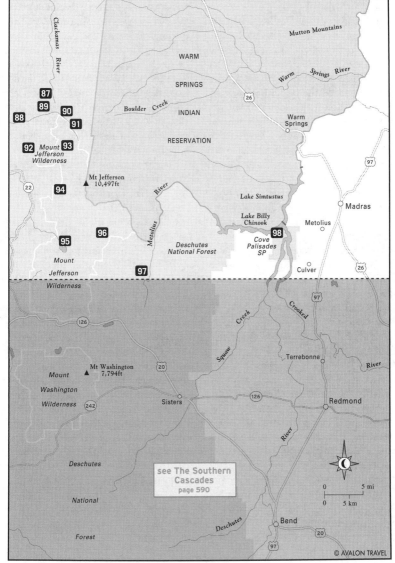

1 LEWIS AND CLARK NATURE TRAIL

4.0 mi/2.0 hr 🏃🏃₁ ⛰₆

in the Columbia Gorge in Lewis and Clark State Park

Map 9.1, page 453

In 1805, Lewis and Clark, nearly to their exploration's goal of the Pacific Ocean and the mouth of the Columbia River, arrived at the banks of Sandy River. They tried to cross it and found themselves sinking, and thus named it the Quicksand River. The name didn't stick, and neither did they—they eventually made it to the Oregon coast and sighted the destination President Jefferson had sent them to. Today you can explore this boundary area between the Cascade Mountains and the Willamette Valley on an easy nature trail that tours white oak, Oregon crabapple, and bigleaf maple woods dotted with flowers like Oregon grape root. A second trail leads to Broughton's Bluff, a popular climbing area, but it's a rocky trail best done on dry days.

The Lewis and Clark Nature Trail begins in the main entrance area. The unnamed, unmaintained Broughton's Bluff climber's trailhead is south from the lot on a gravel path. It switchbacks up to the base of the cliffs.

User Groups: Hikers and dogs. No horses or mountain bikes allowed. No wheelchair facilities.

Permits: Permits are not required. Parking and access are free.

Maps: You can purchase a Trails of the Columbia Gorge Map from Geo-Graphics. For a topographic map, ask the USGS for Camas.

Directions: From Portland, drive east on I-84 to Exit 18 and follow signs less than 0.1 mile to Lewis and Clark State Park.

Contact: Oregon Parks and Recreation Department, 1115 Commercial Street NE, Salem, OR, 97301, 800/551-6949, www.oregonstateparks.org.

2 LATOURELL FALLS

2.3 mi/1.0 hr 🏃🏃₁ ⛰₈

east of Gresham in the Columbia River Gorge

Map 9.1, page 453 **BEST (**

For an introduction to the Columbia Gorge, look no further than Guy W. Talbot State Park, a summer estate for the Talbot family until it was donated to the state. What the state—and by extension, you—got was two waterfalls in a beautiful side canyon and a wonderfully green trail along a splashing creek. Of all the waterfalls in the Gorge, this one is closest to Portland and hence the most accessible. And the drive to get there follows the 1922 Columbia River Highway, a historic road that twists and curves along the Columbia. Not to mention it's one of the easiest, and most level hikes of the bunch—bring the whole family.

From the parking area, take the 0.2-mile paved path down for a quick look at 250-foot Latourell Falls, dropping over lichen-encrusted lava cliffs, then go back to the lot and head uphill on the Latourell Falls Trail to the left. This trail climbs 0.3 mile to a viewpoint over the lower falls and continues steadily and easily 0.5 mile to the twisting 100-foot Upper Latourell Falls and a creek crossing. From here, the path follows the opposite shore 0.5 mile, passing a dizzying overlook of the lower falls that is not for the squeamish, and then switchbacks down one final mile to the picnic area of Guy Talbot Park, circling back to the parking area.

User Groups: Hikers and dogs. No horses or mountain bikes allowed. There is a short wheelchair-accessible path to the lower falls.

Permits: Permits are not required. Parking and access are free.

Maps: You can purchase a Trails of the Columbia Gorge Map from Geo-Graphics. For a topographic map, ask the USGS for Bridal Veil.

Directions: From Portland, drive I-84 east to Exit 28 and turn right on the Columbia River Highway, driving 2.8 miles to a lot on the left.

Contact: Oregon Parks and Recreation Department, 1115 Commercial Street NE, Salem, OR, 97301, 800/551-6949, www.oregonstateparks.org.

❸ ANGELS REST
4.4 mi/2.5 hr

east of Gresham in the Columbia River Gorge

Map 9.1, page 453

If there's one thing the Columbia Gorge is famous for it's wind. Just driving into the Gorge on a blustery day can be an exercise in wheel-gripping anxiety. Trees, though, have a way of deadening that wind, but not so on the burned slopes leading to the Angels Rest, a magnificent view over the Gorge and a spot that truly buffets with wind. On the hardest-blowing days, you can stand on this lava tongue and lean into the wind. Believe me, it will hold you.

From the parking area, climb on the Angels Rest Trail 0.6 mile on the Bridal Veil Trail to Coopey Falls, hidden somewhat in the underbrush. From there the trail climbs 1.6 miles to the edge of the Angels Rest; follow the cliff out for stunning views. From here, return the way you came for an easy 4.4-mile round-trip.

User Groups: Hikers and dogs. No horses or mountain bikes allowed. No wheelchair facilities.

Permits: Permits are not required. Parking and access are free.

Maps: You can purchase a Trails of the Columbia Gorge Map from Geo-Graphics. For a topographic map, ask the USGS for Bridal Veil.

Directions: From Portland, drive I-84 east to Exit 28 and park a few hundred yards past the exit at the junction with the Columbia River Highway.

Contact: Oregon Parks and Recreation Department, 1115 Commercial Street NE, Salem, OR, 97301, 800/551-6949, www.oregonstateparks.org.

❹ WAHKEENA FALLS LOOP
5.0 mi/2.5 hr

east of Gresham in the Columbia River Gorge

Map 9.1, page 453   **BEST (**

The Columbia Gorge offers an amazing network of trails off the beaten path—though it is true that some of those paths are well beaten, particularly on weekends. This trail is one of them, but don't let that dismay you. With fortitude, and an early start, you can beat the crowds and visit five waterfalls, a massive spring, and deep woods with towering Douglas firs and tiny calypso orchids. Wahkeena Creek is almost a continual waterfall itself, and Multnomah Creek hosts not only the famous Multnomah Falls, but two others besides that higher up on the trail.

From the lot, head up the paved Wahkeena Trail 0.2 mile to a stone bridge beneath 242-foot Wahkeena Falls, a triple cascade in a lava slot that comes crashing down with a vengeance. The next 1.4 miles climbs the canyon, passing the base of Fairy Falls and a left-hand spur trail, the 419, continuing to a junction with Trail 415 to Angels Rest. For a short side trip, head right on the 415 trail a short distance to see the massive spring that gives birth to Wahkeena Creek, then head back to the junction. Continue uphill on the Wahkeena Trail 0.3 mile to a four-way junction and stay straight on the Wahkeena Trail. In 0.9 mile, the trail reaches a junction at Multnomah Creek; go left along the creek 1.8 miles to the base of Multnomah Falls and the historic lodge. From here, go to the left on the Gorge Trail paralleling the Columbia Highway for the 0.8-mile return to your car.

User Groups: Hikers and dogs. No horses or mountain bikes allowed. The steep but paved path to Wahkeena Falls provides wheelchair access.

Permits: Permits are not required. Parking and access are free.

Maps: You can purchase a Trails of the Columbia Gorge Map from Geo-Graphics. For a topographic map, ask the USGS for Bridal Veil.

Directions: From Portland, drive I-84 east to Exit 28 and turn left on the Columbia River Highway for 2.6 miles to the Wahkeena Falls Picnic Ground pullout on the left.

Contact: Columbia Gorge National Scenic Area, 902 Wasco Avenue, Suite 200, Hood River, OR, 97031, 541/308-1700.

5 MULTNOMAH FALLS
2.2–3.6 mi/1.0–2.0 hr   🥾1 ⛰8

east of Gresham in the Columbia River Gorge

Map 9.1, page 453

Most famous of all the falls in Oregon is perhaps Multnomah—it's not only the tallest, at 542 feet, but nothing rivals its unparalleled beauty. The stone bridge just below the first tier is one of the most photographed places in the state. It's also one of the most heavily visited areas in the state; it's not uncommon to find hundreds of people here at a time, many of them making the steep switchback climb to the top of the falls and the observation deck at the water's edge. To escape the crowds, all you need to do is go higher and farther than that for even more waterfalls along the creek.

From the lot, duck under the highway and train tracks through a tunnel and under a bridge to the Multnomah Lodge. Continue past the viewpoint up the paved Multnomah Falls Trail to the stone bridge at the base of the upper falls. By now you've gone 0.5 mile. To continue to the top, follow the paved path up a long series of switchbacks 0.6 mile to a junction; head right and down along the creek on this paved path to the viewpoint high above the lodge. To add another 1.4 miles and two waterfalls to your hike, continue upstream to the junction with the Wahkeena Trail (see *Wahkeena Falls Loop* listing in this chapter).

User Groups: Hikers and dogs. No horses or mountain bikes allowed. The paved path to the stone bridge provides wheelchair access.

the bridge at Multnomah Falls

© SEAN PATRICK HILL

Permits: Permits are not required. Parking and access are free.

Maps: You can purchase a Trails of the Columbia Gorge Map from Geo-Graphics. For a topographic map, ask the USGS for Bridal Veil.

Directions: From Portland, drive I-84 east to the Multnomah Falls turnoff at Exit 31 into the lot.

Contact: Columbia Gorge National Scenic Area, 902 Wasco Avenue, Suite 200, Hood River, OR, 97031, 541/308-1700.

6 ONEONTA GORGE AND HORSETAIL FALLS
2.7 mi/1.5 hr   🥾2 ⛰9

east of Gresham in the Columbia River Gorge

Map 9.1, page 453

The Columbia Gorge, as impressive as it is, isn't the only gorge around here. Take the Oneonta Gorge, for instance, a narrow slot sliced into sheer volcanic rock extending back more than a mile into the cliffs. On a summer day, with the right clothes and footwear, it's possible to wade back into the gorge to a secret waterfall. The more common way to see this gorge is to climb up and around it, passing numerous falls and crossing a crazily high bridge on your way to a triple waterfall falling on Oneonta Creek.

The hike begins at 176-foot Horsetail Falls, climbing the cliffs to the Gorge Trail. Turn right on the Gorge Trail and continue up to 80-foot Ponytail Falls, which the trail ducks behind, and a viewpoint over the Columbia River. The trail follows the creek and switchbacks down to a steel bridge over two falls, the lower one careening into the Oneonta Gorge. All this takes place in the first 1.3 miles.

At a junction on the far side of the bridge, go left on the Oneonta Trail, climbing steadily up 0.9 mile to 120-foot Triple Falls, pouring over a basalt lip. Just beyond lies a bridge and an area to stop and explore. To make a loop of the trail, head back down to the junction by the high bridge, this time going left to stay on the Oneonta Trail. In the next 0.9 mile, the trail descends to another viewpoint, then gradually returns to the highway. Keep right at a junction with the Gorge Trail, going 0.2 mile back to the highway, then following the highway east toward the mouth of the Oneonta Gorge—a designated botanical area—and a partially renovated tunnel through which the old highway once passed. The walk along the highway is a short 0.5 mile back to the Horsetail lot.

User Groups: Hikers and dogs. No mountain bikes or horses allowed. No wheelchair facilities.

Permits: Permits are not required. Parking and access are free.

Maps: You can purchase a Trails of the Columbia Gorge Map from Geo-Graphics. For a topographic map, ask the USGS for Multnomah Falls.

Directions: From Portland, drive I-84 east to Exit 35 for Ainsworth Park and follow the Columbia Highway to the right 1.5 miles to the Horsetail Falls Trailhead parking area. **Contact:** Columbia Gorge National Scenic Area, 902 Wasco Avenue, Suite 200, Hood River, OR, 97031, 541/308-1700.

7 OXBOW PARK
3.5 mi/2.0 hr

southeast of Gresham on the Sandy River

Map 9.1, page 453

Just a short ways past the bustle of highways and shopping centers that is Gresham lies this jewel of a park along an oxbow on the Sandy River. There are 1,200 acres of quiet woods, browsing deer, an ancient forest, and cobbled beaches on the river curving around Alder Ridge—all awaiting exploration. Along the way, you'll see anglers, campgrounds, and likely an osprey or two hunting fish in the river. A few stretches of trail may be wiped out when you visit due to winter storms; they don't seriously disrupt these hikes, since the network of trails and a few paved roads gives easy portage around the destruction. On top of that, you'll see firsthand what effect massive rains have on this ever-changing landscape. Kids will love it here, as the trails are easy and fun.

There are so many options for hiking, it's hard to say where to begin. The lot at Area C makes as good a spot as any, so start there and follow the trail out of the lot into the woods toward the river. At a junction, head right 0.5 mile through the woods, staying left at all junctions, until you reach the large lot and group picnic area. From here, you'll be able to see the huge washout the river slope suffered, taking many large trees and a half-mile length of trail with it. Head for the road, crossing it and heading up a gravel road. Go uphill to a junction on the left and head down into the woods for 0.8 mile. At the next junction, go right 0.2 mile, then left 0.2 mile toward the river. At a trail junction near a group camping site, and if the trail is mended, you can follow the river 0.6 mile around the oxbow, passing a stone beach and some impressive washouts (if not, pay attention to your map, adjusting as you go). From the junction marked "M," continue along the river 0.4 mile to the boat ramp. At this point, you'll have to use the road for 0.8 mile along the campsites, heading downstream. When you return to the picnic area "A," you can head back into the woods to return to your car.

User Groups: Hikers and dogs. Horses and mountain bikes on designated trails only. Paved portions of the park are wheelchair accessible.

Permits: Permits are not required. A fee of $4 per car is collected at the entrance. An annual pass is $40.

Maps: A brochure and map is available at the entrance gate or online at www.oregonmetro.gov. For a topographic map, ask the USGS for Sandy.

Directions: From I-205, take Exit 19 and go east on Division Street. Cross Burnside Street in Gresham and continue as the road becomes Oxbow Parkway. After 13 miles turn left at a four-way junction and follow park signs 1.4 miles to the entrance. Continue along the river to the first trail parking area, marked "C," on the left.

Contact: Metro Regional Center, 600 NE Grand Avenue, Portland OR, 97232, 503/797-1700.

8 LARCH MOUNTAIN CRATER
6.0 mi/3.0 hr 🥾3 ⛰8

above Multnomah Falls in the Columbia River Gorge

Map 9.1, page 453

Sherrard Point, at 4,055 feet, has a commanding view of the Columbia River Gorge, several Cascade peaks, and the distant city of Portland. It also looks down into the remnants of its volcanic crater, ground out by glaciers and the headwaters of Multnomah Creek. For a firsthand look at the crater, including its

Sherrard Point from Larch Mountain Crater

© SEAN PATRICK HILL

marshy core where bog orchids thrive, you'll have to climb down and into the heart of this ancient mountain.

From the parking lot, the trail to Sherrard Point begins to the left of a signpost. Follow this obvious paved path to a junction and head right and steeply uphill, finally climbing a row of stairs to the impressive overlook. Then head back down, but this time follow the right-hand junction that heads into a picnic area, then head downhill on the Larch Mountain Trail to the right down a cathedral-like wooded ridge. After 1.5 miles, the trail crosses a dirt road, and in another 0.4 mile connects with a spur trail, Multnomah Creek Way. Take this trail to the right for 0.2 mile, then at a junction with the Multnomah Way Trail, go to the right again, following the young Multnomah Creek into the crater. This 2.5-mile section skirts the boggy meadows with views to Sherrard Point's massive volcanic plug. The trail makes use of an old logging road then joins the Oneonta Trail. Go right up the ridge 0.9 mile, where avalanche lilies bloom in spring right out of the snow. When the trail reaches the Larch Mountain Road, head to the right on the paved road 0.3 mile back to the lot.

User Groups: Hikers, dogs, horses, and mountain bikes. No wheelchair facilities.

Permits: Permits are not required. A federal Northwest Forest Pass is required to park here; the cost is $5 a day or $30 for an annual pass. You can buy a day pass at the trailhead, at ranger stations, or through private vendors.

Maps: You can purchase a Trails of the Columbia Gorge Map from Geo-Graphics. For a topographic map, ask the USGS for Multnomah Falls.

Directions: From Portland, drive I-84 east to the Corbett exit (Exit 22), and drive one mile uphill to Corbett. Turn left on the Columbia River Highway for two miles and fork right on Larch Mountain Road for 12 miles to its end.

Contact: Columbia Gorge National Scenic Area, 902 Wasco Avenue, Suite 200, Hood River, OR, 97031, 541/308-1700.

🄈 MILO MCIVER STATE PARK
6.0 mi/2.0 hr   🏃1 ⛰7

northwest of Estacada off Highway 211

Map 9.1, page 453

There's more to this state park than Frisbee golf, a fish hatchery, and an annual Civil War re-enactment. A woodsy loop trail sets out from the fish hatchery in the southern day-use area and follows a path along the Clackamas River, shared by equestrians. Because this park receives the national average for rainfall, winter is not the best time to go, unless you like hiking in the mud. The Nature Trail continues past views of the Clackamas River to the northern day-use area, connecting to loops with the Maple Ridge Trail and Cedar Knoll Trail.

User Groups: Hikers, dogs, and horses. No mountain bikes allowed. Paved portions of the trail are wheelchair accessible.

Permits: Permits are not required. A $3 day-use fee is collected at the camping entrance, or you can get an annual Oregon Parks and Recreation pass for $25; contact Oregon Parks and Recreation, 800/551-6949.

Maps: For a free park brochure, call Oregon Parks and Recreation, 800/551-6949, or download a free map at www.oregonstateparks.org. For a topographic map, ask the USGS for Estacada.

Directions: From Estacada, drive OR 211 south toward Molalla one mile, following signs to McIver Park and the fish hatchery. The trail heads around the hatchery to the right.

Contact: Oregon Parks and Recreation Department, 1115 Commercial Street NE, Salem, OR, 97301, 800/551-6949, www.oregonstateparks.org.

🄉 OLD BALDY
7.7 mi/4.0 hr   🏃3 ⛰8

east of Estacada in Mount Hood National Forest

Map 9.1, page 453

In 1999, a group of environmental activists barricaded the access road to Old Baldy, protesting the cutting of old-growth trees here. After a standoff with the Forest Service, the timber sale buyers decided to back out, and all is at peace again. Now you can visit Old Baldy along an ancient route predating the Forest Service through groves of noble fir. Though the peak itself, once the site of a fire lookout, is now largely overgrown and viewless, there is a cliff-edge viewpoint along the way with views to Mount Hood and Mount Adams.

From the Baldy Trailhead, go left on the Baldy Trail and follow it 2.9 miles, rounding Githens Mountain. At a crest, near a rock cairn, head to the right 30 yards to the cliff viewpoint. Returning to the trail, continue 0.9 mile to 4,200-foot Old Baldy.

User Groups: Hikers, dogs, horses, and mountain bikes. No wheelchair facilities.

Permits: Permits are not required. Parking and access are free.

Maps: For a map of the Mount Hood National Forest, contact the Mount Hood National Forest Headquarters, 16400 Champion Way, Sandy, OR, 97055, 503/668-1700. For a topographic map, ask the USGS for Wildcat Mountain.

Directions: From I-205 near Oregon City, take Exit 12 and drive east toward Estacada 18 miles. Drive through town and continue 1.6 miles on Highway 224. Just beyond milepost 25, turn left on Surface Road for 1.1 mile and turn right on Squaw Mountain Road. Follow this paved road, which becomes Road 4614, for 14.4 miles. Park on a pullout on the right, and at the end of a short path find the Old Baldy Trailhead.

Contact: Mount Hood National Forest, Clackamas River Ranger District, 595 NW Industrial Way, Estacada, OR, 97023, 503/630-6861.

11 TUMALA MOUNTAIN
4.4 mi/2.5 hr   🥾2 ⛰8

east of Estacada in Mount Hood National Forest

Map 9.1, page 453

Near the headwaters of both the North Fork Clackamas River and the South Fork Eagle Creek, the mountain formerly known as Squaw Mountain rises 4,770 feet above the Salmon-Huckleberry Wilderness. This is the site of an old fire watchtower, of which only an old concrete staircase remains, and the view of Mount Hood and Mount Jefferson is unimpeded, as is the view down to the Tumala Lakes Basin. As of 2001, the Oregon State Legislature called for the removal of the word "Squaw" from all place names, and the Oregon Geographic Names Board has worked to replace that antiquated and derogatory name with the word "Tumala," a Chinook word meaning "tomorrow" or "afterlife."

From the Fanton Trailhead, located in an old clear-cut, climb 0.7 mile through an old-growth forest, passing a marsh and primitive campsite. At the Old Baldy Trail, turn right

for 0.6 mile, then right again at the next junction. Climb to the peak up 0.4 mile of trail and finally along an old service road, going to the left on this rutted track.

User Groups: Hikers, dogs, horses, and mountain bikes. No wheelchair facilities.

Permits: Permits are not required. Parking and access are free.

Maps: For a map of the Mount Hood National Forest, contact the Mount Hood National Forest Headquarters, 16400 Champion Way, Sandy, OR, 97055, 503/668-1700. For a topographic map, ask the USGS for Estacada.

Directions: From I-205 near Oregon City, take Exit 12 and drive east toward Estacada 18 miles. Drive through town and continue 1.6 miles on Highway 224. Just beyond milepost 25, turn left on Surface Road for 1.1 miles and turn right on Squaw Mountain Road. Follow this paved road, which becomes Road 4614, for 13.4 miles. Turn right on a gravel road to the Fanton Trailhead.

Contact: Mount Hood National Forest, Clackamas River Ranger District, 595 NW Industrial Way, Estacada, OR, 97023, 503/630-6861.

12 SHEEPSHEAD ROCK
2.8 mi/1.5 hr   🥾1 ⛰7

east of Estacada in Mount Hood National Forest

Map 9.1, page 453

If it wasn't timber thieves and sheepherders threatening these forests in the early 1900s, it was fire. The Forest Service built a guard station atop The Plaza, a wide plateau, in order to thwart the people, and a fire watchtower atop nearby Salmon Mountain to thwart the flames. Now the whole area is within the Salmon-Huckleberry Wilderness, all accessible by the Plaza Trail. An easy destination is Sheepshead Rock, a barren stony outcrop atop mighty cliffs.

From the trailhead, go right for 1.4 miles along the Plaza Trail, which joins an old road at the guard station site, then continues. The trail descends from the plateau, and just before it switchbacks back up, a side trail to the right leads to a scramble up Sheepshead Rock.

User Groups: Hikers, dogs, and horses. No mountain bikes allowed. No wheelchair facilities.

Permits: A free self-issue Wilderness Permit is required and is available at the trailhead. Parking and access are free.

Maps: For a map of the Mount Hood National Forest and the Salmon-Huckleberry Wilderness, contact the Mount Hood National Forest Headquarters, 16400 Champion Way, Sandy, OR, 97055, 503/668-1700. For a topographic map, ask the USGS for Three Lynx.

Directions: From I-205 near Oregon City, take Exit 12 and drive east toward Estacada 18 miles. Drive through town and continue 6.5 miles on Highway 224. Across from Promontory Park, turn left at a sign for Silver Fox RV Park and go left onto Road 4610. Follow this road 18.4 miles, forking left at 7.1 miles, right at eight miles, and left at 17 miles. Watch for a trailhead sign on the left and park at the Twin Springs Campground a hundred yards beyond on the right. Walk back to the trailhead.

Contact: Mount Hood National Forest, Zigzag Ranger District, 70220 East Highway 26, Zigzag, OR, 97049, 503/622-3191.

13 MEMALOOSE LAKE AND SOUTH FORK MOUNTAIN
4.6 mi/2.5 hr   👤2 ⛰8

southeast of Estacada in Mount Hood National Forest

Map 9.1, page 453

Less than an hour from Portland, you'll feel as if you're deep in the mountains. Memaloose Lake sits beneath South Fork Mountain in what remains of an ancient cirque from the Ice Age, and now plays home to salamanders and huckleberries. The lake is as family-friendly as it gets, but for a challenge you can continue on to the top of the mountain with views of nine Cascade peaks—a rarity, for sure.

From the trailhead, the Memaloose Lake Trail climbs modestly over 1.3 miles, switchbacking at its end down to the lake. To climb South Fork Mountain on an unmaintained trail, don't confuse it with the spur trails leading to the shores and campsites around the lake, but continue to the left up 700 feet in 1.0 mile.

User Groups: Hikers, dogs, horses, and mountain bikes. No wheelchair facilities.

Permits: Permits are not required. Parking and access are free.

Maps: For a map of the Mount Hood National Forest, contact the Mount Hood National Forest Headquarters, 16400 Champion Way, Sandy, OR, 97055, 503/668-1700. For a topographic map, ask the USGS for Wanderers Peak.

Directions: From I-205 near Oregon City, take Exit 12 and drive east toward Estacada 18 miles. Drive through town and continue 9.2 miles on Highway 224. Between mileposts 33 and 34, go right across a bridge onto Memaloose Road 45 and drive 11.2 miles. Keep right on a gravel road for one more mile to a trailhead on the left.

Contact: Mount Hood National Forest, Clackamas River Ranger District, 595 NW Industrial Way, Estacada, OR, 97023, 503/630-6861.

14 CLACKAMAS RIVER
7.8 mi one-way/4.0 hr   👤2 ⛰8

southeast of Estacada in Mount Hood National Forest

Map 9.1, page 453

This breezy trail follows the rough and tumbling Clackamas River on a great day's journey. Along the way, you'll pass a couple of waterfalls, including Pup Creek Falls in a side canyon, and The Narrows, where the river squeezes through a gorge between two pieces of a lava flow, narrowing the river to a thin whitewater rush. Though the trail parallels the highway, the road is on the far shore.

The trailside has some great up-and-down hauls through dense woods and even passes a couple beaches.

From the Fish Creek Trailhead, follow the trail along the river, rounding a bend, for 3.6 miles. At that point, there is a side trail to the right leading in 200 yards to a viewpoint of Pup Creek Falls. Continue on the main trail 1.3 miles to The Narrows. From there, the trail continues on for three miles to an upper trailhead at Indian Henry Campground.

User Groups: Hikers and dogs. Horses and mountain bikes not allowed. No wheelchair facilities.

Permits: Permits are not required. A federal Northwest Forest Pass is required to park here; the cost is $5 a day or $30 for an annual pass. You can buy a day pass at the trailhead, at ranger stations, or through private vendors.

Maps: For a map of the Mount Hood National Forest, contact the Mount Hood National Forest Headquarters, 16400 Champion Way, Sandy, OR, 97055, 503/668-1700. For a topographic map, ask the USGS for Three Lynx.

Directions: From I-205 near Oregon City, take Exit 12 and drive east toward Estacada 18 miles. Drive through town and continue 14.4 miles on Highway 224. Past milepost 39, after crossing the second green bridge, turn right on Fish Creek Road 54. Follow this road 0.2 mile, cross the Clackamas River, then park at a big lot on the right. To reach Indian Henry Campground, stay left on OR 224, following the river seven miles. Follow signs for Indian Henry Campground straight on Road 4620 for 0.6 mile and park in a lot on the right across from the campground entrance.

Contact: Mount Hood National Forest, Clackamas River Ranger District, 595 NW Industrial Way, Estacada, OR, 97023, 503/630-6861.

15 RIVERSIDE NATIONAL RECREATION TRAIL

8.0 mi/3.0 hr

southeast of Estacada in Mount Hood National Forest

Map 9.1, page 453

The Riverside Trail is only one of three in the Mount Hood Forest to be designated a National Recreation Trail. It's outstanding natural beauty is due to thick forests of Douglas fir and red cedar, and the fact that the river provides companionship for the trail's whole length. It's worth it to hike the whole thing in one burst.

From the trailhead, the trail goes in two directions. To the left, it ambles down 1.4 miles to a beach and its terminus at the Riverside Campground. To the right, it extends out 2.6 miles along cliffs, over creeks, down to a beach, down to a nice pool, and to a fine viewpoint over the river, before continuing along the Oak Grove Fork to its end at the Rainbow Campground.

User Groups: Hikers, dogs, and mountain bikes. Horses not allowed. No wheelchair facilities.

Permits: Permits are not required. A federal Northwest Forest Pass is required to park here; the cost is $5 a day or $30 for an annual pass. You can buy a day pass at the trailhead, at ranger stations, or through private vendors.

Maps: For a map of the Mount Hood National Forest, contact the Mount Hood National Forest Headquarters, 16400 Champion Way, Sandy, OR, 97055, 503/668-1700. For a topographic map, ask the USGS for Fish Creek Mountain.

Directions: From I-205 near Oregon City, take Exit 12 and drive east toward Estacada 18 miles. Drive through town and continue 26 miles on Highway 224 to the Ripplebrook Bridge. Turn right onto Road 46 for 1.8 miles to a Riverside Trailhead sign and a parking lot on the right.

Contact: Mount Hood National Forest, Clackamas River Ranger District, 595

NW Industrial Way, Estacada, OR, 97023, 503/630-6861.

16 NESMITH POINT AND ELOWAH FALLS

3.0-9.8 mi/1.5-5.0 hr   🏃3   ⛰8

west of Cascade Locks in the Columbia River Gorge

Map 9.2, page 454

Two very different hikes launch from Yeon State Park, named for one of the principal architects of the historic Columbia River Highway. The first views 289-foot Elowah Falls from both the bottom and the top, making use of a unnerving but fenced cliff-ledge trail to climb over Elowah to Upper McCord Creek Falls. The second climbs steeply up a dry gorge to Nesmith Point, almost 4,000 feet above the trailhead, and provides absolutely stunning views to the mountains on the far side of the Columbia River.

To hike to the falls, take the left-hand Trail 400 from the parking lot 0.4 mile to a junction. Two trails lead from here: The first goes 0.4 mile to the left to a footbridge at the base of Elowah Falls; the second heads up the cliff face 0.7 miles to 60-foot Upper McCord Falls, with sweeping views from the dynamite-blasted ledge along the cliff.

To climb to Nesmith Point, take the right-hand junction from Yeon Park on Trail 428. The first 0.9 mile climbs steadily through the forest. At a junction with the Gorge Trail by a creek, head left. From here, the trail climbs 2,300 feet in only 2.4 miles, reaching its crest at a saddle with excellent views. Continue on this ridgeline trail 1.3 miles, passing a spring along the way, turning uphill through a forest of towering trees not unlike being in a massive cathedral. The trail joins an old road, so go right up 0.3 mile to a cliff-edge view and the site of an

Columbia River Gorge from Nesmith Point

old watchtower, with one building's ruins still collapsing into the ground.

User Groups: Hikers and dogs. No mountain bikes or horses allowed. No wheelchair facilities.

Permits: Permits are not required. Parking and access are free.

Maps: You can purchase a Trails of the Columbia Gorge Map from Geo-Graphics. For a topographic map, ask the USGS for Tanner Butte.

Directions: From Portland, drive I-84 east and take Exit 35 for Ainsworth Park, and turn left toward Dodson for 200 feet, then turn right onto Frontage Road. Follow Frontage Road 2.1 miles to a pullout on the right.

Contact: Oregon Parks and Recreation Department, 1115 Commercial Street NE, Salem, OR, 97301, 800/551-6949, www.oregonstateparks.org.

❿ WAHCLELLA FALLS

1.8 mi/1.0 hr

west of Cascade Locks in the Columbia River Gorge

Map 9.2, page 454

Once the stretch of Columbia River Highway ends, it's easy to miss off-the-beaten-path spots like Wahclella Falls. It's unfortunate, because this double-plunge waterfall tumbling into the canyon where massive boulders line Tanner Creek is unique and worth a visit. The Wahclella Falls Trail sets out on an old road that becomes a trail beyond an old dam, heading into the canyon 0.9 mile along Tanner Creek. Watch for a side falls along the way. The trail comes to a junction, the beginning of a short loop. Go left to reach the base of the falls, a pounding cataract, then cross the creek on a footbridge, passing a small cave and the giant boulders left from a landslide decades ago. The trail crosses the creek again on a footbridge and climbs to rejoin the original trail. Head left to return to the lot.

User Groups: Hikers and dogs. No horses or mountain bikes allowed. No wheelchair facilities.

Permits: Permits are not required. A federal Northwest Forest Pass is required to park; the cost is $5 a day or $30 for an annual pass. You can buy a day pass at the trailhead, at ranger stations, or through private vendors.

Maps: You can purchase a Trails of the Columbia Gorge Map from Geo-Graphics. For a topographic map, ask the USGS for Tanner Butte.

Directions: From Portland, drive I-84 east and take Exit 40 for the Bonneville Dam. At the intersection, keep right and then stay to the right again for the parking area.

Contact: Columbia Gorge National Scenic Area, 902 Wasco Avenue, Suite 200, Hood River, OR, 97031, 541/308-1700.

⓲ WAUNA VIEWPOINT

3.8 mi/2.0 hr

west of Cascade Locks in the Columbia River Gorge

Map 9.2, page 454

Two sections of the Columbia River Highway are abandoned but open as a State Trail. Paralleling the interstate that eventually made this highway obsolete, the old highway is open to hikers and bikers, and provides access to other trails, including a viewpoint of Wauna Point, a challenging climb. For an easy day, you can hike out the old highway and back, a two-mile walk that hugs Tooth Rock on a parapet-like section of the road. Either way, this stretch of old road accesses the Wauna Viewpoint nicely.

Beginning at the Tooth Rock Trailhead, follow the paved path 0.2 mile to a junction. Stay straight on the old highway another 0.8 mile to the road's end at a stone stairway.

For a different hike from the same trailhead, try Wauna Viewpoint. Follow the old highway from the Tooth Rock Trailhead to the junction and go right 0.4 mile on a poorly marked spur trail toward Wauna. Take the next trail to the right, heading uphill 0.1 mile to an old roadbed that marks the Gorge Trail. Stay left, going uphill to find the continuation of the trail. Follow the trail to the left another 0.4 mile. Then go right at a sign for Wauna Viewpoint, plodding up the switchbacks to the 1,050-foot viewpoint near a powerline base. From here you can spot Mount Adams in Washington. Head back the way you came.

User Groups: Hikers and dogs. Mountain bikes allowed on paved trails only. No horses allowed. Paved portions are wheelchair accessible.

Permits: Permits are not required. Parking and access are free.

Maps: You can purchase a Trails of the Columbia Gorge Map from Geo-Graphics. For a topographic map, ask the USGS for Bonneville Dam.

Directions: From Portland, drive I-84 east and

take Exit 40 for the Bonneville Dam. At the intersection, keep right and then turn left for the parking area.

Contact: Oregon Parks and Recreation Department, 1115 Commercial Street NE, Salem, OR, 97301, 800/551-6949, www.oregon-stateparks.org, and Columbia Gorge National Scenic Area, 902 Wasco Avenue, Suite 200, Hood River, OR, 97031, 541/308-1700.

19 EAGLE CREEK
12.0 mi/7.0 hr

west of Cascade Locks in the Columbia River Gorge

> **Map 9.2, page 454**   **BEST (**

Eagle Creek is surely one of the best hikes in Oregon—and it's one of the oldest, built in the 1910s as part of the Columbia River Highway project. You'll pass six waterfalls in all, and for the finale you'll walk behind Tunnel Falls through a little cave carved out of the cliff wall. The whole route is nothing short of spectacular, and there's ample opportunity to backpack as well, with several woodsy group camping areas along the way. Of course, parts of the trail are perilous, walking alongside sheer cliffs with naught but a cable handrail to ease the anxiety. Almost every year, it seems, someone falls into the canyon and needs to be rescued, or worse. Keep an eye on kids and dogs, and the trip will be one for posterity.

From the trailhead, head upstream on the Eagle Creek Trail. At 1.5 miles, a side trail leads to a viewpoint of Metlako Falls, and at 2.1 miles a side trail leads down to Punchbowl Falls, a great place to spot water ouzels, little grey birds that spend much of their time underwater and darting in and out of waterfalls looking for insects. Returning to the trail, the next 1.2 miles brings you to the first high bridge, crossing not only a creek but a faultline. From here, it's 0.4 mile farther to Tenas Camp, then another mile to Wy-East Camp, and finally another 0.6 mile to Blue Grouse Camp. Once you've passed Blue Grouse

Camp, it's only 0.7 mile to Tunnel Falls, and if you're not yet tired out, head around the bend a short distance to reach another falls and a good lunch spot. Return as you came.

User Groups: Hikers and dogs. No horses or mountain bikes allowed. No wheelchair facilities.

Permits: Permits are not required. A federal Northwest Forest Pass is required to park here; the cost is $5 a day or $30 for an annual pass. You can buy a day pass at the trailhead, at ranger stations, or through private vendors.

Maps: You can purchase a Trails of the Columbia Gorge Map from Geo-Graphics. For a topographic map, ask the USGS for Bonneville Dam.

Directions: From Portland, drive I-84 east and take Exit 41 for Eagle Creek. At the intersection, keep right for one mile to the parking area.

Contact: Columbia Gorge National Scenic Area, 902 Wasco Avenue, Suite 200, Hood River, OR, 97031, 541/308-1700.

20 RUCKEL RIDGE
9.6 mi/5.0 hr

west of Cascade Locks in the Columbia River Gorge

> **Map 9.2, page 454**

Ruckel Creek Trail may not be appropriately named, since it provides only two glimpses of Ruckel Creek. But what this trail accomplishes is far more ambitious: a demanding climb to the Benson Plateau, where trails go off in all directions like the strands of a spider's web. Along the way, you'll pass mysterious pits that could be 1,000 years old, most likely vision quest sites for young Native American men. The rest is what my friend used to call a "death march" up the rugged ridge into the Hatfield Wilderness area with views to Table Mountain and Mount Adams.

From the trailhead in the Eagle Creek Campground, follow the Gorge Trail east 0.7 mile east, following the paved old Columbia River Highway for a spell. Cross Ruckel Creek on a picturesque stone bridge and head to the right on the Ruckel Creek Trail, which quickly becomes a thigh-burner. In 0.3 mile, you'll enter a moss-covered rockslide area, where you'll find the pits. Touch nothing and remove nothing; these sites are federally protected. The next 1.5 miles is steep, arriving at a viewpoint at 2,000 feet. After this, the trail affords a break for 1.5 miles through a fairly level, grassy slope before climbing again steeply for the remaining 0.8 mile. Once on top, walk through the woods to a trail fork, and go right to visit Ruckel Creek. Return as you came.

User Groups: Hikers and dogs. No wheelchair facilities.

Permits: Permits are not required. A federal Northwest Forest Pass is required to park here; the cost is $5 a day or $30 for an annual pass. You can buy a day pass at the trailhead, at ranger stations, or through private vendors.

Maps: You can purchase a Trails of the Columbia Gorge Map from Geo-Graphics. For a topographic map, ask the USGS for Bonneville Dam.

Directions: From Portland, drive I-84 east and take Exit 41 for Eagle Creek. At the intersection, keep right and then turn left into the parking area.

Contact: Columbia Gorge National Scenic Area, 902 Wasco Avenue, Suite 200, Hood River, OR, 97031, 541/308-1700.

21 DRY CREEK FALLS
4.8 mi/2.0 hr   🏃1 ⛰7

south of Cascade Locks in Mount Hood National Forest

Map 9.2, page 454

There's a sign for the Pacific Crest Trail on the Bridge of the Gods, a long steel bridge spanning the Columbia River. How else would through-hikers get over that river? Just off the road here, the beginning of the Oregon stretch of the PCT starts into the forest. Within a few miles is the first footbridge over rushing water, the misnamed Dry Creek. Hikers may not realize that

the old road leading off the PCT and upstream comes to a 50-foot waterfall pouring through a slot in lumpy lava flows. Don't let the early stage of the trail fool you; this is actually a quiet walk through some deep fir woods.

From the trailhead, head south on the PCT, away from the Bridge of the Gods, going under I-84 and briefly up a dirt road, following PCT signs typically nailed to trees (and a telephone pole). The trail spurs to the left off the road. After 1.2 miles, cross an old powerline road and continue into the woods. After 0.9 mile, the trail crosses Dry Creek, but take the road to the right up 0.3 mile to the base of the falls and an abandoned diversion dam that, if anything, adds charm to this spot.

User Groups: Hikers, dogs, and horses. No mountain bikes allowed. No wheelchair facilities.

Permits: Permits are not required. A federal Northwest Forest Pass is required to park here; the cost is $5 a day or $30 for an annual pass. You can buy a day pass at the trailhead, at ranger stations, or through private vendors.

Maps: You can purchase a Trails of the Columbia Gorge Map from Geo-Graphics. For a topographic map, ask the USGS for Bonneville Dam and Carson.

Directions: From Portland, drive I-84 east to the Cascade Locks (Exit 44) and follow signs for the Bridge of the Gods. Just before the tollbooth for the bridge, turn right into a parking area. The trail begins across the road.

Contact: Columbia Gorge National Scenic Area, 902 Wasco Avenue, Suite 200, Hood River, OR, 97031, 541/308-1700.

22 HERMAN CREEK TO INDIAN POINT
8.0-8.4 mi/4.0-4.5 hr   🏃3 ⛰8

east of Cascade Locks in the Columbia River Gorge

Map 9.2, page 454

Herman Creek Trail is a bit of a misnomer, since you'll have to go 4.2 miles just to get to a point on the water. The destination, though, is a truly lovely and untrammeled spot on the confluence of Casey and Herman Creeks. On the way, you'll pass tiger lilies in summer and a side creek with a nice waterfall. This trail is also the access point for a killer climb to Indian Point, a promontory high above the Columbia River and sweeping views.

For the hike above Herman Creek, begin from the campground, climbing through a boulder field on the Herman Creek Trail 0.6 mile to a junction with the Herman Bridge spur. Go left 0.7 mile, staying on the Herman Creek Trail, where the trail eventually joins an old road. At the next junction, site of Herman Camp, go to the right to stay on Herman Creek, keeping right at the next junction as well, for 2.6 miles. After that, you'll reach a second camp and a junction of trails; an unmarked side trail to the right goes down the canyon 0.3 mile to the confluence.

For the Indian Point climb, begin from the campground, climbing through the boulder field 0.6 mile to a junction with the Herman Bridge spur. Go left 0.7 mile, where the trail eventually joins the old road. At the next junction, site of Herman Camp, go left up the Gorton Creek Trail and climb steadily for 2.6 miles to a junction. Continue 50 yards up the Gorton Creek Trail and take an unmarked side trail to the left 0.1 mile to Indian Point. Return to the junction and go left down the Cutoff Trail 0.6 mile to the Nick Eaton Trail, going right on this trail down a steep ridge for two miles. At the junction with the old road, follow it back to Herman Camp, then return to the right down the road as you came to the Herman Creek campground.

User Groups: Hikers, dogs, and horses. No mountain bikes allowed. No wheelchair facilities.

Permits: A free self-issue Wilderness Permit is required and is available on the trail. A federal Northwest Forest Pass is required to park here; the cost is $5 a day or $30 for an annual pass. You can buy a day pass at the trailhead, at ranger stations, or through private vendors.

Maps: You can purchase a Trails of the Columbia Gorge Map from Geo-Graphics. For a topographic map, ask the USGS for Carson.

Directions: From Portland, drive I-84 east to Cascade Locks (Exit 44), driving through town for two miles. At the next on-ramp for I-84, go straight onto a road marked "To Oxbow Fish Hatchery" and follow this road two miles to a Forest Service complex, and turn right into the Herman Creek Campground entrance to a parking area at the end of the road. In the winter, the gate is closed, but you can park off the road near the gate and walk in to the campground.

Contact: Columbia Gorge National Scenic Area, 902 Wasco Avenue, Suite 200, Hood River, OR, 97031, 541/308-1700.

23 STARVATION CREEK FALLS

2.5 mi/1.0 hr

east of Cascade Locks in the Columbia River Gorge

Map 9.2, page 454

Located just off I-84, nestled in a canyon beneath Starvation Ridge, is a 186-foot waterfall on Starvation Creek. The creek is named for an 1884 disaster; a train was stranded in the snow for weeks here, and the passengers were paid to help dig it out as they waited for food to arrive.

It's easy enough to walk to Starvation Creek Falls from the lot along a paved stretch of the out-of-use section of the Columbia River Highway. But there are more falls back in those hills above the freeway, and a somewhat demanding hike visits them all.

After visiting Starvation Creek Falls, head west on the paved Mount Defiance Trail skirting the highway, following signs for Mount Defiance. At a junction with the Starvation Ridge Cutoff Trail in 0.3 mile, stay to the right for 0.6 mile, passing Cabin Creek Falls and Hole-in-the-Wall Falls. These falls were a bizarre undertaking by highway workers in

1938 to prevent Warren Creek Falls from constantly flooding out the highway. They fixed this by tunneling the creek right through a cliff—quite a feat.

The trail climbs to a junction, and it's worth it to head right on the Mount Defiance Trail a short distance for a peak at Lancaster Falls, which falls right down to the trail. Go back to the junction and head uphill to the right on the Warren Creek Trail. In the course of an unbelievable mile, the trail fords Warren Creek and climbs to high meadows overlooking the Gorge and traces some precarious cliffs. At the Starvation Ridge Cutoff Trail, head to the left and down an incredibly steep 0.3 mile to return to the old highway site, heading to the right to return to the Starvation Creek Falls lot.

User Groups: Hikers and dogs. No mountain bikes or horses allowed. Paved areas of the park are wheelchair accessible.

Permits: Permits are not required. Parking and access are free.

Maps: You can purchase a Trails of the Columbia Gorge Map from Geo-Graphics. For a topographic map, ask the USGS for Mount Defiance.

Directions: From Cascade Locks, drive 10 miles east on I-84 to the Starvation Creek trailhead at Exit 55.

Contact: Oregon Parks and Recreation Department, 1115 Commercial Street NE, Salem, OR, 97301, 800/551-6949, www.oregon-stateparks.org, and Columbia Gorge National Scenic Area, 902 Wasco Avenue, Suite 200, Hood River, OR, 97031, 541/308-1700.

🔲 MOUNT DEFIANCE AND STARVATION RIDGE

11.4 mi/1 day   🥾5   ⛰️8

east of Cascade Locks in the Columbia River Gorge

Map 9.2, page 454

Mount Defiance is one of the most difficult hikes in the entire state of Oregon, so let's just say that right off the bat. Are you ready for a rough-and-tumble challenge in the highest degree? Then climb this monster of a trail—with a nearly 5,000-foot elevation gain—to the peak rising from the Hatfield Wilderness. Talk about views. This being the highest point in the Columbia Gorge, you'll see Cascade peaks ringing you in. For a real day of it, try an exhausting but ultimately rewarding loop trail down Starvation Ridge. Don't let words like "Defiance" and "Starvation" get you down, but give yourself a full day to tackle this one.

Following signs for Mount Defiance, hike along the highway for the first mile on the Mount Defiance Trail, keeping right at junctions and passing two waterfalls. After the second junction with the Warren Creek Trail, continue to the right toward Mount Defiance, passing Lancaster Falls and charging up the mountain 3.9 miles on switchbacks and through the woods to a junction with the Mitchell Point Trail, which will serve as the return route. Go uphill 0.2 mile to the next junction, and take the Mount Defiance Trail to the right, overlooking Bear Lake and the Hatfield Wilderness. In one mile, you'll arrive at the peak.

To head down, pass the tower and look for an old trail sign. Follow this trail down 0.8 mile, crossing a road twice, then go downhill at the next junction 0.2 mile, then head right 0.8 mile along the Mitchell Trail, reaching Warren Lake. Continue forward, watching for a junction and turning left onto the Starvation Ridge Trail, for a total of 3.7 miles. Near the bottom, take the right-hand Starvation Cutoff Trail, steeply switchbacking 0.3 mile, then going right on the Mount Defiance Trail 0.3 mile back to the lot.

User Groups: Hikers and dogs. No mountain bikes or horses allowed. No wheelchair facilities.

Permits: A free self-issue Wilderness Permit is required and is available on the trail. Parking and access are free.

Maps: You can purchase a Trails of the

Columbia Gorge Map from Geo-Graphics. For a topographic map, ask the USGS for Mount Defiance.

Directions: From Cascade Locks, drive 10 miles east on I-84 to the Starvation Creek trailhead at Exit 55.

Contact: Columbia Gorge National Scenic Area, 902 Wasco Avenue, Suite 200, Hood River, OR, 97031, 541/308-1700.

25 WYGANT PEAK
8.5 mi/5.5 hr   👥4 ⛰8

east of Cascade Locks in the Columbia River Gorge

Map 9.2, page 454

Two prominent points rise above a small rest area on I-84: 1,200-foot Mitchell Point and 2,144-foot Wygant Peak. The trail up 1.1 miles to Mitchell is relatively easy; it's a hardier hike to get to forested Wygant Peak, but along the way there are great views over the Gorge and a loop-trail option along Perham Creek. What makes it hardy is that, for the most part, this trail is not maintained, meaning that you'll be ducking under fallen trees and hopping over some collapsed trail. Use caution. What's most frustrating is how much longer it takes when you have to bushwhack your way along the route.

From the lot, head back down the road to a gated road, following the clearly marked Wygant Trail one mile along both trail and a stretch of the old Columbia River Highway to a junction. Stay straight on the Wygant Trail for 1.6 miles, crossing Perham Creek and topping a viewpoint before climbing to the Chetwood Trail. To climb Wygant, go right 1.7 miles past a few good viewpoints to the peak.

Returning 1.7 miles to the junction, you can either return as you came or try some adventure by going right on the Chetwood Trail for 1.5 mile, crossing Perham Creek higher up in its canyon, before returning to the Wygant Trail via the Perham Loop Trail.

footbridge on the **Wygant Trail**

When you hit the Wygant, go right to return to the car. Be aware that this extra loop is every bit as unmaintained as the Wygant, and the creek crossing should be done when the water is low.

User Groups: Hikers and dogs. No mountain bikes or horses allowed. Paved areas of the park are wheelchair accessible.

Permits: Permits are not required. Parking and access are free.

Maps: You can purchase a Hood River map from Geo-Graphics. For a topographic map, ask the USGS for Mount Defiance.

Directions: From Cascade Locks, drive 14 miles east on I-84 to Exit 58 to the Lausman State Park rest area.

Contact: Oregon Parks and Recreation Department, 1115 Commercial Street NE, Salem, OR, 97301, 800/551-6949, www.oregonstateparks.org.

26 MOSIER TWIN TUNNELS
4.5 mi one-way/2.0 hr   🏃1 ⛰8

east of Hood River in the Columbia River Gorge

Map 9.2, page 454   **BEST (**

The old Columbia River Highway sat abandoned for decades—until 1995, when stretches of it were restored to become part of the state trail system. The stretch between the city of Hood River and the town of Mosier is perfect for a long bike ride or an easy hike—excepting, perhaps, the wind, which is famous in the Columbia Gorge.

The real treasures here are a couple of tunnels that took two years to build. For an easy visit to the tunnels, start on the Mosier side and go as far as you'd like: to the County Line Overlook, a viewpoint over Koberg Beach State Wayside, or all the way to the Hood River trailhead. By the time you get east of Hood River you're in a new landscape of basalt rock and oak and ponderosa pine, differing dramatically from the more lush western Gorge.

From the Mosier parking area, follow a paved path to the gated road that marks the trail's entrance. From here it's a 0.7-mile walk to the Mosier Twin Tunnels and their sturdy roof, built to withstand massive rockfall. In another 0.9 mile, you'll reach the County Line Overlook on the border of Wasco and Hood River Counties. Yet another 0.8 mile beyond that is a 0.2-mile side trail out on a cliff to the overlook of Koberg Beach. From here, it's another 1.9 miles to the trail's end.

User Groups: Hikers, dogs, and mountain bikes. No horses allowed. The Historic Columbia Highway Trail is entirely wheelchair accessible, and there is a separate parking area for wheelchair users.

Permits: Permits are not required. A $3 day-use fee is collected at the park entrance, or you can get an annual Oregon Parks and Recreation pass for $25; contact Oregon Parks and Recreation, 800/551-6949.

Maps: For a map of the Historic Columbia River Highway State Trail, contact Oregon Parks and Recreation Department, 800/551-6949, www.oregonstateparks.org. For a topographic map, ask the USGS for White Salmon and Hood River.

Directions: Drive east of Hood River five miles on I-84 to the Mosier exit (Exit 69). Go south from the exit 0.2 mile to Mosier and turn left on Rock Creek Road for 0.7 mile to the Hatfield Trailhead on the left. For the western trailhead, take I-84, exit 64, and follow Government Camp signs for 0.3 mile. At a stop sign, go left on Old Columbia River Drive for 1.3 miles to road's end.

Contact: Oregon Parks and Recreation Department, 1115 Commercial Street NE, Salem, OR, 97301, 800/551-6949, www.oregonstateparks.org.

27 TOM MCCALL PRESERVE
5.6 mi/3.0 hr   🏃2 ⛰7

east of Hood River in the Columbia River Gorge

Map 9.2, page 454

More than 300 varieties of plants grow on the dramatic oak grasslands above the Columbia River and Rowena Dell. Thanks to The Nature Conservancy, this fabulous preserve—named for former Oregon Governor McCall, a conservationist—is open to everyone. Spring and early summer mark some of the showiest wildflower shows anywhere, though poison oak has a grip here, too. Lava flows and ash deposits coupled with massive floods have produced this strange mound-and-swale topography that baffles even the experts on that sort of thing. Here you'll find meadowlarks, the Oregon state bird, as well as canyon wrens, Pacific chorus frogs, and mule deer. Flowers include grass widows, prairie stars, lupine, Indian paintbrush, balsamroot, milk vetch, shooting stars, and waterleaf, several of which are found only in the Gorge.

Two trails lead out from the Rowena Crest Viewpoint. Opposite the highway from the parking area, a sign marks the lower plateau trail, an easy 2.2-mile round-trip that visits two ponds and several viewpoints. The upper trail to Tom McCall Point leads uphill for 1.7 miles to the 1,722-foot knob overlooking the eastern Gorge.

User Groups: Hikers only. No dogs, horses, or mountain bikes allowed. No wheelchair facilities.

Permits: Permits are not required. Parking and access are free.

Maps: Brochures are typically available at the trailhead. For a topographic map, ask the USGS for White Salmon.

Directions: Drive east of Hood River five miles on I-84 to the Mosier exit (Exit 69) and follow "Scenic Loop" signs 6.6 miles to the Rowena Crest Viewpoint.

Contact: The Nature Conservancy, 821 SE 14th Street, Portland, OR, 97214, 503/802-8100.

28 WAHTUM LAKE
4.1 mi/2.5 hr

south of Hood River in the Hatfield Wilderness

Map 9.2, page 454

Hiking the entire length of the Eagle Creek Trail (see *Eagle Creek* listing in this chapter) is one way to get to Wahtum Lake, but it requires a backpack and several days. There's an easier way: You can start right from the deep blue lake itself and follow the Pacific Crest Trail to a viewpoint on the rocky bluffs of Chinidere Mountain, looking out to Tanner Butte, the Benson Plateau, and five Cascade peaks.

From the Wahtum Lake Campground, take the Wahtum Express Trail down 0.2 mile to the lake. Turn right on the Pacific Crest Trail, rounding the lake through the Hatfield Wilderness and going 1.6 miles to a junction, going left. Then go right and uphill past a "Chinidere Mountain" sign up a steep 0.4 mile to the former lookout site. To return via the loop, head down to the PCT, go left 100 yards, and continue right 0.9 mile on the Chinidere Mountain Trail. You'll pass campsites and cross a creek, then join the Eagle Creek Trail. Stay to the left at this junction and the PCT

junction, going another 0.4 mile and passing more campsites along the lakeshore. At the final junction, go right on the Wahtum Express to return 0.2 mile to the car.

User Groups: Hikers, dogs, and horses. No mountain bikes allowed. No wheelchair facilities.

Permits: A free self-issue Wilderness Permit is required and is available at the trailhead. A federal Northwest Forest Pass is required to park here; the cost is $5 a day or $30 for an annual pass. You can buy a day pass at the trailhead, at ranger stations, or through private vendors.

Maps: You can purchase a Trails of the Columbia Gorge Map from Geo-Graphics. For a topographic map, ask the USGS for Wahtum Lake.

Directions: Drive I-84 east of Portland to West Hood River at Exit 62, driving 1.1 miles into Hood River. Turn right on 13th Street, and follow signs for Odell for 3.4 miles. Cross the Hood River Bridge and turn right on a fork past Tucker Park for 6.3 miles. Fork right again toward Dee, cross the river, and turn left toward Lost Lake for 4.9 miles. Turn right at a "Wahtum Lake" sign and follow Road 13 for 4.3 miles, then go right on Road 1310 for six miles to the Wahtum Lake Campground.

Contact: Columbia Gorge National Scenic Area, 902 Wasco Avenue, Suite 200, Hood River, OR, 97031, 541/308-1700.

29 BEAR LAKE AND MOUNT DEFIANCE
6.4 mi/ 3.5 hr

south of Hood River in the Hatfield Wilderness

Map 9.2, page 454

The grueling way up Mount Defiance (see *Mount Defiance and Starvation Ridge* listing in this chapter) isn't for everyone; this is a far easier way to the top, and one that visits pretty little Bear Lake along the way. It's so shallow and warm in summer that it's perfect for a quick swim.

Follow the Mount Defiance Trail to a junction and go right for 0.5 mile. A left-hand trail at the next junction leads 0.8 mile to Bear Lake. Continuing on the Mount Defiance Trail 0.9 mile, the path comes to another junction; go right 0.2 mile to the peak. To make a loop of it, with a view down to Bear Lake, walk past the tower and look for an old trail sign for the Mount Defiance Trail. Follow this trail down 0.8 mile, crossing a road twice, then go left on an unmarked trail one mile, rounding the peak. This will bring you back to the Mount Defiance Trail, which you can follow 1.4 miles back to the road.

User Groups: Hikers, dogs, and horses. No mountain bikes allowed. No wheelchair facilities.

Permits: A free self-issue Wilderness Permit is required and is available on the trail. Parking and access are free.

Maps: You can purchase a Trails of the Columbia Gorge Map from Geo-Graphics. For a topographic map, ask the USGS for Mount Defiance.

Directions: Drive I-84 east of Portland to West Hood River at Exit 62, driving 1.1 miles into Hood River. Turn right on 13th Street, and follow signs for Odell for 3.4 miles. Cross the Hood River Bridge and turn right on a fork past Tucker Park for 6.3 miles. Fork right again toward Dee, cross the river, and turn right toward Rainy Lake. Follow paved Punchbowl Road for 1.4 miles and continue on gravel Road 2820 for 10 miles to a sign for Mount Defiance Trail on the right.

Contact: Columbia Gorge National Scenic Area, 902 Wasco Avenue, Suite 200, Hood River, OR, 97031, 541/308-1700.

30 BALD BUTTE
8.2 mi/5.0 hr 🥾4 ⛰8

south of Hood River in Mount Hood National Forest

Map 9.2, page 454

Not to be confused with the plethora of other Bald Buttes out there, this one has the required old lookout site to provide a sweeping view of the Hood River Valley and nearby Mount Hood, then clear out into the Washington Cascades: St. Helens, Rainier, and Adams. Not bad for a hike that'll make you work for it, gaining 2,300 feet in elevation when all is said and done. Making use of the popular horse-and-bike trail on Surveyor's Ridge, this peak still remains fairly off-the-map.

Take the Oakridge Trail 2.5 miles from the grassy meadow into the fir and oak forest and climb the switchbacks. Turn left on the Surveyor's Ridge Trail for 0.9 mile then stay straight on a dirt road another 0.7 mile to the summit.

User Groups: Hikers, dogs, mountain bikes, and horses. No wheelchair facilities.

Permits: Permits are not required. Parking and access are free.

Maps: For a map of the Mount Hood National Forest, contact Mount Hood National Forest Headquarters, 16400 Champion Way, Sandy, OR, 97055, 503/668-1700. For a topographic map, ask the USGS for Parkdale.

Directions: From I-84 at Hood River, take Exit 64 and follow Highway 35 south for 14.8 miles. Turn left on Smullen Road 0.3 mile, then turn left on a gravel road 0.1 mile to the trailhead.

Contact: Mount Hood National Forest, Hood River Ranger District, 6780 Highway 35, Parkdale, OR, 97041, 541/352-6002.

31 LOST LAKE
3.2 mi/1.5 hr 🥾1 ⛰7

south of Hood River in Mount Hood National Forest

Map 9.2, page 454

Located on the north slope of Mount Hood, this lake has long been a popular destination for travelers. The Hood River tribe knew about it, naming it "Heart of the Mountains." A resort and campground are there now, and the lakeshore has been restored after years of heavy use. In just over three miles, you can treat yourself to stunning views of Mount Hood and Lost Lake Butte, watching for high-elevation birds along the water. The 3.4-mile shoreline loop trail can be taken in either direction, and a junction near a group camp leads to Lost Lake Butte (see *Lost Lake Butte,* next listing).

User Groups: Hikers and dogs. Mountain bikes and horses not allowed. Parts of the trail are wheelchair accessible.

Permits: Permits are not required. There is a day-use fee of $7 collected at the entry booth.

Maps: For a map of the Mount Hood National Forest, contact Mount Hood National Forest Headquarters, 16400 Champion Way, Sandy, OR, 97055, 503/668-1700. For a topographic map, ask the USGS for Bull Run Lake.

Directions: From Exit 62 in Hood River, drive 1.1 miles into town, turn right on 13th Street and follow signs for Odell for five miles. Cross a bridge and fork right past Tucker Park for 6.3 miles, then fork right again toward Dee and follow signs 14 miles to Lost Lake. Drive past the Lost Lake entry booth, go toward the store, and follow the lake to the right to a picnic area at the end of the road.

Contact: Mount Hood National Forest, Hood River Ranger District, 6780 Highway 35, Parkdale, OR, 97041, 541/352-6002.

32 LOST LAKE BUTTE
3.8 mi/2.0 hr

south of Hood River in Mount Hood National Forest

Map 9.2, page 454

Rising over a thousand feet above picturesque Lost Lake, this butte of the same name has a character all its own. Hiking its viewless forested slopes will eventually lead to an unimpeded view of Mount Rainier, Mount Adams, and Mount Hood. Along the way, you'll find beargrass blooms in summer and rhododendron blossoms in spring.

This hike begins from Campground Loop

B, climbing 1.9 miles up the forested slope to some easy switchbacks at the top. The best views are from the remains of an old watchtower.

User Groups: Hikers and dogs. Mountain bikes and horses not allowed. Parts of the trail are wheelchair accessible.

Permits: Permits are not required. There is a day-use fee of $7 collected at the entry booth.

Maps: For a map of the Mount Hood National Forest, contact Mount Hood National Forest Headquarters, 16400 Champion Way, Sandy, OR, 97055, 503/668-1700. For a topographic map, ask the USGS for Bull Run Lake.

Directions: From Exit 62 in Hood River, drive 1.1 miles into town, turn right on 13th Street and follow signs for Odell for five miles. Cross a bridge, and fork right past Tucker Park for 6.3 miles, then fork right again toward Dee and follow signs 14 miles to Lost Lake. Drive past the Lost Lake entry booth, go toward the store, and follow the lake to the right to a picnic area at the end of the road.

Contact: Mount Hood National Forest, Hood River Ranger District, 6780 Highway 35, Parkdale, OR, 97041, 541/352-6002.

33 WEST ZIGZAG MOUNTAIN
11.0 mi/8.0 hr   🏃4 ⛰9

north of Zigzag in the Mount Hood Wilderness

Map 9.2, page 454

Just above the town of Zigzag, the border of the Mount Hood Wilderness begins at the base of Zigzag Mountain, so big it becomes two peaks: East and West. Tackling West Zigzag is no mean feat, as the trail climbs nearly 3,000 feet in only 2.3 miles, then heads out over the ridge to a lookout site. Still, this well-graded trail won't totally break you; it'll just strengthen your calves a bit.

The first 1.3 miles of the Zigzag Mountain Trail switchback up steeply. The next 2.3 miles climbs as well, to a high point of 4,300 feet. After that, the next 1.9 miles provides some views over the mountains, coming to the old lookout site atop some rocky cliffs.

User Groups: Hikers, dogs, and horses. No mountain bikes allowed. No wheelchair facilities.

Permits: A free self-issue Wilderness Permit is required and is available at the trailhead. Parking and access are free.

Maps: For a map of the Mount Hood National Forest, contact Mount Hood National Forest Headquarters, 16400 Champion Way, Sandy, OR, 97055, 503/668-1700. A map of the Mount Hood Wilderness is available from Geo-Graphics. For a topographic map, ask the USGS for Rhododendron.

Directions: Drive east of Portland 42 miles on U.S. 26 to Zigzag, turning left onto East Lolo Pass Road for 0.4 mile. Turn right on East Mountain Drive for 0.2 mile, keeping right at a fork. After 0.5 mile, watch for a sign on the left for the Zigzag Mountain Trail and park on the shoulder.

Contact: Mount Hood National Forest, Zigzag Ranger District, 70220 East Highway 26, Zigzag, OR, 97049, 503/622-3191.

34 EAST ZIGZAG MOUNTAIN
8.0 mi/5.0 hr   🥾3   ⛰9

north of Zigzag in the Mount Hood Wilderness

Map 9.2, page 454

Like West Zigzag Mountain, East Zigzag Mountain provides some immense views over the surrounding country. The difference, though, is that this trail isn't quite as difficult. It's still difficult, just not bone-crushingly so. What you'll find is a ramble through Devil's Meadow, a side trail to Cast Lake, and high-alpine country looking out over the Mount Hood Wilderness.

From the Burnt Lake Trailhead, follow signs for Devil's Meadow. The Burnt Lake Trail follows an old road into this abandoned campground, going 2.6 miles to a junction, the start of the loop. Follow "Burnt Lake" signs to the right, going 1.4 miles to a junction atop a ridge.

Go left one mile, passing the East Zigzag summit at 4,971 feet and arriving at a junction with the Cast Creek Trail, heading to the left. The next junction leads to Cast Lake on the right, which will add 1.2 miles to your round-trip mileage. Continuing on the Zigzag Mountain Trail, you'll reach a junction with the Devil's Tie Trail; take this left-hand turn for 0.4 mile to return to Devil's Meadow, then go right the remaining 2.6 miles back to the trailhead.

User Groups: Hikers and dogs. No horses or mountain bikes. No wheelchair facilities.

Permits: A free self-issue Wilderness Permit is required and is available at the trailhead. Parking and access are free.

Maps: For a map of the Mount Hood National Forest, contact Mount Hood National Forest Headquarters, 16400 Champion Way, Sandy, OR, 97055, 503/668-1700. A map of the Mount Hood Wilderness is available from Geo-Graphics. For a topographic map, ask the USGS for Government Camp.

Directions: Drive east of Portland 47 miles on U.S. 26 to the village of Rhododendron. Turn left on Road 27 for 0.6 mile. Turn left on gravel Road 207 for 4.5 miles until it ends; this road is rough, so cars should take it slow.

Contact: Mount Hood National Forest, Zigzag Ranger District, 70220 East Highway 26, Zigzag, OR, 97049, 503/622-3191.

35 BURNT LAKE
6.8 mi/3.5 hr   🥾2   ⛰8

northeast of Zigzag in the Mount Hood Wilderness

Map 9.2, page 454

The area around Burnt Lake burned once and left massive hollowed-out cedar stumps. It's a heavily visited spot in the Mount Hood Forest, and rightfully so: It reflects nearby Mount Hood and is ringed in by big trees and a half-mile loop trail. Along the way, the nearly hidden Lost Creek Falls lie a bit off the trail and East Zigzag Mountain looms overhead like a great wall.

From the Burnt Lake Trailhead, follow the trail between two creeks—Burnt Lake Creek and Lost Creek—for 2.4 miles, crossing Burnt Lake Creek and arriving at a side trail to the left leading down to Lost Creek Falls. Continue on the main trail another mile to arrive at the shore of Burnt Lake.

User Groups: Hikers and dogs. No horses or mountain bikes allowed. No wheelchair facilities.

Permits: A free self-issue Wilderness Permit is required and is available at the trailhead. A federal Northwest Forest Pass is required to park here; the cost is $5 a day or $30 for an annual pass. You can buy a day pass at the trailhead, at ranger stations, or through private vendors.

Maps: For a map of the Mount Hood National Forest, contact Mount Hood National Forest Headquarters, 16400 Champion Way, Sandy, OR, 97055, 503/668-1700. A map of the Mount Hood Wilderness is available from Geo-Graphics. For a topographic map, ask the USGS for Government Camp.

Directions: Drive east of Portland 42 miles on U.S. 26 to Zigzag. Turn left on East Lolo Pass Road, following this route 4.2 miles and turn right on Road 1825 for 0.7 mile. Turn right across the Sandy River Bridge and continue on Road 1825 another 2.1 miles to the entrance for Lost Creek Campground. Go left on a gravel road 1.4 miles to its end at a parking area.

Contact: Mount Hood National Forest, Zigzag Ranger District, 70220 East Highway 26, Zigzag, OR, 97049, 503/622-3191.

RAMONA FALLS
7.1 mi/3.5 hr   🏃2 ⛰8

northeast of Zigzag in the Mount Hood Wilderness

Map 9.2, page 454

The Sandy River flows from Mount Hood and tumbles down a rocky bed. It's not filled with sand, though early pioneers thought it was. Actually, the milky color of many young mountain rivers is due to glacial silt.

This fine loop travels upstream to Ramona Falls, a 120-foot drop in a lovely fern-draped glen of columnar basalt. If the bridge is out when you visit (as it has been in the past), you will have to ford the Sandy River; this is easiest and safest late in the summer, when the water drops and exposes stones to cross over.

From the trailhead, head up the Sandy River 1.4 miles to a crossing. After fording the river, turn right on the PCT Horse Trail for 1.5 miles to a junction with the Pacific Crest Trail, and go left 0.5 mile to reach the falls on Ramona Creek. At the next junction just beyond the waterfall, continue left for 1.8 miles on the PCT, then take a left turn for 0.5 mile to return to the Sandy River crossing, fording it then going right the remaining 1.4 miles to the lot.

User Groups: Hikers, dogs, and horses. No mountain bikes allowed. No wheelchair facilities.

Permits: A free self-issue Wilderness Permit is required and is available at the trailhead. A federal Northwest Forest Pass is required to park here; the cost is $5 a day or $30 for an annual pass. You can buy a day pass at the trailhead, at ranger stations, or through private vendors.

Maps: For a map of the Mount Hood National Forest, contact Mount Hood National Forest Headquarters, 16400 Champion Way, Sandy, OR, 97055, 503/668-1700. A map of the Mount Hood Wilderness is available from Geo-Graphics. For a topographic map, ask the USGS for Bull Run Lake.

Directions: From Portland, drive U.S. 26 east toward Mount Hood 42 miles. At Zigzag, turn left onto East Lolo Pass Road and go 4.2 miles, then turn right on Road 1825. Drive 0.7 mile and turn right across the Sandy River. Continue 1.8 miles on Road 1825 and go left on Road 100 for 0.5 mile to a parking area at the end of the road.

Contact: Mount Hood National Forest, Zigzag Ranger District, 70220 East Highway 26, Zigzag, OR, 97049, 503/622-3191.

37 YOCUM RIDGE

16.2 mi/10.0 hr   ₥5 △10

northeast of Zigzag in the Mount Hood
Wilderness

Map 9.2, page 454

The meadows on Yocum Ridge are the definition of "alpine country." Set beside the Sandy
Glacier on the slopes of Mount Hood, the
source of the Sandy River, this makes for one
of the most spectacular views on the mountain. The ascent is as arduous as the scenery
is spectacular: You'll need to climb 3,800
feet from the Sandy River to get to this lush
viewpoint.

From the trailhead, head up the Sandy
River 1.4 miles to a crossing. After fording
the river, turn right on the PCT Horse Trail
for 1.5 miles to a junction with the Pacific
Crest Trail, and go left 0.5 mile to reach the
falls on Ramona Creek. At the next junction
just beyond the waterfall, turn right on the
Timberline Trail. Follow this trail 0.6 mile
to a right-hand junction up the Yocum Ridge
for 4.7 miles.

User Groups: Hikers, dogs, and horses. No
mountain bikes allowed. No wheelchair
facilities.

Permits: A free self-issue Wilderness Permit
is required and is available at the trailhead.
A federal Northwest Forest Pass is required
to park here; the cost is $5 a day or $30 for
an annual pass. You can buy a day pass at
the trailhead, at ranger stations, or through
private vendors.

Maps: For a map of the Mount Hood Na-
tional Forest, contact Mount Hood National
Forest Headquarters, 16400 Champion Way,
Sandy, OR, 97055, 503/668-1700. A map of
the Mount Hood Wilderness is available from
Geo-Graphics. For a topographic map, ask the
USGS for Mount Hood North.

Directions: From Portland, drive U.S. 26
east toward Mount Hood 42 miles. At Zigzag, turn left onto East Lolo Pass Road and
go 4.2 miles, then turn right on Road 1825.
Drive 0.7 mile and turn right across the Sandy

River. Continue 1.8 miles on Road 1825 and
go left on Road 100 for 0.5 mile to a parking
area at the end of the road.

Contact: Mount Hood National Forest, Zigzag Ranger District, 70220 East Highway 26,
Zigzag, OR, 97049, 503/622-3191.

38 MCNEIL POINT

8.8 mi/5.0 hr   ₥4 △10

northeast of Zigzag in the Mount Hood
Wilderness

Map 9.2, page 454

In the 1930s, the Civilian Conservation Corps
built a series of beautiful stone shelters encircling Mount Hood along the Timberline Trail.
Only three remain, and the loftiest must surely
be the one on McNeil Point, named for Portland newspaperman Fred McNeil. The climb
to the towering plateau is every bit as amazing,
circling Bald Mountain, ascending through
thick huckleberry fields, and finally following
a towering ridge to some alpine ponds and the
6,100-foot plateau edge. But be careful: The
scenery here is so spectacular that you may
want to move into the cabin like a modern-day
Thoreau and never leave again.

Start by climbing on the Top Spur Trail
up 0.5 mile to the Pacific Crest Trail, going
right at a junction, then left at the next aside
a big map board. Follow the Timberline Trail
2.3 miles, staying to the right on Timberline
and hiking the ridge high above the roaring
Muddy Fork. At 5,300 feet, you'll pass a faint
side trail, but stay on the main Timberline
Trail another 0.6 mile, passing a couple of
ponds and the end of the Mazama Trail to a
junction. Head up this trail to the right, following a ridge up a mile to the stone shelter
high atop McNeil Point. Return the way you
came.

User Groups: Hikers, dogs, and horses. No
mountain bikes allowed. No wheelchair
facilities.

Permits: A free self-issue Wilderness Permit
is required and is available at the trailhead.

A federal Northwest Forest Pass is required to park here; the cost is $5 a day or $30 for an annual pass. You can buy a day pass at the trailhead, at ranger stations, or through private vendors.

Maps: For a map of the Mount Hood National Forest, contact Mount Hood National Forest Headquarters, 16400 Champion Way, Sandy, OR, 97055, 503/668-1700. A map of the Mount Hood Wilderness is available from Geo-Graphics. For a topographic map, ask the USGS for Mount Hood North.

Directions: From Portland, drive U.S. 26 east toward Mount Hood 42 miles. At Zigzag, turn left onto East Lolo Pass Road and go 4.2 miles, then turn right on Road 1825. In 0.7 mile, go straight on Road 1828 and follow signs for "Top Spur Trail" for 7.1 miles to a parking pullout on the gravel road.

Contact: Mount Hood National Forest, Zigzag Ranger District, 70220 East Highway 26, Zigzag, OR, 97049, 503/622-3191.

39 MAZAMA TRAIL TO CAIRN BASIN

8.6 mi/5.0 hr   🏃4 ⛰9

northeast of Zigzag in the Mount Hood Wilderness

Map 9.2, page 454   **BEST (**

This difficult trail is maintained by the Mazamas, Portland's oldest outdoors club. In 1894, the Mazamas (155 men and 38 women in all) climbed this mountain to its peak to elect their first president. Now you can get a sense of what brought them here. The trail climbs massive Cathedral Ridge to the glassy tarns and wildflower meadows on Mount Hood. The stone shelter in Cairn Basin is a good destination—with views of the forests, meadows, and peak of Mount Hood. You can make this short backpacking trip, too, by pitching your tent at Cairn Basin.

The path is straightforward, if steep. From the trailhead, climb the Mazama Trail one mile to the Mount Hood Wilderness sign atop a series of switchbacks. Continue 2.7 miles to this trail's terminus with the Timberline Trail. To the right is a short walk to a couple mountain tarns. Continue to the left, where a right-hand junction leads to McNeil Point (see *McNeil Point,* previous listing), or continue on to the left to Cairn Basin, a total of 0.6 mile from the end of the Mazama Trail.

User Groups: Hikers and dogs. No horses or mountain bikes allowed. No wheelchair facilities.

Permits: A free self-issue Wilderness Permit is required and is available at the trailhead. Parking and access are free.

Maps: For a map of the Mount Hood National Forest, contact Mount Hood National Forest Headquarters, 16400 Champion Way, Sandy, OR, 97055, 503/668-1700. A map of the Mount Hood Wilderness is available from Geo-Graphics. For a topographic map, ask the USGS for Mount Hood North.

Directions: From Portland, drive U.S. 26 east toward Mount Hood 42 miles. At Zigzag, turn left onto East Lolo Pass Road and go 10.5 miles to Lolo Pass. Turn right on McGee Creek Road 1810 for 5.5 miles and turn right on gravel Road 1811 for 2.5 miles to a parking pullout.

Contact: Mount Hood National Forest, Hood River Ranger District, 6780 Highway 35, Parkdale, OR, 97041, 541/352-6002.

40 CAIRN BASIN VIA VISTA RIDGE

7.9 mi/4.0 hr   🏃3 ⛰9

north of Hood River in the Mount Hood Wilderness

Map 9.2, page 454

The stone shelter at Cairn Basin is set among some towering old-growth trees, near meadows and picturesque views of Mount Hood's enormous peak and the Ladd Glacier. This loop trail also leads through two other mountain meadows: Wy'East Basin (an ancient Native American name for this iconic mountain)

© SEAN PATRICK HILL

view of Mount Hood from Eden Park

and Eden Park. You can easily get water from nearby Ladd Creek, making this a good destination for backpacking. Vista Ridge Trail is easier than the nearby Mazama Trail and has views to distant peaks to boot.

Start up the Vista Ridge Trail 0.4 mile, and keep right at a junction, climbing Vista Ridge for 2.1 miles. At the next junction, head to the left 0.3 mile to arrive at the edge of Wy'East Basin. Then go right on the Timberline Trail 1.1 rambling miles with excellent views to Cairn Basin. Just past the stone shelter, take a right-hand trail down a steep slope to Eden Park, continuing to the Vista Ridge Trail, a total of 1.5 miles. Then go left to return the way you came.

User Groups: Hikers and dogs. No horses or mountain bikes allowed. No wheelchair facilities.

Permits: A free self-issue Wilderness Permit is required and is available at the trailhead. Parking and access are free.

Maps: For a map of the Mount Hood National

Forest, contact Mount Hood National Forest Headquarters, 16400 Champion Way, Sandy, OR, 97055, 503/668-1700. A map of the Mount Hood Wilderness is available from Geo-Graphics. For a topographic map, ask the USGS for Mount Hood North.

Directions: From Portland, drive U.S. 26 east toward Mount Hood 42 miles. At Zigzag, turn left onto East Lolo Pass Road and go 10.5 miles to Lolo Pass. Turn right on McGee Creek Road 1810 for 7.7 miles to Road 18. Continue on this paved road 3.2 miles and turn right on Road 16, then follow "Vista Ridge Trail" signs nine miles up Road 16 and Road 1650 to the trailhead.

Contact: Mount Hood National Forest, Hood River Ranger District, 6780 Highway 35, Parkdale, OR, 97041, 541/352-6002.

41 ELK COVE
8.0 mi/5.0 hr   🥾 3 ⛰ 9

north of Hood River in the Mount Hood Wilderness

Map 9.2, page 454

Elk Cove, a magnificent meadow on the slopes of Mount Hood, is not only an amazing destination for a day trip but a great spot to camp. Indeed, many people do spend the night here—such as ambitious backpackers who tackle the entire length of the Timberline Trail, which circles Mount Hood, visiting an array of unforgettable spots. The trail to Elk Cove starts fairly high up the mountain, making it one of the easier destinations on Mount Hood.

The popular hike to Elk Cove from the Cloud Cap Campground is officially closed due to massive flooding on the Timberline Trail. Check with the US Forest Service before attempting this route. The following description is another way to get to Elk Cove from the Vista Ridge Trail.

Start up the Vista Ridge Trail 0.4 mile, and keep right at a junction, climbing Vista Ridge for 2.1 miles. At the next junction, head to the left 0.3 mile to arrive at the edge of Wy'East Basin. Then go left on the Timberline Trail; in just under a mile, you'll reach Elk Cove's meadows and the junction with the Elk Cove Trail.

User Groups: Hikers and dogs. No horses or mountain bikes allowed. No wheelchair facilities.

Permits: A free self-issue Wilderness Permit is required and is available at the trailhead. A federal Northwest Forest Pass is required to park here; the cost is $5 a day or $30 for an annual pass. You can buy a day pass at the trailhead, at ranger stations, or through private vendors.

Maps: For a map of the Mount Hood National Forest, contact Mount Hood National Forest Headquarters, 16400 Champion Way, Sandy, OR, 97055, 503/668-1700. A map of the Mount Hood Wilderness is available from Geo-Graphics. For a topographic map, ask the USGS for Mount Hood North.

Directions: From Portland, drive U.S. 26 east toward Mount Hood 42 miles. At Zigzag, turn left onto East Lolo Pass Road and go 10.5 miles to Lolo Pass. Turn right on McGee Creek Road 1810 for 7.7 miles to Road 18. Continue on this paved road 3.2 miles and turn right on Road 16, then follow "Vista Ridge Trail" signs nine miles up Road 16 and Road 1650 to the trailhead.

Contact: Mount Hood National Forest, Hood River Ranger District, 6780 Highway 35, Parkdale, OR, 97041, 541/352-6002.

42 COOPER SPUR

6.8 mi/4.0 hr   3 9

north of Hood River in the Mount Hood Wilderness

Map 9.2, page 454

From Cloud Cap Campground, this trail climbs to one of three CCC-built stone shelters on the flanks of Mount Hood, this one on a windswept ridge populated by a few whitebark pines, the highest-growing

tree in Oregon. But the fun has only started. A steady climb over the gravely ridge of the Cooper Spur leads to an impressive view of Mount Hood and the Eliot Glacier, which on a good summer day can be heard cracking and shifting under its own massive weight. Views extend far out to Mount Jefferson and north to the peaks of the Washington Cascades. Be sure to bring sunblock and a wide-brimmed hat; there's no protection up here from the relentless sun.

From the Cloud Cap Campground, head to the Timberline Trail and go left, following it up some small gorges 1.2 miles to a four-way junction. Go right onto the Cooper Spur Trail 0.1 mile to the Cooper Spur stone shelter. Continue on this trail 2.6 miles to get up the Cooper Spur to a saddle, where a rock is carved with a 1910 commemoration for a Japanese climbing party.

User Groups: Hikers and dogs. No horses or mountain bikes allowed. No wheelchair facilities.

Permits: A free self-issue Wilderness Permit is required and is available at the trailhead. A federal Northwest Forest Pass is required to park here; the cost is $5 a day or $30 for an annual pass. You can buy a day pass at the trailhead, at ranger stations, or through private vendors.

Maps: For a map of the Mount Hood National Forest, contact Mount Hood National Forest Headquarters, 16400 Champion Way, Sandy, OR, 97055, 503/668-1700. A map of the Mount Hood Wilderness is available from Geo-Graphics. For a topographic map, ask the USGS for Mount Hood North.

Directions: From Highway 35 on the east side of Mount Hood, between mileposts 73 and 74, go west on Cooper Spur Road for 3.3 miles to Tilly Jane Junction, and turn left on Road 3512 to go 10.3 miles to the Cloud Cap Campground.

Contact: Mount Hood National Forest, Hood River Ranger District, 6780 Highway 35, Parkdale, OR, 97041, 541/352-6002.

43 CLOUD CAP VIA POLALLIE RIDGE

6.0 mi/3.5 hr　　　🏃3　⛰7

on the northeast slope of Mount Hood

Map 9.2, page 454

Atop a timbered knoll high on the flanks of Mount Hood is the Cloud Cap Inn, built in 1889 and listed on the National Register of Historic Places. Though the historic chalet is accessible by road, there's an old ski trail that leads there—making it that much more of a destination. Along the way, the trail passes the deep and scoured Polallie Canyon, with side trail options to the Cooper Spur and the stone shelter on its flanks (see *Cooper Spur,* previous listing). You'll also pass just behind the Tilly Jane Campground and its 1924 cookhouse and old amphitheater.

From the trailhead, hike 2.6 miles up Tilly Jane Ski Trail and along the Polallie Canyon to Tilly Jane Campground, then head to the right on a 0.5-mile spur trail to Cloud Cap Campground. From here, go to the road and follow it up a short distance to views from the old inn. Head back to Tilly Jane and follow the sign for "Tilly Jane #600A" to the Polallie Ridge Trail for a return loop.

User Groups: Hikers and dogs. No horses or mountain bikes allowed. No wheelchair facilities.

Permits: Permits are not required. Parking and access are free.

Maps: For a map of the Mount Hood National Forest, contact Mount Hood National Forest Headquarters, 16400 Champion Way, Sandy, OR, 97055, 503/668-1700. For a topographic map, ask the USGS for Mount Hood North.

Directions: From Highway 35 on the east side of Mount Hood, between mileposts 73 and 74, go west on Cooper Spur Road for 3.3 miles to Tilly Jane Junction, and turn left on Road 3512 to go 1.4 miles to a trail sign on the left.

Contact: Mount Hood National Forest, Hood River Ranger District, 6780 Highway 35, Parkdale, OR, 97041, 541/352-6002.

44 WILDCAT MOUNTAIN AND MCINTYRE RIDGE

10.0 mi/5.5 hr　　　🏃4　⛰8

southeast of Sandy in Mount Hood National Forest

Map 9.2, page 454

The long McIntyre Ridge, alternately easy and steep, climbs to Wildcat Mountain and its overgrown former watchtower site. But the ridge has great views of the Mount Hood country from its meadows, looking over the Salmon-Huckleberry Wilderness and out to nearby Huckleberry Mountain.

From the McIntyre Ridge Trailhead, the path begins its climb through acres of huckleberry fields and forest 2.1 miles to the first clear viewpoint. Another 0.8 mile leads to a fine mountain meadow with awesome views, though the trails meander every which way here. The next 1.6 miles heads out into another large meadow to a junction with the Douglas Trail. Go left and up for 0.5 mile to the 4,480-foot summit of Wildcat Mountain.

User Groups: Hikers, dogs, and horses. No mountain bikes allowed. No wheelchair facilities.

Permits: A free self-issue Wilderness Permit is required and is available at the trailhead. Parking and access are free.

Maps: For a map of the Mount Hood National Forest and the Salmon-Huckleberry Wilderness, contact Mount Hood National Forest Headquarters, 16400 Champion Way, Sandy, OR, 97055, 503/668-1700. For a topographic map, ask the USGS for Wildcat Mountain.

Directions: From Portland, drive U.S. 26 toward Mount Hood. At 11 miles past Sandy, turn right onto East Wildcat Creek Road for 1.5 miles. Note that the BLM has closed the road to McIntyre Ridge from this point for the time being; contact the Forest Service for updates and for information on other access points. To hike into the trailhead from here, stay on the larger road at all forks for three miles. The McIntyre Ridge Trailhead is after the last stretch of deeply rutted road.

Contact: Mount Hood National Forest, Zigzag Ranger District, 70220 East Highway 26, Zigzag, OR, 97049, 503/622-3191.

45 WILDWOOD RECREATION SITE/BOULDER RIDGE/ HUCKLEBERRY MOUNTAIN
1.5-11.6 mi/1.0-6.0 hr

southeast of Sandy off U.S. 26

Map 9.2, page 454

A network of trails here spans the Wildwood Recreation Site and the Salmon-Huckleberry Wilderness, located along the Wild and Scenic Salmon River. There's plenty to do here, including fishing, swimming, wildlife-watching, and a number of short loop trails. It's also the gateway to a challenging loop up Boulder Ridge to the summit of Huckleberry Mountain and back down again. If you're camping with a group of people and you have two cars, I recommend a shuttle to tackle Boulder Ridge; otherwise, the loop requires you to hike a long ways down roads and highways. If you try this loop, you'll follow the deep Cheeney Creek canyon and pass the abandoned shaft of the Bonanza Mine. If you have the kids, you can make it an easy day and stick to the easier Wildwood Trails.

The Wildwood loops are an easy 1.5 mile altogether and are all-accessible. To try the loops, or part of them, follow either the 0.7-mile Wetland Trail or the 0.8-mile Streamwatch Loop, which both begin at the trailhead parking area.

For a more challenging day, take the Wetland Trail loop 0.3 mile to the right to the Boulder Ridge Trail. This path climbs steeply up Boulder Ridge, passing two viewpoints 4.3 miles to a junction with the Plaza Trail. Turn right and go up another mile to a crest on Huckleberry Mountain. Another 0.5 mile follows the ridge to the Bonanza Trail. This, or any point before, would be a fine turn-around point.

If you've arranged for a shuttle, go left on the Bonanza Trail, following it down the mountain 2.4 miles to the mine shaft near a creek, and the remaining 2.7 miles to the end of the trail, fording a creek at the end.

User Groups: Hikers and dogs. No horses or mountain bikes allowed. Wildwood Trails are wheelchair accessible.

Permits: Permits are not required. The BLM charges a $5 parking fee at the site.

Maps: For a map of the Mount Hood National Forest and the Salmon-Huckleberry Wilderness, contact Mount Hood National Forest Headquarters, 16400 Champion Way, Sandy, OR, 97055, 503/668-1700. For a topographic map, ask the USGS for Rhododendron and Wildcat Mountain.

Directions: Follow U.S. 26 past Sandy 15.4 miles, and turn south into the Wildwood Recreation Site. To shuttle a car for the Bonanza Trail, drive U.S. 26 another mile east of Wildwood to a stoplight at Welches and turn right on Welches Road for 1.3 miles, staying left at a fork, and driving 0.7 mile to another junction, heading straight across a one-lane bridge. Take the second gravel street to the left and follow East Grove Lane to a fork. The road closed by a cable is the start of the Bonanza Trail. The Wildwood Trails begin in the Recreation Area.

Contact: Bureau of Land Management, Salem District Office, 1717 Fabry Road SE, Salem, OR, 97306, 503/375-5646, and Mount Hood National Forest, Zigzag Ranger District, 70220 East Highway 26, Zigzag, OR, 97049, 503/622-3191.

46 HUNCHBACK MOUNTAIN
4.2-9.0 mi/2.0-4.5 hr

at Zigzag in the Salmon-Huckleberry Wilderness

Map 9.2, page 454

How did Hunchback Mountain get its name? I have two guesses: one is the general hunching shape of the mountain itself, easily discernable from the highway, and the other is the way you feel when you're going up this beast. Yes, Hunchback Mountain is steep, steep, steep, and coming down is no easier. The nine-mile round-trip out to the Great Pyramid is an ample day's journey. There are good viewpoints along the way, and once you're on top of the ridge things get a bit easier. A bit.

From the trailhead, climb on Hunchback Mountain Trail, a steep path, for 2.1 harsh, switchbacking miles to a viewpoint on some sheer rimrock just inside the wilderness boundary. In another 0.3 mile, a side trail leads to the big, jumbled "Viewpoint Rockpile"—another great view. Another 1.1 miles leads to the "Viewpoint Helispot 260," though as far as I know no helicopter has landed here in a long time. Another mile past that leads to a side trail by a junction leading out to a viewpoint on the 4,030-foot Great Pyramid, overlooking the Salmon River canyon. Though Devil's Peak is farther on, this is a good spot to turn around; the trail sharply drops in elevation after this, only to rise again later.

User Groups: Hikers and dogs. No mountain bikes or horses allowed. No wheelchair facilities.

Permits: A free self-issue Wilderness Permit is required and is available at the trailhead. Parking and access are free.

Maps: For a map of the Mount Hood National Forest and the Salmon-Huckleberry Wilderness, contact Mount Hood National Forest Headquarters, 16400 Champion Way, Sandy, OR, 97055, 503/668-1700. For a topographic map, ask the USGS for Rhododendron.

Directions: From Portland, drive 42 miles east on U.S. 26 to the Zigzag Ranger Station in Zigzag. Turn left into a large parking lot by the trailhead.

Contact: Mount Hood National Forest, Zigzag Ranger District, 70220 East Highway 26, Zigzag, OR, 97049, 503/622-3191.

47 CASTLE CANYON
1.8 mi/1.0 hr

north of Rhododendron in the Mount Hood Wilderness

Map 9.2, page 454

This fun trail leads to some colossal rock formations. You'll climb up about 800 feet in 0.9 mile to reach the jagged spires of Castle Canyon, and you'll have the opportunity to scramble up and play around on the peaks and ridges looking out far over the valleys below. But be careful: These cliffs are high. If you bring pets or children, be sure to keep them close.

User Groups: Hikers and dogs. No horses or mountain bikes. No wheelchair facilities.

Permits: Permits are not required. Parking and access are free.

Maps: For a map of the Mount Hood National Forest, contact Mount Hood National Forest Headquarters, 16400 Champion Way, Sandy, OR, 97055, 503/668-1700. A map of the Mount Hood Wilderness is available from Geo-Graphics. For a topographic map, ask the USGS for Rhododendron.

Directions: Drive east of Portland 44 miles on U.S. 26 to the village of Rhododendron, and turn left on East Littlebrook Lane. Keep left on the paved road 0.3 mile and turn left on the gravel road, following Barlow Road Route for 0.4 mile to a trailhead sign on the right. Park on the shoulder.

Contact: Mount Hood National Forest, Zigzag Ranger District, 70220 East Highway 26, Zigzag, OR, 97049, 503/622-3191.

48 HIDDEN LAKE
4.0 mi/2.0 hr

north of Government Camp in Mount Hood National Forest

Map 9.2, page 454

The name is appropriate enough, as this mountain lake is secreted on an access trail to the Mount Hood Wilderness. Though the lake has no views to speak of, it's circled with pink rhododendrons. Think of this easy-in, easy-out four-mile loop trail as a destination in and of itself, or as a way into the Zigzag Canyon and Paradise Park areas of the Mount Hood Wilderness. From the trailhead, follow the Hidden Lake Trail.

User Groups: Hikers, dogs, and horses. No mountain bikes allowed. No wheelchair facilities.

Permits: A free self-issue Wilderness Permit is required and is available at the trailhead. A federal Northwest Forest Pass is required to park here; the cost is $5 a day or $30 for an annual pass. You can buy a day pass at the trailhead, at ranger stations, or through private vendors.

Maps: For a map of the Mount Hood National Forest, contact Mount Hood National Forest Headquarters, 16400 Champion Way, Sandy, OR, 97055, 503/668-1700. A map of the Mount Hood Wilderness is available from Geo-Graphics. For a topographic map, ask the USGS for Mount Hood South and Government Camp.

Directions: From Portland, drive U.S. 26 toward Mount Hood. At 4.1 miles east of the town of Rhododendron, turn left on Road 2639 for two miles to the trailhead.

Contact: Mount Hood National Forest, Zigzag Ranger District, 70220 East Highway 26, Zigzag, OR, 97049, 503/622-3191.

49 ZIGZAG CANYON AND PARADISE PARK

4.4-12.3 mi/2.5-8.0 hr   🏔5 ⛰10

from Timberline Lodge in the Mount Hood Wilderness

Map 9.2, page 454   **BEST (**

Some of the most dramatic alpine territory in the Pacific Northwest is easily accessible from the classic Timberline Lodge, a gem of a building on the slopes of Mount Hood. The Pacific Crest Trail passes by the lodge on its way around the mountain and on toward the

Paradise Park on Mount Hood

© SEAN PATRICK HILL

Columbia Gorge, and it is this access that opens up the high meadows of Paradise Park and the deep, glacier-carved gorge of Zigzag Canyon. This is some serious hiking: Take lots of water and stamina and be prepared for unforgettable mountain country. You can take the trail in bits or as a 12-plus mile-escapade; either way you'll be circling the mountain on one of the most famous trails in the country. Bring a camera.

From Timberline Lodge, you can either walk the road past the lodge, which turns to trail, or follow the PCT, which runs behind the lodge; either way, in 0.7 mile both paths meet beyond the last ski lift. From here, hike 1.5 miles down and out of the gravelly Little Zigzag Canyon and on to the lip of massive Zigzag Canyon, a good turnaround point for the less ambitious.

From here, it's a 1.5-mile crossing down and back up from the 700-foot-deep canyon, but it's a pleasure along the way—with wildflowers, shady woods, and a waterfall upstream from the crossing of the Zigzag River. Once out of the canyon, the loop begins through the meadows of Paradise Park. Go right on an uphill climb leading to the boulder-strewn meadows of this unparalleled scenic area, a 2.4-mile walk through heaven. After the trail slopes back down to the PCT, go left for 2.4 miles, passing lovely waterfalls along the way, to return to the beginning of the loop and the return trail.

User Groups: Hikers, dogs, and horses. No mountain bikes allowed. No wheelchair facilities.

Permits: A free self-issue Wilderness Permit is required and is available at the trailhead. Parking and access are free.

Maps: For a map of the Mount Hood National Forest, contact Mount Hood National Forest Headquarters, 16400 Champion Way, Sandy, OR, 97055, 503/668-1700. A map of the Mount Hood Wilderness is available from Geo-Graphics. For a topographic map, ask the USGS for Government Camp and Mount Hood South.

Directions: From Portland, drive U.S. 26 toward Mount Hood for 54 miles. Past Government Camp, turn left for six miles at the sign for Timberline Lodge. Park in the lot.

Contact: Mount Hood National Forest, Zigzag Ranger District, 70220 East Highway 26, Zigzag, OR, 97049, 503/622-3191.

50 SILCOX HUT
2.2 mi/2.0 hr   🥾3 ⛰9

at Timberline Lodge on Mount Hood

Map 9.2, page 454

President Franklin D. Roosevelt showed up in 1937 for the dedication of Timberline Lodge, an incredible work of art that made use of some of the best Northwest artists and artisans. The building was a Works Progress Administration project during the Great Depression; it's received much care and attention over the years, leaving a legacy of beauty. These days you can visit, eat here, or even stay

overnight. Just above the lodge is the Silcox Hut, which was at the top of the Magic Mile Chairlift from 1939 to 1962, until it sat idle for 30 years. Today it operates in the style of a classic European chalet, and you can hike here for views extending south to Mount Jefferson and the Three Sisters.

Start by following the paved path along the right-hand side of Timberline Lodge and turn right on the Pacific Crest Trail, crossing a gully, then heading uphill 1,100 feet on the Mountaineer Trail to Silcox Hut—a total of one mile. Descend a different way by heading over to the top of the Magic Mile Chairlift and following the service road down 1.2 miles back to the lodge.

User Groups: Hikers and dogs. No horses or mountain bikes allowed. No wheelchair facilities.

Permits: Permits are not required. Parking and access are free.

Maps: For a map of the Mount Hood National Forest, contact Mount Hood National Forest Headquarters, 16400 Champion Way, Sandy, OR, 97055, 503/668-1700. For a topographic map, ask the USGS for Mount Hood South.

Directions: From Portland, drive U.S. 26 toward Mount Hood for 54 miles. Past Government Camp, turn left for six miles at the sign for Timberline Lodge. Park in the lot.

Contact: Mount Hood National Forest, Zigzag Ranger District, 70220 East Highway 26, Zigzag, OR, 97049, 503/622-3191.

51 TIMBERLINE TRAIL
40.7 mi/4-5 days   🥾5 ⛰10

in the Mount Hood Wilderness

Map 9.2, page 454

Up for a backpacking adventure? Want to see the best that Mount Hood has to offer, including Zigzag Canyon, Paradise Park, Ramona Falls, Bald Mountain, Cairn Basin, Wy'East Basin, Elk Cove, and the Cooper Spur? The Timberline Trail circles Mount

Hood, almost completely in a wilderness area, with easy access from historic Timberline Lodge. Crossing meadows rich with wildflowers, gorges carved by prehistoric glaciers, mountain hemlock forests—and passing snowfields, waterfalls, and views in every direction—this is one of the most breathtaking trails in Oregon.

Due to a flood and landslide in 2006, a major crossing was swept away at the Eliot Branch of the Hood River, leaving behind an insurmountable gorge where the trail once was. The Forest Service has closed this portion of the trail and expressly forbids trying to cross it, though for the determined it is possible to circumvent the disaster by detouring on a number of trails between Elk Cove and Cloud Cap. Please use care, avoid the dangerous washout, and contact the Forest Service for updates on the condition of the trail.

There are numerous access points, the most popular being Timberline Lodge, Cairn Basin, the Mazama Trail, and Cloud Cap (see listings in this chapter).

User Groups: Hikers, dogs, and horses. No mountain bikes allowed. No wheelchair facilities.

Permits: A free self-issue Wilderness Permit is required and is available at the trailhead. Parking and access are free.

Maps: For a map of the Mount Hood National Forest, contact Mount Hood National Forest Headquarters, 16400 Champion Way, Sandy, OR, 97055, 503/668-1700. A map of the Mount Hood Wilderness is available from Geo-Graphics. For a topographic map, ask the USGS for Mount Hood North.

Directions: From Portland, drive U.S. 26 toward Mount Hood for 54 miles. Past Government Camp, turn left for six miles at the sign for Timberline Lodge. Park in the lot.

Contact: Mount Hood National Forest, Zigzag Ranger District, 70220 East Highway 26, Zigzag, OR, 97049, 503/622-3191, or Hood River Ranger District, 6780 Highway 35, Parkdale, OR, 97041, 541/352-6002.

52 ELK MEADOWS
6.8 mi/3.0 hr   2   8

north of Hood River in the Mount Hood Wilderness

Map 9.2, page 454

This unassuming entrance to the Mount Hood Wilderness leads to two of its most famous spots: the sweeping Elk Meadow, rimmed in by trees and shadowed by Mount Hood itself; and Gnarl Ridge, a deep canyon carved from the mountain's flanks. Though camping is prohibited within Elk Meadow in order to protect vegetation, there are camping spots back in the trees along a 1.2-mile perimeter trail, and there's a shelter used by cross-country skiers in the winter season.

From the trailhead, walk one mile on the Elk Meadows Trail to a junction, going to the right for 0.6 mile and entering the Mount Hood Wilderness. At a second junction, go straight and cross Newton Creek, then switchback up one mile to a four-way junction. Going to the right leads out to Elk Mountain; to the left, Lamberson Butte and Gnarl Ridge. Go straight a short 0.2 mile to the Elk Meadows perimeter trail, which you can hike clockwise or counterclockwise, avoiding the trails that radiate away from the meadow.

User Groups: Hikers, dogs, and horses. No mountain bikes allowed. No wheelchair facilities.

Permits: A free self-issue Wilderness Permit is required and is available at the trailhead. A federal Northwest Forest Pass is required to park here; the cost is $5 a day or $30 for an annual pass. You can buy a day pass at the trailhead, at ranger stations, or through private vendors.

Maps: For a map of the Mount Hood National Forest, contact Mount Hood National Forest Headquarters, 16400 Champion Way, Sandy, OR, 97055, 503/668-1700. A map of the Mount Hood Wilderness is available from Geo-Graphics. For a topographic map, ask the USGS for Badger Lake.

Directions: From Portland, drive U.S 26 to

Mount Hood and take Highway 35 toward Hood River for 8.3 miles. Go 1.5 miles past the Mount Hood Meadows turnoff and turn left on the Clark Creek Sno-Park loop for 0.3 mile to the second pullout.

Contact: Mount Hood National Forest, Hood River Ranger District, 6780 Highway 35, Parkdale, OR, 97041, 541/352-6002.

53 EAST FORK HOOD RIVER
4.6 mi/2.0 hr   🚶1 ⛰7

on the East Fork Hood River

Map 9.2, page 454

Portions of the East Fork Hood River Trail remain flood damaged from a massive landslide that occurred in November 2006, but this northernmost section is still fine. Just contact the US Forest Service before you go. This stretch of trail is quite popular with mountain bikers, who can make short work of it in only a few hours. But hikers are different, having a bit more length to deal with, but they get to glide along a riverbank that effectively drowns out any highway noise. The main access point is the Pollalie Trailhead; from here, going left leads 1.1 miles to a junction with the Tamanawas Trail, and going 0.6 miles further leads to a river crossing to the East Fork Trailhead, but the bridge was wiped out in a 2006 flood. Should the rest of the East Fork Trail reopen, it will continue to a lower trailhead and a sandy stretch near the defunct Robinhood Campground.

User Groups: Hikers, dogs, and mountain bikes. Horses not allowed. No wheelchair facilities.

Permits: A free self-issue Wilderness Permit is required and is available at the trailhead. A federal Northwest Forest Pass is required to park here; the cost is $5 a day or $30 for an annual pass. You can buy a day pass at the trailhead, at ranger stations, or through private vendors.

Maps: For a map of the Mount Hood National Forest, contact Mount Hood National Forest

Headquarters, 16400 Champion Way, Sandy, OR, 97055, 503/668-1700. For a topographic map, ask the USGS for Dog River and Badger Lake.

Directions: Drive Highway 35 on the east side of Mount Hood about 8.5 miles south from the junction with U.S. 26 to the Pollallie Trailhead on the left.

Contact: Mount Hood National Forest, Hood River Ranger District, 6780 Highway 35, Parkdale, OR, 97041, 541/352-6002.

54 TAMANAWAS FALLS
5.6 mi/2.0 hr   🚶2 ⛰8

in the Mount Hood National Forest

Map 9.2, page 454

This 100-foot waterfall on the flanks of Mount Hood is named Tamanawas for the Chinook Indian word meaning "spiritual guardian." Cascading in a curtain over a water-carved grotto, these falls certainly are guarding the wilderness beyond. Hiking to this spot is easy and the walk along Cold Spring Creek makes it that much better. Making a loop of it won't add too much time and effort, and you'll be rewarded by the Polallie Overlook, which looks over a vast canyon carved by a 1980 flash flood that took out both the forest and the highway. Such is the power of Mother Nature in these mountains.

To get to the falls, cross the river and head right on the East Fork Trail for 0.6 mile, then left at a junction for 0.9 mile to a junction, which will be the start of the loop. Continue 0.4 mile, crossing the creek and arriving at the falls. Head back to the junction, this time going left if you want to try the loop. You'll go up and over a ridge and down 1.6 miles to a side trail on the left for the Polallie Overlook, then continue on to a junction at the Polallie Trailhead. Stay to the right, following the highway and the river 1.7 miles back to the trailhead.

User Groups: Hikers and dogs. No horses or mountain bikes allowed. No wheelchair facilities.

Permits: Permits are not required. A federal Northwest Forest Pass is required to park here; the cost is $5 a day or $30 for an annual pass. You can buy a day pass at the trailhead, at ranger stations, or through private vendors.

Maps: For a map of the Mount Hood National Forest, contact Mount Hood National Forest Headquarters, 16400 Champion Way, Sandy, OR, 97055, 503/668-1700. For a topographic map, ask the USGS for Dog River.

Directions: Drive Highway 35 on the east side of Mount Hood to the East Fork Trailhead near milepost 72.

Contact: Mount Hood National Forest, Hood River Ranger District, 6780 Highway 35, Parkdale, OR, 97041, 541/352-6002.

55 BADGER LAKE VIA GUMJUWAC SADDLE
5.4-11.5 mi/3.0-7.0 hr

east of Mount Hood in the Badger Creek Wilderness

Map 9.2, page 454

First of all, let it be said that not just any old car can make it to the Gumjuwac Saddle; only vehicles with clearance should attempt this. If you're driving one of those little economy cars, start at the Highway 35 trailhead instead, located between mileposts 68 and 69. Either way, the destination here is Badger Lake. But there are a myriad of ways to get here. You could take the easy route on the Divide Trail, which leads 2.5 miles straight from the Gumjuwac Saddle to the Badger Creek Trail; a left and a right on this trail will bring you to the shore and an old campground. And there are plenty more ways than that, including following Gumjuwac Creek and Badger Creek on a 6.7-mile loop, or the Gunsight Trail, passing Gunsight Butte on an 8.5-mile loop with the Divide Trail, or the big 11.5-mile difficult trek from Highway 35.

User Groups: Hikers, dogs, and horses. No mountain bikes allowed. No wheelchair facilities.

Permits: A free self-issue Wilderness Permit is required and is available at the trailhead. Parking and access are free.

Maps: For a map of the Mount Hood National Forest or the Badger Creek Wilderness, contact Mount Hood National Forest Headquarters, 16400 Champion Way, Sandy, OR, 97055, 503/668-1700. For a topographic map, ask the USGS for Badger Lake.

Directions: From Highway 35 on the east side of Mount Hood, between mileposts 70 and 71, go east on Dufur Mill Road 44 for 3.8 miles, then turn right on High Prairie Road 4410. Go 4.7 miles, staying always uphill, to a T-junction where the road goes from gravel to dirt. Go right on Bennett Pass Road 3550 for 1.9 very rugged miles to the trailhead by a large sign.

Contact: Mount Hood National Forest, Barlow Ranger District, 780 NE Court Street, Dufur, OR, 97021, 541/467-2291.

56 LOOKOUT MOUNTAIN
2.4 mi/1.0 hr

east of Mount Hood in Mount Hood National Forest

Map 9.2, page 454

Not nearly as well known as the nearby Mount Hood Wilderness, the Badger Creek Wilderness provides the same rugged country and sweeping views, especially from 6,525-foot Lookout Mountain, whose views encompass Mount Rainier to the Three Sisters. For the ambitious, this trail can be extended along the Divide Trail stretching along a row of craggy palisades with a side trail down to scenic Oval Lake.

The Lookout Mountain Trail begins on an old road through the sub-alpine meadows of High Prairie, heading across through wildflowers and up a long switchback to the Divide Trail. Go right to the summit, a 1.2-mile walk in all. To continue on the Divide Trail, go 1.4 mile to a junction. Going left and down 0.2 mile takes you to Oval Lake, but staying on the Divide Trail another 0.3 mile brings you to a viewpoint on Palisade Point.

User Groups: Hikers, dogs, and horses. No mountain bikes allowed. No wheelchair facilities.

Permits: A free self-issue Wilderness Permit is required and is available at the trailhead. A federal Northwest Forest Pass is required to park here; the cost is $5 a day or $30 for an annual pass. You can buy a day pass at the trailhead, at ranger stations, or through private vendors.

Maps: For a map of the Mount Hood National Forest or the Badger Creek Wilderness, contact Mount Hood National Forest Headquarters, 16400 Champion Way, Sandy, OR, 97055, 503/668-1700. For a topographic map, ask the USGS for Badger Lake.

Directions: From Highway 35 on the east side of Mount Hood, between mileposts 70 and 71, go east on Dufur Mill Road 44 for 3.8 miles, then turn right on High Prairie Road 4410. Go 4.7 miles, staying always uphill, to a T-junction where the road goes from gravel to dirt. Go left on High Prairie Road 200 yards and park at the trailhead on the right.

Contact: Mount Hood National Forest, Barlow Ranger District, 780 NE Court Street, Dufur, OR, 97021, 541/467-2291.

57 BALL POINT
2.0-7.0 mi/1.0-3.5 hr

east of Mount Hood in the Badger Creek Wilderness

Map 9.2, page 454

Heading east into the Badger Creek Wilderness, you begin to cross into another ecosystem and climate. Things here on the eastern slope of the Cascades are a bit drier, and you're more likely to find these pine-oak grasslands, where big showy balsamroots burst in summer. From atop Ball Point, you'll overlook everything from Cascade peaks as far as Mount Jefferson and the Three Sisters to the distant farmlands of Eastern Oregon.

The School Canyon Trail to Ball Point is an easy one-mile climb to a saddle, but it's worth it while you're here to continue on another 2.6 miles to a viewpoint at a helispot with a camping spot nearby and a spring. Views overlook Little Badger Creek, and its namesake trail switchbacks steeply down to it, running four miles to Road 2710—along the way you'll pass an old mine. The School Canyon Trail continues on to Flag Point. If this is too far in its entirety, you can turn back at any time.

User Groups: Hikers, dogs, and horses. No mountain bikes allowed. No wheelchair facilities.

Permits: A free self-issue Wilderness Permit is required and is available at the trailhead. Parking and access are free.

Maps: For a map of the Mount Hood National Forest or the Badger Creek Wilderness, contact Mount Hood National Forest Headquarters, 16400 Champion Way, Sandy, OR, 97055, 503/668-1700. For a topographic map, ask the USGS for Flag Point and Friend.

Directions: From Portland, drive U.S. 26 beyond Mount Hood. After milepost 68, at a sign for Wamic, turn left on Road 43 and drive six miles. Turn right on Road 48 and go 15.2 miles, then turn left on Road 4810 and follow signs to Bonney Crossing Campground. After 0.2 mile, stay right on Road 4810 and go another 1.9 miles, then go right on Road 4811 for 1.2 miles, and turn right on the rough gravel road 2710 for 6.7 miles, going toward Tygh Valley. Turn left on Road 27 for 2.1 miles to a pullout and sign on the left for the School Canyon Trail.

Contact: Mount Hood National Forest, Barlow Ranger District, 780 NE Court Street, Dufur, OR, 97021, 541/467-2291.

58 DOUGLAS CABIN TRAIL
8.0 mi/4.5 hr

east of Mount Hood in the Badger Creek Wilderness

Map 9.2, page 454

The Douglas Cabin Trail traverses the Badger Creek Wilderness, offering access to a number of spots. The destination is the Flag Point Lookout, which—unlike other lookouts in this region—is sometimes staffed (when it's not, it's available for rental). You'll have to climb 1,200 feet to get to the lookout, and 60 more feet to get up to the top of the lookout itself, but the views of Mount Hood and the surrounding area are tremendous. Built in 1973, this observation cabin sits atop a timber pole tower that itself sits atop 5,650-foot Flag Point Butte. You can reach the cabin via a straight shot on the Douglas Cabin Trail, hitting 4,820-foot Gordon Butte along the way.

User Groups: Hikers, dogs, and horses. No mountain bikes allowed. No wheelchair facilities.

Permits: A free self-issue Wilderness Permit is required and is available at the trailhead. Parking and access are free.

Maps: For a map of the Mount Hood National Forest or the Badger Creek Wilderness, contact Mount Hood National Forest Headquarters, 16400 Champion Way, Sandy, OR, 97055, 503/668-1700. For a topographic map, ask the USGS for Flag Point.

Directions: From Portland, drive U.S. 26 beyond Mount Hood. After milepost 68, at a sign for Wamic, turn left on Road 43 and drive six miles. Turn right on Road 48 and go 15.2 miles, then turn left on Road 4810 and follow signs to Bonney Crossing Campground. After 0.2 mile, stay right on Road 4810 and go another 1.9 miles, then go right on Road 4811 for 1.2 miles, and turn right on the rough gravel road 2710 for 5.6 miles, and go left for 3.5 miles. (Note: The access road is gated October 1 to May 1.)

Contact: Mount Hood National Forest,

Barlow Ranger District, 780 NE Court Street, Dufur, OR, 97021, 541/467-2291.

59 BADGER CREEK
11.4-23.8 mi/6 hr-2 days

east of Mount Hood in the Badger Creek Wilderness

Map 9.2, page 454

By the time Badger Creek makes its way from the alpine forests of nearby Mount Hood to the sagebrush deserts of Eastern Oregon, it crosses a diverse array of landscapes with a variety of attendant plant life. At the beginning of the Wilderness area just above Bonney Crossing, the trail along Boulder Creek passes through an area of white oak, ponderosa pine, Western red cedar, and grand fir. Flowers along the way include the rare lady's slipper orchid, trilliums, balsamroot, larkspur, twinflowers, and white prairie stars—all in a gorgeous canyon with opportunities for long hikes all the way to Badger Lake.

The Badger Creek Trail sets out across the road from the Bonney Crossing Campground, heading in 5.7 miles to the confluence with Pine Creek, a good destination for the day. Return the way you came. If you're backpacking, consider going the rest of the way to Badger Lake, an additional 6.2 miles upstream (see *Badger Lake via Gumjuwac Saddle* listing in this chapter).

User Groups: Hikers, dogs, and horses. No mountain bikes allowed. No wheelchair facilities.

Permits: A free self-issue Wilderness Permit is required and is available at the trailhead. A federal Northwest Forest Pass is required to park here; the cost is $5 a day or $30 for an annual pass. You can buy a day pass at the trailhead, at ranger stations, or through private vendors.

Maps: For a map of the Mount Hood National Forest or the Badger Creek Wilderness, contact Mount Hood National Forest Headquarters, 16400 Champion Way, Sandy, OR, 97055,

503/668-1700. For a topographic map, ask the USGS for Flag Point.

Directions: From Portland, drive U.S. 26 beyond Mount Hood. After milepost 68, at a sign for Wamic, turn left on Road 43 and drive six miles. Turn right on Road 48 and go 15.2 miles, then turn left on Road 4810 and follow signs to Bonney Crossing Campground. After 0.2 mile, stay right on Road 4810 and go another 1.9 miles, then go right on Road 4811 for 1.2 miles, and turn right on the rough gravel road 2710 for 1.8 miles. The trail is on the left, but you will need to park in the lot along the entrance road to Bonney Crossing Campground and walk to the trailhead on Road 2710.

Contact: Mount Hood National Forest, Barlow Ranger District, 780 NE Court Street, Dufur, OR, 97021, 541/467-2291.

60 SALMON BUTTE
8.8 mi/5.0 hr

south of Zigzag in the Salmon-Huckleberry Wilderness

Map 9.2, page 454

Here's a straightforward trail whose view is anything but. From the peak of Salmon Butte, you'll look far out over the Salmon River Canyon to massive Mount Hood. Not only that, but you'll see Mount Jefferson and the Three Sisters on the Oregon side, and Mount Adams, Mount St. Helens, and Mount Rainier on the Washington side. No wonder they put a lookout here, though all that remains are bits and pieces.

From behind the gate, head up the Salmon Butte Trail 4.4 miles, connecting on the old road at the top and following it uphill to the summit. The trail is a single-shot with no junctions, up to the 4,900-foot peak and back.

User Groups: Hikers, dogs, and horses. No mountain bikes allowed. No wheelchair facilities.

Permits: A free self-issue Wilderness Permit is required and is available at the trailhead. A federal Northwest Forest Pass is required to park here; the cost is $5 a day or $30 for

an annual pass. You can buy a day pass at the trailhead, at ranger stations, or through private vendors.

Maps: For a map of the Mount Hood National Forest and the Salmon-Huckleberry Wilderness, contact Mount Hood National Forest Headquarters, 16400 Champion Way, Sandy, OR, 97055, 503/668-1700. For a topographic map, ask the USGS for High Rock.

Directions: Drive east of Portland 42 miles on U.S. 26 to Zigzag. Turn south on Salmon River Road, following the paved road 4.9 miles to a bridge. Crossing the bridge, follow the gravel road 1.7 miles to a pullout on the left.

Contact: Mount Hood National Forest, Zigzag Ranger District, 70220 East Highway 26, Zigzag, OR, 97049, 503/622-3191.

61 SALMON RIVER TO DEVIL'S PEAK
15.7 mi one-way/1-2 days

south of Zigzag in the Salmon-Huckleberry Wilderness

Map 9.2, page 454

Just beyond civilization and a busy highway, the Salmon River extends into a deep wilderness area and roars beneath Hunchback Mountain through a canyon of its own making. The river rumbles far below the trail, and the view, once it opens up, is staggering. Atop Devil's Peak, rising off Hunchback, an old fire watchtower provides a good destination, not to mention a rugged climb. Hike the river or turn this one into a loop, but either way the route is good for backpacking.

From the trailhead, head into the old-growth forest following the Salmon River Trail for 3.6 miles, passing the primitive Rolling Riffle Camp, to arrive at a stupendous viewpoint high above the canyon and looking out over the mountains of the Salmon-Huckleberry Wilderness. Return as you came, or continue on another 2.5 miles, passing another campsite on Goat Creek, to a junction. Turn left and uphill for 2.0 miles on the Kinzel Lake Trail to reach a car campground on said lake. Continue to Road 2613, go left on the Hunchback Trail to arrive at Devil's Peak, a total of 1.6 miles. To complete a strenuous loop, continue on the Hunchback Trail another 2.4 miles and go left on the Green Canyon Way Trail, descending 3.3 miles back to the road. Go left 0.3 mile to return to your vehicle via the road.

User Groups: Hikers and dogs. No horses or mountain bikes allowed. No wheelchair facilities.

Permits: A free self-issue Wilderness Permit is required and is available at the trailhead. A federal Northwest Forest Pass is required to park here; the cost is $5 a day or $30 for an annual pass. You can buy a day pass at the trailhead, at ranger stations, or through private vendors.

Maps: For a map of the Mount Hood National Forest and the Salmon-Huckleberry Wilderness, contact Mount Hood National Forest Headquarters, 16400 Champion Way, Sandy, OR, 97055, 503/668-1700. For a topographic map, ask the USGS for Rhododendron, High Rock, and Wolf Peak.

Directions: Drive east of Portland 42 miles on U.S. 26 to Zigzag. Turn south on Salmon River Road, following the paved road 4.9 miles to a pullout on the left before a bridge.

Contact: Mount Hood National Forest, Zigzag Ranger District, 70220 East Highway 26, Zigzag, OR, 97049, 503/622-3191.

62 DEVIL'S PEAK LOOKOUT
8.2 mi/4.5 hr   🧍3 ⛰8

south of Zigzag in Mount Hood National Forest

Map 9.2, page 454

The use of airplanes largely made fire watchtowers irrelevant, so most federal agencies removed most of them. Most, but not all. Some remain staffed year after year, and some remain as great rest stops for hikers—or even for camping. The Devil's Peak Lookout is kept unlocked for hikers. Volunteers keep it looking good, and will continue to do so if you do your

share. There is no outhouse here, so you'll have to make like you're backpacking, packing out all trash and toilet paper.

The trail is simple: a 4.1-mile climb up the Cool Creek Trail to a junction, meeting up with the Hunchback Trail (go right, then left at the next junction to the tower). Along the way there are some views to Mount Hood. Do this trail as an alternative to hiking in on the Salmon River Trail (previous listing).

User Groups: Hikers and dogs. No horses or mountain bikes allowed. No wheelchair facilities.

Permits: Permits are not required. Parking and access are free.

Maps: For a map of the Mount Hood National Forest, contact Mount Hood National Forest Headquarters, 16400 Champion Way, Sandy, OR, 97055, 503/668-1700. For a topographic map, ask the USGS for Government Camp.

Directions: Drive east of Portland 42 miles on U.S. 26 to Zigzag. Go 1.4 miles east of Zigzag and turn right on Still Creek Road, following this road 2.6 miles to the end of the pavement and an additional 0.3 mile on gravel to the crossing of Cool Creek. About 300 yards farther, watch on the right for a "Cool Creek Trail" sign and park here.

Contact: Mount Hood National Forest, Zigzag Ranger District, 70220 East Highway 26, Zigzag, OR, 97049, 503/622-3191.

63 LAUREL HILL
1.0-9.4 mi/0.5-4.0 hr

west of Government Camp in Mount Hood National Forest

Map 9.2, page 454

In what seems like a distant past, Oregon Trail pioneers came trundling into Oregon in their covered wagons. For the longest time, all they could do on the last stretch was to raft the Columbia River, which then (before being dammed) was a rugged and dangerous roller-coaster ride. In 1845, Sam Barlow laid out his version of a new trail, which brought pioneers over Mount Hood to a nondescript knoll called Laurel Hill. Actually, it was anything but nondescript to the pioneers; on one cliff-edge, they had to lower their wagons down by a rope winched around the trees. Those trees still bear the burn marks, and you can see them for yourself, along with bits of the old wagon trail, on a series of trails around Laurel Hill. You can also hike an abandoned stretch of the old 1921 Mount Hood Highway, ducking through a tunnel on the way to Little Zigzag Falls.

The "wagon chute" is an easy one-mile round-trip walk from Highway 26 near a big historic marker sign just before milepost 51. Park along the highway and take the path to the top of the cliff, following the old Oregon Trail. You'll see quickly enough why the pioneers were so frustrated.

For a more extensive hike, start from the upper trailhead for the Pioneer Bridle Trail and follow the trail for 1.4 miles to the old tunnel, and turn right on the abandoned road. From here, it's 0.3 mile to the waterfall, following this road to the trail on the right. From the tunnel, you can continue on the Pioneer Bridle Trail another 0.4 mile to a junction that will lead you to the left and over busy Highway 26 to the Wagon Chute trail, and beyond this junction the trail continues another 2.3 miles.

User Groups: Hikers, dogs, and horses. No mountain bikes allowed. No wheelchair facilities.

Permits: Permits are not required. A pass is not required to park at the historic marker on U.S. 26, but for the Pioneer Brindle Trailhead a federal Northwest Forest Pass is required to park; the cost is $5 a day or $30 for an annual pass. You can buy a day pass at the trailhead, at ranger stations, or through private vendors.

Maps: For a map of the Mount Hood National Forest, contact Mount Hood National Forest Headquarters, 16400 Champion Way, Sandy, OR, 97055, 503/668-1700. For a topographic map, ask the USGS for Government Camp.

Directions: To reach the upper trailhead, drive on U.S. 26 from Portland toward Mount Hood. Between mileposts 52 and 53, turn left off the highway onto Road 522 (across from the Mount Hood Ski Bowl entrance) for 0.2 mile to the lot for the Glacier View Sno-Park.

Contact: Mount Hood National Forest, Zigzag Ranger District, 70220 East Highway 26, Zigzag, OR, 97049, 503/622-3191.

64 MIRROR LAKE
3.2 mi/1.5 hr   👫1 ⛰8

west of Government Camp in Mount Hood National Forest

Map 9.2, page 454

It's easy to see how popular this trail is; its parking area is along the highway and it's always bursting at the seam. This trail ascends the oddly named Tom Dick & Harry Mountain to an amazing viewpoint of Mount Hood, the enormous Zigzag Valley, and little Mirror Lake, which you'll pass along the way named Mirror. Use is regulated at Mirror Lake, and only six designated campsites are available. From the peak, you'll be able to visit only one peak out of three; the other two are protected for peregrine falcons.

From the trailhead, cross Camp Creek above Yocum Falls and climb the Mirror Lake Trail 1.4 miles to Mirror Lake. A 0.4-mile loop trail circles the lake. If you're continuing to the 4,920-foot peak, stay right and climb another 1.8 miles to the viewpoint.

User Groups: Hikers and dogs only. No horses or mountain bikes allowed. No wheelchair facilities.

Permits: Permits are not required. A federal Northwest Forest Pass is required to park here; the cost is $5 a day or $30 for an annual pass. You can buy a day pass at the trailhead, at ranger stations, or through private vendors.

Maps: For a map of the Mount Hood National Forest, contact Mount Hood National Forest Headquarters, 16400 Champion Way, Sandy, OR, 97055, 503/668-1700. For a topographic map, ask the USGS for Government Camp.

Directions: From Portland, drive U.S. 26 towards Mount Hood. Between mileposts 51 and 52, park along the south shoulder of the highway at the trailhead.

Contact: Mount Hood National Forest, Zigzag Ranger District, 70220 East Highway 26, Zigzag, OR, 97049, 503/622-3191.

65 TWIN LAKES
5.0-9.1 mi/2.5-5.0 hr

south of Mount Hood in Mount Hood National Forest

Map 9.2, page 454

Just off the Wapinitia Pass, the Frog Lake Sno-Park offers wintry access to the Pacific Crest Trail where it curves near the old Barlow Road and a ridge and butte named for old Barlow, too. In a big glacial valley, a modern campground sits in for an old pioneer campground, and is still named Devil's Half Acre today. You can see these sites from Palmateer Point, a good destination on a fun loop that passes the two Twin Lakes, with options for swimming and exploring for all ages.

From the Frog Lake Sno-Park lot, follow the PCT 1.4 miles to a right-hand junction. Go right 0.7 mile to Lower Twin Lake, a good destination for a short walk. A 0.9-mile trail circles the lake. Continue beyond the lake another 1.4 miles on the Palmateer Point Trail, passing the smaller Upper Twin Lake and cliffs with views of Mount Hood. From here, continue 0.6 mile to the right and go right 0.3 mile to the Point. To complete the loop, return to the Palmateer Trail and continue to the right 0.9 mile to the junction with the PCT, and go left 3.5 miles back to the lot.

User Groups: Hikers, dogs, and horses. No mountain bikes allowed. No wheelchair facilities.

Permits: Permits are not required. A federal Northwest Forest Pass is required to park here; the cost is $5 a day or $30 for an annual pass. You can buy a day pass at the trailhead, at ranger stations, or through private vendors.

Maps: For a map of the Mount Hood National Forest, contact Mount Hood National Forest Headquarters, 16400 Champion Way, Sandy, OR, 97055, 503/668-1700. For a topographic map, ask the USGS for Mount Hood South.

Directions: From Government Camp, drive eight miles east on U.S. 26 to milepost 62, turning left into Frog Lake Sno-Park.

Contact: Mount Hood National Forest, Barlow Ranger District, 780 NE Court Street, Dufur, OR, 97021, 541/467-2291.

66 WHITE RIVER FALLS
0.6 mi/0.25 hr

north of Maupin on the White River

Map 9.2, page 454

By the time you're out roaming in the dry landscapes east of the Cascade Mountains, things get real distant from one another. You have to travel out quite a ways to get to a place like the small state park on the White River, but once you're there you'll find a lot to investigate. For one thing, you've got a three-tiered waterfall on the White River plunging over a basalt shelf into a canyon on its way to the Deschutes River. You'll also find an abandoned powerhouse that supplied Wasco and Sherman Counties with power from 1910 until 1960. There are also a couple beaches and an oak bench, but some of these areas should only be hunted by the most intrepid of explorers willing to endure poison oak and a rugged canyon mouth.

The trail from the parking lot is a simple 0.3-mile descent to a number of viewpoints and the old powerhouse. From there, you could go farther over the course of a mile through pungent sagebrush to a beach and oak grove. The trail to the mouth, however, is a fainter path yet, another 1.2 miles to a beach on the Deschutes beneath a railroad span.

User Groups: Hikers and dogs only. No mountain bikes or horses. Paved trails are wheelchair accessible.

Permits: Permits are not required. Parking and access are free.

Maps: For a topographic map, ask the USGS for Maupin.

Directions: From Highway 197 near milepost 34 between The Dalles and Maupin, go east on Highway 216 for four miles towards Sherars Bridge to the White River Falls State Park entrance on the right.

Contact: Oregon Parks and Recreation Department, 1115 Commercial Street NE, Salem, OR, 97301, 800/551-6949, www.oregonstateparks.org.

67 ROCK LAKES
7.7 mi/3.0 hr

southeast of Estacada in Mount Hood National Forest

Map 9.2, page 454

In the high country between the Roaring and Clackamas Rivers, these Ice Age–carved lakes glisten in the sun. Getting there is the hard part, as you'll have to endure some crummy roads; but once there you'll be privy to meadows, forested lakes, glacier-scoured country, and an impressive rock outcrop called High Rock.

From the Frazier Turnaround, head to the right-hand Serene Lake Trail and go 0.8 mile to a junction. A mere 0.2 mile to the left is Middle Rock Lake, and you can follow the shore back to a higher and smaller lake beyond. The main trail continues to the right and to Lower Rock Lake, with its sunken logs and tree-lined shores. Stay on the main trail another 2.1 miles to Serene Lake, a larger lake with cliffs diving into the water. To do the full loop, continue another 0.9 mile through woods and up to the plateau. Go left on the Grouse Point Trail for 1.8 miles past viewpoints to Cache Meadow, the remains of an old guard station, and a four-way junction. Stay left on the Grouse Point Trail at this and the next junction as you climb out of the bowl, the trail leveling out finally on the 2.1-mile return to the Frazier Turnaround.

User Groups: Hikers, dogs, horses, and mountain bikes. No wheelchair facilities.

Permits: Permits are not required. Parking and access are free.

Maps: For a map of the Mount Hood National Forest, contact Mount Hood National Forest Headquarters, 16400 Champion Way, Sandy, OR, 97055, 503/668-1700. For a topographic map, ask the USGS for High Rock.

Directions: From Oregon City on I-205, take Exit 12 and go 18 miles east toward Estacada. Go through Estacada and continue 26 miles on Highway 224 to the bridge at Ripplebrook. Go left on Road 57 toward Timothy Lake for 7.4 miles, then turn left on Road 58 for 6.9 miles toward High Rock, then left on Abbott Road 4610 for 1.3 miles. Go straight on the unmaintained dirt Road 240 at the sign for Frazier Fork for 4.4 miles, then keep left at a fork by Frazier Fork campground and go 0.2 mile to the end of the road.

Contact: Mount Hood National Forest, Clackamas River Ranger District, 595 NW Industrial Way, Estacada, OR, 97023, 503/630-6861.

68 TIMOTHY LAKE
12.0 mi/6.0 hr

south of Mount Hood in Mount Hood National Forest

Map 9.2, page 454   **BEST (**

The Pacific Crest Trail follows the eastern shoreline of this tremendous lake within eyeshot of Mount Hood. The 1,500-acre lake is maintained as parkland by Portland General Electric because of the PGE-run dam at its far end. There are a host of campgrounds around it, including a primitive spot to pitch a tent at Meditation Point, not to mention windsurfing and fishing. There's also plenty to see while hiking the loop around the lapping shores, making this an ideal outing for the family.

From Little Crater Campground, start off on the 0.3-mile connection trail to the PCT, passing Little Crater Lake. Go left on the PCT another 0.3 mile, following Crater Creek to the junction of the loop trail. To follow the PCT, head to the left 3.6 miles, passing views to the mountain. At the next junction, stay along the lakeshore for another thre miles, passing through the many campgrounds to a crossing of the lake's outlet on a log boom. Continue 1.2 miles along the shore to a 0.3-mile side trail out to Meditation Point, then the remaining three miles to the end of the loop.

User Groups: Hikers, dogs, horses, and mountain bikes. There are several wheelchair access points.

Permits: Permits are not required. Parking and access are free.

Maps: For a map of the Mount Hood National Forest, contact Mount Hood National Forest Headquarters, 16400 Champion Way, Sandy, OR, 97055, 503/668-1700. For a topographic map, ask the USGS for Timothy Lake.

Directions: From Portland, drive U.S. 26 toward Mount Hood. Drive past Wapinitia Pass 3.4 miles to a turnoff between mileposts 65 and 66. At a sign for Timothy Lake, turn onto Skyline Road 42 for four miles. Turn right on Abbott Road 58 for 1.4 miles to Little Crater Campground and park at the far end of the campground loop by the trail sign.

Contact: Mount Hood National Forest, Barlow Ranger District, 780 NE Court Street, Dufur, OR, 97021, 541/467-2291.

69 LOWER DESCHUTES RIVER
4.2-8.0 mi/2.0-4.0 hr   🏃2 ⛰️6

east of The Dalles in Deschutes River State Recreation Area

Map 9.3, page 455

An old railroad once ran along this penultimate stretch of the Deschutes River before it joins at last with the Columbia River at the easternmost edge of the Columbia River Gorge National Scenic Area. Now the railroad is gone, but the grade remains, and its path through this dry, rocky land is now a state park with many options for hiking, both easy and more challenging. Along the river, three rapids—Moody, Rattlesnake, and Colorado—tumble through this sagebrush-dotted canyon. For something a bit more wild, there are also a number of trails between the old railroad grade and the river. The bike path makes for good mountain biking, as well as easy hiking.

The railroad grade is the easiest, and makes for an eight-mile out-and-back trail to Gordon Canyon and an old corral. A loop trail up the bluff begins 1.4 miles out and heads up the canyon to a high viewpoint near Ferry Springs, then connects back down, about 2.5 miles in all. Other trails skirt the riverbank, some dropping down to beaches on the river and close-up views of the rapids.

User Groups: Hikers, dogs on leash only, horses, and mountain bikers. Limited wheelchair access.

Permits: Permits are not required. Parking and access are free.

Maps: For a free park brochure, call Oregon Parks and Recreation, 800/551-6949, or download a free map at www.oregonstateparks.org. For a topographic map, ask the USGS for Wishram and Emerson.

Directions: Drive past the Dalles Dam on I-84 to Exit 97 for Deschutes Park. Follow park signs two miles on Highway 206, and after crossing the Deschutes River turn right into the park. Park at the last lot.

Contact: Oregon Parks and Recreation Department, 1115 Commercial Street NE, Salem, OR, 97301, 800/551-6949, www.oregonstateparks.org.

70 TABLE ROCK
7.6 mi/3.5 hr   🏃2 ⛰️8

east of Salem in Table Rock Wilderness

Map 9.4, page 456

This small, seemingly insignificant wilderness area in the Cascade Mountains actually claims two formidable rock outcrops: Rooster

Rock and 4,881-foot Table Rock, which is entirely climbable and has views to spare. You'll see 10 full Cascade Peaks from here, and all you'll have to do is make it around a couple landslides. These woods are rich with Douglas fir and western hemlock and are home to two endangered plants: Oregon sullivantia and the Gorman's aster. You may even spot the elusive spotted owl.

Getting to the trailhead is part of the hike, as two landslides damaged the road quite a bit, making it impassable for all but on foot. Park before the first landslide and hike in 1.3 miles to the trailhead on the right. From there, climb 1.9 miles on the Table Rock Trail to a junction. To the left, 0.4 mile, is access to the peak of Table Rock, a good destination in and of itself with views north to Mount Rainier and west to the Willamette Valley. If you're up for more, go to the right after bagging the peak for 1.4 miles to view the sheer lava cliffs of Rooster Rock.

User Groups: Hikers, dogs, and horses. No mountain bikes. No wheelchair facilities.

Permits: A free self-issue Wilderness Permit is required and is available at the trailhead. Parking and access are free.

Maps: For a map of the Mount Hood National Forest, contact Mount Hood National Forest Headquarters, 16400 Champion Way, Sandy, OR, 97055, 503/668-1700. For a topographic map, ask the USGS for Rooster Rock.

Directions: From Molalla (east of I-5 at Woodburn), drive 0.5 mile on Highway 211 toward Estacada, and turn right on South Mathias Road for 0.3 mile, then left on South Feyrer Park Road for 1.6 miles, then right on South Dickey Prairie Road for 5.3 miles. At a junction with South Molalla Forest Road, turn right and cross the Molalla River and follow this paved road 12.8 miles to a fork, and go left on Middle Fork Road for 2.6 miles, then right at a sign for Table Rock Wilderness. After two miles, go left, following wilderness pointers. Go the last 2.4 miles to the landslide.

Contact: Bureau of Land Management, Salem District Office, 1717 Fabry Road SE, Salem, OR, 97306, 503/375-5646.

🟦7🟦1 WHETSTONE MOUNTAIN
4.8 mi/2.5 hr

southeast of Estacada in Bull of the Woods Wilderness

Map 9.4, page 456

Here's an easy way to get into the high country, overlooking the dense forests of the Opal Creek Wilderness and Bull of the Woods Wilderness. This moderately paced trail up Whetstone Mountain has views extending from Mount Rainier to the Three Sisters, with Mount Jefferson a prominent viewpoint. The mountain, like many others in the region, was a Native American site for vision quests. Find your own peace of mind here in this easy summit.

From the trailhead, head into the old-growth woods 1.3 miles on the Whetstone Mountain Trail, passing a little pond that is one of the sources for Whetstone Creek. At a junction, go right on a faint path for 1.1 miles, turning right at a signboard for the summit trail. You'll see the Bull of the Woods Lookout, and clear out over the Willamette Valley to the Coast Range.

User Groups: Hikers, dogs, and horses. No mountain bikes allowed. No wheelchair facilities.

Permits: A free self-issue Wilderness Permit is required and is available at the trailhead. Parking and access are free.

Maps: For a map of the Mount Hood National Forest, contact Mount Hood National Forest Headquarters, 16400 Champion Way, Sandy, OR, 97055, 503/668-1700. For a topographic map, ask the USGS for Battle Ax.

Directions: From I-205 near Oregon City, take Exit 12 and go east 18 miles to Estacada. Go through town and continue 26 miles on Highway 224 to the Ripplebrook bridge. Go straight on Road 46 for 3.6 miles, turn right on Road 63 for 3.5 miles, and turn right on

Road 70 for nine miles. Then follow signs for the Whetstone Mountain Trail, going left on Road 7030 for 5.6 miles, then right on Road 7020 for 0.7 mile. Just prior to the end of the road, turn left onto Road 028 to a parking area.

Contact: Mount Hood National Forest, Clackamas River Ranger District, 595 NW Industrial Way, Estacada, OR, 97023, 503/630-6861.

72 BAGBY HOT SPRINGS
3.0 mi/1.5 hr   👥1   ⛰6

south of Estacada in Mount Hood National Forest

Map 9.4, page 456

The hike into Bagby Hot Springs is pleasant enough without its famous destination: a series of bathhouses that channel the thermal spring water down a series of flumes into cedar tubs. Really, it defies short explanation, and the trail in is a lovely walk through springtime rhododendron flowers and white trilliums along the Hot Springs Fork of the Collawash River. There's also a historic Guard Station being restored to its early 20th-century glory. From the trailhead, cross Nohorn Creek and follow the Bagby Trail into the woods 1.5 miles, crossing the Fork, and arriving at the hot springs complex. This trail continues into the Bull of the Woods Wilderness and its many destinations.

User Groups: Hikers and dogs. No horses or mountain bikes allowed. No wheelchair facilities.

Permits: Permits are not required. A federal Northwest Forest Pass is required to park here; the cost is $5 a day or $30 for an annual pass. You can buy a day pass at the trailhead, at ranger stations, or through private vendors.

Maps: For a map of the Mount Hood National Forest, contact Mount Hood National Forest Headquarters, 16400 Champion Way, Sandy, OR, 97055, 503/668-1700. For a topographic map, ask the USGS for Bagby Hot Springs.

Directions: From I-205 near Oregon City, take Exit 12 and go east 18 miles to Estacada. Go through town and continue 26 miles on Highway 224 to the Ripplebrook bridge. Go straight on Road 46 for 3.6 miles, turn right on Road 63 for 3.5 miles, and turn right on Road 70 for six miles to a parking lot on the left.

Contact: Mount Hood National Forest, Clackamas River Ranger District, 595 NW Industrial Way, Estacada, OR, 97023, 503/630-6861.

73 PANSY LAKE
2.3 mi/1.0 hr   👥1   ⛰8

south of Estacada in Bull of the Woods Wilderness

Map 9.4, page 456

This easy exploration of the Bull of the Woods Wilderness visits green Pansy Lake, named for a nearby mining claim called the Pansy Blossom Mine, where Robert Bagby mined copper. Though the claim is a thing of the past, you can make a claim to a beautiful meadowed basin beneath Pansy Mountain, with options for camping and further hiking.

The easiest access is to follow the Pansy Lake Trail in from the road 0.9 mile to a junction. A right-hand trail goes into Pansy Basin on an abandoned trail. The left-hand trail goes promptly uphill to another junction; go straight 0.2 mile to Pansy Lake, where you can follow the trail to the right along the lakeshore.

User Groups: Hikers, dogs, and horses. No mountain bikes allowed. No wheelchair facilities.

Permits: A free self-issue Wilderness Permit is required and is available at the trailhead. Parking and access are free.

Maps: For a map of the Mount Hood National Forest, contact Mount Hood National Forest Headquarters, 16400 Champion Way, Sandy, OR, 97055, 503/668-1700. For a topographic map, ask the USGS for Bull of the Woods.

Directions: From I-205 near Oregon City, take Exit 12 and go east 18 miles to Estacada. Go through town and continue 26 miles on Highway 224 to the Ripplebrook bridge. Go straight on Road 46 for 3.6 miles, turn right on Road 63 for 5.6 miles, and turn right on Road 6340 for 7.8 miles, following signs for Pansy Basin Trail. Turn right on Road 6341 for 3.5 miles and park at a pullout on the right side. The trail begins across the road.

Contact: Mount Hood National Forest, Clackamas River Ranger District, 595 NW Industrial Way, Estacada, OR, 97023, 503/630-6861.

🔢74 BULL OF THE WOODS LOOKOUT
6.4 mi/3.5 hr   🏃7 ⛰9

south of Estacada in Bull of the Woods Wilderness

Map 9.4, page 456

This trail passes Pansy Lake (see previous listing) but continues up to the 1942 Bull of the Woods Lookout, which is sometimes staffed. It then follows a loop up and down a mountain cradling little Dickey Lake. Views extend out to Mount Jefferson, and to many more as well.

Follow the Pansy Lake Trail in from the road 0.9 mile to a junction. The right goes into Pansy Basin on an abandoned trail; take the left-hand trail, which goes promptly uphill to another junction. This time go straight 0.2 mile to Pansy Lake, taking the left-hand trail another 0.8 miles toward Twin Lakes. At the next junction, go uphill to the left on the Mother Lode Trail 1.9 miles, going left at a signed junction onto the Bull of the Woods Trail to the lookout tower. To complete the loop, continue past the tower 1.1 miles to a barely marked junction, then descend 1.3 miles on the Dickey Lake Trail, passing a short side trail to Dickey Lake, back to the Pansy Lake Trail, staying right at junctions back to the road.

User Groups: Hikers, dogs, and horses. No mountain bikes allowed. No wheelchair facilities.

Permits: A free self-issue Wilderness Permit is required and is available at the trailhead. Parking and access are free.

Maps: For a map of the Mount Hood National Forest, contact Mount Hood National Forest Headquarters, 16400 Champion Way, Sandy, OR, 97055, 503/668-1700. For a topographic map, ask the USGS for Bull of the Woods.

Directions: From I-205 near Oregon City, take Exit 12 and go east 18 miles to Estacada. Go through town and continue 26 miles on Highway 224 to the Ripplebrook bridge. Go straight on Road 46 for 3.6 miles, turn right on Road 63 for 5.6 miles, and turn right on Road 6340 for 7.8 miles, following signs for Pansy Basin Trail. Turn right on Road 6341 for 3.5 miles and park at a pullout on the right side. The trail begins across the road.

Contact: Mount Hood National Forest, Clackamas River Ranger District, 595 NW Industrial Way, Estacada, OR, 97023, 503/630-6861.

🔢75 DICKEY CREEK
11.0 mi/5.5 hr   🏃4 ⛰8

south of Estacada in Bull of the Woods Wilderness

Map 9.4, page 456

Want to visit an old-growth forest? Try the groves along the wilderness of Dickey Creek. To get here, you must hike *down* first, an unwelcome prospect for many. Still, the lakes you'll find back in these woods in the carved-out flanks of Big Slide Mountain make it worth the price of admission.

The Dickey Creek Trail begins as an old road then changes to trail, the first 0.8 mile heading down nearly 500 feet into an old-growth grove of Douglas fir. From here you'll pass a pond and follow Dickey Creek 2.1 miles to a crossing. Now you'll begin climbing nearly 1,400 feet in 2.6 miles to the shore of

Big Slide Lake, with the mountain looming above. There are campsites and a small island to explore, and the Bull of the Woods Lookout is on the ridge above.

User Groups: Hikers, dogs, and horses. No mountain bikes allowed. No wheelchair facilities.

Permits: A free self-issue Wilderness Permit is required and is available at the trailhead. Parking and access are free.

Maps: For a map of the Mount Hood National Forest, contact Mount Hood National Forest Headquarters, 16400 Champion Way, Sandy, OR, 97055, 503/668-1700. For a topographic map, ask the USGS for Bull of the Woods.

Directions: From I-205 near Oregon City, take Exit 12 and go east 18 miles to Estacada. Go through town and continue 26 miles on Highway 224 to the Ripplebrook bridge. Go straight on Road 46 for 3.6 miles, turn right on Road 63 for 5.6 miles, and turn right on Road 6340 for 2.8 miles following signs for Dickey Creek Trail. Turn left on Road 140 for one mile, and turn right at a T-junction 0.5 mile to the trailhead at road's end.

Contact: Mount Hood National Forest, Clackamas River Ranger District, 595 NW Industrial Way, Estacada, OR, 97023, 503/630-6861.

76 HAWK MOUNTAIN
10.4 mi/5.0 hr

south of Estacada in Mount Hood National Forest

Map 9.4, page 456

There is something romantic about a fire watchtower, with isolation and nature combining to form a kind of idyllic life. It took a certain kind of person to live alone on a mountaintop for a summer. There are many books written by authors who did this, from Jack Kerouac to Edward Abbey. With new techniques for spotting fires, however, many of these lookouts have been abandoned and many of the original structures lost—this lonely cabin atop Hawk Mountain remains, however. Today you can visit this cabin, look out over Mount Jefferson, and get a sense of how lookouts lived. This trail up Rho Ridge (short for "Rhododendron") crosses two meadows and provides a first-hand look.

From the Graham Pass trailhead, follow the Rho Ridge Trail 1.1 miles, connecting with abandoned Road 33, to a junction with Road 270. Go right for one mile, staying right at a junction with Road 280 and left at a junction with Road 290. Take a right on the continuation of the trail along Rho Ridge for 2.7 miles, crossing another dirt road, to Round Meadow. A left-hand trail leads 0.4 mile to the old lookout cabin atop Hawk Mountain.

User Groups: Hikers, dogs, horses, and mountain bikes. No wheelchair facilities.

Permits: Permits are not required. Parking and access are free.

Maps: For a map of the Mount Hood National Forest, contact Mount Hood National Forest Headquarters, 16400 Champion Way, Sandy, OR, 97055, 503/668-1700. For a topographic map, ask the USGS for Breitenbush Hot Springs.

Directions: From I-205 near Oregon City, take Exit 12 and go east 18 miles to Estacada. Go through town and continue 26 miles on Highway 224 to the Ripplebrook bridge. Go straight on Road 46 for 3.6 miles, turn right on Road 63 for 8.8 miles. At a sign for Graham Pass, turn left on Road 6350 for 1.2 miles, then go right for 4.5 miles on the gravel road, then fork left staying on Road 6350. In one mile, park in a lot at a four-way junction.

Contact: Mount Hood National Forest, Clackamas River Ranger District, 595 NW Industrial Way, Estacada, OR, 97023, 503/630-6861.

⁷⁷ LITTLE NORTH SANTIAM RIVER
9.0 mi/4.0 mi

northeast of Mill City in Willamette National Forest

Map 9.4, page 456

Cascading through a boulder-lined bed, this tributary of the Santiam watershed flows through old-growth forests and over waterfalls squeezing between the lava canyon. The 4.5-mile Little North Santiam Trail, built by volunteers from Salem, sometimes scrambles down to swimming holes and beaches and ends at a campground upstream. Go as far as you like and return as you came; there's plenty to see.

From Elkhorn Road, start in 0.7 mile to a side trail down to a series of waterfalls. From here, a 2.6-mile stretch crosses Winter Creek and climbs to 1,800 feet and back down to a series of inaccessible pools and a beach. The final 1.2 miles crosses Cedar Creek and ends at the Shady Grove Campground.

User Groups: Hikers, dogs, and bicycles. No horses allowed. No wheelchair facilities.

Permits: Permits are not required. A federal Northwest Forest Pass is required to park here; the cost is $5 a day or $30 for an annual pass. You can buy a day pass at the trailhead, at ranger stations, or through private vendors.

Maps: For a map of the Willamette National Forest, contact Willamette National Forest Headquarters, 3106 Pierce Parkway, Suite D, Springfield, OR, 97477, 541/225-6300. For a topographic map, ask the USGS for Lyons.

Directions: Drive east from Salem on OR 22 for 23 miles to Mehama and turn left on Little North Fork Road for 14.5 miles. Beyond milepost 13, turn right on Elkhorn Drive, cross the river, and 0.4 mile later park on the left at a pullout.

Contact: Willamette National Forest, Detroit Ranger District, HC73, Box 320, Mill City, OR, 97360, 503/854-4239.

⁷⁸ HENLINE MOUNTAIN
5.6 mi/4.0 hr

northeast of Mill City in Opal Creek Wilderness

Map 9.4, page 456

From the lookout site beneath Henline Mountain, the ridges and peaks of the Cascades ripple into the distance like frozen waves, their folded ridges flowing down to the Little North Santiam River. The lookout site is not on the peak of Henline, but who's counting? A 1.1-mile trail, rough as it is, continues past this lookout to the 4,650-foot peak, but the view from this destination is in itself worth the climb. This is also an initial foray into the Opal Creek Wilderness.

Prepare to climb steadily and steeply for the 2.8-mile trail to the old lookout point. You'll gain 2,200 feet in this short distance, so give yourself plenty of time.

User Groups: Hikers and dogs. No horses or mountain bikes allowed. No wheelchair facilities.

Permits: A free self-issue Wilderness Permit is required and is available at the trailhead. Parking and access are free.

Maps: For a map of the Willamette National Forest, contact Willamette National Forest Headquarters, 3106 Pierce Parkway, Suite D, Springfield, OR, 97477, 541/225-6300. For a topographic map, ask the USGS for Elkhorn.

Directions: Drive east from Salem on OR 22 for 23 miles to Mehama and turn left on Little North Fork Road for 16.3 miles to a fork. Go to the left on Road 2209 for one mile and park on the right near the trailhead.

Contact: Willamette National Forest, Detroit Ranger District, HC73, Box 320, Mill City, OR, 97360, 503/854-4239.

79 OPAL CREEK
7.1 mi/2.5 hr

northeast of Mill City in Opal Creek Wilderness

Map 9.4, page 456 **BEST (**

Let's just say the Opal Creek Wilderness is famous to some and infamous to others. Author David Seideman's 1993 book, *Showdown at Opal Creek: The Battle for America's Last Wilderness* amply details the 1980s controversy over the designation of this area as wilderness. What ensued here involved armed standoffs between federal agencies and the owners of the private land that stood between the National Forest and the proposed logging area, which houses some enormous stands of Douglas fir and Western red cedar. Senator Mark Hatfield stepped in to protect the area and it has now been preserved. The mining town back here called Jawbone Flats, where the owners made their stand, remains, and now that the furor is over ,the whole town has become the Opal Creek Ancient Forest Research Center. This trail follows the original road along the Little North Santiam River, passing an abandoned mill, slipping into the mining town, and setting off along Opal Creek towards the wilderness area.

From the locked gate, follow the old dirt road 3.5 miles. You'll scurry along some amazing half-bridges, where the road clings to the cliff-face, then arrive at the site of the Merton Mill and its hodgepodge of lumber bric-a-brac, and a side trail down to Sawmill Falls. You'll pass Slide Falls on the way, too. At Jawbone Flats, take a right-hand junction to a footbridge over heavily photographed Opal Pool. To return via a loop, go right for 1.4 miles back to a crossing over the river and return via the road. To extend your trip, however, you can go left on the Opal Creek Trail 1.5 miles to a stand of enormous red cedars that are staggering to see. The trail eventually reaches Beachie Creek and peters out.

User Groups: Hikers and dogs. No horses or mountain bikes allowed. No wheelchair facilities.

Permits: A free self-issue Wilderness Permit is required and is available at the trailhead. Parking and access are free.

Maps: An Opal Creek Wilderness map is available from Geo-Graphics. For a map of the Willamette National Forest, contact Willamette National Forest Headquarters, 3106 Pierce Parkway, Suite D, Springfield, OR, 97477, 541/225-6300. For a topographic map, ask the USGS for Battle Ax.

Directions: Drive east from Salem on OR 22 for 23 miles to Mehama and turn left on Little North Fork Road for 16.3 miles to a fork. Go to the left on Road 2209 for 4.2 miles and park on the shoulder at the locked gate.

Contact: Willamette National Forest, Detroit Ranger District, HC73, Box 320, Mill City, OR, 97360, 503/854-4239.

80 FRENCH CREEK RIDGE
8.2 mi/3.5 hr

north of Detroit in Opal Creek Wilderness

Map 9.4, page 456

This long ridge over the Opal Creek Wilderness passes a number of rock formations and peaks on its way to Mount Beachie, entering stands of rare Alaska cedar and offering views to Mount Jefferson, craggy Three-Fingered Jack, and the Three Sisters.

From the message board, start into the forest on the French Creek Ridge Trail, passing Marten Buttes, for 2.4 miles to a series of rock formations at a pass. Ignoring a side trail to the right, continue 1.7 miles past a pond and through a brush-lined path to the viewpoint on Mount Beachie.

User Groups: Hikers, dogs, and horses. No mountain bikes allowed. No wheelchair facilities.

Permits: A free self-issue Wilderness Permit is required and is available at the trailhead. Parking and access are free.

Maps: An Opal Creek Wilderness map is available from Geo-Graphics. For a map of the Willamette National Forest, contact

Willamette National Forest Headquarters, 3106 Pierce Parkway, Suite D, Springfield, OR, 97477, 541/225-6300. For a topographic map, ask the USGS for Battle Ax.

Directions: Drive 50 miles east of Salem on OR 22 to Detroit Lake. Just before the Breitenbush River turn left on French Creek Road 2223 and go 4.2 miles to a fork at pavement's end. Go right on Road 2207 for 3.7 miles and park at a large lot on the right.

Contact: Willamette National Forest, Detroit Ranger District, HC73, Box 320, Mill City, OR, 97360, 503/854-4239.

81 BATTLE AX
5.6-6.4 mi/3.0-3.5 hr   🥾3   ⛰9

north of Detroit in Bull of the Woods Wilderness

Map 9.4, page 456

This mountain has such a rugged name, don't you think? Some say it's because of its sharp shape, others because of a brand of chewing tobacco around during the time of the gold prospectors. Either way, it's earned its moniker. This peak, the tallest in the Bull of the Woods Wilderness, has views extending as far as Diamond Peak in the southern Cascades and Mount Hood to the north. Beneath it, Elk Lake looks like a big puddle among the trees. Atop its rocky peak, a profusion of alpine flowers root down and thrive.

After parking at the fork in the road approaching Elk Lake Campground, walk the remaining 0.4 mile of road to the trailhead on the right. Strike out on the Bagby Hot Springs Trail for two miles, passing a number of ponds and steadily climbing to a junction. Go left 1.3 miles to the 5,558-foot peak of Battle Ax. To make a loop of this hike, continue forward and descend the mountain down a series of switchbacks 1.5 mile to the end of the road at Beachie Saddle. Walk the road back down 0.8 mile to the trailhead, then the remaining distance to your vehicle.

User Groups: Hikers, dogs, and horses. No mountain bikes allowed. No wheelchair facilities.

Permits: A free self-issue Wilderness Permit is required and is available at the trailhead. Parking and access are free.

Maps: An Opal Creek Wilderness map is available from Geo-Graphics. For a map of the Willamette National Forest, contact Willamette National Forest Headquarters, 3106 Pierce Parkway, Suite D, Springfield, OR, 97477, 541/225-6300. For a topographic map, ask the USGS for Battle Ax.

Directions: Drive 50 miles east of Salem on OR 22 to Detroit Lake. Cross the Breitenbush River and turn left on paved Road 46 for 4.4 miles to a sign for Elk Lake. Turn left on Road 4696 for 0.8 mile, then turn left onto Road 4697 and go 4.7 miles, then turn left yet again at a sign for Elk Lake. The next two miles are rough and difficult. At a fork for the Elk Lake Campground, passenger cars without clearance should park and hikers will need to continue on foot up the road another 0.4 mile to the trailhead. However, high-clearance vehicles can continue up the road and park on the shoulder.

Contact: Willamette National Forest, Detroit Ranger District, HC73, Box 320, Mill City, OR, 97360, 503/854-4239.

82 PHANTOM BRIDGE
4.6 mi/2.0 hr   🥾2   ⛰8

north of Detroit in Willamette National Forest

Map 9.4, page 456

This rare and intimidating rock arch spans a 50-foot-deep gorge that will unnerve even the bravest. Maybe just a view of it is enough. The trail itself stretches away from French Creek Ridge, rounding Dog Rock and Cedar Lake before climbing to the arch. Below, the Opal Creek Wilderness drifts into the distance, with Opal Lake, source of the creek, within view.

Park in the lot at the end of Road 2223 and walk back down the road about 100 feet to the trailhead. In 1.3 miles you'll arrive at

Cedar Lake and a junction. Go left up the ridge another 0.7 mile to an old trailhead lot, then continue the remaining 0.3 mile to the Phantom Bridge.

User Groups: Hikers, dogs, horses, and mountain bikes. No wheelchair facilities.

Permits: Permits are not required. Parking and access are free.

Maps: For a map of the Willamette National Forest, contact Willamette National Forest Headquarters, 3106 Pierce Parkway, Suite D, Springfield, OR, 97477, 541/225-6300. For a topographic map, ask the USGS for Battle Ax.

Directions: Drive 50 miles east of Salem on OR 22 to Detroit Lake. Just before the Breitenbush River, turn left on French Creek Road 2223 and go 4.2 miles to a fork at pavement's end. Go right on Road 2207 for 3.7 miles and park at a large lot on the right.

Contact: Willamette National Forest, Detroit Ranger District, HC73, Box 320, Mill City, OR, 97360, 503/854-4239.

shore to the left 0.3 mile to see the outlet creek and waterfall.

User Groups: Hikers, dogs, and mountain bikes. No horses allowed. No wheelchair facilities.

Permits: Permits are not required. Parking and access are free.

Maps: For a map of the Willamette National Forest, contact Willamette National Forest Headquarters, 3106 Pierce Parkway, Suite D, Springfield, OR, 97477, 541/225-6300. For a topographic map, ask the USGS for Battle Ax and Detroit.

Directions: Drive 50 miles east of Salem on OR 22 to Detroit Lake. Just before the Breitenbush River turn left on French Creek Road 2223 and go 4.2 miles to a fork at pavement's end. Fork left onto Road 2223 for 3.9 miles, watching carefully for a post on the left that marks the trailhead. Park on the right.

Contact: Willamette National Forest, Detroit Ranger District, HC73, Box 320, Mill City, OR, 97360, 503/854-4239.

83 DOME ROCK AND TUMBLE LAKE

5.2 mi/2.5 hr

north of Detroit in Willamette National Forest

Map 9.4, page 456

From the edge of Detroit Reservoir, the Tumble Ridge Trail heads straight into the neighboring mountains, climbing steeply to the spire of Needle Rock and the vista of Dome Rock. Hidden up Tumble Creek is Tumble Lake, with a waterfall. Though you could hike in this way, there is an easier point of entry that makes for a quicker hike to these sights.

From the upper trailhead on Road 2223, go in 0.4 mile to a junction. To access Dome Rock, go left 0.5 mile to a second junction, then left another 0.5 mile to the 4,869-foot peak. To access Tumble Lake, go right at this first junction, crossing a meadow down into a gully for 1.2 miles to the shore. Follow the

84 STAHLMAN POINT

5.0 mi/2.5 hr   [🚶1] [⛰8]

south of Detroit Reservoir in Willamette National Forest

Map 9.4, page 456

If you're in the area and looking for a quick view of the surrounding country, incorporating the Detroit Reservoir and Mount Jefferson, head up this fairly easy 2.5-mile trail that climbs 1,300 feet to an old lookout site. Below, sailboats drift on the massive lake and the mountain broods in the distance. Watch for fish-hunting osprey, which nest in the area.

User Groups: Hikers and dogs. No horses or mountain bikes allowed. No wheelchair facilities.

Permits: Permits are not required. Parking and access are free.

Maps: For a map of the Willamette National Forest, contact Willamette National Forest Headquarters, 3106 Pierce Parkway, Suite D,

Springfield, OR, 97477, 541/225-6300. For a topographic map, ask the USGS for Detroit.
Directions: Drive 50 miles east of Salem on OR 22 to the town of Detroit. Go 2.5 miles east of town, then turn right on Blowout Road 10 for 3.5 miles to the large parking area on the left side of the road.
Contact: Willamette National Forest, Detroit Ranger District, HC73, Box 320, Mill City, OR, 97360, 503/854-4239.

85 COFFIN MOUNTAIN LOOKOUT
3.0 mi/2.0 hr

south of Detroit in Willamette National Forest

> Map 9.4, page 456

From a distance, it's easy to see how Coffin Mountain got its name. This square and prominent peak atop a wall of cliffs certainly resembles a giant's final resting place, but those cliffs are deceptive; along the backside, an easy trail climbs to a staffed lookout tower—a 16-square-foot box that, if you're lucky, you may be able to visit. You'll see why these fire towers are still staffed on the way up: the trail passes through an old burn being repopulated by young noble fir and sub-alpine fir. From the trailhead, follow the old bulldozer road and finally trail up 1.5 miles to the peak.
User Groups: Hikers, dogs, and mountain bikes. No horses allowed. No wheelchair facilities.
Permits: Permits are not required. Parking and access are free.
Maps: For a map of the Willamette National Forest, contact Willamette National Forest Headquarters, 3106 Pierce Parkway, Suite D, Springfield, OR, 97477, 541/225-6300. For a topographic map, ask the USGS for Coffin Mountain.
Directions: Drive east of Salem 69 miles on OR 22. Beyond Marion Forks 2.9 miles, go right on Straight Creek Road for 4.2 miles to

a sign for Coffin Mountain Trailhead, and turn right for 3.8 miles on Road 1168 to the trailhead sign and parking area on the left.
Contact: Willamette National Forest, Detroit Ranger District, HC73, Box 320, Mill City, OR, 97360, 503/854-4239.

86 BACHELOR MOUNTAIN
3.8 mi/2.5 hr

south of Detroit in Willamette National Forest

> Map 9.4, page 456

Just beyond the towering cliffs of Coffin Mountain sits the slightly higher Bachelor Mountain. By coupling this trail with the Coffin Mountain Lookout hike (previous listing), both peaks are easy to bag in a single day (or even in a couple of hours). This trail traverses the Buck Mountain Burn, which in the 1970s reduced many of the trees to the white snags you see today.

From the trailhead, follow the ridge 1.2 miles to a junction with the Bruno Meadows Trail. Stay to the left and climb the final 0.7-mile rocky path up 500 feet to the peak.
User Groups: Hikers, dogs, horses, and mountain bikes. No wheelchair facilities.
Permits: Permits are not required. Parking and access are free.
Maps: For a map of the Willamette National Forest, contact Willamette National Forest Headquarters, 3106 Pierce Parkway, Suite D, Springfield, OR, 97477, 541/225-6300. For a topographic map, ask the USGS for Mount Bruno.
Directions: Drive east of Salem 69 miles on OR 22. Beyond Marion Forks 2.9 miles, go right on Straight Creek Road for 4.2 miles to a sign for Coffin Mountain Trailhead, and turn right for 4.5 miles on Road 1168 then turn left on Road 430, driving 0.5 mile to its end.
Contact: Willamette National Forest, Detroit Ranger District, HC73, Box 320, Mill City, OR, 97360, 503/854-4239.

87 OLALLIE LAKE AND POTATO BUTTE

7.2 mi/3.0 hr

east of Detroit in Olallie Lakes Scenic Area

Map 9.5, page 457

A long stretch of power lines marks the boundary for the Olallie Lake Scenic Area, and the transformation to this lake-strewn plateau is abrupt. The Olallie Lake Scenic Area sits in the shadow of Mount Jefferson and offers many options for hiking. To start into the Scenic Area from the west, try this hike; it passes four big lakes and a couple smaller ones, finally topping it off with 5,280-foot Potato Butte, with views over the dense forest to the towering peak of Jefferson.

From the road, the Red Lake Trail crosses a clear-cut and joins a dirt road. Go left a short distance, then right on a spur road to find the continuation of the trail. Once you go under the power lines, you enter the Scenic Area. The first 1.6 miles of the trail reaches Red Lake. The next 1.3 miles passes Averill, Wall, and Sheep Lakes and arrives at a junction. Go left 0.7 mile past a few small ponds and up several steep switchbacks to the top of Potato Butte.

User Groups: Hikers, dogs, horses, and mountain bikes. No wheelchair facilities.

Permits: Permits are not required. Parking and access are free.

Maps: For a map of the Mount Hood National Forest, contact Mount Hood National Forest Headquarters, 16400 Champion Way, Sandy, OR, 97055, 503/668-1700. For a topographic map, ask the USGS for Olallie Butte.

Directions: From I-205 near Oregon City, take Exit 12 and go east 18 miles to Estacada. Go through town and continue 26 miles on Highway 224 to the Ripplebrook bridge. Go straight on Road 46 for 26.7 miles toward Detroit. Beyond the turnoff for Olallie Lake 4.9 miles, turn left on Road 380 for 0.9 mile to a point where the road becomes unmaintained. From Salem, follow OR 22 east to Detroit and go left on Breitenbush Road 46

for 18.2 miles to the right-hand turnoff for Road 380.

Contact: Mount Hood National Forest, Clackamas River Ranger District, 595 NW Industrial Way, Estacada, OR, 97023, 503/630-6861.

88 SOUTH BREITENBUSH GORGE

6.2 mi/2.0 hr

east of Detroit on the South Breitenbush River

Map 9.5, page 457

The South Breitenbush River comes roaring down from the flanks of Mount Jefferson into this cool, green old-growth forest. Long ridges tower over the water, including nearby Devils Peak. At one point in the forest, the light pours down through a large swath of blowdown, the trees leveled by a 1990 windstorm. But the forest goes on, and in the midst of a particular glade the river squeezes into a 40-foot gorge running along for 100 yards. Fallen trees crisscross the lava walls, making for precarious bridges suitable, at best, for small mammals. The gorge is a perfect destination, though continuing onward will eventually bring you to Roaring Creek—another great turnaround point—and the slopes of Jefferson itself.

Begin at the site of an historic guard station, descending into the forest to the river, heading upstream for 1.2 miles, crossing the North Fork Breitenbush along the way, to a trail junction. Go straight along the river another 1.4 miles to a sign and spur trail on the right for "South Breitenbush Gorge." To continue on to Roaring Creek is only another 0.5 mile up the trail, and it's worth it for views of both the river and this lovely creek.

User Groups: Hikers and dogs. No horses or mountain bikes allowed. No wheelchair facilities.

Permits: Permits are not required. Parking and access are free.

Maps: For a map of the Willamette National Forest, contact Willamette National Forest

Headquarters, 3106 Pierce Parkway, Suite D, Springfield, OR, 97477, 541/225-6300. For a topographic map, ask the USGS for Breitenbush Hot Springs.

Directions: Drive 50 miles east of Salem on OR 22 to Detroit. Cross the Breitenbush River and turn left on Road 46 for 11.2 miles. Turn right on a gravel road and after 0.3 mile park on the left at the site of the old guard station.

Contact: Willamette National Forest, Detroit Ranger District, HC73, Box 320, Mill City, OR, 97360, 503/854-4239.

89 TOP LAKE AND DOUBLE PEAKS
5.3 mi/3.0 hr   🏃1 ▲8

east of Detroit in Olallie Lakes Scenic Area

Map 9.5, page 457

The 6,000-year-old remnant of a glacier-carved plateau has left mile after mile of lakes scattered across the Olallie Lake Scenic Area like pearls from a broken necklace. To see for yourself, try this loop past several lakes to Double Peaks, a 5,998-foot summit towering above the lake basin and looking out to Olallie Butte and Mount Jefferson.

Follow the Red Lake Trail 1.1 miles through mountain hemlocks and lodgepole pines, keeping right at a junction to Timber Lake, to Top Lake and a three-way junction. Go left 0.4 mile, switchbacking up to the Pacific Crest Trail and then going left to Cigar Lake. At the next junction, leave the PCT and go right steeply up 0.8 mile to Double Peaks. To return via the loop, go back to the PCT, following it left 0.5 mile past Cigar Lake to a four-way junction with the Red Lake Trail. Stay straight on the PCT another 1.4 miles to the road at Head Lake, going right 0.3 mile back to the car.

User Groups: Hikers, dogs, and horses. No mountain bikes allowed. No wheelchair facilities.

Permits: Permits are not required. Parking and access are free.

Maps: For a map of the Mount Hood National Forest, contact Mount Hood National Forest Headquarters, 16400 Champion Way, Sandy, OR, 97055, 503/668-1700. For a topographic map, ask the USGS for Olallie Butte.

Directions: From I-205 near Oregon City, take Exit 12 and go east 18 miles to Estacada. Go through town and continue 26 miles on Highway 224 to the Ripplebrook bridge. Go straight on Road 46 for 21.8 miles toward Detroit. Turn left on Road 4690 at the Olallie Lake turnoff, following this road 8.1 miles, turning right on Road 4220 for 5.1 miles, turning right at an intersection with the Olallie Lake Resort. Go 0.3 mile to a message board on the right for the Red Lake Trail and park on the shoulder. From Salem, follow OR 22 east to Detroit and go left on Breitenbush Road 46 for 23.5 miles to the Olallie Turnoff.

Contact: Mount Hood National Forest, Clackamas River Ranger District, 595 NW Industrial Way, Estacada, OR, 97023, 503/630-6861.

90 MONON LAKE
3.9 mi/2.0 hr   🏃1 ▲7

northeast of Detroit in Olallie Lakes Scenic Area

Map 9.5, page 457

Olallie Lake is a popular destination and rightfully so. With its big campgrounds and unparalleled view of nearby Olallie Butte, it makes for a great destination. But nearby Monon Lake, the second-biggest lake after Olallie, has its own beauty. Unfortunately, a 2001 fire blackened the shores of this scenic lake, but it is slowly recovering as the undergrowth begins its triumphant resurgence. These mountains, after all, evolved with forest fires, so you can get an edifying look at how a forest regenerates, even after such a devastating burn as this one.

From the campground, go 0.5 mile to the right along Olallie Lake to a junction with the Olallie Lake Trail, going right. You'll pass

Nep-Te-Pa and Mangriff Lakes and arrive at Monon Lake. Go right for a 2.9-mile loop around the lake, with 0.3 mile of it on the road, then rejoin the Olallie Trail. At the last junction, you can go left to return to the car or extend the day by going right 0.4 mile along Olallie Lake to another junction. Going left extends this trail another 0.9 mile to the Paul Dennis Campground; going right heads 0.4 mile into the Warm Springs Reservation to the shore of Long Lake.

User Groups: Hikers, dogs, horses, and mountain bikes. No wheelchair facilities.

Permits: Permits are not required. Parking and access are free.

Maps: For a map of the Mount Hood National Forest, contact Mount Hood National Forest Headquarters, 16400 Champion Way, Sandy, OR, 97055, 503/668-1700. For a topographic map, ask the USGS for Olallie Butte.

Directions: From I-205 near Oregon City, take Exit 12 and go east 18 miles to Estacada. Go through town and continue 26 miles on Highway 224 to the Ripplebrook bridge. Go straight on Road 46 for 21.8 miles toward Detroit. Turn left on Road 4690 at the Olallie Lake turnoff, following this road 8.1 miles, turning right on Road 4220 for seven miles, turning left at the Peninsula Campground entrance and following signs for the boat ramp. From Salem, follow OR 22 east to Detroit and go left on Breitenbush Road 46 for 23.5 miles to the Olallie Turnoff.

Contact: Mount Hood National Forest, Clackamas River Ranger District, 595 NW Industrial Way, Estacada, OR, 97023, 503/630-6861.

91 PARK RIDGE

7.4 mi/5.0 hr

east of Detroit in Mount Jefferson Wilderness

Map 9.5, page 457

Jefferson Park is one of the most spectacular places in the Cascade Mountains. Don't let the word "Park" fool you though, for this is no city park with picnic tables. Rather, "Park" designates a mountain meadow, and this one is unsurpassed for its beauty, especially in early summer when the flower show begins. There are a number of ways in, and this one—despite the final two miles of rough roads—comes in from the north, up and over Park Ridge and down to Russell Lake and the jeweled expanse of lakes, alpine scenery, and islands of wind-swept trees. There's even a side trail to climb 6,095-foot Pyramid Butte on the way.

From the trailhead, follow the Pacific Crest Trail to the left for 0.6 mile to a junction. To continue to Jefferson Park, stay on the PCT for five miles to cross over Park Ridge and arrive at Russell Lake and the meadows. For a climb up Pyramid Butte, go right 1.1 miles, then right again to the peak. Coming back down, go one mile, staying right and rejoining the PCT.

User Groups: Hikers, dogs, and horses. No mountain bikes allowed. No wheelchair facilities.

Permits: A free self-issue Wilderness Permit is required and is available at the trailhead. Parking and access are free.

Maps: You can purchase a Mount Jefferson Wilderness Map from Geo-Graphics. For a map of the Mount Hood National Forest and the Mount Jefferson Wilderness, contact Mount Hood National Forest Headquarters, 16400 Champion Way, Sandy, OR, 97055, 503/668-1700. For a topographic map, ask the USGS for Olallie Butte Mount Jefferson.

Directions: From I-205 near Oregon City, take Exit 12 and go east 18 miles to Estacada. Go through town and continue 26 miles on Highway 224 to the Ripplebrook bridge. Go straight on Road 46 for 21.8 miles toward Detroit. Turn left on Road 4690 at the Olallie Lake turnoff, following this road 8.1 miles, turning right on Road 4220 for 10.5 miles, noting that the final two miles of this road are extremely rough and require high-clearance vehicles. Past Breitenbush Lake, turn left to the Pacific Crest Trail lot. From Salem, follow OR 22 east to Detroit and go left on

Breitenbush Road 46 for 23.5 miles to the Olallie turnoff.

Contact: Mount Hood National Forest, Clackamas River Ranger District, 595 NW Industrial Way, Estacada, OR, 97023, 503/630-6861.

92 TRIANGULATION PEAK
4.2 mi/2.0 hr   🥾1 ⛰9

east of Detroit in Mount Jefferson Wilderness

Map 9.5, page 457

A fitting name for a peak on which a fire watchtower once stood, Triangulation Peak offers an impressive view of Mount Jefferson not only from its peak, but from the mouth of a secret cave accessible by a cross-country scramble over the flanks of the peak. Along the way, the trail passes the towering monolith of Spire Rock and enters a series of alpine meadows covered with fish-filled lakes. For intrepid travelers, this trail also provides access deeper into Mount Jefferson Wilderness Area.

From the trailhead, start out 1.5 easy miles on the Triangulation Trail paralleling an old road and entering the Wilderness area. At a junction by Spire Rock's pillar, which rises from the trees and tempts rock climbers, go right to climb the remaining 500 feet and 0.6 mile. To find Boca Cave, beware of steep cliffs and watch your step. From the peak, hike down to a saddle and go right and cross-country to a second and lower peak. From here, a scramble trail descends along the right of a rock outcrop. The path ends at a cliff edge. Go to the right around the cliff and descend a steep forested slope to a 100-foot-deep cavern with a view of Mount Jefferson.

User Groups: Hikers, dogs, and horses. No mountain bikes allowed. No wheelchair facilities.

Permits: A free self-issue Wilderness Permit is required and is available at the trailhead. Parking and access are free.

Maps: You can purchase a Mount Jefferson Wilderness Map from Geo-Graphics. For a map of the Willamette National Forest and the Mount Jefferson Wilderness, contact Willamette National Forest Headquarters, 3106 Pierce Parkway, Suite D, Springfield, OR, 97477, 541/225-6300. For a topographic map, ask the USGS for Mount Bruno.

Directions: Drive 56 miles east of Salem on OR 22. One mile past Idanha, turn left on McCoy Creek Road 2233 for 9.2 miles. At a building, go right and continue 1.3 miles and park at spur Road 635. The trailhead is 100 feet down the spur road.

Contact: Willamette National Forest, Detroit Ranger District, HC73, Box 320, Mill City, OR, 97360, 503/854-4239.

93 JEFFERSON PARK
10.2 mi/5.0 hr   🥾3 ⛰10

south of Detroit in Mount Jefferson Wilderness

Map 9.5, page 457   BEST (

By far one of the most beloved places in Oregon, Jefferson Park is an alpine dream. Wildflowers dot the seemingly endless expanses of meadows, spotted here and there by mountain lakes and islands of wind-bent trees. Looming above it is Oregon's second-highest mountain, 10,497-foot Mount Jefferson. There are a number of ways into Jeff Park, as it's known, and this route is by far one of the most scenic. Climbing through an old-growth forest, the trail has expansive views of the mountain as it climbs and crosses the Sentinel Hills, passing rock fields where pikas dart in and out of their dens, and arriving at a virtual wonderland of lakes and undulating land.

The Whitewater Trail is easy to follow, climbing through the forest 1.5 miles to a junction. Go right along the Sentinel Hills 2.7 miles to a junction with the Pacific Crest Trail, then follow it 0.9 mile to the start of Jefferson Park. If you continue on the PCT another 0.7 mile, you'll come to Russell Lake, and side trails lead to other lakes: Scout, Rock, Bays, and Park.

User Groups: Hikers, dogs, and horses. No

mountain bikes allowed. No wheelchair facilities.

Permits: You can purchase a Mount Jefferson Wilderness Map from Geo-Graphics. A free self-issue Wilderness Permit is required and is available at the trailhead. A federal Northwest Forest Pass is required to park here; the cost is $5 a day or $30 for an annual pass. You can buy a day pass at the trailhead, at ranger stations, or through private vendors.

Maps: For a map of the Willamette National Forest and the Mount Jefferson Wilderness, contact Willamette National Forest Headquarters, 3106 Pierce Parkway, Suite D, Springfield, OR, 97477, 541/225-6300. For a topographic map, ask the USGS for Mount Jefferson.

Directions: Drive 61 miles east of Salem on OR 22. Beyond Detroit about 10 miles and between mileposts 60 and 61, turn left on Whitewater Road 2243 and drive 7.4 miles to its end at a parking area.

Contact: Willamette National Forest, Detroit Ranger District, HC73, Box 320, Mill City, OR, 97360, 503/854-4239.

94 PAMELIA LAKE AND GRIZZLY PEAK

10.0 mi/5.0 hr

south of Detroit in Mount Jefferson Wilderness

Map 9.5, page 457

This popular trail has become, in the last umpteen years, too popular. What could it be? The stroll along Pamelia Creek? The shores of Pamelia Lake, with staggering Mount Jefferson reflected in its waters? Or possibly the side hike up domineering Grizzly Peak? Alas, it is all of these. To deal with the onslaught of hikers, the Forest Service requires hikers to obtain a free permit in advance. This helps to ease the congestion and allow for this fragile area, especially the lakeshore, to recover from overuse.

The first 2.2 miles of trail follow Pamelia Creek into the dense forest. At a junction you

have several options. Go straight to the lakeshore, and you can circle it to the right for a view of Mount Jefferson. Go right at the junction following a sign for Grizzly Peak to climb 2.8 miles to the 5,799-foot summit.

User Groups: Hikers, dogs, and horses. No mountain bikes allowed. No wheelchair facilities.

Permits: A free Limited Entry Permit is required for overnight and day visits to the Pamelia Lake area; contact the USFS for information. A federal Northwest Forest Pass is required to park here; the cost is $5 a day or $30 for an annual pass. You can buy a day pass at the trailhead, at ranger stations, or through private vendors.

Maps: You can purchase a Mount Jefferson Wilderness Map from Geo-Graphics. For a map of the Willamette National Forest and the Mount Jefferson Wilderness, contact Willamette National Forest Headquarters, 3106 Pierce Parkway, Suite D, Springfield, OR, 97477, 541/225-6300. For a topographic map, ask the USGS for Mount Jefferson.

Directions: Drive 62 miles east of Salem on OR 22. Beyond Detroit about 12 miles, between mileposts 62 and 63, turn left on Pamelia Road 2246 for 3.7 miles to the trailhead lot at the end of the road.

Contact: Willamette National Forest, Detroit Ranger District, HC73, Box 320, Mill City, OR, 97360, 503/854-4239.

95 MARION LAKE AND MARION MOUNTAIN

11.2 mi/5.5 hr

east of Marion Forks in Mount Jefferson Wilderness

Map 9.5, page 457

Like nearby Pamelia Lake, this popular lake in the Mount Jefferson Wilderness shows obvious signs of overuse. The trail is well trammeled, and on a summer day you can expect to have company. None of this makes this big lake any less lovely. Anglers ply the waters, hikers climb over boulders to views of Three-Fingered Jack, and campers linger in the woods on cool mornings. Marion Lake isn't the only destination; you'll also see Marion Falls and Marion Mountain (did I mention this is Marion County?) along this hike. Granted, for some parts you will have to enter the notorious B&B Complex Burn, a devastating fire that roared through this wilderness in 2003, reducing much of it to ash.

The first 2.2 miles on the Marion Lake Trail are an easy walk through the forest, passing Lake Ann and its subterranean outlet. At a junction, go right on the Marion Lake Outlet Trail for 0.6 mile, watching on the right for the 0.2-mile side trail down to Marion Falls. At the next junction, you have a choice: left for a 0.7-mile trail along Marion Lake, which connects to a left-hand 0.3-mile trail back toward Lake Ann; or, if you're feeling sturdy, to the right, crossing Marion Creek and heading toward Marion Mountain on the Blue Lake Trail. The first mile enters the burn. At a pond-side junction, go right on the Pine Ridge Trail for 0.8 mile to a fork and a small sign for Marion Mountain. The remaining 0.8 mile climbs to the site of an old lookout with views to Three-Fingered Jack and Mount Jefferson.

User Groups: Hikers, dogs, and horses. No mountain bikes allowed. No wheelchair facilities.

Permits: A free self-issue Wilderness Permit is required and is available at the trailhead. A federal Northwest Forest Pass is required to park here; the cost is $5 a day or $30 for an annual pass. You can buy a day pass at the trailhead, at ranger stations, or through private vendors.

Maps: You can purchase a Mount Jefferson Wilderness Map from Geo-Graphics. For a map of the Willamette National Forest and the Mount Jefferson Wilderness, contact Willamette National Forest Headquarters, 3106 Pierce Parkway, Suite D, Springfield, OR, 97477, 541/225-6300. For a topographic map, ask the USGS for Marion Lake.

Directions: Drive 66 miles east of Salem on OR 22 to Marion Forks. Between mileposts 66 and 67 turn left on Marion Creek Road 2255 and drive 5.4 miles to the lot at road's end.

Contact: Willamette National Forest, Detroit Ranger District, HC73, Box 320, Mill City, OR, 97360, 503/854-4239.

96 CARL LAKE AND SOUTH CINDER PEAK
9.4-13.4 mi/4.5-6.0 hr

north of Sisters in Mount Jefferson Wilderness

Map 9.5, page 457

In 2003, the massive B&B Complex Fire (actually two forest fires that merged into one epic conflagration) swept through the Mount Jefferson Wilderness, torching many beloved places. Still, many areas were spared, including rock-rimmed Carl Lake. This camping-friendly lake also gives access to a number of great hikes, astonishing huckleberry fields, and a momentous view from the barren South Cinder Peak.

From the trailhead, march into the burned area which ends before the 1.9-mile walk to Cabot Lake and its side trail. From here the trail begins to switchback up into the high country, passing several ponds on the 2.8-mile walk to Carl Lake. Circle the lake for a variety of perspectives on the surrounding mountain country. The hike from here to South Cinder Peak is a challenge, requiring a 1.5-mile climb past Shirley Lake and along a deep valley to the Pacific Crest Trail. Go left on the PCT for 0.2 mile, then follow a path up the red cinder butte for views to Mount Jefferson and south to the Three Sisters.

User Groups: Hikers, dogs, and horses. No mountain bikes allowed. No wheelchair facilities.

Permits: A free self-issue Wilderness Permit is required and is available at the trailhead. A federal Northwest Forest Pass is required to park here; the cost is $5 a day or $30 for an annual pass. You can buy a day pass at the trailhead, at ranger stations, or through private vendors.

Maps: You can purchase a Mount Jefferson Wilderness Map from Geo-Graphics. For a map of the Deschutes National Forest and Mount Jefferson Wilderness, contact Deschutes National Forest Headquarters, 1001 SW Emkay Drive, Bend, OR, 97702, 541/383-5300.For a topographic map, ask the USGS for Marion Lake.

Directions: Drive 12 miles west of Sisters on U.S. 20 to a "Wilderness Trailheads" sign near milepost 88. Drive north on Jack Lake Road 12 for 4.4 miles and turn left on Road 1230 for 1.6 miles to pavement's end and seven miles on gravel to road's end at a large lot.

Contact: Deschutes National Forest, Sisters Ranger District, P.O. Box 249, Sisters, OR, 97759, 541/549-7700.

97 METOLIUS RIVER
5.4 mi/2.0 hr

north of Sisters in Deschutes National Forest

Map 9.5, page 457

The Metolius River rushes aboveground at 50,000 gallons a minute from an underground spring at the base of Black Butte. From there, the river makes a full display of itself with its ethereal blues and white water rushing through a forest of ponderosa pine and Douglas fir, where eagles wait in the branches for a chance at fish. This trail passes among songbirds amid some real scenery: islands of flowers entirely growing on fallen logs and a cascade of springs—including a waterfall splashing right out of the rock.

The easy West Metolius Trail is out-and-back from the Lower Canyon Creek Campground, heading 2.7 miles downstream to Wizard Falls and a fish hatchery. You can continue this hike as far downstream as far as you'd like, and can even cross the river and explore the opposite shore along a trail there, though there is no loop available in the form

of a second bridge to return you to the starting point.

User Groups: Hikers and dogs. No horses or mountain bikes allowed. No wheelchair facilities.

Permits: Permits are not required. Parking and access are free.

Maps: For a map of the Deschutes National Forest, contact Deschutes National Forest Headquarters, 1001 SW Emkay Drive, Bend, OR, 97702, 541/383-5300. For a topographic map, ask the USGS for Candle Creek.

Directions: Drive U.S. 20 west of Sisters nine miles, passing Black Butte. Near milepost 91, turn right at a sign for Metolius River and drive onto Road 1419 for 4.8 miles. At a stop sign, go straight on Road 1420 another 3.3 miles and turn right at a sign for Canyon Creek Campground, driving one mile to the end of the road.

Contact: Deschutes National Forest, Sisters Ranger District, P.O. Box 249, Sisters, OR, 97759, 541/549-7700.

98 COVE PALISADES STATE PARK
7.2 mi/2.5 hr

southwest of Madras in Cove Palisades State Park

Map 9.5, page 457

In a dramatic canyon where three rivers—the Deschutes, the Crooked, and the Metolius—meet, an impressive array of cliff walls nestle the combined flow into the massive Lake Billy Chinook reservoir. One way to get the views of two arms of the canyon and The Island (actually a peninsula, whose towering plateau-expanse makes it the next best thing to an island) is to hike the Tam-A-Lau Trail to The Peninsula, a broad desert atop a plateau with views over Cove Palisades State Park. If you're lucky, you can spot the bald eagles that roost nearby, and on a clear day you'll certainly see Mount Jefferson on the horizon.

From the lot, follow the Tam-A-Lau Trail

0.5 mile through massive tumbled boulders, crossing the two entrance roads to a junction, going to the right. The next 1.3 miles climbs the canyon wall up a series of switchbacks to a junction with some old roads. Keep to the left and follow the trail along the lip of The Peninsula 1.2 miles to the tip above the strange formation of Steamboat Rock. For a longer loop, follow this trail around the plateau another 2.4 miles, returning to the Tam-A-Lau Trail.

User Groups: Hikers and dogs only. No wheelchair facilities.

Permits: Permits are not required. A $3 day-use fee is collected at the parking entrance, or you can get an annual Oregon Parks and Recreation pass for $25; contact Oregon Parks and Recreation, 800/551-6949.

Maps: For a free park brochure, call Oregon Parks and Recreation, 800/551-6949 or download a free map at www.oregonstateparks.org. For a topographic map, ask the USGS for Round Butte Dam.

Directions: Drive 15 miles north of Redmond on U.S. 97, going up and over Culver Butte, to a sign for The Cove State Park. Follow the Culver Highway and signs for the park into the canyon. Follow this road over a suspension bridge above the Crooked River, passing a turnout for the Crooked River Petroglyph, the park headquarters, and campgrounds. Turn right at a sign for the Tam-A-Lau Trail. Park in the big lot at the end of the road.

Contact: Oregon Parks and Recreation Department, 1115 Commercial Street NE, Salem, OR, 97301, 800/551-6949, www.oregonstateparks.org.

NORTHEASTERN OREGON

BEST HIKES

◖ **Short Backpacking Trips**
Strawberry Lake and Little Strawberry Lake,
 page 581.

The Oregon Trail spans this area of the state,

crossing a rugged landscape of high deserts and mountains on its way to the paradise of the Willamette Valley. The Blue Mountains comprise several small ranges splayed across the region: the Wallowas, the Ochocos, and the Strawberries. Each differs in its flavor and coloring, but all are among the oldest ranges in the Western United States, having risen from the ocean floor millions upon millions of years ago. Over the top of this landscape are the massive Columbia River basalt lava flows that oozed from a giant crack in the earth, spreading across three states and all the way to the Pacific Ocean. This makes for a series of plateaus cut deep by the local rivers: the Walla Walla, the Umatilla, and the John Day.

A number of famed wilderness areas provide great hiking in northeastern Oregon, including the Eagle Cap Wilderness, an island of granite rising above Hells Canyon, as well as the Strawberry Mountain Wilderness, a range of the Blue Mountains. Rivers get their due, too, including those in the North Fork Umatilla, Wenaha-Tucannon, and North Fork John Day Wildernesses. Though quickly accessible to the towns that dot this region, they are off the beaten path for residents of the major metropolitan areas of Western Oregon. Backpacks are a must.

There's plenty to love here: forests of western larch, golden in autumn; rivers where prospectors still pan for gold; Wallowa Lake, once home to the Nez Perce tribe; and Hell's Canyon, among the deepest ravines in the United States. Looking for solitude? Look no further: in northeastern Oregon, you'll have the chance for real seclusion. Watch for elk herds as you explore, and you'll see why many of the pioneers lay down their burdens in this region and called it home.

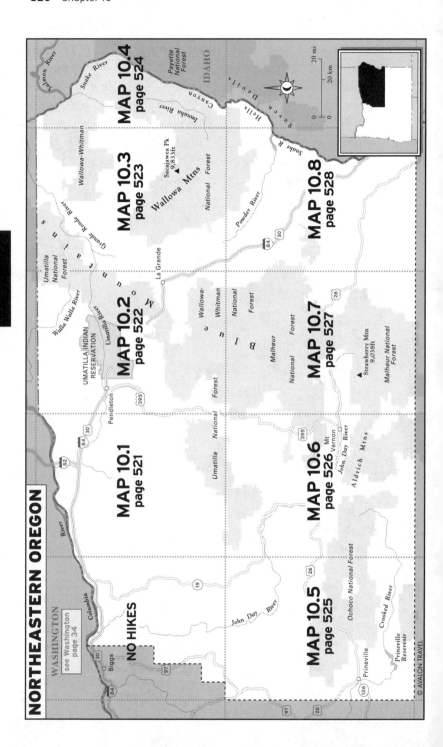

NORTHEASTERN OREGON

WASHINGTON
see Washington
page 34

NO HIKES

MAP 10.1
page 521

MAP 10.2
page 522

MAP 10.3
page 523

MAP 10.4
page 524

MAP 10.5
page 525

MAP 10.6
page 526

MAP 10.7
page 527

MAP 10.8
page 528

IDAHO

Payette National Forest

Salmon River

Snake River

Wallowa-Whitman

Imnaha River

Hells Canyon

Seven Devils

Sacajawea Pk
9,833ft

Wallowa Mtns

National Forest

Snake R.

Powder River

Grande Ronde River

Umatilla National Forest

Walla Walla River

Umatilla River

La Grande

B l u e M o u n t a i n s

UMATILLA INDIAN
RESERVATION

Pendleton

Wallowa-Whitman National Forest

Malheur National Forest

Strawberry Mtn
9,038ft

Malheur National Forest

Mt Vernon

John Day River

Aldrich Mtns

Umatilla National Forest

Columbia River

Biggs

John Day River

Ochoco National Forest

Crooked River

Prineville

Prineville Reservoir

20 mi

20 km

© AVALON TRAVEL

Map 10.1

Hikes 1-3
Pages 529-530

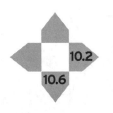

10.2

10.6

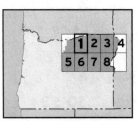

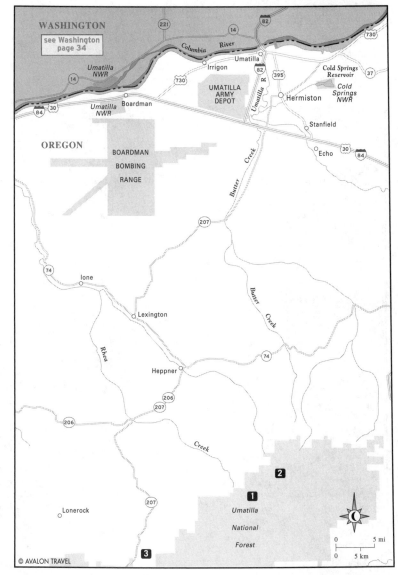

WASHINGTON

see Washington page 34

Umatilla NWR

Columbia River

Umatilla

Irrigon

UMATILLA ARMY DEPOT

Umatilla R.

Cold Springs Reservoir

Cold Springs NWR

Hermiston

Umatilla NWR

Boardman

OREGON

BOARDMAN

BOMBING

RANGE

Stanfield

Echo

Butter Creek

Ione

Butter Creek

Lexington

Rhea

Heppner

Creek

Lonerock

Umatilla

National

Forest

© AVALON TRAVEL

0   5 mi

0   5 km

Map 10.2

**Hikes 4-10
Pages 530-534**

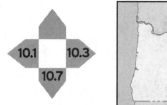

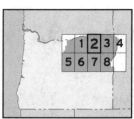

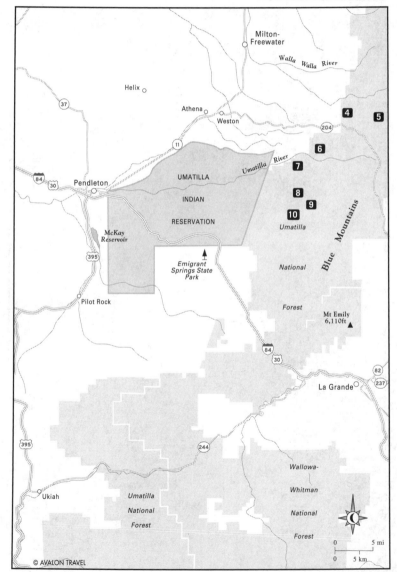

Map 10.3

Hikes 11-41
Pages 534-555

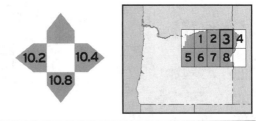

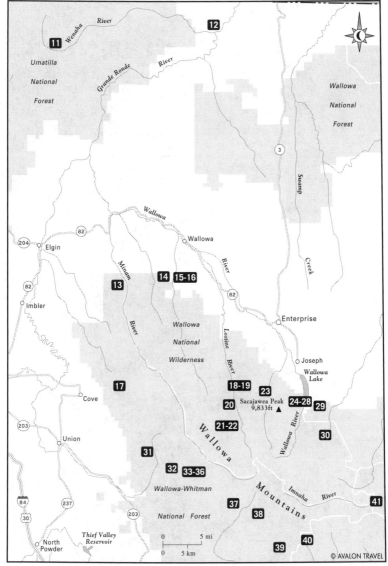

Map 10.4

Hikes 42-48
Pages 556-560

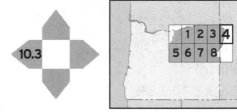

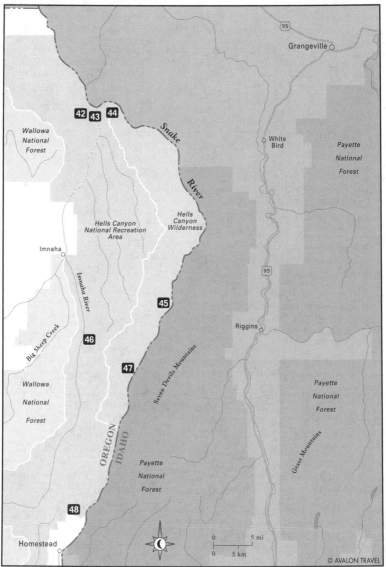

Map 10.5

Hikes 49-54
Pages 561-564

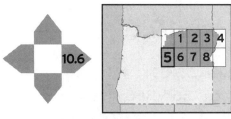

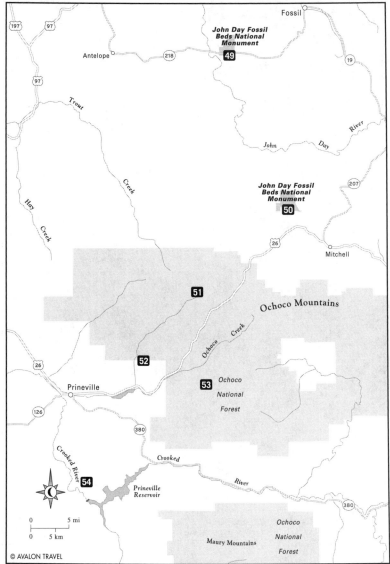

Map 10.6

Hikes 55-59
Pages 564-566

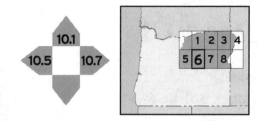

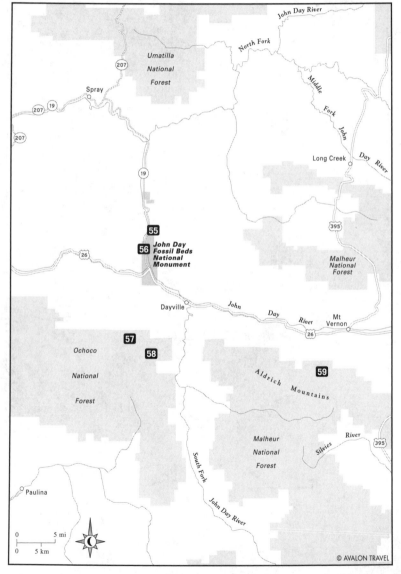

Map 10.7

Hikes 60-90
Pages 567-584

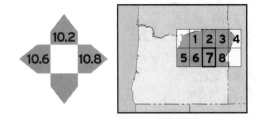

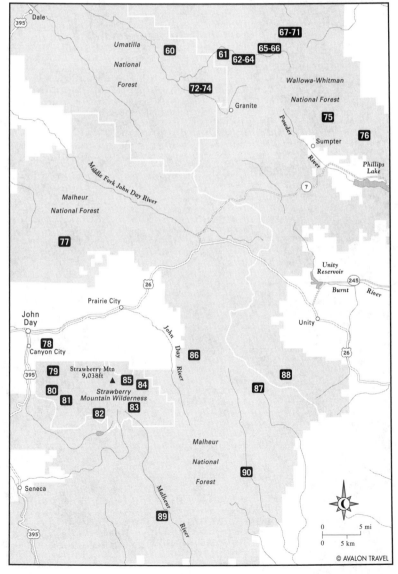

Map 10.8

Hike 91
Page 585

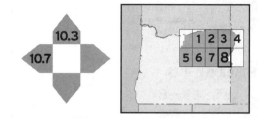

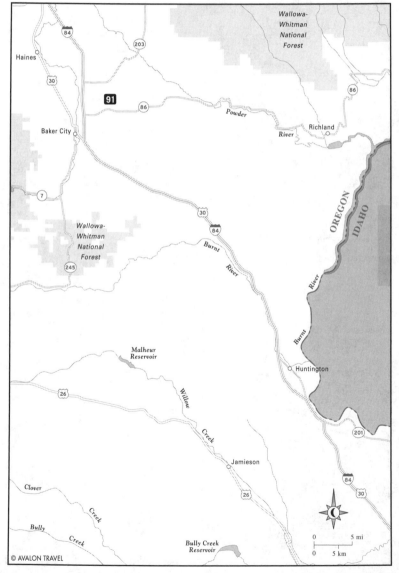

1 BALD MOUNTAIN

7.5 mi/3.0 hr   🏃2 ⛰7

south of Heppner in Umatilla National Forest

Map 10.1, page 521

Morrow County, Oregon, may not strike anyone as a place to go hiking, but there's plenty of history (both natural and man-made) here. The Smith Ditch was built by the Civilian Conservation Corps in the 1930s as a way to bring irrigation to the area. The Gibson Cave's history goes back much further; Native Americans used the cave within the last thousand years, and a man named Gibson made this cave his home during the Great Depression, building a wall with a window at the mouth of the cave, and bringing in a cot, wood-burning stove, kerosene lamps, and other assorted furniture, some of which he built. You won't find anyone living there today, of course. This trail loops nicely, connecting with a few others in the area.

From the Coalmine Day Use Area, follow the Bald Mountain Trail 0.2 mile to the Smith Ditch. Another mile brings you to the Gibson Cave. Though the trail ends in a saddle between Little Bald Mountain and Bald Mountain, you can extend this trail to a loop by following the Hells Half Acre Trail 2.5 miles to Cutsforth Park, then taking the Willow Creek Trail 2.5 miles back to the Coalmine Day Use Area.

User Groups: Hikers, dogs, and horses or mountain bikes allowed. No wheelchair facilities.

Permits: Permits are not required. Parking and access are free.

Maps: For a map of the Umatilla National Forest, contact the Umatilla National Forest, 2517 SW Hailey Avenue, Pendleton, OR, 97801, 541/278-3716. For a topographic map, ask the USGS for Arbuckle.

Directions: From Heppner, drive one mile south on Highway 207 to Willow Creek Road. Follow Willow Creek Road 23 miles south to the Coalmine Day Use Area.

Contact: Umatilla National Forest, Heppner Ranger District, P.O. Box 7, Heppner, OR, 97836, 541/676-1987.

2 COPPLE BUTTE TRAIL

12.5 mi/6.5 hr   🏃2 ⛰7

south of Heppner in Umatilla National Forest

Map 10.1, page 521

This trail makes an ideal mountain biking excursion, but there are opportunities for backpacking here, too—not to mention views of Mount Hood and Mount Adams from the eastern side of the Cascade Range. A profusion of trails reaches out from this area, making this a good entry point into the Blue Mountains of Morrow County. The elevation gain is nearly zero, following a ridgeline for 6.25 miles with views from Copple Butte, and nearby Texas Butte and the watchtower at Madison Butte. Hike bits of it, or make it a grand daylong excursion.

User Groups: Hikers, dogs, horses, and mountain bikes. No wheelchair facilities.

Permits: Permits are not required. Parking and access are free.

Maps: For a map of the Umatilla National Forest, contact the Umatilla National Forest, 2517 SW Hailey Avenue, Pendleton, OR, 97801, 541/278-3716. For a topographic map, ask the USGS for Madison Butte.

Directions: From Heppner, drive one mile south on Highway 207 to Willow Creek Road. Follow Willow Creek Road/County Road 678 for about 23 miles to FS Road 21. Follow FS Road 21 for 3.5 miles to Ditch Creek Guard Station and turn right on Road 050. Continue to the "Road Closure" sign at a corral, then go 1.25 miles across Martin Prairie to Texas Road 5350. Cross the road and follow a dirt road to a wooden gate. The trail begins here.

Contact: Umatilla National Forest, Heppner Ranger District, P.O. Box 7, Heppner, OR, 97836, 541/676-9187.

❸ BULL PRAIRIE LAKE
0.5 mi/0.25 hr

south of Heppner in Umatilla National Forest

Map 10.1, page 521

This little lake in northeastern Oregon, 28 acres in all and 20 feet at its maximum depth, makes for a quiet day. No motorboats are allowed on the lake, but anglers cast from the docks for rainbow and brook trout. If you're camping here or doing some of the other trails in the area, consider this for an easy walk for the family in the cool shade of big pine trees.

User Groups: Hikers and dogs. No horses or mountain bikes. No wheelchair facilities.

Permits: Permits are not required. Parking and access are free.

Maps: For a map of the Umatilla National Forest, contact the Umatilla National Forest, 2517 SW Hailey Avenue, Pendleton, OR, 97801, 541/278-3716. For a topographic map, ask the USGS for Madison Butte.

Directions: From Heppner, drive 40 miles south on Highway 207. Turn left onto FS Road 2039 at a sign for Bull Prairie Recreation Area, driving one mile to the recreation area on the right. Access points are scattered around the lake.

Contact: Umatilla National Forest, Heppner Ranger District, P.O. Box 7, Heppner, OR, 97836, 541/676-9187.

❹ SOUTH FORK WALLA WALLA RIVER
6.6-19.0 mi/3.0 hr-2 days

southeast of Milton-Freewater in Umatilla National Forest

Map 10.2, page 522

The Walla Walla River—its name means "little river"—slithers through its deep canyon (almost 2,000 feet in places) from a point high in the Blue Mountains. You can access the river from trailheads at its opposite ends, but the Rough Fork Trail descends roughly in the middle, allowing you to follow the river in either direction; if you go too far downstream, though, you'll quickly run into gas-powered motorbikes. It's more worth your while to stay in the more rugged middle point, where you can visit a box canyon and camping is possible.

From the Rough Fork Trailhead, descend into the canyon through forests and meadows for 3.3 miles to a footbridge over the South Fork Walla Walla. From here, you'll reach the junction with the South Fork Walla Walla Trail, a 19-mile trail. Return the way you came or continue on for a longer hike. Upstream the trail leads 7.5 miles to the Deduct Trailhead, and downstream continues 11.5 miles, passing Box Canyon, Bear Creek, and the Table Springs Trail before ending at a Forest Service road. Hike in either direction, and return via the Rough Fork Trail.

User Groups: Hikers, dogs, horses, and mountain bikes. No wheelchair facilities.

Permits: Permits are not required. Parking and access are free.

Maps: For a map of the Umatilla National Forest, contact the Umatilla National Forest, 2517 SW Hailey Avenue, Pendleton, OR, 97801, 541/278-3716. For a topographic map, ask the USGS for Jubilee Lake, Tollgate, and Bone Springs.

Directions: From I-84 at Pendleton, take Exit 210 and follow signs to Milton-Freewater on Highway 11 for 20.5 miles. After milepost 20, turn right at a sign for Elgin, then go left on Tollgate Road/Highway 204 for 19.9 miles. Turn left on Road 64 toward Jubilee Lake. Follow Road 64 north 13.5 miles to a fork, going left toward Walla Walla on Road 64. Go another 1.7 miles, then go left on Road 6403 (possibly unmarked) for 1.5 miles to a meadow at a junction. Fork right on an unmarked road 200 yards to a parking lot.

Contact: Umatilla National Forest, Walla Walla Ranger District, 1415 West Rose, Walla Walla, WA 99863, 509/522-6290.

5 JUBILEE LAKE NATIONAL RECREATION TRAIL

2.6 mi/1.0 hr 🥾1 ⚠7

northeast of Tollgate in Umatilla National Forest

Map 10.2, page 522

Jubilee Lake was created by a dam in 1968, and the trail around it is designated a National Recreation Trail. It makes a good camping and fishing spot, certainly, but also a relatively wild hiking spot. You can make an easy day of it with the family if you're staying the night. The trail loops 2.6 miles around the lake, crossing the dam and sometimes making use of old dirt roads along the way; just stay along the lakeshore and you can't go wrong.

User Groups: Hikers and dogs only. No horses or mountain bikes allowed. The trail is designed for barrier-free access.

Permits: Permits are not required. There is a $5 day-use fee collected at the fee booth.

Maps: For a map of the Umatilla National Forest, contact the Umatilla National Forest, 2517 SW Hailey Avenue, Pendleton, OR, 97801, 541/278-3716. For a topographic map, ask the USGS for Jubilee Lake.

Directions: From I-84 at Pendleton, take Exit 210 and follow signs to Milton-Freewater on Highway 11 for 20.5 miles. After milepost 20, turn right at a sign for Elgin, then go left on Tollgate Road/Highway 204 for 19.9 miles. Turn left on Road 64 toward Jubilee Lake. Follow Road 64 north 11.5 miles and turn right into the Jubilee Campground for 0.6 mile to the fee booth, then 0.2 mile to the boat ramp parking. The trail begins at the parking lot.

Contact: Umatilla National Forest, Walla Walla Ranger District, 1415 West Rose, Walla Walla, WA 99863, 509/522-6290.

6 LICK CREEK TO GROUSE MOUNTAIN

7.8 mi/3.5 hr 🥾3 ⚠7

southeast of Tollgate in North Fork Umatilla Wilderness

Map 10.2, page 522

Climbing a steep creek canyon into the North Fork Umatilla Wilderness, the Lick Creek Trail heads a mere 2.3 miles but climbs 1,800 feet through open stands of timber and native grasslands. Expect solitude. At a junction at the top of the ridge, the Lick Creek Trail continues its final mile to the right, but to the left a faint side trail leads 1.6 miles to a viewpoint at Grouse Mountain.

User Groups: Hikers, dogs, and horses. No mountain bikes allowed. No wheelchair facilities.

Permits: A free self-issue Wilderness Permit is required and is available at the trailhead. Parking and access are free.

Maps: For a map of the Umatilla National Forest and the North Fork Umatilla Wilderness, contact the Umatilla National Forest, 2517 SW Hailey Avenue, Pendleton, OR, 97801, 541/278-3716. For a topographic map, ask the USGS for Bingham Springs and Blalock Mountain.

Directions: To access the lower trailhead, take Exit 216 off I-84 south of Pendleton. Go north on Market Road/OR 331 for 1.9 miles to Mission-Cayuse Road, and go right for 1.6 miles, then go left on Cayuse Road for 11.2 miles. After milepost 15, turn right onto Bingham Road and follow it 14.7 miles. The trailhead is on the left.

Contact: Umatilla National Forest, Walla Walla Ranger District, 1415 West Rose, Walla Walla, WA 99863, 509/522-6290.

◻7 NORTH FORK UMATILLA RIVER

9.1 mi one-way/1-2 days 🏃3 ⛰7

east of Pendleton in North Fork Umatilla Wilderness

Map 10.2, page 522

Northeastern Oregon is a matter of lava, specifically the massive Columbia River basalt flows that poured out over this region over the course of millions of years. The Columbia Plateau was left behind, and rivers like the Umatilla slowly but surely carved their way, leaving steep canyons in the flat-as-a-pancake tablelands. For an exploration of one of these canyons, follow the North Fork Umatilla River into a wilderness area of cottonwood trees and red alders, which crowd the shores, and Douglas fir and Grand fir higher up. The lower part of the trail is popular and fairly easy, but it's the upper reaches where you'll find the most solitude, as well as exquisite views of the drainage.

From the trailhead, follow the North Fork Umatilla River and Trail 2.7 miles to a crossing of Coyote Creek and a campsite. Ignoring an unmaintained spur trail to the left, continue 1.6 miles along the river, then ascend Coyote Ridge over the next 2.8 miles. From a high point on the ridge, continue another two miles to an upper trailhead at Road 041, climbing 2,000 feet above the river.

User Groups: Hikers, dogs, and horses. No mountain bikes allowed. No wheelchair facilities.

Permits: A free self-issue Wilderness Permit is required and is available at the trailhead. Parking and access are free.

Maps: For a map of the Umatilla National Forest and the North Fork Umatilla Wilderness, contact the Umatilla National Forest, 2517 SW Hailey Avenue, Pendleton, OR, 97801, 541/278-3716. For a topographic map, ask the USGS for Bingham Springs.

Directions: To access the lower trailhead, take Exit 216 off I-84 south of Pendleton. Go north on Market Road/OR 331 for 1.9 miles to Mission-Cayuse Road, and go right for 1.6 miles, then go left on Cayuse Road for 11.2 miles. After milepost 15, turn right onto Bingham Road and follow it 15.7 miles. The trailhead is on the left. To reach the upper trailhead, drive west of Tollgate 1.2 miles on State Highway 204 and turn left on FS Road 3719. Follow this road about 1.5 miles and turn right on Road 040. After 0.6 mile, go right at a junction for 0.1 mile, then right 0.2 mile on Road 041 to road's end at the Coyote Ridge Trailhead.

Contact: Umatilla National Forest, Walla Walla Ranger District, 1415 West Rose, Walla Walla, WA 99863, 509/522-6290.

◻8 NINEMILE RIDGE

6.8 mi one-way/4.0 hr 🏃3 ⛰7

east of Pendleton in North Fork Umatilla Wilderness

Map 10.2, page 522

The North Fork Umatilla Wilderness has a quality of remoteness about it that draws people from the western part of the state, but for Eastern Oregonians, this may as well be their backyard. Ninemile Ridge rises above the Umatilla drainage enough so that the foliage changes dramatically from a deep fir forest to the sparse ponderosa pine stands and finally into grasslands and wildflower meadows. But it's a difficult climb, ascending more than 2,000 feet to a cairn at the summit, and ambling onward to an upper trailhead at Road 31. If you plan on backpacking, bring plenty of water, as there is no drinkable water along the way.

From the trailhead, go 200 feet to a four-way junction and take the left-hand Ninemile Ridge Trail, and in 0.1 mile go right toward the wilderness boundary. In two miles, the trail climbs out of the fir forests and into the pines, ascending nearly 1,200 feet to the start of the ridge. The next 1.6 miles climbs nearly 1,000 feet to the cairn marking the 4,568-foot summit. From here the trail continues along Ninemile Ridge 3.6 miles, joining the abandoned road that is the Umatilla Rim Trail for 0.7 mile to the upper trailhead at Road 31.

User Groups: Hikers, dogs, and horses. No mountain bikes allowed. No wheelchair facilities.

Permits: A free self-issue Wilderness Permit is required and is available at the trailhead. Parking and access are free.

Maps: For a map of the Umatilla National Forest and the North Fork Umatilla Wilderness, contact the Umatilla National Forest, 2517 SW Hailey Avenue, Pendleton, OR, 97801, 541/278-3716. For a topographic map, ask the USGS for Bingham Springs and Andies Prairie.

Directions: To access the lower trailhead, take Exit 216 off I-84 south of Pendleton. Go north on Market Road/OR 331 for 1.9 miles to Mission-Cayuse Road, and go right for 1.6 miles, then go left on Cayuse Road for 11.2 miles. After milepost 15, turn right onto Bingham Road and follow it 16.1 miles. Turn left on a rocky spur road 0.2 mile to a parking lot at road's end. For the upper trailhead, start from Tollgate and drive 8 miles south (or 14 miles north of Elgin) on State Highway 204 and turn west on FS Road 31. Go 2 miles and turn right on Road 3100-320 for 0.1 mile, then left on to Road 3100-330. After 2 miles, come to the end of the road at Shamrock Springs. The badly marked trail and trailhead are located 100 yards west of the springs.

Contact: Umatilla National Forest, Walla Walla Ranger District, 1415 West Rose, Walla Walla, WA 99863, 509/522-6290.

🖲 BUCK CREEK

5.5 mi/2.5 hr

east of Pendleton in North Fork Umatilla Wilderness

Map 10.2, page 522

The Buck Creek Trail certainly makes use of the creek, crossing and recrossing it up to 30 times along the way. Thus, you'll want to avoid this trail in the high spring runoff. But come summer, you'll be hopping the little creek easily, though you should wear a good pair of boots or shoes you can get wet. From the upper trailhead, it is possible to form a loop with the Buck Mountain Trail (see *Buck Mountain,* next listing) for a 12.2-mile loop. Note that the upper reaches of this trail cross clear-cuts and burned areas and may not make for the most scenic stretch.

From the trailhead, go 200 feet to a four-way junction and continue straight along Buck Creek. After three miles, the trail climbs 2.5 miles up a ridge and ends at the upper Lake Creek Trailhead at Road 3150.

User Groups: Hikers, dogs, and horses. No mountain bikes allowed. No wheelchair facilities.

Permits: A free self-issue Wilderness Permit is required and is available at the trailhead. Parking and access are free.

Maps: For a map of the Umatilla National Forest and the North Fork Umatilla Wilderness, contact the Umatilla National Forest, 2517 SW Hailey Avenue, Pendleton, OR, 97801, 541/278-3716. For a topographic map, ask the USGS for Bingham Springs.

Directions: To access the lower trailhead, take Exit 216 off I-84 south of Pendleton. Go north on Market Road/OR 331 for 1.9 miles to Mission-Cayuse Road, and go right for 1.6 miles, then go left on Cayuse Road for 11.2 miles. After milepost 15, turn right onto Bingham Road and follow it 16.1 miles. Turn left on a rocky spur road 0.2 mile to a parking lot at road's end. For the upper trailhead, from the town of Weston drive east on Highway 204 for 15.3 miles, turning right on McDougall Camp Road 3715 and driving 3.4 miles to its end at the trailhead.

Contact: Umatilla National Forest, Walla Walla Ranger District, 1415 West Rose, Walla Walla, WA 99863, 509/522-6290.

10 BUCK MOUNTAIN

6.5 mi/3.5 hr 🚶4 ⛰7

east of Pendleton in North Fork Umatilla Wilderness

Map 10.2, page 522

It is possible to make a loop of this trail with the Buck Creek hike (see *Buck Creek,* previous listing), though you'll have to cross a few logging roads and clear-cuts to do it. Nevertheless, you'll traverse the North Fork Umatilla Wilderness and afford yourself some views of this canyon country.

From the trailhead, hike in 200 feet to a four-way junction and go right on the Buck Mountain Trail. The trail climbs 2,100 feet in 2.2 miles before leveling off along the rim and mountain meadows for 4.3 miles to the upper trailhead for Buck Creek. At the peak, you will have a panoramic view of the surrounding country.

User Groups: Hikers, dogs, and horses. No mountain bikes allowed. No wheelchair facilities.

Permits: A free self-issue Wilderness Permit is required and is available at the trailhead. Parking and access are free.

Maps: For a map of the Umatilla National Forest and the North Fork Umatilla Wilderness, contact the Umatilla National Forest, 2517 SW Hailey Avenue, Pendleton, OR, 97801, 541/278-3716. For a topographic map, ask the USGS for Bingham Springs.

Directions: To access the lower trailhead, take Exit 216 off I-84 south of Pendleton. Go north on Market Road/OR 331 for 1.9 miles to Mission-Cayuse Road, and go right for 1.6 miles, then go left on Cayuse Road for 11.2 miles. After milepost 15, turn right onto Bingham Road and follow it 16.1 miles. Turn left on a rocky spur road 0.2 mile to a parking lot at road's end. For the upper trailhead, from the town of Weston drive east on Highway 204 for 15.3 miles, turning right on McDougall Camp Road 3715 and driving 3.4 miles to its end at the trailhead.

Contact: Umatilla National Forest, Walla Walla Ranger District, 1415 West Rose, Walla Walla, WA 99863, 509/522-6290.

11 UPPER WENAHA RIVER

9.0 mi round-trip or 31.4 mi one-way/5.0 hr–6 days 🚶3 ⛰8

east of Pendleton in Wenaha-Tucannon Wilderness

Map 10.3, page 523

The Wenaha River covers quite a stretch of this little corner of Oregon nestled up to the Washington border. To do this river at a stretch requires endurance and a love of getting wet since you'll have to ford the river and side creeks at points. Then there are the rattlesnakes and high summer temperatures, but after all, this is the high-and-dry country. On the other hand, numerous bars along the river afford good camping spots, and the canyon itself is rugged and phenomenally beautiful, particularly as it crosses the Wenaha-Tucannon Wilderness, with its western larch trees, orchids, and wild mushrooms. This trail descends, so just remember that what goes down must come back up.

From the historic guard station at Timothy Springs, start out on the Wenaha Trail. In the first two miles, the trail crosses two creeks and follows the South Fork Wenaha River. At the third creek crossing, look for a waterfall upstream from the crossing. After 0.3 mile, the trail fords the 20-foot-wide river. If you decide to cross, continue 2.2 miles up and down a cliff face, crossing a small creek and reaching the second major ford of Milk Creek, which makes a good turnaround point. If you continue, the trail goes on 5.7 miles to Wenaha Forks, 14.8 miles from there to Crooked Creek, then 4.1 miles to the National Forest boundary and 2.3 final miles to the town of Troy.

User Groups: Hikers, dogs, and horses. No mountain bikes allowed. No wheelchair facilities.

Permits: A free self-issue Wilderness Permit is required and is available at the trailhead. Parking and access are free.

Maps: For a map of the Umatilla National Forest, contact the Umatilla National Forest, 2517 SW Hailey Avenue, Pendleton, OR,

97801, 541/278-3716. For a topographic map, ask the USGS for Wenaha Forks.

Directions: From I-84 at Pendleton, take Exit 210 and follow signs to Milton-Freewater on Highway 11 for 20.5 miles. After milepost 20, turn right at a sign for Elgin, then go left on Tollgate Road/Highway 204 for 19.9 miles. Turn left on Road 64 toward Jubilee Lake. Follow Road 64 north 13.5 miles. Two miles past Jubilee Lake, go right at a fork onto Road 6413 toward Troy, going 11.8 miles to a T-junction. Go left, staying on Road 6413 for 1.8 miles, then go left on Road 6415 for 6.9 miles to Timothy Springs Campground on the right. Turn right and stay on the middle road for 0.2 mile to a message board at the Wilderness boundary.

Opposite trailhead the same as Lower Wenaha River: From La Grande on I-84, take exit 261 and follow signs toward Enterprise, driving on Highway 82 for 65 miles. In Enterprise, turn left on First Street/Highway 3 for 35 miles to a sign for Flora, and turn left three miles to the ghost town of Flora, and continue 11.3 miles from paved road to a steep, one-lane gravel road and cross the Grande Ronde River. After the bridge, turn left for two miles to the town of Troy. Just before the downtown, turn right on Bartlett Road toward Pomeroy, going 0.4 mile to a pullout at a switchback. The trailhead is behind the message board.

Contact: Umatilla National Forest, Pomeroy Ranger District, 71 West Main Street, Pomeroy, WA 99347, 509/843-1891.

12 LOWER WENAHA RIVER
12.8 mi/6.5 hr

west of Troy in Umatilla National Forest

Map 10.3, page 523

There are numerous access points to the Wenaha River, and the tiny town of Troy marks the lower stretch. From here, the trail heads into the whitewater canyon, passing ponderosa pine, mariposa lilies, and poison oak.

Undaunted, it follows the canyon walls into the Wenaha-Tucannon Wilderness, making for a long backpacking or horseback trip up to the historic guard station at Timothy Springs. For an easier day-hike, or a short backpacking trip, Crooked Creek makes a good destination point.

From the trailhead, hike the Wenaha Trail 2.3 miles upstream along the river to the National Forest boundary. From here, elevation gain is minimal. The next 4.1 miles continues to viewpoints and rimrock cliff overhangs to a junction; go left to a footbridge crossing of Crooked Creek and campsites. If you continue on, it is 14.8 miles to Wenaha Forks, and another 10.2 to Timothy Springs.

User Groups: Hikers, dogs, and horses. No mountain bikes allowed. No wheelchair facilities.

Permits: Permits are not required unless entering the wilderness area, where a free self-issue Wilderness Permit is required and is available on the trail. Parking and access are free.

Maps: For a map of the Umatilla National Forest, contact the Umatilla National Forest, 2517 SW Hailey Avenue, Pendleton, OR, 97801, 541/278-3716. For a topographic map, ask the USGS for Troy.

Directions: From La Grande on I-84, take exit 261 and follow signs toward Enterprise, driving on Highway 82 for 65 miles. In Enterprise, turn left on First Street/Highway 3 for 35 miles to a sign for Flora, and turn left three miles to the ghost town of Flora, and continue 11.3 miles from paved road to a steep, one-lane gravel road and cross the Grande Ronde River. After the bridge, turn left for two miles to the town of Troy. Just before the downtown, turn right on Bartlett Road toward Pomeroy, going 0.4 mile to a pullout at a switchback. The trailhead is behind the message board.

Opposite trailhead the same as Upper Wenaha Trail: From I-84 at Pendleton, take Exit 210 and follow signs to Milton-Freewater on Highway 11 for 20.5 miles. After milepost 20, turn right at a sign for Elgin, then go left on Tollgate Road/

Highway 204 for 19.9 miles. Turn left on Road 64 toward Jubilee Lake. Follow Road 64 north 13.5 miles. Two miles past Jubilee Lake, go right at a fork onto Road 6413 toward Troy, going 11.8 miles to a T-junction. Go left, staying on Road 6413 for 1.8 miles, then go left on Road 6415 for 6.9 miles to timothy Springs Campground on the right. Turn right and stay on the middle road for 0.2 mile to a message board at the Wilderness boundary.

Contact: Umatilla National Forest, Pomeroy Ranger District, 71 West Main Street, Pomeroy, WA 99347, 509/843-1891.

13 MINAM RIVER FROM ROCK SPRINGS TRAILHEAD
8.4 mi/4.0 hr

northeast of La Grande in Eagle Cap Wilderness

Map 10.3, page 523

Making your way to the Minam River is difficult. No matter how you do it, you'll still have to descend into a 2,500-foot-deep canyon in the heart of the Eagle Cap Wilderness—and get back out. The Rock Springs Trail offers one of the most desirable entries to the canyon; it leads to the confluence of the mighty Minam River with the Little Minam River at a point where a few log cabin ruins mark an abandoned lodge. From the top of the canyon, the land stretches out like folds in a sleeve, but soon enough dives into the depths of the rimrock.

The trail almost immediately heads downhill into a forest of lodgepole pine, grand fir, subalpine fir, and western larch for 3.4 miles, coming to two good viewpoints of the canyon before dropping steeply into the final pitch of the canyon. Near the bottom, the trail comes to a junction; to the right is the Little Minam River Trail, which follows this river to the Moss Springs Trailhead 12 miles upstream (see *Little Minam River* in this chapter). To access the Minam River, go right past the abandoned lodge buildings, passing a more obvious trail on the right and continuing through the

meadow. This path leads 0.8 mile along the river to a ford, far too cold and swift for hikers to attempt fording, so return as you came.

Otherwise, the nearest place to cross is to head 5.5 miles on the Little Minam River, then go right 1.1 miles to the old Reds Horse Ranch and cross to the other side there, from which you can follow the river upstream to Minam Lake.

User Groups: Hikers, dogs, and horses. No mountain bikes allowed. No wheelchair facilities.

Permits: A free self-issue Wilderness Permit is required and is available at the trailhead. Parking and access are free.

Maps: A contour map of the Wallowa Mountains is available from Imus Geographics. For a map of the Wallowa-Whitman National Forest, contact the Wallowa-Whitman National Forest Headquarters, P.O. Box 907, 1550 Dewey Avenue, Baker City, OR, 97814, 541/523-6391. For a topographic map, ask the USGS for Minam.

Directions: From the La Grande Exit 261 off I-84, follow Highway 82 toward Wallowa Lake for eight miles to Alicel. Turn right on Alicel Lane, and stay on this road through several turns and bends for four miles. Turn right on Gray's Corners Road for one mile and turn left on an unmarked gravel road that heads uphill. In 10.2 miles cross a bridge and turn left on Road 62, going 6.8 miles to a fork. Go right, continuing on Road 62 for three miles to the Rock Springs Trailhead. The trailhead is about 200 yards farther down the road.

Contact: Wallowa-Whitman National Forest, Eagle Cap Ranger District, 88401 Highway 82, Enterprise, OR, 97828, 541/426-5546.

14 STANDLEY CABIN
10.2 mi/4.5 hr

south of Wallowa in Eagle Cap Wilderness

Map 10.3, page 523

The Standley Guard Station was used as the site for range studies in the early 1900s, and though it is not open for public use it is in remarkably good condition. The cabin is the destination on this hike along Standley Ridge, which passes through burned woods and fields of fireweed into the Eagle Cap Wilderness.

From the Bearwallow Trailhead, follow the Standley Trail along the ridge. In 0.8 mile, the trail passes Bald Knob, and 1.7 miles later moves into the burn, staying in the midst of the snags and fireweed for 1.6 miles to the Dobbins Creek Trail junction, which gives you the option of heading down four miles to the Bear Creek Guard Station (see *Bear Creek,* next listing). Instead, continue on: 0.9 mile past Dobbins Creek Trail junction, you'll reach the cabin and a spring. From the cabin, you'll have your pick of three different directions to hike into the wilderness for days of adventure.

User Groups: Hikers, dogs, and horses. No mountain bikes allowed. No wheelchair facilities.

Permits: A free self-issue Wilderness Permit is required and is available at the trailhead. Parking and access are free.

Maps: A contour map of the Wallowa Mountains is available from Imus Geographics. For a map of the Wallowa-Whitman National Forest, contact the Wallowa-Whitman National Forest Headquarters, P.O. Box 907, 1550 Dewey Avenue, Baker City, OR, 97814, 541/523-6391. For a topographic map, ask the USGS for Mount Moriah.

Directions: From the La Grande Exit 261 off I-84, follow Highway 82 toward Wallowa Lake for 35 miles. Turn right on Big Canyon Road 8270 for 10.8 miles, then go left on primitive Road 050 for 6.9 miles, staying on the main road at junctions. Park at the Bearwallow Trailhead at road's end.

Contact: Wallowa-Whitman National Forest, Eagle Cap Ranger District, 88401 Highway 82, Enterprise, OR, 97828, 541/426-5546.

⏹5 BEAR CREEK

10.0 mi/4.5 hr

south of Wallowa in Eagle Cap Wilderness

Map 10.3, page 523

This fairly easy trail accesses the vast Eagle Cap Wilderness, with opportunities to connect to other trails in this wilderness area, or just to fish the stream. Bear Creek rolls through open country, pine stands, and dense fir forests. Cottonwood trees stand tall along the creek. Where Goat Creek joins Bear Creek, the historic Bear Creek Guard Station sits quietly in a meadow. Though locked to the public, there are plenty of campsites nearby. From there, the wilderness is at your fingertips.

From the trailhead and Boundary Campground, follow Bear Creek upstream 4.3 miles to the junction with the Goat Creek Trail. There are campsites in the woods here. Proceed on the Bear Creek Trail 0.7 mile to the cabin. In another 0.5 mile, another junction leads up 4.4 miles to Standley Ridge (see *Standley Cabin,* previous listing).

User Groups: Hikers, dogs, and horses. No mountain bikes allowed. No wheelchair facilities.

Permits: A free self-issue Wilderness Permit is required and is available at the trailhead. A federal Northwest Forest Pass is required to park here; the cost is $5 a day or $30 for an annual pass. You can buy a day pass at the trailhead, at ranger stations, or through private vendors.

Maps: A contour map of the Wallowa Mountains is available from Imus Geographics. For a map of the Wallowa-Whitman National Forest, contact the Wallowa-Whitman National Forest Headquarters, P.O. Box 907, 1550 Dewey Avenue, Baker City, OR, 97814, 541/523-6391. For a topographic map, ask the USGS for Fox Point.

Directions: From the La Grande Exit 261 off I-84, follow Highway 82 toward Wallowa Lake 46.5 miles to the town of Wallowa. Turn right toward North Bear Creek Road, which becomes Road 8250, for 8.2 miles. Go straight on Road 040, following signs for Boundary Campground, another 0.8 mile past the campground to the trailhead at road's end.

Contact: Wallowa-Whitman National Forest, Eagle Cap Ranger District, 88401 Highway 82, Enterprise, OR, 97828, 541/426-5546.

16 HUCKLEBERRY MOUNTAIN

3.8–16.0 mi/2.0 hr–2 days 🥾3 ⛰7

south of Wallowa in Wallowa-Whitman National Forest

Map 10.3, page 523

This wonderfully rough trail, following an old cattle trail, arduously climbs to an old lookout site on Huckleberry Mountain, whose open grasslands fill with flowers in July and provide views down to the Lostine Canyon and Bear Creek. Although the trail crosses Little Bear Creek at the outset, water is scarce after that—unless you plan on following the trail six miles farther along the ridge to Little Storm Lake. You may find a good use here for your route-finding skills, as the trail is rougher than average and faint in places. Even the road to get there is a bit rough; with a high-clearance vehicle you can drive straight to the trailhead through a gate open July 15 through September 15. If you're not in the mood for busted shocks, simply park in Little Bear Saddle and walk in, adding one mile round-trip to your hike.

If need be, park at the intersection of Road 8250 and Road 160. Follow Road 160 by foot or vehicle up 0.5 mile to the trailhead on the left. The Huckleberry Mountain Trail climbs relentlessly from here 1.9 miles and 1,850 feet to the lookout site atop Huckleberry Mountain. This makes a good turnaround point. But the trail continues along the ridge and into the Eagle Cap Wilderness, where wilderness permits are required. Follow the trail six miles, dropping down to 7,200-foot elevation Little Storm Lake.

User Groups: Hikers, dogs, and horses. No

aspens in the Wallowa Mountains

© SEAN PATRICK HILL

mountain bikes allowed. No wheelchair facilities.

Permits: Permits are not required unless entering the Eagle Cap Wilderness, where a free permit can be filled out at the wilderness boundary. Parking and access are free.

Maps: A contour map of the Wallowa Mountains is available from Imus Geographics. For a map of the Wallowa-Whitman National Forest, contact the Wallowa-Whitman National Forest Headquarters, P.O. Box 907, 1550 Dewey Avenue, Baker City, OR, 97814, 541/523-6391. For a topographic map, ask the USGS for Lostine.

Directions: From the La Grande Exit 261 off I-84, follow Highway 82 toward Wallowa Lake 46.5 miles to the town of Wallowa. Turn right on North Bear Creek Road, which becomes Road 8250, for 8.2 miles. Go left, following signs for Huckleberry Trail, another 7.4 miles. At a fork in Little Bear Saddle, turn right on Road 160 for 0.5 mile to the trailhead. If the gate is closed or if you have a low-clearance vehicle, park at the intersection and follow the hiking directions in the hike description.

Contact: Wallowa-Whitman National Forest, Eagle Cap Ranger District, 88401 Highway 82, Enterprise, OR, 97828, 541/426-5546.

17 LITTLE MINAM RIVER
15.2 mi/2 days 🥾4 ⛰8

east of La Grande in Eagle Cap Wilderness

Map 10.3, page 523

Like the Rock Springs Trail to the Minam River, this trail along the Little Minam River drops into a canyon spiked with western larch, subalpine fir, and grand fir, and visits an unused lodge and the Reds Horse Ranch, a former dude ranch that is currently closed but maintained by volunteers. With camping available along the Minam River, and three creeks along the way for water, this makes a good overnighter.

From the trailhead lot, pass by the Lodgepole Trail and instead take the trail behind the message board, which immediately forks. Go left on the Horse Ranch Trail, gradually climbing down into the canyon. In 1.4 miles, the trail crosses Horseshoe Creek then begins following the Little Minam River for three miles to a bridge over the Little Minam. Stay left after the bridge, following the river then leaving it 2.1 miles to a pass. The trail to the left leads to the Rock Springs Trail; go straight 1.1 miles to the bridge over the Minam River and the old dude ranch.

User Groups: Hikers, dogs, and horses. No mountain bikes allowed. No wheelchair facilities.

Permits: A free self-issue Wilderness Permit is required and is available at the trailhead. A federal Northwest Forest Pass is required to park here; the cost is $5 a day or $30 for an annual pass. You can buy a day pass at the trailhead, at ranger stations, or through private vendors.

Maps: A contour map of the Wallowa Mountains is available from Imus Geographics. For a map of the Wallowa-Whitman National Forest, contact the Wallowa-Whitman National Forest Headquarters, P.O. Box 907, 1550 Dewey Avenue, Baker City, OR, 97814, 541/523-6391. For a topographic map, ask the USGS for Mount Moriah.

Directions: From the La Grande Exit 261 off I-84, follow Highway 82 toward Wallowa Lake for 1.8 miles, then go straight on East 1st Street, which becomes Highway 237, for 14 miles to the town of Cove. In Cove, follow the highway on Main Street to where it turns right, then go left on French Street, following signs for Moss Creek Campground. The road becomes Mill Creek Lane then Road 6220; follow this road 9.1 miles to the campground. The last seven miles of this road are steep and rough. Go right into the campground for 0.3 mile to the trailhead parking area at the end of a loop.

Contact: Wallowa-Whitman National Forest, Eagle Cap Ranger District, 88401 Highway 82, Enterprise, OR, 97828, 541/426-5546.

18 STEAMBOAT LAKE LOOP
29.3 mi/3 days 🥾5 ⛰10

south of Wallowa in Eagle Cap Wilderness

Map 10.3, page 523

If there is one thing the Eagle Cap Wilderness is famous for, it's lakes. In this corner of the wilderness, lakes abound, creeks tumble over the trails, and two major rivers, the Lostine and the Minam, have their headwaters here. This rough-and-tumble rocky mountain stretch makes for a mighty loop, backpacker and horse train worthy. Midweek, you may not see many people; there are far more popular areas in the wilderness, so you can really get away for days here. Along the way, you'll pass Chimney, John Henry, Steamboat, and Swamp Lakes—all camping friendly. Watch for elk, deer, and bear.

To hike the full loop, start at the Bowman Trailhead and climb into a forest of lodgepole pine, fir, and spruce 3.6 miles and 2,000 feet to a junction in Brownie Basin. Chimney Lake and the Laverty Lakes are 1.5 miles to the right and Hobo Lake is 1.6 mile farther on. For the loop, continue on the Bowman Trail 1.1 miles up to Wilson Pass, then switchback down 1.2 miles to a junction in Wilson Basin. John Henry Lake is 0.5 mile to the left and makes a good camping site for the first night.

From this junction, continue 1.2 mile over the Wilson Basin, then go left across a creek at a junction, continuing 2.5 miles to a three-way junction in North Minam Meadows. Go left toward Copper Creek, following the North Minam River 5.3 miles to Steamboat Lake, a good spot to camp for a second night; if not here, go 1.7 miles farther to Swamp Lake, passing a right-hand 1.8-mile spur trail to Long Lake. All three lakes are set in a granite basin.

Continue past Swamp Lake 1.7 miles to the uplands, then go left along the Copper Creek Trail 3.4 miles to a meadow, then 1.6 miles to a junction, staying left along the West Lostine River for 2.8 descending miles to the Two Pan Trailhead. From here, the walk back to the Bowman Trailhead is along the Lostine River Road 3.2 miles, but there are three developed campgrounds along the way, Shady Campground being the closest in 0.5 mile.

User Groups: Hikers, dogs, and horses. No mountain bikes allowed. No wheelchair facilities.

Permits: A free self-issue Wilderness Permit is required and is available at the trailhead. A federal Northwest Forest Pass is required to park here; the cost is $5 a day or $30 for an annual pass. You can buy a day pass at the trailhead, at ranger stations, or through private vendors.

Maps: A contour map of the Wallowa Mountains is available from Imus Geographics. For a map of the Wallowa-Whitman National Forest, contact the Wallowa-Whitman National Forest Headquarters, P.O. Box 907, 1550 Dewey Avenue, Baker City, OR, 97814, 541/523-6391. For a topographic map, ask the USGS for North Minam Meadows and Steamboat Lake.

Directions: From the La Grande Exit 261 off I-84, follow Highway 82 toward Wallowa Lake for 55 miles to Lostine. Where the highway turns left in town, go straight on Lostine River Road for 12.2 miles to the Lostine Guard Station, and continue on gravel another 2.9 miles to the Bowman Trailhead on the right. To find the Two Pan Trailhead, continue 3.2 miles on the Lostine River Road to road's end.

Contact: Wallowa-Whitman National Forest, Eagle Cap Ranger District, 88401 Highway 82, Enterprise, OR, 97828, 541/426-5546.

19 FRANCES LAKE

18.2 mi/2 days

south of Wallowa in Eagle Cap Wilderness

Map 10.3, page 523

The Frances Lake Trail offers some amazing views of Twin Peaks and Marble Point, and looks out over the Lostine Canyon to Chimney and Hobo Lakes (see *Steamboat Lake Loop* in this section). It's an arduous 3,300-foot climb to a high pass, then another nearly 1,000-foot drop to the lake itself. Climb switchback after switchback, following this trail 9.1 miles to the lake; be sure to carry adequate water. Because of the lack of water on the trail, the best place to camp is Frances Lake itself. Be sure to refill your bottles there.

User Groups: Hikers, dogs, and horses. No mountain bikes allowed. No wheelchair facilities.

Permits: A free self-issue Wilderness Permit is required and is available at the trailhead. A federal Northwest Forest Pass is required to park here; the cost is $5 a day or $30 for an annual pass. You can buy a day pass at the trailhead, at ranger stations, or through private vendors.

Maps: A contour map of the Wallowa Mountains is available from Imus Geographics. For a map of the Wallowa-Whitman National Forest, contact the Wallowa-Whitman National Forest Headquarters, P.O. Box 907, 1550 Dewey Avenue, Baker City, OR, 97814,

541/523-6391. For a topographic map, ask the USGS for North Minam Meadows and Chief Joseph Mountain.

Directions: From the La Grande Exit 261 off I-84, follow Highway 82 toward Wallowa Lake for 55 miles to Lostine. Where the highway turns left in town, go straight on Lostine River Road for 12.2 miles to the Lostine Guard Station, and continue on gravel another 2.9 miles to the Bowman Trailhead on the right.

Contact: Wallowa-Whitman National Forest, Eagle Cap Ranger District, 88401 Highway 82, Enterprise, OR, 97828, 541/426-5546.

20 MAXWELL LAKE

7.6 mi/4.5 hr

south of Wallowa in Eagle Cap Wilderness

Map 10.3, page 523

If the long hikes into the alpine wonder of the Eagle Cap Wilderness aren't your bag, consider the short—but by no means easy—trail to Maxwell Lake. Although some steepness will shorten your breath, Maxwell Lake itself will take your breath away. Nestled in a granite, glacier-carved basin above the Lostine River, the lake awaits at the end of the trail.

From the trailhead, descend to the river crossing and begin upward for 2.8 miles on the series of long, steady switchbacks known as the Maxwell Lake Trail. The next 0.8 mile climbs steeply to a pass, then descends 0.2 mile to the lakeshore and trail's end.

User Groups: Hikers, dogs, and horses. No mountain bikes allowed. No wheelchair facilities.

Permits: A free self-issue Wilderness Permit is required and is available at the trailhead. A federal Northwest Forest Pass is required to park here; the cost is $5 a day or $30 for an annual pass. You can buy a day pass at the trailhead, at ranger stations, or through private vendors.

Maps: A contour map of the Wallowa Mountains is available from Imus Geographics. For a map of the Wallowa-Whitman National

Forest, contact the Wallowa-Whitman National Forest Headquarters, P.O. Box 907, 1550 Dewey Avenue, Baker City, OR, 97814, 541/523-6391. For a topographic map, ask the USGS for North Minam Meadows.

Directions: From the La Grande Exit 261 off I-84, follow Highway 82 toward Wallowa Lake for 55 miles to Lostine. Where the highway turns left in town, go straight on Lostine River Road for 12.2 miles to the Lostine Guard Station, and continue on gravel another 5.6 miles to the Maxwell Lake Trailhead on the right.

Contact: Wallowa-Whitman National Forest, Eagle Cap Ranger District, 88401 Highway 82, Enterprise, OR, 97828, 541/426-5546.

21 MINAM AND MIRROR LAKES LOOP

11.6-17.7 mi/7.5 hr-2 days

south of Wallowa in Eagle Cap Wilderness

Map 10.3, page 523

The West Lostine River meanders through high mountain meadows between grassy banks, flanked by steep ridges and fed by Minam Lake. Less than a mile above that lake is little Blue Lake, walled in by stupendous cliffs. These two lakes make a good day trip, but if you're interested in a longer loop for backpacking you can continue over a high pass between two forks of the Lostine River to Mirror Lake, with the emblematic Eagle Cap peak towering above it, and return through some lovely meadows along the East Lostine River.

To head to Minam Lake, start off on the Minam Lake/West Fork Lostine River Trail (aka Two Pan Trail), keeping right at the first junction. Climb steadily 2.8 miles, keeping left at the Copper Creek junction. In another 1.5 miles, cross the river and continue 1.5 miles to the head of Minam Lake. In 0.8 mile the trail reaches the top of the lake at an earthen dam. To head to Blue Lake, follow the trail across the dam and climb 0.9 mile.

For a longer backpacking trip, start at the head of Minam Lake and follow a Lake Basin sign to the left and up 1.9 miles to the 8,560-foot Minam Pass, then down 1.3 miles on the far side. When you reach the two cairns marking a four-way junction, you can go straight on Trail 1661 to Mirror Lake. Going left follows the East Lostine River on the East Fork Trail through vibrant meadows 7.1 miles back to the Two Pan Trailhead (see *Mirror Lake and Eagle Cap,* next listing).

User Groups: Hikers, dogs, and horses. No mountain bikes allowed. No wheelchair facilities.

Permits: A free self-issue Wilderness Permit is required and is available at the trailhead. A federal Northwest Forest Pass is required to park here; the cost is $5 a day or $30 for an annual pass. You can buy a day pass at the trailhead, at ranger stations, or through private vendors.

Maps: A contour map of the Wallowa Mountains is available from Imus Geographics. For a map of the Wallowa-Whitman National Forest, contact the Wallowa-Whitman National Forest Headquarters, P.O. Box 907, 1550 Dewey Avenue, Baker City, OR, 97814, 541/523-6391. For a topographic map, ask the USGS for Steamboat Lake and Eagle Cap.

Directions: From the La Grande Exit 261 off I-84, follow Highway 82 toward Wallowa Lake for 55 miles to Lostine. Where the highway turns left in town, go straight on Lostine River Road for 12.2 miles to the Lostine Guard Station, and continue on gravel another 6.1 miles to the Two Pan Trailhead at road's end.

Contact: Wallowa-Whitman National Forest, Eagle Cap Ranger District, 88401 Highway 82, Enterprise, OR, 97828, 541/426-5546.

22 MIRROR LAKE AND EAGLE CAP

19.6 mi/1-2 days   🏃5 ⛺10

south of Wallowa in Eagle Cap Wilderness

Map 10.3, page 523

From the Lostine River meadows, Eagle Cap looms. At 9,572 feet, it's the centerpiece of

its namesake wilderness and dominates the skyline for this whole part of the Wallowa Mountains (though it's not the tallest peak in the area—that prize is reserved for Sacajawea, followed by the Matterhorn). What Eagle Cap has, though, is a 360-degree view of the surrounding range, down to lakes, ridges, and river valleys extending away from its point in all directions.

In one straight shot, this trail follows the East Lostine River to Mirror Lake, set beneath Eagle Cap's cliffs like an ornament. To climb Eagle Cap, plan this as a backpacking trip; you'll be grateful for the time and the rest required.

From the Two Pan Trailhead, follow the left-hand fork on the East Fork Lostine River Trail, passing a waterfall in 0.8 mile. In the next two miles, the trail switchbacks up over 1,000 feet to a series of ponds, then rolls along the Lostine Meadows nearly effortlessly for 2.3 miles to a river crossing, then climbs two miles across the meadows and up more switchbacks to a junction. To visit or camp at Mirror Lake, go left at the cairn 0.3 mile. To continue to Eagle Cap, go right at the cairn instead, then left at the next junction a short distance down the trail, then continue 2.7 miles, keeping left at every junction, climbing nearly 2,000 feet to the peak, where you'll find a summit register to leave your name.

User Groups: Hikers, dogs, and horses. No mountain bikes allowed. No wheelchair facilities.

Permits: A free self-issue Wilderness Permit is required and is available at the trailhead. A federal Northwest Forest Pass is required to park here; the cost is $5 a day or $30 for an annual pass. You can buy a day pass at the trailhead, at ranger stations, or through private vendors.

Maps: A contour map of the Wallowa Mountains is available from Imus Geographics. For a map of the Wallowa-Whitman National Forest, contact the Wallowa-Whitman National Forest Headquarters, P.O. Box 907, 1550 Dewey Avenue, Baker City, OR, 97814,

541/523-6391. For a topographic map, ask the USGS for Steamboat Lake and Eagle Cap.

Directions: From the La Grande Exit 261 off I-84, follow Highway 82 toward Wallowa Lake for 55 miles to Lostine. Where the highway turns left in town, go straight on Lostine River Road for 12.2 miles to the Lostine Guard Station, and continue on gravel another 6.1 miles to the Two Pan Trailhead at road's end.

Contact: Wallowa-Whitman National Forest, Eagle Cap Ranger District, 88401 Highway 82, Enterprise, OR, 97828, 541/426-5546.

23 HURRICANE CREEK AND ECHO LAKE
15.4 mi/8.0 hr

south of Enterprise in Eagle Cap Wilderness

Map 10.3, page 523

With plenty of water, spectacular views, and the chance to see bighorn sheep, mountain goats, and elk, plus side trips to a waterfall on Fall Creek and the cliff-rimmed Echo Lake, the Hurricane Creek entrance to the Eagle Cap Wilderness is one of the best. Views reach to the peaks of Eagle Cap, Matterhorn, and Sacajawea, and the trail follows in the shadow of massive granite and limestone cliffs clear down to wildflower meadows.

From the trailhead, follow Hurricane Creek 0.1 mile to a side-trail junction. A mere 0.2 mile up this trail is a viewpoint of Fall Creek Falls (this trail continues 3.8 difficult miles up the creek, almost 4,000 feet elevation gain, passing an old mine and fading out before Legore Lake beneath Twin Peaks). Follow Hurricane Creek 4.6 miles, crossing Slick Rock Creek Gorge after three miles. After Granite Creek, a side trail to the right climbs the canyon wall 1.9 miles up Granite Creek to the lip and a small pond. From here, cross the trailless meadow to find the trail, which continues 1.1 miles, climbing to Echo Lake.

To continue into the wilderness, stay on Hurricane Creek, fording Billy Jones Creek and Hurricane Creek, and follow trails branching off to the Wallowa Lake Trailhead and the Two Pan Trailhead.

User Groups: Hikers, dogs, and horses. No mountain bikes allowed. No wheelchair facilities.

Permits: A free self-issue Wilderness Permit is required and is available at the trailhead. A federal Northwest Forest Pass is required to park here; the cost is $5 a day or $30 for an annual pass. You can buy a day pass at the trailhead, at ranger stations, or through private vendors.

Maps: A contour map of the Wallowa Mountains is available from Imus Geographics. For a map of the Wallowa-Whitman National Forest, contact the Wallowa-Whitman National Forest Headquarters, P.O. Box 907, 1550 Dewey Avenue, Baker City, OR, 97814, 541/523-6391. For a topographic map, ask the USGS for Chief Joseph Mountain and Eagle Cap.

Directions: From the La Grande Exit 261 off I-84, follow Highway 82 toward Wallowa Lake for 65 miles to Enterprise. Just past downtown, where the highway goes left toward Joseph, follow a Hurricane Creek sign onto Hurricane Creek Road 8205, following it 9.1 miles to the trailhead at road's end.

Contact: Wallowa-Whitman National Forest, Eagle Cap Ranger District, 88401 Highway 82, Enterprise, OR, 97828, 541/426-5546.

24 ICE LAKE AND THE MATTERHORN
15.0-18.8 mi/9.0 hr-2 days

south of Joseph in Eagle Cap Wilderness

Map 10.3, page 523

High in the Eagle Cap Wilderness, sparkling Ice Lake lies in a basin beneath the Matterhorn, the Wallowa Mountain's second-highest peak. At 9,826 feet, it nearly commands the view here—but for nearby Sacajawea, which tops Matterhorn by just 12 feet. Getting there is the trick: you'll climb three sets of steep switchbacks just to get to the lake, following

Adam Creek as it tumbles over the ridges and two waterfalls on its way to the West Fork Wallowa River. The climb to the Matterhorn itself requires stamina, though this is certainly a non-technical climb, heading up 2,000 feet in 1.5 miles.

Begin at the Wallowa Lake Trailhead and follow the West Fork Wallowa River Trail 0.3 mile, then stay to the left and continue along the river 2.5 miles. Following a sign for Ice Lake, go right and begin the climb. The first 2.2 miles climbs over 1,100 feet up two sets of switchbacks to a viewpoint for an Adam Creek waterfall. The next 2.5 miles climbs 1,250 feet up the canyon wall past another waterfall and to the plateau of Ice Lake. A trail circles the lake for 1.7 miles.

To climb Matterhorn, stay to the right around the lake 0.4 mile to an inlet creek on the far side, and follow a faint trail up 1.5 miles to the peak on an obvious ridge.

User Groups: Hikers, dogs, and horses. No mountain bikes allowed. No wheelchair facilities.

Permits: A free self-issue Wilderness Permit is required and is available at the trailhead. Parking and access are free.

Maps: A contour map of the Wallowa Mountains is available from Imus Geographics. For a map of the Wallowa-Whitman National Forest, contact the Wallowa-Whitman National Forest Headquarters, P.O. Box 907, 1550 Dewey Avenue, Baker City, OR, 97814, 541/523-6391. For a topographic map, ask the USGS for Joseph, Aneroid Lake, and Eagle Cap.

Directions: From the La Grande Exit 261 off I-84, follow Highway 82 toward Wallowa Lake for 78 miles through Enterprise and on to Joseph. Go one mile along Wallowa Lake to the Wallowa Lake Trailhead at road's end.

Contact: Wallowa-Whitman National Forest, Eagle Cap Ranger District, 88401 Highway 82, Enterprise, OR, 97828, 541/426-5546.

25 LAKES BASIN LOOP
27.3 mi/2 days   👣 5   △ 10

south of Joseph in Eagle Cap Wilderness

Map 10.3, page 523

The Lakes Basin of the Eagle Cap Wilderness is the most famous spot in all this wilderness and as such is heavily used. Yet, with the amount of endurance it takes to get here, you can almost be assured that the difficulty will weed out the tenderfeet (but not the horses), leaving only sure-footed backpackers to lay claim to this area. High atop a plateau with views to Eagle Cap itself, six major lakes are within reach, though "within reach" depends on your stamina. This is a backpacker's dream, for certain. Choose a lake or two and continue on in any direction; from here, you can follow the West Fork Wallowa River, or head to Hurricane Creek, the Lostine River forks, and on to Eagle Cap itself.

From the Wallowa Lake Trailhead, follow the West Fork Wallowa River 6.1 miles to Sixmile Meadow, a possible camping spot, and a junction. To go on to the Lake Basin, go right, cross the river on a footbridge, and climb 3.1 miles to Horseshoe Lake. The trail splits here, and comes together again in one mile. If you go to the left, you'll follow Horseshoe Lake and pass little Lee Lake. At the end of the loop, go right 0.5 mile to Douglas Lake. Follow the left-hand trail two miles to Moccasin Lake, then go left again 2.7 miles, climbing up and over steep Glacier Pass, to cliff-rimmed Glacier Lake, high in an alpine bowl beneath Eagle Cap. Follow the trail down an outlet creek two miles to Frazier Lake, then stay to the left and follow it 1.8 miles, fording the Wallowa Fork, to the next junction, and keep left 2.2 miles to return to Sixmile Meadow.

User Groups: Hikers, dogs, and horses. No mountain bikes allowed. No wheelchair facilities.

Permits: A free self-issue Wilderness Permit is required and is available at the trailhead. Parking and access are free.

Maps: A contour map of the Wallowa

Mountains is available from Imus Geographics. For a map of the Wallowa-Whitman National Forest, contact the Wallowa-Whitman National Forest Headquarters, P.O. Box 907, 1550 Dewey Avenue, Baker City, OR, 97814, 541/523-6391. For a topographic map, ask the USGS for Joseph, Aneroid Lake, and Eagle Cap.

Directions: From the La Grande Exit 261 off I-84, follow Highway 82 toward Wallowa Lake for 78 miles through Enterprise and on to Joseph. Go one mile along Wallowa Lake to the Wallowa Lake Trailhead at road's end.

Contact: Wallowa-Whitman National Forest, Eagle Cap Ranger District, 88401 Highway 82, Enterprise, OR, 97828, 541/426-5546.

26 CHIEF JOSEPH MOUNTAIN
11.8-15 mi/6.0-8.0 hr   🏃5 ⛰9

south of Joseph in Eagle Cap Wilderness

Map 10.3, page 523

The peak that towers above long and beautiful Wallowa Lake is named for the patriarch of the Nez Perce's Wallowa band. In 1877, chased by the U.S. Army, he led his people on a daring flight to Canada, a flight that eventually ended in surrender. The mountain stands as a monument to his endurance, and the sturdy hiker can climb to a knoll on the side of this rugged peak and look out over the lands once loved by the Nez Perce tribes. This is a steep and challenging climb, though there are opportunities to rest beside a few waterfalls and several viewpoints over Wallowa Lake. There are two ways to climb this trail: The first is from the Wallowa Lake Trailhead, which makes for a daunting 15-mile day. If you prefer to knock off three miles, opt instead to begin from the state park, climbing a steep 0.9 mile to join the main trail. (Note that a washout may have wrecked the trail at BC Creek; check with the Forest Service to see if the trail has been repaired. If not, head to the state park trailhead and start from there instead.)

From the Wallowa Lake Trailhead, start to the right for 0.3 mile, then go right on the Chief Joseph Mountain Trail for one mile to cross the West Fork Wallowa River's gorge and climb to a viewpoint of two falls on BC Creek. Continue along the edge of the mountain 1.2

Chief Joseph Mountain in the Wallowas

© SEAN PATRICK HILL

miles to where the State Park Trail joins from the left. The next 1.1 miles stays level, then climbs the remaining 3.9 miles through steep meadows beneath the mountain. Though there is no trail to the peak, you can climb atop a knoll near where the trail ends for a view of Mount Howard and the Wallowa country.

From Wallowa Lake State Park, find campsite B-25 and follow this trail 0.9 mile up to join the Chief Joseph Trail. Go left 1.2 miles to see the falls, or right to head to the mountain.

User Groups: Hikers, dogs, and horses. No mountain bikes allowed. No wheelchair facilities.

Permits: A free self-issue Wilderness Permit is required and is available at the trailhead. Parking and access are free.

Maps: A contour map of the Wallowa Mountains is available from Imus Geographics. For a map of the Wallowa-Whitman National Forest, contact the Wallowa-Whitman National Forest Headquarters, P.O. Box 907, 1550 Dewey Avenue, Baker City, OR, 97814, 541/523-6391. For a topographic map, ask the USGS for Chief Joseph Mountain.

Directions: From the La Grande Exit 261 off I-84, follow Highway 82 toward Wallowa Lake for 78 miles through Enterprise and on to Joseph. Go one mile along Wallowa Lake to the Wallowa Lake Trailhead at road's end. For the State Park trailhead, turn instead into the Wallowa Lake State Park entrance one mile before the end of the road, parking at the boat ramp lot.

Contact: Wallowa-Whitman National Forest, Eagle Cap Ranger District, 88401 Highway 82, Enterprise, OR, 97828, 541/426-5546.

27 WEST FORK WALLOWA RIVER TO HAWKINS PASS
24.0 mi/2 days   5   10

south of Joseph in Eagle Cap Wilderness

Map 10.3, page 523

If you're in the mood to follow the West Fork Wallowa River as far as you can go, beyond even Ice Lake and the Lakes Basin, consider walking it all the way to its end at Hawkins Pass. Follow the river 10.1 miles to Frazier Lake, then go left the remaining 1.9 miles to Hawkins Pass. From there, you can fan out farther into the wilderness area at whim.

User Groups: Hikers, dogs, and horses. No mountain bikes allowed. No wheelchair facilities.

Permits: A free self-issue Wilderness Permit is required and is available at the trailhead. Parking and access are free.

Maps: A contour map of the Wallowa Mountains is available from Imus Geographics. For a map of the Wallowa-Whitman National Forest, contact the Wallowa-Whitman National Forest Headquarters, P.O. Box 907, 1550 Dewey Avenue, Baker City, OR, 97814, 541/523-6391. For a topographic map, ask the USGS for Joseph, Aneroid Lake, and Eagle Cap.

Directions: From the La Grande Exit 261 off I-84, follow Highway 82 toward Wallowa Lake for 78 miles through Enterprise and on to Joseph. Go one mile along Wallowa Lake to the Wallowa Lake Trailhead at road's end.

Contact: Wallowa-Whitman National Forest, Eagle Cap Ranger District, 88401 Highway 82, Enterprise, OR, 97828, 541/426-5546.

28 ANEROID LAKE
12.0 mi/7.0 hr   4   9

south of Joseph in Eagle Cap Wilderness

Map 10.3, page 523

Two forks of the Wallowa River fall into big Wallowa Lake, and this trail follows the East Fork. Once the trail passes the wilderness boundary, the river deepens—and it even enters a gorge for a distance. Anglers ply the waters of Roger and Aneroid Lakes, beneath a range of mountains: Mount Howard, Bonneville Mountain, Aneroid Mountain, and East Peak. If you're curious as to what "aneroid" means, it's a kind of barometer, and one that a surveyor brought here in 1897 to measure the elevation. If you're backpacking, you can continue on this trail up and over Dollar Pass and visit the Bonny Lakes, or to Tenderfoot Pass to find the North Fork Imnaha River.

From the Wallowa Lake Trailhead, take the left-hand trail to the East Fork Wallowa River. Switchback up 0.8 miles, ignoring both a service road to the left and a horse trail to the right, then continue one mile up the river to a dam. Follow the river into the wilderness for 2.1 miles to a bridge crossing, and continue on the far side along a deep gorge and into meadows for 1.7 miles to Roger Lake. From here, Aneroid Lake is just ahead, and the trail rises 0.4 mile to overlook the lake.

User Groups: Hikers, dogs, and horses. No mountain bikes allowed. No wheelchair facilities.

Permits: A free self-issue Wilderness Permit is required and is available at the trailhead. Parking and access are free.

Maps: A contour map of the Wallowa Mountains is available from Imus Geographics. For a map of the Wallowa-Whitman National Forest, contact the Wallowa-Whitman National Forest Headquarters, P.O. Box 907, 1550 Dewey Avenue, Baker City, OR, 97814, 541/523-6391. For a topographic map, ask the USGS for Aneroid Lake.

Directions: From the La Grande Exit 261 off I-84, follow Highway 82 toward Wallowa Lake for 78 miles through Enterprise and on to Joseph. Go one mile along Wallowa Lake to the Wallowa Lake Trailhead at road's end.

Contact: Wallowa-Whitman National Forest, Eagle Cap Ranger District, 88401 Highway 82, Enterprise, OR, 97828, 541/426-5546.

29 MOUNT HOWARD

1.9-5.5 mi/1.0-2.5 hr

south of Joseph in Wallowa-Whitman National Forest

Map 10.3, page 523

The view from Mount Howard is amazing, for sure, but you have to be willing to pay to get to the top. What you get for your money is a 3,700-foot ride on a gondola to the grassy summits of this 8,241-foot peak. The gondola operates from mid-May to September 30, and takes 15 minutes to climb to its perch above long, blue Wallowa Lake. You can even have lunch at the Summit Grill. After that, strike out over the meadows for views of all the major peaks: Eagle Cap, the Matterhorn, and scores of others, including East Peak, which you can head towards on a trail that enters the Eagle Cap Wilderness.

From the tramway, hike clockwise around the trails to see the Valley Overlook, the Summit, and the Royal Purple Overlook, a 1.9-mile loop. For a longer hike, head south from the summit cross-country to a pass and an old trail that heads 0.8 mile over the ridge to a grassy saddle at the wilderness boundary. From there, follow cairns to rejoin the trail for one mile to its end at a spring.

User Groups: Hikers only. No dogs, horses, or mountain bikes allowed. The Wallowa Lake Tramway gondola is wheelchair accessible, though the summit trails are not maintained for wheelchairs.

Permits: Permits are not required. The Wallowa Lake Tramway costs $24 for adults, $21 for seniors, $18 for students, and $11 for children aged 4–11.

Maps: A contour map of the Wallowa Mountains is available from Imus Geographics. For a map of the Wallowa-Whitman National Forest, contact the Wallowa-Whitman National Forest Headquarters, P.O. Box 907, 1550 Dewey Avenue, Baker City, OR, 97814, 541/523-6391. For a topographic map, ask the USGS for Joseph.

Directions: Take exit 261 off I-84 in La Grande and follow Highway 82 for 77 miles to Joseph. Continue through town to Wallowa Lake, following it toward the state park. Go past the state park entrance 0.3 mile and park on the left at the Wallowa Lake Tramway.

Contact: Wallowa-Whitman National Forest, Eagle Cap Ranger District, 88401 Highway 82, Enterprise, OR, 97828, 541/426-5546; Wallowa Lake Tramway, 59919 Wallowa Lake Highway, Joseph, OR, 541/432-5331.

30 BONNY LAKES AND IMNAHA DIVIDE

7.8-16.3 mi/4.0 hr-2 days 🏃4 ⛰8

south of Joseph in Eagle Cap Wilderness

Map 10.3, page 523

The Tenderfoot Trailhead is underutilized and barely mentioned in hiking books, on outdoors websites, or even on the Forest Service's trail list. This should be a clue as to the relative use of this trail. Yet it provides access to the Big Sheep Basin, Tenderfoot Pass, the Imnaha Divide, and a set of three secret lakes: the two shallow but lovely Bonny Lakes and Dollar Lake, set on the high plateau of Dollar Pass. Granted, the trail sets off on a 1989 burn, but quickly enters into the high country of the Eagle Cap Wilderness through a huge valley along a fork of Big Sheep Creek. Though the lakes make good destinations, backpackers can make a loop of it by heading over two passes and following the Imnaha Divide. You really can't go wrong in this rugged and rocky landscape.

From the trailhead, cross the wilderness boundary and stay left at a junction, continuing 1.1 miles on the Tenderfoot Wagon Trail to a ford of Big Sheep Creek. Stay to the left and continue 1.2 miles to a junction with the Bonny Lakes Trail, the start of the loop. Go right up the valley 1.6 miles along the creek to reach the Bonny Lakes. In another 1.7 miles, the trail leaves the valley and climbs to Dollar Pass; if you head due south cross-country across the meadows for 0.3 mile you'll reach Dollar Lake.

To continue on the loop, stay on the main trail from Dollar Pass and continue 0.9 mile to a junction; to the right, Aneroid Lake is one mile away (see *Aneroid Lake* listing in this chapter). Go left 1.5 miles on the North Fork Imnaha Trail #1814, climbing 700 feet to Tenderfoot Pass and descending to another trail junction. Continue to the left on the North Fork Imnaha River Trail for 1.5 miles, then head left on the Tenderfoot Trail over the Imnaha Divide for 2.7 miles to a high pass. From here, the trail drops down 700 feet over 1.2 miles to complete the loop; go to the right, staying right at all junctions 2.3 miles back to the Tenderfoot Trailhead.

User Groups: Hikers, dogs, and horses. No mountain bikes allowed. No wheelchair facilities.

Permits: A free self-issue Wilderness Permit is required and is available at the trailhead. Parking and access are free.

Maps: A contour map of the Wallowa Mountains is available from Imus Geographics. For a map of the Wallowa-Whitman National Forest, contact the Wallowa-Whitman National Forest Headquarters, P.O. Box 907, 1550 Dewey Avenue, Baker City, OR, 97814, 541/523-6391. For a topographic map, ask the USGS for Aneroid Mountain.

Directions: From Joseph, head east on the Hells Canyon Byway and follow Imnaha Highway 8.3 miles to a sign for Salt Creek Summit, then go right on Wallowa Mountain Road 39 for 13 miles. After a creek crossing, turn right on Road 100 for 3.2 miles to the Tenderfoot Trailhead.

Contact: Wallowa-Whitman National Forest, Eagle Cap Ranger District, 88401 Highway 82, Enterprise, OR, 97828, 541/426-5546.

31 CATHERINE CREEK MEADOWS

8.6 mi/4.0 hr 🏃2 ⛰7

east of La Grande in Eagle Cap Wilderness

Map 10.3, page 523

At some places in the Eagle Cap Wilderness, you may run into grazing sheep or cattle. Catherine Creek Meadows is one of those places, and you'll also be able to poke around a century-old log cabin with graffiti dating back at least to 1944. Backpackers, take note: From these meadows, you can head just about anywhere into the wilderness, as no less than six trails fan out in all directions from the creek.

The trail begins at the campground message board and follows North Fork Catherine Creek 3.8 miles upstream and into the Eagle Cap Wilderness. In the meadows, a rock cairn marks a faded trail to the right that climbs 2.8 miles to Meadow Mountain. In 0.3 mile, the trail forks; go to the right 200 yards to find the old cabin, or continue straight to cross the creek to a junction. Go right to continue up this creek another 3.9 miles to a junction with trails leading to Burger Pass and the Minam River; head left out of the canyon to access trails to Moss Springs Trailhead, the Jim White Trail, the Lodgepole Trail, and the Little Minam River.

User Groups: Hikers, dogs, and horses. No mountain bikes allowed. No wheelchair facilities.

Permits: A free self-issue Wilderness Permit is required and is available at the trailhead. A federal Northwest Forest Pass is required to park here; the cost is $5 a day or $30 for an annual pass. You can buy a day pass at the trailhead, at ranger stations, or through private vendors.

Maps: A contour map of the Wallowa Mountains is available from Imus Geographics. For a map of the Wallowa-Whitman National Forest, contact the Wallowa-Whitman National Forest Headquarters, P.O. Box 907, 1550 Dewey Avenue, Baker City, OR, 97814, 541/523-6391. For a topographic map, ask the USGS for China Cap.

Directions: From La Grande, go south on I-84 to Exit 265, going left on Highway 203 and following it 14 miles to Union. In Union, turn left on Beakman Street and follow Highway 203 for 11.4 miles. Turn left on Catherine Creek Lane/Road 7785 for 6.1 miles to the Catherine Creek Trailhead on the right.

Contact: Wallowa-Whitman National Forest, Eagle Cap Ranger District, 88401 Highway 82, Enterprise, OR, 97828, 541/426-5546.

32 BURGER PASS

8.8 mi/4.5 hr

southeast of Union in Eagle Cap Wilderness

Map 10.3, page 523

A long ridge connects two distinctive high points in this dusty wilderness: Burger Butte

and China Cap. Not only that, but it straddles two very different landscapes: one of granite and one a plateau of basalt lava. The trail that leads there is dusty with volcanic ash, the result of a long history of explosive eruptions that blanketed this former Pacific island worn down by glaciers. Yes, these mountains are really that old.

Follow the Elk Creek Alternate Trail from the message board 0.7 mile to a clear-cut and a junction with the Elk Creek Trail. Continue to the right on an ash-strewn trail 1.3 miles to a switchback, entering the granite landscape. Follow a plateau along a ridge 1.6 miles, crossing the Middle Fork Catherine Creek, to a junction with the China Ridge Trail. Go right along the base of China Cap, steadily climbing the ridge for 0.8 mile to Burger Pass. From here, the trail switchbacks down 300 feet to Burger Meadows in 0.6 mile at a junction. To the left, the trail leads to the Minam River and Tombstone Lake; to the right, Sand Pass and the Mule Peak Lookout.

User Groups: Hikers, dogs, and horses. No mountain bikes allowed. No wheelchair facilities.

Permits: A free self-issue Wilderness Permit is required and is available at the trailhead. A federal Northwest Forest Pass is required to park here; the cost is $5 a day or $30 for an annual pass. You can buy a day pass at the trailhead, at ranger stations, or through private vendors.

Maps: A contour map of the Wallowa Mountains is available from Imus Geographics. For a map of the Wallowa-Whitman National Forest, contact the Wallowa-Whitman National Forest Headquarters, P.O. Box 907, 1550 Dewey Avenue, Baker City, OR, 97814, 541/523-6391. For a topographic map, ask the USGS for China Cap.

Directions: From La Grande, go south on I-84 to Exit 265, going left on Highway 203 and following it 14 miles to Union. In Union, turn left on Beakman Street and follow Highway 203 for 11.4 miles. Turn left on Catherine Creek Lane/Road 7785 for 4.2 miles, then go right on Road 7787 for 3.9 miles, then left at a fork for 0.3 mile to the Buck Creek Trailhead on the right.

Contact: Wallowa-Whitman National Forest, Eagle Cap Ranger District, 88401 Highway 82, Enterprise, OR, 97828, 541/426-5546.

33 EAGLE CREEK TO TOMBSTONE AND DIAMOND LAKES
18.0 mi/2 days   🥾5 ⛰8

northeast of Baker City in Eagle Cap Wilderness

Map 10.3, page 523

More power to the backpackers, as this trail is anything but a day hike. The long route to Tombstone Lake is a relentless climb at points up long switchbacks into the Eagle Cap Wilderness, but that's no reason to turn back. Just beyond Tombstone is Diamond Lake. Pick a lake and drop the tent, and enjoy the walk along West Eagle Creek while it lasts, with its forest of rare Engelmann spruce and Wallowa-friendly western larch and grand fir.

The West Eagle Loop Trail starts out on an old road, but quickly becomes trail. Pass the meadows and enter the forest in 0.4 mile, coming to a junction with the Fake Creek Trail. Continue to the left on West Eagle Creek 0.7 mile and ford the creek. Continue 1.8 miles, fording the creek again and then climbing to a junction. Go left toward Tombstone Lake for 5.5 miles, switchbacking steeply up an 8,200-foot pass and dropping down 770 feet to the large lake. Just 0.5 mile beyond this and 0.2 mile to the right is Diamond Lake.

User Groups: Hikers, dogs, and horses. No mountain bikes allowed. No wheelchair facilities.

Permits: A free self-issue Wilderness Permit is required and is available at the trailhead. A federal Northwest Forest Pass is required to park here; the cost is $5 a day or $30 for an annual pass. You can buy a day pass at the trailhead, at ranger stations, or through private vendors.

Maps: A contour map of the Wallowa Mountains is available from Imus Geographics. For a map of the Wallowa-Whitman National Forest, contact the Wallowa-Whitman National Forest Headquarters, P.O. Box 907, 1550 Dewey Avenue, Baker City, OR, 97814, 541/523-6391. For a topographic map, ask the USGS for Bennet Peak.

Directions: From La Grande, go south on I-84 to Exit 265, going left on Highway 203 and following it 14 miles to Union. In Union, turn left on Beakman Street and follow Highway 203 for 14.2 miles. Following a sign for West Eagle, go left on increasingly rough Road 77 for 15.7 miles to the West Eagle Trailhead on the left.

Contact: Wallowa-Whitman National Forest, Eagle Cap Ranger District, 88401 Highway 82, Enterprise, OR, 97828, 541/426-5546.

34 ECHO AND TRAVERSE LAKES
13.2 mi/7.0 hr   🥾5 ⛰8

northeast of Baker City in Eagle Cap Wilderness

Map 10.3, page 523

Like the trail to Tombstone Lake, this trail follows West Eagle Creek into a forest of grand fir, western larch, and the rare Engelmann spruce. Only this trail stays on the creek, following it up nearly 2,300 feet to a pair of alpine lakes—Echo and Traverse—rimmed in by steep precipices and towering peaks and lined with blooms of phlox and mountain heather.

The West Eagle Loop Trail starts out on an old road, but quickly becomes trail. Pass the meadows and enter the forest in 0.4 mile, coming to a junction with the Fake Creek Trail. Continue to the left on West Eagle Creek 0.7 mile and ford the creek. Continue 1.8 miles, fording the creek again and then climbing to a junction. Continue to the right, climbing another 1,000 feet in 2.4 miles to Echo Lake, and another 500 feet in 1.3 miles to Traverse Lake. For the ambitious, the trail climbs another 700 feet to Wenker Pass, allowing for longer backpacking adventures.

User Groups: Hikers, dogs, and horses. No mountain bikes allowed. No wheelchair facilities.

Permits: A free self-issue Wilderness Permit is required and is available at the trailhead. A federal Northwest Forest Pass is required to park here; the cost is $5 a day or $30 for an annual pass. You can buy a day pass at the trailhead, at ranger stations, or through private vendors.

Maps: A contour map of the Wallowa Mountains is available from Imus Geographics. For a map of the Wallowa-Whitman National Forest, contact the Wallowa-Whitman National Forest Headquarters, P.O. Box 907, 1550 Dewey Avenue, Baker City, OR, 97814, 541/523-6391. For a topographic map, ask the USGS for Bennet Peak.

Directions: From La Grande, go south on I-84 to Exit 265, going left on Highway 203 and following it 14 miles to Union. In Union, turn left on Beakman Street and follow Highway 203 for 14.2 miles. Following a sign for West Eagle, go left on increasingly rough Road 77 for 15.7 miles to the West Eagle Trailhead on the left.

Contact: Wallowa-Whitman National Forest, Eagle Cap Ranger District, 88401 Highway 82, Enterprise, OR, 97828, 541/426-5546.

35 EAGLE CREEK LAKES LOOP

19.0 mi/2-3 days

northeast of Baker City in Eagle Cap Wilderness

Map 10.3, page 523

Backpackers can rejoice over Eagle Creek, as this loop—which follows two branches of the creek—visits not only waterfalls, but four or more lakes, depending on what you're up for (for side trips, see *Lookingglass and Bear Lakes,* next listing). This is a demanding loop, calling for over 4,000 feet of elevation gain in nearly 20 miles, but there's water and plenty

of options for camping along the way, and a connection to trails leading to the Minam River and Traverse Lake. Enjoy the scenery as you walk in the glare of towering peaks along Eagle Creek.

Begin on the Main Eagle Trail, crossing a landslide and crossing the creek in 0.6 mile. In 1.9 miles, the trail crosses the creek again, and 0.5 mile later reaches a junction just beyond Copper Creek Falls, the start of the loop. Go left on the Bench Trail, which climbs steeply 1.5 miles, then crosses Bench Canyon Creek to the right and continues 0.8 mile to Arrow Lake (with Heart Lake to the right along the way, accessed by a cross-country jaunt). Continue above Arrow Lake over a 7,880-foot pass to a junction, keeping right. Go another 1.6 miles to a higher pass at 8,170 feet and descend 700 feet in two miles into the Eagle Creek Canyon and small Cached Lake. Descend further into meadows one mile to a junction; the left-hand trail climbs 350 feet in 1.1 miles to scenic Eagle Lake behind a dam. Return to the main trail and continue descending along Eagle Creek 1.8 miles to Eagle Creek meadow. At the next junction, stay to the right 1.4 miles, passing Bench Canyon Falls and completing the loop.

User Groups: Hikers, dogs, and horses. No mountain bikes allowed. No wheelchair facilities.

Permits: A free self-issue Wilderness Permit is required and is available at the trailhead. A federal Northwest Forest Pass is required to park here; the cost is $5 a day or $30 for an annual pass. You can buy a day pass at the trailhead, at ranger stations, or through private vendors.

Maps: A contour map of the Wallowa Mountains is available from Imus Geographics. For a map of the Wallowa-Whitman National Forest, contact the Wallowa-Whitman National Forest Headquarters, P.O. Box 907, 1550 Dewey Avenue, Baker City, OR, 97814, 541/523-6391. For a topographic map, ask the USGS for Eagle Cap.

Directions: From La Grande, go south on I-84

to Exit 265, going left on Highway 203 and following it 14 miles to Union. Turn left on Highway 203 for 21 miles to Medical Springs. Turn east on Eagle Creek Drive, following signs for Boulder Park for 1.6 miles, forking left on Big Creek Road 67. In 14.6 miles, go left on Road 77 for 0.8 mile, then straight on Road 7755 for 3.7 miles to road's end at the Main Eagle Trailhead.

Contact: Wallowa-Whitman National Forest, Eagle Cap Ranger District, 88401 Highway 82, Enterprise, OR, 97828, 541/426-5546.

36 LOOKINGGLASS AND BEAR LAKES
14.0 mi/7.0 hr   🏃4 ⛰8

northeast of Baker City in Eagle Cap Wilderness

Map 10.3, page 523

If a long backpacking trip up the Eagle Creek and Bench Creek drainages (see previous listing) are too much for you, try a slightly easier route to a pair of alpine lakes high above Eagle Creek. With endurance, this hike can be done in a day—though it's also possible to backpack it. Lookingglass Lake is actually a reservoir, dammed for irrigation. Bear Lake remains in its pristine state. Both are accessible from the same trail, with two waterfalls and the gorgeous Eagle Creek Meadow along the way.

Begin on the Main Eagle Trail, crossing a landslide and crossing the creek in 0.6 mile. In 1.9 miles, the trail crosses the creek again, and 0.5 mile later reaches a junction just beyond Copper Creek Falls. Go right and stay on the Eagle Creek Trail another 1.4 miles, passing Bench Canyon Falls to the left and climbing steadily to Eagle Creek Meadow, hemmed in by stunning peaks. At a junction, go right on the Bear Lake Trail for one mile, fording Eagle Creek and climbing over 650 feet to a junction. To the right, a 1.7-mile trail crests a high point of 7,530 feet and descends 200 feet to Lookingglass Lake. To reach Bear Lake, continue straight 0.4 mile to Little Culver Lake, and finally 0.6 mile to Bear Lake.

User Groups: Hikers, dogs, and horses. No mountain bikes allowed. No wheelchair facilities.

Permits: A free self-issue Wilderness Permit is required and is available at the trailhead. A federal Northwest Forest Pass is required to park here; the cost is $5 a day or $30 for an annual pass. You can buy a day pass at the trailhead, at ranger stations, or through private vendors.

Maps: A contour map of the Wallowa Mountains is available from Imus Geographics. For a map of the Wallowa-Whitman National Forest, contact the Wallowa-Whitman National Forest Headquarters, P.O. Box 907, 1550 Dewey Avenue, Baker City, OR, 97814, 541/523-6391. For a topographic map, ask the USGS for Krag Peak.

Directions: From La Grande, go south on I-84 to Exit 265, going left on Highway 203 and following it 14 miles to Union. Turn left on Highway 203 for 21 miles to Medical Springs. Turn east on Eagle Creek Drive, following signs for Boulder Park for 1.6 miles, forking left on Big Creek Road 67. In 14.6 miles, go left on Road 77 for 0.8 mile, then straight on Road 7755 for 3.7 miles to road's end at the Main Eagle Trailhead.

Contact: Wallowa-Whitman National Forest, Eagle Cap Ranger District, 88401 Highway 82, Enterprise, OR, 97828, 541/426-5546.

37 HIDDEN LAKE
16.4 mi/2 days   🏃4 ⛰8

northeast of Baker City in Eagle Cap Wilderness

Map 10.3, page 523

Glaciers, more than anything, scoured and shaped the Wallowa Mountains, creating stunning scenery. Hidden Lake is flanked by such rugged peaks, as is the entire hike along the East Fork Eagle Creek. This is a demanding day hike; backpackers may fare better.

From the gated road, follow the East Fork Eagle Creek into the canyon. In 2.5 miles, watch for a waterfall on the left. After gradually climbing four miles, the trail comes to a junction. Go left at a cairn, fording the creek and climbing nearly 1,000 feet in 1.7 miles to paradisiacal Hidden Lake, passing Little Moon Lake along the way.

Eagle Creek Trail continues up the creek another 0.9 mile to a junction. To the left, connector trails fan out to the Minam River, Minam Lake, and the Frazier Pass; to the right, the trail climbs 3.3 miles to Horton Pass, then splits—the left goes 1.3 mile to Mirror Lake, the right up 1.5 mile to the peak of Eagle Cap.

User Groups: Hikers, dogs, and horses. No mountain bikes allowed. No wheelchair facilities.

Permits: A free self-issue Wilderness Permit is required and is available at the trailhead. A federal Northwest Forest Pass is required to park here; the cost is $5 a day or $30 for an annual pass. You can buy a day pass at the trailhead, at ranger stations, or through private vendors.

Maps: A contour map of the Wallowa Mountains is available from Imus Geographics. For a map of the Wallowa-Whitman National Forest, contact the Wallowa-Whitman National Forest Headquarters, P.O. Box 907, 1550 Dewey Avenue, Baker City, OR, 97814, 541/523-6391. For a topographic map, ask the USGS for Bennet Peak.

Directions: Just north of Baker City on I-84, take exit 302 and follow Highway 86 east for 23.2 miles. At a sign for Sparta just beyond milepost 23, go left and uphill on Sparta Lane for 4.9 miles, then go left on East Eagle Creek Road for 5.8 miles to a five-way junction. Go left on Empire Gulch Road 7015 for 4.8 miles, cross a bridge, then go left on Road 77 for 2.8 miles. Fork right on East Eagle Road 7745 for 6.4 miles, passing the Eagle Creek Trailhead sign and continuing 0.8 mile to road's end at the East Eagle Trailhead.

Contact: Wallowa-Whitman National Forest, Eagle Cap Ranger District, 88401 Highway 82, Enterprise, OR, 97828, 541/426-5546.

38 CRATER LAKE
11.8 mi/7.0 hr   🏃4 ⛰8

northeast of Baker City in Eagle Cap Wilderness

Map 10.3, page 523

Not to be confused with Crater Lake National Park in the southern Oregon Cascades, this lake is not set in a crater at all, but in a basin ground out by prehistoric glaciers. But the granite walls rising up around this clear lake will make you feel as if you've entered a crater.

From the turnaround parking loop, begin on the Little Kettle Creek Trail 0.1 mile, going left at a junction with the equestrian trail. The next 3.5 miles climbs thousands of feet to the lip of a ridge and crosses a creek. The trail then continues 2.3 miles through meadows, crossing a rockslide and passing smaller ponds, and finally arriving at Crater Lake. A 0.7-mile trail circles the lake and connects with a 0.3-mile spur trail to a junction with two trails, one leading to Tuck Pass, the other to Cliff Creek.

User Groups: Hikers, dogs, and horses. No mountain bikes allowed. No wheelchair facilities.

Permits: A free self-issue Wilderness Permit is required and is available at the trailhead. A federal Northwest Forest Pass is required to park here; the cost is $5 a day or $30 for an annual pass. You can buy a day pass at the trailhead, at ranger stations, or through private vendors.

Maps: A contour map of the Wallowa Mountains is available from Imus Geographics. For a map of the Wallowa-Whitman National Forest, contact the Wallowa-Whitman National Forest Headquarters, P.O. Box 907, 1550 Dewey Avenue, Baker City, OR, 97814, 541/523-6391. For a topographic map, ask the USGS for Krag Peak.

Directions: Just north of Baker City on I-84, take exit 302 and follow Highway 86 east for 23.2 miles. At a sign for Sparta just beyond milepost 23, go left and uphill on Sparta Lane for 4.9 miles, then go left on East Eagle Creek

Road for 5.8 miles to a five-way junction. Go left on Empire Gulch Road 7015 for 4.8 miles, cross a bridge, then go left on Road 77 for 2.8 miles. Fork right on East Eagle Road 7745 for 6.4 miles, passing the Eagle Creek Trailhead sign and continuing 0.8 mile to road's end at the East Eagle Trailhead.

Contact: Wallowa-Whitman National Forest, Eagle Cap Ranger District, 88401 Highway 82, Enterprise, OR, 97828, 541/426-5546.

39 SUMMIT POINT LOOKOUT
2.0 mi/1.0 hr   👫1 ⛰8

northeast of Baker City in Wallowa-Whitman National Forest

Map 10.3, page 523

Set above the sagebrush meadows, this lookout tower affords views of the Elkhorn Range, the Wallowas, and the slopes falling down to Hell's Canyon. It's an easy hike, perhaps even a warm-up for the longer Pine Lakes tour described below. From the gate, follow the old road 0.7 mile, then go left 0.3 mile to the lookout on its 7,006-foot perch.

User Groups: Hikers, dogs, and horses. No mountain bikes allowed. No wheelchair facilities.

Permits: A free self-issue Wilderness Permit is required and is available at the trailhead. A federal Northwest Forest Pass is required to park here; the cost is $5 a day or $30 for an annual pass. You can buy a day pass at the trailhead, at ranger stations, or through private vendors.

Maps: A contour map of the Wallowa Mountains is available from Imus Geographics. For a map of the Wallowa-Whitman National Forest, contact the Wallowa-Whitman National Forest Headquarters, P.O. Box 907, 1550 Dewey Avenue, Baker City, OR, 97814, 541/523-6391. For a topographic map, ask the USGS for Jimtown.

Directions: Drive two miles north of Baker City on I-84 to Exit 302, and follow Highway 86 east toward Halfway for 49 miles.

Driving six miles beyond Richland, past milepost 48, go left on Road 77 following signs for Summit Point Lookout. In 11 miles, at a four-way junction, go right on the steep Road 7715 for 4.8 miles to the Summit Point Trailhead.

Contact: Wallowa-Whitman National Forest, Eagle Cap Ranger District, 88401 Highway 82, Enterprise, OR, 97828, 541/426-5546.

40 PINE LAKES
16.2-24.0 mi/2-4 days   👫4 ⛰9

northeast of Baker City in Eagle Cap Wilderness

Map 10.3, page 523

Day hikers can head toward Pine Lakes, though the distance and nearly 3,000-foot elevation gain makes it a daunting day. There are easier destinations along the way: Little Eagle Meadows, for one, and a series of passes with views to 8,643-foot Cornucopia Peak to the east. Nip Pass or Tuck Pass are easy goals, but if you're headed for Pine Lakes, two lush lakes set beneath steep cliffs, you'd better pack some camping gear; you'll need to rest for the way back. On the other hand, why go back? The trail continues on in a number of directions to the Cornucopia Trailhead and Crater Lake. For a killer 24-mile loop, continue on along Pine Creek, visiting the ruins of an old gold-mining boomtown.

Behind the gate, follow the old road in 0.7 mile then stay left at a junction. Follow the Cliff Creek Trail 2.2 miles along the ridge and past a fence to reach Little Eagle Meadows. At a junction, go left along a steep slope 1.7 miles to Nip Pass, and another 0.5 mile to Tuck Pass and a junction. If you're going to Pine Lakes, go right here on the Pine Lakes Trail, climbing another 300 feet in 0.8 mile to a higher pass, then continue 2.2 miles past little Cirque Lake to the two Pine Lakes.

From here, you can continue on a long loop around Cornucopia Mountain, passing falls at the outlet of the Pine Lakes and switchbacking down to Pine Creek, going 5.3

miles to a bridge crossing, then 1.1 miles to another crossing, and the last mile to a road. Go 0.3 mile to the Cornucopia Trailhead, the end of the Pine Lakes Trail. Continue 0.9 mile down this road, then onto a dirt road to the right past the ruins of the boomtown. Turn right, following an old road 0.9 mile, then connecting with the trail to the left, going 3.5 miles and passing a cowboy cabin to return to Little Eagle Meadows and the Cliff Creek Trail.

User Groups: Hikers, dogs, and horses. No mountain bikes allowed. No wheelchair facilities.

Permits: A free self-issue Wilderness Permit is required and is available at the trailhead. A federal Northwest Forest Pass is required to park here; the cost is $5 a day or $30 for an annual pass. You can buy a day pass at the trailhead, at ranger stations, or through private vendors.

Maps: A contour map of the Wallowa Mountains is available from Imus Geographics. For a map of the Wallowa-Whitman National Forest, contact the Wallowa-Whitman National Forest Headquarters, P.O. Box 907, 1550 Dewey Avenue, Baker City, OR, 97814, 541/523-6391. For a topographic map, ask the USGS for Krag Lake.

Directions: Drive two miles north of Baker City on I-84 to Exit 302, then follow Highway 86 east toward Halfway for 49 miles. Driving six miles beyond Richland, past milepost 48, go left on Road 77 following signs for Summit Point Lookout. In 11 miles, at a four-way junction, go right on the steep Road 7715 for 4.8 miles to the Summit Point Trailhead.

Contact: Wallowa-Whitman National Forest, Eagle Cap Ranger District, 88401 Highway 82, Enterprise, OR, 97828, 541/426-5546.

41 SOUTH FORK IMNAHA RIVER

11.4-34.6 mi/7.0 hr-3 days 🏃4 ⛰8

north of Richmond in Eagle Cap Wilderness

Map 10.3, page 523

The Imnaha River follows an old fault line; at a point, the fault opens up to allow the river to squeeze through a slot canyon. The result is the Blue Hole, 50 feet deep and emptying out onto a pebbled beach. Farther up the river is another gorge and Imnaha Falls. If it's a long trip you're looking for, this is as good an entry point as any to the Eagle Cap Wilderness and its many trails. The South Fork Imnaha Trail carries on farther to Hawkins Pass (see *West Fork Wallowa River to Hawkins Pass* listing in this chapter) near the river in a forest of Douglas fir and grand fir, but in 0.8 mile enters an old burn. In 1.2 miles the trail forks; go left to descend to the Blue Hole and its beach. Then continue upstream over a bluff; in 3.3 miles, you'll hear the water rushing through a second gorge. Continue 0.4 mile beyond and watch for a trail to the left that overlooks Imnaha Falls. This makes a good turnaround point for a day trip.

For a multi-day trip, you can head to either Tenderfoot of Hawkins Pass. After Imnaha Falls, continue 0.6 mile straight at a junction and go another 0.5 mile to a fork. To the right is the North Fork Imnaha Trail, which continues another 8.9 miles up to 8,500-foot Tenderfoot Pass; to the left, the South Fork continues another 10.5 miles to 8,330-foot Hawkins Pass.

User Groups: Hikers, dogs, and horses. No mountain bikes allowed. No wheelchair facilities.

Permits: A free self-issue Wilderness Permit is required and is available at the trailhead. A federal Northwest Forest Pass is required to park here; the cost is $5 a day or $30 for an annual pass. You can buy a day pass at the trailhead, at ranger stations, or through private vendors.

Maps: A contour map of the Wallowa

Mountains is available from Imus Geographics. For a map of the Wallowa-Whitman National Forest, contact the Wallowa-Whitman National Forest Headquarters, P.O. Box 907, 1550 Dewey Avenue, Baker City, OR, 97814, 541/523-6391. For a topographic map, ask the USGS for Deadman Point.

Directions: From Joseph, head east on the Hells Canyon Byway and follow Imnaha Highway 8.3 miles to a sign for Halfway, then go right on Wallowa Mountain Road 39 for 32 miles. Turn right on Road 3960 and go nine miles to the Indian Crossing Campground and park by the restroom on the right.

Contact: Wallowa-Whitman National Forest, Eagle Cap Ranger District, 88401 Highway 82, Enterprise, OR, 97828, 541/426-5546.

42 EUREKA VIEWPOINT
7.2-15.4 mi/4.0 hr-2 days 🏃3 ⛰9

in Hells Canyon National Recreation Area

Map 10.4, page 524

From the historic Buckhorn Lookout, the land folds and ripples into the incredible distances of Hell's Canyon. The Snake River carves its way through this long furrow more than 4,000 feet below, making tangible the fact that Hells Canyon is deeper than the Grand Canyon. You can hike down into these depths—but be careful not to overtax your strength, keep track of your water, and avoid the high heat of summer. For backpackers, this is one way to get to the bottom and the Eureka Bar, though even that is a long, hard journey with poison oak along the way. For day hikers, it's best to climb down to a stunning viewpoint along the way, watching for the Imnaha River Canyon and Hat Point on the horizon.

You'll be amazed that people lived here and somehow managed to work the land. The trail follows the abandoned Eureka Wagon Road Trail, an old logging road that once supplied timber to a now defunct town in the bottom of the canyon. Along the descent, you'll pass the ruins of a cabin and an old mineshaft. At the Eureka Bar on the Snake River itself, you can see some of the ruins of that town, mainly the old Stamp Mill. Respect the history of the area and touch nothing.

From the parking area, walk back up Road 780 for 0.2 mile, then take the rough road to the right 1.2 miles to a gate (this road can be driven with a high-clearance vehicle). Follow the Cemetery Ridge Trail 0.5 mile through sparse trees and wildflowers to a fork at a saddle. Go right and follow the Eureka Wagon Road Trail 1.4 miles, staying to the left at a junction with the Tulley Creek Trail, down 750 feet to a wire fence in Spain Saddle. Cross the fence and continue 0.6 mile and another 350 feet down to a second fence and a viewpoint of the Snake River. To reach the Eureka Viewpoint, continue 1.1 miles and another 530 feet down to a rock cairn where the trail turns right. Head off-trail toward the lava formations and climb to the left to the ridgeline for views of the Snake River.

From here, the Eureka Bar still lies 2,500 feet below. Where the trail turned right at the cairn, it continues down 2.5 miles to Eureka Creek, and another 1.6 miles to the Snake River, an arduous journey not recommended for day hikes.

User Groups: Hikers, dogs, horses, and mountain bikes. No wheelchair facilities.

Permits: Permits are not required. Parking and access are free.

Maps: For a map of the Hells Canyon National Recreation Area, contact Wallowa Mountains Visitor Center, 88401 Highway 82, Enterprise, OR, 97828, 541/426-5546. For a topographic map, ask the USGS for Deadhorse Ridge.

Directions: From Enterprise, drive 3.5 miles east on Highway 82 and turn north at a sign for Buckhorn Spring onto Crow Creek Road for 1.2 miles, then go right and continue on Crow Creek Road for 4.2 miles. Go right on Zumwalt Road, which becomes Road 46, for 32.5 miles. At a sign for Buckhorn Overlook, go right on Road 780 for 0.3 mile to a junction, staying straight and to the right at the next two forks to road's end at the overlook parking area.

Contact: Hells Canyon National Recreation Area, 88401 Highway 82, Box A, Enterprise, OR, 97828, 541/523-1315.

43 EUREKA BAR

9.8 mi/4.0 hr   3 ▲8

in Hells Canyon National Recreation Area

Map 10.4, page 524

Though the Eureka Bar can be reached by starting from the Buckhorn Overlook, it is a terribly arduous journey that makes more cause for misery than anything, despite the scenery. From the Imnaha River, though, it's an easier trail. But the road to get to the Cow Creek Bridge, where the trail begins, is what makes this trail a challenge. A long, hard drive down a rocky road makes this a true test of patience. Give yourself at least an hour for the 15-mile drive. It will make it all the more ludicrous to find the ruins of Eureka, an old mining town on the Snake River that didn't last much past its 1899 inception.

The trail begins at 1,200 feet elevation on the Imnaha River, descending the white-water river 4.2 miles to a cobble beach on the Snake River. Go to the left and downstream to visit the Stamp Mill ruins and old mineshaft. The trail along the river peters out after 0.7 mile at Eureka Creek.

User Groups: Hikers, dogs, horses, and mountain bikes. No wheelchair facilities.

Permits: Permits are not required. Parking and access are free.

Maps: For a map of the Hells Canyon National Recreation Area, contact Wallowa Mountains Visitor Center, 88401 Highway 82, Enterprise, OR, 97828, 541/426-5546. For a topographic map, ask the USGS for Deadhorse Ridge.

Directions: From downtown Joseph, follow the Imnaha Highway and signs for Hells Canyon Scenic Byway 29 miles to the town of Imnaha. Turn left on Lower Imnaha Road for 6.6 miles to Fence Creek, where pavement ends and the

rocky, rutted dirt road begins. Follow this road 15 miles to the Cow Creek Bridge over the Imnaha River. Turn left on a spur road to the parking area.

Contact: Hells Canyon National Recreation Area, 88401 Highway 82, Box A, Enterprise, OR, 97828, 541/523-1315.

44 SNAKE RIVER TRAIL VIA DUG BAR

8.6-48.0 mi/4.5 hr-6 days

    4 ▲10

in Hells Canyon Wilderness Area

Map 10.4, page 524

Once you are in depths of Hells Canyon, the rest seems easy by comparison. The Snake River Trail follows the canyon and the river through a designated wilderness area. With loop options and dispersed campsites along the river, it's a dream for backpackers and horseback riders. Wildflowers adorn the shores, and the rushing water follows the whole way, though the trail does at points leave the river to climb up and over the bluffs. Pay attention to water sources, rattlesnakes, poison ivy, and ticks along the way. Be sure to purchase a good map for the far-too-long-to-explain trail mileages here. A popular place to start is Dug Bar, since the trailhead itself is on the river and requires no climb in and out of the canyon—just prepare to allow two full hours to descend on the road into the canyon.

From Dug Bar, an easy day hike visits the mouths of Dug and Deep Creeks. From the parking lot, walk back up the road and turn left on the Snake River Trail, heading to a high viewpoint and continuing along a ridge 2.2 miles to Dug Creek. Head left, watching for poison oak, for 1 mile to the Snake River. If you're not winded yet, continue upstream 1.1 mile, passing good camping sites, to the mouth of Deep Creek. Return as you came.

User Groups: Hikers, dogs, and horses. No mountain bikes allowed. No wheelchair facilities.

Permits: A free self-issue Wilderness Permit is required and is available at the trailhead. Parking and access are free.

Maps: For a map of the Hells Canyon National Recreation Area, contact Wallowa Mountains Visitor Center, 88401 Highway 82, Enterprise, OR, 97828, 541/426-5546. For a topographic map, ask the USGS for Cactus Mountain.

Directions: From downtown Joseph, follow the Imnaha Highway and signs for Hells Canyon Scenic Byway 29 miles to the town of Imnaha. Turn left on Lower Imnaha Road for 6.6 miles to Fence Creek, where pavement ends and the rocky, rutted dirt road begins. Follow this road 25.4 miles to road's end at a boat launch and campground. Park beside the restroom. The trail begins back 150 feet on the road.

To begin the trail from the far opposite end, one must first climb into the canyon 10.1 miles from the Saddle Creek Trailhead. From downtown Joseph, follow the Imnaha Highway and signs for Hells Canyon Scenic Byway 29 miles to the town of Imnaha. Turn right on Upper Imnaha Road, following signs for Halfway. Drive 13 miles to a fork before a bridge and turn left on Road 4230. Drive 2.9 miles to the Saddle Creek Trailhead lot at road's end. Follow the Saddle Creek Trail to the Snake River, following the canyon downstream on the Snake River Trail toward Dug Bar.

Contact: Hells Canyon National Recreation Area, 88401 Highway 82, Box A, Enterprise, OR, 97828, 541/523-1315.

45 HAT POINT TO SNAKE RIVER

15.4 mi/10.0 hr-2 days   🏃5 ⛰9

in Hells Canyon National Recreation Area

Map 10.4, page 524

Atop a 6,910-foot ridge sits Hat Point lookout tower, a cabin atop a 90-foot tower that overlooks the magnificent Hells Canyon. A full 5,600 feet below lies the Snake River, carving its way through these canyonlands. Far down there lies the mouth of Saddle Creek, a destination for the most rugged hiker. If this hike sounds daunting, it is: For every one of those 5,600 feet you climb down, you will have to climb back up. Two days may be required for this one. Along the way, you'll find stunning viewpoints and an old cabin open to the public—as well as fields of poison oak.

Begin on the Hat Point Trail, going 0.2 mile across a meadow. Stay right and switchback down 3.5 miles through a Douglas fir forest, descending 2,200 feet to a junction. To the right on the High Trail lies the cabin. To continue down the canyon, go left at this junction and veer right at the next fork, following signs for Snake River. The next 0.3 mile follows a bench with views to Idaho's mountains, then begins to descend into Smooth Hollow. The next 1.2 miles drops 1,000 feet and peters out near an old corral. Go toward the cairn with a signpost in it, then head to the right, passing a viewpoint and switchbacking down 2.1 miles and 2,200 feet to the Snake River and Snake River Trail. To the right 0.4 mile is Saddle Creek.

User Groups: Hikers and dogs only. No horses or mountain bikes allowed. There are wheelchair facilities at the Hat Point Observation area.

Permits: A free self-issue Wilderness Permit is required and is available at the trailhead. A federal Northwest Forest Pass is required to park here; the cost is $5 a day or $30 for an annual pass. You can buy a day pass at the trailhead, at ranger stations, or through private vendors.

Maps: For a map of the Hells Canyon National Recreation Area, contact Wallowa Mountains Visitor Center, 88401 Highway 82, Enterprise, OR, 97828, 541/426-5546. For a topographic map, ask the USGS for Hat Point.

Directions: From downtown Joseph, follow the Imnaha Highway and signs for Hells Canyon Scenic Byway 29 miles to the town of Imnaha. Go straight through town onto Hat Point Road 4240. Climb steeply for five miles, then continue 17.6 miles to the parking area at Hat Point. Park at the first parking area at a sign for the trailhead.

Contact: Hells Canyon National Recreation Area, 88401 Highway 82, Box A, Enterprise, OR, 97828, 541/523-1315.

46 FREEZEOUT SADDLE
5.6-12.0 mi/4.0 hr-7.5 hr 🥾3 ⛰8

in Hells Canyon National Recreation Area

Map 10.4, page 524

Hung above Hells Canyon and flanked by two ridges is Freezeout Saddle, named for the nearby creek that tumbles through the dark forests along its banks. But the trail itself sets out into ponderosa pine stands with views first out to the canyon walls of the Imnaha River, then to the Wallowas, and finally to the depths of Hell's Canyon and the Seven Devils Mountains in Idaho. For a longer hike, head up Summit Ridge into the Hells Canyon Wilderness, following it back to the trailhead on a meandering trip through wildflower meadows and past a cowboy camp.

The Saddle Creek Trail heads to the left from the lot on gentle switchbacks, climbing nearly 2,000 feet over 2.8 miles through meadows and ponderosa pines. At the four-way junction in Freezeout Saddle, go right for the loop. Hike 4.2 miles through meadows along Summit Ridge, then at a junction go right on an old road 0.4 mile, staying right at a fork, until the path peters out. Go downhill toward a rock cairn and signpost, and turn right on this trail. In 0.4 mile pass Marks Cabin, and in 0.2 mile stay left at a fork. The trail descends 2,200 feet down the ridge for 1.9 miles to a junction. Go right, descending another 1,000 feet in two miles to the trailhead.

User Groups: Hikers, dogs, and horses. No mountain bikes allowed. No wheelchair facilities.

Permits: Permits are not required. A federal Northwest Forest Pass is required to park here; the cost is $5 a day or $30 for an annual pass.

Hells Canyon from Freezeout Saddle

© SEAN PATRICK HILL

You can buy a day pass at the trailhead, at ranger stations, or through private vendors.

Maps: For a map of the Hells Canyon National Recreation Area, contact Wallowa Mountains Visitor Center, 88401 Highway 82, Enterprise, OR, 97828, 541/426-5546. For a topographic map, ask the USGS for Hat Point.

Directions: From downtown Joseph, follow the Imnaha Highway and signs for Hells Canyon Scenic Byway 29 miles to the town of Imnaha. Turn right on Upper Imnaha Road, following signs for halfway. Drive 13 miles to a fork before a bridge and turn left on Road 4230. Drive 2.9 miles to the Saddle Creek Trailhead lot at road's end.

Contact: Hells Canyon National Recreation Area, 88401 Highway 82, Box A, Enterprise, OR, 97828, 541/523-1315.

47 STUD CREEK

2.4 mi/1.0 hr

in Hells Canyon National Recreation Area

Map 10.4, page 524

The 330-foot-tall Hells Canyon Dam stands like a fortress on the Snake River, damming 20 miles of its flow into a giant reservoir. Just above the shores is the Hells Canyon Wilderness, some of the most rugged and wild terrain in the Northwest. This easy jaunt passes mock orange and sumac—not to mention poison ivy—from a visitors center to the mouth of Stud Creek, with views of the monolithic walls of Hells Canyon in all its natural glory along the way. You can visit an archeological site nearby, a shallow hole where a Native American pit house once stood. Don't plan on extending your trip: towering cliffs simply block any further opportunity to go forward. If you're looking for more, there is a 0.2-mile trail leading from the dam on the Idaho side down to Deep Creek and the dam's outlet tunnel.

From the visitors center, head to the boat dock and follow a walkway to the trail. In one mile you'll reach the cobble beach at the mouth of Stud Creek; the trail ends 0.2 mile later.

User Groups: Hikers and dogs only. No horses or mountain bikes allowed. No wheelchair facilities.

Permits: Permits are not required. Parking and access are free.

Maps: For a map of the Hells Canyon National Recreation Area, contact Wallowa Mountains Visitor Center, 88401 Highway 82, Enterprise, OR, 97828, 541/426-5546. For a topographic map, ask the USGS for Squirrel Prairie.

Directions: From Baker City, go north on I-84 to Exit 302. From the exit, drive Highway 86 east 65 miles to Oxbow. Follow Road 454 and signs to Hells Canyon Dam 23 miles. Cross the dam and drive 1.1 miles to the visitors center parking lot at road's end. The trail begins at the boat dock.

Contact: Hells Canyon National Recreation Area, 88401 Highway 82, Box A, Enterprise, OR, 97828, 541/523-1315.

48 HELLS CANYON RESERVOIR

8.6 mi/3.0 hr

in Hells Canyon National Recreation Area

Map 10.4, page 524

Although this hike follows the Hells Canyon Reservoir, formed by the 330-foot dam downstream, it still makes for a rugged trip through the wilderness area. Side creeks pour in one after another and side trails roam deeper into the canyon's highlands. Some of those trails have been washed out, but the 32-Point Trail continues onward.

From road's end, start on the Hells Canyon Reservoir Trail by a message board. Cross Copper Creek, and continue 0.9 mile to cross Nelson Creek. In another 0.9 mile the trail crosses McGraw Creek; go left here 0.4 mile to a waterfall, but beyond this the trail is washed out and abandoned. Return to the main trail and continue 0.6 mile to the junction with the 32-Point Trail; long-distance backpackers can continue on this trail 8.2 miles to Buck Point Lookout and Road 3965. The Reservoir Trail goes beyond this junction 0.2 mile to Spring Creek, then is abandoned, though hikers with path-finding skills can continue 1.9 mile to its end at Leep Creek.

User Groups: Hikers, dogs, and horses. No mountain bikes allowed. No wheelchair facilities.

Permits: A free self-issue Wilderness Permit is required and is available at the trailhead. Parking and access are free.

Maps: For a map of the Hells Canyon National Recreation Area, contact Wallowa Mountains Visitor Center, 88401 Highway 82, Enterprise, OR, 97828, 541/426-5546. For a topographic map, ask the USGS for White Monument.

Directions: From Baker City, go north on I-84 to Exit 302. From the exit, drive Highway 86 east 65 miles to Oxbow. Go left onto Homestead Road and follow it nine miles to its end.

Contact: Hells Canyon National Recreation Area, 88401 Highway 82, Box A, Enterprise, OR, 97828, 541/523-1315.

49 CLARNO PALISADES
0.6 mi/0.5 hr 🥾1 ⛰7

west of Fossil in the John Day Fossil Beds

Map 10.5, page 525

Prehistoric Oregon was not at all the place we see today. Before the Cascade Mountains rose, what is now Eastern Oregon went through several incarnations: marshy jungle, wild savanna. Some of the animals and plants that thrived here—including saber-toothed cats, miniature horses, and the dawn redwood—did so for a long time. But when the Cascade Mountains rose up in volcanic pyrotechnic displays of ash and fire, those living things were buried and fossilized. The John Day Fossil Beds is a great place to find fossils. At the Clarno Palisades, massive mudslides buried forests instantaneously, and you can see some of the fossilized trunks buried in the solidified mud and ash. Two trails, an easy 0.6-mile walk altogether, investigate the towering walls, all that remains of those prehistoric flows. A fossil loop invites you to explore the 44-million-year-old mud flows with branch and leaf fossils, and an uphill climb takes you to a viewpoint of an arch high on the rock wall. Remember to take nothing from the area!

User Groups: Hikers and dogs on leash only. No horses or mountain bikes allowed. No wheelchair facilities.

Permits: Permits are not required. Parking and access are free.

Maps: For a brochure, contact John Day Fossil Beds National Monument, 32651 Highway 19, Kimberly, OR, 97848, 541/987-2333. For a topographic map, ask the USGS for Clarno.

Directions: From The Dalles, drive I-84 east to Biggs (Exit 104) and turn south on U.S. 97 for 59 miles. When you reach Shaniko, turn left on Highway 218 for 26 miles, passing Antelope and Clarno. Cross the John Day River and continue three miles to a pullout on the left.

Contact: John Day Fossil Beds National Monument, 32651 Highway 19, Kimberly, OR, 97848, 541/987-2333.

50 PAINTED HILLS
2.6 mi/1.5 hr 🥾1 ⛰8

northwest of Mitchell in the John Day Fossil Beds

Map 10.5, page 525

In the distant past, 33-million-years-ago to be precise, powerful volcanoes forever changed the landscape of Eastern Oregon. The volcanic ash that fell here settled layer on layer, each with a different mineral content. After eons of erosion, what remains are the Painted Hills, eerily colorful mounds colored red, yellow, black—striped by manganese, iron, and other minerals. Four easy trails visit one of the most photographed places in Oregon, along with a few other interesting side trips to fossil-strewn mounds and mounds of claystone. Bring a camera, and choose a day with good light. But be sure to stay on all paths: these treasures are easily damaged.

All four trails in the Painted Hills Unit are close together and easy. The Painted Hills Overlook Trail is 0.3 mile, and the nearby Carroll Rim Trail climbs to a high viewpoint up 400 feet and 0.8 mile. Two other nearby trails, the Painted Cove Trail and the Leaf Hill Trail, are 0.2-mile loops.

User Groups: Hikers and dogs on leash only. No horses or mountain bikes allowed. The 0.2-mile Leaf Hill Loop is wheelchair accessible.

Permits: Permits are not required. Parking and access are free.

Maps: For a brochure, contact John Day Fossil Beds National Monument, 32651 Highway 19, Kimberly, OR, 97848, 541/987-2333. For a topographic map, ask the USGS for Painted Hills.

Directions: From the town of Mitchell on U.S. 26, drive four miles west to Burnt Ranch Road and turn right, going six miles to Bear Creek Road. Turn left on Bear Creek Road for 1.2 miles to the Painted Hills Overlook Area for the trailheads to Carroll rim and the Painted Hills. Continue another 0.7 mile on Bear Creek Road to a junction; the Leaf Hill Loop is 1.1 miles to the left, and the Painted Cove Trail is 0.5 mile to the right.

Painted Hills in the John Day Fossil Beds

Contact: John Day Fossil Beds National Monument, 32651 Highway 19, Kimberly, OR, 97848, 541/462-3961.

51 MILL CREEK WILDERNESS
16.8 mi/7.5 hr   🏃3 ⛰️8

northeast of Prineville in Mill Creek Wilderness

Map 10.5, page 525

In 2000, a devastating fire roared through the Mill Creek Wilderness just north of the city of Prineville. Much of the forest has recovered, and now black morels sprout up among the snags and still-standing ponderosa pines. Twin Pillars Trail heads into a wilderness area, fording the creek 10 times on its way up to the Twin Pillars, a pair of distinctive rock formations towering above the creek. Watch for ticks along the way.

From the trailhead parking at Wildcat Campground, start on Twin Pillars Trail. The trail follows the creek 2.9 miles, fording it nine times, but watch for newer trails that avoid the fords. Stay to the left at a junction with the Belknap Trail. After the 10th ford, continue 2.6 miles and 1,400 feet up to a signed viewpoint of Twin Pillars. From here, the trail continues 2.6 miles farther to a junction with Road 27.

User Groups: Hikers, dogs, and horses. No mountain bikes allowed

Permits: A free self-issue Wilderness Permit is required and is available at the trailhead. Parking and access are free.

Maps: For a map of the Ochoco National Forest, contact Ochoco National Forest, 3160 NE 3rd Street, Prineville, OR, 97754, 541/416-6500. For a topographic map, ask the USGS for Steins Pillar.

Directions: From Prineville, drive 10 miles east on U.S. 26. Beyond milepost 28, turn left on Mill Creek Road and go 10.7 miles.

Contact: Ochoco National Forest, Lookout Mountain Ranger District, 3160 NE 3rd Street, Prineville, OR, 97754, 541/416-6500.

52 STEINS PILLAR

4.0 mi/2.0 hr

northeast of Prineville in Ochoco National Forest

Map 10.5, page 525

The Ochoco Mountains represent one of the westernmost terminuses of the Blue Mountain Range. This easy trail follows a ponderosa pine and bitterbrush slope to views of the Three Sisters, heading to 350-foot Steins Pillar, a rhyolitic ash column that hard-core rock climbers challenge themselves to top. For the hiker, there is an amazing rock outcrop beside the pillar to explore, and you can hike to the bottom of the pillar where the trail officially ends. From the trailhead, follow the one-way Steins Pillar Trail two miles to the base of Steins.

User Groups: Hikers, dogs, horses, and mountain bikes. No wheelchair facilities.

Permits: Permits are not required. Parking and access are free.

Maps: For a map of the Ochoco National Forest, contact Ochoco National Forest, 3160 NE 3rd Street, Prineville, OR, 97754, 541/416-6500. For a topographic map, ask the USGS for Steins Pillar.

Directions: From Prineville, drive 10 miles east on U.S. 26. Beyond milepost 28, turn left on Mill Creek Road and go 6.7 miles. At a sign for Steins Pillar Trailhead, go right across a bridge on Road 500 for two miles to a turnaround.

Contact: Ochoco National Forest, Lookout Mountain Ranger District, 3160 NE 3rd Street, Prineville, OR, 97754, 541/416-6500.

53 LOOKOUT MOUNTAIN

7.0 mi/3.0 hr

east of Prineville in the Ochoco National Forest

Map 10.5, page 525

Lookout Mountain earns its name in two ways: one, it was the site of a long-since removed fire lookout; two, the view is awesome.

From this peak, you'd think there was nothing but mountains, with the Three Sisters in the west, and the foothills of the Ochocos rolling away from the base of the colossal cliffs. Along the way, the trail passes stunning wildflower meadows with views to Big Summit Prairie, climbs a long slope to the lookout site, and finally descends to an abandoned cinnabar mine. Look at this mine from a distance, but don't go near it; old mines are dangerous.

If you parked at the lower lot, take the right-hand trail that goes up 0.9 mile to the upper trailhead. From the upper lot, start on the far-left Trail 808, which climbs through cool woods for one mile and tops the plateau. The next 3.2 miles travels through beautiful spring prairies, crosses Brush Creek, then begins the climb up the slope to the peak. Stay right at the junctions. From the 6,926-foot lookout site, the trail to the left goes 1.2 mile along the edge of the cliffs to a viewpoint. Otherwise, go straight on Trail 808, following it down 0.2 mile to a shelter, then stay left at a junction with Trail 808A for 2.6 miles, descending through deep woods to the Independent Mine and the lot.

User Groups: Hikers, dogs, horses, and mountain bikes. No wheelchair facilities.

Permits: Permits are not required. Parking and access are free.

Maps: For a map of the Ochoco National Forest, contact Ochoco National Forest, 3160 NE 3rd Street, Prineville, OR, 97754, 541/416-6500. For a topographic map, ask the USGS for Lookout Mountain.

Directions: From Prineville, drive 17 miles east on U.S. 26 then fork right on Ochoco Creek Road. Go 8.2 miles to the Ranger Station then right on Road 42 for 6.8 miles. Turn right on Road 4205 at a sign for Independent Mine. Go 100 yards to a parking area on the left for the Round Mountain Trail, or up 0.9 mile farther to an upper trailhead on Road 4205.

Contact: Ochoco National Forest, Lookout Mountain Ranger District, 3160 NE 3rd Street, Prineville, OR, 97754, 541/416-6500.

54 CHIMNEY ROCK

2.8 mi/1.0 hr

south of Prineville on the Prineville Reservoir

Map 10.5, page 525

If you didn't know it was there, this fork of the Crooked River, snaking its way through a burnished desert canyon, would elude you. And many people don't know it's there, since it's far off the beaten path. The drive through the canyon alone is worth every minute; but for a bird's-eye view, the easy Rim Trail climbs a dry wash to a high bench and out to Chimney Rock, with its blooms of bitterroot and views to the Three Sisters in the west.

From the trailhead, walk into the dry gulch for 0.7 mile, then climb up to the head of a dry waterfall and continue 0.7 mile along the rimrock to the 40-foot-tall Chimney Rock, standing 500 feet over the river below.

User Groups: Hikers, dogs, horses, and mountain bikes. No wheelchair facilities.

Permits: Permits are not required. Parking and access are free.

Maps: For a brochure of the Lower Crooked Wild and Scenic River, contact the Bureau of Land Management, Prineville District, 3050 NE 3rd Street, Prineville, OR, 97754, 541/416-6700, or go to www.or.blm.gov/prineville. For a topographic map, ask the USGS for Stearns Butte.

Directions: From Prineville, head south on Main Street, which becomes Road 27 for 16.6 miles. At a sign for chimney Rock Recreation Site, park on the left side of the road at a sign for Rim Trail.

Contact: Bureau of Land Management, Prineville District, 3050 NE 3rd Street, Prineville, OR, 97754, 541/416-6700.

55 BLUE BASIN OVERLOOK

4.0 mi/2.0 hr

northwest of Dayville in the John Day Fossil Beds

Map 10.6, page 526

Of all the strange formations left behind by the prehistoric volcanoes, mudslides, and ash deposits in what is now the John Day Fossil Beds, Blue Basin has to be the strangest. Blue Basin derives all its ghostly colors from colored ash. "Blue" may not be the best word to describe it; perhaps "Green Basin" would be better. Squabbling aside, what you'll find here is a box canyon entirely draped in blue-green ash deposits, like something from a fantasy film. Even the creek is a muddy green, as it slowly erodes the basin. Two great trails offer two ways to see it.

From the parking lot, follow the green creek on the Island in Time Trail leading to the right. In 0.2 mile, the trail splits; go left first, staying on the Island Trail 0.4 miles to see the interior of the basin and a few replicas of a fossilized saber-toothed cat and giant tortoise. Then return to the junction and go right, looping around the Overlook Trail for three miles to return to the lot.

User Groups: Hikers and dogs on leash only. No horses or mountain bikes allowed. No wheelchair facilities.

Permits: Permits are not required. Parking and access are free.

Maps: For a brochure, contact John Day Fossil Beds National Monument, 32651 Highway 19, Kimberly, OR, 97848, 541/987-2333. For a topographic map, ask the USGS for Picture Gorge West.

Directions: From the town of Mitchell on U.S. 26, drive 35 miles east into Picture Gorge, then turn left on Highway 19, going five miles to the Blue Basin parking lot on the right.

Contact: John Day Fossil Beds National Monument, 32651 Highway 19, Kimberly, OR, 97848, 541/987-2333.

56 SHEEP ROCK TRAILS
2.0 mi/1.0 hr   🏃1 ⛰7

northwest of Dayville in the John Day Fossil Beds

Map 10.6, page 526

The Sheep Rock unit of the John Day Fossil Beds has a number of impressive sights. If you're driving from Highway 26, east or west, you'll pass through Picture Gorge, a three-armed canyon where Native American petroglyphs are hidden on the high rocks. Sheep Rock is a story told in layers, as the John Day River carved through successive epochs of stone, leaving Sheep Rock a striped monument of different lava flows and formations. Located just above the historic James Cant Ranch, the 0.5-mile Sheep Rock Overlook Trail will give you a first-hand look, and the nearby 0.5-mile River Trail offers a view of the John Day River. Just across Highway 19, at the Condon Paleontology Center, a 0.5-mile trail leads to a view of the John Day River Valley.

Farther north on Highway 19, past the Island in Time Trail (see *Blue Basin Overlook,* previous listing), two more trails are worth a stop: the 0.25-mile Flood of Fire Trail, which crosses a ridge for a view of the basalt-rimmed John Day River Valley, and the 0.25-mile Story in Stone Trail, with its touchable exhibits along a basin of blue-green claystone.

User Groups: Hikers and dogs on leash only. No horses or mountain bikes allowed. The River Trail and Story in Stone Trail are wheelchair accessible.

Permits: Permits are not required. Parking and access are free.

Maps: For a brochure, contact John Day Fossil Beds National Monument, 32651 Highway 19, Kimberly, OR, 97848, 541/987-2333. For a topographic map, ask the USGS for Mount Misery.

Directions: From Dayville, drive five miles west on U.S. 26 to Highway 19. Turn right and go two miles to the John Day Fossil Beds National Monument sign at the James Cant Ranch and turn right and go to the parking lot and the trailheads for the River Trail and Sheep Rock Overlook, or to the left into the Thomas Condon Paleontology Center for the Condon Overlook Trail. Then go another seven miles north on Highway 19 for the Story in Stone and Flood of Fire Trails.

Contact: John Day Fossil Beds National Monument, 32651 Highway 19, Kimberly, OR, 97848, 541/987-2333.

57 ROCK CREEK TO SPANISH PEAK
16.0 mi/7.5 hr   🏃3 ⛰7

south of Dayville in Ochoco National Forest

Map 10.6, page 526

The Ochoco Mountains are one of the loneliest of mountain ranges. They sit just about in the middle of the state near Post, a little town that is the geographic center of Oregon. Rock Creek Trail is one of the few trails out this way, and you'll likely find solitude here to spare. Once you wander away from the road, you'll enter a wilderness that fits the definition if not the designation. Some of the people who found their way back here include those who built the Waterman Ditch, a late-1800s flume that supplied placer gold miners with water to wash gold from the hillsides. An abandoned cabin on Fir Tree Creek testifies to their presence, as well. The trail sets out in lodgepole pines, and if you go far enough you'll find stands of ponderosa pines at a saddle beneath Spanish Peak, crossing the imaginatively named First and Second Creeks. Climbing to the top of Spanish Peak is an option.

The Rock Creek Trail descends 500 feet and 2.4 miles from the trailhead to the start of the Waterman Ditch, then continues to follow it 1.4 level miles to the cabin ruins, crossing Fir Tree Creek. In 3.2 miles, the trail crosses Second Creek then First Creek and reaches the saddle beneath 6,871-foot Spanish Peak. The trail ends one mile ahead at the end of public land. The trail to the right begins a climb of Spanish Peak. To do that, follow this trail 4.5 miles, climbing 1,700 feet to a fork. Go left 0.8 mile, connecting with a road, and following it up to the peak.

User Groups: Hikers, dogs, and mountain bikes. No horses allowed. No wheelchair facilities.

Permits: Permits are not required. Parking and access are free.

Maps: For a map of the Ochoco National Forest, contact Ochoco National Forest, 3160 NE 3rd Street, Prineville, OR, 97754, 541/416-6500. For a topographic map, ask the USGS for Six Corners and Antone.

Directions: From Prineville, drive east on U.S. 26 for one mile and turn right on the Paulina Highway 59.5 miles east. Turn left on South Beaver Creek Road for 7.7 miles. At a sign for Wolf Creek Campground, go left on Road 42 for 1.5 miles, then go straight on Road 3810 for 3.2 miles, keeping right at a junction to stay on 3810 for 3.9 more miles, then right on Road 38 for 1.5 miles. At a junction, go straight on Road 38 for 1.7 miles to the Rock Creek Trailhead on the left.

Contact: Ochoco National Forest, Paulina Ranger District, 7803 Beaver Creek Road, Paulina, OR, 97751, 541/477-6900.

58 BLACK CANYON WILDERNESS
21.8 mi/2 days   🥾4 ⛰️8

south of Dayville

Map 10.6, page 526

The Black Canyon Wilderness encompasses many different wilds, from the high meadows of the Ochoco Mountains to the sagebrush flats of the high desert. Because the lower end of this trail demands a ford of the South Fork John Day River, which is difficult, if not impossible at certain times of the year, another option is needed. Boeing Field, with its outrageous displays of big mules ear daisies, offers an easy 0.5-mile entry to the canyon itself. Along the way, backpackers will find ample opportunity to camp, and day hikers can take in the scenery, poke around a ruined cabin, and get their feet wet numerous times—almost too numerous to count. The crossings get more

difficult as the creek descends, getting deeper, until it at last reaches the John Day.

From Boeing Field, head down the trail 0.5 mile and cross Owl Creek. To the right, 1.5 miles upstream, is the Black Canyon Trail's official beginning at Road 5840, but go left two miles (the cabin is hidden in a series of meadows along the way to the left) to Black Creek. Cross the creek here and continue 1.4 miles to a second crossing. From here, the trail crosses and re-crosses the creek five more times in the next 0.9 mile. From there, the trail stays on the bank another 4.3 miles, then fords the by-now-deeper creek 10 times in 1.8 mile before arriving at the South Fork John Day River.

User Groups: Hikers, dogs, and horses. No mountain bikes allowed. No wheelchair facilities.

Permits: A free self-issue Wilderness Permit is required and is available at the trailhead. Parking and access are free.

Maps: For a map of the Ochoco National Forest, contact Ochoco National Forest, 3160 NE 3rd Street, Prineville, OR, 97754, 541/416-6500. For a topographic map, ask the USGS for Wolf Mountain.

Directions: From Prineville, drive east on U.S. 26 for one mile and turn right on the Paulina Highway 59.5 miles east. Turn left on South Beaver Creek Road for 7.7 miles, then fork right for 1.3 miles. Turn left on Road 5810 for 11.1 miles to a pullout on the left and the Boeing Field Trailhead.

Contact: Ochoco National Forest, Paulina Ranger District, 7803 Beaver Creek Road, Paulina, OR, 97751, 541/477-6900.

59 FIELDS PEAK AND MCCLELLAN MOUNTAIN
9.8 mi/5.0 hr   🥾3 ⛰️8

southeast of Dayville in Malheur National Forest

Map 10.6, page 526

The largely barren Fields Peak has at least one thing going for it: set between the Strawberry

Mountains to the east and the Cascades to the west, it is the highest point between them. It takes in an enormous view. The trail up Fields Peak goes on to McClellan Mountain, a quiet and steady walk to another nearby peak, only 300 feet shorter, requiring an easy cross-country ramble up a grassy ridge. As there are no trees here to offer shade, be sure to bring ample water, sunblock, and a hat.

From the trailhead, climb 500 feet in 0.7 mile to Bitterroot Ridge, then continue uphill 600 feet and 0.8 mile to a junction. To climb Fields Peak, follow the wide path to the left 0.8 mile to the 7,362-foot peak. To continue to McClellan Mountain, return to the junction and follow the trail over a number of passes 2.2 miles to a meadow. Where the trail appears to end, follow the ridge east to the 7,043-foot peak of McClellan Mountain. The trail continues along the mountainside past meadows, leading 9.2 miles to the Riley Creek Trailhead.

User Groups: Hikers, dogs, horses, and mountain bikes. No wheelchair facilities.

Permits: Permits are not required. Parking and access are free.

Maps: For a map of the Malheur National Forest, contact Malheur National Forest, 431 Patterson Bridge Road, John Day, OR, 97845, 541/575-3000. For a topographic map, ask the USGS for Big Weasel Springs and McClellan Mountain.

Directions: From Dayville, drive east on U.S. 26 for 13 miles, then turn south on Fields Creek Road 21. Follow this road 8.6 miles to a sign for Fields Peak, and turn left on Road 115 for 0.4 mile, then turn right at a junction onto Road 2160 for 0.1 mile, then left on Road 041 for 1.2 miles to road's end at the McClellan Mountain Trailhead.

Contact: Malheur National Forest, Blue Mountain Ranger District, 431 Patterson Bridge Road, P.O. Box 909, John Day, OR, 97845, 541/575-3000.

60 WINOM CREEK
8.0-10.2 mi/4.0-5.0 hr

southeast of Ukiah in North Fork John Day Wilderness

Map 10.7, page 527

Comprising a massive part of the Blue Mountain range, the Winom Frazier OHV Complex has more than 140 miles of trail for off-road vehicles to roar into the forest. Just to the south, though, Winom Creek cascades through the North Fork John Day Wilderness, where all motorized vehicles are banned. Though a fire burned through here, the trail is well maintained and comprises a loop that returns via a nearby campground for a tour of the Blue Mountain region.

From the trailhead, the South Winom Trail heads out four miles and climbs 1,650 feet to its end along the creek, home to brook trout, redband trout, and bull trout. To make a slightly longer loop, turn left on the Big Creek Trail and go 4.5 miles to a tie trail on the left. Follow this 1.2 miles, then follow the campground road back 0.5 mile to the parking area.

User Groups: Hikers, dogs, and horses. No mountain bikes allowed. No wheelchair facilities.

Permits: A free self-issue Wilderness Permit is required and is available at the trailhead. Parking and access are free.

Maps: For a map of the Umatilla National Forest and the North Fork John Day Wilderness, contact Umatilla National Forest, 2517 SW Hailey Avenue, Pendleton, OR, 97801, 541/278-3716. For a topographic map, ask the USGS for Pearson Ridge and Kelsay Butte.

Directions: From Ukiah, drive 22.6 miles south on the Blue Mountain Scenic Byway/Road 52 and turn right on Road 440 for 0.7 mile. At a fork for South Winom Campground, go left 0.2 mile to a pullout on the right. The trailhead is across the road.

Contact: Umatilla National Forest, North Fork John Day Ranger District, P.O. Box 158, Ukiah, OR, 97880, 541/427-3231.

61 NORTH FORK JOHN DAY RIVER

**5.2 mi–22.9 mi one-way/
2.0 hr–2 days**

northwest of Granite in North Fork John Day Wilderness

Map 10.7, page 527

In the riverbed of the North Fork John Day, mica sparkles and glistens like gold. No wonder so many miners have active claims here: watch for their tin signs nailed to the trees. Better yet, poke around some of the cabins, especially the "Bigfoot Hilton," a dilapidated miner's cabin that makes for a possible camp, though it may prove too rustic for some. Along the trail, western larches turn their own brand of gold in the autumn; it's the only conifer to lose its needles in winter. For an easy exploratory day trip or overnighter, consider fording the river at Crane Creek and returning via a loop. Otherwise, you can go on down the canyon as far as you like.

From the North Fork Trailhead, start off 0.1 mile then go to the right-hand trail. Cross Trail Creek and head into the canyon. In 2.5 miles, the trail comes to Trout Creek and the old miner's cabin on the right. Continue 4.0 miles down the river to the junction with the Crane Creek Trail. For a short loop, go left 0.2 mile to the river, fording it here. Then follow the Crane Creek Trail 4.1 miles to the Crane Creek Trailhead, then go left on the North Crane Trail back to the campground. For those wanting to continue on the North Fork John Day, continue on the remainder of this 22.9-mile trail to its end at the Big Creek Campground on dirt Road 5506.

User Groups: Hikers, dogs, and horses. No mountain bikes allowed. No wheelchair facilities.

Permits: A free self-issue Wilderness Permit is required and is available at the trailhead. A federal Northwest Forest Pass is required to park here; the cost is $5 a day or $30 for an annual pass. You can buy a day pass at the trailhead, at ranger stations, or through private vendors.

Maps: For a map of the Umatilla National Forest and the North Fork John Day Wilderness, contact Umatilla National Forest, 2517 SW Hailey Avenue, Pendleton, OR, 97801, 541/278-3716. For a topographic map, ask the USGS for Desolation Butte and Olive Lake.

Directions: From Baker City, go south on Main Street/Highway 7 toward John Day for 25 miles and turn right toward Sumpter on the Sumpter Valley Highway 220, continuing 20 miles to the town of Granite. Take Road 73 north nine miles to a stop sign, and turn left into the North Fork John Day Campground. Drive to the far end and the trailhead parking area.

To shuttle a car at Big Creek Campground, drive 14 miles south of Ukiah on U.S. 395 and go left on Road 55, following it for 5 miles. Go straight onto Road 5506, whose first 6.5 miles is gravel and remaining 6 miles is unmaintained dirt, to the trailhead at road's end.

Contact: Umatilla National Forest, North Fork John Day Ranger District, P.O. Box 158, Ukiah, OR, 97880, 541/427-3231.

62 BALDY LAKE

13.4 mi/7.0 hr

west of Baker City in North Fork John Day Wilderness

Map 10.7, page 527

This corner of the North Fork John Day Wilderness is hemmed in by granite cliffs, through which Baldy Creek makes its way to the North Fork John Day. At the head of one of those creek arms, fed by springs, Baldy Lake lies still and clear beneath Mount Ireland. The trail switchbacks up the path of an old power line that brought electricity to the gold miners working nearby.

Cross the North Fork John Day River and go 1.1 miles to a crossing of Baldy Creek. Ford Bull Creek and cross a patch of burned woods, then cross Baldy Creek again and head five miles up the canyon and 1,300 feet up in elevation to a junction. Stay right and go another 0.2 mile to Baldy Lake. Continue 0.4 mile around the lake to explore the shore and see the springs, but turn around from here; after this, the trail climbs a difficult one mile to its end at the upper Baldy Lake Trailhead, whose long and difficult drive doesn't make for a good shuttle.

User Groups: Hikers, dogs, and horses. No mountain bikes allowed. No wheelchair facilities.

Permits: A free self-issue Wilderness Permit is required and is available at the trailhead. Parking and access are free.

Maps: For a map of the Wallowa-Whitman National Forest and the North Fork John Day Wilderness, contact the Wallowa-Whitman National Forest Headquarters, P.O. Box 907, 1550 Dewey Avenue, Baker City, OR, 97814, 541/523-6391. For a topographic map, ask the USGS for Mount Ireland.

Directions: From Baker City, drive 19 miles north on I-84 to Exit 285. Following Anthony Lakes signs, go 3.9 miles west on North Powder River Lane, then left 0.7 mile on Ellis Road, then right 6.5 miles on Anthony Lakes Highway. Continue on Road 73 for 12.7 miles to a sign for the Baldy Creek Trail, turning left on Road 380 to its end at a parking area.

Contact: Wallowa-Whitman National Forest, Baker City Ranger District, 3165 10th Street, Baker City, OR, 97814, 541/523-4476.

63 MOUNT IRELAND AND DOWNIE LAKE
6.6-9.2 mi/3.0-4.0 hr

west of Baker City in Wallowa-Whitman National Forest

Map 10.7, page 527

Perched on 8,321-foot Mount Ireland, a fire lookout tower (staffed in summer) peers over into a corner of the North Fork John Day Wilderness and the Baldy Lake basin, and as far out as the Elkhorn Range and Wallowa Mountains. Along the way, a side trail leads to seldom-visited Downie Lake, a calm track of water bounded in buy subalpine fir and lodgepole pine.

Cross the berm and head up 0.2 mile on old Road 130 to a junction. Go left on Road 132 to find the Mount Ireland sign, then follow this old road 0.3 mile to where it becomes a trail. Continue 0.8 miles, cross Road 142, then climb 0.9 mile to a junction. To the left, the trail climbs 800 feet in 1.1 miles to the lookout at Mount Ireland.

Though this makes for a good hike in itself, it's worth it to extend the trip to visit Downie Lake. Coming back down from Mount Ireland to the junction, continue straight. The trail seems to disappear, but picks up 100 feet to the left and continues down 750 feet in elevation and 0.7 mile to a junction. Go left 0.1 miles at a sign for Downie Lake, then right 0.5 mile past two ponds to Downie Lake. Return as you came.

User Groups: Hikers, dogs, horses, and mountain bikes. No wheelchair facilities.

Permits: Permits are not required. Parking and access are free.

Maps: For a map of the Wallowa-Whitman National Forest and the North Fork John Day Wilderness, contact the Wallowa-Whitman National Forest Headquarters, P.O. Box 907, 1550 Dewey Avenue, Baker City, OR, 97814, 541/523-6391. For a topographic map, ask the USGS for Mount Ireland.

Directions: From Baker City, go south on Main Street/Highway 7 toward John Day for 25 miles and turn right toward Sumpter on the Sumpter Valley Highway 220, continuing 12.2 miles over the Grant County Line. Go right on bumpy Road 7370 at a sign for Mount Ireland LO for 0.6 mile, veering left to continue another 1.8 miles on this road, then left again for 0.6 mile to a fork with Road 100. Go right 0.3 mile and park at the "Mt Ireland LO Trail" sign.

Contact: Wallowa-Whitman National Forest, Baker City Ranger District, 3165 10th Street, Baker City, OR, 97814, 541/523-4476.

64 PEAVY TRAIL

7.2 mi/3.5 hr   🚶3 ⛰6

west of Baker City in North Fork John Day
Wilderness

Map 10.7, page 527

The Peavy Cabin, which is available for rent,
sits at a high pass on the Elkhorn Range—
providing options to explore every which way
on the Elkhorn Range, part of which lies in
the North Fork John Day Wilderness. From
the cabin, the Peavy Trail climbs 1,700 feet to
the Elkhorn Crest Trail, connecting at Cracker
Saddle. For a loop, follow the Crest Trail left
3.4 miles to Nip and Tuck Pass, then continue
left one mile to the Cunningham Trail, going
left 2.8 miles back to the cabin.

User Groups: Hikers, dogs, and horses. No
mountain bikes allowed. No wheelchair
facilities.

Permits: A free self-issue Wilderness Permit
is required and is available at the trailhead.
Parking and access are free.

Maps: For a map of the Wallowa-Whitman
National Forest and the North Fork John Day
Wilderness, contact the Wallowa-Whitman
National Forest Headquarters, P.O. Box 907,
1550 Dewey Avenue, Baker City, OR, 97814,
541/523-6391. For a topographic map, ask
the USGS for Crawfish Lake and Anthony
Lakes.

Directions: From Baker City, drive 19 miles
north on I-84 to Exit 285. Following Anthony
Lakes signs, go 3.9 miles west on North Powder River Lane, then left 0.7 mile on Ellis
Road, then right 6.5 miles on Anthony Lakes
Highway. Continue on Road 73 22.2 miles,
then turn left on Road 380 for three miles
to its end.

Contact: Wallowa-Whitman National Forest,
Baker City Ranger District, 3165 10th Street,
Baker City, OR, 97814, 541/523-4476.

65 CRAWFISH LAKE

6.0 mi/2.5 hr   🚶1 ⛰7

west of Baker City in Wallowa-Whitman
National Forest

Map 10.7, page 527

An easy hike into the North Fork John Day
Wilderness follows the Crawfish Lake Trail
through lodgepole pine woods to a pleasant
lake beneath the Lakes Lookout. Though it
crosses a 1989 burn in places, the trail also
follows intact woods and meadows. Perfect
for swimming, the lake also has a big granite
outcrop for relaxing and taking in the view.

From the trailhead, follow the trail 1.4 miles
to Crawfish Lake, passing through the burn
along the way. The trail follows the lake 0.3
mile, then continues along an edge of the wilderness and finally along Crawfish Creek for
1.3 mile to a lower trailhead.

User Groups: Hikers, dogs, and horses. No
mountain bikes allowed. No wheelchair
access.

Permits: A free self-issue Wilderness Permit
is required and is available at the trailhead.
Parking and access are free.

Maps: For a map of the Wallowa-Whitman
National Forest and the North Fork John Day
Wilderness, contact the Wallowa-Whitman
National Forest Headquarters, P.O. Box 907,
1550 Dewey Avenue, Baker City, OR, 97814,
541/523-6391. For a topographic map, ask the
USGS for Crawfish Lake.

Directions: From Baker City, drive 19 miles
north on I-84 to Exit 285. Following Anthony
Lakes signs, go 3.9 miles west on North Powder River Lane, then left 0.7 mile on Ellis
Road, then right 6.5 miles on Anthony Lakes
Highway. Continue on Road 73 for 15 miles,
and turn left on Road 216 at a sign for Crawfish Lake. Go 0.25 mile into a parking area.

Contact: Wallowa-Whitman National Forest,
Baker City Ranger District, 3165 10th Street,
Baker City, OR, 97814, 541/523-4476.

66 THE LAKES LOOKOUT
1.4 mi/1.0 hr

west of Baker City in Wallowa-Whitman
National Forest

Map 10.7, page 527

The Anthony Lakes area in the Blue Mountains has a plethora of hikes. Here's a start: a gentle climb to a viewpoint and the site of an old lookout tower, long gone. From the trailhead, climb an easy 0.7-mile trail, gaining 700 feet, to a view of the lake-strewn landscape below.

User Groups: Hikers and dogs. No horses or mountain bikes permitted. No wheelchair access.

Permits: Permits are not required. Parking and access are free.

Maps: For a map of the Wallowa-Whitman National Forest, contact the Wallowa-Whitman National Forest Headquarters, P.O. Box 907, 1550 Dewey Avenue, Baker City, OR, 97814, 541/523-6391. For a topographic map, ask the USGS for Anthony Lakes.

Directions: From Baker City, drive 19 miles north on I-84 to Exit 285. Following Anthony Lakes signs, go 3.9 miles west on North Powder River Lane, then left 0.7 mile on Ellis Road, then right 6.5 miles on Anthony Lakes Highway. Continue on Road 73 for 15.4 miles, and turn left on Road 210. Follow this rutted and rocky road 1.6 miles, then right 0.3 mile at a junction, then left to a parking area at the trailhead.

Contact: Wallowa-Whitman National Forest, Baker City Ranger District, 3165 10th Street, Baker City, OR, 97814, 541/523-4476.

67 ANTHONY LAKE TO HOFFER LAKES
3.0 mi/1.5 hr

west of Baker City in Wallowa-Whitman
National Forest

Map 10.7, page 527

Lying at the foot of the Elkhorn Range, Anthony Lake is a popular destination. With its historic guard station, its campgrounds, boat ramp, even a ski area, this is a well-known area to traverse, especially if you're going to circle the lake by foot. The lake is also an entryway to other lakes as well, including the two Hoffer Lakes, an easy distance away. Start by circling Anthony Lake, then strike out along Parker Creek to the two marshy lakes with their wildflower meadows.

Set out from the pavilion to Anthony Lake, and follow the lakeshore left 0.3 mile. Pass the boat ramp, and continue 0.3 mile to a junction. To visit Hoffer Lakes, go left along Parker Creek 0.6 mile to the first lake, where side trails lead to the second. To see the meadows, continue along the main trail 0.5 mile to an old service road. Return as you came to Anthony Lake, and continue left along its shore 0.4 mile back to the parking area.

User Groups: Hikers, dogs on leash only, and horses. No mountain bikes allowed. No wheelchair access.

Permits: Permits are not required. Parking and access are free.

Maps: For a map of the Wallowa-Whitman National Forest, contact the Wallowa-Whitman National Forest Headquarters, P.O. Box 907, 1550 Dewey Avenue, Baker City, OR, 97814, 541/523-6391. For a topographic map, ask the USGS for Crawfish Lake and Anthony Lakes.

Directions: From Baker City, drive 19 miles north on I-84 to Exit 285. Following Anthony Lakes signs, go 3.9 miles west on North Powder River Lane, then left 0.7 mile on Ellis Road, then right 6.5 miles on Anthony Lakes Highway. Continue on Road 73 for 10.2 miles to the Anthony Lake Campground on the left. Follow the entrance road, forking right then parking on the left at a picnic gazebo.

Contact: Wallowa-Whitman National Forest, Baker City Ranger District, 3165 10th Street, Baker City, OR, 97814, 541/523-4476.

68 DUTCH FLAT SADDLE LOOP

8.2 mi/4.0 hr

west of Baker City in Wallowa-Whitman National Forest

Map 10.7, page 527

Anthony Lake is popular for camping, skiing, and boating, and is a haven for hiking. With its link to the Elkhorn Crest Trail and a section of the North Fork John Day Wilderness, this epic day-hike—or backpacking trip—circles around Angell Peak and Gunsight Mountain, with a passage above Crawfish Meadow and side-trip options to Dutch Flat Lake and Lost Lake.

Set out from the pavilion to Anthony Lake, and follow the lakeshore left 0.3 mile. At a boat ramp, take the Black Lake Trail on the left 0.5 mile past Lilypad Lake to the Elkhorn Crest Trail. Stay on the Elkhorn Crest Trail, keeping left at a junction to Black Lake itself, and continue 2.1 miles around Gunsight Mountain and Angell Peak, climbing 1,000 feet to Angell Pass. Enter the wilderness here, and in 0.6 mile the trail descends 300 feet to Dutch Flat Saddle and a junction. Go right on the Crawfish Basin Trail and continue through the wilderness and out again 2.5 miles to a road. Follow the road 0.1 mile, staying left at a junction and continuing 0.3 mile to a pass. Take an unmarked trail to the right 0.1 mile to another road, then go right on that road 0.3 mile to the Hoffer Lakes Trail. Follow the trail 1.1 miles back to Anthony Lake, then go left on the shore 0.4 mile back to the parking area.

User Groups: Hikers, dogs on leash only, and horses. No mountain bikes allowed. No wheelchair access.

Permits: A free self-issue Wilderness Permit is required and is available on the trail. Parking and access are free.

Maps: For a map of the Wallowa-Whitman National Forest, contact the Wallowa-Whitman National Forest Headquarters, P.O. Box 907, 1550 Dewey Avenue, Baker City, OR,

97814, 541/523-6391. For a topographic map, ask the USGS for Anthony Lakes.

Directions: From Baker City, drive 19 miles north on I-84 to Exit 285. Following Anthony Lakes signs, go 3.9 miles west on North Powder River Lane, then left 0.7 mile on Ellis Road, then right 6.5 miles on Anthony Lakes Highway. Continue on Road 73 for 10.2 miles to the Anthony Lake Campground on the left. Follow the entrance road, forking right then parking on the left at a picnic gazebo.

Contact: Wallowa-Whitman National Forest, Baker City Ranger District, 3165 10th Street, Baker City, OR, 97814, 541/523-4476.

69 BLACK LAKE

2.4 mi/1.0 hr

west of Baker City in Wallowa-Whitman National Forest

Map 10.7, page 527

Lilypad and Black Lakes are set in the same forested landscape as big, popular Anthony Lake, but they don't get nearly the recognition. If you're camping up here with the kids, take this delightful day trip away from the crowds and the boats and head for some woodsy quiet.

Set out from the pavilion to Anthony Lake, and follow the lakeshore left 0.3 mile. At a boat ramp, take the Black Lake Trail on the left 0.5 mile past Lilypad Lake to the Elkhorn Crest Trail. Stay on the Elkhorn Crest Trail a short distance, then go right and climb 100 feet in 0.4 mile to Black Lake. To make a loop of it, return to the Elkhorn Trail and follow it to the left, staying on that trail 0.5 mile to a trailhead on Road 73. Take the next trail to the left back 0.3 mile to the campground and to the parking area.

User Groups: Hikers, dogs on leash only, and horses. No mountain bikes allowed. No wheelchair access.

Permits: Permits are not required. Parking and access are free.

Maps: For a map of the Wallowa-Whitman

National Forest, contact the Wallowa-Whitman National Forest Headquarters, P.O. Box 907, 1550 Dewey Avenue, Baker City, OR, 97814, 541/523-6391. For a topographic map, ask the USGS for Anthony Lakes.

Directions: From Baker City, drive 19 miles north on I-84 to Exit 285. Following Anthony Lakes signs, go 3.9 miles west on North Powder River Lane, then left 0.7 mile on Ellis Road, then right 6.5 miles on Anthony Lakes Highway. Continue on Road 73 for 10.2 miles to the Anthony Lake Campground on the left. Follow the entrance road, forking right then parking on the left at a picnic gazebo.

Contact: Wallowa-Whitman National Forest, Baker City Ranger District, 3165 10th Street, Baker City, OR, 97814, 541/523-4476.

🔟 ELKHORN CREST NATIONAL RECREATION TRAIL

22.8 mi one-way/2 days 5 ⛰10

west of Baker City in Wallowa-Whitman National Forest

Map 10.7, page 527

The highest-elevation trail in the Blue Mountains runs north–south through the glaciated granite landscape of the Elkhorn Range. Lake after lake falls along the subalpine route, with views to the Blue Mountains and the Wallowas. Deer, elk, and mountain goats live in this high country, and much of the trail traverses the North Fork John Day Wilderness. The trail can be accessed from either end, or a shuttle can be arranged to make the whole run.

The northern end of the trail sets out from the trailhead on Road 73 near Anthony Lake, climbing 3.2 miles to Dutch Flat Saddle and into the wilderness, passing Black Lake and affording access to Dutch Flat Lake. In 1.9 miles, it reaches Nip and Tuck Pass, with access to Lost Lake and Meadow Lake. The next 3.4 miles rounds Mount Ruth and reaches Cracker Saddle, with access to

Summit Lake (see *Elkhorn Crest Lakes,* next listing). The trail then leaves the wilderness and follows a long 9.5-mile slope, passing old mining prospects and rounding Rock Creek Butte. At the junction with Twin Lakes (see *Twin Lakes* listing in this chapter), the trail completes its traverse on an easy 3.8 miles to Marble Pass.

User Groups: Hikers, dogs, and horses. Mountain bikes not allowed in wilderness area. No wheelchair facilities.

Permits: A free self-issue Wilderness Permit is required and is available on the trail. A federal Northwest Forest Pass is required to park here; the cost is $5 a day or $30 for an annual pass. You can buy a day pass at the trailhead, at ranger stations, or through private vendors.

Maps: For a map of the Wallowa-Whitman National Forest, contact the Wallowa-Whitman National Forest Headquarters, P.O. Box 907, 1550 Dewey Avenue, Baker City, OR, 97814, 541/523-6391. For a topographic map, ask the USGS for Elkhorn Peak.

Directions: For the north access, begin in Baker City, driving 19 miles north on I-84 to Exit 285. Following Anthony Lakes signs, go 3.9 miles west on North Powder River Lane, then left 0.7 mile on Ellis Road, then right 6.5 miles on Anthony Lakes Highway. Continue on Road 73 for 9.9 miles to the Elkhorn Crest Trailhead on the left. For the south access, start in Baker City at exit 304 on I-84. Drive west on Campbell Street 1.5 miles, then turn right on 10th Street for 1.1 mile. At a flashing yellow light, turn left on Pocahontas Road for 7.6 miles, following signs for Marble Creek Picnic Area. Go straight on Marble Creek Road 8.1 miles to a pass and the Elkhorn Crest Trail. The final four miles of Marble Creek Road require vehicles with high clearance.

Contact: Wallowa-Whitman National Forest, Baker City Ranger District, 3165 10th Street, Baker City, OR, 97814, 541/523-4476.

71 ELKHORN CREST LAKES

24.8 mi/3 days   👥5 ⛰9

west of Baker City in Wallowa-Whitman
National Forest

Map 10.7, page 527

The northernmost section of the Elkhorn
Crest National Recreation Trail has the most
water. Along the way, spur trails lead to three
subalpine lakes: Dutch Flat, Lost, and Summit. For backpackers, these three lakes offer
great camping—the only catch is getting
there. To reach the ultimate destination, the
high-set Summit Lake, requires 2,600 feet of
elevation gain. But the other two are along the
way, easily accessible from trail passes.

The trail sets out from nearby Anthony
Lake, climbing 3.2 miles and 750 feet to Dutch
Flat Saddle and into the wilderness, passing
Black Lake along the way (see *Black Lake* listing in this chapter). At the four-way junction
of Dutch Flat Saddle, you'll see Dutch Flat
Lake below to the east; take the left-hand trail
down 1.1 miles to access it. Continue south on
the Elkhorn Trail, passing the Cunningham
Trail, for 1.9 miles to Nip and Tuck Pass. Just
beyond this narrow slot in the rock, go left
1.3 miles to Lost Lake. For Summit Lake, the
largest and prettiest, continue on the Elkhorn
Trail 3.4 miles to Cracker Saddle, crossing an
old ghost town dirt road, and go left 1.5 mile
to Summit Lake.

User Groups: Hikers, dogs, and horses. No
mountain bikes allowed. No wheelchair
facilities.

Permits: A free self-issue Wilderness Permit is
required and is available on the trail. A federal
Northwest Forest Pass is required to park here;
the cost is $5 a day or $30 for an annual pass.
You can buy a day pass at the trailhead, at
ranger stations, or through private vendors.

Maps: For a map of the Wallowa-Whitman National Forest, contact the Wallowa-Whitman
National Forest Headquarters, P.O. Box 907,
1550 Dewey Avenue, Baker City, OR, 97814,
541/523-6391. For a topographic map, ask the
USGS for Elkhorn Peak and Anthony Lakes.

Directions: Begin in Baker City, driving 19
miles north on I-84 to Exit 285. Following
Anthony Lakes signs, go 3.9 miles west on
North Powder River Lane, then left 0.7 mile
on Ellis Road, then right 6.5 miles on Anthony Lakes Highway. Continue on Road 73
for 9.9 miles to the Elkhorn Crest Trailhead
on the left.

Contact: Wallowa-Whitman National Forest,
Baker City Ranger District, 3165 10th Street,
Baker City, OR, 97814, 541/523-4476.

72 GRANITE CREEK

6.6 mi/2.5 hr   👥2 ⛰7

northwest of Granite in North Fork John Day
Wilderness

Map 10.7, page 527

For an introductory tour of gold mining country, look no further than Granite Creek. As in
other areas in and around the North Fork John
Day Wilderness, there are still active claims.
The ponderosa pine–lined canyon leads down
to the North Fork John Day River, where trails
branch out in all directions into the wilderness. You'll pass a handy spring along the way,
bubbling out of a pipe. Note the mica that
sparkles in the riverbed like gold. For a tour
of the devastation of mining, simply loop back
on an old mining road that passes old ruins,
active claims, and a few miners' shacks.

Follow the Granite Creek Trail 1.3 miles
to a junction, staying to the right 0.6 mile
to the first footbridge over Granite Creek.
Continue 1.4 miles along Granite Creek to
the John Day River, crossing Lake Creek and
Snowshoe Spring on the way, and passing the
Lake Creek Trail on the left. The John Day
River makes a good turnaround point, but
longer hikes can be extended along the John
Day itself. The Granite Creek Trail ends at
the North Fork John Day Trail, so you can
return the way you came. To the right, the
North Fork John Day Trail follows the river
13.6 miles to its end at the North Fork John
Day Campground.

Across the river and to the left, the river trail ambles 11 miles to its opposite end.

User Groups: Hikers, dogs, and horses. No mountain bikes allowed. No wheelchair facilities.

Permits: A free self-issue Wilderness Permit is required and is available at the trailhead. A federal Northwest Forest Pass is required to park here; the cost is $5 a day or $30 for an annual pass. You can buy a day pass at the trailhead, at ranger stations, or through private vendors.

Maps: For a map of the Umatilla National Forest and the North Fork John Day Wilderness, contact Umatilla National Forest, 2517 SW Hailey Avenue, Pendleton, OR, 97801, 541/278-3716. For a topographic map, ask the USGS for Desolation Butte.

Directions: From Baker City, go south on Main Street/Highway 7 toward John Day for 25 miles and turn right toward Sumpter on the Sumpter Valley Highway 220, continuing 20 miles to the town of Granite. Go left on Road 10 for 1.5 miles, then right on Road 1035 for 4.6 miles, then left on Road 010 for 0.2 mile to the parking area before the gate. The trail begins behind the gate.

Contact: Umatilla National Forest, North Fork John Day Ranger District, P.O. Box 158, Ukiah, OR, 97880, 541/427-3231.

7.3 LOST CREEK AND SADDLE RIDGE

16.2 mi/8.0 hr

southeast of Dale in Umatilla National Forest

Map 10.7, page 527

Olive Lake is certainly popular, with its campground and boat ramp, but just beyond its shoreline lies a swath of the North Fork John Day Wilderness in a remote stretch of the Greenhorn Mountains. This big loop passes a marsh on Lake Creek, ambles along Saddle Ridge, then follows Lost Creek past Ben Harrison Peak through swales marked only by cairns. Along the way, the trail follows an old

redwood pipeline that once carried water to the nearby Fremont Powerhouse.

From Lost Creek Trailhead, go 0.2 mile to a junction and go right on the Saddle Camp Trail along an old pipeline. In 1.5 miles, cross a hill and arrive at a junction, going left. In 0.7 mile, the trail reaches the terminus of the Upper Reservoir marsh, and continues 1.9 miles and 800 feet up to Saddle Camp and a trail junction. Stay left for two miles along Saddle Ridge to Dupratt Spring Pass and a dirt road. Follow the Lost Creek Trail, an old roadbed 50 yards to the left of a cairn, 2.3 miles to another junction, staying left in the pass. Over the course of the next 2.7 miles the trail vanishes in a series of five meadows; watch for cairns and/or blazes along the way to find the trail again. At the final junction, go straight 0.2 mile to the trailhead.

User Groups: Hikers, dogs, and horses. No mountain bikes allowed. No wheelchair facilities.

Permits: A free self-issue Wilderness Permit is required and is available on the trail. A federal Northwest Forest Pass is required to park here; the cost is $5 a day or $30 for an annual pass. You can buy a day pass at the trailhead, at ranger stations, or through private vendors.

Maps: For a map of the Umatilla National Forest, contact Umatilla National Forest, 2517 SW Hailey Avenue, Pendleton, OR, 97801, 541/278-3716. For a topographic map, ask the USGS for Olive Lake.

Directions: From downtown Baker City, drive south on Main Street (which becomes Highway 7) for 25 miles. Turn right on Highway 220 toward Sumpter and go 20 miles to Granite. Turn left on Road 10 for 3.6 miles, then fork right on Road 10 where it becomes gravel. Go 8.1 miles to the Lost Creek Trailhead on the right.

Contact: Umatilla National Forest, North Fork John Day Ranger District, P.O. Box 158, Ukiah, OR, 97880, 541/427-3231.

74 OLIVE LAKE
2.7-6.5 mi/1.0-3.0 hr

southeast of Dale in Umatilla National Forest

Map 10.7, page 527

You could tour Olive Lake by starting at the campground on the lake itself, and if you're so inclined then follow the directions below to the Lake Creek Trailhead, but go 0.8 mile farther up Road 10 and go left on Road 480 to the lake. From here you can start at the boat ramp and take an easy 2.7-mile walk around the lake.

If you're in the mood for something longer, adding 3.8 miles to the trip, follow a wooded hike from a different trailhead. Start at the Lost Creek Trailhead, going 0.2 mile to a junction, then right on the Saddle Camp Trail along an old pipeline. In 1.5 miles, cross a hill and arrive at a junction, going right 0.2 mile to a road, then left on a short trail to the campground. Now follow the lakeshore in either direction for its 2.7-mile loop, quickly leaving the campground behind in favor of lodgepole pine woods. Make your way back to the start of the loop and return as you came to the Lost Creek Trailhead.

User Groups: Hikers, dogs, horses, and mountain bikes. No wheelchair facilities.

Permits: Permits are not required. A federal Northwest Forest Pass is required to park here; the cost is $5 a day or $30 for an annual pass. You can buy a day pass at the trailhead, at ranger stations, or through private vendors.

Maps: For a map of the Umatilla National Forest and the North Fork John Day Wilderness, contact Umatilla National Forest, 2517 SW Hailey Avenue, Pendleton, OR, 97801, 541/278-3716. For a topographic map, ask the USGS for Olive Lake.

Directions: From downtown Baker City, drive south on Main Street (which becomes Highway 7) for 25 miles. Turn right on Highway 220 toward Sumpter and go 20 miles to Granite. Turn left on Road 10 for 3.6 miles, then fork right on Road 10 where it becomes gravel. Go 8.1 miles to the Lost Creek Trailhead on the right.

Contact: Umatilla National Forest, North Fork John Day Ranger District, P.O. Box 158, Ukiah, OR, 97880, 541/427-3231.

75 SOUTH FORK DESOLATION CREEK
15.6 mi/7.5 hr

southeast of Dale in Umatilla National Forest

Map 10.7, page 527

South Fork Desolation Creek Trail is a good option for reaching Saddle Ridge (*Lost Creek and Saddle Ridge* is another way, see listing in this chapter) as well as entering the North Fork John Day Wilderness. This trail begins on Forest Service Road 45 and passes through the Vinegar Hill-Indian Rock Scenic Area, climbing 2,200 remote miles into the Greenhorn Range. From the trailhead, travel seven miles through a valley to the old Portland Mine. The trail completes its final 0.8 mile in the shadow of the Saddle Ridge, leading to Dupratt Spring Pass. From there, you arrive at a junction with the Blue Mountain Trail and the Lost Creek Trail, where you can head off along Lost Creek or up Saddle Ridge toward the junction to Olive Lake.

User Groups: Hikers, dogs, horses, and mountain bikes. No wheelchair facilities.

Permits: Permits are not required. A federal Northwest Forest Pass is required to park here; the cost is $5 a day or $30 for an annual pass. You can buy a day pass at the trailhead, at ranger stations, or through private vendors.

Maps: For a map of the Umatilla National Forest and the North Fork John Day Wilderness, contact Umatilla National Forest, 2517 SW Hailey Avenue, Pendleton, OR, 97801, 541/278-3716. For a topographic map, ask the USGS for Desolation Butte.

Directions: From downtown Baker City, drive south on Main Street (which becomes Highway 7) for 25 miles. Turn right on Highway 220 toward Sumpter and go 20 miles to Granite. Turn left on Road 10 for 3.6 miles, then fork right on Road 10 where it becomes gravel. Go 14.9 miles and turn left on Road 45 for one mile to the trailhead pullout on the right; the trail is on the left.

Contact: Umatilla National Forest, North Fork John Day Ranger District, P.O. Box 158, Ukiah, OR, 97880, 541/427-3231.

76 TWIN LAKES
6.2–10.2 mi/3.0–5.0 hr

west of Baker City in Wallowa-Whitman National Forest

Map 10.7, page 527

There are two ways to reach Twin Lakes: the southern access for the Elkhorn Crest Trail (see *Elkhorn Crest National Recreational Trail* listing in this chapter) or from this easier road, more suitable for your everyday car. The lakes themselves are cupped in an unbelievable bowl of rock, with the head of Rock Creek Butte—the highest point in the Blue Mountains at 9,106 feet—rising above it all, and equally dominating 8,931-foot Elkhorn Peak towering as well. Should you take the easier road in, you'll have a shorter hike but a steeper climb, but it's worth it to continue up and out of the valley to the Crest Trail, and amble along as long as you'd like. If you do, consider making this an excellent backpacking trip.

The Twin Lakes Trail climbs steeply for 3.1 miles along Lake Creek to Lower Twin Lake. At the far end, follow a user trail 0.2 mile to smaller Upper Twin Lake. Return as you came, or continue on the main trail one mile from Twin Lakes switchbacks up to a saddle on the Elkhorn Crest Trail.

From the junction with the Elkhorn Crest Trail, it's 3.8 miles to the right to trail's end at the Marble Pass Trailhead, and 1 mile to the left are viewpoints of Rock Creek Butte, which hovers above the Twin Lakes like a sentinel. Beyond this, the entire length of the trail stretches onward to Anthony Lake.

User Groups: Hikers, dogs, horses, and mountain bikes. No wheelchair facilities.

Permits: Permits are not required. Parking and access are free.

Maps: For a map of the Wallowa-Whitman National Forest, contact the Wallowa-Whitman National Forest Headquarters, P.O. Box 907, 1550 Dewey Avenue, Baker City, OR, 97814, 541/523-6391. For a topographic map, ask the USGS for Elkhorn Peak.

Directions: From downtown Baker City, drive east on Main Street, which becomes Highway 7, for 23.3 miles. Past Phillips Lake and between mileposts 28 and 29, go right on Deer Creek Road for 4.2 miles, then go straight on Road 030 for 3.8 miles to road's end at the trailhead.

Contact: Wallowa-Whitman National Forest, Baker City Ranger District, 3165 10th Street, Baker City, OR, 97814, 541/523-4476.

77 MAGONE LAKE AND MAGONE SLIDE
2.5 mi/1.5 hr

north of John Day in Malheur National Forest

Map 10.7, page 527

This pine-lined lake, popular with anglers, was born when an 1860s landslide apparently dammed up Lake Creek, creating this 5,000-foot elevation lake. Magone Lake is named for an Army major who stocked the lake by carrying buckets of fish on his shoulders. Rainbow and brook trout now feed in the lake, and bear, elk, deer, and cougar occasionally come to visit. The two-mile loop around Magone Lake makes for an easy walk; if you're up for more, cross the road to the trailhead for the Magone Slide, a 1.0-mile climb up and back down the landslide.

User Groups: Hikers and dogs only. No horses or mountain bikes. The hard-packed dirt trail around Magone Lake is wheelchair accessible in dry weather.

Permits: Permits are not required. Parking and access are free.

Maps: For a map of the Malheur National Forest, contact Malheur National Forest, 431

Patterson Bridge Road, John Day, OR, 97845, 541/575-3000. For a topographic map, ask the USGS for Magone Lake.

Directions: From John Day, drive U.S. 26 east 9.5 miles. Turn left on Road 18 for 13 miles, then turn left on Road 3620 for 1.2 miles, and right on road 3618 for 1.5 miles to the Magone Lake day-use area on the left.

Contact: Malheur National Forest, Blue Mountain Ranger District, P.O. Box 909, 431 Patterson Bridge Road, John Day, OR, 97845, 541/575-3000.

78 CANYON MOUNTAIN
11.4-29.0 mi/7.0 hr-2 days 🥾4 ⛰8

south of Canyon City in Strawberry Mountain Wilderness

Map 10.7, page 527

Driving the road into this trailhead, you'll wonder how Canyon City miners managed to get up here to mine the gold that was discovered here. The Strawberry Mountains are one of the farthest terminuses of gold in the Blue Mountain Range, but some 10,000 miners showed up here in 1862. Today, this part of Oregon is relatively quiet and rarely visited. It may even be possible to have this mountain to yourself.

From the trailhead, climb the Canyon Mountain Trail 750 feet and 1.6 miles to a crossing of Little Pine Creek, then gently climb 1.7 miles past a viewpoint in a high meadow with springs to Dog Creek, then another 2.2 miles to Dean Creek. This makes a good turnaround point, though the trail continues on 5.2 miles to the Joaquin Miller Trail and another 3.8 miles to the East Fork Canyon Creek Trail, where a backpacking spot is available at the Hotel De Bum Camp (see *East Fork Canyon Creek* hike in this chapter).

User Groups: Hikers, dogs, and horses. No mountain bikes. No wheelchair facilities.

Permits: Permits are not required. Parking and access are free.

Maps: For a map of the Malheur National

Forest and Strawberry Mountain Wilderness, contact Malheur National Forest, 431 Patterson Bridge Road, John Day, OR, 97845, 541/575-3000. For a topographic map, ask the USGS for Canyon Mountain.

Directions: From John Day, drive two miles south on U.S. 395 to Canyon City. Turn left on Main Street, which becomes Road 52, and drive 1.9 miles, then turn right on Gardner Road 77. In 0.3 mile, veer right. At the next fork, go straight onto the gravel road for 2.2 miles, which becomes very steep at times. Where the gravel ends in a saddle, go straight on a dirt road 200 feet to a pine tree with a blaze, then go left 300 feet to road's end at the trailhead for Canyon Mountain Trail.

Contact: Malheur National Forest, Blue Mountain Ranger District, P.O. Box 909, 431 Patterson Bridge Road, John Day, OR, 97845, 541/575-3000.

79 PINE CREEK
21.0 mi/2 days 🥾3 ⛰8

southeast of John Day in Strawberry Mountain Wilderness

Map 10.7, page 527

There are many entrances to the Strawberry Mountain Wilderness, a band of mountains that lifts from the prairies of Eastern Oregon like a great groundswell. This trail heads into the wilderness 10.5 miles, gaining a steady 800 feet in elevation. The trail heads to a spine of the wilderness, switchbacking up to a pass over Bald Mountain, then heads down to Wildcat Basin. Along the way, there is access to many trails: Canyon Mountain, East Fork Canyon Creek, Indian Creek, Onion Creek, and Buckhorn Meadows.

User Groups: Hikers, dogs, and horses. No mountain bikes allowed. No wheelchair facilities.

Permits: Permits are not required. Parking and access are free.

Maps: For a map of the Malheur National Forest and Strawberry Mountain Wilderness, contact Malheur National Forest, 431 Patterson Bridge Road, John Day, OR, 97845, 541/575-3000. For a topographic map, ask the USGS for Pine Creek Mountain.

Directions: From Prairie City, drive 6.5 miles west on U.S. 26 and turn left on Pine Creek Road/County Road 54. Follow this road 8.5 miles to road's end and the trailhead.

Contact: Malheur National Forest, Blue Mountain Ranger District, P.O. Box 909, 431 Patterson Bridge Road, John Day, OR, 97845, 541/575-3000.

80 JOAQUIN MILLER TRAIL
11.6 mi/8.0 hr   🚶4 ⛰8

south of Canyon City in Strawberry Mountain Wilderness

Map 10.7, page 527

Before setting out on this trail, it's good to get a sense of who Joaquin Miller was. A true man of the West, a former gold miner, Pony Express rider, and newspaper writer, he settled down to a law practice in nearby Canyon City in the 1860s, during the height of the gold rush, and eventually became a poet before moving on to Oakland, California. What's left of Miller is the cabin he built in town—now part of the Grant County Historical Museum—and this namesake trail, whose stately ponderosa pines are part of the Canyon Creek Natural Area. This steep and rugged trail, worthy of its name, climbs to a high crest and connects to three other trails in the wilderness. This trail climbs 3,250 dry feet, so bring plenty of water.

Start on the Joaquin Miller Trail, which reaches a fence and the wilderness boundary in 0.3 mile. Continue into the wilderness meadows and woods two miles to a junction with the Tamarack Creek Trail. Go left to stay on the Miller Trail and climb 2,000 feet to the Joaquin Miller Crest, passing Tamarack Creek itself, the only water source on this trail, in 1.8 miles. Continue 1.5 miles to a ridge crest. To see the view of the John Day Valley,

scramble 0.2 mile up this slope. This makes a good turnaround point, though the trail ends at the Canyon Mountain Trail only 0.7 mile farther up.

User Groups: Hikers, dogs, and horses. No mountain bikes. No wheelchair facilities.

Permits: Permits are not required. Parking and access are free.

Maps: For a map of the Malheur National Forest and Strawberry Mountain Wilderness, contact Malheur National Forest, 431 Patterson Bridge Road, John Day, OR, 97845, 541/575-3000. For a topographic map, ask the USGS for Canyon Mountain.

Directions: From John Day, drive south on U.S. 395 for 9.7 miles and turn left on County Road 65 for 2.9 miles. Turn left on Road 6510 and keep left on this road for five miles to the Joaquin Miller Trailhead.

Contact: Malheur National Forest, Blue Mountain Ranger District, P.O. Box 909, 431 Patterson Bridge Road, John Day, OR, 97845, 541/575-3000.

81 EAST FORK CANYON CREEK
4.4-20.3 mi/2.0 hr-2 days 🚶4 ⛰7

south of Canyon City in Strawberry Mountain Wilderness

Map 10.7, page 527

The Canyon Creek Natural Area features park-like stands of ponderosa pine, not to mention cottonwood and dogwood trees. A few creeks meander by, and camping spots crop up along the trail. For a day hike, head in as far as you like, or challenge yourself to hike the whole trail, even looping around Indian Creek Butte before returning. For backpackers, this is one of many entrances to the Strawberry Mountain Wilderness, following this deep gouge carved out by the East Fork of Canyon Creek.

From the trailhead, the East Fork Canyon Creek Trail climbs easily in 2.2 miles to the first camp at Yokum Corrals, to the right on a fork, and in another 0.3 mile connects to the

Tamarack Trail. Stay on the main trail 0.4 mile to ford Brookling Creek, then another 1.1 miles to Bingham Camp. The next 3.3 miles climb 1,200 feet to the Hotel de Bum Camp at the headwaters of the creek. The trail continues one mile to a junction that begins the loop. To climb gradually, go left 1.3 mile to the Canyon Mountain Trail, then right 0.9 mile around Indian Creek Butte, then right again for 0.9 mile to the Table Mountain Trail, then right 0.6 mile back to the East Fork Canyon Creek Trail.

User Groups: Hikers, dogs, and horses. No mountain bikes. No wheelchair facilities.

Permits: A free self-issue Wilderness Permit is required and is available at the trailhead. Parking and access are free.

Maps: For a map of the Malheur National Forest and Strawberry Mountain Wilderness, contact Malheur National Forest, 431 Patterson Bridge Road, John Day, OR, 97845, 541/575-3000. For a topographic map, ask the USGS for Canyon Mountain.

Directions: From John Day, drive south on U.S. 395 for 9.7 miles and turn left on County Road 65 for 2.9 miles. Turn left on Road 6510 and keep left on this road for 1.6 miles, then turn right on Road 812 for 2.8 miles to a parking lot at road's end.

Contact: Malheur National Forest, Blue Mountain Ranger District, P.O. Box 909, 431 Patterson Bridge Road, John Day, OR, 97845, 541/575-3000.

82 WILDCAT BASIN AND THE BADLANDS

6.9 mi/3.5 hr

south of Canyon City in Strawberry Mountain Wilderness

Map 10.7, page 527

The Roads End Trail begins where the road ends only for cars; for the hiker, the 1.5-mile trail is still an old road, though it leads to spectacular views of the Indian Creek Basin and also makes the shortest route to nearby Strawberry Mountain. It's also a quick way to get to some amazing alpine and wildflower territory. A 1996 fire cleared the forest but opened up sunlight for the wildflower gardens proliferating here. Erosion has cleared off the rock, too, exposing ash deposits left millions of years ago in two "badlands"—really, a series of striated outcrops set amidst pines and firs. This loop visits two ash badlands along the way.

Follow the Roads End Trail, actually an old roadbed, 1.2 miles to a junction. To the right, Strawberry Mountain is 2.4 miles away. Go left 0.3 mile to another junction. Go left 1.6 miles past a series of badlands to Wildcat Basin and its spring and campsites. At a junction, go right on the Pine Creek Trail one mile. Go right on the Indian Creek Trail 0.2 mile, then right 1.1 miles past another series of badlands to finish the loop. Then go left 0.3 mile and right on the Roads End Trail to return to the trailhead.

User Groups: Hikers, dogs, and horses. No mountain bikes. No wheelchair facilities.

Permits: A free self-issue Wilderness Permit is required and is available at the trailhead. Parking and access are free.

Maps: For a map of the Malheur National Forest and Strawberry Mountain Wilderness, contact Malheur National Forest, 431 Patterson Bridge Road, John Day, OR, 97845, 541/575-3000. For a topographic map, ask the USGS for Strawberry Mountain.

Directions: From John Day, drive south on U.S. 395 for 9.7 miles and turn left on County Road 65 for 13.6 miles. At a four-way intersection, go left on Road 16 for 2.5 miles, then left on Road 1640 for 9.6 miles and park near a switchback at a sign for the Roads End Trail.

Contact: Malheur National Forest, Blue Mountain Ranger District, P.O. Box 909, 431 Patterson Bridge Road, John Day, OR, 97845, 541/575-3000.

83 SKYLINE TRAIL
9.4 mi/5.0 hr

south of Prairie City in Strawberry Mountain Wilderness

Map 10.7, page 527

Potentially, there are three ways to get to the Skyline Trail; you connect to it from the Strawberry Campground, heading toward alpine Slide Lake, where you can continue with backpack on into the high country. Another, quicker route is from one of two trailheads, but it's the westernmost trailhead that leads to both Slide Lake and High Lake, which sits in a glaciated basin below Indian Spring Butte and the Rabbit Ears, a pair of prominent spires on a high ridge dividing this basin from the Strawberry Lakes.

The Skyline Trail descends 500 feet and 1.3 miles to High Lake, with a loop trail to campsites leading to the left. Continue past the Lake Creek Trail to the right and continue on the Skyline Trail 1.6 miles, climbing to a high pass. From here, descend 1.3 miles to a junction (note that this route can be covered with snow late into the summer). At the junction, go right to Slide Lake, with its one-mile loop around the shore. From here the Skyline Trail continues 0.5 mile to a junction that leads toward Strawberry Lake; go right to stay on the Skyline, which continues 12.3 miles to its end at Road 101.

User Groups: Hikers, dogs, and horses. No mountain bikes. No wheelchair facilities.

Permits: A free self-issue Wilderness Permit is required and is available at the trailhead. Parking and access are free.

Maps: For a map of the Malheur National Forest and Strawberry Mountain Wilderness, contact Malheur National Forest, 431 Patterson Bridge Road, John Day, OR, 97845, 541/575-3000. For a topographic map, ask the USGS for Roberts Creek and Logan Valley East.

Directions: From John Day, drive south on U.S. 395 for 9.7 miles and turn left on County Road 65 for 13.6 miles. At a four-way

intersection, go left on Road 16 for 2.5 miles, then left on Road 1640 for 10 miles to the end of the road and the Skyline Trailhead.

Contact: Malheur National Forest, Prairie City Ranger District, P.O. Box 337, Prairie City, OR, 97869, 541/820-3800.

84 STRAWBERRY LAKE AND LITTLE STRAWBERRY LAKE
6.6 mi/3.0 hr

south of Prairie City in Strawberry Mountain Wilderness

Map 10.7, page 527   **BEST (**

As dry as the Strawberry Wilderness can be, it's amazing that there are such beautiful lakes—and a waterfall, too. A must-hike for day-hikers and backpackers alike, this trail heads in to two lakes, one large and one small, in a glaciated valley high in the Strawberry Mountain Wilderness. The bigger Strawberry Lake was formed by a thousand-year-old landslide, creating a perfect mirror of the rugged mountains surrounding it; the creek that feeds it runs mostly underground, hidden by the landslide.

From the parking area, head up the Strawberry Lake Trail one mile to a junction, go right 0.3 mile, then right again to Strawberry Lake. A trail loops around the lake; go right 0.9 mile along the west shore for views. At the far end, continue right 0.9 mile, climbing 600 feet to Strawberry Falls and a junction. Go left 0.4 mile to Little Strawberry Lake.

User Groups: Hikers, dogs, and horses. No mountain bikes. No wheelchair facilities.

Permits: A free self-issue Wilderness Permit is required and is available at the trailhead. Parking and access are free.

Maps: For a map of the Malheur National Forest and Strawberry Mountain Wilderness, contact Malheur National Forest, 431 Patterson Bridge Road, John Day, OR, 97845, 541/575-3000. For a topographic map, ask the USGS for Strawberry Mountain.

Directions: From U.S. 26 in Prairie City,

drive 0.5 mile south on South Bridge Street, then continue right on Bridge Street, which becomes County Road 60 and then FS Road 6001, for 10.7 miles to road's end at Strawberry Campground.
Contact: Malheur National Forest, Prairie City Ranger District, P.O. Box 337, Prairie City, OR, 97869, 541/820-3800.

85 ONION CREEK TO STRAWBERRY MOUNTAIN
7.2 mi/4.5 hr

south of Prairie City in Strawberry Mountain Wilderness

Map 10.7, page 527

The namesake of Strawberry Mountain Wilderness is a 9,038-foot brown peak surrounded by rugged, glacier-torn cirques and cliffs that fall down to a sagebrush plain stretching for miles. At that height, its no wonder the old lookout cabin blew away a piece at a time. Now it's inhabited only by wildflowers growing from the steep-pitched shale. A steep, relatively unused trail to the peak of Strawberry Mountain will cost you 10 miles round-trip and 4,000 feet elevation gain, but there is an easier way from a back route up the Onion Trail.

Follow the Roads End Trail, actually an old roadbed, 1.2 miles to a junction. Go right to the Onion Creek Trail 1.3 miles to a junction, continuing on the Onion Creek Trail to the left another 0.7 mile, climbing steadily up to a junction on the mountain itself, then climb to the left up the final 0.4 mile.
User Groups: Hikers, dogs, and horses. No mountain bikes. No wheelchair facilities.
Permits: A free self-issue Wilderness Permit is required and is available at the trailhead. Parking and access are free.
Maps: For a map of the Malheur National Forest and Strawberry Mountain Wilderness, contact Malheur National Forest, 431 Patterson Bridge Road, John Day, OR, 97845, 541/575-3000. For a topographic map, ask the USGS for Strawberry Mountain.

Directions: From John Day, drive south on U.S. 395 for 9.7 miles and turn left on County Road 65 for 13.6 miles. At a four-way intersection, go left on Road 16 for 2.5 miles, then left on Road 1640 for 9.6 miles and park near a switchback at a sign for the Roads End Trail.
Contact: Malheur National Forest, Prairie City Ranger District, P.O. Box 337, Prairie City, OR, 97869, 541/820-3800.

86 REYNOLDS CREEK
3.2 mi/1.5 hr

south of Prairie City in Malheur National Forest

Map 10.7, page 527

This lower-elevation trail will allow for some spring hiking months before the rest of the Blue Mountains emerge from the snow. This easy hike follows Reynolds Creek into the Baldy Mountain Wildlife Emphasis Area and heads for a rock arch and mysterious petroglyphs. Simply follow this trail 1.4 miles to its end at a waterfall on Reynolds Creek and a dry side creek. You'll have to set out cross-country farther up the Reynolds Creek Canyon to find the arch 0.2 mile beyond.
User Groups: Hikers, dogs, horses, and mountain bikes. No wheelchair facilities.
Permits: Permits are not required. Parking and access are free.
Maps: For a map of the Malheur National Forest, contact Malheur National Forest, 431 Patterson Bridge Road, John Day, OR, 97845, 541/575-3000. For a topographic map, ask the USGS for Isham Creek and Bates.
Directions: From Prairie City, follow County Road 62 for 7.5 miles, then turn left on Road 2635 for 4.3 miles to the Reynolds Creek Trail parking area on the right.
Contact: Malheur National Forest, Prairie City Ranger District, P.O. Box 337, Prairie City, OR, 97869, 541/820-3800.

87 LITTLE MALHEUR RIVER
14.8 mi/7.5 hr   👣3 ⛰7

southwest of Unity in Monument Rock Wilderness

Map 10.7, page 527

The little-known Monument Rock Wilderness in the Blue Mountains is just wild enough to bring out the wildlife and make hiking a bit more adventurous. The trail along the headwaters of the Little Malheur River crosses the river on bridgeless fords seven times from end to end, a relatively short trail that can be done in a single day (or more if you're looking for escape from the crowds). Old-growth western larch grow along the trail, and meadows are filled with columbine and alders. When you find Lunch Creek, you can decide if it's the right spot to live up to its name.

The upper trailhead follows Elk Flat Creek 2.2 miles through meadows and stands of trees to a crossing of the Little Malheur. Over the next 2.6 miles, the trail fords the river four more times before fording South Bullrun Creek, then continues another 2.6 miles past two more crossings to its end at the lower trailhead.

User Groups: Hikers, dogs, and horses. No mountain bikes. No wheelchair facilities.

Permits: A free self-issue Wilderness Permit is required and is available at the trailhead. Parking and access are free.

Maps: For a map of the Malheur National Forest and Monument Rock Wilderness, contact Malheur National Forest, 431 Patterson Bridge Road, John Day, OR, 97845, 541/575-3000. For a topographic map, ask the USGS for Flag Prairie.

Directions: From Prairie City, follow County Road 62 for eight miles, then turn left on Road 13 for 11.7 miles. Next turn left on Road 1370 at a sign for Little Malheur River, keeping left for five miles to the parking area and trailhead sign.

Contact: Malheur National Forest, Prairie City Ranger District, P.O. Box 337, Prairie City, OR, 97869, 541/820-3800.

88 MONUMENT ROCK
5.6 mi/2 hr   👣2 ⛰7

southwest of Unity in Monument Rock Wilderness

Map 10.7, page 527

Monument Rock is a strange rock cairn that sits atop a 7,736-foot peak. No one knows who built it—probably not Native Americans, but perhaps miners or sheepherders. Regardless of its origin, you can find Monument Rock with a little bushwhacking into a wilderness that's home to deer, elk, badgers, and the rare wolverine. Though a fire passed through here in 1989, the area is recovering. Along this trail, there are opportunities to visit two viewpoints at the Table Rock Lookout and Bullrun Rock, as well as a trip to visit the mysterious cairn.

From the trailhead, enter the Monument Rock Wilderness by crossing the dirt berm to start out on an old road for 0.6 mile, keeping left at a junction and continuing another 1.1 miles to a junction marked by a post. To climb Bullrun Rock, go left 0.4 mile along the road to a wire fence, then climb to the left to the 7,873-foot peak.

To continue to Monument Rock, go right at the post instead, crossing a gate in the wire fence and continuing 0.2 mile to a small rock cairn at a junction in burned woods. Turn left on a faint path to a pass and follow the ridge to the right, climbing a steep slope and heading over a mountaintop to Monument Rock itself.

If you're up for adding another 1.6 mile to your day, then return to your car and walk the rest of the way up Road 1370, too steep and rugged for passenger cars, to the summer-staffed Table Rock Lookout.

User Groups: Hikers, dogs, and horses. No mountain bikes. No wheelchair facilities.

Permits: A free self-issue Wilderness Permit is required and is available at the trailhead. Parking and access are free.

Maps: For a map of the Malheur National Forest and Monument Rock Wilderness, contact Malheur National Forest, 431 Patterson Bridge Road, John Day, OR, 97845,

541/575-3000. For a topographic map, ask the USGS for Bullrun Rock.

Directions: From Prairie City, follow County Road 62 for eight miles, then turn left on Road 13 for 11.7 miles. Next turn left on Road 1370 at a sign for Little Malheur River, keeping left for 5.9 miles, then turn right at a sign for Table Rock Lookout, staying on Road 1370 for 0.2 mile to a fork. Take the rough and rocky left-hand fork for 3.8 slow miles to a message board and parking area along the road.

Contact: Malheur National Forest, Prairie City Ranger District, P.O. Box 337, Prairie City, OR, 97869, 541/820-3800.

89 MALHEUR RIVER NATIONAL RECREATION TRAIL
7.6 mi one-way/3.0 hr   🥾2 ⛰7

southeast of Prairie City in Malheur National Forest

Map 10.7, page 527

The Malheur River carves its way through a gorge along this National Recreation Trail stretch from a sketchy road crossing at Malheur Ford to the meadows of Hog Flat, where it's possible to spot pronghorn antelope. Along the way, numerous creeks join the flow from rugged side canyons. Starting from the campground at Malheur Ford, follow the river downstream 7.6 miles to its end, where it leaves the river and climbs the canyon wall to Hog Flat and Road 142.

User Groups: Hikers, dogs, horses, and mountain bikes. No wheelchair facilities.

Permits: Permits are not required. Parking and access are free.

Maps: For a map of the Malheur National Forest, contact Malheur National Forest, 431 Patterson Bridge Road, John Day, OR, 97845, 541/575-3000. For a topographic map, ask the USGS for Dollar Basin.

Directions: From John Day, drive 9.7 miles south on U.S 395 and turn left on County Road 65, which becomes Road 15, for 13.6 miles to a four-way intersection. Turn left on Road 16 for 5.3 miles, then turn right on Road 1643. Follow signs for Malheur River for nine miles to a fork and go left on Road 1651 for 1.3 miles to a parking area at Malheur Ford. For a shuttle, head back down 1.3 miles from Malheur Ford on Road 1651 and go left on Road 1653 for 6.5 miles, then left on Road 142 for 1.4 miles to its end.

Contact: Malheur National Forest, Prairie City Ranger District, P.O. Box 337, Prairie City, OR, 97869, 541/820-3800.

90 NORTH FORK MALHEUR RIVER AND CRANE CREEK
12.4-18.6 mi one-way/2 days
🥾3 ⛰7

south of Prairie City in Strawberry Mountain Wilderness

Map 10.7, page 527

One of the first forty rivers in Oregon to be designated "Wild and Scenic," this 12-mile stretch of the North Fork Malheur is a scenic dream with old-growth ponderosa pine, rugged canyon walls, and steep talus slopes. This lightly used trail starts high and ends low, drinking in Crane Creek along the way. You'll cross the river immediately at the trailhead, then follow it down through a Wild and Scenic River stretch along the west side of the river, descending 850 feet and 12.4 miles to its end on private land. Access to this end of the trail is poor, and the Forest Service recommends beginning and ending at the main trailhead.

Another option for an extended hike begins at Crane Crossing. The Crane Creek Trail connects to the North Fork Malheur 2.8 miles down from the trailhead and climbs back into the mountains 1,100 feet and 6.5 miles up a woodsy valley, following the historic roadbed of the Dalles Military Road. This trail is also accessible from an upper trailhead.

User Groups: Hikers, dogs, and horses. No mountain bikes. No wheelchair facilities.

Permits: A free self-issue Wilderness Permit

is required and is available at the trailhead. Parking and access are free.

Maps: For a map of the Malheur National Forest and Strawberry Mountain Wilderness, contact Malheur National Forest, 431 Patterson Bridge Road, John Day, OR, 97845, 541/575-3000. For a topographic map, ask the USGS for Stemler Ridge.

Directions: For the North Fork Malheur Trail, start in Prairie City, follow County Road 62 for eight miles, then turn left on Road 13 for 16.2 miles, then right on Road 16 for 2.2 miles. Turn right on Road 1675 for four rough miles, passing the North Fork Campground, to the trailhead.

To start on the upper trailhead for Crane Creek, start in Prairie City and follow Road 62 south for 23 miles to Summit Prairie. Stay left on Road 16 another 4.5 miles, then turn right on Road 1663 for one mile to Crane Creek and go left to a gate, the start of the trail.

Contact: Malheur National Forest, Prairie City Ranger District, P.O. Box 337, Prairie City, OR, 97869, 541/820-3800.

91 OREGON TRAIL INTERPRETIVE CENTER
2.6 mi/1.0 hr

east of Baker City off Highway 86

Map 10.8, page 528

Remarkably, some stretches of the Oregon Trail are preserved—nowhere better than the path below Flagstaff Hill at the Oregon Trail Interpretive Center. Paved paths, as well as a few unpaved stetches, make it easy year-round to visit an old mining site, Panorama Point, an old railroad grade, and finally down to the two ruts of the great Oregon Trail itself—complete with a covered wagon. You'll quickly see why many pioneers plopped down and said, this place will do: In the distance, the Blue Mountains rise as a formidable wall to any further progress. Baker City was founded this way, amidst the sagebrush desert of far Eastern Oregon.

After the short walk to the old Flagstaff Mine, continue one mile over Flagstaff Hill on the paved path to Panorama Point, then continue down 0.6 mile to a junction. Go straight to a bench and the covered wagon set down on the Oregon Trail. A 0.3-mile loop connects to the Eagle Valley Railroad Grade Loop Trail and continues across the paved trail on a 0.9-mile unpaved trail back to the interpretive center.

User Groups: Hikers only. No dogs, horses, or mountain bikes allowed. The 1.5-mile paved path to the Oregon Trail is wheelchair accessible.

Permits: Permits are not required. Entrance fees from April to October are $8 for two days, and $5 for two days from November to March ($4.50/$3.50 for seniors). Youth aged 15 and under are free.

Maps: A brochure map is available at the center. For a topographic map, ask the USGS for Virtue Flat.

Directions: Drive north of Baker City on I-84 to Exit 302 and drive five miles east on Highway 86 to the Oregon Trail Interpretive Center entrance road on the left.

Contact: National Historic Oregon Trail Interpretive Center, 22267 Highway 86, P.O. Box 987, Baker City, OR, 97814, 541/523-1843.

THE SOUTHERN CASCADES

© SEAN PATRICK HILL

BEST HIKES

◖ **Hikes for Kids**
Shevlin Park, **page 629.**

◖ **Hikes for Views**
The Obsidian Trail, **page 621.**
Green Lakes via Fall Creek, **page 625.**

◖ **Hikes Through Old-Growth Forests**
Lookout Creek Old-Growth Trail, **page 605.**

◖ **Self-Guided Nature Walks**
Lava Cast Forest, **page 663.**

◖ **Hikes for Waterfalls**
Sahalie and Koosah Falls, **page 604.**
Deschutes River Trail/Dillon and Benham Falls,
    page 660.

◖ **Wheelchair-Accessible Trails**
Natural Bridge and the Rogue Gorge, **page 675.**

The Cascade Mountains, extending from British

Columbia to California, make their breathtaking sweep straight through the center of the state and are home to a series of fantastic volcanic peaks and dense, old-growth forests. Here you can hike along mountain rivers, visit fire watchtowers, or climb into alpine meadows lush with summer flowers. Reach some of the highest elevations in Oregon, including a non-technical – but difficult – climb of South Sister, Oregon's third-highest peak. Don't forget Crater Lake National Park, one of the prides of the state.

To the southwest, the Siskiyou Mountains feel more like California: Open forests of ponderosa pine, a rugged granite landscape, and whitewater stretches of the Rogue River lie in an entirely different and drier climate. In this billions-of-years-old landscape, you'll find rattlesnakes, mountain lions, and the California pitcher plant, a bug-devouring oddity found in these mountains.

In these two zones, you'll find the majority of Oregon's claim to the Pacific Crest Trail. This well-maintained path traverses the edge of the Siskiyou Mountains before cutting over to the Cascades, where it passes through a bevy of wilderness areas and the national park, and along innumerable streams and lakes. Many of the trails in this section use the PCT as an entry point or a destination in and of itself. And if you like mountains, the PCT brushes by all the biggies: Mount Jefferson, Three Fingered Jack, Mount Washington, the Three Sisters, Diamond Peak, Mount Thielsen, and Mount McLoughlin. You'll skirt Crater Lake, the Sky Lakes, Odell Lake, and Waldo Lake.

Just remember that weather is finicky in these mountains. Snow typically buries many of the trails from late November until as late as July, at least for high elevations. But there is plenty of surrounding area to explore, and year-round trails abound in the foothills both east and west of the divide.

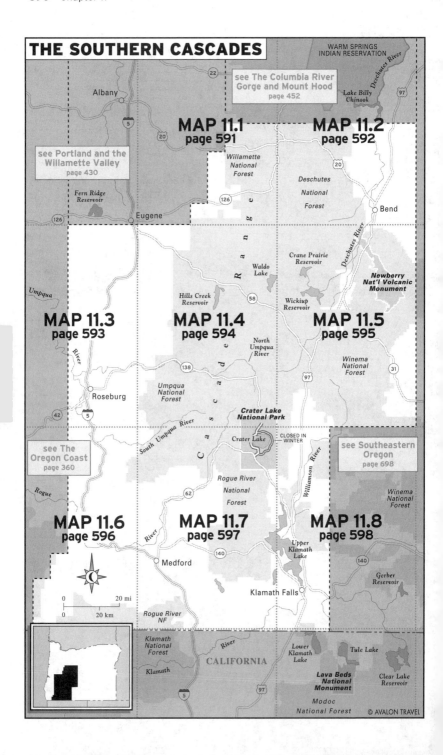

THE SOUTHERN CASCADES

WARM SPRINGS
INDIAN RESERVATION

see The Columbia River
Gorge and Mount Hood
page 452

Albany

see Portland and the
Willamette Valley
page 430

MAP 11.1
page 591

MAP 11.2
page 592

Lake Billy
Chinook

*Willamette
National
Forest*

*Deschutes
National
Forest*

Fern Ridge
Reservoir

Eugene

Bend

Crane Prairie
Reservoir

*Newberry
Nat'l Volcanic
Monument*

Waldo
Lake

Umpqua

Hills Creek
Reservoir

Wickiup
Reservoir

MAP 11.3
page 593

MAP 11.4
page 594

MAP 11.5
page 595

North
Umpqua
River

*Winema
National
Forest*

Roseburg

*Umpqua
National
Forest*

South Umpqua River

*Crater Lake
National Park*

see The
Oregon Coast
page 360

Crater Lake

CLOSED IN
WINTER

see Southeastern
Oregon
page 698

Rogue

*Winema
National
Forest*

Rogue River
National
Forest

MAP 11.6
page 596

MAP 11.7
page 597

MAP 11.8
page 598

Upper
Klamath
Lake

Gerber
Reservoir

0   20 mi

0   20 km

Medford

Rogue River
NF

Klamath Falls

Klamath
National
Forest

River

Lower
Klamath
Lake

Tule Lake

Clear Lake
Reservoir

Klamath

CALIFORNIA

*Lava Beds
National
Monument*

Modo
National Forest

© AVALON TRAVEL

Map 11.1

Hikes 1-19
Pages 599-610

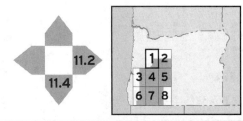

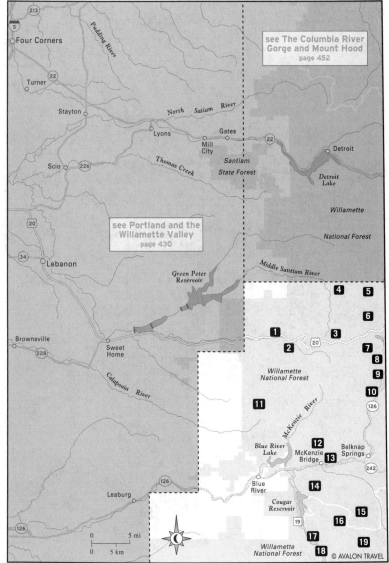

see The Columbia River Gorge and Mount Hood
page 452

see Portland and the Willamette Valley
page 430

Four Corners

Turner

Stayton

Lyons

Mill City

Gates

Detroit

Scio

Santiam State Forest

Detroit Lake

North Santiam River

Pudding River

Thomas Creek

Willamette

National Forest

Lebanon

Brownsville

Sweet Home

Green Peter Reservoir

Middle Santiam River

Calapooia River

Willamette National Forest

McKenzie River

Blue River Lake

McKenzie Bridge

Belknap Springs

Blue River

Leaburg

Cougar Reservoir

Willamette National Forest

0   5 mi
0   5 km

© AVALON TRAVEL

Map 11.2

Hikes 20-47
Pages 610-629

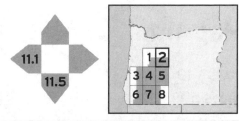

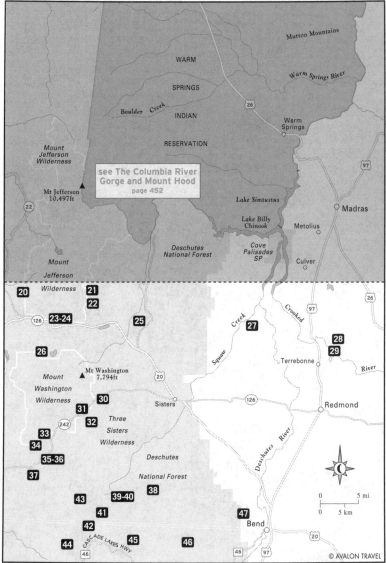

Mutton Mountains

WARM

SPRINGS

Warm Springs River

Boulder Creek

INDIAN

26

Warm Springs

97

RESERVATION

Mount Jefferson Wilderness

see The Columbia River Gorge and Mount Hood page 452

Mt Jefferson 10,497ft

22

Lake Simtustus

Madras

Lake Billy Chinook

Metolius

Deschutes National Forest

Cove Palisades SP

Culver

Mount Jefferson

20 Wilderness

21

22

126 23-24

25

26

27

97

Crooked Creek

28

29

Squaw Creek

Terrebonne

River

Mount Washington Wilderness

Mt Washington 7,794ft

20

126

Redmond

30

Sisters

31

32

Three Sisters Wilderness

242

33

34

35-36

Deschutes River

37

Deschutes National Forest

38

43

39-40

47

41

Bend

42

44 CASCADE LAKES HWY 45

46

46

20

97

46

0   5 mi
0   5 km

© AVALON TRAVEL

Map 11.3

Hike 48
Page 629

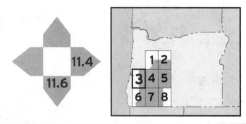

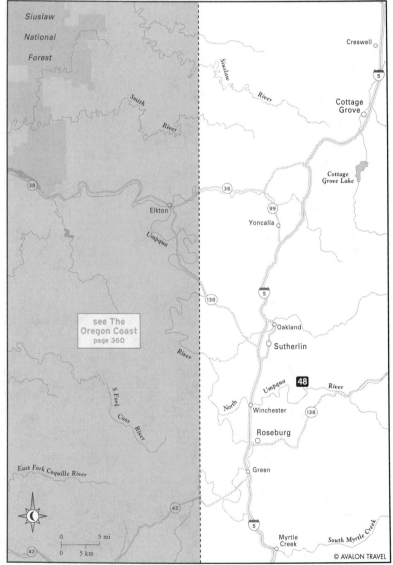

Siuslaw National Forest

Creswell

Cottage Grove

Cottage Grove Lake

Smith River

Elkton

Yoncalla

Umpqua

see The Oregon Coast page 360

Oakland

Sutherlin

North

Umpqua River

Winchester

Roseburg

S Fork Coos River

Green

East Fork Coquille River

Myrtle Creek

South Myrtle Creek

0 5 mi
0 5 km

© AVALON TRAVEL

Map 11.4

Hikes 49-93
Pages 630-658

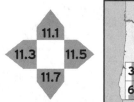

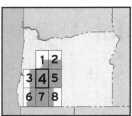

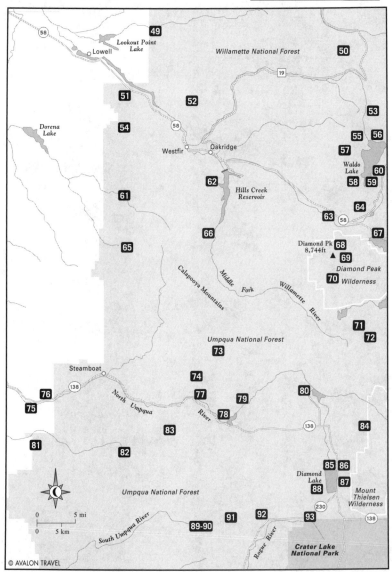

Map 11.5

Hikes 94-108
Pages 659-667

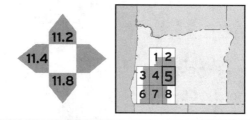

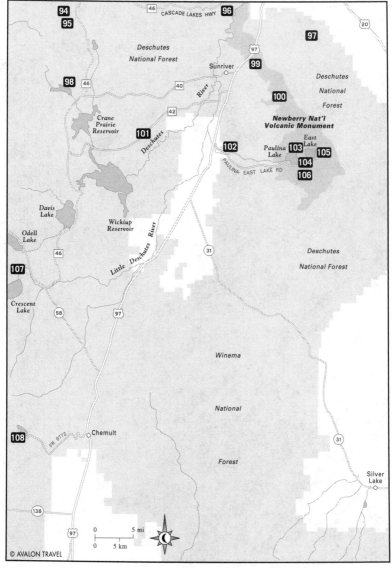

Map 11.6

Hikes 109-119
Pages 668-673

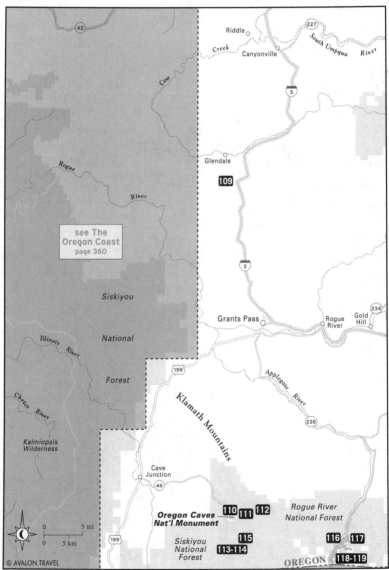

Map 11.7

Hikes 120-156
Pages 674-692

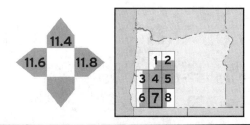

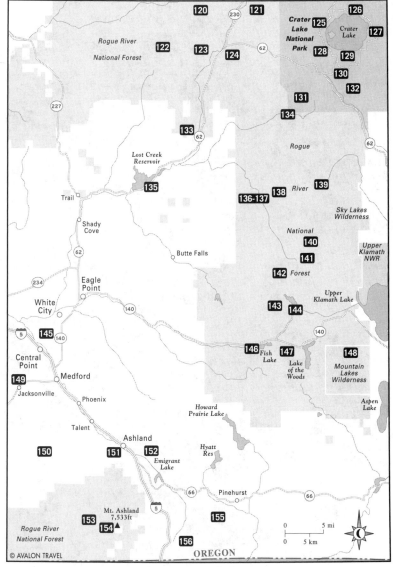

Map 11.8

Hikes 157-158
Page 693

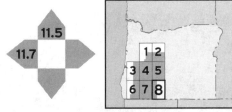

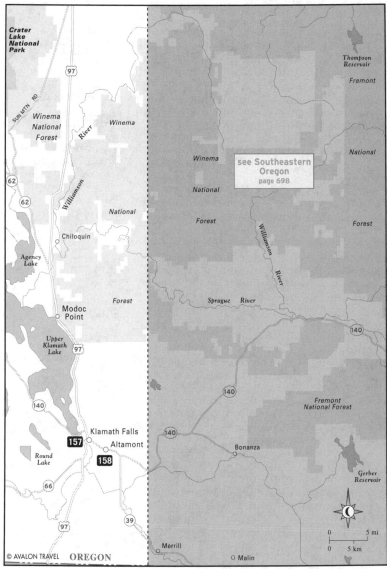

1 ROOSTER ROCK

4.2–6.6 mi/1.5–4.0 hr

west of Santiam Pass in Menagerie Wilderness

Map 11.1, page 591

This towering pillar of basalt and andesite is a popular destination for rock climbers, as are many of the spires in the Menagerie Wilderness: Rabbit Ears, Turkey Monster, Chicken Rock, The Eggs, The Siamese Twins, and the Royal Arch, to name a few. Each is a challenge in its own right. If you're not the mountain-climbing type but want to see what all the fuss is about, there are two ways in.

The shorter but harsher route is up the Rooster Rock Trailhead, climbing 1.6 miles up 1,500 feet to the junction with the Trout Creek Trail. From here, go right up 0.5 mile to a viewpoint near Rooster Rock.

The longer, but somewhat more gradual way, is from the Trout Creek Trailhead, climbing 1,600 feet over a distance of 2.8 miles to the Rooster Rock Trail, heading to the left and uphill the remaining 0.5 mile.

User Groups: Hikers and dogs. No horses or mountain bikes allowed. No wheelchair facilities.

Permits: A free self-issue Wilderness Permit is required and is available at both trailheads. Parking and access are free at the Rooster Rock Trailhead. A federal Northwest Forest Pass is required to park at the Trout Creek Trailhead; the cost is $5 a day or $30 for an annual pass. You can buy a day pass at the trailhead, at ranger stations, or through private vendors.

Maps: For a map of the Willamette National Forest and the Mount Jefferson Wilderness, contact Willamette National Forest Headquarters, 3106 Pierce Parkway, Suite D, Springfield, OR, 97477, 541/225-6300. For a topographic map, ask the USGS for Upper Soda.

Directions: From Sweet Home, go east on U.S. 20 for 21 miles just past Trout Creek Campground near milepost 49. Park at a pullout on the north side of the highway. The Rooster Rock Trailhead is 2.6 miles farther east on U.S. 20 at a pullout.

Contact: Willamette National Forest, Sweet Home Ranger District, 4431 Highway 20, Sweet Home, OR, 97386, 541/367-5168.

2 SANTIAM WAGON ROAD

4.8 mi round-trip or 19.5 mi one-way/2.5 hr–2 days

west of Santiam Pass in Willamette National Forest

Map 11.1, page 591

This stretch of the historic Santiam Wagon Road is famous not only for its history of travelers between the cattle farms of the Willamette Valley and the mining towns of Eastern Oregon, but also for a 1905 Transcontinental automobile race in which the new-fangled horseless carriages descended the steep mountains with trees tied to the autos to slow their descent of Sevenmile Hill. Some sections of the wagon trail are remarkably well preserved, while others become a jumble of logging roads. The trail can be taken in a series of segments, each with its own flavor. The entire stretch extends from the westernmost trailhead on U.S. 20 across from the Mountain House Restaurant to the easternmost trailhead at Fish Lake near the Santiam Pass, 19.5 miles in all.

The easiest and most historic route is from the trailhead across from the Mountain House Restaurant to House Rock, a 4.8-mile round-trip hike to a boulder that dwarfs everything around it and that served as shelter for entire pioneer families. Hike in 2.0 miles from Highway 20 along the most intact section of the old wagon road to the beginning of the loop, then head in either direction 0.8 mile around House Rock, located in the House Rock Campground.

To extend this segment to an 11.8-mile round-trip, continue from the loop on the Santiam Wagon Road to a viewpoint knoll atop Sevenmile Hill overlooking a canyon. Continue from the House Rock Campground 0.8 mile east to a gate, following the old wagon route. Go 0.3 mile to the left on Road 2044, cross the river, then turn right at the next gate to continue 2.3 mile to the knoll. If you continue one more mile, you will arrive at the Sevenmile Trailhead, where there are dispersed campsites. Otherwise, return as you came, bypassing the loop by staying to the left as you near the campground.

You could also start the hike by parking at the House Rock Campground, walking the 0.8-mile loop around House Rock and continuing on to the Sevenmile Knoll 3.4 miles past the loop, returning as you came.

Of course, you could continue further. The 4.2-mile stretch between Sevenmile Trailhead and Tombstone Pass has views to Iron Mountain, but the next 6.5-mile segment between Tombstone Pass and Hackleman Creek Road is not as interesting, as it follows newer roads that supplanted the original wagon road. The final 3.6-mile segment, however, follows an intact portion of the road to the trail's end at Fish Lake, where you'll find a historic guard station; note that parking is not allowed at Fish Lake, so park at the Hackleman Creek Road trailhead instead.

User Groups: Hikers, dogs, and horses. Mountain bikes allowed on some segments. No wheelchair facilities.

Permits: Permits are not required. Parking and access are free at the trailhead across from Mountain House Restaurant, House Rock Campground, and Hackleman Creek Road. A federal Northwest Forest Pass is required to park at the Sevenmile Trailhead; the cost is $5 a day or $30 for an annual pass. You can buy a day pass at the trailhead, at ranger stations, or through private vendors.

Maps: For a map of the Willamette National Forest and the Mount Jefferson Wilderness, contact Willamette National Forest Headquarters, 3106 Pierce Parkway, Suite D, Springfield, OR, 97477, 541/225-6300. For a topographic map, ask the USGS for Harter Mountain and Echo Mountain.

Directions: To begin the hike at Mountain House Restaurant, drive east from Sweet Home about 23 miles to the old restaurant between mileposts 52 and 53, going just beyond it to a parking area by a green gate on the south shoulder. To begin at House Rock Campground, drive east of Sweet Home 25 miles on U.S. 20 and turn right at a sign for House Rock Campground for 0.2 mile, then right again at the campground entrance for 0.2 mile to the trailhead. To reach the Sevenmile Trailhead, drive east of Sweet Home about 30.3 miles on U.S. 20 and turn right on spur Road 024, driving to the trailhead at road's end. The easternmost trailhead is on Hackleman Creek Road 2672, about 40 miles east of Sweet Home on U.S. 20; turn right onto Road 2672 and follow signs to the trailhead on the left.

Contact: Willamette National Forest, Sweet Home Ranger District, 4431 Highway 20, Sweet Home, OR, 97386, 541/367-5168.

3 IRON MOUNTAIN
3.4 mi/1.5 hr   🏃2 ⛰9

west of Santiam Pass in Willamette National Forest

Map 11.1, page 591

Despite its sturdy name, Iron Mountain is most famous for its wildflowers. With more than 300 species of flowering plants—including steer's head, scarlet gilia, glacier lilies, and blue flax—this peak is a designated Special Interest Area. Much of the trail follows Cone Peak, which will amaze and delight you with its array of summer colors. Bring a camera. You can visit the staffed lookout tower atop Iron Mountain's dangerous peaks. Be careful! One staffer fell to his death, and the entire tower blew off once in a winter storm. Stay away from the edge and keep a close eye on kids and dogs.

For the full loop, start at the Tombstone Pass Trailhead and go toward the nature trail and follow this 0.6 mile, crossing the highway. From here, the trail climbs 800 feet through stands of rare Alaska cedar into the meadows for 1.8 miles. From the meadows, you'll see Iron Mountain. Continue 1.5 miles along the trail to a junction. Go left and uphill, a steep 650-foot climb in 0.7 mile to the watchtower. To return, go back down Iron Mountain and take two lefts, then continue down one mile, crossing the highway again, to the Santiam Wagon Road Trail, going left 0.3 mile back to the Tombstone lot.

User Groups: Hikers and dogs. No horses or mountain bikes allowed. No wheelchair facilities.

Permits: Permits are not required. A federal Northwest Forest Pass is required to park here; the cost is $5 a day or $30 for an annual pass. You can buy a day pass at the trailhead, at ranger stations, or through private vendors.

Maps: You can purchase a Middle Santiam Wilderness Map from Geo-Graphics. For a map of the Willamette National Forest and the Mount Jefferson Wilderness, contact Willamette National Forest Headquarters, 3106 Pierce Parkway, Suite D, Springfield, OR, 97477, 541/225-6300. For a topographic map, ask the USGS for Harter Mountain.

Directions: Drive east of Sweet Home 36 miles on U.S. 20, parking at Tombstone Pass between mileposts 63 and 64.

Contact: Willamette National Forest, Sweet Home Ranger District, 4431 Highway 20, Sweet Home, OR, 97386, 541/367-5168.

4 MIDDLE SANTIAM RIVER
13.0 mi/7.0 hr   🥾3 ⛰7

northwest of Santiam Pass in Willamette National Forest

Map 11.1, page 591

Virtually hidden in the Cascade foothills beyond a maze of logging roads, the Middle Santiam Wilderness encompasses everything great about the Oregon Cascades. Of course, negotiating this area of rain-gorged creeks means several crossings without bridges. In low water, you may be able to cross on logs. If no logs are there to help, wading shoes

will help. Some of the road that skirts this wilderness area was utterly demolished in a series of landslides, extending your journey somewhat. Nevertheless, you could take this trail as far as you'd like: the Shedd Camp Shelter, Pyramid Creek, or distant Donaca Lake all make excellent destinations, depending on your endurance.

From the Chimney Peak Trailhead, it's an easy 0.7 mile to the shake-roofed shelter and the Middle Santiam River, with 20-foot Shelter Falls. From here you'll have to cross the river and continue 0.3 mile to a junction with the South Pyramid Creek Trail. Stay left another two miles to another crossing on Pyramid Creek. If you're going on, continue 0.8 mile and cross Road 2041, then head into the wilderness area for 2.7 miles to Donaca Lake, which was dammed long ago by a massive landslide—look for boulders and snags of dead trees in the lake. Return as you came.

User Groups: Hikers, dogs, and horses. No mountain bikes allowed. No wheelchair facilities.

Permits: A free self-issue Wilderness Permit is required and is available at the trailhead. Parking and access are free.

Maps: You can purchase a Middle Santiam Wilderness Map from Geo-Graphics. For a map of the Willamette National Forest and the Mount Jefferson Wilderness, contact Willamette National Forest Headquarters, 3106 Pierce Parkway, Suite D, Springfield, OR, 97477, 541/225-6300. For a topographic map, ask the USGS for Harter Mountain.

Directions: From Sweet Home, drive 24 miles east on U.S. 20. Just beyond milepost 52, turn left on Soda Fork Road 2041 and stay on this road for eight miles to a six-way junction. Go straight, staying on Road 2041 for another 4.5 miles to a three-way fork. Take the middle Road 646 for 0.6 mile to its end at a lot for the Chimney Peak Trail.

Contact: Willamette National Forest, Sweet Home Ranger District, 4431 Highway 20, Sweet Home, OR, 97386, 541/367-5168.

⑤ THE PYRAMIDS
4.0 mi/2.0 hr

northwest of Santiam Pass in Willamette National Forest

Map 11.1, page 591

Why go to Egypt when you can just come visit Oregon's version of the pyramids? These glaciated peaks in the Old Cascades, a mountain range far younger than the bigger, snow-clad peaks, provide a view stretching from Mount Hood in the north to Diamond Peak in the south. The climb to Middle Pyramid crosses terrain ranging from woodland slopes to wildflower meadows. Vanilla leaf, bleeding hearts, columbine, and the tall white lily stalks of hellebore keep you company along the way.

From the trailhead, cross a creek to the Old Cascades Crest Trail and go right uphill for 1.8 miles, steeply climbing switchbacks near the end. At a saddle, head uphill on a fainter path 0.2 mile to the 5,618-foot peak and the site of an old watchtower. Straddled between North and South Pyramid, you'll have views of the whole countryside.

User Groups: Hikers and dogs. No horses or mountain bikes allowed. No wheelchair facilities.

Permits: Permits are not required. Parking and access are free.

Maps: For a map of the Willamette National Forest and the Mount Jefferson Wilderness, contact Willamette National Forest Headquarters, 3106 Pierce Parkway, Suite D, Springfield, OR, 97477, 541/225-6300. For a topographic map, ask the USGS for Coffin Mountain.

Directions: From Salem, drive 77 miles east on OR 22. Between mileposts 76 and 77, go right on Lava Lake Meadow Road 2067 and follow this route 1.9 miles. Cross Park Creek and turn right, following a sign for the Pyramids Trail. Follow Road 560 for 3.5 miles to its end at a parking lot.

Contact: Willamette National Forest, Sweet Home Ranger District, 4431 Highway 20, Sweet Home, OR, 97386, 541/367-5168.

⑥ CRESCENT MOUNTAIN
8.6 mi/4.5 hr

west of Santiam Pass in Willamette National Forest

Map 11.1, page 591

This aptly named mountain is just what it says it is: an enormous crescent-shaped bowl rimmed by a mighty peak, cradling little Crescent Lake and its outlet creek. The views from up here encompass Three-Fingered Jack, Mount Washington, and the Three Sisters. To get to the peak, and the last remnants of a watchtower, you'll cross a broad meadow on the Old Cascades Crest Trail to the 5,750-foot summit.

Follow the Old Cascades Crest Trail 1.1 miles to a crossing of Maude Creek then begin to climb for the next 3.2 miles to Crescent Mountain's high point along a ridge of subalpine fir and mountain hemlock.

User Groups: Hikers, dogs, and horses. No mountain bikes allowed. No wheelchair facilities.

Permits: Permits are not required. Parking and access are free.

Maps: For a map of the Willamette National Forest and the Mount Jefferson Wilderness, contact Willamette National Forest Headquarters, 3106 Pierce Parkway, Suite D, Springfield, OR, 97477, 541/225-6300. For a topographic map, ask the USGS for Echo Mountain.

Directions: Drive east of Sweet Home 43 miles on U.S. 20. Near milepost 71, turn left on Lava Lake Road for one mile, then left on Road 508 for 0.7 mile to a trailhead lot.

Contact: Willamette National Forest, Sweet Home Ranger District, 4431 Highway 20, Sweet Home, OR, 97386, 541/367-5168.

7 BROWDER RIDGE
8.4 mi/5.0 hr

west of Santiam Pass in Willamette National Forest

Map 11.1, page 591

Amazing views, mountain wildflower meadows, old-growth forests... why don't people come here more often? Why ask? This summit-topping trail commands views of the Southern Cascade peaks from Jefferson to the Three Sisters, and if you're lucky you might not see another soul.

From the Gate Creek Trailhead, climb 3.1 miles up nearly 1,600 feet to a junction. Go right here, up another 0.9 mile and 250 feet along Browder Ridge. A cross-country summit is possible by climbing the last 0.2 mile the remaining 300 feet to a summit.

User Groups: Hikers, dogs, and horses. No mountain bikes allowed. No wheelchair facilities.

Permits: Permits are not required. Parking and access are free.

Maps: For a map of the Willamette National Forest and the Mount Jefferson Wilderness, contact Willamette National Forest Headquarters, 3106 Pierce Parkway, Suite D, Springfield, OR, 97477, 541/225-6300. For a topographic map, ask the USGS for Tamolitch Falls.

Directions: Drive east of Sweet Home 41 miles on U.S. 20. Near milepost 68, go south on Hackelman Creek Road for 1.7 miles, then turn right on Road 1598 for 2.8 miles to the trailhead.

Contact: Willamette National Forest, Sweet Home Ranger District, 4431 Highway 20, Sweet Home, OR, 97386, 541/367-5168.

8 CLEAR LAKE
5.4 mi/2.5 hr

southwest of Santiam Pass in Willamette National Forest

Map 11.1, page 591

The source of the wild McKenzie River is the cold Clear Lake, fed by a giant spring emerging from an ancient lava flow. The lake itself was once a forest: the lava flow dammed an ancient river and flooded this tree-filled hollow, creating a kind of ghost forest of preserved white snags beneath the calm water. This is also the topmost stretch of the McKenzie River Trail, but you can do it in a loop around the lake. You'll pass picturesque views of the lake and the mountains, and be able to spot a variety of wildflowers in the forest.

Start at the Clear Lake Resort, heading north on the trail. The first 1.5 miles curves around Ikenick Creek and meets with the sometimes dry Fish Lake Creek. In another 0.5 mile you'll come to the massive springs that feed the lake. The next 2.2 miles crosses the lava flows and passes the campground before reaching a junction. To the left, the McKenzie River Trail heads to the waterfalls, but to continue the loop go right the last 1.2 miles to the lot, watching for views to the Three Sisters and Mount Washington.

User Groups: Hikers, dogs, and bicycles. No horses allowed. No wheelchair facilities.

Permits: Permits are not required. Parking and access are free.

Maps: For a map of the Willamette National Forest, contact Willamette National Forest Headquarters, 3106 Pierce Parkway, Suite D, Springfield, OR, 97477, 541/225-6300. For a topographic map, ask the USGS for Tamolitch Falls.

Directions: Drive east on OR 126 from McKenzie Bridge 20 miles. Between mileposts 3 and 4, turn east at the Clear Lake Resort sign, driving the paved loop road 0.4 mile to the parking lot.

Contact: Willamette National Forest, McKenzie River Ranger District, 57600 McKenzie Highway, McKenzie Bridge, OR, 97413, 541/822-3381.

🟓 SAHALIE AND KOOSAH FALLS
2.6 mi/1.0 hr   🥾1 ⛰9

south of Clear Lake on the McKenzie River

Map 11.1, page 591   BEST (

In the Chinook language, a Native American trade jargon that gives many local places their colorful names, both "Sahalie" and "Koosah" mean sky or heaven—which makes these two dramatic waterfalls aptly named, as they are without a doubt two of the most beautiful waterfalls in all of Oregon. What formed them is a series of lava flows from the nearby Cascades, over which the river plunges twice before it slows behind the dam at the Carmen Reservoir. The convenient pullout and viewpoint at Sahalie Falls offers access to an excellent loop around both falls, so you can see them from opposite sides of the river. You'll also see the forest, lava outcrops, and spring trilliums and calypso orchids along the way.

From the lot, walk down to the viewpoint of double-plumed Sahalie Falls, then head downstream to the left, descending easily to sheer Koosah Falls in 0.5 mile. Keep going another 0.4 mile to the road, cross the bridge to the right, and head to the right again on the spur trail, arriving at the junction with the McKenzie River Trail. The next 1.3 miles passes the waterfalls again before arriving at an upper footbridge. Go right over the bridge, then right again for the 0.4-mile return to the pullout.

User Groups: Hikers, dogs, and bicycles. No horses allowed. There is wheelchair access to the overlook at Sahalie Falls.

Permits: Permits are not required. Parking and access are free.

Maps: For a map of the Willamette National Forest, contact Willamette National Forest

Koosah Falls on the McKenzie River

© SEAN PATRICK HILL

Headquarters, 3106 Pierce Parkway, Suite D, Springfield, OR, 97477, 541/225-6300. For a topographic map, ask the USGS for Tamolitch Falls.

Directions: Drive 19 miles east of McKenzie Bridge on OR 126. Near milepost 5, go left into the Sahalie Falls Overlook parking area.

Contact: Willamette National Forest, McKenzie River Ranger District, 57600 McKenzie Highway, McKenzie Bridge, OR, 97413, 541/822-3381.

🔟 TAMOLITCH POOL
4.2 mi/2.0 hr   🥾1 ⛰8

north of McKenzie Bridge on the McKenzie River

Map 11.1, page 591

The upper reaches of the McKenzie River were shaped by a series of 6,000-year-old lava flows that poured down from the area around Mount

Washington, shifting, damming, and even covering the river. In the stretch above Tamolitch Pool—a Chinook word for "bucket"—the McKenzie River actually runs underground for three miles, ending at this strangely empty waterfall. At the base of the seeming invisible falls, a pool composed of colors simply unimaginable lies still as the sky, a haunting blue and emerald green. At the edge of this silent pool, the river roars to life, cascading on its long journey from the mountains. A beautiful walk in a rugged canyon, this is an excellent hike for kids you want to impress.

From the Trail Bridge Reservoir road 655, head north on the McKenzie River Trail for 2.1 miles to reach the viewpoint of Tamolitch Pool, then return as you came.

User Groups: Hikers, dogs, and bicycles. No horses allowed. No wheelchair facilities.

Permits: Permits are not required. Parking and access are free.

Maps: For a map of the Willamette National Forest, contact Willamette National Forest Headquarters, 3106 Pierce Parkway, Suite D, Springfield, OR, 97477, 541/225-6300. For a topographic map, ask the USGS for Tamolitch Falls.

Directions: Drive 14 miles east of McKenzie Bridge on OR 126 to Trailbridge Reservoir, and turn left at a sign for the Trailbridge Campground. Cross the bridge and turn right on Road 655. After 0.3 mile, park at a trailhead sign.

Contact: Willamette National Forest, McKenzie River Ranger District, 57600 McKenzie Highway, McKenzie Bridge, OR, 97413, 541/822-3381.

🔢11 TIDBITS MOUNTAIN
4.0 mi/2.0 hr   🥾2   ⛰8

north of Blue River in Willamette National Forest

Map 11.1, page 591

You couldn't ask much more of a hike: views to the snow-capped peaks of the Three Sisters and all the way down to the Willamette Valley, even a close-up view of one of Tidbits' two peaks. Old-growth forests line the trail, as do flowering rhododendrons and beargrass, a type of lily, and big Cascade lilies. On top, the trail passes the ruins of an old Forest Service shelter and the remains of a stairway that you won't need to get to the top.

From the trailhead, the Tidbits Mountain Trail climbs steadily 1.3 miles to a saddle with both the shelter ruins and a trail junction. Continue to the left 0.5 mile, nearly circling Tidbits Mountain, to a four-way junction. Go left and climb 0.2 mile to the summit. You can explore around the peak a bit, too.

User Groups: Hikers, dogs, horses, and mountain bikes. No wheelchair facilities.

Permits: Permits are not required. Parking and access are free.

Maps: For a map of the Willamette National Forest, contact Willamette National Forest Headquarters, 3106 Pierce Parkway, Suite D, Springfield, OR, 97477, 541/225-6300. For a topographic map, ask the USGS for Tidbits Mountain.

Directions: From Springfield, drive 44 miles east on OR 126, passing Blue River. Near milepost 44, turn left onto Road 15, following signs for Blue River Reservoir and going 4.8 miles. At pavement's end, continue on Road 1509 for 8 miles, passing a water tank, then go left on steep Road 877 for 0.2 mile to a left-hand spur parking area.

Contact: Willamette National Forest, McKenzie River Ranger District, 57600 McKenzie Highway, McKenzie Bridge, OR, 97413, 541/822-3381.

🔢12 LOOKOUT CREEK OLD-GROWTH TRAIL
7.0 mi/3.5 hr   🥾2   ⛰6

north of McKenzie Bridge in Willamette National Forest

Map 11.1, page 591   BEST (

The H. J. Andrews Experimental Forest in the Blue River drainage is part of an ecological research program of Oregon State University and the National Science Foundation. This rugged trail enters a forest of old-growth Douglas fir, red cedar, and Pacific yew. Feel blessed that Oregon has preserved places like this for future generations; indeed, this is the whole purpose of the Experimental Forest.

Cross Lookout Creek and head into the woods. If you're looking for a turnaround point, a 3,000-foot rock pinnacle marks the 1.6-mile mark. Otherwise, it's another 1.9 miles to the end of the trail at an upper trailhead on the 1506 road.

User Groups: Hikers and dogs. No horses or mountain bikes allowed. No wheelchair access.

Permits: Permits are not required. Parking and access are free.

Maps: For a map of the Willamette National Forest, contact Willamette National Forest Headquarters, 3106 Pierce Parkway, Suite D, Springfield, OR, 97477, 541/225-6300. For a topographic map, ask the USGS for Tamolitch Falls.

Directions: From Eugene, drive 40 miles east on OR 126 to Blue River, then go beyond town three miles to FS Road 15. Turn left and go four miles to Lookout Creek Road 1506, turning right and driving seven miles to the parking area.

Contact: Willamette National Forest, McKenzie River Ranger District, 57600 McKenzie Highway, McKenzie Bridge, OR, 97413, 541/822-3381.

⃞⃞ MCKENZIE RIVER NATIONAL RECREATION TRAIL

26.5 mi one-way/2 days 　🏃3 　⛰9

between Clear Lake and McKenzie Bridge in Willamette National Forest

Map 11.1, page 591

Backpackers rejoice! This amazing stretch of the Wild and Scenic McKenzie River is brimming with not only day trips, but excellent opportunities for extended hikes. With maintained campgrounds along the way—and more primitive spots, if you can find them—it's tempting to do the whole trail. Along the way you'll find white-water rapids, hot springs, waterfalls, and lava fields culminating in the river's source at lovely Clear Lake. Access points abound along the way (see *Clear Lake, Sahalie and Koosah Falls,* and *Tamolitch Pool* listings in this chapter) and you're never too far from the road, though once you set out you'll find yourself worlds away.

Some basic mileage numbers: From the start of the trail to the McKenzie Ranger Station, a route paralleling the highway, is one mile. From the Ranger Station to Belknap Hot Springs, a private resort where you can pay to swim, is 3.9 miles, with Paradise Campground in-between. From Belknap to the natural hot springs at Deer Creek is five miles; you'll cross the river on a road and arrive at Deer Creek Road. From Deer Creek to the campground at Trail Bridge Reservoir is 3.3 miles. From Trail Bridge to Tamolitch Pool is 3.9 miles. From Tamolitch to Carmen Reservoir is 3.4 miles (along this stretch the river runs underground). From Carmen to the crossing of Highway 126, passing both Sahalie and Koosah Falls is two miles. From the highway to the upper trailhead, passing Clear Lake and Coldwater Cove Campground is four miles.

User Groups: Hikers, dogs, and bicycles. No horses allowed. No wheelchair facilities.

Permits: Permits are not required. Parking and access are free.

Maps: For a map of the Willamette National Forest, contact Willamette National Forest Headquarters, 3106 Pierce Parkway, Suite D, Springfield, OR, 97477, 541/225-6300. For a topographic map, ask the USGS for Tamolitch Falls.

Directions: To get to the lower trailhead at McKenzie Ranger Station, go 2.2 miles east of McKenzie Bridge on OR 126 and park at the station. To get to the upper trailhead, drive east on OR 126 from McKenzie Bridge about 21 miles, passing the entrance for Clear Lake Resort to the well-marked trailhead on the right.

Contact: Willamette National Forest, McKenzie River Ranger District, 57600 McKenzie Highway, McKenzie Bridge, OR, 97413, 541/822-3381.

🖪 CASTLE ROCK
2.0–11.4 mi/1.0–6.0 hr   ₂ ⚠₈

south of Blue River in Willamette National Forest

Map 11.1, page 591

There are two main ways to climb Castle Rock: the easy way and the hard way. It's a matter of both distance and elevation gain, but the end point is the same: an excellent view down to the McKenzie River canyon and east to the Three Sisters. The peak itself, the remnant of a long-extinct volcano, has sheer cliffs at the summit, and you can look down into the peaks of the Douglas fir trees. To try the easy hike, follow the driving directions and head up the trail a mere mile to the summit.

For the difficult hike, you'll start at a lower trailhead. Once on Kings Road, instead of turning onto Road 480, continue 1.3 miles past it to the trailhead on the right. From here, the King Castle Trail sets off four miles, crosses Road 480, continues up 0.7 mile through a clear-cut, then arrives at the upper trailhead, with its remaining mile to the top.

User Groups: Hikers, dogs, horses, and mountain bikes. No wheelchair facilities.

Permits: Permits are not required. Parking and access are free.

Maps: For a map of the Willamette National Forest, contact Willamette National Forest Headquarters, 3106 Pierce Parkway, Suite D, Springfield, OR, 97477, 541/225-6300. For a topographic map, ask the USGS for McKenzie Bridge.

Directions: From Springfield, drive 45 miles east on OR 126 and turn right onto the Aufderheide Road 19. At the next fork in 0.5 mile, stay straight onto Road 410, and in another 0.4 mile go left onto Kings Road 2639 for 0.5 mile. Turn right on Road 480 and continue uphill 5.8 miles to road's end at the upper trailhead.

Contact: Willamette National Forest, McKenzie River Ranger District, 57600 McKenzie Highway, McKenzie Bridge, OR, 97413, 541/822-3381.

🖪 OLALLIE MOUNTAIN/ OLALLIE RIDGE
7.2–12.2 mi/4.0–6.0 hr   ₃ ⚠₈

south of McKenzie Bridge in Three Sisters Wilderness

Map 11.1, page 591

When all is said and done, the Olallie Trail stretches 9.7 miles end to end, making this a great option for backpackers (another trailhead is located 6.0 miles away at Horsepasture Saddle; see *Horsepasture Mountain and Olallie Ridge* listing in this chapter). From this trail, you can bushwhack to a hidden lake, find the remains of an old guard station in Olallie Meadows, and climb to one of only two lookouts left in this wilderness, a 14-square-foot cabin with stunning views. Not only that, but the door is usually unlocked, opening it up for backpackers. You'll find the big metal fire locator still there, and the panoramic view is unequalled.

From Pat Saddle Trailhead, enter the Three Sisters Wilderness on the Olallie Trail. In 0.5 mile, cross Mosquito Creek (heading off-trail and upstream 0.2 mile leads to Wolverine Lake, but use your route-finding skills). Continue on the Olallie Trail 1.6 miles to a pass and junction. Head right 1.5 miles and up 700 feet to the lookout for a 7.2 mile round-trip hike, returning as you came.

Other options for extended trips abound. From the lookout tower, return to the Olallie Trail junction. Going right 0.9 mile farther leads to the guard station ruins in Olallie Meadows. In another 0.6 mile past the meadows, a left-hand junction goes 10.2 miles to Horse Lake, and the Bear Flat Trail heads to the right, making for a potential loop around Olallie Mountain by following it 6.9 miles to a junction with the French Pete Creek Trail, then heading right 2.9 mile back to the Pat Saddle Trailhead.

User Groups: Hikers, dogs, and horses. No mountain bikes allowed. No wheelchair facilities.

Permits: A free self-issue Wilderness Permit is required and is available at the trailhead. Parking and access are free.

Maps: A map of the Three Sisters Wilderness is available for purchase from Geo-Graphics. For a map of the Willamette National Forest, contact Willamette National Forest Headquarters, 3106 Pierce Parkway, Suite D, Springfield, OR, 97477, 541/225-6300. For a topographic map, ask the USGS for French Mountain.

Directions: From Springfield, drive 45 miles east on OR 126 and turn right onto the Aufderheide Road 19. At the next fork in 0.5 mile, go right on Road 19 for 10 miles to the French Pete Trailhead on the left. To begin at the top, start at the Pat Saddle Trailhead: From Springfield, drive 45 miles east on OR 126 and turn right onto the Aufderheide Road 19. At the next fork in 0.5 mile, go right on Road 19 for 2.8 miles to the reservoir. Turn left across the Cougar Dam on Road 1993 for 2.6 miles, then fork left and stay on Road 1993 another 11.3 miles to the Pat Saddle Trailhead on the left.

Contact: Willamette National Forest, McKenzie River Ranger District, 57600 McKenzie Highway, McKenzie Bridge, OR, 97413, 541/822-3381.

16 HORSEPASTURE MOUNTAIN AND OLALLIE RIDGE
2.8 mi/1.0 hr   👥1 ⛰8

south of McKenzie Bridge in Willamette National Forest

Map 11.1, page 591

One entry to the Three Sisters Wilderness is Olallie Ridge, which leads up to the boundary just before Olallie Mountain. Only the mountain retains the name Horsepasture—named because horseback wilderness rangers once camped here. The camp is long gone, though huckleberries—once harvested by Native Americans in the area—remain. Olallie, in fact, is a Chinook word for "berry."

For views as far as Mount Jefferson and Mount Hood, go left from the trailhead up 1.4 miles to the 5,660-foot summit. This easy hike also offers access to the Olallie Trail, which extends six miles from the Horsepasture Saddle to the Pat Saddle Trailhead.

User Groups: Hikers, dogs, horses, and mountain bikes. No wheelchair facilities.

Permits: Permits are not required. Parking and access are free.

Maps: A map of the Three Sisters Wilderness is available for purchase from Geo-Graphics. For a map of the Willamette National Forest, contact Willamette National Forest Headquarters, 3106 Pierce Parkway, Suite D, Springfield, OR, 97477, 541/225-6300. For a topographic map, ask the USGS for French Mountain.

Directions: From Springfield, drive 50 miles east on OR 126 to McKenzie Bridge. Cross the river and turn right on Horse Creek Road 2638 for 1.7 miles. Turn right on Road 1993 for 8.6 miles and park at the Horsepasture Trailhead on the right.

Contact: Willamette National Forest, McKenzie River Ranger District, 57600 McKenzie Highway, McKenzie Bridge, OR, 97413, 541/822-3381.

17 FRENCH PETE CREEK
9.8 mi one-way/4.0 hr   👥3 ⛰7

south of Cougar Reservoir in Three Sisters Wilderness

Map 11.1, page 591

This lovely mountain creek makes a good day hike and provides entrance to the high country. In 1.7 miles, the French Pete Trail reaches the first ford. The next 1.3 miles runs along the opposite shore to a second ford. Beyond this the trail is not maintained, but runs another 1.8 miles to the five-mile marker. From here, continue another 4.8 miles to the Pat Saddle Trailhead, following Pat Creek rather than French Pete.

User Groups: Hikers, dogs, and horses. No mountain bikes allowed. No wheelchair facilities.

Permits: A free self-issue Wilderness Permit is required and is available at the trailhead. Parking and access are free.

Maps: A map of the Three Sisters Wilderness is available for purchase from Geo-Graphics. For a map of the Willamette National Forest, contact Willamette National Forest Headquarters, 3106 Pierce Parkway, Suite D, Springfield, OR, 97477, 541/225-6300. For a topographic map, ask the USGS for Cougar Reservoir.

Directions: From Springfield, drive 45 miles east on OR 126 and turn right onto the Aufderheide Road 19. At the next fork in 0.5 mile, go right on Road 19 for 10 miles to the French Pete Trailhead on the left.

Contact: Willamette National Forest, McKenzie River Ranger District, 57600 McKenzie Highway, McKenzie Bridge, OR, 97413, 541/822-3381.

18 REBEL ROCK
12.3 mi/7.0 hr 4 8

south of Cougar Reservoir in Three Sisters Wilderness

Map 11.1, page 591

One of two lookouts left in the Three Sisters Wilderness (the other is on Olallie Mountain), Rebel Rock Lookout is perched on a 5,000-foot promontory overlooking Mount Bachelor. You won't spot this from the wooded trail, however, so you'll have to be alert for its spur trail. This loop as a whole is a great entrance to the Three Sisters country, with a trail veering off at Rebel Rock (which is not where the tower is, actually) into the deeper wilderness. This loop, though, is nothing to sneeze at: it will require some fortitude, as it travels more than 12 miles and climbs 3,300 feet along the way.

Start on the Rebel Creek Trail to the left at the trailhead, crossing two bridges and a true old-growth forest in the first 1.1 miles. The next 4.6 miles climbs away from the creek and up the canyon slope and into hemlock woods to a junction. Go right on the Rebel Rock Trail for 1.8 miles, watching to the left for the pillar of Rebel Rock. Watch for four rock cairns on the left and a faint path; follow this a short distance to the lookout. Continue on the main trail 0.5 mile to a viewpoint of the Three Sisters and Mount Jefferson. The trail descends to a meadow and continues the remaining 4.3 miles following Trail Creek back to the trailhead.

User Groups: Hikers, dogs, and horses. No mountain bikes allowed. No wheelchair facilities.

Permits: A free self-issue Wilderness Permit is required and is available at the trailhead. Parking and access are free.

Maps: A map of the Three Sisters Wilderness is available for purchase from Geo-Graphics. For a map of the Willamette National Forest, contact Willamette National Forest Headquarters, 3106 Pierce Parkway, Suite D, Springfield, OR, 97477, 541/225-6300. For a topographic map, ask the USGS for Chucksney Mountain and Grasshopper Mountain.

Directions: From Springfield, drive 45 miles east on OR 126 and turn right onto the Aufderheide Road 19. At the next fork in 0.5 mile, go right on Road 19 for 13 miles to the Rebel Creek Trailhead on the left.

Contact: Willamette National Forest, McKenzie River Ranger District, 57600 McKenzie Highway, McKenzie Bridge, OR, 97413, 541/822-3381.

19 LOWDER MOUNTAIN
5.6 mi/3.0 hr

south of McKenzie Bridge in Three Sisters
Wilderness

Map 11.1, page 591

From the summit of Lowder Mountain, you
will see mountains from the Three Sisters to
Mount Hood. You can camp on the plains
atop the peak, with its sheer drop over the
cliffs down to inaccessible Karl and Ruth
Lakes, nearly 2,000 feet below. If you choose
to camp here, be sure to bring enough water.

From the trailhead, head to the left on the
Lowder Mountain Trail (the right-hand trail
goes to a quaking aspen swamp) and go uphill,
passing through three view-laden meadows in
the first two miles. At a junction, go left and
climb steeply up a series of switchbacks for 0.5
mile. When you reach the plain, go another
0.3 mile, almost to the forest, then turn uphill
0.2 mile to the cliffs.

User Groups: Hikers, dogs, and horses. No
mountain bikes allowed. No wheelchair
facilities.

Permits: A free self-issue Wilderness Permit
is required and is available at the trailhead.
Parking and access are free.

Maps: A map of the Three Sisters Wilderness is
available for purchase from Geo-Graphics. For
a map of the Willamette National Forest, contact Willamette National Forest Headquarters,
3106 Pierce Parkway, Suite D, Springfield,
OR, 97477, 541/225-6300. For a topographic
map, ask the USGS for French Mountain.

Directions: From Springfield, drive 45 miles
east on OR 126 and turn right onto the Aufderheide Road 19. At the next fork in 0.5 mile,
go right on Road 19 for 2.8 miles to the reservoir. Turn left across the Cougar Dam on
Road 1993 for 2.6 miles, then fork left and
stay on Road 1993 another 9.2 miles to the
Lowder Mountain Trailhead on the right.

Contact: Willamette National Forest, McK-
enzie River Ranger District, 57600 McKenzie Highway, McKenzie Bridge, OR, 97413,
541/822-3381.

20 DUFFY AND MOWICH LAKES
8.8-11.8 mi/4.5-6.0 hr

west of Three Fingered Jack in Mount
Jefferson Wilderness

Map 11.2, page 592

Like all the Cascade Mountain wilderness
areas, Mount Jefferson's flanks are studded
with beautiful mountain lakes of all shapes
and sizes. In 2003, the unfortunate B&B
Complex Fire roared through this area, reducing much of the forest to snags and ash. Don't
let that stop you: This area is still untouched
in places, and the lakes are as cool and clear
as ever. Two lakes lie along this entrance to
backpacking adventures: Duffy Lake, below
the pointed peak of Duffy Butte, and Mowich
Lake, with one side untouched by fire. From
little Alice Lake you can climb Red Butte and
continue on to the Eight Lakes Basin. Or, you
can head to nearby Santiam Lake for a stunning view of Three Fingered Jack.

From the trailhead, follow the Duffy Trail
along the North Santiam River bed up 3.3
miles, staying left at a junction, to Duffy
Lake. From here, continue along Duffy Lake,
keeping to the left 1.1 miles to Mowich Lake,
then another mile to Alice Lake. An obvious
cross-country path climbs 0.5 mile up Red
Butte here. From there, the Blue Lake Trail
continues on to Eight Lakes Basin.

For a look at the alpine meadows around
Santiam Lake, source of the North Santiam
River, start from the outlet of Duffy Lake and
go 0.2 mile to a spur trail on the right, following it one mile to Santiam Lake at the bottom
of Three Fingered Jack's long slope from its
craggy heights.

User Groups: Hikers, dogs, and horses. No
mountain bikes allowed. No wheelchair
facilities.

Permits: A free self-issue Wilderness Permit
is required and is available at the trailhead.
Parking and access are free.

Maps: You can purchase a Mount Jefferson
Wilderness Map from Geo-Graphics. For a

map of the Willamette National Forest and the Mount Jefferson Wilderness, contact Willamette National Forest Headquarters, 3106 Pierce Parkway, Suite D, Springfield, OR, 97477, 541/225-6300. For a topographic map, ask the USGS for Santiam Junction.

Directions: From Salem, drive 76 miles east on OR 22. Near milepost 76, turn east on Big Meadows Road 2267 for three miles to road's end.

Contact: Willamette National Forest, Detroit Ranger District, HC73, Box 320, Mill City, OR, 97360, 503/854-4239.

21 ROCKPILE LAKE

10.8-13.2 mi/4.0-6.0 hr

north of Three Fingered Jack in Mount Jefferson Wilderness

Map 11.2, page 592

The 2003 B&B Complex Fire truly devastated this area, so you'll need to confirm trail conditions before hiking in these parts. Rockpile Lake Trail follows the massive Bear Valley steadily up to the Pacific Crest Trail and little Rockpile Lake, with access in either direction to great views along the Cascade Crest. If trails are in working order, it is possible to do a great loop around Bear Valley, stopping by little Minto Lake along the way.

From the trailhead follow the Rockpile Lake Trail to the right. In 0.3 mile, stay left at a junction, then stay left again in another 2.3 mile. From the second junction, climb steadily for 2.8 miles up 1,000 feet to the Pacific Crest Trail and Rockpile Lake to the right. Return as you came.

If the loop trail is open, and if you'd like to follow some stunning vistas along this high ridge, head south on the PCT for 3.4 miles to Minto Lake on the right. To the left, the Bear Valley Trail descends 4.4 miles into huckleberry groves and past Bear Valley Lake to the trailhead.

User Groups: Hikers, dogs, and horses. No mountain bikes allowed. No wheelchair facilities.

Permits: A free self-issue Wilderness Permit is required and is available at the trailhead. Parking and access are free.

Maps: You can purchase a Mount Jefferson Wilderness Map from Geo-Graphics. For a map of the Deschutes National Forest and the Mount Jefferson Wilderness, contact Deschutes National Forest Headquarters, 1001 SW Emkay Drive, Bend, OR, 97702, 541/383-5300. For a topographic map, ask the USGS for Marion Lake.

Directions: From Sisters, drive 12 miles west on U.S. 20 to about milepost 88. Turn right on Road 12 at a sign for Mount Jefferson Wilderness Trailheads. Drive north 3.7 miles on Road 12 and continue straight on Road 1230 for 1.5 miles, then turn left on Road 1234 for 0.8 mile. Turn right on Road 1235 for 3.9 miles to road's end.

Contact: Deschutes National Forest, Sisters Ranger District, P.O. Box 249, Sisters, OR, 97759, 541/549-7700.

22 CANYON CREEK MEADOWS

7.5 mi/4.0 hr

east of Three Fingered Jack in Mount Jefferson Wilderness

Map 11.2, page 592

For a worthy alpine meadow experience, and to get a look at a glacial-silt lake among an array of wildflowers, the Canyon Creek Meadows is it. By the grace of nature, the meadows were spared by the 2003 fire that decimated other parts of the wilderness, including the area around Jack Lake and the trailhead here. Did I mention you will also be standing beneath the towering crags of Three Fingered Jack? The creek begins in a cirque in the bowl of the mountain, surrounded by gravel walls. This trail, going from burn to forest to meadow to alpine rockfall, even a pitch to a saddle with a view over the mountain range to the south, allows you to visit just about every kind of ecosystem in this range. The meadows, too, are suitable for backpacking.

From Jack Lake, head up the Wasco Lake Trail 0.4 mile to a junction. Here the trail splits into the Canyon Creek Meadows Loop, and the USFS asks that you go to the left first, and return on the opposite loop. So go left 1.7 miles, leaving the burn and reaching the lower meadow. Go left another 1.5 miles, reaching the upper meadow and an alpine wonderland. If you follow the trail to the end, you'll climb a ridge above the meadows, climbing steeply to the saddle on the shoulder of the mountain. When you return, go left at the loop junction. Head 0.9 mile along the creek to a junction. If you'd like to visit Wasco Lake, go left 0.7 mile, watching for the waterfalls off the trail. Then return to this junction and go right 1.5 miles back to Jack Lake.

User Groups: Hikers, dogs, and horses. No mountain bikes allowed. No wheelchair facilities.

Permits: A free self-issue Wilderness Permit is required and is available at the trailhead. A federal Northwest Forest Pass is required to park here; the cost is $5 a day or $30 for an annual pass. You can buy a day pass at the trailhead, at ranger stations, or through private vendors.

Maps: You can purchase a Mount Jefferson Wilderness Map from Geo-Graphics. For a map of the Deschutes National Forest and the Mount Jefferson Wilderness, contact Deschutes National Forest Headquarters, 1001 SW Emkay Drive, Bend, OR, 97702, 541/383-5300. For a topographic map, ask the USGS for Three Fingered Jack.

Directions: From Sisters, drive 12 miles west on U.S. 20 to about milepost 88. Turn right on Road 12 at a sign for Mount Jefferson Wilderness Trailheads. Drive north 3.7 miles on Road 12 and continue straight on Road 1230 for 1.5 miles, then turn left on Road 1234 and going five miles to the trailhead at Jack Lake Campground.

Contact: Deschutes National Forest, Sisters Ranger District, P.O. Box 249, Sisters, OR, 97759, 541/549-7700.

⧉ PACIFIC CREST TRAIL TO THREE FINGERED JACK
10.5 mi/5.5 hr

south of Three Fingered Jack in Mount Jefferson Wilderness

Map 11.2, page 592

Three Fingered Jack is a dark-hued volcanic core that resembles a frightening fortress. It rises abruptly from the surrounding mountains and practically begs rock climbers to try their luck. Most likely, one look will make you lose all nerve. Instead, this Pacific Crest Trail stretch offers a commanding look at this massive peak, and an entrance to the Mount Jefferson Wilderness. The forest was burned here in a 2003 fire, but that opened up the views as this trail follows the ridgeline. From the PCT trailhead, follow the PCT north 5.2 miles to a close-up viewpoint of the mountain. From there, you can return the way you came—or continue on as far as you like.

User Groups: Hikers, dogs, and horses. No mountain bikes allowed. No wheelchair facilities.

Permits: A free self-issue Wilderness Permit is required and is available at the trailhead. A federal Northwest Forest Pass is required to park here; the cost is $5 a day or $30 for an annual pass. You can buy a day pass at the trailhead, at ranger stations, or through private vendors.

Maps: You can purchase a Mount Jefferson Wilderness Map from Geo-Graphics. For a map of the Willamette National Forest and the Mount Jefferson Wilderness, contact Willamette National Forest Headquarters, 3106 Pierce Parkway, Suite D, Springfield, OR, 97477, 541/225-6300. For a topographic map, ask the USGS for Three Fingered Jack.

Directions: The trailhead is located 20 miles west of Sisters on U.S. 20 at the Santiam Pass, accessible from either Sisters to the east or Eugene/Springfield/OR 126 or OR 22/Salem to the east.

Contact: Willamette National Forest, Detroit Ranger District, HC73, Box 320, Mill City, OR, 97360, 503/854-4239.

24 BERLEY AND SANTIAM LAKES
10.2 mi/4.5 hr

south of Three Fingered Jack in Mount Jefferson Wilderness

Map 11.2, page 592

The original trail to these lakes, which began at the ruins of the abandoned Santiam Lodge, was permanently closed after the 2003 wildfire that decimated this section of the Mount Jefferson Wilderness. There is another way to get to the two rock-rimmed tarns known as the Berley Lakes and to picturesque Santiam Lake at the base of Three Fingered Jack. This trail runs along a section of the Skyline Trail.

From the PCT trailhead on U.S. 20, go north 1.2 miles to a left-hand junction and go left 0.5 mile on this connector trail. Then go right 1.5 miles on the Santiam Lake Trail and watch for an unmarked turnoff to the left heading 0.3 mile to and along the lower and larger Berley Lake; follow this trail to another side trail and find the upper lake. Return to the Santiam Trail and go left another 1.9 miles to a right-hand turnoff for Santiam Lake.

User Groups: Hikers, dogs, and horses. No mountain bikes allowed. No wheelchair facilities.

Permits: A free self-issue Wilderness Permit is required and is available at the trailhead. A federal Northwest Forest Pass is required to park here; the cost is $5 a day or $30 for an annual pass. You can buy a day pass at the trailhead, at ranger stations, or through private vendors.

Maps: You can purchase a Mount Jefferson Wilderness Map from Geo-Graphics. For a map of the Willamette National Forest and the Mount Jefferson Wilderness, contact Willamette National Forest Headquarters, 3106 Pierce Parkway, Suite D, Springfield, OR,

97477, 541/225-6300. For a topographic map, ask the USGS for Santiam Lake.

Directions: The trailhead is located 20 miles west of Sisters on U.S. 20 at the Santiam Pass, accessible from either Sisters to the east or Eugene/Springfield/OR 126 or OR 22/Salem to the east.

Contact: Willamette National Forest, Detroit Ranger District, HC73, Box 320, Mill City, OR, 97360, 503/854-4239.

25 BLACK BUTTE
3.8 mi/2.5 hr

north of Sisters in Deschutes National Forest

Map 11.2, page 592

Set aside to the east of the bulk of the Cascades, Black Butte seems an oddball mountain. For one thing, this dominant 6,436-foot butte retains its perfectly symmetrical shape, a huge rounded mound set near peaks far more eroded than its stern face. This has less to do with age than with weather: the peaks to the west create a rainshadow that has largely kept this mountain from being weathered. This makes for a fairly easy climb, which explains why Black Butte hosts one of the few surviving fire watchtowers in the Cascade Mountains, with a view worth a summer spent spotting fires. Atop Black Butte, you can check out the old cupola-style lookout and get a glimpse of the new one. A second lookout built by the Civilian Conservation Corps in 1934 was destroyed in a storm. Beyond the edges of the peak, you'll have an expansive view of the Cascades, Green Ridge, and the Metolius River far below.

The trail is a straightforward lunge for the peak up 1.9 miles of trail that climbs steadily, even steeply at times. Follow it through the ponderosa pine forests onto the open prairies of wildflowers.

User Groups: Hikers, dogs, and horses. No mountain bikes allowed. No wheelchair facilities.

Permits: A federal Northwest Forest Pass is

© SEAN PATRICK HILL

historic Black Butte lookout

required to park here; the cost is $5 a day or $30 for an annual pass. You can buy a day pass at the trailhead, at ranger stations, or through private vendors.

Maps: For a map of the Deschutes National Forest contact Deschutes National Forest Headquarters, 1001 SW Emkay Drive, Bend, OR, 97702, 541/383-5300. For a topographic map, ask the USGS for Black Butte.

Directions: From Sisters, drive 5.5 miles west on U.S. 20 to Green Ridge Road 11. Turn right and follow this road north 3.8 miles, then turn left on Road 1110, following it 5.1 miles uphill to the parking area at road's end.

Contact: Deschutes National Forest, Sisters Ranger District, P.O. Box 249, Sisters, OR, 97759, 541/549-7700.

26 PATJENS LAKES
6.0 mi/3.0 hr   🏃2 ⛰8

at Big Lake in Mount Washington Wilderness

Map 11.2, page 592

Big Lake earns its name and makes for a destination for car campers and, in the winter,

cross-country skiers. For hikers, adventure lies beyond the big lake in the Mount Washington Wilderness, with meadows, ponds, slopes of bracken ferns, and the Patjens Lakes hidden nicely back in Hidden Valley, with its view of Mount Washington's spire. The Patjens Lake Loop Trail follows the shore of Big Lake too, past a beach and towards views of broad and flat-topped Hayrick Butte. For backpackers, this makes a good entry into this little-explored wilderness.

From the trailhead, follow signs for Patjens Lakes, staying right at the first junction and left at the second for 1.8 miles to a saddle. Continue 1.7 miles into the midst of the lakes, the third of four being a perfect place to stop and eat. Continue 1.5 miles through Hidden Valley to a beach on Big Lake, going left along the shore one mile back to the trailhead.

User Groups: Hikers, dogs, and horses. No mountain bikes allowed. No wheelchair facilities.

Permits: A free self-issue Wilderness Permit is required and is available at the trailhead. Parking and access are free.

Maps: For a map of the Willamette National

Forest and the Mount Washington Wilderness, contact Willamette National Forest Headquarters, 3106 Pierce Parkway, Suite D, Springfield, OR, 97477, 541/225-6300. For a topographic map, ask the USGS for Clear Lake.

Directions: Drive U.S. 20 to the Santiam Pass and turn south on Big Lake Road four miles to a trailhead on the right.

Contact: Willamette National Forest, McKenzie River Ranger District, 57600 McKenzie Highway, McKenzie Bridge, OR, 97413, 541/822-3381.

27 ALDER SPRINGS
6.0 mi/2.5 hr

northeast of Sisters in Crooked River National Grassland

Map 11.2, page 592

The creek formerly known as "Squaw Creek" is now called "Whychus Creek," derived from a Sahaptin word meaning "the place we cross the water." It's a fitting name for this hike, since you'll have to ford the creek to travel this trail in a remote canyon down to its confluence with the Deschutes River. Along the way the trail passes a dry waterfall and a massive spring that flows out of a cliff and down through a grove of alder into the main creek. At the confluence, note the incredible rock formations high on the canyon walls, and watch for more springs.

From the trailhead, go downhill on the Alder Springs Trail to a junction in 0.2 mile, continuing to the right for 1.2 miles along the canyon rim and finally down to the creek itself. Ford the creek and continue 1.6 miles downstream on the opposite shore to the confluence of the Deschutes and its massive, water-smoothed boulders.

User Groups: Hikers and dogs on leash only. No horses or mountain bikes. No wheelchair facilities.

Permits: Permits are not required. Parking and access are free.

Maps: For a topographic map, ask the USGS for Steelhead Falls.

Directions: From Sisters, drive east on U.S. 20 and veer left on OR 126 toward Redmond. Go 4.6 miles and turn left on Goodrich Road for 8.1 miles. At milepost 7, go left on Road 6360 through a green gate (remember to close the gate behind you). Go 4.1 miles and turn right at an Alder Springs sign, going 0.8 mile to road's end.

Contact: Crooked River National Grassland, 813 SW Highway 97, Madras, OR, 97741, 541/475-9272.

28 GRAY BUTTE
4.8-7.1 mi/2.5-3.0 hr

north of Redmond in Crooked River National Grassland

Map 11.2, page 592

The lopsided pyramid that looms behind the crags of Smith Rock State Park is Gray Butte, and this not-well-known trailhead offers a free entrance to Smith Rock State Park (see next listing). From the saddle between the butte and the ridge that gently slopes down to the Crooked River canyon, this vista-rich trail looks out over the desert and Cascade Mountains and crosses a pass where you can find rare bitterroot flowers in spring. The root of these tiny flowers provided Native Americans with a valuable food.

From the Gray Butte Saddle Trailhead, follow the trail away from Gray Butte 1.4 miles to a pass. Pass by the dirt roads and continue one mile to the dirt Burma Road. You can continue on an unofficial trail to a viewpoint and along the ridge into Smith Rock, a 1.5-mile walk to the Crooked River.

A longer tour, perhaps better for mountain bikes, especially in summer, loops for a 7.1-mile ride around Gray Butte itself. From the Gray Butte Saddle Trailhead, go back to the four-way junction and go straight on a dirt road. The trail crosses this road, circling the butte. The longest stretch of walking trail goes 3.4 mile to the left, ending at the McCoin Orchard Trailhead. From here follow Road 57 down 0.7 mile, veering right on Road 5710 for 1.4 miles, then going right again on Road 5720 over the cattle guard and veering off on the trail to the right for the remaining 1.6 miles.

User Groups: Hikers, dogs, horses, and mountain bikes. No wheelchair facilities.

Permits: Permits are not required. Parking and access are free.

Maps: For a topographic map, ask the USGS for Gray Butte.

Directions: From Redmond, drive six miles north on U.S. 97 to Terrebonne and a sign for Smith Rock State Park. Turn east on Smith Rock Way for 5.9 miles to a junction, and go left on Lone Pine Road for 3.4 miles. At a sign for Gray Butte Trailhead go left on Road 5720 for 1.6 miles to a four-way junction. Turn left and park on the right by the trailhead.

Contact: Crooked River National Grassland, 813 SW Highway 97, Madras, OR, 97741, 541/475-9272.

29 SMITH ROCK STATE PARK

3.7-6.3 mi/1.5-3.5 hr 🥾3 ⛰9

north of Redmond

Map 11.2, page 592

In a state rich with state parks, Smith Rock ranks in the upper echelon. Simply put, this is one of Oregon's most magnificent parks, an intense land of river canyon, rock formations, wildlife, and ponderosa pines. What makes it famous is its allure to rock climbers, and on any given spring, summer, or fall day—sometimes even winter, one of the best times to hike here—you're sure to see climbers on the many dizzying walls. The kingpin of these climbs is the welded tuff ash formation known as Monkey Face, which, from the right angle, resembles exactly that. Within view of all the climbing, aeries of golden eagles nestle in the cliff faces. Deer wander here, as do coyote and other animals. And arcing gracefully through it all is the Crooked River, oxbowing around this one-of-a-kind rock formation. You can easily spend a full day here, or two, and a walk-in campground for backpackers and climbers makes that a temptation. Two hikes crown the

Smith Rock State Park

© SEAN PATRICK HILL

park and visit everything you could want to see. Just be aware of the dangers here; people have died in this park by falling from the cliffs. Play it safe and stay on the trail.

To climb over Misery Ridge and visit Monkey Face close up, start from the parking area and descend 0.4 mile into the canyon and cross the footbridge. Continue to the left and up the Misery Ridge Trail 0.5 mile up staircases and a steep trail to the crest. Follow the trail to a junction, where a left-hand user trail goes down a ridge to a view of Monkey Face. You should not attempt this if you are afraid of heights. Continue on the Misery Ridge Trail down the opposite side of the ridge on a long series of steep switchbacks, then along the cliffs above the river to a junction with the river trail, 0.7 mile in all. From here you can explore at whim; going left along the river 1.7 miles will bring you back to the footbridge and the remaining 0.4 mile to the lot.

For a longer walk, hike 0.4 mile to the footbridge and follow the river downstream 2.2 miles, passing the climbing walls and huge boulders. Past Monkey Face and at a huge boulder, turn right up a path climbing a steep gully, following it 1.5 miles up and along the ridge to the Burma Road. From the road, going straight leads to Gray Butte (see listing in this chapter). For the loop, go right on Burma Road and descend back into the canyon 0.7 mile to the trail junction on the right, and follow this trail 1.1 mile back to the footbridge and the remaining 0.4 mile back to the parking lot.

User Groups: Hikers and dogs on leash only. No horses or mountain bikes. No wheelchair facilities.

Permits: Permits are not required. A $3 day-use fee is collected at a self-serve kiosk, or you can get an annual Oregon Parks and Recreation pass for $25; contact Oregon Parks and Recreation, 800/551-6949.

Maps: For a free park brochure, call Oregon Parks and Recreation, 800/551-6949, or download a free map at www.oregonstateparks.org. For a topographic map, ask the USGS for Gray Butte.

Directions: From Redmond, drive six miles north on U.S. 97 to Terrebonne and a sign for Smith Rock State Park. Turn east on Smith Rock Way and follow signs 3.3 miles to the parking area.

Contact: Oregon Parks and Recreation Department, 1115 Commercial Street Northeast, Salem, OR, 97301, 800/551-6949, www.oregonstateparks.org.

🔟 PACIFIC CREST TRAIL TO LITTLE BELKNAP CRATER

5.2 mi/2.5 hr   👥2 ⛰9

in the McKenzie Pass in Mount Washington Wilderness

Map 11.2, page 592

If you want to get a sense of what walking on a barren planet like, say, Mars is like (especially after the photographs from that red planet), all you have to do is walk onto the McKenzie Pass. At first view of these lava fields, it's hard not to be shocked. You'll feel a certain awe here, as the size of these flows staggers the imagination. You'll have a whole new respect for those that built the Pacific Crest Trail, carving its route over the black, jumbled basalt. You'll also get a sense of what volcanics really look like up close. An easy tour heads out onto the flow toward the Little Belknap Crater. Atop its knob, a series of lava caves plunge into the peak, and the views extend to far bigger Belknap Crater and Mount Washington and the Sisters. With a sharp eye you can spot "lava bombs"—which solidified in the shapes of tears as they were hurled through the air. Bring plenty of sunblock and water on this trail, especially in summer.

From the PCT trailhead, head north. The trail begins at the foot of a forested island in the lava, then crosses a second island, the trail heading 2.4 miles to the Little Belknap Crater. A cairn marks the right-hand side trail that climbs 0.2 mile up the crater. The PCT continues on along the base of Mount Washington and rises to the Santiam Pass.

User Groups: Hikers, dogs, and horses. No mountain bikes allowed. No wheelchair facilities.

Permits: A free self-issue Wilderness Permit is required and is available at the trailhead. A federal Northwest Forest Pass is required to park here; the cost is $5 a day or $30 for an annual pass. You can buy a day pass at the trailhead, at ranger stations, or through private vendors.

Maps: For a map of the Deschutes National Forest and the Mount Washington Wilderness, contact Deschutes National Forest Headquarters, 1001 SW Emkay Drive, Bend, OR, 97702, 541/383-5300. For a topographic map, ask the USGS for Mount Washington.

Directions: From McKenzie Bridge, drive east on OR 126 to the McKenzie Pass Highway 242. Follow the highway to a trailhead sign near milepost 77. From Sisters, drive OR 242 west 0.5 mile beyond the McKenzie Pass.

Contact: Deschutes National Forest, Sisters Ranger District, P.O. Box 249, Sisters, OR, 97759, 541/549-7700.

31 BLACK CRATER
7.4 mi/4.0 hr   🥾4 ⛰9

in the McKenzie Pass in Three Sisters Wilderness

Map 11.2, page 592

From the town of Sisters, the massive silhouette of Black Crater is imposing and dominant on the skyline. This monumental volcanic peak, carved into 500-foot-cliffs atop its peak by Ice Age glaciers, is a killer climb. From the top, you'll secure a view extending from Mount Hood to the Three Sisters atop a windswept peak of stunted, whitebark pine—one of the best views of the High Cascades anywhere.

The Black Crater Trail climbs 2,500 feet in 3.7 miles, crossing a glacier-carved valley on the crater's flank then climbing steeply up switchbacks to the craggy peak.

User Groups: Hikers, dogs, and horses. No

mountain bikes allowed. No wheelchair facilities.

Permits: A free self-issue Wilderness Permit is required and is available at the trailhead. A federal Northwest Forest Pass is required to park here; the cost is $5 a day or $30 for an annual pass. You can buy a day pass at the trailhead, at ranger stations, or through private vendors.

Maps: A map of the Three Sisters Wilderness is available for purchase from Geo-Graphics. For a map of the Deschutes National Forest and the Three Sisters Wilderness, contact Deschutes National Forest Headquarters, 1001 SW Emkay Drive, Bend, OR, 97702, 541/383-5300. For a topographic map, ask the USGS for Black Crater.

Directions: From Sisters, drive west on the McKenzie Pass Highway 242. Between mileposts 80 and 81, turn left into the Black Crater Trailhead parking area.

Contact: Deschutes National Forest, Sisters Ranger District, P.O. Box 249, Sisters, OR, 97759, 541/549-7700.

32 PACIFIC CREST TRAIL TO MATTHIEU LAKES
6.0 mi/3.0 hr   🥾2 ⛰7

in the McKenzie Pass in Three Sisters Wilderness

Map 11.2, page 592

Although you could enter the Three Sisters Wilderness at the McKenzie Pass trailhead for the Pacific Crest Trail, that would result in a longer walk over black, jagged lava. A closer trailhead reaches the PCT quickly and sets out north for a loop around the two Matthieu Lakes. The northern lake is set in a deep forest, but the southern lake, the smaller one, is set high in Scott Pass with views to North Sister. Both of these lakes make for good camps (though regulations require that camps be 250 feet from the shore), and the swimming here is exquisite. It also makes for a launching point to other explorations including the Scott Trail and the mountains themselves.

From the Lava Camp Trailhead, set out toward the PCT for 0.2 mile and go left. Follow the PCT 0.7 mile to a junction. Get the high ground out of the way and go to the left on the PCT for 2.1 miles, with views down to North Matthieu Lake. At the next junction, go left on the PCT toward Scott Pass and South Matthieu Lake. To continue farther, note that the next junction splits; to the left, access to distant Green Lakes, and to the right the PCT continues toward Yapoah Crater and the Scott Trail. To return, go back to the junction before South Matthieu and go left 0.7 mile on the North Matthieu Lake Trail to reach the lower lake. Continue 1.4 miles to return to the PCT and the 0.9 mile back to the trailhead.

User Groups: Hikers, dogs, and horses. No mountain bikes allowed. No wheelchair facilities.

Permits: A free self-issue Wilderness Permit is required and is available at the trailhead. A federal Northwest Forest Pass is required to park here; the cost is $5 a day or $30 for an annual pass. You can buy a day pass at the trailhead, at ranger stations, or through private vendors.

Maps: A map of the Three Sisters Wilderness is available for purchase from Geo-Graphics. For a map of the Deschutes National Forest and the Three Sisters Wilderness, contact Deschutes National Forest Headquarters, 1001 SW Emkay Drive, Bend, OR, 97702, 541/383-5300. For a topographic map, ask the USGS for North Sister.

Directions: From Sisters, drive west on the McKenzie Pass Highway 242. Near milepost 78, turn left at a sign for Lava Lake Camp and follow Road 900 for 0.3 mile, then turn right for the PCT parking.

Contact: Deschutes National Forest, Sisters Ranger District, P.O. Box 249, Sisters, OR, 97759, 541/549-7700.

33 HAND LAKE AND OLD MCKENZIE WAGON ROAD
2.6 mi/1.0 hr 🏃1 ⛰7

in the McKenzie Pass in Mount Washington Wilderness

Map 11.2, page 592

Though you can visit Hand Lake via the Benson Trail (see *Benson Lake and Scott Mountain,* next listing), it's easy to get there from the highway trailhead. This way you can spend a little time here exploring this strange lake that pools up against a rugged lava flow, and a piece of the old McKenzie Wagon Road chipped through that same flow by John Craig in 1871, meant to be a shortcut. You'll have to go off trail to find it, but with a landmark as substantial as this lava flow it presents no problem.

The stretch of hike goes an easy 0.5 mile along the Hand Lake Trail into the wilderness to the Hand Lake Shelter, with its view of Hand Lake and two of the Three Sisters. At a junction, go right (the left leads to Scott Lake and its campground) and walk 0.6 mile along the lake and lava flow. Watch for a series of rock cairns and the 15-foot-wide berth in the flow to the right. Cross on this old wagon road then follow the flow to the right, eventually finding Hand Lake again in one mile. Return the 0.5 mile to the trailhead.

User Groups: Hikers, dogs, and horses. No mountain bikes allowed. No wheelchair facilities.

Permits: A free self-issue Wilderness Permit is required and is available at the trailhead. Parking and access are free.

Maps: For a map of the Willamette National Forest and the Mount Washington Wilderness, contact Willamette National Forest Headquarters, 3106 Pierce Parkway, Suite D, Springfield, OR, 97477, 541/225-6300. For a topographic map, ask the USGS for North Sister.

Directions: From McKenzie Bridge, drive east on OR 126 to the McKenzie Pass Highway 242. Follow the highway to a trailhead sign between mileposts 72 and 73. From Sisters, drive OR 242 west 4.5 miles beyond the McKenzie Pass.

Contact: Willamette National Forest, McKenzie River Ranger District, 57600 McKenzie Highway, McKenzie Bridge, OR, 97413, 541/822-3381.

34 BENSON LAKE AND SCOTT MOUNTAIN
8.2-9.7 mi/4.0-4.5 hr   🥾3   ⛰9

in the McKenzie Pass in Mount Washington Wilderness

Map 11.2, page 592

When summer in the Central Oregon desert heats up, it's good to know that easy respite lies in any one of the mountain lakes strewn over the Cascade Crest. Benson Lake, for one, is a swimmer's dream: cold, clear, and deep. Beyond Benson Lake are even more lakes, the congregation of little pools known as the Tenas Lakes, set atop a plateau with a view out over the western range. If that's not enough of a day, try climbing Scott Mountain for an amazing view over the lava-rubble fields of the McKenzie Pass, with a perfect view of six Cascade peaks. To lengthen the trail even further, you can link to a loop past Hand Lake (see *Hand Lake and Old McKenzie Wagon Road,* previous listing) for a 9.7-mile jaunt that's great for backpacking.

Start out from the lot at Scott Lake and follow the Benson Trail straight for 1.4 miles to broad Benson Lake. In another 1.1 miles, the trail reaches a left-hand spur to the Tenas Lakes, a series of lovely rock bowls. To climb Scott Mountain, continue on 0.9 mile, staying right at a junction leading to The Knobs, to another junction on Scott Mountain itself. From here, go left and up 300 feet and 0.7 mile to the peak. This makes a fine turnaround point for the 8.2-mile hike, but you could continue on the Benson Trail another 1.8 miles to a junction, then go right 1.6 miles to Hand Lake, and continue to the right past

the shelter for the remaining 1.5 miles to Scott Lake, making for a 9.7-mile loop.

User Groups: Hikers, dogs, and horses. No mountain bikes allowed. No wheelchair facilities.

Permits: A free self-issue Wilderness Permit is required and is available at the trailhead. A federal Northwest Forest Pass is required to park here; the cost is $5 a day or $30 for an annual pass. You can buy a day pass at the trailhead, at ranger stations, or through private vendors.

Maps: For a map of the Willamette National Forest and the Mount Washington Wilderness, contact Willamette National Forest Headquarters, 3106 Pierce Parkway, Suite D, Springfield, OR, 97477, 541/225-6300. For a topographic map, ask the USGS for Linton Lake.

Directions: From McKenzie Bridge, drive east on OR 126 to the McKenzie Pass Highway 242. Follow the highway to a sign for Scott Lake between mileposts 71 and 72 and turn left, following Road 260 for 1.5 miles to its end. From Sisters, drive OR 242 west 5.6 miles beyond the McKenzie Pass.

Contact: Willamette National Forest, McKenzie River Ranger District, 57600 McKenzie Highway, McKenzie Bridge, OR, 97413, 541/822-3381.

35 SCOTT TRAIL TO FOUR-IN-ONE CONE
9.0 mi/5.0 mi   🥾3   ⛰8

in the McKenzie Pass in Three Sisters Wilderness

Map 11.2, page 592

The Scott Trail was blazed by Captain Felix Scott, who arduously led a wagon train across this volcanic landscape in 1862. This modern hiking trail follows his route and leads backpackers into the Three Sisters Wilderness, opening up their own world of exploration. Hike across a lava flow erupted from the Four-in-One Cone, four cinder cones with a view of North and Middle Sister and the surrounding

© SEAN PATRICK HILL

Sunshine Meadows in the Three Sisters Wilderness

volcanic landscape. You can also go farther and connect to the Pacific Crest Trail. Keep in mind that this trail is largely exposed to the sun—bring adequate water, headgear, and sunblock.

From the trailhead, cross the McKenzie Pass Highway and start on the Scott Trail, staying left at the first junction (the right leads to the Obsidian Trailhead and Frog Camp) and continue 2.7 miles. The next 1.4 miles crosses a rugged lava flow and the forested island in its midst, then arrives at a cairn beside the cinder cones. Climb to the left for a view of the mountains, 0.4 mile along the Four-in-One Cone's rim. From the cairn, it is another 0.8 mile up the Scott Trail to its junction with the PCT.

User Groups: Hikers, dogs, and horses. No mountain bikes allowed. No wheelchair facilities.

Permits: A free self-issue Wilderness Permit is required and is available at the trailhead. Parking and access are free.

Maps: A map of the Three Sisters Wilderness is available for purchase from Geo-Graphics. For a map of the Willamette National Forest and the Three Sisters Wilderness, contact Willamette National Forest Headquarters, 3106 Pierce Parkway, Suite D, Springfield, OR, 97477, 541/225-6300. For a topographic map, ask the USGS for North Sister.

Directions: From McKenzie Bridge, drive east on OR 126 to the McKenzie Pass Highway 242. Follow the highway to a sign for Scott Lake between mileposts 71 and 72 and turn left, then right into a parking area. From Sisters, drive OR 242 west 5.6 miles beyond the McKenzie Pass.

Contact: Willamette National Forest, McKenzie River Ranger District, 57600 McKenzie Highway, McKenzie Bridge, OR, 97413, 541/822-3381.

36 THE OBSIDIAN TRAIL
12.0 mi/6.0 hr   🚶3 ⛺10

west of McKenzie Pass in Three Sisters Wilderness

Map 11.2, page 592   **BEST (**

The Obsidian Trail in the Three Sisters Wilderness sees a multitude of visitors—including those who come to climb 10,047-foot Middle Sister, Oregon's fourth-highest mountain. Because of the trail's popularity, the Forest Service requires a special permit that can be attained in advance from the McKenzie Ranger Station. What makes it such a desirable destination are the meadows known as Sunshine, which offer some of the rarest landscape to be found anywhere. The trail passes 4.1 miles through deep forests and over jagged rivers of lava fields that poured down from nearby Collier Cone. Volcanic black glass abounds here, making it obvious how this trail acquired its name. Atop the Obsidian Cliffs, the alpine plateau sparkles with acres of glittering chips. You'll pass 20-foot Obsidian Falls tumbling into a forest that by late summer is full of the mop-head blooms of western pasque flower, known as "old man of the mountain." From the Sunshine Meadows around Glacier Creek, climbers ascend to summit Middle Sister. Backpacking and camping affords many opportunities for day trips. To the south lie the Linton Meadows, the Wickiup Plain, and South Sister. To the north, the PCT crosses the ridge of Little Brother and deep lava flows to the volcanic moonscape beneath North Sister and a steep climb up the Collier Cone.

Starting from the McKenzie Pass Highway, go 4.1 miles on the Obsidian Trail through forests and over lava fields. Immediately after crossing the White Branch Creek, take a right at a junction, staying on the Obsidian Trail for 1.7 miles. Once on the PCT, turn left for 1.4 miles to continue to Sunshine. A 0.7-mile spur trail heading downhill along Glacier Creek completes the loop, returning to the last 4.1-mile stretch of the Obsidian Trail back to the trailhead.

User Groups: Hikers, dogs, and horses. No mountain bikes allowed. No wheelchair facilities.

Permits: A Limited Entry Permit is required for overnight and day visits to the Pamelia Lake area; contact the USFS for information. A federal Northwest Forest Pass is required to park here; the cost is $5 a day or $30 for an annual pass. You can buy a day pass at the trailhead, at ranger stations, or through private vendors.

Maps: A map of the Three Sisters Wilderness is available for purchase from Geo-Graphics. For a map of the Willamette National Forest and the Three Sisters Wilderness, contact Willamette National Forest Headquarters, 3106 Pierce Parkway, Suite D, Springfield, OR, 97477, 541/225-6300. For a topographic map, ask the USGS for North Sister.

Directions: From McKenzie Bridge, drive east on OR 126 to the McKenzie Pass Highway 242. Follow the highway to a sign for the Obsidian Trail between mileposts 70 and 71 and turn right 0.4 mile into a parking area. From Sisters, drive OR 242 west 6.2 miles beyond the McKenzie Pass.

Contact: Willamette National Forest, McKenzie River Ranger District, 57600 McKenzie Highway, McKenzie Bridge, OR, 97413, 541/822-3381.

37 PROXY FALLS/ LINTON LAKE
4.8 mi/2.5 hr

west of McKenzie Pass in Three Sisters Wilderness

Map 11.2, page 592

There's a reason you may have trouble finding parking here. These two easy hikes into the Three Sisters Wilderness are located just off the beautiful and heavily traveled McKenzie Pass Highway (a gateway to many fantastic hikes). That's no reason to pass up these two hikes, though, and their relative brevity makes it a good idea to do both.

The one-mile Proxy Falls loop should be hiked counterclockwise, as per Forest Service request; the loop visits Lower Proxy Falls, a tall cascade over a lava wall, and Upper Proxy Falls, which ends abruptly in a pool without a visible outlet (the water travels underground from here).

The Linton Lake Trail enters the woods and heads 1.4 miles to the edge of the lake at an ancient lava flow. You can continue 0.5 mile farther along the lakeshore to a beach. In the distance you can hear Linton Falls tumbling out of the hills.

User Groups: Hikers and dogs. No horses or mountain bikes. No wheelchair facilities.

Permits: A free self-issue Wilderness Permit is required and is available at the trailhead. A federal Northwest Forest Pass is required to park here; the cost is $5 a day or $30 for an annual pass. You can buy a day pass at the trailhead, at ranger stations, or through private vendors.

Maps: A map of the Three Sisters Wilderness is available for purchase from Geo-Graphics. For a map of the Willamette National Forest and the Three Sisters Wilderness, contact

Willamette National Forest Headquarters, 3106 Pierce Parkway, Suite D, Springfield, OR, 97477, 541/225-6300. For a topographic map, ask the USGS for Linton Lake.

Directions: From McKenzie Bridge, drive east on OR 126 to the McKenzie Pass Highway 242. For the Proxy Falls Trailhead follow this highway nine miles, and park on the roadside between mileposts 64 and 65. For the Linton Lake Trailhead, drive another 1.6 miles past Proxy Falls and park on the left. From Sisters, drive OR 242 west 13.5 miles beyond the McKenzie Pass.

Contact: Willamette National Forest, McKenzie River Ranger District, 57600 McKenzie Highway, McKenzie Bridge, OR, 97413, 541/822-3381.

38 CAMP LAKE AND CHAMBERS LAKES
14.2 mi/7.0 hr 🚶4 ⛰10

southwest of Sisters in Three Sisters Wilderness

Map 11.2, page 592

Although this trail starts out hot and dry in a viewless, lodgepole pine forest, all that quickly changes. Soon enough the trail traverses one of the most stunning landscapes in the state, ambling along beneath North and Middle Sister, with views to South Sister and Broken Top. The heights are breathtaking, and the destination of Camp Lake, set in the alpine saddle between Middle and South Sister, is almost too beautiful to bear. It's hard to exaggerate this place's wonder—and to know that you could go even farther into the wilderness (with a map and compass, of course), and head for the trail-less Chambers Lakes higher in the saddle, makes this a true wilderness destination.

Start on the Pole Creek Trail, going 1.4 miles to a junction that heads to Scott Pass. Stay left and continue 0.6 mile to Soap Creek. At the junction here, go right (the left heads for Green Lakes) another 2.6 miles. At this point, a side trail to the left leads 0.8 mile

down to Demaris Lake, a possible side trip. Otherwise, continue 2.5 miles to trail's end at Camp Lake. To find the Chambers Lakes, watch for user trails and consult your map.

User Groups: Hikers, dogs, and horses. No mountain bikes allowed. No wheelchair facilities.

Permits: A free self-issue Wilderness Permit is required and is available at the trailhead. Parking and access are free.

Maps: A map of the Three Sisters Wilderness is available for purchase from Geo-Graphics. For a map of the Deschutes National Forest and the Three Sisters Wilderness, contact Deschutes National Forest Headquarters, 1001 SW Emkay Drive, Bend, OR, 97702, 541/383-5300. For a topographic map, ask the USGS for North Sister.

Directions: From Sisters, drive 1.4 miles west of Sisters on Highway 242 then turn left on Road 15 for 10.5 miles, following signs for the Pole Creek Trailhead.

Contact: Deschutes National Forest, Sisters Ranger District, P.O. Box 249, Sisters, OR, 97759, 541/549-7700.

39 PARK MEADOW
7.6 mi/4.0 hr 🚶2 ⛰8

southwest of Sisters in Three Sisters Wilderness

Map 11.2, page 592

This unassuming trail beneath the Tam McArthur Rim is a back door to the very popular Green Lakes area (see *Green Lakes via Broken Top Trail* and *Green Lakes via Fall Creek* listings in this chapter). Park Meadow lies in the midst of thick woods with views to the nearby mountains. But the trail continues on, and with some path-finding skills you may be able to find nearly invisible Golden Lake nearly a mile off the trail, and could follow a series of tarns on the flanks of Broken Top.

The beginning of the Park Meadow Trail follows an old road 1.1 miles along the Snow Creek Ditch. Once the trail proper begins, it descends 2.7 miles to Whychus Creek (stay straight at a four-way intersection along the way). From here it's 1.1 miles to Park Meadow, fed by Park Creek, which is fed, in turn, by the Bend Glacier on Broken Top. From here the trail continues to Green Lakes, and following it you could wander off trail to the south to find Golden Lake with its impressive views, a waterfall, and sky-reflecting tarns high on the mountain.

User Groups: Hikers, dogs, and horses. No mountain bikes allowed. No wheelchair facilities.

Permits: A free self-issue Wilderness Permit is required and is available at the trailhead. Parking and access are free.

Maps: A map of the Three Sisters Wilderness is available for purchase from Geo-Graphics. For a map of the Deschutes National Forest and the Three Sisters Wilderness, contact Deschutes National Forest Headquarters, 1001 SW Emkay Drive, Bend, OR, 97702, 541/383-5300. For a topographic map, ask the USGS for Broken Top.

Directions: From Sisters, go south on Elm Street, which becomes Road 16, for 14.3 mostly paved miles to the Park Meadow Trailhead.

Contact: Deschutes National Forest, Sisters Ranger District, P.O. Box 249, Sisters, OR, 97759, 541/549-7700.

TAM MCARTHUR RIM
9.4 mi/4.0 hr   🥾3   ⛰9

southwest of Sisters in Three Sisters Wilderness

Map 11.2, page 592

Tam McArthur Rim is the rim of a massive, long-dead volcano. It's far higher than most mountains in the state, making this is one of the best viewpoints in Oregon, with vistas as far as Mount Adams in Washington State—and everything in between. The rim itself drops impressively over 500-foot cliffs to the lakes below, and at the far end of the ridge lies Broken Top. With care, you can extend this hike along that ridge, which gets narrower

© SEAN PATRICK HILL

North Sister from the Tam McArthur Rim

as you go, to a hidden lake beneath the steep slope of craggy Broken Top.

From the trailhead, climb the Tam McArthur Rim Trail steadily through the woods nearly 600 feet and 0.7 mile to the rim. Continue 1.8 miles to a right-hand junction, which leads to an overlook on a long tongue of lava. From here, continue 2.2 miles, the trail becoming increasingly faint, to the lava plug of Broken Hand. The trail traverses the left side and continues on to the mountain itself, but only the sure-footed should attempt it.

User Groups: Hikers, dogs, and horses. No mountain bikes allowed. No wheelchair facilities.

Permits: A free self-issue Wilderness Permit is required and is available at the trailhead. A federal Northwest Forest Pass is required to park here; the cost is $5 a day or $30 for an annual pass. You can buy a day pass at the trailhead, at ranger stations, or through private vendors.

Maps: A map of the Three Sisters Wilderness is available for purchase from Geo-Graphics. For a map of the Deschutes National Forest and the Three Sisters Wilderness, contact Deschutes National Forest Headquarters, 1001 SW Emkay Drive, Bend, OR, 97702, 541/383-5300. For a topographic map, ask the USGS for Broken Top.

Directions: From Sisters, go south on Elm Street, which becomes Road 16, for 15.7 mostly paved miles to the trailhead on the left.

Contact: Deschutes National Forest, Sisters Ranger District, P.O. Box 249, Sisters, OR, 97759, 541/549-7700.

41 GREEN LAKES VIA BROKEN TOP TRAIL

9.6 mi/5.5 hr

west of Bend in the Three Sisters Wilderness

Map 11.2, page 592

Getting to this trailhead requires one of the worst drives possible. Since you'll have to contend with badly rutted and steep dirt roads, washouts, shock-busting potholes, you'll want to drive something with clearance and you'll want to take it slow. The Broken Top Trail passes before the colossal crater of its namesake mountain, a desolate and rocky castle surrounded by meadows of wildflowers so intense you'd never think the two belonged together. Larkspur, columbine, and other varieties dot these high alpine meadows. Views extend out to Mount Bachelor and more distant peaks.

From the trailhead, follow the Broken Top Trail, not taking any side trails, until you reach Green Lakes in 4.8 miles. Watch for the Cayuse Crater along the way, a cinder vent along the trail at the end of a long ridge. Return as you came.

User Groups: Hikers, dogs on leash only, and horses. No mountain bikes allowed. No wheelchair facilities.

Permits: A free self-issue Wilderness Permit is required and is available at the trailhead.

A federal Northwest Forest Pass is required to park here; the cost is $5 a day or $30 for an annual pass. You can buy a day pass at the trailhead, at ranger stations, or through private vendors.

Maps: A map of the Three Sisters Wilderness is available for purchase from Geo-Graphics. For a map of the Deschutes National Forest and the Three Sisters Wilderness, contact Deschutes National Forest Headquarters, 1001 SW Emkay Drive, Bend, OR, 97702, 541/383-5300. For a topographic map, ask the USGS for Broken Top.

Directions: From Bend, drive 23.7 miles west on the Cascade Lakes Highway and turn right at a sign for Todd Lake onto Road 370. After 0.5 mile, continue on Road 370 (the gate stays closed most of the year) for 3.5 terrible miles to Road 380, going left on this road 1.3 miles to its end at the Broken Top Trailhead.

Contact: Deschutes National Forest, Bend-Fort Rock Ranger District, 1230 NE 3rd Street, Suite A-262, Bend, OR, 97701, 541/383-4000.

42 GREEN LAKES VIA FALL CREEK

8.4-11.4 mi/4.5-6.0 hr

west of Mount Bachelor in Three Sisters Wilderness

Map 11.2, page 592 **BEST (**

Whereas other areas of the Three Sisters Wilderness are virtually empty, this trail—leading to what has to be one of the most beautiful places in the world—almost never is. The three Green Lakes lie in a valley between South Sister and Broken Top, with unparalleled views of both. To get there, you'll follow the loud and vivacious Fall Creek, which tumbles and tumbles on its way down, almost an endless waterfall; when it does level out, you'll pass a massive obsidian flow that glows in the sun. No wonder it's so popular.

This area has seen a lot of visitor damage over the years, so make sure you camp at a designated area marked by a post and stick to marked trails. You could do this trip in an out-and-back fashion, or make a loop of it using the Broken Top and Soda Creek Trails (recommended if you're backpacking).

From the trailhead, follow the Fall Creek Trail two miles, stay straight at a junction, and continue 2.2 miles to the next junction. Crest a rise and you'll see the Green Lakes, which you can visit by continuing another 1.2 miles. Return to the junction with the Broken Top Trail. You can return as you came or go left toward Broken Top for 2.7 miles, then right at a sign for Fall Creek Trailhead for 0.8 mile, then follow the Soda Creek Trail to the right down 3.7 miles to the lot.

User Groups: Hikers, dogs on leash only, and horses. No mountain bikes allowed. No wheelchair facilities.

Permits: A free self-issue Wilderness Permit is required and is available at the trailhead. A federal Northwest Forest Pass is required to park here; the cost is $5 a day or $30 for an annual pass. You can buy a day pass at the trailhead, at ranger stations, or through private vendors.

Maps: A map of the Three Sisters Wilderness is available for purchase from Geo-Graphics. For a map of the Deschutes National Forest and the Three Sisters Wilderness, contact Deschutes National Forest Headquarters, 1001 SW Emkay Drive, Bend, OR, 97702, 541/383-5300. For a topographic map, ask the USGS for Trout Creek Butte and Broken Top.

Directions: From Bend, drive 26.4 miles west on the Cascade Lakes Highway and turn right at a Green Lakes Trailhead sign to a parking area.

Contact: Deschutes National Forest, Bend-Fort Rock Ranger District, 1230 NE 3rd Street, Suite A-262, Bend, OR, 97701, 541/383-4000.

43 SOUTH SISTER SUMMIT
11.0-12.6 mi/1-2 days   🥾5 ⛰10

west of Mount Bachelor in Three Sisters Wilderness

Map 11.2, page 592

Of all the alpine climbs you could do in Oregon, and of all the peaks you could bag without needing equipment or real mountaineering expertise, South Sister is king. At the same time, you must make serious considerations and take precautions. Altitude sickness affects some more than others, and this trail will lift you 10,358 feet into the atmosphere on Oregon's third-highest mountain. You'll need all day to do it, too; starting early is never a bad idea. The most direct route—and most challenging—begins at the Devil's Lake Trailhead. It's easy to turn this into a backpacking multi-day pitch simply by securing a campsite near Moraine Lake, a little lake with a big view of South Sister and nearby Broken Top. Hike up, pitch a tent, and gather your strength: You'll need it. Be safe and check the weather before attempting an ascent. Any clouds are usually bad clouds. Also, a note on dogs: Because cinders are sharp and can badly cut a dog's paws, it's best to spare them this climb.

From the Devil's Lake Trailhead, climb 1.5 miles on the South Sister climbing trail, heading up a gully, gradually growing steeper, to a four-way junction at the first view of South Sister. To the right, the 0.8-mile side trail leads down to Moraine Lake, where camping is regulated (choose a spot marked with a post). To continue on the climb, go forward up the climber's trail 1.8 miles to the head of the canyon on the right. The next 1.1 miles climbs steeply up the mountain before arriving at a lake beneath the Lewis Glacier. The final grinding slog is up 0.7 mile of sliding cinder to the rim. Once at the top, follow the rim counter-clockwise 0.4 mile to the summit. From here, you'll see half the state of Oregon and, in the crater, Teardrop Pool—the highest lake in Oregon.

User Groups: Hikers, dogs on leash only, and horses. No mountain bikes allowed. No wheelchair facilities.

Permits: A free self-issue Wilderness Permit is required and is available at the trailhead. A federal Northwest Forest Pass is required to park here; the cost is $5 a day or $30 for an annual pass. You can buy a day pass at the trailhead, at ranger stations, or through private vendors.

Maps: A map of the Three Sisters Wilderness is available for purchase from Geo-Graphics. For a map of the Deschutes National Forest and the Three Sisters Wilderness, contact Deschutes National Forest Headquarters, 1001 SW Emkay Drive, Bend, OR, 97702, 541/383-5300. For a topographic map, ask the USGS for South Sister.

Directions: From Bend, drive 28.5 miles west on the Cascade Lakes Highway and turn left at a Devil's Lake Trailhead sign to a parking area.

Contact: Deschutes National Forest, Bend-Fort Rock Ranger District, 1230 NE 3rd Street, Suite A-262, Bend, OR, 97701, 541/383-4000.

44 SISTERS MIRROR LAKE AND WICKIUP PLAIN

8.3-11.3 mi/4.0-5.0 hr

west of Mount Bachelor in the Three Sisters Wilderness

Map 11.2, page 592

The Pacific Crest Trail passes breathtakingly close to South Sister, the third-highest mountain in Oregon, via the broad Wickiup Plain. In this alpine wonderland, you'll see expansive lava flows, smaller peaks, craters, and rolling meadows. It is strange, really, to find this corner of the Three Sisters Wilderness so bereft of crowds. This loop trail leads to backpacking sites near a bundle of lakes, the most well known of which is Sisters Mirror Lake; it somewhat reflects nearby South Sister, whose rounded crown peeks over the tree line. A small peninsula juts out into the lake, but camping is banned in this one spot. Instead, poke around some of the side trails to find plenty of other spots nearby.

From the trailhead, go 0.4 mile on the Mirror Lakes Trail to a four-way junction, staying straight for 2.7 miles to the PCT. The trail crosses Sink Creek and passes several ponds and Kokostick Butte. At the PCT, go left 0.2 mile along Sisters Mirror Lake. To find the other lakes, Lancelot and Denude, go back to the north shore and follow a user trail 0.4 mile. To make a loop from the Wickiup Plain, return to the four-way junction just north of Mirror Lake and continue north on the PCT. In 0.2 mile, you have a choice. For the shorter loop along the edge of the plain, go right here for 1.4 miles to the Wickiup Plains Trail, right at the next junction for one mile, then right again for 1.6 miles along the Elk-Devils Trail to the first four-way junction; go left 0.4 mile back to the lot. For a longer hike, continue on the PCT another 1.6 miles into the Wickiup meadows toward Le Conte Crater, beside the shimmering lava rock mesa. At a junction, go right towards Devil's Lake for 1.1 miles, then straight on the Wickiup Plains Trail for 0.5 mile, continuing left on this path for one mile. Now follow signs for Elk Lake to the right for 1.6 miles, and finally take the final left to return to the Mirror Lakes Trailhead.

User Groups: Hikers, dogs, and horses. No mountain bikes allowed. No wheelchair facilities.

Permits: A free self-issue Wilderness Permit is required and is available at the trailhead. A federal Northwest Forest Pass is required to park here; the cost is $5 a day or $30 for an annual pass. You can buy a day pass at the trailhead, at ranger stations, or through private vendors.

Maps: A map of the Three Sisters Wilderness is available for purchase from Geo-Graphics. For a map of the Deschutes National Forest and the Three Sisters Wilderness, contact Deschutes National Forest Headquarters, 1001 SW Emkay Drive, Bend, OR, 97702, 541/383-5300. For a topographic map, ask the USGS for South Sister.

Directions: From Bend, drive 29.8 miles west

on the Cascade Lakes Highway and turn right at a Trailhead sign to a parking area.

Contact: Deschutes National Forest, Bend-Fort Rock Ranger District, 1230 NE 3rd Street, Suite A-262, Bend, OR, 97701, 541/383-4000.

45 TUMALO MOUNTAIN
3.6 mi/2.5 hr

west of Bend in Deschutes National Forest

Map 11.2, page 592

This fairly straightforward climb offers views of surrounding peaks, but is far easier to climb than the others—though it is a 1,200-foot gain in elevation in less than two miles. The view down into Tumalo's eroded crater makes it worth it. From the Sno-Park, follow the Tumalo Mountain Trail up 1.8 miles to the peak.

User Groups: Hikers and dogs only. No horses or mountain bikes allowed. No wheelchair facilities.

Permits: No permits are required. Parking and access are free.

Maps: For a map of the Deschutes National Forest, contact Deschutes National Forest Headquarters, 1001 SW Emkay Drive, Bend, OR, 97702, 541/383-5300. For a topographic map, ask the USGS for Broken Top.

Directions: From Bend, drive 21.7 miles west on the Cascade Lakes Highway and turn right at the Dutchman Flat parking area.

Contact: Deschutes National Forest, Bend-Fort Rock Ranger District, 1230 NE 3rd Street, Suite A-262, Bend, OR, 97701, 541/383-4000.

46 TUMALO FALLS
6.8 mi/3.5 hr

west of Bend in Deschutes National Forest

Map 11.2, page 592

The people who call Bend home are lucky to live such a short distance from such incredible beauty. Here, for instance, at the end of a long paved road into the forest is not one, but several waterfalls on Tumalo Creek, which flows all the way down to Bend, passing through Shevlin Park. In 1979, a wildfire started by a campfire burned off six-square-miles of stately trees. It's amazing how much the forest has recovered, and this hike doesn't stay long in the burn before getting into the good high-country forests.

Follow the South Fork Trail 0.2 mile to the right to find the top of 97-foot Tumalo Falls. Continue along the creek another 3.2 miles, passing four sets of waterfalls along the way. At a junction, go left on the Swampy Lakes Trail 2.1 miles on a high ridge (note that this trail enters the Bend Watershed, and that animals and mountain bikes are not allowed). Then follow the Bridge Creek Trail to the left 1.3 miles back to the lot.

User Groups: Hikers, dogs, horses, and mountain bikes. No mountain bikes or animals allowed in the Bend Watershed. There is a wheelchair-accessible trail to an overlook of Tumalo Falls.

Permits: A federal Northwest Forest Pass is required to park here; the cost is $5 a day or $30 for an annual pass. You can buy a day pass at the trailhead, at ranger stations, or through private vendors.

Maps: For a map of the Deschutes National Forest, contact Deschutes National Forest Headquarters, 1001 SW Emkay Drive, Bend, OR, 97702, 541/383-5300. For a topographic map, ask the USGS for Tumalo Falls.

Directions: From the west side of Bend, follow Skyliner Road 9.8 miles to its end at the OMSI camp, and turn right on dirt Road 4603 for 3.4 miles to the picnic area and trailhead.

Contact: Deschutes National Forest, Bend-Fort Rock Ranger District, 1230 NE 3rd Street, Suite A-262, Bend, OR, 97701, 541/383-4000.

47 SHEVLIN PARK
4.7-5.0 mi/2.0-2.5 hr   🏃₁ 📐₇

west of Bend

Map 11.2, page 592   **BEST (**

Suffice it to say that this has to be one of the country's best city parks—and it's not even in the city. Instead, it stretches out in a canyon along Tumalo Creek, a cold mountain river that passes under stately ponderosa pine, quaking aspen, Douglas fir, and Engelmann spruce. In spring and summer, wildflowers abound here, and you could spend all day trying out side trails, looking up gulches, and exploring farther up Tumalo Creek, where a biking trail leads all the way to Tumalo Falls. But for an easy start, try this loop trail that follows the canyon rim in a scenic loop around all the park's perks. The burn the trail passes over is the result of a 1990 forest fire that just missed destroying the forested canyon. Already, trees are growing back strong.

From the lot, head toward the creek on the Shevlin Loop Trail along the stand of aspen trees, crossing the creek on a footbridge and climbing the ridge to the burn. After the first 0.9 mile, the trail meets an old road. Follow this road a bit, then head back onto trail for one mile, dropping down into the canyon to a side creek flowing past enormous boulders. Cross the creek and continue 0.6 mile through denser woods of Douglas fir to a crossing of Tumalo Creek. Continue over the old road (though going left follows the creek back a ways into National Forest land) and follow this trail along the opposite side of the canyon 1.5 miles to the top of Red Tuff Gulch and a supply yard. Then walk the final 0.7 mile back to your vehicle.

For another walk, this one along the creek, follow the 2.5-mile Tumalo Creek Trail out-and-back; it passes footbridges connecting to the Loop Trail, a covered bridge, and historic Fremont Meadows before launching into the National Forest.

User Groups: Hikers, dogs on leash only, and mountain bikes. No horses allowed. Paved portions of the park are wheelchair accessible.

Permits: No permits are required. Parking and access are free.

Maps: For a downloadable map, go to www.bendparksandrec.org. For a topographic map, ask the USGS for Shevlin Park.

Directions: From downtown Bend, follow Newport Avenue (which becomes Shevlin Park Road) 3.9 miles. Just after crossing Tumalo Creek, turn left at a bend in the road and park in the first lot.

Contact: Bend Parks and Recreation, 200 NW Pacific Park Lane, Bend, OR, 97701, 541/389-7275.

48 NORTH BANK DEER PRESERVE
6.9 mi/3.5 hr   🏃₂ 📐₈

north of Roseburg on the North Umpqua River

Map 11.3, page 593

The Columbia white-tailed deer once roamed widely in Western Oregon, but by the 1970s populations had dwindled to two pockets: one on the Columbia River, and the other along this bend of the Umpqua River. This 10,000-acre former ranch is now a wildlife preserve where you can certainly see wildlife, not to mention an assortment of landscapes from rolling forests and oak savannah to giant madrone trees and creek-carved chasms. The trail rises and falls, climbing two knobs high above the preserve. Watch for pennyroyal, blue-eyed grass, mariposa lilies, and cat's ear. Note that chiggers are a problem here, so wear long pants.

From the west access, hike straight onto an old road and up 1.8 miles to the 1,480-foot peak of South Knob. A right-hand trail leads to Whistler's Overlook over the Umpqua River, a good place to spot osprey, and will add three miles round-trip to your hike. From South Knob continue 1.5 miles over Middle Ridge to 1,816-foot Middle Knob. Keep going another 0.5 mile, sticking to the left, to a saddle. From here, go left for 2.3 miles through woods along Chasm Creek to a road. Turn left on the road for 0.8 mile back to the car, going to the left of the gate for the last stretch of trail.

User Groups: Hikers, horses, and bicycles. Dogs are discouraged. No wheelchair facilities.

Permits: Permits are not required. Parking and access are free.

Maps: For a topographic map, ask the USGS for Winchester and Oak Creek Valley.

Directions: From Roseburg, drive I-5 north four miles to Winchester (Exit 129). Turn left toward Wilbur for two miles, then turn right on North Bank Road for 5.5 miles. Beyond a gated road on the left, watch for a gravel lot on the left.

Contact: Bureau of Land Management, Roseburg District, 777 NW Garden Valley Boulevard, Roseburg, OR, 97471, 541/440-4930.

49 FALL CREEK NATIONAL RECREATION TRAIL
9.0–13.7 mi one-way/3.0 hr–2 days
🥾2 🏕7

southeast of Eugene in Willamette National Forest

Map 11.4, page 594

Open all year, this forested hike follows Fall Creek through a lush riparian zone, passing side streams and a small cave once used by Native Americans. A good beginning is to hike a nine-mile section of the trail to what was formerly a 90-foot log bridge, now gone. There is a primitive campsite about halfway out, which could make for a good backpacking spot. There are many access points along the way, but a good stretch begins at the westernmost point in an old-growth forest, and soon traverses out over a 2003 burn on its way upstream. With the bridge out about 9.5 miles upstream, it is possible to access the higher trailhead from the upper stretches of Road 18, hiking downstream to an old-growth grove on Marine Creek.

From the trailhead at the Dolly Varden Campground, follow the creek 2.9 miles through an old-growth forest of ferns and firs along the forested bank to a footbridge at Timber Creek. Along the way, the trail sometimes drops to gravel beaches and to a swimming hole two miles in. After the footbridge, the trail enters the burn from the 2003 Clark Fire, continuing another 0.6 mile to Road 18. Go left across the bridge, and continue upstream on the trail on the far side. In 1.1 miles, the trail passes the cave on Slick Creek and a possible camping area. Continuing another 0.4 mile, the trail forks; to the right is the Bedrock Campground, but the bridge to it is gone. Stay left, going 0.7 mile up a series of switchbacks to a junction with the Jones Creek Trail on the left, closed due to fire damage. The Fall Creek Trail exits the burn, staying high above the creek for one mile, then descending to the creekside again for 3.3 miles to gravel road 1828. This makes the best turnaround point, though continuing 0.5 mile on the trail will bring you to the spot the bridge once spanned, but the bridge being out and the creek being unfordable here makes this a fine ending.

The final 4.2 miles of trail beyond the missing bridge can be reached from Road 1833.

User Groups: Hikers and dogs only. No horses or mountain bikes allowed. No wheelchair facilities.

Permits: Permits are not required. Parking and access are free.

Maps: For a map of the Willamette National Forest, contact Willamette National Forest Headquarters, 3106 Pierce Parkway, Suite D, Springfield, OR, 97477, 541/225-6300. For a topographic map, ask the USGS for Saddleblanket Mountain.

Directions: From Eugene, drive east on Highway 58 for 14 miles and turn left across Dexter Reservoir at the covered bridge. Take Jasper-Lowell Road 2.8 miles through Lowell, following signs for Fall Creek. Turn right on Big Fall Creek Road for 10.3 miles, parking at a trail sign on the right just before the Dolly Varden Campground. To shuttle this as a 9-mile one-way walk, continue past the Dolly Varden Campground 8 miles and turn left on Road 1828 to the trailhead.

To reach the uppermost trailhead, follow Road 18 past Dolly Varden Campground another 12 miles, turn right on Road 1833 and cross a bridge. The trailhead is on the left.

Contact: Willamette National Forest, Middle Fork Ranger District, 46375 Highway 58, Westfir, OR, 97492, 541/782-2283.

50 CHUCKSNEY MOUNTAIN
10.3 mi/5.5 hr   🏃3 ⛰8

northeast of Oakridge in Willamette National Forest

Map 11.4, page 594

From the peak of Chucksney Mountain, views extend to the Three Sisters, Broken Top, and Mount Bachelor in the east. The meadows atop the peak are home to wildflowers such as pearly everlasting, coneflower, and larkspur. You'll work for this peak, though, as you climb 2,000 feet in less than five miles, but on the way down the trail visits the headwaters of Box Canyon Creek and follows the stream down.

From the horse camp trailhead, follow the trail in 0.3 mile, keeping right at all junctions until you reach the Chucksney Mountain Loop Trail. Go right on this trail for 2.4 miles to a side trail on the right with views of the eastern peaks. Continue 0.6 mile to a crest, then switchback down into a large cirque and back out again for 1.7 miles to the 5,600-foot summit. Continue across the meadowed ridge 1.4 miles to the Grasshopper Trail. Go left for one mile to the meadows at the headwaters of Box Canyon Creek, then another 2.6 miles back down to the end of the loop, turning right 0.3 mile back to the horse camp.

User Groups: Hikers, dogs, horses, and mountain bikes. No wheelchair facilities.

Permits: Permits are not required. Parking and access are free.

Maps: For a map of the Willamette National Forest, contact Willamette National Forest Headquarters, 3106 Pierce Parkway, Suite D, Springfield, OR, 97477, 541/225-6300. For a topographic map, ask the USGS for Chucksney Mountain.

Directions: From Blue River, drive four miles east on OR 126 to Road 19 and turn south for 25.5 miles to Box Canyon Horse Camp. From Westfir, drive 32 miles north on Road 19 to Box Canyon Horse Camp.

Contact: Willamette National Forest, McKenzie River Ranger District, 57600 McKenzie Highway, McKenzie Bridge, OR, 97413, 541/822-3381.

51 GOODMAN CREEK AND EAGLE'S REST
13.4 mi/6.0 hr   🏃3 ⛰7

south of Lookout Point Reservoir in Willamette National Forest

Map 11.4, page 594

This popular trail is popular for several reasons: It's easily accessible from the Eugene/Springfield area, it's an easy hike for families, and it passes through an old-growth forest along Goodman Creek to a pretty waterfall and swimming hole. Continuing beyond the lower part of the trail on to Eagles Rest, passing a marshy swale of skunk cabbage and a shelter, you'll leave the crowds behind and make for a view over the Lost Creek Valley, standing high above the Lookout Point Reservoir.

From the trailhead, stick to the right-hand junction after 0.2 mile and follow the Goodman Creek arm of the Lookout Point Reservoir. In 1.8 miles, watch for an unmarked trail to the left leading to the waterfall and swimming hole. To continue on to Eagles Rest stay on the Goodman Trail, crossing the creek and continuing 1.2 miles along the creek, then crossing a side creek and climbing the next mile to a road crossing and the Eagles Rest Trailhead. Climb 700 feet over 1.5 miles of second-growth woods to the Ash Swale Shelter by its boggy marsh. Continue 0.3 mile up, cross another road, then ascend the final 0.7 mile to the rocky peak of Eagles Rest.

User Groups: Hikers, dogs, horses, and mountain bikes. No wheelchair facilities.

Permits: Permits are not required. Parking and access are free.

Maps: For a map of the Willamette National Forest, contact Willamette National Forest Headquarters, 3106 Pierce Parkway, Suite D, Springfield, OR, 97477, 541/225-6300. For a topographic map, ask the USGS for Mount June.

Directions: From Eugene, follow Highway 58 east to milepost 21, and park on the right at a trailhead sign.

Contact: Willamette National Forest, Middle Fork Ranger District, 46375 Highway 58, Westfir, OR, 97492, 541/782-2283.

52 TIRE MOUNTAIN
7.6 mi/3.0 hr   🏃2 ⛰8

north of Oakridge in Willamette National Forest

Map 11.4, page 594

On the large, flat top of Tire Mountain a fire watchtower once stood atop a platform on a topped tree. The mountain itself is named for a nearby creek, which in turn was named for a wagon wheel someone left there. Today the trail accessing this mountain is part of the Eugene to Pacific Crest Trail system, which quite handily connects that nearby city to the mountains. Along this trail, wildflower meadows spread out over the ridge and views open to the distant Cascade peaks.

From the left side of the road, start up the Alpine Trail, going 1.2 miles into an old-growth forest then a meadow at 4,000 feet with views to the Three Sisters, Mount Bachelor, and Diamond Peak. At the junction, go right on the easy and level Tire Mountain Trail for two miles, crossing another steep mountainside meadow and two smaller meadows

on the way to the peak. A side trail to the left leads 0.6 mile to the 4,329-foot summit.

User Groups: Hikers, dogs, horses, and mountain bikes. No wheelchair facilities.

Permits: Permits are not required. Parking and access are free.

Maps: For a map of the Willamette National Forest, contact Willamette National Forest Headquarters, 3106 Pierce Parkway, Suite D, Springfield, OR, 97477, 541/225-6300. For a topographic map, ask the USGS for Westfir East and West.

Directions: From Eugene, follow Highway 58 east 30 miles then go left toward Westfir for 0.3 mile. At a three-way junction, go left 1.8 miles toward Westfir to a red covered bridge and go straight on Road 19 for 4.5 miles. Turn left on Road 1912 for 6.8 miles to Windy Pass, going straight onto Road 1910 for 0.3 mile, then right on Road 1911 for 0.4 mile to the Alpine Trail on the left.

Contact: Willamette National Forest, Middle Fork Ranger District, 46375 Highway 58, Westfir, OR, 97492, 541/782-2283.

53 ERMA BELL LAKES
8.4 mi/4.5 hr   🏃2 ⛰8

northeast of Oakridge in Three Sisters Wilderness

Map 11.4, page 594

This trail has every right to be heavily used: Located just inside the Three Sisters Wilderness, the trail crosses Skookum Creek (Chinook for "powerful"), and loops around five major lakes, including the three Erma Bell Lakes, the lower and middle of which are joined by a waterfall falling over a rock ledge. As for the lakes themselves, they are wonderfully wild and without the usual trampling of shoreline trails. This doesn't mean there's no camping to be had, though it is prohibited on Lower Erma Bell Lake. Respect the rules and stay at least 200 yards away from lakeshores when pitching a tent.

From the Skookum Creek Campground, cross the creek and head into the wilderness on the Erma Bell Lake Trail 0.6 mile to a junction. Follow the right-hand main trail 1.1 miles to Lower Erma Bell Lake, another 0.4 mile past the waterfall to Middle Erma Bell Lake, and another 0.7 mile to Upper Erma Bell Lake on the right. Continue 0.7 mile to a junction, staying left on the Erma Bell Trail (the right-hand trail goes less than a mile past Mud Lake and Edna Lake to the Taylor Burn Campground). In another 0.7 mile, begin the loop by staying left on the Williams Lake Trail, then go 0.4 mile to Williams Lake. From here the trail gradually descends 2.4 miles through forest to the Irish Mountain Trail junction. Stay to the left another 0.3 mile to Otter Lake, then finish the loop in 0.3 mile. Return to Skookum Creek by going right 0.6 mile.

User Groups: Hikers, dogs, and horses. No mountain bikes allowed. The trail to Lower Erma Bell Lake is wheelchair accessible.

Permits: A free self-issue Wilderness Permit is required and is available at the trailhead. A federal Northwest Forest Pass is required to park here; the cost is $5 a day or $30 for an annual pass. You can buy a day pass at the trailhead, at ranger stations, or through private vendors.

Maps: A map of the Three Sisters Wilderness is available for purchase from Geo-Graphics. For a map of the Willamette National Forest and Three Sisters Wilderness, contact Willamette National Forest Headquarters, 3106 Pierce Parkway, Suite D, Springfield, OR, 97477, 541/225-6300. For a topographic map, ask the USGS for Waldo Mountain.

Directions: From McKenzie Highway 126, turn south on Road 19 toward the Cougar Reservoir for 25.6 miles. Pass Box Canyon Guard Station and go left on Road 1957 to Skookum Campground. The trail begins from the campground parking lot.

Contact: Willamette National Forest, Middle Fork Ranger District, 46375 Highway 58, Westfir, OR, 97492, 541/782-2283.

54 MOUNT JUNE AND HARDESTY MOUNTAIN
9.6–10.0 mi/5.0 hr

south of Lookout Point Reservoir in Willamette National Forest

Map 11.4, page 594

The name Hardesty Mountain has a certain ring to it, mostly because you have to be pretty hardy to attempt this steep climb. Eugene hikers slog up Hardesty Mountain Trail when they need a real bout of exercise. You'll find, though, that Hardesty has no views, the old lookout site being overgrown with trees. If you begin at Mount June, though, you'll traverse from one peak to the next and passing the 50-foot block of Sawtooth Rock with its shallow cave.

To climb Hardesty Mountain the tough way, start at the Highway 58 trailhead, keeping to the left at the junction in 0.2 mile. This Hardesty Mountain Trail climbs 3,300 feet in 4.8 miles to the summit, passing the Eula Ridge Trail on the left near the top. The final 0.2 mile goes to the left where the trail meets the Cutoff Trail on the right. Return as you came.

To start from Mount June, follow the Mount June Trail 0.7 mile. At a junction, climb 0.5 mile to the left to top 4,618-foot Mount June, which has views extending as far as Mount Hood. Return to the main trail and continue to the right another 0.7 mile on the Sawtooth Trail. Go right one mile through a wildflower meadow past the spire to another junction after some switchbacks, and stay left on the Sawtooth Trail another 2.2 miles to a three-way junction. From here, it is possible to do a short loop around the peak of Hardesty Mountain, going left 0.2 mile on the Hardesty Cutoff Trail, then right over the peak, then right another 0.2 mile back to the Sawtooth Trail. Return as you came.

User Groups: Hikers, dogs, and horses. No mountain bikes allowed. No wheelchair facilities.

Permits: Permits are not required. Parking and access are free.

Maps: For a map of the Umpqua National Forest, contact Umpqua National Forest, 2900 NW Stewart Parkway, Roseburg, OR, 97470, 541/672-6601; for a map of the Willamette National Forest, contact Willamette National Forest Headquarters, 3106 Pierce Parkway, Suite D, Springfield, OR, 97477, 541/225-6300. For a topographic map, ask the USGS for Mount June.

Directions: For the lower trailhead to Hardesty Mountain, start from Eugene and follow Highway 58 east to milepost 21, and park on the right at a trailhead sign. For the upper trailhead to Mount June, follow Highway 58 east from Eugene 11.4 miles to the Dexter Dam and turn right toward Lost Creek. After 3.7 miles, keep left onto Eagles Rest Road, following this road 7.8 miles to a fork. Keep left on Road 20-1-14 for 6.1 miles and turn left on Road 1721 for 0.1 mile, then left on Road 941 for 0.4 mile to the trailhead sign on the right.

Contact: Umpqua National Forest, Cottage Grove Ranger District, 78405 Cedar Park Road, Cottage Grove, OR, 97424, 541/767-5000; Willamette National Forest, Middle Fork Ranger District, 46375 Highway 58, Westfir, OR, 97492, 541/782-2283.

55 EDDEELEO LAKES
9.2-16 mi/4.0 hr-2 days   🥾3 ⛰7

north of Waldo Lake in Waldo Lake Wilderness

Map 11.4, page 594

The strange name of these lakes is not so strange when you separate the syllables into three names: Ed, Dee, and Leo. These were three Forest Service workers who carried in fish to these lakes to stock them. The two lakes that carry their names are still being fished today. Lined up along the base of long Winchester Ridge, along with three other lakes, these lakes are jewels along a stone wall. Extending this trip makes for a good backpacking jaunt to Waldo Lake, the very large namesake of this wilderness area.

To begin, follow the Winchester Trail 0.8 mile, then take a left turn at a junction for 0.3 mile, then go right at the Blair Lake Trail junction for 1.1 miles to reach Lower Quinn Lake and another junction leading to Taylor Burn Campground. Stay right on the Six Lakes Trail to visit the lakes. The first mile passes a loop on the right to Upper Quinn Lake and arrives at the head of aptly named Long Lake. Follow this lake for most of the next 1.4 miles to the edge of Lower Eddeeleo Lake, and another 1.5 miles to Upper Eddeeleo. This can serve as a turnaround point.

If you're backpacking, continue 2.7 miles to the Waldo Shore Trail, then go south to Elbow Lake for 2.4 miles. At Elbow Lake, turn right on Trail 3585 for 0.8 mile, then right at the next junction on a cutoff trail for 300 yards, then left toward Waldo Mountain for 0.5 mile, then right on the Winchester Ridge Trail for 5.7 miles back to the Winchester Trail junction, then left 0.8 mile back to the trailhead.

User Groups: Hikers, dogs, and horses. No mountain bikes allowed. No wheelchair facilities.

Permits: A free self-issue Wilderness Permit is required and is available at the trailhead. Parking and access are free.

Maps: For a map of the Willamette National Forest and Waldo Lake Wilderness, contact Willamette National Forest Headquarters, 3106 Pierce Parkway, Suite D, Springfield, OR, 97477, 541/225-6300. For a topographic map, ask the USGS for Waldo Mountain.

Directions: From Highway 58 at Oakridge, turn north on Crestview Street for 0.2 mile to East 1st Street, going right. Follow this road, which becomes Salmon Creek Road 24, for 11 miles, then veer left on Road 2417 for 10.9 miles. Turn left at Road 254 for 0.3 mile, following signs for Winchester Trail. Park on the right at a parking lot.

Contact: Willamette National Forest, Middle Fork Ranger District, 46375 Highway 58, Westfir, OR, 97492, 541/782-2283.

56 RIGDON LAKES
8.0 mi/4.0 hr

north of Waldo Lake in Waldo Lake Wilderness

Map 11.4, page 594

Though the 1996 fires that burned through the north shore of Waldo Lake made the area a ghostly version of a forest, it does not follow that the area is off-limits. Burns have their own beauty and after time manage to regenerate. To access the Rigdon Lakes, you'll follow the 10-square-mile Waldo Lake, nearly surrounded by wilderness, on your way to Rigdon Butte and the lakes in its shadow. As long as you're here, why not make a loop of it? Visit Lake Kiwa and return on the far side of the butte, to the lake's outlet, the headwaters of the North Fork Middle Fork Willamette River—a mouthful, I know.

From the North Waldo Trailhead head west, ignoring a horse trail on the right, but noting instead a one-mile shoreline trail on the left that rejoins the main trail 0.7 mile later on the North Waldo Trail. Continue on this easy shoreline walk one mile past numerous ponds to the Rigdon Lakes Trail on the left. Go left 0.7 mile to Upper Rigdon Lake, circled on the far side by a user trail connecting to a 0.6-mile climb of Rigdon Butte. The final 1.3 miles of the Rigdon Lakes Trail passes Lower Rigdon Lake, Lake Kiwa, and little Ernie Lake before joining the Wahanna Trail. Go left at this junction 1.3 miles through the burned woods to a junction; go straight to the head of this fork of the Willamette. Otherwise, turn left and go 1.3 miles back along Waldo Lake to the beginning of the loop, then 1.7 miles back to the campground.

User Groups: Hikers, dogs, and horses. No mountain bikes allowed. No wheelchair facilities.

Permits: A free self-issue Wilderness Permit is required and is available at the trailhead. A federal Northwest Forest Pass is required to park here; the cost is $5 a day or $30 for an annual pass. You can buy a day pass at the trailhead, at ranger stations, or through private vendors.

Maps: For a map of the Willamette National Forest and Waldo Lake Wilderness, contact Willamette National Forest Headquarters, 3106 Pierce Parkway, Suite D, Springfield, OR, 97477, 541/225-6300. For a topographic map, ask the USGS for Waldo Mountain.

Directions: From Highway 58 go three miles west of the Willamette Pass and turn north on Road 5897 toward Waldo Lake for 13 miles to the North Waldo Campground. Park at a sign for the Waldo Lake Trail.

Contact: Willamette National Forest, Middle Fork Ranger District, 46375 Highway 58, Westfir, OR, 97492, 541/782-2283.

57 WALDO MOUNTAIN LOOKOUT
7.9–8.8 mi/4.0–5.0 hr

northwest of Waldo Lake in Waldo Lake Wilderness

Map 11.4, page 594

Waldo Lake, at 10 square miles, is so large that it's hard to get a sense of scale when you're standing on the shoreline. From the lookout atop Waldo Mountain, though, you'll have clear view down to the sparkling water and nearby peaks, including The Twins, Maiden Peak, Fuji Mountain, Diamond Peak, and the distant Three Sisters. The 1957 cabin, staffed in summer, is listed on the National Historic Lookout Register. A figure eight of trails on this mountain's flanks passes through a wildflower meadow, with a side trip to the pair of Salmon Lakes and a 20-foot waterfall. A number of loops are possible, so a map is essential in this wilderness area.

From the trailhead, enter the forest of big grand fir and hemlock for 200 yards to a junction, staying left on the Waldo Mountain Trail. The trail climbs gradually 1.9 miles up through beargrass plumes and sub-alpine trees to a T-junction, where you'll continue up one mile and almost 600 feet to the 6,357-foot summit. From here there are two ways to get down and form one of two loops.

The first way down is to return down the peak the way you came for one mile, keeping left at the next two junctions for 1.2 miles to Waldo Meadows and a T-junction. To return to the car, go right 2.5 miles on the Waldo Meadows Trail back to the trailhead. To find Upper and Lower Salmon Lakes, go left 100 feet to a signed trail on the right, going down 0.5 mile to the Upper Lake.

The second way down from the mountain, a longer loop, requires you to continue up and over the far side of the peak, descending 1.4 miles to a junction (ignore the left-hand Winchester Ridge Trail along the way). At the intersection, with Lake Chetco nearby to the left, instead go right 1.7 miles to Waldo Meadows, staying right at junctions to Elbow Lake and the Salmon Lakes, then continuing as above 2.5 miles back to the trailhead.

User Groups: Hikers, dogs, and horses. No mountain bikes allowed. No wheelchair facilities.

Permits: A free self-issue Wilderness Permit is required and is available at the trailhead. Parking and access are free.

Maps: For a map of the Willamette National Forest and Waldo Lake Wilderness, contact Willamette National Forest Headquarters, 3106 Pierce Parkway, Suite D, Springfield, OR, 97477, 541/225-6300. For a topographic map, ask the USGS for Waldo Mountain.

Directions: From Highway 58 at Oakridge, turn north on Crestview Street for 0.2 mile to East 1st Street, going right. Follow this road, which becomes Salmon Creek Road 24, for 11 miles, then veer left on Road 2417 for six miles. Turn right on Road 2424 and go 3.7 miles to the trailhead.

Contact: Willamette National Forest, Middle Fork Ranger District, 46375 Highway 58, Westfir, OR, 97492, 541/782-2283.

58 LILLIAN FALLS AND KLOVDAHL BAY

7.6 mi/4.5 hr

west of Waldo Lake in Waldo Lake Wilderness

Map 11.4, page 594

Access to the western shore of Waldo Lake can be a long journey if you start from the eastern shore, where the road and campgrounds are. A backdoor entrance along Black Creek is just as easy, and opens up the network of trails inside the wilderness area bordering the shoreline. A short, easy jaunt leads to Lillian Falls, and a longer more rugged hike climbs to Klovdahl Bay on the eastern shore. Oddly, neither Black Creek, Nettle Creek, nor Klovdahl Creek are outlets for Waldo Lake—it has only one outlet in its northwestern corner; the creeks in this area slip away, fed instead by winter snows. But one Simon Klovdahl tried in 1912 to dynamite a tunnel from Waldo to the Black Creek Canyon, an irrigation and hydroelectric power scheme that failed.

Start out on the trail along Black Creek, climbing easily for 1.2 miles to the base of Lillian Falls. From here the trail switchbacks up 0.7 mile and begins to climb more fiercely, leveling off in a valley along Nettle Creek then climbing again to Klovdahl Creek and above the Waldo shore for 1.9 miles before descending to the Waldo Lake Trail and Klovdahl Bay.

User Groups: Hikers, dogs, and horses. No mountain bikes all owed. No wheelchair facilities.

Permits: A free self-issue Wilderness Permit is required and is available at the trailhead. Parking and access are free.

Maps: For a map of the Willamette National Forest and Waldo Lake Wilderness, contact Willamette National Forest Headquarters, 3106 Pierce Parkway, Suite D, Springfield, OR, 97477, 541/225-6300. For a topographic map, ask the USGS for Waldo Lake.

Directions: From Highway 58 at Oakridge, turn north on Crestview Street for 0.2 mile to East 1st Street, going right. Follow this road, which becomes Salmon Creek Road 24, for 11 miles, keeping right at a Y-junction and staying on Road 24 for another 3.2 miles, then going straight on Road 2421 for 8.2 miles to road's end.

Contact: Willamette National Forest, Middle Fork Ranger District, 46375 Highway 58, Westfir, OR, 97492, 541/782-2283.

59 WALDO LAKE SHORE
21.5 mi/2-3 days

on Waldo Lake north of Willamette Pass

Map 11.4, page 594

The best way to circumnavigate huge Waldo Lake, the second-largest freshwater lake in Oregon, is by mountain bike, and many do attempt its single-track challenge. The 21-plus-mile Jim Weaver Loop Trail mostly follows the lakeshore, though for a substantial portion it ducks a bit away from the lake into deep woods that are heavy with huckleberries in the late summer. This is also a backpacker's dream; there are camps aplenty dispersed along the shore, as well as secluded beaches reachable only by foot or boat. On top of that, the side trails radiate out from the northern, western, and southern shore into the Waldo Lake Wilderness, a maze of peaks and lakes good for extended trips. The Jim Weaver Trail is best accessed from either the Shadow Bay Campground or North Waldo Campground. Watch for bikes along the way!

User Groups: Hikers, dogs, horses, and mountain bikes. No wheelchair facilities.

Permits: Permits are not required. A federal Northwest Forest Pass is required to park here; the cost is $5 a day or $30 for an annual pass. You can buy a day pass at the trailhead, at ranger stations, or through private vendors.

Maps: For a map of the Willamette National Forest and Waldo Lake Wilderness, contact Willamette National Forest Headquarters, 3106 Pierce Parkway, Suite D, Springfield, OR, 97477, 541/225-6300. For a topographic map, ask the USGS for Waldo Lake.

Directions: To find the Shadow Bay Trailhead, drive Highway 58 three miles west of the Willamette Pass to milepost 59 and turn on Road 5897 for 6.7 miles, following signs for Waldo Lake. Turn left into the Shadow Bay Campground, continuing two miles to the boat ramp parking. To find the North Waldo Trailhead, continue 6.3 miles farther on Road 5897 to the North Waldo Campground and park at the Waldo Lake Trailhead.

Contact: Willamette National Forest, Middle Fork Ranger District, 46375 Highway 58, Westfir, OR, 97492, 541/782-2283.

60 THE TWINS
6.6 mi/3.0 hr

east of Waldo Lake in Willamette National Forest

Map 11.4, page 594

The peak of The Twins, with its distinct dual volcanic flanks and crater, is easy enough to spot from the east or west. Accessible from the Pacific Crest Trail, this 7,360-foot peak offers an outstanding view of Waldo Lake to the west, the Three Sisters to the north, and Diamond Peak to the south. The trail is an easy one-shot climb from the trailhead: Ascend the first 450 feet through lodgepole pine and mountain hemlock forest in 1.6 miles to the PCT junction, and continue straight 1.7 miles and 1,160 feet to the north summit. With a bit of path-finding, you can explore the crater and top the south summit as well.

User Groups: Hikers, dogs, horses, and mountain bikes. No wheelchair facilities.

Permits: Permits are not required. A federal Northwest Forest Pass is required to park here; the cost is $5 a day or $30 for an annual pass. You can buy a day pass at the trailhead, at ranger stations, or through private vendors.

Maps: For a map of the Willamette National Forest, contact Willamette National Forest Headquarters, 3106 Pierce Parkway, Suite D, Springfield, OR, 97477, 541/225-6300. For a topographic map, ask the USGS for The Twins.

Directions: Drive Highway 58 three miles past the Willamette Pass to milepost 59 and turn on Road 5897 for 6.2 miles, following signs for Waldo Lake. Park at the Twin Peaks Trailhead on the right.

Contact: Willamette National Forest, Middle Fork Ranger District, 46375 Highway 58, Westfir, OR, 97492, 541/782-2283.

61 BRICE CREEK
5.5-7.5 mi one-way/2.5-3.5 hr
👫2 ⚠7

east of Cottage Grove in Umpqua National Forest

Map 11.4, page 594

In the Cascade Mountains above Cottage Grove, this lovely rushing creek bounds out of the forest in a forested canyon. Rain or shine, this trail is accessible all year, and it even has some primitive campsites along Road 22, not to mention bigger campgrounds and a backpacking spot along the far side of the creek. The trail stays on the far side of the creek away from the road, making for a quiet hike. There is also the option at the upper reach of the trail to loop around the two Trestle Creek Falls, adding two miles to the trip.

From the lower trailhead, follow the creek upstream 1.5 miles along the canyon and into old-growth forest. Ignore a side trail over the creek that goes to the Cedar Creek Campground, and continue 2.6 miles, passing a series of waterfalls over a rock shelf and the primitive Boy Scout Camp to another bridge crossing to the Lund Park Campground. The trail continues upstream 0.6 mile to the beginning of the loop. Going straight along the creek another 0.5 mile leads to Trestle Creek (for an interesting side-trip, follow a left-hand trail up 0.3 mile to a view of the lower falls). Continue another 0.3 mile up the Brice Creek Trail to its end at the upper trailhead.

A loop option leading to two waterfalls is also available at Trestle Creek. From the upper trailhead, this 3.4-mile loop makes for an easier trip that can be coupled with a longer excursion downstream on the Brice Creek Trail. At the end of the Brice Creek Trail at the upper trailhead, note the side trail going uphill. Following this steep trail up nearly 1,000 feet you'll reach the Upper Trestle Creek Falls, pass behind them, and descend another mile to the Brice Creek Trail. Go left to return to the upper trailhead, passing the side trail to the lower waterfall, or go right for any length along the remaining 4.7 miles of the Brice Creek Trail.

User Groups: Hikers, dogs, and horses. No mountain bikes allowed. No wheelchair facilities.

Permits: Permits are not required. Parking and access are free.

Maps: For a map of the Umpqua National Forest, contact Umpqua National Forest, 2900 NW Stewart Parkway, Roseburg, OR, 97470, 541/672-6601. For a topographic map, ask the USGS for Rose Hill.

Directions: To find the lower trailhead, drive I-5 south of Eugene to Cottage Grove (exit 174), and follow signs east to Dorena Lake on Row River Road, which becomes Road 22, for 21.7 miles to a parking lot on the right. For the upper trailhead at the Trestle Creek Falls Loop, continue past the lower trailhead on Road 22 for another 5.5 miles to the next bridge and parking for the trailhead.

Contact: Umpqua National Forest, Cottage Grove Ranger District, 78405 Cedar Park Road, Cottage Grove, OR, 97424, 541/767-5000.

62 LARISON CREEK
12.6 mi/6.0 hr
👫3 ⚠7

on Hills Creek Reservoir in Willamette National Forest

Map 11.4, page 594

This easy trail up Larison Creek weaves its way into some pretty stunning old-growth above the Hills Creek Reservoir. Douglas fir, red cedar, and the fabled yew trees—which Native Americans used for bows—all grow here.

You'll find a primitive campsite and a waterfall as you enter this deep, green canyon.

The trail begins along Larison Cove, an arm of the Hills Creek Reservoir; hillsides here are livid with poison oak. After 1.5 miles, the Larison Creek Trail reaches the end of the cove and a camping and picnic area. The trail then climbs gradually another 1.5 miles to a small waterfall and pool on the left. The next 2.2 miles leaves the creek and crosses a clear-cut before returning to the creek, crossing it near a creek fork. The last 1.1 miles climbs steeply up to trail's end at a dirt road. Return as you came.

User Groups: Hikers, dogs, horses, and mountain bikes. No wheelchair facilities.

Permits: Permits are not required. A federal Northwest Forest Pass is required to park here; the cost is $5 a day or $30 for an annual pass. You can buy a day pass at the trailhead, at ranger stations, or through private vendors.

Maps: For a map of the Willamette National Forest, contact Willamette National Forest Headquarters, 3106 Pierce Parkway, Suite D, Springfield, OR, 97477, 541/225-6300. For a topographic map, ask the USGS for Oakridge.

Directions: From Oakridge, drive 1.8 miles east on Highway 58. Between mileposts 37 and 38, turn south toward Hills Creek Dam on Road 23. In 0.5 mile, turn right on Road 21 for 3.3 miles to the trailhead on the right.

Contact: Willamette National Forest, Middle Fork Ranger District, 46375 Highway 58, Westfir, OR, 97492, 541/782-2283.

63 SALT CREEK FALLS AND VIVIAN LAKE

8.0 mi/4.0 hr 🏃3 ⛰9

in the Willamette Pass in Diamond Peak Wilderness

Map 11.4, page 594

Fall Creek, Diamond Creek, and Salt Creek— talk about waterfalls. Salt Creek Falls, showering over a basalt flow 286 feet into the canyon below,

Vivian Lake in Diamond Peak Wilderness

are the second highest in Oregon. Diamond Creek Falls and the double-tiered Fall Creek Falls also grace this trail into Diamond Peak Wilderness. At the top lies muddy-bottomed Vivian Lake, with its towering white pine trees and view of nearby Mount Yoran, a volcanic plug dominating the skyline. Besides flowering rhododendrons, huckleberries grow in such profusion along this trail that it's doubtful you'll get anywhere quickly, but watch out as you're stumbling through the bushes like a hungry bear—ground wasps call this area home, and I can attest that they pack quite a sting.

From the lot for Salt Creek Falls, take a quick tour of the observation trail on the north side of the creek. Then go upstream and cross a footbridge. At a junction, go right on the Diamond Creek Falls Trail for 1.8 miles along the canyon rim, passing strangely named Too Much Bear Lake and a viewpoint of a tall waterfall streaming into Salt Creek's canyon. To see Diamond Creek Falls, take a right-hand signed side trail down 0.2 mile to see the 100-

foot fan-shaped falls. Return to the main trail and keep to the right, switchbacking up to a junction. Go right and begin steadily climbing along Fall Creek on the Vivian Lake Trail. In 1.3 miles, the trail reaches two viewpoints of Fall Creek Falls. The next mile is a more gradual grade, coming to a side trail on the right leading to Vivian Lake. From here, backpackers can continue on to Notch Lake and other trail connections into Diamond Peak Wilderness. For a return loop, return on the Vivian Lake Trail down 2.3 miles to the junction, this time going right 1.2 miles back to Salt Creek.

User Groups: Hikers, dogs, and horses. No mountain bikes allowed. No wheelchair facilities.

Permits: A free self-issue Wilderness Permit is required and is available at the trailhead. A federal Northwest Forest Pass is required to park here; the cost is $5 a day or $30 for an annual pass. You can buy a day pass at the trailhead, at ranger stations, or through private vendors.

Maps: For a map of the Willamette National Forest, contact Willamette National Forest Headquarters, 3106 Pierce Parkway, Suite D, Springfield, OR, 97477, 541/225-6300. For a topographic map, ask the USGS for Diamond Peak.

Directions: From Oakridge, drive Highway 58 east to milepost 57 and turn right at a sign for Salt Creek Falls. Follow this paved road to the parking lot at its end.

Contact: Willamette National Forest, Middle Fork Ranger District, 46375 Highway 58, Westfir, OR, 97492, 541/782-2283.

64 FUJI MOUNTAIN
3.0–11.2 mi/1.5–4.0 hr   🏃4 ⛰9

south of Waldo Lake in Waldo Lake Wilderness

Map 11.4, page 594

The dominant peak of Fuji Mountain has a lot going for it. At 7,144 feet, it towers above the surrounding countryside, and with its 360-degree view of the surrounding Cascade Mountains, it has quite the stupendous view, reaching as far as the peak of Mount Hood in the north to Mount Thielsen in the south. The view also extends clear across monumental Waldo Lake, the reason this made a great lookout point long ago.

For the easier trailhead off Road 5883, follow the trail into the forest 0.3 mile to a junction and turn left on the Fuji Mountain Trail. The trail gets gradually steeper, climbing 1.2 miles to the peak.

For the more difficult climb, start from the trailhead on Road 5897, climbing one mile on the Fuji Mountain Trail to the forested plateau. In another two miles, the trail reaches Birthday Lake (warm in summer and a great place for a cool-down swim on the way down the mountain). In another 0.4 mile, it passes little Verde Lake on the left and comes to a junction. Go left 100 feet to a second junction, going right one mile and climbing to the junction with the Road 5883 spur trail. Keep right, and continue 1.2 miles to the top.

User Groups: Hikers, dogs, and horses. No mountain bikes allowed. No wheelchair facilities.

Permits: A federal Northwest Forest Pass is required to park here; the cost is $5 a day or $30 for an annual pass. You can buy a day pass at the trailhead, at ranger stations, or through private vendors.

Maps: For a map of the Willamette National Forest, contact Willamette National Forest Headquarters, 3106 Pierce Parkway, Suite D, Springfield, OR, 97477, 541/225-6300. For a topographic map, ask the USGS for Waldo Lake.

Directions: To find the shorter trail, begin in Oakridge and drive 15 miles east on Highway 58 to Eagle Creek Road 5883, between mileposts 50 and 51. Turn left on Road 5897 for 10.3 miles to the trailhead on the left. For the more difficult trail, continue on Highway 58 to milepost 59, and turn left on Road 5897, following signs for Waldo Lake. In two miles, park on the left at the trailhead.

Contact: Willamette National Forest, Middle Fork Ranger District, 46375 Highway 58, Westfir, OR, 97492, 541/782-2283.

65 BOHEMIA MOUNTAIN
1.6 mi/1.0 hr

east of Cottage Grove in Umpqua National Forest

Map 11.4, page 594

If you think the road to Bohemia Mountain is long and rough, imagine what it must have been like for the miners who once lived in Bohemia City. This old mining town, now one of Oregon's many ghost towns, sits at the base of its namesake mountain. Residents drilled the Musick Mine looking for gold, which was discovered here by a Czech immigrant in 1863. Only one building remains: the old post office, visible from the peak. You can make your way to it, being careful not to cross any private land, by bushwhacking down a hillside and heading for the last remnant of a town that operated from 1880 to 1930.

Follow the Bohemia Mountain Trail up 0.8 mile and 700 feet to the peak, where views stretch from Mount Shasta in the south to Mount Hood in the north. If this isn't enough for you, you can return to the Bohemia Saddle and follow the road one mile up to the watchtower on Fairview Peak.

User Groups: Hikers and dogs only. No horses or mountain bikes allowed. No wheelchair facilities.

Permits: Permits are not required. Parking and access are free.

Maps: For a map of the Umpqua National Forest, contact Umpqua National Forest, 2900 NW Stewart Parkway, Roseburg, OR, 97470, 541/672-6601. For a topographic map, ask the USGS for Fairview Peak.

Directions: Drive I-5 south of Eugene to Cottage Grove (Exit 174) and follow signs east to Dorena Lake on Row River Road, which becomes Road 22, for 30.5 miles. Turn right on Road 2212 at a sign for Fairview Peak and go 8.4 miles to Champion Saddle, then turn left on Road 2460. Follow this steep and rough road 1.1 miles to a junction in Bohemia Saddle. Park at the saddle and walk 100 yards to the left to the Bohemia Mountain Trail.

Contact: Umpqua National Forest, Cottage Grove Ranger District, 78405 Cedar Park Road, Cottage Grove, OR, 97424, 541/767-5000.

66 MIDDLE FORK WILLAMETTE RIVER
33.1 mi one-way/3 days

south of Hills Creek Reservoir in Willamette National Forest

Map 11.4, page 594

The Hills Creek Reservoir catches all of the Middle Fork Willamette River, the main branch of this colossal and important Oregon river. With plenty of established campgrounds along the way, it's possible to spend days here exploring the trail in segments. Backpackers may be tempted to try it in longer stretches along any of the points between the reservoir and Timpanogas Lake, the river's headwaters. Along the way are a series of springs—Chuckle Springs and Indigo Springs—that add to the river's bulk. With all the mixed stands of conifers, wildflowers, and waterfalls, there's plenty to see and explore. The total elevation gain for the trail is 4,000 feet, so plan ahead with a map.

The trail segments are as follows: Sand Prairie to Road 2127, 5.1 miles; Road 2127 to Road 2133, 5.2 miles; Road 2133 to 2143, 4.7 miles; Road 2143 to Indigo Springs, three miles; Indigo Springs to 2153, including Chuckle Springs, 6.8 miles; Road 2153 to Road 2154, 7.1 miles; Road 2154 to Timpanogas Lake, 0.3 mile; from Timpanogas Lake to the Pacific Crest Trail, 4.5 miles.

User Groups: Hikers, dogs, and horses. No mountain bikes allowed in wilderness area. No wheelchair facilities.

Permits: A free self-issue Wilderness Permit is required to enter the uppermost section in Waldo Lake Wilderness and is available at the trailhead; otherwise, permits are not required. Parking and access are free.

Maps: For a map of the Willamette National Forest, contact Willamette National Forest Headquarters, 3106 Pierce Parkway, Suite D, Springfield, OR, 97477, 541/225-6300. For a topographic map, ask the USGS for Rigdon Point.

Directions: To find the lower trailhead from Oakridge, drive 1.8 miles east on Highway 58. Between mileposts 37 and 38, turn south toward Hills Creek Dam on Road 23. In 0.5 mile, turn right on Road 21 for 11 miles to the Sand Prairie Campground access. Along this route are many trailheads for the Middle Fork Willamette River Trail, including points at Roads 2120, 2127, 2133, 2143, 2153, and Timpanogas Lake. The uppermost trailhead is found at the Timpanogas Campground: From the lower trailhead, continue on Road 21 another 2.5 miles and turn left on Timpanogas Road 2154, following signs for Timpanogas Lake for 9.3 miles to the campground and a trailhead parking area on the right.

Contact: Willamette National Forest, Middle Fork Ranger District, 46375 Highway 58, Westfir, OR, 97492, 541/782-2283.

67 ROSARY LAKES AND MAIDEN PEAK

5.4–19.0 mi/2.0 hr-2 days 🥾5 ⛰9

in the Willamette Pass in Willamette National Forest

Map 11.4, page 594

Of all the peaks in the Waldo Lake area, none stands higher than 7,818-foot Maiden Peak, easily visible from afar for its long, sloping sides and prominent spire near the summit. Looming above Odell Lake, it seems a daunting climb, yet a number of trails crisscross its flanks, including the Pacific Crest Trail, the main access point. Along the way, the trail passes the picturesque Rosary Lakes, a shelter, and little Maiden Lake.

Start by going north on the PCT for 2.7 gradual miles to Rosary Lakes, switchbacking up just before the lakes. Pass the three lakes over 1.4 miles, then keep straight on the PCT, climbing to Maiden Saddle. Keep right on the PCT and continue 1.8 miles to the log cabin Maiden Peak Shelter, built by the Eugene Nordic Club and Forest Service crews during the 1990s. Continue another 0.7 mile on the PCT to a junction. To climb Maiden Peak, turn right here on the Maiden Peak Trail, which climbs 1,700 feet in 2.7 miles to a left-hand, 0.3-mile summit trail climbing the final 300 feet to the crater. Return to the Maiden Peak Trail and continue forward on it to make a loop, descending 1,200 feet in 1.7 miles to a junction, going right toward Maiden Lake. After 0.6 mile, pass the lake and continue 2.3 miles back to the PCT. Go left to return to the highway and parking lot.

User Groups: Hikers, dogs, and horses. No mountain bikes allowed. No wheelchair facilities.

Permits: Permits are not required. Parking and access are free.

Maps: For a map of the Willamette National Forest, contact Willamette National Forest Headquarters, 3106 Pierce Parkway, Suite D, Springfield, OR, 97477, 541/225-6300. For a topographic map, ask the USGS for Willamette Pass and Odell Lake.

Directions: From Oakridge, drive east on Highway 58 to the Pacific Crest Trail lot 0.3 mile east of the Willamette Pass Ski Area.

Contact: Deschutes National Forest, Crescent Ranger District, 136471 Highway 97 North, P.O. Box 208, Crescent, OR, 97733, 541/433-3200.

68 DIVIDE LAKE

8.0 mi/4.0 hr 🥾3 ⛰8

southeast of Hills Creek Reservoir in Diamond Peak Wilderness

Map 11.4, page 594

It's hard to say if Divide Lake is a secret, but not many people seem to go there. For

Mount Yoran and Divide Lake

through-hikers on the Pacific Crest Trail, it lies hidden behind the long wall of the Cascade Divide. The Divide Lake Trail itself is somewhat remote, lying west of Diamond Peak at the far end of a long, lonely drive. The trailhead, awash in huckleberries, seems a good sign that this is something special. And it is. The views of Diamond Peak, so close it's startling, provide ever-present company, and views extend to the north out to the Three Sisters. At the end of the trail, huddled beneath the massive volcanic plug of Mount Yoran, is Divide Lake, a perfect pond for camping and swimming. You can continue up the trail and climb out on the Cascade Divide, a wall that abruptly ends at a steep precipice where you can stand with a foot in two watersheds.

Start on the Vivian Lake Trail, going 0.8 mile to Notch Lake, a lovely series of ponds rimmed with mountain heather. Just 0.2 mile past these lakes, go right on the Mount Yoran Trail for three miles (steep at times) to Divide Lake, perfect for a backpacking camp. From here, the trail switchbacks 0.8 mile up and over the Cascade Divide to meet the PCT.

User Groups: Hikers, dogs, and horses. No mountain bikes allowed. No wheelchair facilities.

Permits: A free self-issue Wilderness Permit is required and is available at the trailhead. Parking and access are free.

Maps: For a map of the Willamette National Forest, contact Willamette National Forest Headquarters, 3106 Pierce Parkway, Suite D, Springfield, OR, 97477, 541/225-6300. For a topographic map, ask the USGS for Diamond Peak.

Directions: To find the lower trailhead from Oakridge, drive 1.8 miles east on Highway 58. Between mileposts 37 and 38, turn south toward Hills Creek Dam on Road 23. Stay on Road 23 for 19.5 miles to a pass at Hemlock Butte. Turn left on a spur road to the trailhead parking area.

Contact: Willamette National Forest, Middle Fork Ranger District, 46375 Highway 58, Westfir, OR, 97492, 541/782-2283.

69 YORAN LAKE
12.0 mi/6.0 hr

south of Odell Lake in Diamond Peak Wilderness

Map 11.4, page 594

For travelers on Highway 58, one of the most beautiful sights is the view of Diamond Peak rising above enormous Odell Lake. Here's a chance at a much closer view, with long, red Diamond Peak lifting above clear and glassy, tree-rimmed Yoran Lake, a clear and glassy lake. There are plenty of opportunities here for backpackers to take a load off for the night—and there's more than one lake to choose from. Scattered along the Pacific Crest Trail are a bevy of beautiful lakes, each with its own personality: Midnight, Arrowhead, Hidden, and Lils, and a number of small ponds to boot. If you come in via the Pacific Crest Trail, you'll have to bushwhack your way a few hundred yards to big Yoran Lake, where you can continue on a loop past very lovely Karen Lake, then descend along Trapper Creek through thick woods of white pine, Douglas fir, and rhododendron.

The trail begins at Pengra Pass on the Pacific Crest Trail. Go toward Midnight Lake, 1.4 miles into the woods. Continue on the PCT a steady 3.2 miles past Arrowhead Lake on the right and Hidden Lake on the left, with views of Diamond Peak ahead. When you reach Lils Lake, go just beyond it and point your compass true south, passing the lake and a small pond, crest a rise, cross a meadow, and then find the lakeshore of Yoran Lake. Follow the left side of the lake past some campsites to its far end and the Yoran Lake Trail. Head left on the trail to stop by Karen Lake, continuing 4.3 miles to a junction. Go left one mile, eventually joining the dirt road back to Pengra Pass.

User Groups: Hikers, dogs, and horses. No mountain bikes allowed. No wheelchair facilities.

Permits: A free self-issue Wilderness Permit is required and is available at the trailhead. Parking and access are free.

Maps: For a map of the Deschutes National Forest, contact Deschutes National Forest Headquarters, 1001 SW Emkay Drive, Bend, OR, 97702, 541/383-5300. For a topographic map, ask the USGS for Willamette Pass.

Directions: From Oakridge, drive east on Highway 58. West of Willamette Pass 0.5 mile, turn right at a sign for Gold Lake Sno-Park onto Abernethy Road for one mile. Fork left on Road 300, and in another 0.2 mile fork left on a dirt road and park 200 yards down this road at a sign for Midnight Lake.

Contact: Deschutes National Forest, Crescent Ranger District, 136471 Highway 97 North, P.O. Box 208, Crescent, OR, 97733, 541/433-3200.

70 DIAMOND PEAK
12.0 mi/1 day

south of Hills Creek Reservoir in Diamond Peak Wilderness

Map 11.4, page 594

Of all the peaks in the Central Oregon Cascades, Diamond Peak seems the most unassuming. Due to its relative anonymity and distance from major urban areas, this wilderness area does not see the crowds that other areas of the forest do. This is to the benefit of not only the area, but also the hiker and backpacker who comes here. There is much to love about Diamond Peak Wilderness: quiet lakes, stately forests, and, of course, the long and graceful peak that sits in the center of it all. What's more, you can summit 8,744-foot Diamond Peak via a little known climber's trail on its south ridge. Along the way, there are opportunities for resting at two lovely and untrammeled lakes. If you do choose to climb the mountain, come prepared with a map, compass, and path-finding skills. What you'll find on top are views over Waldo Lake, the Three Sisters, Mount Jefferson, and far off, the tip of Mount Hood.

Start off on the Rockpile Trail 1.3 miles to a four-way junction, continuing straight another 1.2 miles, passing the Diamond Rockpile ridge on the left. At the next intersection, either way leads to a lake; to the left 0.2 mile is the larger Marie Lake, and to the right, the main trail continues to a right-hand side trail to little Rockpile Lake. Continue on the main trail 0.5 mile to reach the Pacific Crest Trail. Go left for 1.2 miles to a sharp right-hand turn on a corner atop an open ridge—if you have a GPS device, mark this spot. A series of rock cairns guides climbers up to tree line, then follow the ridge up and over the false summit one mile from the PCT. The next section follows a hogback and is sketchy—be careful. This route arrives at the true summit in 0.4 mile. Return as you came. For those not at ease with the climb, you can continue hiking along the PCT along the slope of Diamond Peak.

User Groups: Hikers, dogs, and horses. No mountain bikes allowed. No wheelchair facilities.

Permits: A free self-issue Wilderness Permit is required and is available at the trailhead. Parking and access are free.

Maps: For a map of the Willamette National Forest, contact Willamette National Forest Headquarters, 3106 Pierce Parkway, Suite D, Springfield, OR, 97477, 541/225-6300. For a topographic map, ask the USGS for Diamond Peak.

Directions: To find the lower trailhead from Oakridge, drive 1.8 miles east on Highway 58. Between mileposts 37 and 38, turn south toward Hills Creek Dam on Road 23. In 0.5 mile go right on Road 21, staying on this route for 29.2 miles. In 0.4 mile past Indigo Springs Campground, go left on Pioneer Gulch Road 2149 for 3.5 miles, then right on Rockpile Road 2160 for 2.3 miles to a sign for the Rockpile Trail, parking beyond the trailhead on the right shoulder.

Contact: Willamette National Forest, Middle Fork Ranger District, 46375 Highway 58, Westfir, OR, 97492, 541/782-2283.

71 WINDY LAKES
11.2 mi/5.0 hr

south of Crescent Lake in Oregon Cascades Recreation Area

Map 11.4, page 594

Just south of Diamond Peak Wilderness is the largely unknown Oregon Cascades Recreation Area. You'd be hard pressed to find any other area in these mountains with so many lakes and ponds. The real jewels are at the end of the trail, where the Windy Lakes fan out below the massive wall of Cowhorn Mountain. Many of these lakes are deep, great for swimming, and certainly make great camping spots. Just be aware that early summer brings mosquitoes.

Begin on the Meek Lake Trail, crossing Summit Creek in 0.2 mile and arriving at Meek Lake in another 0.3 mile. From there the trail ambles into a pond-strewn forest for most of the next 2.4 miles. At a junction, go left to continue toward Windy Lakes (the right-hand junction heads to Summit Lake). After 1.6 miles the trail reaches North Windy Lake, and a right-hand side trail leads down to East Windy Lake. At the intersection with the Crescent Lake Trail, go right toward South Windy Lake. In 0.9 mile the trail skirts East Windy, passes another lake, then reaches its end at South Windy Lake. Return as you came.

User Groups: Hikers, dogs, horses, and mountain bikes.

Permits: Permits are not required. Parking and access are free.

Maps: For a map of the Deschutes National Forest, contact Deschutes National Forest Headquarters, 1001 SW Emkay Drive, Bend, OR, 97702, 541/383-5300. For a topographic map, ask the USGS for Cowhorn Mountain.

Directions: Drive Highway 58, going seven miles east of the Willamette Pass to Crescent Junction, turning right on Road 60 for 2.2 miles. At an intersection, turn right to stay on this road for another five miles. Turn right on dirt Road 6010 to Summit Lake. Follow this road 3.9 miles to the Meek Lake Trail on the left.

Contact: Deschutes National Forest, Crescent Ranger District, 136471 Highway 97 North, P.O. Box 208, Crescent, OR, 97733, 541/433-3200.

72 COWHORN MOUNTAIN LOOP
11.9 mi/6.0 hr

south of Hills Creek Reservoir in Willamette National Forest

Map 11.4, page 594

Two mountain peaks, worn down by time, stand sentry over the source of the Middle Fork Willamette River. In their shadow, Timpanogas and Indigo Lakes glisten in the light. Sawtooth Mountain stands more than 1,000 feet above Indigo Lake, but the goal here is

Cowhorn Mountain, which once really did have a horn (it fell off in a 1911 storm). A magnificent loop climbs to the Pacific Crest Trail and scrambles to the 7,664 peak of Cowhorn with its amazing view north to the Three Sisters and south to Crater Lake.

Begin by following the Indigo Lake Trail 0.7 mile to a junction, staying to the left another 1.2 miles to Indigo, where a one-mile trail circles the lake. Continue on the main trail up a series of steady-climbing switchbacks 1.7 miles to a pass. To the right, a climber's trail heads up two miles and 600 feet to Sawtooth Mountain. Go left on the Windy Pass Trail 2.1 miles to a junction; to climb to the peak of Cowhorn go right 0.3 mile to the Pacific Crest Trail, then right on the PCT 0.3 mile to a scramble trail by a rock cairn following a ridge up the steep climb 0.4 mile. To descend on the loop, return to the Windy Pass Trail and go right and down 2.7 miles to a junction, and turn left toward Timpanogas Lake for 1.1 miles. At the lake, go right 0.4 mile back to the campground.

User Groups: Hikers, dogs, and mountain bikes. No horses allowed. No wheelchair facilities.

Permits: Permits are not required. Parking and access are free.

Maps: For a map of the Willamette National Forest, contact Willamette National Forest Headquarters, 3106 Pierce Parkway, Suite D, Springfield, OR, 97477, 541/225-6300. For a topographic map, ask the USGS for Cowhorn Mountain.

Directions: To find the lower trailhead from Oakridge, drive 1.8 miles east on Highway 58. Between mileposts 37 and 38, turn south toward Hills Creek Dam on Road 23. In 0.5 mile, turn right on Road 21 for 31.2 miles. Turn right on Timpanogas Road 2154, going 9.3 miles to the Timpanogas Campground on the left. Drive into the campground and watch for the trailhead sign on the right.

Contact: Willamette National Forest, Middle Fork Ranger District, 46375 Highway 58, Westfir, OR, 97492, 541/782-2283.

⁊⁊ BULLPUP LAKE AND BULLDOG ROCK
1.4–7.0 mi/1.0–3.5 hr

north of North Umpqua River in Umpqua National Forest

Map 11.4, page 594

The Calapooya Mountains form a high divide between the watershed of the North Umpqua and the Willamette Rivers. One entry point to this heavily eroded lava mountain range is via Bullpup Lake, an easy destination in itself, with a shake-roofed shelter on the shore and towering andesite cliffs above it. Top that slope and the views quickly extend out to the Cascade Range, and you can go on farther to the Bear Camp Shelter, passing Bulldog Rock along the way.

The initial hike extends only 0.4 mile to Bullpup Lake and the shelter, and you can circle the lake on a 0.6-mile loop. At the far end of that loop (going left is the shortest, at 0.2-mile) you can continue up the slope and on the Bulldog Rock Trail 2.8 miles to a view of Bulldog Rock, and another 2.2 miles beyond that to the Bear Camp Shelter.

User Groups: Hikers, dogs, horses, and mountain bikes. No wheelchair facilities.

Permits: Permits are not required. Parking and access are free.

Maps: For a map of the Umpqua National Forest, contact Umpqua National Forest, 2900 NW Stewart Parkway, Roseburg, OR, 97470, 541/672-6601. For a topographic map, ask the USGS for Chiltcoot Mountain and Reynolds Ridge.

Directions: From Roseburg, drive east on OR 138 for 38.4 miles and turn left on Steamboat Creek Road for 10.4 miles to a fork. Go right on Bend Creek-Washboard Road 3817 for 2.2 miles, then right on Road 3850 for 5.6 miles, then left on Road 200 for 0.1 mile, and finally left on Road 300 for four miles to the trail parking area on the right.

Contact: Umpqua National Forest, North Umpqua Ranger District, 18782 North Umpqua Highway, Glide, OR, 97443, 541/496-3532.

74 ILLAHEE ROCK LOOKOUT
1.4 mi/1.0 hr

north of Boulder Creek Wilderness in Umpqua National Forest

Map 11.4, page 594

Not one, but two fire lookout towers are set atop 5,382-foot Illahee Rock. The newer one was built in 1958, and its 40-foot-high lookout is staffed each summer. The older one is a cupola-style lookout building, built in 1925 and housed in a lightning cage. This easy 1.4-mile round-trip climbs 500 feet to the towers, with high-point views extending out over a number of Cascade peaks.

User Groups: Hikers, dogs, horses, and mountain bikes. No wheelchair facilities.

Permits: Permits are not required. Parking and access are free.

Maps: For a map of the Umpqua National Forest, contact Umpqua National Forest, 2900 NW Stewart Parkway, Roseburg, OR, 97470, 541/672-6601. For a topographic map, ask the USGS for Illahee Rock.

Directions: From Roseburg, drive 47 miles on OR 138 and turn left on Illahee Road 4760 for eight miles. Go straight on Road 100 for 1.3 miles, then left on the steep and rocky Road 104 to its end.

Contact: Umpqua National Forest, North Umpqua Ranger District, 18782 North Umpqua Highway, Glide, OR, 97443, 541/496-3532.

75 NORTH UMPQUA NATIONAL RECREATION TRAIL
3.5–79.0 mi/1–10 days

east of Roseburg on the North Umpqua River

Map 11.4, page 594

Just past Idleyld Park in the canyon of the North Umpqua River begins a trail and backpacking adventure. The North Umpqua National Recreation Trail follows the river 79 miles, passing waterfalls, rapids, and

Toketee Falls on the North Umpqua River

© SEAN PATRICK HILL

gorges, crossing creeks, and meeting up with several side trails leading to old homesteads and shelters. You can even access hot springs along the way. The trail follows the river up to its headwaters at Maidu Lake high in the Cascades, with many access points along the good steady trip. You'll pass through unique forests of sugar pine, Shasta red fir, and incense cedar. Be sure to contact the USFS and BLM about trail conditions; at the time of this writing, the Calf Segment is closed due to unsafe conditions.

The Umpqua Trail is segmented into sections suitable for day hikes or backpacking trips. The Swiftwater Trailhead accesses the 15.5-mile Tioga section along the south bank of the river, ending at the Wright Creek Trailhead. From here, it's 5.5 miles to the Mott Trailhead, then 5.0 miles to the Panther Trailhead. The next 3.7-mile section to Calf Creek Trailhead is closed as of now. The 3.6-mile section to Marsters Trailhead is open, however. From here, the trail follows the north bank of the river 4.1 miles through the Jessie Wright section to the Soda Springs Trailhead, then the longer 9.6-mile Deer Leap section to the Toketee Lake Trailhead. From here the trail leaves Highway 138, going 3.5 miles to the Hot Springs Trailhead, and on 13.0 miles into the strangely named Dread and Terror Section to the White Mule Trailhead, another 6.3 miles through the Lemolo section to the Kelsay Valley Trailhead, and finally 9.0 miles through the Maidu segment to the Digit Point Trailhead and the end of the trail.

User Groups: Hikers, dogs, horses, and mountain bikes. No wheelchair facilities.

Permits: Permits are not required. Parking and access are free for most trailheads, excepting Umpqua Hot Springs.

Maps: For a map of the Umpqua National Forest, contact Umpqua National Forest, 2900 NW Stewart Parkway, Roseburg, OR, 97470, 541/672-6601. For a topographic map, ask the USGS for Old Fairview, Mace Mountain, Steamboat, Illahee Rock, Toketee Falls, Lemolo Lake, Tolo Mountain, and Burn Butte.

Directions: To access the Tioga Trailhead, the westernmost entry for the North Umpqua Trail, follow OR 138 east from Roseburg 22 miles. One mile past Idleyld Park, turn right at a "Swiftwater Park" sign, cross the river, and park at the Tioga Trailhead. Trailheads are numerous along Highway 138 and Forest Service Road 3401.

Contact: Bureau of Land Management, Roseburg District, 777 NW Garden Valley Boulevard, Roseburg, OR, 97471, 541/440-4930, or Umpqua National Forest, 2900 NW Stewart Parkway, Roseburg, OR, 97470, 541/672-6601.

76 SUSAN CREEK FALLS AND FALL CREEK FALLS

3.8 mi/1.5 hr

east of Roseburg on the North Umpqua River

Map 11.4, page 594

If you're in the area of the North Umpqua River and looking for a place to stretch your legs or just take in the fresh air, try these two waterfalls just off Highway 138. The 70-foot Susan Creek Falls tumble over the canyon wall, on top of which is a fenced area of Indian mounds, where tribes reputedly held vision quests for their youth. A bit further east is Fall Creek Falls, with a side trail leading to a columnar basalt outcrop called Jobs Garden. Both trails are easily hiked together, though from two different trailheads.

The Susan Creek Falls Trail sets out 0.7 mile up to a viewpoint of the trail, and continues 0.3 mile to the top of the canyon and the Indian mounds. The Fall Creek Falls Trail climbs 0.9 mile to the top of the falls, with a side trail to Jobs Garden at the 0.3-mile mark.

User Groups: Hikers and dogs only. No horses or mountain bikes. Susan Creek Falls is wheelchair accessible.

Permits: Permits are not required. Parking and access are free.

Maps: For a topographic map, ask the USGS for Old Fairview and Mace Mountain.

Directions: To access Susan Creek Falls, drive east of Roseburg 28.3 miles on OR 138 to the Susan Creek Recreation Area lot on the right. To access Fall Creek Falls, drive another 3.9 miles east of Susan Creek on OR 138 and park at a trailhead sign on the left.

Contact: Bureau of Land Management, Roseburg District, 777 NW Garden Valley Boulevard, Roseburg, OR, 97471, 541/440-4930, or Umpqua National Forest, North Umpqua Ranger District, 18782 North Umpqua Highway, Glide, OR, 97443, 541/496-3532.

77 BOULDER CREEK

8.0-21.6 mi/3.0 hr-2 days

north of the North Umpqua River in Boulder Creek Wilderness

Map 11.4, page 594

Above the North Umpqua River, this low-elevation wilderness area is open year-round and makes for excellent backpacking. There is camping available on a plateau of ponderosa pines at the top of the Boulder Creek canyon. From this plateau, trails radiate in all directions; hike into this area to get a taste of what these mountains offer.

Go under the giant pipe and head up the Pine Bench Trail 0.4 mile, then go left 1.5 miles to top Pine Bench. Once you reach another trail junction, go right 0.4 mile to a viewpoint with a spring and camping area. Continue on 1.7 miles to a crossing of Boulder Creek, a good turnaround point. Backpackers can follow the Boulder Creek Trail another 6.8 miles, fording the creek three times then grinding uphill on a series of switchbacks to its end. Return as you came.

User Groups: Hikers, dogs, and horses. No mountain bikes allowed. No wheelchair facilities.

Permits: A free self-issue Wilderness Permit is required and is available at the trailhead. Parking and access are free.

Maps: For a map of the Umpqua National Forest and Boulder Creek Wilderness, contact Umpqua National Forest, 2900 NW Stewart Parkway, Roseburg, OR, 97470, 541/672-6601. For a topographic map, ask the USGS for Illahee Rock.

Directions: From Roseburg, drive 54.7 miles east on OR 138. Between mileposts 54 and 55, turn left at a sign for Spring Creek then immediately left on Soda Springs Road, following this gravel road 1.4 miles to a trailhead parking area on the left.

Contact: Umpqua National Forest, Diamond Lake Ranger District, 2020 Toketee Ranger Station Road, Idleyld Park, OR, 97477, 541/498-2531.

78 TOKETEE AND WATSON FALLS
1.4 mi/0.5 hr 👣1 ⛰8

west of Toketee Ranger Station in Umpqua National Forest

Map 11.4, page 594

These two easy trails head to two of the Umpqua Canyon's most famous falls. Toketee Falls is a heavily photographed (and heavily visited) plunge along the North Umpqua River, the water spills in two tiers, one falling 40 feet into a bowl and the other 80 feet over a notch in some of the most beautiful examples of hexagonal columnar basalt anywhere. From the trailhead, you'll head 0.8 mile out and back to a viewpoint overlooking this deep gorge.

You'll see Watson Falls, the highest in southwest Oregon, not from the top but from the bottom of the 272-foot plunge. Watson makes a fun 0.6-mile loop and passes a viewpoint at the base of the falls.

User Groups: Hikers and dogs only. No wheelchair facilities.

Permits: Permits are not required. Parking and access are free.

Maps: For a map of the Umpqua National Forest and Boulder Creek Wilderness, contact Umpqua National Forest, 2900 NW Stewart Parkway, Roseburg, OR, 97470, 541/672-6601. For a topographic map, ask the USGS for Illahee Rock.

Directions: To access Toketee Falls, drive 58.6 miles east of Roseburg on OR 138 and turn north on Toketee-Rigdon Road 34. Turn left at each junction for 0.4 mile to a parking area. To access Watson Falls, drive 60.9 miles east of Roseburg on OR 138 and turn south on Fish Creek Road 37 to a lot on the right.

Contact: Umpqua National Forest, Diamond Lake Ranger District, 2020 Toketee Ranger Station Road, Idleyld Park, OR, 97477, 541/498-2531.

79 UMPQUA HOT SPRINGS
0.6 mi/0.25 hr

north of Toketee Ranger Station in Umpqua National Forest

Map 11.4, page 594

Along this stretch of the North Umpqua River Trail, a spur heads off to one of the most famous hot springs in Oregon: the sheltered pool of Umpqua Hot Springs. A number of pools have been dug into the orange travertine deposits that form this cascading cliff down to the North Umpqua River and its old-growth forests. Recently, the bridge has been removed over the river, but by the time of this publication it may have already been replaced. If not, you can hike in from a trailhead on Road 3401 just before the road crosses the river, which adds 1.6 miles to the hike but also adds a profusion of spring-flowering rhododendron bushes.

From the lot, follow the trail toward the river to a crossing and up the hill for 0.1 mile. At the junction, go right 0.2 mile to the shelter atop the cliff and the hot springs. The hot springs are clothing-optional.

User Groups: Hikers only. No wheelchair facilities.

Permits: Permits are not required. A federal Northwest Forest Pass is required to park here; the cost is $5 a day or $30 for an annual pass. You can buy a day pass at the trailhead, at ranger stations, or through private vendors.

Maps: For a map of the Umpqua National Forest and Boulder Creek Wilderness, contact Umpqua National Forest, 2900 NW Stewart Parkway, Roseburg, OR, 97470, 541/672-6601. For a topographic map, ask the USGS for Illahee Rock.

Directions: Drive 58.6 miles east of Roseburg on OR 138 and turn north on Toketee-Rigdon Road 34. Keep left along the lake and continue two miles, forking right on Thorn Prairie Road to a large lot on the left.

Contact: Umpqua National Forest, Diamond Lake Ranger District, 2020 Toketee Ranger Station Road, Idleyld Park, OR, 97477, 541/498-2531.

80 LEMOLO FALLS
3.4 mi/1.5 hr

north of Toketee Ranger Station in Umpqua National Forest

Map 11.4, page 594

On this upper reach of the North Umpqua Trail, near the oddly named Dread and Terror Ridge, the river plunges over 100-foot Lemolo Falls and into a canyon. This woodsy hike begins at the spot the trail crosses Road 2610. Start the section of trail south of the road, crossing a canal. In 1.7 miles you'll reach a viewpoint of the falls, then continue another 0.7 mile to a footbridge crossing of the river. From here, the trail continues on another 10 miles towards the Umpqua Hot Springs.

User Groups: Hikers, dogs, horses, and mountain bikes. No wheelchair facilities.

Permits: Permits are not required. Parking and access are free.

Maps: For a map of the Umpqua National Forest, contact Umpqua National Forest, 2900 NW Stewart Parkway, Roseburg, OR, 97470, 541/672-6601. For a topographic map, ask the USGS for Lemolo Lake.

Directions: Drive east of Roseburg 70 miles on OR 138 and turn north on Road 2610 towards Lemolo Lake Recreation Area. After five miles cross the dam and go left on Road 2610 for 0.6 mile to a parking area.

Contact: Umpqua National Forest, Diamond Lake Ranger District, 2020 Toketee Ranger Station Road, Idleyld Park, OR, 97477, 541/498-2531.

81 WOLF CREEK FALLS
2.6 mi/1.0 hr

southeast of Glide on the Little River

Map 11.4, page 594

The so-called "Land of Umpqua" (as the tourism advertisements like to call it) is, above all, a land of waterfalls. There are so many waterfalls feeding the North Umpqua River Canyon that it would be quite impossible to do them all even in a week's time. But here and there, you can catch some of the finest. The 70-foot Wolf Creek Falls feeds the Little River and makes for a good 2.6-mile in-and-out hike from the trailhead. In the rainy season, the falls really pound, but in the dryer months you'll get a chance to see some of the carved-out bedrock beneath the plunge.

User Groups: Hikers and dogs only. No wheelchair facilities.

Permits: Permits are not required. Parking and access are free.

Maps: For a topographic map, ask the USGS for Red Butte.

Directions: From Roseburg, drive east on OR 138 toward Glide. At milepost 16, go right on Little River Road for 10.4 miles and park at the Wolf Creek Trail parking on the right.

Contact: Bureau of Land Management, Roseburg District, 777 NW Garden Valley Boulevard, Roseburg, OR, 97471, 541/440-4930.

82 HEMLOCK LAKE

7.2 mi/3.5 hr

southeast of Glide in Umpqua National Forest

Map 11.4, page 594

Beyond the reservoir of Hemlock Lake lie some of the most beautiful alpine meadows in this part of the world. Hellebore, also known as corn lily, bloom their tall sprouts in a series of meadows dotted by Douglas fir and Shasta red fir. In the Yellow Jacket Glade you'll find shooting stars (the flower, not the falling stardust) and trilliums, and in other sections you'll see marsh marigolds, yellow fawn lilies, bunchberry, and violets.

Starting on the Hemlock Creek Trail you'll quickly come to a junction; go right then left on the Yellow Jacket Loop Trail for a 1.1-mile tour of Hemlock Meadows. At a junction, it's worth it to go right up 0.8 mile to 5,310-foot Flat Rock with its views of the rim of Crater Lake, Diamond Peak, Mount Thielsen, and Mount Bailey. Head back to Yellow Jacket and go right at the junction through Yellowjacket

Glade, continuing 2.9 miles along a viewpoint ridge and paralleling Road 625 to the next junction, heading left on the faint path and passing Dead Cow Lake. Stay left at the next two junctions for 1.6 miles, reaching the shore of Hemlock Lake and returning to the parking area.

User Groups: Hikers, dogs, horses, and mountain bikes. No wheelchair facilities.

Permits: Permits are not required. Parking and access are free.

Maps: For a map of the Umpqua National Forest, contact Umpqua National Forest, 2900 NW Stewart Parkway, Roseburg, OR, 97470, 541/672-6601. For a topographic map, ask the USGS for Quartz Mountain.

Directions: Drive east of Roseburg on OR 138 to milepost 16 and turn right on Little River Road, which becomes Road 27. Follow this road 18.8 miles on pavement and 11.5 miles on gravel to Hemlock Lake, crossing the dam to an intersection and the trailhead.

Contact: Umpqua National Forest, North Umpqua Ranger District, 18782 North Umpqua Highway, Glide, OR, 97443, 541/496-3532.

83 TWIN LAKES AND TWIN LAKES MOUNTAIN

3.2-5.4 mi/1.5-3.0 hr

south of the North Umpqua River in Umpqua National Forest

Map 11.4, page 594

If you are a novice backpacker, or just want a quick trip, or are camping with kids, make Twin Lakes your destination. Once you're settled in and the tent is pitched, you can ramble off on a couple side trails: Twin Lakes Mountain, for example, is a fairly easy climb to a viewpoint above the lakes that also looks out over the Cascade Mountains. You can also just circle the lakes to find a couple old shelters. Beyond lies the largely roadless Boulder Creek Wilderness.

From the trailhead, hike in 0.6 mile on

the Twin Lakes Trail to a junction, with a viewpoint of three Cascade peaks along the way. Turn right then a quick left for 0.3 mile to an old shelter. To the right at this junction are six campsites with picnic tables, and this Twin Lakes Loop Trail joins a loop around the larger of the two lakes, 0.7 mile in all. At the far end of the lake, a spur trail joins a 0.7-mile loop trail around the smaller lake, with another log shelter along the way.

To climb Twin Lakes Mountain head back from the old shelter on the larger lake toward the parking area. At the junction, go right and then stay right for 1.1 miles to a viewpoint. Another 0.6 mile and this trail ends at Road 530.

User Groups: Hikers, dogs, horses, and mountain bikes. No wheelchair facilities.

Permits: Permits are not required. Parking and access are free.

Maps: For a map of the Umpqua National Forest, contact Umpqua National Forest, 2900 NW Stewart Parkway, Roseburg, OR, 97470, 541/672-6601. For a topographic map, ask the USGS for Twin Lakes Mountain.

Directions: From Roseburg, drive 49 miles east on OR 138. Cross the North Umpqua River on Marsters Bridge and go right on Wilson Creek Road 4770, following this gravel road nine miles to the trailhead parking at road's end.

Contact: Umpqua National Forest, North Umpqua Ranger District, 18782 North Umpqua Highway, Glide, OR, 97443, 541/496-3532.

84 TIPSOO PEAK

6.2 mi/2.5 hr   🥾2 ⛰9

northeast of Diamond Lake in Mount Thielsen Wilderness

Map 11.4, page 594

Nearby Crater Lake National Park and Diamond Lake attract a lot of tourists, but this alpine area begs for exploration. Just inside Mount Thielsen Wilderness is 8,034-foot Tipsoo Peak, a pretty substantial peak with the accompanying view it deserves. What's more, this trail leads right to its summit with a breathtaking view of the alpine territory around it, including the pumice plains dotted with clumps of trees, not to mention a view of peaks extending from Mount Shasta in California to the Three Sisters in Central Oregon, with Mount Thielsen's domineering spire clearly marking the centerpiece of this wilderness.

The Tipsoo Peak Trail itself is a single track heading up 3.1 miles to the summit. It is possible, with a compass, to hike cross-country across Tipsoo Meadow 0.5 mile to the Pacific Crest Trail. From there, Maidu and Miller Lakes are five miles to the north, Howlock Meadows only 1.6 miles south, and the access to the Mount Thielsen climbing trail five miles beyond that.

User Groups: Hikers, dogs, and horses. No mountain bikes allowed. No wheelchair facilities.

Permits: A free self-issue Wilderness Permit is required and is available at the trailhead. A federal Northwest Forest Pass is required to park here; the cost is $5 a day or $30 for an annual pass. You can buy a day pass at the trailhead, at ranger stations, or through private vendors.

Maps: For a map of the Umpqua National Forest and Mount Thielsen Wilderness, contact Umpqua National Forest, 2900 NW Stewart Parkway, Roseburg, OR, 97470, 541/672-6601. For a topographic map, ask the USGS for Mount Thielsen.

Directions: Drive east of Roseburg 75 miles on OR 138. Near milepost 75, turn east on Cinnamon Butte Road 4793 and go 1.7 miles. Go straight on Wits End Road 100 for 3.2 miles to a Tipsoo Trail sign on the right.

Contact: Umpqua National Forest, Diamond Lake Ranger District, 2020 Toketee Ranger Station Road, Idleyld Park, OR, 97477, 541/498-2531.

85 DIAMOND LAKE

11.5 mi/5.0 hr

on Diamond Lake in Umpqua National Forest

Map 11.4, page 594

It's easy to see why 3,015-acre Diamond Lake is one of the most popular destinations in the area, even more so than nearby Crater Lake National Park. Two mountains hover at opposite sides above the placid waters: Mount Thielsen and Mount Bailey. There are hundreds of campsites along the lake—well-established car campsites, needless to say—and picnic areas and boat ramps. There are, too, a few side trails to little Teal Lake and Horse Lake. All in all, the Diamond Lake Trail is a good trail if you're staying here. Plus, the entire route is paved, making it accessible to all and a good route for bikes. And if you're in the mood for a swim, Diamond Lake's 20-foot average depth means it warms up quickly, unlike so many of the other Cascade high-mountain lakes.

You can go either way along the loop trail. The east side follows routes through the large Diamond Lake Campground for most of its 3.8 miles to the South Shore Picnic Area. The south side continues 1.9 miles to a crossing of Road 4795, with side trails to two small lakes and along Silent Creek. The west side of the lakeshore is mostly private land, and the trail goes 2.9 miles above the road, but with views to Mount Thielsen. After crossing the road again near Thielsen View Campground and going another 1.2 miles to the road crossing at Lake Creek. The final uninterrupted stretch travels 1.7 miles along the north shore back to the lodge.

User Groups: Hikers, dogs, and mountain bikes. No horses allowed. The paved lakeshore loop is wheelchair accessible.

Permits: Permits are not required. Parking and access are free.

Maps: For a map of the Umpqua National Forest, contact Umpqua National Forest, 2900 NW Stewart Parkway, Roseburg, OR, 97470, 541/672-6601. For a topographic map, ask the USGS for Diamond Lake.

Directions: To find the Diamond Lake Lodge, drive east of Roseburg 78.6 miles east on OR 138 to a sign for Diamond Lake, and turn right on Road 6592, following signs for the Lodge, turning right and going past a boat ramp to the parking area.

Contact: Umpqua National Forest, Diamond Lake Ranger District, 2020 Toketee Ranger Station Road, Idleyld Park, OR, 97477, 541/498-2531.

86 THIELSEN CREEK AND HOWLOCK MOUNTAIN

11.4-15.7 mi/6.0-8.0 hr

northeast of Diamond Lake in Mount Thielsen Wilderness

Map 11.4, page 594

A series of meadows in the Mount Thielsen Wilderness lie strewn along Thielsen Creek and the Pacific Crest Trail, and the hardy hiker can visit one, two, or all three of them in a single hike. Along the way, there's plenty to see in this alpine country, including Mount Thielsen itself looming above this country like a church spire. The Howlock Mountain Trail provides the opportunity for a long loop, with extended opportunities for backpacking available, too.

The Howlock Mountain Trail starts at the trailhead, ducking through a tunnel under the highway, and continuing 1.1 miles to a junction with the Spruce Ridge Trail. Stay left on the Thielsen Creek Trail another 2.4 miles through a hot, dusty country of lodgepole pines and manzanita bushes to Timothy Meadows and Thielsen Creek. To continue on to Thielsen Meadow, go right 2.2 miles along Thielsen Creek to the junction of the Pacific Crest Trail.

From here, you can return as you came, or for an outstanding loop, go north and left on the PCT for three miles along the base of Howlock Mountain to Howlock Meadows, then left 3.5 miles back to Timothy Meadows.

User Groups: Hikers, dogs, and horses. No mountain bikes allowed. No wheelchair facilities.

Permits: A free self-issue Wilderness Permit is required and is available at the trailhead. A federal Northwest Forest Pass is required to park here; the cost is $5 a day or $30 for an annual pass. You can buy a day pass at the trailhead, at ranger stations, or through private vendors.

Maps: For a map of the Umpqua National Forest and Mount Thielsen Wilderness, contact Umpqua National Forest, 2900 NW Stewart Parkway, Roseburg, OR, 97470, 541/672-6601. For a topographic map, ask the USGS for Mount Thielsen.

Directions: From Roseburg, drive 78.6 miles east on OR 138 to a sign for Diamond Lake, and turn right on Road 6592 for 0.3 mile to a parking area on the left.

Contact: Umpqua National Forest, Diamond Lake Ranger District, 2020 Toketee Ranger Station Road, Idleyld Park, OR, 97477, 541/498-2531.

87 MOUNT THIELSEN
10.0 mi/6.0 hr   🥾5 ⛰10

northeast of Diamond Lake in Mount Thielsen Wilderness

Map 11.4, page 594

Mount Thielsen's peak, a towering 9,182 feet in the sky, has earned the nickname "Lightning Rod of the Cascades" for no uncertain reason. What was once an 11,000-foot-high volcano has been whittled down by glaciers to its single lava plug, an andesite core left after 100,000 years. What you'll find on the peak are the lightning-melted spots of fulgurite, a re-crystalized glassy rock that pocks the summit boulders. Named for a pioneer railroad engineer, Thielsen is no climb for the weak-hearted. It demands endurance, stamina, sureness of hands, and outright skill; the final ascent is a dangerous technical climb that requires ropes and climbing partners to aid you.

Any ascent past the topmost ledge, a Class 4 rock climb, is done at your own risk. *Only experienced climbers should attempt this final pitch.* Should you make it, you'll find a canister summit register at the top.

From the Mount Thielsen Trailhead, climb 1.4 miles into the forest, staying right at a junction with the Spruce Ridge Trail, and continuing another 2.4 miles into the Wilderness Area to a junction with the PCT. To attempt the summit, continue straight up the ridge 1.2 miles on a climber's trail, spiraling to the right around the eastern ledge at the base of the 80-foot peak. The drop from this ledge to the east is thousands of feet, a dizzying view down to the deserts of Eastern Oregon. *Do not climb to the peak without rock climbing experience; rockfall and exposure make this pitch dangerous.* To ascend to the peak requires climbing up the series of cracks and fissures in the rock, wedging your way up to the peak. To be sure, the peak is an unnerving experience and only for the stout-hearted. The shoulder beneath the peak has expansive views across the Cascade Range, down into Crater Lake, and out over Diamond Lake to the west.

User Groups: Hikers only. Dogs are not recommended. Horses can access the PCT from the nearby Howlock Mountain Trailhead. No mountain bikes allowed. No wheelchair facilities.

Permits: A free self-issue Wilderness Permit is required and is available at the trailhead. A federal Northwest Forest Pass is required to park here; the cost is $5 a day or $30 for an annual pass. You can buy a day pass at the trailhead, at ranger stations, or through private vendors.

Maps: For a map of the Umpqua National Forest and Mount Thielsen Wilderness, contact Umpqua National Forest, 2900 NW Stewart Parkway, Roseburg, OR, 97470, 541/672-6601. For a topographic map, ask the USGS for Mount Thielsen.

Directions: From Roseburg, drive 81.6 miles east on OR 138 to a large trailhead parking area on the left.

Contact: Umpqua National Forest, Diamond Lake Ranger District, 2020 Toketee Ranger Station Road, Idleyld Park, OR, 97477, 541/498-2531.

88 MOUNT BAILEY
9.8 mi/5.0 hr

west of Diamond Lake in Umpqua National Forest

Map 11.4, page 594

The Mount Bailey National Recreation Trail follows what in winter becomes a Nordic trail. Blue diamonds lead the way to some alpine ski runs on this dome-shaped mountain above Diamond Lake. But in summer, this mountain makes a fairly easy summit—no gear or technical expertise required. All you'll need is a little stamina to make it up the crater rim to an 8,368-foot view of the Cascade Mountains in all directions. From Road 300, the trail climbs steadily up 2.2 miles to cross another dirt road, then begins to really climb up the mountain's ridge for 2.7 miles and up 2,300 feet to the south summit with its small crater and finally the true summit.

User Groups: Hikers and dogs only. No wheelchair facilities.

Permits: Permits are not required. Parking and access are free.

Maps: For a map of the Umpqua National Forest, contact Umpqua National Forest, 2900 NW Stewart Parkway, Roseburg, OR, 97470, 541/672-6601. For a topographic map, ask the USGS for Diamond Lake.

Directions: Drive east of Roseburg 78.6 miles on OR 138 to a sign for Diamond Lake, and turn right on Road 6592, following this road to the South Shore Picnic Area. Turn right on Road 4795 for 1.7 miles and turn left on Road 300 for 0.4 mile to a parking area.

Contact: Umpqua National Forest, Diamond Lake Ranger District, 2020 Toketee Ranger Station Road, Idleyld Park, OR, 97477, 541/498-2531.

89 BUCKEYE AND CLIFF LAKES
3.4-8.9 mi/1.5-4.5 hr

in the Rogue-Umpqua Divide Wilderness

Map 11.4, page 594

In this 16- to 25-million-year-old mountain range, the forest has had time to get a foothold in this lovely bottom of high lakes. Even a massive landslide that befell this valley when Grasshopper Mountain collapsed 1,000 years ago has been repaired by the trees. Beneath what is left of that mountain, Buckeye and Cliff Lakes warm in the afternoon sun and invite backpackers. Being so close to Fish Lake (see next listing), you can easily turn this into a multi-day trip. For a different entry into the Rogue-Umpqua Divide Wilderness, try starting this trail from the Skimmerhorn Trailhead. You'll climb to a high meadow above the lakes.

To access the Lakes Trail from the Skimmerhorn Trailhead, hike in 0.2 mile and keep left at the first junction, going another 0.7 mile and keeping right at the next junction with the Indian Trail. After 0.1 mile go left at the next junction with the Acker Divide Trail for 0.4 mile, arriving at Buckeye Lake. In 0.3 mile arrive at Cliff Lake. From here, you can return as you came.

To continue on a longer loop to Grasshopper Mountain, continue another 0.3 mile past Cliff Lake to a junction. Now go right on the Grasshopper Trail and climb onto a high plateau of mixed conifer for one mile to Grasshopper Meadow. A right-hand junction leads 0.6 mile and 300 feet up to Grasshopper Mountain and good views. Going straight here leads to a junction with the Acker Divide Trail; go right on this trail and down 0.9 mile to a trailhead near Road 550 and go right, continuing on the Acker Divide Trail. In 0.4 mile find Mosquito Camp; continue on 1.7 miles, passing Little Fish Lake, and rejoining the Lakes Trail. Go left one mile to the trailhead.

User Groups: Hikers, dogs, and horses. No mountain bikes allowed. No wheelchair facilities.

Permits: A free self-issue Wilderness Permit is required and is available at the trailhead. Parking and access are free.

Maps: For a map of the Umpqua National Forest and Rogue-Umpqua Divide Wilderness, contact Umpqua National Forest, 2900 NW Stewart Parkway, Roseburg, OR, 97470, 541/672-6601. For a topographic map, ask the USGS for Buckeye Lake.

Directions: From Roseburg, drive 25 miles north on I-5 to the Canyonville exit 98, following signs towards Crater Lake. In Canyonville, turn east on 3rd Street and follow this road, which becomes the Tiller-Trail Highway, 23.3 miles to Tiller. Go through town and turn left on Road 46 for 24.2 miles, then go right on Road 2823. Follow Skimmerhorn Trailhead signs for 2.4 miles to a right turn on Road 2830 and go 3.9 miles. Turn left on Road 600 for 1.8 miles to road's end at the trailhead.

Contact: Umpqua National Forest, Tiller Ranger District, 27812 Tiller Trail Highway, Tiller, OR, 97484, 541/825-3201.

90 FISH LAKE
12.6 mi/7.0 hr

in the Rogue-Umpqua Divide Wilderness

Map 11.4, page 594

This loop serves as an introduction to the Rogue-Umpqua Divide Wilderness, following a rugged landscape where the key word is "Highrock"—as in Highrock Creek, Highrock Meadow, and Highrock Mountain. Fish Lake, true to its name in regards to the fish, is a good destination for backpackers, as there are several camping sites along the lake, and access to a multitude of lakes and trails beyond. Take this trail up the dramatic andesite cliff-strewn backbone of Rocky Ridge for a peak experience.

From the Beaver Swamp Trailhead take the right-hand Beaver Swamp Trail in 1.5 miles to Fish Lake, staying left at a junction. When you reach the lake, go left around the lake and continue on the Fish Lake Trail past camping spots 1.3 miles

to a junction, staying left again for another three miles to the lovely Highrock Meadows beneath Highrock Mountain. At the next junction, go left on the Rogue Umpqua Divide Trail toward Rocky Ridge, staying left at a junction in 0.4 mile and continuing up the steep climb for 3.2 miles, over Standoff Point and several viewpoints. Keep left at the next junction and descend past more viewpoints 3.2 miles to the trailhead

User Groups: Hikers, dogs, and horses. No mountain bikes allowed. No wheelchair facilities.

Permits: A free self-issue Wilderness Permit is required and is available at the trailhead. Parking and access are free.

Maps: For a map of the Umpqua National Forest and Rogue-Umpqua Divide Wilderness, contact Umpqua National Forest, 2900 NW Stewart Parkway, Roseburg, OR, 97470, 541/672-6601. For a topographic map, ask the USGS for Buckeye Lake.

Directions: From Roseburg, drive 25 miles north on I-5 to the Canyonville exit (Exit 98), following signs towards Crater Lake. In Canyonville, turn east on 3rd Street and follow this road, which becomes the Tiller-Trail Highway, 23.3 miles to Tiller. Go through town and turn left on Road 46 for 24.2 miles, then go right on Road 2823. Follow Fish Lake Trailhead signs for 2.4 miles to a right turn on Road 2830 and go 3.9 miles, then go left on Road 2840 for 0.5 mile. Continue past the Fish Lake Trailhead another 4.6 miles to the Beaver Swamp Trailhead.

Contact: Umpqua National Forest, Tiller Ranger District, 27812 Tiller Trail Highway, Tiller, OR, 97484, 541/825-3201.

91 RATTLESNAKE MOUNTAIN
5.2–5.6 mi/3.0 hr

in the Rogue-Umpqua Divide Wilderness

Map 11.4, page 594

In the heart of the Rogue-Umpqua Divide Wilderness, the wildflowers of Fish Creek

Valley see few visitors, which is fortunate for the intrepid explorer looking for a little quiet time. The meadows along Fish Creek are only the beginning; above them, a loop trail reaches Windy Gap and its awesome views, and a side trail climbs Rattlesnake Mountain, second highest in the Rogue Umpqua Divide Wilderness, with views out to nearby Mount Thielsen, Mount Scott, Mount Bailey, and Mount McLoughlin.

From the Happy Camp Trailhead, follow Fish Creek 0.7 mile along the Rogue Umpqua Divide Trail to a junction and go left on the Whitehorse Meadow Trail, climbing along a creek one mile to Windy Gap and a four-way junction. The right-hand Rattlesnake Way Trail (also known as the Rattlesnake Mountain Trail) climbs one mile and 1,000 feet to a viewpoint on Rattlesnake Mountain. Return as you came, for 5.6 miles in all.

For a loop option, which turns out to be 0.4 mile shorter, go back to Windy Gap and take the Castle Creek Trail, which heads along the ridge 0.4 mile to a junction. Go left, staying on Trail 1576, to descend 1.1 miles back to Happy Camp.

User Groups: Hikers, dogs, and horses. No mountain bikes allowed. No wheelchair facilities.

Permits: A free self-issue Wilderness Permit is required and is available at the trailhead. Parking and access are free.

Maps: For a map of the Umpqua National Forest and Rogue-Umpqua Divide Wilderness, contact Umpqua National Forest, 2900 NW Stewart Parkway, Roseburg, OR, 97470, 541/672-6601. For a topographic map, ask the USGS for Fish Mountain.

Directions: From Roseburg, drive east on OR 138, and between mileposts 60 and 61 turn right on Fish Creek Road 37 for 13 miles. Turn right on Incense Cedar Loop Road 800 for 3.5 miles, then right on Fish Creek Valley Road 870 for 4.2 miles to a "Rogue-Umpqua Trail" sign on the right. Park 100 yards farther down the road.

Contact: Umpqua National Forest, Diamond Lake Ranger District, 2020 Toketee Ranger Station Road, Idleyld Park, OR, 97477, 541/498-2531.

92 MUIR CREEK TO BUCK CANYON
15.0-22.8 mi/7.0 hr-2 days
🏃3 ⛺8

in the Rogue-Umpqua Divide Wilderness
Map 11.4, page 594

The relatively uncrowded Rogue-Umpqua Divide Wilderness is a must-do for the backpacking crowd. About the only visitors this area sees in the summer are the cows that are allowed to graze here. But don't let that dissuade you: This trail up Muir Creek and into Buck Canyon opens a door to numerous backpacking sites, beautiful meadows, and Buck Canyon. From here you can traverse out to other areas like Rattlesnake Mountain and Hershberger Mountain. This trail system begins within a stone's throw of a paved highway, yet you'd never know it was there. With some path-finding skills, you can make your way in a loop around theis wilderness and bushwhack a bit back to your car.

Starting from the highway, follow the Muir Creek Trail 2.7 miles to an overlook of Muir Falls, then continue one mile, keeping left at a junction, then 1.4 miles, keeping left at another trailhead junction. From here hike 1.6 miles into Buck Canyon and Hummingbird Meadows. The next junction has a right-hand turn to cross the creek and pass Wiley Camp; from here the main trail continues to follow Muir Creek another 0.8 mile past some falls, the crumbling Devil's Slide, and an upper meadow. For a day's exploration, this is adequate. Backpackers can continue on another 3.9 miles for three more camps and the Alkali Meadows and connections to trails fanning out from there.

User Groups: Hikers, dogs, and horses. No mountain bikes allowed. No wheelchair facilities.

Permits: A free self-issue Wilderness Permit is required and is available at the trailhead. Parking and access are free.

Maps: For a map of the Rogue River National Forest and the Rogue-Umpqua Divide Wilderness, contact the Rogue River-Siskiyou National Forest, 3040 Biddle Road, Medford, OR, 97504, 541/618-2200. For a topographic map, ask the USGS for Fish Mountain.

Directions: From Medford, drive 57 miles east on OR 62, going left onto Highway 230 for 10.3 miles. Just before the Muir Creek Bridge, park in a lot on the left.

Contact: Rogue River National Forest, Prospect Ranger District, 47201 Highway 62, Prospect, OR, 97536, 541/560-3400.

93 BOUNDARY SPRINGS AND UPPER ROGUE RIVER TRAIL

5.0-18.6 mi/2.0 hr-1 day 🥾2 ⛰️8

on the Upper Rogue River and in Crater Lake National Park

Map 11.4, page 594

From a massive series of springs just inside the boundary of Crater Lake National Park, the Rogue River begins its journey through the southern Cascade Mountains. Almost immediately, the river sets out into a forested canyon, plunging over Rough Rider Falls and No Name Falls. From there, the trail goes on and on, allowing for a long backpacking adventure along several access points. For a sampling of the Rogue's wonders, start from the easy pullout at the head of the canyon. Then you can plan out a longer trip along the Upper Rogue River Trail, following this Wild and Scenic River from the Crater Rim to the town of Prospect.

To see the Boundary Springs, follow the Upper Rogue River Trail in from the Crater Rim Viewpoint lot 0.5 mile to a junction. Go left on the Boundary Springs Trail 1.9 miles to the springs. Return as you came, or continue on to the viewpoint.

To descend instead into the Rogue Canyon and hike the uppermost segment of this famous trail, begin from the same trailhead, following the Upper Rogue Trail, and go to the right from this first junction. In 4.2 miles you'll march along the canyon rim and reach Rough Rider Falls, and in another 2.2 you'll go into the canyon itself to see No Name Falls. A final stretch of the trail continues through the forest another 1.7 miles to a lower trailhead at the Hamaker Campground.

The entire length of the Upper Rogue River Trail is 47.9 miles, with numerous access points along the way. Contact the Rogue River-Siskiyou National Forest (www.fs.fed.us/r6/rogue-siskiyou) for maps and information.

User Groups: Hikers and dogs only. No horses or mountain bikes allowed. No wheelchair facilities.

Permits: Permits are not required. Parking and access are free.

Maps: For a map of the Rogue River National Forest, contact the Rogue River-Siskiyou National Forest, 3040 Biddle Road, Medford, OR, 97504, 541/618-2200. For a topographic map, ask the USGS for Pumice Desert West and Hamaker Butte.

Directions: To reach the upper trailhead, start from Medford, drive 57 miles on OR 62 and continue on Highway 230 for 18.6 miles to the Crater Rim Viewpoint on the right. For the lower trailhead, go north on 230 approximately 14 miles from the junction with Highway 62. Turn right on Road 6530, and follow it one mile to Road 900. Continue 0.5 mile on Road 900. The trail begins east of the Hamaker Campground.

Contact: Rogue River National Forest, Prospect Ranger District, 47201 Highway 62, Prospect, OR, 97536, 541/560-3400.

94 HORSE LAKE
7.2-8.8 mi/4.0-4.5 hr

west of Mount Bachelor in the Three Sisters Wilderness

Map 11.5, page 595

In the stretches of the Three Sisters Wilderness south of the peaks themselves, the landscape is a dense forest punctuated by lakes. No wonder they call the main access road the Cascade Lakes Highway; this entire area east of the Cascade Divide is rife with ponds and lakes, many suitable for swimming. Starting from big Elk Lake, a superb loop trail passes through the forests to visit Horse Lake with its rocky peninsula, then returning past two smaller lakes, Colt and Sunset. Be prepared to walk through a burn, resulting from fire that torched this area in 1999.

From the trailhead, start on the right-hand Horse Lake Trail, immediately entering the wilderness area. In 1.3 miles, the trail crosses the Pacific Crest Trail. Continue straight on the Horse Lake Trail two miles to a T-junction with a sign for Horse Lake. After viewing the lake, you have a choice; to continue on the loop, go south from this junction toward Dumbbell Lake 0.1 mile, stay left at the next junction, and continue 0.3 mile to another junction, going to the left toward Sunset Lake.

To circle Horse Lake on a loop, however, go forward to the lake and to the right instead and watch for a side trail which circles the lake over 1.7 miles, keeping left at a junction 0.3 mile after the peninsula until you reach another junction. Go right toward Dumbbell Lake 0.3 mile, then go left away from Dumbbell Lake, going toward Sunset Lake instead.

Both options bring you to the same place. Now, to continue from either of these two options, start down the trail toward Sunset Lake, watching on the left for a faint trail to Colt Lake, and just beyond a trail to the right for Sunset Lake. Stay on this main trail 1.3 miles to a junction with the PCT. Go left on the PCT for 1.2 miles, then right on the Island Meadow Trail one mile back to the trailhead.

User Groups: Hikers, dogs, and horses. No mountain bikes allowed. No wheelchair facilities.

Permits: A free self-issue Wilderness Permit is required and is available at the trailhead. A federal Northwest Forest Pass is required to park here; the cost is $5 a day or $30 for an annual pass. You can buy a day pass at the trailhead, at ranger stations, or through private vendors.

Maps: A map of the Three Sisters Wilderness is available for purchase from Geo-Graphics. For a map of the Deschutes National Forest and the Three Sisters Wilderness, contact Deschutes National Forest Headquarters, 1001 SW Emkay Drive, Bend, OR, 97702, 541/383-5300. For a topographic map, ask the USGS for South Sister.

Directions: From Bend, drive the Cascades Lake Highway 32.7 miles west to the Elk Lake Trailhead on the right, following the 0.3-mile spur road to the parking area.

Contact: Deschutes National Forest, Bend-Fort Rock Ranger District, 1230 NE 3rd Street, Suite A-262, Bend, OR, 97701, 541/383-4000.

95 SIX LAKES TRAIL
2.0-19.0 mi/1.0 hr-1 day

southwest of Mount Bachelor in the Three Sisters Wilderness

Map 11.5, page 595

There are so many lakes along the Six Lakes Trail that it's hard to say which six give the trail its name. You'll pass two big ones, Blow and Doris, right off, then continue into a virtual maze of lakes both big and small. Bring a map and a backpack, and have your pick. Two other obvious goals are Cliff Lake and Mink Lake, both with rustic shelters. The Pacific Crest Trail curves right through this basin, allowing access to other hikes in the area, including Horse Lake and Sisters Mirror Lake to the north. Consider this hike either as a straight in-and-out, or with the possibility for a number of loops.

From the Six Lakes Trailhead, follow the trail one mile to Blow Lake, and another 1.4 miles to Doris Lake. In another 0.9 mile, stay right at a junction, climb a pass and descend to the PCT in 2.1 miles. Go left on the PCT 1.6 miles to an unmarked side trail on the left to Cliff Lake's shelter, just before a junction to Porky Lake. To continue to Mink Lake, leave the PCT and go right toward Porky Lake 1.6 miles, then left to Mink Lake's old shelter. A loop trail around Mink Lake is 2.6 miles.

From here, possibilities for loops can be done a number of ways. From Mink Lake, go right away from Porky Lake, then stay left on the main trail 1.2 miles to the PCT. Go left on the PCT 2.2 miles, passing five lakes to return to Cliff Lake. Another way is to leave Mink Lake towards Porky Lake, then go left 1.2 miles to Goose Lake, then right for 2.2 miles past smaller lakes to the PCT. Go straight to return to the trailhead.

User Groups: Hikers, dogs, and horses. No mountain bikes allowed. No wheelchair facilities.

Permits: A free self-issue Wilderness Permit is required and is available at the trailhead. A federal Northwest Forest Pass is required to park here; the cost is $5 a day or $30 for an annual pass. You can buy a day pass at the trailhead, at ranger stations, or through private vendors.

Maps: A map of the Three Sisters Wilderness is available for purchase from Geo-Graphics. For a map of the Deschutes National Forest and the Three Sisters Wilderness, contact Deschutes National Forest Headquarters, 1001 SW Emkay Drive, Bend, OR, 97702, 541/383-5300. For a topographic map, ask the USGS for Elk Lake and Packsaddle Mountain.

Directions: From Bend, drive the Cascades Lake Highway 34.7 miles west to the Six Lakes Trailhead on the right, following the spur road to the parking area.

Contact: Deschutes National Forest, Bend-Fort Rock Ranger District, 1230 NE 3rd Street, Suite A-262, Bend, OR, 97701, 541/383-4000.

96 DESCHUTES RIVER TRAIL/DILLON AND BENHAM FALLS

4.4-17.4 mi/2.0 hr-1 day   👥3   ⛰9

southwest of Bend in the Deschutes National Forest

Map 11.5, page 595	BEST (

The city of Bend is blessed to have this Upper Deschutes River Trail. From here, the river makes its way to the center of town, languidly flowing behind a dam, creating Mirror Pond, but in the ponderosa pine forests of the lower Cascades, the river is a pounding cataract of falls and eddies, and at other times gentle as a pond. The landscape is one of lava flows, which constantly force the river into its shapes and drops—the remnants of a massive flow from nearby Lava Butte. It is possible to do the trail up and down in a day, and shuttling is easy enough; along the way, too, are a number of access points, making for combinations of hikes leading to the best points: Lava Island Falls and the Lava Island Cave, Dillon Falls and Ryan Ranch Meadow, and the absolutely beautiful Benham Falls.

From the Meadow picnic area, climb 0.5 mile on the Deschutes River Trail to a slough, keeping left along the river 0.6 mile to the cave and Lava Island Falls. Continue 1.1 woodsy miles to a view of Big Eddy Rapids, and another 1.1 miles to the Aspen Picnic Area. The next 0.9 mile enters pine woods and climbs to a viewpoint of Dillon Falls' long cascade. Follow the road to Ryan Ranch Meadows, with views to the lava on the opposite shore, and continue 2.3 miles to the Slough Day-Use Area. The next 1.5 miles climbs into cooler, denser woods and arrives at Benham Falls overlook. From here, the trail follows an old logging railroad grade 0.7 mile to a crossing of the Deschutes, arriving at the Benham West Day-Use Area, with a few more loop trails angling into the woods to an old mill site.

User Groups: Hikers, dogs on leash only, horses, and mountain bikes uphill only. The

Big Eddy Rapids, Dillon Falls, and Benham Falls West Area are wheelchair accessible.

Permits: Permits are not required. A federal Northwest Forest Pass is required to park here; the cost is $5 a day or $30 for an annual pass. You can buy a day pass at the trailhead, at ranger stations, or through private vendors.

Maps: For a map of the Deschutes National Forest, contact Deschutes National Forest Headquarters, 1001 SW Emkay Drive, Bend, OR, 97702, 541/383-5300. For a topographic map, ask the USGS for Benham Falls.

Directions: From Bend, take the Cascades Lake Highway 6.2 miles west to a sign for Meadow Day Use Area and turn left on gravel FS Road 100 for 1.3 miles to the road's end for the lower trailhead. To access other sites, continue another 1.6 mile on Cascade Lakes Highway then turn left on Conklin Road/Road 41. Go 2.6 miles and turn left on Road 4120 for 0.5 mile, then right on Road 4120 for 3.1 miles to the trailhead at road's end.

Contact: Deschutes National Forest, Bend-Fort Rock Ranger District, 1230 NE 3rd Street, Suite A-262, Bend, OR, 97701, 541/383-4000.

97 NEWBERRY LAVA TUBES
0.4-1.2 mi/1.0-2.0 hr   🏃2 ⛰8

east of Bend in the Deschutes National Forest

Map 11.5, page 595

These trails require hiking underground. "Spelunking" gives an impression of clambering around in chambers, but that's not what Central Oregon caves are about—although you can do that too. These volcanic-formed caves are "lava tubes," formed when rivers of lava from nearby Newberry Caldera cooled on top, but left the lava flowing underneath. In time, the lava drained and left these rounded wormholes descending

under the basalt roofs. Three caves along China Hat Road in the dry, burned forests east of Bend are open for walking—come prepared with warm clothes and a flashlight with plenty of batteries. Boyd Cave is shortest, Skeleton Cave a little longer. The Wind Cave is most difficult, but has a skylight, which is how the bats enter—thus, Wind Cave is closed from November to late April to protect their habitat.

The Boyd Cave is the easiest at 0.2 mile. Simply descend the stairs and follow the broad cave back to its low ceiling. The Skeleton Cave is more ambitious; go down the stairs and hike in 0.4 mile to a junction. The left tunnel peters out in a short distance, though you can get on your belly and go farther. The right path continues another 0.2 mile to its end. Wind Cave is most difficult of all, requiring climbing and descending massive jumbles of boulders 0.1 mile to the skylight room, and continuing 0.5 mile to its end.

User Groups: Hikers only. No dogs, horses, or mountain bikes allowed. No wheelchair facilities.

Permits: Permits are not required. Parking and access are free.

Maps: For a map of the Deschutes National Forest, contact Deschutes National Forest Headquarters, 1001 SW Emkay Drive, Bend, OR, 97702, 541/383-5300. For a topographic map, ask the USGS for Kelsey Butte.

Directions: Drive four miles south of Bend on U.S. 97 and turn left on China Hat Road 18. In nine miles, turn left at a sign for Boyd Cave. Another 0.5 mile beyond this turn, go left on Road 1819 for 1.6 miles to the Skeleton Cave. Another two miles east on China Hat, turn left at a sign for Wind Cave and park at the lot.

Contact: Deschutes National Forest, Bend-Fort Rock Ranger District, 1230 NE 3rd Street, Suite A-262, Bend, OR, 97701, 541/383-4000.

98 MUSKRAT LAKE CABIN
10.0–11.2 mi/3.5–4.0 hr

north of Cultus Lake in Three Sisters Wilderness

Map 11.5, page 595

At this southeastern corner of the Three Sisters Wilderness, you'll be lucky to see anyone. Sure, it's far from the peaks, but close as it is to popular Cultus Lake, a wind-whipped lake high on the divide, visitors just don't seem to wander down here. The Winopee Trail follows the shore of this massive lake for a stretch, with possibilities for backpacking, then dives into the wilderness to access a number of lakes. The two large Teddy Lakes are an easy side trip, but the goal is a decrepit cabin on Muskrat Lake; it once was suitable for camping—with a stove, a loft, windows, and cupboards—but vandals have rendered unusable. It's worth a visit though, as this corner of the wilderness is quiet and deep.

Follow the Winopee Trail 2.9 miles along the shore of Cultus Lake, keeping left at the first junction to Corral Lakes, then heading right toward Winopee Lake 0.7 mile to a junction. To the right, two Teddy Lakes lie along a 0.6-mile trail. Continue left 1.4 miles to reach the cabin at Muskrat Lake.

User Groups: Hikers, dogs, and horses. No mountain bikes allowed. No wheelchair facilities.

Permits: A free self-issue Wilderness Permit is required and is available at the trailhead. A federal Northwest Forest Pass is required to park here; the cost is $5 a day or $30 for an annual pass. You can buy a day pass at the trailhead, at ranger stations, or through private vendors.

Maps: A map of the Three Sisters Wilderness is available for purchase from Geo-Graphics. For a map of the Deschutes National Forest and the Three Sisters Wilderness, contact Deschutes National Forest Headquarters, 1001 SW Emkay Drive, Bend, OR, 97702, 541/383-5300. For a topographic map, ask the USGS for Irish Mountain.

Directions: From Bend, drive the Cascades Lake Highway 44 miles west to the Cultus Lake Resort on the right. Turn right on Road 4635 for 1.8 miles, then go right on Road 100 toward the campground, keeping right on a Dead End road and parking at the trailhead in 0.5 mile.

Contact: Deschutes National Forest, Bend-Fort Rock Ranger District, 1230 NE 3rd Street, Suite A-262, Bend, OR, 97701, 541/383-4000.

99 LAVA RIVER CAVE
2.2 mi/1.5 hr

southeast of Bend in the Newberry National Volcanic Monument

Map 11.5, page 595

Like Boyd, Skeleton, and Wind Caves (see *Newberry Lava Tubes* listing in this chapter), the Lava River Cave is a lava tube, only this one is the queen bee. A full 1.1 miles long, it actually goes beneath Highway 97, and features a double-tiered cave and strange formations of the Sand Garden that form castles on the floor as Mount Mazama ash leaks in from above. You may find crowds here visiting such notable places as Echo Hall and Low Bridge Lane, but it's worth joining the fray to see one of Oregon's treasures. The cave makes for an easy excursions, and guided tours are available.

User Groups: Hikers only. No dogs, horses, or mountain bikes. No wheelchair facilities.

Permits: Permits are not required. A federal Northwest Forest Pass is required to park here; the cost is $5 a day or $30 for an annual pass. You can buy a day pass at the trailhead, at ranger stations, or through private vendors. Lanterns can be rented for $2.

Maps: For a map of the Deschutes National Forest, contact Deschutes National Forest Headquarters, 1001 SW Emkay Drive, Bend, OR, 97702, 541/383-5300. For a topographic map, ask the USGS for Lava Butte.

Directions: From Bend, drive 11 miles south on U.S. 97 and turn left at a sign for Lava

River Cave. Between May and October, you can drive 0.3 mile to the fee booth; the rest of the year the road is gated, but you can walk it.

Contact: Deschutes National Forest, Bend-Fort Rock Ranger District, 1230 NE 3rd Street, Suite A-262, Bend, OR, 97701, 541/383-4000.

100 LAVA CAST FOREST
1.0 mi/1.0 hr

southeast of Bend in the Newberry National Volcanic Monument

Map 11.5, page 595   **BEST (**

Make this a destination if you're touring the entire Lava Lands complex. Lava Cast Forest makes an interesting educational outing with the kids, or if you're looking to entertain visitor—if they can stand the awful washboard gravel road to get there. This easy, paved one-mile loop crosses the lava landscape of the Newberry Caldera's eruption, with views to that great shield volcano itself. The "lava casts" are actually stone cast of ancient trees—when the lava pooled around them and cooled, the tree it embraced burned and left perfect casts, some wells in the ground deep enough to stand in up to your chest, or in some cases knocked them over, leaving tubes and tunnels you can look through horizontally.

User Groups: Hikers and dogs. No horses or mountain bikes allowed. The entire trail is wheelchair accessible.

Permits: Permits are not required. A federal Northwest Forest Pass is required to park here; the cost is $5 a day or $30 for an annual pass. You can buy a day pass at the trailhead, at ranger stations, or through private vendors.

Maps: For a map of the Deschutes National Forest, contact Deschutes National Forest Headquarters, 1001 SW Emkay Drive, Bend, OR, 97702, 541/383-5300. For a topographic map, ask the USGS for Lava Cast Forest.

Directions: From Bend, drive 13.2 miles south on U.S. 97 and turn left on Road 9720,

following this miserable road nine miles to its end at the trailhead.

Contact: Deschutes National Forest, Bend-Fort Rock Ranger District, 1230 NE 3rd Street, Suite A-262, Bend, OR, 97701, 541/383-4000.

101 FALL RIVER
7.0 mi/3.0 hr

southwest of Sunriver in the Deschutes National Forest

Map 11.5, page 595

Fall River is amazingly quiet and absolutely lovely. It seems only anglers appreciate its charm, but bird-lovers and hikers should, too. This easy hike follows the river up and down along its bends and riffles, right up to the point where the river emerges from the ground in its entirety. Just above this massive spring sits the quiet Fall River Guard Station (another possible place to begin the hike, though you'll be following old user trails to get to the main trail). Near the campground, a footbridge crosses a deep pool and leads to a reflective spot at a bench, a good place to admire the pines and listen to the water birds.

The main trail begins behind campsite #8, ambling 2.4 miles downstream for a stretch following an old road, before petering out near private land. From the picnic area of the campground, hike down to the footbridge. On the opposite side, go left 0.4 mile to the viewpoint. Cross the bridge once more, and set out upstream to the left to make your way 0.7 mile to the springs behind the guard station.

User Groups: Hikers, dogs, horses, and mountain bikes. No wheelchair facilities.

Permits: Permits are not required. Parking and access are free.

Maps: For a map of the Deschutes National Forest, contact Deschutes National Forest Headquarters, 1001 SW Emkay Drive, Bend, OR, 97702, 541/383-5300. For a topographic map, ask the USGS for Pistol Butte.

Directions: From Bend, drive 16 miles south

on U.S. 97 and turn right on Vandevert Road, following signs for Fall River. In one mile, turn left on South Century Drive for 0.9 mile, then right on Road 42 for 9.7 miles. Just before milepost 13, turn left and park in the Fall River Campground.

Contact: Deschutes National Forest, Bend-Fort Rock Ranger District, 1230 NE 3rd Street, Suite A-262, Bend, OR, 97701, 541/383-4000.

102 PAULINA CREEK TRAIL
9.2-17.0 mi/5.0 hr-2 days   👥3   ⛰8

east of LaPine in the Deschutes National Forest

Map 11.5, page 595

Paulina Creek, fed by Paulina Lake in the collapsed volcano of the Newberry Caldera, falls in a double plume over the lip of the crater and begins a long descent down to the Deschutes River. A trail follows it through burned woods and out to a viewpoint of not only the uppermost falls, but two others as well. At the right time of year, expect to see salmon meandering beneath those massive top falls, thick enough you'd think you could walk over them. Two trailheads give access to the whole stretch—one going up, and one coming down. A shuttle is easy enough, as both trailheads start of the main road. If you do shuttle, you could easily start from the top and make your way to the bottom.

From the Paulina Falls Picnic Area, take the left trail and follow it 0.2 mile to a viewpoint. After this great view of the double falls, return to the junction and head upstream 0.3 mile to a road at the mouth of Paulina Lake. Go left, crossing the bridge, then go left to access the creek trail. In 3.3 miles you'll reach a lower falls, and in another 2.4 miles reach the falls at McKay Crossing with a campground to the right down the road. The last 2.8 miles continues to a crossing, joins an old road, and ends at the Ogden Trailhead.

From the Ogden Trailhead, a loop option is available. From the Ogden Camp, head back up a trail and take a short spur trail to the right, then follow gravel road 2120 for 2.8 miles upstream. Cross a road and continue 5.0 miles on what is now trail. Watch for mountain bikes! This trail returns to the lot at the Paulina Creek Falls Overlook.

User Groups: Hikers, dogs, horses, and mountain bikes. No wheelchair facilities.

Permits: Permits are not required. Parking and access are free from the Ogden Camp Trailhead, but a federal Northwest Forest Pass is required to park at the Paulina Falls Trailhead; the cost is $5 a day or $30 for an annual pass. You can buy a day pass at the trailhead, at ranger stations, or through private vendors.

Maps: For a map of the Deschutes National Forest, contact Deschutes National Forest Headquarters, 1001 SW Emkay Drive, Bend, OR, 97702, 541/383-5300. For a topographic map, ask the USGS for Paulina Peak and Anns Butte.

Directions: From Bend, drive 22 miles south on U.S. 97 and turn left on Road 21 toward the Newberry Caldera. For the Ogden Trailhead, follow Road 21 for 2.8 miles and turn left at the Ogden Group Camp and park at the lot for the Peter Skene Ogden Trail. For the Paulina Falls Viewpoint, continue on Road 21 for 9.4 miles and turn left into the Paulina Falls Picnic Area.

Contact: Deschutes National Forest, Bend-Fort Rock Ranger District, 1230 NE 3rd Street, Suite A-262, Bend, OR, 97701, 541/383-4000.

103 PAULINA LAKE
8.6 mi/3.0 hr   👥2   ⛰8

in the Newberry National Volcanic Monument

Map 11.5, page 595

The Newberry Caldera is rather like a small Crater Lake, though Newberry's crater is filled with not one but two lakes: Paulina and East. Paulina Lake has a trail around it, and it's quite a walk. The trail passes a smaller crater, a pumice cone, an obsidian flow, and a lakeside hot spring. For pretty much the whole hike, Paulina Peak is a massive presence at the south side of the water. This leisurely hike is the longest in the Newberry Caldera National Volcanic Monument, and is a must-do for day-hikers, campers, and even backpackers.

From the trailhead, set out along the lakeshore to the left. In 1.2 miles the trail crosses an obsidian lava flow and comes to a camping area on the right. In another 1.4 miles the trail passes more camping sites and a beach where hot springs bubble. The next 1.7 miles follows the lakeshore through the woods before arriving at the Paulina Lake Lodge. Continue on the trail, crossing the bridge over Paulina Creek, then continuing along the lakeshore 2.4 miles, passing two campgrounds. The trail crosses the entrance road to Little Crater Campground and climbs to the peak of Little Crater, then descends 1.9 miles back to the trailhead.

User Groups: Hikers and dogs. No horses or mountain bikes allowed. No wheelchair access.

Permits: Permits are not required. A federal Northwest Forest Pass is required to park here; the cost is $5 a day or $30 for an annual pass. You can buy a day pass at the trailhead, at ranger stations, or through private vendors.

Maps: For a map of the Deschutes National Forest, contact Deschutes National Forest Headquarters, 1001 SW Emkay Drive, Bend, OR, 97702, 541/383-5300. For a topographic map, ask the USGS for Paulina Peak.

Directions: From Bend, drive 22 miles south on U.S. 97 and turn left on Road 21 toward the Newberry Caldera. Follow Road 21 for 14.5 miles and turn left at the Little Crater Campground and follow this road 0.9 mile to the trailhead at road's end.

Contact: Deschutes National Forest, Bend-Fort Rock Ranger District, 1230 NE 3rd Street, Suite A-262, Bend, OR, 97701, 541/383-4000.

104 BIG OBSIDIAN FLOW
0.8 mi/0.5 hr　　　　　🏃1　⬜8

in the Newberry National Volcanic Monument

Map 11.5, page 595

Breathtakingly short but nonetheless breathtaking, this terribly easy 0.8-mile trails loops into Oregon's most recent volcanic eruption, a sweeping and swirling flow of obsidian, a black volcanic glass that shines in the sun. When doing any of the other hikes in the Newberry Volcanic National Monument, make sure to include this one.

User Groups: Hikers only. No dogs, horses, or mountain bikes. No wheelchair facilities.

Permits: Permits are not required. A federal Northwest Forest Pass is required to park here; the cost is $5 a day or $30 for an annual pass. You can buy a day pass at the trailhead, at ranger stations, or through private vendors.

Maps: For a map of the Deschutes National Forest, contact Deschutes National Forest Headquarters, 1001 SW Emkay Drive, Bend, OR, 97702, 541/383-5300. For a topographic map, ask the USGS for East Lake.

Directions: From Bend, drive 22 miles south on U.S. 97 and turn left on Road 21 toward the Newberry Caldera. Follow Road 21 for 14.8 miles and turn right into the Obsidian Trail parking lot.

Contact: Deschutes National Forest, Bend-Fort Rock Ranger District, 1230 NE 3rd Street, Suite A-262, Bend, OR, 97701, 541/383-4000.

105 CINDER HILL AND THE DOME
1.4-7.2 mi/0.5-3.5 hr　　🏃2　⬜8

in the Newberry National Volcanic Monument

Map 11.5, page 595

The Newberry Caldera—a National Volcanic Monument—is well worth exploring. It's also a great place to camp. Whether you're here overnight or just for the day, make it a big day and hike as much of it as you can. There are plenty of short trails, and the trail to The Dome ranks high up there: the easy 0.7 mile climbs up to its crater rim with views to the Cascade peaks and Fort Rock Valley.

For a longer hike, climb to Cinder Hill, following its trail up 900 feet in 1.8 miles to the Crater Rim Trail, a long, hot, and dusty trail used primarily by mountain bikers. Go right 1.1 miles to Cinder Hill's peak, with its view to the Cascade Mountains and down to East Lake.

User Groups: Hikers and dogs. No horses allowed. Mountain bikes allowed only on the Crater Rim Trail. No wheelchair facilities.

Permits: Permits are not required. A federal Northwest Forest Pass is required to park here; the cost is $5 a day or $30 for an annual pass. You can buy a day pass at the trailhead, at ranger stations, or through private vendors.

Maps: For a map of the Deschutes National Forest, contact Deschutes National Forest Headquarters, 1001 SW Emkay Drive, Bend, OR, 97702, 541/383-5300. For a topographic map, ask the USGS for East Lake.

Directions: From Bend, drive 22 miles south on U.S. 97 and turn left on Road 21 toward the Newberry Caldera. Follow Road 21 for 17.4 miles to a junction. To go to The Dome, go right following Road 21 for 2.5 miles, and park on the right at The Dome Trailhead. To go to Cinder Hill, turn left at the junction 1.8 miles to Cinder Hill Campground. Continue 0.3 mile to the trailhead at road's end, or if the gate is closed park there and walk.

Contact: Deschutes National Forest, Bend-Fort Rock Ranger District, 1230 NE 3rd Street, Suite A-262, Bend, OR, 97701, 541/383-4000.

106 PAULINA PEAK

6.0 mi/4.0 hr

in the Newberry National Volcanic Monument

Map 11.5, page 595

At 7,984 feet, Paulina Peak is not only the highest point on the rim of the Newberry Caldera, but it's pretty much the highest point in the entire area. Thus, views extend from the Fort Rock Valley to the Cascade peaks, with the entire caldera below it, including the pudding-like surface of the Big Obsidian Flow, and the shimmering Paulina and East Lakes. Thing is, the road goes right to the top for this stunning view, so most people drive up. But you can climb it on foot, if you're up for a trail with an 8 percent grade that climbs 1,500 feet in only two miles. You'll feel, if not whipped, victorious at having achieved a view stretching from Mount Adams in Washington State to Mount Shasta in California on your own merits and heels.

Beginning at the Paulina Peak Trailhead, start out on the Crater Rim Trail. At the 2.7-mile mark, continue straight on the main trail. In 0.3 mile past this junction, the trail reaches the peak and overlook.

User Groups: Hikers, dogs, and horses. No mountain bikes allowed. No wheelchair facilities.

Permits: Permits are not required. A federal Northwest Forest Pass is required to park here; the cost is $5 a day or $30 for an annual pass. You can buy a day pass at the trailhead, at ranger stations, or through private vendors.

Maps: For a map of the Deschutes National Forest, contact Deschutes National Forest Headquarters, 1001 SW Emkay Drive, Bend, OR, 97702, 541/383-5300. For a topographic map, ask the USGS for Paulina Peak.

Directions: From Bend, drive 22 miles south on U.S. 97 and turn left on Road 21 toward the Newberry Caldera. Follow Road 21 for 13.2 miles and turn right at the visitors center. The trailhead is 50 feet before the vistors center on the right side of the road.

Contact: Deschutes National Forest, Bend-Fort Rock Ranger District, 1230 NE 3rd Street, Suite A-262, Bend, OR, 97701, 541/383-4000.

107 FAWN LAKE, PRETTY LAKE, AND STAG LAKE
6.8-7.3 mi/3.0-4.0 hr 🏃2 ⚠️7

north of Crescent Lake in Diamond Peak Wilderness

Map 11.5, page 595

Many of the stretches in the Diamond Peak Wilderness are dominated by dry, lodgepole pine forests, but there are points of beauty. In view of the nearly 7,000-foot Redtop Mountain, and slightly higher Lakeview Mountain, Fawn Lake is a jewel in this wilderness, though its popularity shows on the dusty, well-trodden path. For more seclusion, continue on the Pretty Lake, or take any number of side trails on your map to nearby Saddle and Stag Lakes, or even to big Odell Lake.

Start on the Fawn Lake Trail, crossing Road 60 and a horse trail, continuing straight 3.4 miles to Fawn Lake. At the lake, go left along the shore and continue 0.6 mile to Pretty Lake on the left. From here, the trail is not maintained; it descends into confusing woods 2.5 miles back to the Fawn Lake Trail. To visit Stag Lake, go back to Fawn Lake then continue around the lake, staying left past the Fawn Lake Trail, then left again 0.2 mile beyond that. Climb gradually for one mile, then go right 0.4 mile to this trail's end at Stag Lake beneath Lakeview Mountain.

User Groups: Hikers, dogs, and horses. No mountain bikes allowed. No wheelchair facilities.

Permits: A free self-issue Wilderness Permit is required and is available at the trailhead. Parking and access are free.

Maps: For a map of the Deschutes National Forest, contact Deschutes National Forest Headquarters, 1001 SW Emkay Drive, Bend, OR, 97702, 541/383-5300. For a topographic map, ask the USGS for Odell Lake.

Directions: From Crescent Junction on OR 58, go west on Road 60 for 2.2 miles, then turn right toward the campgrounds for 0.3 mile to Crescent Lake Campground. Turn left into the campground and then right into a lot at the Fawn Lake Trailhead.

Contact: Deschutes National Forest, Crescent Ranger District, 136471 Highway 97 North, P.O. Box 208, Crescent, OR, 97733, 541/433-3200.

108 MILLER AND MAIDU LAKES
5.1-8.4 mi/1.5-4.0 hr 🏃2 ⚠️7

at Miller Lake and in the Mount Thielsen Wilderness

Map 11.5, page 595

Two lakes are the goal of this hike, one inside and one outside the Mount Thielsen Wilderness. The Pacific Crest Trail intersects the trail and opens up routes farther into the wilderness area and also along the beginning of the North Umpqua Trail. Broad Miller Lake is a world apart from little Maidu Lake, where the Forest Service removed a shelter to help protect the area.

From Digit Point Campground, you can circle Miller Lake in either direction, a total of 5.1 miles. At the western end of the lake, by Evening Creek, a side trail launches up a cliff 2.1 miles to the PCT junction, continuing on as the North Umpqua Trail 0.8 mile to Maidu Lake, headwaters of the North Umpqua, at which point there is a one-mile loop around the lake.

If you feel like going farther, continue on the North Umpqua Trail another 1.2 miles to a junction. Take the trail to the left, a 0.7-mile loop around Lucile Lake.

User Groups: Hikers, dogs, and horses. Mountain bikes allowed around Miller Lake only. No wheelchair facilities.

Permits: A free self-issue Wilderness Permit is required and is available at the trailhead. Parking and access are free.

Maps: For a map of the Umpqua National Forest and Mount Thielsen Wilderness, contact Umpqua National Forest, 2900 NW Stewart Parkway, Roseburg, OR, 97470, 541/672-6601. For a topographic map, ask the USGS for Worden and Burn Butte.

Directions: From Bend, drive 65 miles south on U.S. 97 to the town of Chemult. Between mileposts 202 and 203, go west on Road 9772, following signs for Chemult Recreation Site. Go 12.5 miles to road's end at Digit Point Campground and park at the picnic loop.

Contact: Umpqua National Forest, Diamond Lake Ranger District, 2020 Toketee Ranger Station Road, Idleyld Park, OR, 97477, 541/498-2531.

109 WOLF CREEK PARK
3.8 mi/2.0 hr

northwest of Grants Pass

Map 11.6, page 596

If you've driven the long stretch of I-5 through southern Oregon, you'll know that breaks are few and far between. If you *really* want to get out and move, Josephine County's Wolf Creek Park is located so close to the interstate you'll be amazed you never knew it was there. By stretching your legs, I mean stretching them up Jack London Peak to a 2,800-foot viewpoint. You've got to hand it to those who name things: West Coast writer Jack London would have appreciated this rugged climb above the little stagecoach town of Wolf Creek, where he once spent the night.

After walking across the dam, start climbing steadily up 1.9 miles to the highest viewpoint. From there, you could walk the rest of the trail as desired 0.6 mile to its end at a dirt road.

User Groups: Hikers and dogs. No horses or mountain bikes allowed. No wheelchair facilities.

Permits: Permits are not required. A $2-per-car day-use pass is required, or you can purchase a $25 annual pass.

Maps: For a topographic map, ask the USGS for Glendale.

Directions: From I-5, 18 miles north of Grants Pass, take Wolf Creek Exit 76 and drive 0.9 mile to the park at the end of Main Street.

Contact: Josephine County Parks, 125 Ringuette Street, Grants Pass, OR, 97527, 541/474-5285.

110 OREGON CAVES NATIONAL MONUMENT
1.0-9.3 mi/1.0-3.5 hr

east of Cave Junction in the Siskiyou National Forest

Map 11.6, page 596

Established as a National Monument in 1909, the Oregon Caves are certainly one of the state's treasures. A one-mile tour of the caves (fee required) visits what was originally an island reef scraped up from the ocean floor by the advancing North American Plate. What is left is a series of marble rooms and calcite drippings forming stalagmites and stalactites. Just outside, a 3.8-mile loop trail heads through a Siskiyou Mountains forest to one of Oregon's largest Douglas fir trees. Other trails head out to No Name Creek and along Cave Creek, adding a total of 5.5 miles to the hikes you can do here in a day.

User Groups: Hikers only. Dogs are not allowed. No wheelchair facilities.

Permits: Permits are not required. There is a fee to enter the caves. Parking and access are otherwise free.

Maps: For a topographic map, ask the USGS for Oregon Caves.

Directions: From Grants Pass, drive U.S. 199 south 29 miles to Cave Junction and follow Oregon Caves signs east on Highway 46 for 20 miles to the turnaround lot.

Contact: Oregon Caves National Monument, 19000 Caves Highway, Cave Junction, OR, 97523, 541/592-2100, ext. 262.

111 STURGIS FORK/ BOUNDARY TRAIL

4.8 mi/3.5 hr 👫2 ⛰7

east of Oregon Caves in the Rogue River National Forest

Map 11.6, page 596

This simple but beautiful hike offers access to a number of backpacking areas: Grayback Mountain, the Oregon Caves National Monument, and the Red Buttes Wilderness. The trail passes through groves of Grand fir and meadows of blooming corn lily, rising to a 6,420-foot viewpoint over the Siskiyou Mountains. From here, the Boundary Trail continues on three miles to Grayback Mountain. From the Sturgis Fork Trail, you could also head 5.7 miles to Sucker Creek Gap.

From the trailhead go in 0.7 mile along the Sturgis Fork, keeping right at a junction and going 0.3 mile on the Boundary Trail to the next junction, again staying right on the Boundary Trail and climbing 0.8 mile through a lush meadow to a pass. From here, it's a 500-foot climb up 0.6 mile to a viewpoint, the turnaround point for this hike. The trail continues three miles to Grayback Mountain (see next listing). Head back to the Sturgis Fork Trail junction to return; from here, the Boundary Trail continues 5.7 miles to Sucker Creek Gap (see *Sucker Creek and Swan Mountain* listing in this chapter).

User Groups: Hikers, dogs, horses, and mountain bikes. No wheelchair facilities.

Permits: Permits are not required. A federal Northwest Forest Pass is required to park here; the cost is $5 a day or $30 for an annual pass. You can buy a day pass at the trailhead, at ranger stations, or through private vendors.

Maps: For a map of the Rogue River National Forest, contact the Rogue River-Siskiyou National Forest, 3040 Biddle Road, Medford, OR, 97504, 541/618-2200. For a topographic map, ask the USGS for Carberry Creek.

Directions: From Grants Pass follow signs to Murphy south for 6.5 miles, continuing on Highway 238 for 11.5 miles to milepost 18. At the Applegate Bridge, go south on Thompson Creek Road for 11.9 miles. Turn right on Road 1020 for 3.7 miles, then fork right on rocky Road 600 for 0.6 mile, then fork left and uphill for 0.1 mile to the trailhead at road's end.

Contact: Rogue River-Siskiyou National Forest, Applegate Ranger District, 6941 Upper Applegate Road, Jacksonville, OR, 97530, 541/899-3800.

112 GRAYBACK MOUNTAIN

4.8 mi/3.0 hr 👫2 ⛰8

east of Oregon Caves in the Rogue River National Forest

Map 11.6, page 596

Like the nearby Sturgis Fork hike (see previous listing), the Boundary Trail passes right through this region of meadows and mountains. Hovering above these tree-edged meadows is the 7,048-foot peak of Grayback Mountain, with its panoramic view from the Pacific Ocean to Mount Shasta, and from Mount McLoughlin to the Illinois River Valley. At the base of the mountain, a historic cabin and a rustic snow shelter sit in the meadows at the head of O'Brien Creek. The trail is easy enough, and the meadows make for good camping, but for a real adventure you can go cross-country and scramble your way to the top.

From the Upper O'Brien Creek Trailhead, climb nearly 1,000 feet in only one mile, following O'Brien Creek. At the first junction, you can go in two directions: 0.3 mile to the left is the Grayback Snow Shelter and the Krause Log Cabin, and above them the Grayback Meadows; to the right, the trail climbs another mile to the Boundary Trail. Both routes can get you to Grayback Mountain: from the Krause Cabin, head cross-country through the meadows 0.4 mile to the Boundary Trail, then head up the mountain for 0.7 mile; from the junction of the O'Brien Trail and the Boundary Trail, jog a bit to the left then head up the mountain on an unofficial path.

User Groups: Hikers, dogs, horses, and mountain bikes. No wheelchair facilities.

Permits: Permits are not required. Parking and access are free.

Maps: For a map of the Rogue River National Forest, contact the Rogue River-Siskiyou National Forest, 3040 Biddle Road, Medford, OR, 97504, 541/618-2200. For a topographic map, ask the USGS for Grayback Mountain.

Directions: From Grants Pass, follow signs to Murphy south for 6.5 miles and continue on Highway 238 another 11.5 miles to the bridge at Applegate. Turn south on Thompson Creek Road for 11.9 miles, and at a pass turn right at a sign for O'Brien Creek Trail onto Road 1005, following this road 2.3 miles to road's end at the trailhead.

Contact: Rogue River-Siskiyou National Forest, Applegate Ranger District, 6941 Upper Applegate Road, Jacksonville, OR, 97530, 541/899-3800.

113 BOLAN MOUNTAIN
3.4 mi/2.0 hr   🏃2 ⚠7

south of Oregon Caves in the Siskiyou National Forest

Map 11.6, page 596

A perfect place for a lookout, Bolan Mountain has a view of the surrounding Siskiyou Mountains and Mount Shasta, as well as a view down to the Illinois Valley and even the Pacific Ocean. Starting from a campground on Bolan Lake, the trail climbs over 800 feet to the rentable Bolan Mountain Lookout.

From the campground, climb 500 feet in one mile on the Bolan Lake Trail to a junction. Go left an easy 0.5 mile to the lookout road, heading left up the final 0.2 mile.

User Groups: Hikers, dogs, and horses. No wheelchair facilities.

Permits: Permits are not required. Parking and access are free.

Maps: For a map of the Rogue River National Forest, contact the Rogue River-Siskiyou National Forest, 3040 Biddle Road, Medford, OR, 97504, 541/618-2200. For a topographic map, ask the USGS for Oregon Caves.

Directions: Drive 35.5 miles south of Grants Pass on U.S. 199. Between mileposts 35 and 36 turn east on Waldo Road, going five miles then straight onto Happy Camp Road for 12.5 miles to a pass, turning left at a sign for Bolan Lake. At the next two junctions fork uphill, and at the 1.8-mile mark fork downhill to the right. After another 2.4 miles go left onto Road 040 and down 1.8 miles to the campground. Park at the trailhead message board.

Contact: Rogue River-Siskiyou National Forest, Wild Rivers Ranger District, 2164 NE Spalding Avenue, Grants Pass, OR, 97526, 541/471-6500.

114 TANNEN LAKES AND TANNEN MOUNTAIN
2.6-8.3 mi/1.0-4.5 hr   🏃3 ⚠8

south of Oregon Caves in Red Buttes Wilderness

Map 11.6, page 596

Two lakes lie in cliff-rimmed cirques beneath Tannen Mountain and the beginning of the Boundary Trail, all of it in the Red Buttes Wilderness. It's so easy to get to Tannen Lake, you'll want to keep going to East Tannen Lake. From there the wilderness opens up, and the possibilities await. The forest you'll pass through gives rise to Douglas fir, tanoak native to these southern mountains, and incense cedar.

From the Tannen Lake Trailhead hike in 0.4 mile to Tannen Lake. Go left another 0.9 mile to East Tannen Lake, a good turnaround point. Or continue 0.6 mile, passing a left-hand trail to another trailhead, and continue 1.5 miles to the Boundary Trail (and passing the left-hand trail to Sucker Creek). Go to the right on the Boundary Trail 1.1 miles, climbing steeply to the meadows of Tannen Mountain. Head right up to the summit and its amazing views over the Klamath Mountains and ocean, and all the way to Mount Shasta. To make this a loop using roads and a compass, continue 0.5 mile to trail's end at Road 570. Go right 0.9 mile to the Sundown Gap pullout and follow an abandoned road into the meadows, then head due east through both meadows and woods to Tannen Lake and the return trail.

User Groups: Hikers, dogs, and horses. No mountain bikes allowed. No wheelchair facilities.

Permits: A free self-issue Wilderness Permit is required and is available at the trailhead. Parking and access are free.

Maps: For a map of the Rogue River National Forest and the Red Buttes Wilderness, contact the Rogue River-Siskiyou National Forest, 3040 Biddle Road, Medford, OR, 97504, 541/618-2200. For a topographic map, ask the USGS for Oregon Caves.

Directions: Drive 35.5 miles south of Grants Pass on U.S. 199. Between mileposts 35 and 36 turn east on Waldo Road, going five miles then straight onto Happy Camp Road for 12.5 miles to a pass, and turn left at a sign for Tannen Lakes. At the next two junctions fork uphill, and at the 1.8-mile mark fork downhill to the right. After another 2.4 miles go right 3.3 miles to a fork and keep left for 1.4 miles. Watch for the trailhead sign and park 100 yards farther down the road.

Contact: Rogue River-Siskiyou National Forest, Wild Rivers Ranger District, 2164 NE Spalding Avenue, Grants Pass, OR, 97526, 541/471-6500.

115 SUCKER CREEK AND SWAN MOUNTAIN

6.4–9.8 mi/3.0–5.0 hr 3 ▲8

south of Oregon Caves in Red Buttes Wilderness

Map 11.6, page 596

The Red Buttes Wilderness draws right up to the boundary of California, making this one of the southernmost hikes in Oregon. In fact, from here you could well hike right into the next state. But before you leave, why not backpack into the Sucker Creek Shelter? From here you can visit a little cirque lake and follow the Boundary Trail up to the shoulder of Swan Mountain, making your way up its manzanita-strewn ridge to the 6,272-foot peak.

From the trailhead, follow Sucker Creek up 1.7 miles to a junction, staying to the right another 1.2 miles to a spring and the Sucker Creek Shelter. At the junction with the Boundary Trail, you have two options. You could go straight another 0.2 mile, then right along a faint path to visit Cirque Lake. Or you could go left on the Boundary Trail, climbing 500 feet to a pass, then making your way up the ridge to the left to the peak of Swan Mountain.

User Groups: Hikers, dogs, and horses. No mountain bikes allowed. No wheelchair facilities.

Permits: A free self-issue Wilderness Permit is required and is available at the trailhead. Parking and access are free.

Maps: For a map of the Rogue River National Forest and the Red Buttes Wilderness, contact the Rogue River-Siskiyou National Forest, 3040 Biddle Road, Medford, OR, 97504, 541/618-2200. For a topographic map, ask the USGS for Oregon Caves.

Directions: From Grants Pass, drive U.S. 199 south 29 miles to Cave Junction and follow Oregon Caves signs east on Highway 46 for 13.3 miles. Where the highway switchbacks left, turn right on Road 4612. Follow Road 4612 for 9.9 miles, forking right at the first two forks, then going straight on Road 098. In another 3.6 miles pass a left-hand fork and park 0.1 mile farther at a trail sign on the right.

Contact: Rogue River-Siskiyou National Forest, Wild Rivers Ranger District, 2164 NE Spalding Avenue, Grants Pass, OR, 97526, 541/471-6500.

116 MILLER LAKE

3.9 mi/2.0 hr   🥾1 ⛰7

east of Oregon Caves in Rogue River National Forest

Map 11.6, page 596

With Grayback Mountain looming in the distance, this lonely trail runs all by its lonesome over a remote section of the Siskiyous. That being said, there's plenty here to see, including two lakes, a stand of Brewer's weeping spruce, and a view to Mount Shasta from a high pass. You'll also find old-growth Douglas fir, Shasta red fir, and huckleberries.

From the trailhead, follow the new Miller Lake Trail in 0.7 mile to the cliff-rimmed Miller Lake. Go to the right over an earthen dam to follow the trail to the right into the forest, passing the spruce stand and continuing up to Upper Miller Lake and the viewpoint. Then descend 1.1 miles to the shore of Miller Lake, and return as you came.

User Groups: Hikers, dogs, and horses. No mountain bikes allowed. No wheelchair facilities.

Permits: Permits are not required. Parking and access are free.

Maps: For a map of the Rogue River National Forest, contact the Rogue River-Siskiyou National Forest, 3040 Biddle Road, Medford, OR, 97504, 541/618-2200. For a topographic map, ask the USGS for Grayback Mountain.

Directions: From Grants Pass, follow signs to Murphy 6.5 miles and continue on Highway 238 another 11.5 miles to the bridge at Applegate. Turn south on Thompson Creek Road for 11.9 miles, and at a pass turn right at a sign for Miller Lake onto Road 1020 for 4.5 miles. At the next junction, go straight onto Road 400 for 3.5 miles to road's end.

Contact: Rogue River-Siskiyou National Forest, Applegate Ranger District, 6941 Upper Applegate Road, Jacksonville, OR, 97530, 541/899-3800.

117 COLLINGS MOUNTAIN

10.3 mi/5.0 hr   🥾3 ⛰7

on Applegate Lake in Rogue River National Forest

Map 11.6, page 596

If there is one famous resident of Oregon, it must be Bigfoot. He (or she) is such a local icon around the Northwest that it's not uncommon to hear a few jokes passed around here and there, even some serious discussion about where the famed hairy Sasquatch may be. The first sighting in the Siskiyous was reported in 1895, and in 1975 a research group built a Bigfoot Trap here above Applegate Lake. Though the trap is somewhat overgrown in poison oak and the caretaker's cabin worn down by time, the trail to Collings Mountain, passing an old mine, is steady as ever. Looping up and around the mountain's summit and descending down to a run along Applegate Lake, this makes for a fine excursion through woods of scrub oak, madrone, and white pine.

From Hart-Tish Park, head uphill and across the road 0.6 mile on the Collings Mountain Trail to the weird Bigfoot Trap with its steel door and thick cell. The next 3.4 miles passes an old prospector's test prospect shaft and ambles along the mountain before arriving at the 3,625-foot summit at a grassy peak. Then descend 2.9 miles to the Watkins Campground and follow the Da-Ku-Be-Te-De Trail along the shore of Applegate Lake for 3.4 miles back to Hart-Tish.

User Groups: Hikers, dogs, horses, and mountain bikes. No wheelchair facilities.

Permits: Permits are not required. Parking and access are free.

Maps: For a map of the Rogue River National Forest, contact the Rogue River-Siskiyou National Forest, 3040 Biddle Road, Medford, OR, 97504, 541/618-2200. For a topographic map, ask the USGS for Carberry Creek.

Directions: From Jacksonville, head west on Highway 238 for eight miles to Ruch, then turn south following Upper Applegate signs for 15.9 miles. At one mile past the Applegate

Dam, turn right into Hart-Tish Recreation Area and park in the lot on the right.

Contact: Rogue River-Siskiyou National Forest, Applegate Ranger District, 6941 Upper Applegate Road, Jacksonville, OR, 97530, 541/899-3800.

118 APPLEGATE LAKE

17.8 mi/2 days

west of Ashland in Rogue River National Forest

Map 11.6, page 596

Though this "lake" is actually a reservoir, its position in the fir, pine, and madrone forests of the Siskiyou Mountains affords it respect. Plus, with the lake being the size it is, you can spend an entire day exploring its shoreline. The trail makes for a good bike ride, too, and some of it follows paved roads. Watch for fish-hunting osprey and three-leafed poison oak. Primitive campsites along the way make this a good backpacking trek.

From French Gulch, head out for a 4.7-mile excursion around a peninsula on the Payette Trail. After jostling along some old mining prospect roads for part of this stretch, continue on the Payette Trail another 4.5 miles along the lake, passing two primitive camps at Harr Point and Tipsu Tyee before arriving at the Manzanita Trailhead. From here, follow a dirt road 1.7 miles to the Seattle Bar picnic area, then continue around the lake on the paved road 1.4 miles to the Watkins Campground. Head into the campground and connect with the Da-Ku-Be-Te-De Trail for 4.3 miles along the shore to the dam. Cross the dam and follow the paved road 1.2 miles back to French Gulch.

User Groups: Hikers, dogs, and mountain bikes. No horses allowed. No wheelchair facilities.

Permits: Permits are not required. Parking and access are free.

Maps: For a map of the Rogue River National Forest or a brochure for Applegate Lake, contact the Rogue River-Siskiyou National Forest,

3040 Biddle Road, Medford, OR, 97504, 541/618-2200. For a topographic map, ask the USGS for Squaw Lakes.

Directions: From Jacksonville, head west on Highway 238 for eight miles to Ruch, then turn south following Upper Applegate signs for 14.9 miles. Turn left over the dam for 1.2 miles and park at the French Gulch Trailhead lot on the right.

Contact: Rogue River-Siskiyou National Forest, Applegate Ranger District, 6941 Upper Applegate Road, Jacksonville, OR, 97530, 541/899-3800.

119 STEIN BUTTE

9.4 mi/5.5 hr

east of Applegate Lake in Rogue River National Forest

Map 11.6, page 596

From this motorcycle trail, which climbs steadily, even relentlessly, toward a lookout site on Stein Butte, you will see over the border and into California. By the time you've come this far south into Oregon, you're practically in another kind of region matching California anyway: the Oregon state tree of Douglas fir begins to blend in with California natives black oak, canyon live oak, madrone, knobcone pine, and Jeffrey pine. The lookout that the Civilian Conservation Corps built in 1936 is gone, but despite the towering manzanita bushes on the ridge, the view to Mount Shasta and Mount McLoughlin is unimpeded.

From the Seattle Bar Trailhead, you will climb the Stein Butte Trail 2,400 feet in 4.7 miles to the 4,400-foot peak of Stein Butte. Take in the views of Applegate Lake, then return as you came.

User Groups: Hikers, dogs, horses, and mountain bikes. No wheelchair facilities.

Permits: Permits are not required. Parking and access are free.

Maps: For a map of the Rogue River National Forest, contact the Rogue River-Siskiyou National Forest, 3040 Biddle Road, Medford,

OR, 97504, 541/618-2200. For a topographic map, ask the USGS for Squaw Lakes.

Directions: From Jacksonville, head west on Highway 238 for eight miles to Ruch, then turn south following Upper Applegate signs for 18.8 miles. At a junction past the Watkins Campground, go left 0.9 mile to the Seattle Bar Trailhead parking area.

Contact: Rogue River-Siskiyou National Forest, Applegate Ranger District, 6941 Upper Applegate Road, Jacksonville, OR, 97530, 541/899-3800.

120 HERSHBERGER MOUNTAIN AND CRIPPLE CAMP

5.8-13.4 mi/3.0 hr-2 days 🥾2 ⛰7

in the Rogue-Umpqua Divide Wilderness

Map 11.7, page 597

From Pup Prairie in the Rogue-Umpqua Divide Wilderness, the backpacker and day tripper both can find their way into the marshes and mountains, with trails leading out in all directions. In the distance, Highrock Mountain rises into the thin air, and atop Hershberger Mountain an old fire watchtower, listed on the National Register of Historic Places, looks out as far as the snow-topped Cascade peaks, and nearby the towering spires of the Rabbit Ears. For a start, you can visit the lookout one of two ways: by driving or hiking 0.5 mile to the end of Road 530. From there, a metal staircase and trail lead to the cupola-style lookout.

To hike into the wilderness, start from the road's switchback following the Acker Divide Trail to the left, descending through woods to the meadows of columbine, larkspur, coneflower, paintbrush, and bluebells. After 1.6 miles the trail meets up with the Rogue-Umpqua Divide Trail. Go right another 0.8 mile into aptly named Toad Marsh to the Cripple Camp and the 1937 shelter amidst incense cedars and tiger lilies. From here, it is possible to backpack farther to Buckeye Lake,

Fish Lake, and the Highrock Meadows for a 13.4-mile loop that returns to the Hershberger Mountain Trailhead.

User Groups: Hikers, dogs, and horses. No mountain bikes allowed. No wheelchair facilities.

Permits: A free self-issue Wilderness Permit is required and is available at the trailhead. Parking and access are free.

Maps: For a map of the Rogue River National Forest and the Rogue-Umpqua Divide Wilderness, contact the Rogue River-Siskiyou National Forest, 3040 Biddle Road, Medford, OR, 97504, 541/618-2200. For a topographic map, ask the USGS for Fish Mountain.

Directions: From Medford, drive 57 miles east on OR 62, going left onto Highway 230 for 0.9 mile, then turning left across the Rogue River onto Road 6510 for 6.2 miles. Next, turn right on Road 6515 for 9.2 miles, then turn left on Road 530 for 1.8 miles and park at a switchback.

Contact: Rogue River National Forest, Prospect Ranger District, 47201 Highway 62, Prospect, OR, 97536, 541/560-3400.

121 NATIONAL CREEK FALLS

0.8 mi/0.5 hr 🥾1 ⛰7

west of Crater Lake in Rogue River National Forest

Map 11.7, page 597

Traveling through the mountains between Medford and Crater Lake? Why not stop and see an impressive waterfall that drops in two 80-foot drops over a basalt ledge in a deep green forest? People have been stopping here for years—as far back as the 1860s, when the gold miners dropped in for a rest. From the trailhead, it's an easy 0.4-mile walk through grand fir, white pine, and hemlock to the base of the falls on National Creek.

User Groups: Hikers and dogs only. No wheelchair facilities.

Permits: Permits are not required. Parking and access are free.

Maps: For a map of the Rogue River National Forest, contact the Rogue River-Siskiyou National Forest, 3040 Biddle Road, Medford, OR, 97504, 541/618-2200. For a topographic map, ask the USGS for Hamaker Butte.

Directions: From Medford, drive 57 miles east on OR 62 and then go left on Highway 230. After six miles, go right on Road 6530 for 3.7 miles, then right on Road 300 to road's end.

Contact: Rogue River National Forest, Prospect Ranger District, 47201 Highway 62, Prospect, OR, 97536, 541/560-3400.

122 ABBOTT BUTTE
7.2 mi/4.0 hr

in the Rogue-Umpqua Divide Wilderness

Map 11.7, page 597

From this entry into the Rogue-Umpqua Divide Wilderness, the backpacking choices seem unlimited. Start by exploring the abandoned lookout on Abbott Butte and the enormous rock formation of the Elephant Head, a good destination for that first backpacking camp. In summer, expect to see plumes of beargrass lilies, balsamroot, and monkeyflower.

The Rogue Umpqua Divide Trail sets out around Quartz Mountain, paralleling the abandoned road to the lookout. In 1.4 miles, it reaches Windy Gap, and in 1.3 miles crosses the service road to Abbott Butte. At this point and to the right, up one mile and a little over 300 feet, is the lookout, whose tower shelters its little cabin. Continue 0.3 mile on the Rogue Umpqua Divide Trail and go 1.6 miles to Elephant Head Pond, bypassing a Cougar Butte Trail junction, and the towering Elephant Head. Just 0.3 mile beyond the pond is Saddle Camp, a good place to pitch a tent. From there, the Divide Trail continues into the wilderness area.

User Groups: Hikers, dogs, and horses. No mountain bikes allowed. No wheelchair facilities.

Permits: A free self-issue Wilderness Permit

is required and is available at the trailhead. Parking and access are free.

Maps: For a map of the Rogue River National Forest and the Rogue-Umpqua Divide Wilderness, contact the Rogue River-Siskiyou National Forest, 3040 Biddle Road, Medford, OR, 97504, 541/618-2200. For a topographic map, ask the USGS for Abbott Butte.

Directions: From Medford, drive east on OR 62, and between mileposts 51 and 52 turn left on Woodruff Meadows Road 68, staying on this road at all junctions for 4.9 miles of pavement and 7.4 miles of gravel. At the pass by a large national forest sign, park on the right for the Rogue-Umpqua Divide Trail.

Contact: Umpqua National Forest, Tiller Ranger District, 27812 Tiller Trail Highway, Tiller, OR, 97484, 541/825-3201.

123 NATURAL BRIDGE AND THE ROGUE GORGE
2.4-8.2 mi/1.0-3.0 hr

on the Rogue River in Rogue River National Forest

Map 11.7, page 597   BEST (

As the Rogue River plunges through its canyon, it sometimes squeezes itself into some pretty tight spaces. The Rogue Gorge is one such place, with deep, fern-draped cliffs dropping 100 feet to the river. Even stranger is the Natural Bridge, where the river goes underground, or more precisely, beneath an ancient lava flow for a distance of 200 feet, with the water spouting out of blowholes along the way. You can easily see both sights from near the parking area, but why not make a longer hike out of it? This is, after all, the Upper Rogue River Trail, and it's worth exploring at length.

From the Natural Bridge viewpoint, head on the left-hand trail to a crossing. Follow this trail to a viewpoint of the Natural Bridge—you can even walk out on the sturdy flow itself. From here, you can continue on the trail to a second footbridge, crossing it and going right back to the car to make a 2.4-mile loop. But if you are ready for a longer hike, go left after the footbridge instead, reaching the Union Creek Campground in 1.7 miles and the Gorge viewpoint in 1.2 miles. The trail continues another 0.4 mile to a campground and ends. Return as you came.

User Groups: Hikers and dogs. No horses or mountain bikes allowed. Paved viewpoints are wheelchair accessible.

Permits: Permits are not required. Parking and access are free.

Maps: For a map of the Rogue River National Forest, contact the Rogue River-Siskiyou National Forest, 3040 Biddle Road, Medford, OR, 97504, 541/618-2200. For a topographic map, ask the USGS for Union Creek.

Directions: Drive OR 62 east of Medford 55 miles and turn left at a sign for Natural Bridge Campground. Keep left for 0.7 mile to the parking area.

Contact: Rogue River National Forest, Prospect Ranger District, 47201 Highway 62, Prospect, OR, 97536, 541/560-3400.

124 UNION CREEK
8.2 mi/3.5 hr   🥾2 ⛰7

west of Crater Lake in Rogue River National Forest

Map 11.7, page 597

Near the Union Creek Resort, which was used in the past by Jack London and Herbert Hoover, this woodsy trail of old-growth fir and Pacific yew heads up nearby Union Creek to a pair of small waterfalls. Start out east on the Union Creek Trail for 3.3 miles to reach the first waterfall, an eight-foot drop, then continue 0.8 mile to 10-foot Union Creek Falls.

User Groups: Hikers and dogs. No horses or mountain bikes allowed. No wheelchair facilities.

Permits: Permits are not required. Parking and access are free.

Maps: For a map of the Rogue River National Forest, contact the Rogue River-Siskiyou

National Forest, 3040 Biddle Road, Medford, OR, 97504, 541/618-2200. For a topographic map, ask the USGS for Hamaker Butte.

Directions: From Medford, drive OR 62 east 56 miles to Union Creek and park on the right at a pullout by the trailhead.

Contact: Rogue River National Forest, Prospect Ranger District, 47201 Highway 62, Prospect, OR, 97536, 541/560-3400.

125 THE WATCHMAN AND THE DEVIL'S BACKBONE
5.6 mi/2.0 hr   🥾1 ⛰9

in Crater Lake National Park

Map 11.7, page 597

Two hikes fan out along the Crater Lake rim to two distinctive viewpoints. One climbs to the Watchman Lookout with its views over the caldera, and the other circles Hillman Peak to viewpoints of the Devil's Backbone, a volcanic dike left when magma seeped into a crack in ancient Mount Mazama.

From the pullout, go right to climb to The Watchman. Take the trail 0.4 mile to a junction, then to the left and up 0.4 mile to the 8,013-foot peak. For the Devil's Backbone viewpoint, go left from the trailhead and circle Hillman Peak following a two-mile trail to two viewpoints over sparkling Crater Lake below.

User Groups: Hikers only. No dogs, horses, or mountain bikes allowed. No wheelchair facilities.

Permits: Permits are not required unless backcountry camping. A $10 fee, good for seven days, is collected at the entrance stations.

Maps: For a map of Crater Lake National Park, contact Crater Lake National Park, P.O. Box 7, Crater Lake, OR, 97604, 541/594-3000, or for a free downloadable map go to www.nps.gov/crla. For a topographic map, ask the USGS for Crater Lake West.

Directions: Drive four miles north on Rim Drive from Rim Village, or 2.2 miles south of the junction with the north entrance road to the pullout parking area.

Contact: Crater Lake National Park, P.O. Box 7, Crater Lake, OR, 97604, 541/594-3000.

126 CLEETWOOD COVE/ WIZARD ISLAND
4.7 mi/2.0-4.0 hr

in Crater Lake National Park

Map 11.7, page 597

Welcome to Crater Lake, one of the most incredible places in the country. This is Oregon's sole National Park, and a stunning one at that. The remnant of a massive volcanic blast, this collapsed caldera slowly filled with abundant snowfall and rain to form this 1,943-foot-deep shimmering lake that casts a ghostly blue hue into the deep. The Cleetwood Cove Trail is the only trail to access the lake itself, but from here you can take a private boat on a 45-minute tour out to Wizard Island to continue your hike; you'll pay $26 for adults and $15.50 for kids to get there, and more if you're dropped off.

From the rim, hike down the switchbacking 1.1-mile trail to Cleetwood Cove and catch the boat to Wizard Island. On Wizard Island, two trails explore this cinder cone: a 0.4-mile trail heads to the left to a lava flow and Fumarole Bay, and a 1.1-mile trail climbs to the crater, with a 0.3-mile loop around the peak.

User Groups: Hikers only. No dogs, horses, or mountain bikes allowed. No wheelchair facilities.

Permits: Permits are not required unless backcountry camping. A $10 fee, good for seven days, is collected at the entrance stations.

Maps: For a map of Crater Lake National Park, contact Crater Lake National Park, P.O. Box 7, Crater Lake, OR, 97604, 541/594-3000, or for a free downloadable map go to www. nps.gov/crla. For a topographic map, ask the USGS for Crater Lake East and West.

Directions: From Rim Village, drive clockwise on Rim Drive 10.6 miles to the trailhead. From the north entrance, go left at Rim Drive 4.6 miles.

Contact: Crater Lake National Park, P.O. Box 7, Crater Lake, OR, 97604, 541/594-3000.

127 MOUNT SCOTT
5.0 mi/3.5 hr

in Crater Lake National Park

Map 11.7, page 597

When Mount Mazama blew its top 7,700 years ago, it decimated the surrounding landscape and left the massive crater that is Crater Lake. The highest point remaining is Mount Scott, Oregon's 10th-tallest mountain. The hike to this peak is actually quite easy. The goal is a fire watchtower that overlooks the whole panoramic scope of the National Park and beyond.

From the trailhead, this well-graded trail sets out 2.5 miles up Mount Scott, climbing 1,000 feet to the peak. From the peak, look for Klamath Lake, Mount Shasta, Mount McLoughlin, Mount Thielsen, and the Three Sisters.

User Groups: Hikers only. No dogs, horses, or mountain bikes allowed. No wheelchair facilities.

Permits: Permits are not required unless backcountry camping. A $10 fee, good for seven days, is collected at the entrance stations.

Maps: For a map of Crater Lake National Park, contact Crater Lake National Park, P.O. Box 7, Crater Lake, OR, 97604, 541/594-3000, or for a free downloadable map go to www. nps.gov/crla. For a topographic map, ask the USGS for Crater Lake East.

Directions: From Rim Village, drive counterclockwise on Rim Drive 11 miles to a parking pullout. From the north entrance, go left on East Rim Drive 13 miles to the trailhead.

Contact: Crater Lake National Park, P.O. Box 7, Crater Lake, OR, 97604, 541/594-3000.

128 LIGHTNING SPRING/ DISCOVERY POINT/ DUTTON CREEK LOOP

13.1 mi/7.0 hr 🥾3 ⛰️8

in Crater Lake National Park

Map 11.7, page 597

Though the Pacific Crest Trail has some of the most scenic views in the Cascade Mountains, its path through Crater Lake National Park is quite hidden. It passes a few miles away from the rim, thus missing Discovery Point, where it is believed that the Hillman prospecting party first saw the lake in 1853. This strenuous hike goes from the rim to the PCT, connecting with a few campsites at Lightning Spring and along Dutton Creek, passing Discovery Point on the very lip of the volcano itself.

From Rim Village, set out north along the rim for 1.3 miles to Discovery Point and continue 1.2 miles to the third pullout. Cross the road and head to the Lightning Springs Trailhead. In 0.8 mile, you'll reach a series of backcountry campsites. Continue 3.2 miles to the PCT and go left 4.2 miles through a lodgepole forest to a junction on Dutton Creek. Turn left to go 2.4 miles back to the Rim Village.

User Groups: Hikers only. Horses allowed on the PCT only. No dogs or mountain bikes allowed. No wheelchair facilities.

Permits: Permits are not required unless backcountry camping. A $10 fee, good for seven days, is collected at the entrance stations.

Maps: For a map of Crater Lake National Park, contact Crater Lake National Park, P.O. Box 7, Crater Lake, OR, 97604, 541/594-3000, or for a free downloadable map go to www. nps.gov/crla. For a topographic map, ask the USGS for Crater Lake West.

Directions: The trail begins in the large parking lot in Rim Village.

Contact: Crater Lake National Park, P.O. Box 7, Crater Lake, OR, 97604, 541/594-3000.

129 GARFIELD PEAK

3.4 mi/1.5 hr 🥾2 ⛰️9

in Crater Lake National Park

Map 11.7, page 597

Named for Teddy Roosevelt's Secretary of the Interior, who created this National Park in 1902, this 8,054-foot peak set high on Castle Crest overlooks a series of pretty meadows and the Phantom Ship, a rock formation forever adrift in Crater Lake. From the visitors center, set out east toward Crater Lake Lodge for 0.2 mile, then continue up Castle Crest for 1.5 miles to the peak.

User Groups: Hikers only. No dogs, horses, or mountain bikes allowed. No wheelchair facilities.

Permits: Permits are not required unless backcountry camping. A $10 fee, good for seven days, is collected at the entrance stations.

Maps: For a map of Crater Lake National Park, contact Crater Lake National Park, P.O. Box 7, Crater Lake, OR, 97604, 541/594-3000, or for a free downloadable map go to www. nps.gov/crla. For a topographic map, ask the USGS for Crater Lake East and West.

Directions: The trail begins in the large parking lot in Rim Village.

Contact: Crater Lake National Park, P.O. Box 7, Crater Lake, OR, 97604, 541/594-3000.

130 ANNIE CREEK AND GODFREY GLEN

2.7 mi/1.0 hr 🥾1 ⛰️8

in Crater Lake National Park

Map 11.7, page 597

Two easy hikes explore canyons carved out of the flank of Crater Lake's massive volcano. Since they're located close to one another, it's worth it to hike both. Annie Creek's 1.7-mile loop follows a glacier-carved canyon with a series of ash pinnacles left over from the 7,700-year-old eruption. Godfrey Glen's one-mile loop looks over Munson Creek's canyon and its haunting pillars of solidified ash.

User Groups: Hikers only. No dogs, horses, or mountain bikes allowed. No wheelchair facilities.

Permits: Permits are not required unless backcountry camping. A $10 fee, good for seven days, is collected at the entrance stations.

Maps: For a map of Crater Lake National Park, contact Crater Lake National Park, P.O. Box 7, Crater Lake, OR, 97604, 541/594-3000, or for a free downloadable map go to www. nps.gov/crla. For a topographic map, ask the USGS for Union Peak.

Directions: To see Annie Creek, start from the park entrance on OR 62, driving 0.3 mile toward Rim Village and turning right at a sign for Mazama Campground. Park at the store and walk to camping area C; the trailhead begins behind site C-11. To see the Godfrey Glen, go past the Mazama Campground and drive toward Rim Village an additional 2.1 miles, turning right at a sign for Godfrey Glen Nature Loop.

Contact: Crater Lake National Park, P.O. Box 7, Crater Lake, OR, 97604, 541/594-3000.

131 UNION PEAK
11.0 mi/6.0 hr   👣5 ⛰9

in Crater Lake National Park

Map 11.7, page 597

This trail heads to 7,709-foot Union Peak, making this the most challenging hike in Crater Lake National Park. Union Peak is the oldest mountain in the park; it's a heavily eroded volcanic plug rising above forests of lodgepole pine and mountain hemlock growing from deep layers of pumice. This hike is bit off the beaten path, and it makes use of the Pacific Crest Trail. Note that there is no water on this trail, so bring plenty to cover this long trip.

Set out on the PCT for 2.9 miles along an old fire road. In a pumice plain, go right on the Union Peak Trail 2.6 miles to the peak, switchbacking steeply at the end.

User Groups: Hikers only. Horses allowed on the PCT only. No dogs or mountain bikes allowed. No wheelchair facilities.

Permits: Permits are not required unless backcountry camping. A $10 fee, good for seven days, is collected at the entrance stations.

Maps: For a map of Crater Lake National Park, contact Crater Lake National Park, P.O. Box 7, Crater Lake, OR, 97604, 541/594-3000, or for a free downloadable map go to www. nps.gov/crla. For a topographic map, ask the USGS for Union Peak.

Directions: Drive 72 miles east of Medford on OR 62 to a summit about one mile west of Mazama Village. Park at a Pacific Crest Trail side road on the right.

Contact: Crater Lake National Park, P.O. Box 7, Crater Lake, OR, 97604, 541/594-3000.

132 CRATER PEAK
6.2 mi/3.0 hr   👣3 ⛰9

in Crater Lake National Park

Map 11.7, page 597

High above the Sun Notch, and with views extending to a host of Cascade peaks and Klamath Lake, Crater Peak is host to high meadows of summer lupine where elk browse in summer. Atop the peak is a volcanic crater filled in with the pumice and ash left from Mazama's violent explosion. From the Vidae Falls Picnic Area, the trail climbs 1,000 feet up 3.1 miles to the crater atop this overlook peak. Once atop the volcanic crater, you can loop 0.4 mile to inspect this long-dead peak.

User Groups: Hikers only. No dogs, horses, or mountain bikes allowed. No wheelchair facilities.

Permits: Permits are not required unless backcountry camping. A $10 fee, good for seven days, is collected at the entrance stations.

Maps: For a map of Crater Lake National Park, contact Crater Lake National Park, P.O. Box 7, Crater Lake, OR, 97604, 541/594-3000, or for a free downloadable map go to www.nps.gov/crla. For a topographic map, ask the USGS for Crater Lake East and Maklaks Crater.

Directions: From Rim Village, follow Rim Drive East 2.9 miles to the Vidae Falls Picnic Area on the right.

Contact: Crater Lake National Park, P.O. Box 7, Crater Lake, OR, 97604, 541/594-3000.

133 TAKELMA GORGE
5.2 mi/2.0 hr   👣1 ⛰8

on the Rogue River in Rogue River National Forest

Map 11.7, page 597

If you don't have the time to hike large stretches of the Upper Rogue River, but prefer something shorter, a walk where a fanny pack would be enough for an outing, try the Takelma Gorge. This mile-long surge through a 150-foot-deep lava slot comes close to the final stretch of this long trail, and provides an exciting series of views into the Rogue's chasm.

From the Woodruff Bridge picnic area, go downstream 1.6 miles to the beginning of the chasm, then continue one mile farther along the stunning viewpoints to a switchback down to a beach on a much calmer section. This makes a good turnaround point, but beyond that, the river trail continues about 8.5 miles to its end at North Fork Park.

User Groups: Hikers and dogs. No horses or mountain bikes allowed. No wheelchair facilities.

Permits: Permits are not required. Parking and access are free.

Maps: For a map of the Rogue River National Forest, contact the Rogue River-Siskiyou National Forest, 3040 Biddle Road, Medford, OR, 97504, 541/618-2200. For a topographic map, ask the USGS for Hamaker Butte.

Directions: Drive east of Medford on OR 62 and between mileposts 51 and 52 turn left on Woodruff Meadows Road for 1.7 miles. Turn left into the Woodruff Bridge picnic area.

Contact: Rogue River National Forest, Prospect Ranger District, 47201 Highway 62, Prospect, OR, 97536, 541/560-3400.

134 RED BLANKET FALLS AND STUART FALLS
10.0 mi/4.5 hr   👣3 ⛰7

south of Crater Lake in Sky Lakes Wilderness

Map 11.7, page 597

At the southern border of Crater Lake National Park lies the Sky Lakes Wilderness, with three major basins of lakes and the peak of Mount McLoughlin to claim as its territory. At the northwestern corner, this trail enters in so close to the national park that you'll pass a 1902 corner marker; after that, you'll follow Red Blanket Creek into its canyon, reaching two waterfalls and a lush huckleberry meadow. From there, the trail heads in two directions to the Pacific Crest Trail, with access to Crater Lake and the Sky Lakes.

The first 2.9 miles of the trail follows Red Blanket Creek to Red Blanket Falls and a junction. To head to Stuart Falls, go left up one mile to another junction, then left again another 0.4 mile. From this point, it is 2.8 miles to the PCT. Return 0.4 mile to the junction and this time go left 0.8 mile on the Stuart Falls Trail to the next junction. Staying to the left heads 2.7 miles to the PCT; go right for a 1.6-mile loop through Lucky Meadow. This Lucky Camp Trail returns to Red Blanket Falls.

User Groups: Hikers, dogs, and horses. No mountain bikes allowed. No wheelchair facilities.

Permits: A free self-issue Wilderness Permit is required and is available at the trailhead. Parking and access are free.

Maps: For a map of the Rogue River National Forest and Sky Lakes Wilderness, contact the Rogue River-Siskiyou National Forest, 3040 Biddle Road, Medford, OR, 97504, 541/618-2200. For a topographic map, ask the USGS for Union Peak.

Directions: Drive east of Medford 45 miles on OR 62 and turn right toward Prospect for 0.7 mile. In town, turn left on Butte Falls Road for one mile, then left on Red Blanket Road for 0.4 mile. At a fork, go left on Road 6205 for 11.4 miles to road's end at a parking area.

Contact: Rogue River National Forest, Prospect Ranger District, 47201 Highway 62, Prospect, OR, 97536, 541/560-3400.

135 LOST CREEK LAKE
5.0-18.7 mi/2.0 hr-2 days 🏃3 🏔7

on the Rogue River in Stewart State Park

Map 11.7, page 597

Stewart State Park is a busy park with lots of visitors and lots of things to do: biking, camping, swimming, boating, you name it. It so happens that the majority of the nearby Lost Creek Lake Reservoir is not only quieter, but provides opportunities for backpacking, making use of three remote camping spots. The Grotto makes an easy destination from Lewis Road, and is actually quite a sight: This box canyon of basalt and green ash left over from the volcanic explosion of Crater Lake is an easy side excursion.

To begin, set out from Lewis Road on the trail. In 0.9 mile you'll reach the first primitive camp, Fire Glen Camp. Another 1.5 miles leads to a right-hand side trail up 0.1 mile to the Grotto overlook. The next 3.4 miles heads to a crossing of Lost Creek, passing Sugar Pine Camp along the way. The next 3.8 miles starts around the opposite shore, passing Four Corners Camp and arriving at a boat ramp at Takelma Park. Here the trail continues 1.4 miles, crossing the dam. The next 2.8 miles heads to the state park, passing through it for 3.6 miles. The final stretch is all on paved roads, following Highway 62 to the left over Peyton Bridge 0.3 mile, then going left on Lewis Road for the last mile.

User Groups: Hikers and dogs. No horses allowed. Trails in Stewart State Park are wheelchair accessible and suitable for mountain biking.

Permits: Permits are not required. Parking and access are free.

Maps: For a topographic map, ask the USGS for McLeod and Cascade Gorge.

Directions: Drive east of Medford 35.5 miles on OR 62. After crossing a bridge over Lost Creek Lake turn left on Lewis Road for one mile to the Lewis Road Trailhead on the left.

Contact: Oregon Parks and Recreation Department, 1115 Commercial Street Northeast, Salem, OR, 97301, 800/551-6949, www.oregonstateparks.org.

136 UPPER SOUTH FORK ROGUE RIVER
12.0 mi/6.0 hr   🏃3 🏔7

southeast of Prospect in Rogue River National Forest

Map 11.7, page 597

The South Fork of the Rogue River is a young river, not as wide as you might suspect, but this section of trail follows it through some substantial trees and large logs along the shore, plus a few gravel bars thrown in for good measure. You'll also find Pacific yew, which Native Americans used for bows because of its flexibility. Along this trail you'll cross several creeks, as well.

From the trailhead, start out upriver on the South Fork Trail, a primitive and seldom-maintained trail. In 0.7 mile you'll cross Big Ben Creek; avoid the side trail on the left leading to a campground. Continue on 4.4 miles, crossing Sam Creek, Wickiup Creek, and Little Billie Creek to a crossing of Road 800. The last 0.9 mile of trail continues to an upper trailhead on Road 37. From here, backpackers can follow nearby Road 720 southeast one mile to the trailhead for the Blue Lake Trail and the Sky Lakes Wilderness.

User Groups: Hikers and dogs. No horses or mountain bikes allowed. No wheelchair facilities.

Permits: Permits are not required. Parking and access are free.

Maps: For a map of the Rogue River National Forest and Sky Lakes Wilderness, contact the Rogue River-Siskiyou National Forest, 3040 Biddle Road, Medford, OR, 97504,

541/618-2200. For a topographic map, ask the USGS for Cascade Gorge.

Directions: From Medford, drive 14.5 miles east on OR 62 and turn right on the Butte Falls Highway for 15 miles to the town of Butte Falls. Go straight one mile then left at a sign for Prospect for nine miles. Turn right on Lodgepole Road for 8.5 miles. Go past South Fork Campground 0.5 mile to a parking area on the right.

Contact: Rogue River National Forest, Butte Falls Ranger District, 47201 Highway 62, Prospect, OR, 97536, 541/865-2700.

137 LOWER SOUTH FORK ROGUE RIVER
13.6-14.0 mi/6.0-7.0 hr   🏃3 ⛰7

southeast of Prospect in Rogue River National Forest

Map 11.7, page 597

The lower stretch of trail on the South Fork of the Rogue River is accessible to mountain bikes. It also provides a glimpse of many sugar pine trees, including one particularly large one on a short side trail. This section of trail ambles over creeks and through woods down to its end at a diversion dam.

Cross the road from the parking area and take the South Fork Trail along the river 1.6 miles to the left-hand side trail; a short 0.2-mile walk crosses Road 3775 and visits the giant sugar pine. The remaining 5.2 miles follows the river down to the dam.

User Groups: Hikers, dogs, and mountain bikes. No horses allowed. No wheelchair facilities.

Permits: Permits are not required. Parking and access are free.

Maps: For a map of the Rogue River National Forest and Sky Lakes Wilderness, contact the Rogue River-Siskiyou National Forest, 3040 Biddle Road, Medford, OR, 97504, 541/618-2200. For a topographic map, ask the USGS for Cascade Gorge.

Directions: From Medford, drive 14.5 miles east on OR 62 and turn right on the Butte Falls Highway for 15 miles to the town of Butte Falls. go straight one mile then left at a sign for Prospect for nine miles. Turn right on Lodgepole Road for 8.5 miles. Go past South Fork Campground 0.5 mile to a parking area on the right.

Contact: Rogue River National Forest, Butte Falls Ranger District, 47201 Highway 62, Prospect, OR, 97536, 541/865-2700.

138 SEVEN LAKES TRAIL
8.4-10.4 mi/3.5-5.0 hr   🏃4 ⛰9

east of Prospect in Sky Lakes Wilderness

Map 11.7, page 597

The Sky Lakes Wilderness is heaven for backpackers and horses, with many opportunities to camp throughout the area. The Seven Lakes Basin, one of the more popular spots, has camps aplenty—just as long as you camp where the USFS asks you to, which means paying attention to posted camp spots. Horses are required to camp at designated areas, are banned from grazing, and are not allowed within 200 feet of lakeshores, unless on trails or near designated watering spots. If this sounds like a lot of information, don't let it dissuade you. It's only to keep the area as pristine as possible. To enter from the west, the Seven Lakes Trail climbs over a pass into a water-dotted landscape that is best viewed from nearby Devils Peak, accessible from the Pacific Crest Trail.

The Seven Lakes Trail sets out from behind a guardrail into the wilderness. At 0.7 mile, go right and continue 2.8 miles, passing Frog Lake, to a pass. Here the trail splits: Take the left trail down 0.2 mile to the basin. At the next junction, going left on the Alta Lake Trail leads to half-mile-long Alta Lake with its campsites. Going straight passes South Lake and Cliff Lake in 1.5 miles; another left-hand trail connects to three more lakes. Continue 0.4 mile to the PCT. For a climb up Devils Peak, turn right on the PCT for 2.5 miles, then heading right up the peak. Head back down and continue on the PCT another 0.6 mile to a junction. Go right on a 1.3-mile spur trail to return to the pass over Seven Lakes.

User Groups: Hikers, dogs, and horses. No mountain bikes allowed. No wheelchair facilities.

Permits: A free self-issue Wilderness Permit is required and is available at the trailhead. Parking and access are free.

Maps: For a map of the Rogue River National Forest and Sky Lakes Wilderness, contact the Rogue River-Siskiyou National Forest, 3040 Biddle Road, Medford, OR, 97504, 541/618-2200. For a topographic map, ask the USGS for Devil's Peak.

Directions: From Medford, drive 14.5 miles east on OR 62 and turn right on Butte Falls Highway for 15 miles to the town of Butte Falls. Go straight one mile and turn left toward Prospect for nine miles, then right on Lodgepole Road 34 for 8.5 miles. Continue straight on Road 37 for 0.4 mile, then go right on Road 3780 for 4.1 miles to a parking area on the left.

Contact: Rogue River National Forest, Butte Falls Ranger District, 47201 Highway 62, Prospect, OR, 97536, 541/865-2700.

139 SEVEN LAKES BASIN VIA SEVENMILE/PCT
11.4-17.3 mi/6.0-9.0 hr

east of Prospect in Sky Lakes Wilderness

Map 11.7, page 597

The eastern entrance to this mythic landscape of lakes visits the same area as the Seven Lakes Trail (see previous listing) but is both longer and easier. For one, you won't have the elevation gain. Plus, you'll be in the headwaters of the Middle Fork Rogue River, including Sevenmile Marsh. From here, you can also walk the shore of Cliff Lake with its views to Devils Peak, and you can climb Devils Peak for a world-class view of the lake country.

Start on the Sevenmile Trail for 1.8 miles,

and go right on the Pacific Crest Trail for 2.7 miles. At the next junction, you can create a 2.4-mile loop past Grass Lake, Middle Lake, and Cliff Lake by going right then staying left for the next three junctions. To climb Devils Peak stay on the PCT another 3.2 miles up to a high pass, climbing the peak to the right. If you want to expand this loop to a 17-plus-mile hike, continue on the PCT 0.6 mile to a junction and go right 1.3 miles on a spur trail to a second pass, connecting with the Seven Lakes Trail. Then go right and stay on this trail for 1.7 miles back to the PCT.

User Groups: Hikers, dogs, and horses. No mountain bikes allowed. No wheelchair facilities.

Permits: A free self-issue Wilderness Permit is required and is available at the trailhead. Parking and access are free.

Maps: For a map of the Rogue River National Forest and Sky Lakes Wilderness, contact the Fremont-Winema National Forest, 1301 South G Street, Lakeview, OR, 97630, 541/947-2151. For a topographic map, ask the USGS for Devils Peak.

Directions: Drive north from Klamath Falls on OR 62 to Fort Klamath, near milepost 90. Turn west on Nicholson Road and go straight 3.9 miles. Go left on Road 3300 at a sign for Sevenmile Trailhead for 0.4 mile, then go right on Road 3334 to road's end.

Contact: Winema National Forest, Klamath Falls Ranger District, 2819 Dahlia Street, Klamath Falls, OR, 97601, 541/883-6714.

140 SKY LAKES FROM NANNIE CREEK TRAIL
12.8-16.7 mi/6.0-8.0 hr

west of Klamath Lake in Sky Lakes Wilderness

Map 11.7, page 597

The Sky Lakes Basin has a challenging side, and this trail is it. This section of lakes huddles around imposing Luther Mountain like jewels flung across the forest. The Nannie Creek Trail will get you there, but once you're there it's up to you to wander around and lose yourself in the landscape. Here are a couple of hikes, both rigorous, to get you warmed up.

The Nannie Creek Trail heads out on a ridge for 2.4 miles to Puck Lakes on the right, and another 1.9 miles to a junction with the Snow Lakes Trail. To hit the main course, go left 1.4 miles passing numerous ponds to a junction. Here you can go 0.5 mile to the right to Margurette Lake, then form a loop: go left 0.2 mile to Trapper Lake, then left at the junction of the Cherry Creek Trail 0.7 mile to Donna and Deep lakes to complete the loop.

For a climb around Luther Mountain, instead go right at Margurette Lake, climbing heartily up 2.8 miles to the PCT. Go right on the PCT for 1.1 miles, then right on the Snow Lakes Trail 2.3 miles back to the Nannie Creek Trail, passing little tarns along the way. Return on the Nannie Creek Trail.

User Groups: Hikers, dogs, and horses. No mountain bikes allowed. No wheelchair facilities.

Permits: A free self-issue Wilderness Permit is required and is available at the trailhead. Parking and access are free.

Maps: For a map of the Rogue River National Forest and Sky Lakes Wilderness, contact the Fremont-Winema National Forest, 1301 South G Street, Lakeview, OR, 97630, 541/947-2151. For a topographic map, ask the USGS for for Pelican Butte.

Directions: From Klamath Falls, go west on Highway 140 for 25 miles. Between mileposts 43 and 44, go north on Westside Road for 12.2 miles, then left on Road 3484 for 5.2 miles to road's end.

Contact: Winema National Forest, Klamath Falls Ranger District, 2819 Dahlia Street, Klamath Falls, OR, 97601, 541/883-6714.

141 SKY LAKES FROM COLD SPRINGS TRAILHEAD
6.9 mi/3.0 hr   🏃3 ⛰8

west of Klamath Lake in Sky Lakes Wilderness

Map 11.7, page 597

The Sky Lakes Basin is a picture-perfect mesh of ponds and lakes. For an easy entrance into its wonders—visiting Heavenly Twin Lakes, with its view of Luther Mountain, and Isherwood Lake, as well as Lakes Florence, Liza, Elizabeth, and Notasha—try this easy loop.

From the Cold Springs Trailhead, head in 0.6 mile to a junction. For the quickest walk through the lodgepole and hemlock woods, go right on the South Rock Creek Trail for 1.8 miles to the next junction. To the left, a 0.3-mile spur connects to a shorter loop with the cold Springs Trail and runs between the heavenly Twin Lakes. For a longer loop among far more lakes, go right 0.4 mile along the lakeshore to the Sky Lakes Trail, then left at the next junction 0.8 mile past the rest of the lovely lakes. At the next junction, go right 0.3 mile, then left on the Cold Springs Trail 2.4 miles back to the car.

User Groups: Hikers, dogs, and horses. No mountain bikes allowed. No wheelchair facilities.

Permits: A free self-issue Wilderness Permit is required and is available at the trailhead. Parking and access are free.

Maps: For a map of the Rogue River National Forest and Sky Lakes Wilderness, contact the Fremont-Winema National Forest, 1301 South G Street, Lakeview, OR, 97630, 541/947-2151. For a topographic map, ask the USGS for Pelican Butte.

Directions: From Medford, drive east 6 miles on OR 62, then right on Highway 140 to milepost 41, and turn north on Road 3651; watch for Cold Springs Trailhead sign. Go 10.1 miles to its end at the Cold Springs Trailhead.

Contact: Winema National Forest, Klamath Falls Ranger District, 2819 Dahlia Street, Klamath Falls, OR, 97601, 541/883-6714.

142 BLUE LAKE BASIN
7.4-11.0 miles/3.0-6.0 hr

north of Mount McLoughlin in Sky Lakes Wilderness

Map 11.7, page 597

Sky Lakes seems a fitting name for a wilderness that hosts lakes so pure they seem to hold their own sky. From some of the shores of these lakes, the true sky seems magnificently large, endless, spanning from one horizon to another. Perhaps this is what Judge John Waldo thought as he passed through here with a horse party in 1888. He left his mark carved into a large Shasta red fir on the shore of Island Lake, a spot you can visit on this fabulous hike.

Take the Blue Canyon Trail 2.3 miles, passing Round Lake, to Blue Lake. Go right at the junction with the South Fork Trail and continue 0.3 mile to the next junction (with a horse camp on the left). Go left and continue 2.9 miles on the Blue Canyon Trail, passing access points to large Horseshoe Lake and Pear Lake, then watching for an unmarked side trail to the left, leading to Waldo's signature and the shore of Island Lake. Another 0.4 mile beyond this trail is the junction with the Badger Lake Trail, and a right turn there leads 0.2 mile to the Pacific Crest Trail.

User Groups: Hikers, dogs, and horses. No mountain bikes allowed. No wheelchair facilities.

Permits: A free self-issue Wilderness Permit is required and is available at the trailhead. Parking and access are free.

Maps: For a map of the Rogue River National Forest and Sky Lakes Wilderness, contact the Rogue River-Siskiyou National Forest, 3040 Biddle Road, Medford, OR, 97504, 541/618-2200. For a topographic map, ask the USGS for Pelican Butte.

Directions: From Medford, drive 14.5 miles east on OR 62 and turn right on Butte Falls Highway for 15 miles to the town of Butte Falls. Go straight one mile and turn left toward Prospect for nine miles, then right on Lodgepole Road 34 for 8.5 miles. Continue straight on Road 37 for 7.4 miles, then turn left on Road 3770 for 5.3 miles to a pullout on the right.

Contact: Rogue River National Forest, Butte Falls Ranger District, 47201 Highway 62, Prospect, OR, 97536, 541/865-2700.

143 MOUNT MCLOUGHLIN
10.6 mi/6.0 hr

west of Klamath Lake in Sky Lakes Wilderness

Map 11.7, page 597

After years of having hikers climb helter-skelter to this 9,495-foot peak, the Forest Service finally laid out a trail. Bring plenty of water and sunscreen and prepare for a rugged, demanding climb, but also a view of half the state of Oregon, and far into California. Named for the Hudson Bay Company leader at Fort Vancouver, this mountain is one of the best non-technical climbs in the state. Just be sure to stay on the trail—even with such a view of the surrounding area, it's easy to get lost.

Cross the Cascade Canal and climb one mile to the Pacific Crest Trail. Follow the PCT uphill and to the right for 0.4 mile, passing a right-hand side trail to Freye Lake, then leaving the PCT on the climber's route to the left. For 1.5 miles the trail is steady before it hurtles upwards the remaining 2.4 miles, heading above tree line, with the final half gaining 1,300 feet.

User Groups: Hikers, dogs, and horses. No mountain bikes allowed. No wheelchair facilities.

Permits: A free self-issue Wilderness Permit is required and is available at the trailhead. A federal Northwest Forest Pass is required to park at the Trout Creek Trailhead; the cost is $5 a day or $30 for an annual pass. You can buy a day pass at the trailhead, at ranger stations, or through private vendors.

Maps: For a map of the Rogue River National Forest and Sky Lakes Wilderness, contact the Fremont-Winema National Forest, 1301 South G Street, Lakeview, OR, 97630, 541/947-2151.

For a topographic map, ask the USGS for Mount McLoughlin.

Directions: From Klamath Falls, go west on Highway 140 to milepost 36, and just beyond it turn right on Road 3661 for 2.9 miles, then left on Road 3650 for 0.2 mile to a parking lot.

Contact: Winema National Forest, Klamath Falls Ranger District, 2819 Dahlia Street, Klamath Falls, OR, 97601, 541/883-6714.

144 FOURMILE LAKE TO LONG LAKE
9.0-14.0 mi/4.0-7.0 hr   🏃3 ⛰7

west of Klamath Lake in Sky Lakes Wilderness

Map 11.7, page 597

Fourmile Lake is bordered on nearly every side by the Sky Lakes Wilderness, through which the Pacific Crest Trail glides by on a relatively level trail. This large lake, with its view of the pyramid-like Mount McLoughlin, offers access to a number of lakes in the Wilderness Area. The route can be extended to a 14-mile loop, though much of it passes through viewless woods and leaves the lakes behind for quite a while.

From the Fourmile Trailhead, head left for 0.8 mile, crossing Road 3661, then left on the Badger Lake Trail, which crosses the Cascade Canal. Now the trail heads into the Wilderness Area, arriving at Badger Lake in 1.8 miles and Long Lake in another 1.9 miles, passing Horse Creek Meadow along the way. This is the last of the lakes this trail sees, but to continue on a wide loop, head farther down the trail 1.6 miles to the PCT, going left. Follow the PCT 5.4 miles, then turn left on the Twin Ponds Trail for 2.5 miles, passing one last lake, and arriving back at the Fourmile Trailhead.

User Groups: Hikers, dogs, and horses. No mountain bikes allowed. No wheelchair facilities.

Permits: A free self-issue Wilderness Permit is required and is available at the trailhead. Parking and access are free.

Maps: For a map of the Rogue River National Forest and Sky Lakes Wilderness, contact the Fremont-Winema National Forest, 1301 South G Street, Lakeview, OR, 97630, 541/947-2151. For a topographic map, ask the USGS for Lake of the Woods North.

Directions: From Klamath Falls, go west on Highway 140 to milepost 36, and just beyond it turn right on Road 3661 for 5.7 miles to Fourmile Campground. Follow signs for the trailhead.

Contact: Winema National Forest, Klamath Falls Ranger District, 2819 Dahlia Street, Klamath Falls, OR, 97601, 541/883-6714.

145 TABLE ROCKS
2.8-5.4 mi/1.0-2.5 hr   🏃1 ⛰8

north of Medford

Map 11.7, page 597

The two formations known as the Table Rocks, rising like fortresses above the Rogue River, seem out of place in this valley. They were, in fact, used as fortresses by the Takelma tribe against the U.S. Army, which came for them when they attacked settlers and gold miners in 1853. These mesas are the remnants of a 9.6-million-year-old lava flow, standing 800-feet-high and capped with tough andesite. Atop the plateaus you'll find scrub oak grasslands and a profusion of wildflowers, which is why The Nature Conservancy built the trail on Lower Table Rock, now a nature preserve. In fact, a rare fairy shrimp—federally listed as threatened—is found in the vernal pools atop the mesa.

To climb Upper Table Rock, you need ascend only 720 feet up a 1.1-mile trail to the viewpoints. The trail to Lower Table Rock is longer; it sets off 1.6 miles across the valley floor, then goes up cliffs studded with black oak and madrone to the mesa. From there, you can hike out to two viewpoints: one just 0.4 mile to the left, and the other 1.1 miles down an old airstrip to a viewpoint. You'll catch views of the Crater Lake rim, Mount McLoughlin, and the Rogue River.

User Groups: Hikers. Dogs not allowed on Lower Table Rock. No horses or mountain bikes allowed. No wheelchair facilities.

Permits: Permits are not required. Parking and access are free.

Maps: For a topographic map, ask the USGS for Sams Valley.

Directions: For Lower Table Rock, return to Table Rock Road and turn right, continuing to milepost 10. Turn left on Wheeler Road 0.8 mile to a parking spur on the left. For Upper Table Rock, take the I-5 north of Medford to Exit 33 for Central Point, driving east on Biddle Road for one mile. Turn left on Table Rock Road for 5.2 miles and turn right on Modoc Road for 1.5 miles to the trailhead lot on the left.

Contact: Bureau of Land Management, Medford Office, 3040 Biddle Road, Medford, OR, 97504, 541/618-2200.

146 FISH LAKE AND THE HIGH LAKES TRAIL
12.7 mi one-way/7.0 hr 🏃3 ⛰7

south of Mount McLoughlin in Rogue River National Forest

Map 11.7, page 597

This fairly new trail makes for a great bike ride or an extended hike. Of course, it can be broken up into segments starting from either Fish Lake or Lake of the Woods. The trail crosses the Cascade Crest and largely follows a massive lava flow erupted from Brown Mountain, which occupies the horizon here like a sentry. An easy 6.6-mile round-trip hike follows the shore of Fish Lake and joins the High Lakes Trail at its far end, and it's here that this description begins.

From the Fish Lake Trailhead, walk in 0.6 mile to a junction near the Fish Lake Dam. Go left and follow the main trail 3.7 miles through an old clear-cut, crossing a road and passing the Fish Lake Resort, and following the Fish Lake shore to the Fish Lake Campground and the start of the High Lakes Trail.

In one mile the trail crosses the Pacific Crest Trail. From here, it's 4.8 miles to Lake of the Woods, following the edge of the Brown Mountain Lava Flow (see next listing) to a visitors center. The trail continues along the edge of the lake for 0.8 mile to the Aspen Point Picnic Area, and continues across a big meadow 1.8 miles to the upper trailhead at the Great Meadow Recreation Site.

User Groups: Hikers, dogs, and bicycles. No horses allowed. No wheelchair facilities.

Permits: Permits are not required. Parking and access are free.

Maps: For a map of the Rogue River National Forest and Sky Lakes Wilderness, contact the Rogue River-Siskiyou National Forest, 3040 Biddle Road, Medford, OR, 97504, 541/618-2200. For a topographic map, ask the USGS for Mount McLoughlin.

Directions: To access the Fish Lake Trailhead, drive east of Medford 35 miles on Highway 140. Between mileposts 28 and 29, turn south on Road 37. In 0.5 mile turn left at the trailhead parking. To access the Lake of the Woods Trailhead, park in a lot on Highway 140 between mileposts 37 and 38.

Contact: Rogue River-Siskiyou National Forest, Ashland Ranger District, 645 Washington Street, Ashland, OR, 97520, 541/552-2900.

147 BROWN MOUNTAIN
5.8 mi/2.0 hr 🏃2 ⛰7

south of Mount McLoughlin in Rogue River National Forest

Map 11.7, page 597

The Brown Mountain Lava Flow spilled quite a mess here, and the builders of the Pacific Crest Trail, which crosses it, had to dynamite their way through. Now the rugged landscape is being pioneered by chinkapin oak and a variety of lichens. Bring water, as summer sun can make a lava field a simmering experience.

From the trailhead, hike in 0.2 mile and go left on the Pacific Crest Trail. In 0.4 mile cross Highway 140 and continue 0.2 mile to a junction with the High Lakes Trail, going straight. Within the next two miles, you will cross the largest part of the flow and arrive at a high point, with views to Mount McLoughlin along the way. If you continue on, you can travel 5.8 miles to the Brown Mountain Trail, which does not climb the mountain but rather goes around it.

User Groups: Hikers, dogs, and horses. No mountain bikes allowed. No wheelchair facilities.

Permits: Permits are not required. Parking and access are free.

Maps: For a map of the Rogue River National Forest and Sky Lakes Wilderness, contact the Rogue River-Siskiyou National Forest, 3040 Biddle Road, Medford, OR, 97504, 541/618-2200. For a topographic map, ask the USGS for Brown Mountain.

Directions: From Medford, drive Highway 140 to a pullout on the left between mileposts 32 and 33, at a sign for Summit Sno-Park. The trail starts at this parking area.

Contact: Rogue River-Siskiyou National Forest, Ashland Ranger District, 645 Washington Street, Ashland, OR, 97520, 541/552-2900.

148 MOUNTAIN LAKES WILDERNESS LOOP

17.1 mi/1-2 days

west of Klamath Lake in the Mountain Lakes Wilderness

Map 11.7, page 597

At only six square miles, the exact size of a township, this is surely one of the smallest wilderness areas there is. This pocket remains as it was since 1964: a stunning terrain of mountainous country hovering over Upper Klamath Lake. Glaciers have carved this area, a collapsed volcano not unlike that of Crater Lake, into towering cliffs, lake basins, and eroded volcanic cones. Piercing a lateral moraine, the grit swept to the sides by glaciers, the trail follows a path of ponderosa pine, Shasta red fir, and white fir into an alpine landscape that just

begs for a backpacker or two—but no more than 10 at a time, according to regulations. Even though this is one of the first designated Wilderness Areas in the country, it remains quite a secret to the public.

Follow the Varney Creek Trail 4.4 miles, with views of Mount Harriman, to a fork at the beginning of the loop. If you're backpacking, go left on the Mountain Lakes Loop Trail to the lakes. You'll reach Lake Como in 0.7 mile, and larger Lake Harriette 1.2 miles beyond that; both are suitable for camping. From Lake Harriette, continue 1.5 miles up to a high pass and go right (the left trail dead-ends at South Pass Lake). In 0.4 mile you'll pass a side route up Aspen Butte, a one-mile cross-country climb to an old lookout site at 8,208 feet. Continuing on the loop, stay straight on the main trail for 2.7 miles to a pass on White-face Peak, passing both an unmaintained trail and the Clover Creek Trail on the left. At the peak, go right (the other path leads to Road 3660 on the Mountain Lakes Trail, descending 2,000 feet and past Lake Waban) to finish the loop, heading 1.4 miles down to Zeb and Eb Lakes. In another 0.4 mile, you'll meet with the Varney Creek Trail; go left to return to the trailhead.

User Groups: Hikers, dogs, and horses. No mountain bikes allowed. No wheelchair facilities.

Permits: A free self-issue Wilderness Permit is required and is available at the trailhead. Parking and access are free.

Maps: For a map of the Rogue River National Forest and Sky Lakes Wilderness, contact the Fremont-Winema National Forest, 1301 South G Street, Lakeview, OR, 97630, 541/947-2151. For a topographic map, ask the USGS for Lake of the Woods North.

Directions: From Klamath Falls, drive 21 miles west on Highway 140. Between mileposts 46 and 47, turn south on Road 3637 at a Varney Creek Trailhead sign, following this road 1.8 miles. Turn left on Road 3664 for 1.9 miles to its end.

Contact: Winema National Forest, Klamath

Falls Ranger District, 2819 Dahlia Street, Klamath Falls, OR, 97601, 541/883-6714.

149 JACKSONVILLE WOODLANDS
1.0-8.0 mi/1.0-2.5 hr 🚶2 ⛰7

in Jacksonville

Map 11.7, page 597

The little city of Jacksonville is designated a National Historic Landmark, a true distinction here in Oregon. This former mining town at the foot of the Siskiyous is charming in its own right, and retains much of its 1886 allure, a leftover from when the railroad abandoned this area and the gold ran out. The woodlands that lie just outside it add to the ambiance. In 1989, citizens of this little red-brick town rallied to preserve the area, and the result is this 20-parcel forest intersected by eight miles of trail, following Jackson Creek, touring old mining ruins, and climbing to a 1,900-foot summit over the town.

From the lot set out 0.8 mile along Jackson Creek on the Zigler Trail. To climb to the summit of Panorama Point, head up 0.7 mile on the Jackson Forks and Rich Gulch Trails. After the viewpoint, the Rich Gulch Trail heads to Rich Gulch, where gold was discovered in 1852, passing some old mining tailings and a side trail to the Chinese Diggings, where the Chinese teams did some of the most extensive diggings. The trail ends at Oregon Street and heads 0.6 mile back to town. From here you can even tour the historic town itself, well worth the trip, then return along C Street to the lot.

User Groups: Hikers, dogs, and mountain bikes. No horses allowed. No wheelchair facilities.

Permits: Permits are not required. Parking and access are free.

Maps: Maps are available at the trailhead and online at www.jvwoodlands.org. For a topographic map, ask the USGS for Medford West.

Directions: From I-5, take the Medford exit (Exit 30) and follow signs seven miles west to Jacksonville on Highway 238. Turn right on C Street and go to its end at a visitors center lot. **Contact:** Jacksonville Woodlands Association, P.O. Box 1210, Jacksonville, OR, 97530, info@jvwoodlands.org.

150 STERLING MINE DITCH
4.7 mi /2.0 hr 🚶1 ⛰7

south of Jacksonville

Map 11.7, page 597

In 1854, just three years after gold was discovered at Jacksonville, miners struck it big at Sterling Creek. After panning gold from the creek, they went after the gold in the surrounding gravel slopes. To achieve this, Chinese laborers built a nearly 27-mile ditch to carry water from the Little Applegate River to these hills. The ditch remained in use from 1877 well into the 1930s. Now that the gold is gone, only the oak and pine forests and open grasslands are left, and a large segment of the ditch has been converted into a trail. Five trailheads—Little Applegate, Tunnel Ridge, Bear Gulch, Wolf Gap, and Deming Gulch—access the ditch trail, but Tunnel Ridge Trailhead offers the middle access with a short loop, and springtime offers a wildflower show to accompany the history. Of course, this trail can be taken for much longer journeys as well.

There are many entry points along Little Applegate Road, so why not start out easy? For an initial 4.7-mile loop, start at the Tunnel Ridge Trailhead and hike in one mile to the junction with the Sterling Mine Tunnel. From here, you could go right one-way for 5.1 miles to the Little Applegate Trailhead, another option. But head left, where you'll pass an old tunnel and continue 2.1 miles on the Sterling Ditch to a junction. Here you could go left 1.0 mile to the Bear Gulch Trailhead, then left along the road 0.6 mile to Tunnel Ridge Trailhead, completing the short 4.7-mile loop. To continue on the Ditch however, go right at this junction as far as you'd like. Another 1.6 miles leads to a junction, where going right leads 1.5 miles to the Wolf Gap Trailhead, and left heads the remaining 7.8 miles to the Deming Gulch Trailhead and the end of the trail.

User Groups: Hikers, dogs, horses, and mountain bikes. No wheelchair facilities.

Permits: Permits are not required. Parking and access are free.

Maps: For a topographic map, ask the USGS for Sterling Creek.

Directions: From Medford, follow Highway 238 through Jacksonville to the town of Ruch. Turn south at a sign for Upper Applegate and continue 2.9 miles and turn left on Little Applegate Road for 9.7 miles to the Tunnel Ridge Trailhead parking on the right.

Contact: Bureau of Land Management, Medford Office, 3040 Biddle Road, Medford, OR, 97504, 541/618-2200.

151 LITHIA PARK
2.8 mi/1.0 hr

in Ashland

Map 11.7, page 597

Ashland's idyllic Lithia Park certainly ranks high among city parks. Once the site of a water-powered sawmill, this parkland now stretches along Ashland Creek through some fairly wild territory—just watch out for poison oak. There are spots to pause and reflect on stone beaches or footbridges, flowers to admire, and a sense of peace that radiates from this little town, home to the Oregon Shakespeare Festival, whose stages are nearby. If you dare, you can even take a drink from the fountains of bubbly Lithia Springs water, which is the other thing Ashland is famous for. The 2.8-mile loop follows both sides of the creek, intersecting along a series of footbridges, so you can go as far as you like. Along the way, you can circle little Meyer Lake and Black Swan Lake and follow the creek up as far as Reservoir Park.

User Groups: Hikers and dogs. No horses or mountain bikes allowed. Paved portions of the park are wheelchair accessible.

Permits: Permits are not required. Parking and access are free.

Maps: For a topographic map, ask the USGS for Ashland.

Directions: From I-5, take either Ashland exit (Exit 14 or 19) and follow signs for City Center and Lithia Park.

Contact: Ashland Parks and Recreation, 340 South Pioneer Street, Ashland, OR, 97520, 541/488-5340.

152 GRIZZLY PEAK
5.4 mi/2.0 hr

east of Ashland

Map 11.7, page 597

Grizzly Peak broods over the town of Ashland and I-5 with views to the snowy cap of Mount Ashland from what was once a forested plateau until a 2002 fire swept over the western face. If anything, it opened up the view even more, and the Grizzly Peak Trail is still a fine walk along the edge to three excellent viewpoints of Mount Shasta, Pilot Rock, and Emigrant Lake.

Climb 1.2 miles to the junction, the beginning of the loop. Go left 0.3 mile to a side spur to the viewless summit and continue 0.8 mile out onto the burn to two viewpoints. Continue along the western face 0.7 mile to a view of Ashland, then return 1.2 miles to the first junction.

User Groups: Hikers, dogs, horses, and mountain bikes. No wheelchair facilities.

Permits: Permits are not required. Parking and access are free.

Maps: For a topographic map, ask the USGS for Grizzly Peak and Rio Canyon.

Directions: From I-5, take the southern Ashland exit (Exit 14) and go east on Highway 66 for 0.7 mile, then turn left on Dead Indian Memorial Highway for 6.7 miles. Turn left again on Shale City Road for three miles, then left on Road 38-2E-9.2 and after 0.8 mile go straight through a three-way junction, continuing 0.9 mile to road's end.

Contact: Bureau of Land Management, Medford Office, 3040 Biddle Road, Medford, OR, 97504, 541/618-2200.

153 WAGNER BUTTE
10.4 mi/6.0 hr

south of Ashland in Rogue River National Forest

Map 11.7, page 597

For panoramic views of the Rogue and Little Applegate Valleys and the mountains that surround them, try this mountain named for early settler Jacob Wagner, who operated a flour mill in nearby Ashland—which you'll get a view of, too. A few pieces remain of an old lookout tower on the 7,140-foot peak, which was intentionally burned down by smokejumpers in 1972. The trail passes the Sheep Creek Slide, where 400,000 tons of soil went crashing down four miles to the Little Applegate River in a 1983 thunderstorm. Now a wealth of wildflowers are pioneering the slopes.

The Wagner Butte Trail begins steep, then gets easier for the first 2.4 miles, crossing the slide along Sheep Creek. Then the trail climbs steeply through sagebrush, gaining nearly 500 feet in 0.9 mile to the Wagner Glade Gap. The final 1.9 miles passes through quaking aspen stands and mountain mahogany, and by a piped spring before its pitch over boulders to the summit.

User Groups: Hikers and dogs only. No horses or mountain bikes. No wheelchair facilities.

Permits: Permits are not required. Parking and access are free.

Maps: For a map of the Rogue River National Forest, contact the Rogue River-Siskiyou National Forest, 3040 Biddle Road, Medford, OR, 97504, 541/618-2200. For a topographic map, ask the USGS for Siskiyou Peak and Talent.

Directions: From I-5 take exit 21 for Talent and go 0.4 mile west on Valley View Drive and turn left on Old Highway 99 for another 0.4 mile. Turn right on Rapp Road and go 1.1 miles to a stop sign, continuing straight on Wagner Creek Road for 6.5 miles, going from paved road to gravel. Go left on Road 22, heading 2 miles to the trailhead parking on the right.

Contact: Rogue River-Siskiyou National Forest, Ashland Ranger District, 645 Washington Street, Ashland, OR, 97520, 541/552-2900.

154 MOUNT ASHLAND MEADOWS AND GROUSE GAP
6.8 mi/3.0 hr

south of Ashland in Rogue River National Forest

Map 11.7, page 597

The tallest peak in the Siskiyou Range is also the most popular. Mount Ashland is the sole ski area in this part of the state, and winter finds Mount Ashland Meadows a destination for the downhill crowd. In summer, it's another story: The meadows are dominated by bursts of lupine, larkspur, sneezeweed, aster, yarrow, and paintbrush. Granite rock formations, stands of grand fir and Shasta red fir, and views to Mount Shasta itself on the California horizon make this stretch of the Pacific Crest Trail worth exploring. It's also part of the final stretch of the PCT before it enters California at the Siskiyou Gap. You can even climb Mount Ashland itself, but it's an easy and short hike up a dirt road.

At the trailhead, cross the road and head on the PCT into the forest for 0.5 mile to the beginning of the meadows. In another 1.1 miles the trail crosses a road and continues 1.8 miles to Grouse Gap and another road leading to a picnic shelter. Here you'll end this hike with a stunning view of Mount Shasta.

User Groups: Hikers, dogs, and horses. No mountain bikes allowed. No wheelchair facilities.

Permits: Permits are not required. Parking and access are free.

Maps: For a map of the Rogue River National Forest, contact the Rogue River-Siskiyou National Forest, 3040 Biddle Road, Medford, OR, 97504, 541/618-2200. For a topographic map, ask the USGS for Mount Ashland.

Directions: From I-5, take Ashland Exit 6 and follow Mount Ashland Ski Area signs. After 0.7 mile, go right on Mount Ashland Road 20 for 7.2 miles and park at a pullout on the right.

Contact: Rogue River-Siskiyou National Forest, Ashland Ranger District, 645 Washington Street, Ashland, OR, 97520, 541/552-2900.

155 PILOT ROCK
1.2 mi/1.0 hr   🏃1 ⛰8

south of Ashland in Cascade Siskiyou National Monument

Map 11.7, page 597

Pilot Rock is aptly named, as it's what pioneers steered by to cross the Siskiyou Pass between California and Oregon. This basalt remnant of a 30-million-year-old lava flow formed of weird, geometric pillars and columns is a destination for serious rock climbers. With the Pacific Crest Trail running just below it, hikers can get close to the rock as well—though climbing it is not recommended. Stay away from that tempting ledge, too—it ends at a cliff.

From the lot, cross the road and head east on the PCT 0.2 mile to a side trail, following this up 0.4 mile to Pilot Rock. For a longer hike, consider continuing on the PCT another 6.5 miles to Soda Mountain (see next listing).

User Groups: Hikers and dogs only. No horses or mountain bikes allowed. No wheelchair facilities.

Permits: Permits are not required. Parking and access are free.

Maps: For a topographic map, ask the USGS for Siskiyou Pass.

Directions: From I-5, take the Ashland Exit 6 and follow Mount Ashland signs along Highway 99, and in 0.7 mile go under the freeway and follow Highway 99 for 1.2 more miles. Turn left on Pilot Rock Road 40-2E-33 and go 2.8 miles to a parking area on the right.

Contact: Bureau of Land Management, Medford Office, 3040 Biddle Road, Medford, OR, 97504, 541/618-2200.

156 SODA MOUNTAIN
4.2 mi/2.5 hr   🏃1 ⛰8

south of Ashland in Cascade Siskiyou National Monument

Map 11.7, page 597

The Cascade-Siskiyou National Monument is a biologically diverse area that creates a kind of bridge between its two namesake mountain ranges. The trees create a strange mix of white oak, cedar, and grand fir, and the big sunflower-like arrowleaf balsamroots thrive the slopes. Atop 6,089-foot Soda Mountain a staffed watchtower looks over Mount Shasta, the Klamath River Canyon, and the Trinity Alps.

Take the Pacific Crest Trail to the right toward Soda Mountain for 1.1 miles to a left-hand junction. Follow this spur 0.2 mile to a road, and go right 0.8 mile to the peak.

User Groups: Hikers, dogs, and horses. No mountain bikes allowed. No wheelchair facilities.

Permits: Permits are not required. Parking and access are free.

Maps: For a topographic map, ask the USGS for Soda Mountain.

Directions: From I-5, take the Ashland Exit 14 and go east on Highway 66 for 15 miles. Turn right on Soda Mountain Road 39-3E-32.3 and go 3.7 miles to a trailhead by power lines.

Contact: Bureau of Land Management, Medford Office, 3040 Biddle Road, Medford, OR, 97504, 541/618-2200.

157 LINK RIVER NATURE TRAIL

4.8 mi/2.0 hr

in Klamath Falls

Map 11.8, page 598

Odd thing about Klamath Falls is that there aren't actually any waterfalls, at least not since the dam on the Link River silenced them. These falls once fell from the outlet of Upper Klamath Lake, the stupendously large inland lake where thousands of birds pass through on their migrations. Though the Link River is now itself a kind of lake, cormorants and pelicans still frequent the water, and this nature trail strides its length between Upper Klamath Lake and Lake Ewauna.

From the trailhead, follow the river through a canyon, crossing a canal and passing a steel staircase to a gauging station and the shore for 1.7 miles. Pass the power station and Favell Museum, go left on Main Street, then continue 0.4 mile to a 0.6-mile loop on the Wingwatchers Trail.

User Groups: Hikers and dogs on leash only. No horses or mountain bikes. The Wingwatchers Trail is wheelchair accessible.

Permits: Permits are not required. Parking and access are free.

Maps: For a topographic map, ask the USGS for Klamath Falls.

Directions: Drive U.S. 97 for one mile north of downtown Klamath Falls and take the Lakeshore Drive exit, following Nevada Avenue onto lakeshore Drive for 0.8 mile. Cross the Link River and turn left into a parking area for the Nature Trail.

Contact: Klamath County Department of Tourism, 1451 Main Street, Klamath Falls, OR, 97601, 541/884-0666.

158 OC&E WOODS LINE LINEAR STATE PARK

6.6-82.0 mi/2.0 hr-5 days

east of Klamath Falls on Highway 140

Map 11.8, page 598

In the great "Rails to Trails" movement, the OC&E Woods Line State Trail is a triumph. A full 82 miles long, this old logging railroad of the Oregon, California, and Eastern Line has been transformed into a linear park that has something for everybody. The first 7.1 miles are paved, and the rest lies a bit more rugged, passing the Sprague River, little towns, and ending at the Sycan Marsh, an avid spot for bird-watchers.

An easy introduction to the trail is the first 3.3-mile segment, which begins in Klamath Falls and ends at Highway 39. Because it is in town, this section is busy with bikers, joggers, and walkers. If you want a longer day on the paved portion, continue to the town of Olene 3.8 miles away, passing through countryside with views of Mount Shasta along the way.

Beyond Olene, the trail is less improved but enters the southern Oregon landscape in full force. The next 24.2 miles passes through old farming communities and juniper and sagebrush country. The end of this stretch reaches the Switchbacks Trailhead, where restrooms and camping are available. In the next 5.5 miles the trail reaches the Sprague River, following it 12.5 miles to the Sycan Siding Trailhead.

Here the trail splits. To the right, one path continues along the Sprague River 14 miles to the town of Bly, the official end of the trail. The left-hand trail crosses the river and heads out for 18.7 miles, following Five Mile Creek for a stretch, before arriving at the Horse Glade Trailhead, another spot to camp. The trail continues 14.2 miles, passing the 400-foot-long Merritt Creek Trestle to its end at Sycan Marsh, a spot renowned for waterfowl and wildlife.

User Groups: Hikers, dogs, horses, and mountain bikes. The eight-mile stretch from Klamath Falls to the town of Olene is paved and wheelchair accessible.

Permits: Permits are not required. Parking and access are free.

Maps: For a free park brochure, call Oregon Parks and Recreation, 800/551-6949, or download a free map at www.oregon-stateparks.org. For a topographic map, ask the USGS for Klamath Falls, Altamont, Bonanza, Sprague River East, Beatty, Bly, Sycan Marsh, and Ferguson Mountain.

Directions: To get to the Klamath Falls paved trailhead, begin on Main Street in downtown Klamath Falls and go east on South 5th Street/OR 39, continuing onto South 6th Street, for 1.6 miles. Turn right on Washburne Way for 0.4 mile, then left on Crosby Avenue 0.2 mile to the trailhead.

For the Switchbacks Trailhead, drive north of Olene 12.5 miles to Bliss Road and go north 12.3 miles to the trailhead in the National Forest, to the left on Road 22. For the Sprague River Trailhead, continue 4.1 miles on Bliss Road to the town of Sprague River, then go left on Main Street less than a mile to the trailhead. For trail's end, drive 44.3 miles east on Highway 140 to the town of Bly. Go right 1.1 miles on Edler Street, left 0.5 mile on Gerber Ranch Road, and left 0.8 mile toward the OC&E State Trail.

Contact: Oregon Parks and Recreation Department, 1115 Commercial Street Northeast, Salem, OR, 97301, 800/551-6949, www.oregonstateparks.org.

SOUTHEASTERN OREGON

BEST HIKES

◖ Short Backpacking Trips
Big Indian Gorge, **page 720.**

In the rugged and remote Oregon Outback, the

desert landscape dominates. The vast region of this seldom-traveled corner of the state is dominated by the high-desert landscape, a region of sagebrush steppes and western juniper stands carved through by prehistoric canyons, some dry and some still cradling their rivers. But don't let the word "desert" fool you; this landscape is anything but deserted. Pronghorn antelope wander the range of the Hart Mountain Wildlife Refuge, and bighorn sheep skirt the cliffs of Steens Mountain. Wildflowers spread for miles over the plateaus and golden eagles wheel in the skies. The farther you go, the more tremendous the scenery.

There are the occasional odd landscapes, too. The Newberry Caldera rises just south of Bend, a 60-mile wide shield volcano cupping two lakes, massive obsidian lava flows, and waterfalls. The Owyhee River carves its way through one of the deepest canyons in North America. With so much to see, it's essential to go prepared. Lots of water, a wide-brimmed hat, and plenty of sunscreen are essential for a good trip. Try to avoid the dead of summer and the hottest part of the day. Desert hikes can make for excellent fall, winter, and spring hikes as well, especially when the rest of the Oregon mountains are snowed in for most of the year. You'll also find access to colorful hot springs, one of the classic Oregon topographical features.

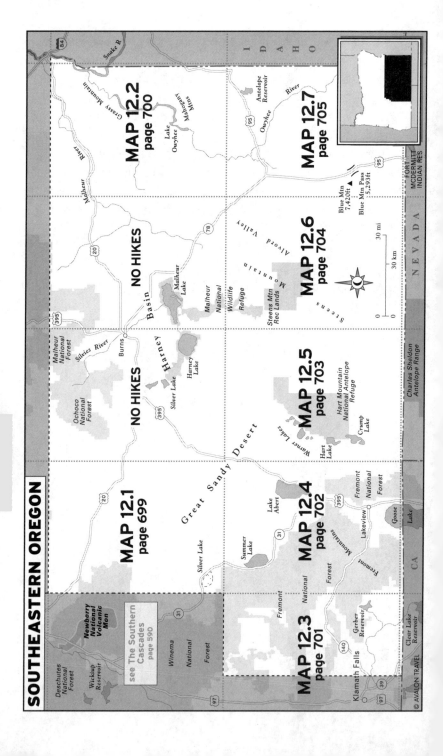

SOUTHEASTERN OREGON

MAP 12.1
page 699

MAP 12.2
page 700

MAP 12.3
page 701

MAP 12.4
page 702

MAP 12.5
page 703

MAP 12.6
page 704

MAP 12.7
page 705

NO HIKES

NO HIKES

see The Southern
Cascades
page 590

Map 12.1

Hikes 1-5
Pages 706-708

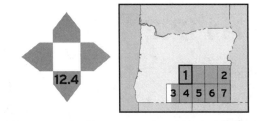

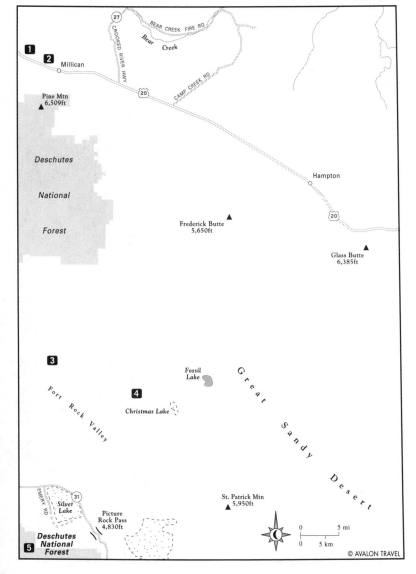

Map 12.2

Hikes 6-7
Page 709

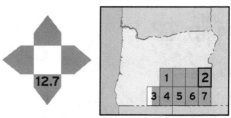

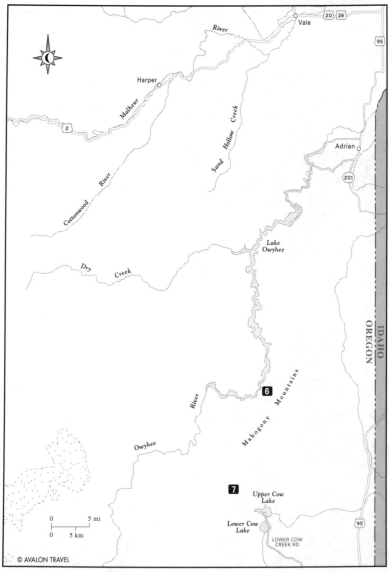

Map 12.3

Hikes 8-9
Page 710

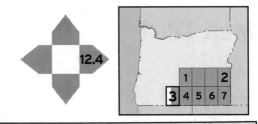

12.4

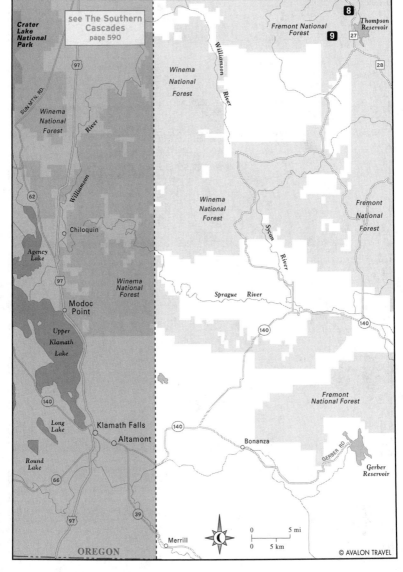

Crater Lake National Park

see The Southern Cascades page 590

Winema National Forest

Williamson River

Fremont National Forest

8

9

Thompson Reservoir

27

28

97

SUN MTN. RD.

Winema National Forest

River

62

Williamson River

Chiloquin

Agency Lake

97

Winema National Forest

Winema National Forest

Sycan River

Sprague River

Fremont National Forest

140

140

Modoc Point

Upper Klamath Lake

140

Long Lake

Klamath Falls

Altamont

140

Bonanza

GERBER RD.

Gerber Reservoir

Round Lake

66

97

39

Merrill

OREGON

0   5 mi
0   5 km

© AVALON TRAVEL

Map 12.4

Hikes 10-17
Pages 711-715

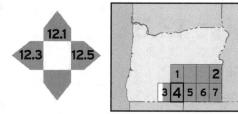

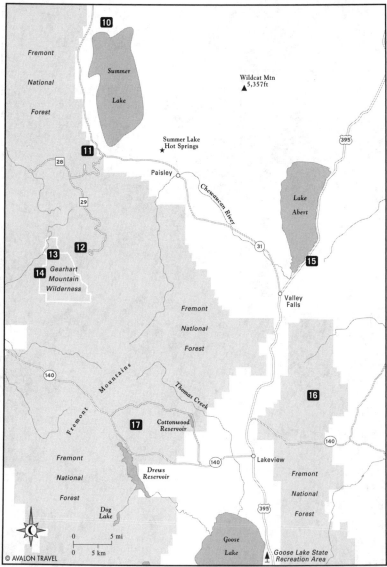

Map 12.5

Hikes 18-21
Pages 715-718

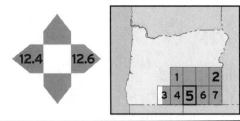

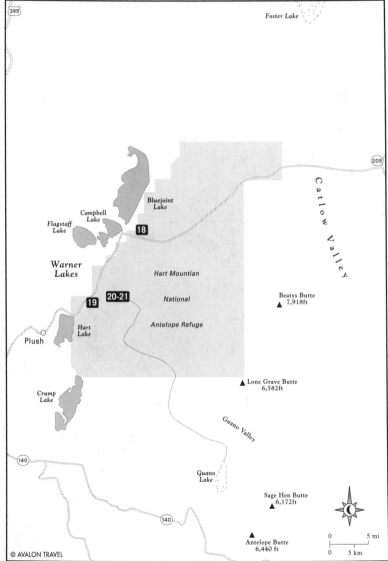

Map 12.6

Hikes 22-28
Pages 718-722

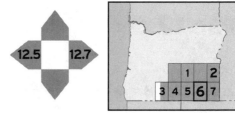

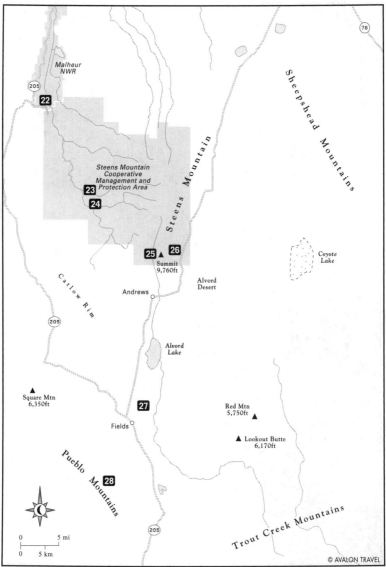

Map 12.7

Hike 29
Page 723

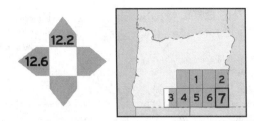

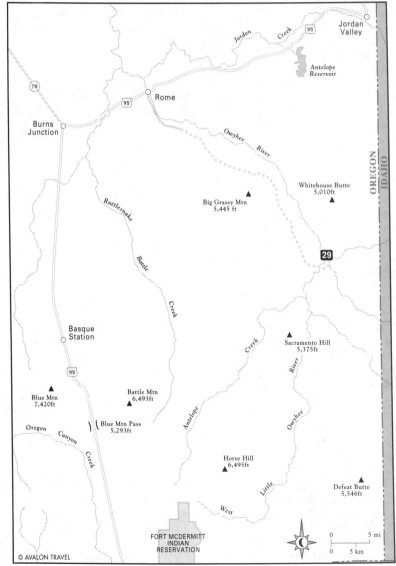

◼ THE BADLANDS
11.0-12.7 mi/3.5-4.0 hr

in the Badlands Wilderness Study Area
southeast of Bend

Map 12.1, page 699

Just 12 miles southeast of Bend, the Badlands is a quiet refuge. In this wilderness study area, the largely flat sagebrush and juniper landscape has some strange formations that break up the seeming monotony. Flatiron Rock and Badlands Rock are outcrops of cracked rock, the remnants of "pressure ridges." The desert is home to an array of plants and flowers, as well as coyote, jackrabbits, raptors, and other animals. Note that Badlands Rock is closed from March through August to protect raptor nesting sites.

From the Flatiron Trailhead, take the right-hand Flatiron Trail 1.3 miles to a fork with the Homestead Trail. Keep left, then take a right at an intersection with the Ancient Juniper Trail. Turn left at a third intersection and continue on for 1.6 miles to Flatiron Rock. When you return 1.6 miles to the jumble of intersections, you can return as you came for a 5.8-mile round-trip. For a slightly longer hike, consider veering right on the Ancient Juniper Trail at the first intersection, which returns 2 miles to the trailhead for a 6.5-mile round-trip.

The second hike begins from the Badlands Rock Trailhead. Head 0.3 mile, passing the Homestead Trail on the left, to a fork, then keep left and continue 2.8 miles along this old road to the great gaping crater of Badlands Rock. Return as you came.

User Groups: Hikers, dogs, horses, and mountain bikes. No wheelchair facilities.

Permits: Permits are not required. Parking and access are free.

Maps: For a brochure and map of the Badlands Wilderness Study Area, contact Bureau of Land Management, Prineville District Office, 3050 NE Third Street, Prineville, OR, 97754, 541/416-6700, or go to www.blm.gov/or/districts/prineville. For a topographic map, ask the USGS for Horse Ridge and Alfalfa.

Directions: For the Flatiron Trail, drive east of Bend for 16 miles on U.S. 20 and park at the trailhead on the left. For the Badlands Rock Trailhead, continue east on U.S 20 for 1.5 miles. At the bottom of a long decline, turn left on a gravel road and cross a cattle guard. Go straight past the gravel piles on a paved road one mile, parking at a signboard for the Badlands Rock Trail on the left.

Contact: Bureau of Land Management, Prineville District Office, 3050 NE Third Street, Prineville, OR, 97754, 541/416-6700.

◼ DRY RIVER CANYON
6.0 mi/2.0 hr

in the Badlands Wilderness Study Area southeast of Bend

Map 12.1, page 699

It's hard to believe, but the vast deserts east of Horse Ridge were once the bed of a massive, inland lake. During the Ice Age, those shores lapped against the ridge and finally found a fault, and the entire lake drained through what is now Dry River Canyon, a slot where Native Americans once fished along the long-extinct river. Though Highway 20 follows the canyon up and over Horse Ridge with a pullout to view it, the only real way to experience it is to see it firsthand. As you walk the canyon, notice how it deepens, and how the walls change color with different lava flows and algae. Plowing through groves of sagebrush and mountain mahogany, the trail comes upon massive ponderosa pines, which seem somehow out of place here. There is also a lower segment of the canyon from a different trailhead, where the river dug a smaller canyon, but one with aged and barely perceptible petroglyphs. Take care not to touch anything, and be aware of the seasonal closure (Feb. 1– Aug. 31) for the upper canyon stretch to protect nesting raptors.

To hike the larger upper canyon, start from the parking area and follow the remaining dirt road to where it becomes trail. Follow the trail three miles to the top end of the canyon, where it ends at a fence marking private land. For the lower canyon, start from the Badlands Rock Trail and go 0.3 mile to a fork. Go right 0.9 mile along an old road. Where the road drops down to a series of big boulders, leave the road and go right into the canyon mouth, a 0.3-mile walk through the 40-foot-deep canyon.

User Groups: Hikers only. No dogs, horses, or mountain bikes allowed. No wheelchair facilities.

Permits: Permits are not required. Parking and access are free.

Maps: For a topographic map, ask the USGS for Horse Ridge.

Directions: Drive east of Bend for 17.6 miles on U.S. 20. At the bottom of a long decline, turn left on a gravel road and cross a cattle guard. For the upper canyon, turn right into a Highway Department gravel pile storage lot, go to the far side and follow the dirt road 0.8 mile toward the canyon to a fork and park on the right by the cliff. For the lower canyon, cross the cattle guard and go straight past the gravel piles on a paved road one mile, parking at a signboard for the Badlands Rock Trail on the left.

Contact: Bureau of Land Management, Prineville District Office, 3050 NE Third Street, Prineville, OR, 97754, 541/416-6700.

🖪 FORT ROCK
1.7 mi/1.0 hr

southeast of LaPine in Fort Rock State Park

Map 12.1, page 699

Once an inland lake, the Fort Rock Valley now is a stretch of desert wandering as far as you can see into the distances of vast tablelands. Evidence of this ancient lake can be seen on the wave-lapped stone of Fort Rock, the remnants of a massive volcano that later was transformed into an island. Ancient peoples used a nearby cave for shelter, where in 1938 archeologists unearthed a pair of sandals made of sagebrush bark, estimated at some 9,000 to 13,000 years old.

For a tour of Fort Rock, take the short paved route from the picnic area to a dirt path, 0.1 mile in all, to the cliff face. Follow an old road 0.6 mile through the interior of Fort Rock, keeping right at all junctions. At a four-way junction, an

Fort Rock State Park

easy 0.2-mile jog to the right leads to a viewpoint of the Fort Rock Cave. Returning to the junction, go straight 0.4 mile back to the lot.

User Groups: Hikers, dogs, horses, and mountain bikes.

Permits: Permits are not required. Parking and access are free.

Maps: For a topographic map, ask the USGS for Fort Rock.

Directions: From Bend, drive 29 miles south on U.S. 97 and turn left on OR 31. Follow this highway 29.2 miles and turn left on Fort Rock Road for 6.5 miles. At a sign for Fort Rock State Park, turn left on Cabin Lake Road/ County Road 5-11 for one mile, then left on Cow Cave Road/County Road 5-11A for 0.6 mile to the park entrance on the right.

Contact: Oregon Parks and Recreation Department, 1115 Commercial Street Northeast, Salem, OR, 97301, 800/551-6949, www.oregonstateparks.org.

4 CRACK-IN-THE-GROUND
1.0–2.0 mi/0.5–1.0 hr 🥾₁ ⛰₇

north of Christmas Valley

Map 12.1, page 699

Like nearby Fort Rock Valley, Oregon's Christmas Valley is a desert landscape of caves, lava flows, windswept sand dunes, and dry lakes. Just beyond the Four Craters lava flow, a strange shifting of the earth after the eruption created a long fissure aptly named Crack-in-the-Ground. Inside, it's easy to see how the crack formed, as the canyon walls are like puzzle pieces. You'll notice right away the temperature change, too; the crack stays amply cool even in summer, which is why homesteaders had picnics down here and made ice cream from the snow they found lingering here even in summer.

Follow the Crack-In-The-Ground Trail 0.2 mile to the beginning of the canyon. At a split in the trail, go right into the slot as far as you'd like. The other trail at the junction follows the crack from the rim, crossing it through a gap twice and continuing on the rim to its end.

User Groups: Hikers and dogs only. No horses or mountain bikes. No wheelchair facilities.

Permits: Permits are not required. Parking and access are free.

Maps: For a topographic map, ask the USGS for Crack-in-the-Ground.

Directions: From Bend, drive 29 miles south on U.S. 97 and turn left on OR 31. Follow this highway 29.2 miles and turn left on Fort Rock Road for 12.3 miles, following County Road 5-10 to the right another 10.2 miles. After the road twists through a couple turns, turn left on Christmas Valley Highway for 11 miles. Turn left at a sign for Crack-in-the-Ground and follow this gravel road 7.2 miles to a signed parking lot on the left. The trail begins across the road.

Contact: Bureau of Land Management, Lakeview District Office, 1301 South G Street, Lakeview, OR, 97630, 541/947-2177.

5 HAGER MOUNTAIN
8.0 mi/4.0 hr 🥾₃ ⛰₇

south of Silver Lake in Fremont National Forest

Map 12.1, page 699

Whereas other peaks crowned with fire lookouts get tons of visitors, this is not the case with the more remote Hager Mountain. You can ascend 7,185-foot Hager via the Fremont Trail in an eight-mile out-and-back hike, or choose from two other trailheads if you'd prefer a longer or shorter route. Along the way, ponderosa pines, big yellow balsamroots and Indian paintbrush line the path to the staffed lookout tower, which is rentable during the rest of the year. On a clear day, views reach from Mount Shasta in California to Mount Jefferson in the north.

From Road 28, begin gradually on the Fremont Trail 0.7 mile, crossing Road 012 at the second trailhead. The trail continues its steady climb 0.8 mile to a junction on the left to the third trailhead. Stay right and continue climbing on the Fremont Trail 1.1 miles and 650 feet to a junction. Go right 1.4 miles to the lookout.

User Groups: Hikers, dogs, horses, and mountain bikes. No wheelchair facilities.

Permits: Permits are not required. Parking and access are free.

Maps: For a map of the Fremont National Forest, contact Fremont-Winema National Forest Headquarters, 1301 South G Street, Lakeview, OR, 97630, 541/947-2151. For a topographic map, ask the USGS for Hager Mountain.

Directions: Drive 29 miles south from Bend on U.S. 97 and turn left onto OR 31. Go 47 miles and turn right on Road 28 for 9.3 miles to the Hager Mountain Trailhead pullout on the left. Park and walk back along the road to the trail. To find the higher trailhead, continue 0.2 mile on Road 28 and turn left on Road 012, going 1.2 miles to a trail sign, or even 0.8 mile farther to a parking area on the right. Each trailhead accesses the Fremont Trail directly.

Contact: Fremont National Forest, Silver Lake Ranger District, Highway 31, P.O. Box 129, Silver Lake, OR, 97638, 541/576-2107.

6 LESLIE GULCH
7.0 mi/2.5 hr

northwest of Jordan Valley on the Owyhee Reservoir

Map 12.2, page 700

Bring your camera, as Leslie Gulch, an Oregon landmark, is one of the most spectacular areas of the state. Easily drivable, this narrow canyon of volcanic tuff formations, rare plants, and wildlife slips down to the Owyhee Reservoir and the Slocum Campground and makes for a good drive punctuated with several easy hikes. Whether you visit for the day or spend the night, these short hikes can be done in a single day. Drive down to the Slocum Campground to start the first hike, then backtrack up the canyon to each sight.

The honeycomb cliffs and gulches of Leslie Gulch are home to not only rare wildflowers found only in this canyon (Packard's blazing star and Etter's groundsel), but California bighorn

sheep, elk, bobcats, as well as birds like the rock wren and chukar. Each of these hikes offers an opportunity to spot something rare among the amazing geology of this ash-flow tuff.

From Slocum Campground, begin by following a primitive trail 1.3 miles up the Slocum Gulch, home to seasonal Slocum Creek, which flows in this ever-narrowing canyon. Then drive up Leslie Gulch 2.35 miles to an unmarked 0.6-mile trail on the left into Timber Gulch, with its scenic rock formations. Driving 1.25 miles beyond that, park on the left for the 0.8-mile Juniper Gulch Trail, which makes for an easy walk beneath overhanging cliffs—just don't go any further than is safe. Finally, drive one more mile up Leslie Gulch and park at a turnaround by a gate and follow this old road into Dago Gulch, a fortress of green ash and stone pillars, 0.8 mile to a gate, beyond which lies private land.

User Groups: Hikers and dogs only. No horses or mountain bikes allowed. No wheelchair facilities.

Permits: Permits are not required. Parking and access are free.

Maps: For a topographic map, ask the USGS for Rooster Comb.

Directions: From Jordan Valley, drive north on U.S. 95 for 27 miles and turn left on Succor Creek Road for 8.4 miles. At a junction, continue left on Succor Creek Road 1.8 miles, then go left on Leslie Gulch Road 14.5 miles. The Slocum Campground is at road's end at the Owyhee Reservoir.

Contact: Bureau of Land Management, Vale District Office, 100 Oregon Street, Vale, OR, 97918, 541/473-3144.

7 COFFEEPOT CRATER
1.0 mi/0.5 hr

northwest of Jordan Valley in the Jordan Craters Lava Beds

Map 12.2, page 700

Before you even think of coming here, check the weather. Wet weather makes many Eastern Oregon roads impassable, and both winter weather and the dead of summer can be inordinately harsh. If you make it, you'll find a 9,000-year-old eruption that leaked lava over 27 square miles. A row of "spatter cones," blocks of lava that acted as vents for hot gases, snake away from Coffeepot Crater and its easy loop trail overlooking the cracked and pitted lava flow. Dogs are not recommended as rough lava can severely hurt their paws.

From the lot, follow the trail to the right of the sign 0.3 mile up to the crater rim and a spur trail leading into the crater itself. Continue around the rim 0.2 mile back to the car, and take a side trail 0.2 mile out to the row of spatter cones.

User Groups: Hikers only. Dogs are not recommended. No horses or mountain bikes allowed. No wheelchair access.

Permits: Permits are not required. Parking and access are free.

Maps: For a topographic map, ask the USGS for Jordan Craters North.

Directions: From Jordan Valley, drive north 8.3 miles on U.S. 95. Turn west onto Cow Creek Road and go 11.4 miles to a fork, following signs for Jordan Craters. At a fork, go right 6.7 miles. At the next fork, go left on a bad road 5.9 miles to yet another fork. Fork left 1.5 miles, then fork left again 1.4 miles to the a parking lot at road's end.

Contact: Bureau of Land Management, Vale District Office, 100 Oregon Street, Vale, OR, 97918, 541/473-3144.

8 SILVER CREEK/ FREMONT TRAIL
4.4-18.1 mi/1.5-6.0 hr   🥾3 ⛰️7

southwest of Silver Lake in Fremont National Forest

Map 12.3, page 701

The Fremont National Forest, named for explorer Captain John Fremont, who traversed this area in 1843, has only one trail, the Fremont Trail, though at 147 miles it is no mere footpath. It traverses this dry mountain country, home to stands of ponderosa pine, topping peaks and following creeks along the way. For a shorter, or even longer stretch of the Fremont Trail, strike out along Silver Creek into an ash-strewn land dusted with the volcanic blasts of Mount Mazama nearly 8,000 years ago. Watch not only for spring wildflowers, but mosquitoes and ticks.

This section of the Fremont Trail begins near the campground entrance and crosses Road 27, then heads one mile to the creek. The next 1.2 miles follows the West Fork Silver Creek to a bridge near the North Fork, an easy day hike. To continue, cross the creek on another bridge and continue along the North Fork Silver Creek and leave the canyon behind, marching into lodgepole pine woods 2.6 miles on the Fremont Trail to a road crossing, then continuing another 3.2 miles to the Antler Trailhead.

User Groups: Hikers, dogs, horses, and mountain bikes. No wheelchair facilities.

Permits: Permits are not required. Parking and access are free.

Maps: For a map of the Fremont National Forest, contact Fremont-Winema National Forest Headquarters, 1301 South G Street, Lakeview, OR, 97630, 541/947-2151. For a topographic map, ask the USGS for Bridge Creek Draw and Partin Butte.

Directions: Drive 29 miles south from Bend on U.S. 97 and turn left onto OR 31. Go 46.6 miles and turn right on Road 27 for 10.4 miles to the Silver Creek Marsh Campground.

Contact: Fremont National Forest, Silver Lake Ranger District, Highway 31, P.O. Box 129, Silver Lake, OR, 97638, 541/576-2107.

9 YAMSAY MOUNTAIN/ FREMONT TRAIL
17.2 mi/1 day   🥾4 ⛰️8

southwest of Silver Lake in Fremont National Forest

Map 12.3, page 701

Yamsay Mountain is the westernmost terminus of the 147-mile Fremont Trail. With views extending over the Fort Rock Valley, the peaks of the Cascades, and even as far as Mount Shasta in California, the 8,196-foot peak is a worthy goal. This is hot, dry country, so come prepared. Begin at the Antler Trailhead for a relatively easy approach. You can also take a short detour to see some volcanic rock pillars, adding only 0.5 mile to the overall hike.

To see the pillars, take the far right-hand trail from the lot, heading one mile to the rock pillars, and continuing 0.3 mile to the Fremont Trail. Go right, climbing 1,000 feet in 4.1 miles to Antler Springs and a four-way junction. Continue straight into mountain hemlock woods and then whitebark pine another 3.9 miles to the summit. To return, follow the Fremont Trail all the way back to the Antler Trailhead, turning left into the lot just before Road 038.

User Groups: Hikers, dogs, horses, and mountain bikes. No wheelchair facilities.

Permits: Permits are not required. Parking and access are free.

Maps: For a map of the Fremont National Forest, contact Fremont-Winema National Forest Headquarters, 1301 South G Street, Lakeview, OR, 97630, 541/947-2151. For a topographic map, ask the USGS for Yamsay Mountain.

Directions: Drive 29 miles south from Bend on U.S. 97 and turn left onto OR 31. Go 46.6 miles and turn right on Road 27 for 9.4 miles and turn right for 2.6 miles on Road 2804. Follow signs for the Antler Trailhead, and go left on Road 7645 for 4.8 miles, then left on Road 036, keeping right at all junctions, for 2.2 miles to the Antler Trailhead parking area on the right.

Contact: Fremont National Forest, Silver Lake Ranger District, Highway 31, P.O. Box 129, Silver Lake, OR, 97638, 541/576-2107.

10 SUMMER LAKE WILDLIFE REFUGE

9.2 mi/3.0 hr

east of Fremont National Forest on Summer Lake

Map 12.4, page 702

When Captain John C. Fremont first spotted this lake from snowy Winter Ridge, he named it after the fact that it appeared a sunny oasis in December 1843. Beginning in 1944, Oregon Department of Fish and Wildlife bought more than 18,000 acres of this desert marshland—an important stopover for migratory birds on the Pacific flyway—to provide habitat for birds as diverse as pelicans, stilts, curlews, mallards, geese, and swans. The best time to come is from March to May, when those migratory birds come through. For a couple wildlife-viewing hikes, use the old dike roads that lead out on the marsh. Mosquitoes can be a problem here, to say the least.

From the Windbreak Campground, head out on the gated dike road for two miles, passing numerous viewpoints. At Summer Lake, the road turns right for 0.5 mile on the Gold Dike to trail's end. For a second hike, start from the Bullgate Campground and follow this dike road 2.1 miles to Summer Lake.

User Groups: Hikers, dogs on leash only, horses, and mountain bikes. The camping areas at Windbreak Dike and Bullgate Dike are wheelchair accessible.

Permits: Permits are not required. Parking and access are free.

Maps: For a downloadable map of Summer Lake Wildlife Area, go to www.dfw.state.or.us/resources/visitors/summer_lake_wildlife_area.asp. For a topographic map, ask the USGS for Summer Lake.

Directions: From Bend, drive south on U.S. 97 for 29 miles and turn left on OR 31 toward Silver Lake. Drive 70 miles to the town of Summer Lake, turning left into the wildlife refuge headquarters. Follow Wildlife Viewing Area signs to a gravel road, going 1.6 miles to a junction. To reach the Windbreak Dike, go right 0.9

mile to the Windbreak Campground. To go to the Bullgate Dike, go left 1.3 miles.

Contact: Oregon Department of Fish and Wildlife, Summer Lake Wildlife Area, 53447 Highway 31, Summer Lake, OR, 97640, 541/943-3152.

🔟🔟 WINTER RIDGE/ FREMONT TRAIL

3.4-10.2 mi/1.0-3.5 hr   🥾₁ ⛰₈

north of Bly in Fremont National Forest

Map 12.4, page 702

First, don't be confused by the name. Though Captain John C. Fremont officially named this fault-block ridge "Winter Ridge," locals insist on calling it Winter Rim. Either way, you'll agree with both the locals and the explorers that this is something to see. Below the ridge, Summer Lake bakes in summer heat, with the occasional dust devil whipped up on the yellow alkaline flats. The trail along the ridge is part of the 147-mile Fremont Trail, which crosses the Fremont National Forest and connects to many trails in this section.

From the parking area, head toward the rim and follow the Fremont Trail north 1.7 miles through big pines and big stumps to a viewpoint accessible by going off-trail. In another 0.7 mile, take a detour left 0.3 mile through a meadow of quaking aspen and corn lily to Currier Spring. Continue on the main trail 1.4 miles; from here, it is not well marked, but you can continue out along the ridge another 0.7 mile to a viewpoint, and continue as far as you'd like. From the trailhead, it is also possible to follow the trail south along the rim.

User Groups: Hikers, dogs, horses, and mountain bikes. No wheelchair facilities.

Permits: Permits are not required. Parking and access are free.

Maps: For a map of the Fremont National Forest, contact Fremont-Winema National Forest Headquarters, 1301 South G Street, Lakeview, OR, 97630, 541/947-2151. For a topographic map, ask the USGS for Harvey Creek.

Directions: Drive 29 miles south from Bend on U.S. 97 and turn left onto OR 31. Go 82 miles and turn right on Road 29, continuing up 9.5 miles to a junction. Go right on Road 2901 and in 0.1 mile park on the right at a trailhead sign.

Contact: Fremont National Forest, Paisley Ranger District, Highway 31, P.O. Box 67, Paisley, OR, 97636, 541/943-3114.

🔟🔟 CAMPBELL AND DEAD HORSE LAKES LOOP TRAIL

7.4 mi/3.0 hr   🥾₂ ⛰₇

south of Summer Lake in Fremont National Forest

Map 12.4, page 702

Set down in a lodgepole pine forest, these two lakes shimmer like mirrors in their alpine, glacier-carved basins. From the rims above, there are views extending out to the Winter Rim, Abert Rim, Hart Mountain, and even distant Steens Mountain. Below, the view reveals lakes bounded by thick trees. As with many trails in this area, you might not see anyone else on the trail with you.

Begin at Campbell Lake on the Lakes Loop Trail, passing a pond and going 0.2 mile to a junction. Go left 1.3 miles to begin the loop, climbing 500 feet up the Campbell Rim. At the next junction, go right along the rim 1.5 miles to another junction. For a short loop, go right here 1.9 miles back to Campbell Lake. For the full loop to Deadhorse Lake, continue forward one mile, then go right at the next junction and down 1.1 miles to Deadhorse. To avoid hiking through campgrounds and on the road, go left 0.6 mile along the lakeshore to an uphill junction on the left. Go up, cross the road, and continue 0.4 mile to a junction with the shorter loop spur, going left 1.3 miles back to Campbell Lake.

User Groups: Hikers, dogs, horses, and mountain bikes. No wheelchair facilities.

Permits: Permits are not required. Parking and access are free.

Maps: For a map of the Fremont National Forest, contact Fremont-Winema National Forest Headquarters, 1301 South G Street, Lakeview, OR, 97630, 541/947-2151. For a topographic map, ask the USGS for Lee Thomas Crossing.

Directions: From Bend, drive south on U.S. 97 for 29 miles and turn left on OR 31 toward Silver Lake. Drive 47 miles to Silver Lake and turn right on Road 28. Go 18 miles to a T-junction, and go left on Road 28 for 34 miles. Turn right on Road 033 for 1.9 miles and turn left into Campbell Lake Campground, driving 0.5 mile to the trailhead parking area on the left.

Contact: Fremont National Forest, Paisley Ranger District, Highway 31, P.O. Box 67, Paisley, OR, 97636, 541/943-3114.

13 BLUE LAKE

5.6-12.8 mi/3.0-6.0 hr

north of Bly in Fremont National Forest

Map 12.4, page 702

This popular and pretty lake is also an entrance to the rarely visited Gearhart Mountain Wilderness. You can hike to 7,031-foot Blue Lake, or head up farther to The Notch, the gateway to the peak of Gearhart (see *Gearhart Mountain,* next listing). Thus, it is possible to make this lake a backpacking waystation for a summit of 8,370-foot Gearhart.

From the North Fork Sprague Trailhead, climb 700 feet up 2.4 miles on the Gearhart Mountain Trail to Blue Lake, then circle it on a 0.8-mile loop. The trail continues four miles to The Notch and continues 1.3 miles to a high saddle, from where it is possible to climb the mountain itself.

User Groups: Hikers, dogs, and horses. No mountain bikes allowed. No wheelchair facilities.

Permits: A free self-issue Wilderness Permit is required and is available at the trailhead. Parking and access are free.

Maps: For a map of the Fremont National

Forest and the Gearhart Mountain Wilderness, contact Fremont-Winema National Forest Headquarters, 1301 South G Street, Lakeview, OR, 97630, 541/947-2151. For a topographic map, ask the USGS for Lee Thomas Crossing.

Directions: From Bend, drive south on U.S. 97 for 29 miles and turn left on OR 31 toward Silver Lake. Drive 47 miles to Silver Lake and turn right on Road 28. Go 18 miles to a T-junction, and go left on Road 28 for 36.2 miles. Turn left on Road 3411 for six miles, then left on Road 3372 for two miles, then right on Road 015 for 1.5 miles to the North Fork Sprague Trailhead.

Contact: Fremont National Forest, Bly Ranger District, Highway 140, P.O. Box 25, Bly, OR, 97622, 541/353-2427.

14 GEARHART MOUNTAIN

12.0 mi/7.0 hr

north of Bly in Gearhart Mountain Wilderness

Map 12.4, page 702

The Gearhart Mountain area is a landscape of lava. The mountain itself is a long outcrop of lava, and the trail spanning it passes a series of haunting pillars, a palisade of andesite pinnacles. Near the top, the trail enters a series of lovely meadows at the headwaters of Dairy Creek. Though the official trail doesn't reach the top, the ambitious can summit the mountain by trailblazing up to the ridge for views extending over handfuls of Cascade peaks.

From the parking area, follow the Gearhart Mountain Trail 0.7 mile into The Palisades. Continue into the forest of pine and white fir for four miles, passing The Dome and arriving at a saddle. The trail continues past a right-hand trail fork and below the peak and into the meadows 1.3 miles to The Notch, where the trail continues down to Blue Lake (see previous listing). If you're looking to climb the peak, be prepared to route-find and use your hands if necessary to make your way to the ridge. Return to the saddle, and head northwest 0.2 mile to the ridge, following it 1.3 miles to the summit.

User Groups: Hikers, dogs, and horses. No mountain bikes allowed. No wheelchair facilities.

Permits: A free self-issue Wilderness Permit is required and is available at the trailhead. Parking and access are free.

Maps: For a map of the Fremont National Forest and the Gearhart Mountain Wilderness, contact Fremont-Winema National Forest Headquarters, 1301 South G Street, Lakeview, OR, 97630, 541/947-2151. For a topographic map, ask the USGS for Lee Thomas Crossing.

Directions: From Bend, drive south on U.S. 97 for 29 miles and turn left on OR 31 toward Silver Lake. Drive 47 miles to Silver Lake and turn right on Road 28. Go 18 miles to a T-junction, and go left on Road 28 for 40 miles. Turn right on Road 34 for 10.4 miles, and turn right toward Corral Creek Campground on Road 012 for 1.5 increasingly rough miles to road's end at the Lookout Rock Trailhead.

Contact: Fremont National Forest, Bly Ranger District, Highway 140, P.O. Box 25, Bly, OR, 97622, 541/353-2427.

15 ABERT RIM
3.6 mi/3.0 hr 🏃4 ⛰8

north of Lakeview on Lake Abert

Map 12.4, page 702

From Lake Abert, the great fault-block mountain of Abert Rim is absolutely imposing. The enormous fault scarp extends 30 miles along a lake teeming with wildlife. Despite its monstrous size, the Abert Rim is, in fact, climbable—though perhaps "scramble-able" is the word to use. This challenging climb hauls itself up 2,000 feet to a high promontory for outstanding views of the surrounding country.

From the Wildlife Viewing parking area, where you're sure to spot a plethora of waterfowl, cross the highway and head into the

sagebrush to find an old roadbed. Go left on it 0.1 mile to a rain tank. For the next 1.5 miles, you'll need to weave your way up the canyon of Juniper Creek through sagebrush, a meadow, a boulder field, and thick mountain mahogany. Near the top, keep to the right along the rimrock wall. When you reach a stand of ponderosa pines at the top, go right along the rim 0.2 mile to a viewpoint.

User Groups: Hikers only. Dogs not recommended. No mountain bikes or horses allowed. No wheelchair facilities.

Permits: Permits are not required. Parking and access are free.

Maps: For a topographic map, ask the USGS for Lake Abert South.

Directions: Drive north from Lakeview on U.S. 395 for 30 miles. Between mileposts 84 and 85, park at the Wildlife Viewing Area pullout.

Contact: Bureau of Land Management, Lakeview District Office, 1301 South G Street, Lakeview, OR, 97630, 541/947-2177.

16 CROOKED CREEK/ FREMONT TRAIL
8.2-13.8 mi/4.0-6.5 hr 🏃3 ⛰7

north of Lakeview in Fremont National Forest

Map 12.4, page 702

The Fremont Trail, not entirely finished in places, nevertheless spans an ambitious 147 miles across the dry and rocky regions of Eastern Oregon. This section along Crooked Creek once had a lower trailhead, and still does despite the washed-out road. This higher trailhead has the benefit of sweeping views to Drake Peak, Light Peak, and Twelvemile Peak, as well as quaking aspen and ponderosa pine groves, but also follows a rugged canyon downhill—every bit down is another bit up. Be sure to keep this in mind!

From the trailhead, cross the road and start on the Fremont Trail. In 0.6 mile cross a road and continue on the Fremont Trail, crossing two forks of Crooked Creek, then starting down 1,000 feet into the canyon in two miles to a ford. For an easy 8.2-mile round trip, turn back here. Otherwise, do one of two things: Ford the creek to connect with an old road, or stay on this bank and bushwhack downstream 0.2 mile to meet the road. From here, the trail descends downstream along the old road 2.6 miles to the Mill Trailhead.

User Groups: Hikers, dogs, horses, and mountain bikes. No wheelchair facilities.

Permits: Permits are not required. Parking and access are free.

Maps: For a map of the Fremont National Forest, contact Fremont-Winema National Forest Headquarters, 1301 South G Street, Lakeview, OR, 97630, 541/947-2151. For a topographic map, ask the USGS for Crook Peak.

Directions: Drive north from Lakeview on U.S. 395 for five miles and go east on Highway 140 for 8.5 miles. Turn left on North Warner Road 3615 for 10.6 miles to the South Fork Crooked Creek Trailhead on the right.

Contact: Fremont National Forest, Lakeview Ranger District, 18049 Highway 395, Lakeview, OR, 97630, 541/947-3334.

🔳 COUGAR PEAK AND COTTONWOOD MEADOW LAKE
3.6-7.6 mi/1.0-4.0 hr

west of Lakeview in Fremont National Forest

Map 12.4, page 702

Cottonwood Meadow Lake, actually a reservoir, is circled by campgrounds and feeder creeks. A trail entirely circles it, making use of the roads at points. The trail also connects to a climb of Cougar Peak after a ramble along Cougar Creek on an abandoned road. The view from the old lookout site stretches right into California along massive Goose Lake and Mount Shasta. Circle the lake, climb the peak, or do both.

From the Cottonwood Trailhead, start one mile on the trail to an intersection with a road. The two hikes fan out from here. To circle the

lake, go straight over the road and continue on the trail uphill one mile and down to Cottonwood Creek and a junction. Go straight and continue another mile past the dam to a junction of roads. Go straight on Road 3870 to return 0.6 mile to the car.

To climb Cougar Peak, go left at the first junction along an old road-turned-trail 1.5 miles along Cougar Creek. Cross a road and start up an old, rough road 0.2 mile, then veer to the left on the hiker route for 1.1 miles to the 7,919-foot peak.

User Groups: Hikers, dogs, horses, and mountain bikes. No wheelchair facilities.

Permits: Permits are not required. Parking and access are free.

Maps: For a map of the Fremont National Forest, contact Fremont-Winema National Forest Headquarters, 1301 South G Street, Lakeview, OR, 97630, 541/947-2151. For a topographic map, ask the USGS for Cougar Peak.

Directions: Drive east of Klamath Falls on Highway 140 for 74 miles and turn left on Road 3870 toward Cottonwood Meadow for 6.1 miles. Where the pavement ends, turn left into the Cottonwood Trailhead lot.

Contact: Fremont National Forest, Lakeview Ranger District, 18049 Highway 395, Lakeview, OR, 97630, 541/947-3334.

🔳 PETROGLYPH LAKE
5.0 mi/2.5 hr

in the Hart Mountain National Antelope Refuge

Map 12.5, page 703

The area now designated as the Hart Mountain National Antelope Trail has been used by people for centuries, and you'll find remnants of those old cultures still. Mysterious petroglyphs dot the landscapes of Eastern Oregon, along with the occasional arrowhead and glittering piles of obsidian chippings left from their construction. Like many hikes in the Hart Mountain Refuge, the hike to Petroglyph Lake has no actual trail. It's a cross-country jaunt that leads up to a stunning viewpoint over the Warner lakes from Poker Jim Ridge, where on a good day, you may be able to spot bighorn sheep. Just below the crest of this ridge, partially hidden by a lava wall, is Petroglyph Lake, so named because its lava wall is painted with ancient rock drawings. Route-finding skills will come in handy, but the route is fairly straightforward.

From the parking area, cross the main road and head north and uphill toward the ridge for about one mile. When you reach the crest, continue north along the ridge 1.2 miles to a viewpoint on a knoll. Then look downhill to the east to spot two lakes; head for the one on the right. Proceed 0.8 mile downhill, working toward the left-hand shore. The lake will vanish into the desert as you approach. When you reach it, walk 0.5 mile along the long wall of drawings. At a dirt road, head back across the desert, southwest and toward the massive Warner Peak for 1.5 miles; you'll spot the road and your car as you get closer.

User Groups: Hikers and dogs on leash only. No horses or mountain bikes allowed. No wheelchair facilities.

Permits: Free self-issue permits are required only for backpackers, and are available at the visitors center. Parking and access are free.

Maps: For a brochure and map of the Hart Mountain Wildlife Refuge, contact Hart Mountain National Antelope Refuge, P.O. Box 111, Lakeview, OR, 97630, 541/947-2731, or download at www.fws.gov/sheldonhartmtn/Hart/index.html. For a topographic map, ask the USGS for Campbell Lake.

Directions: Drive north of Lakeview on U.S. 395 for five miles then turn east on Highway 140 for 16 miles. Go toward Plush, turning left on Road 3-13 for 20 miles to the town of Plush. Continue 0.8 mile through town and turn right on Road 3-12 toward Hart Mountain for 21.6 miles and park beside a right-hand dirt road with a sign for Hilltop Reservoir.

Contact: U.S. Fish and Wildlife Service, Hart Mountain National Antelope Refuge, P.O. Box 111, Lakeview, OR, 97630, 541/947-2731.

🔟🟨 DEGARMO CANYON

1.4–9.4 mi/0.5–5.0 hr

in the Hart Mountain National Antelope Refuge

Map 12.5, page 703

On a high plateau rising above the Warner Lakes, the Hart Mountain Wildlife Refuge's high desert landscape is home to some serious wildlife, including the pronghorn antelope and bighorn sheep. Notched in the side of this colossal wall is DeGarmo Canyon, which climbs DeGarmo Creek past a waterfall and up to the vast steppe of the refuge. The canyon is surprisingly and refreshingly lush, and makes for a good introduction to desert ecology. Be aware that the upper stretches of the canyon don't have trails, but connect to other trails at the DeGarmo Notch.

Follow the trail into the canyon mouth past a small waterfall upstream to a shallow creek crossing, then continue 0.7 mile to trail's end at a far larger waterfall. Though you could return as you came, watch on the right just before the waterfall for a steep scramble route. Head up and around the waterfall cliffs, and past another lava flow 500 feet to an obvious trail. If you choose to loop back to the parking area, go left 0.9 mile along the canyon. The trail switchbacks down and becomes lost in sagebrush, but it's easy to spot your car and go cross-country.

If you choose to go farther up the canyon, go right on the upper trail instead for 1.8 miles to where the pine trees and the trail ends. But it's easy to cross the meadows, following the creek one mile to an old road on the left leading to Hart Mountain Hot Springs (3.4 miles) or another 0.6 mile farther to the DeGarmo Notch at a quaking aspen stand.

User Groups: Hikers, dogs on leash only. No horses or mountain bikes allowed. No wheelchair facilities.

Permits: Free self-issue permits are required only for backpackers, and are available at the visitors center. Parking and access are free.

Maps: For a brochure and map of the Hart Mountain Wildlife Refuge, contact Hart

Mountain National Antelope Refuge, P.O. Box 111, Lakeview, OR, 97630, 541/947-2731, or download at www.fws.gov/sheldonhartmtn/Hart/index.html. For a topographic map, ask the USGS for Hart Lake.

Directions: Drive north of Lakeview on U.S. 395 for five miles then turn east on Highway 140 for 16 miles. Go toward Plush, turning left on Road 3-13 for 20 miles to the town of Plush. Continue 0.8 mile through town and turn right on Road 3-12 toward Hart Mountain for 9.2 miles to just before a sign for DeGarmo Canyon, and turn right on a dirt road. Follow this road 0.5 mile, keeping right then left to stay on the main road. Park at road's end.

Contact: U.S. Fish and Wildlife Service, Hart Mountain National Antelope Refuge, P.O. Box 111, Lakeview, OR, 97630, 541/947-2731.

20 HART MOUNTAIN HOT SPRINGS TO WARNER PEAK

11.1 mi/6.0 hr 3 8

in the Hart Mountain National Antelope Refuge

Map 12.5, page 703

Hart Mountain Hot Springs simmer up out of the ground at a comfortable temperature, a great dip on a chilly night if you're camping in the nearby campground—the only campground in the refuge. It's also a great place to start a hike. Looming above the hot springs and little oasis of trees that is the campground, 8,017-foot Warner Peak broods, sometimes holding snow in its lees well into summer. An absolute maze of trails leads to the radio tower on the peak, but easy routes abound if you utilize the old roads in this upper corner of the refuge.

From the springs, cross the meadow on an old road toward the campground, about 0.2 mile. When you come to the Barnhardi Road, go right 0.3 mile to a gate. Continue following the road one mile to a junction, keeping left. In another 0.9 mile, watch for the Barnhardi

Hart Mountain National Antelope Refuge

© SEAN PATRICK HILL

Cabin to the right up the creek. Head for the cabin, then follow the creek uphill 0.9 mile to the DeGarmo Notch. From here, head cross-country two miles to the left up the open ridge to Warner Peak's summit. Return as you came.

User Groups: Hikers, dogs on leash only, and horses. Mountain bikes allowed only on main roads only. No wheelchair facilities.

Permits: Free self-issue permits are required only for backpackers, and are available at the visitors center. Parking and access are free.

Maps: For a brochure and map of the Hart Mountain Wildlife Refuge, contact Hart Mountain National Antelope Refuge, P.O. Box 111, Lakeview, OR, 97630, 541/947-2731, or download at www.fws.gov/sheldonhartmtn/Hart/index.html. For a topographic map, ask the USGS for Warner Peak.

Directions: Drive north of Lakeview on U.S. 395 for five miles then turn east on Highway 140 for 16 miles. Go toward Plush, turning left on Road 3-13 for 20 miles to the town of

Plush. Continue 0.8 mile through town and turn right on Road 3-12 toward Hart Mountain for 24 miles to the refuge headquarters. Turn right on Blue Sky Road for 4.5 miles to a parking area to the right by the bathhouse.

Contact: U.S. Fish and Wildlife Service, Hart Mountain National Antelope Refuge, P.O. Box 111, Lakeview, OR, 97630, 541/947-2731.

21 DEGARMO NOTCH
7.7 mi/4.0 hr   👣2 🏕7

in the Hart Mountain National Antelope Refuge

Map 12.5, page 703

This trail follows DeGarmo Creek up to the DeGarmo Notch, a grassy saddle of aspen trees part way up a 2,000-foot wall. Day hikers can make a loop out of it, returning by a different route altogether. Backpackers can explore this stretch of the sagelands, hiking to the notch and then continuing into the canyon (see *DeGarmo Canyon* listing in this chapter). The trail to the DeGarmo Notch requires a bit of cross-country hiking, so route-finding skills will prove valuable.

From the hot springs, cross the meadow on an old road toward the campground, about 0.2 mile. When you come to the Barnhardi Road, go right 0.3 mile to a gate. Continue following the road one mile to a junction, keeping left. In another 0.9 mile, watch for the Barnhardi Cabin to the right up the creek. Head for the cabin, then follow the creek uphill 0.9 mile to the DeGarmo Notch. Follow the creek into the canyon 0.6 mile, and go right at a canyon fork on an old road. Follow this track 0.7 mile to a ridge crest, then descend to the right on a road 1.1 miles back to Barnhardi Road, then left 1.5 miles back to the hot springs.

User Groups: Hikers, dogs on leash only, and horses. Mountain bikes allowed only on main roads only. No wheelchair facilities.

Permits: Free self-issue permits are required only for backpackers, and are available at the visitors center. Parking and access are free.

Maps: For a brochure and map of the Hart Mountain Wildlife Refuge, contact Hart Mountain National Antelope Refuge, P.O. Box 111, Lakeview, OR, 97630, 541/947-2731, or download at www.fws.gov/sheldonhartmtn/ Hart/index.html. For a topographic map, ask the USGS for Hart Lake.

Directions: Drive north of Lakeview on U.S. 395 for five miles then turn east on Highway 140 for 16 miles. Go toward Plush, turning left on Road 3-13 for 20 miles to the town of Plush. Continue 0.8 mile through town and turn right on Road 3-12 toward Hart Mountain for 24 miles to the refuge headquarters. Turn right on Blue Sky Road for 4.5 miles to a parking area to the right by the bathhouse.

Contact: U.S. Fish and Wildlife Service, Hart Mountain National Antelope Refuge, P.O. Box 111, Lakeview, OR, 97630, 541/947-2731.

22 DONNER UND BLITZEN RIVER
2.8 mi/1.0 hr   👣1 🏕7

south of Burns on Steens Mountain Loop Road

Map 12.6, page 704

The Malheur Wildlife Refuge is fed by the lazy, marshy Donner und Blitzen River, which has its headwaters in the nearby Steens Mountain Wilderness Area. Mosquitoes are vicious in early summer, so be prepared. The river, whose name means "thunder and lightning" in German, was named by Army Colonel George Curry, who led battles in the Bannock Indian War in 1864—ultimately banishing the defeated tribes who once occupied this desert country to reservations in Burns and Yakima. Two short trails are accessible from a trailhead in the Page Springs Campground.

The easiest trail sets off to the right 0.7 mile along the Donner und Blitzen River. The second trail begins to the left at a Nature Trail sign, heading up a side canyon 0.5 mile, then turns left to the rim and descends 0.7 mile back to the campground. Walk the last 0.2 mile to the left to return to the trailhead.

User Groups: Hikers and dogs only. No horses or mountain bikes allowed. No wheelchair facilities.

Permits: Permits are not required. Parking and access are free.

Maps: For a topographic map, ask the USGS for Frenchglen and Page Springs.

Directions: From Burns, drive east on Highway 78 for 1.7 miles, then turn right on Highway 205 for 61 miles to Frenchglen. Turn left on Steens Mountain Loop for 2.9 miles, crossing the river, to a fork. Go right into the Page Springs Campground entrance, staying to the right for 0.6 mile to the trailhead.

Contact: Bureau of Land Management, Burns District Office, 28910 Highway 20 West, Hines, OR, 97738, 541/573-4400.

23 LITTLE BLITZEN RIVER
5.6-17.0 mi/2.0 hr-3 days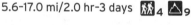

southeast of Burns in Steens Mountain Wilderness

Map 12.6, page 704

Steens Mountain is open precious little time out of the year, and this road is usually gated from November to May. But when it's open, it's incredible. One of Oregon's newest designated wilderness areas, Steens Mountain offers plenty to explore. The fault-block mountain is sheared through by enormous glacier-carved gorges, one of them being the canyon of the Little Blitzen River, which feeds into the larger Donner und Blitzen River. If you're looking for a backpacking trip in the Steens, this is it: With the longest trek possible away from roads, you'll have the opportunity to camp in a deep river canyon. Day-hikers can sample two stretches, one a short walk to the Donner und Blitzen passing the historic Riddle Ranch. The longer hike is far more adventurous, requiring a creek crossing (best done in summer when the water is low), a mile of cross-country trekking, and a cumulative climb of 1,800 feet.

The trail to the Donner und Blitzen begins at the Riddle Ranch (though cars with low clearance will have to park down the road at the gate, and walk the remaining 1.3 miles). Cross the footbridge to the house, then take a trail behind an outhouse 1.5 miles to the river.

For the Little Blitzen Gorge Trail, cross the Steens Mountain Loop road from the trailhead and go 100 yards farther up the road to the trail on the left. Go one mile to a ford, and continue 2.1 miles into meadows and pools along the river. Continue one mile up the canyon to reach 4-Mile Camp. This makes a good turnaround, but hikers can continue 4.5 rougher miles, passing two waterfalls before the trail ends.

User Groups: Hikers, dogs, and horses. No mountain bikes allowed. No wheelchair facilities.

Permits: Permits are not required. Parking and access are free.

Maps: For a topographic map, ask the USGS for Tombstone Canyon and Fish Lake.

Directions: From Burns, drive east on Highway 78 for 1.7 miles, then turn right on Highway 205 for 61 miles to Frenchglen. Continue another 10 miles on this highway and turn left on Steens Mountain Loop Road. Drive 19.2 miles to a junction. To visit the Donner und Blitzen, follow a sign for Riddle Ranch and turn left 1.3 mile to a gate open Thursday through Sunday, mid-June through October. If your car has clearance, you can continue the last 1.3 miles to road's end at the ranch. For the Little Blitzen Canyon, continue 0.8 mile on the Steens Mountain Loop to the Little Blitzen Trailhead on the right.

Contact: Bureau of Land Management, Burns District Office, 28910 Highway 20 West, Hines, OR, 97738, 541/573-4400.

24 BIG INDIAN GORGE
8.2 mi/4.0 hr   🥾3 ⛺9

southeast of Burns in Steens Mountain
Wilderness

Map 12.6, page 704   **BEST (**

A spectacular 2,000-foot gorge carved into the side of the Steens Mountain is the bed of Big Indian Creek, lined with quaking aspen and cottonwood trees, and excellent for camping. It is said that long after the Bannock Indian War of 1864, the local tribes still came to this canyon to camp and race horses. Now it is as quiet as anything you can imagine, with only the wind in the willow leaves and the swift creek following you. Though the approach is on an arid plain following a dirt road, even that has its share of views as far as Hart Mountain in the west. Once the canyon begins, it swallows you up.

From the South Steens Campground, follow the old road behind the gate 1.9 miles to a woodsy ford of Big Indian Creek. In another 0.2 mile, ford Little Indian Creek near a falls. Watch for a ruined cabin in another 0.4 mile, then continue into the gorge 0.6 mile to the final crossing of Big Indian Creek. In another mile, the trail curves with the canyon to a long stretch with views to the Steens summit. The trail continues another 2.4 miles to a camping spot before the trail peters out, though hiking is still entirely possible another 1.6 miles to a series of creek forks.

User Groups: Hikers, dogs, and horses. No mountain bikes allowed. No wheelchair facilities.

Permits: Permits are not required. Parking and access are free.

Maps: For a topographic map, ask the USGS for Fish Lake.

Directions: From Burns, drive east on Highway 78 for 1.7 miles, then turn right on Highway 205 for 61 miles to Frenchglen. Continue another 10 miles on this highway and turn left on Steens Mountain Loop Road. Drive 19.5 miles on the Steens Mountain Loop to the South Steens Campground on the right. Take the second entrance and drive all the way to the far end, parking at a gate.

Contact: Bureau of Land Management, Burns District Office, 28910 Highway 20 West, Hines, OR, 97738, 541/573-4400.

© SEAN PATRICK HILL

Big Indian Gorge in Steens Mountain Wilderness

25 STEENS MOUNTAIN SUMMIT AND WILDHORSE LAKE

2.4 mi/1.0 hr

southeast of Burns on Steens Mountain

Map 12.6, page 704

Oregon's highest-elevation road drives nearly to the top of 9,733-foot Steens Mountain, and all around the roadbed lies the wilderness area designated by Congress in 2000. Late snows can keep the final pitch to the summit blocked well into July, so be sure to call ahead to confirm conditions. Along the way, the road passes viewpoints of the Kiger Gorge and East Rim, making this a dramatic drive. At the end, hike up an easy trail to the summit and down into a basin that holds Wildhorse Lake, one of Oregon's highest. The views from Steens reach as far as you can see, over the yellow alkali Alvord Basin and beyond.

To head to the summit, take the left trail up 0.4 mile to the radio buildings. To go to Wildhorse Lake, take the right-hand trail 1.2 miles and down 1,100 feet to the shore.

User Groups: Hikers, dogs, and horses. No mountain bikes allowed. No wheelchair facilities.

Permits: Permits are not required. Parking and access are free.

Maps: For a topographic map, ask the USGS for Wildhorse Lake.

Directions: From Burns, drive east on Highway 78 for 1.7 miles, then turn right on Highway 205 for 61 miles to Frenchglen. Turn left on Steens Mountain Loop for 24.5 miles to a four-way junction. Go left at a Wildhorse Lake for two rough miles to the trailhead at road's end.

Contact: Bureau of Land Management, Burns District Office, 28910 Highway 20 West, Hines, OR, 97738, 541/573-4400.

26 PIKE CREEK CANYON

5.4 mi/3.0 hr

north of Fields on the east face of Steens Mountain

Map 12.6, page 704

On the eastern side of Steens Mountain, you can truly get a sense of the desert. Spread out like a great yellow carpet, the Alvord Playa bakes in the sun to a cracked landscape where virtually nothing can grow. Even the creeks don't know what to do here; they just run down to the lip of this desert and disappear. Such is the fate of Pike Creek, but if you find the creek higher up, it's wonderfully cold and clear, and it has its own path into a steep and narrow canyon among the ruins of old mines.

From a giant boulder at the upper campground, cross the creek and follow an old mining road up and to the right. This path climbs one mile and nearly 500 feet to a second creek crossing, then climbs steeply 300 feet in 0.4 mile to the end of the road. From here, you can go to the road's highest point and follow a series of cairns and faint paths up another 1.3 miles and nearly 600 feet to the Pike Knob, which cleanly divides two forks of the creek.

User Groups: Hikers, dogs, and horses. No mountain bikes allowed. No wheelchair facilities.

Permits: Permits are not required. Parking and access are free.

Maps: For a topographic map, ask the USGS for Alvord Hot Springs.

Directions: From Fields, follow Highway 205 north 1.3 miles and continue to the right on gravel Fields-Follyfarm Road for 24 miles along the mountain, then turn left over a cattle guard on an unmarked dirt road. Park here unless you have a high-clearance vehicle, then continue 0.6 mile up this rough road to the camping area.

Contact: Bureau of Land Management, Burns District Office, 28910 Highway 20 West, Hines, OR, 97738, 541/573-4400.

27 BORAX HOT SPRINGS
3.0 mi/1.0 hr   👫1 ⚠️8

northeast of Fields

Map 12.6, page 704

Oregon is hot spring country, and the Steens Mountain area is particularly rife with hot water cauldrons. People swim in the Alvord Springs, and visit Mickey Springs, but the Borax Springs are something else altogether—far too hot to touch. Instead, they have an unmatched beauty due to the phenomenal colors that grow in the pools. This Nature Conservancy–protected area is also the site of Borax Lake, an ancient arsenic-laced pond that's home to the borax chub (an endangered species that lives nowhere else). The trail also passes huge, rusting boiling vats for a borax company that once mined the white alkaline soils all around. Stay away from the pools themselves! The edges can be dangerous and unstable, so keep children close at hand. You'll want to wear sunglasses here, since the ground can be so bright it can hurt your eyes.

Cross the wire gate and follow the road 0.4 mile past the Lower Borax Lake Reservoir to a junction, staying right another 0.5 mile past the rusting vats to Borax Lake. Continue to the left 0.6 mile past a series of the strange, boiling springs, the last two beyond a fence.

User Groups: Hikers only. No dogs, horses, or mountain bikes allowed. No wheelchair facilities.

Permits: Permits are not required. Parking and access are free.

Maps: For a topographic map, ask the USGS for Borax Lake.

Directions: From Fields, follow Highway 205 north 1.3 miles and continue to the right on gravel Fields-Follyfarm Road for 0.4 mile, then go right onto a dirt powerline road for 2.1 miles. Turn left at the first fork and go 1.8 miles to road's end at a wire gate. The trail starts behind the fence.

Contact: The Nature Conservancy, 821 SE 14th Avenue, Portland, OR, 97214, 503/802-8100.

28 PUEBLO MOUNTAINS
7.2 mi/3.0 hr   👫3 ⚠️8

south of Fields near the Nevada border

Map 12.6, page 704

There are people in this world known as desert rats. They enjoy seemingly stark landscapes with a lack of trees, trails, and water. If you're one of those, then this is the trail for you. Still, mule deer thrive here, and you'll come upon wildflowers and willows, with side trips to the Van Horn Basin and Pueblo Mountain in what is easily the most remote and least known range in Oregon. Part of a 2,000-mile desert trail, this stretch will test your endurance. Bring plenty of water and hike early in the day if you can.

From the trailhead at the first cairn, follow the old road 0.6 mile and veer into the left-hand valley. The "trail" is marked almost entirely by rock cairns, spaced within sight of each other. Continuing 1.0 mile past several cairns brings you to a 6,900-foot saddle. In two miles, the trail reaches a 7,790-foot high point before continuing on toward Nevada and the town of Denio, 13 miles away—but for the unprepared day-hiker, it's safest to turn back here.

User Groups: Hikers, dogs, and horses. No mountain bikes allowed. No wheelchair facilities.

Permits: Permits are not required. Parking and access are free.

Maps: For a Pueblo Mountains Desert Trail map, contact Bureau of Land Management, Burns District Office, 28910 Highway 20 West, Hines, OR, 97738, 541/573-4400, or contact the Desert Trail Association, P.O. Box 34, Madras, OR, 97741, www.thedeserttrail.org/index.html. For a topographic map, ask the USGS for Van Horn Basin.

Directions: From Fields, drive south on Highway 205 for 3.1 miles to a sign for Domingo Pass. Turn right here across a cattle guard onto a gravel road for 3.8 miles. At a fork, go right 0.5 mile. At the next fork, go left 0.2 mile, crossing another cattle guard. At the third fork go left and stay going straight for 0.9 mile to a 90-degree turn to the left. Turn left at this corner and go 1.25 miles to a rock cairn at a side road to the right.

Contact: Bureau of Land Management, Burns District Office, 28910 Highway 20 West, Hines, OR, 97738, 541/573-4400.

29 THREE FORKS HOT SPRINGS

4.2-7.2 mi/2.0-3.0 hr   🏃🏃 2 ⛰ 8

south of Rome in the Owyhee River Canyon

Map 12.7, page 705

Loneliest of all, the trail to Three Forks Hot Springs lies in the farthest and most remote corner of Oregon. Even the road there feels vast and never-ending. And the road down into the canyon is nothing to sneeze at either; it's a slow 1.5 miles over very primitive road to get to the Owyhee River and its fantastic canyon. If you come in spring, you may catch some boaters going by, as this is a popular rafting river. As summer progresses, though, the river drops dramatically; still, you'll have to wade a number of times to get to the hot spring pool fed by a pouring waterfall from a warm creek in a side canyon.

From the parking area, go to the boat ramp and walk to the left and upstream along the river, fording the North Fork Owyhee River. On the far side, stay along the shore and follow an old wagon road two miles along the river. After a few twists, you'll begin to see and smell the warm water flowing over the trail—look across to find the big springs. Where a road comes down to the shore, ford the river (sometimes knee-deep, sometimes ankle-deep) to a gravel bar on the far side, then follow the old road up to a bridgeless crossing to the hot springs.

User Groups: Hikers and dogs. No horses or mountain bikes allowed. No wheelchair facilities.

Three Forks Hot Springs on the Owyhee River

© SEAN PATRICK HILL

Permits: Permits are not required. Parking and access are free.

Maps: For a topographic map, ask the USGS for Three Forks.

Directions: From Burns, drive Highway 78 east 93 miles to Burns Junction and go left on U.S. 95 for 30.5 miles, passing the hamlet of Rome and crossing the Owyhee River. At a sign for Three Forks, turn right on Three Forks Road and go 27.6 miles to a T-junction. Go right 2.7 miles to an old corral and park here. If you have a vehicle with high clearance, continue down the canyon wall 1.4 miles to a junction, then go right 0.1 mile toward the lone outhouse.

Contact: Bureau of Land Management, Vale District Office, 100 Oregon Street, Vale, OR, 97918, 541/473-3144.

RESOURCES

NATIONAL FORESTS

United States Forest Service lands provide access to a great deal of the Pacific Northwest's hikes, including everything from remote wilderness areas to public campgrounds. Camping is generally allowed anywhere unless specifically prohibited, as it is in sensitive wilderness areas or places where camping is restricted to preexisting sites. To escape the crowds, and to perhaps find real solitude, the national forests are your best bet.

Many Forest Service trails traverse areas with limited water, so always be sure to bring plenty if you're hiking in a dry area. Likewise, many remote Forest Service campgrounds have no water and no toilet facilities. For campgrounds like these, there is usually no fee or reservation required. For established campgrounds with drinking water and more elaborate facilities, there is nearly always a modest fee. Campgrounds at higher elevations are subject to closure during winter months.

Dogs are permitted in national forests, though it is strongly recommended that they be under total verbal control by the owner. The leading cause of lost pets in the wild is through chasing wildlife. In some places leashes on dogs are required.

Some areas require special permits, and wilderness areas almost always do. These free self-issue permits are usually obtainable at either the trailhead or the wilderness boundary. They are required between the Friday of Memorial Day weekend and October 31 for all groups that enter the wilderness.

Northwest Forest Pass

Many sites require a Northwest Forest Pass for each vehicle parked at a designated trailhead. Daily passes are $5; annual passes are available for $30. You can purchase the Northwest Forest Pass at any Forest Service ranger station or at many, but not all, of the trailheads. Retail outlets, especially outdoors stores, frequently carry them as well. For a list of businesses, go to www.fs.fed.us/r6/passespermits/vendors. php. You can also order passes online at www.

naturenw.org. For phone orders, call 800/270-7504. Checks should be made payable to the USDA Forest Service.

Golden Eagle Passports will be honored in lieu of Northwest Forest Passes until they expire, and the Golden Age and Golden Access Passports are valid for the pass holder's lifetime. Parking is free in the national forests on two "free days": National Trails Day in June and Public Lands Day in September. A pass is not required on those days.

A current list of sites requiring the Northwest Forest Pass is online at www.fs.fed.us/r6/passespermits/sites.shtml. Recreation passes do not cover fees for winter Sno-Parks, cabin rentals, or developed campgrounds, and are not substitutes for climbing or wilderness permits. Recreation passes are not valid at concessionaire-operated day-use sites, though many honor passes through discounts at Forest Service campgrounds.

National Forest Reservations

Reservations at popular campgrounds, horse camps, and group camps are made by a reservation system. Reservations can be made online at www.recreation.gov or by calling 877/444-6777. Individual campsites can be reserved up to 240 days in advance of arrival, and group sites up to 360 days in advance. There is a nonrefundable fee of $9 for reservations; major credit cards are accepted. Holders of Golden Age or Golden Access passports receive a 50 percent discount for single-family campsites. Some forests, such as the Deschutes National Forest, authorize private concessionaires by a Special Use Permit to manage campgrounds; contact the national forest offices for details. Camping longer than 14 consecutive days at the same spot is generally not allowed.

National Forest Maps

National Forest maps detail access roads, hiking trails, campgrounds, and lakes, and are generally about $9. Orders can be placed by phone directly by calling the supervisor's office for each individual National Forest. You can also purchase select topographic wilderness maps from the Forest Service by contacting U.S. Forest Service, National Forest Store, P.O. Box 8268, Missoula, MT, 59807, 406/329-3024, fax 406/329-3030, www.nationalforeststore.com. You can also purchase maps from Discover Your Northwest at www.discovernw.org.

FOREST SERVICE INFORMATION

Forest Service personnel are helpful when it comes to trail and road information. Phone in advance of your trip for the best service, though you can also visit their offices during the week. For specific information on a particular national forest, contact the following offices:

Washington

COLVILLE NATIONAL FOREST
www.fs.fed.us/r6/colville

Newport Ranger District
315 N. Warren
Newport, WA 99156
509/447-7300

Republic Ranger District
650 E. Delaware Ave.
Republic, WA 99166
509/775-7400

Sullivan Lake Ranger District
12641 Sullivan Lake Rd.
Metaline Falls, WA 99153
509/446-7500

Three Rivers Ranger District, Colville Ranger Station
765 S. Main
Colville, WA 99114
509/684-7000

Three Rivers Ranger District, Kettle Falls Ranger Station
255 W. 11th Ave.
Kettle Falls, WA 99141
509/738-7700

GIFFORD PINCHOT NATIONAL FOREST
www.fs.fed.us/r6/gpnf

Cowlitz Valley Ranger District
10024 U.S. 12
P.O. Box 670
Randle, WA 98377
360/497-1100

Mount Adams Ranger District
2455 Hwy. 141
Trout Lake, WA 98650
509/395-3400

MOUNT BAKER–SNOQUALMIE NATIONAL FOREST
www.fs.fed.us/r6/mbs

Darrington Ranger District
1405 Emens Ave. N.
Darrington, WA 98241
360/436-1155

Glacier Public Service Center
Glacier, WA 98244
360/599-2714

Mount Baker Ranger District Office
810 Hwy. 20
Sedro-Woolley, WA 98284
360/856-5700 ext. 515

Skykomish Ranger District
74920 NE Stevens Pass Hwy.
P.O. Box 305
Skykomish, WA 98288
360/677-2414

Snoqualmie Ranger District, Enumclaw Ranger Station
450 Roosevelt Ave. E.
Enumclaw, WA 98022
360/825-6585

**Snoqualmie Ranger District,
North Bend Ranger Station**
902 SE North Bend Way, Bldg. 1
North Bend, WA 98045
425/888-1421

Verlot Public Service Center
33515 Mountain Loop Hwy.
Granite Falls, WA 98252
360/691-7791

OKANOGAN NATIONAL FOREST
www.fs.fed.us/r6/oka

Methow Valley Ranger District
24 W. Chewuch Rd.
Winthrop, WA 98862
509/996-4003

Tonasket Ranger District
1 W. Winesap
Tonasket, WA 98855
509/486-2186

OLYMPIC NATIONAL FOREST
www.fs.fed.us/r6/olympic

Forks Ranger District
437 Tillicum Lane
Forks, WA 98331
360/374-6522

Hoodsport Ranger District
150 N. Lake Cushman Rd.
P.O. Box 68
Hoodsport, WA 98548
360/877-2021

Quilcene Ranger District
295142 U.S. 101 S.
P.O. Box 280
Quilcene, WA 98376
360/765-2200

Quinault Ranger District
353 South Shore Rd.
P. O. Box 9
Quinault, WA 98575
360/288-2525

UMATILLA NATIONAL FOREST
www.fs.fed.us/r6/uma

Pomeroy Ranger District
71 W. Main
Pomeroy, WA 99347
509/843-1891

WENATCHEE NATIONAL FOREST
www.fs.fed.us/r6/wenatchee

Chelan Ranger District
428 W. Woodin Ave.
Chelan, WA 98816-9724
509/682-2576

Cle Elum Ranger District
803 W. 2nd St.
Cle Elum, WA 98922
509/852-1100

Entiat Ranger District
2108 Entiat Way
P.O. Box 476
Entiat, WA 98822
509/784-1511

Lake Wenatchee Ranger District
22976 Hwy. 207
Leavenworth, WA 98826
509/763-3103

Leavenworth Ranger District
600 Sherbourne
Leavenworth, WA 98826
509/548-2550

Naches Ranger District
10237 Hwy. 12
Naches, WA 98937
509/653-1401

Oregon

Columbia Gorge National Scenic Area
902 Wasco Avenue, Suite 200
Hood River, OR 97031
541/308-1700
www.fs.fed.us/r6/columbia

Crooked River National Grassland
813 SW Highway 97
Madras, OR 97741
541/475-9272
www.fs.fed.us/r6/centraloregon

Deschutes National Forest
1001 SW Emkay Drive
Bend, OR 97702
541/383-5300
www.fs.fed.us/r6/centraloregon

Fremont-Winema National Forest
1301 South G Street
Lakeview, OR 97630
541/947-2151
www.fs.fed.us/r6/frewin

Hells Canyon National Recreation Area
88401 Highway 82, Box A
Enterprise, OR 97828
541/523-1315
www.fs.fed.us/r6/w-w

Malheur National Forest
431 Patterson Bridge Road
John Day, OR 97845
541/575-3000
www.fs.fed.us/r6/malheur

Mount Hood National Forest
16400 Champion Way
Sandy, OR 97055
503/668-1700
www.fs.fed.us/r6/mthood

Newberry Volcanic National Monument
1001 SW Emkay Drive
Bend, OR 97702
541/383-5300
www.fs.fed.us/r6/centraloregon

Ochoco National Forest
3160 NE 3rd Street
Prineville, OR 97754
541/416-6500
www.fs.fed.us/r6/centraloregon

Oregon Dunes National Recreation Area
4077 SW Research Way
P.O. Box 1148
Corvallis, OR 97339
541/750-7000
www.fs.fed.us/r6/siuslaw

Rogue River-Siskiyou National Forest
3040 Biddle Road
Medford, OR 97504
541/618-2200
www.fs.fed.us/r6/rogue-siskiyou

Siuslaw National Forest
4077 SW Research Way
P.O. Box 1148
Corvallis, OR 97339
541/750-7000
www.fs.fed.us/r6/siuslaw

Umatilla National Forest
2517 SW Hailey Avenue
Pendleton, OR 97801
541/278-3716
www.fs.fed.us/r6/uma

Umpqua National Forest
2900 NW Stewart Parkway
Roseburg, OR 97470
541/672-6601
www.fs.fed.us/r6/umpqua

USDA Forest Service
Pacific Northwest Region
333 SW 1st Street
P.O. Box 3623
Portland, OR 97208-3623
503/808-2468
fax 503/808-2210
www.fs.fed.us/r6

Wallowa-Whitman National Forest
P.O. Box 907
1550 Dewey Avenue
Baker City, OR 97814
541/523-6391
www.fs.fed.us/r6/w-w

Willamette National Forest
3106 Pierce Parkway, Suite D
Springfield OR, 97477
541/225-6300
www.fs.fed.us/r6/willamette

NATIONAL PARKS

Washington

MOUNT RAINIER NATIONAL PARK
**Longmire Wilderness
Information Center**
Tahoma Woods, Star Route
Ashford, WA 98304
360/569-4453

**White River Wilderness
Information Center**
70004 Highway 410 E.
Enumclaw, WA 98022
360/569-2211 x6030

NORTH CASCADES NATIONAL PARK
Golden West Visitor Center
Stehekin, WA
360/854-7365, ext. 14

**Marblemount Wilderness
Information Center**
7280 Ranger Station Rd.
Marblemount, WA 98267
360/854-7245

OLYMPIC NATIONAL PARK
Olympic Wilderness Information Center
600 E. Park Ave.
Port Angeles, WA 98362-6798
360/565-3130

Oregon

Oregon has one major National Park, the amazing Crater Lake. Though campgrounds are not as numerous as at other National Parks, there are spots available at Crater Lake Lodge and Mazama Village Motor Inn; reservations are strongly recommended and can be made through Xanterra Parks & Resorts at 541/830-8700. Half the campsites at Mazama Campground are on a reservation system and can be attained by calling 888/774-2728. Expect to pay an entrance fee of $10 per car, good for seven days. For an additional fee, a Golden Eagle sticker can be added to the National Parks Pass, which in turn eliminates fees for many sites managed by the Forest Service, U.S. Fish and Wildlife, and Bureau of Land Management. Discounts are available for holders of the Golden Age and Golden Access passports, including a 50 percent reduction of individual camping fees and a waiver of park entrance fees.

Oregon also has a number of National Historic Trails, National Monuments, and National Historic Parks.

Crater Lake National Park
P.O. Box 7
Crater Lake, OR 97604
541/594-3000
www.nps.gov/crla

**John Day Fossil Beds
National Monument**
32651 Highway 19
Kimberly, OR 97848
541/987-2333
www.nps.gov/joda

Lewis and Clark National Historic Park
92343 Fort Clatsop Road
Astoria, OR 97103-9197
503/861-2471
www.nps.gov/lewi

National Park Service
Pacific West Region

One Jackson Center
1111 Jackson Street, Suite 700
Oakland, CA 94607
510/817-1304
www.nps.gov

Oregon Caves National Monument
19000 Caves Highway
Cave Junction, OR 97523
541/592-2100, ext. 262
www.nps.gov/orca

STATE PARKS

The Pacific Northwest has some of the best state parks systems in the nation. From the coast to the mountains to the deserts, there are numerous day-use areas, campgrounds, and hiking trails. Many campgrounds offer drive-in campsites, showers and bathrooms, interpretive tours, even yurts. Reservations are always a good idea, especially in the high summer season.

If you're looking for a good camping spot, be sure to call ahead and make reservations, as they can go quickly and months in advance. Fees are reasonable, and some state parks have walk-in camping for free.

State Park Reservations

WASHINGTON

**Washington State Parks
and Recreation Commission**
1111 Israel Rd. SW
Olympia, WA 98504-2650
360/902-8844 (information) or
360/902-8500 (State Parks Pass)
www.parks.wa.gov

OREGON

Half of Oregon State Parks campgrounds accept campsite reservations, and the rest are first-come, first-served. Reservations may be made from two days to nine months in advance. Reservations for Oregon State Parks are made through Reserve America by phone at 800/452-5687 or online at www.reserveamerica.com. A reservation fee of $8 is charged for a campsite. Major credit cards are accepted by phone and online, but generally not at the parks themselves. The charge is based on one vehicle, and additional vehicles are charged more.

For general information about Oregon State Parks, contact:

**Oregon Parks and
Recreation Department**
1115 Commercial Street NE
Salem, OR 97301
800/551-6949
www.oregon.gov/oprd/parks/index.shtml

BUREAU OF LAND MANAGEMENT

The Bureau of Land Management (BLM) manages many trails and primitive campsites in Washington and Oregon, including forest and desert areas. The BLM is also the manager for the Steens Mountain Wilderness. For specific information on a particular area, contact the following offices:

Washington
Bureau of Land Management
Spokane District Office
1103 N. Fancher St.
Spokane, WA 99212-1275
509/536-1200

Oregon
Burns District Office
28910 Highway 20 West
Hines, OR 97738
541/573-4400
www.blm.gov/or/districts/burns

Coos Bay District
1300 Airport Lane
North Bend, OR 97459
541/756-0100
www.blm.gov/or/districts/coosbay

Eugene District Office
2890 Chad Drive
Eugene, OR 97440
541/683-6600
www.blm.gov/or/districts/eugene

Lakeview District Office
1301 South G Street
Lakeview, OR 97630
541/947-2177
www.blm.gov/or/districts/lakeview

Medford Office
3040 Biddle Road
Medford, OR 97504
541/618-2200
www.blm.gov/or/districts/medford

Prineville District
3050 NE 3rd Street
Prineville, OR 97754
541/416-6700
www.blm.gov/or/districts/prineville

Roseburg District
777 NW Garden Valley Boulevard
Roseburg, OR 97471
541/440-4930
www.blm.gov/or/districts/roseburg

Salem District Office
1717 Fabry Road SE
Salem, OR 97306
503/375-5646
www.blm.gov/or/districts/salem

Vale District Office
100 Oregon Street
Vale, OR 97918
541/473-3144
www.blm.gov/or/districts/vale

PARKS, RECREATION AREAS, AND OTHER RESOURCES

State Forests
OREGON
Oregon Department of Forestry
2600 State Street
Salem, OR 97310
503/945-7200
fax 503/945-7212
www.oregon.gov/ODF/index.shtml

Santiam State Forest
North Cascade Unit
22965 North Fork Road SE
Lyons, OR 97358
503/859-4344
fax 503/859-2158
www.oregon.gov/ODF/northcascade/santiam-stateforest.shtml

Tillamook State Forest
Forest Grove District Office
801 Gales Creek Road
Forest Grove, OR 97116
503/357-2191,
egov.oregon.gov/ODF/TSF/about_us.shtml

City/County/Regional Park Departments
OREGON
Ashland Parks and Recreation
340 South Pioneer Street
Ashland, OR 97520
541/488-5340
www.ashland.or.us/SectionIndex.asp?SectionID=426

City of Eugene Parks
99 W 10th Avenue, Suite 340
Eugene, OR 97401
541/682-5333
www.eugene-or.gov/portal/server.pt

Josephine County Parks
125 Ringuette Street
Grants Pass, OR 97527
541/474-5285
www.co.josephine.or.us

Lane County Parks
90064 Coburg Road
Eugene, OR 97408
541/682-2000
www.lanecounty.org/Parks/laneParks.htm

Linn County Parks and Recreation
3010 SW Ferry Street
Albany, OR 97322
541/967-3917
www.co.linn.or.us/parks/index.html

**North Clackamas Parks
and Recreation District**
9101 SE Sunnybrook Boulevard
Clackamas, OR 97015
503/794-8041
www.clackamas.us/ncprd

**Oregon Parks and
Recreation Department**
1115 Commercial Street NE
Salem, OR 97301
800/551-6949
www.oregonstateparks.org

Portland Parks and Recreation
1120 SW 5th Avenue, Suite 1302
Portland, OR 97204
503/823-PLAY (503/823-7529)
www.portlandonline.com/parks

**Washington County Facilities
Management**
169 North 1st Avenue, MS 42
Hillsboro, OR 97124
503/846-8715
www.co.washington.or.us/Support_Servic-
es/Facilities/Parks/index.cfm

Regional, State,
and Federal Offices
WASHINGTON
Monument Headquarters
(Gifford Pinchot National Forest)
42218 NE Yale Bridge Rd.
Amboy, WA 98601
360/449-7800
Mount Margaret Backcountry: 360/449-
7871
Climbing Info: 360/449-7861

**Mount St. Helens-Johnston
Ridge Observatory**
24000 Spirit Lake Hwy.
Toutle, WA 98649
360/274-2140

**Mount St. Helens National
Volcanic Monument**
www.fs.fed.us/gpnf/mshnvm

Seattle City Parks and Recreation
100 Dexter Ave. N.
Seattle, WA 98109
206/684-4075
www.cityofseattle.net/parks

**Washington Department
of Fish and Wildlife**
201 N. Pearl St.
Ellensburg, WA 98926
509/925-6746
6653 Road K NE
Moses Lake, WA 98837
509/765-6641

**Washington Department
of Natural Resources**
P.O. Box 47001
Olympia, WA 98504-7001
360/902-1375

OREGON
Cape Perpetua Visitor Center
2400 Highway 101
Yachats, OR 97498
541/547-3289

Metro Regional Center
600 NE Grand Avenue
Portland OR 97232
503/797-1700
www.oregonmetro.gov

**National Historic Oregon
Trail Interpretive Center**
22267 Highway 86
P.O. Box 987
Baker City, OR 97814
541/523-1843

Oregon Department of Fish and Wildlife
3406 Cherry Avenue NE
Salem, OR 97303
800/720-ODFW (800/720-6339) or
503/947-6000
www.dfw.state.or.us

**Oregon Dunes National
Recreation Area Visitors Center**
855 Highway Avenue
Reedsport, OR 97467
541/271-6019
U.S. Fish and Wildlife Service
1849 "C" Street NW
Washington, DC 20240
www.fws.gov

U.S. Geological Survey
Branch of Information Services
P.O. Box 25286, Bldg. 810, MS 306
Federal Center
Denver, CO 80225
888/ASK-USGS (888/275-8747) or 303/202-4700
www.usgs.gov

MAP SOURCES

Washington
Green Trails
P.O. Box 77734
Seattle, WA 98177
206/546-MAPS (206/546-6277)
www.greentrails.com

Outdoor Recreation Information Center
in the Seattle REI Building
222 Yale Ave. N.
Seattle, WA 98109-5429
206/470-4060

USGS Information Services
Box 25286
Denver, CO 80225
www.store.usgs.gov

Oregon
Geo-Graphics
18860 SW Alerwood Drive
Beaverton, OR 97006
503/591-7635
www.geo-graphicsmaps.com

Imus Geographics
P.O. Box 161
Eugene, OR 97440
www.imusgeographics.com

U.S. Forest Service
Attn: Map Sales
P.O. Box 8268
Missoula, MT 59807
406/329-3024
fax 406/329-3030
www.fs.fed.us/recreation/nationalforeststore

U.S. Geological Survey
Branch of Information Services
P.O. Box 25286, Federal Center
Denver, CO 80225
303/202-4700 or 888/ASK-USGS
(888/275-8747)
fax 303/202-4693
www.usgs.gov

HIKING CLUBS AND GROUPS

Washington
Cascade Chapter of Sierra Club
180 Nickerson St.
Ste. 202
Seattle, WA 98109-1631
206/378-0114
www.cascade.sierraclub.org

Cascadians of Yakima, WA
www.cascadians.org

Mazamas
527 SE 43rd Ave.
Portland, OR 97209
503/227-2345
www.mazamas.org

Mountaineers
7700 Sand Point Way NE
Seattle, WA 98115
206/521-6000
www.mountaineers.org

Mountains-to-Sound Greenway
911 Western Ave.
Ste. 523
Seattle, WA 98104
206/382-5565
www.mtsgreenway.org

Pacific Northwest Trail Association
24854 Charles Jones Memorial Circle, Unit #4
North Cascades Gateway Center
Sedro-Woolley, WA 98284
877/854-9415
www.pnt.org

Washington Trails Association
2019 3rd Ave.
Ste. 100
Seattle, WA 98121
206/625-1367
www.wta.org

Oregon
Bergfreunde
10175 SW Barbur Boulevard, Suite 100-BB
Portland, OR 97219
503/245-8543
www.bergfreunde.org

Chemeketans
P.O. Box 864
Salem, OR 97308
www.chemeketans.org

Friends of the Columbia Gorge
522 SW 5th Avenue, Suite 720
Portland, OR 97204
503/241-3762
gorgefriends.org

Mazamas
527 SE 43rd Avenue
Portland, OR 97215
503/227-2345
www.mazamas.org

Obsidians
P.O. Box 322
Eugene, OR 97440
503/344-1775
www.obsidians.org

Oregon Sierra Club
1821 SE Ankeny Street
Portland, OR 97214
503/238-0442
oregon.sierraclub.org

Pacific Crest Trail Association
5250 Date Avenue, Suite L
Sacramento, CA 95841
916/349-2109
www.pcta.org

Trails Club of Oregon
P.O. Box 1243
Portland, OR 97207
503/233-2740
www.trailsclub.org

Index

www.moon.com

DESTINATIONS | ACTIVITIES | BLOGS | MAPS | BOOKS

MOON.COM is ready to help plan your next trip! Filled with fresh trip ideas and strategies, author interviews, informative travel blogs, a detailed map library, and descriptions of all the Moon guidebooks, Moon.com is all you need to get out and explore the world—or even places in your own backyard. While at Moon.com, sign up for our monthly e-newsletter for updates on new releases, travel tips, and expert advice from our on-the-go Moon authors. As always, when you travel with Moon, expect an experience that is uncommon and truly unique.

MOON IS ON FACEBOOK—BECOME A FAN!
JOIN THE MOON PHOTO GROUP ON FLICKR

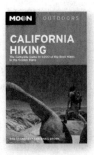

MOON PACIFIC NORTHWEST HIKING

Avalon Travel
a member of the Perseus Books Group
1700 Fourth Street
Berkeley, CA 94710, USA
www.moon.com

Editors: Tiffany Watson, Elizabeth Hollis Hansen
Series Manager: Sabrina Young
Copy Editors: Maura Brown, Ellie Winters
Graphics and Production Coordinator:
    Domini Dragoone
Cover Designer: Domini Dragoone
Interior Designer: Darren Alessi
Map Editors: Albert Angulo, Mike Morgenfeld
Cartographers: Kat Bennett, Brice Ticen
Illustrations: Bob Race

ISBN-13: 978-1-59880-099-9
ISSN: 1082-0760

Printing History
1st Edition – 1999
6th Edition – May 2010
5 4 3

Text © 2010 by Scott Leonard and
    Sean Patrick Hill.
Maps © 2010 by Avalon Travel.
All rights reserved.

KEEPING CURRENT

We are committed to making this book the most accurate and enjoyable hiking guide to the Pacific Northwest. You can rest assured that every trail in this book has been carefully reviewed in an effort to keep this book as up-to-date as possible. However, by the time you read this book, some of the fees listed herein may have changed and trails may have closed unexpectedly.

If you have a favorite gem you'd like to see included in the next edition, or see anything that needs updating, clarification, or correction, please drop us a line. Send your comments via email to feedback@moon.com, or use the address above.